Milltown

A HISTORY

First published 2023 by Eastwood Books
Dublin, Ireland
www.eastwoodbooks.com
www.wordwellbooks.com

First edition

Eastwood Books is an imprint of the Wordwell Group.

The Wordwell Group is a member of Publishing Ireland, the Irish Publishers' Association.

Eastwood Books
The Wordwell Group
Unit 9, 78 Furze Road
Sandyford
Dublin, Ireland

ISBN: 978-1-913934-41-5 (Hardback)

British Library Cataloguing in Publication Data.
A catalogue record for this book is available from the National Library of Ireland and the British Library.

Design by Fiacra McCarthy
Printed in Spain by Graficas Castuera

Milltown

A HISTORY

DAVID COSTELLO

For Gerald

Contents

Illustrations and Maps

MAPS

Map 4. 'An Actual Survey of the County of Dublin, on the same scale as those of Middlesex, Oxford, Barks, & Buckinghamshire, by John Rocque; 1760' (author's collection)

Map 5. 'A Plan of the City Suburbs and Environs of Dublin by John Rocque ... with additions and improvements by Mr Bernard Scale 1773' (author's collection)

Map 6. 'A survey of part of the River Dodder between Milltown and Clonskeagh done for Geo. Thompson Esq, by J.L. 1812 Nov' (image courtesy of the National Library of Ireland)

Map 7. 'A map of the woollen factory at Milltown, County Dublin belonging to Burke, esq. Surveyed By Jn. Longfield, 1821' (image courtesy of the National Library of Ireland)

Map 8. 'A survey of the demesne of Fairyland at Milltown in the County of Dublin belonging to W.C. Hogan esq by J Longfield, 1821' (image courtesy of the National Library of Ireland)

Map 9. OSI, Boundary Department, Sketch map of the parish of Donnybrook in the Barony of Rathdown and County of the City of Dublin, 23 August 1830 (courtesy of the National Archives of Ireland)

Map 10. 'Map of the lands of Roebuck in the Parish of Taney, Barony of Rathdown and County of Dublin Made by order of The Right Hon and the Hon the Commissioners of His Majesty's Woods Forests Land Revenues Works and Buildings by Brassington and Gale, 1832' (courtesy of the National Archives of Ireland)

Map 11. 'A map of premises on the north side of the River Dodder between the turn of the road from Rathmines to Milltown and Classon's Bridge, 1833' (courtesy of the National Archives of Ireland)

Map 12. 'Map of premises at Milltown for Mr Rooke by William Longfield, 1838' (image courtesy of the National Library of Ireland)

Map 13. 'A survey of ground at Milltown for Miss Hunt, 1839' (image courtesy of the National Library of Ireland)

Map 14. Map of Milltown village appended to lease dated 4 July 1837 Robert Dry to Patrick Hackett (courtesy of the National Archives of Ireland)

Map 15. OSI, Co. Dublin, Sheet 22, six inches to one statute mile, surveyed in 1837 and corrected in 1843, showing the boundaries of the Church of Ireland Parish of Milltown and the civil townlands of Milltown and Rathmines South (courtesy of RCB Library, Dublin D6/64)

Map 16. Town Plan of Milltown village, *c.* 1850 (courtesy of the Valuation Office)

Map 17. OSI, City of Dublin, Rathmines and Rathgar and Pembroke Townships, Sheet XXII.8 (2nd ed.), five feet to one statute mile, surveyed in 1865 and revised in 1889 (courtesy of UCD Digital Library, with permission of OSI)

Map 18. OSI, City of Dublin, Rathmines and Rathgar Township, Sheet XXII.18, five feet to one statute mile, surveyed in 1878 and revised in 1882 (courtesy of UCD Digital Library, with permission of OSI)

Map 19. OSI, City of Dublin, Rathmines and Rathgar Township, Sheet XXII.28, five feet to one statute mile, surveyed in 1879 and revised in 1882 (courtesy of UCD Digital Library, with permission of OSI)

Map 20. OSI, Co. Dublin, Dublin/Rathdown/ Uppercross, Sheet XII.4, 25 inches to one statute mile (edition of 1911), surveyed in 1837, revised in 1908 (author's collection)

Map 21. OSI, Co. Dublin, Dublin/Rathdown, Sheet 22. IV, 25 inches to one statute mile (edition of 1938), surveyed in 1837, revised in 1936 (author's collection)

Map 22. Map prepared for the Milltown Village Area Compulsory Purchase Order 1952, 5982A (copyright Dublin City Council)

MAPS

Map 1. Down Survey, 'The Barony of 1/2 Rathdown in the County of Dublin by Williem Farrand and Williem Storck', 1655

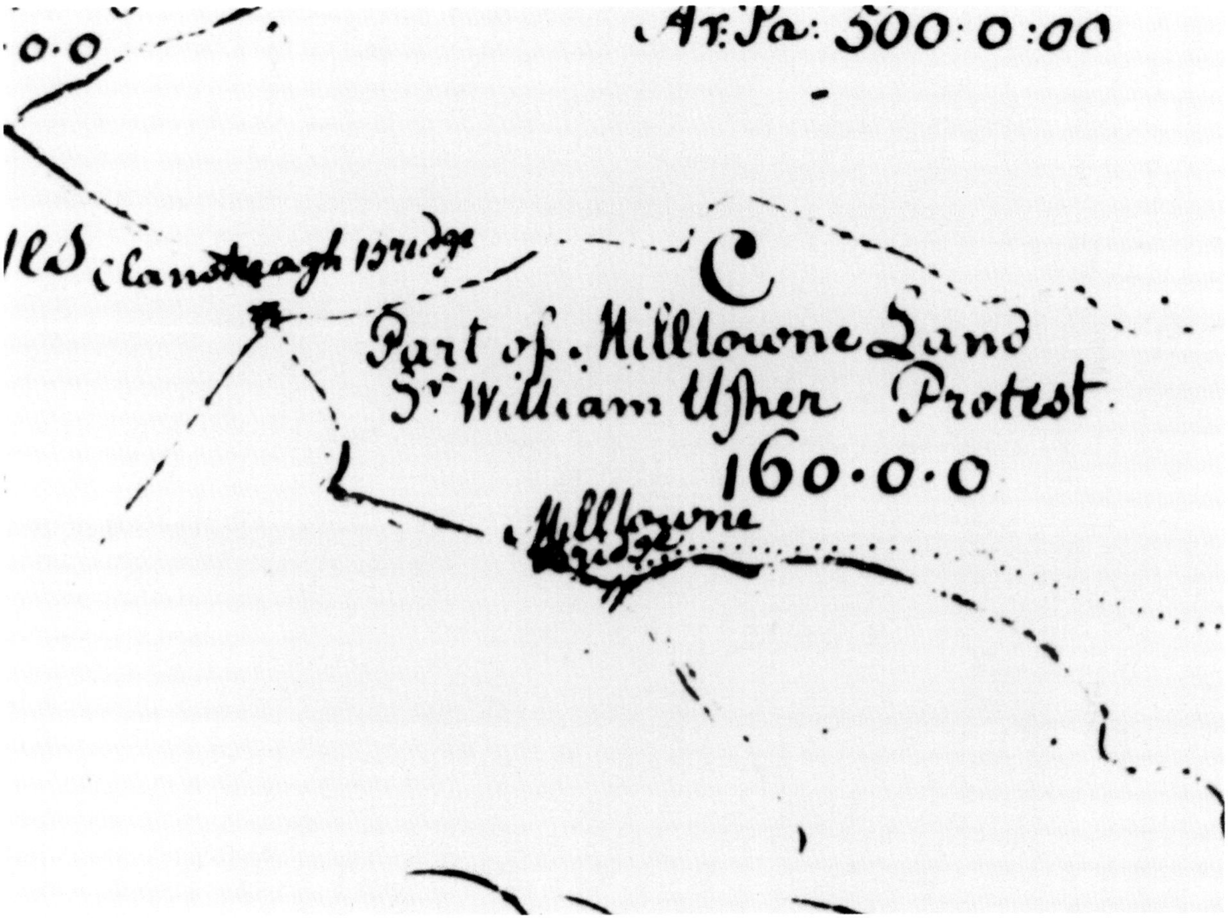

Map 2. Down Survey, 'The Parishes of Doonabrooke & Tannee in the 1/2 Barony of Rathdowne by Wm Farrand', 1655

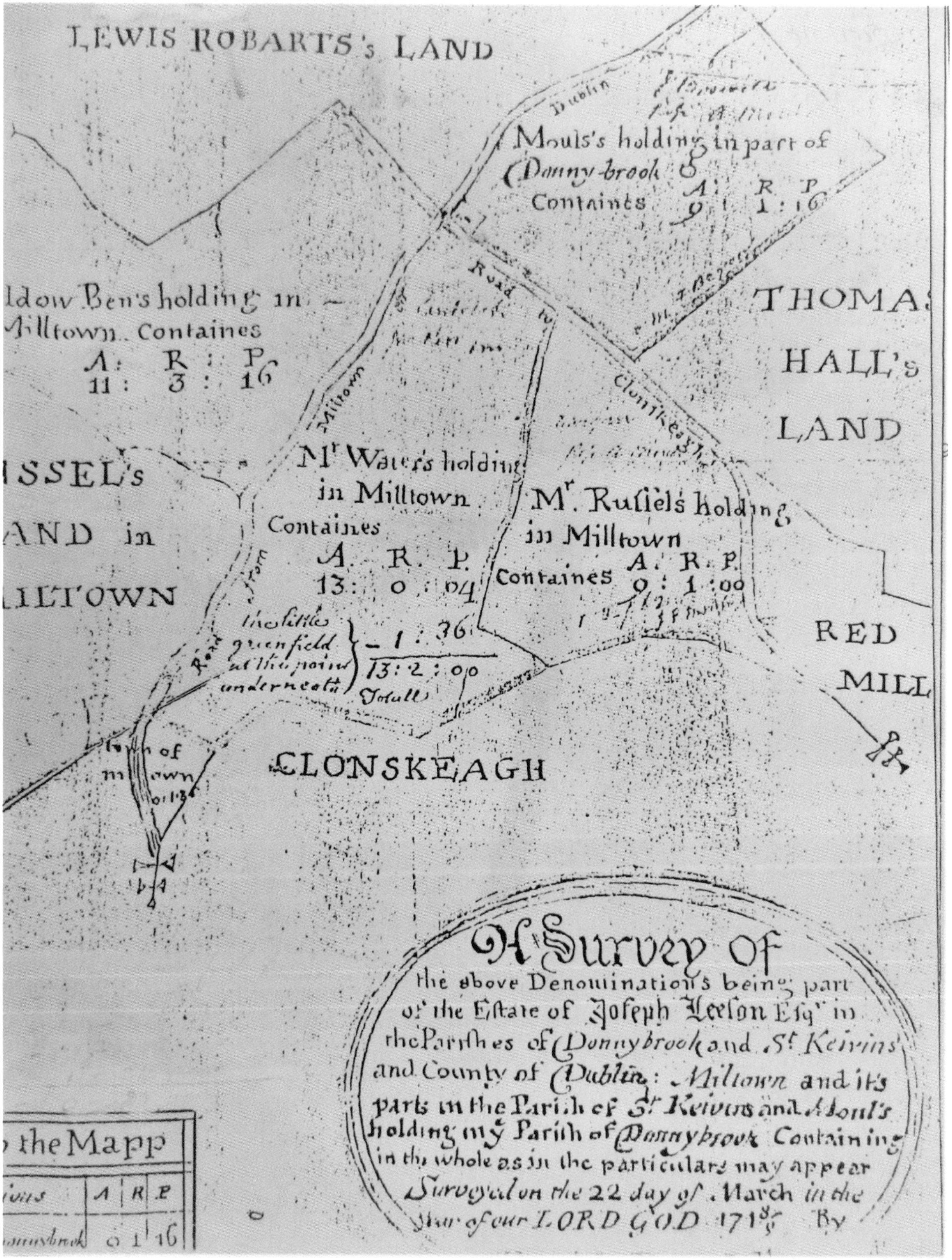

Map 3. 'A Survey of the above Denominations being part of the Estate of Joseph Leeson Esq in the Parishes of Donnybrook and St. Kevins and County of Dublin: Miltown and its parts in the Parish of St. Kevins and Mouls holding in the Parish of Donnybrook Containing in the whole as in the particulars may appear Surveyed on the 22 day of March in the year of our Lord God 1718/9' (courtesy of the late Danny Parkinson)

Map 4. 'An Actual Survey of the County of Dublin, on the same scale as those of Middlesex, Oxford, Barks, & Buckinghamshire, by John Rocque; 1760' (author's collection)

Map 5. 'A Plan of the City Suburbs and Environs of Dublin by John Rocque ... with additions and improvements by Mr Bernard Scale 1773' (author's collection)

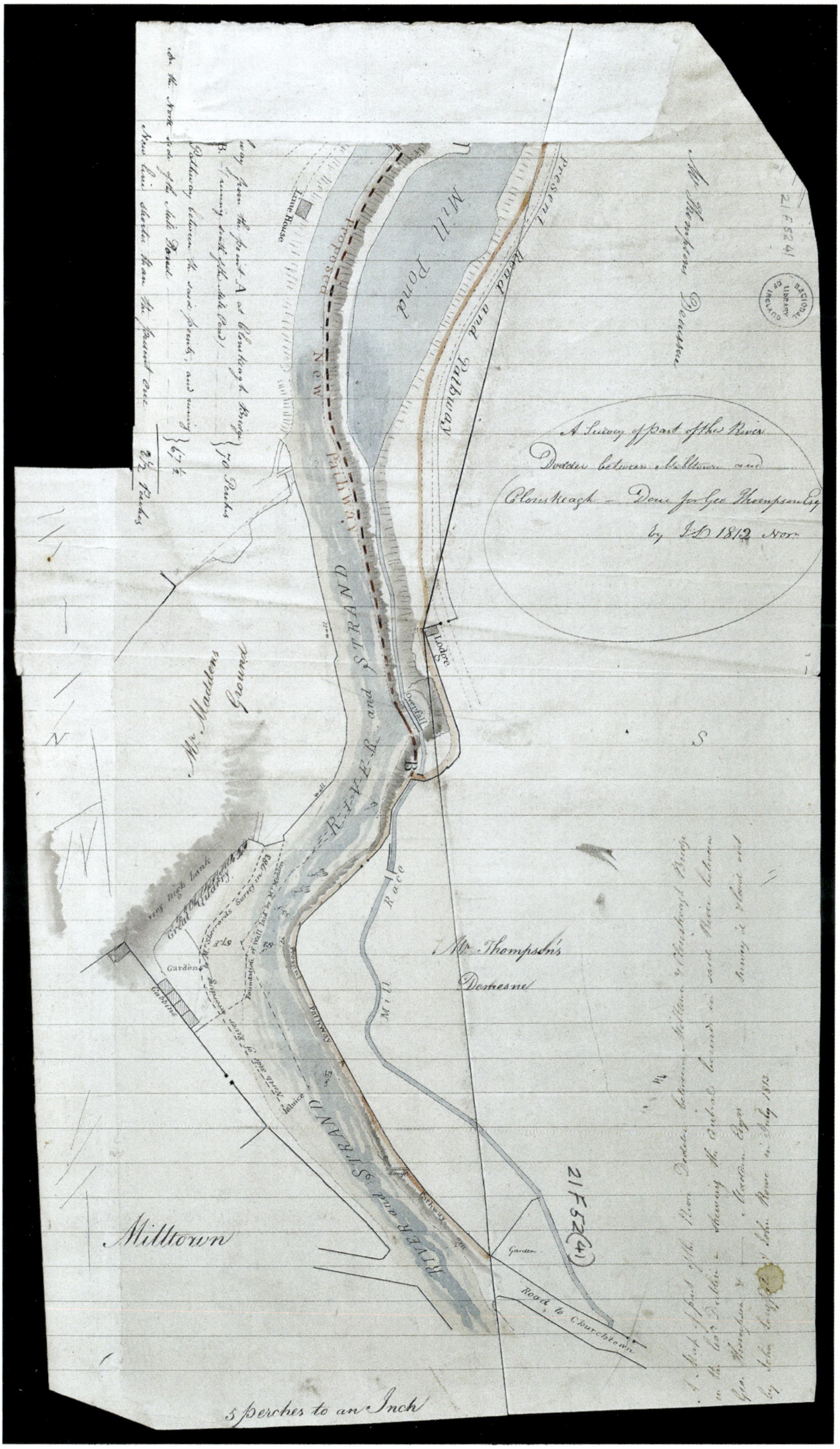

Map 6. 'A survey of part of the River Dodder between Milltown and Clonskeagh done for Geo. Thompson Esq, by J.L. 1812 Nov' (image courtesy of the National Library of Ireland)

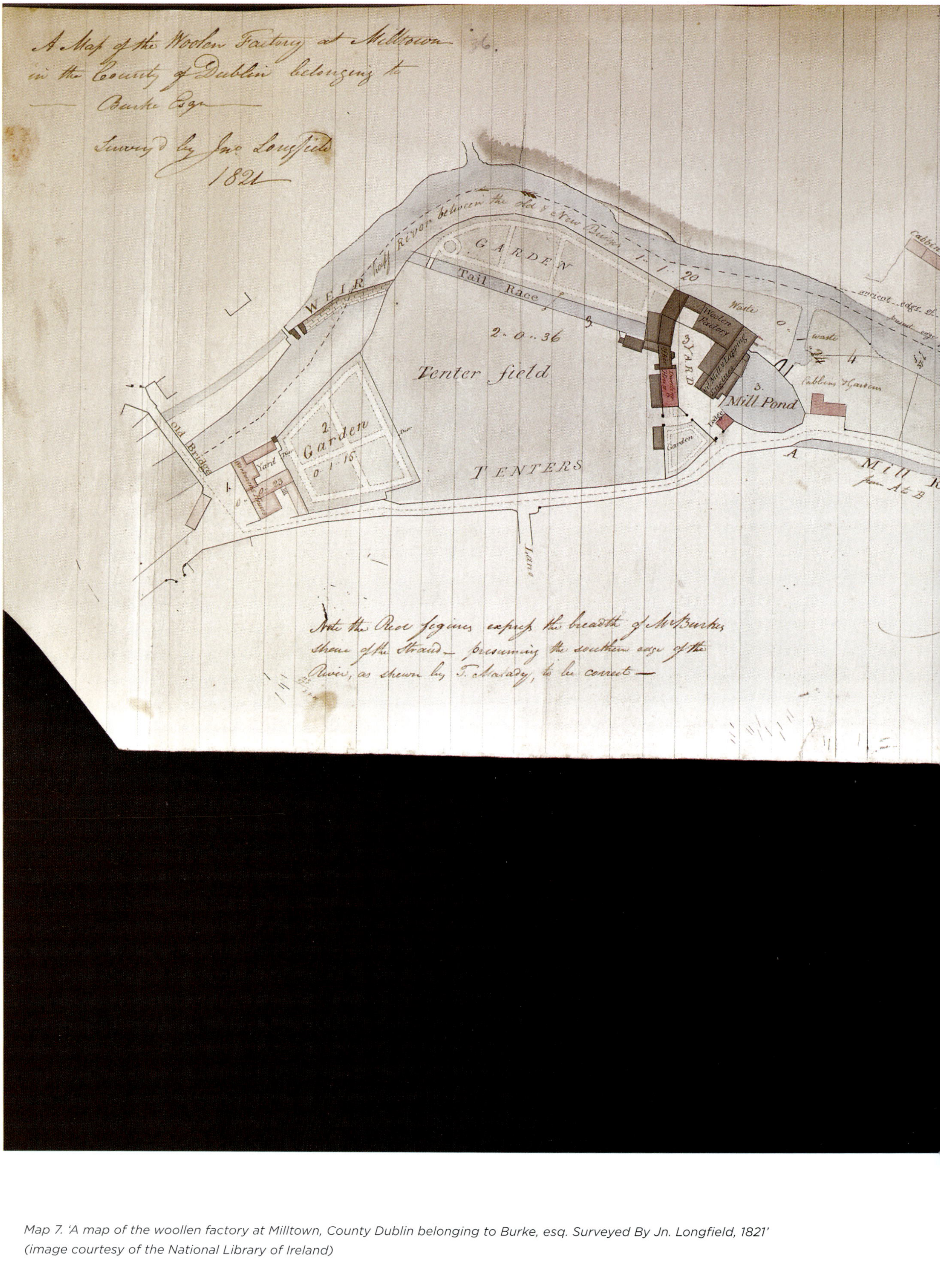

Map 7. 'A map of the woollen factory at Milltown, County Dublin belonging to Burke, esq. Surveyed By Jn. Longfield, 1821' (image courtesy of the National Library of Ireland)

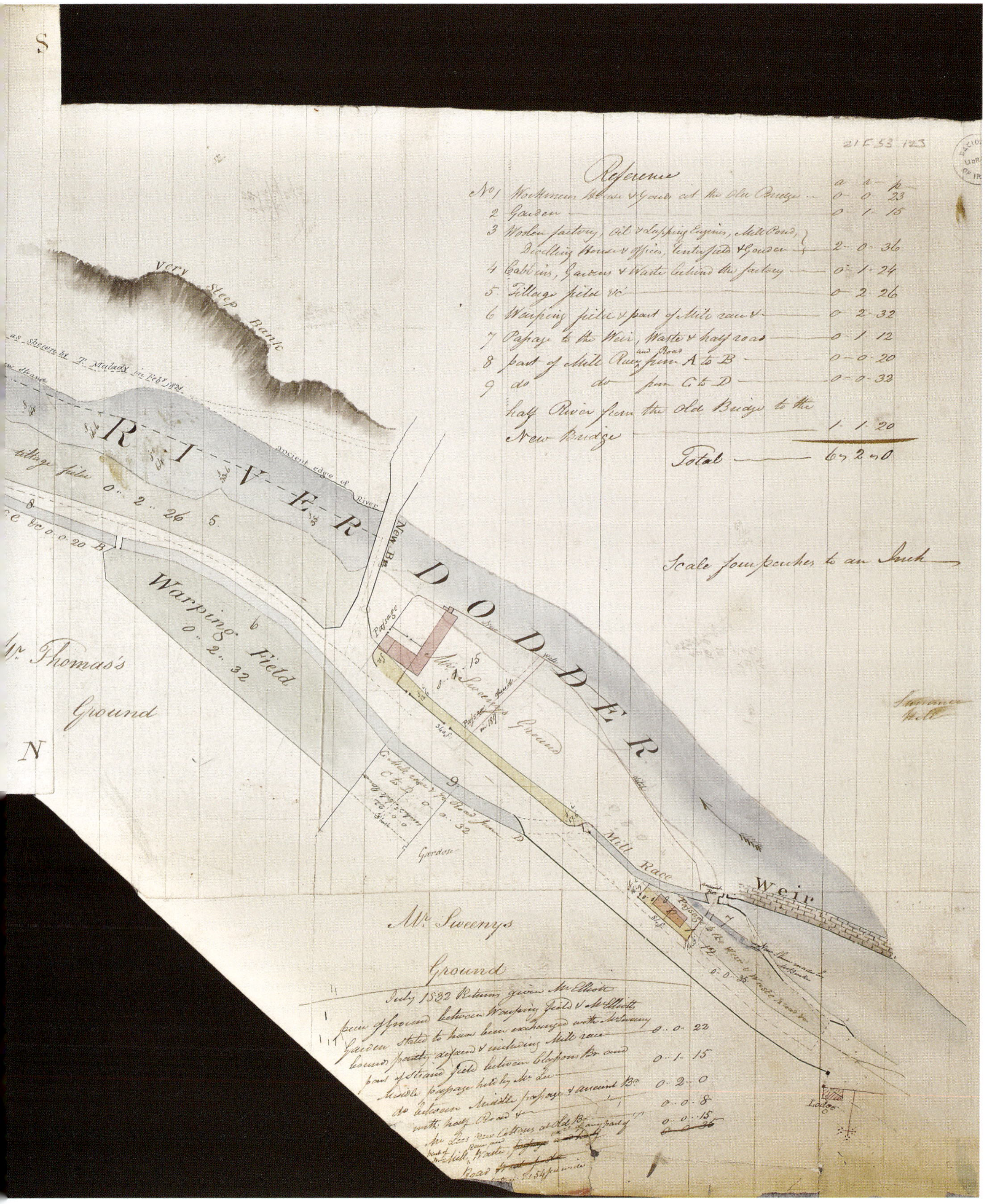
Reference
No 1 Workmens House & Garden at the Old Bridge — 0 - 0 - 23
2 Garden — 0 - 1 - 15
3 Woolen factory, Oil & Lapping Engines, Mill Pond, Dwelling House & offices, Tenter field & Garden — 2 - 0 - 36
4 Cabbins, Gardens & Waste behind the factory — 0 - 1 - 24
5. Tillage field &c — 0 - 2 - 26
6 Warping field & part of Mill race & — 0 - 2 - 32
7 Passage to the Weir, Waste & half road — 0 - 1 - 12
8 part of Mill Race and Road from A to B — 0 - 0 - 20
9 do do from C to D — 0 - 0 - 32
half River from the Old Bridge to the New Bridge — 1 - 1 - 20
Total — 6 - 2 - 0
Scale four perches to an Inch
Very Steep Bank
RIVER DODDER
ancient edge of River
New Br.
tillage field 0 .. 2 .. 26 5
Warping Field 0 .. 2 .. 32
Mr Thomas's Ground
Passage
Mill Race
Weir
Lodge
Mr Sweenys Ground
S
N

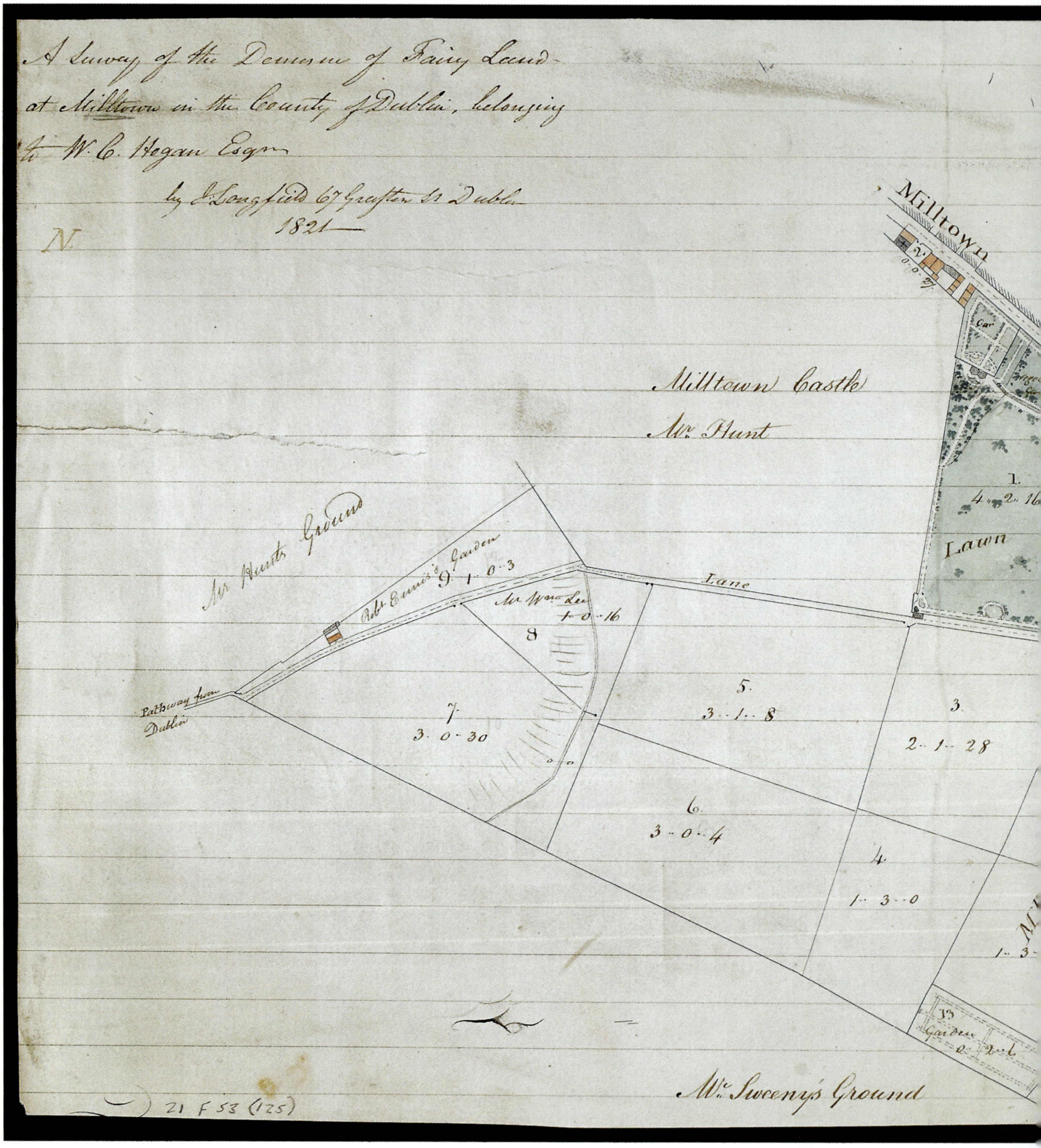

Map 8. *'A survey of the demesne of Fairyland at Milltown in the County of Dublin belonging to W.C. Hogan esq by J Longfield, 1821' (image courtesy of the National Library of Ireland)*

No.	Description	a r p	
1.	House, Offices, Lawn & Gardens &c &c	4·2·16	
2	Chapel holding & Tenements	0·0·27	
3	Meadow	2·1·28	
4	do	1·3·0	
5	do including the Lane	3·1·8	
6	do	3·0·4	
7	do	3·0·30	
8	do let to Mr Wm Lee	1·0·16	
9	House & Garden let to Robt Ennis	1·0·3	20·2·12
10	do & Shrubberies let to Mr Thomas	0·2·16	
11	Meadow do	2·0·30	
12	do do	1·3·22	
13	Garden do	0·2·6	5·0·34
	Total		25·3·6

10 perches to an Inch

Map 9. OSI, Boundary Department, Sketch map of the parish of Donnybrook in the Barony of Rathdown and County of the City of Dublin, 23 August 1830 (courtesy of the National Archives of Ireland)

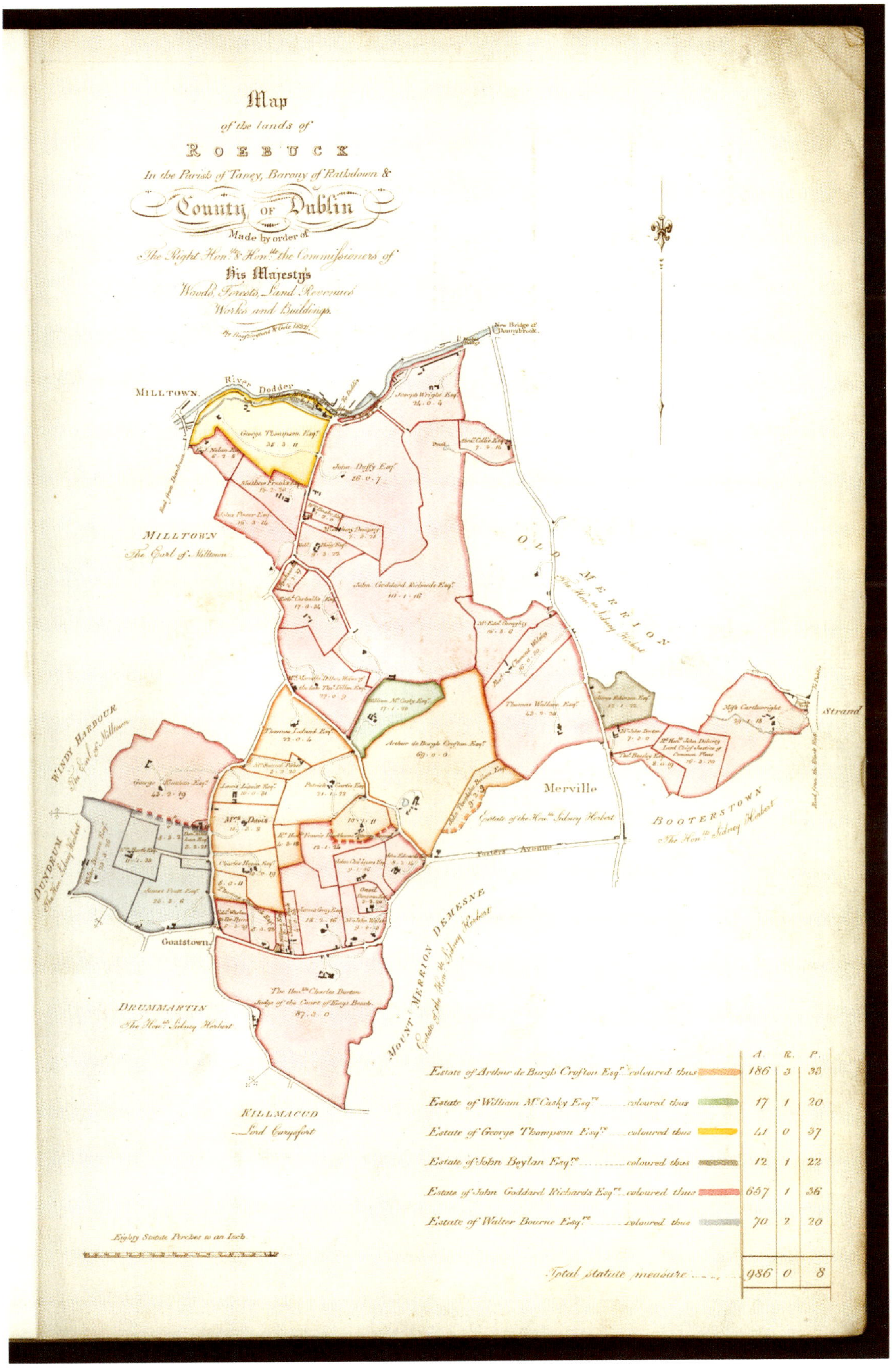

Map 10. 'Map of the lands of Roebuck in the Parish of Taney, Barony of Rathdown and County of Dublin Made by order of The Right Hon and the Hon the Commissioners of His Majesty's Woods Forests Land Revenues Works and Buildings by Brassington and Gale, 1832' (courtesy of the National Archives of Ireland)

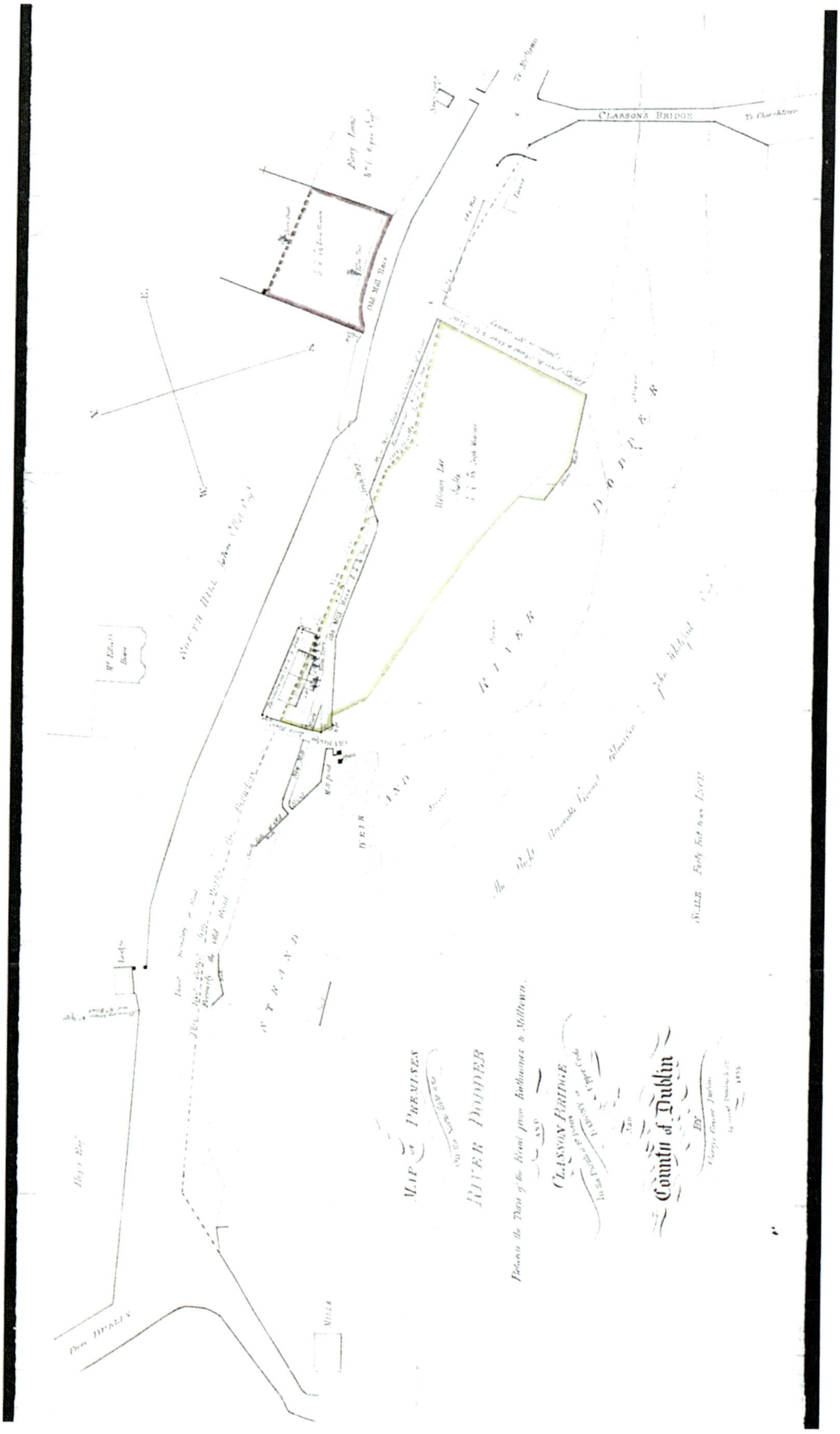

Map 11. 'A map of premises on the north side of the River Dodder between the turn of the road from Rathmines to Milltown and Classon's Bridge, 1833' (courtesy of the National Archives of Ireland)

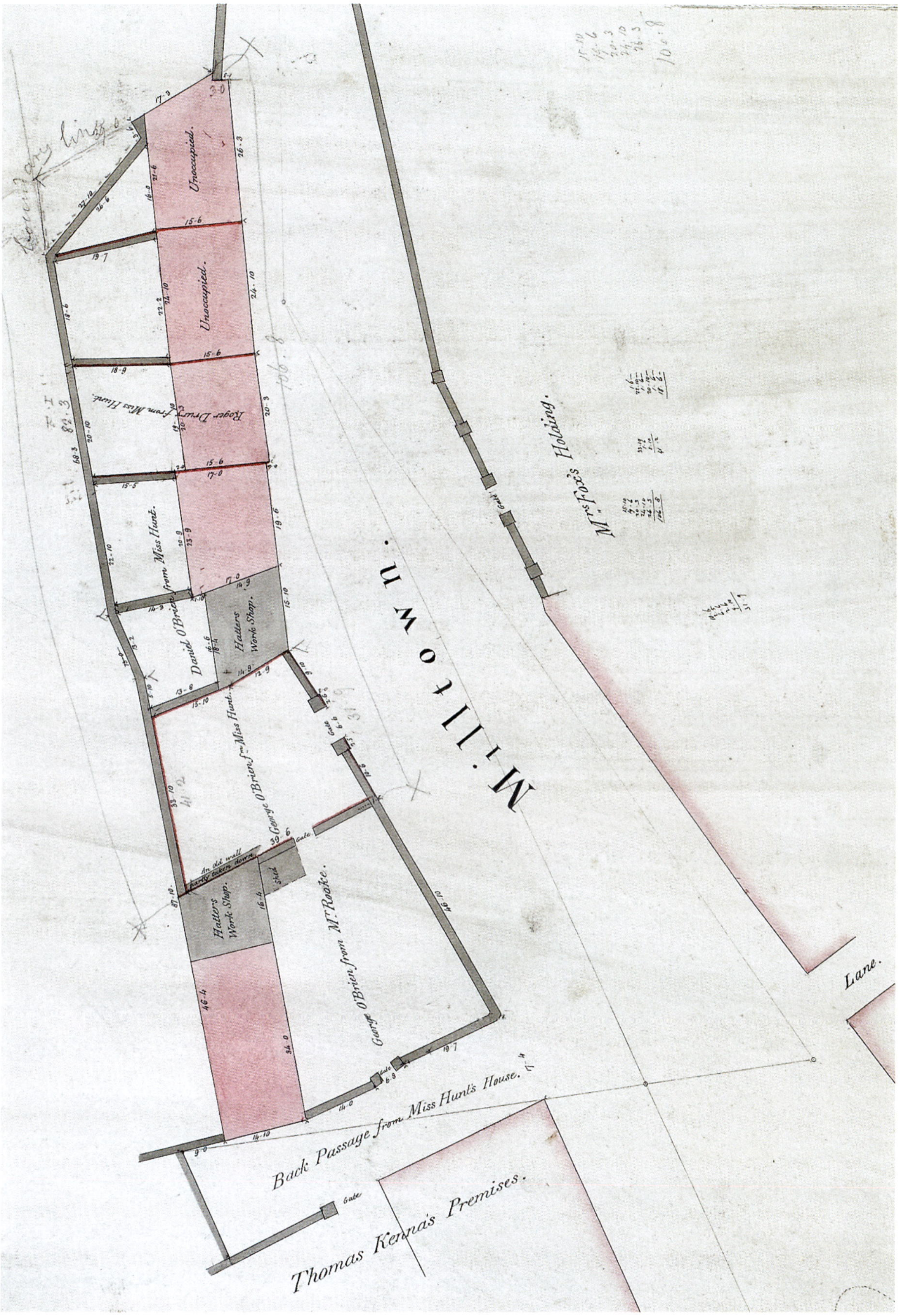

Map 12. 'Map of premises at Milltown for Mr Rooke by William Longfield, 1838' (image courtesy of the National Library of Ireland)

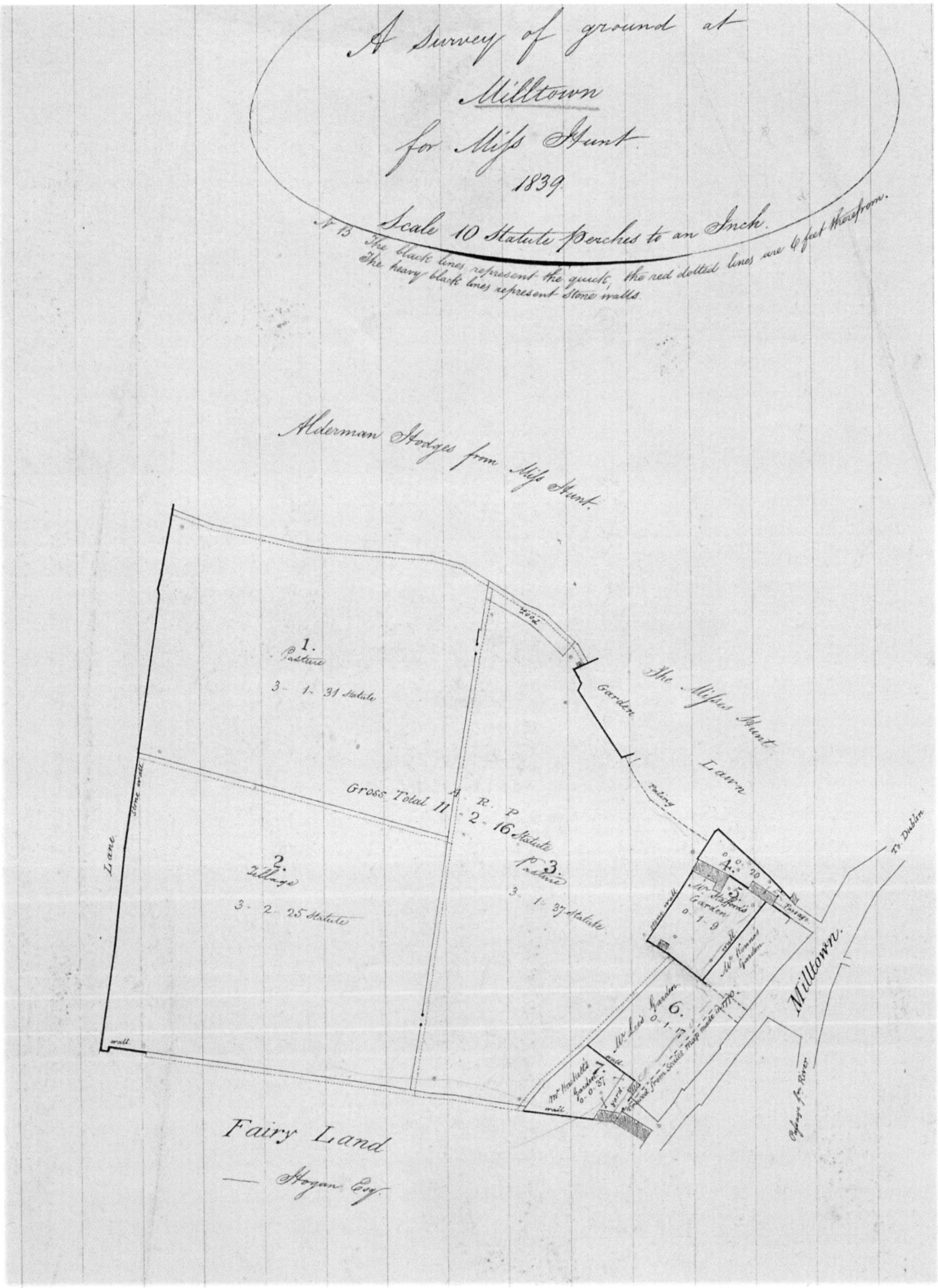

Map 13. 'A survey of ground at Milltown for Miss Hunt, 1839' (image courtesy of the National Library of Ireland)

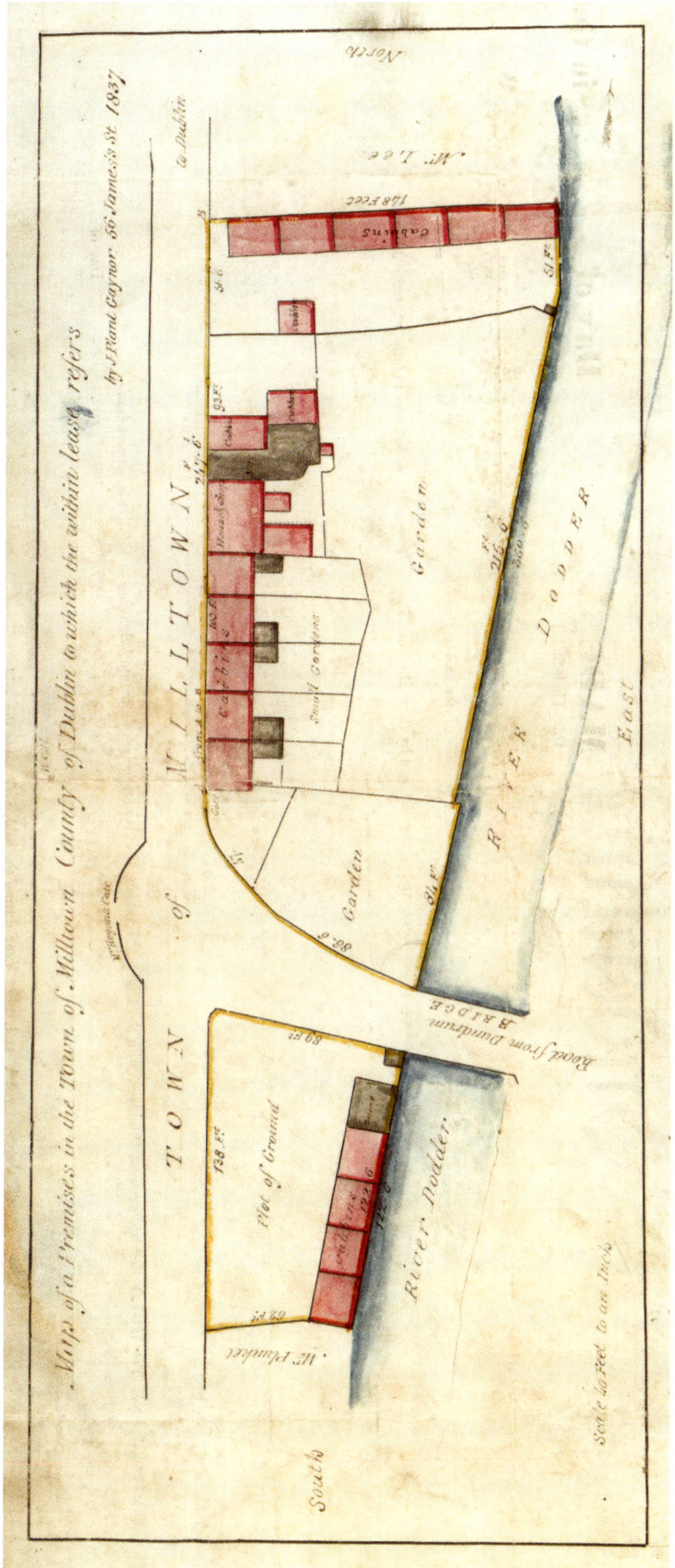

Map 14. Map of Milltown village appended to lease dated 4 July 1837 Robert Dry to Patrick Hackett (courtesy of the National Archives of Ireland)

Map 15. OSI, Co. Dublin, Sheet 22, six inches to one statute mile, surveyed in 1837 and corrected in 1843, showing the boundaries of the Church of Ireland Parish of Milltown and the civil townlands of Milltown and Rathmines South (courtesy of RCB Library, Dublin D6/64)

Woodville
Belmon
Sandford Cottage
Milltown Park
C L O N S K
Sandford Hill
Sandford Grove
68
Mount Prospect
Milltown Cottage
Milltown Colonnade
Green Mount
L T O W N
185
2
13
Elmfield
Milltown Ho.
Milltown Castle
Milltown Hill
Aqueduct
Thompson's Tower
Milltown
R.C. Chapel
Chapel of Ease
Clonskeagh Castle
Fairy Land
Milltown Lodge
Blue Hill
Richmond Hill
Cloth Mill
Casino

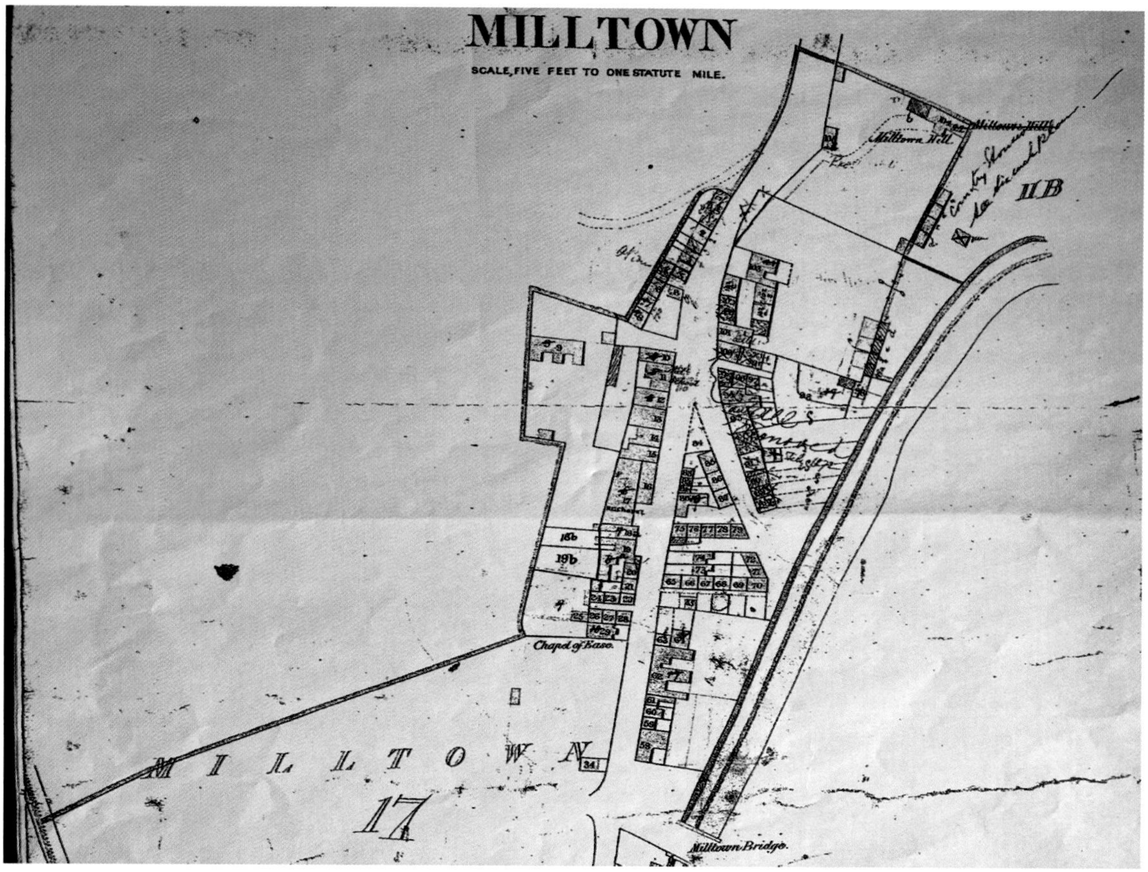

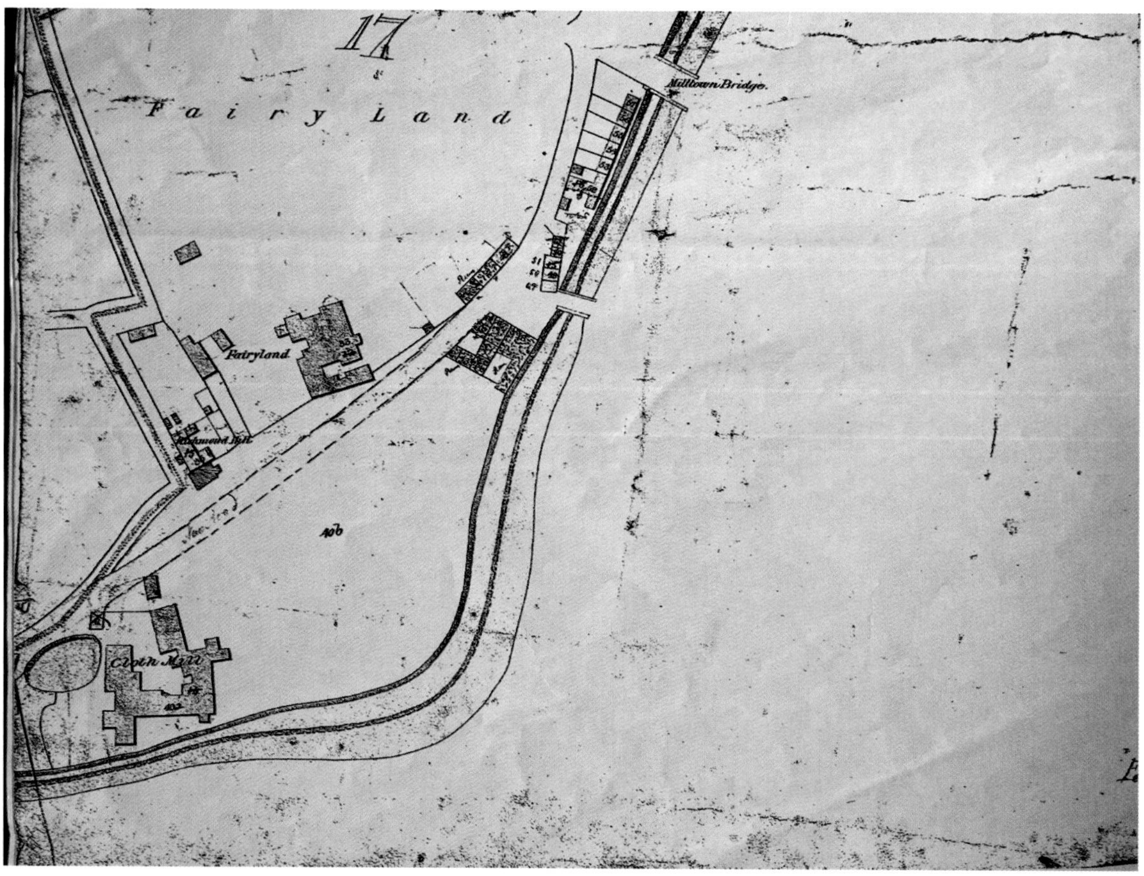

Maps 16a (above) and 16b (below). Town Plan of Milltown village, c. 1850 (courtesy of the Valuation Office)

Map 17. OSI, City of Dublin, Rathmines and Rathgar and Pembroke Townships, Sheet XXII.8 (2nd ed.), five feet to one statute mile, surveyed in 1865 and revised in 1889 (courtesy of UCD Digital Library, with permission of OSI)

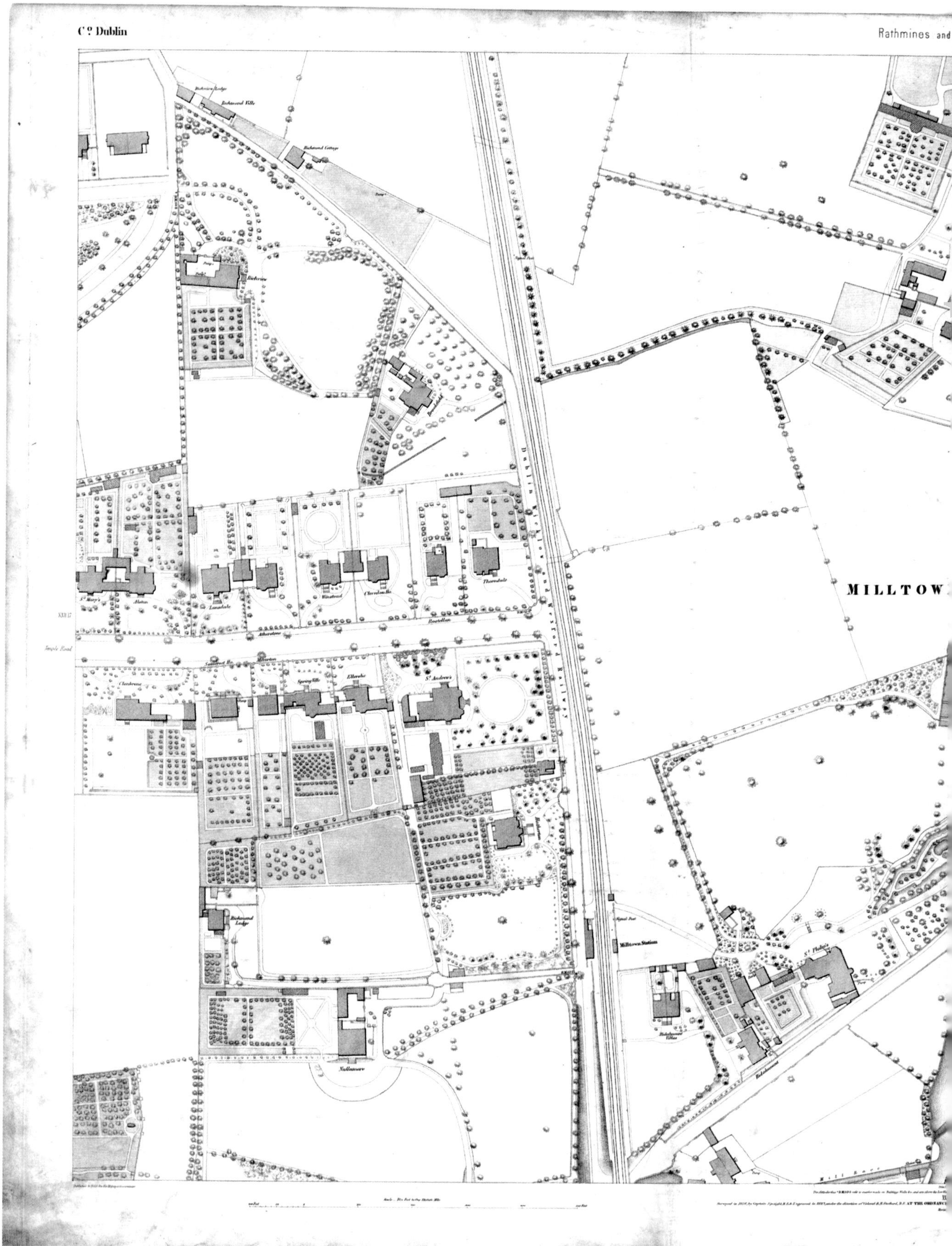

Map 18. OSI, City of Dublin, Rathmines and Rathgar Township, Sheet XXII.18, five feet to one statute mile, surveyed in 1878 and revised in 1882 (courtesy of UCD Digital Library, with permission of OSI)

Milltown Hill
Old Quarry
Mill Pond
River Dodder
Elm Hall
Milltown Ho.
Milltown Lodge
Mill Pond

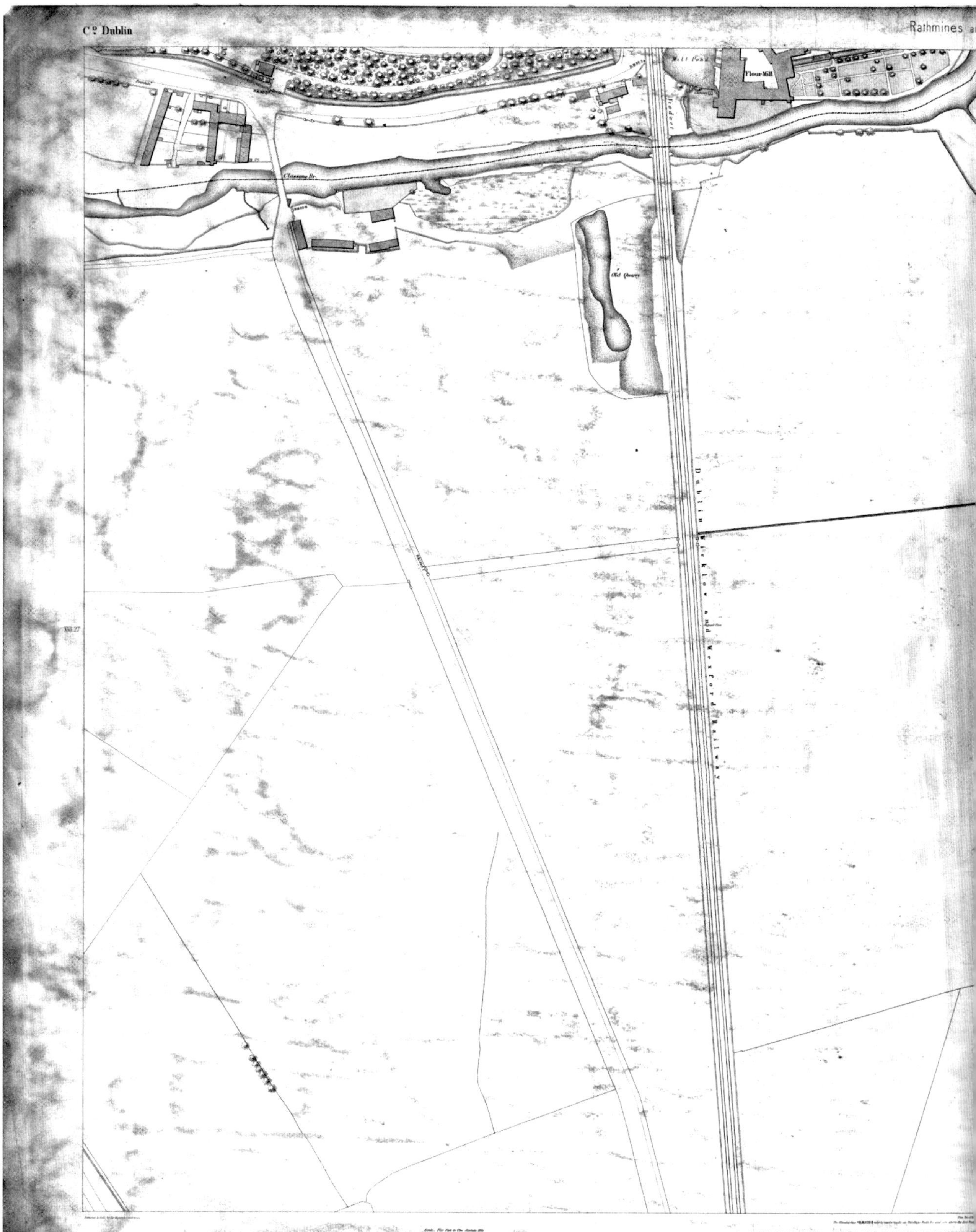

Map 19. OSI, City of Dublin, Rathmines and Rathgar Township, Sheet XXII.28, five feet to one statute mile, surveyed in 1879 and revised in 1882 (courtesy of UCD Digital Library, with permission of OSI)

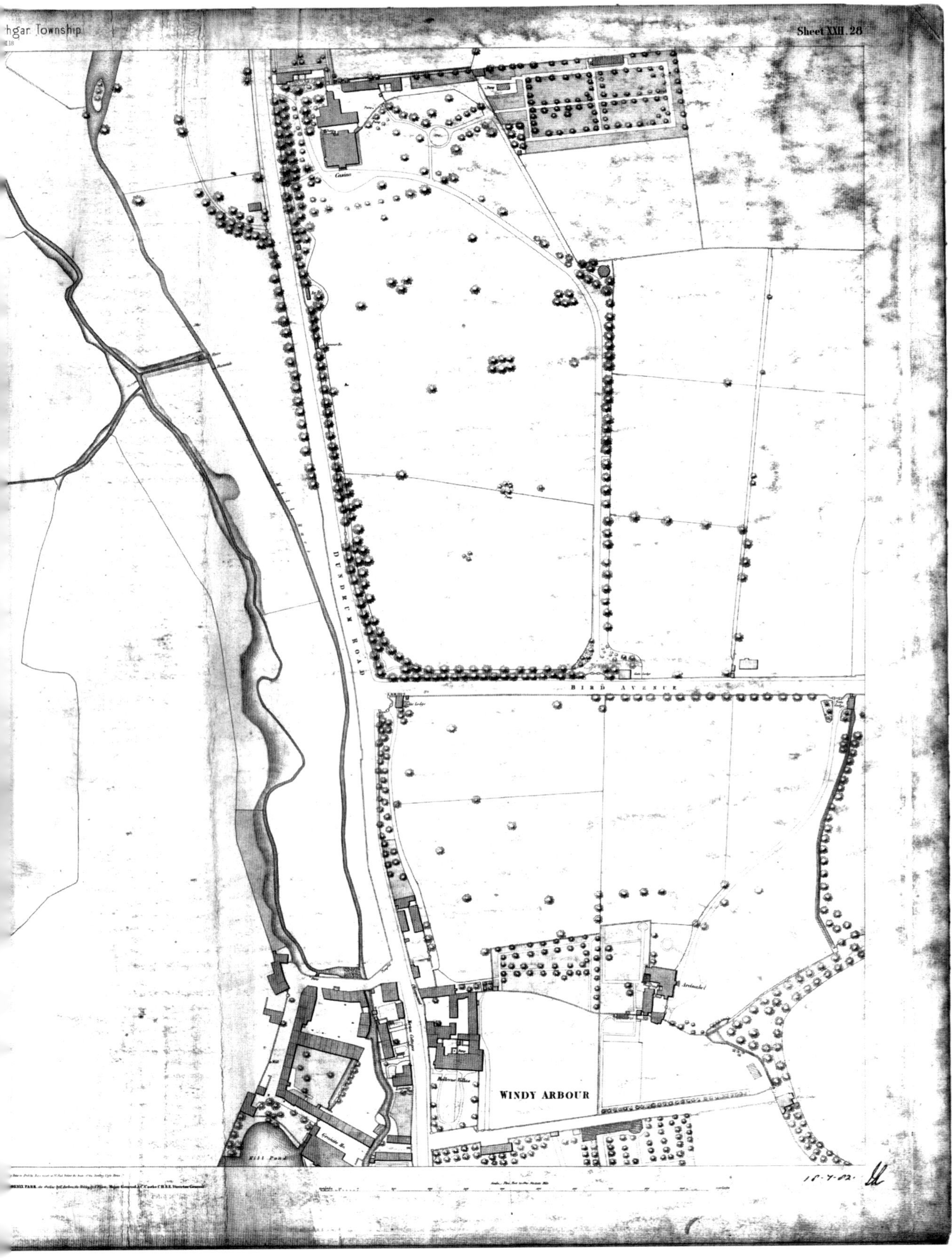
hgar Township
Sheet XXII. 28
DUNDRUM ROAD
BIRD AVENUE
WINDY ARBOUR
18-7-82

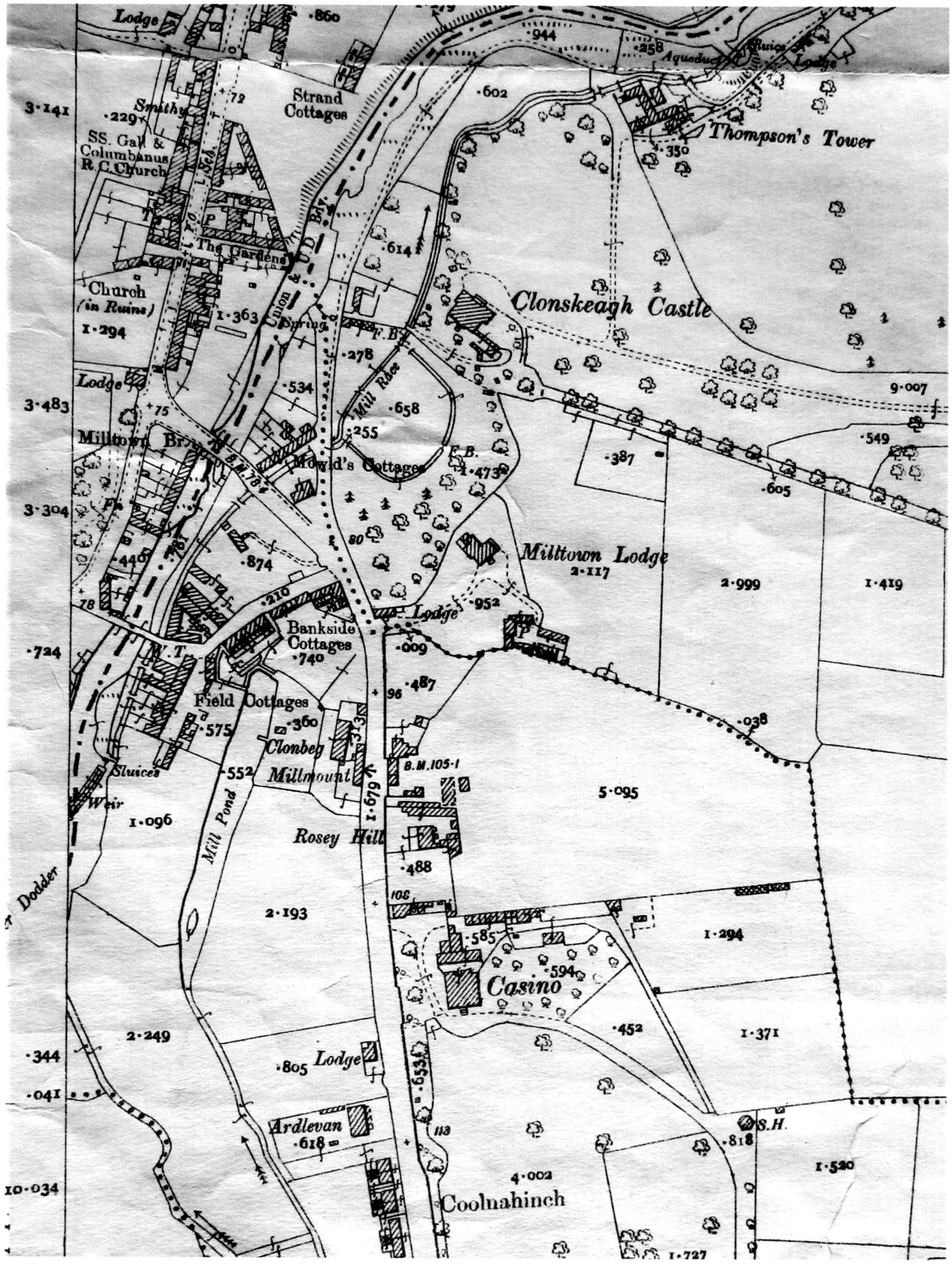

Map 20. OSI, Co. Dublin, Dublin/Rathdown/Uppercross, Sheet XII.4, 25 inches to one statute mile (edition of 1911), surveyed in 1837, revised in 1908 (author's collection)

Map 21. OSI, Co. Dublin, Dublin/Rathdown, Sheet 22. IV, 25 inches to one statute mile (edition of 1938), surveyed in 1837, revised in 1936 (author's collection)

Map 22. Map prepared for the Milltown Village Area Compulsory Purchase Order 1952, 5982A (copyright Dublin City Council)

Acknowledgements

For over 25 years I have harboured an ambition to write a history of Milltown, county Dublin both to satisfy my own curiosity and to publicise this part of south county Dublin whose past has largely remained hidden and ignored in comparison to its neighbouring villages.

The challenge of researching a new historical subject meant that I had to visit and investigate primary source material in numerous private and public institutions, and seek the assistance and professionalism of the people who staff these places. I cannot express my appreciation enough to the dozens of people who helped me over the years and who displayed kindness to me and enthusiasm for my project. Suffice to say, the staff of our national cultural institutions, such as the National Library of Ireland, the National Archives of Ireland and the Irish Architectural Archive, to name but three, are critically important custodians of our national heritage, without whom books such as this could not be written. I would like to thank the staff in the South Dublin Library, the Valuation Office and the Registry of Deeds for their assistance with locating records specific to Milltown. The archivists of University College Dublin, the Society of Jesus and the Representative Church Body were all unfailingly helpful, and responded promptly to my questions and copying requests. It is perhaps invidious to single out any specific individuals in this context, but I would like to make two exceptions. Dr Mary Clarke at Dublin City Archives provided invaluable help with locating material and providing copies of maps and copyright permissions. Mr Tom Kennedy in the legal department of Dublin City Council went way beyond the call of duty with his help in locating housing files and assisting with copying important material related to the development of public housing in Milltown after the Second World War.

Over the years I have had the benefit of learning about life in old Milltown first hand through conversations with many local people who grew up in or who have lived in Milltown for many decades, and who generously shared their memories and photographs. Special thanks are due to Tommy Feerick, Barry Farrell, Benny McGuirk, Mary Long (née Doyle), Bernadette Sheehan (née Purcell) and Anne O'Beirne. I would also like to thank my neighbour Shirley McKenna who very kindly shared her collection of legal records of old Milltown properties, and Sheila Dubel and Taffy Farrington for their hospitality and for permission to photograph their historic homes. The same gratitude is due to Larry Ryan of B&A Research & Insight who kindly facilitated my visit to, and photography of, Milltown House. I would like to pay a special tribute to my late cousin-in-law Fergus Armstrong and late custodian of Clonskeagh Castle, whose interest, support and encouragement I very much appreciated over the years, and who sadly cannot be with us to enjoy the story of our neighbourhood.

I owe a great deal of gratitude to many people who read draft chapters and gave me very useful and insightful comments and feedback. In particular I would like to thank most sincerely Michael Laffan and Colom Lennon for their expertise in reviewing sample chapters, and for their ongoing mentoring and encouragement over morning coffees and lunches. Thank you to Annette Fortune who proofread some chapters and encouraged me with my writing. I also persuaded some of my close friends to read draft chapters and respond with their initial impressions, which were (diplomatically) positive. Thanks guys! I have received helpful advice and encouragement on the daunting process of publishing from various friends and contacts, including Brian Blennerhassett and Anna Farmar. In this regard I am truly grateful that Wordwell Publishing agreed to take on my book, and I must thank Ronan Colgan, and the Wordwell team for their help, courtesy and professionalism during the publication process.

It goes without saying that I sincerely apologise if I have failed to thank people who deserved to be. My only explanation is that so many people have helped me over many years with this project that I have shamefully forgotten some of them as I write this. In a book of this size there will inevitably be some mistakes and factual inaccuracies for which I am solely responsible and for which I apologise.

This book would never have been written had I not taken the decision in 2016 to resign from my employment and devote myself full-time to researching and writing up Milltown. Like the French Revolution, it is perhaps too early to say if leaving a well-paid and pensionable position in one of Ireland's leading law firms was a wise move. Either way, I would like to thank my friends, brothers and sisters, brothers-in-law and especially my mother, for their love and support. I hope this book repays your patience and faith in me.

September 2022

List of Abbreviations

BMH	Bureau of Military History
CARD	Calendar of Ancient Records of Dublin
DMP	Dublin Metropolitan Police
IGPA	Irish Genealogy Projects Archives
IPP	Irish Parliamentary Party
IRA	Irish Republican Army
MAI	Military Archives of Ireland
NAI	National Archives of Ireland
NLI	National Library of Ireland
OS	Ordnance Survey
OSI	Ordnance Survey of Ireland
QRO	Quit Rent Office
RCB	Representative Church Body
RD	Registry of Deeds
RIC	Royal Irish Constabulary
RDC	Rural District Council
RSAI	Royal Society of Antiquaries of Ireland
ISSLT	Irish Sailors' and Soldiers' Land Trust
UCD	University College Dublin
UDC	Urban District Council
VO	Valuation Office
WS	Witness Statement

Introduction

This book sets out the history of Milltown, a southern suburb of Dublin which straddles the River Dodder in the modern postal districts of Dublin 6 and Dublin 14, and which falls under the municipal jurisdiction of Dublin City Council and Dún-Laoghaire Rathdown County Council. Immediately adjacent to Milltown lie the suburbs of Clonskeagh to the east, Windy Arbour to the south, Dartry/Rathmines to the west, and Ranelagh to the north.

Windy Arbour apart, all of the aforementioned Dublin villages have been the subject of detailed local history studies. Surprisingly, given the increasing interest in local history, there has heretofore been no published history of Milltown. The reasons for this are not clear, but the fact that Milltown suffered the loss of its old village and the dispersal of its tightknit local community in the 1950s is probably a major factor. These events possibly reinforced a mistaken long-held belief that very little of Milltown's history could be recovered. More importantly, the pre-eminent local historian of County Dublin, Francis Elrington Ball, devoted less than four pages to Milltown out of his eight-volume work written in the first and second decades of the twentieth century. Furthermore, with the exception of Robert Emmet, who lived sporadically in Milltown at his parents' country villa (Casino) in the 1790s, Milltown has not produced a locally born person or a long-term resident of national renown. Much more recently, Milltown has been dismissed as 'a nondescript County Dublin village', a perception which this book firmly aims to dispel.[1]

GEOGRAPHICAL EXTENT OF MILLTOWN

While researching and writing this book the most frequent query I have been asked was 'Where is Milltown?' As it turns out, this is a very pertinent question and one that is not easy to answer. The place-name 'Milltown' has been in use in this area of south Dublin since the mid-thirteenth century. Over the past 770 years the district called Milltown has expanded and contracted in line with changes in topography, local government, ecclesiastical and civil jurisdictions, suburban development, and the personal designation of inhabitants, who from time to time claimed a closer affinity or identity with a neighbouring district. The ebb and flow of these factors are explained and discussed in detail in the appropriate sections of the relevant chapters. Suffice to say, the task of corralling Milltown between neat, easily distinguished boundaries is impossible, and always has been

1 William Laffan and Kevin Mulligan, *Russborough: A great Irish house, its families and collections* (Blessington, 2014), p. 25.

For the purpose of this book, then, I have designated the core area of Milltown to encompass both sides of Milltown Road from its eastern junction with Sandford/Eglinton/Clonskeagh roads to its junction with Lower Churchtown Road at Classon's Bridge, which marks the western end of the Milltown Road shortly before the roadway seamlessly changes to Dartry Road. For readers unfamiliar with the area there is a YouTube video taken using a dash camera in 2014, which starts on Dartry Road at the bottom of Orwell Park, travelling in a north-easterly direction along the Milltown Road as far as its junction with Sandford Road.[2] The area on both sides of the Dundrum Road from Milltown Bridge to Bird Avenue/Windy Arbour also forms an important part of the historical narrative. From medieval times that district, which was then called Boley Major (from which the townland of Farranboley derives), was included as part of Milltown, long before the emergence of the small village of Windy Arbour in the early nineteenth century and the expansion of suburban Clonskeagh in the twentieth century.

An important difference between the landholdings on the north and south banks of the River Dodder at Milltown was that the land on the north bank was part of the civil barony of Uppercross, whereas the land on the south bank of the Dodder was part of the civil barony of Rathdown. Both of these baronies maintained separate legal, political, ecclesiastical, health and administrative jurisdictions, which became more comprehensive and complex from the mid-nineteenth century onwards. The existence of two different civil and municipal authorities was a major obstacle to providing integrated housing and infrastructure for the inhabitants of Milltown who lived on either side of the River Dodder.

The civil townland boundary sometimes creates inconvenient obstacles for the local historian because in the nineteenth and early twentieth centuries official data were recorded separately for each civil townland. Thus, there can be gaps and differences in the historical data sets that hinder the study of the social and economic relationships of the environs of Milltown as a whole on both sides of the River Dodder. To take one example, the district fronting the east side of the Dundrum Road from Milltown Bridge, today comprising the apartment complexes at Dodderbank and Milltown Grove, Dodder Bridge Road, the Whitebeam and Whitethorn housing estates and Maple Road, all formed part of the Trimleston estate, and was included in the civil townland of Roebuck in the nineteenth century.[3] Conversely, the area comprising the Churchfields housing estate and adjacent properties on both sides of the Dundrum Road at Mount St Marys/Emmet House and St Luke's Crescent and beyond to Windy Arbour formed part of the original Leeson estate in the civil townland of Farranboley.

---

2 https://www.youtube.com/watch?v=oR3DTUgMDDw&list=LLMy85jvA9esueJsFExsFrFw&index=184&t=0s (accessed 21 November 2019) or search YouTube under 'Dash Cam Ireland Milltown Road, Dublin'.

3 The Trimleston estate was originally owned by the Barnewall family, Barons of Trimlestown, whose title was Lord Trimlestown. In modern times their lands in south Dublin are referred to as the Trimleston estate.

STRUCTURE OF THIS BOOK

This book of 16 chapters is predominantly arranged on a thematic basis rather than using a chronological timeline. Each chapter is divided using sub-headings to assist the reader in navigating each section or in browsing specific subjects of interest. In adopting this approach my ambition is that the book appeals to both the generalist and the specialist historians who, on the one hand, may be interested in Milltown for its own sake or, on the other hand, wish to learn how national events and trends impacted on this small village in County Dublin. Specialist historians may hopefully find it useful to consider how Milltown's experience compares with other villages or, more broadly, with the national picture pertaining to their area of expertise.

The first three chapters discuss early human settlement in Milltown and cover successive historical epochs ending at the turn of the eighteenth century. The information presented in these chapters draws on archaeological discoveries in Milltown and its vicinity and a number of medieval records. Livestock rearing, particularly cattle, was a major part of the local economy for centuries up until the 1950s, and this activity features prominently throughout this book. There is a surprising amount of information available about Milltown in the seventeenth century deriving from the 1641 Depositions, the Down Survey of the 1650s and the registers of St Kevin's and St Peter's parishes which record the names of people living in Milltown from the 1670s onwards. At this time a vibrant village began to emerge in Milltown as part of the prosperity and expansion enjoyed by Dublin after the catastrophe of the Cromwellian interregnum. The availability of multiple historical data sources from the eighteenth century onwards permits more varied subject matter to be researched and presented in separate chapters. These deal with the topographical, political, economic, environmental and social history of Milltown over the last 300 years. In this regard, investigations into the development of the Leeson estate in Milltown in the eighteenth century and the origins of industrial activity along the banks of the River Dodder at Milltown have yielded considerable information, which is presented here for the first time. The very high turnover in industrial businesses in Milltown, particularly in the textile industry, highlights the wider economic forces that millowners were subjected to. More specifically, by the middle of the nineteenth century excessive water extraction from the River Dodder was causing economic stress on millowners, and was one of a number of factors which led to the decline and eventual cessation of water-powered milling activity on the Dodder in Milltown by about 1880.

The growth of the state in nineteenth-century Ireland and its intrusion into the daily lives of the local population has left an abundance of official records which, for the most part, are stored in the National Archives of Ireland. These archives facilitate the analysis of the impact of national events and institutions at local level. It is thus possible to devote chapters to the impact on the lives of Milltown's inhabitants of all-island events such as the introduction of national primary education in 1832, the Great Famine of 1845–50 and the Fenian Rising of 1867. These topics are complemented by studies of contemporary events specific to Milltown's experience, such as the arrival of the Sisters of Charity in 1879, the incorporation of Milltown into the Rathmines township in 1880 and the establishment of the Dublin Laundry Company in 1887 (of which only a redbrick chimney remains). These three arrivals ushered in new social and economic conditions to Milltown and they form an important backdrop to its late nineteenth- and early twentieth-century history. Milltown's place in national and local politics during the period 1880–1930 is examined in three chapters, one of which is devoted to the activities of one of Milltown's most influential inhabitants of the late nineteenth century, Thomas Hackett, a landlord, publican and local politician who has left the largest remaining historical legacy of all of Milltown's native-born inhabitants.

The revolutionary decade, 1913–23, is one of the most studied periods of Irish history. The centenaries of many important events that occurred during that decade coupled with the digitisation of the records of the Military Archives of Ireland and the Bureau of Military History have reinvigorated further studies of the impact of this period on local Irish communities. It is natural, then, that this book includes a detailed investigation of the revolutionary period in Milltown from both the nationalist (later republican) and unionist perspectives.

The events which make up the revolutionary decade, 1913–23, overlapped with the outbreak of the First World War (the Great War) and its aftermath. It is regrettable that Irish historiography has until very recently neglected the impact of the Great War from an Irish domestic and social perspective. In the not-so-distant past, research on this subject had been largely the preserve of a small number of military historians, genealogists and individual family members with a curiosity about deceased Irish ancestors and veterans who fought in the Great War. However, historians such as Pádraig Yeates and Richard Grayson are beginning to redress the balance as far as Dublin is concerned.[4] Identifying men from a particular locality who fought in the Great War is challenging due to the sheer number of soldiers involved in the conflict and the uneven distribution of data in the surviving records. It is also fair to say that information is more readily available about the unfortunate soldiers who were killed in the Great War than about those who survived and returned home, many of whom were physically or mentally injured (or both), to face civilian life in a hostile environment. For their sake, I have attempted to describe the impact of the Great War on Milltown and compiled a roll of honour of the inhabitants who fought in the conflict. In both cases the results are far from complete but can hopefully be the foundations for future research on this sensitive period in Irish history.

No history of Milltown would be complete without a comprehensive review of the housing conditions that the inhabitants had to put up with for decades in the twentieth century, despite frequent promises of new housing schemes from the Rathmines Urban District Council and its counterpart on the south bank of the River Dodder, the Rathdown No. 1 Rural District Council, and their successors Dublin Corporation and Dublin County Council. Unlike their

4 Pádraig Yeates, *A City in Wartime: Dublin 1914–18* (Dublin, 2011); Richard S. Grayson, *Dublin's Great Wars: The First World War, the Easter Rising and the Irish Revolution* (Cambridge, 2018).

much-studied city counterparts in Dublin's slum tenements, the villagers living beside the Dodder in Milltown and Classon's Bridge had to live with the threat of inundation by the river. Thankfully, a considerable amount of fascinating material on this important social topic has survived, and it forms the basis of the penultimate chapter of this book. The final chapter contrasts with the chronic housing problems of Milltown, as it describes the two dozen or so villas and large houses that were built in Milltown and its vicinity in the eighteenth and nineteenth centuries.

Finally, I must apologise for the fact that there is no chapter devoted to sport in Milltown, a surprising omission given that for decades in the twentieth century Milltown was synonymous with Shamrock Rovers Football Club, while Milltown Golf Club is one of Dublin's well-known golf clubs. Excellent histories of these prominent clubs have already been published.[5] Regardless, it would be impossible to include a history of all of the sporting activity in Milltown in this local study. To illustrate the point, hockey has been played continuously in Milltown on the grounds of Alexandra College since the 1890s. Instead, I have attempted to record some of the more ephemeral sports clubs and sporting events that took place in Milltown in the late nineteenth and early twentieth century, as part of the overview of social changes that took place during that period.

TOPOGRAPHY, ROADS AND LANDMARKS

Having given an overview of the subject matter contained in this local history book, it is appropriate at this juncture to introduce the most important features in the landscape that appear throughout this work. One of Dublin's best-known rivers, the Dodder, has influenced the history of Milltown for centuries and is a key physical landmark today. From time immemorial a fording point on the river Dodder facilitated the transportation of people and livestock across the river. The fording point was originally sited on the shallow point of the river behind the public carpark opposite the Wilde and Green delicatessen in Milltown. A tributary of the Dodder, the River Slang (also known as the Dundrum River), enters the Dodder on its south bank about 100 metres upstream of the large weir behind the Shanagarry apartment complex. The River Slang rises to the west of the Ballinteer Road and, having been augmented by the Ticknock River, flows through the villages of Dundrum and Windy Arbour on the west side of the Dundrum Road. This small river is largely unknown because over the years it has been extensively culverted and, like the River Poddle, very little of it remains above ground. The River Slang was very important in medieval times because it was less turbulent than the River Dodder, and so its watercourse could be more easily harnessed to power watermills. It is no coincidence that the first mills in Milltown were powered by a millrace taken off the River Slang in the thirteenth century.

5 Paul Doolan and Robert Goggins, *The Hoops: A history of Shamrock Rovers* (Dublin, 1993); Eamonn Beale, Dermot Gilleece, John Redmond, *Milltown Golf Club: An illustrated centenary history 1907–2007* (Dublin, 2007).

Four bridges span the River Dodder at Milltown. The oldest, which still stands and is known as the Packhorse Bridge, was most likely erected in the late sixteenth century. Less than 100 metres to the east of the Packhorse Bridge, the main vehicular bridge (Milltown Bridge) crosses the Dodder onto the Dundrum Road. It was built in about 1817 and widened in the 1970s. Classon's Bridge, which spans the Dodder beside the popular Dropping Well pub, was almost certainly built in the first or second quarter of the eighteenth century, as it is shown on Rocque's Survey of County Dublin which was published in 1760 (Map 4). It too was widened in 1928 after having been damaged during the War of Independence. Milltown's most imposing landmark, the limestone viaduct which today carries the track for the Luas trams, was built in 1850 when the railway line from Harcourt Street to Bray was being laid down. The viaduct is known locally as the Nine Arches bridge.

The Milltown Road is one of Dublin's oldest thoroughfares. Its origins are unknown but it undoubtedly formed part of the pre-Norman road network that linked the Norse settlement in Dublin with its agricultural hinterland and the important ecclesiastical settlement at Taney. Up until the late eighteenth century the entire route from Camden Street to Milltown was called the Milltown Road. It was only with the gradual building of houses along the road out of the city's suburbs coupled with the naming of new thoroughfares in the period 1780–1830, including Charlemont Street, Ranelagh Road and Sandford Road, that Milltown Road assumed its current geographical limits at its northern end at Sandford Road, a name which dates from the 1820s.

Up until the early eighteenth century virtually all of the traffic leaving the city using the Milltown Road would have been travelling to south Dublin or north Wicklow, crossing by the Dodder ford at Milltown or the Packhorse Bridge, and making its way along the Dundrum Road. At some unknown date in the early to mid-eighteenth century Milltown Road was extended westwards beyond the Packhorse Bridge towards Rathmines and Rathgar. The road now called the Lower Churchtown Road was almost certainly built in the first or second quarter of the eighteenth century, as evidenced by old deeds relating to the Leeson estate. It is also depicted on Rocque's map of 1760. Over the course of the nineteenth century that part of the Milltown Road and the district westward of Classon's Bridge on the north bank of the River Dodder became known as Dartry Road and Upper Rathmines respectively, which are relatively new developments in historical terms.

In addition to Milltown Road, a narrow pedestrian lane, also commencing at the top of Camden Street and called the Milltown Path, headed in a south-easterly direction towards Milltown, emerging a few metres to the west of the Packhorse Bridge. Like the Milltown Road, over the course of the nineteenth century the Milltown Path was built up, and parts of it were named Mount Pleasant Avenue, Belgrave Square East and Palmerston Road. After the arrival of the railway in 1850, the portion of the Milltown

Path closest to Milltown village was realigned to the west of the railway line and renamed Richmond Avenue South. The railway, informally named by Dubliners 'the Harcourt Street line', closed down in 1958.

The modern Clonskeagh Road on the city side or north bank of the River Dodder was laid out in the 1780s; however, a small village and a mill on the north bank of the Dodder had existed in Clonskeagh for hundreds of years previously. Before the new Clonskeagh Road was laid out, a narrow laneway, called the Clonskeagh Lane, branched off the Milltown Road and led down a steep embankment (behind where Ramleh Close is now) to a fording point in the River Dodder at Clonskeagh. As early as 1603 a bridge spanned the Dodder in Clonskeagh, which was probably contemporaneous with the Packhorse Bridge in Milltown. Of more importance is the fact that the Clonskeagh Lane formed part of the ancient boundary between the civil jurisdiction of Dublin city and the extensive landholding of the archbishops of Dublin, who owned and controlled Milltown in the medieval era, when it was part of a large farming district called the manor of St Sepulchre. From medieval times up until the early nineteenth century Clonskeagh Lane was included in the route of the annual (later triennial) perambulation of Dublin city's boundaries, a custom called 'riding the franchises'. Clonskeagh Lane also served as a boundary for barony, municipal, parish and townland jurisdictional purposes. A residual part of this ancient boundary survives today in Prospect Lane, opposite the entrance to the Jesuits' headquarters in Milltown Park.

Finally, Eglinton Road was constructed in 1855.[6] Until then, Milltown was connected to Donnybrook by Belmont Avenue, which was originally called Coldblow Lane, and which can be dated as far back as 1708 although it is probably considerably older.[7]

Many illustrations of maps are employed in this book. In addition, readers are encouraged to visit the Ordnance Survey of Ireland's (OSI's) website, where it is possible to view the OSI's archive of digitised ordnance survey (OS) maps of Milltown over a 100-year period from about 1840 to 1936.[8] If this approach is adopted readers will be able to view and magnify the roads and rivers mentioned in the text. More usefully, it will also allow the reader to locate historical buildings and industrial infrastructure – most of which no longer exists – and compare it with what stands on the ground now.

DIRECTIONS AND COMPASS POINTS

Directions given throughout this book use the four cardinal points of the compass in an attempt to make it easier for the reader, especially one more familiar with the area, to visualise the location under discussion. Thus,

6 *Freeman's Journal*, 4 May 1855, p. 4.

7 Beaver H. Blacker, *Brief sketches of the parishes of Donnybrook and Booterstown* (Dublin, 1874), p. 125.

8 http://geohive.maps.arcgis.com/apps/webappviewer/index.html?id=9def898f708b47f19a8d8b7088a100c4 (accessed 25 November 2019).

references to the north side of Milltown Road or to the north bank of the River Dodder refer to those parts which lie on the Dublin city side of the road or the river respectively. Conversely, references to the south side of Milltown Road refer to the area lying between it and the River Dodder and references to the south bank of the River Dodder encompass the district lying in the Dún Laoghaire-Rathdown County Council (formerly Dublin County Council and before that the Rathdown No. 1 RDC). Generally speaking, Milltown Road and the River Dodder are aligned in an east-west direction from Clonskeagh to Dartry and references in this context to those compass points should be construed accordingly. In the same vein, as one travels out of Milltown on the Dundrum Road the area to the left is on the east side of the road while the area on the right is on the west side of the road. That said, neither the River Dodder nor the roads in Milltown follow straight lines and so they do not neatly align to the four cardinal points of the compass. As a result, a small number of old deeds quoted in the text use a different set of compass points in describing eighteenth- or nineteenth-century landholdings. For example, a deed may refer to the city side of the Milltown Road as being on the west side of Milltown Road. Any confusion caused is unavoidable.

A BRIEF NOTE ON SOURCE MATERIAL

The development of the Internet and the resulting digitisation of Irish historical records over the last 25 years has revolutionised the study of history and opened up research opportunities that would have been impossible a generation ago. This book relies heavily on these developments. In particular, the availability online of newspapers dating back to the mid-eighteenth century permits highly detailed and forensic investigations into all aspects of Irish history. The genealogical website of the National Archives of Ireland provides free access to many important records, including the 1901 and 1911 censuses and a register of wills since 1858.[9] Websites designed for genealogical research such as www.irishgenealogy.ie provide free access to civil and Church records of births, baptisms, marriages and burials.[10] Combining this data with the Griffith's Valuation and the decennial census returns it is possible to build up a profile of the individuals and families who lived in the old village of Milltown at the turn of the twentieth century. The website www.Findmypast.ie provides online access and weblinks to a very comprehensive collection of Irish historical records deposited in archives throughout Ireland and the United Kingdom.[11] This website has been essential for much of my research; however, access to its records is by subscription only.

On the other hand, researching land ownership and real estate transactions is much more challenging because the historical data have

9 https://genealogy.nationalarchives.ie/ (accessed 27 November 2019).

10 https://www.irishgenealogy.ie/en/ (accessed 27 November 2019).

11 https://www.findmypast.ie/ (accessed 27 November 2019).

not been digitised. In most cases, the historian must attend the Registry of Deeds or the Valuation Office in Dublin, and undertake considerable time (and physical effort in the Registry of Deeds) to uncover the information being sought, assuming it is available. Despite these difficulties, hugely valuable historical data are contained in the aforementioned offices and these have been used extensively in the chapters discussing the origins of the Leeson estate in Milltown, the mills on the River Dodder and the villa residences of the eighteenth and nineteenth centuries.

THE PROBLEM OF PRICE INFLATION

Prices and different units of currency are referred to extensively throughout this book. This creates an insoluble problem as regards converting historical price data to their twenty-first-century equivalents. This is because the currency and monetary denominations used in Ireland over the last 200 years have been restructured on several occasions and no accurate price inflation calculator exists to convert very old prices and units of currency to present day values in euro. The Central Statistics Office website has an inflation calculator that covers the period January 1922 to date but it only works in euro. The calculator does, however, provide the rate of inflation in the consumer price index over the timeline used in the calculation to convert the old price to the current price in euro. Given these difficulties, the (unsatisfactory) approach is to provide a few examples of historical rates of pay so that these can be compared with prices quoted in the text in order to try and give some meaning and context to the contemporary figure quoted. In the 1670s the daily wage for an agricultural labourer was four pence (4*d.*), which rate had increased to about 6½*d.* by the 1770s. On the eve of the Great Famine in 1845, daily wages ranging from 6*d.* to 8*d.* a day were common for agricultural labourers, and by the 1890s their wages were of the order of one shilling (1*s.*) and 8*d.* a day. The daily wages for builders' labourers in mid-eighteenth-century Dublin were 1*s.*[12] In 1796 daily wages of workmen in Dublin Corporation's store yard were increased from 13*d.* to 16*d.*[13] A century later, the maximum weekly wages for workmen in the Rathmines township were 15*s.*, an amount which they struggled to get by on.[14]

Slightly higher up the social scale, at the turn of the nineteenth century, the lowest-paid clerks in the Irish civil service were paid about £50 per annum, while porters and messengers received about £25 to £30 per annum. An army captain was paid £172 a year and a Church of Ireland curate in the diocese of Dublin was usually paid about £75 a year.[15] Nonetheless, these rates varied and the distinctions between the salary

12 L.M. Cullen, 'Economic development, 1691–1750' in T.W. Moody and W.E. Vaughan (eds), *A new history of Ireland, iv: Eighteenth century Ireland 1691–1800* (Oxford, 1986), pp. 186–7.

13 Calendar of ancient records of Dublin (19 vols, Dublin, 1889–1944), xiv, pp. 442–3 (hereafter CARD).

14 *Irish Independent*, 26 July 1897, p. 6.

15 R.B. McDowell, *The Irish Administration 1801–1914* (London, 1964), pp. 11–12.

levels sometimes became blurred. For example, in 1818 the annual salary of a messenger in the Chancellor of the Exchequer's Office was £80 with gratuities.[16] Eighty years later, in 1899 an office clerk living in Rathmines had an annual income of £100 out of which he paid £30 a year to rent a small terraced house.[17]

SUMMARY

As a long-term resident of Milltown, the omission in the local history of south Dublin's villages provided me with a unique opportunity and a challenge. This publication includes the fruits of my research. It is also the first large-scale stand-alone book on the history of Milltown and as such, it has been a great privilege to undertake this work. The amount of information contained in the following pages may appear surprising to some or tedious to others. Unlike Péig Sayers, this book does not have to be read in its entirety from cover to cover! Readers are encouraged to pick at their leisure a topic or a chapter that appeals to them, or one which arouses the most curiosity. Above all else I hope you enjoy reading this book. ■

---

16 NAI, CSO/RP/1818/831.

17 *Rathmines News*, 4 March 1899, p. 4.

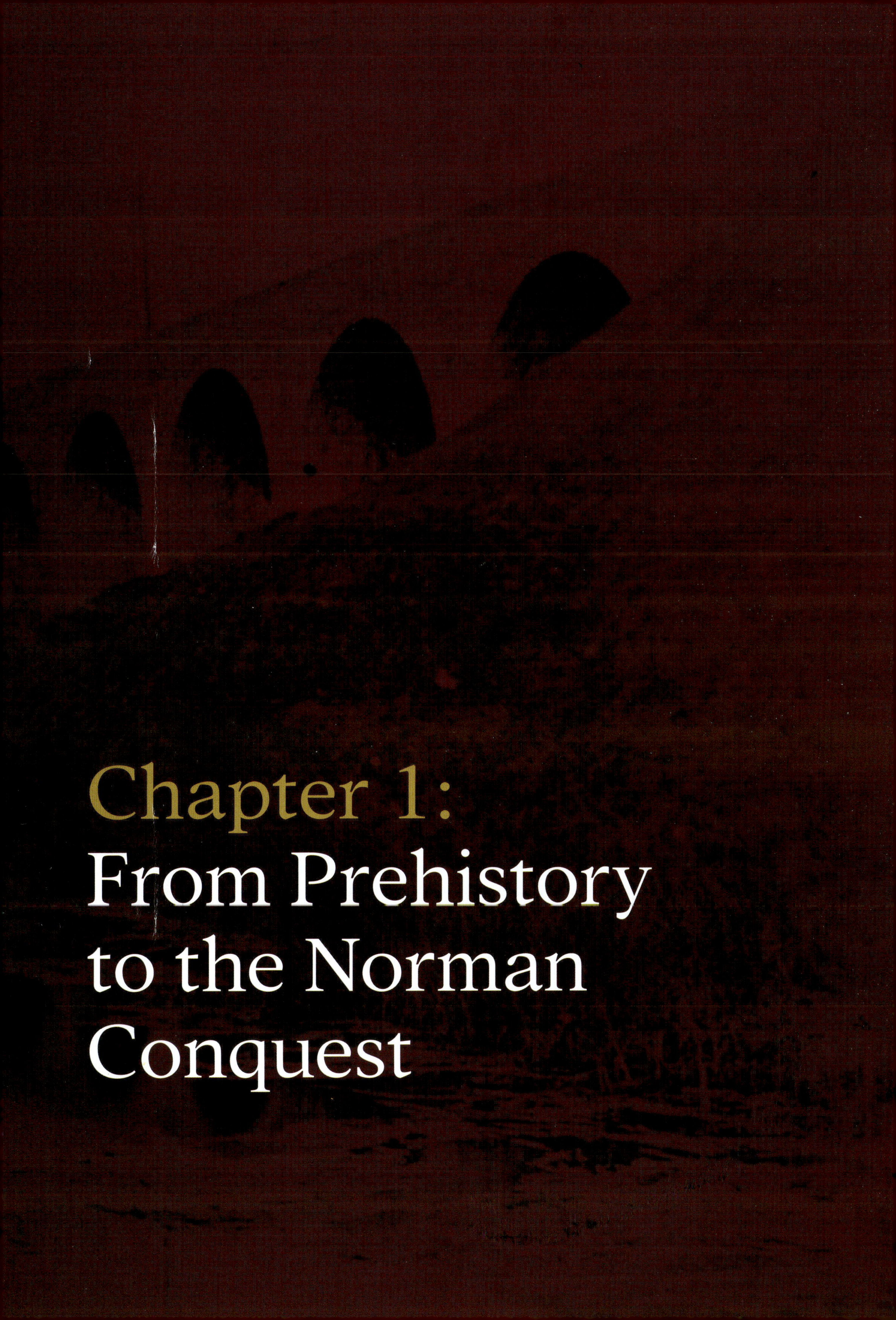

Chapter 1: From Prehistory to the Norman Conquest

Chapter 1: From Prehistory to the Norman Conquest

INTRODUCTION

This chapter investigates evidence for the earliest human settlement in Milltown and its vicinity, progressing through the Celtic, Christian and Viking eras, and ending with the arrival of the Normans in Ireland in the third quarter of the twelfth century. An important part of this story is how the pre-Norman developments contributed to Milltown becoming an important long-term fording point of the River Dodder in the context of the wider pastoral economy which was dominated by cattle farming.

THE PREHISTORIC ERA

The first humans arrived in the south-east of County Dublin at the end of the Mesolithic (middle stone age) period, about 5,000–3,300 BC. These people would have been attracted by the variety of flora and fauna available on the river estuaries and delta sites such as the Rivers Liffey and Dodder. The archaeological record of Mesolithic activity in the Dublin bay area is very scant due to the fact that this coastal area has been farmed and built up over subsequent millennia. Unearthing finds from this period in Dublin is made even more difficult by the fact that the main tool of early Mesolithic societies is the microlith, a very small pointed stone/flint scraping tool. Small numbers of these implements have been found at Dalkey Island, Dún Laoghaire, Rathfarnham and Loughlinstown, which provide evidence of small-scale settlement along the rivers and streams of south Dublin.[1] In recent years ancient fish traps dating to the Mesolithic era have been found during building works on the River Liffey at Spencer Dock, these finds reinforcing the importance of riverside/estuarine locations to our earliest ancestors.[2]

---

1 Geraldine Stout and Matthew Stout, 'Patterns in the Past: County Dublin 5,000 BC to 1,000 AD' in F.H.A. Allen and Kevin Whelan (eds), *Dublin City and County: From Prehistory to Present* (Dublin, 1992), p. 6; Christiaan Corlett, *Antiquities of old Rathdown* (Bray, 1999), pp. 8–11.

2 Moriarty, C. 2011, 'Dublin the Prehistoric City' in *Irish Archaeology.ie* http://irisharchaeology.ie/2011/05dublin-the-prehistoric-city/ (accessed 31 January 2017).

One of the indicators of early human coastal settlement is the shell midden. A shell midden was built up by discarded shellfish consumed by hunter gatherers who settled in transitory fashion close to the seashore. Shell middens have been excavated in Dalkey Island and at Sutton, in north Dublin.[3] In the early nineteenth century George Thompson, the owner of Clonskeagh Castle, made the following discovery, as reported in Lewis's *Topographical Dictionary of Ireland:*

> *Clonskeagh Castle, the handsome residence of G. Thompson, Esq., affords fine views of the city and bay of Dublin, with the adjacent mountains; it was built by H. Jackson, who acted a prominent part in the disturbances of 1798. On digging in front of the mansion, a few years since, a layer of muscle shells, about three feet thick, and imbedded in clay, was found about eight feet below the surface.*[4]

The location of the find is on the south bank of the River Dodder, behind the boundary wall of Clonskeagh Castle at the Milltown end, and close to the Dundrum Road. Although the report refers to the front of the mansion, the exact find spot is impossible to determine because the entrance front of Clonskeagh Castle changed in the nineteenth century.[5] To compound matters, any remaining archaeology would have been disturbed either when the Whitebeam/Whitethorn housing estate was laid out in the 1930s or when the apartment developments at Milltown Grove and Dodderbank were built in the late twentieth and early twenty-first centuries.

It is impossible to say what the significance and age of the shell deposits were, but their depth – 8 feet below ground level – points to considerable antiquity. It is tempting to suggest, however tentatively, that the nineteenth-century discovery at Clonskeagh Castle was of a prehistoric shell midden. There is no archaeological evidence to support this theory, unfortunately. Realistically, the shell deposit may be of much more recent historical origin, for example, human refuse related to quarrying activity on the banks of the River Dodder.

NEOLITHIC AND BRONZE AGES

We are on firmer ground when it comes to Neolithic (new stone age) settlement in the Milltown area, an era characterised by the permanent settlement of farmers with domesticated animals, and employing pottery and sophisticated stone tools. In the late 1960s the gardener of 68 Eglinton Road found a very fine polished stone adze (axe head) while landscaping the rear garden (Pl.1).[6] Although this find's location is nearer to Donnybrook than Milltown, the find spot is close to the River Dodder and is sufficiently proximate to Milltown to merit inclusion here. The finder, John Neville, donated his find to the National Museum of Ireland which confirmed to him that 'the adze head is probably of Neolithic date *c.* 3500–200 BC'.[7] Subsequent research carried out by the museum has opined that the Eglinton Road axe is of Scandinavian origin (i.e. a *Linearbandkeramik* stone axe) dating

3 Michael J. O'Kelly, *Early Ireland: An Introduction to Irish Prehistory* (Cambridge, 1989), p. 28; Stout, 'Patterns in the Past', pp. 5–7; Corlett, *Antiquities of old Rathdown*, p. 8.

4 Samuel Lewis, *Topographical Dictionary of Ireland* (2 vols, Dublin, 1837), i, p. 376 (entry for Clonskeagh).

5 Alistair Rowan, *Clonskeagh Castle, Dublin: An architectural history and assessment of the house* (undated research paper privately commissioned by the owners of Clonskeagh Castle in the early twenty-first century), p. 11.

6 Personal communication with the author from the late John Neville of 8 Beatty's Avenue, Ballsbridge, Dublin 4; National Museum of Ireland, file no. 1A/27/1998, find registration number 2009: 255.

7 Letter in author's possession dated 3 July 1998 from Mary Cahill, Assistant Keeper Irish Antiquities Division of the National Museum of Ireland, to John Neville.

Plate 1. Neolithic stone axe found at 68 Eglinton Road, Donnybrook, Dublin 6 (image reproduced with the kind permission of the National Museum of Ireland)

to the early Neolithic period (4500–3600 BC).[8] The museum's file records that Neville had told archaeologist Nessa O'Connor that when he was landscaping the garden there had been a number of small boulders and a flagstone/capstone which may subsequently have been incorporated as an ornamental feature. Whatever the adze's origins, it is undoubtedly a fine specimen that belonged to a high-status individual, and raises the intriguing possibility that a prosperous Neolithic community with foreign trade links settled on the banks of the River Dodder in the Clonskeagh/Donnybrook area in prehistoric times. Stone axes have also been found in Dundrum, Monkstown and Dún Laoghaire, reinforcing such a proposition.[9]

During the Bronze Age metal-workers in Ireland became highly skilled in metal working in gold and bronze. By about 700 BC Irish gold-smiths were producing some of the most spectacular and accomplished pieces of work.[10] The evidence of Bronze Age settlement in Milltown is more comprehensive than that pertaining to earlier epochs but that evidence derives from nineteenth- and early twentieth-century second-hand reports which are impossible to verify now. A bronze palstave (axe), apparently found in Milltown in the nineteenth century, is illustrated in an early academic text book of Bronze Age implements.[11] Unfortunately, it has not proved possible to find out how or where the item was uncovered or, more importantly, where the palstave is currently deposited notwithstanding enquiries made by the author in the National Museum. In the context of the other Irish palstaves, Evans opined that:

8 National Museum of Ireland, file no. 1A/27/1998, find registration number 2009: 255.

9 Corlett, *Antiquities of Rathdown*, p. 15.

10 Corlett, *Antiquities of Rathdown*, pp. 28–9.

11 John Evans, *The ancient bronze implements, weapons, and ornaments of Great Britain and Ireland* (London, 1881), p. 104.

> *The most remarkable feature of the Milltown example is a projecting, slightly curved spike or neb placed near the top of the blade rather above the position usually occupied by the loop. At first sight it looks like an imperfect loop, but, on examination, it is evident that the casting is perfect; and, on consideration, it seems clear that this projection would serve quite as well as a loop for receiving a cord to hold the blade back upon its haft, while for the actual tying it would be more convenient, as the cord would have merely to be passed over a hook, and not to be threaded through a loop.*[12]

Evans's discussion, interesting as it is, is completely overshadowed by a later unsubstantiated report of a very significant Bronze Age discovery at Milltown Castle in the nineteenth century. The second find is mentioned in a general history of the River Dodder which appeared in serialised form in the local newspaper, the *Rathmines News and Dublin Lantern*, in the winter of 1901–2.[13] The author of the Dodder history was a poet and local historian called John Christopher FitzAchary.[14] The following passage extracted from FitzAchary's history of the Dodder at Milltown is, if accurate, truly remarkable:

> *Many weapons of richly ornamented bronze were found in the time of the former owner [of Milltown Castle], and more recently a discovery was made which, if turned to account, might have proved advantageous to somebody. While they were digging a deep sewer to drain off the surplus waters of the Dodder, one of the workmen came upon a quantity of what were apparently rusty old rings. He showed them to the proprietress, but in her estimation they seemed so utterly worthless that she desired them to be thrown back into the sewer again. In a day or two afterwards she went down to where the workmen were excavating the sewer, when in her presence another ring, and of a similar design, was dug up and on being handed to her, she desired the labourer to hit it with his pickaxe. The blow broke the ring, and the metal of which it was composed appearing of that rich and almost copper coloured yellow, which is to be found now only in old brooches and miniature frame mountings of the end of the eighteenth or early part of the nineteenth century, she took it into Dublin, and showed it to her jeweller, who pronounced it to be pure gold. An immediate search was then made for the rings that, at her suggestion, had been thrown away – some sixty or seventy – but not a trace of them was ever afterwards found.*[15]

FitzAchary's historical information – at least as far as Clonskeagh and Milltown are concerned – is in the author's experience accurate, and therefore creditable. FitzAchary's reference to the proprietress of Milltown Castle is significant because contemporary directories and maps confirm that a Miss Charlotte Hunt lived in Milltown Castle in the mid-nineteenth century.[16] Even if we discount or downgrade the likelihood of the rings being made of precious metal – their tarnished appearance and sheer number would seem to militate against them being made of gold – FitzAchary's report is important.[17] If we accept that the rings were of ancient origin and made

12 Evans, *The ancient bronze implements*, pp. 103–4.

13 John Christopher FitzAchary, 'The Dodder; its history, traditions, and associations', *Rathmines News and Dublin Lantern*, November 1901–January 1902 (hereafter cited as the *Rathmines News*).

14 Appreciation of FitzAchary in the *Rathmines News*, 25 January 1902.

15 *Rathmines News*, 14 December 1901, p. 3.

16 Lewis, *Topographical Dictionary of Ireland*, ii, p. 370 (entry for Milltown); see also Map 13.

17 The importance was acknowledged in the *Dublin City Development Plan 1991* (Dublin Corporation, 1991), List 7/Table 14.3.7, 'Documented Archaeological Sites Outside the Zone of Archaeological Interest', p. 280, where Milltown is recorded as a find spot for archaeological objects.

of bronze, it raises the possibility that they were deliberately deposited in the River Dodder as a votive offering.

At the start of his account FitzAchary mentions that 'many weapons of richly ornamented bronze' were found at Milltown Castle during Ms Hunt's occupancy. It is thus possible that the palstave find discussed by Evans in 1881 was also uncovered in the vicinity of Milltown Castle.

At this point, it is appropriate to refer briefly to other historical discoveries of Bronze Age artefacts that were located within a couple of miles of Milltown. Fragments of gold ribbon torques and a gold spindle ring were unearthed in Donnybrook in the nineteenth century.[18] In nearby Rathfarnham, three Bronze-Age socketed axes were uncovered.[19] More significantly bearing in mind FitzAchary's report of the Milltown discovery, is the fact that a gold hair ornament was found in the mid-nineteenth century by a labourer screening gravel extracted from the River Dodder at Rathfarnham. On a separate occasion only a few years apart from the first find, a small gold ribbed ring was unearthed in Rathfarnham.[20] Taken together, the discovery and survival of the Bronze Age objects in Donnybrook and Rathfarnham add to the likelihood that similar antiquities were found in Milltown in the nineteenth century, as reported by Evans and FitzAchary, notwithstanding their subsequent loss.

There is an unusual set of circumstances which probably aided the casual discoveries and reporting of antiquities in Milltown, Donnybrook and Rathfarnham in the nineteenth century. Three important late eighteenth- and early nineteenth-century antiquarians and Irish scholars, Major General Charles Vallencey, Town Major Henry Sirr and Reverend James Henthorn Todd, lived for a time in Milltown, Ranelagh and Clonskeagh respectively. Colonel (later General) Charles Vallencey lived in a villa called Prospect on Milltown Road in the 1780s,[21] Town Major Sirr lived in Elm Park House in Ranelagh from about 1810 to the mid-1820s[22] and Reverend James Henthorn Todd lived in Vergemount House (now the site of the Clonskeagh Hospital campus) in the 1840s and 1850s.[23] The fact that Sirr, a great collector of Irish antiquities which were subsequently bought by the Royal Irish Academy after his death, was living close to Milltown for several years may have led to increased awareness among the local labouring population of the value of reporting any finds, especially if they could expect to be rewarded. Aside from Sirr's acquisitiveness, a commercial trade in Irish antiquities had developed in Ireland by the middle of the nineteenth century, and finds such as those at Rathfarnham were occasionally reported in the press.[24]

A postscript to the nineteenth-century Bronze-Age discoveries in Milltown is to be found in the UCD Department of Folklore's collection of oral history. This unique record of oral history was collected throughout Ireland by national school children from their elderly relatives in the 1930s. In the folklore report for Milltown, there are two stories which specifically refer to buried treasure. The first account was told to schoolboy Noel Dowling by his seventy-seven-year-old grandfather, W. Dowling, who lived in 2 Byrne's Cottages in Milltown village:

---

18 E.C.R. Armstrong, *Catalogue of Irish gold ornaments in the collection of the Royal Irish Academy* (Dublin, 1920), pp. 64, 97.

19 Corlett, *Antiquities of Rathdown*, p. 30.

20 Corlett, *Antiquities of Rathdown*, p. 29.

21 Monica Nevin, 'General Charles Vallencey 1725–1812', *Journal of the Royal Society of Antiquaries of Ireland*, 123 (1993), p. 39.

22 Deirdre Kelly, *Four Roads to Dublin: The History of Ranelagh, Rathmines and Leeson Street* (Dublin, 1995), p. 54.

23 Martin Holland, *Clonskeagh: A Place in History* (Dublin, 2007), pp. 382–87.

24 C. Stephen Briggs, 'Dealing with Antiquities in 19th Century Dublin', *Dublin Historical Record*, xxxi, no. 4 (September 1978), pp. 146–8; *Belfast Mercury*, 8 September 1857, p. 3.

> *A long time ago there was treasure supposed to be hidden in Palmerston Park. It was buried by the Danes because when they made raids, they had to leave some of their loot behind. When it was heard of many attempts were made to discover it, but without success for the real spot in which it was hidden was not known, as Palmerston is a big place. The chief seekers were the people in the vicinity. The treasure consisted of gold and sacred vessels which were taken out of the churches and schools one of them being in Milltown.*[25]

A second anonymous narrator in the folklore collection for Milltown recalled that:

> *A light has often been seen rising at the road in Clonskeagh and following a course along the Dodder inside the castle wall. My father and some men and women of the village have seen it which is supposed to be a fairy light guarding a treasure.*[26]

While the two oral histories quoted above recount events that are obviously fictional (buried treasure and fairies are common themes in Irish folklore) there is a possibility that the antiquarian discoveries of the nineteenth century were imprinted in the popular memories of the Milltown inhabitants who, over time, embellished them with more exotic and less plausible explanations.

EARLY CHRISTIAN SETTLEMENT

The introduction of Christianity to Ireland in the fifth century coupled with an increase in population in the south-eastern part of county Dublin (equivalent to the Dún Laoghaire-Rathdown County Council area) in the second half of the first millennium has left a significant mark on that landscape, especially in the form of ecclesiastical remains.[27] The two main settlement types of early medieval society in south-east Dublin, which will be discussed presently, are the monastic church and the secular settlement called a ringfort or rath, meaning earthen rampart.[28]

The earliest landscape record of human settlement in Milltown is of a rath, which reportedly existed until the early nineteenth century on the south bank of the River Dodder close to the Packhorse Bridge. The rath is mentioned in D'Alton's *History of County Dublin*, where D'Alton very briefly states that, 'This village [Milltown] gives the title of Earl to the family of Leeson: it formerly exhibited one of the ancient raths not now visible.'[29] A little more detail is forthcoming in the *Parliamentary Gazetteer of Ireland* which notes that, 'To the left of the bridge across the Dodder [i.e. Packhorse Bridge], at the village, is a rath or ancient fort, now nearly obliterated.'[30] A deed from 1797 records the assignment of a field containing 1 acre and 30 perches plantation measure, part of the lands of Milltown in the parish of Taney 'then called and known by the name of Bawn field', and bounded on the north-west by the River Dodder and on the south by the road leading from Milltown Bridge [Packhorse Bridge] to the Dundrum Road [where Bankside Cottages are now].[31] In the 1820s a two-storey house, called Bawn House, was built on part of Bawn field and occupied

25 UCD, Department of Folklore, County Dublin Book 795, Milltown, Uppercross, County Dublin, p. 45.

26 UCD, Department of Folklore, County Dublin Book 795, Milltown, Uppercross, County Dublin, p. 49.

27 Stout, 'Patterns in the Past', p. 13.

28 Stout, 'Patterns in the Past' pp. 13–16; Aidan O'Sullivan, Finbar McCormick, Thomas R. Kerr and Lorcan Harney, *Early Medieval Ireland, AD 400–1100* (Dublin, 2013), p. 50.

29 John D'Alton, *A History of the County of Dublin* (Dublin, 1838), p. 798.

30 *Parliamentary Gazetteer of Ireland, 1844–45* (3 vols, Dublin, 1846), ii, p. 771.

31 RD 511/8/327979.

a site of approximately an acre and a half immediately to the right of the current Milltown Bridge (built *c.* 1817) on the south bank of the river on the Dundrum Road (Map 18).[32]

A second archaeological feature of indeterminate age is recorded on sheet 22 of the first edition of the County Dublin six-inch Ordnance Survey (OS) map, which was surveyed in 1837 and corrected in 1843 (Map 15). The map depicts two circles at the edge of a field containing the letter 'N' on which part of the Ramleh Park estate is now built. This representation was typically used by the nineteenth-century OS map and boundary surveyors to denote the site of a 'fort', which was used as a generic term to include raths as well as fortified earthworks.[33] The Dublin City Development Plan for 1991 listed this potential archaeological site incorrectly as being located in Clonskeagh as opposed to Milltown.[34] Given the evidence discussed above the cartographical representation is more likely to be of a single or double ditch rath, but site identification is impossible given the lack of any archaeological evidence. The fact that the site is not recorded on any of the later OS maps, particularly the five-foot scale series of 1878 (Map 17), must raise a doubt as to whether there was any rath in the Ramleh Park area of Milltown.

A third man-made feature recorded on a nineteenth-century manuscript map provides tentative evidence of a possible early medieval site on the north bank of the River Dodder. In 1821 the owner of an extensive demesne named Fairyland, W.C. Hogan, commissioned a map of his property which contains a circular earthwork feature which is described as a 'Moat' (Map 8).[35] Fairyland demesne, later renamed St Philip's, is now part of the grounds of the Alexandra College girls' secondary school opposite Milltown Bridge on the city side of the River Dodder. The name Fairyland suggests the existence of a rath, which was frequently associated with fairies in popular folklore. However, it is possible that the earthwork was a much more modern feature constructed in the eighteenth century as part of the development of the demesne.

Having established that one or possibly more raths existed in Milltown in the early medieval period it is necessary to discuss these settlements in a broader geographic context. There are at least four place names that incorporate the word 'rath' and which are adjacent or close to Milltown: Rathmines, Rathgar, Rathfarnham to the west and south, and Roebuck to the south-east. Although the name Milltown and the rath place-names were formally assigned to those districts by the government when the country was being mapped by the OS office in the 1820s and 1830s, these topographical names occur in medieval sources and are often indicators of much older human activity.[36] The example of Roebuck, a townland of some 800 statute acres, derives from the word 'Rabo' which itself is an anglicisation of the Irish 'Rathnabó', meaning the rath of the cows. The reference to cattle is significant as it gives a clue to the economy of the early medieval settlers of Milltown and adjacent districts. Additional evidence of cattle farming is provided by the townland adjacent to Roebuck, Farranboley, which encompasses the land on both sides of the Dundrum Road from Milltown Bridge to Windy Arbour. Farranboley means the grass of the booley lands. Booleying is a pastoral farming practice whereby animals are brought out to

32 RD 766/432/519967, RD 803/273/542009. The origins of Bawn House are discussed in more detail in a subsequent chapter. Al Hussain House now occupies the site where Bawn House stood.

33 Jacinta Prunty, *Maps and map-making in local history* (Dublin, 2004), pp. 173–4.

34 'Dublin City Development Plan 1991', List 7/Table 14.3.7, *Documented Archaeological Sites Outside the Zone of Archaeological Interest*, p. 277.

35 'A survey of the demesne of Fairyland at Milltown in the County of Dublin belonging to W.C. Hogan esq by J. Longfield, 1821' (NLI, Longfield estate maps, MS 21 F. 53/125).

36 Charles McNeill (ed.), *Calendar of Archbishop Alen's Register* c. *1172–1534* (Dublin, 1950), pp. 103, 170–3, 234.

pasture in upland areas in the summer and brought back down to lowland areas in the winter.[37] During the early medieval period there were no mills in Milltown so this district must have had an earlier place-name, now lost or as yet unidentified.[38]

Archaeologists are uncertain why raths appeared in great numbers throughout Ireland in the seventh and eighth centuries and what their primary purpose was.[39] It has been suggested by some historians that the primary aim of these enclosures was to defend cattle, which was the basis of wealth at that time, and to protect against cattle raiding, which behaviour was a form of a political competition among young men.[40] Another related argument postulates that raths emerged at a time of increased cattle production facilitated by advanced dairying techniques of the early medieval period, which in turn created conditions conducive to growth in food and population.[41] Certainly, the place-name evidence cited above supports the theory that cattle were an important part of the economy in Milltown and its hinterland. It is notable that the Milltown rath on the south bank of the River Dodder would have had additional defensive protection by the River Slang and its steep ravine against cattle raids on its south-western flank.

The second type of human settlement which emerged in the early medieval period was the church or monastic settlement. Milltown is located between two such settlements, Donnybrook (Domhnach-broc – or the church of St Broc) and Taney (Teach Naithí – Nahi's house). Of the two, we have much more information about Taney thanks to recent archaeological excavations which took place in 2007 on the grounds of Notre Dame secondary school on the Upper Churchtown Road, about a mile and a half south of Milltown.[42] St Nahi is thought to have been a bishop who lived in the sixth century.[43] The first phase of human settlement and activity at Taney dates from the late seventh to early tenth century and began with the erection of a single defensive ditch and palisade, later augmented by an outer ring of concentric defensive ditches.[44] Over 50 per cent of the cattle, sheep and pig bone fragments from the medieval period have been identified as cattle bones.[45] The bone analysis suggests that cattle were reared, slaughtered and consumed within the vicinity of St Nahi's church within a dairy-based economy in the early medieval period.[46]

---

37 See for example a letter from the Dublin Laundry Company to T.P. Hackett of Milltown, where, in reference to the fencing of their respective grazing lands in Farranboley, the writer states that 'the last of the cattle will today be withdrawn for the winter': NAI, Business Records 56, Dublin Laundry Company, Correspondence Book In, 1895–1902, 11 December 1901.

38 The place-name Milltown is first recorded in the mid-thirteenth century: McNeill (ed.), *Calendar of Archbishop Alen's Register*, p. 103.

39 O'Sullivan et al., *Early Medieval Ireland*, pp. 74–7; Stout, *Patterns in the Past*, pp. 16–19.

40 O'Sullivan et al., *Early Medieval Ireland*, p. 209.

41 O'Sullivan et al., *Early Medieval Ireland*, p. 77.

42 Edmond O'Donovan, 'Early Christian and medieval excavations at Teach Naithí: The changing morphology of a church site in Dundrum, County Dublin' in Sean Duffy (ed.), *Medieval Dublin XXII* (Dublin, 2012), pp. 9–93; Edmond O'Donovan, 'Early Christian Remains at St Nahi's Church, Churchtown Upper' in Christiaan Corlett (ed.), *Unearthing the Archaeology of Dún Laoghaire-Rathdown* (Dublin, 2013), pp. 91–4; Edmond O'Donovan, 'Medieval Remains at St Nahi's Church, Churchtown Upper' in Corlett (ed.), *Unearthing the Archaeology of Dún Laoghaire-Rathdown*, pp. 129–32.

43 O'Donovan, 'Excavations at Teach Naithí', p. 13.

44 O'Donovan, 'Excavations at Teach Naithí', p. 50.

45 O'Donovan, 'Excavations at Teach Naithí', p. 84.

46 O'Donovan, 'Excavations at Teach Naithí', p. 85.

FORDING THE DODDER

The human activity and settlement patterns of the early medieval period described above created the need for a vital function which must have arisen at Milltown long before its proto-industrial phase, namely, to provide a safe (or, more accurately, a safer) crossing of the River Dodder for humans and their livestock. This function is appropriate given the name of the river, which was called Dothra in Old Irish, an adjective which has been interpreted to mean 'turbulent' or 'violent', although the origins and meaning of the word remain uncertain.[47]

The bed of the River Dodder is particularly shallow about 100 metres downstream of Milltown Bridge beside the public car park on the north bank and the river walk on the south bank. This is where the first crossing of the Dodder at Milltown was established. This part of the river continued to be used as a convenient fording point down to the nineteenth century despite the erection of three stone bridges in successive periods from the sixteenth to the nineteenth centuries – Packhorse Bridge, Classon's Bridge and Milltown Bridge. This begs the question as to where the people were travelling to and from and what roads or paths, if any, existed in the early medieval period. These questions are impossible to answer with any certainty but a network of paths or primitive trackways must have grown up between the larger ecclesiastical centres as the population and economy of south Dublin flourished in the early medieval period. This transport network would have facilitated trading in livestock (cattle was the dominant currency at that time), increasingly so after the arrival of the Vikings in Dublin in the ninth century. The site archaeologist at Taney, Edmond O'Donovan, has noted that the Taney site is close to the top of a natural ridge overlooking the River Slang valley and on an important north-south routeway.[48]

VIKING INFLUENCES

The permanent settlement of Vikings (Norsemen) in Dublin in the ninth century had a pervasive and prolonged impact on the political and cultural development of the surrounding areas to the north and south of the River Liffey. For example, at Taney a large defensive U-shaped ditch was dug in the eighth or ninth century coinciding with the first Viking settlement in Dublin.[49] Evidence of Viking cultural influences at Taney – and by extension at Milltown – was also provided by the discovery of two grave-slabs in the graveyard at St Nahí's, which are part of a group of grave slabs known as Rathdown Slabs. These slabs are only found in the barony of Rathdown, which encompasses south-east County Dublin beyond the River Dodder. The carvings of the granite stone slabs feature abstract designs of Viking origin, consisting of a combination of cup-marks, concentric circles, radiating lines, vertical central bands and, occasionally, crosses.[50]

About two miles to the east of Milltown, off Ailesbury Road, Donnybrook, the burial of a Viking warrior laid to rest among scores of other corpses was discovered in 1878. Obviously, the burial could not have been accurately dated given the lack of modern technology and the fact that the site was not scientifically excavated. It was therefore assumed at the time that the Viking had died in battle nearby along with the other people buried with him.[51] However, a much more recent

47 Christopher Moriarty, *Down the Dodder* (Dublin, 1991), p. 10.

48 O'Donovan, 'Excavations at Teach Nathi', p. 51.

49 O'Donovan, 'Early Christian Remains at St Nahi's Church', p. 93.

50 O'Donovan, 'Excavations at Teach Naithí', p. 15; Elizabeth O'Brien, 'Churches of South-East County Dublin, Seventh to Twelfth Century' in G. MacNiocaill and P.F. Wallace (eds), *Keimelia, Studies in medieval archaeology and history in memory of Tom Delaney* (Galway, 1988), pp. 508–10.

51 William Frazer, 'Description of a Great Sepulchral Mound at Aylesbury', *Proceedings of the Royal Irish Academy*, 2C (1880), pp. 29–55.

and sophisticated appraisal of the burial suggests that the Viking was deliberately and peacefully buried in a pre-existing Christian cemetery and, possibly, that he was part of the garrison of an outlying Viking fort near Donnybrook.[52] The location has potentially added significance because the River Dodder was a political boundary which marked the northernmost territorial influence of the native Cualu Leinster tribe in the ninth century.[53] Later, as the Viking settlement in Dublin grew, the hinterland outside the town came under the political control of the Norsemen, and the region became known as *Dyflinarskiri* or Dublin shire.[54] Modern research and archaeological evidence suggests that *Dyflinarskiri* extended as far south as Dalkey or possibly Cherrywood in south Dublin and as far west as the modern county border with Kildare.[55] Thus Milltown was firmly under the political control of the Dublin Norsemen from about the early tenth century.

By the first half of the eleventh century Christianity had become the dominant religion of the Dublin political elites, as shown by King Sitric's pilgrimage to Rome in 1028, his foundation of Christ Church Cathedral, and the establishment of the diocese of Dublin at much the same time.[56] These developments had long-term jurisdictional and administrative repercussions because the archbishops of Dublin acquired substantial tracts of land throughout the hinterland of Dublin before the Norman invasion of the late twelfth century. These landholdings were likely to have been acquired as donations from wealthy Norse or Hiberno-Norse citizens.

In summary, in the early medieval period Milltown was incorporated into a wider, more complex society with an economic and cultural identity seemingly quite specific to south-east County Dublin and, from the ninth or tenth century onwards, increasingly influenced and controlled by Viking Dublin. The importance of an economy based on cattle resulted in the building of earthwork settlements (such as raths) on the banks of the Dodder at Milltown and a permanent fording point of the river at Milltown. Later, as will be discussed in the next chapter, Milltown and its hinterland were absorbed into ecclesiastical ownership in the eleventh or twelfth century, becoming part of the Dublin archbishop's manor of St Sepulchre. This situation remained unchanged for several hundred years, albeit with fluctuations in de facto control by the Church of the manor's outlying areas. ■

52 John Bradley, 'Some reflections on the problem of Scandinavian settlement in the hinterland of Dublin during the ninth century' in John Bradley and others (eds), *Dublin in the Medieval World: Studies in Honour of Howard B. Clarke* (Dublin, 2009), pp. 55, 59–60.

53 Bradley, 'Scandinavian settlement', p. 55.

54 The Icelandic sagas called Dublin's hinterland 'Dyflinarski': Angret Simms and Patricia Flanagan, 'Villages in county Dublin: Their Origins and Inheritance' in Aalen and Whelan (eds), *Dublin City and County: From Prehistory to Present* (Dublin, 1992), p. 89.

55 O'Sullivan et al., *Early Medieval Ireland*, pp. 134–5.

56 E.E. O'Donnell, *The Annals of Dublin* (Dublin, 1987), p. 49; Paul MacCotter, 'The church lands of the diocese of Dublin: Reconstruction and history' in Sean Duffy (ed.), *Medieval Dublin XIII* (Dublin, 2013), p. 93.

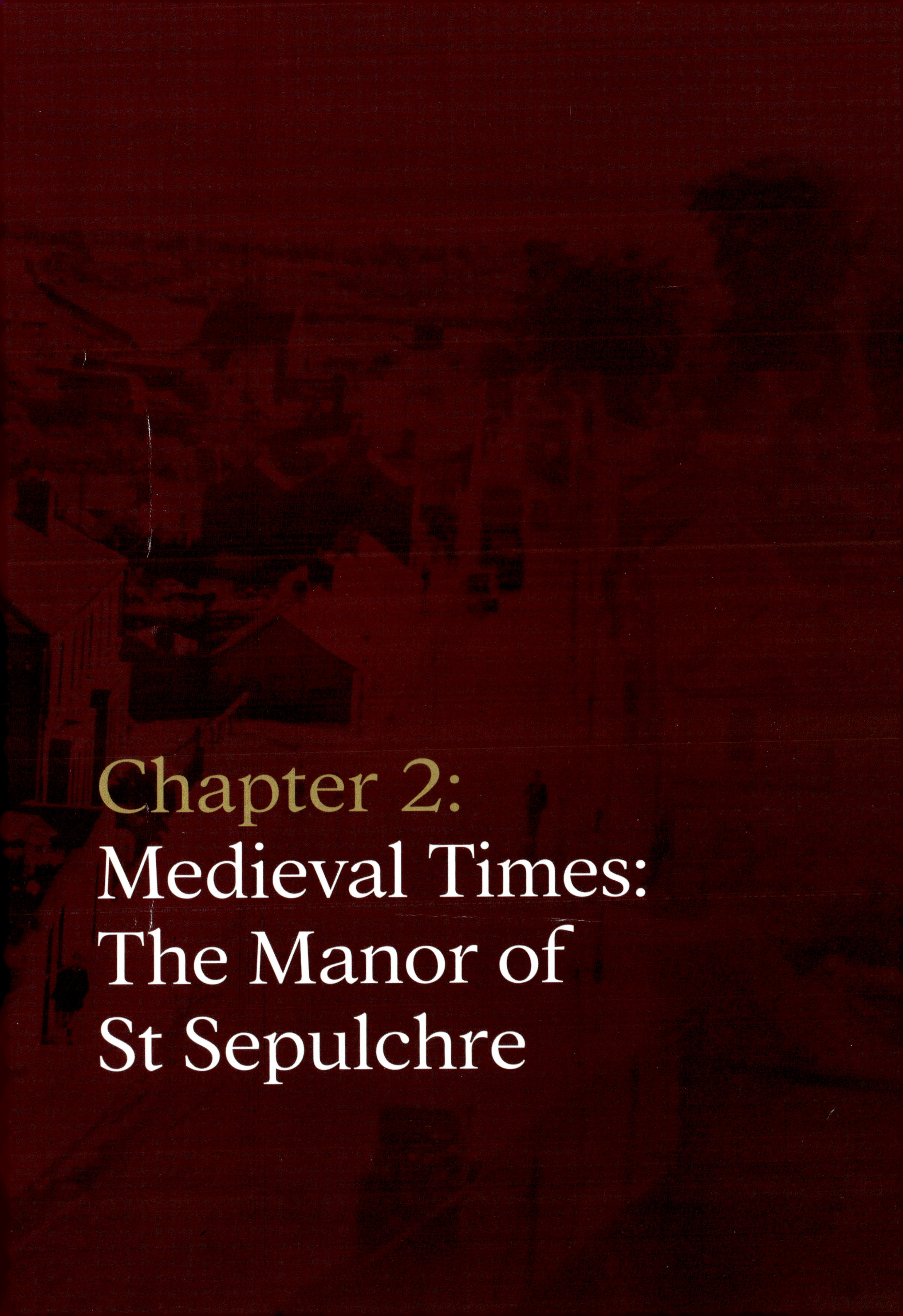

Chapter 2: Medieval Times: The Manor of St Sepulchre

Chapter 2:
Medieval Times: The manor of St Sepulchre

INTRODUCTION

Due to the transcription of several medieval manuscript sources by nineteenth- and twentieth-century archivists and historians we can begin to piece together information about some of Milltown's inhabitants and their experiences. Recent excavations at Dundrum Castle and Taney church, two miles to the south of Milltown, will be discussed as the detailed archaeological reports provide physical evidence to complement the written sources. I will also consider Milltown in the broader political context of the struggle between the dispossessed native Irish and the citizens of Dublin, which over time saw a contraction of the local economy and the creation of an unstable marcher[1] district south of the River Dodder.

BOUNDARY DEVELOPMENTS

An important consequence of the Norman takeover of Dublin in 1170 was the granting of charters by King Henry II and his son John, Lord of Ireland, whereby the city of Dublin was granted to merchants from Bristol. To encourage and incentivise the new settlers in Dublin, the charters gave the merchants the same liberties and free customs that they had previously enjoyed in their native Bristol. The Normans respected the existing property rights of the Irish Church and did not seek to dispossess any of the lands held by the archbishop of Dublin. Arising from these developments, the Dublin civic authorities marked out the boundaries of the city's jurisdiction, or liberties as they were called. This initiated the practice of the mayor and his officials perambulating the boundaries of the city's liberties on a triennial basis, a custom known as 'riding the franchises' or 'riding the fringes' in contemporary Dublin slang.

An important boundary to be delineated was that between the city's liberties and the lands and liberties of the archbishop of Dublin. We are solely concerned with that part of the boundary affecting the archbishop's manor of St Sepulchre, which ran from the River Dodder at Clonskeagh to

1 The term 'march' or 'marcher' derives from the old English 'mearc' meaning boundary, and in this context refers to the borderlands separating the Norman settlers from the native Irish and outlaws who lived beyond the control of the Norman lordship in Dublin.

Milltown Road and northwards back towards the city. This part of the boundary was described in a written record of the riding of the franchises in 1603, as follows:

> *... and then tornid southward by the myll pound [millpond] upon the land of Donabroke, soe farr as it went neer the bridge of Clonskeyghe; and then tornid west uppon the just meare [boundary walk] of Donabroke, deviding the lands of Donabroke and Mylton, and soe keapte on upon the uttermost meare of Donabroke, leaving all the land thereof within them uppon their righte hand, alongst by the high waye side [Milltown/ Sandford Road] leading to Dublin ...*[2]

A couple of interesting facts emerge from this account. By the beginning of the seventeenth century at the latest, there was a bridge over the Dodder at Clonskeagh. This stone bridge, which was probably built in the sixteenth century, had two arches. It was replaced by a new single-span bridge in the early nineteenth century, between 1807 and about 1820, during which period both the old and the new bridges were painted in pen and ink by the artist Cecilia Margaret Nairn.[3] Secondly, the territorial division at Clonskeagh and Milltown was delineated by a boundary walk (the 'just meare of Donabroke') which could be traversed by men on horseback. This pathway was called the Clonskeagh Lane in the eighteenth and nineteenth centuries.

In 1835 a royal commission was set up to investigate the municipal corporations of Ireland and report to parliament. A footnote in an appendix to the report describes the form of riding the franchises, which includes an early nineteenth-century description of the city's boundaries at Clonskeagh and Milltown:

> *... along by the south-east boundary of the Half-moon Field, to the south corner of the weir in the River Dodder, along said river to the bridge of Clonskeagh, and under the eastmost arch therof to the mill of Clonskeagh, and through said mill. From thence to the end of a lane, called Clonskeagh Lane, and along said lane to Milltown Road, along said road northward near the house of John Rivett, and through the gardens to the Swan Water ...* [4]

A short time earlier, in 1830, the Ordnance Survey Ireland's (OSI's) boundary department had drawn up a sketch map of the civil parish of Donnybrook as part of their preparations for compiling the maps for the country-wide six-inch OS, which for Dublin was surveyed in 1837. Fortunately, the parish map for Donnybrook is preserved in the National Archives and so it is possible to compare the boundary of the city's liberties at Clonskeagh with the previous written descriptions, and with current landmarks (Map 9). The boundary is marked on the map by a red line on the south bank of the River Dodder at Clonskeagh Bridge and thereafter by a red dotted line where the boundary crosses the river at the Clonskeagh iron mills on the south bank and onto the north bank about 100 metres upstream (west) of Clonskeagh Bridge. The boundary runs behind what are now the back gardens of Ramleh Close and the boundary wall of the grounds of Clonskeagh Hospital. It then veers left onto Prospect Lane,

---

2 John T. Gilbert (ed.), CARD, i, p. 192 (Dublin, 1889).

3 Cecilia Margaret Nairn (née Campbell), *Old Clonskeagh Bridge* and *Clonskeagh Bridge* (NLI, Prints and Drawings 1969 TX 26); *Old Bridge at Clonskeagh*, unsigned and undated hand coloured etching *circa.* 1800–1820 (NLI, Prints and Drawings, ET A354); *Grand Jury Presentments, Dublin: Accounts of All Sums presented to be raised off the City of Dublin by the different term Grand Juries from the year 1807 inclusive, to the 1st January 1821*, p. 4, H.C. 1821 (477), xx, 325. £500 was presented at the 1806 Michaelmas sessions of the Grand Jury for the County of the City of Dublin to build a new bridge at Clonskeagh, but there seems to have been a delay of several years before the new bridge was actually built.

4 *Appendix to the First Report of the Commissioners appointed to inquire into the corporations in Ireland: Report on the City of Dublin, Part 1*, p. 2, H.C. 1835 (25), xxvii.

which ends at a T-junction with Milltown Road opposite the entrance to the Jesuit headquarters at Milltown Park. The boundary turns right and then continues along Milltown Road and Sandford Road back towards the city.

One of the cottages shown on the north bank of the River Dodder at Clonskeagh still survives today, a short distance west of the car park of Clonskeagh House (formerly O'Shea's public house and now called Farmer Browns). Up until about the middle of the nineteenth century there was a pathway connecting Milltown Road with the River Dodder at Clonskeagh, called the Clonskeagh Lane. It will be seen from the boundary map that the cartographer described the city boundary as being in 'the centre of the old road'. Clonskeagh Lane fell into disuse when the new Clonskeagh Road to the north and east was laid out in the late eighteenth century. Clonskeagh Lane continued in use as a cul-de-sac to provide access to an eighteenth-century farmhouse called 'Prospect', hence its current name, Prospect Lane.

The historical importance of Prospect Lane is twofold. Firstly, it is a fortuitous survivor of a very old part of the local transport network used since medieval times to delineate the boundaries of the city's liberties. Secondly, Prospect Lane separated the Baronies of Uppercross (to the west) and Dublin (to the east), the civil parishes of St Peter and Donnybrook, the townlands of Clonskeagh (to the east) and Milltown (to the west), and from 1880 the lane separated the Rathmines and Rathgar township from the Pembroke township until these two urban district councils (as they had become in 1898) were taken over by Dublin Corporation in 1930.[5]

DEVELOPMENT OF THE MANOR OF ST SEPULCHRE

One of the most significant properties belonging to the Dublin archbishopric at the time of the Norman invasion was the manor of St Sepulchre, which was located to the south of the medieval city. The name 'St Sepulchre' is related to the Third Crusade, a time when it was fashionable to dedicate churches to the holy sepulchre. St Sepulchre was the senior manor of the archbishopric and contained the archbishop's palace, parts of which still survive within the building fabric of Kevin Street Garda station.[6]

At its greatest extent St Sepulchre's manor is estimated to have contained up to 3,071 statute acres made up of substantial landholdings in the modern parishes of St Catherine, St Nicholas Without, St Peter, Donnybrook, Taney and Crumlin. Of particular relevance for the study of Milltown, the manor's territory included (among many others) the modern townlands of Cullenswood, Ranelagh North, Ranelagh South, Sallymount, Rathmines East, Rathmines South, Rathmines West, Rathmines Great, Rathmines Little, Churchtown Lower, Churchtown Upper, Milltown, Farranboley and part of Clonskeagh.[7]

The thirteenth century was sufficiently peaceful to allow the extensive manor of St Sepulchre to thrive and become a valuable source of income for the archbishop of Dublin. During this period of growth the archbishop established a manor farm within the greater manor of St Sepulchre, called

5 *Parliamentary Gazetteer of Ireland*, i, p. 463, ii, p. 771; The Rathmines and Rathgar (Milltown Extension) Act 1880 (43 & 44 Vict., 2 August 1880), section 2.

6 Howard B. Clarke, 'Urbs et suburbinem: Beyond the walls of medieval Dublin' in Conleth Manning (ed.), *Dublin and beyond the Pale: Studies in honour of Patrick Healy* (Wicklow, 1998), pp. 53–4; Christine Casey, *The Buildings of Dublin* (Yale, 2005), pp. 636–7.

7 Paul MacCotter, 'The church lands of the diocese of Dublin: Reconstruction and history' in Sean Duffy (ed.), *Medieval Dublin XIII* (Dublin, 2013), p. 84; Jocelyn Otway-Ruthven, 'The church lands of medieval county Dublin' in J.A. Watt, J. Morral and F.X. Martin (eds), *Medieval Studies presented to Aubrey Gwynn* (Dublin, 1961), pp. 57, 72–3.

Colonia, which was a prebend[8] in St Patrick's cathedral.[9] The manor of Colonia comprised 271 medieval acres (about 680 statute acres)[10] and included among its lands the area called Cullenswood to the north of Milltown.[11] The archbishop of Dublin had a residence here in the thirteenth century consisting of a chamber with adjoining chapel, a stone hall roofed with shingles and a kitchen built of timber with a garden. There was also a grange, a granary, stables and a fishery.[12]

In the 1850s the archivist and historian Sir William Betham delivered a paper to the Royal Irish Academy describing the accounts for the archbishop's manors in the 1270s, including the accounts for the 'Manor of Coloyne' (Colonia).[13] The accounts were prepared in the following circumstances. When the archbishop of Dublin, Fulk de Sandford, died in 1271 the holy office was vacant for seven years and during that time Thomas de Chaddisworth was made custodian of the Church's temporalities (ecclesiastical income derived from secular sources). De Chaddisworth's accounts of receipts and discharge from the archbishop's manors were recorded in a medieval manuscript known as a pipe roll, subsequently destroyed when the Four Courts was burned in 1922, but which had been transcribed by Betham in the 1850s.[14] The accounts for Colonia[15] (see table on p.18) provide an interesting insight into everyday life in the manor close to Milltown in the twelfth century:

On the expense side of the accounts £37 and 12*s*. were incurred in bailiffs' fees, repairs to houses and mills, and other sundry expenses.[16]

The largest source of income, £195 and 18*s*., was made up of rent from three distinct classes of tenants, freeholders, betaghs and cottagers. Betaghs were tenants of Irish origin whom historians believe may have occupied distinct townlands in the manor, such as the townland of Farranboley (called Boley Maior in medieval texts), which is on the south bank of the River Dodder at Milltown.[17] Betaghs lived in family groups and apparently cultivated their land in common.[18]

Below the betaghs in status were the cottars who held very small holdings of less than an acre.[19] Cottars usually performed labour services for their land, for example two days a year reaping crops

8 A prebend is the entitlement of a clergyman to share in the revenues and a vote in the assembly of cannons called the chapter.

9 James Mills, 'Notices of the manor of St Sepulchre, Dublin, in the fourteenth century', *Journal of the Royal Society of Antiquaries of Ireland*, 19 (1889), p. 33.

10 The acre used in medieval times was much bigger than the statute and the Irish plantation acre, perhaps being 2.5 times a statute acre, although local variations probably applied: Otway-Ruthven, 'Anglo Irish agriculture', p. 3.

11 Margaret Murphy and Michael Potterton, *The Dublin region in the Middle Ages: Settlement, land-use and economy* (Dublin, 2010), pp. 76, 289. Some historians interchange the names St Sepulchre and Colonia which mistakenly gives the impression they are one and the same place.

12 Murphy and Potterton, *The Dublin region in the Middle Ages*, pp. 76, 173; Mills, 'Notices of the manor of St Sepulchre', p. 33.

13 William Betham, 'On the Account of Thomas de Chaddisworth, Custodee of the Temporalities of the Archbishop of Dublin', *Proceedings of the Royal Irish Academy*, 5C (1850–53), pp. 145–62.

14 Betham, 'Account of Thomas de Chaddisworth', p. 149.

15 Betham, 'Account of Thomas de Chaddisworth', pp. 155–6.

16 Betham, 'Account of Thomas de Chaddisworth', p. 161.

17 Mills, 'Notices of the manor of St Sepulchre', p. 34; Jocelyn Otway-Ruthven, 'The organization of Anglo-Irish agriculture in the middle ages', *Journal of the Royal Society of Antiquaries of Ireland*, 81, no. 1 (1951), pp. 12–13.

18 Murphy and Potterton, *The Dublin region in the Middle Ages*, p. 187.

19 Murphy and Potterton, *The Dublin region in the Middle Ages*, p. 189.

MANOR OF COLOYNE

The said Master Thomas rendered an account of the manor of Coloyne for the same period [1271–1276], as follows:

	POUNDS	SHILLINGS	PENCE
Of the rents of the freeholders, betaghs, and cottagers of the said manor	195	18	0
Of the demesnes there located and set to farm	110	3	1
Of the meadows there	19	18	0
Of the pastures there	26	15	6
Of the rent of three mills there	51	0	0
Of the gardens there	12	12	0
Of the boll beer and alewyte	16	4	9
Of the rents of horsewshoeing	0	6	6
Of the portion of salmon fishery	6	0	0
Of the service and work of the betagh and cottagers	9	6	4
Of underwood sold	4	1	5
Of one seldar newly levied	1	0	0
Of chimney rent	0	2	0
Of the rent of Close of Weymill	2	3	6
Of stubble sold	0	2	0
Of perquisites of the fairs on the day of the Invention of Holy Cross	8	0	10
Of the perquisites of the court there	22	19	8¼
Of the issue of the mill which was Robert de Weymill'	1	2	11½
Summa	**487**	**16**	**6¾**

and another two days in the year either hoeing or haymaking, in addition to paying a modest rent.[20] During recent excavations at Taney, archaeologists found the remains of a foundation trench of a rectangular house ten metres long, probably dating to the late twelfth or early thirteenth century. All the evidence indicated that the Taney site represented a farm originally occupied by one of the betaghs or cottars of the manor.[21]

The importance of cattle to the economy of Milltown in the early medieval period has been discussed earlier, but according to a recent analysis and national reappraisal of archaeological evidence, the dominant position of cattle began to decline from about AD 800 onwards in some parts of the country, coincidental with an increase in mill building.[22] The pace of such changes is difficult to evaluate but cattle were eventually replaced as the dominant agricultural product so that by about 1300 an average of 74 per cent of total land in the Dublin region was used for arable purposes, with the actual figure for arable land in Colonia put at 61 per cent.[23] Food made from grain crops was an important part of medieval people's diet in which bread and ale predominated, particularly among the labouring classes. Grain was also required to feed medieval Dublin. Throughout the parts of the country which were under Norman control, grain was grown to supply local urban centres and exported to England. From the reign of King Edward I onwards, grain was required to victual royal armies.[24] The growth in cultivation of grain crops, particularly wheat, saw a big increase in the number of corn mills, which were necessary for processing the wheat into flour. Manorial tenants were legally bound to grind their corn in the lord's mill.[25] These developments bring us to the origins of milling at Milltown.

THE ORIGINS OF THE PLACE-NAME MILLTOWN AND THE LOCATION OF ITS FIRST MILL

The first written reference to Milltown can be dated to 1257–63 when a sworn investigation was made at St Sepulchre's palace into the operation of the law (legal articles) on the archbishop's manor. Details of the investigation were transcribed in a sixteenth-century calendar of ancient ecclesiastical and manorial documents compiled by Archbishop Alen in the 1530s, now called the *Calendar of Archbishop Alen's Register*. This historically very valuable calendar was edited by the historian Charles McNeill in 1947 prior to its publication by the Royal Society of Antiquaries of Ireland in 1950.[26]

Milltown is mentioned in the context of the jury's investigation into the ninth article of the law which governed crimes affecting Englishmen living on the manor, as the following terse quote explains:

20 Otway-Ruthven, 'Anglo-Irish agriculture', pp. 12–13.

21 Edmond O'Donovan, 'Medieval Remains at St Nahi's Church, Churchtown Upper' in Christiaan Corlett (ed.), *Unearthing the Archaeology of Dún Laoghaire-Rathdown* (Dublin, 2013), p. 130; Edmond O'Donovan, 'Early Christian and medieval excavations at Teach Naithi: The changing morphology of a church site in Dundrum, County Dublin' in Sean Duffy (ed.), *Medieval Dublin XXII* (Dublin, 2012), p. 43.

22 Aidan O'Sullivan, Finbar McCormick, Thomas R. Kerr and Lorcan Harney, *Early Medieval Ireland, AD 400–1100* (Dublin, 2013), p. 210.

23 Murphy and Potterton, *The Dublin region in the Middle Ages*, pp. 287–9.

24 Murphy and Potterton, *The Dublin region in the Middle Ages*, pp. 474–7.

25 Angret Simms and Patricia Flanagan, 'Villages in county Dublin: Their Origins and Inheritance' in Aalen and Whelan (eds), *Dublin City and County: From Prehistory to Present* (Dublin, 1992), p. 93.

26 Charles McNeill (ed.), *Calendar of Archbishop Alen's Register* c. *1172–1534* (Dublin, 1950).

As to the ninth article, Archbishop Fulk's predecessors frequently took redemption for an Englishman's death: for instance, in Archbishop L's time [Archbishop Henry of London, archbishop of Dublin 1213–28] William Miller (Molendinar) of Milltown (Molneton) and his sons, Richard and Ralph, were taken for Ralph the miller's death, who was killed in their presence by Heymarthus, because they did not detain the latter. Taken and imprisoned they made a fine in the archbishop's court ...[27]

From this very short reference we can confirm that a mill had been built by at least the early twelfth century in the district which became known as Milltown and that the manor was populated by persons of different ethnic backgrounds. The deceased miller, Ralph, was apparently of English origin and as the ninth article of the law only discusses crimes involving Englishmen this shows that different rules applied to the native Irish betaghs living on the manor. In this regard, the murder of an Irishman was not considered a felony under Norman law as applied in Ireland.[28]

The next issues to consider are what type of mill was used at Milltown and where it was located. There is no doubt that the medieval mill at Milltown was located on the south bank of the River Dodder and was water powered, either by water from the River Slang (also called the Dundrum River) or from the River Dodder. The two most common types of mill used in the early medieval period are the horizontal overshot watermill, where water powering the mill falls from a height onto a wheel of wooden paddles aligned horizontally below, and the vertical undershot watermill, where the base of the wheel is set into the natural flow of the stream or millrace, with the kinetic energy driving the mill wheel.[29]

The question of which type of mill was used first in Milltown is a moot point, but a strong argument can be made that the structure was a horizontal overshot watermill powered by water taken off the River Slang on elevated ground above the south bank of the Dodder. The attraction of this theory is that it would have been easier for the mill engineers of the time to harness water power from the River Slang as opposed to taking water from the larger and more turbulent River Dodder. At some point, the water flow of the River Slang was augmented by water taken off the Little Dargle and Ticknock rivers above Dundrum, which supports the theory that the Slang was used to power a grain mill at Milltown, among other places.[30] Cartographic support is also provided by Rocque's Survey of County Dublin, published in 1760, where what appears to be a millrace is shown above the words '2 Miles' (Map 4), and by subsequent OS maps (Map 19).

Much later, a weir was constructed across the Dodder at Milltown (Pl. 2) to provide additional water power for mills at Clonskeagh on the south bank of the river but that weir cannot be dated with any certainty prior to the third quarter of the eighteenth century, when its millrace was definitively depicted on Bernard Scale's map of 1773 (Map 5).

The topography of the south bank of the River Dodder and its tributary, the River Slang, underwent huge changes in the mid-twentieth century. Unfortunately, this makes it impossible to identify the site of the first mill at Milltown or to confirm its power source. In the 1950s the millpond and millraces were filled in and the River Slang was buried deep under ground in a culvert (which discretely discharges into the Dodder at a bend in the river on the south bank below the playground)

27 McNeill, *Archbishop Alen's Register*, p. 103.

28 Murphy and Potterton, *The Dublin region in the Middle Ages*, p. 188.

29 Murphy and Potterton, *The Dublin region in the Middle Ages*, pp. 416–21; Aidan O'Sullivan, Finbar McCormick, Thomas R. Kerr and Lorcan Harney, *Early Medieval Ireland, AD 400–1100* (Dublin, 2013), pp. 203–9; Don McEntee and Michael Corcoran, *The Rivers Dodder and Poddle: Mills, Storms, Droughts and the Public Water Supply* (Dublin, 2016), pp. 94–6.

30 McEntee and Corcoran, *The Rivers Dodder and Poddle*, pp. 47–9.

Plate 2. Weir on the River Dodder at Milltown, 2015 (author's collection)

as part of extensive landscaping associated with Dublin Corporation's new housing programme at St Luke's Crescent and St Colombanus estate off the Dundrum Road. All remains of the derelict mill complexes located at the end of and opposite Bankside Cottages were removed, so that apart from nineteenth-century cartographic evidence, very few physical traces of their locations remain now. We can, however, speculate as to the medieval mill's location by reference to a tantalising description contained in a lease referring to 'the ancient millrace', whereby Joseph Leeson (the earl of Milltown's grandfather) leased the following property to Edward Allen on 21 March 1718:

> *33 acres 3 roods and 4 perches of land being part of Milltown lands together with the passage cross Milltown bottom leading to the said two fields next to Churchtown lands which said passage was to consist of 60 feet broad ... excepting out of the said demise forever unto Joseph Leeson and his heirs the ancient millrace and water course that leads to the iron mill of Milltown and liberty to make a millrace through any part of the premises for the conveniency of a new mill to be erected; rent sixty pounds sterling.*[31]

More intriguingly, the reference to the 'iron mill of Milltown' appears to be a transcribing error made by a clerk in the Registry of Deeds at the time the memorial was drawn up because when the original lease – not the memorial – was quoted in a sale of the earl of Leeson freehold es-

31 RD 23/139/12909.

tate in 1856, the conveyancer observed that the lease contained a reservation to the lessor of the 'ancient millrace and water course that leads to the Grain Mill of Milltown'.[32]

Nineteenth-century OS maps show two separate mill complexes (the later one closest to the Dodder bank originating in the 1720s) at the end of and opposite Bankside Cottages respectively, with a millrace supplying water from one complex to the other (Maps 15 & 18). Nonetheless, the references in the 1718 deed to the ancient millrace leading to the grain mill at Milltown and the Churchtown lands prove that the medieval mill was built on the south bank of the River Dodder.

In short, based on the very limited topographical and documentary evidence available, medieval milling activity in Milltown is likely to have begun in the twelfth or early thirteenth century a short distance to the south-west of Bankside Cottages before the point where the River Slang enters the Dodder, i.e. between the Dundrum Road and the viaduct now carrying the Luas tram, often referred to as the 'Nine Arches', to use well-known modern landmarks.

POLITICAL AND MILITARY DEVELOPMENTS

In general terms, the Norman colonisation of the late twelfth and early thirteenth centuries was not violently resisted by the population living in the hinterland of Dublin, whose everyday lives and occupations continued uninterrupted albeit that for some inhabitants their servile status changed in line with the introduction of Norman laws and manorial customs. Essentially, there was a political takeover of the secular *Dyflinskiri* territory by the Norman elites via Royal grants of land at the expense of the Norse political elite, but the archbishop's lands were left unmolested.[33]

There was, apparently, one notorious exception to this peaceful state of affairs. On Easter Monday 1209 a large unarmed group of Dublin merchants of Bristolian origin went out to Cullenswood to celebrate the feast day. There, the group was ambushed and massacred by disaffected Irish tribesmen from the Dublin and Wicklow mountains. The truth of what happened on that fateful day is impossible to determine because the earliest surviving written record of the event dates to the sixteenth century. What is beyond doubt is that the incident (subsequently called 'Black Monday') was solemnly commemorated on an annual basis down to the mid-seventeenth century. This involved a military parade by the mayor of Dublin and armed officials to Cullenswood on the anniversary of the massacre where the citizens reaffirmed their identity and issued a show of strength to their Irish enemies, who had become formidable adversaries by the beginning of the fourteenth century.[34]

A possible and rather peculiar record of Black Monday is preserved in the first edition of the six-inch OS map depicting farmland to the west of Milltown Road and village, which is called 'The Bloody Fields' (Map 15).[35] The late historian of Ranelagh and Rathmines, Deirdre Kelly, opined that the name was a reference to the Battle of Rathmines of 1649.[36] I am inclined to discount

32 NAI, Landed Estates Court Rental, 'Particulars and Conditions of Sale of the free simple estates of the Earl of Milltown on 8 January 1856', lot 58.

33 For example, the lands of Rabo (Roebuck) were successively granted by King Henry II and King John to Thomas and Robert de St Michael respectively: James Mills, 'The Norman settlement in Leinster – The cantreds near Dublin', *Journal of the Royal Society of Antiquaries of Ireland*, 2, no. 4 (1894), p. 167.

34 Declan Johnston, 'Black Monday: The power of myth in medieval Dublin' in Sean Duffy (ed.), *Medieval Dublin XIII* (Dublin, 2013), pp. 139–49.

35 OSI, Co. Dublin, Sheet 22, six inches to one statute mile, surveyed in 1837 and corrected in 1843.

36 Kelly, *The Four Roads to Dublin*, p. 23.

that theory because, relatively speaking, there was little bloodshed at the Battle of Rathmines, which was infamous for the cowardice of the Royalists. Furthermore, in the 1860s, the editor of the Dublin Builder linked the 'Bloody Fields' with the massacre of Black Monday.[37] The puzzling thing is that the toponym is not found in any maps or newspapers prior to the early nineteenth century when the Bloody Fields were incorporated into the civil townland of Milltown in the late 1830s. We can tell from contemporary newspaper reports that Victorian Dubliners were familiar with the name and the area it covered, but why did the Bloody Fields only become a place-name of public record in the 1830s?[38] The question must remain unanswered, but in any event the infamous name was short-lived. In 1850, the new railway was cut through the Bloody Fields and when their owner, Lord Palmerston (Prime Minister in the 1850s), began to develop his estate in Upper Rathmines in the 1860s the name was, unsurprisingly, dropped.[39] By the 1880s the Bloody Fields were built over by Palmerston Road, Palmerston Park and Cowper Road, among others.

Returning to medieval politics, by around 1270 relationships between the Dublin administration and the native Irish O'Toole and O'Byrne clans living in the upland areas of Wicklow had broken down, irretrievably as it turned out. The exact causes of the trouble are unknown. Historians have speculated that a prominent factor was the vacancy in the death of Archbishop Fulk de Sandford in 1271, which led to an aggressive pursuit of rents/taxation by the archbishop's agents (such as John de Chaddisworth) on his Wicklow manors during the vacancy in the archbishopric. At the same time, a deterioration in the weather was a major cause of widespread famine which forced the native Irish living on the marginal uplands of Wicklow to rebel against the government and plunder the rich grain and livestock manors of south Dublin.[40] The changed conditions of the 1270s saw endemic raids and warfare waged by the Wicklow native Irish (frequently joined by rogue elements among the Norman marcher settlers) against the inhabitants of the fertile agricultural lands of south Dublin for the next 300 years. The new military situation resulted in the creation of a marcher or frontier district south of the River Dodder populated by a resilient interconnected group of families called Walsh, Howell, Harold, Lawless and Archbold, who were drawn from a mixture of Scandinavian, Welsh and English ethnic backgrounds.[41]

An example of how bad the situation had become in Milltown by the early fourteenth century is revealed by a detailed investigation made of the manor of St Sepulchre in 1326:

> *At Thanahy [Taney] and le Miltoun are certain tenants, English and Irish, holding four score acres, 3d. [an acre] a year in peace, nothing in war. There are 40 acres waste and untilled for want of tenants, extended at nothing because nothing can be got from them; there were four cottages now waste for want of tenants, no value.*[42]

---

37 *Dublin Builder*, 15 March 1861, p. 12.

38 *Freeman's Journal*, 21 December 1842, p. 3.

39 *Freeman's Journal*, 31 August 1850.

40 J.F. Lydon, 'Medieval Wicklow – A Land of War' in Ken Hannigan and William Nolan (eds), *Wicklow History and Society* (Dublin, 1994), p. 158; Emmet O'Byrne, 'Cultures in contact in the Leinster and Dublin marches, 1170–1400' in Sean Duffy (ed.), *Medieval Dublin V* (Dublin, 2004), pp. 122–3; Emmet O'Byrne, 'A much disputed land: Carrickmines and the Dublin marches' in Sean Duffy (ed.), *Medieval Dublin IV* (Dublin, 2003), p. 236.

41 Christopher Maginn, 'English marcher lineages in south Dublin in the late middle ages', *Irish Historical Studies*, 34, no. 134 (November, 2004), pp. 113–36.

42 McNeill, *Archbishop Alen's Register*, p. 171.

Things were just as bad at Colonia and 'Boly Maior' (Farranboley):

> *At Colonia, there is a hall with stone walls, now thrown down, a chamber for the archbishop with chapel adjoining; these are roofed with shingles and of no value ... There were a kitchen built of timber, a grange, a stable and a granary roofed with boards, now altogether thrown down.*
>
> *At Colonia, 16 acres, pasture, 16d. a year and no more for want of beasts, and most of the pasture is near evil-doers; 66 acres of wood, no value either for letting in grazing for selling underwood, because wholly wasted.*
>
> *At Boley maior are three tenements of farmers who hold betaghs' land, 21 acres 1 stang, 6d. an acre in time of peace but of no value in time of war; 41 acres 3 stangs, usually held by betaghs, because the betaghs are undone by evil-doers, and so the land is extended at no value either in grazing or otherwise.*[43]

That such a desolate picture existed so close to the medieval town shows how beleaguered the Norman administration in Dublin had become by the 1320s. This was due to a number of factors. Dublin and the Norman administration at large had been greatly weakened by the effects of the Bruce invasion of 1315/1316. Shortly afterwards the population suffered from the effects of a severe island-wide famine and plague in the years 1316–18. In addition, the administration's revenue had been adversely affected since the late thirteenth century due to excessive taxation and purveyance demands from Edward I to fund and supply his Scottish campaigns.[44] Thus the 'evil-doers' south of Dublin could take full advantage of the manor's plight with impunity.

Despite the violent conditions some tenants continued to farm at Colonia in 1326 – crops had to be sown regardless of the dangers as otherwise the population would starve:

> *At Colonia there are this year in one sowing 50 acres arable, sown under plough with wheat, extended at 3d. an acre, 12s. 6d. a year; there are in sowing 48 acres sown with oats this year under plough, at 3d. an acre, 12s.; in another sowing 68 acres, fallow, extended at 1d. an acre, 5s. 8d. and no more, as the land is exhausted and poor. There are of the same lands in the hands of farmers four score acres, 40s. a year, at 6d. an acre.*[45]

The remarks about the land being exhausted and poor are noteworthy because they show that the tenants were under pressure to farm the manor land intensively in the agricultural areas closest to Dublin. The normal farm management and crop rotation systems practiced in peaceful times had been abandoned or modified due to the crises of the second decade of the fourteenth century. In short, law and order had broken down on the manor in Milltown and Farranboley in the 1320s so it became critical to grow food on the home farm at Colonia which was closer to the security of Dublin.

The importance of Milltown as a fording point of the River Dodder from early times has previously been discussed. This is supported by a reference to the high way to Milltown in an undated letter, apparently dating to the fifteenth century. The road to Milltown is mentioned in a request made by the archbishop of Dublin to the lord mayor to confirm the ownership of a property called the 'Hoch ley' (the meaning of which is unknown) lying between the roads to Milltown and Colonia:

---

43 McNeill, *Archbishop Alen's Register*, p. 170.

44 James Lydon, *The Lordship of Ireland in the Middle Ages* (2nd edition, Dublin, 2003), pp. 101–5, 118.

45 McNeill, *Archbishop Alen's Register*, p. 170.

that ye Hoch ley that lyeth between the two high ways yt goeth to Colon and Milton may be knowen to be kept as part of the Archbi'pps demayn and to the intent hit might be emparked and not lye waste (as hit doth now) or else to shew lawfull cause why hit ought not to be soe[46]

INHABITANTS OF MILLTOWN IN THE MEDIEVAL PERIOD

There are only a handful of references in the medieval documents to the names of people who lived in Milltown. I have previously mentioned the Englishman, Ralph Miller, who operated the corn mill in the early twelfth century. During the reign of Richard II, a detailed rental of St Sepulchre's manor was compiled in 1382 which lists the names of the principal tenants living on the manor. Thus we find that a man named Philip Irrych held 26 acres at Milltown for a term of 24 years at a yearly rent of 13*s*., or 6*d*. an acre.[47] In the same rental, a tenant by the name of Henry Brygge (also spelt Brugg'es or Brige in other documents) held 40 acres in Milltown at a rent of 13*s*. 4*d*. (i.e. 4*d*. an acre) together with 2 acres in a place described as 'Kylraschi (alias Inch, where the Vicar of S. Kevin's has tithes – by the Doder and the mill)'. The location of Kylraschi is unclear but it must either be beside Milltown or represent a place within the townland of Milltown. The difference in the annual rents paid by Irrych and Brygge may perhaps be explained by the quality of the lands being let or the length of the leases.

Henry Brygge is mentioned again in a deed dated 14 April 1399, when 'Henry Brugg'es of Milton' witnessed a lease of 9 acres of land in Rathmines.[48] A third reference to the Brygge family occurs in an undated entry in Archbishop Alen's register which records the grant of a lease of 4 acres of land called Culecroftyn lying just south of Donnybrook:

Bartholomew de Hodges and Ysolda Ball, his wife, have given to John Russell, son of Geoffrey the miller, 4 acres of arable land called Culecroftyn, lieing between William le Brige's land on the south and the land of Douenaghbroke [Donnybrook] on the north: rent 3 1/2d. an acre to the chief lord at the due terms, and 1d. a year to William Brige for all service.[49]

It is likely that the Brygges were of Flemish origin (as indicated by the alternative spelling Brugg'es) and that Henry Brygge was a senior free tenant of the manor, as evidenced by the fact that he was literate and that he witnessed a deed with his signature. The transactions quoted above show that the rents at Milltown had recovered to or exceeded their peacetime rates of the early fourteenth century, and that there was a market for land in Milltown in the last two decades of the fourteenth century.

MILLTOWN CASTLE

Despite the more benign circumstances in Milltown at the turn of the fifteenth century, defence and security issues had, since the early thirteenth century, been a continuous concern to the inhabitants of south Dublin, and would remain so until the seventeenth century. The obvious example of this closest to Milltown is Dundrum Castle (still standing but now dwarfed by the shopping centre), erected to the south of the Church's lands at Taney (Churchtown) in the early thirteenth century by royal grantees. The first custodians of Dundrum Castle held their lands by military or

46 McNeill, *Archbishop Alen's Register*, p. 234.

47 Mills, 'Notices of the manor of St Sepulchre', p. 124.

48 McNeill, *Archbishop Alen's Register*, p. 234.

49 McNeill, *Archbishop Alen's Register*, p. 305.

knight service from the king, and were required to supply one armed horseman for each 'knight's fee' if they were summoned to go on military campaign with the king.[50] As an aside, during excavations at Dundrum Castle archaeologists found two thirteenth-century iron arrowheads which provide physical proof supporting the documentary evidence of the castle's military functions.[51] Over time the knight's fee was commuted for a monetary payment so that in 1272 the knight's fee for Dundrum had been replaced by a payment of 40s., which was a considerable sum of money.[52] For unknown reasons the early Norman castle was abandoned and allowed to fall into ruin during the period between 1490 and 1590, following which the castle was completely rebuilt by the Fitzwilliam family.[53]

At some point in the later medieval period, probably in the fifteenth century, a fortified dwelling was built in Milltown. The first edition of the six-inch OS map shows the structure – a square building called Milltown Castle – beside Milltown House (Map 15). Shortly after acquiring Milltown House in 1879, Tooke Cumming Luscombe sold Milltown Castle to the Sisters of Charity in 1880 and the nuns demolished the castle to make way for their Victorian novitiate building, which in 2003 was converted into 15 private apartments called Convent Hall, as part of the Mount St Anne's redevelopment complex.[54]

Apart from knowing its location, we have very little detail about the castle. No visual records of it have apparently survived, except for a very small symbolic depiction on a Down Survey barony map from about 1655 (Map 1).[55] In 1901 local historian John Christopher FitzAchary published his personal recollections of Milltown Castle in the Rathmines News. This report is the only written description we have of the structure:

> *Milltown Castle, when we last saw it, was in thorough repair, and the arched guard room had been transformed into a very spacious and excellent kitchen, and an improved close-range occupied the space where in olden times, the former occupants were delighted with the big wooden logs that blazed upon the hearth. A fine old stone staircase led us to the upper apartments. When it was deemed expedient to raise the ceilings of the upper rooms, it was, of course, necessary to remove the ancient roof, and it was found to be a work of great labour. The walls turned out to be about five feet thick, and so well was the masonry work done that, like in the old fortalices that we have met with in the 'Kingdom of Kerry', the mortar proved almost harder than the stone. The hill on which the castle is built presents all the appearance of an entrenchment.*[56]

In 1725 a lease of 13 acres including 'the castle of Milltown and the new dwelling house, messuage[57] or tenement thereunto adjoining' was granted to Hugh Johnston of Dublin for 41

50 Mills, 'The Norman settlement in Leinster', p. 173; Francis Elrington Ball, *The history of the county of Dublin* (8 parts, Dublin, 1903–20), ii, pp. 66–7.

51 Elizabeth O'Brien, 'Excavations at Dundrum Castle' in Christiaan Corlett (ed.), *Unearthing the Archaeology of Dún Laoghaire-Rathdown* (Dublin, 2013), p. 116.

52 Mills, 'The Norman settlement in Leinster', p. 173.

53 O'Brien, 'Excavations at Dundrum Castle' pp. 114–15.

54 RD 1880/42/282; Irish Sisters of Charity, *Milltown in Brief... 1879–1995*, Circular Letter 26 April 1995; *Sunday Times*, 30 March 2003.

55 Down Survey, 'The Barony of 1/2 Rathdown in the County of Dublin by Williem Farrand and Williem Storck', http://downsurvey.tcd.ie/down-survey-maps.php#bm=Rathdown&c=Dublin (accessed 9 December 2019).

56 *Rathmines News*, 14 December 1901.

57 A messuage is a term used in deeds to signify a dwelling-house and its immediate surrounding property including outbuildings.

years.[58] The castle is mentioned briefly in 1837 when it was the residence of the Misses Hunt, and described as the 'partly repaired edifice of Milltown Castle'.[59] The castle was assessed in 1845 for the Griffith's Valuation, when it was occupied by the Rev. R.G.L. McGhee, but unfortunately there are no revealing comments about the structure, apart from the surveyor recording that its dimensions were 46 feet long, 29 feet wide and 20 feet tall. The surveyor assigned the building with the quality letter b -, meaning that it was deteriorated by age and in imperfect repair. Other parts of the complex, including a cellar, were recorded as old but in repair.[60] Two years later, in 1847, another surveyor recorded in the observations section of his notebook that the property was 'called Milltown Castle [with] land attached', a regrettably short and enigmatic comment.[61]

One of the old access points to the castle is visible on a nineteenth-century estate map of Milltown village (Map 12). That entrance is now a pedestrian walkway between the Wilde and Green delicatessen and St Broc's sheltered housing building (formerly St Anne's secondary school). The footpath leads uphill to the Mount St Anne's apartment complex close to where the castle stood originally.

We do not know when Milltown was built or for whom, but we can make some tentative suggestions based on a fifteenth-century grant of land at Taney. In 1414, Archbishop Thomas Cranley granted Thomas Locum a 50-year lease of a messuage and 80 acres in Taney at a yearly rent of 43*s*. 4*d*. (i.e. 6½*d*. per acre) for the first 30 years and thereafter at 50*s*. per annum for the remaining 20 years of the term.[62] Crucially, Locum was required to build at his own cost a sufficient house of stone, ditched and embattled, 18 feet by 26 feet within the walls, and 40 feet high below the battlement. At the end of the term Locum was required to surrender the premises with the haggard and gardens sufficiently enclosed. The archbishop could re-enter the premises if the fortified house was not built within four years. It is not unreasonable to assume that a lease with similar conditions was granted in the fifteenth century by the archbishop to the senior tenant of Milltown. In any event, Milltown Castle must have had additional defensive functions apart from being a fortified residence. The castle was deliberately built on an elevated site overlooking the valley of the River Dodder and the ford at Milltown. A photograph taken in 1951 by local photographer Tommy O'Neill from the top of St Anne's national school building – itself situated within about 100 metres of the original site of the castle – gives a very good idea of what the view must have been like from the parapet of Milltown Castle (Pl. 3). In the fifteenth century there would have been clear uninterrupted views towards the mountains in the background, the road to Dundrum in the middle distance and the fording point of the Dodder in the immediate foreground.

We know that the vulnerability of bridges and fording points on the River Liffey was of great concern to the Irish parliament in medieval times, as the following extract from 1455 explains:

> *Irish enemies and English rebels coming by night ... sometimes between the water of the Liffey between Lucan and Clontarf onto Fingal, rob, kill and destroy the liege people of the King so that the parts of Fingal are likely to be finally destroyed unless remedy be ordained thereupon.*[63]

---

58 RD 44/351/29734.

59 Lewis, *Topographical Dictionary of Ireland*, ii, p. 370.

60 NAI, VO OL50945, House Book for Milltown Village 1845, no. 96.

61 NAI, VO, OL70089, Quarto Book, Townland of Milltown 1847, p. 211.

62 McNeill, *Archbishop Alen's Register*, pp. 237–8.

63 H.F. Berry (ed.), *Statute rolls of the parliament of Ireland, reign of Henry VI* (Dublin, 1910), p. 315.

Plate 3. Milltown Village, c. 1951 (courtesy of Mary Long)

Accordingly, orders were made for the inhabitants of Fingal to assist in stopping up all fords and building trenches 'upon whatever land it may be, from the bridge of Dublin to the island of Clontarf'. The work was overseen by several prominent lay and clerical landowners, including the archbishop of Dublin.[64]

Although the defensive measures do not mention the River Dodder, undoubtedly the raiders were able to cross the river unimpeded on their way to the Liffey crossing points and beyond to plunder Fingal. Milltown Castle may therefore have been built or later strengthened to secure the fording point on the Dodder at Milltown. It is hardly co-incidental that a defensive structure, parts of which still survive in the grounds of Simmonscourt Castle, was built close to the crossing point on the south bank of the River Dodder below Donnybrook.

LOSS OF CONTROL BY THE CHURCH

In the mid-fifteenth century concerns too were being raised about the loss of control of the archbishop's lands in south Dublin, such as the manors of Shankill and Tallaght. Recitals in a statute of 1460 explain that these marginal lands had been lost not only because of raids by Irish enemies and English rebels, but because over time the archbishop had sold or leased the lands to parties who

64 Berry (ed.), *Statute rolls of Henry VI*, p. 315.

had no legal obligation to defend the land or who neglected to fulfil their defensive duties.[65] When archbishop Michael Tregury attempted to take control of these lands later in the 1460s he was violently resisted – to such extent that Tregury was taken prisoner and abused in captivity – by the marcher families occupying the lands, namely, the Harolds, the Walshes and the O'Byrnes.[66] Later still, a statute of 1488 defined the boundary dividing the territory fully controlled by Dublin city and that controlled or influenced by the marcher families to the south and west, as running from along the coast from Dalkey to Merrion and then south-west following the River Dodder and beyond as far as Saggart and Rathcoole.[67] On occasion, national politics impacted negatively on the region too. When King Henry VII removed the earl of Kildare as Justiciar (Lord Lieutenant), Kildare responded in 1492 by ordering his political satellite clients in the Dublin march to create havoc in an attempt to thwart the king.[68]

CONCLUSION

The medieval period in Milltown was marked by periods of prosperity and warfare as the political relationships between the Palesmen and the Gaelic natives ebbed and flowed. The introduction of the organised manorial system of farming controlled by the archbishop of Dublin brought its own stability, prosperity and routines too. Nonetheless, at the end of the fifteenth century Milltown was on the boundary of a volatile area in circumstances which must have made life very difficult for the ordinary inhabitants trying to farm their land and pay their rents. This situation was to become more complicated by the Reformation and its attempted implementation throughout the island of Ireland by the Tudor and Stuart monarchies of England in the sixteenth and seventeenth centuries. ■

65 Áine Foley, *The Royal Manors of Medieval Dublin: Crown and Community* (Dublin, 2013), p. 179.

66 Maginn, 'English marcher lineages', p. 130.

67 Maginn, 'English marcher lineages', p. 134.

68 Maginn, 'English marcher lineages', p. 134.

Chapter 3:
The Era of the Tudor and Stuart Monarchies

Chapter 3: The Era of the Tudor and Stuart Monarchies

INTRODUCTION

This chapter charts the transition from the late medieval period to the early modern era in Milltown, a time of unprecedented political and religious upheaval in Ireland. There is very little historical information from the sixteenth century specific to Milltown, apart from a contemporary description of quarrying activities, which will be mentioned presently. The historical record for Milltown improves greatly in the following century. Although the 1640s were a devastating decade in Irish history, the Cromwellian conquest left us with a wealth of contemporary records which, in the case of Milltown, shine a light on some of its principal inhabitants. The survival of the parish registers of the Protestant parishes of St Peter and St Kevin, which date back to the third quarter of the seventeenth century, has greatly assisted in mapping out the accelerated growth in the population of Milltown that occurred as part of the transformation of Dublin city after the restoration of the Stuart monarchy in 1660.

CHANGES IN LAND OWNERSHIP AND OCCUPANCY

In the early sixteenth century the senior tenant of the archbishop's lands at Milltown was Robert Talbot of Belgard, who held a castle, two messuages and 160 acres in Milltown together with 5 acres in Churchtown.[1] Talbot's property in Milltown included the townland of 'Boley Maior' (Farranboley), according to a note made by Archbishop Alen when he was editing the diocesan property calendar in the early 1530s.[2]

Robert Talbot's principal residence was at Belgard Castle near Clondalkin which was built on lands belonging to the archbishop of Dublin. The Talbot family of Belgard, which was a branch of the Talbot family anciently settled at Malahide Castle, held extensive lands scattered throughout

1 Margaret C. Griffith, *Calendar of Inquisitions formerly in the office of the Chief Remembrancer of the Exchequer prepared from the MSS of the Irish Record Commission* (Dublin, 1991), pp. 148–50.

2 Charles McNeill (ed.), *Calendar of Archbishop Alen's Register c. 1172–1534*, (Dublin, 1950), p. 172 at footnote 5: 'Talbot is now tenant; anciently called Bolytown'.

County Dublin. Robert was heavily involved in the political machinations of the time concerning the feud between the FitzGerald earls of Kildare and the Butler earls of Ormond and this may have caused his death in 1523. On Robert Talbot's death his Milltown property passed to his son Reginald Talbot. Reginald married Rose Luttrell in 1536 and granted Milltown to Simon Luttrell and others as part of his marriage settlement with Rose. Later on, in 1553, Reginald created a trust under his will in which he bequeathed his lands in Milltown and 5 acres in Dundrum to his son John for life.[3] It is very unlikely that the Talbots ever lived in Milltown given that their principal residence was at Belgard Castle. Instead, the Talbots would have sublet their Milltown and Churchtown properties to local families such as the Lawlesses and Walshes who occupied and farmed the lands.

The Talbot property transactions at Milltown were part of a wider trend affecting territory originally in the firm ownership and oversight of the archbishop of Dublin but which over time passed into the *de facto* control of the archbishop's tenants. The process by which this trend occurred and the reasons for it are rather complicated. Nonetheless, a brief explanation is necessary at this point because it provides the background to the acquisition of land in Milltown in the seventeenth and eighteenth centuries by the Dublin merchant families of Ussher and Leeson, which will be discussed later.[4]

The critical issue was that the archbishop of Dublin did not own the diocesan lands outright but only held a life interest in those lands. Archbishops with materialistic ambitions sought to increase their own income and those of their families by creating long leaseholds and making transfers of land, a legal procedure called alienation. By way of example, in 1604 Archbishop Loftus leased a property for 61 years, the lease to begin on the expiry of another 61-year lease made in 1593, with the result that the property was alienated from the control of the see until 1715, assuming the leases ran their full terms. Once a long lease was granted to a tenant, the tenant or his successors could sell on the lease by way of assignment (possibly on multiple occasions over the term of the lease) with the result that the property and its tenants passed out of the direct control and supervision of the Church for very long periods, thereby considerably weakening the connection between the archbishop and his estates. The government was slow to deal with the situation and it was not until 1634 that an act was passed by the Irish parliament which restricted episcopal leases to maximum terms of 21 years and 40 years for agricultural and urban land respectively. But by then much damage had been done by excessive alienation and the negative effects were difficult to undo, notwithstanding the limited success of some tenacious clergymen in the post-Restoration period of the seventeenth century.[5]

In addition to the problems caused by excessive alienation, old customary tenures such as copyhold, which required the payment of only a very small head rent, continued to operate on the archbishop's estates well into the nineteenth century.[6] An instance of this came to light in 1856 when the earl of Milltown put up his freehold estates for sale. The earl's estates included properties in Milltown and Donnybrook which he held in fee subject to 'a chief rent of five pounds late currency, which has been paid to the archbishop of Dublin and his predecessors from time

3 Ball, *History of county Dublin, iii* (Dublin, 1905), pp. 15–16; Griffith, *Calendar of Inquisitions*, pp. 148–50 (inquisition post mortem of alienations by Reginald Talbot, 23 October 1556).

4 Raymond Refaussé and Mary Clark, *A catalogue of the maps of the estates of the archbishop of Dublin 1654–1850* (Dublin, 2000) where the topic is very well explained by Raymond Gillespie in his historical introduction at pp. 21–36.

5 Refaussé & Clark, *A catalogue of the maps of the estates of the archbishop of Dublin*, pp. 22, 24, 28.

6 Refaussé & Clark, *A catalogue of the maps of the estates of the archbishop of Dublin*, p. 24.

immemorial'. The deed creating the chief rent had long since been lost by 1856 and it was a condition of the sale that 'the purchaser shall not be at liberty to object by reason thereof'. One of the freehold properties for sale in Milltown (lot 56) sold for £2,700; the condition that lot 56 indemnify the other lots previously subject to chief rent was of immaterial concern given the value of the land.[7]

In practical terms, therefore, from the mid-sixteenth century onwards (i.e. from the Talbot tenancy of Milltown) it is more appropriate to refer to the senior ecclesiastical tenant of Milltown as the owner as he had *de facto* control over the use and disposal of the property with few, if any, legal obligations to the archbishop of Dublin apart from the payment of a small annual rent.

The succeeding ownership of Milltown after the Talbots is difficult to trace. This is because there is a complete lack of ecclesiastical and private property records for Milltown for the 150-year period between the inquisition post mortem of Reginald Talbot's property in 1556 and the creation of the Registry of Deeds in 1707. To partially fill this gap historians are reliant on three incomplete civil and cartographic records commissioned as part of the Cromwellian and Stuart land resettlement of Ireland, namely, the Civil Survey (1654), the Down Survey (1655–6) and the Books of Survey and Distribution (c. 1663).

The Civil Survey and the *Books of Survey and Distribution* record that at the time of the Irish rebellion of 1641, 60 acres of land described as being part of Churchtown, in the parish of Taney, half barony of Rathdown were held by Sir William Ussher as part of his inheritance. This land was bounded on the east with Roebuck, on the south with Dundrum, on the west with Rathfarnham, and on the north with Milltown. In short, the district of Milltown situated on the south bank of the River Dodder (also known as Farrenboley) was, in the mid-seventeenth century, part of the parish of Taney in the half barony of Rathdown, and was included as part of Churchtown's lands in the Civil Survey.[8] These facts are confirmed by the Down Survey parish map for Donnybrook and Taney but with the difference that Ussher is stated as owning 160 acres of land, which equates exactly to the amount of land which Robert Talbot held in Milltown in the early sixteenth century (Map 2).[9]

The part of Milltown located on the north bank of the River Dodder was, in the mid-seventeenth century, part of the parish of St Kevin in the barony of Newcastle and Uppercross. According to the *Books of Survey and Distribution*, in 1641 Sir Adam Loftus held land in Milltown amounting to 193 acres, 3 roods and 8 perches.[10] The same document records that Peter Barnewell was the owner of an identical quantity of land in Milltown lying in the parish of Rathfarnham.[11] The latter entry was made in error, as shown by the fact that Milltown was not included in the Rathfarnham parish boundary description accompanying the Down Survey map.[12]

Ussher and Loftus were both Protestants and their religious background was instrumental in their acquisition of property in Milltown.

7 NAI, Landed Estates Court Rental, 'Particulars and Conditions of Sale of the free simple estates of the Earl of Milltown on 8 January 1856'; *Freeman's Journal*, 12 January 1856, p. 3.

8 Robert C. Simington, *The Civil Survey of County Dublin AD 1654–1656* (Dublin, 1945), pp. 262–3; Books of Survey and Distribution for the Parish of Taney, Half Barony of Rathdown, County Dublin, (NLI, MS 714, folio 47, Microfilm P7382A).

9 Down Survey, The Parishes of Doonabrooke & Tannee in the 1/2 Barony of Rathdown by Wm Farrand', http://downsurvey.tcd.ie/down-survey-maps.php#bm=Rathdown&c=Dublin&p=Donnybrook+and+Taney (accessed 9 December 2019).

10 Simington, *Civil Survey of Dublin*, p. 308.

11 Simington, *Civil Survey of Dublin*, p. 302.

12 Simington, *Civil Survey of Dublin*, p. 302.

THE USSHER AND LOFTUS FAMILIES

The Usshers were an old Dublin mercantile family with many branches throughout the city and county. Part of the lands of Donnybrook came into Ussher hands through marriage with the Fitzwilliams in 1524. Sometime later the Usshers built an impressive Tudor residence for themselves called Donnybrook Castle, which was something of a misnomer as it was built with comfort in mind – it had 13 hearths in the 1660s – without any fortification. The Usshers were part of a small group of leading civic families of Dublin who embraced the Tudor reformation of the second half of the sixteenth century. In contrast, the Tudor reformation was rejected by the majority of the old Norman colonist families of Dublin city and of the Pale – often referred to as the old English to distinguish them from the sixteenth-century English Tudor immigrants referred to as the new English. The Ussher family prospered under the Tudor and Stewart administrations and the Usshers' enthusiastic adoption of the new state religion was central to their rising fortunes.[13] Thus William Ussher of Donnybrook was knighted in 1603 and in 1613 he was returned as a member of parliament for the borough of Wicklow.[14] Ussher married well, for his first wife was a daughter of Archbishop Adam Loftus of Rathfarnham. Sir William Ussher died at a very advanced age in 1637 and was succeeded by his grandson, Sir William Ussher the younger (William the elder's son and heir Arthur had sometime previously drowned while attempting to cross the River Dodder during a flood).[15]

Impressive as the ascent of the Usshers was, it was eclipsed by the success of the Loftus family, and Adam Loftus in particular, who had come to Ireland as chaplain to the earl of Essex when the latter was appointed lord lieutenant in the 1560s. Loftus was a highly intelligent and well-educated man who had distinguished himself at Cambridge University. He was also extremely ambitious and he used his many talents for political and material self-aggrandisement. During a highly successful career, he was to be appointed successively as dean of St Patrick's cathedral, archbishop of Armagh and Dublin, and lord chancellor of Ireland, the last position which he held for 24 years. Like his son-in-law, Sir William Ussher, Loftus was a supporter of Trinity College which was founded in 1592. Following the failed rebellion of James Eustace, the 3rd Viscount Baltinglass, in 1580, the lands of Rathfarnham reverted to the crown. In the meantime, Loftus had been soliciting lands forfeited during the Desmond rebellion but the crown instead granted him Baltinglass's lands in Rathfarnham in 1582. Within two years of acquiring Rathfarnham Loftus built the imposing fortified house, Rathfarnham Castle, which still stands to this day and is in the care of the Office of Public Works.[16] In October 1582 Loftus was given a grant of lands in Donnybrook which were formerly part of All Hallows estate.[17]

Loftus's acquisitiveness was greatly resented by his political opponents and in 1592 he was accused of making favourable grants of archiepiscopal lands to his relations.[18] From a procedural point of view the chapter (governing body) of Christ Church Cathedral was required to confirm episcopal leases made by the archbishop but there is no official record of any leases for Milltown

13 Ball, *History of county Dublin*, ii (Dublin, 1903), pp. 50–3; Colm Lennon, *The lords of Dublin in the age of the Reformation* (Dublin, 1989), pp. 273–4; David Dickson, *Dublin: The making of a capital city* (Dublin, 2014), pp. 36–9.

14 NLI, Genealogical Office, MS U 26 G.O. 469; Calendar of the state papers relating to Ireland, 1611–1614 (London), p. 114.

15 Ball, *History of county Dublin*, ii, p. 51.

16 Ball, *History of county Dublin, ii*, pp. 117–20.

17 Lennon, *Lords of Dublin*, p. 97.

18 Refaussé and Clark, *A catalogue of the maps of the estates of the archbishop of Dublin*, p. 24.

being granted or confirmed during the period 1574 to 1634.[19] Nonetheless, the evidence points to Adam Loftus having used his position to acquire the district of Milltown on both sides of the River Dodder for himself and his son-in-law, William Ussher, in the late sixteenth century.

The local impact of these two Protestant proprietors is hard to judge but there is strong evidence that Ussher, and Loftus in particular, favoured persons of the same religious persuasion when subletting their lands.[20] Such a policy would be consistent with Adam Loftus's antipathy towards Catholicism, as exemplified in 1584 when Loftus, as lord chancellor, was centrally involved in the nine-month trial, torture and execution of the Catholic archbishop of Cashel, Dr Dermot O'Hurley.[21] Some years later, a religious survey carried out by Archbishop Bulkely in 1630 revealed that about 40 and 60 people were attending divine service in the Church of Ireland parishes of Donnybrook and Rathfarnham respectively. In contrast, there were only two householders in Taney parish that regularly attended divine service. Bulkely's survey also reported on Catholic religious practice in the area and noted that mass was said by a Fr John Cahill in Donnybrook and its adjoining parishes, including the towns of Merrion, Dundrum and Balally.[22] There is no mention of mass being said in Milltown because there were insufficient numbers of Catholics living there in the early seventeenth century due to Ussher's and Loftus's policy of promoting a Protestant tenantry. Indeed, it is unlikely that the area around the fording point of the Dodder at Milltown was sufficiently built up in the early seventeenth century to constitute the nucleus of the village that grew up there in the second half of the seventeenth century, a point which is discussed later in this chapter.

The creation of a Protestant interest at Milltown and Donnybrook in the late sixteenth and early seventeenth centuries was mirrored by developments to the west of Milltown, at Rathmines. In the 1630s Rathmines came into the ownership of Sir George Radcliffe who was a friend and confidant of the lord lieutenant, the earl of Strafford. Radcliffe built a large Jacobean mansion worth £7,000 on a site where Palmerston Villas and Cowper Villas are now. Radcliffe and his mansion were badly impacted by the political and military turmoil of the 1640s – Radcliffe was imprisoned in London in 1640 and his mansion was burnt down in 1642. The house was later rebuilt on a smaller scale with six hearths, which was recorded on the Down Survey barony map of 1655 (Map 1).[23]

LAW AND ORDER IN THE SIXTEENTH CENTURY

By creating a marcher district in south and west County Dublin inhabited by strong Norman settler families such as Walsh, Harold and Lawless, the Dublin authorities hoped to contain or mitigate the worst effects of their Irish enemies, the O'Byrnes and the O'Tooles. This strategy did not always work out as planned because the temptation of rogue elements of the marcher families to 'go native' and plunder their neighbours was sometimes too hard to resist. This is starkly illustrated by a petition made to the Irish parliament in 1563:

19 Refaussé & Clark, *A catalogue of the maps of the estates of the archbishop of Dublin*, p. 22; Raymond Gillespie (ed.), *The first chapter act book of Christ Church Cathedral, Dublin, 1574–1634* (Dublin, 1997).

20 As regards Loftus this view is also supported by Professor William J. Smyth of UCC: William J. Smyth, 'Exploring the social and cultural topographies of sixteenth and seventeenth century county Dublin' in F.H.A. Allen and Kevin Whelan (eds), *Dublin City and County: From Prehistory to Present* (Dublin, 1992), p. 136.

21 C. Scantlebury SJ, 'Rathfarnham Castle', *Dublin Historical Record*, xxii, no.1 (February 1951), p. 22.

22 'Archbishop Bulkeley's report on the diocese of Dublin, 1630', *Irish Ecclesiastical Record*, 5, (Dublin, 1869), p. 148.

23 Ball, *History of county Dublin, ii, pp. 101, 105–6*; Down Survey, 'The Barony of 1/2 Rathdowne in the County Dublin by Williem Farrand and Williem Storck', http://downsurvey.tcd.ie/down-survey-maps.php#bm=Rathdown&c=Dublin (accessed 9 December 2019).

> *Whereas William Harrold, esquire, came with diverse persons in warlike manner to Balally, Dundrum, Mulchanstown and Leopardstown in the march of the county of Dublin, the 20th day of August last past, and there feloniously killed eight of the King's subjects, and pillaged the said villages, and feloniously took with them 200 cows, 40 heifers, and 100 sheep.*[24]

After considering the petition and coming to the conclusion that Harrold 'is a fugitive and keeps no certain residence in any place, and is not amendable to Common Law', parliament issued a proclamation for him to surrender to the authorities to answer the charges made against him and in default Harrold would be attainted as a felon and his land and property forfeit.[25]

Despite these outbreaks of violence ordinary life continued and disputes were resolved without recourse to violence. The right to operate courts independent of crown and municipal jurisdiction was part of the liberties reserved to the archbishop of Dublin in the twelfth century. This episcopal independence was the origin of the archbishop's manor court of St Sepulchre. A transcript of the court's proceedings for the years 1586 to 1590 has survived, some of which mention litigants living in Milltown.[26]

On 21 June 1587 a case was heard at St Sepulchre between Alison Lawless of Little Bray against Edmond Walsh of Milltown, Belina Talbot his wife and Thomas Lawless, executors, in a dispute concerning the will of John Lawless of Milltown, and an unpaid legacy of £30 sterling bequeathed by John to one of his daughters. It subsequently transpired on 24 October 1587 that Edmond Walsh of Milltown and John Walsh of Little Bray agreed to enter into a bond of £40 each and to abide by the outcome of arbitration in relation to the dispute over John Lawless's will. The arbitrators were John Talbot of Crumlin, John Durning of Dublin, Theobald Walsh of Carrickmines and John Walsh of Balally.[27] In an unrelated case, an Edward Walsh of Milltown was appointed to serve on a 12-man jury on 21 June 1587.[28] The association with Milltown of old marcher families such as Lawless and Walsh is interesting because it indicates the degree to which the district had become integrated with the south Dublin march at the end of the sixteenth century before the letting policies of the Usshers and Loftuses had taken effect.

INFRASTRUCTURAL DEVELOPMENTS

The physical legacy of sixteenth- and seventeenth-century Milltown is recorded by an old stone bridge erected across the River Dodder about 80 metres upstream from the modern vehicular bridge at the junction of Milltown Road and the Dundrum Road. This ancient bridge has for years been known locally as the Packhorse Bridge (Pl. 51). On an early nineteenth-century estate map (Map 7) the bridge is called the 'Old Bridge' to distinguish it from the 'New Bridge', i.e. Classon's Bridge beside The Dropping Well pub, which was built in the eighteenth century and later repaired and widened in 1928.

No information about the Packhorse Bridge's builder or its date of construction has survived. The bridge is depicted on the Down Survey parish map which was drawn up in 1655 so the bridge must have been built in the early seventeenth century at the latest (Map 2). A bridge of similar design and

24 Henry F. Berry (ed.), *Statute Rolls of the Parliament of Ireland first to twelfth years of King Edward the fourth* (Dublin, 1914), pp. 67–9.

25 Berry, *Irish Statute Rolls*, pp. 67–9.

26 Herbert Wood, *The Court Book of the Liberty of St Sepulchre* (Dublin, 1930).

27 Wood, *The Court Book of St Sepulchre*, pp. 25, 44–5.

28 Wood, *The Court Book of St Sepulchre*, p. 26.

Plate 51. Old Bridge House and the Packhorse Bridge, Milltown, c. 1960 (author's collection)

proportions existed in Clonskeagh in 1603 and it is possible that the Packhorse Bridge was erected at the same time as the Clonskeagh Bridge, possibly in the second half of the sixteenth century.[29] There is a potential mention of the Packhorse Bridge among the memoirs of the Elizabethan lord lieutenant, Sir Henry Sidney. The reference occurs in Sydney's account of the bizarre escape of Sir Edmund Butler from Dublin Castle in 1575, whence Sir Edmund:

> *came to the bridge of the water of the Dodder, a mile and a half distant from the Castle of Dublin and there what mad joy soever took him in the head I cannot tell, he went into the river and there stood (as he constantly after affirmed) the most part of that cold and long night in the water up to the chin. From thence he crept away ... and was conducted into the county of Kilkenny and was secure.*[30]

This bridge could be either the Packhorse Bridge or one of the other bridges over the Dodder at Clonskeagh or Rathfarnham. The reference to the short distance of one and a half miles from Dublin Castle makes the Packhorse Bridge the most likely candidate, particularly if the Milltown Path, which is depicted prominently on Rocque's 1760 survey of County Dublin (Map 4), existed in the sixteenth century. Coincidentally, local folklore from the early twentieth century

29 CARD, i (Dublin, 1895), p. 192; NLI Prints and Drawings 1969 TX 26, *Old Clonskeagh Bridge* and *Clonskeagh Bridge*, pen and ink drawings by Cecilia Margaret Nairn née Campbell.

30 Peter O'Keeffe and Tom Simington, *Irish Stone Bridges: History and Heritage* (1st edition, Dublin, 1991), p. 213.

held that Henry and Arthur O'Neill and Hugh Roe O'Donnell, future lord of Ticonnell, crossed the Packhorse Bridge on making their way to Wicklow after their escape from Dublin Castle in 1591 and stayed overnight at an inn beside the bridge before pressing on to Wicklow the next day in a snow storm.[31]

Assuming then that the Packhorse Bridge was built in the sixteenth century this raises the question of who may have built it. There are no references to the bridge among the Dublin city or Dublin diocesan records. This suggests that the bridge was built by a private individual. If this is the case then the Packhorse Bridge may have been built by one of the major tenants of the archbishop who leased land in Milltown at various times in the sixteenth century, such as the Talbots of Belgard, the Usshers of Donnybrook and the Loftuses of Rathfarnham. There is no evidence that the bridge was ever tolled.

The Packhorse Bridge has justifiably been described from an engineering perspective as a 'first-class job'.[32] The bridge has two arches and was originally wide enough to carry horse-drawn vehicles. A third arch was inserted at a later period to allow a millrace to pass underneath the bridge on the south bank of the River Dodder. The foundations were laid on the original limestone bedrock of the River Dodder but over many years the limestone was quarried out around the piers and foundations of the bridge. A pedestrian refuge was built as an extension to one of the bridge's parapet walls to protect pedestrians from animal traffic. When one considers the number of floods the bridge has withstood – especially the Hurricane Charlie flood of 25/26 August 1986 – and its lack of regular maintenance, the Packhorse Bridge is a remarkable survivor.

QUARRYING ACTIVITY

The bedrock of Milltown and the surrounding district is composed of black carboniferous limestone, known locally in Dublin as 'calp', which was quarried extensively along the Dodder from medieval times to the mid-nineteenth century.[33] In 1564–5 calp was extracted from quarries at Milltown and Clonskeagh to provide stones to repair Christ Church Cathedral which had suffered serious damage in April 1562 when parts of its walls and vaults collapsed.[34] The quarrying operations were overseen by Sir Peter Lewis, the proctor of Christ Church. Contemporary accounts and journals kept by Lewis describe stonemasons cutting the stone out of the bed of the River Dodder, which, with great difficulty, had been dammed and diverted for that purpose. The workmen also attempted to quarry stone from the river bank. This was dangerous work. On 15 October 1564 a large bank of earth fell and buried a workman seriously injuring him, while on another occasion an autumnal flood washed away the dam and diversions erected on the river bed.[35]

Once extracted from the Dodder the calp had to be cut into more manageable portions and carted to Christ Church at a cost of 3*s.* 6*d.* a day. These transport costs were mitigated on occasions when,

31 J. Nolan, *Changing Faces* (Dublin, 1982), p. 134.

32 O'Keeffe and Simington, *Irish Stone Bridges*, p. 213. The authors' engineering backgrounds provide a comprehensive description of the bridge from an engineering point of view.

33 G.W. Lamplugh, 'The geology of the country around Dublin' in *Memoirs of the Geological Survey of Ireland*, (London, 1903), pp. 9, 76, 101; Margaret Murphy and Michael Potterton, *The Dublin region in the Middle Ages* (Dublin, 2010), p. 390; *Freeman's Journal*, 26 April 1858, p. 4; *Saunder's Newsletter*, 25 November 1869, p2.

34 Raymond Gillespie (ed.), *The proctor's accounts of Peter Lewis 1564–1565* (Dublin, 1996), pp. 13, 24, 53, 66, 68, 80.

35 James Mills, 'Peter Lewys: His work and workmen', *Journal of the Royal Society of Antiquaries of Ireland*, 31, no. 2 (1901), pp. 102–3; Gillespie, *Proctor's accounts*, p. 53.

as an alternative to quarrying at Milltown, stone was quarried at low tide on the shoreline at Clontarf, because the load could be shipped directly to the cathedral.[36] The effects of quarrying on the bed of the River Dodder can still be seen at Milltown between the Packhorse Bridge and Classon's Bridge.

THE 1641 REBELLION AND THE CROMWELLIAN CONQUEST OF IRELAND

A complex interplay of local, national and international events led to an uprising of Catholics in Ulster in October 1641 which in turn resulted in ten years' strife and bloodshed throughout the country. Milltown was also impacted by these developments, but before discussing them it is necessary to provide a short background to the rebellion in Dublin.

Although the rebels failed in their objective to capture Dublin on 23 October 1641, its southern hinterland – strategically important because of its location between the city and the Wicklow mountains – was the scene of much violence and bloodshed in the early 1640s, most infamously at Carrickmines Castle. Conflict was inevitable because the vast majority of Old English Catholic gentry of the Pale, and in particular those with land in south-east Dublin, eventually threw in their lot with the rebels (the exception being the Fitzwilliams of Merrion). Several factors gave rise to their decision to join the revolt but disaffection caused by the Dublin government's antipathy towards the Old English Catholics coupled with the initial defeat of the Dublin garrison army at Julianstown were critical. More specifically, the old English Catholic proprietors living in south Dublin and north Wicklow were placed in a terrible predicament. On the one hand, at an early stage in the revolt, they were on the receiving end of sectarian cruelty by the Dublin garrison commanded by Sir Charles Coote and, on the other hand, they faced attacks from the O'Toole and O'Byrne clans, whose lands in Wicklow had been the subject of attempted dispossession in the 1630s by the earl of Strafford, Sir Thomas Wentworth. Given all these circumstances it is not surprising that the old English Catholics of south Dublin joined the rebellion. In short, from November 1641 onwards the whole of south Dublin became a zone of guerrilla warfare, with the rebels – who set up their headquarters at Bray – and government forces making plundering sorties throughout south Dublin/north Wicklow, sometimes as close to the city as St Stephen's green in the case of the rebels.[37]

The effects of the rebellion on local inhabitants can be gauged by studying the sworn written depositions made predominantly by the Protestant victims which were collected by the Dublin authorities in the 1640s. For example, a miller living in Milltown in 1641, John Bacon, deposed that on 12 December 1641 a group of about 100 rebels drove away 29 English-bred cows belonging to him. On 22 December 1641 the rebels returned and broke into his house through the slate roof and stole two English horses and five pecks of good wheat. On a third occasion, the rebels broke down the doors of Bacon's house and the adjoining mill house and took away seven English-bred horses and all Bacon's goods and 'household stuff'. Bacon went on to identify some of the raiders, namely, Donnell O'Doyle of Milltown, Donnell Carroll and Donnell Moore both of Churchtown, all of whom Bacon described as labourers, 'who having gotten armour of his majesty's fled therewith to the rebels'. Bacon estimated the value of his losses as being at least £300 sterling. The credi-

36 Murphy and Potterton, *The Dublin region in the Middle Ages*, p. 390.

37 Nicholas Canny, 'What really happened in 1641?' in Jane H. Ohlmeyer (ed.), *Ireland from independence to occupation 1641–1660* (Cambridge, 1995), pp. 24–42; David Costello, 'The political and topographical history of the half barony of Rathdown, county Dublin in the seventeenth century' (MA thesis, University College, Dublin, 1990); Aidan Clarke, *The old English in Ireland, 1625–42* (Dublin, 1966), pp. 177–8; Mark Clinton, Linda Fibiger & Damian Shiels, 'Archaeology of massacre: The Carrickmines mass grave and the siege of March 1642' in David Edwards, Padraig Lenihan & Clodagh Tait (eds), *Age of atrocity: Violence and political conflict in early modern Ireland* (Dublin, 2007), pp. 192–218.

bility of Bacon's report is open to doubt because Bacon had already fled to the safety of his house in Dublin by the time of the first attack and his deposition was entirely based on the second-hand evidence of other informants.[38]

It is of interest that Bacon stocked English-bred livestock and was sufficiently affluent to own a house in Dublin as well as his house in Milltown, which unusually for the time had a slate roof. This suggests that Bacon was probably one of the strong English tenants brought in by Ussher or Loftus to Milltown. The fact that the robberies were allegedly carried out by (amongst others) Irish labourers living in Milltown and Churchtown hints of local tensions that had been building up between the two ethnic groups prior to the rebellion. On the other hand, it may be that the crimes against Bacon were opportunistic ones committed amid the general anarchy prevailing at the time.

In March 1642 the government forces went on an offensive to drive out the rebels, who had occupied the old Norman tower houses in south Dublin, and were disrupting local markets and the city's food supply. One of the rebel bases was at Carrickmines Castle which was the subject of a notoriously bloody siege. The government forces brought artillery to besiege the castle, including heavy duty demi-culverin which were difficult to transport.[39] Thus it is probable that the artillery train crossed the Dodder at Milltown using the Packhorse Bridge and proceeded to Carrickmines via Dundrum.

Sometime later the government decided to billet cavalry at Milltown. The soldiers were likely to have been stationed in Milltown Castle as this was the only fortified building in the locality. The cavalry's orders were to patrol south Dublin and attack any rebels they encountered. From the deposition of Hugh Booth, it appears that the soldiers engaged the rebels on many occasions. On or about 2 June 1643, the commander of the cavalry, Hugh Booth, and seven cavalrymen were ambushed near Merrion by a party of about 35 rebels who were led by a Captain Bernard Talbot. Two of Booth's men were killed in the attack, two escaped and Booth and three of his men (two of whom who were injured in the ambush) were made prisoners and taken to Arklow Castle. One of the soldiers, William Pigeon, was freed as part of a prisoner exchange and another soldier was ransomed for £30. Booth and the fourth prisoner, John Woodyard, were held captive for 22 weeks 'in daily danger of death and in much want and miserie'.[40]

The eventual victory of the parliamentarians in the English Civil War by the middle of the 1640s was an ominous development for the royalist cause in Ireland and the Catholic Confederacy based in Kilkenny. As a result, the latter two groups were forced into an uneasy and ultimately unsuccessful alliance. Dublin had been held by the parliamentarian interest since 1647, but in July 1649 the Marquis (later Duke) of Ormonde attempted to retake the city by laying siege to it with a coalition force of about 10,000 men. Ormonde's army was camped to the south of the city near Rathmines (believed to have been in the area of Palmerston Park) from where they captured Rathfarnham Castle and its small garrison of parliamentarian soldiers on 28 July 1649. The next objective was to occupy Baggotrath Castle in order to prevent the Dublin garrison from grazing their horses on the pastures between Baggotrath and the city's walls. A force of 1,500 soldiers was dispatched from Rathmines on the night of the 1–2 August to occupy Baggotrath Castle but for unknown reasons – incompetence or treachery on the part of the guides has been suggested – the troops did not arrive at their destination (a distance of perhaps one and a half miles) until daybreak, and then only

38 Deposition of John Bacon, 29 January 1641 (TCD, MS 809, fols 295r-295v).

39 Costello, 'The political and topographical history of the half barony of Rathdown', pp. 21–2; Clinton and others, 'Archaeology of massacre', p. 198.

40 Deposition of Hugh Booth, 6 January 1644 (TCD MS 810, fols 230r-230v).

to find that the parliamentarians had substantially dismantled the castle rendering it useless. Ormonde's forces had to secure their exposed position at Baggotrath and they began by erecting ramparts and digging trenches in full view of the city's defenders. This proved fatal because the parliamentary commander, Colonel Michael Jones, seized the initiative and attacked and routed the soldiers at Baggotrath on 2 August 1649, thus starting the Battle of Rathmines which ended in the complete defeat of the royalists.[41]

It is beyond the scope of this chapter to describe the Battle of Rathmines in any great detail save for one incident. The centre of Ormonde's army, which was composed of infantry, was commanded by Colonel Giffard. According to the account of the battle by the historian Francis Elrington Ball, Giffard's infantry was attacked from behind by a troop of Colonel Jones's cavalry 'which approached them by a lane which ran from Milltown to what is now the Ranelagh road' and attacked in front by a party of Colonel Jones's cavalry.[42] It is impossible to say where the location of the attack was by reference to modern geographic locations – it could have been along the current Prospect Lane/Milltown Road/Sandford Road – but what is beyond doubt is that the battlefield theatre encompassed a wide area of farmland and lanes stretching westwards from Baggotrath Castle to Rathmines and Milltown as far as the River Dodder over which the parliamentarians pursued and attacked the fleeing royalists.[43]

Apart from the number of royalists killed – put at 600 by the royalists and 4,000 by the parliamentarians – the battle was a disaster for Ormonde and the Catholic cause in Ireland because it allowed Cromwell to land unopposed in Dublin at Ringsend on 14 August 1649.[44] The might of the Cromwellian military machine after the sacking of Drogheda on 11 September 1649 – one contemporary report stated that the heads of 16 executed royalist officers were sent to Dublin and stuck on pikes on the approach roads to the city – must have created considerable fear and apprehension among the remaining Catholic population in and around Dublin.[45] As it happened, Cromwell's army arrived almost at the doorstep of Milltown on 22 September 1649 when Cromwell chose Donnybrook to muster his forces for his campaigns in Munster and south Leinster. The army which camped overnight in Donnybrook was made up of four regiments of light horse, four regiments of dragoons and four regiments of foot.[46] Cromwell's short stay in Donnybrook gave rise to two incidents recorded in the local folklore of Milltown and Rathfarnham. It is asserted that there was a mass-house in Milltown on the site of the current church of St Columbanus and St Gall and that it escaped destruction because the Cromwellians thought the building was a private residence.[47] While it is plausible that some Cromwellian soldiers passed

---

41 Ball, *History of county Dublin*, ii, pp. 47–8, 102–5; Francis Elrington Ball, 'The Battle of Rathmines', *Journal of the Royal Society of Antiquaries of Ireland*, 32, no. 3 (1902), pp. 246–56; Weston St John Joyce, *The neighbourhood of Dublin* (2nd edition, Dublin, 1913), pp. 182–90.

42 Ball, 'The Battle of Rathmines', p. 255.

43 See also C.H. Firth (ed.), *The Memoirs of Edmund Ludlow Lieutenant-General of the Horse in the Army of the Commonwealth of England 1625–1672* (Oxford, 1894), i, p. 230, where Ludlow records that Jones captured some of Ormonde's infantry who had taken refuge in Rathmines Castle, which originally stood where Palmerston Park is now.

44 Ball, 'The Battle of Rathmines', p. 256; Dickson, *Dublin: The making of a capital city*, pp. 70–1.

45 John Morrill, 'The Drogheda massacre in Cromwellian context' in David Edwards, Padraig Lenihan & Clodagh Tait (eds), *Age of atrocity: Violence and political conflict in early modern Ireland* (Dublin, 2007), p. 256.

46 Ball, *History of county Dublin*, ii, p. 53.

47 Rev. Michael G. Murray, 'The Story of Milltown' in *Souvenir of the Blessing and Dedication of the Church of the Immaculate Virgin Mary of the Miraculous Medal at Clonskeagh* (Dublin, 1957), unpaginated.

through Milltown on their way to or from the Donnybrook camp, there is no evidence of any mass-house in Milltown in the seventeenth century and, as previously explained, the number of Catholic inhabitants in Milltown in the first half of the seventeenth century was likely to have been small.

The other piece of local folklore is that Cromwell spent a night at Rathfarnham Castle and held a council of war in an adjacent building (since demolished) called Cromwell's Court.[48] Again, this story is almost certainly inaccurate. It may be that Cromwell was confused in the folklore with one of the many military incidents that are recorded to have taken place at Rathfarnham Castle over the course of its history. This debate is certainly not over because archaeological excavations in one of the castle's basement towers in 2014 resulted in the discovery of a seventeenth-century breast plate which had been pierced by a musket ball.[49]

To add to the dislocation caused by warfare, Dublin and its hinterland suffered periodic outbreaks of bubonic plague in the early 1650s. The cumulative effects of these catastrophes have led one historian to estimate conservatively that there was a mortality rate of at least 14 per cent in south county Dublin during the period 1649–52.[50] Nonetheless, despite the turmoil of the 1640s and early 1650s, Milltown was in a better position to stage a recovery from the mid-1650s onwards because the district was unaffected by the Cromwellian confiscations of the 1650s and the Stuart land ownership changes of the 1660s. Thus, Milltown continued to be controlled by the Ussher and Loftus families after the restoration of Charles II as king of England in 1660 until the close of the seventeenth century.[51]

When William Petty's cartographers were mapping the barony of Newcastle and Uppercross in the mid-1650s they noted that many of the Dodder's mills from Rathfarnham to Ringsend had been destroyed during the late wars but that some had been recently repaired.[52] It is likely that one of those repaired was John Bacon's mill at Milltown because Loftus or Ussher would have been in a position to arrange for this to happen as soon as the security situation in Milltown had improved.

The effects of Adam Loftus's policy of creating a Protestant tenantry is revealed again in the results of a nationwide poll tax of 1660/1661 in which the number of persons aged 15 years and over living in Milltown, parish of St Kevin, barony of Uppercross (i.e. the Loftus lands on the city side of the Dodder) was 19, 14 of whom were of English origin and five who were of Irish origin.[53] The number of adults returned for the Loftus lands at Rathfarnham, half barony of Rathdown, was 39, 23 of whom were of English origin and 16 of whom were of Irish origin.[54] Conversely, the neighbouring districts of Donnybrook, Churchtown, Dundrum and Roebuck all returned comfortable majorities of Irish inhabitants.[55]

48 Scantlebury, 'Rathfarnham Castle', p. 25.

49 'New Discoveries at Rathfarnham Castle', *Archaeology Ireland*, 28, no. 4, issue 110 (Winter 2014), pp. 4–5.

50 Pádraig Lenihan, 'War and Population, 1649–52', *Irish Economic and Social History*, 24 (1997), pp. 9–11, 16.

51 Ball, *History of county Dublin*, ii, pp. 53, 112.

52 Simington, *Civil Survey of Dublin*, p. 289.

53 Séamus Pender (ed.), *A census of Ireland circa 1659 with a new introduction by William J Smyth* (Dublin, 2002), p. 380. Smyth argues that the document is not a census but is a poll tax return for 1660.

54 Pender, *Census of Ireland*, p. 377.

55 Pender, *Census of Ireland*, pp. 365, 381.

PROSPERITY AND THE EMERGENCE OF CONSUMERISM

As noted above, in the space of about 70 years from 1560 to 1630 Milltown and its immediate hinterland came to be controlled by extremely powerful and wealthy families who built large mansions at Donnybrook, Rathfarnham and Rathmines and introduced a strong Protestant tenantry to their lands. The October 1641 rebellion put an abrupt halt to the prosperity that was undoubtedly experienced by a small cohort of inhabitants of Milltown and their neighbours in Donnybrook, Rathmines and Rathfarnham – the deposition of the Milltown miller, Hugh Bacon, shows how well-off he was, and he was not at the top of the social pyramid.

The prosperity enjoyed by Bacon and the wealthier inhabitants is tantalisingly revealed by two very small but significant objects dug up in the late twentieth century in the gardens of houses at 8 Clonskeagh Road and 68 Eglinton Road, which had originally been fields located only a few hundred metres to the north-east of Clonskeagh/Prospect Lane. The earlier of the two items is a tobacco clay pipe bowl which was found by the author in the back garden of 8 Clonskeagh Road/ 4 St James's Terrace (Pl. 4). The extremely small clay pipe dates from the early seventeenth century, a time when tobacco was a very expensive and luxurious commodity. The clay pipe was almost certainly imported from England, which raises the possibility that one of Ussher's English Protestant tenants had taken up the smoking habit. Certainly, smoking seems to have become more widespread and popular by the late seventeenth century judging by the large numbers of clay pipe bowls and stem fragments found in Rathfarnham Castle.[56]

The second object is a fragment of a glass wine bottle with a seal of a bishop's mitre with the initials WP above which was found by John Neville at 68 Eglinton Road, Donnybrook and is now in the author's possession (Pl. 5).[57] According to archaeological experts at the Museum of London, the bottle was made in London in the mid-seventeenth century by a William Paget or a William Proctor, each of whom owned pubs called the mitre tavern. The experts' opinion is that the bottle was commissioned by William Proctor of Wood Street. The WP seal is the most common seal design found archaeologically in London, and examples have also been found on colonial sites on the east coast of America.[58] How a mid-seventeenth-century wine bottle from London came to be discarded near Donnybrook is a mystery. It would be sensationalist – and very likely incorrect – to link the bottle with Cromwell's camp at Donnybrook of 22 September 1649. The bottle's origins are likely to be more prosaic: it may have belonged to the occupants of Donnybrook Castle which was within 400 metres of the find site. Coincidentally, a number of late seventeenth-century wine bottles bearing the seal of Adam Loftus were found during excavations of Rathfarnham Castle which, along with numerous other luxury items recovered, are indicative of the sophisticated consumer culture that grew up quickly in post-restoration Dublin and spread to the city's hinterland of which Milltown was an integral part.[59]

Other seventeenth-century items found close to Milltown provide a contrast to the luxuries consumed by the inhabitants of Donnybrook and Rathfarnham Castles. These are three brass halfpenny tokens dated 1672 which were found on separate occasions in the gardens of 8 Clonskeagh Road and 68 Eglinton Road (Pl. 6).[60] The three tokens were issued by a Michael Wilson, a Dublin

56 Antoine Giacometti and Alva MacGowan, *Rathfarnham Castle Excavations 2014* (Dublin, 2015), p. 99.

57 Personal communication with John Neville, since deceased.

58 E-mail correspondence between the author and Nigel Jeffries of the Museum of London Archaeology, 8 June 2015.

59 'New Discoveries at Rathfarnham Castle', pp. 4–5.

60 The coins were found on separate occasions by John Neville and the author in the late twentieth century.

Plate 4. Clay pipe bowl, early seventeenth century (author's collection)

Plate 5. Wine bottle seal, mid-seventeenth century (author's collection)

Plate 6. Brass halfpenny tokens, 1672 (author's collection)

butcher, because there was no officially authorised small denomination coinage in circulation in Ireland at that time. The void was met by merchants who issued their own low denomination trade tokens notwithstanding official proclamations forbidding such practice.[61] The tokens would have been in the possession of local labourers who were farming the fields where the coins were lost. It is a remarkable coincidence that two of the coins were found on the same property on two separate occasions. The close proximity of the Clonskeagh Road coins to each other (originally in one field) may indicate that in the late seventeenth century the land was used for more labour-intensive farming such as tillage or meadowing rather than animal husbandry.

THE EMERGENCE OF A VILLAGE AT MILLTOWN

It is impossible to state with any certainty when human settlement by the banks of the Dodder at Milltown became sufficiently nucleated to be termed a village, due to a complete lack of evidence prior to the mid-seventeenth century. From about 1660 onwards information becomes available from separate sources which indicate that Milltown had developed into a village by the banks of the Dodder by the last quarter of the seventeenth century.

As previously noted, the number of persons aged fifteen years and over living in Milltown, parish of St Kevin, barony of Uppercross (i.e. the Loftus lands on the city side of the Dodder) in 1660/1661 was 19.[62] This is the only base record available from which to make assumptions as to the population of Milltown in 1660 and its growth thereafter. In order to estimate the number of all inhabitants an eminent historical geographer has suggested that the number of adults be multiplied by 2.5, which for Milltown gives a figure of 47.5 persons in 1660/1661.[63]

61 Edward Colgan, *For want of good money: The story of Ireland's coinage* (Bray, 2003), pp. 130, 132; An identical token was discovered at Rathfarnham Castle: Giacometti & McGowan, Rathfarnham Excavations, pp. 101–2.

62 Pender, *Census of Ireland*, p. 380.

63 William J. Smyth, 'Society and settlement in seventeenth century Ireland: The evidence of the "1659 Census"' in W.J. Smyth and K. Whelan (eds), *Common Ground: Essays on the historical geography of Ireland* (Cork, 1988), p. 56.

Undoubtedly, Milltown grew quickly in the post-Restoration period in line with the increase in the city's population. In this regard, it has been estimated that the population of Dublin city doubled in about 20 years from the 1660s to the 1680s due to an influx of migrants from the provinces and from England.[64]

The impact of the city's growth on Milltown's population in the later decades of the seventeenth century can be traced in the register of births and deaths for the Protestant parishes of St Peter and St Kevin.[65] These two parishes and a portion of St Stephen's parish united in 1680 as the single united parish of St Peter.[66] For example, during the period 1674 (the year of the first entry for Milltown) to 1689, the parish register records a total of 25 deaths and baptisms for people who were living in Milltown; for the decade 1690 to 1699 that figure had increased to 31. The list of the Milltown residents recorded in the register reveals a wide variety of surnames (and spellings), some common and others much less so: Barker, Ben\Benn, Bishop, Blunt, Carton\Cartane\Charton, Chamberlain, Classon\Glasson, Clyeburne, Coffy, Connell, Cooke, Cormock, Crag, Davies, Delaney, Dillon, Freemen, Francisco, Fyan, Fellow, Hill, Hendrick, Jewitt, Lee, Pagett, Parris, Randal, Reany, Robarts, Reily, Richardson, Rozine, Scot, Smedlock, Syberry\Sybry, Throsdell, Thorp, Wall, Waters, Wade and Ward. Note that the data derive from one Protestant parish only. Other inhabitants of Milltown – including Catholics – would have been baptised or buried in other parishes such as Donnybrook or Taney so the number of families living in Milltown in the late seventeenth century was undoubtedly greater than those recorded in the register for St Peter's parish.

Some of the local families listed in the St Peter's parish register intermarried, which is not surprising. For example, Thomas Lee, whose family was farming in Milltown in the late seventeenth century, married a Mary Waters in 1715. Mary was likely to have been a daughter of John Waters who was manufacturing paper in Milltown in 1711 and who died in 1715.[67] In addition, families can be traced into the eighteenth century by examining property transactions which from 1708 were registered in the Registry of Deeds. Edward and Joan Coffy [*sic*] of Milltown are recorded as having had three children, Mary, Hannah and William, who were baptised on 30 July 1692, 22 November 1693 and 18 July 1694 respectively.[68] In 1724 a piece of ground commonly known as 'Coffee's [*sic*] garden leading upon the left hand of the castle near the two ash trees' was leased by John Magennis, a market gardener of Milltown, to John Benn of Milltown, victualler.[69] A Robert and Jane Benn were living in Milltown in the 1680s.[70] By the 1720s Jane, who had been widowed, was in possession of 12 acres of land on the north side of Milltown Road, roughly where Milltown Park and the Abbeyfield and Glenmalure Park housing estates stand now (Map 3). [71]

---

64 Dickson, *Dublin: The making of a capital city*, pp. 91–2.

65 James Mills, *The register of the Parish of St Peter and St Kevin 1669–1761* (Parish Register Society of Dublin, 1911).

66 James Mills, *The register of the Parish of St Peter and St Kevin 1669–1761* (Parish Register Society of Dublin, 1911).

67 Report of the Deputy Keeper of the Public Records of Ireland, *Index to the Act or Grant Books, and to original Wills, of the Diocese of Dublin 1272–1858*, Appendix to the 26th Report (Dublin, 1894), p. 519; Mills, *Register of St Peter & St Kevin*, pp. 206, 236; NAI, Thrift genealogical abstracts, bundle 15, no. 3696; RD 8/218/2640.

68 Mills, *Register of St Peter & St Kevin*, pp. 132, 137, 141.

69 RD 50/303/33112.

70 Mills, *Register of St Peter & St Kevin*, p. 99.

71 RD 49/49/30653.

Plate 7. Weir on the River Dodder, Classon's Bridge, Milltown c. 1900 (image courtesy of the National Library of Ireland)

By the late seventeenth and early eighteenth centuries milling activity at Milltown began to diversify beyond the essential requirement to grind corn. In 1711 Joseph Leeson granted a lease to John Waters of Milltown, paper maker, and to his son Edward, a printer, for a paper mill which was formerly a tuck mill (tuck or fulling mills were used to clean and beat raw wool prior to its being woven into cloth).[72] The mill, which was powered by the weir on the River Dodder behind the carpark of The Dropping Well pub (Pl. 7), was located on the north bank of the River Dodder (Map 7) where the Shanagarry apartment complex is now. The obsolete tuck mill, which had probably been established in the third quarter of the seventeenth century before the introduction of restrictions on exports of wool to England in 1699, marked the beginning of industrial activity on the banks of the Dodder at Milltown that was to continue for the next 200 years or so and which characterised the locality in the eighteenth and nineteenth centuries.

CONCLUSION

In many ways the experiences of Milltown during the sixteenth and seventeenth centuries mirrored those which were occurring on a national level, as Milltown fell under the control of the Tudor *nouveau-riche* gentry, clergymen and their tenantry. The district and its inhabitants suffered considerably during the wars of the 1640s but, due to its close proximity to Dublin city, Milltown was able to take advantage of the economic growth of the city in the Restoration period post 1660. Although there is insufficient evidence available before that date to confirm the existence or extent of nucleated settlement on the banks of the River Dodder at Milltown, it is beyond doubt that a village existed at that location by the third quarter of the seventeenth century. Analysis of property records in the Registry of Deeds dating back to first decade of the eighteenth century provides additional support for the view that Milltown can be characterised as a village from the late seventeenth century onwards. These transactions are discussed in detail in the next chapter. ■

72 RD 8/218/2640; NAI, Landed Estates Court Rental, vol. 38, no. 3, 'Particulars and Conditions of Sale of the Freehold Estate of the Earl of Milltown to be sold on 8 January 1856', lot 59.

Chapter 4: The Development of the Leeson Estate in the Eighteenth Century

Chapter 4: The Development of the Leeson Estate in the Eighteenth Century

INTRODUCTION

This chapter investigates the impact of the Leeson family and its influence on the development of Milltown in the eighteenth century through reviewing the nine leases whereby the Leesons let their large freehold estate in Milltown in the early and mid-eighteenth century, and the subsequent sub-lettings and assignments to middlemen made by the first Leeson tenants. Thanks to the Registry of Deeds, which began recording property transactions in 1708, it is possible to build up a comprehensive set of very detailed data about life in Milltown in the 1700s and the various landholdings, buildings and their occupants. The emergence, too, of numerous newspapers in Dublin reveals new social and economic details about Milltown that are not available for previous centuries. Collectively, these data sources help to explain how an ambitious and wealthy family transformed Milltown over the course of 50 years or so in the eighteenth century.

THE RISE OF THE LEESON DYNASTY

Towards the close of the seventeenth century, the Loftus family disposed of their property in Milltown. The exact timing of the disposal is uncertain because it predated the setting up of the Registry of Deeds in 1707.[1] Nonetheless, the change in ownership is likely to have occurred after the death at the siege of Limerick of Colonel Adam Loftus (grandson of Sir Adam Loftus of Rathfarnham who died in the 1660s) in 1691 following which the Loftus estate subsequently devolved by marriage to the Wharton family who were absentee landlords.[2] Similarly, in 1701 the Usshers sold off their properties in Donnybrook and appear to have disposed of their interests in

1 The Registry of Deeds was established to prevent fraudulent land transactions in the wake of the Williamite land confiscations of the 1690s, but registration was not compulsory.

2 Ball, *History of county of Dublin*, ii (Dublin, 1903) pp. 128–30.

Milltown by 1707.[3] Thus, after a tumultuous century and a quarter lasting from the late sixteenth century to the beginning of the eighteenth century, the Loftus and Ussher families disappear from Milltown's history. So, who replaced the once powerful Loftus and Usshers in Milltown? In short, Milltown was taken over by an ambitious Dublin brewing family by the name of Leeson. The Leesons were to have a pervasive impact on the growth of Milltown in the eighteenth century but before discussing those developments, it is appropriate to review the background to the Leeson family's acquisition of the freehold estate of Milltown.

The first of the Leeson family, Hugh Leeson, came to Ireland in the 1640s as part of the English army sent over to Dublin to suppress the 1641 Rebellion. At the end of the hostilities Hugh Leeson left the army and entered business, establishing himself as firstly a butcher and then as a brewer, proving successful at the latter activity. Hugh married the daughter of Alderman Richard Tighe, who was twice Lord Mayor of Dublin, thus enhancing his social status. This in turn enabled Leeson to further his business interests, which among other things, included substantial property developments on the south side of St Stephen's Green. Hugh Leeson died in 1700 and was succeeded in the brewery business by his son Joseph Leeson (1660–1741), who was made a freeman of Dublin in 1696. Joseph Leeson was an enthusiastic property speculator who used the profits of his brewing business to invest in substantial house building and property lettings in Dublin city and its suburbs.[4]

By the 1740s the Leesons had sold the brewery business as part of their ascent to the ranks of the gentry. On his death in 1741 Joseph Leeson was succeeded by his sole surviving son, Joseph Leeson the younger, who was born in 1711 (Pl. 8). It was during Joseph Leeson the younger's lifetime (he died in 1783) that the Leeson family achieved its greatest wealth and status. This Joseph built Russborough house in Blessington (building commenced in 1742), entered the Irish House of Commons in 1749 as the MP for Rathcormack, and was successively ennobled as baron of Russborough (1756), Viscount Russborough (1760) and the 1st earl of Milltown (1761).[5] It was while canvassing for a peerage in 1751 that Leeson asked that his title be:

> *changed from that it was formerly intended and instead of Russborough in the County of Wicklow, to be Milltown in the County of Dublin. This my friends think more proper as it is the name of a now flourishing town which came to me from my grandfather.*[6]

The degree to which Milltown had become a flourishing town by the 1750s will be discussed presently but first it is appropriate to set out the geographic location of the Leeson estate in Milltown.

The property transactions recorded in the Registry of Deeds provide compelling evidence that Hugh Leeson and Joseph Leeson the elder had acquired all bar one portion of their Milltown estate before 1707 (the year in which the Registry of Deeds was established) because there is only one memorial after 1707 that records Joseph Leeson the elder purchasing land in Milltown. In 1714 Joseph Leeson bought Thomas Lee senior's property in Milltown from his heirs and assigns Thomas Lee junior,

3 NAI, Landed Estates Court Rental, vol. 38, no. 3, 'Particulars and Conditions of Sale of the Freehold Estate of the Earl of Milltown to be sold on 8 January 1856'.

4 Laffan and Mulligan, *Russborough* (Blessington, 2014), pp. 13–25.

5 Laffan and Mulligan, *Russborough*, pp. 22, 31, 39; John Lodge, *The Peerage of Ireland* (Dublin, 1789), iii, pp. 124–6.

6 Letter from Joseph Leeson to Sir Robert Wilmot, 15 July 1751 (Derbyshire Record Office, D3155/WH/3442).

Plate 8. Portrait of Joseph Leeson, later 1st earl of Milltown (1711–1783), by Antony Lee, 1735, NGI.698 (photo © National Gallery of Ireland)

Thomas Russell, Thomas Blackham and Katherine Blackham (alias Lee) for £275.[7] Apart from this transaction the Leesons are likely to have acquired some of their land in Milltown before 1700 (the year Hugh Leeson died). In any event, from 1711 onwards Joseph Leeson the elder began leasing extensive premises, mills, farmland and other properties in Milltown.

The extent of the Leeson property interests in Milltown can be gauged from legal documents drawn up when the Leeson freehold estate was put up for sale in the encumbered estates court on 8 January 1856.[8] The data for Milltown have been summarised in tabular form below with an estimate of the current locations compared with the contemporary locations mentioned in the legal documents, which will be described in greater detail presently.

The data need to be explained to appreciate their value and limitations. When Hugh and Joseph Leeson were buying up property in Milltown and its vicinity there were only three narrow lanes and one main road in existence – the Milltown Path (now subsumed by Richmond Avenue South), Coldblow Lane (Belmont Avenue), Clonskeagh Lane (Prospect Lane) and the Milltown/Dundrum Road – and two narrow bridges spanning the Dodder at Milltown (the Packhorse Bridge) and at Clonskeagh. With the exception of the village beside the Dodder ford at the bottom of Milltown Hill the area was completely rural, made up of a patchwork of large enclosed fields with a few small cabins and farmhouses.

Very fortunately, a map of some of Joseph Leeson's property on Milltown Road which was surveyed on 22 March 1718 has survived (Map 3).[9] The late Donnybrook historian, Daniel Parkinson, kindly gave the author a photocopy of part of the original map. Unfortunately, Danny had not kept a record of where he acquired his copy of the map and despite many efforts to track down its location, its current ownership and location remains a mystery.[10] Notwithstanding the absence of some of the detail, the map contains much interesting information about Milltown 300 years ago. As far as the author is aware, no other maps of the Leeson estate in Milltown have survived. The absence of specific surveys of the Leeson estate in Milltown and its environs (in contrast with the Pembroke and Trimleston estates) make it very difficult to identify the locations of properties described in the leases with complete precision. This is especially so given the profound changes to the topography and infrastructure which have taken place over the last 300 years (see table overleaf).

---

7 Registry of Deeds, Dublin (henceforth RD) 13/193/5576, RD 13/194/5577. Apparently, a descendant of the Milltown Lee family, Anne Lee, married Arthur Guinness junior of the Guinness brewing family in 1793, from which issue Sir Benjamin Lee Guinness was named: http:gallot.co.nz/Guinness/ArthurGuinness.htm (accessed 7 July 2006); Frederic Mullally, *The Silver Salver* (London, 1981), p. 15.

8 NAI, Landed Estates Court Rental, vol. 38, no. 3, 'Particulars and Conditions of Sale of the Freehold Estate of the Earl of Milltown to be sold on 8 January 1856'. The total number of properties put up for sale amounted to 119 lots spread over Dublin city and six counties, nine lots (51–9) of which related to freehold property in Milltown.

9 *A Survey of the above Denominations being part of the Estate of Joseph Leeson Esq in the Parishes of Donnybrook and St. Kevins and County of Dublin: Miltown [sic] and its parts in the Parish of St. Kevins and Mouls holding in the Parish of Donnybrook Containing in the whole as in the particulars may appear Surveyed on the 22 day of March in the year of our Lord God 1718/9.* The surveyor's name is not clear from the photocopy in the author's possession.

10 In addition to online searches, the author made enquiries of the Dublin City Council archivist and the map librarian of Trinity college neither of whom knew where the original map is stored. Note that Irish/plantation acre measurements are used so the equivalent amount in statute acres is considerably larger.

Table 1. Long leases granted by the Leeson estate during the eighteenth century at Milltown

Contemporary location	Quantity in statute & (Irish/ plantation) acres A. R. P.	Yearly rent in current (1856) & (old) money £ *s.* *d.*	Renewal fine in current money (1856) £ s. d.	Tenure	Estimated current location
Meadow land on the west side of Prospect Lane, Donnybrook civil parish, Clonskeagh townland (Lot 51)	15 0 23 (9) (1) (16)	29 10 9 (32) (0) (0)	14 15 4 (6 months' rent)	Lease for lives 27 April 1753 to Anne Mowlds	Palmerston Grove, Millbrook village, Mount Sandford, St James's Terrace, Connaught Terrace and parts of Clonskeagh & Eglinton roads
Meadow land and farmhouse on the south side of Clonskeagh/Prospect Lane, St Peter's civil parish, Milltown townland (Lot 52)	9 1 0 (9) (1) (0)	29 10 9 (32) (0) (0)	14 15 4 (6 months' rent)	Lease for lives 27 April 1753 to Anne Mowlds	Crannagh, Ramleh Close and parts of Ramleh Park
Demesnes of Casino, Bloomfield & another house etc., Taney civil parish, Farranboley townland (Lot 53)	75 0 17 (46) (1) (19)	98 8 5 (106) (12) (6)	49 4 2 (6 months' rent)	Lease for lives 28 February 1754 to George Mowlds	Churchfields & Mount St Marys, Dundrum Road, Clonskeagh parish church, Gledeswood House/Avenue/Park, part of Bird Avenue
Several residences & houses in Milltown and land on the south side of Milltown Road, St Peter's civil parish, Milltown townland (Lot 54)	21 3 18 (13) (2) (0)	36 18 5 (40) (0) (0)	9 4 7 (6 months' rent)	Lease for lives 22 January 1725 to John Kerr, senior	South side of Milltown Road from Prospect Lane to the green opposite Milltown church inc. Grove House apartments, Greenfields, Ramleh Villas, Ramleh Park, Milltown shopping centre, the Old House, Milltown Hill, Geraldine Terrace, Strand Cottages, public carpark & Scullys Field
Milltown Colonnade, another dwelling house and other land forming part of Milltown Park, St Peter's civil parish, Milltown townland (Lot 55)	19 1 30 (12) (0) (0)	40 8 6 (not stated)	Not stated but probably 6 months' rent	Lease for lives 9 April 1741 to Robert Harris converted to a fee farm grant in 1850	North side of Milltown Road inc. Garrynure, Milltown Colonnade, Abbeyfield and part of Milltown Park
Several residences, demesnes, houses & cabins in Milltown, St Peter's civil parish, Milltown townland (Lot 56)	83 0 03 (51) (1) (7)	129 4 7 (140)(0)(0) plus head rent to archbishop of Dublin 4 12 3	64 12 3 (6 months' rent)	Lease for lives 22 September 1720 to Edward Allen	Adjacent to the previous lot on north side of Milltown Road from the former BMW garage to Alexandra College inc. Glenmalure Park, Elm House, Elm Grove House, Mt St Anne's, Milltown Catholic church, shops and apartments on main road; also includes the park on the north bank of the River Dodder as far as the Shanagarry apartments
A building formerly used as an iron mill, several houses, meadow land and other premises on the south bank of the River Dodder, Taney civil parish, Farranboley townland (Lot 57)	17 0 10 (10) (2) (6)	36 18 5 (40) (0) (0)	18 9 2 (6 months' rent)	Lease for lives 25 April 1764 to James Tandy and Thomas Kavanagh	Open space beside the Packhorse Bridge inc. Al Hussain House, Bankside Cottages, Thorncliffe apartments and part of the Dodder park; area on the west side of Dundrum Road inc. St Luke's Crescent, Ardlevan, Coolnahinch, Millmount Cottages/Terrace, Farrenboley Cottages & part of the Dodder park to the rear of those properties
Two houses and pasture land between the Dundrum Road and the Lower Churchtown Road, Taney civil parish, part of Rathmines Great townland (Lot 58)	54 2 33 (33) (3) (4)	55 7 8 (60) (0) (0)	27 13 0 (6 months' rent)	Lease for lives 21 March 1718 to Edward Allen	The north side of the Lower Churchtown Road from Classon's Bridge to the Windy Arbour Luas stop, including all of the houses opposite Milltown Golf Club, Patrick Doyle Road and St Columbanus housing estate
Mill, houses, buildings, cabins and three acres of land near Milltown Bridge, St Peter's civil parish, part of Milltown and Rathmines South townlands (Lot 59)	3 0 0 (not stated)	36 18 5 (40) (0) (0)	18 9 2 (6 months' rent)	Lease for lives 30 November 1717 to Edward Watters	Area on the north bank of the Dodder from the Packhorse Bridge westwards to the weir behind The Dropping Well pub and bounded by the road to Dartry and Rathmines and the River Dodder

PLANTATION ACRES AND STATUTE ACRES

Another complication is that an archaic unit based on the Irish or plantation acre was used to measure property in the eighteenth century and early nineteenth century. The Irish acre was replaced in the nineteenth century by the smaller English or statute acre, which was used by the cartographers of the Irish OS office. There is a significant difference in size between the two units: one English/statute acre equals 0.617347 Irish/plantation acres whereas one Irish/plantation acre equals 1.619835 English/statute acres. Thus, it is often difficult to match a written description of property in a lease using Irish acres with property delineated in the later OS maps which use statute acres, let alone match the description with the modern environment. The statute acre figure has been inserted in column 2 of the table with the Irish acre figure included in parenthesis below. Finally, the acre was subdivided into measurements of roods and perches – four roods to an acre and 40 roods to one perch.[11]

Despite these challenges, it is possible to identify with an acceptable degree of accuracy the current locations (in column 6 of the table) of the nine Milltown landholdings that were put up for sale in 1856 by the earl of Milltown. By reference to modern locations the Leeson freehold estate in Milltown can roughly be broken down as follows:

- From opposite the junction of Sandford Road and Belmont Avenue (its north-eastern extremity) including part of the Jesuit headquarters at Milltown Park and westwards along both sides of Milltown Road including the area between the Dodder and Clonskeagh on the south side of the road and the land on the north side of Milltown Road, including parts of the Milltown Park, Gonzaga College and Alexandra College campuses as far as the Luas tramline (its northern extremity)

- From Milltown Bridge on both sides of the road to Dartry and Rathmines as far as the River Dodder weir in the park behind The Dropping Well pub (its north-western extremity)

- From Milltown Bridge along both sides of the Dundrum Road (with the exception of a very small area on the east side of the Dundrum Road from Milltown Bridge to the entrance to the Churchfields housing estate) as far as Windy Arbour (its southern extremity) and the Lower Churchtown Road (its south-western extremity)

- From the junction of the Dundrum Road and Bird Avenue incorporating the housing estates on both sides of Bird Avenue to the junction with the Clonskeagh Road (its north-eastern extremity)

- From the junction of Milltown Road with the Lower Churchtown Road at Classon's Bridge to the Windy Arbour Luas stop, including all of the houses opposite Milltown Golf Club on the north side of the Lower Churchtown Road as far as the Luas stop, Patrick Doyle Road and St Columbanus housing estate

- As previously explained, this extensive area acquired by the Leesons originated from the much larger medieval landholdings of Milltown and Farranboley. Accordingly, the district identified today with Milltown is considerably smaller than it was several centuries ago (Maps 2 & 10).

11 Brian Nugent, *A guide to the 18th century records in the Irish Registry of Deeds* (Corstown, 2012), pp. 23–4. English/statute acres are quoted wherever possible as this unit was used by the OS in the nineteenth and twentieth centuries; however, there are occasions when only the Irish acreage is available, for example, when quoting from eighteenth-century deeds and newspapers.

CURRENCY DIFFERENCES

Rent was charged in a currency unit of pounds, shillings (20*s.* to the pound) and pence (12*d.* to 1*s.* or 240*d.* to the pound) which predated the introduction of decimal currency in 1971. An additional complication is that for almost 400 years the Irish pound was valued at less than the English pound, so the practice with legal documents in the eighteenth and early nineteenth centuries was either to distinguish between the Irish pound value and the English pound value or to include both. In 1701 the difference between the two currencies was fixed so that 13 Irish pence equated to one English shilling and 13 Irish pounds equated to 12 English pounds. The system of separate currencies for Ireland and England ended when the Irish pound was abolished in 1826.[12] Column 3 of the table shows the English pound (the legal currency when the properties were sold in 1856) with the old Irish currency in parenthesis. Due to space constraints the currency amounts have been rounded down to the nearest penny where fractions of a penny occur in the rental.

THE COMPLICATIONS OF LEGAL TENURE AND SECURITY

An explanation regarding the tenure of the properties listed in the table (at column 5) and the system of renewal fines (at column 4) is needed. Eighteenth- and nineteenth-century land law and conveyancing practice was very different and complicated by modern standards. The data for each of the nine lots put up for sale in Milltown in the 1850s include mandatory details of the legal tenure under which the tenant held his interest in the land. Over the passage of time numerous legal transactions affected all of the properties both before and after the date of the original tenant's lease from Joseph Leeson. These included subletting on short-term leases (of which there were very many), property subdivisions, surrenders and assignments of leases, mortgages, charges and judgements over property. In particular, eighteenth-century trade depended on extensive and informal networks of credit and debt. Success in business frequently depended on the quality of a person's credit network. In buoyant times, merchants were tempted to expand their credit relative to their capital base and were thus vulnerable to economic downturns.[13] Such transactions meant that at any given time there was a multitude of often competing legal and personal interests affecting many of the properties, as shall be shown later.[14]

In simple terms, the position is best understood using the analogy of a pyramid, with Joseph Leeson (the freeholder and head landlord) at its top and the property occupier (a junior tenant on a weekly lease or a lodger) at its base. The pyramid's mid-section comprises multiple layers of intermediate tenants and landlords (middlemen) some of whom held leases renewable forever, while others held short-term or determinable leasehold estates. In addition, other legal interests such as rent charges (annuities), family trusts, mortgages, and debts frequently encumbered the property.

The renewal fine was a fixed monetary charge that applied to a specific type of lease known as a lease for lives renewable forever. Legally, leases for lives renewable forever were classed as freehold tenure. This type of lease was commonly used to convey property in the eighteenth and first half of the nineteenth century. The important difference between the lease for lives renewable forever and a fixed-term lease was that the former was a lease of indefinite duration. In short, the lessor leased the property to the lessee who held the property for the duration of

12 Nugent, Registry of Deeds, p. 33; Colgan, *For want of good money*, pp. 176, 187.

13 David Kelly, 'The conditions of debtors and insolvents in eighteenth century Dublin' in David Dickson (ed.), *The Gorgeous Mask, Dublin 1700–1850* (Dublin, 1987), p. 98.

14 Kelly, 'The conditions of debtors' in Dickson (ed.), *The Gorgeous Mask*, p. 98.

the lifetimes of specific persons named in the lease, usually three in number. On the death of each of the named lives the lessee was required to pay a renewal fee to the lessor – which in the case of the Leeson leases amounted to six months' rent – and execute a new deed appointing a new named life to replace the one who had died. This process could, in theory, be repeated indefinitely, hence the term 'lease for lives renewable forever'. In practice, legal complications frequently arose with such leases when, for example, the named lives were not replaced after they died and as a result arears of renewal fines built up. As part of a radical overhaul of Irish property law in the wake of the Famine, the lease for lives renewable forever was abolished by the Renewable Leasehold Conversion Act of 1849 which, among other things, facilitated the conversion of such leases to fee farm grants. In practical terms, a fee farm grant was easier to administer and involved the payment of an annual fee farm rent (now commonly known as ground rent) to the grantor.[15]

The majority of the parties to property transactions involving credit had little or no personal connection with the building or locality in question. Identifying the important and discounting the irrelevant transactions, many of which are recorded in the Registry of Deeds (in the form of a summary of the original deed, called a memorial), is a time-consuming exercise. The approach I have adopted in this chapter is to bundle the transactions into separate strands relating to specific buildings, locations and activities, and to quote from those memorials that best describe the topographical, architectural and social history of Milltown village and its surrounding farms in the eighteenth century.[16]

ESTATE PRACTICE IN THE EIGHTEENTH CENTURY

The leasing strategies used by landowners to improve their estates varied widely in their complexities and outcomes. In some cases, landlords were restricted in the management of their estates by existing tenurial arrangements, restrictive covenants and by dependence on professional land agents.[17] The sample of nine long leases from Milltown is too small to be able to make any firm conclusions as regards estate planning by Hugh and Joseph Leeson. In so far as any estate policy can be dimly ascertained for the Leesons' farmland investments on the south side of the city, the Leeson practice seems to have been to grant leases for lives renewable for ever to strong famers such as the extended Mowlds family (originally spelt Mouls or Moules, but from the mid-eighteenth century onwards the surname was consistently spelt as Mowlds or Moulds). The Mowlds family had become well established as dairy farmers in Donnybrook by the turn of the eighteenth century.[18] Besides 18 plantation acres on the north-eastern end of Milltown, the Mowlds were granted leases of over 38 plantation acres in Cullenswood and Cullensfarm in 1741 (today part of Rathmines and Harold's Cross), 86 plantation acres at south Milltown/Windy Harbour (1734) and over 71 plantation acres in Churchtown (1754).[19]

15 For an excellent explanation of the arcane subject of eighteenth- and nineteenth-century conveyancing law see Edmund R. Digues La Touche, *The Law of Landlord and Tenant as administered in Ireland* (2nd Edition, 2 vols, Dublin, 1869).

16 The history of the mills and villas of Milltown are discussed in separate chapters.

17 B.J. Graham and L.J. Proudfoot, *Urban Improvement in Provincial Ireland 1700–1840*, Irish Settlement Studies No. 4 (The Group for the Study of Irish Historic Settlement, 1994), pp. 42–50.

18 RD 48/187/31299. On 18 May 1730 John Mouls and Elizabeth Thomas were married at Donnybrook: Blacker, *Brief sketches of the parishes of Donnybrook and Booterstown*, p. 274.

19 NAI, Landed Estates Court Rental, vol. 38, no. 3, 'Particulars and Conditions of Sale of the Freehold Estate of the Earl of Milltown to be sold on 8 January 1856', lots 51, 52, 53, 60, 61; RD 77/455/54333, RD 248/557/160861.

The Mowlds family multiplied and prospered throughout the eighteenth century and they became embedded in the farming and social fabric of Milltown for nearly 200 years, particularly on the south bank of the Dodder along the east side of the Dundrum Road.[20] Interestingly, the Mowlds eschewed riskier investments in industrial businesses on the Rivers Dodder and Slang, and their prudence undoubtedly contributed to the family's longevity in the district.

A contemporary expert writing in 1801, Lieutenant Joseph Archer, observed that farms in County Dublin were held under a variety of tenures; chiefly freehold, some for lives renewable forever, others for three lives only, and others for 31 years.[21] Archer's observations reflect the experience and practice in Milltown, but of more interest are his comments about a new custom whereby leases were granted to a tenant in return for a large lump-sum payment with a commensurate reduction in the annual rent. This upfront payment was called the entry fine, and should not to be confused with the renewal fine that applied on the death of the named life in the lease for lives renewable forever. Archer was highly critical of the entry fine:

> *Most of the leases are of an old date, and, of course, the holders of them derive great advantages. The oldest leases have been taken without a fine. It is now customary to demand a sum in hand, and to set at a lower rent in proportion, in which case it is commonly given for lives renewable for ever. It is assuredly a great check to agricultural improvements, to pay a fine; it lessens the farmer's capital, and, when paid, occasions an indolence in most tenants, that makes them careless of improvements.*[22]

Archer's criticisms of the entry fine were echoed by his contemporary critic, Hely Dutton, who made the following observations on the practice:

> *Mr Archer very justly reprobates the too general mode of taking fines; in addition to the destructive effects pointed out by him, I must add the injury the national character sustains; for I have frequently heard Englishmen exclaim against this practice, as tending to stamp us with the character of swindlers. So firmly has this custom taken root, that now, if a man has only a stable, at £6 a year, he will ask a fine. It is ridiculous enough to see advertisements stuck up in waste lots of ground; 'This ground to be let in lots for building without a fine': so far from demanding a fine, I think it would be much more reasonable to say, 'This ground will be let for building, rent free for two years.' I am convinced this would stimulate many to build, that are prevented by having to pay two years rent and very often more, before they can set their houses, besides the money expended in building.*[23]

It is impossible to know how prevalent the use of the entry fine was in Milltown since it was not compulsory to record the entry fine in the memorials lodged in the Registry of Deeds. If the practice was as common as contended by Archer and Dutton then this could have been a factor in the decline in building activity in Milltown village which began during the last quarter of the eighteenth century.

---

20 There are scores of transactions relating to the Mowlds family's activities in Milltown recorded in the Registry of Deeds, newspapers and elsewhere over a period of nearly 200 years that could form the subject of a separate history.

21 Joseph Archer, *Statistical Survey of the County of Dublin with observations on the means of improvement; drawn up for the consideration, and by order of the Dublin Society* (Dublin, 1801), p. 64.

22 Archer, *Statistical Survey of Dublin*, p. 65.

23 Hely Dutton, *Observations on Mr Archer's Statistical Survey of the County of Dublin* (Dublin, 1802), pp. 85–6.

DAIRY FARMING AND THE IMPORTANCE OF FODDER

Many of the leases quoted in this chapter concern the letting of meadow and pasture to dairymen. This is unsurprising given the demand for pasture for dairy cows and hay fodder for the numerous horses used to transport people and goods. Resulting from this demand, good grassland in the vicinity of Dublin could be let at between £2 and £10 per acre, yielding up to 4 cwt (203 kilograms) of hay per acre.[24] Dublin Corporation was one of the biggest consumers of hay because it had dozens of draught animals to feed. In July 1746 the Corporation owned 63 cart horses which required 1,500 loads of hay to feed annually at a cost of between £5 5*s.* and £5 10*s.* a score.[25]

Cows were let to dairymen at annual rents from £5 or £6 per cow. On average, a cow required between one and one-and-a-half acres of medium-quality grassland in order to produce up to 8 quarts (about 9 litres) of milk a day in summer and 5 quarts (about 5½ litres) a day in winter, but abuses such as adulterating milk with water were widespread.[26]

After James Classon died in 1778 his executors advertised that 'about 200 loads of excellent, well saved hay ... with horses, cows, carts, cars and household furniture' would be auctioned at his house and farm of 12 acres at Rathmines.[27]

The importance of hay in the farming practiced in Milltown and its vicinity is illustrated by contemporary newspaper advertisements from time to time:

> *Hay to be sold by auction, on Monday the 26th November, 1781, on the lands of Milltown, near the bridge, three ricks of well saved hay, about 500 loads of which will be sold either in the whole or by the rick, as the bidders shall think proper. The sale to begin at eleven o'clock on said day, and continue till all is sold. Dated this 19th day of November 1781.*[28]

> *Prospect Hall, near Milltown. To be let from 25th day of March next, for any term of years, or lives renewable forever, as may be agreed on, 21 acres of choice meadow land, divided into five fields, enclosed almost all round with a six feet stone wall, with a good house, garden and offices:*

> *For good air and extensive prospects no situation can excel it. For Particulars inquire at Healy's, No. 122, Stephen's green ... N.B. Between five and six hundred loads of choice well saved hay, the growth of the above land, to be sold by private contract, by said Healy. Three months' credit will be given on approved bills.*[29]

> *To be sold by auction on the premises, tomorrow, the 10th instant August [1784], the crop now standing on the lands of Churchtown, near Milltown, in the County of Dublin, about two miles from the city, late in the possession of Mr George Moulds, about 19 acres of excellent meadow, fit for mowing. The sale to begin precisely at 12 o'clock*[30]

24 R.A. Butlin, 'Agriculture in County Dublin in the late eighteenth century', *Studia Hibernica*, 9 (1969), p. 99. CWT is an abbreviation for 'hundredweight', a British imperial and US customary unit of weight or mass equal to 112lbs and 100lbs respectively.

25 CARD, ix (Dublin, 1902), pp. 210–11, 214.

26 Butlin, 'Agriculture in County Dublin', p. 99; Archer, *Statistical Survey of Dublin* (Dublin, 1801), pp. 58–61.

27 *Saunders's Newsletter*, 19 March 1778, p. 3.

28 *Saunders's Newsletter*, Tuesday 20 November 1781, p. 4.

29 *Saunders's Newsletter*, 9 March 1784, p. 4.

30 *Saunders's Newsletter*, Monday 9 August 1784, p. 3.

To be set for 21 years, either in the whole or in two divisions, about 19 acres of meadow, near Milltown, in the county of Dublin, divided into eight fields. Apply to Mr Ledsam, as above.[31]

To be sold by auction, by the sheriff of the County of Dublin, on Thursday the 25th day of January [1787] instant, by virtue of two writs of fieri-facias issued in these causes, near the Defendant's [John Moulds] house at Milltown, one large rick of hay the property of the Defendant. The sale to begin at twelve o'clock in the forenoon of the said day. Dated this 22nd day of January, 1787.[32]

Three of the advertisements quoted above emphasise that the hay has been 'well saved'. According to one contemporary critic writing in 1802, hay was often carelessly stacked and left too long in the fields and as a result:

It is not infrequent to see upwards of a foot at the bottom of the cock quite spoiled by this neglect; this to some of our great hay farmers is no loss, as, with all the bad and refuse hay of the farm, it is (if not reserved for the cows, which deserve the sweetest and best hay of the farm) lapped up in the inside of each roll of hay, and loaded for Smithfield. The frauds that are practiced in loading hay for this market call loudly for redress.[33]

Hay mowing provided employment for the local farm labourers. At the turn of the nineteenth century it cost, depending on the quality of the grass, between 6*s*. 6*d*. and 10*s*. to mow an acre of hay crop. At harvest-time, labourers worked from sun-rise to sun-set, but farm labourers typically worked a 12-hour day beginning at 6 a.m., with a half an hour for breakfast and one hour for dinner.[34]

During the course of the eighteenth century it appears that the Irish breeds of cattle were being slowly replaced by imported breeds and crosses. Dairy herds near Dublin comprised mostly English and Dutch breeds, with a few native Kerries.[35] Some cattle were particularly valuable to a dairyman and if a prized cow strayed or was stolen, its owner resorted to offering significant rewards for the cow's return by placing advertisements in the daily newspapers:

Stolen or strayed, off the lands of Rathmines, near Milltown, two new-calved cows, one of them yellow, with lloby [sic] horns, and R.F. on one of them, with a few white spots on her rump, and a white udder, rising seven years old; the other also yellow, with a white stripe down her back, and a brown muzzle, with wide horns, about eight years old, and a white belly. Whoever will bring said cows, or give intelligence to John Lapham, at Milltown, where they can be had, shall be paid one guinea reward; and if stolen, six guineas, to be paid on conviction of the person or persons who stole the same – November 25, 1781. John Lapham.[36]

Stolen or Strayed, on Friday night the 29 May [1784], from the lands of Milltown, a large red and white springing cow, five years old, each horn branded T.A. and one of them branded T.B. Whoever brings said

---

31 *Saunders's Newsletter*, Saturday 19 August 1786, p. 3. In 1790 Ledsam acquired a plot of ground on the north side of Milltown village main street with road frontage of 191 feet previously occupied by John Lapham, dairyman and farmer: RD 416/120/275477.

32 *Freeman's Journal*, 20 January 1787, p. 1.

33 Dutton, *Observations on Mr Archer's Statistical Survey*, p. 77.

34 Archer, *Statistical Survey of Dublin*, p. 113.

35 Butlin, 'Agriculture in County Dublin', p. 100.

36 *Saunders's Newsletter*, 30 November 1781, p. 3.

cow to Mr Thomas Andrews, No. 110, Coombe, shall be paid two guineas reward and no questions asked; or if stolen, five guineas for the thief or thieves, on conviction, over and above the reward of 20 guineas offered by the gentlemen of the Rathfarnham and Milltown Association.[37]

It is difficult to say how effective these advertisements were. Notwithstanding that the notices could only be read by the small percentage of the population who were literate, the fact that such losses were advertised in the press with significant rewards might suggest that successful recoveries were possible. As a deterrence to such crimes, the punishment for stealing cattle and sheep was hanging or transportation.[38]

Despite the theft of his cow, Thomas Andrews remained committed to Milltown. In 1790 he took a lease from Ann Elizabeth Mowlds of the field on the north-west corner of Bird Avenue at the junction with the Dundrum Road containing two acres, one rood and 28 perches.[39] A year later, in September 1791, Andrews was elected as an alderman of Dublin.[40] By that time Andrews was renting the villa on the Dundrum Road called Casino (later called Mount St Marys and now known as Emmet House) together with eight and a half plantation acres, which he had acquired from George Frederick Mowlds in 1782, and which Andrews subsequently assigned along with the two-acre corner field to Dr Robert Emmet on 18 April 1792.[41]

COLDBLOW: A DEFUNCT PLACE-NAME

The origin of the name 'Coldblow' is obscure, but it most likely refers to the exposed position of the lane that runs east-west from Donnybrook to the Milltown Road, which would have been subjected to cold easterly winds in winter. The earliest surviving written record of the name Coldblow is on a gravestone in Donnybrook graveyard that memorialises Ellen and William Hall of Coldblow who died in 1708 and 1711 respectively.[42] This proves that the place-name must have been in common usage in the seventeenth century. Although Coldblow was included in the parish of Donnybrook it was never an officially recognised or mapped district, and so it is impossible to be precise about its extent and its boundaries. It appears from eighteenth- and nineteenth-century deeds and estate maps that Coldblow's core area of about 30 plantation acres extended to the north and south sides of Belmont Avenue, the western side of Sandford Road and Milltown Road including land which until 2019 comprised the Jesuit headquarters at Milltown Park, Norwood Park, Cherryfield Avenue and Hollybank Avenue. It also included farmland on the eastern sides of Clonskeagh Road and Eglinton Road.[43]

The name Coldblow was used by at least three different houses in the eighteenth and early nineteenth century, two of which were located at the top of Belmont Avenue (then called Coldblow

37 *Saunders's Newsletter*, 3 June 1784, p. 3.

38 Brian Henry, *Dublin Hanged: Crime, law enforcement and punishment in late eighteenth century Dublin* (Dublin, 1994), pp. 101, 113.

39 RD 495/50/321029.

40 CARD, xiv (Dublin, 1909), pp. 216–17. Andrews became Lord Mayor in 1798: CARD, xv (Dublin, 1911), p. 45.

41 RD 345/228/232935, RD 453/133/289401.

42 Blacker, *Brief sketches of the parishes of Donnybrook and Booterstown*, p. 125.

43 RD 47/290/30640, RD 173/497/117055, RD 437/33/281750; *Pue's Occurrences*, 6 December 1757 p. 4; 'A survey of part of the lands of Donnybrook by John Longfield, 1823' (NLI, Longfield map collection, MS 21 F.28); NAI, Landed Estates Court Rental, vol. 123, no. 41, 'Rental & Particulars of Sale of Properties in Dublin to be sold on 5 May 1876 for William Radcliff', lot 16.

Lane) and the other on the far side of Sandford Road (then called Milltown Road). The extensive farmland bordering the north-eastern end of Milltown Road (later part of Sandford Road) was, in the early eighteenth century, farmed by the Roberts family, whose presence there can be traced back to 1674.[44] On the Leeson estate map of 1718, the landholding is called 'Lewis Robarts's [*sic*] land', but this did not form part of the Leeson freehold estate (Map 3). This property was originally part of a 30-acre farm called 'Luntsland', which was included among the landholdings of Donnybrook parish.[45]

In 1725 Lewis Roberts granted a lease to Robert Roberts of a house and 10 plantation acres of farmland.[46] This house was the original Coldblow House, and was located at the very top of Coldblow Lane (renamed Belmont Avenue) on the corner with Milltown Road (later Sandford Road). In the third quarter of the eighteenth century it was inhabited successively by Lawrence Byrne and a Dr Radcliff.[47] This property predated its namesake on the west side of Sandford Road and should not be confused with Milltown Park. The original Coldblow House was demolished and replaced by 132/134 Sandford Road in the late 1870s.

Having concluded the preliminary observations and explanations it is now appropriate to discuss in detail the development of the Leeson estate in sub-parcels which, for ease of reference, align with modern landmarks.

GROWTH OF MILLTOWN VILLAGE

The most valuable portion of Joseph Leeson's property portfolio in Milltown was a substantial landholding amounting to over 51 plantation acres (83 statute acres). This comprised almost entirely agricultural land (30 acres of meadow and 21 acres, 1 rood and 7 perches of pasture) on the north-west side of the Milltown Road as far as the boundary with Rathmines lands (which today roughly equates to the Luas tram track) together with houses and cabins in Milltown village (including Milltown Castle) and some market gardens and offices. All of this holding was located on the north bank of the River Dodder in the Church of Ireland parish of St Peter.[48]

By a lease for lives renewable forever of 22 September 1720 Joseph Leeson granted the entire holding of 51 acres, 1 rood and 7 perches to Edward Allen, gentleman. No information is available about Edward Allen or why Leeson granted him the property. The demised property also included 'the castle, houses, cow houses, stables and garden thereon'. Curiously, Leeson retained 'a thatched cabin which is adjoining Edward Water's mill' (Edward Water's mill lay on the north bank of the River Dodder where the Shanagarry apartments are now). The named lives in the lease included two local residents, Thomas Doyle, son of Thomas Doyle of Milltown, blacksmith, and Isaac Burgess, son of John Burgess of Milltown, dairyman. The annual rent was significant, £140 (old currency), increased by £5 per acre for every acre or part acre should the lessee plough the land or convert it to tillage. There was a covenant in the lease requiring Allen to plant trees in accordance with legislation enacted in 1699 to encourage tree planting in order to mitigate the severe shortage of timber in Ireland that had arisen by the turn of the eighteenth century. This legislation required landowners and leaseholders of land worth £10 per annum to

44 Mills, *Register of St Peter & St Kevin*, p37.

45 RD 496/437/320007.

46 RD 56/522/39033

47 *Pue's Occurrences*, 6 December 1757, p. 4; *Saunders's Newsletter*, 5 May 1773, p. 2; 11 March 1782, p. 4; 1 February 1785, p. 2.

48 NAI, Landed Estates Court Rental, vol. 38, no. 3, 'Particulars and Conditions of Sale of the Freehold Estate of the Earl of Milltown to be sold on 8 January 1856', lot 56.

plant 10 trees of four years growth every year until 1730.[49] The absence of arable land is consistent with the historic importance in Milltown and its wider vicinity of dairying and the provision of fodder for the city's horses.

Another noticeable recurring feature in the eighteenth-century leases is the involvement of senior members of Dublin Corporation in property deals in Milltown from the 1730s onwards. At this time, the Corporation was controlled by an exclusive self-perpetuating Protestant oligarchy comprising the Lord Mayor (elected annually from the 24 aldermen) and 24 aldermen (elected for life from the sheriff's peers (past sheriffs)) who formed the upper house of a bicameral governing body. The lower house was composed of the two sitting sheriffs, the sheriff's peers (not exceeding 48) and 96 representatives of the city's 24 guilds (later increased to 25).[50] Critically, to qualify for election as a city sheriff the individual (a freeman of the city) had to own real or personal estate of at least £2,000 in value, so in practice the lord mayor and aldermen were all extremely wealthy individuals.[51] As will be outlined below, at various stages from the 1730s onwards city aldermen such as William Walker, John Adamson, Percival Hunt the elder, Percival Hunt the younger and Thomas Andrews held substantial property interests in Milltown. The Recorder of Dublin, Thomas Morgan, also invested in Milltown in the second quarter of the eighteenth century.[52]

Building activity in Milltown village during the second and third quarters of the eighteenth century was concentrated on the north side of the main street in an area that today stretches from the former St Anne's secondary school building (now St Broc's sheltered housing) to the entrance gate to St Alexandra College. This is borne out by contemporary leases and from studying Rocque's Survey of County Dublin of 1760 (Map 4) and Bernard Scale's update of Rocque's map carried out in 1773 (Map 5). Accordingly, the north side of the village main street will be discussed first and the south side of the main street thereafter.

THE NORTH SIDE OF THE MAIN STREET THROUGH MILLTOWN VILLAGE

Joseph Leeson's principal tenant, Edward Allen, died sometime before January 1725. In September 1725 Allen's executors granted a sublease of 41 years to Hugh Johnston of a substantial property portfolio comprising Milltown Castle, a substantial new house beside the castle with a garden, stables, coach house and almost 13 plantation acres of land.[53] Johnston was appointed a justice of the peace for Dublin in 1727. He continued to live in Milltown until 1733 when he sold his lease to Isaac Dobson of Dublin for £160.[54] Johnston's residency, although short, is an early indication that the gentry class were, from the second quarter of the eighteenth century onwards, beginning to favour Milltown as a location to reside in.

49 RD 27/221/16698; NAI, Landed Estates Court Rental, vol. 38, no. 3, 'Particulars and Conditions of Sale of the Freehold Estate of the Earl of Milltown to be sold on 8 January 1856', lot 56; J.G. Simms, 'The establishment of protestant ascendancy, 1691–1714', in T.W. Moody and W.E. Vaughan (eds), *A new history of Ireland, iv: Eighteenth century Ireland 1691–1800* (Oxford, 1986), p. 15.

50 Sean Murphy, 'The Corporation of Dublin 1660–1760', *Dublin Historical Record*, xxxviii, no. 1 (December 1984), p. 22; CARD, xix (Dublin, 1944), pp. 355–6.

51 The property qualification for sheriffs was introduced by legislation in 1760: *Appendix to the First Report of the Commissioners appointed to inquire into the corporations in Ireland, presented to both Houses of Parliament, Report on the city of Dublin, part one* [C 25], House of Commons, 1835, xxvii, pp. 11–12.

52 RD 166/533/112471. The Recorder of Dublin or City Judge was the Corporation's legal adviser and was elected to office for life by the aldermen and the commons house of the Corporation: CARD, xix (Dublin, 1944), p. 356.

53 RD 44/351/29734.

54 Ball, *History of county Dublin*, ii, p. 113.

Some of the land beside Milltown Castle was sublet to market gardeners to grow vegetables for sale locally and to supply the Dublin market. On 5 February 1724 John Magennis of Milltown, gardener, entered into an agreement with John Benn of Milltown, victualler (grocer) to grant a lease to Benn of ground for a term of 30 years at £3 per annum of:

> *a piece or parcel of ground commonly known by the name of Coffee's [sic] garden leading upon the left hand of the castle near the two ash trees and from thence down to the ditch of Doyle's garden and on the east joining the road and to the back of the cabins, two of which were then empty and to that part wherein Cullen then dwelt.*[55]

The Coffey family lived in Milltown in the 1690s, appearing very briefly in the St Peter's parish records of that time, whereas the Benn family put down firm roots in Milltown in the 1680s and flourished.[56] As for Maggenis, he seems to have run into financial difficulties for in 1726, the last mention of him in connection with Milltown, he mortgaged his house and a piece of ground called 'the pigeon garden' to John French of Dublin for £28 15*s*.[57] Some years later, Milltown House was built on the pigeon garden in the mid-eighteenth century.[58]

A considerable amount of social and genealogical information can be gathered from another lease granted to John Benn in 1731 by Walter Allen (Edward Allen's son and heir) of the following property:

> *All that one house, stable and nine pin alley fronting the great road leading from Dublin to Milltown Bridge [Packhorse Bridge] in the possession of the said John Benn and also one other house or cabin late in the possession of Mary Fellows, deceased, and tenanted by James Barry, miller, together with the yard or backside and garden behind the said houses mearing and bounding on the north and west with a stone wall enclosing the castle of Milltown in the possession of Hugh Johnston esq and partly on the south with a field now possessed by Michael Fleming and partly with a garden in the possession of Thomas Doyle, smith, and on the east with the high road aforementioned together with a gateway or passage leading from the house of John King, carman, to a house on the east part of the premises by the said deed of lease demised, To Hold the said premises from 25 March 1731 for the lives of John Benn, John Benn junior his son, and Michael Fleming of Milltown, farmer paying yearly to Walter Allen for the said house lately in the possession of Mary Fellows the rent of one pound sterling and for all the other premises the rent of seven pounds sterling payable half yearly together with a yearly duty of one quart of brandy or rum with instructions to be made into punch and drank at the house and premises hereby demised.*[59]

The local historical and social value of this lease cannot be over-emphasised. The reference to a nine-pin alley is the first record of recreational activity in Milltown and shows that a community spirit was well developed in Milltown by the early eighteenth century. The condition requiring John Benn to produce a quart of brandy or rum punch every year for consumption on his premises is either another example of Milltown's community spirit at work or perhaps an arcane piece of licensing law. In any event, Benn was an enterprising man who used sponsorship to promote his business, for on 15 June 1728 Benn placed the following newspaper advertisement in the *Dublin Weekly Journal*:

55 RD 50/303/33112.

56 Mills, *Register of St Peter & St Kevin*, pp. 99, 132, 137, 141.

57 RD 50/340/33274.

58 RD 1869/17/208. The history of Milltown House is discussed in Chapter 15.

59 RD 69/11/46932.

> *On Monday next there is a saddle and bridle race to be run from John Benn's at Milltown, to the Cock in Cavan's port [Kevin Street], and back again, by any grass horse, mare or gelding, that does not exceed six pounds in value, each horse, mare or gelding that runs for the said saddle and bridle, the owners to pay two British shillings before starting, to the said John Benn, the first horse that comes in to have the saddle, the second the bridle.*[60]

A further indication of Benn's prosperity is shown by a lease dated 24 December 1734 whereby he gifted for life 'the house or tenement situate in Milltown where John Beard then dwelt' to his sister and brother-in-law Anne and Philip Hughes 'in consideration of the love and affection which he bore to his sister' at the yearly rent of one peppercorn.[61] This was a generous Christmas present for Anne but whether it was at John Beard's loss is unknown.

The record of the other residents' names and occupations in the Allen lease of 1731 is invaluable too because it is not available in any other source material. These people would more than likely have held their property on short-term leases which are not recorded in the Registry of Deeds.[62] Some of the individuals named in the lease such as Thomas Doyle and James Barry were probably Catholics. As such, they suffered from major disadvantages under the penal laws for most of the eighteenth century. For example, under the 'Popery Act' of 1704 Catholics were not entitled to buy land or hold a lease of more than 31 years duration.

Further building and subdividing of landholdings on the north side of the village main street continued throughout the second quarter of the eighteenth century as the Allens continued to sublet plots suitable for development. Two subtenants, the Rickissons and the Cassons, were responsible for much of the building that took place in the 1740s and 1750s.[63]

Richard Rickisson was a freeman of Dublin and an attorney (barrister) practising in the Court of Exchequer and the Tholsel Court. He also acted as one of the water bailiffs of Dublin city in 1748.[64] On 14 March 1748 John Selling Allen, who had bought out his brother Walter's leasehold interest in Milltown in 1741 for £500, let to Richard Rickisson (then in his possession) five houses or tenements fronting 'the great road from Dublin to Milltown Bridge' (the Packhorse Bridge) together with one cabin in the possession of John King fronting the road. Rickisson's lease was for three lives renewable forever but the low annual rent of £9 10*s.* suggests that he had to pay a large sum of money for his lease or that he was being compensated for having expended money building the five houses.[65]

In November 1749 Richard Rickisson sublet building ground on the village main street to James Rickisson, presumably Richard's brother, on which two houses or tenements were then being built.[66] Richard died in 1752 and his two daughters, Margaret and Ann, petitioned Dublin corporation 'praying the city's favour'. In response, the corporation agreed to pay the petitioners half of the dues and perquisites that had accrued to the succeeding water bailiff, John Ussher, since Richard Rickisson's death.[67]

---

60 *Dublin Weekly Journal,* 15 June 1728 (no. 168, p. 662); Benn is misspelt as 'Burr' in Ball's *History of county Dublin,* ii, p. 113.

61 RD 93/392/66029.

62 Since registration was not compulsory, only longer-term leases of 31 years or more tended to be registered.

63 RD128/124/86272, RD 148/385/100017, RD 167/197/11944, RD 167/198/111945, RD 167/198/111946.

64 CARD, viii (Dublin, 1901), pp. 194, 313.

65 RD 102/427/71612, RD 148/21/98296.

66 RD 139/165/93571.

67 CARD, x (Dublin, 1903), pp. 25-6.

In 1754 Margaret and Ann Rickisson sublet 'the old house wherein John Benn formerly lived and the forge adjoining the same' for 31 years to Thomas Donnellan of Milltown, who was a gardener, at an annual rent of £4 2*s*. 6*d*.[68] The Donnellan family prospered and in the 1780s and 1790s John Donnellan, who was described as a farmer, was dealing in property in Milltown and held a 77-year lease of over 20 statute acres of farmland divided into six fields.[69] By this time too the Donnellan family could afford a headstone in Taney churchyard, which recorded the deaths of John's wife Catherine in 1792 aged forty-six and three of their children who died young.[70]

Unlike the Donnellans, the Rickissons may have fallen on hard times or over-extended themselves – if not in Milltown then perhaps in other speculative investments – because in 1757 Margaret Rickisson mortgaged the five houses to a Mathew Staunton who in turn assigned his mortgage in 1763 to George Sparks.[71]

The Casson family first appear in Milltown when a Dublin merchant, John Casson, was granted a lease of 49 years by Alderman William Walker in October 1746 of a house, garden and outbuildings located off the north side of the village main street. The lease mentions some quirky details, such as that the demised property included 'the cheas [*sic*] house and stable adjoining the said Walker's coach house and also two coal holes behind Casson's dump as the same are now held and enjoyed by and in the possession of John Casson'.[72] It became clear from a later deed of 1791 that the word 'cheas' was an archaic spelling of the word 'chaise', a two-wheeled horse-drawn carriage, and was not a reference to a cheese house![73] John Casson's house, a detached building with a garden and offices, was situated off the north side of the main street of Milltown on a site that is now occupied by the Wilde and Green delicatessen and its carpark to the rear. In 1845 Casson's house, by then called Gillstown, was inhabited by Hugh Thomas Stafford, who leased it and its garden from Miss Hunt.[74] The property was subsequently renamed Turret House at some time prior to its demolition by the Sisters of Charity not long after they acquired it, along with Milltown Castle, in 1880 (Map 16a/9 and Map 18).[75]

In June 1747, Joseph Leeson's tenant, John Selling Allen, leased an adjacent plot of ground to John Casson which had lately been occupied by the local blacksmith, Thomas Doyle. Casson was required under the terms of his 48-year lease to separate this second plot from Allen's property by erecting an 8-foot-high wall made of limestone and sand. Casson was also required to build a new shed and workshop for the blacksmith who had been discommoded by Casson. Allen reserved the right to use the new limestone wall for future building operations that he or his subtenants might undertake but strictly on the condition that no windows would overlook Casson's property and that 'the water be carried off from any buildings made on said wall that the same may not fall into the said demised ground'.[76]

---

68 RD 173/74/115449.

69 RD 369/149/246761, RD 446/110/287840; *Saunders's Newsletter*, 27 May 1786, p. 4.

70 Francis Elrington Ball and Everard Hamilton, *The Parish of Taney* (Dublin, 1895), p. 47.

71 RD 222/129/147380.

72 RD 124/208/84348.

73 RD 466/110/287840.

74 NAI, VO, OL52714, House Book for Milltown Village 1845, no. 55; Thom's Directory 1848, p. 855.

75 VO, Cancellation Books, Parish of St Peter, South Dublin Union, Electoral Division of Rathmines, 1873–87, vol. 2, bk. 1, p. 196, plot 9; RD 1880/42/282.

76 RD 128/124/86272. A householder had no right to discharge the rainwater into his neighbour's property: La Touche, *The Law of Landlord and Tenant in Ireland*, i, p. 370.

On 4 February 1754 Allen leased two separate plots of land to John Casson's son George, one of which included 'the four new stone houses then lately built thereon by George Casson with liberty to quarry stones'.[77] On the same day, George Casson executed another lease for 99 years concerning a pair of 4-acre fields that were bounded on the west by a stone wall separating the fields from the lands of Rathmines.[78] Two years later Casson surrendered this lease to his landlord, John Selling Allen.[79] The reasons for this are unknown but possibly Casson could not turn a quick profit from building on or subletting the two fields, and so had to surrender his lease. In any event, by 1766 George Casson had died and the sole executor of his estate, his brother Joseph Casson (described as a cooper of Dublin) sold the Casson leases to a Daniel Sweeney of Dublin, gentleman, for £250.[80]

Another lease from John Selling Allen, this time to William Dixon, public notary, and executed on 2 September 1751, disposed a development site with over 300 feet of road frontage on the western end of Milltown village (where Alexandra College entrance gate is now). The description of the property is notable as it refers among other things to a new road from the village main street to the Packhorse Bridge:

> *the parcel of ground lying on the west side of the new road leading from the town of Milltown to Milltown Bridge [Packhorse Bridge] containing in front along the new road from the south gable end of Thomas Doyle's forge to a gateway or passage of sixteen feet wide intended to lead from the road to land in the occupation of the representatives of Alderman William Walker, three hundred and eighteen feet and in the rere with the wall which divides the same from land in the occupation of the representatives of Alderman Walker and Mr George Casson and with liberty of quarrying and carrying away stones and resting and bearing timber as therein mentioned.*[81]

The reference to the 'new road' from the town of Milltown to Milltown Bridge (Packhorse Bridge) is puzzling, particularly as Allen's lease of 14 March 1748 to Richard Rickisson refers to the 'great road from Dublin to Milltown Bridge'.[82] Indeed, it is extremely unlikely that the main road was not extended westwards beyond the fording point to the Packhorse Bridge when the bridge was originally built. If this was actually the case it would suggest that the Packhorse Bridge was originally built solely to facilitate pedestrian and animal traffic travelling to and from the city using the narrow Milltown Path (realigned in the nineteenth century and now part of Richmond Avenue South), which seems implausible. Perhaps the reference to the new road in the 2 September 1751 lease should be interpreted as reference to a new, improved road, which replaced the pre-existing road through the village arising from the new building developments in the village.

By the mid- to late 1750s John Selling Allen had fallen behind with his rent to Joseph Leeson. Consequently, on 21 January 1760 Joseph Leeson obtained possession of his property and a judgement in his favour for arrears of rent totalling £490 plus costs. The upshot of this was that a complicated trust was set up to pay off the arrears of rent and costs owed to Leeson over seven years.

---

77 RD 167/197/111944, RD 167/197/111945.

78 RD 167/198/11945.

79 RD 170/187/120052.

80 RD 247/253/161481.

81 RD 148/385/100017.

82 RD 148/21/98296.

This arrangement was guaranteed and administered by Alderman Percival Hunt the younger of Dublin whereby Allen assigned the arrears of rent due to him from his undertenants to Hunt.[83]

The demise of the Allen fortunes and those of his tenants put a break on the development of the north side of the village main street. A likely cause of this change in fortunes was a series of bank failures in the 1750s beginning in March 1754 which were the cause of stagnation of trade and credit, and which ruined many families.[84] A lack of records in the Registry of Deeds covering the north side of Milltown village strongly indicates that no significant building work took place at this location after 1760. Instead, small infill developments of terraced cottages and cabins occurred on a piecemeal basis into the nineteenth century.[85]

Percival Hunt and John Hunt were merchants in Bride Street who traded with the American colonies in the 1740s.[86] The Hunt family feature prominently in the affairs of Dublin Corporation in the second and third quarters of the eighteenth century during which time Percival Hunt the elder and Percival Hunt the younger were both city aldermen.[87] In 1755 Percival Hunt the younger was elected as Lord Mayor for the 1755–6 term and later stood unsuccessfully as an MP for Dublin in 1761.[88] The Hunt connection with Milltown originates with a mortgage dated 23 February 1754 when the Recorder of Dublin, Thomas Morgan, conveyed to Alderman Percival Hunt the elder 'part of the lands and houses of Milltown subject to the proviso of redemption contained in the deed'.[89] Some 13 years later, in 1763, Alderman Percival Hunt the younger bought out the Morgan legal interests in Milltown for £750 when the lands were auctioned by the master of the High Court to discharge the outstanding debts owed by Thomas Morgan (by then deceased), to Alderman Percival Hunter the elder, also deceased.[90] In the same year John Selling Allen leased Milltown Castle together with 15 acres and 21 perches plantation measure to Percival Hunt.[91] Over time, the Hunts acquired legal interests in most, if not all, of the Allen's property on the north side of the main street of Milltown.

Percival Hunt the younger served on the Corporation's committee responsible for the city's water supply in the 1760s but resigned as alderman in 1771, probably due to advancing years.[92] By that stage, Hunt was living in a large villa close to the village (probably Milltown House), where he died in 1776.[93]

The Allen leasehold interest in Milltown became further fragmented by a complicated long-standing family dispute, which ended in Edward Allen's three surviving granddaughters each acquiring one third of their grandfather's residual Milltown property in a family settlement drawn up

---

83 RD 203/492/136431. The annual rent due to Leeson was £140 so the arrears totalled over three years' rent.

84 Dickson, *Dublin: The making of a capital city*, p. 180.

85 These include Lee's Lane and a pair of terraced houses called Castleview.

86 *Pue's Occurrences*, 8 April 1749, p. 3.

87 See for example, CARD, viii (Dublin, 1901), pp. 437, 438, 499; CARD, x (Dublin, 1903), p. 461.

88 CARD, x (Dublin, 1903), p. 461; *Dublin Courier*, 8 May to 11 May 1761, p. 2.

89 RD 166/533/112471. Morgan held four separate properties in Milltown comprising both fields and tenements that he had acquired by various assignments and subleases: RD 173/293-96/120550.

90 RD 223/163-4/147771.

91 RD 223/28/146305.

92 CARD, xi (Dublin, 1904), p. 350; CARD, xii (Dublin, 1905), pp. 163–4.

93 RD 166/533/112471; *Dublin Courier*, 7 April 1766, p. 2; Saunders's Newsletter, 24–6 August 1774, p. 1; 16 October 1776, p. 1; *Freeman's Journal*, 12 October 1776, p. 3.

in 1786.[94] Prior to that settlement, the three Allen granddaughters and their spouses had in 1779 mortgaged their legal interests to counsellor-at-law John Percival Hunt, the son of Alderman Percival Hunt the younger, for £600. The mortgage was repaid in 1787 at a cost of over £765.[95] John Percival Hunt continued to reside in Milltown and was living there in 1808.[96]

THE SOUTH SIDE OF THE MAIN STREET THROUGH MILLTOWN VILLAGE

The south side of the main road through Milltown village was, during the eighteenth century, much less developed than the north side of the street. This was because the land on the south side of the village main street formed the flood plain of the River Dodder and was frequently subject to flooding. Drownings occasionally resulted when travellers risked their lives attempting to cross the rain-swollen river at its fording point, notwithstanding that in one case the locals advised them to cross by the Packhorse Bridge.[97] The low-lying area beside the fording point of the river was known locally in Milltown in the nineteenth and twentieth centuries as 'The Strand', a name which is preserved today by a terrace of cottages called Strand Terrace (located behind the Milltown Hill apartment complex). Originally, the few eighteenth-century houses on the south side of the village main street had long back gardens, some over 140 feet long, stretching down to the River Dodder. In contrast, the houses on the north side of the village main street had no rear gardens because the ground rose very steeply immediately behind the buildings, as it still does today.

On the Leeson estate map of 1718, 'The Strand' is described as 'the little green field at the point underneath' containing 1 rood and 36 perches (Map 3). This description suggests that there were no buildings on this small plot of ground; however, Rocque's map of 1760 shows three buildings on either side of the roadway as it veers to the left towards the River Dodder and its fording point (Map 4). One of these properties may have been an Inn owned by a Felix McManus who, in March 1737, was granted a lease for 31 years by John Kerr of Dublin, gentleman, of the following property:

> *all that messuage, garden, houses or plot or parcel of ground in Milltown ... containing three roods of ground or thereabouts bounded on the north with Mr Cole's stone wall, on the east with the river of Milltown, on the south and west with the street in Milltown.*[98]

McManus was also required to pay his landlord £4 per annum and 'one pot of green peas yearly or four shillings in lieu thereof'.[99] John Kerr had been granted a lease for lives renewable forever by Joseph Leeson in 1725, thus Kerr was seeking to extract a profit by subletting to McManus.[100] In due course Kerr's lease was acquired by William Cole, junior, who in 1768, leased a small triangular plot of one rood and three perches to John Barker of Milltown, which was described as follows:

> *that triangular piece of ground with the houses and cabins erected thereon situate in the town of Milltown late in the possession of Ephraim Thwaites .... to hold during the lives of his Majesty King George*

94 RD 378/507/254038.

95 RD 392/502/259749.

96 *Dublin Evening Post*, 2 April 1808, p. 2.

97 *Pue's Occurrences*, 6 January 1756, p. 2; *Dublin Evening Post*, 12 October 1782, p. 2.

98 RD 89/277/63175.

99 McManus probably had a vegetable garden behind his inn stretching to the banks of the River Dodder.

100 RD 47/307/30741.

the third, the said William Cole and of Ann Cole his daughter and the survivors of them ... at the yearly rent of eighteen pounds.[101]

Returning briefly to the Allen family who had invested heavily in Milltown in the 1750s, the three Allen sisters (the granddaughters of Edward Allen the original Leeson tenant) and their spouses granted a lease for lives renewable forever in January 1788 to Samuel Dixon, shoemaker, and husband of Mary Allen. Among the property of 19 perches extent (about an eighth of an acre) conveyed to Samuel Dixon was 'one cabin and a garden late in the possession of Darby Nowlan now occupied by the said John Brady shoemaker and also one other cabin formerly in the possession of the widow Ghest'. The annual rent was a modest £9 2*s.*[102] This property would have been slightly further west of the small triangle of 1 rood and 3 perches originally occupied by Barker. Although the transaction was an insignificant one, the personal details recorded in the memorial deed are invaluable because they contain the names and occupations of the working-class men and women who lived in Milltown village in the late eighteenth century, whose existence would otherwise be unknown.

Another interesting lease from the same period reveals the relationships that existed in the wider communities of Milltown, Clonskeagh and Donnybrook towards the end of the eighteenth century. A Christopher Sheil of Milltown, described as a cabinet maker, granted a lease for 31 years to Peter Byrne, a Donnybrook farmer, on 15 October 1788 of:

All that and those that piece or parcel of ground with the house or cabin built thereon situate, lying and being on the east side of the road leading through the town of Milltown containing in length in front one hundred and twenty six feet and ranging in the rere with the slip or passage to the River Dodder ... at the yearly rent of six pounds.

The lease was witnessed by William Eustace, John Carbery and Samuel Thomas, all of whom were living in Clonskeagh and working as paper manufacturers.[103]

The description of the properties in the pair of leases of 1788 contrasts with the relative prosperity of the north side of the main street as developed by the Cassons and the Rickissons in the 1740s and 1750s. The two leases quoted above also suggest that the less affluent people of Milltown were more likely to live on the south side of the main street. This is borne out by an advertisement dating from 1795 whereby the firm of Martin and Company, pawnbrokers, offered to let or sell their freehold concern in Milltown comprising the following properties:

A plot of ground on which J. McMahon has built a house – rent £4
A house and garden occupied by a solvent tenant – rent £14
A small slate house and garden – rent £4 and 11s.
Four small slate houses with gardens let by the year – rent £4 and 11s. each
and a large new-built house which, containing six rooms, a kitchen, coal-hole, and small dairy, a good yard, and large walled-in garden, full cropped, and well planted with choice young fruit trees; also, a

101 RD 265/220/174912. The deed was witnessed by local blacksmith James Rose. Barker sold on his lease 17 months later for £42 10s. (RD 284/25/182988).

102 RD 396/106/260493.

103 RD 409/131/266767.

> *potato garden, now planted, containing near half an acre, with room for building twenty small houses, and allowing gardens to each. Plenty of sand, and a quantity of stones on the premises.*[104]

Martin and Company's annual rent was £18 4*s*. but as a landlord they received £40 15*s*. from their tenants, thereby earning an annual profit of £22 11*s*.[105] Further details of these properties are provided by a lease for lives renewable forever dated 10 June 1792 whereby Stephen Martin of Dublin, perfumer, leased to George Osborn of Dublin, apothecary, the following property (property 2 in the 1795 advertisement) at an annual rent of £14:

> *all that plot or piece of ground being part of the lands of Milltown situate lying and being in the County of Dublin containing in front to the high road sixty two feet ten inches, in breath in the rere from wall to wall including the half of both walls fifty four feet and from front to rere one hundred and forty six feet, bounded on the front by the high road, on the rere by the River Dodder, on the south by a house and garden inhabited by Mr Martin [probably property 3 in the 1795 advertisement] and on the north by a house and garden in the possession of James McMahon, bricklayer [property 1 in the 1795 advertisement].*[106]

The large newly built house had presumably been built by Stephen Martin or by Martin and Company in the early 1790s. It later became a pub and a grocery store, which was owned by the Hackett family for over a century during the nineteenth and early twentieth centuries.[107] A postcard dating from about 1910 shows a scene that had remained largely unchanged since the 1790s (Pl. 9). Today, the Martin property is taken up by the public park by the River Dodder on both sides of Milltown Bridge, which cut through the landholding in about 1817 when the new main bridge for the Dundrum Road was built to replace the Packhorse Bridge (Map 14).[108]

THE EASTERN END OF MILLTOWN ROAD IN THE FIRST HALF OF THE EIGHTEENTH CENTURY

The topography of the eastern end of Milltown Road at the beginning of the eighteenth century would be unrecognisable to the modern eye. Clonskeagh Road and Eglinton Road did not exist and the area on both sides of the Milltown Road was laid out in fields that were predominantly used for cattle pasture and meadowing.[109] Only two physical features that existed before the eighteenth century have survived. The first is a right-hand bend in what was then solely called the Milltown Road and is now a major right-hand junction at Sandford Road and Milltown Road. The deviation in the road is marked on eighteenth-century maps of the area and is of ancient origin (Map 4). The bend may originate from an important physical or territorial boundary that existed at that spot when the archbishop of Dublin's land was being marked out from the Liberties of Dublin in the late twelfth century. The second ancient physical feature of this district

104 *Saunders's Newsletter*, 26 May 1795, p. 2.

105 *Saunders's Newsletter*, 26 May 1795, p. 2.

106 NAI, MS 999/355/1/1.

107 Lease dated 4 July 1837 Robert Dry to Patrick Hackett (NAI, MS 999/355/1/10).

108 A presentment was passed in 1816 to build a new bridge at Milltown at a cost of £1,662 6s.: Ball and Hamilton, *Parish of Taney*, p. 222.

109 Clonskeagh Road was laid out in the 1790s, almost certainly by John Crosthwaite of Vergemount House: RD 437/33/281750 (Deed, 9 May 1791 Duignan to Crosthwaite). Eglinton Road was laid out by Edward Wright of Donnybrook in the early 1850s: *Freeman's Journal* 4 May 1855, p. 4.

Plate 9. Postcard of Milltown Village looking east, c. 1910 (courtesy of Mary Long)

that has survived since the seventeenth century is Clonskeagh Lane (now Prospect Lane), which, as noted in Chapter 2, also separated the Liberties of Dublin from the lands belonging to the archbishop of Dublin.

MILLTOWN ROAD FROM THE JUNCTION WITH CLONSKEAGH ROAD TO THE CORNER OF PROSPECT LANE

The area immediately opposite Milltown Park on the south side of Milltown Road from the junction with Clonskeagh Road to the corner of Prospect Lane was farmed by the Mowlds family and their subtenants throughout the eighteenth century.

The northernmost point of the Leeson estate map of 1718 (Map 3) marks the sharp right-hand bend in the Milltown Road at the current four-way junction with Sandford Road, Eglinton Road and Clonskeagh Road. The area to the north called 'Lewis Robarts's Land' has been discussed earlier under Coldblow. The 'Road to Clonskeagh' still partly exists today as Prospect Lane, now a cul-de-sac that terminates at Palmerston Grove.

The plot described as 'Mouls's holding in part of Donnybrook' containing 9 plantation acres, 1 rood and 16 perches was historically part of the lands of Donnybrook and was included in the Church of Ireland parish of that name. The area is today completely built over by Palmerston Grove, Millbrook village, Mount Sandford, St James's Terrace, Connaught Terrace, and by Clonskeagh and Eglinton roads that later bisected the original fields at their north-eastern ends.

The 9 acres, 1 rood and 16 perches changed hands several times over the course of the late eighteenth and early nineteenth centuries. The current Clonskeagh Road was laid out across the north-eastern end of this plot in the 1790s by John Crosthwaite, a wealthy Dublin jeweller who built a villa and several terraced houses on the new Clonskeagh Road called Vergemount in the 1790s and 1800s.[110] In 1855 the ground was purchased by a Dublin draper, James Boswell, who in the 1860s built St James's Terrace (now noss 2–24 Clonskeagh Road) and a villa called St James. St James was demolished in May 1989 and the Mount Sandford town houses built on the site.[111]

PROSPECT LANE

The land on the west of Prospect Lane (marked 'Road to Clonskeagh' on the 1718 Leeson estate map) described as 'Mr Russell's holding in Milltown' containing 9 acres and 1 rood is now largely built on by the Ramleh Park and Ramleh Close housing estates. The holding includes waste land at a site called Scully's Field (formerly part of the Milltown quarry) and undeveloped land adjacent to the River Dodder close to the carpark of the Clonskeagh House pub. The River Dodder marks the southern boundary of this landholding.

The field of 9 acres and 1 rood on the south side of the road to Clonskeagh, together with John Moules's holding of 9 acres 1 rood and 16 perches on the north side of the road in the parish of Donnybrook, was let by Joseph Leeson by lease dated 28 July 1720 for three lives renewable forever to 'John Moules senior of Donnybrook, dairyman', at an annual rent of £52.[112] The lives named in the lease were John Moules junior, Robert Moules and William Moules. The total area of John Moules's combined landholding in Milltown in 1720 was thus 18 acres, 2 roods and 16 perches.

By a subsequent lease of 27 April 1753 Joseph Leeson replaced the 28 July 1720 lease of 18 acres, 2 roods and 16 perches with a new lease to Anne Mowlds, widow of John Mowlds of Milltown and daughter-in-law of the first lessee, John Moules senior of Donnybrook. The named lives in the lease included Anne's grandsons John and William, the first and second sons of her son Thomas Mowlds.[113] Anne had four children who survived to adulthood, George, Thomas, Edward and Anne junior. George and Thomas acquired separate landholdings from Joseph Leeson along the Dundrum Road at Farranboley/Windy Harbour, Edward died unmarried and Anne Mowlds junior married a James Classon, who held 69 acres of farmland in Rathmines.[114]

In the eighteenth century Anne Mowlds senior lived in a farmhouse with a garden situated on the north-east side of Prospect Lane and the corner of Milltown Road (now the carpark for Millbrook Court apartments). A small square can faintly be picked out on the bottom left-hand corner of the 'Mouls field' marking out the farmhouse from the field (Map 3). The farmhouse is also recorded on John Rocque's Survey of County Dublin of 1760 (Map 4). In 1765 Anne Mowlds senior let her Milltown property of 18 acres, 2 roods and 16 perches jointly to her son George and son-in-law James Classon for £87 per annum while reserving the farmhouse on the corner of Prospect Lane and Milltown Road to herself for her lifetime. Simultaneously, George Mowlds and his brother-in-law James Classon agreed to partition the property so that George kept the 9-acre, 1-rood field on

---

110 RD 437/33/281750, RD 617/393/424857; NAI, Landed Estates Court Rental, vol. 32, no. 53, 'Rental and Particulars of part of the lands of Coldblow and Clonskeagh to be sold on 12 December 1854 for John Clarke Crosthwaite'.

111 Copy of a Deed of Fee Farm Grant dated 14 December 1855 in the author's possession; *Irish Builder*, No. 76, p. 30, 15 February 1863; Irish Times, 8 October 1988.

112 RD 48/187/31299. Although John Moules is described as living in Donnybrook it is very likely that he resided in the farmhouse on the north side of the corner of Clonskeagh (Prospect) Lane and Milltown Road, which was just inside the Donnybrook parish boundary (Map 9).

113 RD 161/97/107750, RD 234/550/154987.

114 RD 248/557/160861, RD 234/550/154987, RD 317/90/210308.

the south side of Prospect Lane and his brother-in-law got the 9 acres, 1 rood and 16 perches on the north side of Prospect Lane bounding Milltown Road (minus the farm house). The two men also agreed to pay equally the annual rent due to Anne Mowlds and thereafter to pay equally the £64 head rent due to Joseph earl of Milltown.[115] James Classon, whose principal farming activities were based in Rathmines, subsequently leased his holding on Milltown Road in 1768 for 31 years to a William Connor of Dublin at an annual rent of £68, thereby making a profit of £24 10*s.* during the lifetime of his mother-in-law.[116]

Sometime after Anne Mowlds senior died her son George leased the farmhouse and garden on the corner of Prospect Lane and Milltown Road to a widow named Margaret Ryan in 1765 for 31 years at an annual rent of £11 7*s.* 6*d.* By 1785 three more dwelling houses had been built on this plot of land, which by then had come into the possession of John Mowlds of Churchtown, eldest son of the late Thomas Mowlds. He, in turn, assigned his lease to John Dowling for £50 for the remainder of the term (11 years).[117] Succeeding generations of the Mowlds family seem to have held considerable sentimental value for their ancestral farmhouse on the corner of Prospect Lane and Milltown Road. When the Crosthwaite interest was sold in 1856, the rental particulars noted that the farmhouse and garden 'has been retained by the lessee of the original lease of 1753, and has never been parted by them'.[118] Thereafter, the property disappears completely from the records and successive OS maps.

The area to the east of the Mowlds family holdings on either side of Prospect Lane – on the 1718 Leeson estate map called 'Thomas Hall's Land' (Map 3) – was farmed by a dairyman of that surname who lived on Coldblow Lane.[119] This land was adjacent to Clonskeagh and was included in the parish of Donnybrook. It did not form part of the Leeson estate. Thomas Hall died in 1744 and was buried in the family plot in Donnybrook graveyard, along with his parents, wife and several descendants.[120] In the 1790s and early 1800s this land was developed into a small country estate originally called Virgemount (now spelled Vergemount) by John Crosthwaite, a wealthy Dublin watchmaker who also laid out the current Clonskeagh Road and built the terrace of houses called Vergemount beside Ashton's pub. Vergemount, Vergemount Hall, Vergemount Park and Clonskeagh Hospital, all of which are located on the current Clonskeagh Road, occupy the Hall's land now.[121]

Finally, the area on the right-hand side of the map at the bottom of Clonskeagh Lane called the Red Mill was part of the lands of Clonskeagh. Clonskeagh was part of Lord Trimlestown's manor of Roebuck and at that time (1718) was leased to farmers William Madden of Clonskeagh and James Madden of Harold's Cross.[122] For centuries water powered industry was carried on at the site of the Red Mill on the north bank of the Dodder (beside Ashton's pub on Clonskeagh Road

115 RD 234/550/154987.

116 RD 256/469/169732.

117 RD 299/122/197629, RD 370/30/246447.

118 Griffith Valuation, Primary Valuation of Tenements, Townland of Clonskeagh, 5 September 1848; NAI, Landed Estates Court Rental, vol. 32, no. 53, 'Rental and Particulars of part of the lands of Coldblow and Clonskeagh to be sold on 12 December 1854 for John Clarke Crosthwaite', lot 3.

119 RD 47/290/30640; Blacker, *Brief sketches of the parishes of Donnybrook and Booterstown*, p. 125.

120 Blacker, *Brief sketches of the parishes of Donnybrook and Booterstown*, p. 125

121 Martin Holland, *Clonskeagh: A place in history* (Dublin, 2007), pp. 132–8; RD 436/75/281751, RD 437/33/281750, RD 556/323/369963, RD 617/393/424857.

122 RD 41/158/25143.

and behind Clonskeagh Terrace) and only ceased when the Smurfit papermill closed in the first decade of this century. The Smurfit site is currently being redeveloped for a private housing development called The Papermill.

THE NORTH SIDE OF MILLTOWN ROAD FROM OPPOSITE PROSPECT LANE TO MOUNT ST ANNE'S

The Leeson estate map of 1718 shows that the land on the north side of Milltown Road from opposite Prospect Lane as far as Mount St Anne's, was occupied by the widow Benn and by a Mr Russell (?), who presumably is the same person who rented the 9 acres and 1 rood on the south side of the road to Clonskeagh. No records about Russell's activities in Milltown have survived. In the early eighteenth century the 'widow Benn's holding in Milltown' of 11 plantation acres, 3 roods and 16 perches was occupied by Jane Benn, the mother of the enterprising Milltown grocer, John Benn. By 1725 Jane Benn no longer occupied this land (presumably she had died) and in January of that year Joseph Leeson let the property to George Guines [*sic*] of Milltown, dairyman, at the yearly rent of £40.[123]

This holding changed hands again, for on 8 April 1741 Joseph Leeson executed a lease to Robert Harris of Dublin, inn keeper, of 'part of the lands of Milltown lately held by William Doyle containing twelve acres'.[124] Two months later, on 6 June 1741, Harris sublet 4 acres of his land for a term of 50 years to the Dublin banker, David Digges La Touche, junior, who at that time held land to the south-west side of the 4 acre plot.[125] The 4 acres comprised a large parcel of land described in contemporary deeds as measuring 359 feet fronting the north side of Milltown Road. Maps in the Jesuit archives confirm that the La Touche's 4-acre property on the north side of Milltown Road included land which became Shamrock Rover's grounds (now Glenmalure Square) and land which until recently was occupied by the Murphy & Gunn BMW dealership and the Gonzaga College rugby fields.[126] Twenty-five years later David La Touche junior bought out the Harris leasehold from Robert Harris's widow and her second husband by way of assignment in 1766.[127]

By the 1760s the La Touches held 3 separate parcels of land on both sides of Milltown Road under various mortgages, subleases and assignments: firstly, 3 roods and 18 perches near Milltown village acquired by David La Touche senior from Edward Allen in 1731 (on which Elm House was built); secondly, the 4 acres on the north side of Milltown Road (Glenmalure Square, the former BMW garage and part of Gonzaga College rugby fields) together with a house, garden and stables acquired in 1766 by David La Touche junior, and thirdly, two fields on the south side of Milltown Road comprising 6 acres, 1 rood and 27 perches (part of the Ramleh Park estate) given as security for a mortgage to William Cole senior in 1742.[128] In 1769 La Touche disposed of all three of his Milltown landholdings to a Dublin jeweller, Francis Smith, for £1,000, a very large sum for the time.[129]

123 RD 49/49/30653.

124 RD 102/337/71029.

125 RD 102/457/71781.

126 'Map of lands at Elm Hall, Milltown Co. Dublin' dated October 1923 (Jesuit Archives, IE IJA/FM/Mill). The BMW garage site (9-14 Milltown Road) was sold in late 2020 to Rohan Holdings for €7 million: *Irish Times*, 16 December 2020, p. 21. It is currently occupied (2022) by Autovision Motor Company.

127 RD 315/330/211605.

128 RD 310/632/208230; 'Milltown Park and some of its owners', pp. 5–7.

129 RD 275/106/175335.

By 1749 Robert Harris had moved to Kildare at which time Henry Doyle, presumably a son of William Doyle, was farming part of the Harris 12-acre holding at Milltown. In the same year, Harris granted Doyle a lease for 31 years for a house and garden together with 8 acres, 2 roods and 23 perches.[130] In 1756 Doyle had become indebted to a Dublin brewer, Francis McMahon, for £50 and was forced to assign his lease to him.[131]

Complicating matters further, Harris mortgaged his property in Milltown for £400 in 1752 to a Dublin merchant, Robert Tighe, subject to a right of redemption after six months.[132] Harris fell behind in his repayments to Tighe, who in turn was indebted to another Dublin merchant, James Varcilles for over £1,800, so Tighe assigned the Harris mortgage to Varcilles in 1755.[133] As noted previously, a series of bank failures in the 1750s which disrupted trade and credit facilities may have been the cause of Harris's and Tighe's difficulties.

The various leasehold interests in the old Harris lands continued to multiply and turn over during the eighteenth century. Towards the end of that century, the 12-acre holding became part of an enlarged Milltown Park demesne along with other lands to the west that originally formed part of the Lewis Roberts' Coldblow estate (now comprising Norwood Park, Sandford Road, Cherryfield Avenue and Hollybank Avenue).[134] A small part of the original Harris lands fronting Milltown Road was developed for housing in 1836, when Milltown Colonnade and Milltown Cottage (now Garrynure townhouses) were built as a speculative venture by George FitzJames Russell, a son-in-law of the owner of Milltown Park, Dr Francis Hodgkinson.[135] The Leeson freehold interest in the 12 acres (19 acres, 1 rood and 30 perches statute measure) was included in the encumbered estates court sale of 1856 at lot 55.[136]

Moving further westwards along the Milltown Road, the plot on the edge of the Leeson estate map of 1718, which is partly obscured but is apparently identified as 'Russell's Land in Milltown', formed part of the 51 acres leased to Edward Allen by Joseph Leeson in 1720.[137] In 1731 Edward Allen's son, Walter, leased land on the north side of the main road through the village adjacent to Milltown Castle to John Adamson of Dublin, merchant, which included:

> *all that piece of ground part of which is called the pigeon garden and some other grounds, the castle garden wall being part of the recited lands situate on the east side of Milltown Castle, on the west to the six acres part of the lands, on the north to the widow Benn's holding and on the east to the King's high road together with the houses thereon which was formerly in the possession of John Magennis, gardener, and now in the occupation of John Adamson.*[138]

---

130 RD 133/302/91139.

131 RD 181/85/120021.

132 RD 158/153/105296.

133 RD 196/24/128929.

134 'Milltown Park and some of its owners', pp. 7–9.

135 Original lease dated 6 December 1836 (Jesuit Archives, IE IJA/FM/Mill/ 6/12/1836); 'Milltown Park and some of its owners', pp. 10–11.

136 NAI, Landed Estates Court Rental, vol. 38, no. 3, 'Particulars and Conditions of Sale of the Freehold Estate of the Earl of Milltown to be sold on 8 January 1856', lot 55.

137 NAI, Landed Estates Court Rental, vol. 38, no. 3, 'Particulars and Conditions of Sale of the Freehold Estate of the Earl of Milltown to be sold on 8 January 1856', lot 56.

138 RD 69/29/47040. The Adamson family retained an interest in this property throughout the eighteenth century and by 1787 it was held by Anne Adamson of Dublin, who was unmarried: RD389/540/257641.

The type of business carried out by Adamson is unknown, but he was sufficiently wealthy to advance a loan of £500 to Dublin Corporation in 1740, and was later elected as an alderman in 1744.[139]

Adamson built a house and stable on part of his holding in Milltown and subsequently let the buildings to Alderman William Walker of Dublin dated 5 July 1736.[140] The description of the property set out in the 1736 lease is important because three separate houses are mentioned in the deed, one of which (Elm Hall opposite the shops at the top of the hill on Milltown Road) is still standing today:

> *that lot of ground situate on the road leading from Dublin to Milltown ... containing in front to the road sixty feet or thereabouts together with a new house and stable built thereon bounded on the south and west by Mr Johnston's wall [i.e. the wall separating the new house from Milltown Castle grounds] and on the north side bounded by a stone wall ... and also, all that house and garden then in the said John Adamson's possession being part of the said recited lands situate between the last-mentioned premises and a house and garden belonging to Mr David La Touche.*

Almost immediately, Walker sold the above property to Luke Mercer of Dublin, gentleman, for £300 on 15 July 1736. In modern parlance Walker 'flipped it on' to Mercer, who Walker had lined up before taking the lease from Adamson.[141] The subsequent development and ownership of the property quoted from the 5 July 1736 lease is very difficult to follow but David La Touche's house and garden became the Elm Hall demesne (later Elm House) which was acquired by the Jesuits in 1884.[142]

THE SOUTH SIDE OF MILLTOWN ROAD FROM PROSPECT LANE TO THE PUBLIC CAR PARK OPPOSITE MILLTOWN CATHOLIC CHURCH

This area is depicted on the Leeson estate map as comprising 13.5 Irish/plantation acres and was in 1718 occupied by Edward Waters. Waters also operated the new paper mill on the north bank of the River Dodder close to the Packhorse Bridge where the Shanagarry apartments are now.[143] The 13.5 acres was a valuable piece of property with plenty of development potential given the extensive road frontage to Milltown Road. The availability of building materials in the Milltown quarry (which formed part of this landholding) was a bonus too. In the mid-eighteenth century 11 acres of this property was divided into small meadow fields and advertised as being 'delightfully situated for building'.[144]

For whatever reason, Edward Waters did not prosper and in 1725 Joseph Leeson let the 13.5 acres to John Kerr senior, gentleman, of Dublin for lives renewable forever at a yearly rent of £40.[145] A penalty applied whereby the annual rent was to increase by £5 per acre for every acre or part acre should the lessee plough the land or convert it to tillage. The lease also included a clause of first refusal to Leeson if Kerr decided to dispose of his lease, a condition requiring Kerr

---

139 CARD, ix (Dublin, 1902), pp. 58, 414.

140 RD 85/42/58964.

141 RD 86/59/59039.

142 'Milltown Park and some of its owners', p. 12. The history of Elm House is set out in Chapter 15.

143 RD 20/158/10143.

144 *Faulkner's Dublin Journal*, 25 April 1747, p. 2.

145 RD 47/307/30741.

to plant trees and, curiously, a clause of view.[146] As far as can be ascertained from the limited descriptions in the contemporary leases, the only substantial building on the 13.5 acres in 1725 was a large detached house, subsequently named Geraldine House, the history of which is discussed in Chapter 15. The lease to John Kerr did not turn out well for Joseph Leeson. Kerr was an absentee landlord and his subleasing activities caused numerous problems for the Leesons and for Kerr's tenants as the following saga shows.[147]

In 1731 John Kerr granted a sublease to William Cole senior of Dublin, merchant, of the following property for the same term as his lease from Joseph Leeson at a modest annual rent of £5:

> *all that dwelling house and garden situate in Milltown where William Hewston, gardener [i.e. market gardener], lately dwelt meared and bounded on the north with a quickset ditch, on the east with the river of Milltown, on the south with the old ditch between the said holding and the tenement now held by Timothy Byrne, which said mearing is set out in a straight line from the angle in the wall in the street in Milltown by the ash tree in the said old ditch, and on the west meared with the high road or street in Milltown.*[148]

One of the conditions of Cole's lease was that Cole could quarry such amount of stone as he should have occasion to use in building and improving the premises – which he did – without having to pay for the stone used as building material.[149]

As previously noted, in 1737 John Kerr granted a house and 3 roods to the Milltown innkeeper, Felix McManus, which was adjacent to William Cole senior's house (according to the lease it was bounded on the north with Mr Cole's stone wall).[150] This was the second subletting by John Kerr following his sublease to William Cole. Kerr then sublet a house on half an acre of land to Theodosius Stone for £3 rent per annum on a 21-year lease from 25 March 1742. Kerr's fourth and final transaction was a lease from year to year to Robert Chambers of two cabins and about 12 acres of farmland at an annual rent of £30.[151] It is noteworthy that a much higher rent was charged by Kerr for the 12 acres of farmland than for all of the houses combined. To summarise, by 1742 John Kerr had divided the 13.5 acres, which he had leased from Joseph Leeson in 1725, into four separate sub-tenancies.

Problems soon arose because John Kerr was only making a profit of £2 after paying his rent to Joseph Leeson. By 1743 Kerr was in arrears with his rent and Joseph Leeson (son of Joseph Leeson the original lessor) instituted ejectment proceedings against Kerr. In the meantime, William Cole senior, who had spent £800 on building works in compliance with the covenants in his lease, had also mortgaged his new house in Milltown to David La Touche senior in September 1742.[152] Cole

146 NAI, Landed Estates Court Rental, vol. 38, no. 3, 'Particulars and Conditions of Sale of the Freehold Estate of the Earl of Milltown to be sold on 8 January 1856', lot 54.

147 RSAI, Francis Elrington Ball MSS, vol. 4, p. 64. The details were also recorded by Ball from two eighteenth-century Exchequer bills but he did not use the information in his history of county Dublin.

148 RD 70/178/47905.

149 RD 111/64/75630: recital in a mortgage from Cole to La Touche, 27 September 1742.

150 RD 89/277/63175; RSAI, Francis Elrington Ball MSS, vol. 4, p. 64.

151 RSAI, Francis Elrington Ball MSS, vol. 4, p. 64. Note that apart from Theodosius Stone's house and a couple of cabins (small labourers' cottages) the entire area on the south side of Milltown Road from Prospect Lane to Geraldine House was open farmland in the early eighteenth century.

152 RSAI, Francis Elrington Ball MSS, vol. 4, p. 64. The nature of Cole's improvements is unrecorded; RD 111/64/75630. The mortgage was subsequently paid off but not formally vacated from the Cole title until 1776: RD 310/632/208230.

initiated a counterclaim in May 1743 against Joseph Leeson, John Kerr and Kerr's three subtenants. Cole died in February 1745 and so his widow Hannah Cole instituted new proceedings in July 1745.[153] The upshot of this was that in April 1747 John Kerr assigned all his interests in the 13.5 acres to John Watson in trust for Hannah Cole.[154] This property was acquired later by William and Hannah Cole's son, William Cole junior.

As with his father, misfortune befell William Cole junior. In 1784 Cole was forced to sell his entire interest in Milltown to David FitzGerald to satisfy a judgement of the master's court of Chancery in a case taken against William Cole junior by a Luke Heron.[155] The names Geraldine House and Geraldine Terrace derive from David FitzGerald's ownership of the 13.5 acres in 1784. The FitzGerald family retained a leasehold interest in Milltown when the 13.5 acres was put up for sale in 1856 as part of the Leeson freehold estate as lot 54.[156] As well as the 13.5 acres, in 1786 David FitzGerald acquired another field on the south side of Prospect Lane from George Mowlds amounting to 5 acres 2 roods and 17 perches. This field seems to have been subdivided out of the 9 acres and 1 rood that George Mowlds had acquired from his mother in 1765.[157]

The imbroglios involving John Selling Allen, John Kerr and William Cole in Milltown in the mid-eighteenth century illustrate the complications that frequently arose with property speculation, and the difficulties caused for landlords and tenants alike when things went badly wrong.

THE LEESON ESTATE ON THE LOWER CHURCHTOWN ROAD

In the early eighteenth century the land on the south bank of the River Dodder where Classon's Bridge and the Lower Churchtown Road are now was very sparsely populated, comprising as it did very large open fields that had not yet been subdivided into smaller units. This is evident in a conveyance which took place on 21 March 1718 whereby Joseph Leeson granted a lease for lives renewable for ever to Edward Allen of land on the south bank of the River Dodder comprising:

> *33 acres, 3 roods and 4 perches of land being part of Milltown lands together with the passage across Milltown bottom leading to the said two fields next to Churchtown lands which said passage was to consist of sixty foot broad in the narrowest part ... excepting ... unto Joseph Leeson and his heirs the ancient millrace and water course that leads to the grain mill of Milltown and liberty to make a millrace through any part of the premises for the convenience of a new mill to be erected.* [158]

As discussed earlier, Joseph Leeson also granted Edward Allen the valuable holding of Milltown village and farmland totalling 51 acres 1 rood and 7 perches plantation measure in 1720.[159] However, the focus here is on the part of the grant that refers to 'the passage across Milltown bottom

---

153 RSAI, Francis Elrington Ball MSS, vol. 4, p. 64.

154 RD 124/482/85522.

155 RD 360/417/244131.

156 NAI, Landed Estates Court Rental, vol. 38, no. 3, 'Particulars and Conditions of Sale of the Freehold Estate of the Earl of Milltown to be sold on 8 January 1856', lot 54.

157 RD 234/550/154987, RD 381/86/251367.

158 RD 23/139/12909. The memorial record in the Registry of Deeds refers to the 'iron mill of Milltown' but this is a transcript error as the original lease quoted in 1856 refers to the 'grain mill of Milltown': NAI, Landed Estates Court Rental, vol. 38, no. 3, 'Particulars and Conditions of Sale of the Freehold Estate of the Earl of Milltown to be sold on 8 January 1856', lot 58.

159 RD 27/221/16698.

leading to the said two fields next to Churchtown lands which said passage was to consist of 60 foot broad in the narrowest part ...'

The wording of the memorial deed is ambiguous. It suggests either the passage had been built across Milltown bottom prior to the signing of the lease or that a passage 60 feet wide was to be built in the future, presumably by Edward Allen. The annual rent of £60 for this substantial plot of over 33 plantation acres on the south bank of the River Dodder was proportionately less expensive than the annual rent of £140 payable by Allen for his holding of 51 plantation acres on the north bank of the River Dodder. The difference in the rent between the two landholdings might be explained by the fact that the land at Milltown bottom was less accessible, and so needed to be improved by Allen expending money to lay out the new road of 60 feet in breadth.

The new roadway was laid out and it is shown quite prominently on Rocque's Survey of the County of Dublin, which was published in 1760 (Map 4). That map shows Classon's Bridge spanning the River Dodder to the west of Milltown village with a road proceeding in a straight line for about half a mile and then taking a sharp turn to the left (east). The road continues in a straight line eastward for another quarter of a mile or so, crossing the River Slang, until it joins the Dundrum Road. The first (straight) part of the road (now the Lower Churchtown Road) survives as far as the original sharp left-hand turn (now the site of the Windy Arbour Luas stop). The road was extended south towards Dundrum and the Upper Churchtown Road in the late 1820s.[160] In contrast, that part of the original road from the left-hand eastwards turn to Windy Arbour fell out of use by the early nineteenth century, assuming that the road had originally been laid out as shown on Rocque's map.[161]

ORIGINS OF THE CLASSON FAMILY AND CLASSON'S BRIDGE

Three separate deeds from 1731 executed by John Selling Allen of Milltown identify the 33 acres, 3 roods and 4 perches as being 'part of Milltown lands called Glassons and Greens land'.[162] No information is available about Glasson and Green's activities in Milltown because they do not appear among the records for Milltown in the Registry of Deeds. A William Glasson of Milltown was baptised at St Peter's Church on 9 May 1715 and his father William Glasson is presumably the same person referred to in the deeds.[163] The surname Glasson is very similar to two other surnames which appear in the mid-eighteenth-century records of Milltown, the Cassons (active in Milltown village) and the Classons (farming in Rathmines). Given that surnames were often misspelt or used with spelling variations, the Glassons, the Cassons and the Classons may not be distinct separate families and could originally have emanated from a single eponymous ancestor. This brings us to the origins of the Classon family in Milltown and their association with Classon's Bridge, which today spans the River Dodder at the junction of Milltown Road and Lower Churchtown Road beside The Dropping Well pub.

In the early twentieth century the pre-eminent local historian, Francis Elrington Ball, opined that the original bridge spanning the Dodder beside The Dropping Well pub was erected by John Clas-

160 *Dublin Evening Mail*, 17 November 1828, p. 8, which has a joke at the expense of the earl of Milltown: 'Why is the new road to Dundrum like the Kildare-street Club? Because it is improved by getting rid of Milltown'.

161 The sharp turn in the road towards Windy Arbour is not shown on Taylor's map of the Environs of Dublin of 1816 or on any subsequent map.

162 RD 65/457/46388, RD 66/295/46363, RD 67/278/46173.

163 Baptismal records for St Peter's Church (Church of Ireland) contained on the website Irishgenealogy.ie.

son, who owned a mill for grinding wood.[164] Ball was mistaken because John Classon acquired his first lease in Milltown in 1764, by which time Classon's Bridge had already been built and recorded on Rocque's Survey of County Dublin (Map 4).[165] The more likely candidate as the bridge builder is James Classon, who in 1748 was granted a lease by Viscount Palmerston for 51 years of approximately 69 plantation acres in Rathmines.[166] According to a deed of 1856, the demesne of South Hill (now the South Hill housing estate on the north side of the Milltown Road opposite The Dropping Well pub) was originally part of James Classon's lands. Critically, this proves that James's lands were immediately beside the spot where Classon's Bridge was built. [167] If James Classon was related to the Glasson named in the 1731 lease then that provides further evidence supporting the case that the Classon or Glasson families were responsible for building the bridge over the Dodder. Furthermore, James Classon was associated with the other large farming family in Milltown, the Mowlds. As previously noted, in 1765 Anne Mowlds senior let her Milltown property of 18 acres, two roods and 16 perches jointly to her son George and her son-in-law James Classon.[168] James made his will in 1776 whereby he left his property jointly to his three daughters, Ruth (who subsequently married John Pasly [*sic*] of Dublin, printer), Anne (remained unmarried and made her will in Rathmines in 1807) and Grace (who subsequently married William Le Maistre of Dublin, cabinet maker), and appointed Thomas Mowlds of Rathmines and John Classon of Eustace Street as his executors.[169] The relationship between James and John Classon is not known but most likely they were brothers.

Returning to Glassons and Greens land, John Selling Allen sold his interest in 1760 to the Rev. John Foster.[170] The property changed hands at least once more, for in 1799 Glassons and Greens land, which was by then 'called and known by the name of Windy Harbour', was sold to Morris Hime of Dublin for £1,210 9*s.* 4*d.* The sale also included 12 acres of land called 'Farrenenowell otherwise Fryarsland otherwise Lartnegar' which in the nineteenth century formed the small townland of Friarland, which is situated on the west side of the Goatstown Road opposite its junction with Roebuck Road.[171]

When the earl of Leeson sold his freehold interest in Glassons and Greenes land in 1856, the Hime family were still *in situ* as the chief tenant, and this property of 54 acres, 2 roods and 33 perches statute measure (originally 33 acres, 3 roods and 4 perches plantation measure) was described in the encumbered estates court rental as 'lying on the south side by Lot 53 [the demesnes of Bloomfield and Casino on Bird Avenue], and adjoining Churchtown and Rathmines, comprising two houses, and some excellent land'.[172]

From this description it would appear that when the first edition of the six-inch OS map was being drawn up in the 1830s, the bulk of Glassons and Greens land was included in the civil town-

164 Ball, *History of County Dublin*, ii, p. 112.

165 RD 246/324/158097.

166 RD 357/274/240334.

167 RD 1856/34/247.

168 RD 234/550/154987.

169 RD 357/274/240334; Report of the Deputy Keeper of the Public Records of Ireland, *Index to the Act or Grant Books, and to original Wills, of the Diocese of Dublin 1272–1858*, Appendix to the 26th Report (Dublin, 1894), pp. 187, 620.

170 RD 202/589/135899. The purchase price is not recorded in the memorial.

171 RD 522/376/342660; OSI, Co. Dublin, Sheet 22, six inches to one statute mile, surveyed in 1837 and corrected in 1843.

172 NAI, Landed Estates Court Rental, vol. 38, no. 3, 'Particulars and Conditions of Sale of the Freehold Estate of the Earl of Milltown to be sold on 8 January 1856', lot 58.

land of Rathmines Great which in total covers an area of 88 acres, 2 roods and 15 perches statute measure on the south bank of the River Dodder at Classon's Bridge.[173] A few years later, under the Griffith's Valuation, Rathmines Great was divided into two separate rateable plots on either side of the Lower Churchtown Road. The plot which lay to the east of the road, comprising 50 acres, 2 roods and 30 perches, contained the bulk of the original Glassons and Greens landholding. A second (smaller) portion of Glassons and Greens land lying to the east between the River Slang and the Dundrum Road at Windy Arbour was incorporated into the civil townland of Farranboley (Map 19). This conjectural mid-nineteenth-century location of Glassons and Greens land is, however, complicated by the fact that Viscount Palmerston is recorded as the immediate lessor of the entire townland of Rathmines Great by the Griffith's Valuation of 1849, raising the possibility that both peers (Palmerston and Milltown) had separate distinct legal interests in landholdings which partly overlay each other.[174] The lack of contemporary maps and estate records for the Palmerston and Leeson estates on the south bank of the River Dodder at Milltown, Windy Arbour and Classon's Bridge greatly hinders the identification process.

THE LEESON ESTATE ON THE SOUTH BANK OF THE DODDER AT MILLTOWN BRIDGE

Before discussing the developments that took place on the Leeson estate on the south bank of the River Dodder it is necessary to outline some of the boundaries that applied to this area, starting with the River Dodder at Milltown main street. As explained previously, since time immemorial the River Dodder was forded at a shallow point in the river where the carpark is situated, opposite Milltown Catholic church. The trackway began its ascent on the south bank of the river beside the modern apartments of Dodderbank and Milltown Grove, and thereafter the road continued more or less in a straight line to Dundrum parallel with the River Slang. All of the land on the south bank of the Dodder between the fording point at Milltown and Donnybrook was open farmland, which was owned by the Lord Trimlestown, whose family, the Barnewalls, had held their land from the crown in an almost unbroken succession since medieval times.[175] Lord Trimlestown's landholding opposite Milltown village on the south bank of the Dodder formed the north-western extremity of the large civil townland of Roebuck comprising 814 statute acres.[176]

The extent of the Leesons' landholding on the south bank of the River Dodder, all of which fell within the Church of Ireland and civil parish of Taney, is shown on a map of the Trimleston estate at Roebuck which was drawn up in 1832 (Map 10).[177] From studying the eighteenth-century leases and the Trimleston map it is clear that the Leeson estate in the eighteenth century included all of the nineteenth-century civil townland of Farranboley and a sizeable portion of the adjacent nineteenth-century civil townland of Churchtown Lower to the south. In the nineteenth century these two townlands collectively amounted to 320 statute acres, encompassing all of the district called 'Windy Harbour' (now Windy Arbour), a placename that was introduced in the 1760s.[178]

173 OSI, Co. Dublin, Sheet 22, six inches to one statute mile, surveyed in 1837 and corrected in 1843.

174 Griffith's Valuation, Primary Valuation of Tenements, Co. Dublin, Barony of Rathdown, Parish of Taney, Townland of Rathmines Great, 1849, p. 151.

175 Ball, *History of county Dublin*, ii, p. 77.

176 OSI, Co. Dublin, Sheet 22, six inches to one statute mile, surveyed in 1837 and corrected in 1843.

177 'Report and Valuation of the Lands of Roebuck in the County of Dublin by Brassington and Gale, 1832' (NAI, QRO/4/3/28).

178 The earliest mention of Windy Harbour I could find occurs in the *Freeman's Journal* of 2 October 1764, p. 3.

Thus, there is an identifiable continuity in territorial units originating with the medieval ecclesiastical townlands of Milltown south of the Dodder and Boley minor, continuing through the seventeenth-century ownership of the Usshers of Donnybrook, and ending with the Leeson estate. That said, only 75 statute acres from Farranboley townland was put up for sale by the earl of Leeson in 1856.[179] The discrepancy could be explained on the basis that the Leesons had disposed of parts of their estate in the south Milltown/north Churchtown area prior to 1856, or had decided at that time not to sell their entire landholding in that district. The discrepancy needs to be investigated further.

We turn now to two large grants made by Joseph Leeson to John and Thomas Mowlds in 1734 and 1754 respectively, neither of which were included in the 1856 sale of the Leeson freehold estate. The first grant was made by the original Joseph Leeson (who died in 1741) to John Moulds of Milltown, farmer, of a lease for lives renewable forever dated 25 October 1734, comprising 86 plantation acres of farmland, as follows:

> *the thirty two acres of meadow and fourteen acres, one rood and sixteen perches of pasture part of the lands of Milltown with the dwelling house and stable and garden thereon, and also that part of Churchtown alias Taney lying on the left hand [sic] of the great road that leads from Dublin to Dundrum the same containing forty acres, two roods and ten perches, also a thatched dwelling house and barn bounding on the north to Milltown land aforesaid, to the east to Lord Trimlestown's land, to the south to Dundrum, and on the west to a small vein of Talbot's land and the great road that leads from Dublin to Dundrum all in the parish of Taney and Barony of Rathdown then in the possession of the said John Mowlds ... at the yearly rent of one hundred and fifty-five pounds.*[180]

Among the four lives named in the lease of 1734 were John's sons George, Thomas and Edward.[181] It is notable that there were only two farmhouses of any note on the two properties. The mention of 'a small vein of Talbot's land' in the description of the western boundary of the demised property is fortuitous because it reveals local memory harking back 200 years to when Richard Talbot held the medieval townland of Farranboley as principal tenant of the archbishop of Dublin in the early sixteenth century.[182]

A gravestone in Donnybrook graveyard records the death of John Mowlds of Churchtown, who died on 4 March 1787 aged forty-three. This individual is likely to have been a son of John Moulds of Milltown who was granted the 86 acres in 1734. John is buried with his wife, Susanna, and their children Henrietta, Susanna and Charlotte.[183] This branch of the family seems to have prospered prior to John's relatively early death because a death notice was inserted into the newspaper in 1783 advising of the death at Churchtown of Miss Charlotte Moulds, daughter of John Moulds,

---

179 NAI, Landed Estates Court Rental, vol. 38, no. 3, 'Particulars and Conditions of Sale of the free simple estates of the Earl of Milltown on 8 January 1856', lot 53.

180 RD 77/455/54333. This John Moulds was almost certainly the son of John Mouls senior of Donnybrook who rented land on the east side of Prospect Lane off Milltown Road from Joseph Leeson in 1720: RD 48/187/31299.

181 RD 77/455/54333.

182 See the discussion at the beginning of Chapter 3.

183 Blacker, *Brief sketches of the parishes of Donnybrook and Booterstown*, p. 129; Danny Parkinson, Donnybrook Graveyard (Dublin, 1993), p. 60 (Headstone C93); http://www.igp-web.com/IGPArchives/ire/dublin/photos/tombstones/donnybrook/mowlds1871gph.jpg (accessed 22 September 2017).

esquire.[184] The death of John Moulds was also reported in the press, which noted that he was 'sincerely lamented by all who had the pleasure of his acquaintance'.[185]

The second large grant was made on 11 March 1754 when Joseph Leeson the second, later the earl of Milltown, granted a lease to Thomas Mowlds of Milltown (the second son of John Moulds, of Milltown and grandson of John Mouls of Donnybrook) of 70 acres 1 rood and 2 perches of land in Churchtown.[186] A large landholding equating exactly to the Thomas Mowlds landholding in Churchtown was advertised for sale in 1800 by the Right Hon. Lord Frankfort, which referred to 'the lands of lower Churchtown, near Milltown'. The public were advised that: 'the present occupiers have it now in their power to avail themselves of an opportunity to renew their respective leases'. The advertisement went on to say that:

> *there is running through those grounds a fine stream of water [the River Slang], which might be used to very great advantage, there being a paper and a bleaching mill to improve and extend, for which good encouragement will be given.* [187]

The mention of the River Slang near Milltown suggests that the Frankfort property was located in an area of lower Churchtown that over time came to be identified with the new place name of Windy Harbour (now Windy Arbour).[188] It is unclear how this territory came into the possession of Lord Frankfort, but a deed of 1826 mortgaging the Leeson estate for £5,000 included: 'that part of the town and lands of Churchtown belonging to Joseph Earl of Milltown containing by estimation 80 acres'.[189]

The Trimleston estate map of Roebuck identifies Windy Harbour as being in the ownership of the earl of Milltown (Map 10). This suggests that the Mowlds' intermediate legal interest in Churchtown had passed to Lord Frankfort who thereby become a subtenant of Leeson, but this needs to be clarified.

THE LEESON ESTATE ON THE NORTH-EASTERN SIDE OF THE DUNDRUM ROAD

As well as granting a substantial landholding in Churchtown to Thomas Mowlds, Joseph Leeson granted a large parcel of land on 28 February 1754 to George Mowlds (the eldest son of John and Anne Moulds of Milltown and a grandson of John Moules of Donnybrook) comprising 46 acres, 1 rood and 19 acres (included as lot 53 in the 1856 sale of the Leeson freehold).[190] This large block of farmland included extensive road frontage along the east side of the Dundrum Road as far as Windy Arbour (later incorporated into the nineteenth-century civil townland of Farranboley) and was bounded on the north and east by the western extremity of the Trimleston estate (later

---

184 *Hibernian Journal*, 17 January 1783, p. 3.

185 *Saunders's Newsletter*, Monday 5 March 1787, p. 1, where his death is recorded as having taken place at Milltown. Contemporary newspapers use the spelling Moulds whereas the gravestone (erected in 1849) uses the spelling Mowlds.

186 RD 248/557/160861.

187 *Freeman's Journal*, 20 December 1800, p. 1. As previously discussed, the Churchtown lands are not mentioned in the 1856 landed estates court sale of the Leeson freehold estate.

188 *Freeman's Journal*, 2 October 1764, p. 3.

189 RD 811/460/546996.

190 NAI, Landed Estates Court Rental, vol. 38, no. 3, 'Particulars and Conditions of Sale of the Freehold Estate of the Earl of Milltown to be sold on 8 January 1856', lot 53.

incorporated into the nineteenth-century civil townland of Roebuck). In the second half of the eighteenth century the Milltown and Churchtown properties changed hands several times between members of the extended Mowlds families – on at least two occasions as part of separate trust and marriage settlement transactions – so that at times the identities of both the properties and the parties become blurred and confusing.[191] In addition, George Mowlds of Milltown and his son George Frederick sublet their extensive holdings at Milltown to dairy farmers and Dublin merchants in transactions which are too numerous to detail here.[192] The essential point is that the extended Mowlds family controlled an extensive area south of Milltown village throughout the eighteenth century.

George Mowlds was the most prominent member of the extended Mowlds family in the second half of the eighteenth century. In 1767 George Mowlds was listed among the four freeholders living in Milltown who were eligible to vote, which gives some indication of the wealth and status he had achieved by that time.[193] A few years later, in 1776, Dublin Corporation awarded a scavenging contract to George Mowlds of Milltown which required him to clean a specific section of the city's streets every Tuesday and Friday.[194] Why Mowlds sought such work is not clear, but it is possible that he used the refuse and dung collected from the city's streets to fertilise his farmland in advance of the grazing season, as suggested by the following advertisement which he placed in *Saunders's Newsletter* the following year:

> *This day are opened forty acres of excellent meadow, part of the lands of Dundrum; there is water in every field. Horses 3s. 6d. and cows at 2s. a week; no disordered beast, bridle or saddle will be received. Gentlemen may be assured the greatest care will be taken of their horses etc. apply to Mr Mowlds, Milltown, where horses will be received, or at the fields of Churchtown.*[195]

Contemporary advocates of agricultural improvement, such as Heley Dutton, deplored the fact that farmers' haycarts returned empty from Dublin city after delivering their load of hay, when best practice dictated that they should have returned home to their farms with a load of dung from the city's streets.[196]

In 1767 the marriage was announced of David Bell and Miss Mary Mowlds of Milltown, who was a daughter of George Mowlds. Bell was noted as an eminent draper in Francis Street while Mary was described as 'an agreeable young lady with a handsome fortune'.[197] Unfortunately, the marriage later broke down over a dispute concerning money and an annuity due to David Bell as part of Mary's marriage settlement. In June 1783 Mary Bell placed the following notice in the newspaper:

---

191 RD 276/456/179205, RD, 282/446/184809, RD 294/507/195553, RD 295/474/197630, RD 380/595/258099, RD 510/257/330639.

192 The Registry of Deeds name index books record at least 24 separate transactions for George Mowlds during the period 1758–85 involving two generations of the family with the Christian name George.

193 'List of Freeholders in Dublin, 1767' (NAI, MS M/4912).

194 *Saunders's Newsletter*, 18 October 1776, p. 3. His father 'George Moulds of Donnybrook' had been awarded a similar contract for £123 in the early 1750s: CARD, x (Dublin, 1903), pp. 126–7.

195 *Saunders's Newsletter*, 23 June 1777, p. 3.

196 Dutton, *Observations on Mr Archer's Statistical Survey*, p. 78.

197 *Belfast Newsletter, 4 August 1767.*

I do hereby caution the public from treating with any person for the purchase, or in any sort incumbering any part of the town and lands of Milltown and Churchtown, in the County of Dublin, and Smoot's Court, alias Symon's Court, in the County of the City of Dublin, now or late in the possession of Mr George Mowlds, as I, and my children have a considerable charge upon said lands and premises under my marriage settlement, for the establishment of which I am now preparing a bill to be filed in the High Court of Chancery. Dated 20 June 1783. Mary Bell.[198]

In September 1783, Mary's husband David Bell inserted a much longer notice whereby (among other things) he cautioned the public on his own behalf and on behalf of the creditors of his late father-in-law, George Mowlds, from accepting any assignment or mortgage of any part of the lands of Milltown or Churchtown, which were subject to a charge of £500 and considerable arrears of interest plus an annuity of £30.[199] The following month Bell inserted another notice specifically addressed to the Mowlds' tenants in Milltown:

Whereas I David Bell, late of Tallaght, in the County of Dublin, esq, am entitled to an annuity, rent or charge of thirty pounds per annum to be issuing and payable to me out of the town and lands of Milltown, in the County of Dublin, from the death of George Mowlds, of Milltown, aforesaid (now deceased) under and by virtue of certain articles, bearing date the 11 day of July 1767 executed on or previous to my intermarriage with Mary Mowlds, daughter of the said George Mowlds, which articles were immediately after duly registered. Now I the said David Bell do hereby caution the several tenants of the said town and lands of Milltown, from paying the said thirty pounds per annum to any person but me on my order, or the trustees entitled by said settlement to receive the same for the uses and trustees therein, as I am determined to take such steps as I am advised for the recovery of the said rent charge or annuity. Given under my hand this 2nd day of October 1783.[200]

The family dispute was not resolved and, relations between Mary and her husband David having broken down, on 5 October 1784 they executed a deed of separation.[201] To add to the family's woes, two judgements for a debt of £800 had issued against the estate of George Mowlds and his son George Frederick Mowlds sometime prior to 19 July 1787.[202] This fact explains notices placed in the newspapers in October and November 1787 advertising two houses for letting or sale.[203] In one of the advertisements George Frederick Mowlds is described as an attorney – his father had earned enough money to educate George Frederick for a professional career.[204] This

198 *Saunders's Newsletter*, 21 June 1783.

199 *Saunders's Newsletter*, 27 September 1783.

200 *Saunders's Newsletter*, 14 October 1783. The memorial transcription of the marriage settlement of July 1767 could not be located in the Registry of Deeds despite an extensive search.

201 RD 364/56/242996.

202 RD 380/595/258099.

203 *Saunders's Newsletter*, 26 October 1787, p. 4; 20 November 1787, p. 4. The properties were subsequently sublet to various tenants but the Mowlds retained their freehold interest in their 2 April 1765 lease until the late nineteenth century: NAI, Landed Estates Court Rental, vol. 140, no. 32, 'Particulars and Conditions of Sale of part of the lands of Milltown by George Frederick Mowlds on 3 December 1880'.

204 *Saunders's Newsletter*, 26 October 1787 p. 4.

marked the beginning of a minor legal dynasty with a number of George Mowlds senior's descendants practising as solicitors in Dublin in the nineteenth century.[205]

THE LEESON ESTATE ON BIRD AVENUE

Bird Avenue was laid out through land which formed part of the large landholding of the Leeson estate on the east side of the Dundrum Road (Map 10).[206] The origins of Bird Avenue can be traced to the early 1780s and to an advertisement which appeared in the *Hibernian Journal* in 1781:

> *To be sold, the interest in a lease for three lives renewable forever, of upwards of four acres of lands of Milltown in the County of Dublin, in the avenue leading from Milltown Road [i.e. the Dundrum Road] to Roebuck, about two miles from Dublin, subject to a small annual rent. The situation is delightful for building on, being well supplied with water and commanding a most beautiful and extensive prospect. For particulars apply to Mr Meredith, Crampton-court. N.B. There are two fronts to said lands, one to Milltown, and the other to the road leading to Roebuck.*[207]

The name subsequently given to the avenue and by which it is known to this day, Bird Avenue, originated in a lease dated 6 April 1782 whereby John Bird of Dublin, gentleman, for the consideration of £150 granted a lease for lives renewable forever to William Cathcart of Dublin, gentleman of:

> *all that part of the lands of Milltown in the parish of Taney ... containing five acres, one rood and eight perches together with the new dwelling house and offices thereto belonging erected on the said lands and all and singular the fixtures and yards to hold from 1 November 1781 ... for the yearly rent of sixty pounds.*[208]

The new house was named Bloomville (later renamed Bloomfield and subsequently Gledeswood) and was included in the sale of the Leeson freehold estate in 1856 as lot 53.[209] The grounds of Bloomville have long since been built on – the houses on the south side of Bird Avenue and Gledeswood Avenue and Gledeswood Park occupy the site now – but the house still survives. Its many occupants – one of whom, Clotworthy Macartney, acted as a solicitor for the earl of Milltown when he sold his freehold estate in 1856 – have been recorded by Martin Holland in his history of Clonskeagh.[210]

Ralph Meredith continued to deal in property on the new Bird Avenue in the 1780s. In 1785 John Mowlds of Churchtown sold his legal interest to Ralph Meredith of Dublin of a field containing 2 acres, 1 rood and 20 perches plantation measure 'at the corner of the avenue leading from Milltown to Roebuck being part of the lands of Milltown'. The purchase price paid by Meredith

---

205 Thom's Directory for 1854 at p. 1150 lists George Frederick Mowlds and Henry Mowlds, solicitors, both of 7 Montague Street, Dublin and William T. Mowlds, solicitor, of 53 Bishop Street, Dublin.

206 'Report and Valuation of the Lands of Roebuck in the County of Dublin by Brassington and Gale, 1832' (NAI, QRO/4/3/28).

207 *Hibernian Journal*, 17 January 1781, p. 2.

208 RD 342/538/231418.

209 NAI, Landed Estates Court Rental, vol. 38, no. 3, 'Particulars and Conditions of Sale of the Freehold Estate of the Earl of Milltown to be sold on 8 January 1856', lot 53, where the demesne is called Bloomfield.

210 NAI, Landed Estates Court Rental, vol. 38, no. 3, 'Particulars and Conditions of Sale of the Freehold Estate of the Earl of Milltown to be sold on 8 January 1856', vol. 38, no. 3; Martin Holland, *Clonskeagh: A place in history* (Dublin, 2007), pp. 193–6.

was an inexplicably expensive £200.[211] This field is now part of the Catholic University School's playing fields at the north-western end of Bird Avenue.

A second villa was built at the extreme eastern end of Bird Avenue at the junction with the Clonskeagh Road in the 1780s or 1790s. On 31 July 1783 George Grant of Dublin, cabinet maker, granted a lease for lives renewable forever to John Edwards of part of the lands of Milltown containing 4 acres and 1 rood, 3 acres of which were lately in the possession of Thomas Andrews, and which were bounded on the east and south 'by the passage called the avenue' (Bird Avenue) at an annual rent of £28 13*s*.[212] The lease reserved various rights and entitlements to the earl of Milltown, thus providing confirmation that the land granted to John Edwards was part of the Leeson estate. Sometime between the execution of the lease in 1783 and the mortgaging of the lands for £300 in 1796, Edwards had 'erected and built a dwelling house and made several lasting and valuable improvements' to the premises.[213] John Edwards' house, named Oaklawn in the nineteenth century and now called Farranboley House, is still standing today at the junction of Bird Avenue and Clonskeagh Road, albeit on much smaller grounds of about a third of an acre.[214]

The third villa built on Bird Avenue towards the end of the eighteenth century was located off the south-western side of the road and is called Farranboley Cottage on the first edition of the six-inch OS map of 1837.[215] The origins of Farranboley Cottage can be traced to a lease for lives renewable forever of 3 May 1794 from brothers William, John and Thomas Beeby (or Bibby) to Nicholas Hunt of Dublin, clothier, of:

> *the two fields or park containing six acres [plantation measure], three roods and twenty five perches with the dwelling house and outhouses, offices, stabling and garden now made and erected thereon and all other improvements made on said premises which are part of the lands of Milltown in the parish of Taney ...*[216]

On 14 April 1798 Hunt subleased the property to a Robert Fyan of Dublin, merchant, who in turn let it to Robert Billing in December 1805. As with the other Bird Avenue leases, the 1798 lease reserved various rights and entitlements to the earl of Milltown, thereby confirming that Farranboley Cottage and its grounds were part of the Leeson estate.[217] This house had many name changes throughout its history and is currently called The Manor. The Manor was built in a typical box Georgian style and is at present extant and in good repair. It is accessible from Bird Avenue through Beechwood Drive.[218]

The final property that falls for consideration as part of the review of the Leeson estate lies just beyond Bird Avenue on the Clonskeagh Road, which later formed the demesne of Roebuck

211 RD 378/560/254201.

212 RD 503/266/323588 (recital in a mortgage deed).

213 RD 503/266/323588; NAI, Landed Estates Court Rentals, vol. 118, no. 88, 'Particulars and Conditions of Sale of part of the lands of Farranboley on 7 May 1875'.

214 Lisney Estate Agents brochure, October 1991; Holland, *Clonskeagh*, pp. 186–9.

215 OSI, Co. Dublin, Sheet 22, six inches to one statute mile, surveyed in 1837 and corrected in 1843.

216 RD 485/349/305740.

217 NAI, Landed Estates Court Rental, vol. 56, no. 12, 'In the matter of the estate of Anne Fyan, owner, Rental and Particulars of Part of the Lands of Milltown to be sold on 28 June 1859'.

218 Holland, *Clonskeagh*, pp. 191–3.

House.[219] On 12 April 1765 John Mowlds granted a lease for lives renewable forever to Peter Le Maistre, of 4 acres, 1 rood and 12 perches plantation measure of the lands of Milltown. As with the Oaklawn property, the lease reserved rights to the earl of Milltown, thus providing confirmation that the land was part of the Leeson estate. On the same day and subsequently on 30 April 1767, John Mowlds granted two separate leases of 2 acres, 1 rood and 12 perches and 4 acres, 2 roods and 9 perches plantation measure respectively to George Grant. The following year, in April 1768, John Mowlds granted a further 3 roods and 38 perches to Peter Le Maistre. These four separate plots of land leased to Peter Le Maistre and George Grant bordered the Trimleston estate at Roebuck. Eventually, the four plots from the Leeson estate were amalgamated with 16 aces, 3 roods and 14 perches statute measure of land to the north, which was part of the Trimleston estate, thus making up Roebuck House and its demesne.[220]

The Trimleston estate map shows that the Roebuck House demesne was bisected by the boundary between the Leeson and Trimleston estates with the house (which was then occupied by John Power of Power's Whiskey), lying just inside the Leeson estate boundary (Map 10). The history of Roebuck House and its interesting occupants is recounted in Martin Holland's history of Clonskeagh.[221]

OVERVIEW AND SUMMARY

This chapter has attempted to set out in detail the significant eighteenth-century landowners in Milltown, with particular emphasis on the Leeson estate and its chief subtenants, together with a discussion on the growth of Milltown village. Despite the valuable data available in the Registry of Deeds and contemporary newspapers, it is impossible to completely reconstruct the Leeson estate in Milltown and its vicinity without detailed estate and deed maps showing boundaries and sub-tenancies. This is especially true for the Leeson estate located on the south bank of the River Dodder. Nonetheless, the volume of information available from sources such as the Registry of Deeds and contemporary newspapers enables a much more detailed picture of Milltown to be drawn up compared with previous centuries. Succeeding chapters will review social life, industrial development and the advent of the 'big house' in Milltown in the eighteenth and nineteenth centuries. ■

219 Roebuck House is located less than 100 metres south-west of the Clonskeagh entrance to the Belfield campus at UCD. The house is now surrounded by modern town houses and a 1960s' development called Embassy Lawn.

220 NAI, Landed Estates Court Rental, vol. 68, no. 67, 'Rental and Particulars of Milltown and Roebuck, known as Roebuck House, to be sold on 26 June 1863'. The sale included a separate plot of the property to the north-east which was originally part of the Trimleston estate as depicted on the estate map of 1832 (Map 10).

221 Holland, *Clonskeagh*, pp. 175–9.

Chapter 5:
Aspects of Social Life and Prosperity in Eighteenth-century Milltown

Chapter 5:
Aspects of Social Life and Prosperity in Eighteenth-century Milltown

INTRODUCTION

This chapter examines a handful of subjects which, at first glance, are unrelated. The purpose of bringing together disparate social history topics such as property advertising, health, intermarriage, crime, transport and communications is to emphasise the prosperity and prominence that Milltown enjoyed as a Dublin suburb in the second half of the eighteenth century. Milltown's popularity was, of course, relative compared with other fashionable contemporary suburbs such as Booterstown and Blackrock. Even so, the prosperity and gaiety that prevailed in the eighteenth century contrasts markedly with the poverty and obscurity that befell Milltown in the nineteenth century, and so this brief golden age for Milltown deserves to be explored in its own right.

SOCIAL ACTIVITY IN MILLTOWN VILLAGE IN THE 1750S

The mini building boom that took place in the main street of Milltown in the second quarter of the eighteenth century was accompanied by a lively social scene, as described in the following notice placed in *Pue's Occurrences* on 18 July 1758:

> *To be run at Milltown near Dublin, on Tuesday the 25 day of July, a pair of plate spurs, by any horse, mare or gelding that never started [i.e. had never raced before] for the value of twenty shillings. Each [entrant] paying half a crown entrance and half a crown to the winner. No less than four to start. A shift to be run for by girls; the first to have the shift; the second to get two shillings two pence, the third to get one shilling seven and a half pence and the fourth one shilling and one penny. A cap and a ribbon to be danced for. All disputes to be decided by the gentlemen then present. The horses to be entered at the Phoenix at Milltown the day before the running or pay double entrance at the post.*[1]

1 *Pue's Occurrences*, 18 July 1758, p. 2.

A very exclusive gentlemen's club called the Florists' Club of Dublin, whose objects were to encourage and promote ornamental horticulture in Ireland, was active for about 20 years in the mid-eighteenth century.[2] Membership was restricted to a small coterie of wealthy establishment figures of the day, including the bankers David La Touche senior and junior who, as revealed in Chapter 15, held property in Milltown at various times in the eighteenth century as part of their policy of protecting their capital by investing in urban leaseholds and freeholds.[3] In practice the members preferred to meet up in convivial circumstances as a dining club, so much so that in 1757 the club introduced a fine of a half crown for any member who turned up to a meeting without a flower![4] From time to time members held so-called extraordinary meetings at various up-market dining venues, where minutes were rarely taken. In spite of this, the Florists' Club's minute book records that extraordinary meetings took place at Mr Hoey's in Milltown on at least three occasions in the 1750s.[5]

A well-to-do family called Bayly rented a country villa in Milltown in the 1740s and early 1750s. A diary was kept by Mrs Katherine Bayly, the wife and later widow of Mr John Bayly, who held an obscure post in the Court of Exchequer, at Dublin Castle.[6] The name and location of the Bayly's house in Milltown is unknown, but there is evidence indicating that it may have been a large house situated on the corner of Prospect Lane and Milltown Road known originally as Mount Prospect and later called Grove House.[7] In 1745 the Baylys bought a number of articles to furnish their house and, while residing there, they attended divine service in Donnybrook. The Baylys were well-off members of Dublin society and they could afford to pay for private entertainment for their young children, as the following diary entry shows: 'For seeing legerdemain tricks at Milltown, 3*s*. 4*d*.' [8] One Sunday in August 1748 Mr Bayly's garden in Milltown was robbed, probably while the family were attending church in Donnybrook. In response, Bayly offered a reward of one guinea to anyone who provided information leading to the conviction of the robbers.[9]

These reports reveal that by the middle of the eighteenth century Milltown was attracting very well-heeled people to live and socialise there. At the same time, considerable building was going on in the village and expensive villas were being built on the outskirts along the Milltown Road. Thus, it was not inaccurate for Joseph Leeson to describe Milltown as a flourishing town in 1751, and it was perfectly understandable for him to choose it for his title when he was canvassing for a peerage. Milltown at that time cannot be dismissed as a 'nondescript County Dublin village'.[10]

---

2 E. Charles Nelson, 'The Dublin Florists' Club in the Mid-eighteenth Century', *Garden History*, 10, no. 2 (Autumn 1982), pp. 142–8; Minute Book of the Florists' Club of Dublin (RIA, MS 24E37).

3 Minute Book of the Florists' Club of Dublin; RD 128/199/86582; David Dickson and Richard English, 'The La Touche Dynasty' in David Dickson (ed.), *The Gorgeous Mask, Dublin 1700–1850* (Dublin, 1987), p. 18.

4 Nelson, 'The Dublin Florists' Club', p. 142.

5 Minute Book of the Florists' Club of Dublin, 3 July 1752, 17 June 1753, 16 June 1758 (RIA, MS 24E37).

6 H.F. Berry, 'Notes from the diary of a Dublin lady in the reign of George II', *Journal of the Royal Society of Antiquaries of Ireland*, 28 (1898), pp. 141–54. The diary was destroyed in 1922 in the Four Courts explosion.

7 RD 128/199/86582 (Lease dated 9 September 1747).

8 Berry, 'Notes from the diary of a Dublin lady', p. 143.

9 *Faulkner's Dublin Journal*, 30 August 1748, p. 2.

10 See Laffan and Mulligan, *Russborough*, pp. 25, 128, 370 where they speculate as to why Leeson chose Milltown for his title.

APOGEE OF POPULARITY

Judging by the number and nature of the property advertisements in *Saunders's Newsletter* from the 1770s onwards, Milltown reached the height of its popularity as a residential district for the upper classes in the last quarter of the eighteenth century. One of the reasons for this was the availability of several well-sited and appointed large detached houses for short-term or long-term letting on the high ground above the village and on the main approach roads. They included villas called Coldblow (Milltown Park), Mount Prospect (Grove House), Milltown Hill (Prospect/The Old House), Milltown House (Mount St Anne's), Elmfield (Elm House), Fairyland (St Philip's), Richmond Hill (Rydalmount) and Casino. The history of these properties is laid out in a separate chapter, but for now attention is given to some of the more eye-catching advertisements.

One of the earliest notices for property letting in Milltown village dates to the mid-1770s and was written in an upbeat style that characterised the advertising format of the time:

> *To be set in Milltown, for a term of years as may be agreed upon, an exceedingly good house, with all necessary offices, a large garden stocked with choice wall and fruit trees in full bearing; the whole is fit for the immediate reception of a gentleman; it would answer well for a tea house or tavern. Apply to Mr John Keogh at Milltown, who will close with a solvent tenant immediately, as he intends soon to leave the Kingdom, or to Mr William Bushe, at his Starch and Blue Warehouse, Back Lane, who is empowered to set the place. A servant attends to show it. Milltown, June 20th, 1774.*[11]

John Keogh had married Elizabeth Humphrey of Sion, County Carlow, in 1772. The following year the couple assigned their Sion property (Elizabeth's dowry) to William Bushe, so John and Elizabeth may have been planning for some time to emigrate.[12] The potential uses suggested for their property in Milltown – a gentleman's residence, a tea house or tavern – show that the local economy was maintaining its ability to sustain or grow its hospitality sector to meet demand in the 1770s, having, as noted earlier, previously attracted an exclusive gentlemen's club whose members dined in Milltown on a number of occasions in the 1750s.[13]

The house and demesne called Coldblow, later renamed Milltown Park, was advertised in April 1776 for letting by the year or for the summer season:

> *To be let on Milltown Road, opposite Clonskeagh Lane [now Prospect Lane], a large convenient house, with coach house, stable, and a large garden; it is pleasantly situated, and commands a most delightful prospect of the harbour of Dublin. Application to be made to Mr James McDonnell, No. 10, Strand. A person attends to show the house.*[14]

A quirky advertisement appeared in the same newspaper three months later in July 1776 when lodgings were offered to rent in Milltown:

> *To be set at Milltown (but a short walk from Dublin, in a remarkable [sic] good air) a handsome dining room and bed chamber, with a neat room above stairs, all genteelly furnished, together with the use of a*

11 *Saunders's Newsletter*, Wednesday 22–Friday 24 June 1774, p. 3.

12 RD 299/118/197623. This deed of assignment was witnessed by John Bourne of Milltown.

13 Minute Book of the Florists' Club of Dublin, 3 July 1752, 17 June 1753, 16 June 1758 (RIA, MS 24E37).

14 *Saunders's Newsletter*, Friday 12–Monday 15 April 1776, p. 4.

kitchen, to a small family, for 12 guineas by the year. Inquire of Mr Williams, Notary Public, Castle Street. The reason of setting it so cheap, is for the pleasure of their company.[15]

By the 1780s Milltown had, as advertised, become genteel enough to attract nobility to live in the very best villas that were available, as a pair of notices indicate:

Lost, on Sunday last the 22nd inst. April [1781], between Lady Kingsland's gate at Milltown and Mount Merrion Hill, a plain double cased silver watch, made by Young Martin, Dublin, with gold hands, a common dog couple steel chain, and two brass keys, one of them broken, and a seal with a family arms engraved thereon. Whoever has found said watch, and will bring it to said Young Martin, Inns quay, Dublin, shall receive one guinea reward and no questions asked. No greater reward will be offered. April 24, 1781.[16]

A house, etc on the top of the descent going into Milltown, inhabited for some years by Lady Cox, at present by Mr Heron; the situation cannot be excelled for health or beauty; to be let for any term, furnished or unfurnished.[17]

The following newspaper notice illustrates Milltown's pecking order among the desirable suburbs on the south side of Dublin in the 1790s:

Wanted immediately, in the neighbourhood of Booterstown, Donnybrook, Ranelagh, or Milltown, and for which a reasonable fine and rent will be given, a tolerable house and garden, with one or two acres of land, for any term not under ten years. Application to be made to Mr Stapleton, No. 74, Dame Street.[18]

MILLTOWN AS A HEALTH RESORT

From about the middle of the eighteenth century some of the wealthier citizens of Dublin began leaving the city to reside temporarily in the suburbs for the sake of their health. There were a number of reasons for this, but the main one was that the air in the city was extremely polluted by domestic coal fires, industrial activity such as glass, brick and lime works, and by rotting street refuse.[19] In 1770 an act was passed to prohibit the burning of bricks within two miles of the city's street lamps, and the following year legislation was enacted to prevent the building of lime kilns 'within the publick [*sic*] lamps of the city of Dublin or the liberties thereof'.[20] It is unsurprising, therefore, that contemporary newspaper advertisements for short-term lettings in Milltown extolled the purity of the air and the beautiful views of the mountains and Dublin bay. A house called Prospect Hall near Milltown was advertised to be let from 25 March 1784 on a lease for years or lives renewable forever; the lessor, John Healy, averring that 'For good air and extensive prospects no situation can excel it.'[21]

---

15 *Saunders's Newsletter*, Wednesday 31 July–Friday 2 August 1776, p. 2.

16 *Saunders's Newsletter*, 27 April 1781, p. 4.

17 *Saunders's Newsletter*, 12 April 1794, p. 4.

18 *Saunders's Newsletter*, 14 October 1793, p. 3.

19 Diarmuid Ó Gráda, *Georgian Dublin: The forces that shaped the city* (Cork, 2015), pp. 110–11, 263–4.

20 'An Act to prevent the pernicious practice of burning bricks within the city of Dublin, or neighbourhood thereof' (11 Geo. IIII, c. 6 (Dublin, 1770)), 'An Act for preventing the erecting of lime kilns in the city of Dublin, or the suburbs thereof' (12 Geo. III, c. 28 (Dublin, 1771)).

21 *Saunders's Newsletter*, 9 March 1784, p. 4.

More specifically, the district south of Milltown at Dundrum, Goatstown and Carrickmines was noted for its production of goats' milk, which was prescribed by the city's physicians for their patients. According to the celebrated naturalist John Rutty writing in 1772:

Goats' whey deserves to be considered as a medicine, which, as goats abound on the mountainous parts of the country, our physicians have of late learned to order their chronical patients in the neighbourhood of Dublin, instead of dismissing them to the mountains of Mourne, and for this purpose good lodgings have lately provided at Carrickmayne [sic], and also the whey has been drank at Dundrum, a distance of only three miles from the city.[22]

Aside from day trippers, people who came to Milltown for health reasons had the option to stay for a short period over the summer season or they could rent a house for a longer period if they wished, as the following advertisements from 1778 and 1785 illustrate:

To be set for the Summer, furnished, or on other terms. A house, with coach house and stable, and beautiful garden, in Milltown, not two miles from Dublin; the situation not to be excelled; the garden noted for the choiceness of its fruits; with a greenhouse and hot house in which the finest grapes are produced.[23]

To be let, a neat house beautifully situated on the hill of Milltown, near the bridge. It commands a most extensive prospect of the sea, the mountains, and the improvements in that neighbourhood, with a large garden, stable, and any number of acres that may be agreeable. There is a convenience of goats whey, and a fine pathway through the fields to Camden Street, computed to be not more than a mile and a quarter, inquire of John Percival Hunt, esq, at his house in Ship Street or of John Donnellan, at his house in Milltown. If the house be not shortly taken the owner will furnish from two to four rooms to accommodate lodgers for the remaining part of the season.[24]

Advertisements such as these attracted the gentry and nobility to reside in Milltown temporarily: on 6 May 1783 the newspapers reported that the Viscountess St Lawrence had given birth to a daughter there.[25] There are no records in the Registry of Deeds of the St Lawrences owning property in Milltown at this time so the Viscountess may have been staying in one of the villas on a short-term letting for the period of her confinement.

Unfortunately, not all of the people with bad health recovered when they went to Milltown for fresh air and goats' whey. Some obituary notices in the newspapers from the 1760s and 1770s record deaths occurring in Milltown in a perfunctory manner without any explanation of the circumstances:

Deaths: At Milltown near this city, Benjamin Mountney, esq, one of the surveyors of the custom house quay.[26]

Died: A few days ago, at Milltown, Thomas Vokes, esq, counsellor at law.[27]

---

22 John Rutty, *An Essay towards a Natural History of County Dublin* (Dublin, 1772), p. 272.

23 *Saunders's Newsletter*, 17 April 1778, p. 4.

24 *Saunders's Newsletter*, 6 July 1784, p. 4.

25 *Dublin Journal*, 6 May 1783, p. 1.

26 *Pue's Occurrences*, 7 June 1757, p. 2.

27 *Freeman's Journal*, 19 March 1765, p. 3.

Died: Near Milltown, the wife of Nicholas Smith of Limerick, esq.[28]

Died: A few days ago, at Milltown, Mr Miller of Coppinger's lane, cabinet maker.[29]

As far as one can tell, none of these people had family or property connections with Milltown and it is impossible to tell if the readership already knew that the deceased had been sick or had gone to Milltown for treatment.

The standard of medicine practised by doctors in eighteenth- and nineteenth-century Ireland was for the most part very primitive and ineffective, and indeed the treatments prescribed by doctors were often very harmful to their patients.[30] This did not discourage doctors from boasting about their abilities. For example, Dr Rowley of Stephen Street, Dublin wrote to the *Leinster Journal* to report several cures he had effected on his patients, among whom was Mr Debaust of Milltown Road, who was cured of 'apoplexy and loss of sight'.[31] In 1811 a Dr Ryan, described as an 'oculist', moved his practice to Dublin from London. Within the space of two months of his arrival, Dr Ryan claimed to have restored the sight of 20 blind persons and cured 40 'obstinate diseases of the eye'. In his written address to the public, Dr Ryan reported on several cases where he had restored his patients' loss of sight, including the case of Robert Quirk of Milltown who had previously worked as a gardener:

This man lost his sight ten years back, and was considered by the most skilful, and [by] Mr Adams, as hopeless; on the 19th day of the treatment he declared; in the presence of – Watson, esq, 10 Charlemont row, [that] he could see the cattle across the meadow.[32]

The final word on this subject is left to the *Dublin Penny Journal,* which more accurately reported in 1833 that the ancient castle of Rathmines had been fitted out as a boarding house for invalids 'and, unfortunately, is seldom empty'.[33]

INTERMARRIAGE AMONG LOCAL LANDOWNERS

The previous chapter reviewed the development of the Leeson estate in Milltown and introduced some of the important tenants to the historical narrative. It is worth briefly examining the inter-relationships that developed among the prominent families who farmed and invested in land in Milltown, such as the Mowlds, the Classons and the Le Maistres, as it further illuminates the attraction of the district in the third quarter of the eighteenth century.

Sometime in the mid-eighteenth century James Classon married Anne Mowlds of Milltown. In 1765 Anne Mowlds senior let her Milltown property of 18 acres, 2 roods and 16 perches jointly to her son George and son-in-law James Classon, whose principal farming activities were based in Rathmines. James Classon subsequently appointed Thomas Mowlds of Rathmines as one of his executors in 1777.[34]

---

28 *Freeman's Journal*, 18 February 1766, p. 2.

29 *Freeman's Journal*, 6 July 1773, p. 4.

30 Ó Gráda, *Georgian Dublin*, pp. 147–51.

31 *Finn's Leinster Journal*, 19 December 1772, p. 3.

32 *Saunders's Newsletter*, 31 August 1811, p. 3.

33 *Dublin Penny Journal, no. 63, vol. 2*, 14 September 1833, p. 82.

34 RD 234/550/154987, RD 357/274/240334.

On 12 April 1765, John Moulds of Milltown granted a lease of 4 acres, 1 rood and 12 perches of the lands of Milltown to Peter Le Maistre, and by deed poll dated 1 April 1768, John Moulds granted a further plot containing 3 roods and 38 perches to Peter Le Maistre. These two plots later formed part of the Roebuck House demesne on the Clonskeagh Road.[35] At the same time, in the 1760s and 1770s Peter Le Maistre was purchasing building plots on George's Lane (later South Great George's Street) from Dublin Corporation. [36]

Peter Le Maistre died sometime before 1777 and was succeeded by his eldest son and heir at law, William.[37] William Le Maistre married Grace Classon, the daughter of James and Anne Classon (née Mowlds) of Rathmines, in 1783.[38] William was a cabinetmaker by trade and was one of the masters of the corporation of joiners.[39] Under the terms of her marriage settlement, Grace Classon conveyed her one-third share of her inheritance to William Le Maistre and Henry Le Maistre. If she survived her husband, she would be paid a pension of £40 per annum.[40]

Henry Le Maistre was a watchmaker, goldsmith and jeweller, whose business was based initially in Kevin Street, before relocating successively to nos 89 and 90 Dame Street.[41] In 1778 Henry married Margaret Mowlds of Milltown.[42] This was probably an advantageous match for both parties. Margaret was marrying into the luxury end of retailing and Henry was marrying into the gentleman farming class and gaining access to land and the social cachet that went with it. In 1786, the two families inserted a rather curious lost property notice in *Saunders's Newsletter*:

> *Dropped, this day, between the top of Milltown hill and the George at Milltown, County Dublin, a plain double case silver watch, with a steel chain and a fourpenny piece to it (the property of a poor man), maker's name Pierre Marechal, not numbered. Whoever brings it to Mr John Mowlds, Milltown, or Mr Henry Le Maistre, of Kevin Street, watch maker, will receive half a guinea reward. If offered for sale, it is requested it may be stopped, and information sent as above. August 29, 1786.*[43]

Who was the poor man? Did he own the watch and the fourpenny piece, or only the fourpenny piece; if he owned the watch, how could he afford such a luxury?

35 NAI, Landed Estates Court Rental, vol. 68, no. 67, 'Rental and Particulars of Milltown and Roebuck, known as Roebuck House, to be sold on 26 June 1863'.

36 CARD, xi (Dublin, 1904), p. 359, xii, pp. 60, 183–4.

37 CARD, xii (Dublin, 1905), p. 498.

38 Report of the Deputy Keeper of the Public Records of Ireland, *Index to the Act or Grant Books, and to original Wills, of the Diocese of Dublin 1272–1858*, Appendix to the 26th Report (1894), p. 522.

39 *Saunders's Newsletter*, 28 April 1786, p. 3.

40 RD/357/274/240334, RD 234/550/154987.

41 *Dublin Evening Post*, 29 January 1789; 25 February 1792, p. 2; *Saunders's Newsletter*, 9 November 1793, p. 3; 24 July 1794, p. 3; 17 July 1795, p. 3.

42 Report of the Deputy Keeper of the Public Records of Ireland, *Index to the Act or Grant Books, and to original Wills, of the Diocese of Dublin 1272–1858*, Appendix to the 26th Report (1894), p. 620.

43 *Saunders's Newsletter*, 30 August 1786, p. 3.

William and Henry Le Maistre had a brother, Philip, who set himself up as public notary in 1786, having previously acted as a clerk for Ralph Meredith prior to setting up on his own.[44] Unlike his two brothers, Philip Le Maistre did not have any familial connections with Milltown. Regardless, Philip Le Maistre was familiar with the Dublin property market, and in his professional capacity as a public notary he was in a position to provide credit and investment facilities:

> *Philip Le Maistre, public notary, respectively informs his friends and the public, that he has commenced business in house No. 13 Crampton Court, where he transacts all manner of notarial business with the greatest fidelity and punctuality. The sum of £1,500 and £1,000 to be laid out in purchase of ground rents or well secured profit rents, and £500 to be lent on a mortgage. Application to be made to Philip Le Maistre, public notary, No. 13 Crampton Court.*[45]

John Ledsam of no. 4 Palace Street was another public notary who was active in the Milltown property market in the 1780s. In 1781 he acted as agent for George Frederick Mowlds when the latter was letting two houses on the east side of the Milltown to Dundrum Road, which were later named Rosy Hill and Casino.[46]

THE FIRST POST OFFICE IN MILLTOWN

On 31 March 1774 the Postmaster General announced that the Penny Post Office would be extended to the suburbs of Dublin that lay within four miles of the city. The new suburban postal service required correspondents to pay one penny on the receipt of a letter and to pay another penny for delivery to 14 specified receiving houses in 13 suburban locations.[47] The announcement explained in detail how the new postal arrangements would operate:

> *The letters will be dispatched from the General Penny Post Office in Dublin once every day, (Sundays excepted) viz. at 10 o'clock in the morning, and the letter carriers will return in time, that the letters they bring from the country [i.e. the suburban receiving houses], may be distributed in Dublin by evening delivery. Letters from England and the country of Ireland, directed to persons residing within the above-mentioned distance from Dublin [four miles], will be forwarded by the Penny Post, on the payment of one penny, over and above the rates of postage due for the conveyance of such letters to the General Post Office Dublin, and letters from England and the Country of Ireland, will be taken in at the receiving houses, on payment of one penny for each. Receiving houses will be established at the following places, where letters may be put in every day, (Sundays excepted) from 8 in the morning till 10 at night, on the before-mention terms.*

It was implicit that the locations of the chosen receiving houses had a sufficient nucleus of literate inhabitants who thus would be inclined to use the postal service. On the south side of Dublin receiving houses were established in Ringsend, Booterstown, Blackrock, Rathfarnham,

44 In 1765 Ralph Meredith 'and Philip Lemaister his clerk' witnessed the memorial of a deed executed by John Mowlds of Churchtown and George Mowlds of Milltown: RD 309/586/207363.

45 *Saunders's Newsletter*, 20 November 1786, p. 3.

46 *Saunders's Newsletter*, 3 April 1781, p. 3; 19 August 1786, p. 3; RD 416/120/275477; NAI, Landed Estates Court Rental, vol. 140, no. 32, 'Rental and Particulars of part of the lands of Milltown, known on the Ordnance Survey as part of the lands of Farranboley, containing 8a 0r 33p statute measure to be sold on 3 December 1880'.

47 *Saunders's Newsletter*, 11 April 1774, p. 3.

Kilmainham and Milltown. The list is interesting for the names of the places that were left out – Rathmines, Ranelagh, Donnybrook and Sandymount – which were apparently not deemed sufficiently developed in the 1770s to qualify for a post office. In contrast, Milltown was given two receiving houses, one in the charge of Mr Egan, tailor, and the other in the charge of Mr Swan, gardener. Thus, it would seem that there was insufficient post to justify the appointment of full-time suburban postmasters, hence the Postmaster General appointed local people to act as receivers of mail on a part-time basis. Interestingly, Milltown was the only location among the 13 suburban villages that had more than one receiving house and postmaster.[48] Reflecting the growth of Dublin's suburbs over the succeeding 40 years, the number of suburban receiving houses was increased in 1811 from 13 to 29, at which stage Dundrum, Rathmines, Ranelagh, Donnybrook and Sandymount had been added to the list of receiving houses.[49]

CRIME: BURGLARY, ROBBERY AND ASSAULT

In November 1753 a William Kalendar was sentenced to be flogged from Milltown to Dundrum for having taken part in the rescue of a prisoner in the city. Kalendar did not survive his punishment and he died a few days later in Newgate Prison, leaving a widow and five children to fend for themselves. The local historian Francis Elrington Ball recorded this unsavoury event in his history of county Dublin in 1903.[50] Ball lived on Sydenham Road, Dundrum, and acted as a justice of the peace at the local petty sessions court in Dundrum at the turn of the twentieth century.[51] Ball dispensed summary justice for various misdemeanours committed by the local inhabitants of Milltown living on the south bank of the Dodder, which lay outside the jurisdiction of the city's courts but inside the Dundrum Petty Sessions' jurisdiction.[52]

The popularity of Milltown as a healthy residential district for Dublin's wealthier inhabitants resulted in crimes (particularly burglaries) being committed there. The outlying villages within walking distance of Dublin were particularly vulnerable to violent crime too because of their isolation from the city centre.[53] Additionally, there was no formal prosecution service to prosecute offences under criminal law. This meant that cases of theft or violence required the victim to notify the authorities, assemble witnesses and present the evidence in court.[54] In practice, the local gentry were forced to take action themselves during periods when crime was particularly bad in their neighbourhoods.

Reports of crime occurring in Milltown start to appear in the press from the late 1760s, increasing in frequency in the 1780s, before declining to a handful of reported incidents in the 1790s. This trend accords with extensive research into crime in Dublin in the late eighteenth century carried out by eighteenth-century historians Brian Henry and Diarmuid Ó Gráda.[55]

Alderman Percival Hunt the younger, who, as noted previously, lived in Milltown in the third quarter of the eighteenth century, was actively involved in combatting crime as a justice of the

48 *Saunders's Newsletter*, 11 April 1774, p. 3.

49 *Saunders's Newsletter*, 4 November 1811, p. 3.

50 Ball, *History of county Dublin*, ii, p. 113, citing Pue's Occurrences.

51 Thom's Directory for 1900, p. 1612.

52 For example, the *Rathmines News*, 4 March 1897, reported that Thomas Richardson of Milltown was summonsed for failing to pay his county cess (local rates imposed on occupiers of property) and that Ball was one of the magistrates sitting on the bench that day.

53 Henry, *Dublin Hanged*, pp. 126–7.

54 Ó Gráda, *Georgian Dublin*, pp. 123–4.

55 Henry, *Dublin Hanged*, pp. 13–15; Ó Gráda, *Georgian Dublin*, Chapter 5.

peace.[56] Hunt recaptured a gaol breaker, Edward Bryan, who was apprehended in Milltown in 1766.[57] On another occasion, in 1769 Hunt committed Barnaby Cunningham to Kilmainham Gaol charged with throwing stones at a gentleman's house on Milltown Road.[58] Five years later, in 1774, Percival Hunt offered a reward for the conviction of garden robbers who were active in the vicinity of Milltown. Such an approach relied on the use of informers, as the notice in *Saunders's Newsletter* explains:

> *The garden of Alderman Hunt, at Milltown, was since the evening of Saturday the 20th inst. Robbed of apples, peaches not ripe, and cabbage, by some person or persons not yet known, who got into said garden by climbing over a high stone wall – among the apples were white and Kentish codlins. In order to bring said robbers to due punishment by law, I promise to pay a reward of 5 guineas, to any person who will inform against, cause to be apprehended, and prosecute to conviction, and one of said robbers; and if said informant, etc should be one who was concerned in said robbery, I will apply for his or her pardon, and also pay him or her the said reward of 5 guineas. N. B. Any person able and inclined to give private and useful information touching said robbery, may depend upon strict secrecy, and to be generously rewarded. Other gardens in the neighbourhood have been lately robbed. Percival Hunt Milltown 21st August 1774.*[59]

A particularly violent incident was reported to have taken place at Robert Tomlinson's house at Milltown in 1779:

> *Yesterday, at noon, a most daring robbery and burglary was committed at the house of Mr Robert Tomlinson, at Milltown, by a set of desperate villains, to the number of fifty or upwards. They fired several shots in the house, and carried off all the plate they could find, and destroyed all the furniture they could not carry off, and wearing apparel etc. They brought their arms in a coffin, covered with a pall as if they had a corpse therein; they consisted of blunderbusses, pistols, etc.*[60]

The use of different types of firearms during the robbery is explained by the fact that such weapons could legally be purchased from the city's gunsmiths' shops or bought from pawnbrokers. To make matters worse, receivers of stolen goods supplied criminal gangs with guns.[61]

Two critical factors were behind an upsurge in crime in Dublin in the 1780s. Firstly, a subsistence crisis seriously impacted on the living conditions for Dublin's poor from 1782 to 1784. Secondly, when the American War of Independence ended in 1783 thousands of troops were demobilised, and this added to the mix of discontented poor in the city.[62] As a result, Dublin's suburban villages were continually plagued by gangs of burglars in the 1780s. In response, the

56 An act of 1760 reorganised Dublin Corporation whereby the lord mayor, sheriffs and aldermen became ex-officio justices of the peace within Dublin city and its liberties: Sean Murphy, 'The Corporation of Dublin 1660–1760', *Dublin Historical Record*, xxxvii, no. 1 (December 1984), p. 32.

57 *Dublin Courier*, 4 April 1766, p. 2.

58 *Freeman's Journal*, 2 May 1769, p. 3.

59 *Saunders's Newsletter*, 24 August 1774, p. 1.

60 *Gentleman's and London Magazine*, 19 August 1779, p. 487, para. 19.

61 Henry, *Dublin Hanged*, p. 99.

62 Henry, *Dublin Hanged*, p. 36.

local gentry established vigilante associations, some of which were armed, to fight crime. The most prominent of these groups was the Blackrock Felons Association.[63]

In December 1782 a notice was published in the *Saunders's Newsletter* asking the inhabitants of the towns of Rathfarnham, Milltown, Rathmines, Crumlin and Tallaght to meet at Laughlin's tavern in Rathfarnham, to consider 'the most effectual method of bringing to justice the perpetrators of the many robberies lately committed, and preventing in future such nightly depredations'.[64] The notice drew a large group of local gentry to Rathfarnham on 9 January 1783, where Sir William Fortick, the High Sheriff of Dublin, who lived on Coldblow Lane (later renamed Belmont Avenue), was appointed chairman. A series of resolutions were passed, the focus of which was to reward informants rather than to actively patrol the countryside.[65] The new association seems to have been ineffective in preventing crime. In February George Frederick Mowlds' house in Milltown was burgled and over £87 in cash was stolen.[66] Rather ironically, Sir William Fortick's home, Belmont House (which was located to the rear of Coldblow House and is still extant)[67] was burgled a few months later in July 1783. Following the burglary, Sir William was obliged to put up a reward of five guineas for the recovery of 'a pair of small screw barrel pocket pistols, steel mounted, made by Collins, Dublin' and some crested silver.[68]

A new local defence force made up of residents from Ranelagh began patrolling the main road from Ranelagh to Milltown in November 1783, a development which met with the enthusiastic approval of *Faulkner's Journal*:

> *Last Saturday began the patrol guard of Ranelagh road, it is formed on such a plan, and executed with so much spirit, that it is highly worthy of imitation. Added to proper arms, they have also adopted the precaution of notice bells and alarm clappers, and a proper watch house; in so much as to make it improbable that any villain can escape in that quarter. The inhabitants of that road deserve the highest commendation for setting so laudable an example to the environs of this widely extended metropolis.*[69]

After 1783 the newspapers are silent about property crimes in Milltown for several years. This may be due to an absence of reporting the crimes rather than because of a marked reduction in burglaries. Admittedly, an increase in the number of hangings and transportations in the mid- to late 1780s, coupled with the introduction of a city police force in 1786 (subsequently abolished in 1795 due to public pressure) and the beginning of the French wars in 1793, all apparently resulted in a significant reduction in crime in Dublin city by the mid-1790s.[70] Despite these developments, the *Belfast Newsletter* published on 22 February 1799 a detailed report about an aggravated burglary that took place at the home of Mr Wight Pike on Milltown

63 Henry, *Dublin Hanged*, pp. 14–15, 128–9; Ball, *History of county Dublin*, ii, pp. 72–3 (for crime in Dundrum).

64 *Saunders's Newsletter*, 28 December 1782, p. 3.

65 *Saunders's Newsletter*, 15 January 1783, p. 3.

66 *Dublin Evening Post*, 15 February 1783, p. 3.

67 After his death, the sale notices for Fortick's house and contents unequivocally confirm that he lived in Belmont House and not in Coldblow House: *Saunders's Newsletter*, 7 August 1789, p. 4; 29 September 1789, p. 3.

68 *Saunders's Newsletter*, 2 July 1783, p. 3.

69 *Faulkner's Dublin Journal*, 6–8 November 1783.

70 Henry, *Dublin Hanged*, pp. 14–15.

Road 'nearly opposite Coldblow Lane'.[71] According to the report, the gang fired at Pike and forced their way into his home; however, a female servant escaped and raised the alarm in Ranelagh. In response:

> *Mr Hooper, and three or four gentlemen of the Stephen's green division, who reside there, and belong to an association of that vicinity, immediately repaired to the above mentioned house, and with a most laudable spirit and activity, assailed the robbers, seized four of them, one of whom they shot in the jaw, and shattered the bone, wounded another, and the remainder fled in various directions.*[72]

One of the captured men became an informer and, as a result, four men were sent to a jury trial charged with committing burglary and robbery at Wight Pike's home.[73] The report of the jury's deliberations in reaching their verdict provides a fascinating insight into conflicting personal and public attitudes to crime and punishment that prevailed in Dublin at that time:

> *The jury went in upon them about three o'clock [on a Friday afternoon], and at four they returned to the box, when instead of giving a verdict, they stated to the court, that they had all agreed save one person, who had refused to accord with them, and to assign any reason for it. The jury were sent back again. They did not return a verdict until eleven o'clock on Sunday, having sat up the whole night in the jury room. At nine o'clock in the morning the judges took their seats on the bench, and at ten, the jury having come out, it was expected they had agreed on a verdict. The judge then asked them had they decided the fate of the prisoners according to their consciences: Forbes, the dissenting juror, said again he had some doubts. The judge immediately replied they must then return to the jury room, where he declared they should stay until Sunday, if they did not agree. They retired accordingly, and at eleven returned a verdict of guilty. The only reason the above mentioned person gave for not agreeing with the rest was, that he did not like a man should be hanged for any crime but murder. This person, we hear, is a schoolmaster, and lives in Glassmanogue. Sentence of death was pronounced upon the prisoners, and they were ordered to be executed on Saturday next.*[74]

Violent crime against the person was a frequent hazard when travelling to and from the city to the suburbs. On 6 May 1772, Edward Moran and William Egan, a Temple Bar publican, were returning to the city from Milltown when they were attacked near the South Circular Road by three armed men who mortally wounded Moran and robbed Egan of a five pound note and a silk handkerchief.[75] There was a happier postscript for Egan, for in September of the following year he married a Miss Catherine Egan of Milltown.[76] It is possible that William had been out at Milltown courting Catherine before he was attacked on his way home to Temple Bar. Prior to her marriage, Catherine lived in a house beside the Packhorse Bridge on the north bank of the River Dodder with her widowed mother, Mary, and her brother William. William Egan was a tailor who, as noted earlier, was ap-

---

71 *Belfast Newsletter*, 22 February 1799, p. 4. Pike's home was almost certainly a detached house called Woodville, which is shown on a manuscript map of 1823 (NLI, Longfield map collection MS 21 F. 28) and on OSI, Co. Dublin, Sheet 22, six inches to one statute mile, surveyed in 1837 and corrected in 1843 (Map 15). Woodville was demolished and replaced by late Victorian terraced houses on Sandford Road beside the entrance gate to Milltown Park.

72 *Belfast Newsletter*, 22 February 1799, p. 4.

73 *Belfast Newsletter*, 22 February 1799, p. 4; *Saunders's Newsletter*, 6 March 1799, p. 1.

74 *Saunders's Newsletter*, 6 March 1799, p. 1.

75 *Freeman's Journal*, 23 May 1772, p. 3.

76 *Finn's Leinster Journal*, 25 September 1773, p. 2.

pointed a receiver for the post office in Milltown.[77]

In March 1773 two men were violently robbed near the Bleeding Horse pub, which was then described as being 'on the Milltown Road'.[78] A few weeks later the newspaper had the pleasure of:

> *assuring the public, that the patrol, some time established on Milltown and Donnybrook roads, have had so good an effect that no person has received the least injury at any hour of the night, since the last audacious attack on two gentlemen near the Bleeding horse, about five weeks ago.*[79]

It seems that the local security patrols set up in south Dublin in the 1770s and 1780s existed on a temporary, *ad hoc* basis, as nothing further is heard of such activity until 1802. In that year the *Freeman's Journal* praised the work carried out by peace officers in patrolling the Rathmines, Milltown and Donnybrook roads until midnight.[80]

All of the accounts thus far relate to victims of crime who had connections with Milltown. Conversely, reports of crimes committed by people from Milltown are rare. In one case, the Commission of Oyer and Terminer[81] sentenced Michael O'Reilly of Milltown to transportation for seven years for stealing two (promissory?) notes valued at 20 guineas, the property of Edward Keogh.[82]

By the late eighteenth century Milltown had its fair share of public houses, some of which were the scenes of various crimes that were reported by the press from time to time. A row broke out in a pub in Milltown on a Sunday afternoon in January 1771 in which the landlord, Mulhall, stabbed a man, mortally wounding him. Mulhall fled the scene and successfully evaded justice.[83] Remarkably, 11 years later the editor of the *Saunders's Newsletter* published an appeal to the Lord Mayor of Dublin to bring Mulhall to justice:

> *Right Hon. The Lord Mayor. We hear that Mulhall, the wigmaker, who some years ago cruelly murdered a poor man in the public house he then kept near Milltown, and against whom the coroner has recorded a verdict for wilful murder, has ever since found refuge in county Wexford, and has been lately seen in Gorey, in said county. It is to be hoped the Volunteers of that country [sic] will exert themselves to apprehending so gross an offender, and give him up to justice.*[84]

The second half of the 1790s was a period of heightened tensions caused by the Napoleonic war with France and the security crises arising from the growth of the United Irishmen movement. As a result of fears for the city's security, in the late 1790s soldiers were stationed on the south side of Dublin at Loughlinstown.[85] To keep the troops occupied, from time to time the authorities em-

77 RD 242/155/156128; *Saunders's Newsletter*, 11 April 1774, p. 3.

78 *Finn's Leinster Journal*, 20 March 1773, p. 2.

79 *Finn's Leinster Journal*, 14 April 1773, p. 6.

80 *Freeman's Journal*, 2 September 1802, p. 4.

81 The Commission of Oyer and Terminer was a criminal court unique to Dublin where indictable crimes (i.e. not misdemeanours) committed in Dublin city and county were tried before two judges of the court of King's Bench with a jury. It was replaced by the Central Criminal Court in 1924.

82 *Dublin Chronicle*, 13 July 1793, vol. 7, no. 972, p. 255.

83 *Finn's Leinster Journal*, 9 January 1771, p. 2.

84 *Saunders's Newsletter*, 29 October 1782, p.2. It is not known if Mulhall was ever arrested and brought to trial.

85 Joyce, *The Neighbourhood of Dublin*, p. 81.

ployed them to suppress after-hours drinking. In September 1797, a party of the Antrim militia were quartered at Mountpleasant, Ranelagh, under the command of Justice Winder. Late one Sunday Justice Winder and his militia:

> *set out at eleven o'clock, and visited the different tippling houses at Milltown, and dispersed a number of idle people of every description whom they found drinking. They then proceeded to Churchtown, and did in like manner. In unlicensed houses they spilled the spirits found, and defaced the vessels used in measuring same. On their return, about half after one, they heard music and dancing in a large new house in Milltown, into which they got admittance after threatening to burst open the door, but all the men who had assembled made their escape out of a back window; however, the soldiers leaped out of the window and apprehended three of the party, who, with several of the idle women who had been dancing and drinking, were marched prisoners and safely lodged for the night. Out of compassion for the youth of the young lads (the oldest not more than fourteen years) and on promise of not transgressing in future, and after reprimanding the women, they were suffered to depart.*[86]

The large new house where the party was taking place was almost certainly a three-storey house on the south side of the village main street that the pawnbrokers Martin and Company had advertised for sale in 1795.[87]

The two criminal accounts quoted above do not reflect well on Milltown's publicans; however, they were not all a bad lot as the following report in *Saunders's Newsletter* shows:

> *Horse supposed to be stolen. Whereas it appears by information upon oath, that a man, genteelly dressed, riding a grey gelding, on Friday the 4th instant, stopped at the house of Pat Kerwin, publican, Milltown, desiring his horse to be put into the stable, and calling for 8s. 8d. to pay a carman, carrying his sister, as he said, going to service to Mr La Touche [at Marlay House, Rathfarnham], but no such car appeared then or after; and the said man being threatened to be brought before a Magistrate for examination by the said Kerwin, made his escape by flight, running through the river at Milltown, and has not since been heard of. He is described to be about 30 years of age, 5 feet 9 inches high, dark complexion, round visage, black beard, straight made, and well looking. The owner of the above horse, on paying the expense of his keeping, etc and proving his property in the beast, may have him, by applying to Justice Ancell, Ranelagh, Dublin. If not claimed in ten days from the date hereof, he will be sold for his expenses. Ranelagh, 7 October, 1799.*[88]

CONTEMPORARY ATTITUDES TO ANTI-SOCIAL BEHAVIOUR: BULL BAITING, FOOTBALL AND DUELLING

The newspapers occasionally carried reports of other forms of anti-social activity occurring in the neighbourhood of Milltown, including bull baiting, football and duelling. In October 1776 the *Freeman's Journal* indignantly reported that 'in the evening [of the 27th], a great number of vagabonds assembled on Milltown Road, where they had a bull beat, to the great annoyance of the inhabitants of that part of the town, and in open violation of the Sabbath'.[89] Bull baiting was very

86 *Saunders's Newsletter*, 27 September 1797, p. 2.

87 *Saunders's Newsletter*, 26 May 1795 p. 2.

88 *Saunders's Newsletter*, 11 October 1799, p. 4.

89 *Freeman's Journal*, 29–31 October 1776, p. 3.

popular with the working-classes in eighteenth-century Dublin.[90] The practice of seizing bulls on their way to market became so chronic that legislation was enacted in 1779 to specifically make such activity an offence. This cruel form of popular entertainment died out in the late 1790s because of the introduction of regulations prohibiting public assembly amid fears of a rebellion by the United Irishmen.[91]

The growth of Sabbatarianism among Protestant zealots in the 1760s was the root cause of a critical report of a football game that took place on a Sunday at Milltown in April 1766, one which attracted a large crowd 'to the great scandal of religion and this metropolis'.[92] In 1804 a new Police Bill gave powers to the superintendent magistrate to fine dairymen (of whom there were several in Milltown) 'in case of the breach of the Sabbath or any other misdemeanour which frequently occurs by their drawing wash, grains, etc, on the Sabbath day at all hours'.[93]

At the other end of the social scale, duelling was prevalent among the upper classes in the eighteenth century as a means of settling real or perceived insults, sometimes with fatal consequences. In November 1728 Joseph Leeson's eldest son and heir, Brice Leeson, was killed in a duel and as a result his younger brother Joseph later became the earl of Milltown.[94] That deaths by duelling were common is proven by the fact that when Dublin Corporation established a publicly funded pension scheme in 1737 the rules provided that no widow's pension would be paid if her husband had died in a duel.[95] The countryside of Roebuck and Clonskeagh was the vicinity of two reported duels in the late eighteenth century. On 4 June 1789 it was reported that, 'On Sunday morning last, a duel was fought near Roebuck Castle, in the County of Dublin, by a Mr H. and a Mr P. when after firing a case of pistols without effect, the affair was amicably adjusted.'[96] A year later, the *Dublin Chronicle* carried a similar story:

> *Yesterday evening a duel was fought in a field belonging to Mr McCarthy, Clonskeagh, between Counsellor W- and Counsellor P-, wherein the latter received a slight wound in the right arm; the seconds then interfered, and reconciled the parties.*[97]

On the other hand, John David Mowlds of Milltown fought a duel in the Phoenix Park in 1805 in which he severely wounded his adversary, Robert Burke of Summerhill.[98] The parties' dispute concerned Burke's alleged breach of promise to marry Mowlds' sister Elizabeth.[99] Nonetheless, from about 1800 the number of reported duelling incidents began to decline as the practice became progressively morally and socially unacceptable.[100]

---

90 See for example, CARD, viii (Dublin, 1901), p. 315, ix (Dublin, 1902), p. 31 for bullbaiting in Smithfield in 1738 and 1741.

91 Anonymous, *Ireland Sixty Years Ago* (3rd edition, Dublin, 1851), pp. 76–7; Henry, *Dublin Hanged*, p. 93.

92 *Faulkner's Dublin Journal*, 12 April 1766 quoted in Ó'Gráda, *Georgian Dublin*, pp. 213–14.

93 CARD, xv (Dublin, 1911), pp. 525–6.

94 James Kelly, *'That Damn'd Thing Called Honour': Duelling in Ireland 1570–1860* (Cork, 1995), p. 52.

95 CARD, viii (Dublin, 1901), p. 229.

96 *Dublin Chronicle*, 4 June 1789, p. 120.

97 *Dublin Chronicle*, 5 June 1790.

98 *Faulkner's Dublin Journal*, 1 June 1805, p. 2.

99 *Dublin Evening Post*, 7 December 1805, p. 2.

100 Kelly, *Duelling in Ireland*, pp. 199, 200, 213.

To conclude this discussion about crime, it is noteworthy that by the turn of the nineteenth century judges and lawyers had replaced the nobility as the most eminent residents of Milltown. In 1801 there were no less than three judges living in Milltown beside one another on the north side of the Milltown Road: Baron Denis George of the Exchequer Court at Coldblow (Milltown Park), Judge Robert Johnson of the Court of Common Pleas at Elmfield (Elm House) and Judge Tankerville Chamberlain of the Kings Bench at Milltown House (Mount St Anne's).[101] George and Chamberlain had distinguished legal careers while Johnson's ended in disgrace. Their careers are included with the histories of their respective residences in Chapter 15. Whether or not the judges deterred crime in Milltown is open to question; on 23 July 1806 Michael Cahill was tried at Kilmainham Quarter Sessions court for stealing a wheelbarrow at Elmfield, the property of Judge Johnson. Fortunately for Cahill, on the direction of the magistrate he was acquitted by the jury because of a legal technicality.[102]

GETTING TO MILLTOWN: ROAD AND TRANSPORT DIFFICULTIES

The district between the city's western suburbs at Kevin Street and Milltown village was, at the turn of the seventeenth century, entirely given over to agriculture, and as a result was very sparsely populated. A map of 1717 depicts three roads radiating out southwards from the Kevin Street area called the Milltown Road, the highway to Cullenswood, and the highway to Rathmines.[103] Throughout the eighteenth century the main road from Kevin Street to Milltown was simply called the Milltown Road, in the same way as the modern N11 dual carriageway from Donnybrook to Stillorgan is called the Stillorgan Road. This means that any imprecise references in contemporary records to events, property or people who lived on 'the Milltown Road' or 'the road to Milltown' are impossible to locate today and thus may have no connection with Milltown village or its immediate vicinity.

Before the introduction of motorised transport, horse riding and travelling on horse-drawn carts entailed considerable risk because of the unpredictable nature of horses, which could stumble and throw off their mount or take fright and bolt. This was an accepted fact of life, just as road traffic accidents are tolerated in the twenty-first century. In the eighteenth century, the newspapers regularly reported accidents on the Milltown/Dundrum Road often but not always involving falls from horses, usually with fatal consequences.[104] For example, in June 1756 John Quinn, the Chairman of Inns Quay Infirmary, died a week after breaking his leg following a fall in the fields leading to Milltown; he was probably walking on the Milltown Path when he fell.[105]

Reflecting its growth, by the late eighteenth century Milltown village was marked prominently on Taylor and Skinners' book of road maps from the 1780s, specifically for the route from Dublin to Powerscourt and Rathdrum.[106] For good measure, an Act of 1786 for wid-

---

101 RD 496/437/32007, RD 456/485/293715, RD 528/4/344352; Archer, *Statistical Survey of Dublin*, p. 108.

102 *Saunders's Newsletter*, 25 July 1806, p. 2.

103 'A Survey of the farm of St Sepulchres surveyed by John Greene in December, 1717', illustrated in Kelly, *The Four Roads to Dublin*, p. 20. The original map is preserved in the Representative Church Body Library.

104 *Pue's Occurrences*, 22 July 1758, p. 2; 26 October 1754; *Belfast Newsletter*, 23 September 1768, p. 2; *Dublin Chronicle*, 11 August 1787, p. 359; 18 April 1789, p. 1216.

105 *Pue's Occurrences*, 15 June 1756, p. 2.

106 George Taylor and Andrew Skinner, *Maps of the roads of Ireland* (2nd edition, Dublin, 1783; reprinted in 1969 by Irish University Press), p. 147.

ening roads in County Dublin listed 'the road from Powerscourt to Dublin, by Dundrum and Milltown' among the great roads of Dublin County.[107]

The grand jury for County Dublin was responsible for maintaining Milltown Road and the bridges spanning the River Dodder. Members of the grand jury were selected at the complete discretion of the county high sheriff (who was a political appointment made by the Lord Lieutenant) from the leading property owners in the county. Catholics were prohibited from serving on grand juries until 1793 but Protestants continued to dominate the grand jury lists after that date partly because of political and religious discrimination and partly due to the concentration of property in Protestant hands. The procedure under which road repairs were authorised and paid for was the presentment system, which originated in 1634 and operated nationally until 1898 when grand juries were replaced by county councils.[108]

The presentment system involved an individual obtaining the prior approval of the grand jury for a road or bridge repair scheme for which an estimated cost had been made and attested by two persons before a justice of the peace. Pressure of business at the grand jury court sittings (known as assizes, and which met twice yearly) meant that the success of a presentment application depended more on the influence of the sponsor than the merits of the proposal. When the works were completed, the grand jury paid the individual the charge authorised at the assizes. The cost of the works was paid out of a local tax known as the county cess (generally shortened to 'cess' and paid by 'cesspayers'). Crucially, the county cess was levied on the occupants of land and not on the land owners. Given that the grand jurors were by definition property owners their actions in granting presentments taxed their tenants and not themselves. Needless-to-say the presentment system was greatly resented by the vast majority of the populace because grand juries were undemocratic and were generally regarded as the most corrupt local authorities in the country.[109] This lamentable state of affairs explains the poor state of the roads in Milltown in the eighteenth and nineteenth centuries. On the other hand, in 1786 the inhabitants of the southside of Dublin successfully opposed the extension of the turnpike toll system of road maintenance that operated on some of the main roads on the north side of Dublin, which might otherwise have improved matters for southside travellers.[110]

Surprisingly, Joseph Archer did not mention the abuses of the grand jury system. Archer maintained that the roads in Dublin County 'are in excellent order, being frequently repaired at a great expense'.[111] This opinion was at odds with contemporary newspaper editorials and with the views expressed by Archer's critic, Hely Dutton, who opined that:

107 'An Act for making, widening, and repairing public roads in the County of Dublin, and for repealing parts of several Acts formerly made for that purpose' (26 Geo. III, c. XIV, s. 22 (Dublin, 1786)).

108 Virginia Crossman, *Local Government in Nineteenth Century Ireland* (Belfast, 1994), pp. 27-8, 93; David Broderick, *Local government in nineteenth century County Dublin: The Grand Jury* (Dublin, 2007), p. 10.

109 Crossman, *Local Government*, pp. 27–9; Broderick, *The Grand Jury*, p. 10. The amount of the cess charged on Taney parish in 1796 was over £438: Ball and Hamilton, *The Parish of Taney*, p. 198.

110 Diarmuid Ó Gráda, 'The rocky road to Dublin: Transport modes and urban growth in the Georgian Age, with particular reference to the turnpike roads', *Studia Hibernica*, 22/23 (1982–3), p. 138.

111 Archer, *Statistical Survey of Dublin*, p. 117.

When a better system of road making is established, the enormous waste of public money, that has taken place, will be truly astonishing; and I am convinced, until a National Board of Roads is established, we never can expect matters to mend; for then the grand cause, grand jury jobbing, will cease, and the conduct be thrown into the hands of scientific and practical road makers.[112]

Over a period of some 70 years the *Freeman's Journal* was consistently outspoken in drawing attention to the poor condition of the Milltown Road and the bridges spanning the River Dodder.[113] Three extracts illustrate how dangerous the roads and bridges often were in the eighteenth century:

The Grand Jury of the county of Dublin are most earnestly intreated [sic] to take proper notice of a dangerous gripe of a ditch, which encroaches on the road from Dublin to Milltown, about fifteen perches on the right hand beyond Coldblow [Lane]. Some time ago a horse and carriage fell therein, and the horse was drowned; and very lately, two young lads driving a cart were overturned therein, and one of them was drowned before sufficient assistance could be had to get him from under the cart; the other with difficulty was saved. The expense to the barony of filling it up can be but trivial, and the great advantage thereby derived to the public is obvious to every traveller going that road.[114]

The shocking condition in which the road from Dublin to Milltown at present appears, is highly disgraceful and extremely dangerous. Within a few yards of Ranelagh, a chasm appears at the side of a ditch, in which several carriages have unavoidably fallen, and the passengers been bruised. Why this road is so shamefully neglected, while improvement is bestowing upon all the other avenues to Dublin, is astonishing, being the high road to Wicklow, Arklow and Wexford, and more necessary to be repaired for the public good, than others upon which great sums are lavishing.[115]

The flood was so great in the River Dodder, on Sunday night, from the incessant rain which fell in the day, that it carried away part of the bridge of Clonskeagh, near Milltown, which had been recently built up, leaving the old part standing, which is no recommendation to modern undertakings.[116]

The same flood also claimed the life of a man on horseback who attempted to cross the Dodder at the fording point in Milltown but was swept away and drowned.[117] In 1807 a presentment was made to the Dublin grand jury to build a new bridge at Clonskeagh at a cost of £535 19*s.* 6*d.*, while nine years later, in 1816, a presentment was passed to build the present bridge over the Dodder at Milltown at a cost of £1,662 and 6*s.*[118]

The constant neglect of the Milltown Road by the Dublin grand jury forced the local inhabitants to repair the road at their own expense in 1811 'for the sake of their lives and properties', according to the indignant report in the *Freeman's Journal*:

112 Dutton, *Observations on Mr Archer's Statistical Survey*, p. 138.

113 *Freeman's Journal*, 17 November 1774, 25 April 1844.

114 *Freeman's Journal*, 17 November 1774, p. 2.

115 *Freeman's Journal*, 10 May 1794, p. 7.

116 *Freeman's Journal*, 25 August 1792, p. 4.

117 *Freeman's Journal*, 28 August 1792, p. 3.

118 Ball and Hamilton, *The Parish of Taney*, p. 222.

We are pleased to see, that Milltown Road is at present undergoing a partial repair; but for this, the public are not obliged to the late Term Grand Jury of the county of Dublin, for we understand the inhabitants are repairing it at their own expense, for the sake of their lives and properties. Two gentlemen are superintending the work, General Arabin and Major Allen, whose activity and great attentions in this very necessary work, highly deserve public thanks. The Grand Jury who refused the presentment for the repair of this road, it is said, are not so much to blame, as was at first imagined, as it is alleged, they were induced to that ungracious conduct, by some jobbers who are interested in the scene of a new road in contemplation at that place, and which they considered would forward their intended plan. Of this plan, however, we do not disapprove, as we consider its adoption would be useful and ornamental; but we reprobate that disgusting avarice, that would render an old public road impassable, for perhaps two or three years, no matter to what injury or inconvenience to the community, because it was conceived it would forward the grasping selfish interests of individuals.[119]

Unfortunately, the repairs undertaken at the expense of the public-spirited inhabitants were not effective because the editor of the *Freeman's Journal* had cause to complain once more the following year:

The high road to Ranelagh and Milltown was never more in a wretched state than at present, notwithstanding that more than £200 was lately expended upon it by the subscription of the inhabitants. It would have been totally impassable but for that temporary repair, and which was made as well as could be effected for such a sum, under the superintendence of General Arabin and Major Allen, to whom the public for such attention are much indebted. We hope no time will be lost in furthering a presentment for the immediate repair of this road. There can be no excuse, the new tax is now collecting for repairing roads in this Barony, and something should be had from the County at Large, being such a general thoroughfare to Wicklow, Wexford, etc in order to ease at once a substantial permanent repair, that in future will not require great trouble to preserve in good order.[120]

Whatever about the accuracy or exaggeration of travellers using the Milltown Road to travel to Wexford – the Donnybrook Road to Bray surely fulfilled that need – there is no doubt that traffic on the Milltown Road would have grown significantly from the 1780s onwards, with a corresponding increase in the wear and tear on the road. Over a period of a quarter of a century commencing in about 1789, the Trimleston estate in Roebuck and Goatstown developed into a prime residential suburb of Dublin during which period at least 25 large villa gentry residences were built on the estate.[121] As noted in the previous chapter, villas were built on Bird Avenue when a link between Dundrum and the Roebuck roads was opened up in the 1780s. In addition, a new road to Clonskeagh was laid out in the 1790s. This act of private enterprise was almost certainly carried out by John Crosthwaite of Vergemount House, who also built a number of semi-detached and terraced houses called Vergemount on Clonskeagh Road in the first decade of the nineteenth century.[122] Public transport first became available to the residents of Milltown and district when

119 *Freeman's Journal*, 15 June 1811, p. 2.

120 *Freeman's Journal*, 6 March 1812, p. 3.

121 'Report and Valuation of the Lands of Roebuck in the County of Dublin by Brassington and Gale, 1832' (NAI, QRO/4/3/28); Maps and Rentals, Schedule of title documents of the Roebuck Estate of Major Richards (NAI, MS 1165/7/9).

122 RD 437/33/281750, RD 436/75/281751, RD 556/323/369963, RD 617/393/424857; Holland, *Clonskeagh A place in history*, pp. 128–38.

a public coach service operating between Dublin, Dundrum and Powerscourt was established in 1816 by Robert Turbett.[123]

Since time immemorial a rough pathway on the south bank of the River Dodder had connected Clonskeagh and Milltown (Map 6), which continues to this day as the foot and cycle pathway linking Milltown Bridge and Clonskeagh Bridge as part of the River Dodder linear park. In 1789 an unsuccessful attempt was made to extinguish this ancient right of way, probably by Henry Jackson who had recently acquired the mill on the south bank of the River Dodder at Clonskeagh from Lord Trimlestown.[124] Fifty-five years later, in 1844, J.G. Richards and George Thompson, successors in title respectively to Trimlestown and Jackson, were refused application by the County Dublin grand jury to close the pathway 'as the road had been there for several years, and that to have it stopped up would be a great inconvenience to the inhabitants of the neighbourhood'.[125]

THE CITY LIBERTIES IN 1767

In 1767 Dublin Corporation undertook a survey of the city's liberties and franchises which were, as we have seen in Chapter 2, perambulated from medieval times in a procession called riding the franchises. The description of the boundary between the city's liberties and the territory belonging to the archbishop of Dublin at Clonskeagh and Milltown is very similar to that of 1603 save that it provides some updated details of properties along the route:

> *From thence [the road to Bray at Donnybrook] across the fields into the road to Clanskeagh [sic] [now Beaver Row] opposite a mill on the river of Donnybrook [on the north bank of the Dodder]. From thence along the said road to the bridge of Clanskeagh, and under the eastmost arch thereof. From thence to the mill of Clanskeagh [on the south bank of the Dodder], and thro' said mill. From thence [crossing the Dodder] to a lane called Clanskeagh lane, and along the said lane [now called Prospect Lane] to Milltown Road. From thence northward to Mr Roberts's house in said road [at this point now Sandford Road]. From thence thro' Mr Roberts's house and garden across the fields to Donnybrook road near a little cabin on the right hand thereof.*[126]

Sometimes the procession became unruly, as this report of an incident which occurred near Coldblow on Monday evening, 31 July 1749 explains:

> *On Monday evening last the Right Hon. The Lord Mayor and Sheriffs, attended by the city officers, went according to custom to throw the dart into the sea, to preserve the bounds of this city, but on their return home the city sword was forcibly carried away by some fellows near Coldblow, against whom we hear [arrest] warrants are issued, but the sword was brought back the next day.*[127]

123 Ball and Hamilton, *The Parish of Taney*, pp. 201–3.

124 *Dublin Chronicle*, 25 July 1789, p. 295; RD 410/399/269912.

125 *Freeman's Journal*, 25 April 1844, p. 3. The newspaper mistakenly refers to Daniel instead of George Thompson, the then owner of Clonskeagh Castle and the landlord of the adjacent iron mills.

126 CARD, xi (Dublin, 1904), p. 489; OSI, Co. Dublin, Sheet 22, six inches to one statute mile, surveyed in 1837 and corrected in 1843 shows the boundary turning north off Sandford Road opposite Anna Villa.

127 *Pue's Occurrences*, 1 August 1749, p. 2.

The final ceremony of riding the franchises took place on Saturday, 10 August 1839.[128] In a reprise of the 1749 procession, the civic sword bearer James Keegan, who had been handed the ceremonial weapon at Clonskeagh, was seriously assaulted in Harcourt Street.[129] Like the famous Donnybrook Fair, this ancient Dublin tradition had outlasted its usefulness.

CONCLUSION

At the turn of the nineteenth century, Joseph Archer considered Milltown to be a large and pleasant village but one that was 'not so much frequented as formerly'.[130] This statement, if accurate, raises two questions. Why did Milltown become a popular suburban destination in the third quarter of the eighteenth century and why did its popularity decline? Some of the answers to the first question have been explored in this chapter and in the previous one: there was a mini building boom in Milltown village in the mid-eighteenth century that coincided with a flourishing hospitality sector that catered for the genteel day trippers from the city such as the Florists' Club of Dublin. A little later, Milltown gained further traction as a health resort for the summer season and became a desirable residence for the gentry who could afford to rent one of the several villas erected in the vicinity in the mid- to late 1700s.

The second question is harder to answer because the decline suggested by Archer's comment was more insidious and is thus more difficult to identify. Certainly, the problems encountered by some of the Leeson estate's subtenants in the 1760s (possibly allied with the use of the entry fine with new leases) hindered large-scale building in the village main street after 1760. The importance of changing fashions cannot be underestimated too, especially as seaside suburbs such as Booterstown and Blackrock were competing with Milltown for the gentry's attentions.

Finally, and perhaps most importantly, quarrying and industrial activity on the banks of the Dodder at Milltown increased significantly from the 1760s onwards. Over time, the influx of dozens of mill workers and their families changed the housing density, social mix and atmosphere of the village from that which existed in the 1750s. It is hardly coincidental that by the turn of the nineteenth century there was a noticeable increase in the frequency of instances wherein pubs in Milltown are mentioned in contemporary newspapers and in property transactions recorded in the Registry of Deeds. These critical developments will be discussed in detail in the following two chapters. ■

---

128 *Freeman's Journal*, 12 August 1839, p. 3.

129 *Freeman's Journal*, 12 August 1839, p. 2.

130 Archer, *Statistical Survey of Dublin*, p. 93.

Chapter 6:
Industrial Development in the Eighteenth and Nineteenth Centuries

Chapter 6: Industrial Development in the Eighteenth and Nineteenth Centuries

INTRODUCTION

This chapter discusses the mills, factories and industrial activity that grew up on the banks of the River Dodder during the eighteenth and nineteenth centuries. To bring clarity to an occasionally confusing history the narrative has been divided into three sections. The first two sections describe the industrial activity that grew up respectively on the north and south banks of the River Dodder from the turn of the eighteenth century. The final section explores the history of quarrying and lime burning which took place on the banks of the River Dodder during the same period.

An examination of eighteenth-century leases shows that by the 1730s the Rivers Dodder and Slang powered two grain mills, a brass mill, an iron mill and a paper mill at Milltown. The ownership and functions of these mills changed frequently with the fluctuating fortunes of the mill owners, especially so in the nineteenth century as will be shown later. That said, iron manufacturing was the most enduring form of industrial activity in Milltown, and to the east at Clonskeagh, from the early eighteenth century until the demise of the Henshaw ironmongery and spade manufacturing works at Clonskeagh in the 1930s. The one constant was the requirement for a reliable source of water to power the machinery.

Unfortunately, there is very little information available concerning the number of people who were employed in the mills and factories in Milltown. The total number of workers employed at any given time is unlikely to have exceeded 100 people, although the use of child labour may have pushed this figure higher on occasion. To compensate for the lack of information, some detail about the working conditions can be found in the newspapers and this is discussed later. The wider effects of the industrialisation of Milltown in the eighteenth and nineteenth centuries, such as on housing and health, are discussed in separate chapters.

A brief explanation about the sourcing of the water to power the mills is necessary. The mills on the north bank of the River Dodder were powered by a weir erected across the

Plate 13. Aerial view of Clonskeagh Castle estate, held by G. & T. Crampton © unknown. Digital content by Dr Joseph Brady, published by UCD Library, University College Dublin http://digital.ucd.ie/view/ucdlib:47143

Dodder on the Milltown Road on a site behind The Dropping Well pub (Maps 7 & 11 and Pl. 7).[1] The mills on the south bank of the river were powered by the River Slang via a millrace which diverted the water from that river at Windy Arbour and fed a millpond at Milltown (Map 19). A second weir at Milltown, which is located a short distance upstream from the Packhorse Bridge opposite the Shanagarry apartments complex (Pl. 2) drew water from the Dodder to power the mills on the south bank of the Dodder at Clonskeagh (Pl. 13). The water was transported to Clonskeagh via a long millrace which ran along the south bank from the Milltown weir to Clonskeagh (Maps 5 & 6). It comes as a surprise to discover that the large weir at Milltown was never used to power machinery in Milltown. Instead, the tailrace from the Milltown mills on the south bank of the River Dodder powered by water taken off the River Slang fed into the millrace leading from the large Milltown weir to Clonskeagh (Map 18). In short, the large millpond at Clonskeagh (Pl. 13) powering the iron mills there was supplied with water sourced from both the River Dodder and the River Slang at Milltown.

MILLING ACTIVITY ON THE NORTH BANK OF THE RIVER DODDER IN THE EARLY EIGHTEENTH CENTURY: DEVELOPMENTS INITIATED BY JOSEPH LEESON

The origins and the development of the extensive Leeson estate at Milltown is dealt with in detail in Chapter 4. As part of those developments, Joseph Leeson granted a lease in 1711

1 RD 20/158/10143, lease dated 13 November 1717 which specifically reserved to Joseph Leeson the 'weir and river between Milltown Bridge [i.e. the Packhorse Bridge] and the orchard'.

to John Waters of Milltown, paper maker, and to his son Edward, a printer, of a paper mill on the north bank of the River Dodder.[2] Sometime prior to 1711, the mill had previously operated as a tuck mill, when it had been in the possession of Alderman William Fownes of Dublin.[3] In addition, Joseph Leeson granted John Waters the 'land, orchard, cabins, watercourses, commodities and appurtenances ... near Milltown Bridge [i.e. the Packhorse Bridge] then in the possession of John Waters', while reserving to himself the 'weir and the river between the said Milltown Bridge and the orchard and all the quarry and mines that are now or shall be in or upon the premises'. Leeson created a right of way for himself or his workmen to cross the lands leased to Waters in order to quarry the limestone (calp) on the banks of the Dodder. Finally, Leeson retained ownership of 'that piece of ground that lies between the said paper mill and the hill that leads down to the paper mill' so that he could build a lime kiln.[4] These concerns all stood on the north bank of the River Dodder.

John Waters died in 1716 and on 30 November 1717, Joseph Leeson granted a new lease to John's son Edward of the same premises, at the same time recording that a lime kiln and a lime house had now been built on the lands reserved to Joseph Leeson in the 1711 lease. The premises leased to Edward Waters were to be held for the lives of Edward, Sarah and Anna Maria Waters at an annual rent of £40, with the right to renew the lease upon payment of a renewal fine of £20.[5] In short, by about 1715 the entire property held by Waters comprised a paper mill, lime kiln, lime house, an orchard, cabins, and 3 plantation acres of land near the Packhorse Bridge at Milltown.[6] The extent of this landholding can be seen in the oldest surviving map of the property which dates to 1821 (Map 7).

By the mid-1720s Edward Waters' papermill had apparently run into difficulty. In February 1724 a lease was granted by William Ford to Robert Randal of Milltown, papermaker, for a term of 60 years at a yearly rent of £10. Under the terms of the lease Randal was required to build a good paper mill and dwelling house, with Ford agreeing to contribute £80 towards the cost of the new buildings. Randal's new papermill was built on the south bank of the River Dodder close to the Packhorse Bridge. It would seem unlikely that Ford would have made Randal build a papermill if Waters' papermill had been working in 1724. These developments suggest that Edward Waters' papermill had ceased operation by the early 1720s, particularly as no mention of him or his papermill occurs after the registration of the 1717 lease.[7]

The old Waters papermill buildings on the north bank of the Dodder were subsequently converted into two corn mills, probably as replacements for the ancient corn mill of Milltown which had stood on the south bank of the River Dodder for centuries.[8] Further evidence is provided by a lease dated 3 April 1731 which refers to a 'house or cabin' in Milltown village

---

2 RD 8/218/2640.

3 Property recital in a mortgage deed of the Leeson estate in 1826: RD 811/460/546996.

4 RD 8/218/2640.

5 Mills, *The register of the Parish of St Peter and St Kevin*, p. 206; RD 20/158/10143.

6 NAI, Landed Estates Court Rental, vol. 38, no. 3, 'Particulars and Conditions of Sale of the Freehold Estate of the Earl of Milltown to be sold on 8 January 1856', lot 59; RD 1856/16/137.

7 RD 62/285/42895. The Registry of Deeds does not list any disposal of the paper mill by Edward Waters; hence, the wider circumstances surrounding the lease to Robert Randall are unknown.

8 170/391/114380.

which was 'tenanted by James Barry, miller'.[9] By the late 1740s the two corn mills were operated successively by John Eustace, Michael Giraty [*sic*] of Milltown, miller, and John Shaw of Dublin, baker.[10] In 1757 a Dublin newspaper reported the death of a local miller, Richard Grady of Milltown, who was found dead in his bed where 'he went seemingly in good health the night before'.[11] Grady does not feature among the property transactions for Milltown registered in the Registry of Deeds at this time but he may, nonetheless, have taken a short-term (31 years or less) sublease of the two corn mills.

THE ARRIVAL OF JOHN CLASSON

John Classon first appears in the public records when his marriage articles were registered in the Registry of Deeds in 1763, which recorded his marriage to a Ms Esther Andrews, the second daughter of a Dublin brewer, Thomas Andrews.[12] Under the terms of their marriage articles, if Esther survived John without issue she was to receive at her election £600 or half of his estate, or one third if they had issue, subject in both cases to 'the just debts of John being first paid'. This proviso would turn out to be critically important for Esther as will be shown presently. In the meantime, John used the dowry which he had received from his father-in-law to buy a 41-year lease of the corn mills at Milltown, in 1764, from John Wallis of Dublin.[13] It is not known why John Classon decided to invest in mills in Milltown but his decision may have been influenced by James Classon (probably John's elder brother) who in 1748 had been granted a lease by Viscount Palmerston of over 69 plantation acres in Rathmines which extended as far as the bridge over the Dodder called Classon's Bridge.[14]

It is apparent from the rent provisions of the lease that Classon intended to invest considerable capital in improving and converting the corn mills and other buildings on the property. For the first year of the lease his annual rent was £40, increasing to £60 from 1765 to 1780 and thereafter to £70. It is worthwhile setting out the three separate parcels of land and properties that Classon took over in 1764 as the wording was repeated for several decades in successive deeds affecting the premises. These comprised:

> *(a) a house and mills, lately two corn mills, together with the lands, orchard, stable, water and water courses behind the said mills leading to the weare [sic] with the appurtenances, lying and being near Milltown, formerly in the possession of John Eustace and late in the possession of Michael Giraghty,*

> *(b) that dwelling house, tenement situate lying and being in Milltown formerly in the tenure and occupation of James Hamill and lately in the possession of John Church and his assigns, with the gardens, stables, coach houses and other buildings and improvements, together with*

9 RD 66/11/46932.

10 RD 170/391/114380.

11 *Pue's Occurrences*, 29 January 1752, p. 2.

12 RD 227/9/145894.

13 RD 246/324/158097.

14 RD 357/274/240334. According to a deed of 1856, the demesne of South Hill (now the South Hill housing estate on the north side of the Milltown Road opposite The Dropping Well pub) was originally part of James Classon's lands: RD 1856/34/247.

(c) all that field or parcel of land as then enclosed and fenced in lying on the west side of the last-mentioned dwelling house containing one acre and three roods [plantation measure] lately held by John Church.[15]

A fourth property was later added to the three holdings listed above, namely, a house, stable and yard which had formerly been occupied by Cornelius Egan and which adjoined the field of 1 acre and 3 roods.[16]

According to contemporary newspaper accounts, the mills that Classon built at Milltown were used to grind wood as part of the process to produce dye for clothing, and also to manufacture oil. The latter activity probably related to the extraction of oil from linseed because Classon later erected mills for this purpose on the River Liffey at Palmerstown.[17] Classon's manufacturing activities were self-financed without recourse to any grant from parliament or subsidy from the Dublin Society.[18] In 1767 Classon raised additional capital of £600 by mortgaging his mills at Milltown, a sum which he repaid in full with interest five years later.[19] Among other improvements at Milltown, Classon built a range wall on the western boundary of his property and a new tail race.[20]

Classon's business continued to prosper in the 1770s and 1780s. Classon executed a new lease at Milltown for 41 years with his landlord John Wallis on 17 May 1781 in which Classon agreed to an increase in his annual rent from £70 to £80. The previous year Classon had placed a newspaper advertisement looking to employ a foreman for his mills at Milltown. The successful applicant was to be 'a discrete sober man, aged about forty or fifty, to oversee a few workmen and take care of other matters that will be delivered into his charge'.[21]

John and Esther lived very comfortably in their town residence at 10 Eustace Street where they employed a coachman and a housemaid.[22] The Classon's domestic servants turned out to be dishonest and in the absence of a professional police force, John Classon inserted the following warning in *Saunders's Newsletter* of 1783:

A caution to the public against two thieving servants. Whereas Michael Delany and Mary his wife, the former employed to drive as post chaise and act as [a] thorough servant, the latter as housemaid, were both detected in the fact, making use of a false key to my wine clear, and other illicit practices. After this warning it is expected no gentleman will employ either of them, and if I can lay hands on them, am determined to prosecute them as far as the law will impower me.[23]

As well as at Milltown, Classon expanded his operations by building new mills at Palmerstown in 1783 which were used to extract oil from linseed. Classon invited dealers in flax seed, particularly those in Ulster who sold their produce to linen manufacturers, to sell their left-over

---

15 RD 246/324/158097. The property in (b), Old Bridge House north, is discussed in Chapter 15.

16 RD 341/178/228027.

17 *Faulkner's Dublin Journal*, 6 November 1783; 23 February 1793, p. 4.

18 *Faulkner's Dublin Journal*, 6 November 1783.

19 RD 253/529/164557, RD 286/514/190146.

20 RD 494/515/336597.

21 *Saunders's Newsletter*, 14 October 1780, p. 3.

22 *Saunders's Newsletter*, 14 October 1780, p. 3.

23 *Saunders's Newsletter*, 3 December 1783, p. 2.

seed to him 'at his house in Eustace Street, where he will give the full value for said seed, for the purpose of extracting oil from it'.[24]

The good times did not last for John and Esther Classon. Eighteenth-century Dublin could experience very sudden short-term fluctuations in its business climate. Businesses and merchants depended on the maintenance of extensive informal networks of credit and debt, and all types of skilled tradesmen and merchants were involved in the borrowing or lending of money. In times of growth, merchants and manufacturers were tempted to expand their businesses or their credit and were exposed when economic circumstances changed.[25] By the early 1790s Classon had got into financial difficulties and in March 1791 he was forced to mortgage his mills at Milltown for £581 to Robert Jenkins. The mortgage deed provided more detail about the type of machinery used at Classon's mills, which were then called logwood mills, and which included:

> *one water wheel with a complete metal engine for rasping dye woods and a water wheel to work a large pair of stones for dye woods and grinding, and another water mill and also a metal press and machinery for manufacturing dye.*[26]

Nine months later in November 1791, John Classon and his two business partners, Thomas and Samuel Classon (probably John's sons), assigned the 17 May 1781 lease to Alderman Thomas Andrews and William Humphrey, who subsequently put their leasehold interest up for auction in April 1793.[27] A further series of transactions took place in 1793. Firstly, the mortgagee Robert Jenkins transferred his mortgage to three merchants, William Rainsford, Walter Burke and Barnaby Mullen, who were clothiers based in Chamber Street, of whom more will be revealed later.[28] Secondly, John Wallis advertised to let the mills for nine months, which were 'lately held by John Classon and now under ejectment for non-payment of rent'.[29] Thirdly, on foot of legal actions brought by Robert Jenkins and other creditors of Classon the city sheriff sold John Classon's title to the Milltown mills for £960 to the aforementioned Chamber Street clothiers, and John Classon was declared bankrupt.[30] It is not clear how the Classons' assignment of November 1791 to Andrews and Humphrey was affected by these legal developments. In any event, the Chamber Street clothiers restarted operations at Milltown in the late autumn of 1793 and placed the following newspaper advertisement in *Saunders's Newsletter*:

> *Oil and Dyestuff mills at Milltown. The public are respectively informed, that they are now at work, and will grind all sorts of spices, drugs, and dyestuffs, at the shortest notice, viz. ginger, pepper, turmeric, galls, bark for stampers, etc in the most complete manner – and that there is for sale a large quantity of linseed oil of the first quality. Inquire at No. 11, Chamber Street. N.B. A large quantity of empty casks to be sold at said mills.*[31]

24 *Faulkner's Dublin Journal*, 6 November 1783.

25 David Kelly, 'The conditions of debtors and insolvents in eighteenth century Dublin' in David Dickson (ed.), *The Gorgeous Mask: Dublin 1700–1850* (Dublin, 1987), p. 98.

26 RD 432/254/280565.

27 RD 435/502/285901; *Saunders's Newsletter*, 3 April 1793, p. 3.

28 RD 467/556/302233 (deed dated 19 May 1793).

29 *Saunders's Newsletter*, 3 July 1793, p. 4.

30 RD 574/413/390937.

31 *Saunders's Newsletter*, 29 October 1793, p. 2; 11 November 1793, p. 2.

In 1798 William Rainsford sold his one-third share of the partnership to Walter Burke and Barnaby Mullen for just under £1,600.[32] Three years later, in 1801, Burke and Mullen were operating three woollen machines, logwood and oil mills at Milltown.[33] In the same year Burke and Mullen surrendered the 17 May 1781 Classon lease to John Wallis, which they had acquired at some stage earlier either from John Classon's assignees or from the city sheriff.[34] In return, John Wallis and Robert Alexander junior granted a new lease for 41 years to Burke and Mullen at an annual rent of £120, which was a 50 per cent increase on the rent charged by the 1781 lease.[35]

Burke and Mullen must have hoped that their title to the Milltown mills was safe once they had executed the new lease with John Wallis. Unfortunately for them this was not the case. John Classon died intestate and his widow Esther (called Hester in later deeds) took out a grant of administration to her late husband's estate, which included considerable debts and probably very few assets. These unhappy circumstances meant that Esther's marriage articles of 1763 were of no value to her in her time of need. Probably because of this, Esther issued legal proceedings against Burke and Mullen in June 1803 claiming that the sale of the Milltown mills by the city sheriff in 1793 should be set aside. The legal wrangling went on for another three years but in a magnanimous example of lawyers foregoing further fees (or cutting their losses!), Esther Classon was advised to settle her case for £600 – the same sum originally provided to her under her marriage articles – as a memorial deed of 10 March 1806 explained:

> *that in order to put an end to the said cause and all further expenses therein and finally debarring same the said Esther Classon by advice and consent of counsel and solicitors in the said cause agreed to dismiss her bill without costs on other side and to convey to said Walter Burke and Barnaby Mullen all her interest and equity of redemption, claims and demands ... for a sum of six hundred pounds.*[36]

The following year Barnaby Mullen agreed to sell his share in the partnership to Walter Burke for £3,000.[37] This paved the way for Walter to bring his sons into the business. On 1 November 1808 Walter Burke executed a new partnership deed with his two sons William and Christopher on condition that they each contributed £3,000 to the new venture and give their father three fifths of the profits. In addition, the Milltown mills were to remain as part of the partnership stock belonging to Walter Burke.[38]

WOOLLEN MANUFACTURE

Although the Burkes' new partnership specifically mentioned the manufacturing of dye stuff and oil at their mills in Milltown, the manufacture of woollen cloth was the more important activity carried on there. By 1800 at least three clothiers had established woollen mills on the River Dodder at Milltown and at Upper Rathmines, an area that later became better known by its unofficial name of Dartry. Aside from Burke and Mullen, clothiers called Nicholas and John Hunt of Braithwaite Street

---

32 RD 494/515/336597.

33 Archer, *Statistical Survey of Dublin*, p. 206.

34 RD 531/576/353600 (surrender dated 18 June 1801).

35 RD 537/434/353599 (lease dated 19 June 1801).

36 RD 574/413/390937.

37 RD 599/214/410912.

38 RD 600/495/412317.

set up new woollen mills on the south bank of the Dodder at Milltown in the 1790s, while in 1801 a Mr Bellwood was operating woollen mills at Upper Rathmines (later known as Darty mills).[39] The mill owners at Milltown and Upper Rathmines specialised in producing a type of woollen clothing called 'blossom naps' and by the third decade of the nineteenth century they had built steam engines to augment the power supplied by the River Dodder, which often proved unreliable in periods of drought.[40] The use of steam engines would not have been possible had there been insufficient demand for the millowners' products because it was expensive to import and transport the coal required to power the steam engines. The move to suburban mills powered by the Rivers Liffey and Dodder from the traditional textile weaving centre in the Dublin Liberties was part of a gradual trend that took place in the late eighteenth and early nineteenth centuries.[41]

A Dublin banking family called Alexander succeeded by marriage to the leasehold interest originally owned by John Wallis in the eighteenth century. In 1812 Robert Alexander junior granted a new 41-year lease to Walter Burke at the yearly rent of £140, an increase of £20 over the 1801 lease.[42] The previous year, Walter had taken a lease of Richmond Hill (Rydalmount) and 5 acres from William Caldwell Hogan at the annual rent of £68 5*s.*[43] Richmond Hill was located on an elevated position above the Milltown Road directly opposite Burke's woollen mills, so he could literally keep an eye on his mills from the comfort of his suburban villa. To all intents and purposes business appeared to be going well for Walter Burke and his two sons. However, as with the Classons 20 years previously, a financial crisis was just around the corner.

The first two decades of the nineteenth century were characterised by extremely volatile and challenging economic conditions for Irish industry, caused by a wide variety of circumstances. Protective tariffs on Irish goods were progressively removed under the terms of the Act of Union up to 1824, which meant that English manufacturers could export cheaper mass-produced goods into Ireland to the detriment of smaller localised industries, particularly those in Dublin's Liberties. The Napoleonic wars also created very challenging trading conditions due to naval blockades of continental Europe. To add to this, there were problems with credit supply which exacerbated the already stressed workforce and their employers. In a lengthy editorial from December 1812, the *Freeman's Journal* portrayed a very difficult situation affecting thousands of working-class Dubliners:

> *We see many thousands of our unfortunate countrymen thrown instantaneously, by the wretched state of trade, into the most appalling misery ... We see the last remains of our commerce, sinking under the want of money and credit among our capitalists; and the Commissioners of Bankruptcy sitting, as if our only Board of Trade! ... But the calamity is not confined to the Liberty. It has spread through all the manufacturers in the woollen branches in the county Dublin – Chapelizod mills, that employed near 1,000 people, are idle. Clondalkin and Blue Bell, employed 700 people, all idle. Rockbrook and other mills adjoining employed 1,000 people, all idle. Rathfarnham, Rathmines, Milltown and Clonskeagh, above 2,000 people, all idle. To be short, we understand the number thrown out of bread, within the last ten days, is computed to amount to THIRTY THOUSAND!*[44]

39 RD 472/550/305739, RD 627/6/428188; Archer, *Statistical Survey of Dublin*, p. 207.

40 *Dublin Evening Post*, 5 October 1830, p. 1; *Irish Times*, 23 December 1864, p. 4; 28 December 1864, p. 4.

41 Dickson, *Dublin: The making of a capital city*, p. 283.

42 RD 648/243/443345; *Burke's Peerage and Baronetage* (London, 1858), p. 18.

43 RD 644/123/441010.

44 *Freeman's Journal*, 17 December 1812, p. 2.

Given this appalling description of the state of the woollen trade in the second decade of the nineteenth century it is not surprising to discover that Walter Burke had had to mortgage his property in Milltown in February 1816 arising from a debt of £931 owed to Richard Sullivan, a Dublin merchant.[45] Obviously, the lack of available credit and capital from commercial banks forced manufacturers like Burke to get by obtaining short-term credit from fellow merchants such as Sullivan. This strategy did not work. By November 1816 Walter Burke and Sons had been declared bankrupt and on 25 November all of the partnership's property in Milltown was put up for auction on 25 November 1816. According to an advertisement in the *Belfast Newsletter*, the Burkes had spent upwards of £10,000 on their mills at Milltown.[46]

Unsurprisingly given the level of debt attached to the property and the difficult economic circumstances prevailing at the time, the mills did not sell. The property was put up for auction once more on 12 April 1817 after yet another postponement. This time the auction advertisement added that the oil mill was capable of making from 500 to 700 gallons of oil per week.[47] It is not clear if the property sold at the auction or was disposed of privately afterwards. In any event, some weeks later, on 25 June 1817, Walter Burke's executor (Walter having died since being declared bankrupt), his five creditors (two of whom lived in the Coombe in the Dublin Liberties), his surviving junior business partners Christopher and Walter Burke junior, and his third son, and heir at law, William Burke, conveyed their respective interests in the Milltown mills to William John Alexander, the brother of the Burkes' landlord, Robert Alexander junior.[48] The memorial deed does not record what consideration was involved in the transaction or whether the Burkes' creditors obtained any financial return. The Alexanders appreciated the need to try and generate some income from their property so Robert and William re-let the mills to William Burke on 16 December 1817 for the duration of the lives of Walter Burke junior and Thomas Burke or for 31 years from 29 September 1817 if the two lives should fail. The new rent to be paid by William Burke was £500 per annum, payable quarterly.[49] There is no obvious explanation for the difference in the rental figure of £500 as compared to the £140 which was charged by Robert Alexander in 1812. The disparity is all the more perplexing given that the years 1815 to 1817 were extremely bad ones nationally due to harvest failures and a depression in agriculture following the end of the Napoleonic wars in 1815.[50] In addition, Irish woollen manufacturers petitioned parliament in 1817 to repeal taxes specific to woollen manufacture, known as alnage, which concerned the regulation of manufacturing standards applicable to cloth weaving. Evidence was given to a select committee of the House of Commons by Jeremiah Haughton, who, as will be revealed shortly, owned a woollen mill in Milltown in the 1830s. Haughton claimed that the alnage regulations were 'totally inconsistent with the present mode of manufacturing, and with the implements of machinery necessary for perfecting the cloth'. In his evidence given on 24 May 1817, Haughton also confirmed that John Hunt and [Walter] Burke

---

45 RD 700/657/480489.

46 *Belfast Newsletter*, 19 November 1816, p. 3.

47 *Saunders's Newsletter*, 17 April 1817, p. 4.

48 RD 717/65/490201.

49 RD 722/392/493528.

50 Dickson, *Dublin: The making of a capital city*, p. 281.

and sons were operating cloth mills in Milltown.[51]

On the subject of cloth-making machinery, the Alexander lease of 16 December 1817 contained a detailed schedule of the plant and machinery used at Burke's mills in Milltown. It is difficult to comprehend the functions of the machinery because of the specialised manufacturing process involved, but some idea of the workings of the mills can be gleaned from the following items:

> *one five-foot scribbler for fine work, one five-foot scribbler for coarse work, one four-foot scribbler without cards, one four-foot scribbler with cards ... one new water wheel for turning the above, one worn out water wheel for turning [an] oil mill ... one fifty spindle billy ... eighteen broad looms ... one old boiler sunk in the ground, one rasping engine, one chipping engine, one pair of dyewood horns, one oil press stamper, one pair of stones for grinding seed ... one oil cistern [to] hold 1,500 gallons ... one tenter fixed in the field 50 yards long, one set of water gates erected at the pond, one set of water gates erected in the garden.*[52]

The cloth woven at Milltown would have been used, among other things, to make the large thick coarse wool coats (called frize coats) universally worn by the Irish peasantry at the time, each of which consumed up to eight yards of woollen cloth.[53] The clothing, dye and oil manufactured at Milltown would have been sold at the Burkes' wholesale business premises in the Dublin Liberties. A Dublin directory for 1818 lists William Burke as a clothier living at 30 Chamber Street and his brother Christopher as living at 20 Chamber Street, where Christopher was described as a clothier, dye wood and oil manufacturer. Their brother Walter junior, also a clothier, was residing at 19 Chamber Street.[54] Indeed, much of the wool produced in Dublin's suburban mills was stored in city warehouses and sold to shops throughout the country to supply the needs of the peasantry.[55]

The first peaceful visit of a British monarch to Ireland occurred in 1821 when King George IV visited the country in that year. The *Freeman's Journal* was encouraged by the prospect of the royal visit and, in complete contrast to the editor's despairing remarks of 1812, made the following optimistic observations:

> *It would seem a rather fortunate circumstance that our national woollen factories should be so situated near to our native beauties and curiosities, that the eyes of our royal and noble visitors, who are shortly expected to this kingdom, will be naturally led to those manufacturing places, and therefore these illustrious strangers will be able to bear testimony to the good demeanour of the people. For in the ride towards the Scalp, we meet the manufacturing village of Milltown, which is highly improved by the trade carried on there, and in the way to the mountain military road, we of course pass through the villages of Rathfarnham and Rockbrook, where the woollen trade is carried on to a good extent, and since its introduction these places are much altered for the better.*[56]

---

51 *Report from the Committee on the Alnage Laws of Ireland: Appendix: Minutes of Evidence*, p. 5, H.C. 1817 (315), viii, 5 (henceforth referred to as the *House of Commons Report on Alnage Laws*). http://www.dippam.ac.uk/eppi/documents/9009/page/203178 (accessed 4 January 2020).

52 RD 722/392/493528. A helpful explanation of some of the machinery and processes involved in textile production can be found in Colin Rynne, *Industrial Ireland 1750–1930: An archaeology* (Cork, 2015), Chapter 8. A scribbler was a specialsit carding machine used in wollen industry. Carding is the process of combing and cleaning raw wool with a sharp toothed tool to distangle the fibres.

53 *House of Commons Report on Alnage Laws*, p. 25.

54 The Treble Almanac 1818, p. 50.

55 Dickson, *Dublin: The making of a capital city*, p. 283.

56 *Freeman's Journal*, 26 June 1821, p. 3.

Plate 10. Nullamore, Classon's Bridge, 2019 (author's collection)

BURKE'S WOOLLEN MILLS, 1821

Perhaps a truer indication of the wellbeing of the woollen trade at Milltown at this time can be gauged by the commissioning of a map by William Burke of his entire mill holding at Milltown in 1821 (Map 7).[57] This unique map is the only known surviving map specifically of mills at Milltown. It also depicts the local topography before changes occurred on the north side of the Milltown Road to Rathmines, beginning with the building of a villa called Nullamore in the 1830s opposite Classon's Bridge (Pl. 10). For these reasons it is worth discussing the map's features in detail.

Starting at the western end of the map, the water is drawn off at the weir and passes along a millrace that crosses under Milltown Road and then runs parallel with the road on its northern side until it turns back in a south-easterly direction under the road into a small millpond. An important detail, which is too small to be viewed in the map reproduced in this book, is a small footbridge that crosses the millrace at right angles to the weir and the millrace. This apparently nondescript feature has added significance because the surveyor added the words 'Ancient Br', thereby signifying that the weir and its infrastructure was considered to be very old in 1821. Taken together with evidence from the Registry of Deeds discussed in Chapter 4, this information supports the view that this weir and the mills on the north bank of the River Dodder date back to the seventeenth century.

Moving eastwards, we come to Classon's Bridge, described as the 'New Bridge' to distinguish it from the older Packhorse Bridge at the map's eastern extremity at Milltown village. The buildings

57 'A map of the woollen factory at Milltown, County Dublin belonging to Burke, esq. Surveyed by Jn. Longfield, 1821' (NLI, Longfield map collection, MS 21 F. 53/123).

Plate 12. Bankside Cottages, Milltown, 2015 (author's collection)

at the corner of Classon's Bridge formed the nucleus of Howe's public house, established in 1831, and now called The Dropping Well. On the far side of the millrace opposite Classon's Bridge is a warping field. Although the term 'warping' is used to describe one of the processes of spinning wool, in this instance the word is used to identify a field which was subjected to deliberate flooding from the River Dodder, in order to deposit mud sediment prior to cultivation.[58]

The heart of the property, the mill complex, comprised several domestic and industrial buildings and water features. A small millpond was fed by the millrace flowing under the Milltown Road at the point marked 'A' on the map. Surplus water could be discharged into the Dodder immediately to the south or used to power the machinery, before being discharged to the north in a tail race that entered the Dodder at a point close to the weir at Milltown. The domestic buildings, coloured pink, are made up of cabins for one or two families fronting the road, the manager's house and a gate lodge. The woollen factory is clearly identified, which is at a right angle to the building containing the oil mill and lapping engines (lapping was one of the technical processes in carding wool). The final detail shows the Packhorse Bridge – called the 'Old Bridge' to distinguish it from Classon's Bridge – and the workmen's houses on the north-west side of the bridge. The millrace on the south bank of the river taken from the Dodder weir closest to Milltown (Pl. 2) passed through a third arch built to the left of the Packhorse Bridge and travelled eastwards to power the iron mills at Clonskeagh.

58 Dutton, *Observations on Mr Archer's Statistical Survey*, p. 90.

The strain of running a textile business in such uncertain economic times took its toll on William Burke and he died at Milltown on 19 August 1823 aged forty-three. He was buried in Taney graveyard with his infant son Christopher.[59] William's widow Mary took over the business on the death of her husband, which suggests that she had some experience running it with her husband before he died. It was not that unusual in the eighteenth and early nineteenth centuries for women to own and manage businesses; it was only from the Victorian period onwards that society disapproved of women participating in commercial activity.[60] Mary's mettle was soon tested when the mills were damaged in a fire one Sunday evening in December 1823. According to the press report, the fire was discovered by a police patrol and 'by the exertions of the police and the inhabitants of the neighbourhood, it was got under [control], but not until much damage was sustained'.[61]

Mary Burke suffered another setback the following year, 1824, when the mills were damaged by a second fire, which also occurred in December, as reported by the *Freeman's Journal*:

> *On Wednesday morning, at four o'clock, a fire was discovered in the wool store and drying stores belonging to the Woollen factory of Mrs Burke, at Milltown, which in a short period, owing to a strong easterly breeze assumed a most alarming appearance. An immediate express was forwarded to the Royal Irish and National Assurance offices, for the engines and men of their respective establishments, who in a short period arrived at the spot, and by their joint exertions, under the directions of Messrs. Darling and Eiffe, succeeded in confining the flames to the buildings where the fire originated, and rescued the adjoining premises from destruction. These concerns we regret were not insured.*[62]

The lack of insurance cover probably reflects a combination of the prohibitive cost of insurance premia for textile mills – and particularly in Mrs Burke's case after the first fire – and the tight margins under which the Burke mills were operating. The mill workers would have been hard hit by the two incidents and no doubt some workers were let go while the damage was being repaired. Some mitigation may have been provided to the Milltown workers when, in 1826, a relief committee was established for the distressed weavers of the Dublin Liberties, which provided employment in repairing the roads in the suburbs of Dublin. In its report of 9 June 1826, a sub-committee reported that 112 weavers had been employed on road works on the 'Milltown and Classon-bridge road' to carry out the following improvements:

> *A road of about 40 perches in length has been widened by an addition of 18 feet, to accomplish which, filling to the average depth of four feet, has been barrowed [sic] from a considerable distance. The stones composing the sustaining wall, making about 300 perches of masonry, have been quarried by the weavers. The reduction of a hill between Milltown and Classon bridge has been also in progress. This work evinces, in a most creditable degree, the docility of the workmen, and their anxiety to meet the bounty of the Committee by a corresponding return of labour.*[63]

59 Ball and Hamilton, *The Parish of Taney* (Dublin 1895), p. 45.

60 Imelda Brophy, 'Women in the Workforce' in David Dickson (ed.), *The Gorgeous Mask: Dublin 1700–1850* (Dublin, 1987), p. 52.

61 *Faulkner's Dublin Journal*, 10 December 183, p. 2.

62 *Freeman's Journal*, 9 December 1824, p. 2.

63 *Freeman's Journal*, 16 June 1826, p. 4. These roadworks were recorded as a 'New Road' on a Valuation Office Town Plan for Milltown dating from 1850 (Map 16b).

From the mid-1820s onwards, the fortunes of the Burke's woollen mills continued to decline in conjunction with the Dublin woollen trade generally. It appears from a newspaper advertisement of 1830 that after the second fire Mrs Burke had sublet the Milltown mills to Jeremiah Haughton, who was one of the pre-eminent woollen merchants of Dublin with extensive operations at Celbridge.[64] In October of that year following Haughton's death a detailed advertisement was placed in the *Dublin Evening Post* and *Saunders's Newsletter*:

> *To be let, for such term as may be agreed on, Milltown Woollen Mills, in the County of Dublin, adjoining Classon's bridge, about two miles from the city, late in the possession of Jeremiah Haughton, deceased, situate on the River Dodder – with a constant supply and fall of water, from 16 to 17 feet; containing water wheel, 18 feet by 10, one do. 12 feet by 4; one steam engine, 24 horse power; five scribblers; five carders; one teaser; one woolley; five slubbing billies; 18 spinning jennies; 30 looms; seven milling stocks; two gigs; one brushing mill; 14 shaving frames; seven knapping mills; 400 yards of tenters; two dye pans, with washing box, all in excellent working order.*
>
> *On the premises are a good dwelling house, gate house, out offices, and several houses for workmen, all in complete order. There are about four Irish or six English statute acres of land, and a good garden, the entire eligibly circumstances, enclosed with a wall from eight to 10 feet high, and well secured. The mills are partly at work, and goods will be received for manufacturing, on application to Mr Wm. Lee, at the mills, who will show them. N.B. The concerns would be let for any purpose not requiring the machinery, which can be disposed of.*[65]

The admission that the mills were only partly at work is revealing. In the same month that the Milltown mills were put up for sale, an editorial in the *Dublin Morning Register* of 6 October 1830 reported that of the 45 woollen manufacturers extant in Dublin and its environs in 1821, only 12 remained in business. The survivors included the Burke/Haughton mill at Milltown and the woollen mill at Upper Rathmines (Dartry), which was owned by Obadiah Willans and sons.[66] Dublin Corporation was conscious of the widespread distress affecting Dublin's industries and established a sub-committee to enquire into the issue with a view to petitioning parliament for relief. On 7 March 1831 the sub-committee made the following sobering findings about the woollen trade in Dublin city and suburbs:

> *The woollen manufactory establishments have been further reduced since the last accounts of 1829. Some improvement however has manifested itself in some of the factories in the environs and county of Dublin, but which are principally employed in a low forced and unprofitable manufacture, but except in the instance of one or more establishments, the woollens manufactured in the Liberties and environs of Dublin appear to be entirely sunk.*[67]

At a first glance, the above findings are to some degree at odds with an optimistic newspaper report 14 months previously, and which concerned the sale of prize cloth by the Haughtons

64 *Saunders's Newsletter*, 15 October 1830, p. 4; *House of Commons Report on Alnage Laws*, p. 4. No transactions concerning Haughton and the Milltown mills could be found in the Registry of Deeds for the 1820s.

65 *Dublin Evening Post*, 5 October 1830, p. 1; *Saunders's Newsletter*, 15 October 1830, p. 4. A 'slubbing billy' was a machine used to produce semi-spun loose threads of wool suitable for use on multi-spindle spinning machine, commonly known as the Spinning Jenny or jenny.

66 *Dublin Morning Register*, 6 October 1830, p. 2.

67 CARD, xviii (Dublin, 1922), p. 491.

and Willans, both of whom, as we have seen, operated woollen mills at Milltown and Upper Rathmines (Dartry) respectively:

> *Sale of Irish Prize Cloths. Yesterday the eight ends of cloth manufactured for Lord Cloncurry's prize of £50 were sold by auction at the Royal Exchange, by Mr Charles Bennett. The entire lot, though manufactured at different mills, was spun from the same wool, grown by Lord Lismore, and sold by Thomas and Luke Dillon. The first piece, which was of a dark Oxford mixture, manufactured by Jeremiah Haughton, to which the prize was awarded, excited great competition, and was knocked down to Messrs. James Wright & Co. of the Leeds Woollen Hall, at the immense price of £5 and 1 shilling per yard. The second lot, manufactured by O. Willans and Sons, was bought by Messrs. Curwan and Hassell, at 30 shillings per yard ... The texture and finish of all were decidedly superior to anything of the kind ever before seen in this country.*[68]

It is impossible to confirm if the prize cloths were made in Milltown or Dartry because the two prize winners also had extensive woollen mills in Rathfarnham, Kilmainham and Celbridge.[69] Even if the Milltown mill workers had won one of the prizes it was of no long-term benefit to them. In January 1831 Mary Burke surrendered her leasehold interest in the Milltown woollen mills to William John Alexander of Caledon, County Tyrone. Dublin solicitor Charles Hogan, a son of William Caldwell Hogan of Fairyland, was a third party to the deed, having had a mortgage over the Burke mills.[70] Shortly after this transaction, William John Alexander and Sir Robert Alexander leased the mills to William Caldwell Hogan of Fairyland.[71]

By 1833 the mills were occupied by another woollen manufacturer, Maurice Harnett, who had also acquired a small triangular plot of land beside the River Dodder at Classon's Bridge in 1831.[72] It is not certain who let the Milltown woollen mills to Harnett but it would appear from recitals in various deeds that they were sublet to him in the late 1820s by William Hogan.[73] The last throw of the dice for the Milltown woollen mills occurred in 1839 when they were acquired by Samuel Moore. Before examining the fortunes of the mills under Moore's ownership it is appropriate to discuss working conditions in the mills.

WORKING CONDITIONS IN THE WOOLLEN MILLS IN THE EARLY NINETEENTH CENTURY

The growth of industrial concerns along the suburban river banks of Dublin in the late eighteenth century can be attributed to many local and much wider causes. One of the more important motives for this relocation was a desire among Dublin's industrial employers to mitigate the worst effects of the city's journeyman associations and their 'combinations', the contemporary term used to describe organised labour and trade unions. For example, after an incident of labour unrest at a factory in Island Bridge in 1826, a senior police magistrate:

---

68 *The Pilot*, 15 January 1830, p. 2.

69 *House of Commons Report on Alnage Laws*, p. 4.

70 RD 871/65/579066. It seems likely that Jeremiah Haughton's death the previous year precipitated this transaction.

71 RD 871/66/579067. The annual rent is not recorded in the transcription of the memorial deed.

72 RD 873/487/580487; NAI, Tithe Aplotment Book, Diocese of Dublin, Parish of St Peter, Ranelagh and Milltown Road, assessed 30 December 1833, http://titheapplotmentbooks.nationalarchives.ie/reels/tab//004625716/004625716_00438.pdf (accessed 24 December 2019). Maurice Harnett's surname is variously spelled 'Hartnett' and 'Hodnett' in several documents and newspapers but I have used 'Harnett' as this was used in the Registry of Deeds and the Tithe Aplotment Book.

73 RD 1833/6/78. The memorial transcript of the sublease to Harnett could not be found in the Registry of Deeds.

> *proceeded shortly after the investigation, at the head of a party of the horse police, to the factories of Mr Osbrey, at Rathgar, Mr Willans, at Milltown, Mr McCaskey's, at Clonskeagh, and Messrs Duffy's at Ballsbridge, and found these places completely quiet and regular.*[74]

After a much more serious outbreak of industrial unrest in the Dublin in 1833, the city's bankers, merchants and traders petitioned the Lord Mayor to convene a meeting:

> *to take into consideration the most effectual means of bringing those persons to justice who committed, and those who were concerned in the barbarous and violent outrages recently committed in our city, arising out of combination.*[75]

Among the several dozen who signed the petition were mill owners Samuel Moore, Maurice Harnett and Obadiah Willans, all of whom owned, or would presently own, factories in Milltown and Rathmines.

When the historian John D'Alton was compiling his history of County Dublin in the late 1830s he felt compelled to digress from the past to comment on the numerous ruined mills and factories he was encountering on his investigations:

> *It may, however, be here remarked, that the failure of so many factories, as are exhibited in ruins in the progress of this work, appears too hastily attributed to the impossibility of coping with English capital and English machinery. If the subject were more coolly investigated, this much to be lamented visitation might be found more referable to the want of skill and attention on the part of the employer, of temperance and honesty on that of his workmen, and of the conviction of their mutual interest, which should exist between both. Hence, those baneful and unkindly combinations, which are too frequently consummated in human blood. The associations of artists and tradesmen to improve the subject of their business, and to maintain their fair station and independent deserts, should not be censured, but when, as too frequently, this connection degenerates into guilty confederacy, blindly demands an increase of wages, which the master cannot afford, or the rejection of a movement of machinery which would multiply his products, then it is but self deception to attribute the fall of manufacturers to any physical inability to maintain them; it is not the want of trade excludes the workman, but the wilful and stubborn ignorance of the workman excludes the trade.*[76]

Since the late eighteenth century there had been a trend towards employing women and children in the textile industries in the city suburbs and wider environs in order to avoid the worst effects of the male-dominated combinations in the city.[77] Women textile workers too were possibly more amenable than their male counterparts to accepting lower wages – sometimes as low as 2*d.* a day – which was also beneficial for the mill owners.[78] The impact of these developments in Milltown will be illustrated shortly.

It is difficult to provide an accurate figure for the number of people employed at the Milltown woollen mills. According to one report from 1837, the Milltown mills under Maurice Harnett

74 *Saunders's Newsletter*, 8 July 1826, p. 2.

75 *Freeman's Journal*, 3 December 1833, p. 2.

76 D'Alton, *History of County Dublin*, pp. 644–5.

77 Dickson, *Dublin: The making of a capital city*, pp. 282–4.

78 Brophy, 'Women in the Workforce', pp. 58–9.

employed about 60 people making low-priced cloth.[79] On the other hand, writing a year later, D'Alton had this to say:

> *the extensive woollen-works of Messrs. Willans are first met with [at Dartry], to which succeeds an establishment of the same kind kept by Messrs. Hodnett [sic], where about eighty are employed, and another (Kennedy's) engaging about fifteen.*[80]

It has not been possible to identify the Kennedy mill in any contemporary records.[81]

The working conditions in the mills were very hard in the early nineteenth century, particularly given the difficult economic circumstances prevailing in Dublin's textile industry, which obliged many employees to work very long hours. The normal working day was of 12 hours duration but it was frequently longer. For example, at midnight one January morning in 1815 a fire broke out in John Hunt's woollen mills on the south bank of the River Dodder at Milltown, allegedly due to the 'carelessness of one of the attendants on the machinery dropping the snuff of a candle into the dry dyewood dust'.[82] The likelihood of fatigue being a contributory factor in the accident was not entertained.

But it was the abuse of child labour that caused much contemporary public concern throughout the United Kingdom. In response to these and other employee health and safety concerns, a succession of factory acts was enacted by parliament throughout the nineteenth century. Of particular interest was an act of 1833 which regulated the employment of children in mills and factories.[83] To summarise very briefly, the Factory Act (among other things):

(a) Prohibited the employment of children under nine years of age
(b) Prohibited the employment of children under the age of thirteen years of age from working more than nine hours a day or 48 hours a week
(c) Prohibited persons under eighteen years of age from working more than 12 hours a day or 69 hours a week
(d) Prohibited persons under eighteen years of age from working between 8.30 p.m. and 5.30 a.m.

subject in each case to a number of limited exceptions. The most relevant exception permitted mill owners to extend the normal hours of work for employees under the age of eighteen by up to three hours a week for a maximum period of six months. This extension was granted to allow employers to make up for inactivity caused by drought or floods. To prevent abuses and evasion by employers, every child under the age of thirteen had to be medically examined by a physician who certified that the child was of the ordinary strength and appearance of a child of at least nine years of age, or the actual age of the child if above the minimum age. The Factory Act also provided for children's meal times, holidays and compulsory school attendance. Finally, the legislation provided for the appointment of four inspectors, who had power to make

79 Lewis, *Topographical Dictionary of Ireland*, ii, p. 370.

80 D'Alton, *History of County Dublin*, p. 798. The reference to Hodnett was an error; it should be Harnett.

81 A John Kennedy from Milltown wrote a letter on the subject of the poor law and low wages, which was published on p. 3 of *The Pilot* newspaper on 9 January 1837. However, none of the contemporary Dublin street directories lists anyone of that name at Milltown.

82 *Freeman's Journal*, 27 January 1815, p. 2.

83 An Act to regulate the labour of children and young persons in the mills and factories of the United Kingdom (3 & 4 Will. IV, c. 103) (29 August 1833) (hereafter cited as the Factory Act).

unannounced visits to factories, and for various offences under the Factory Act to be punishable by imprisonment or the imposition of fines.

The dubious distinction of being the first defendants to be prosecuted under the new Factory Act fell to Obadiah Willans and Maurice Harnett of Rathmines (Dartry) and Milltown woollen mills respectively, in December 1835. Because these were the first prosecutions under the Factory Act the two cases were reported in detail in the press.[84] In the first case, Willans was charged with over-working children by making them labour until 9 p.m. instead of 8.30 p.m. Willans gave the following testimony, as reported by the journalist for the *Freeman's Journal*:

> *The defendant said that the first section of the act regulated the hours of work as stated; but the third section provided that in cases where scarcity of water occurred, so as to delay the works, then, when the supply became sufficient, half an hour a day extra work, within the next six calendar months, was permitted, until the loss were [sic] made good. This was his case. From June last to November, a loss of upwards of fifty hours was incurred, in consequence of then lowness of the water in the River Dodder, on which his establishment was situate. It was to make good the deficiency thus occasioned that he had worked, and that only during one week, the additional half hour. In fact he had only gained five hours out of the number in arrears. Mr Willans declared his wish to be [words missing], not to violate any regulation whatever in the statute.*

After Willans' evidence the factory overseer testified that only three and a half hours of lost time had been made up, albeit he had failed to keep regular written records of the hours worked. The magistrate decided not to convict Willans of any offence and 'recommended that in future such [time] should be regularly kept, so as to be able to ascertain exactly the period lost, and not exceed it in the hours of overwork.'[85]

The case against Maurice Harnett was more serious and uncovered very unsettling behaviour at the Milltown woollen mills. The first charge involved employing three children under the age of twelve beyond the maximum number of hours permitted under the Factory Act. The foreman at the factory, Samuel Hunt, contended that the youngest child was aged at least twelve and a half and the eldest was aged sixteen. His evidence was disputed by the factory inspector, James Webster, who said he was positive from the children's appearance that they were aged under twelve. In addition, the medical certificates had not been properly filled in, which added to the uncertainty surrounding the children's ages.[86] But it was the third charge, that of obstruction by the foreman against Inspector Webster, which revealed disturbing behaviour at the Milltown woollen mills. According to the report in the *Freeman's Journal*:

> *Mr Webster stated that while engaged examining the children in Mr Hartnett's mills, the defendant commenced swearing at them for answering his questions or affording him any information. The children on this left him, and he could not consequently obtain all the knowledge he wished. The penalty with which this offence was punishable under the act was £10. Hunt was admonished by the bench, after which the parties left the office.*[87]

---

84 *Dublin Evening Packet and Correspondent*, 19 December 1835, p. 4; *Freeman's Journal*, 19 December 1835, p. 3; *Saunders's Newsletter*, 19 December 1835, p. 2.

85 *Freeman's Journal*, 19 December 1835, p. 3.

86 *Freeman's Journal*, 19 December 1835, p. 3; Saunders's Newsletter, 1835, p. 2.

87 *Freeman's Journal*, 19 December 1835, p. 3.

Interestingly, the evidence quoted above in the *Freeman's Journal* did not appear in the report contained in Saunders's Newsletter, which only recorded the charge levied against Hunt. This may or may not indicate a deliberate intention on the part of Saunders's Newsletter to edit evidence that was particularly incriminating against the employer. Both newspapers reported that no convictions or penalties were imposed on Willans, Harnett or Hunt because the inspector did not want to sanction the defendants in this instance, seeking instead to appraise them of the law so that it might not be broken in the future.[88]

On a more positive note, in 1834 Maurice Harnett had subscribed 10*s*. to the Rathmines Free School which could accommodate nearly 600 children, some of whom undoubtedly worked in his mills.[89] Whatever about Maurice Harnett's record as an employer, he was active in Dublin's political community, and he campaigned for the repeal of the Act of Union and the removal of discrimination against Catholics.[90] Harnett was also appointed as a collector for Milltown chapel to raise funds for the Daniel O'Connell tribute, which was established to compensate the Liberator from the loss of professional income incurred in pursuit of the national objective of repeal of the union.[91]

Long working hours and bullying foremen were not the only hazards for employees. The mills used large heavy machinery in the woollen manufacturing process which could be extremely dangerous, as the following account from 1828 shows:

> *Dreadful Accident. On Wednesday, a poor man named Bond, who was employed in a cloth factory at Milltown, whilst oiling the axel tree of one of the wheels, his great coat was caught by part of the wheel; the poor man was dragged under it, and in an instant the body was crushed to pieces.*[92]

This is the only reported industrial accident at Milltown found thus far among the nineteenth-century newspaper reports; no doubt many more accidents occurred which never came to the public's attention.

Despite the miserable working conditions, workers were desperate to hold onto their jobs in times of such uneconomic uncertainty. During an outbreak of fever in Milltown in April 1818, the St Peter's parish committee for the prevention of fever reported that a factory operative named Collins was found to be working on 28 March 1818 while labouring under fever. Collins refused to go to hospital so 'the foreman of the factory in which he worked undertook to have his sons, who slept in the same room, separated from him'.[93] The deliberate separation of the sick father from his healthy sons is an interesting detail because at that time the majority of the Irish medical profession adhered to the contagionist theory of epidemic disease. Medical opinion changed in the 1830s with the outbreak of cholera when the medically incorrect theory of miasmatic

---

88 Two days later the magistrates at the Arran Quay police office imposed a fine of £5 – the maximum being £20 – on a Blanchardstown factory owner for breaches of the Factory Act: *Saunders's Newsletter*, 22 December 1835, p. 2.

89 *Freeman's Journal*, 8 February 1834, p. 1.

90 *Freeman's Journal*, 9 July 1825, p. 2.

91 *Freeman's Journal*, 4 November 1833, p. 2.

92 *Drogheda Journal*, 8 March 1828, p. 3. Curiously, this report appears in only one (provincial) newspaper; its reference to a cloth factory confirms the location as almost certainly Milltown, Co. Dublin.

93 *Freeman's Journal*, 3 April 1818, p. 3.

(airborne) dispersal of epidemic disease held sway.[94]

Another reported case of 1826, this time involving lead stolen from Mrs Burke's woollen mill, hints at ugly undercurrents that existed among some of the workers' families. The report in the *Freeman's Journal* is worth quoting in full for the domestic and workplace complexities it revealed:

> *The Commission of Oyer and Terminer – Monday 19 June. At ten o'clock the Honourable Baron Pennefather and the Honourable Justice Torrens having taken their seats on the bench, a county jury was sworn, when Andrew O'Reilly was put to the bar, charged with stealing 3 cwt. [152 kilograms] of lead, from the factory of Mrs Burke, at Milltown, on the night of 6 March last. Mr Bethel stated the case of the jury. The prisoner was in the employment of Mrs Burke, and was about to be dismissed, having received a week's notice to that effect, when on the night laid in the indictment, he entered the factory by one of the windows, and committed the robbery in question. Bridget Roche Sworn and examined. The prisoner came to witness and told her Mr Lee had given him a week's notice; but that he had nicked [sic] him for it, by stealing the lead; he likewise told witness where he had concealed it. Cross examined by Mr Dunn. Is a single woman; is now in custody for fear of being murdered; went to the Magistrate and requested to be taken into custody, as she was afraid of being killed; has four brothers, they are all good characters as far as she knows; has a brother by the name of Nicholas; hears he is now in the hulks [i.e. in custody awaiting transportation]; believes he was tried in this court for selling the lead [Nicholas Roche had been sentenced on 11 April to transportation for seven years for stealing the lead];[95] she gave it to him to sell; she stole it honestly from the prisoner at the bar and gave it to her brother [Nicholas] to sell; never heard her brother was suspected of robbery; has a brother named James; don't [sic] know where he is at present; in March last he was working in the County Dublin; does not know when he left the county; upon her honour it was not James who told her where the lead was buried; it was the prisoner at the bar.*
>
> *James Ryan, sworn, identified the lead. John Bracewell, a boy employed in the factory, proved the prisoner having come to him in the shearing room, and asked him if the window would rise, to which he replied in the affirmative; prisoner then tried the window himself; witness next morning found the window had been opened in the night, and the lead stolen. This witness was cross examined by Mr Dunn, but nothing particular elicited. Richard Bracewell, father to the last witness, examined; the prisoner's business in the factory did not call him into that room. Cross examined by Mr Dunn. There were pieces of cloth in the room, but none of them were taken; they were in an unfinished state.*
>
> *Thomas McKeon met the prisoner and three other persons, James Roche, his wife, and another woman whom he did not know, under Baron George's wall at Milltown [i.e. the demesne wall of Milltown Park on Milltown Road], between seven and eight o'clock on 13 March. Prisoner had a load under his coat.*
>
> *Mr Lee, the overseer of the factory examined. In his cross examination by Mr Dunn, he [Lee] said that Nicholas Roche was tried and convicted at the last Commission for stealing the lead, but it now appeared he was only the receiver. The property being found on him, he [Nicholas Roche] was supposed to have stolen it.*[96] *Mr Dunne – Then you think the Court and Jury decided wrong. Mr Lee – I suppose so. On his further cross examination, he [Lee] said he went to the place where Bridget Roche, the first witness was working, to get her to swear the informations against the prisoner [Andrew O'Reilly]; her mother was then present; he did not offer any money to Roche's mother, but on this occasion the mother*

94 Joseph Robins, *The Miasma: Epidemic and panic in nineteenth century Ireland* (Dublin, 1995), pp. 37, 95–8.

95 *Freeman's Journal*, 12 April 1826, p. 3.

96 Nicholas Roche had been found guilty at the Commission of Oyer and Terminer of 11 April 1826 of stealing the lead and was sentenced to seven years transportation: *Freeman's Journal*, 12 April 1826, p. 3.

threatened to have her daughter's life if she gave evidence against the prisoner. Witness in consequence had her put into the Institution to protect her. Mr Dunn – Was it not that she might be forthcoming at this trial? Mr Lee – It was to protect her life, that she might be allowed to give evidence. Mr Dunn – And then she might be murdered. Baron Pennefather observed that Mr Lee had acted with great propriety, and that he would take care the witness should be protected. Mr Dunn – I hope Mr Lee you will not [sic] take her under your protection. In his further evidence as to the cause of James Roche absconding, Mr Lee said that Roche had beaten his sister-in-law, the wife of Nicholas, in a dreadful manner, and her children, and that a warrant was out against him, which induced him to make off; he heard that Bridget Roche said it was a shame that her brother [Nicholas Roche] should be transported, and the guilty be walking about.

For the defence, several witnesses were examined to prove that Bridget Roche was not entitled to be believed on her oath. The learned Baron Pennefather then charged the jury, who after a few minutes consultation returned a verdict of guilty. In delivering the sentence of the court, the learned judge wished to take this opportunity of declaring publicly that if the witness, Bridget Roche, had come forward in this case to give evidence with a view to saving her brother [Nicholas] from the execution of the sentence which had been awarded against him, that hope must be delusive; there was nothing whatever in the evidence produced on this present trial, that could in the slightest degree impeach the decision of the court in the case of Nicholas Roche. The prisoner was then sentenced to seven years transportation. A conversation then ensued, between the counsel for the prosecution and the bench, with regard to the safety of Bridget Roche; Baron Pennefather said a proper application should be made to have her protected, and at the same time regretted that witnesses should be subjected to such apprehensions for their safety. He directed her to be taken care of in the Institution for the present.[97]

There are all sorts of issues and unanswered questions raised by this unhappy affair which ended very badly for all involved. A couple of points stand out – the prevalence of domestic violence by both sexes – mother against daughter and brother and against sister-in-law – and the involvement of a child employee, John Bracewell, as a key prosecution witness. The account also reveals a more humane side to the foreman, Lee, compared with that of his successor Samuel Hunt.

THE END OF WOOLLEN MANUFACTURE IN MILLTOWN

Maurice Harnett's short time working the woollen mills in Milltown came to an end in the late 1830s, when they were taken over by Samuel Moore, who up until then was manufacturing woollen cloth in Bluebell.[98] Moore installed new modern looms at the Milltown mills and afterwards placed the following advertisement in a number of newspapers:

Woollen manufacture in Ireland. – The first power loom for broad cloth weaving that has ever been introduced into this country has been lately erected at Milltown factory by Mr Moore. Formerly the woollen manufacture was carried on to a considerable extent in Ireland, and it should gratify the favourers of native industry to find an open[ing] still for its encouragement.[99]

97 *Freeman's Journal*, 20 June 1826, p. 3.

98 *Freeman's Journal*, 9 April 1840, p. 2.

99 *Dublin Morning Register*, 26 July 1839, p. 3; *General Advertiser for Dublin, and All Ireland*, 27 July 1839, p. 4; *Northern Whig*, 27 July 1839; p. 4; *Vindicator*, 27 July 1839, p. 4. Moore's new factory suffered flood damage from the River Dodder on 29–30 July 1839: *Dublin Weekly Herald*, 3 August 1839, p. 3.

In addition to the introduction of power looms, Samuel Moore employed hand-loom woollen weavers in Milltown. A report to parliament of 1840 on hand-loom weavers contains very revealing details about the hard lives these men led in the 1830s:

> *Mr Nicholas Hunt, foreman to Mr Moore, woollen manufacturer, Milltown, states: 'Mr Moore employs 30 hand-loom woollen weavers, 16 of these work out [i.e. in their homes], the others in a room in the factory. We are going to make an alteration to get all inside; we prefer having the men employed in a factory; it prevents theft; there is not, however, much theft; nor have we much cause to find fault on this head. With some few exceptions, the weavers are hard-working poor creatures when they can get work to do. For the last three years our men have been kept waiting for warps,*[100] *on an average, 10 weeks in each year. The average earnings per week, including the time they are kept idle, for the year 1836, was 13s. 7 ¾ d.; in 1837, 11s. 6d. per week. I cannot judge of this year [1839], as at the beginning of it we were moving from one factory [Bluebell] to another [Milltown]. We were not doing so much in 1837, which accounts for the decreased earnings of the men. If the men had constant employment they could average from 15s. to 18s. per week, and they should work 14 hours a day to make this.'*[101]

Notwithstanding his employment of hand-loom weavers, Moore's concerns in Milltown were focused on the latest technology in cloth weaving. In an extensive article describing woollen cloth manufacturing in Ireland published in the *Irish Penny Journal* of 24 October 1840, Moore received favourable publicity about his business venture at Milltown:

> *The machinery in the woollen factories of Ireland is certainly inferior to that of our English neighbours, and the decline of the trade renders improvement difficult, if not altogether hopeless. Power looms for the weaving of woollen cloth, so generally at work at the other side of the Channel, have been only this year introduced for the first time to this country by Mr Moore, proprietor of the Milltown factory near Dublin; and that Irish mechanists are not inferior to any others, is evidenced by the fact that the power looms erected at Milltown are vastly superior to those imported, and which were on the most improved construction. Whether the experiment will have any effect in reviving this sinking business, remains to be seen.*[102]

It is not clear what impact the new power looms had on the numbers employed at the mills in Milltown. The article in the *Irish Penny Journal* described the woollen cloth manufacturing process, from raw material to finished product, in great detail. It is obvious from the journalist's description that regardless of the introduction of power looms, considerable manual labour was required to carry out the manufacturing process, which could take between one and two months to complete.[103] In September 1840 31 employees from Moore's woollen mills subscribed to Daniel O'Connell's Repeal Association, which gives some idea of the number of workers employed in the mills.[104]

100 Warps are the threads on a loom over and under which other threads (the weft) are passed to make cloth.

101 *Reports from the Assistant Hand-Loom Weavers Commissioners; viz. Report by C.G. Otway, Esq; on Ireland, Part III*, p. 661, H.C. 1840, (43), xxiii. Nicholas Hunt is listed as 'woollen manufacturer, Milltown mills' in Thom's Directory 1847, but by 1853 Nicholas and his wife and daughter had moved to Manchester, presumably to seek employment in the mills there: *Evening Freeman*, 8 July 1853, p. 2; *Dublin Daily Express*, 15 December 1858, p. 4.

102 *Irish Penny Journal*, 1, no. 17 (24 October 1840), p. 135.

103 *Irish Penny Journal*, 1, no. 17 (24 October 1840), pp. 134–5.

104 *Dublin Morning Register*, 30 September 1840, p. 4.

In the following year, 1841, Samuel Moore was included in a list of supporters and patrons of the College for Civil Engineering in Ireland, which reveals a professional interest in keeping up to date with modern trends and manufacturing methods in his chosen trade.[105] The annual census for the same year recorded that in Milltown townland 32 men and 15 women were working in the clothing industry.[106] All of these people would have worked in Moore's woollen mills apart from George and Daniel O'Brien who were self-employed hatters with workshops on the north side of Milltown main street (Map 12).[107]

In 1845 the surveyors from the Griffith's Valuation visited Moore's mills and recorded very precise details about the machinery at the mills and the power it produced:

> *A good supply of water for six months in the year and 12 hours in the day and an average for the other 6 months (say 6 hours in the day). Waterwheel wood – Diameter 16 feet, buckets 8 feet broad, shouldering 14 inches. Revolves 6 times in a minute – 15 power looms – Mules 576. Billies 150, Spindles, Scribblers and Carders 7, all take about 15 horse power, or no more power is used at the same time.*[108]

The words 'mules', 'billies', 'slubbing billies', 'spindles', 'scribblers' and 'carders' were all part of the specialist terminology used to describe the woollen cloth manufacturing process, and each term and the process it signified was explained in great detail in the *Irish Penny Journal* article of 1840.

Moore's factory premises at Milltown was a large industrial complex (Map 16b/40). Beside the mills, it contained extensive buildings including a house for the manager with an adjoining kitchen and gate lodge, two factory buildings, a press and a weaving shop and store, a cow house and dairy, sheds and offices, a wool store, a forge, a dye house and a privy.[109] All of the buildings at Moore's premises in Milltown were initially rated for local taxation at £55.[110]

The Famine had a devastating impact on Moore's business. The surveyors from the Griffith's Valuation visited his factory again in 1847 and remarked in two separate ledger entries that:

> *July 1st 1847 – I have been at Mr Moore's factory this day, and find there is no work doing. and have been informed that none has been done here since last March [1847], and that the cloth manufactured last year is still on hands. and in consequence of this decline in business I think the above valuation may be reduced to £50 – J Donnelly valuator*[111]
>
> *No trade – nothing done here since the 18th March. Work only 4 days a week during Winter – no prospect of work. Trade is on the decline. No work whatsoever doing here and the cloth manufactured last year is still on hands. In consequence I think the above valuation may be reduced to £50.*[112]

---

105 *Evening Packet*, 11 November 1841, p. 1.

106 Census of Ireland for the year 1841, County Dublin, Barony of Uppercross, Townland of Milltown, pp. 30–1.

107 Thom's Directory 1849, p. 837.

108 NAI, VO, OL52714, House Book for Milltown Village 1845, no. 82.

109 NAI, VO, OL52714, House Book for Milltown Village 1845, p. 559, no. 82.

110 Thom's Directory 1846, p. 1112.

111 NAI, VO, OL52714, House Book for Milltown Village 1845, p. 559, no. 82.

112 NAI, VO, OL70089, Quarto Book for Milltown Village 1847, p. 211, no. 40.

It is unsurprising that the Famine had such a negative effect on Moore's business. The woollen cloth manufactured at Milltown was predominantly made to clothe the Irish peasantry, most of whom by 1847 were desperately trying to survive on what little money they had to buy food or save for the boat ticket to Liverpool and thence to North America. Moore successfully defended an action for ejectment on title in February 1848, but this was only delaying the inevitable.[113] By April 1848 the mills were put up for sale, when the premises was referred to as having been 'lately used as a Woollen Factory'.[114] Further newspaper advertisements, none of which mentioned Moore, appeared over the course of the next 18 months in an attempt to dispose of the remaining machinery and effects.[115] A notice in the *Freeman's Journal* alerting readers to an auction to be held on 11 April 1849 rather poignantly mentioned a four-drawer office desk.[116] The final auction of unsold machinery was held the following September, with everything to be peremptorily sold without any reserve whatsoever.[117]

Although the Woollen Mills had ceased operation in 1848, the gate lodge beside the mill entrance off the Milltown Road (an old but well-repaired structure 19 feet long and 14.5 feet in height, according to the Valuation Office), was let to several tenants and lodgers in the early 1850s.[118] One night in late December 1852 a terrible tragedy befell the occupants of the lodge when a large tree fell through its roof during a particularly violent winter storm, which was 'unparalleled in its violence since the memorable hurricane of 1839':

> *At Dundrum, Roebuck, Milltown, etc, the effects of the storm were not less severe than elsewhere; and we have to record the melancholy fact that three lives were lost at the last mentioned place. On making enquiries we have been informed that between six and seven o'clock on yesterday morning a large tree was overthrown at the Milltown factory, which, falling on the gate house attached thereto, carried down the roof, floor, and walls, burying the inmates, six in number, underneath. Three persons were suffocated under the ruins, and taken out dead – namely, Mrs Ryan, the owner of the lodge, her daughter Margaret Ryan, and her son Philip Ryan. The others – two of whom were lodgers, and the third a daughter of Mrs Ryan's, escaped with a few bruises.*[119]

This accident explains why the gate lodge was subsequently crossed out in manuscript with an 'X' on the Valuation Office town plan for Milltown village (Map 16b/41).

On 8 January 1856 the freehold interest in the Milltown mills formerly operated by Samuel Moore was put up for auction by the earl of Milltown and was bought by the Hogan estate

113 *Freeman's Journal*, 4 February 1848, p. 3. An ejectment on title was usually brought against a tenant who failed or refused to give up possession.

114 *General Advertiser for Dublin, and All Ireland*, 1 April 1848, p. 3.

115 *General Advertiser for Dublin, and All Ireland*, 3 June 1848, p. 2; 31 March 1849, p. 2; *Freeman's Journal*, 29 March 1849, p. 1; 16 September 1849, p. 1

116 *Freeman's Journal*, 29 March 1849, p. 1.

117 *Freeman's Journal*, 16 September 1849, p. 1.

118 NAI, VO, OL50945, House Book for Milltown Village 1845, no. 4; NAI, VO, OL70089, Quarto Book for Milltown Village 1847, p. 211, no. 41. *The Advocate, or Irish Industrial Journal*, 29 December 1852, p. 4.

119 *The Advocate, or Irish Industrial Journal*, 29 December 1852, p. 4; Weekly Telegraph, 1 January 1853, p. 2.

for £930.[120] The Hogan estate already held an extensive freehold estate on the far side of the Milltown Road at Fairyland (St Philip's) and Richmond Hill (Rydalmount).[121] The woollen mills had been unoccupied since the demise of Samuel Moore's business at Milltown. Once the Hogan estate had acquired the Leeson freehold the Hogan estate trustees set about advertising for a tenant for the mills in March 1856:

> *To be let for such terms as may be agreed on the extensive and valuable concerns, with mills and water wheel, formerly used as a woollen factory, situate at Milltown, County Dublin, with a commodious residence, good garden, and about three Irish acres of excellent land. The water from the River Dodder which supplies the mill is abundant, and never failing. The close vicinity to the metropolis, and the Dublin and Wicklow Railway passing close to the property, render this a most desirable situation. Immediate possession can be given.*[122]

The advertisement typically made the best of an unpromising situation. More importantly, the assertion that the River Dodder supplied an abundant and unfailing supply of water was patently untrue. An official report commissioned in 1844 had found that every mill on the Dodder for a period of from two to four months in the year was inoperable for a portion of the day, varying from one quarter to one half of the whole time of labour due to an insufficient flow of water.[123] It took 18 months for the Hogan estate to find a tenant for the derelict woollen mills. In May 1858 the mills were leased to bakers Robert Gibney senior and Robert Gibney junior of Patrick Street, who had recently converted the premises to a flour mill since gaining possession the previous November. The description of the mill premises was now updated in the lease to include mention of the new railway viaduct:

> *All that and those the houses and mill now a flour mill together with the land, orchard, millpond, water, water courses, conveniences and appurtenances ... lying and being between the old bridge of Milltown and the Railway Viaduct in the County of Dublin bounded on the north by the new road then made from said old bridge of Milltown [Packhorse Bridge] to said viaduct, on the south by the River Dodder, on the east by Milltown and on the west by the holding of the Dublin and Wicklow Railway Company, then in the possession of Robert Gibney senior ... to hold to Robert Gibney senior and Robert Gibney junior from 1 November 1857 for one hundred years subject to the yearly rent of seventy five pounds.*[124]

The lease also imposed several interesting covenants on the Gibneys. Firstly, they were required to demolish the old ruinous workmen's houses clustered around the northern end of the Packhorse Bridge within six months of signing the lease. Secondly, the Gibneys were required to expend £750 in repairs and valuable improvements on the premises within 12 months and to insure them every year for £800. To prevent a proliferation of working-class housing on the site, the Gibneys were forbidden to build any cabins or cottages on the grounds except villa residences at least two storeys high on which a minimum of £500 should be expended. In short,

---

120 NAI, Landed Estates Court Rental, vol. 38, no. 3, 'Particulars and Conditions of Sale of the Freehold Estate of the Earl of Milltown to be sold on 8 January 1856', lot 59; RD 1856/16/137.

121 The development of Hogan estate is covered in Chapter 15.

122 *Saunders's Newsletter*, 11 March 1856, p. 4.

123 Robert Mallet, *Report on the proposed formation of reservoirs on the River Dodder* (Dublin, 1844), p. 16.

124 RD 1858/15/80.

only middle-class housing would be permitted. The Gibneys were also forbidden from using the existing chimney for any purposes other than as a flue to a boiler or oven for baking bread, and no steam engine was to be used under any pretext on penalty of £50. Finally, there was a covenant forbidding noisome (malodorous) trades on penalty of £150.[125]

The Gibneys' tenure at the Milltown flour mills was unremarkable (they did not build any speculative middle-class housing fronting the Milltown Road) and in 1887 Robert Gibney junior assigned his lease to the Dublin Laundry Company Limited for £500.[126] The previous year Gibney had received £458 5*s*. from the Rathmines and Rathgar township in compensation for damage caused by the laying of the Dodder valley main sewer through his premises at Milltown.[127] It is possible that the disruption caused by the sewage works influenced Gibney's decision to dispose of the premises to the laundry, once that opportunity arose.

The proprietor of the Dublin Laundry Company, Thomas Edmondson, used the most advanced machinery of the time required for a modern steam laundry. Such a facility required a reliable water supply to operate the boilers and the wooden washing machines. Edmondson dispensed with the large waterwheel that was *in situ* when he took over the Gibney's flour mill as it was no longer needed to power machinery. Instead, Edmondson decided to obtain the required water supply from the River Dodder using the millrace which, as noted earlier, took off the water at the weir behind The Dropping Well pub.[128] Edmondson was in regular correspondence with the residents of the demesnes of Nullamore and South Hill, through which the millrace passed, to ensure that they removed any obstacles such as stones or fallen branches that, from time to time, hindered the flow of water. As a Quaker businessman, Edmondson did not miss the opportunity to charge 30*s*. to fertilise the ground in the adjacent fields with mud removed from the millrace.[129]

When the sluice gate was open the millrace carried a substantial flow of water from the Dodder. This was demonstrated when the Dodder historian, John Christopher FitzAchary, narrowly escaped drowning when he fell in while trying to retrieve his hat, which had blown into the millrace at a location behind the boundary wall of Nullamore, opposite The Dropping Well pub:

> *It [the hat], however, alighted in a mill-race which, at this point, turns under the roadway and into the grounds of Nullamore, the residence of Mr Johnston. He [FitzAchary] immediately crossed the roadway wall, and in endeavouring to stay the progress of his hat in the rapidly flowing water, he unfortunately slipped into the race and immediately found himself submerged to the chin. His efforts to extricate himself proved unavailing, as on the roadside there was nothing but a steep wall, and on the riverside the tufts of grass to which he, in desperation clung, gave way one after another, just as he had got half way out of the water, and as a result, he found himself each time deeper and deeper submerged. At length the howling of a favourite collie dog that accompanied him, attracted the attention of a couple of postmen who were passing just then, and by their assistance, which arrived in the nick of time, he was brought to the bank in a very exhausted condition.*[130]

125 RD 1858/15/80.

126 RD 1887/43/218; Hearn, *Thomas Edmondson*, p. 22.

127 Dublin City Archives, Rathmines and Rathgar UDC papers, UDC 1/List 1/43, Agreement dated 21 June 1886.

128 Hearn, *Thomas Edmondson*, p. 26.

129 NAI, Business Records, DUB 56, Dublin Laundry Company Limited, letter books 1887–1909.

130 *Rathmines News*, 19 August 1899, p. 4.

If nothing else, the story proves that the original surveyors got the gradient spot on when they designed and constructed the weir and millrace. All mention of the millrace disappears after 1908, by which time it had become defunct.[131]

The Dublin Laundry Company's presence at Milltown lasted nearly a century before the company closed down and went into voluntary liquidation in 1983.[132] The laundry site remained derelict for over ten years until Jackson Properties secured planning permission to build the Shanagarry apartment complex on the site in the mid-1990s.[133] As part of the redevelopment, Dublin Corporation created a public path along the bank of the River Dodder behind the apartments and substantially widened the Milltown Road so that both lanes of traffic passed under separate arches of the viaduct, where previously traffic in both directions had to pass under the archway beside the Richmond Avenue South junction.

The experience of the woollen mill at Dartry during the Famine and its immediate aftermath followed a similar path to that of the Milltown woollen mills. In 1845 the surveyors from the Griffith's Valuation visited Dartry Woollen Mills and recorded that they used 26 horse power for six months of the year and 12 hours of the day, declining to 20 horse power for four months of the year. More importantly, the official noted that 'very little work [is] done for the remaining two months'. The six months of declining output was probably caused by a fall-off in business during 1845 or perhaps by low water levels in the River Dodder. The river powered a water wheel which was 20 feet in diameter and 14 feet broad, which revolved six times in a minute. The mill wheel in turn supplied power to six looms with 84 spindles and 13 fulling stocks in the tuck mill.[134]

William Willans, successor to Obadiah Willans at Dartry mills, was anxious to diversify from woollen manufacturing. In 1846 he leased the Dartry woollen mills and adjacent property to Richard Jones, a cotton manufacturer.[135] In 1849 Willans notified the public that he was henceforth confining his business to supplying army and other contracts and as a result he was offering his surplus woollen stock for sale.[136] Things did not fare well for Jones, and his business partnership was dissolved in 1850. As a result, Jones's leasehold of Dartry and the cotton milling machinery were put up for auction and were bought by Thomas Drury who later took up residence in Dartry House.[137]

Cotton spinning seems to have continued sporadically at Dartry until 1876 when Drury advertised that the machinery would be auctioned off as he had recently let the mills to Charles Panter, a paint manufacturer.[138] Three years later a fire broke out at Dartry mills and they were burnt to the ground because, as one newspaper put it, 'no help being at hand but the hand engine of the Rathmines Commissioners, the building was quickly burned down'.[139] A distressed auction

131 *Freeman's Journal*, Tuesday 18 August 1908, p. 8.

132 *Irish Independent*, 8 June 1983, p. 19.

133 *Evening Herald*, 25 January 1994, p. 43; 19 September 1995, p. 23.

134 NAI, VO, OL50936, House Book, Townland of Rathmines South 1845, p. 6, no. 15.

135 Drury Papers (NAI, Small Accessions no. 1/704, D12940); NAI, VO, OL70089, Quarto Book, Townland of Rathmines South 1847, p. 230, no. 31.

136 *Freeman's Journal*, 16 January 1849, p. 1.

137 Drury Papers (NAI, Small Accessions no. 1/704, D12940); *Freeman's Journal*, 17 October 1850, p. 1.

138 *Freeman's Journal*, 7 September 1876, p. 7.

139 *Northern Whig*, 5 December 1879, p. 8; *Freeman's Journal*, 5 December 1879, p. 7.

sale was held of Panter's remaining property at Dartry on 18 December 1879 due to his non-payment of rent, and by the following January he had become bankrupt.[140] The fire at Dartry mills was one of several serious fires to occur in the Rathmines township during the 1870s. As a result of these destructive accidents, the township obtained statutory powers to set up its own fire brigade in August 1880.[141]

In 1895 the Dartry mills were acquired by the Dublin Laundry Company Limited which subsequently repurposed them up for dyeing, dry cleaning and carpet cleaning.[142] These specialist activities continued at Dartry until 1958 when the business relocated down the road to the Milltown laundry site, following which the Dartry premises was acquired by James North and Sons, which specialised in the manufacture of polyvinyl acetate (PVC) garments.[143]

MILLING ACTIVITY ON THE SOUTH BANK OF THE RIVER DODDER IN THE EARLY EIGHTEENTH CENTURY

From the 1720s onwards, the number of manufacturers and their activities on the south bank at Milltown began to increase. The picture is rather complicated because not all of the business relationships or legal interests of the protagonists are ascertainable from the surviving records, nor are the exact locations of the factories and workshops identifiable. In attempting to simplify matters, one must bear in mind that, save possibly for a brief period at the turn of the nineteenth century, there were only two separate mill complexes located on the south bank of the Dodder in the vicinity of the Packhorse Bridge, together with one or two smaller industrial enterprises which did not use water-powered machinery. The premises housing these businesses were frequently demolished and rebuilt or refitted for other purposes, and, as will be discussed later, on one occasion a woollen mill burnt down.

DEVELOPMENTS INITIATED BY JOSEPH LEESON – PAPER MANUFACTURE

As noted earlier, Joseph Leeson granted a lease in 1711 to the Milltown paper makers John and Edward Waters of a paper mill on the north bank of the River Dodder, which had ceased operation by 1724 when Robert Randal established his paper mill on the south bank of the river close to the Packhorse Bridge. Before elaborating on this development, the background to paper manufacture in Milltown may be given briefly. Paper manufacture depended on access to a large urban market, a plentiful supply of rags for making pulp (supplied by the urban poor of Dublin) and clear running water. The third requirement was met by the rivers which rose in the Dublin mountains, such as the Dodder and Owendoher. In the early eighteenth century the process involved cotton and linen rags being fed into a water-powered stamping mill which reduced them to a pulp (hence the requirement to provide 15 hammers in new paper mill built by Randal in 1724). The pulp was further diluted with water which was then spread on to a frame with a wire mesh. The wire mesh was used to create a web of fibrous material to which the rag pulp had now been reduced. The remaining water was drained off the frame and the material was compressed on a screw press to eradicate any residual moisture. Finally, the raw paper was hung up to dry out completely in a specially ventilated loft. As the eighteenth century progressed further improvements were made to the pulping process with the

140 *Freeman's Journal*, 18 December 1879, p. 8; 31 January 1880, p. 3.

141 *Irish Times*, 5 June 1880, p. 7.

142 *Dublin Daily Express*, 14 June 1895, p. 1.

143 *Irish Independent*, 27 February 1958, p. 17; *Dublin Evening Mail*, 5 February 1962, p. 14.

introduction of the 'Hollander' which as a result increased the size of paper mills.[144]

The Randal family had lived in Milltown since the seventeenth century so they knew the area and were presumably aware of the risks and opportunities they were taking on when they agreed terms with William Ford who owned the adjacent brass mill.[145] Randal's lease contains interesting details about the parties' agreement to share the millrace water and is worth quoting as follows:

> *all that piece or parcel of ground as then enclosed adjoining to the said William Ford's brass mill in Milltown together with the benefit of the water two weeks in every three ... and further that the said Robert Randall [sic] shall at his own cost keep the water wheel of the said brass mill in good order and repair ... and also should within three months from the date of the said lease erect a good paper mill with fifteen hammers and a dwelling house, he William Ford to advance towards building the same the sum of eighty pounds. And if William Ford shall use the water more often than one week in every three weeks then Robert Randall shall have the water again as long as William Ford shall enjoy the same above one week in three, and in like manner if Robert Randall shall enjoy the water more often than two weeks in every three weeks then William Ford shall have the water for so long as Robert Randall shall have the same benefit of the said water two parts, and William Ford shall enjoy the same or third part.* [146]

The lease also contained a clause of first refusal which required Randal to offer the premises to Ford first if Randal wanted to sell or dispose of them. Thirteen years later in 1737 Randal and his three sons Robert, John and Anthony surrendered their lease to Roger Ford's successor in title, William Ford, possibly because their business had outgrown their water supply agreement with Ford.[147] Later evidence supports this theory and suggests that the Randals surrendered their lease in Milltown because they wanted to relocate to new premises at Windy Arbour. On 26 October 1754 the death was reported of:

> *Mr John Randal, a paper maker near Milltown, [who] had the misfortune to be thrown from his horse between Dundrum and Milltown, by which he fractured his skull and expired in three hours after. He was a man of very good character.*[148]

Before his unfortunate death John Randal had undoubtedly been making paper in the vicinity of Windy Arbour because a paper mill is located in that area on the River Slang, according to Rocque's Survey of County Dublin (Map 4). At the time, that district was often described in deeds as being part of Milltown or Churchtown lands; the place name 'Windy Harbour' (as Windy Arbour was originally spelt) did not come into common usage until the 1760s.[149]

---

144 Rynne, *Industrial Ireland*, pp. 307–10.

145 Mills, *The register of the Parish of St Peter and St Kevin*, pp. 171, 177 which record the deaths of Mary Randal and Joseph Randal of Milltown in 1703 and 1705 respectively.

146 RD 62/285/42895.

147 RD 88/383/62985.

148 *Pue's Occurrences*, 22 October 1754.

149 *Freeman's Journal*, 2 October 1764.

BRASS AND IRON MILLS

The availability of a reliable power source attracted iron manufacturers to Milltown and Clonskeagh in the eighteenth century. In this industry the water mill powered the bellows and hammers used in the iron-making process during which the iron ore was reduced to a liquid by burning charcoal and employing a continuous blast of air from the water powered bellows. Limestone – another raw material readily available in Milltown and Clonskeagh – was applied to the liquid iron ore as a flux which, combining with the impurities in the furnace, produced slag. The slag floated above the molten metal and could thus be easily drawn off. The molten metal was poured into a sand bed and either cast into so-called pigs (from the shape of the sand bed, hence the term pig iron) or into moulds.[150] Another attraction for iron founders was the availability of sand along the River Dodder at Milltown, which was found to be suitable for casting sheet lead and metal.[151]

As previously noted in Chapter 4 as part of the discussion in the development of the Leeson estate, on 21 March 1718 Joseph Leeson granted a lease to Edward Allen, gentleman, of land on the south bank of the River Dodder of:

> *33 acres, 3 roods and 4 perches of land being part of Milltown lands together with the passage cross Milltown bottom leading to the said two fields next to Churchtown lands which said passage was to consist of sixty foot broad ... excepting ... unto Joseph Leeson and his heirs the ancient millrace and water course that leads to the iron mill of Milltown and liberty to make a millrace through any part of the premises for the convenience of a new mill to be erected.*[152]

Within six years of granting the lease to Allen, Joseph Leeson had followed through with his plans to build a new mill – an iron mill – as evidenced by a lease dated 20 April 1724 from Joseph Leeson to Humphrey French whereby Leeson, for a yearly rent of £50, leased to French:

> *all that the iron mill, head, workhouses and dwelling houses and all that piece or parcel of ground of Milltown bottom containing by estimate 10 acres, 2 roods and 6 perches and also all that little brass mill and millpond all which premises are situate lying and being in Milltown together with all mill streams and mill dams and water courses and appurtenances belonging*[153]

French immediately sublet the brass mill, millpond and the millrace exiting the iron mill to the brass mill to William Ford for a term of 99 years at an annual rent of £10.[154] As noted earlier, Ford granted a lease to John Randal on condition that he build a paper mill and share the water with Ford's brass mill.[155]

150 Rynne, *Industrial Ireland*, p. 112.

151 *Irish Builder*, xii, no. 274, 15 May 1871, p. 121.

152 RD 23/139/12909. As noted previously, the memorial record in the Registry of Deeds refers to the 'iron mill of Milltown' but this is an error as the original lease, which is quoted in the 1856 sale particulars of the Leeson freehold estate, refers to the 'grain mill of Milltown': NAI, Landed Estates Court Rental, vol. 38, no. 3, 'Particulars and Conditions of Sale of the Freehold Estate of the Earl of Milltown to be sold on 8 January 1856', lot 58.

153 RD 42/110/25830.

154 RD 39/393/25843 (lease dated 21 April 1724).

155 RD 62/285/42895.

In summary, by the mid-1720s a brass mill, an iron mill and a paper mill were all operating on the south bank of the River Dodder close to the Packhorse Bridge. The three mills were powered by a shared water supply taken off the River Slang by a millrace located close to Windy Arbour. The water was stored in a millpond in an elevated position close to the mills. The ancient grain mill on the south bank of the Dodder was apparently replaced by two grain mills on the north bank of the River Dodder.

In the mid-eighteenth century the Recorder of Dublin, Thomas Morgan, held an interest in the iron mills in Milltown for a short period. A lease from 1756 refers to:

> *all that tenement opposite the iron mills in Milltown and that piece of ground called the bottoms of Milltown formerly in the possession of Richard Cooke containing about six [plantation] acres and mentioned to have been demised by Alexander Ryves, James Tandy and Mathew French to Thomas Morgan, deceased*[156]

The next occupant of the iron mills did not survive for long either. In December 1759 *Pue's Occurrences* reported that: 'Mr Dogherty who kept the iron works at Milltown near this city was found dead in his bed in the morning to which he went the night before seemingly in good health.'[157]

In 1764 the earl of Milltown leased the following property to two Dublin ironmongers, James Tandy and Thomas Cavanagh:

> *all that the iron mill, millhead, work houses and dwelling houses and all that piece or parcel of ground of Milltown bottom containing by estimation ten acres two roods and six perches [plantation measure] and described in a map and also that piece of ground whereon a brass mill formerly stood and the millpond thereunto belonging ... with all mill streams, mill dams, watercourses and appurtenances.*[158]

The lease granted to Tandy and Cavanagh was for lives renewable forever at an initial rent of £35, rising to £40 on 25 March 1773 and annually thereafter. The tenants were forbidden from using any of the earth or clay for making bricks or tiles, except for building or making improvements to the premises, on pain of a 10-shilling fine for every thousand bricks or tiles that should be sold or carried off the premises. The mills came with a considerable amount of land, equating to over 17 statute acres.[159] As far as one can tell without having sight of the lease map, the 17 acres covered an area stretching from the junction of the Dundrum Road and Bankside Cottages (which were not built until the nineteenth century) on the north and as far as Windy Arbour at Farrenboley Park on the south, bounded on the east by the Dundrum Road and on the west by the River Slang. Crucially, the land included the millrace that was taken off the River Slang at Windy Arbour. That millrace supplied water for the millpond that was located on an elevated position to the south of the Packhorse Bridge and which in turn powered the iron mills (Map 19). The area is now largely built on save for the public green area behind St Luke's Crescent, Millmount Cottages and Coolnahinch on the Dundrum Road.

James Tandy was a wholesale ironmonger who had a warehouse in Cornmarket where he sold

156 RD 173/239/120550.

157 *Pue's Occurrences*, 4 December 1759.

158 RD 228/579/152562.

159 NAI, Landed Estates Court Rental, vol. 38, no. 3, 'Particulars and Conditions of Sale of the Freehold Estate of the Earl of Milltown to be sold on 8 January 1856', lot 58.

iron shovels, coal boxes and frying pans, among other things.[160] Tandy was the father of the radical politician and United Irishman James Napper Tandy.[161] Nothing is known about the ironmonger Thomas Cavanagh. The iron manufactory at Milltown operated for several years as a business partnership made up of James Tandy, Thomas Cavanagh and Michael Reilly. When Reilly died his son sold his father's one third share of the Milltown iron mills to Tandy and Kavanagh for £350 in 1775.[162] James Tandy senior died at his home in Ranelagh in 1790 aged eighty-four following which James Napper Tandy inherited his father's property.[163] According to his biographer, Napper Tandy did not work for long in the ironmongery business, preferring instead the less arduous and more remunerative occupation of land agent and rent collector.[164]

By 1793 Napper Tandy was coming under increasing pressure from the authorities for his radical politics and French republican sympathies, and in March 1793 he skipped bail to avoid trial at the Dundalk spring assizes on trumped up charges, the outcome of which could have had potentially fatal consequences for him. A short while later, Tandy fled the country and sought refuge in London from where he issued letters of instructions to settle his affairs.[165] Before he left Tandy had given a power of attorney to a fellow radical and ironmonger, Henry Jackson, to dispose of his property. Accordingly, on 24 and 25 June 1793 Jackson executed two deeds on behalf of Tandy whereby Tandy disposed of his interest in the Milltown iron mills to either his son or first cousin James Tandy of Dublin.[166]

IRONMONGERS PATRICK POUNDEN AND JOHN HEAVISIDE

Patrick Pounden and John Heaviside were Dublin ironmongers who in the mid-1770s built new iron works at Milltown. In 1777 the two partners obtained a patent 'for the peculiar method of making useful iron of the best quality, from scraps and small pieces, at their new erected iron works at Milltown, near Dublin'.[167] The articles made at Milltown, which included anchors and cart axles, were sold at their foundries in Church Street and Luke Street.

The two partners' leasehold interest in Milltown is not recorded but it is likely that Pounden and Heaviside were granted a long sub-lease from James Tandy, as part of a subdivision of Tandy and Cavanagh's holding. Heaviside was the more prominent of the two men. In 1777 John Heaviside played a critical role in supplying iron ferrules and angle joints that were used in the construction of a new piped water supply in Dublin city.[168] Ten years later, in 1787, Heaviside began making garden pots alongside his scrap iron works in Milltown, as the *Freeman's Journal* explains:

---

160 *Finn's Leinster Journal*, 12 December 1772, p. 3.

161 *Dublin Evening Post*, 17 August 1790, p. 2.

162 RD 308/133/204000.

163 *Dublin Evening Post*, 17 August 1790, p. 2.

164 Rupert J. Coughlan, *Napper Tandy* (Dublin, 1976), pp. 4–5.

165 Coughlan, *Napper Tandy*, pp. 98–103.

166 RD 473/258/300532. The familial relationship between the parties is not stated but Napper Tandy had a son named James and a cousin named James Tandy.

167 *Saunders's Newsletter*, 4 September 1777, p. 4.

168 CARD, xii (Dublin, 1905), pp. 375–6, 463–4, 469, 507.

A very fine bed of clay has been discovered near Milltown, and is now manufacturing by the ingenious Mr Heaviside, in crucibles and garden pots. An improvement, it is reported, has been made in the above manufacture by the before mentioned artist, by which the progress is rendered vastly more easy and short, but full as efficacious.[169]

The following month, Heaviside placed the following advertisement in *Saunders's Newsletter*:

A new pottery is now established at the iron works at Milltown (two miles south of Dublin, on the Kilgobbin road), where Gentlemen and others may be constantly supplied with improved garden pots, stands, etc on the best terms for ready money.[170]

Heaviside's ingenuity was also revealed by his avoidance of the restrictive covenant in the Leeson lease to Tandy and Cavanagh of 1764 which, as we have seen, forbade the manufacture of bricks or tiles using the clay at Milltown. The mention in the advertisement of 'best terms for ready money' reflected the common practice in the eighteenth and early nineteenth centuries of using promissory notes instead of cash in commercial transactions.[171]

Sometime in the late 1780s Heaviside either sublet his iron mills at Milltown or took on a new partner called William Beeby, who had possibly replaced Patrick Pounden. In 1787 the following advertisement was placed in the *Dublin Chronicle*:

The scrap iron forge at Milltown is now completely at work on improved principles, where the public may be supplied with crow, sock, coulter, and beam moulds; anchor arms, palmes and shanks; shoeing iron for horses and carriage wheels of any required dimensions, for which purposes this kind of iron is found to be peculiarly adapted; and all other forms and uses producible by a mill hammer. The iron will be found of the first quality, inferior to none, but superior in general for toughness and durability and the terms reasonable – orders will be received and punctually attended to at the iron foundry, Luke Street, or at Mr William Beeby's, George's Street, George's Quay.[172]

During the turbulent decade of the 1790s Heaviside's iron mill at Milltown was raided by the police who, presumably on foot of a tip-off, were looking for arms and ammunition illegally made there. The report in the *Belfast Newsletter* of 5 March 1793 informed its readers that:

Last Saturday a party of horse under the direction of the Chief Commissioner of Police, marched from this city to the foundry of Mr Heaviside, at Milltown, where they seized a quantity of cannon ball, which on enquiry was found to be the property of [the] Government, and cast by order from the Ordnance board![173]

That the attention of the police should be directed to the iron works at Milltown is unsurprising. Aside from James Napper Tandy, another very prominent United Irishman, Henry Jackson,

169 *Freeman's Journal*, 8 September 1787, p. 3.

170 *Saunders's Newsletter*, 22 October 1787, p. 3.

171 George O'Brien, *The Economic History of Ireland in the eighteenth Century* (Dublin, 1918), pp. 355–6. In 1809 Patrick Gore of Milltown was acquitted of stealing a promissory note for £30 from his former employer, Nicholas Hunt: *Saunders's Newsletter*, 3 November 1809, p. 2.

172 *Dublin Chronicle*, 7 February 1789, p. 1.

173 *Belfast Newsletter*, 5 March 1793, p. 3.

operated iron mills half a mile downstream on the south bank of the Dodder at Clonskeagh.[174] It is possible that Jackson's iron works at Clonskeagh were the intended target of the police raid but that faulty intelligence or directions led them to raid Heaviside's ironworks instead. However, when the 1798 Rebellion broke out in May of that year, a quantity of pike handles was discovered by the military authorities hidden in a hay loft near Milltown.[175]

LINEN PRINTING AT MILLTOWN – JOSEPH CHAPPELL

The demand for printed textiles and personal linen and cotton apparel evolved from a desire for a simple and economical means of superimposing and duplicating patterns on cloth, particularly since embroidery was a very time-consuming process. The fashion for coloured fabrics developed in seventeenth-century France, and later spread throughout Europe. English restrictions on Irish trade, however, forbade the exportation to England of Irish-stained linens. Despite this, the nascent Irish textile printing industry was promoted by the trustees of the Linen Hall in Dublin and by the Dublin Society. From the late 1720s onwards, the banks of the Dodder attracted textile printers who, at various times in the eighteenth century, established printing yards at Ballsbridge, Donnybrook, Milltown and Rathfarnham.[176]

In 1727 the Linen Board gave a grant of just under £29 to Daniel Chappell together with a lease of land and buildings in Ballsbridge to enable him to set up a linen printing yard there. Shortly afterwards, the Linen Board provided Chappell with a second grant of £20 to employ two apprentices, Philip and Joseph Chappell, who presumably were Daniel's sons. The Chappells' business was not a success; there were complaints about their work and the Linen Board washed their hands of him by 1735 stating that they would 'do no more for him or for encouraging his manufacture'.[177]

After a gap of some 36 years Daniel's son Joseph appears on public record in Milltown. In August 1771 the ironmongers James Tandy and Thomas Cavanagh granted a lease for lives renewable for ever to 'Joseph Chappell of Milltown, Linen Printer'. The rent annual rent was £37 10*s.* and the lives named on the lease were Joseph's three sons Daniel, Henry and William.[178] Given that Joseph Chappell entered apprenticeship with his father in 1727 we can assume that he was born sometime between 1710 and 1715, which would mean that Joseph was in his late fifties or early sixties when he took on the lease at Milltown. Of particular interest are the descriptions of property leased to Chappell and the strict regulation of the water supply which he was permitted to use for his printing business:

> *all that the two houses with the stable and coach house and small garden with two acres and twelve perches [plantation measure] of land in Milltown as marked out to Rose's Ground as appeared by map to said deed ... together with such a supply of water from the watercourse belonging to the said James Tandy and Thomas Cavanagh as shall flow or proceed through the bore or pipe of one inch diameter then laid down and fixed into the said watercourse for the supplying of Joseph Chappell with water and Joseph Chappell and his heirs or assigns are in no ways to disturb or remove the same.*[179]

174 For Jackson's activities at Clonskeagh see Martin Holland, *Clonskeagh: A place in history* (Dublin, 2007), pp. 40–7.

175 *Freeman's Journal*, 2 June 1798, p3.

176 Ada K. Longfield, 'History of the Irish Linen and Cotton Printing Industry in the 18th Century', *Journal of the Royal Society of Antiquaries of Ireland*, seventh series, 7, no. 1 (June 1937), pp. 26–56.

177 Longfield, 'History of Irish Linen and Cotton Printing', pp. 32, 52.

178 RD 290/120/189337.The eldest son Daniel set up on his own as a paper stainer (RD 518/221/341235) while Henry joined his father's business (RD 405/451/266853).

179 RD 290/120/189337.

Aside from the availability of a water supply, there is another potential reason why Joseph Chappell chose Milltown to set up his linen printing business. Since 1764 John Classon had been operating a dye wood mill on the north bank of the Dodder directly opposite the site which Chappell had acquired from Tandy and Cavanagh.[180] It is reasonable to assume therefore that Chappell could conveniently source dye for his printing business from Classon's mills.

In June 1775 Joseph's son Henry, who by then was working with his father in Milltown, married a Miss Elizabeth Alcock of Ranelagh.[181] The following month Henry executed a partnership deed with his father whereby they agreed to hold the property in Milltown as tenants in common.[182] In November 1779 Joseph and Henry Chappell took out a six-month term loan of £105 from Daniel Tighe of Carrick, County Westmeath. Tighe, who was related by marriage to Joseph Chappell, was given a mortgage over the Milltown premises as security.[183]

Part of the premises which the Chappells leased from Tandy and Cavanagh included two houses with stables and land, which Henry Chappell later advertised for letting in the 1780s:

> *To be let, in a most pleasing situation, a house with gardens, stable and coach house, all well enclosed, the trees promising a luxuriant harvest. For further particulars apply to Mr Henry Chappell, at Milltown Bridge, who will show the premises.*[184]

> *To be set, a small new house in Milltown, with a good garden, extremely well stocked with fruit trees, in full bearing; the situation very pleasing. For particulars enquire of Mr Read, cutler, in Parliament Street, or Mr Henry Chappell, Milltown.*[185]

Henry and Joseph Chappell were not the only linen printers working in Milltown in the fourth quarter of the eighteenth century. The relaxation of the penal laws commencing with the Relief Act of 1778 meant that Catholics could take out leases for up to 999 years or for five lives, provided that they swore an oath of allegiance to the king which was taken and subscribed in court, and recorded for posterity in the Rolls Office. Although the original rolls perished in the Four Courts fire of 1922 an index of names, trades, addresses and dates of swearing has survived.[186] Among that list is a record of a Michael Bardon, who took the oath of allegiance on 8 February 1779, and whose occupation was described as a linen printer with an address at Milltown.[187] Aside from the fact that Bardon died intestate in 1800[188] no further information about him is forthcoming despite searches in the Registry of Deeds and of contemporary newspapers. The lack of information may indicate that Bardon was an employee of the Chappells rather than an independent linen printer in his own

---

180 RD 246/324/158097; *Faulkner's Dublin Journal*, 6 November 1783; 23 February 1793, p. 4.

181 *Finn's Leinster Journal*, 14 June 1775, p. 2.

182 RD 405/451/266853.

183 RD 405/451/266853. NAI, Crossle genealogical abstracts for Daniel Tighe and Bentham genealogical abstracts of prerogative wills, William Chappell (Phillips manuscripts), T. 1748-86.

184 *Saunders's Newsletter*, 25 June 1781, p. 1.

185 *Saunders's Newsletter*, 9 March 1784, p. 2.

186 Maureen Wall, 'The Catholic Merchants, Manufacturers and Traders of Dublin, 1778–1782', *Reportorium Novum*, ii, no. 2 (1959–1960), pp. 298–323.

187 Wall, 'The Catholic Merchants', p. 303.

188 Longfield, 'History of Irish Linen and Cotton Printing', p. 52; NAI, Prerogative Indexes to Wills and Administrations (testamentary class).

right. Evidence to support this theory is provided by a newspaper notice signed by Joseph and Henry Chappell and 12 linen and calico (white or unbleached cotton) printers in July 1787 which does not mention Michael Bardon. The occasion giving rise to the notice was an industrial dispute (which was successfully suppressed) in a print yard in Ballsbridge:

> *We the several linen and calico printers whose names are hereunto subscribed, do return our most unfeigned thanks to Mrs Mary Kennan, of Ballsbridge, linen and calico printer, for whose spirited and active conduct in a late prosecution carried on by her in suppressing a combination and conspiracy formed against her by her journeymen we feel ourselves much indebted. And we are determined in future to co-operate with each other, as well in punishing any delinquent in the trade, as in rewarding the industry of those whom we shall find most deserving.*[189]

In May 1790 Joseph and Henry Chappell took out another six-month term loan, this time of £350, from William Alcock of Milltown, linen printer.[190] Alcock was Henry Chappell's father-in-law or brother-in-law and he probably had an interest in the Chappells' business in Milltown. As was the usual practice with these transactions, Alcock was given a mortgage over the Milltown premises – as well as a slated house in Churchtown – as security for his loan. The mortgage deed described in similar terms the property leased to the Chappells by Tandy and Cavanagh in 1771 but now included 'all buildings and improvements erected and made by the said Joseph and Henry Chappell and the mill and mill works of the said Joseph and Henry Chappell therein'.[191]

In the 1790s the Chappells were manufacturing printed calico in a variety of different patterns, printed shawls and other printed garments called 'marseiles' (presumably of French origin) and 'cassimer' (cashmere?). They also made plain, striped, spotted and tamboured muslin, which was a lightweight, plain woven cotton cloth. The dyes used for printing the cloth were made from 'yellow berries, gum senica, madder and pearl ashes'.[192] Although the restrictions on exporting printed clothing to England had been lifted in 1779, it was by then too late for Irish goods to compete in the English market. While there is evidence that some Irish-made printed clothing was exported to Spain and Portugal, the vast majority of the Irish goods were produced for domestic consumption.[193]

After his father retired from the business Henry Chappell appears to have entered into partnership with a linen printer called William Styles.[194] By the late 1790s the business had run into difficulties and in 1797 Chappell and Styles went bankrupt. All of their stock on hand and their plant and machinery at Milltown was auctioned on 3 and 24 July of that year.[195] Among other things the auction at Milltown included 'a copperplate printing press, several good prints and grounds, printing tables, colour plans, an indigo mill, boilers and

189 *Saunders's Newsletter*, 31 July 1787, p. 3.

190 RD 420/456/275247.

191 RD 420/456/275247.

192 *Dublin Evening Post*, 29 June 1797, p. 4; *Saunders's Newsletter*, 15 July 1797, p. 3.

193 Longfield, 'History of Irish Linen and Cotton Printing', p. 50.

194 *Saunders's Newsletter*, 27 November 1797, p. 3. Joseph Chappell died on 18 April 1797: NAI, Bentham genealogical abstracts of prerogative wills (Phillips manuscripts), c. 1792–99.

195 *Saunders's Newsletter*, 28 June 1797, p. 3; 18 July 1797, p. 3.

other materials for the printing business, with some household furniture'.[196]

Some 19 months later, on 27 February 1799, the Chappell and Styles' premises was put up for sale. An advertisement in contemporary newspapers provides interesting detail about the printing mills and their location:

> *To be sold by auction, on Wednesday the 27th February, the interest in the lease of the house and large concerns, situated at the foot of Milltown Bridge [Packhorse Bridge], adjoining the iron mills, in the county of Dublin, being a perpetuity, and subject to the small rent of £37 10s. per annum; has been established upwards of 30 years in the calico printing and bleaching business. There needs no comment on the eligibleness [sic] of the situation for that or any other manufactory that requires room, and a constant supply of good water, having a pond in the garden 30 feet high [in elevation]; it would likewise make an excellent brewery or distillery. There is a mill and several out offices, the whole enclosed with a stone wall, so that the purchaser will have scarcely a shilling to lay out on it. There will be sold a quantity of printing utensils worth the attention of printers.*[197]

The outcome of the auction was that the print yard and mills were sold to Nicholas Hunt, a clothier based in Braithwaite Street in the Dublin Liberties, of whom more will be said shortly.[198] Although the print yard was gone there is evidence that small-scale cotton dyeing and printing continued afterwards. From 1802 to 1805 Thomas Balfe of Milltown, who was described as a calico dyer, leased a small plot of ground in Milltown village 'whereon a cabin lately stood wherein the widow Hanahoe formerly resided'.[199]

According to evidence given to a government inquiry of 1836 concerning the condition of the poor in Ireland, the Irish calico industry continued to flourish until 1810 and then began to decline. Tariff protections against cheap cotton imports from England were reduced successively in 1807, 1814 and 1821. As a result, unemployment rose among workers in the Irish calico industry after 1814, in particular, together with a decrease in wages.[200] Despite these worsening conditions, the first edition of the six-inch OS map shows that a Blue Mill (i.e. a dye mill) was located on the south bank of the River Dodder opposite the Packhorse Bridge close to Millmount Lodge, which indicates that cloth dyeing survived in Milltown into the second quarter of the nineteenth century (Map 15).

By 1843 the old Chappell and Styles dyeing business had long since ceased and the industrial premises was in ruins. In that year a successor in title to the Tandy and Cavanagh lease, James Harvey, let their old 2-acre and 12 perches holding to Patrick Hackett of Milltown, which included 'the material of the old dyeing house for the purposes of building'.[201] Hackett subsequently recycled the materials and built eight cottages which, according to the surveyors for the Griffith's Valuation, were supplied with 'a bleaching green or piece of ground for the use of Mr Hackett's tenants'.[202]

196 *Saunders's Newsletter*, 18 July 1797, p. 3.

197 *Saunders's Newsletter*, 23 February 1799, p. 4, which described the property as Millmount House and Demesne.

198 RD 518/221/341235. The deed of assignment dated 31 August 1799 does not record the price paid by Hunt.

199 RD 571/357/386312, RD 577/248/386567.

200 First report from his Majesty's Commissioners for inquiring into the poorer classes in Ireland: Appendix C, Part II, Report on the City of Dublin and Supplement containing answers to queries, with Addenda to Appendix (A), and Communications, *p. 16 (evidence on combination), H.C. 1836 (35),* xxx (hereafter cited as Poor Inquiry, City of Dublin, 1836).

201 RD 1843/15/78.

202 NAI, VO, OL53661, House Book, Townland of Farranboley 1845, no. 2.

NICHOLAS AND JOHN HUNT'S WOOLLEN MILLS

By the middle of the 1790s the manufacture of cheap woollen cloth had become the dominant industrial activity in Milltown. As discussed earlier in this chapter, Walter Burke and Barnaby Mullen had, by 1800, taken over John Classon's mills on the north bank of the River Dodder and refitted them as woollen mills. At much the same time, Nicholas Hunt and his brother John, both of whom had been admitted to the merchant guild of Shearman in 1794, began acquiring premises on the south bank of the River Dodder.[203] The first opportunity for the Hunts arose when John Heaviside decided to lease his property in Milltown. It seems that Heaviside's pottery business at Milltown had ceased by early 1794 – perhaps the clay was exhausted – and he was then described as an iron founder residing at Luke Street.[204] In any event, on 3 May 1794 Heaviside leased the following property and water rights to Nicholas Hunt for 999 years at a modest annual rent of £50:

1. *the spot of ground ... in Milltown wherein a brass mill foundry stood and whereon Samuel Tonge (?) and John Heaviside have since erected a new mill which was lately in the actual possession of John Heaviside, together with the millrace and millpond thereunto belonging,*
2. *three cabins adjoining the said mill and the ground whereon same are built lately in the possession of John Heaviside or his undertenants,*
3. *all the water proceeding from under the mills formerly called plating mills and then in the possession of James Tandy and Thomas Cavanagh,*
4. *all water that shall naturally flow over the waste gates, but always reserving in said ponds as much water as will be necessary for the use of the said plating mill.*[205]

Essentially, this arrangement was a continuation of the original agreement made in 1724 between William Ford and Robert Randal to share the water resource for their respective brass and paper mills. On taking possession of the premises Nicholas Hunt immediately carried out alterations to the new Heaviside mill buildings. Among other things, the alterations included building new walls and laying five joists across the millrace.[206]

Nicholas Hunt decided to relocate closer to Milltown from his city premises so that he could pay closer attention to his new operations. On 3 May 1794 he executed a lease for lives renewable forever with William, John and Thomas Beeby thereby acquiring 6 acres, 3 roods and 25 perches (plantation measure) of land together with a newly built villa, garden, outhouses and stables.[207] This villa, along with its grounds, was located on the south-west side of Bird Avenue at Windy Arbour, and was called Farranboley Cottage in the mid-nineteenth century, subsequently renamed Ardnabel, and is now called The Manor.[208]

Two years later, Nicholas and John Hunt acquired 8 plantation acres which formed part of the original land leased by Lord Milltown to James Tandy and Thomas Cavanagh in 1764. On 17 November 1796 the brothers William, John and Thomas Beeby, together with John

203 Roll of the Freeman of Dublin City, 1774–1824.

204 RD 472/550/305739.

205 RD 472/550/305739.

206 Bryan Bolger Papers, 23 July 1794 (NAI, MS 2/476/15–16).

207 RD 485/349/305740.

208 Holland, *Clonskeagh*, pp. 191–3.

Heaviside, leased the following property to Nicholas and John Hunt for lives renewable forever at the annual rent of £142 10*s.*:

> *that piece or parcel of ground containing by estimation eight acres or thereabouts together with the dwelling house, iron mills, workshops, three cabins and other improvements erected and made thereon then in the possession of Nicholas Hunt and John Hunt … with liberty of using and taking away from [the] stone quarry next adjoining a small piece of ground demised to Joseph Chappell all such stones as they shall have occasion for in building and improving on the said demised premises and also all mill streams, water courses … to the said premises belonging.*[209]

The dwelling house and the 8 acres attached to it were later named Millmount. The property is shown on the first edition of the OS map just off the Dundrum Road behind Bankside Cottages (Map 15). Its land extended southwards as far as Windy Arbour (Map 18).

Although the Beebys had sold their interest in the 8 acres to clothiers Nicholas and John Hunt, that property was subject to other leasehold interests. To take one example, in October 1801 the executor of John Heaviside's estate, William Heaviside, conveyed a 'one undivided moiety' of the 8-acre property to John and Thomas Beeby, a transaction that is difficult to understand given that the Beebys had disposed of their interest in the same property to Nicholas and John Hunt some five years previously.[210]

The fourth and final piece of the Hunt property jigsaw puzzle was the acquisition by Nicholas Hunt of the Chappell and Styles print yard and mills which, as previously noted, took place at an auction of the bankrupts' leasehold property at Milltown on 27 February 1799. When Joseph Archer visited Milltown at the turn of the nineteenth century, he recorded that Mr Hunt worked two woollen machines there.[211]

FIRE AND BANKRUPTCY

From the turn of the nineteenth century John Hunt assumed a greater commercial prominence than his brother Nicholas. Aside from his new woollen manufacturing mills in Milltown, John had extensive woollen mills at Chapelizod. These mills were burnt down in February 1804, and, as they were uninsured, Hunt had to rebuild them at a personal cost of £20,000. Nonetheless, Hunt's business recovered and he went on to receive first prize premiums from the Farming Society of Ireland in three years' succession for the best manufactured clothing made from Irish wool. Further misfortune befell Hunt when he became bankrupt 'due to the unfortunate failures which took place in July 1812'.[212] As a result, Hunt's stock and goods were put up for sale at two separate auctions which were held in Milltown on 11 January and 15 March 1813. Among the items offered for sale were finished and unfinished woollen cloths, dye-stuffs, four horses, two carts, a jaunting car, a cock of good hay, a post chaise and harness, a few articles of household furniture and 'all the machinery of the mills'.[213] However the woollen mills failed to sell because two years prior to John Hunt's bankruptcy, Nicholas and John Hunt had mortgaged their concerns

209 RD 511/476/332956.

210 RD 540/329/355638.

211 Archer, *Statistical Survey of Dublin*, p. 206.

212 *Freeman's Journal*, 27 January 1815, p. 2. The failures probably relate to banking collapses that occurred in that month.

213 *Saunders's Newsletter*, 9 January 1813, p. 4; 8 March 1813, p. 4.

3 roods of land. Hunt's landlord was Miss Frances Nunn Pounden, who presumably was a descendant of John Heaviside's business partner in the 1770s, the ironmonger Patrick Pounden. Six months later John Hunt assigned this lease to the woollen manufacturer, William Burke, who, as noted earlier, owned the woollen mills opposite on the north bank of the River Dodder.[222]

The last legal interest to be sorted out was the mill holding beside the Packhorse Bridge (the site of the old brass mill), which John Heaviside had leased to Nicholas and John Hunt on 3 May 1794, which they subsequently mortgaged to their sister Alicia Law in 1810.[223] In this case John Hunt and Alicia Law assigned their respective legal interests on 28 January 1822 to John Heaviside's son and executor, William Heaviside, who in turn wrote off a considerable amount of rent that was owed to him.[224] In spite of all this, John Hunt seems to have got back into business once again as he is listed in a Dublin directory for 1824 as resident in Donnybrook, under the entry for Woollen Manufacturers.[225]

The extent of the industrial buildings on the south bank of the River Dodder at Milltown in the early nineteenth century can be seen in a pencil drawing made by the artist Samuel Brocas in about 1820 (Pl. 11).[226] The Dodder and the new bridge, which was built about 1817 as part of a realignment of the Dundrum Road, take up the foreground.[227] The two arches of the superseded Packhorse Bridge are just visible in the background through the single arch of the new bridge. The industrial complex to the left of the bridge comprises three buildings. The smoke billowing out from the two chimneys is probably from the coal-fired boilers that were used to heat the water for the cloth dyeing and bleaching process, or possibly indicates the presence of steam powered spinning or weaving machinery.

WILLIAM AND JOHN LEE'S MARBLE WORKS AND SAW MILLS

As soon as William Heaviside had regained possession of the woollen mills lately worked by John Hunt, he leased the premises to William Lee on 31 January 1822. Lee's lease was for 972 years (the remaining term of the Hunts' 999-year lease of 1794) but at a rent of £22 15*s.*[228] The new rent charged to Lee was less than half of what the Hunts had agreed to pay Heaviside in 1794 (£50). This shows that either a decline in the rent attainable for this type of small industrial premises had set in or that the mills had not been rebuilt after the fire of 1816 (or possibly both).

It is unclear what activity William Lee carried on at Milltown in the 1820s and 1830s because of conflicting evidence in contemporary sources. A newspaper advertisement from 1830 mentions him in connection with the letting of the woollen mills on the north bank of the River Dodder which had lately been in the possession of Jeremiah Haughton, whereas two Dublin directories for 1843 record William Lee of Milltown as being both a builder and a millwright and

222 RD 766/158/519694.

223 RD 472/550/305739, RD 627/6/428188.

224 RD 768/594/521330. The deed recited that John Hunt was entitled to Nicholas Hunt's interest in the premises.

225 Pigot & Co. City of Dublin and Hibernian Provincial Directory (Dublin, 1824), p. 93, column 99.

226 Samuel Brocas, *Two figures on a bridge with single arch at Milltown* (NLI, Prints and Drawings, PD 2084 (TX) 1).

227 Ball and Hamilton, *The Parish of Taney*, p. 222.

228 RD 769/43/521379.

a John Lee as being the proprietor of a marble works at Milltown.[229] William Lee served as a poor law warden for the Rathmines electoral division of the South Dublin Union from 1856 to 1872, but records of his activities in that regard have not survived.[230]

The Griffith's Valuation records from 1845 onwards also confirm that John Lee, who was probably William's brother, was in possession of a saw mill in the townland of Farranboley (i.e. on the south bank of the River Dodder) which was rated at £20.[231] Later OS maps locate the saw mill immediately beside the Packhorse Bridge on the north side of the roadway leading from the bridge to the junction with the Dundrum Road, and opposite a flour mill adjacent to Millmount Lodge (Map 18).

Further information on the Lees' activities is provided by two legal transactions dating from 1849. In November of that year John Lee surrendered his lease to William Heaviside, who in turn leased the mills to John Lee for 940 years at the greatly reduced rent of £6 9*s.* 6*d.*, down from £22 15*s.*[232] The new lease granted to John Lee contained several covenants regulating the water supplying his mills and those of Millmount, including one providing that Lee 'should not raise his water gates so as to cause the water in the millpond to raise more than three feet'. This is another example of the importance of shared water rights and their precise regulation between the various millwrights over the eighteenth and nineteenth centuries.

John Lee fitted out the premises as a marble cutting works and saw mills.[233] Lee's choice of business was a sound one. The huge growth in Catholic church building from the mid-nineteenth century onwards coupled with the expansion of middle-class housing in the Rathmines and Pembroke townships created a big demand for marble altars, columns and mantel pieces, all of which would have been prefabricated to specification at Milltown and erected on the building site.

Saw mills were less complicated, not as labour intensive and required less horsepower compared with the complex machinery and steam engines found in the cotton and woollen mills. It is not surprising, therefore, that saw mills replaced the textile mills as the latter began to fail, beginning in the early nineteenth century. For example, when the historian John D'Alton visited Donnybrook in the 1830s he recorded that 'there were formerly cotton and printing mills erected here, which employed a great proportion of the population; they are now, however, idle, and only about fourteen persons find occupation at the saw mills of Messrs. Wright and Stanley'.[234] In contrast, Waldron's cotton works in Rathgar employed about 100 people and the machinery there was powered by a steam engine of 30 horse power and a water wheel of equal force.[235] Even so, Waldron's cotton mills had ceased operation by 1844 and were later replaced by saw mills in 1856.[236]

---

229 *Dublin Evening Post*, 5 October 1830, p. 1; Pettigrew and Oulton's Dublin Almanac and General Register of Ireland, 1843, p. 818. The Post Office and Annual Directory and Calendar for 1843, p. 300.

230 South Dublin Poor Law Union, Board of Guardians Minute Books A9, December 1855–December 1856, p. 350 and A25, January 1872–December 1872.

231 NAI, VO, OL53661, House Book, Townland of Farranboley 1845, no. 11; Griffith's Valuation, Rateable Valuation of Tenements, Co. Dublin, Barony of Rathdown, Parish of Taney, Townland of Farranboley, 1849, p. 149, at entry no. 11.

232 RD 1849/20/261, RD 1849/20/263.

233 For several years after 1843 the Dublin directories list John Lee as being the proprietor of a marble works and saw mills.

234 D'Alton, *History of County Dublin*, p. 803.

235 D'Alton, *History of County Dublin*, p. 779.

236 Mallet, *Report on the proposed formation of reservoirs on the River Dodder*, p. 14. Saunders's Newsletter, 4 December 1856, p. 3.

After John Lee's death his widow Sarah leased the marble works and saw mills to Thomas Patrick Hackett of Milltown at the annual rent of £15, when they were described as 'the old mill and premises adjoining the old bridge at Milltown'.[237] Hackett converted the buildings into a tenement which was known locally as 'marble hall', in reference to its earlier use under John Lee. Hackett was a publican, landlord and local politician, of whom more is revealed in Chapter 12. The old buildings were eventually demolished in the late 1930s and the area is now an open green space beside the Packhorse Bridge opposite Bankside Cottages.

MILLMOUNT LODGE AND ITS MILLS IN THE SECOND HALF OF THE NINETEENTH CENTURY

The Millmount Lodge and its mills experienced a high turnover in its owners, occupants and activities throughout the nineteenth century. This reflected the fact that the property was made up of three components, not all of which complemented each other. First of all, there was the industrial complex which comprised the mills, offices, millpond, millraces and about half a dozen workmen's houses which later made up the terrace called Bankside Cottages. Secondly, there was the residence called Millmount Lodge and its pleasure grounds located on the Dundrum Road (where the Thorncliffe apartments are now). Millmount Lodge was a comfortable, roomy country residence with two kitchens, two parlours, two sitting-rooms and four bedrooms.[238] Thirdly, there was agricultural land attached to the residence which was from time to time let to local farmers. The entirety of this property – for the sake of convenience, hereafter called Millmount – amounted to 8 acres and 1 rood plantation measure or about 13.5 statute acres when it was surveyed privately in the 1830s.[239]

As noted previously, in 1817 Millmount passed to a middleman landlord, tobacconist James Hevey of Thomas Street, following the departure of John Hunt. No information has emerged of who actually occupied the premises as tenant of Hevey or what activity they carried on at the Millmount mills during his ownership. By 1835 Millmount had come into the possession of another middleman, Richard Charles, a Dublin builder with premises off Great Brunswick Street.[240] Charles sublet Millmount to a James Palmer of Milltown. James Palmer was not listed in the contemporary city directories but he may have been connected with John and Robert Palmer who were corn and flour factors operating out of James's Street in 1835.[241] In any event, James Palmer paid £300 consideration to Richard Charles for the lease (i.e. an entry fine) and also agreed to pay an annual rent of £197, reduced to £140 if Palmer subsequently paid Charles a further sum of £570.[242] The economic rationale behind these financial commitments on Palmer's part is lost to history but both parties ultimately made a bad bargain. Three years later, in 1838, Palmer was in arrears of rent of almost £150 and so he surrendered his lease to Charles on condition that Charles gave up his claim for the rent arrears.[243] As soon as Charles regained possession of Millmount, he placed several newspaper advertisements seeking to lease or

237 RD 1881/11/187.

238 *Saunders's Newsletter*, 29 March 1828, p. 4.

239 RD 1835/14/282.

240 RD 1835/14/282; The Post Office Annual Directory and Calendar for 1843, p. 183.

241 Pettigrew and Oulton's Dublin Almanac and General Register of Ireland 1835, p. 111.

242 RD 1835/14/282.

243 RD 1838/1/167.

sell the Millmount complex, which was then described as Milltown Flour and Oatmeal Mills and Kilns. The premises also included six workmen's cottages, machinery for making starch and blue (dye) and a pair of unused mill stones.[244] Richard Charles eventually succeeded in subletting the industrial buildings, but he retained his leasehold interest in Millmount into the mid-1840s and continued to live in the mill-house with his wife and mother.[245]

In November 1840 an advertisement was placed in the *Dublin Evening Mail* informing its readers that the proprietor of the Milltown mills (i.e. Millmount mills) had opened an office for the sale of 'his patent round-cut oatmeal, also cattle and pig food'.[246] The name of the new millwright was not given, but when the surveyor from the Griffith's Valuation visited Millmount in 1845 he recorded that Richard Charles had sublet the mill and forge to Patrick Coghlan, together with some old houses and a yard. Coghlan in turn had sublet a house on the corner of the Dundrum Road and Bankside Cottages (which is still standing directly opposite Milltown Bridge Road with the nameplate 'The Stores') to James Mackey. The surveyor also recorded that Charles retained land attached to an 'old Blue Mill', thereby indicating that calico bleaching, dyeing and printing activity had ceased in Milltown.[247]

Richard Charles was also the landlord of a bark mill and eight cottages at Windy Arbour which were located immediately to the south of Millmount in the adjacent townland of Churchtown Lower. This mill, which was let to Bartholomew Walker, ground bark which was used in the process of tanning leather.[248] This suggests that Charles had deliberately invested in a corridor of land with mills and housing complexes along the River Slang stretching from Windy Arbour to Milltown, and comprising over 20 statute acres according to the Griffith's Valuation. It is possible that Charles envisaged carrying out speculative building along the Dundrum Road from Milltown to Windy Arbour.

Whatever long-term plans Charles may have had for his property in Milltown were brought to an end in May 1845. In that year Charles lost a court case concerning his lease of Millmount. The press report of the case is very brief, merely advising readers that:

> *This was an action of ejectment on the title, brought for recovery of a moiety of the mill, mill-house, and workmen's cottages situate at Milltown ... the Chief Justice directed the jury to find a verdict for the plaintiff for a moiety of the premises, 6d. damages and 6d. costs, which was accordingly found.*[249]

Charles must have been in breach of the terms of his lease, probably a failure to pay his rent. As a result of losing the case Charles disposed of his interest in Millmount and auctioned off a miscellaneous collection of livestock, equipment and household furniture on 29 October 1845.[250]

244 *General Advertiser for Dublin, and All Ireland*, 10 February 1838, p. 3; 31 March 1838, p. 3; 22 October 1838, p. 3.

245 *Freeman's Journal*, 20 December 1842, p. 3.

246 *Dublin Evening Mail*, 11 November 1840, p. 1. The millwright's name is not given.

247 NAI, VO, OL53661, House Book, Townland of Farranboley 1845, no. 3. The first edition of the six-inch OS map records the Blue Mill at this spot as late as 1843 (Map 15).

248 NAI, VO, OL53663, House Book, Townland of Churchtown Lower 1844, nos 1a an 2a; NAI, VO, OL53661, House Book, Townland of Churchtown Lower 1845, p. 12, no. 1; NAI, VO, OL53660, Tenure Book, Townland of Churchtown Lower 1847, no. 1; Bartholomew Wall and Sons operated as tanners at 31 Mill Street in Dublin's liberties: Pettigrew and Oulton's Dublin Almanac and General Register of Ireland 1845, p. 752.

249 *Freeman's Journal*, 12 May 1845, p. 3.

250 *Freeman's Journal*, 28 October 1845, p. 1.

The auction advertisement is worth transcribing in full because it is a reminder of the ubiquity and variety of farm animals which were part and parcel of everyday life in Milltown in the mid-nineteenth century:

> *To be sold by auction, on tomorrow (Wednesday), the 29th October, 1845, on the premises (adjoining Milltown Bridge), in consequence of the proprietor (Mr Charles) having disposed of the concerns, working horses, drays, carts and harness; a donkey with cart and harness, a market cart and a water carriage, a large boxed cart for grains, a winnowing machine, an oat bruiser, field and garden rollers, filed gates, ladders and boilers, a large [hay] rick cover, a few cows, calves, and pigs; a phaeton for one or a pair of horses (to form a close carriage), a set of pair horse harness, a donkey phaeton, a gig, a new side saddle, two saddles and bridles; also some articles of household furniture, antique tables and chairs, large sized Turkey and Brussels carpets, a few paintings, plated tea urn, candlesticks and branches, a water filter, a number of cement ornaments and miscellaneous lots.*[251]

The penultimate item mentioned in the auction advertisement was 'a number of cement ornaments'. When the Millmount mills were being let in 1852 they included an oven for manufacturing cement, which shows that Richard Charles had been using the mills and kilns to make building materials for his business, as well as garden ornaments.[252] Taken in isolation these details are unremarkable, but their interest derives from the fact that in the late nineteenth and early twentieth centuries that part of Milltown which lay on the south bank of the River Dodder adjacent to the Dundrum Road – chiefly around the Packhorse Bridge, Mowlds Cottages, Dew Drop Inn, Bankside Cottages and Hackett's/Field's Cottages – was known locally as 'Concrete' or 'Concrete Town' (Map 22). The 1901 Census described this local district in the following terms: 'Milltown, now known as Concrete Town, stands on the townland of Farranboley, in which its area and valuation are included; its estimated area is 2 acres.' [253] How the name Concrete came to be applied to this part of Milltown village is not recorded in any oral history. It can only be assumed that the name came into local usage as a result of Richard Charles's cement manufacturing at Millmount mills.

According to the Griffith's Valuation for 1849 the landlord who succeeded Richard Charles at Millmount was a man called Mr Heavey, but by 1855 the Valuation Office cancellation books record that the landlord was a Captain William Harvey.[254] It is quite likely that the two individuals were the same person because the first recorded surname of Heavey could subsequently have been corrected to Harvey rather than the actual landlord being replaced by a separate individual. Evidence to support this view is supplied by a lease of 14 June 1852 whereby James William Harvey of Cloyne, County Cork leased Millmount to Thomas James O'Callaghan.[255]

251 *Freeman's Journal*, 28 October 1845, p. 1.

252 Dublin Corporation Archives, Gilbert Library, Pearce Street, Maxwell Weldon Papers, Ms Ar/add/12/236, location G1/01/212 (Box 11).

253 Census of Ireland 1901, County of Dublin, Table VII, housing and population returns for Concrete Town, p. 34 (CD-ROM, Archive CD Books Ireland, Dublin, 2010).

254 Griffith's Valuation, Rateable Valuation of Tenements, Co. Dublin, Barony of Rathdown, Parish of Taney, Townland of Farranboley, 1849, p. 149, at entry no. 3; VO, Cancellation Books, County Dublin, Barony of Rathdown, Parish of Taney, Electoral Division of Dundrum, 1855–1869, p. 68, at entry no. 3a.

255 Dublin Corporation Archives, Gilbert Library, Pearce Street, Maxwell Weldon Papers, Ms Ar/add/12/236, location G1/01/212 (Box 11).

Harvey's claim to fame was that he had fought in the Battle of Waterloo as a sixteen-year-old recruit to the Coldstream Guards.[256]

After Richard Charles left Milltown Millmount was let to James Henderson who continued to operate the saw mill. As the effects of the Great Famine began to take hold in earnest Henderson saw an opportunity and placed the following notice in *Saunders's Newsletter*:

> *To corn factors, etc – Indian Corn. James Henderson begs to announce to the public that he has lately fitted up his mill at Milltown, near Dublin, where he will grind Indian Corn on moderate terms. Every attention paid to punctuality and dispatch. Apply to the above at Millmount Lodge, Milltown, or at his office, 29 Richmond Street.*[257]

Henderson's tenure at Millmount was brief. Apart from being a member of the Orange Order and one of the petitioners who campaigned for the release of the New Irelander William Smith O'Brien following the failed rebellion in 1848, nothing else is known about him.[258]

Henderson had vacated Millmount by 1852 when, as already mentioned, James William Harvey let the property to Thomas James O'Callaghan. Under the terms of his lease O'Callaghan was required to spend £300 on improvements by 14 June 1855 and to insure the buildings for at least £750 each year. In addition, the lease contained a schedule of fixtures and fittings which illustrate the various uses to which the premises had been put during the difficult famine years. Among other things the inventory mentions:

> *two harrowing (?) machines, three bushing machines, three mill stones ... a sawing mill or machine lately used in conjunction with the flour mill for sawing timber, two step ladders, one machine or oven lately used for manufacturing cement and baking bread, water wheel straps, elevators, iron works and other articles and machinery now on said mill concerns.*

Thomas O'Callaghan lived at Millmount for 35 years, during which time he operated a flour mill.[259] O'Callaghan put Millmount and all of its contents up for auction on 19 September 1887, presumably due to his retirement.[260] The next tenants of Millmount were John and Joseph Kelly, the former being recorded as a customs official.[261] All the evidence indicates that the mills attached to Millmount had ceased working after Thomas O'Callaghan's departure as they are no longer mentioned in the Dublin directories.

Millmount changed hands again in the late 1890s but this time its new owners were to make major changes to the property. As mentioned earlier, Thomas Edmondson had bought the old Gibney flour mill on the north bank of the River Dodder in 1887 and established a flourishing steam laundry business there. When in 1898 an opportunity arose to buy a long leasehold interest in Millmount Edmondson took it as he was anxious to acquire property in Milltown

---

256 *Wexford Independent*, 15 March 1873, p. 2.

257 *Saunders's Newsletter*, 20 October 1846, p. 3.

258 William Smith O'Brien Petition, 1848–49 (NAI, MS CRF 1848/O/16).

259 The Thom's Directories for 1860 (p. 1341) and 1882 (p. 1519) describe O'Callaghan as a corn miller.

260 *Dublin Daily Express*, 16 September 1887, p. 8.

261 Thom's Directory 1892, p. 1550.

where he could house his expanding workforce.[262] While Edmondson was negotiating the lease Millmount was subject to several acts of vandalism which prompted Edmondson to write to the Royal Irish Constabulary (RIC) Inspector in Dundrum on 4 February 1898:

> *Dear Sir*
> *We wish to draw your attention to the want of additional police protection in Milltown village on the County side. We are in negotiation for the purchase of the property known as Millmount, which extends from Windy Arbour down to Milltown village. There has been considerable delay in the completion of the legal documents, and we are therefore not in actual possession of the property. The Milltown people appear to have got the notion that the place is derelict, and that they may do as they like in it. The old mill on the premises has been completely ransacked, timber taken from the floor, and roof, doors of the adjoining cottage carried off, and several metal columns carried out of the yard and we are informed sold as old metal in Henshaws in Clonskeagh. The gate lodge also near Windy Arbour has the door and window taken out of it. We will ask you to be good enough to give special instructions for a watch to be kept with a view to detecting and if needful arresting anyone trespassing. If your men would occasionally enter the premises at the top of Milltown hill, and go quietly through into the old mill premises behind, they would likely drop on some of the culprits. Although we are not in actual possession, I am advised on behalf of the owner to appear and prosecute for him. I may add that I do not ever recollect seeing a number of your force in that immediate neighbourhood.*
> *Thanking you in anticipation for your kind attention in the matter. I am yours faithfully,*
> *Thomas Edmondson.*[263]

Shortly after he took possession of Millmount, Edmondson set up Millmount Lodge as a hostel for girls employed in his laundry who, initially, were not recruited from Milltown. In 1903 the property was let by Edmondson to Thomas Ryan at an annual rent of £45. Sometime later, the main house was renamed Clonbeg and, somewhat confusingly, the adjacent buildings retained the name Millmount (Map 20).[264] Thomas Edmondson was a Quaker and this explains why in 1901 he granted a site on the grounds of Millmount just off the Dundrum Road with a 99-year lease to a builder, and co-religionist, called Samuel Roberts. He built a Tudor-style house on the acre of ground called Ardlevin (Map 20).[265] In due course Edmondson demolished what was left of the derelict mill premises beside the Packhorse Bridge and built four terraced houses on the site that are now part of Bankside Cottages (Pl. 12).

Although the mills at Millmount had been demolished at the turn of the twentieth century the old millrace taken off the River Slang at Windy Arbour and the millpond to the west of Bankside Cottages were left in place because they acted as property boundaries and provided water for livestock that grazed on the Millmount grasslands. The water from the millpond continued to discharge into the millrace on the Dodder bank parallel to the river below the Packhorse Bridge, as is confirmed by a picture painted by Harry Kernoff in 1936.[266] The millrace and the millpond

262 Hearn, *Thomas Edmondson*, pp. 22, 80–3.

263 NAI, Business Records, Dub.56, Dublin Laundry Company, letter book 12 February 1898–16 March 1900, p. 983.

264 Hearn, *Thomas Edmondson*, pp. 80–1.

265 *Irish Times*, 29 March 1952, p. 11; NAI, 1911 Census, Form A, residents for house no. 18, Dundrum Road, Dundrum Electoral Division, Parish of Taney, Farranboley townland, Dublin. Ardlevin is now called Chandos.

266 See illustration in McEntee and Corcoran, *The Rivers Dodder and Poddle*, p. 174.

were eventually filled in when the St Luke's Crescent public housing scheme was built in the late 1940s and the area to its rear landscaped as a public open space by Dublin Corporation.

As for Clonbeg, the Dublin Laundry Company retained a residual amount of the original Millmount Lodge pleasure grounds amounting to 1.5 acres.[267] In 1981 the Dublin Laundry Company applied for planning permission to build flats at Clonbeg. It is not clear if the old house had already been demolished but it may well have been, because the planning applications published in the newspapers did not refer to it.[268] Before these development plans were realised the Dublin Laundry Company went into voluntary liquidation in 1983.[269] The Clonbeg site was eventually redeveloped when the Thorncliffe apartment complex was built on the site in the 1990s.

THE DODDER WEIR AT MILLTOWN AND THE CLONSKEAGH IRON MILLS

Sometime in the eighteenth century a large weir was erected across the Dodder about 100 metres upstream of the Packhorse Bridge (Pl.2). The water taken off the Dodder at this weir was not harnessed to power the mills beside the Packhorse Bridge in Milltown, but was used to power mills half a mile away on the south bank of the Dodder at Clonskeagh (Pl. 13). The millrace is shown definitively on Bernard Scale's map of 1773 (Map 5) and its remnants can still be traced at the north side of the Shi'a Islamic centre (Al Hussain House) beside the pedestrian and cycle path.

In 1789 Lord Trimlestown, whose family had owned the manor of Roebuck for hundreds of years, leased 7 plantation acres and the mill and mill holding of Clonskeagh to Henry Jackson for 99 years at an annual rent of £56 17*s.* 6*d.*[270] Jackson's iron manufacturing business in Clonskeagh and his prominence in the United Irishmen movement have been well documented by Martin Holland in his history of Clonskeagh. For the present purpose, it is worth noting that Jackson expended thousands of pounds in improvements at Clonskeagh which included the construction of the largest millpond on the River Dodder and the realignment of the millrace.[271] The size of these works can be appreciated from a map of 1812 which was drawn up for George Thompson, who had taken over the iron mills and Clonskeagh Castle and its grounds in succession to Henry Jackson (Map 6). The extent of the area covered by the Clonskeagh millpond can be seen from an aerial photograph of the Crampton estate at Clonskeagh Castle taken in about 1950 (Pl. 13).

PROBLEMS WITH THE WATER SUPPLY TO THE MILLS

By the second quarter of the nineteenth century the number of water-powered mills and factories on the Rivers Dodder and Slang began to adversely impact on the amount of water power available from those rivers, especially in the summer months. Several of the contemporary newspaper advertisements went out of their way to reassure prospective purchasers of the sufficiency of the water supply, as the following advertisement from 1802 describing conditions on the River Slang illustrates:

> *Mrs Hall of Milltown will set or sell her interest in the paper mill of Windy Arbour, near Dundrum, with six [plantation] acres of land. There is a constant supply of water; Milltown iron*

267 *Irish Independent*, 13 June 1969, p. 31.

268 *Irish Independent*, 27 August 1981, p. 2; Evening Herald, 10 October 1981, p. 5.

269 *Irish Independent*, 8 June 1983, p. 19.

270 RD 410/399/269912.

271 Holland, *Clonskeagh*, pp. 40–6, 358–9. A comparison of the millponds on the nineteenth-century OSI maps show beyond doubt that the millpond at Clonskeagh was the largest on the River Dodder.

> *mills are on it and Dundrum iron mills worked by it. For particulars inquire of James Thorp at the bleach green, Churchtown.*[272]

The availability of a reliable water supply was also emphasised in the following advertisement which appeared when the Clonskeagh iron mills were put up for auction in November 1834, following the death of the proprietor, William McCaskey:

> *The great iron mills of Clonskeagh, which are very extensive, and well-known as the most effective and complete in Ireland, possessing an advantage of being the manor mill, with a never failing supply of water, having in addition to the river Dodder the advantage of the river [Slang] from Mr Mallet's mills of Dundrum, which empties itself into the race at Milltown ... There are two powerful water wheels, each twelve feet diameter by seven feet wide, one twelve feet diameter by five feet wide, and another twelve feet by three, each possessing a head and fall of sixteen feet and upwards together with a spacious pond from which four feet of water may be drawn ...*[273]

Notwithstanding the bullish advertisement, the problem of irregular water supply on the River Dodder had become acute by the 1840s. Accordingly, in 1843 a number of mill owners held a meeting to consider petitioning the Commissioners of Public Works to build a reservoir on the upper part of the River Dodder to supply water for their mills during the summer months, 'the loss of which leaves many persons unemployed'.[274] The meeting culminated in the publication of the Mallet Report in 1844 which among other things recommended that reservoirs be constructed to provide a secure water supply to the mill owners.[275] Mallet's report provided a very factual account of the problems facing all the mill owners on the Dodder and one section in particular is worth quoting:

> *The principal branches of trade carried on upon the stream [the River Dodder] are evidently prosperous, but all the mill owners complain alike of the uncertainty and deficiency of water. The extreme limits of the statements received by me on this subject are, that, for a period of from two to four months in the year, every mill on the river dependent upon its power is thrown idle for a portion of the day varying from one fourth to one half of the whole time of labour. Thus, then, taking an average of all, it is certain that for one fourth of the year the mills are idle for at least three eights of their time for want of water. The results of this cannot fail to be most injurious to business; the utmost precariousness of power exists as a consequence, for every miller is dependent upon the one above him, who throws him idle the moment he shuts down his sluice to accumulate a head, after having exhausted his own temporary supply. Hence the delay and disappointment in the execution of orders, and consequent loss of trade, unproductive payment of rents and charges, and hands [employees] thrown idle, and either paid for time by the humane employer, for which he receives no return, or left to their own scanty resources, and thus their means of subsistence placed literally at the mercy of the elements. In three cases steam engines are employed to relieve this, and in two others they have been contemplated.*[276]

272 *Saunders's Newsletter*, 31 December 1802, p. 4.

273 *Londonderry Sentinel and North West Advertiser*, 1 November 1834, p. 1.

274 *Freeman's Journal*, 28 June 1843, pp. 1, 3.

275 Robert Mallet, *Report on the proposed formation of reservoirs on the River Dodder* (Dublin, 1844).

276 Mallet, *Report on the Dodder*, p. 16.

Plate 14. Packhorse Bridge, Milltown, c. 1890, Charles Russell Collection (courtesy of South Dublin Libraries)

The Mallet report was never implemented and so the unsatisfactory conditions described above continued unabated. This situation occasionally caused conflict among mill owners. For example, millwrights William Laird and Thomas Murray, who had mills at Rathfarnham, went to court in 1850 over the erection of a weir or dam on a small stream of water (probably the Owendoher) near Rathfarnham Bridge. The jury found for the plaintiff but only awarded Laird 6*d.* damages and 6*d.* costs.[277]

A serious threat emerged in 1858 with potentially catastrophic consequences for mill owners at Milltown and Clonskeagh who relied on the River Slang for their water supply. In that year a private bill proposing the building of water works for Kingstown (Dún Laoghaire), was opposed by several land owners and mill owners with farms and businesses on the south side of the city, in what is now the Dún Laoghaire-Rathdown local authority area. An opposition meeting was held in Dundrum on 29 December 1858 which was attended by all of Milltown's mill owners – John Lee, Thomas J. O'Callaghan and Robert Gibney – as well as local landowner George F. Mowlds.

277 *Freeman's Journal*, 14 May 1850, p. 3; *Dublin Evening Packet and Correspondent*, 14 May 1850, p. 1. Similar litigation involving disputed riparian rights on the River Dodder at Donnybrook occurred in 1837: *Freeman's Journal* 2 December 1837, p. 3.

Plate 15. River Dodder and the Henshaw Ironworks, Clonskeagh, c. 1890, Charles Russell Collection (courtesy of South Dublin Libraries)

The meeting heard that the proposed waterworks – which in the end did not go ahead – would cut off the Little Dargle river and the River Slang, thereby destroying the working of 13 mills unless they switched to steam power at a cost of £5,000 per annum.[278]

The large millpond at Clonskeagh (Pl. 13) required a considerable amount of water to be taken off the Dodder at the Milltown weir in order to power the mill wheels. The consequences of this can be seen in a couple of photographs taken one summer morning at Milltown and Clonskeagh in about 1890.[279] In the first photograph the bed of the River Dodder below the Packhorse Bridge at Milltown has almost run dry while the water is being taken off the river at the Milltown weir to fill the Clonskeagh millpond (Pl. 14). Later, after the sluice gates had been closed at the Milltown weir, the normal water flow was restored to the Dodder while the millpond fed the mill wheels at the Clonskeagh ironworks, as shown in the second photo (Pl.

278 *Freeman's Journal*, 30 December 1858, p4; *Dublin Daily Express*, 31 December 1858, p. 2.

279 The photographs are part of a series of views of Glenasmole and the River Dodder valley taken by George Russell in about1890 and which are preserved in South Dublin County Library, Tallaght, as part of the Patrick Healy Collection. The inclusion of the Bohernabreena reservoir dates them no earlier than 1887 when the Rathmines township waterworks became operational.

15). At the time the photograph was taken the iron mills were owned by Alfred Henshaw, who lived in St Philip's in Milltown (now Alexandra College).

The experiences related above contrast with the legal rights and obligations in respect of water (riparian rights) which in theory were enjoyed by the millowners. According to Halsbury's Laws of England:

> *Where a person has acquired the right to abstract water from a natural channel for a particular purpose, he cannot use it for other purposes, or increase the amount he takes. Thus, if he has acquired the right to have a pond replenished from a river, he may cleanse the pond, but he must not enlarge it, so that thereby a greater quantity of water be taken from the river. Similarly, if he has the right to take water by a channel of a certain size, he may not enlarge it so as to divert more water to the prejudice of another proprietor. Every riparian owner may divert the water of a stream for purposes in connexion with his land, or for other purposes; but he is bound to return the water which he has diverted into the stream again before it leaves his land substantially undiminished in volume and unaltered in character; for a lower riparian owner, subject to the rights of an upper owner, is entitled to have the water flowing in the natural bed of the stream come to him unaltered in quality and quantity, and to come to his land in its ordinary and accustomed channel.*[280]

The difficulties with water supply from the Rivers Dodder and Slang were never ameliorated or resolved. It is difficult to gauge what beneficial effects the construction of the Rathmines township waterworks in the Glenasmole valley in the 1880s had on the water supply to the mill owners on the River Dodder, notwithstanding that the lower reservoir was specifically designated to compensate the mill owners by providing 2.45 million gallons per day to the river. Indeed, the year in which the Rathmines water supply commenced, 1887, was one of driest recorded on the Dodder.[281] Writing in 1901, the historian John Christopher FitzAchary remarked that the Dodder at Donnybrook 'seems to be becoming inert, as though it were exhausted by the amount of labour imposed upon it'. [282] By the turn of the twentieth century most of the water-powered mills on the Dodder had ceased operation or had been reconfigured for other purposes not necessitating water power, such as those at Milltown and Dartry which were used for laundry and dry cleaning. Only the Henshaw iron mills at Clonskeagh were possibly still using water-powered machinery in the Edwardian age.

QUARRYING AND LIME PRODUCTION IN MILLTOWN IN THE EIGHTEENTH AND NINETEENTH CENTURIES

The quarrying of calp limestone from the river bed of the Dodder at Milltown in the sixteenth century has been discussed in Chapter 3. This abundance of calp in Milltown and along many other parts of the River Dodder encouraged extensive quarrying operations that were carried on, in some instances, for centuries. Indeed, calp on both sides of the banks of the River Dodder was quarried between Rathgar and Donnybrook at different periods from the sixteenth century to the middle of the nineteenth century and calp quarries are a

280 Earl of Halsbury, *The Laws of England: Being a complete statement of the whole law of England* (1st Edition, London, 1914), vol. XXVII, p. 427 (paragraph 847) and p. 428 (paragraph 853).

281 See Chapter 16 of McEntee and Corcoran, *The Rivers Dodder and Poddle*, for a comprehensive history of this great Victorian engineering project.

282 *Rathmines News*, 21 December 1901.

prominent feature of nineteenth-century OS maps (Maps 15, 18 & 19).[283] In the eighteenth and nineteenth centuries there were at least two quarries in the vicinity of Milltown. The nineteenth-century OS maps show one quarry located on the south bank of the Dodder close to Classon's Bridge on what is now Patrick Doyle Road. The second quarry, which was older and larger, was located on the north bank of the Dodder between Milltown and Clonskeagh at a site now known as Scully's Field (Map 18). The lime kiln adjoining this quarry was built beside the old Clonskeagh Lane where it forded the north bank of the river at a point about 100 metres west of Clonskeagh Bridge (Map 9).[284]

In the eighteenth and nineteenth centuries the Leeson estate deliberately retained control of all quarrying, mining rights and rights of way in their leases to tenants at Milltown. The north bank quarry at Milltown (Scully's Field) was very extensive judging from the OS maps. It too was owned by the Leeson estate in the eighteenth and nineteenth centuries. In 1725 Joseph Leeson set out detailed conditions as to the use of his quarry in a sub-lease as follows:

> *covenant ... against digging for stones, quarrying or raising any stones off the premises save what should be needful and necessary to expend and build on the said premises ... and not otherwise, and in the case they or any of them [lessees] shall make or dig any new quarry, that they shall immediately, before any such quarry shall be made, build a wall of lime and stone along the side of the river of Milltown, so far as such new quarry shall be made, such wall to be of such height, strength and thickness, so as at all times to prevent the river from overflowing, washing away or doing any damage to the said premises ... and in default ... pay the sum of five pounds per annum as an increased rent ...*[285]

In 1772 the natural historian, John Rutty, observed that 'near Milltown Bridge [Packhorse Bridge] was one of the best quarries in the county'. [286] The quarries at Milltown were sometimes operated in a dangerous and reckless manner, as was reported in the newspapers in the 1770s:

> *Last Friday as a labourer was working in a quarry at Milltown, the earth fell upon him, under which he lay a considerable time, and in getting him out a pick was struck in his leg, his jaw bone broke to pieces, and most of the teeth forced out of the sockets, his head and other parts greatly bruised. He is under care of Dr Rowley, and in a fair way of recovery.*[287]
> *The Rathfarnham division of the grand jury of the County Dublin ... have ordered a presentment to be drawn against John Paget, for quarrying under the high road leading from Milltown to Rathmines, and leaving an unguarded perpendicular, a precipice of 30 or 40 feet deep, which passengers are in the utmost danger of falling into.*[288]

283 Holland, *Clonskeagh*, pp. 370–1; G.W. Lamplugh, *The geology of the country around Dublin: Memoirs of the Geological Survey of Ireland* (HMSO, 1903), p. 9.

284 An undated pencil drawing of the lime kiln attributed to the Brocas family of artists is preserved in the NLI: NLI ET A353.

285 NAI, Landed Estates Court Rental, vol. 77, no. 13, 'In the matter of the estate of Maria Moyles, owner, to be sold on 2 March 1880', lot 3 (conditions of sale).

286 John Rutty, *An essay towards a natural history of the county of Dublin* (2 vols, Dublin, 1772), ii, p. 93.

287 *Freeman's Journal*, 5 December 1772, p. 2.

288 *Freeman's Journal*, 7 January 1773, p. 3.

Lime kilns went hand in hand with calp quarries and two kilns were built in Milltown and Clonskeagh in the eighteenth century beside the quarries.[289] Lime kilns were built for agricultural and building purposes, to neutralise acidic soils and to make lime mortar, a bonding agent used in construction. The process of making lime requires limestone with upwards of 50–90 per cent calcium carbonate (its main constituent) and involves burning the stone (calcining) to create calcium oxide, commonly called quicklime. The quicklime is then mixed with water and converted into calcium hydroxide in a process called slaking. Calcium hydroxide (slake lime) is the active ingredient used to neutralise the acidity of soil. The benefits of liming soil can last for several years provided it is not overdone, as otherwise excessive liming exhausts soil nutrients.[290] An enormous amount of lime was, however, required to do the job properly. According to Joseph Archer in 1801:

> *A county Dublin farmer need not hesitate at laying on a hundred and fifty barrels of lime to an acre, each barrel near five cubic feet. I mention this large quantity for one reason, that almost all the limestone I have seen in this county appears of a very impure nature, consequently requires to be used copiously.* [291]

Archer's views were generally supported by his critic, Heley Dutton, who opined in 1802 that:

> *In this county, and, I believe, in general through Ireland, lime is used in such small quantities, as often to be of little benefit: it has been frequently brought into disrepute by being used on poor worn out soils, totally deprived of any of those substances proper for the action of the lime; and not infrequently, on the strength of the liming, another crop is taken from [the] ground, already exhausted by corn crops.*[292]

Essentially, the experts recommended that much more lime needed to be used in order for it to be effective. This may explain why three lime kilns were erected in the late eighteenth century in Clonskeagh and Ranelagh.[293] In 1787 Michael Tisdall of Leeson Street, lime burner, sold his lease of 4 acres, 3 roods and 9 perches of land straddling the townlands of Milltown and Clonskeagh, where he had recently built a lime kiln, to Joseph Madden of Donnybrook, publican, for £160.[294] Tisdall's lime kiln was built on the north bank of the Dodder about 100 metres west of the Clonskeagh Bridge, and is shown on the Thompson map of 1812 (Map 6). The precise locations of the two lime kilns built in Ranelagh in 1793 are unknown although one of them was close to Mount Pleasant Avenue.[295] Lime burning was criticised for the noxious smoke emitted from the kilns and the editor of the *Freeman's Journal* deplored the developments in Ranelagh:

289 RD 8/218/2640, RD 386/361/258792.

290 Rynne, *Industrial Ireland*, p. 157; Muiris O'Sullivan and Liam Downey, 'Lime kilns', *Archaeology Ireland*, 19, no. 2, issue 72 (Summer 2005), p. 21.

291 Archer, *Statistical Survey of the County Dublin*, p. 75.

292 Dutton, *Observations on Mr Archer's Statistical Survey*, p. 93. Neither Archer nor Dutton mention what fuel was typically used to burn the lime in the kilns.

293 RD 386/361/258792; *Freeman's Journal*, 8 October 1793, p. 4.

294 RD 386/361/258792.

295 'Survey of part of the farm of St Sepulchre by Brassington and Greene, 1826' (NAI, MS 2574).

> *Two large lime kilns lately built upon the west side of Milltown Road, near Ranelagh, and now at work, are become a most dreadful annoyance to all that neighbourhood. If execrations could have any effect, the proprietors of these pernicious volcanoes might expect no success in their speculation, as the inhabitants of that neighbourhood are hourly sending them forth in abundance, against those destructive nuisances, and destroyers of their health.*[296]

The nuisance caused by lime kilns in the Dublin area was recognised to a certain extent by legislation which in 1786 forbade the building of lime kilns within 20 yards of a public road in County Dublin.[297] The two Ranelagh lime kilns eventually gave way to the rising property development in that district in the second and third decades of the nineteenth century.

The quarrying and lime manufacturing activity on the south bank of the River Dodder did not last beyond the mid-nineteenth century. A coroner's inquest into a death at the lime kiln in Milltown on the south bank of the River Dodder in December 1842 makes a very brief mention of the lime burner and his son (Patrick Callaghan) which would suggest that the amount of employment at the kiln and the adjacent quarry was relatively modest.[298] A few years later the site was probably rendered useless by the extensive engineering works when the railway viaduct cut across the River Dodder valley in the 1850s. By the mid-1840s the quarrying and lime-burning activity between Milltown and Clonskeagh on the north bank of the Dodder had apparently ceased. In 1847 a surveyor for the Griffith's Valuation noted that seven houses had been built 'in an old quarry a portion of which around the houses is waste and used in common as a yard and for drying clothes'.[299] The mention of drying clothes shows that women living in the cottages were earning their living as washerwomen, some of whom advertised their services.[300]

In the late 1850s the *Dublin Builder* and the *Freeman's Journal* criticised Dublin Corporation for using Welsh slate to pave the city's streets rather than procuring granite or limestone locally, and both papers opined that the limestone available at Milltown was of a sufficient quality to pave Dublin's streets.[301] This publicity seems to have borne fruit, for the Clonskeagh quarry was reopened in 1860. In that year a William Ward of Ballsbridge took a lease for 31 years of 4 acres and 8 perches of property straddling the townlands of Clonskeagh and Milltown comprising the quarry fields and 19 cottages, 15 of which were situated in Clonskeagh townland with the remainder located in Milltown townland.[302] In August 1862 Ward placed an advertisement in the *Freeman's Journal* looking to hire a 'locomotive engine' for pumping water out of the quarry.[303] By November 1862 William's brother Patrick Ward, a lime burner of Bath Avenue, had acquired the lease and he in turn assigned the quarry and cottages for £50 to

296 *Freeman's Journal*, 8 October 1793, p. 4.

297 'An Act for making, widening, and repairing public roads in the County of Dublin, and for repealing parts of several Acts formerly made for that purpose' (26 Geo. III, c. XIV, s. 69 (Dublin, 1786)).

298 *Freeman's Journal*, 20 December 1842, p. 3.

299 NAI, VO, OL70088, Quarto Book, Townland of Milltown, 1847, p. 209, nos 27–33.

300 *General Advertiser for Dublin, and All Ireland*, 29 July 1848, p. 1.

301 *Freeman's Journal*, 26 April 1858, p. 4; *Dublin Builder*, 3 January 1859, p. 3.

302 RD 1860/36/257.

303 *Freeman's Journal*, 5 August 1862.

Thomas Byrne of Simmonscourt.[304] In January of the following year, an insolvent dairyman of Ranelagh, J.J. Carroll, was reported to have worked the quarry in partnership with other persons and a few years later, on 24 November 1869, two workmen were reported to have been injured while blasting stone in the quarry.[305] Following Byrne's death his executors auctioned the quarry lease in March 1878, when it was described as containing:

> *a fourteen horse power engine, boiler, and connections, working a double action pump able to discharge three tons [of] water per minute; weight house and machine, blasting and quarry tools, windlass, cranes, hand pump, lorry etc*[306]

By the early 1880s quarrying and lime-burning activity had apparently ceased completely at Milltown and Clonskeagh. The disused quarry became a considerable source of danger to local children for years afterwards. On 19 December 1886 two local boys, Thomas and Patrick McLoughlin, aged twelve and thirteen respectively, were drowned while playing on ice on the surface of the quarry pond.[307] The two boys were buried in Taney grave yard with their nine-month-old brother John.[308] Ten years later, in November 1896 the Rathmines township commissioners took a lease of the quarry for 10 years to use as a refuse depot and for dumping municipal refuse into the quarry hole.[309] This resulted in heavy traffic of horse and carts turning left off Milltown Road at the bottom of the hill and thence passing the front of Strand Cottages directly opposite the River Dodder which was part of an open space beside the river bank called 'The Strand'. Children played at this dangerous traffic spot and as a consequence three separate child fatalities occurred in August 1899, August 1900 and October 1902.[310] The Rathmines and Rathgar Urban District Council (as it had become in 1898) stopped dumping rubbish at Milltown when the council bought a refuse destructor in 1904, but this was too late for the parents of the deceased children.[311]

The site of the old quarry comprising over 5 acres was purchased by John Scully of 8 Strand Terrace in 1930 and it is from him that the name 'Scully's Field' originated.[312] The site has been derelict waste ground for decades and awaits redevelopment.

CONCLUSION

A wide variety of industrial activity was carried on at Milltown in the eighteenth and nineteenth centuries to supply the growing needs of Dublin. The nature of these activities fluctuated with the fortunes of the entrepreneurs and industrialists who tried to earn a living on the banks of the Dodder. Some businesses were successful and others were failures. An expert witness to the House of Commons Select Committee on Industries (Ireland) Report of

304 RD 1862/35/293 (Assignment dated 1 November 1862).

305 *Saunders's Newsletter*, 29 January 1863, p. 2; 25 November 1869, p. 2.

306 *Freeman's Journal*, 17 March 1878, p. 2.

307 *Freeman's Journal*, 21 December 1886, p. 6.

308 Ball and Hamilton, *Parish of Taney*, p. 50.

309 Recital in a 35-year lease held by Mathew O'Neill of Milltown: RD 1897/47/173. *Rathmines News*, 8 August 1896, p. 3.

310 *Rathmines News*, 12 August 1899, p. 4; 26 August 1899, p. 5; 21 October 1899, p. 5; 4 August 1900, p. 5; 4 October 1902, p. 4.

311 *Rathmines News*, 5 March 1904, p. 3.

312 RD 1930/44/192.

1885 remarked that several years previously there had been 28 mills on the River Dodder but that most of them were now idle.[313] The reasons behind these outcomes need to be explored more fully through a detailed investigation of all the industries which located themselves on the banks of the river and its tributaries during the period under review. Nonetheless, as far as Milltown is concerned, business success or failure can be ascribed to a number of factors. In no particular order of importance these include individual business acumen and entrepreneurship (John Heaviside and Thomas Edmondson), risk taking and problems with credit supply (John Classon and John Hunt), occasions of *force majeure* such as fires (John Hunt and Mrs Burke), floods (Samuel Moore) and droughts (Obadiah Willans), macro-economic events such as the Famine and the removal of protective tariffs (Samuel Moore), obsolescence (especially in the case of quarrying and lime-burning activity) and excessive water extraction from the River Dodder and its tributaries (Henshaw).

Finally, the industrialisation of Milltown which grew apace towards the end of the eighteenth century coincided with it falling out of favour as a residential location of choice for the nobility and gentry, which hitherto had been the case in the mid-eighteenth century. As a result, Milltown became a village predominantly populated by a Catholic working-class who were socially, politically and economically isolated from the Protestant professional classes who lived behind the boundary walls and gate lodges of their big houses perched above the village and further afield on the Dundrum Road. ■

313 Tony Farmar, *Privileged Lives: A social history of middle-class Ireland 1882–1989* (Dublin, 2010), p. 36.

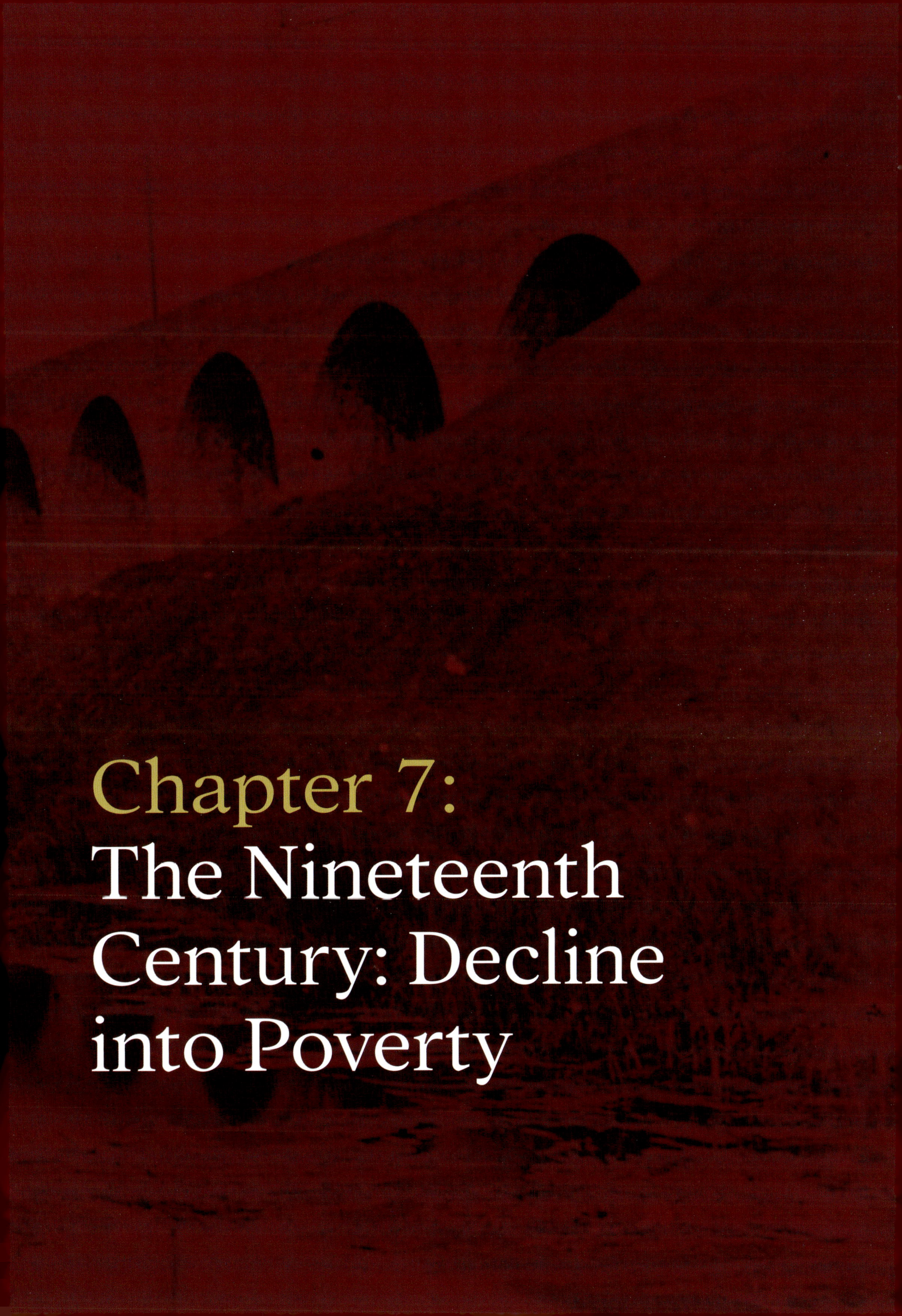

Chapter 7: The Nineteenth Century: Decline into Poverty

Chapter 7: The Nineteenth Century: Decline into Poverty

INTRODUCTION

The prosperity that Milltown benefited from in the eighteenth century in terms of industrial development and villa building was absent in the nineteenth century. Instead, a gradual malaise affected Milltown which in general terms reflected the growing poverty in early nineteenth-century Ireland that culminated in the Great Famine, a subject that is dealt with separately in Chapter 8 as regards its impact on Milltown. Other national developments and events that impinged on Milltown's experience, such as the introduction of the national school system and the Fenian Rising of 1867, are given individual treatment in Chapters 9 and 10.

This chapter reviews national and local events and developments in the political, religious, municipal, health and social spheres which influenced the lives of people living in Milltown. Taken individually and in isolation, each topic is too specialised to be obviously important, but when they are considered collectively one can recognise the emergence of a more sophisticated society and the gradual integration of Milltown into the wider Victorian milieu of the nineteenth century.

THE EARLY YEARS OF THE NINETEENTH CENTURY

Since the late eighteenth century, the working-classes had been settling in increasing numbers in cabins close to the factories and mills along the Dodder and Slang River valleys at Dartry, Classon's Bridge, Milltown, Clonskeagh and Windy Arbour. The emergence of a new suburban proletariat changed the demographics and atmosphere of these districts, which thereby became unequivocally working-class. In the case of Milltown, the increasing numbers of industrial operatives replaced the nobility and gentry who had previously, in the second and third quarters of the eighteenth century, been attracted to the locality for health and recreational purposes. Some indication of this trend can be detected in the property advertisements for Milltown after 1800, in particular those published by the *Saunders's Newsletter* newspaper where there is a noticeable drop off in the frequency of advertisements for villa lettings at Milltown in the first decade of the nineteenth century compared to the last quarter of the eighteenth century.[1]

Signs of stagnation are evident in 1809 when a middleman landlord, a brewer called Michael Lowry, advertised for sale a lease for 900 years of the following property on the south side of the main street in Milltown village:

> *About 200 feet of building ground in Milltown, on which are newly erected two small lodges and a building in the rere fit for a factory, with a walled in garden with the best fruit trees; also a small field laid down with barley and grass seeds.*[2]

Six months later the property was still unsold when a new advertisement advised that the garden was to be sold to clear the ground for building.[3] In the absence of a sale Lowry apparently built several labourers' cottages on the land which he re-advertised in October 1810 as follows:

> *A small garden, with several small houses and buildings in Milltown, near Dundrum, to be let for 900 hundred years. Inquire of M. Lowry, Windsor Ale Brewery, Crane Street, Thomas Stree*

Thus, from the early 1800s small cottages, or cabins as they were contemporaneously called, came to dominate the streetscape and housing stock of Milltown village, particularly on its south side. This trend shows how embedded the middleman landlord system had become in Milltown village by 1800 through fragmentation of holdings and multiple sub-lettings, where the emphasis now was to generate rental income for the middleman via higher-density low-quality housing, without any of the constraints imposed on tenants by the Leeson estate in the early to mid-eighteenth century.

The second decade of the nineteenth century was an extremely volatile and challenging one at both national and local level. As noted in the previous chapter, millwright John Hunt went bankrupt in July 1812 and two years later his premises were destroyed by an accidental fire. Undoubtedly these dismal events caused great privation among the local families who became unemployed as a result of these calamities.

Nationally, 1812 was a year when provisions (basic foodstuffs) were at a very high price. In response, the Protestant parishioners of Taney, which included that part of Milltown on the south bank of the Dodder, organised a relief fund which raised over £184 from the local gentry. In June 1814 the Taney parish select vestry held a meeting to consider what measures could be adopted as might be best calculated to afford the poor permanent relief.[5] Given these reported conditions it is difficult to comprehend the timing of an initiative launched in January 1816 to establish a local savings bank for the poorer classes of Dundrum and its vicinity, as reported in the *Freeman's Journal*:

1 Five separate villa lettings were advertised during the first decade in *Saunders's Newsletter* of 29 July 1803, p. 4; 12 July 1804, p. 3; 11 March 1808, p. 4; 16 March 1809, p. 4; 19 July 1810, p. 4.

2 *Freeman's Journal*, 23 June 1809, p. 9.

3 *Saunders's Newsletter*, 16 December 1809, p. 4.

4 *Saunders's Newsletter*, 20 October 1810, p. 4.

5 Ball and Hamilton, *The Parish of Taney*, pp. 206–7.

Savings Banks. It will be perceived by the following, that the people of Dundrum and its vicinity already enjoy the benefits of one of these admirable institutions. We congratulate them on the circumstance. For the promptitude as well as liberality of the arrangements which have been adopted, great praise is due to the trustees and secretaries, as well as the Rev. Richard Ryan the [Catholic] curate of Taney:- Dundrum Savings Bank will be open every Wednesday from ten o'clock to one for the purpose of enabling servants, labourers, mechanics etc to lay by money on the following terms:

Any sum will be taken
All persons withdraw their money whenever they choose.
When any person's deposits amount to ten shillings, interest will be allowed at the rate of 5 per cent, which will be one halfpenny a month for every ten shillings.
At the end of every year the interest will be added to the principal of each person, and interest allowed for the next year on the whole sum.
N.B. Sixpence a week laid by for twenty years will make forty-three pounds.
Trustees. Thomas Sherlock, esq. Dundrum, W.C. Hogan, esq, Milltown. Secretaries. George Thompson, esq. Clonskeagh Castle, Rev. R. Ryan, Dundrum.[6]

POVERTY, PESTILENCE AND SCANDAL

The hope expressed in the advertisement that individuals might save regularly for a 23-year period was very optimistic, if not naïve, on the part of the promotors given the precariousness of life and livelihoods in nineteenth-century Ireland. This reality was brought home when, following bad weather and a poor harvest in 1816, a national epidemic of typhus and relapsing fever broke out in 1817 which lasted for two years. These highly contagious diseases were spread by lice and aided by the crowding together of the poor, who were badly clad and lived in squalid housing conditions.[7]

The authorities' response to the epidemic in Dublin was to set up parish committees in January 1818 which were required to appoint medical officers to inspect their respective parishes and report back to a general medical committee. Milltown, Clonskeagh and Classon's Bridge were grouped together as number two district of St Peter's parish. The medical officers inspected these locations during the first week of February 1818 and reported back to the general committee as follows:

Milltown. Seven cases of fever occurred of whom two were sent to the House of Industry. There were six houses whose inhabitants required particularly to be cleansed from infection. To five persons straw was ordered; and to three houses white washing. Many of the dwellings were in a very dirty state especially at number 81, an obstructed sewer forming a dangerous nuisance was observed.
Clonskeagh. One case of fever. The houses from no. 1 to no. 15 were in remarkably good order, and the inhabitants cleanly; from no. 15 to no. 25, the houses had bad straw roofs, and were liable to under water from the soaking of dung hills; from no. 15 to no. 40, the inhabitants were in great distress for want of employment; every house in Milltown and Clonskeagh was inspected.
Classon's Bridge. No fever.[8]

---

6 *Freeman's Journal*, 6 January 1816, p. 3.

7 Joseph Robbins, *The miasma: Epidemic and panic in nineteenth century Ireland* (Dublin, 1995), pp. 32, 38–42.

8 *Freeman's Journal*, 6 February 1818, p. 2.

Given that contemporary medical science did not understand how typhus and relapsing fever originated and spread, the treatment prescribed to patients and the remedial actions taken by the authorities could do little to arrest the disease or improve the condition of the infected. In spite of these limitations the local medical officers were able to report a more benign situation at Milltown a month later:

> *No new case of fever. Hannah Tool [sic] and Christian Tool have returned to Milltown convalescent from the House of Industry. Six of this family, which consists of seven individuals, have now suffered under fever within the last two months. This single fact should put the inhabitants of Milltown on their guard against giving credit to the unfounded and deceptive assertions in some of the public prints, that the village has been entirely free of fever.*[9]

The third and final publicly published report of the St Peter's parish committee for the prevention of fever presented mixed conditions prevailing in Milltown during March 1818:

> *Three persons were found labouring under fever in Milltown. 1st, Eleanor Brown, on the 4th of March she was removed to Sir P. Dunne's Hospital and attention paid to disinfecting her clothes and bedding. 2nd. A child in the same family who had mild fever on 20 March and subsequent days and is at present convalescent. 3rd. Collins was found labouring under fever on the 28th; he declined going into hospital; the foreman of the factory in which he worked undertook to have his sons, who slept in the same room, separated from him. Clonskeagh and Classon's Bridge are free from fever.*[10]

By February 1819 the typhus epidemic was on the wane and it petered out later that year. A less severe typhus epidemic broke out in Dublin in 1826 at a time of exceptional unemployment and deprivation in Dublin's Liberties, but there are no records of any illness or fatalities in Milltown at that time.[11]

The poverty and general distress described above led to an increase in reports of burglary and cow stealing in the Milltown area from 1816 onwards, all of which point to a society under social and economic stress.[12] The malign experiences of the second decade of the nineteenth century increased tensions between the poor and the privileged classes of Dublin society which occasionally resulted in outbreaks of violence, as the following report from the *Freeman's Journal* of 1820 illustrates:

> *Last Sunday a very respectable party of our fellow citizens, consisting of several families amounting to upwards of forty persons, mostly females and children, dines at the Dargle in the County Wicklow, and on their return home, when they arrived at Milltown about nine o'clock, were assailed in a dreadful manner by a gang of ruffians who issued without their coats from a dancing house in that village. They instantly attacking the party, dragged them indiscriminately from the coaches and from off the cars and*

9 *Freeman's Journal*, 7 March 1818, p. 3.

10 *Freeman's Journal*, 3 April 1818, p. 3.

11 Robbins, *The miasma*, pp. 59–61.

12 *Freeman's Journal*, 13 March 1816, p. 4 (gang of burglars in Cullenswood); *Saunders's Newsletter*, 4 March 1819, p. 3 (cow stealing and maiming at Dunville, Ranelagh by 'some villains supposed to be from the neighbourhood of Milltown'); *Saunders's Newsletter*, 6 July 1819, p. 2 and 8 July 1819, p. 2 (theft of property at Counsellor John Crosbie Graves' house at Milltown); *Saunders's Newsletter*, 15 December 1820, p. 3 (theft of clothes from Patrick Lynch's cabin in Milltown).

maltreated them in a dreadful way. A few gentlemen who were of the party were beaten and cut most severely, and some of them owed the preservation of their lives to their wives and children who threw themselves on their prostrate bodies. The only cause that can be assigned for this outrage, is an altercation which took place at Windy Harbour between one of the gentleman's servants and a person on the road; and the latter was heard to exclaim, 'before you get to town you shall be well paid.' That this threat had some connection with the outrage may be inferred as before the attack was attempted a whistle was heard three or four times, upon which these fellows rushed out. We understand this affair will [lead to] a legal investigation. Are not dancing and drinking parties in public houses, on the Sabbath day, violations of the law? There is a short path across the fields from Windy Harbour to Milltown.[13]

The social problems associated with excessive alcohol consumption on Sundays by the working class was a particular concern for the middle and professional classes of Dublin. Following the formation of the 'Association for preventing the Profanation of the Lord's Day' in August 1818, the select vestry of St Peter's parish appointed 50 overseers from among 'the respectable inhabitants' of the parish to enforce the Sabbatarian laws then in force, 'particularly by the superintendance over public houses'. William C. Hogan of Fairyland, Milltown, was appointed as an overseer but how he was expected to enforce the law in the absence of an adequate police force was not explained.[14] Depending on one's viewpoint, anti-social behaviour of a different sort took place early one morning in March 1821 when the *Freeman's Journal* reported that 'a pugilistic context took place on Monday morning in Milltown fields at seven o'clock in the presence of several hundred spectators. The parties were Malone, a slater, and Collins, a farrier.'[15] The paper described the 28-minute fight in detail, including the decisive eleventh round in which:

Malone showed his superior mode of fighting by repeatedly planting his hits on his adversary's head, from which blood flowed copiously; the men got into a heavy rally, by which Collins was hit down and did not wish to come any more ... There has not been a better fight witnessed for some time. The good order and decorum that prevailed all through the fight was highly praiseworthy to the spectators who dispersed immediately and seemed to be highly pleased with the fight. Malone intends giving his friends of the Fancy a treat at the Cock Pit, in Clarendon Street, on Monday next, the 19th instant. [16]

The report of the sports journalist could just as easily be replicated today to describe the mixed martial arts phenomena of twenty-first century Ireland.

The 1820s were largely unremarkable as far as the history of Milltown is concerned. In 1900 a claim was made by the author of a history of Dublin's Catholic cemeteries that in the late 1820s land at Milltown was acquired by the Catholic Cemeteries Committee to provide a burial ground for Catholics in the event that capacity ran out at the Golden Bridge cemetery, which had opened in 1828. The catalyst to these acquisitions by the Cemeteries Committee was a Burial Act of 1824 which allowed the internment of Catholics in Church of Ireland cemeteries but forbade Catholic clergy from officiating at the graveside of the burial. Without providing any names or locations the author claimed that after land in Milltown had been acquired, 'an

13 *Freeman's Journal*, 20 July 1820, p. 2.

14 *Freeman's Journal*, 7 September 1818, p. 2.

15 *Freeman's Journal*, 14 March 1821, p. 3.

16 *Freeman's Journal*, 14 March 1821, p. 3.

influential parson in that locality took an active part in obtaining signatures against the scheme. The costly machinery of the Court of Chancery was set in motion; an injunction was granted on the grounds that neighbouring inhabitants objected, the acquired land was abandoned, and the [Catholic Cemeteries] Committee lost heavily on the transaction.'[17] It has proved impossible to prove or disprove this account. Neither the Registry of Deeds, contemporary newspapers nor the correspondence of Daniel O'Connell provide any evidence to support the claim. On the other hand, a potential candidate for the 'influential parson' who supposedly opposed the plan was the Rev. John Clarke Crosthwaite who was living in Vergemount House, Clonskeagh (now the site of Clonskeagh Hospital), in the 1830s.[18] Another remote possibility is that some land in Milltown was acquired by contract (but not subsequently registered) from the earl of Milltown following a publicly advertised sale – apparently aborted – of his Dublin city and county freehold estate in October 1827.[19]

In contrast to the alleged cemetery debacle, a sensational scandal involving a scion of an old Milltown landowning family, George Frederick Mowlds, was the much-publicised elopement of his wife with 23-year-old John Joseph Pim in November 1824. The offending pair were later apprehended in Dunmore, County Waterford, while waiting to flee to England on the steam packet. Pim, who was said to have been at least 10 years younger than his paramour, was lodged in Waterford gaol under both the civil and criminal process. George Frederick Mowlds was reported to have 'received an additional pang from the discovery, that the base betrayer of his peace and happiness, was his bosom friend'.[20]

Mowlds was a practising solicitor who lived at 2 North Cumberland Street. His legal practice frequently took him away from home on circuit which goes some way to explaining the circumstances of his wife's elopement.[21] A decade later, in 1834, George Frederick suffered three occasions of misfortune which ultimately proved fatal to his livelihood. In March of that year a jury awarded damages of £300 against Mowlds in a civil claim for false imprisonment arising from a dispute over legal fees.[22] Then, on 10 May, Mowlds was violently assaulted in a random attack while walking near his office in Dublin.[23] Sometime afterwards, he was dismissed from a position he held in the post office, as a result of which he sought help from Daniel O'Connell. O'Connell responded by presenting a petition on Mowlds' behalf to the House of Commons.[24] The petition had no beneficial affect and in July 1835 O'Connell lodged another petition in the House of Commons on behalf of Mowlds:

17 W.J. FitzPatrick, *History of the Dublin Catholic Cemeteries* (Dublin, 1900), p. 18; S.J. Connolly, 'Union Government, 1812–23' in W.E. Vaughan (ed.), *A new history of Ireland, v: Ireland under the Union 1801–1870* (Oxford, 1989), p. 70.

18 Pettigrew and Oulton's Dublin Almanac and General Register of Ireland 1834, p. 158.

19 *Saunders's Newsletter*, 18 October 1827, p. 4.

20 *Waterford Mail*, 17 November 1824, p. 4; 24 November 1824, p. 1; *Dublin Morning Register*, 17 November 1824, p. 3; *Enniskillen Packet and Erne Chronicle*, 18 November 1824, p. 3; *Saunders's Newsletter*, 19 November 1824, p. 2; *Dublin Evening Mail*, 20 November 1824, p. 4; *Dublin Mercantile and Weekly Adviser*, 22 November 1824, p. 2.

21 *Westmeath Journal*, 5 August 1824, p. 3; *Waterford Mail*, 17 November 1824, p. 4; Pettigrew and Oulton's Dublin Almanac and General Register of Ireland 1835, p. 167.

22 *Dublin Evening Packet and Correspondent*, 22 March 1834, p. 3.

23 *Dublin Observer*, 10 May 1834, p. 8.

24 *Dublin Evening Packet and Correspondent*, 9 August 1834, p. 2.

Mr O'Connell presented a petition from Mr George Frederick Moulds [sic], who had been thirty one years a clerk in the Dublin post-office, and who was dismissed without any reasonable cause, it being alleged that he was in the country attending to his own business as an attorney than that of the post office, whereas his absence was only occasioned by ill health and praying the house for relief.[25]

The second petition was as unsuccessful as the first. Unfortunately, Mowlds couldn't break his run of misfortune and by November 1836 he was bankrupt.[26]

The 1820s and 1830s were at times difficult decades for Dublin merchants and businessmen as well as the poor at large. Coldblow (later renamed Milltown Park) was bought by a timber merchant, Richard Connery, in 1821. About six years later Connery mortgaged the property for £10,000 to Austin Brothers, a London firm of money lenders, but by 1831 he had become bankrupt. Coldblow was eventually sold at a considerable loss in 1833, attracting a bid of only £3,425.[27] When Dublin stockbroker Samuel Bruce died in 1834 his executors put his Milltown Road home, Elmfield (now Elm House), up for sale.[28] Despite the development potential of the ground fronting the main road, Elmfield failed to sell on several occasions, and the property remained on the hands of Bruce's executors for several years until its eventual sale in 1846.[29] By way of a third example, when the Trimleston estate of Roebuck was valued in 1832 the surveyor visited the McCaskey ironworks at Clonskeagh and noted in his report that 'from the declined state of the iron trade in this Country it is presumed the present rent of £52.10.0 would be a fair value for the site if divested of the buildings and improvements'.[30] The decline in the Irish iron trade was attributed by a contemporary iron founder to the removal of protective duties in 1827 and the availability of favourable credit terms from English manufacturers. As a result, the Irish market was flooded with cheap English-made ironmongery.[31]

The years 1832 and 1833 were marked by further outbreaks of devastating infectious disease, in this case cholera, which originated in the Indian sub-continent and spread westwards reaching Dublin in March of 1832. In that year roughly 40 per cent of people in Ireland who contracted cholera – generally caught from contaminated water or food – died but the death rate was as a high as 76 per cent in some areas. One of its early victims was Milltown dairyman, Luke Plunkett, who died on 23 or 24 April 1832. The epidemic reached its peak in the summer and autumn months of 1832 and declined thereafter. Further local outbreaks occurred in 1833 and 1834.[32] A particularly fatal outbreak of cholera occurred in St Mary's parish, Donnybrook, in July 1833 which killed 29 out of 50 infected people within a three-week period.[33] In response, the Sisters of Charity headed by Sister Mary Aikenhead opened a hospital to treat cholera patients which was

25 *Saunders's Newsletter*, 16 July 1835, p. 1.

26 *Saunders's Newsletter*, 18 November 1836, p. 3.

27 *Saunders's Newsletter*, 16 April 1832, p. 4; 'Milltown Park and some of its owners', p. 10.

28 *Saunders's Newsletter*, 12 May 1835, p. 1; RD 1846/5/244.

29 *Saunders's Newsletter*, 30 May 1836, p. 4; RD 1846/5/244.

30 'Report and Valuation of the lands of Roebuck in the County of Dublin by Brassington and Gale, 1832' (NAI, QRO 4/3/28).

31 *Poor Inquiry, City of Dublin, 1836*, Evidence on Combination, p. 28.

32 Robbins, *The miasma*, pp. 62–70, 107; *Dublin Evening Post*, 26 April 1832, p. 3.

33 NAI, Cholera Papers, MS 2/440/8.

funded by private donations from Lords Anglesea and Herbert, among others.[34]

There are no surviving reports of the effects of the cholera epidemic in Milltown but it must be assumed that more local people besides Luke Plunkett died given the poverty and poor housing conditions that existed in the village. As well as the healthcare response to the crisis by the Sisters of Charity, charitable organisations such as the County and City of Dublin Orphan Society and the St Peter's Orphan Society were actively involved in raising funds from the wealthier classes.[35] At a meeting of the County and City of Dublin Orphan Society held in Dundrum on 19 May 1833 a resolution was passed that Messrs Raferty and Carroll be appointed to collect funds 'from the humane and benevolent' in Milltown, Windy Arbour and Clonskeagh to support upwards of 162 cholera orphans.[36] On 29 September 1833 the St Peter's Orphan Society met at Milltown and appointed eight local collectors for Milltown and its adjoining district.[37] It is not clear why two separate orphan charities, both of which seem to have been of Catholic ethos judging by the volunteers' surnames, were concurrently active in the same districts. Another resolution, this time passed by the County and City of Dublin Orphan Society at the parochial school room of Dundrum on 20 April 1834, passed a resolution thanking Messrs Rafferty, Carroll and O'Brien, all of Milltown, for their efficient and valuable services as collectors, and for their kindness in agreeing to continue their support for the charity.[38]

One of the most violent storms in Irish meteorological history took place on the night of 6 January 1839 when a winter storm with hurricane force winds passed over the country, causing colossal damage, injury and loss of life. Fortunately, there were no reported deaths in Milltown despite the extensive reports of damage to property that occurred locally.[39]

DANIEL O'CONNELL AND THE REPEAL CAMPAIGN

National politics during the second quarter of the nineteenth century were dominated by Daniel O'Connell. O'Connell's critical innovation was the creation of a peaceful, political movement which agitated for change by applying external pressure on the government through extra parliamentary lobbying and mass public demonstrations. This movement was sustained by regular contributions from as little as one penny a month, known as the Catholic rent and later, the Repeal rent, which were collected at parishes throughout the country and which were used to fund election campaigns. The success of O'Connell's Catholic Association and its campaign during the 1820s for Catholic emancipation (which it achieved in 1829) raised the confidence of Irish Catholics and their support for constitutional democratic politics as a means of effecting change.

On 3 November 1833 the inhabitants of the Catholic parish of St Mary's and St Peter's, Rathmines, held a meeting at the new free school in Rathmines to support the national tribute, or annuity, for Daniel O'Connell, which had been established to compensate O'Connell for professional income forgone on account of his political activism on behalf of the Irish people.[40]

34 *Poor Inquiry, City of Dublin, 1836*, Communications, p. 25.

35 *Dublin Morning Register*, 2 January 1833, p. 1.

36 *Dublin Weekly Register*, 25 May 1833, p. 1.

37 *Freeman's Journal*, 23 October 1833, p. 2.

38 *Freeman's Journal*, 26 April 1834, p. 1.

39 See for example *The Pilot*, 9 January 1839, pp. 1–2.

40 *Freeman's Journal*, 4 November 1833, p. 2.

Among other things, the meeting resolved that 'the collection be made at the entrance gates of several chapels in this parish, but without interfering with the usual collection for the clergy at the chapel doors' and appointed the following collectors for Milltown chapel: Patrick Hayes, Maurice Harnett, Michael Roche, Michael McGrath, William Boshell, Hugh Mullanphy and Edmund Lawless.[41] As discussed in the previous chapter, Maurice Harnett was the owner of one of the woollen mills on the banks of the River Dodder in Milltown.[42]

The formation of the Precursor Society in 1838 and its successor, the Loyal National Repeal Association of Ireland, in 1840, gave new impetus to the campaign to repeal the Act of Union and to re-establish an Irish parliament in Dublin. At a meeting of the Precursor Society 41 subscribers from Milltown and Rathmines were admitted to the society on 26 March 1839 following their recruitment by Milltown publican, Patrick Hackett, who had raised £2 1*s.* in the process.[43] Hackett proved to be a very diligent recruiter for the repeal association. In July 1840 he enrolled his wife and seven children plus their servant Bridget Ryan as repealers.[44] The following month, Hackett wrote to the association enclosing a list of 24 repealers and advised that, 'there were the names of some Protestants in the list, one of whom is a £50 freeholder of the county, who says he will support at any future election any candidate starting on the repeal interest'.[45] This was an attempt by Hackett to impress his political superiors that the Repeal movement had, in Milltown at least, a broader confessional support which included liberal-minded Protestants.

By 28 September 1840 Patrick Hackett had recruited a total of 95 people from Milltown to the repeal cause.[46] In his letter returning the funds and a list of the subscribers, Hackett commented that:

> *The father of one of these gentlemen, whose name is in the enclosed list, was one of the most extensive and wealthy woollen manufacturers in the Liberty [i.e. the Dublin Liberties]. He kept his carriage, and moved in the first circles of society; but it was before the Union.*[47]

The implication was that the Union had been detrimental to Irish manufacturing, in particular the textile industries that had flourished in the Liberties before 1801.

The Catholic clergy for the most part were enthusiastic supporters of O'Connell's repeal movement with parish priests supporting the repeal campaign at local level.[48] This explains why the annual fundraising meeting of parishioners to appoint collectors for the O'Connell tribute were frequently held at the new Catholic church in Rathmines and chaired by the

41 *Freeman's Journal*, 4 November 1833, p. 2.

42 RD/873/487/580487; NAI, Tithe Aplotment Book, Diocese of Dublin, Parish of St Peter, Ranelagh and Milltown Road, assessed 30 December 1833, http://titheapplotmentbooks.nationalarchives.ie/reels/tab//004625716/004625716_00438.pdf (accessed 24 December 2019).

43 *Dublin Morning Register*, 27 March 1839, p. 3; Freeman's Journal, 30 March 1839, p. 2.

44 *Freeman's Journal*, 1 August 1840, p. 2.

45 *Freeman's Journal*, 27 August 1840, p. 4.

46 *Dublin Morning Register*, 30 September 1840, p. 4.

47 *Dublin Morning Register*, 30 September 1840, p. 4.

48 Oliver MacDonagh, 'The economy and society, 1830–45' in W.E. Vaughan (ed.), *A new history of Ireland, v: Ireland under the Union 1801–1870* (Oxford, 1989), pp. 238–9.

local parish priest, Fr William Stafford. At these annual November meetings, four or five local residents of Milltown were appointed as collectors of the tribute, of whom Patrick Hackett was the most prominent.[49]

The year 1843 marked the high point for the repeal movement with huge 'monster meetings' held nationwide, including one held at Donnybrook fair green on 3 July which attracted a crowd estimated at between 150,000 and 200,000 by one account, or 30,000 'including idle visitors' by another.[50] From time to time during 1843 the pro-repeal newspapers such as *The Nation* and the *Freeman's Journal* published the weekly collections of the repeal rent, including that collected in Milltown by Patrick Hackett. The 14 weekly collections identified for Milltown for 1843 disclose a wide variation in the total amounts collected, ranging from a high of 10*s*. 51/2*d*. to a low of 2*s*. 7*d*.[51] It is impossible to draw any firm conclusions from these statistics except to speculate that the fluctuations may have been caused by the endemic poverty and under-employment experienced by the working-classes of Milltown and districts beyond at that time. On the other hand, on the national level, the total weekly amounts fluctuated considerably during 1843 – having peaked in the third week of June – so external factors were at play too.[52]

Following the cancelation of the Clontarf monster meeting in October 1843 the repeal movement became divided and eventually split over O'Connell's failed political strategy. The emergence of the Young Irelander movement in the mid-1840s was also a catalyst to the split and in January 1847 they launched their own organisation, called the Irish Confederation.[53] Despite their inauspicious timing, the Confederates attracted support from some erstwhile O'Connellite repealers and fifty of their number from Donnybrook and Clonskeagh joined the Irish Confederation in April 1843. Harking back to the memory of the United Irishman and Clonskeagh ironmonger, Henry Jackson, the Clonskeagh Confederates set up their own branch and called themselves the Jackson Club.[54]

The Great Famine catastrophe and the death of O'Connell in 1847 dealt a grievous blow to the repeal movement, whose objects had been pursued by peaceful protest and participation in democratic politics. Local activism in Milltown came to a halt. The Young Irelander, Charles Gavan Duffy, attempted to reinvigorate the repeal movement in Milltown in July 1848 under its new designation, the Irish League, which had replaced both the repeal association and the confederation.[55] However, Patrick Hackett was not involved in this venture and it does not seem to have been a success.[56]

49 *Freeman's Journal*, 22 October 1842, p. 1; 16 November 1844, p. 2; 13 November 1845, p. 2.

50 *Freeman's Journal*, 4 July 1843, p. 4; *Dublin Evening Packet and Correspondent*, 4 July 1843, p. 2.

51 *The Nation*, 11 March 1843, p. 4; 7 October 1843, p. 14.

52 Michael J. Keyes, 'Money and Nationalist politics in nineteenth century Ireland: From O'Connell to Parnell' (PhD thesis, NUI Maynooth, 2009), p. 140.

53 James S. Donnelly, 'A famine in Irish politics' in W.E. Vaughan (ed.), *A new history of Ireland, v: Ireland under the Union 1801–1870* (Oxford, 1989), pp. 357–63.

54 *The Nation*, 8 April 1843, pp. 3, 27.

55 *The Pilot*, 14 July 1848, p. 4. Duffy had planned to attend a meeting in Milltown on a Sunday in July to form a branch of a new organisation called the Irish League. It is uncertain if the meeting took place as Duffy was arrested on Saturday 8 July on his way home to Merton House in Ranelagh: *The Nation*, 15 July 1848, p. 2.

56 The published weekly returns of repeal rent mention Milltown once, in 1850: *Dublin Weekly Register*, 12 January 1850, p. 8.

The futility of armed rebellion was brought home by the abject failure of the Young Ireland rebellion of 29 July 1848, which took place during the height of the Famine. One of the leaders of the failed rebellion was William Smith O'Brien, who was the younger son of Baron Inchiquin. The Barons of Inchiquin were political conservatives and supporters of the Orange Order. O'Brien was convicted of treason and sentenced to death but his sentence was commuted to transportation to Australia following a successful petition signed by over 80,000 people from both sides of the political divide, including members of the Orange Order. Over 42,000 of the petitioners lived in Dublin. The Dublin signatories included over a dozen residents of Milltown, the majority of whom were middle-class and lived in villas surrounding the village. Two of the petitioners, John Lee and James Henderson, signed the petition drawn up by the Orange Institution of Dublin. Obviously, Lee and Henderson were Loyalists and would have opposed Daniel O'Connell and the Repeal movement.[57]

LOCAL TAXATION REFORM – THE GRIFFITH'S VALUATION

During the second quarter of the nineteenth century it became increasingly obvious that existing forms of local taxation in Ireland were inadequate to meet the demands posed by challenging social conditions and to fund the increase in State bureaucracy, such as the Poor Law system which was introduced in 1838. To take one important example, county cess, which was used to pay for roads, bridges and gaols under the grand jury presentment system, was paid entirely by the occupier of the land whereas the poor law rates were shared between the occupier and the immediate lessor, and were paid to the local poor law board of guardians.[58] It thus became critical to identify the occupier and the lessor of property and to introduce scientific and fair methods for valuing land and buildings throughout the entire island. The process of reforming local taxation was a complicated and lengthy affair beginning in 1826 (commencing in earnest in 1844 with the tenement valuation) and spanning four decades. By the late 1840s and early 1850s the entire country had been surveyed by evaluators who assessed or rated every property according to detailed instructions laid down by the commissioner of valuation, Richard Griffith, after whom the whole process was informally named. The results of the initial nationwide valuation survey were published in a series of books printed between 1847 and 1864 and which were called the Primary Valuation. The contents of the Primary Valuation books were compiled by evaluators who had previously visited every townland, town and tenement and recorded detailed data in manuscript notebooks (the most useful being the house, quarto, tenure and field books), many of which survive in the National Archives of Ireland. The house books are particularly valuable because they record the dimensions of every structure, the materials used in its construction and its approximate age and quality. From about 1850 onwards, the Valuation Office began to prepare maps to accompany the Primary Valuation, which were based on the OS six-inch townland maps and the five-foot scale town plans in cities and large towns.[59] There are two early plans for Milltown village dating from the 1850s in the Valuation Office (town plan 17/field sheet

57 Information by Ruth Lawlor on the Findmypast.ie website which includes a search facility for the names and addresses of the petitioners. The original petitions are held in the National Archives of Ireland but are not available for public consultation.

58 For an excellent exposition of Irish local taxation and administration see The Irish Loyal and Patriotic Union, *Local & Centralised Government in Ireland: A sketch of the existing systems* (Dublin, 1888).

59 For a comprehensive explanation of the Griffith's Valuation and its archival material see Frances McGee, *The archives of the valuation of Ireland, 1830–65* (Dublin, 2018).

15). The earliest plan (illustrated at Map 16a/16b) is undated but can nonetheless be assigned to 1850 at the latest because the plan's building plot numbers match the numerical list used in the Griffith Valuation's 'Rateable Valuation of Tenements' for Dublin which was published in 1850.[60] The second town plan has a manuscript date of 6 April 1852 and also has later handwritten insertions and deletions. Nonetheless, both plans are very similar to each other.

The Griffith's Valuation has left a uniquely detailed record of the inhabitants of Milltown and the physical infrastructure of its buildings in the mid-to late 1840s. The marvel is that the majority of the occupants and landlords of virtually every building in the village of Milltown can be identified from Famine times. Subsequent changes in occupancy, land ownership and rateable valuation up to the 1970s (i.e. before the abolition of domestic rates) together with new building developments can be traced in unpublished books called Cancellation Books, which are held by the Valuation Office in the Irish Life Centre in Dublin.[61] The Griffith's Valuation records and the Valuation Office Cancellation Books are the most important records for local historians for the nineteenth and twentieth centuries, and are quoted from extensively throughout this book.[62]

DEMARCATION OF MILLTOWN TOWNLAND

A critical development took place in the third and fourth decades of the nineteenth century when the townlands of the entire island were formally demarcated and mapped for the first edition of the six-inch OS maps which covered the entire country. A comprehensive discussion of the new cartographic townland of Milltown and its geographic boundaries is needed to appreciate the impracticalities which those boundaries caused, and which gradually became apparent over time (Map 15). Critically, the OS townland unit was used as the basis for a whole range of administrative purposes throughout the Victorian era and beyond. For example, the townland unit was used as the basic framework for local taxation (the Griffith's Valuation) from the mid-nineteenth century onwards and was also used for collecting all of the nineteenth and early twentieth century census data.

But while the physical geography of the townlands changed over time the townland borders remained static and inflexible, without having regard to changes in the built environment or the social composition of the residents. This was not a problem for rural Irish townlands but in the expanding suburbs of late nineteenth-century Dublin it created practical difficulties where the old townland boundaries were submerged under terraces of houses, as was especially the case with the western boundary of Milltown townland. This unsatisfactory situation was partially resolved when Dublin Corporation took over Milltown in 1930, but even then, the territory on the south bank of the Dodder remained under the jurisdiction of Dublin County Council.

The background to the reorganisation and mapping of Irish townlands was the dire need for an authoritative up-to-date large-scale survey of all property that would form the basis

60 It is possible to identify the rateable occupant of every property recorded on the town plan by matching the plot numbers to those recorded in the Rateable Valuation of Tenements for County Dublin, Barony of Uppercross, Parish of Taney, Townland of Milltown, pp. 54–6, plots 17/1–17/105. The data can be viewed for free online at https://www.askaboutireland.ie.

61 The public may consult the cancellation books free of charge and, for a small fee, obtain high-quality colour copies of pages relating to a specific property or properties in Dublin city and county.

62 Many of the Griffith's Valuation records are available free online on the websites of the National Archives of Ireland and askaboutireland.ie.

for levying local taxation.[63] The first stage of the process involved the creation of a boundary commission in 1825. The surveyors employed by the boundary commission were required to establish the key boundaries of each townland through a public consultation process, by marking the boundaries on the ground and recording them in field books and, finally, providing the information to the surveyors in charge of the mapping from the OS office in the Phoenix Park. In practice, the demarcation process was time consuming, complicated and often ended up with unsatisfactory results. This was due to the fact that the boundary surveyors had to rely on the collectors of local taxation and landowners to point out the boundaries to the surveyors on the ground and neither party had maps to assist with the process.

The boundary register and sketch map for the parish of Donnybrook, which lies adjacent to Milltown at the ancient Prospect Lane boundary, have survived and are preserved in the National Archives (Map 9).[64] These two archives record in great detail the boundaries between Milltown and Clonskeagh to the east of the former townland and follow the ancient medieval boundary between the civic and ecclesiastical jurisdictions of Dublin which, as noted in previous chapters, were perambulated bi-annually by Dublin's lord mayor and his officials. To recap, this boundary starts at its easternmost point at the River Dodder about 100 metres west of Clonskeagh Bridge and, bisecting a terrace of cottages on the north bank of the river,[65] proceeds in a northerly direction along the old Clonskeagh Lane (now the back of Ramleh Close) and Prospect Lane to the junction with Milltown Road. The boundary continues along Milltown Road and Sandford Road and separates the northern end of Milltown townland from Clonskeagh townland on the east.

The northern boundary of the townland ran from Milltown Road and along the west side of Sandford Road as far as Sandford Terrace (the boundary wall of no. 55 Sandford Road marks the spot today). The area included all of the Milltown Park demesne (previously called Coldblow and subsequently acquired by the Jesuits in 1858), open ground which became Norwood Park (18 semi-detached houses built in 1950), Woodville (built prior to 1837), and a field formerly part of the eighteenth-century Coldblow demesne on which the Edwardian terrace houses on Cherryfield Avenue and Hollybank Avenue now stand (Map 15).[66] In addition, the townland took in the villas and extensive grounds of Sandford Grove and Sandford Hill (now Gonzaga College) which had been built for the Bewley families in the 1820s. The two Sandford villas were owned by the Bewleys until 1949 and thereafter by the Jesuits, who built the boys' primary and secondary school, Gonzaga College, on the grounds.[67]

The inhabitants of the northern area of the new townland of Milltown never identified with

63 The information in this paragraph is taken from Jacinta Prunty, *Maps and map making in local history* (Dublin, 2004).

64 OSI Boundary Department, Sketch map of the Parish of Donnybrook in the Barony of Rathdown and County of the City of Dublin, 23 August 1830 (NAI, VO/3.1584); Boundary Register of Donnybrook Parish in the Barony of Rathdown and County of the City of Dublin, 31 March 1837 (NAI, VO/3.1583). The boundary registers and sketch maps for Taney and St Peter's parishes have not survived.

65 At this point a small parcel of land containing 1 rood and 8 perches containing five cottages and wasteland and forming part of the civil parish of Donnybrook and the civil townland of Clonskeagh was transferred to the Barony of Uppercross: An Act to alter the Number and define the Boundaries of the several Baronies of the County of Dublin (5 & 6 Vict. c. xcvi) (10 August 1842). The reason for this administrative change is unknown but this tiny parcel of land is demarcated on the nineteenth-century OS maps (see Maps 9 & 15) and causes much confusion when researching local taxation and census records for Milltown and Clonskeagh.

66 Griffith's Rateable Valuation of Tenements Co. Dublin, Barony of Uppercross, Parish of St Peter, Townland of Milltown, 1850, p. 53, lots 1 and 2; Kelly, *Four Roads to Dublin*, p. 245; Minutes of the Municipal Council of the City of Dublin, 1949, pp. 162, 250; 'Milltown Park and some of its owners', p. 12.

67 *Gonzaga Record*, 1985, pp. 7–14. The Bewleys vacated the two houses in 1950.

Milltown village and its adjacent farms. From the outlook of geography and social class, the inhabitants of this part of the townland would have been much closer to Ranelagh and middle-class Dublin suburbia than working-class Milltown village and its rural hinterland south of the Dodder.

The River Dodder from Clonskeagh to a point close to the railway viaduct (now carrying the Luas tramline) marked the southern boundary of the new townland of Milltown. This stretch of the Dodder was also the boundary between two baronies. The territory on the north bank of the Dodder was part of the barony of Uppercross while the land on the south bank was part of the barony of Rathdown. These two baronies maintained separate legal, political, ecclesiastical, health and administrative jurisdictions among the civil parishes and townlands which made up each barony.

The western boundary of Milltown townland is most perplexing. The background to the creation of this boundary in the 1830s is as follows. In about 1830 William Hogan of Fairyland demesne (Map 8 – now Alexandra College) developed his landholding to the west of the Milltown Path and he or his first tenants began building Nullamore[68] and other villas called Richview, Brookfield and Richmond Park.[69] At the same time Hogan realigned the Milltown Path so that it ran in front of the villa called Richmond Hill (now Rydalmount, opposite Shanagarry apartments) by creating a dog-leg at the rear of the house. These changes are visible for the first time on the six-inch OS map of 1837–43 (Map 15).

When the boundary commission surveyors were working in Milltown in the 1830s they decided to include all of the farmland on the east side of the Milltown Path – then forming part of 'The Bloody Fields' – in the new Milltown townland plus a small triangular field on the west side of the path (containing the word 'The' on the OS map) and which was enclosed by a stone wall and a ditch on its long and short sides respectively. Their reasons for including land on both sides of the Milltown Path are unknown but whatever they were, the boundary surveyors did not replicate the property boundaries between the two head landlords, the earl of Milltown and Viscount Palmerston, whose landholdings historically lay in Milltown and Rathmines respectively. The upshot was that Viscount Palmerston ended up with land on both sides of the townland boundary of Milltown and Rathmines South.[70] This suggests that the boundary commission's surveyors did not do a particularly good job when they were working in Milltown.

The western boundary of Milltown townland soon became completely outdated when the Dublin, Dundrum and Rathfarnham Railway Company laid out the railway line across Milltown

68 The reason for the adoption of an Irish sounding placename – Nullamore – is unknown. The Irish word *uladh [ulla] means a tomb or cairn: P. W. Joyce, The origin and history of Irish names of places*, i, p. 338. Alternatively, it has recently been suggested that the placename has no plausible Irish etymology and may derive from the Latin words 'nulla mora' meaning 'no delay': Cormac Brady, 'The archaeology of a benchmark. Historical archaeology repeating itself on a Dublin gate pillar', *Archaeology Ireland*, 36, no. 3, issue 141 (Autumn 2022), p. 41.

69 Lewis, *Topographical Dictionary of Ireland*, ii, p. 370; Griffith's Rateable Valuation of Tenements Co. Dublin, Barony of Uppercross, Parish of St Peter, Townland of Rathmines South, 1850, p. 70, lots 5–8; NAI, Landed Estates Court Rental, vol. 33, no. 33, 'In the matter of the estate of the Rev. Smyth Whitelaw Fox, owner and petitioner, to be sold on 29 January 1852' (sale of Richview).

70 'Map and survey of that part of the estate of the Right Hon. Viscount Palmerston situate at Rathmines in the County of Dublin, surveyed in June 1861, by William Gartland' (NLI, MS 16.G.49 (17)); 'Ground design for an arrangement of small villas etc occupying about seventy acres of land situated between Rathmines, Milltown and Sandford in the County of the city of Dublin, the property of the Right Hon. the Viscount Palmerston' (NLI, MS 16.G.49(18) (unsigned and undated)). Both maps are too large and fragile to be photographed. Palmerston held 33 acres in Milltown townland, part of 'The Bloody Fields': Griffith's Rateable Valuation of Tenements Co. Dublin, Barony of Uppercross, Parish of St Peter, Townland of Milltown, 1850, p. 54, lot 6.

and Rathmines South townlands and built the viaduct across the Dodder, which, as will be discussed later, was completed in 1850.[71] In addition, the railway bisected the Milltown Path at a point which is still visible today opposite the Brookfield apartment complex and the Alexandra College hockey pitches on Richmond Avenue South, which at this location replaced the old Milltown Path on the far (eastern) side of the railway.

The farmland to the west of the railway line which was owned by the Hogan and Palmerston estates was developed from the early 1860s onwards, when Temple Road was laid out by the Palmerston and Hogan estates.[72] The boundary line between the two landowners fell respectively between 'Alston' (no. 19) and 'Lonsdale' (no. 21) on the north side of Temple Road and 'Clonbrone' (no. 38) and 'High Cross' (formerly Somerset, no. 40) on the south side, and ran as far as the junction of the Richmond Avenue South with Palmerston Park on the north, and the boundary wall separating South Hill and Nullamore as far as the Milltown Road opposite The Dropping Well pub on the south (Map 18). The original dividing line is visible on the Hogan estate map of 1821 (Map 8); the eastern (Hogan) end of Temple Road bisected the fields marked 5 and 6.

The Hogan estate developed several large detached houses on both sides of Temple Road at its eastern end and granted very long leasehold interests to family members, builders and other investors.[73] The last of William Hogan's children, Elizabeth, died in 'Templeton', Temple Road on 22 December 1888 aged eighty-two.[74] The Hogan estate trust remained active down to the mid-twentieth century and beyond until the various Hogan freehold and leasehold interests in Milltown were sold to new owners, including Dublin Corporation and Alexandra College.[75]

Viscount Palmerston also had very ambitious plans to develop his extensive landholding in Upper Rathmines, which he never got to fully realise.[76] On 18 October 1865 Henry John Temple, 3rd Viscount Palmerston, died without issue. Henry left his estate to Lady Palmerston and after she died in September 1869, the estate devolved to her second son, William Cowper-Temple.[77] It was from these families that many of the roads to the west of the railway line were named. Over time, Temple Road, Temple Gardens, Palmerston Road, Cowper Road, Merton Gardens and the Mageough Home were built across the townlands of Milltown and Rathmines South on the western side of the railway without any impediment by the townland boundaries.[78] In contrast, the impenetrable barrier caused by the railway was evident by the fact that it was not until the Edwardian era that development began on the eastern side of

---

71 *Freeman's Journal*, 31 August 1850, p. 4.

72 'Map and survey of that part of the estate of the Right Hon. Viscount Palmerston situate at Rathmines in the County of Dublin, surveyed in June 1861, by William Gartland' (NLI, MS 16.G.49 (17)).

73 Hogan Estate Trust Deed dated 1 June 1909. 'Ground design for an arrangement of small villas etc occupying about seventy acres of land situated between Rathmines, Milltown and Sandford in the County of the city of Dublin, the property of the Right Hon. the Viscount Palmerston' (NLI, MS 16.G.49(18) (unsigned and undated)).

74 *Weekly Freeman's Journal*, 1 January 1887, p 7.

75 Hogan Estate Trust Deed, dated 1 June 1909.

76 'Ground design for an arrangement of small villas etc occupying about seventy acres of land situated between Rathmines, Milltown and Sandford in the County of the city of Dublin, the property of the Right Hon. the Viscount Palmerston' (unsigned and undated) (NLI, MS 16.G.49(18)).

77 Blacker, *Brief sketches of the parishes of Donnybrook and Booterstown*, p. 469.

78 Kelly, *Four Roads to Dublin*, pp. 227–8. The Post Office Dublin Directory and Calendar for 1908, p. 671.

the railway, with the laying out of Park Drive and Cowper Grove from 1907 onwards, in Milltown townland. Access to these houses was from Ranelagh by Beechwood Avenue or via a pedestrian bridge over the railway at the eastern end of Cowper Road.

The social and political outlook of the inhabitants living on the western side of the railway line was very similar to that of those living on the northern end of Milltown townland on Sandford Road closest to Ranelagh. All of these districts were staunchly upper middle-class, and the residents would have been predominantly of the Protestant faith and of Unionist political persuasion. As far as these residents were concerned, they had nothing in common with the village of Milltown apart from sharing an outdated administrative townland unit. This attitude can be seen in complaints made in relation to postal services, as both Rathmines and Milltown each had a post office. In 1883 a resident of Upper Rathmines complained in a letter to the *Freeman's Journal* about the lack of a post office in the vicinity of Palmerston Park, Cowper Road and Temple Road, which meant that the people living there had to walk down to the post office on the main street in lower Rathmines. The complainant considered this to be a great inconvenience for the people of 'this influential and rising portion of the township'.[79] It had obviously not crossed the correspondent's mind that the Milltown post office was geographically much closer to him than the one in Rathmines, or if he was aware of that fact, he deliberately chose not to shop in Milltown. On the other hand, when the owner of the Dublin Laundry Company and Dartry resident, Thomas Edmondson, called into Milltown post office and couldn't get the stamps he needed – probably large denominations unlike the commonly used halfpenny stamps – he was so irritated that he wrote a letter of complaint to the General Post Office.[80] The final word should be left to Mr W. Carruthers of 10 Palmerston Park who gave evidence to a Local Government Board enquiry into proposals to rearrange the number of wards in the Rathmines UDC in 1904. Carruthers opposed the measures in the belief that if the division into smaller wards returned more artisans, they would not be so competent to deal with the business of the township as better educated businessmen.[81]

In summary, the formal demarcation of Milltown and adjacent townlands in the third decade of the nineteenth century has created difficulties for the local historian. This is particularly so as regards collecting official data for the geographic and historical core of Milltown which spanned both sides of the River Dodder comprising some or all of the four nineteenth-century townlands of Milltown, Roebuck, Farranboley, Rathmines South and Rathmines Great. To take one example, some of the 1901 census forms and all of the 1911 census forms for Cowper Road, Palmerston Road and Temple Gardens do not distinguish between the houses which lie in the townland of Milltown and those which lie in the townland of Rathmines South and so it is impossible to calculate the total number of people living in Milltown townland in 1901 and 1911 from the census data. Thus, as an administrative and a cartographic unit Milltown townland had ceased to have practical value by the turn of the twentieth century, some 70 years after its creation.

MUNICIPAL REFORM – THE SETTING UP OF THE RATHMINES TOWNSHIP

The establishment of the Rathmines township originated from the dissatisfaction of residents of that district in the 1840s over three critical issues. These were a desire on the part of the inhabitants to remain outside the municipal control of Dublin Corporation which had assumed

79 *Freeman's Journal*, 3 May 1883, p. 4.

80 Hearn, *Thomas Edmondson*, p. 153.

81 *Irish Times*, 27 May 1904, p.3.

a pro-repeal political outlook since its reform in 1840, dissatisfaction with the lack of attention given to Rathmines by the grand jury presentment system, and as a consequence, a need to take control over the supply of basic services such as water, lighting, paving and cleaning.[82] By late 1846 sufficient momentum had been generated by dissatisfied ratepayers to promote a private bill, called the Rathmines Improvement Bill, which would achieve the aforementioned aims.[83] In short, the promotors of the Rathmines Improvement Bill wanted the suburban area to the west of the Grand Canal comprising the districts of Rathmines, Mountpleasant, Ranelagh, Cullenswood, Milltown, Rathgar and Harold's Cross to be controlled by a new municipal body called the Rathmines and Rathgar Township. It was required by statute that all local acts be subject to preliminary inquiries. Accordingly, a commission of inquiry was held in Rathmines in February 1847 to consider the merits of the Rathmines Improvement Bill and to hear the arguments of both the promotors of and objectors to the bill.[84]

During the hearing held on 11 February 1847, one of the promotors of the bill, Frederick Stokes, told the enquiry that the average value of houses in Milltown was £12, compared to £31 and £29 for houses in Rathmines and Ranelagh respectively.[85] The low value relative to Rathmines and Ranelagh reflected the fact that by that time Milltown village was made up of modest to poor quality houses and cabins. Evidence was also heard about the lack of sewers on Milltown Road.[86] It was, however, a development which occurred at the hearing held on 17 February 1847 that had profound implications for Milltown. The hearing that day involved the consideration of lists of dissenting ratepayers who wished to be excluded from the Rathmines Improvement Bill. During the course of the proceedings a Francis Hagan presented a list of ratepayers of Milltown who protested against the bill in the following terms:

> *We, the undersigned, landed proprietors and householders residing in the rural districts of Milltown, within the limits sought to be included in the proposed Bill, object to our being so included, as the local circumstances of our properties are such that we neither require the aid as stated therein, nor could the provisions of said Bill be carried into effect so as to benefit us in any degree commensurate with the amount of taxation which would be laid upon our properties. The gentry reside in detached houses at a distance from the high road, with land adjoining under grass or tillage, varying in quality from one to thirty five acres. The town consists of a number of small houses or cottages, and is situated in a valley, with the River Dodder running through, etc. etc.*

Wm. Hodges, J.P., Milltown House	*35 acres*
Wm. C. Hogan, Fairyland, Milltown	*16 acres*
Mary A. Hunt, Milltown Castle	*6 acres*
Charlotte Hunt, Elm Hall	*8 acres*
Wm. T. Hamilton, S. R., Milltown Park	*25 acres*
Jn. Elliott, South Hill, near Classon's Bridge	*16 acres*

82 Séamas Ó Maitiú, *Dublin's Suburban Towns, 1834–1930* (Dublin, 2003), pp. 26–37.

83 *Freeman's Journal*, 14 November 1846, p. 1; *Saunders's Newsletter*, 7 December 1846, p. 3.

84 *Local Acts – Preliminary Inquiries: 9 & 10 Vict. C. 106. Report by A. Hayward and C.P. Brassington on the Rathmines Improvement Bill to the Commissioners of Her Majesty's Woods, Forests, Land Revenues, Works and Buildings*, H.C. 1847 (124), xxvi (hereafter cited as the Rathmines Report), http://www.dippam.ac.uk/eppi/documents/12365/page/305146 (accessed 2 January 2020).

85 Rathmines Report, minutes of evidence taken at Rathmines on 11 February 1847, p. 3.

86 Rathmines Report, minutes of evidence taken at Rathmines on 11 February 1847, pp. 6, 11.

Samuel Moore, Milltown Mills	*6 acres*
W.H. Flemyng, Nullamore, Classon's Bridge	*8 acres*
Wm. Lee, Milltown	*24 houses and cottages*
John Madden, Milltown	*27 statute acres*
Jn. Lee, Milltown	*27 statute acres*[87]

In short, the Milltown petitioners rejected their inclusion in the bill on a cost-benefit analysis. In this regard the bill provided for an assessment of up to 4 shillings in the pound in the first year and 2 shillings in the pound in the second and subsequent years with the possibility of a maximum rate of 4 shillings in the pound with the consent of the ratepayers.[88] In contrast, the poor law rate for the Rathmines division of the South Dublin Union was struck at seven pence-halfpenny in the pound in June 1847.[89]

In response to the Milltown petition, Frederick Jackson agreed on behalf of the promoters to facilitate the removal of Milltown from the bill, explaining that 'all we wanted was to have a proper boundary for the district included in the Bill, and if they will frame such a clause as will give us one, we will winningly strike that district out of it'.[90] The upshot of this was that the townland of Milltown was excluded when the bill became law later that year.

There is no indication that the objectors sought the opinions of, or gave any consideration to, the inhabitants in the village as to their exclusion from the new township. The villagers were among the poorest inhabitants of the townland and would potentially have benefited from the public services that become available when the new township of Rathmines was formally established later in 1847. On the other hand, the ratepayers had legitimate concerns about the unknown level of local taxation which they could be subjected to under the new local municipal regime. In 1843 an amendment to the Poor Law Act of 1838 had made the immediate lessor liable for poor law rates where his property was valued at less than £4.[91] This change impacted on most if not all of the Milltown petitioners. Particularly affected were Samuel Moore, John Madden, the Hunt sisters and the Lee brothers, all of whom owned small cottages in Milltown village or Classon's Bridge for which they were liable for poor law rates.[92] In addition, by 1847, local ratepayers were also subjected to increasing demands from the government to fund famine relief projects such as road works and soup kitchens.[93] When Richmond Hill (later renamed Rydalmount) was advertised to be let in July 1848, one of the stated attractions was that it was 'outside the new taxes' which presumably was a reference to the rates payable under the newly established Rathmines township. established Rathmines township.[94]

87 Rathmines Report, minutes of evidence taken at Rathmines on 17 February 1847, p. 14. The name Francis Hagan may be a mistake and the reference should possibly be to solicitor Frederic Hogan, a son of W.C. Hogan of Fairyland, Milltown.

88 *Freeman's Journal*, 9 April 1847, p. 3.

89 *Freeman's Journal*, 22 June 1847, p. 1.

90 Rathmines Report, minutes of evidence taken at Rathmines on 17 February 1847, p. 13.

91 Gerard O'Brien, 'The Establishment of Poor-Law Unions in Ireland, 1838–43', *Irish Historical Studies*, 23, no. 90 (November 1982), p. 119.

92 Griffith's Valuation, Primary Valuation of Tenements, Co. Dublin, Barony of Uppercross, Parish of St Peter, Townlands of Milltown and Rathmines South, 1847, pp. 57–60, 74.

93 James S. Donnelly, 'The soup kitchens' in W.E. Vaughan (ed.), *A new history of Ireland, v: Ireland under the Union 1801-1870* (Oxford, 1989), p. 313.

94 *General Advertiser for Dublin, and All Ireland*, 29 July 1848, p. 2.

In the circumstances, it is not surprising that a spirit of self-interest prevailed among the landowners of Milltown. That said, a notable absence from the list of objectors to the new township was the Bewley families of Sandford Hill (Joseph Bewley) and Sandford Grove (Samuel Bewley), whose properties totalling 16 acres were located at the northern end of the townland (Map 15).[95] The Bewleys were Quakers, whose adherents were well-known for their public altruism. It is possible that the Bewleys did not support the exclusion of Milltown from the Rathmines township because of the drawbacks this would have on the poorest inhabitants of the townland. This theory is supported by the fact that they successfully sponsored a private bill to include Milltown in the Rathmines and Rathgar township in 1880, a development which will be discussed presently.

The other notable absentee from the objectors' list was Viscount Palmerston who owned 33 acres of farmland on the north-western end of Milltown townland, adjacent to the Bewleys' parkland, in an area known as the Bloody Fields.[96] Lord Palmerston also held an extensive landbank in the neighbouring townland of Rathmines South and benefited after that townland was included in the Rathmines township in 1847, thereby making his land attractive to builders and property speculators. This last point highlights a critical divergence in the fortunes of the two adjacent townlands of Milltown and Rathmines South. Unlike Rathmines South, building activity in Milltown in the north and west of the townland was severely constrained by the townland's exclusion from the Rathmines township in 1847 and, in particular, by the building of the railway line in 1850. In the following decades, the Rathmines township expanded to include the townlands of Rathgar and Sallymount in 1862. During this period too Catholic religious orders acquired the extensive demesnes of Milltown Park (Jesuits in 1858), Milltown House and Milltown Castle (Sisters of Charity in 1878–80) on the outskirts of the village which prevented any intensive building taking place on those extensive landholdings.

It is impossible to know how things would have turned out had Milltown been included in the Rathmines township from the outset in 1847, but at the very least the village would have benefited from access to public services and utilities much sooner than when it eventually was incorporated into the township in 1880.

POLICING AND THE ADMINISTRATION OF JUSTICE

In 1836 policing in Ireland was reorganised into a single centralised police force responsible for the maintenance of law and order over the entire country, with the exception of the cities of Dublin, Belfast and Derry.[97] The metropolitan district of the city of Dublin, which as regards Milltown extended as far as the River Dodder, was policed by the Dublin Metropolitan Police (DMP). The two DMP police barracks closest to Milltown were in Donnybrook, at the bottom of Belmont Avenue, and in Rathmines. Both police stations formed part of the 'E' metropolitan divisional district.[98] The Irish Constabulary (from 1867 onwards, the Royal Irish Constabulary

95 Griffith's Valuation, Primary Valuation of Tenements, Co. Dublin, Barony of Uppercross, Parish of St Peter, Townland of Milltown, 1847, p. 57, lots 4 and 5.

96 Griffith's Valuation, Primary Valuation of Tenements, Co. Dublin, Barony of Uppercross, Parish of St Peter, Townland of Milltown, 1847, p. 57, lot 6.

97 Oliver MacDonagh, 'Ideas and institutions, 1830–45' in W.E. Vaughan (ed.), *A new history of Ireland, v: Ireland under the Union 1801–1870* (Oxford, 1989), p. 213.

98 Pettigrew and Oulton's Dublin Almanac and General Register of Ireland 1839, p. 653; *Freeman's Journal*, 21 December 1842, p. 3; 23 December 1843, p. 3 (murder at Classon's Bridge).

(RIC)) were responsible for law and order on the south bank of the River Dodder. The nearest constabulary barracks to Milltown south of the River Dodder was in Dundrum village. Accordingly, pre-1922 newspaper reports of crimes at Milltown which were investigated by the DMP can be identified as occurring on the north bank of the River Dodder, whereas those investigated by the RIC occurred on the south bank of the river.

The records of the DMP general register for the years 1837–1925 have been digitised and are available to view and search (for a fee) on the Findmypast.ie website. The DMP register contains data on three policemen – Michael Byrne, James Waldron and Patrick Gorman – who were natives of Milltown, and who joined the force during the period 1839–54. Of the three, Patrick Gorman had the most distinguished career, rising from the position of third-class constable to first-class inspector, the rank which he held when he retired on 24 February 1880 on an annual pension of £100.[99] The *Dublin Evening Telegraph* published the following encomium:

> *Inspector Gorman, whose name has been so frequently before the public as one of the most energetic, clever, and indefatigable officers, has retired on pension after a service of over thirty years, which reflected the greatest credit upon him. No officer performed his duty in such a straightforward and manly way as Inspector Gorman.*[100]

Alas for Gorman, his retirement was not a success and in September 1882 he was declared bankrupt.[101] The background to his financial difficulties is not known.

The different policing arrangements on each side of the River Dodder also had consequences for the administration of justice in the nineteenth and early twentieth centuries. Petty crimes committed on the south bank of the river in, for example, Farranboley, Roebuck and Rathmines Great townlands were prosecuted by the RIC at the Dundrum Petty Sessions Court, which was presided over by local justices of the peace. The records of the Dundrum Petty Sessions Court have survived, and these will be referred to from time to time in subsequent chapters. Conversely, petty crimes occurring on the north bank of the river, in Milltown village or at Classon's Bridge in the townland of Rathmines South for example, were prosecuted by the DMP at Dublin city's police courts. These policing arrangements occasionally led to farcical situations. For example, on Saturday nights drunkards who were in breach of the peace in Concrete (where the Dew Drop Inn was located) on the south bank of the River Dodder, fled northwards across Milltown Bridge into the metropolitan police district at the approach of the RIC, and turned back again to Concrete when the DMP appeared in Milltown village.[102]

More serious crimes committed within the DMP's jurisdiction were heard before local courts specific to Dublin city whose names and functions are now obscure, but which were very familiar to Dubliners over 100 years ago. These included the court of quarter sessions which was presided over by the Recorder of Dublin (the chief city magistrate). Serious offences and appeals from the Recorder's court were heard by the commission court, on which two judges of

99 DMP General Register, 1853, p. 94, Patrick Gorman, warrant number 4676, admitted 24 June 1853.

100 *Dublin Evening Telegraph*, 9 March 1880, p. 3. Gorman's actual service was 26 years and 8 months.

101 *Dublin Daily Express*, 13 September 1882, p. 2.

102 *Rathmines News*, 16 January 1904, p. 3.

the superior courts sat.[103] Mention is briefly made of these judicial bodies here because they will be referred to in later chapters in quotations from contemporary press reports of court proceedings.

THE POOR LAW GUARDIANS AND THE WORKHOUSE

The inexorable increase in poverty in Ireland in the second and third decades of the nineteenth century was behind a radical overhaul of the Irish poor law system which saw the introduction of a completely new form of administration by the Poor Relief (Ireland) Act of 1838. Under the new system of relief the entire island was divided into 130 (later 163) poor law unions, which in turn were subdivided into poor law divisions which were later called district electoral divisions. These administrative units were made up of a number of civil townlands. Under the new arrangement, indoor relief in the form of food and lodgings was provided in the union workhouse for the old, invalids, orphans, widows and the most deserving poor. The poor law was administered by a board of guardians whose activities were financed by poor rates levied on both owners and occupiers of land in the specific union. Both groups were given votes but highly rated occupiers were given multiple votes so that in practice the voting system was weighted in favour of the land owners.[104] As the nineteenth century wore on the government assumed increasing responsibility for public health which in turn led to an increase in the powers and duties of the poor law boards. From the mid-nineteenth century onwards, the poor law boards were no longer solely involved in providing social welfare through the workhouse and outdoor relief but had become an increasingly important part of local government. By the 1890s the poor law boards of guardians' areas of responsibility covered a myriad of issues including (among others), the provision of medical (dispensary) services, infectious diseases, nuisance removal, sanitation, diseases in farm animals, river pollution and rural housing for labourers.[105]

The geographical position of Milltown, straddling the River Dodder, resulted in the village being administered by two different unions. The parts of Milltown village and Classon's Bridge lying on the north bank of the River Dodder in the civil townlands of Milltown and Rathmines South respectively were administered by the South Dublin Union, which had its headquarters in James's Street. All of the area on the south bank of the River Dodder, including the civil townlands of Farranboley, Roebuck, Rathmines Great and Rathmines Little, was administered by the Rathdown Union with its workhouse in Loughlinstown (now St Columcille's Hospital). The minute books of the meetings of the guardians for the South Dublin and Rathdown poor law unions have survived and from them we can get an idea of how the poor law impacted on the inhabitants of Milltown during the nineteenth and early twentieth centuries. Limitations of space preclude a full discussion of this topic but some brief observations may nevertheless be made. Of the roughly 120 references to Milltown in the minute books spanning the period 1840 to 1921 which were reviewed, a large majority of the entries concerned human health, sanitation laws and animal health regulations. For example, on 22 September 1870 the Board of Guardians for the South Dublin Union ordered that Mary Tittle of Milltown be prosecuted for failing to abate a nuisance on her property having been served with a notice by the

103 For a detailed explanation of this complicated subject, see R.B. McDowell, 'The Irish courts of law, 1801–1914' in *Irish Historical Studies*, vol. 10, no. 40 (September, 1957), pp. 263–91.

104 Matthew Potter, *The municipal revolution in Ireland: A handbook of urban government in Ireland since 1800* (Dublin, 2011), pp. 84–5; Crossman, Local Government, pp. 43–6.

105 Crossman, *Local Government*, pp. 50–2.

sanitary officer.[106] On 6 July 1885, the guardians approved the admission of Teresa Henderson of Milltown to the South Dublin Union infirmary for medical treatment.[107] Following an outbreak of scarlatina in a tenement building called Marble Hall, which was located beside the Packhorse Bridge in Milltown on the south bank of the River Dodder, the relieving officer of the Rathdown Union reported that he had fumigated the tenement and destroyed the infected bedding, for which he paid 33*s*. in compensation to the inhabitants.[108]

The introduction of the Contagious Diseases (Animals) Act 1878 increased the workload of the poor law guardians because of the numerous city and suburban dairies whose premises and animals fell under the act.[109] This can be seen in many reports of outbreaks of swine fever and respiratory ailments among cattle herds belonging to the farmers of Milltown and Classon's Bridge. To take one case, on 7 January 1891 the guardians of the Rathdown Union read a report from the veterinary inspector who had slaughtered a cow belonging to the herd of George Lambert of Milltown which was found to be infected with tuberculosis and septic poisoning.[110] The same farmer had the misfortune of his pigs becoming infected with swine fever five years later.[111]

Pregnancy outside of marriage was a major taboo with life-changing consequences for the mother and her baby. A small number of the board of guardians' records relate to this issue and reveal the great distress involved. On the evening of 29 October 1897 Mathew Doyle of Classon's Bridge found a deserted male child in a lane off Milltown Road (possibly Prospect Lane) which he brought to the South Dublin Union workhouse.[112] In August 1894 the guardians of the Rathdown Union approved the admission of Mary Price to the workhouse on the recommendation of Reverend Moffatt, the rector of St Philip's Milltown, on account of her having become pregnant.[113]

The operation of the workhouse system and its impact on Milltown will be discussed in detail in Chapter 8 as part of the review of the Great Famine.

GROWTH IN TRANSPORT

The growth in the number of suburban villas on the south side of Dublin city created a demand for more flexible public transport options beyond that of the hired hackney or jaunting car. With this in mind a proposal was put forward in 1816 by Robert Turbett to establish a coach service to run twice daily between Dublin, Dundrum and Enniskerry in the morning and evening. The coaches were designed to accommodate six inside and 12 outside passengers, with the fare charged from Dundrum to Dublin being 1*s*. 3*d*. inside and 10*d* outside.[114] This initiative was a failure and its only mention in the press appeared in March 1817 when the committee of the

106 South Dublin Poor Law Union, Board of Guardians Minute Book A22–A24, January 1869–August 1871, Folio 11, p. 751.

107 South Dublin Poor Law Union, Board of Guardians Minute Book A37–A39, October 1884–June 1886, Folio 13, p. 637.

108 Rathdown Poor Law Union, Board of Guardians Minute Book 97–100, July 1891–September 1893, Folio 17, p. 473.

109 *Freeman's Journal*, 1 October 1878, p. 2.

110 Rathdown Poor Law Union, Board of Guardians Minute Book A96, September 1890–March 1891, Folio 23, p. 335.

111 Rathdown Poor Law Union, Board of Guardians Minute Book A106, September 1895–March 1896, Folio 24, p. 528.

112 South Dublin Poor Law Union, Board of Guardians Minute Book A50, January 1897–December 1897, Folio 9, p. 869.

113 Rathdown Poor Law Union, Board of Guardians Minute Book A103, March 1894–April 1896, Folio 10, p. 418.

114 Ball and Hamilton, *Parish of Taney*, pp. 201–3.

Dundrum and Enniskerry Coach Company sought tenders for supplying horses for its coaches.[115] The development of a network of coach services was also hindered by strong opposition by the Dublin hackneys to such enterprises until 1848 when a new police act facilitated the introduction of privately run omnibus services.[116] Despite these difficulties, an omnibus service to Dundrum which passed through Milltown was promoted in house advertisements in 1844.[117]

The fares for hackney carriages were prohibitively expensive for working-class people. For example, in 1855 the hackney fare from the GPO to Milltown Bridge, a distance of a little over three miles, was 1*s.* 9*d.* one way and 2*s.* 2*d.* return.[118] This explains why, before the introduction of affordable public transport in the late nineteenth century, people walked to their destinations unless they had their own equine transport. The hackney drivers did not always have it easy: in 1840 a hackney driver named Garrett Byrne of Milltown was among several drivers whose vehicles were stripped overnight of their brass plates by thieves.[119]

Pedestrians walking to Milltown from the city centre frequently used the Milltown Path, which was a more direct route than the Ranelagh and Sandford roads. Prior to the development of Belgrave Square and Palmerston Road this path passed through sparsely populated countryside (Map 15). At a certain point between Rathmines and Milltown the path was also known in the mid-nineteenth century as Blackberry Lane, a descriptor which conveys its rural isolation. Walkers were occasionally robbed if they chose to use that route at night. A youth named Edward Wright was assaulted and robbed by three men of bread, butter and a bundle of hay while on his way home to his employer, John Bracken, on the night of 25 July 1850. Bracken lived in a cottage with a small garden on the western side of the grounds of Milltown House fronting Blackberry Lane, which he rented from Alderman William Hodges.[120] Luckily for Wright, two policemen who were patrolling Blackberry Lane heard his cries for help and they later caught one of the culprits.[121]

Despite the occasional dangers to personal safety the Milltown Path began to lose some of its isolation from the late 1850s onwards when the Belgrave and Palmerston roads began to be laid out and developed by builders. In November 1861 a correspondence to the *Dublin Daily Express* urged the Rathmines township commissioners to take the pathway in charge:

> *The pathway from Belgrave road to Milltown and the Dodder is almost the only pleasant walk through the fields open to the public on the south side of the city. It is very much frequented during the Summer months, and it would be a still greater benefit to the public in Winter. But it is now, and will be till next Spring, almost impassable from Belgrave road to Lord Palmerston's fields, where it is elevated and dry ... Mr Plunket, the owner of the new houses on Palmerston road at this end of the path, will, no doubt, soon put his portion of the way in proper order.*[122]

---

115 *Saunders's Newsletter*, 5 March 1817, p. 3.

116 Michael Corcoran, *Through Streets Broad and Narrow: A history of Dublin Trams* (Leicester, 2000), p. 8.

117 *Saunders's Newsletter*, 5 October 1844, p. 4, sale of Richmond Cottage.

118 *Saunders's Newsletter*, 24 December 1855, pp. 3–4.

119 *Freeman's Journal*, 29 July 1840, p. 3.

120 Griffith's Valuation, Rateable Valuation of Tenements, Co. Dublin, Barony of Uppercross, Parish of St Peter, Townland of Milltown, p. 54, lot 13c.

121 *Freeman's Journal*, 27 July 1850, p. 4.

122 *Dublin Daily Express*, 21 November 1861, p. 4.

The extension of horse-drawn trams to Palmerston Road and Clonskeagh Road in 1876 by the Dublin Central Tramways Company helped to connect the extreme west and east ends of Milltown Road with the city's suburban tramway network, thereby further reducing the isolation of those districts.[123] In April 1896 a proposal by the Rathmines, Dundrum and Blackrock Tramway Company to lay down an electric tramline from Milltown to Blackrock via Dundrum, including a tramline from the Clonskeagh Road tram terminus to Palmerston Road via Milltown Road and Dartry Road, was approved (subject to conditions) by the County Dublin Grand Jury and the Rathmines township commissioners, but this new line did not go ahead.[124] Instead, it was the enthusiasm for railway transport in mid-nineteenth-century Ireland which would leave a significant physical impression on Milltown.

THE RAILWAY

In the early 1840s before the onset of the Famine there was huge enthusiasm among the professional and middle classes for railways as both investment and public transport vehicles. To take a local example, Alderman William Hodges of Milltown House was a director of the Dublin and Drogheda Railway Company and the Dublin, Dundrum and Rathfarnham Railway Company in the 1840s.[125] Railways were huge engineering projects that required considerable amounts of investment and political capital – the former to fund the compulsory acquisition of land and for the infrastructure, the latter to ensure that, where necessary, private bills with statutory powers were negotiated through parliament in Westminster. The newspapers of the time published numerous hopelessly optimistic or downright misleading prospectuses seeking investors for grandiose schemes, many of which never progressed beyond the initial publicity or preliminary parliamentary stages. Two examples of this phenomenon from 1845 are worth mentioning because the routes of the proposed railways passed through Milltown. The prospectus for the Dublin, Dundrum and Enniskerry Railway published in June 1845 made some very bold claims to entice investors:

> *The above Railway is intended to start from Harcourt Street, in the city of Dublin, and will reach the town of Enniskerry by a line only eleven and a quarter miles in length. It takes its course through or near the beautiful and important suburbs of Ranelagh, Rathmines, Milltown, and Dundrum: the passenger traffic which, at present, employs several public conveyances, omnibuses, coaches etc, altogether independent of the vast number of hired cars which are constantly passing and repassing between these densely populated localities ... The well-known district traversed by this railway exhibits so dense a population, and so great an intercourse with Dublin, as not to leave a doubt of the certainty of a very large return for the investment of the required capital.*[126]

The contrast between this fictitious description of 'densely populated localities' in south county Dublin – more appropriate for the twenty-first century Luas tramline than pre-Famine Ireland – and the reality of the rural landscape from Ranelagh onwards could hardly be starker. Four months later, on 7 October 1845 a small notice was inserted in the *Freeman's Journal* alerting the public to the Dublin Southern Villa Railway:

123 Corcoran, *Through Streets Broad and Narrow*, p. 19.

124 *Dublin Evening Telegraph*, 20 April 1896, p. 6; *Evening Herald*, 22 April 1896, p. 2.

125 *Saunders's Newsletter*, 29 December 1846, p. 1; *Freeman's Journal*, 12 March 1847, p. 3.

126 *Freeman's Journal*, 19 June 1845, p. 1.

Plate 16. Railway viaduct at Milltown, known locally as 'The Nine Arches', c. 1900 (courtesy of the Irish Architectural Archive)

> *From a point near the end of Aungier Street, in the city of Dublin, to Rathfarnham and Ballyboden, with branches to Tallaght on one side, and on the other to Milltown, Dundrum and through the vale of Shanganagh to join the Bray line. Notice is hereby given, that arrangements are being made to form a company for the purpose of making an atmospheric railway throughout the southern district of county Dublin. A prospectus, with full information and list of the provisional committee, will be published as soon as the requisite preliminaries have been completed.*[127]

Needless to say, the Famine put paid to the most ambitious railway schemes but by the end of the decade progress was being made with laying down the railway which later became known among Dubliners as the Harcourt Street line. In 1847 the Dublin, Dundrum and Rathfarnham Railway Company acquired 3 roods and 25 perches plantation measure at the western end of the Milltown House demesne, where the new railway line would be laid down en route to Dundrum.[128] This company subsequently changed its name twice to the Dublin and Bray Railway Company and then the Dublin, Wicklow and Wexford Railway Company.[129] In August 1850 the company's half-yearly report to shareholders advised them of progress with the construction of the railway, some of which is particularly interesting as regards the building of the railway viaduct at Milltown (Pl. 16):

---

127 *Freeman's Journal*, 7 October 1845, p. 1.

128 RD 1869/17/209, RD 1869/17/210.

129 *Freeman's Journal*, 10 June 1852, p. 2; *Saunders's Newsletter*, 21 July 1865, p. 2.

Your directors cannot conclude this report without referring to the valuable aid granted to the company by Lord Palmerston, who with a liberality and promptness at once marking his desire for local improvement, and a benevolent anxiety for promoting employment in a very distressed neighbourhood, has given possession of his property in the valley of the Dodder river at Milltown, through which the most important work of your line extends itself. Mr Dargan has already actively commenced the viaduct at this point, and the importance of advancing the work, while the dry season exists, which leaves the bed of the river easy to receive the foundation stones of the piers of the bridge, makes the permission granted by his lordship a matter of essential consequence to the company, and deserving of their grateful recognition.[130]

In the same report the engineer advised that:

The Dodder viaduct of 11 arches has been commenced, the foundations of the piers are nearly all taken out, and every effort is being made by the contractors to procure a large supply of the requisite materials, so as to lose no time in having the piers carried up a sufficient height to be out of the reach of the floods, and from recent directions given by Mr Dargan, in person, on the works, to have an increased force of men put on, I see no difficulty to having this extensive work completed within five months.

It is impossible to know if the additional workforce hired to expedite the building of the viaduct was recruited from the many labourers living in Milltown village. At the very least, the Milltown limestone quarries would have been busy and, presumably, some of the men working on the railway would have lodged at Milltown or spent their wages in the village shops and pubs. If, in fact, the railway brought much needed business to Milltown in the early 1850s the benefit only lasted for about 30 months before the engineering works moved further down the line towards Dundrum. In February 1853 the project engineer reported that:

The earthworks between Dundrum and Milltown will be completed next month ... The Dodder viaduct, 360 feet long and 60 feet high, is now ready for the rails. The earthworks between Milltown and Dublin are in a forward state and can be made up in about two months.[131]

The railway was opened to the public on Monday 10 July 1854. On the previous Saturday, the directors laid on three special trains for the company's shareholders who travelled directly from Harcourt Street to Bray – a distance of 12 miles – in under half-an-hour.[132] At this stage there was no station at Milltown, an omission which generated letters to the newspapers requesting that a station be built there.[133] The company eventually built a station at Milltown (where the Luas tram stop is now beside the back entrance to Alexandra College), which opened on 1 May 1860.[134] One of the first station masters appointed to Milltown was a widower called Patrick Healy. He lived with his adult daughter in a neat two-storey station house and was sufficiently remunerated to employ a servant.[135]

130 *Freeman's Journal*, 31 August 1850, p. 4.

131 *Saunders's Newsletter*, 26 February 1853, p. 2.

132 *Freeman's Journal*, 10 July 1854, p. 3.

133 *Saunders's Newsletter*, 27 October 1854, p. 3; 9 June 1855, p. 3.

134 *Freeman's Journal*, 30 April 1860, p. 2.

135 *Saunders's Newsletter*, 19 October 1861, p. 3.

Like all railways, the Dublin, Wicklow and Wexford Railway had its share of accidents and incidents over the years. Even before the station had been opened at Milltown a woman was killed on the line in that neighbourhood one July evening in 1857, and some six years later the Milltown ticket taker was accidentally killed by the night train at Milltown while he was working there, leaving a wife and seven children.[136] Inevitably, there were suicides on the railway line close to Milltown because beyond Ranelagh the line ceased to be elevated and was thus easier to trespass on amid the open farmland.[137] On another occasion Healy, the station master, caught a woman named Mary Armstrong trespassing on the line. Armstrong was prosecuted by the railway company, whose barrister told the court his client was determined to prevent trespassing on the line, but in this instance would not press for a heavy fine because the defendant was a poor woman. Nonetheless, Armstrong was fined 5*s*.[138]

An altogether much more serious incident with potentially catastrophic consequences occurred when an attempt was made to sabotage the railway line between Milltown and Dundrum by Fenian activists. According to the *Freeman's Journal*, on the morning of Saturday 9 March 1867 a railway linesman discovered that an attempt had been made during the night to lift the rails on the line near the Quaker Meeting House on the Lower Churchtown Road (today, the location would be about 200 metres beyond the Windy Arbour Luas tram stop). Although the attempted sabotage of the railway line was unsuccessful, the perpetrators managed to cut the telegraph wires and partially saw off one of the telegraph posts.[139] The timing of this incident is curious. The Fenian Rising took place in Dublin on the night of 5 and 6 March 1867 and was quickly suppressed by the police. But the incident described above is reported to have occurred some two to three days later on the night of 8 and 9 March when the local activists must have known that the Fenian Rising was a lost cause.

On a more mundane note, it was standard practice on the Harcourt Street line for the ticket inspector to check all passengers' tickets when the train stopped at Milltown. Apparently, the process was inefficient and caused delays which in turn saw complaints being made at shareholders' meetings.[140] The vast majority of commuters who used the Harcourt Street line were from the middle-class and professional backgrounds. In addition, the convenience of the new Milltown railway station was highlighted in newspaper advertisements in 1862 for building ground on the Palmerston estate in Upper Rathmines.[141] From time to time, 'cheap tickets for the working classes' were promoted by the railway company. In June 1870 the *Freeman's Journal* advertised third-class tickets for a single journey between Harcourt Street station and Milltown station at a fare of one penny. This low fare targeted working-class men who worked in the city as it only applied to the trains which ran at 7 a.m., 5.25 p.m. and 6.20 p.m.[142] In contrast, third-class return fares from Milltown to Bray on Sundays and Mondays cost 1*s*.[143]

A lack of information makes it difficult to gauge how well the railway was patronised by

136 *Leinster Express*, 18 July 1857, p. 3; Saunders's Newsletter, 29 October 1863, p. 3.

137 *Saunders's Newsletter*, 7 September 1866, p. 3.

138 *Dublin Evening Mail*, 31 October 1861, p. 3.

139 *Freeman's Journal*, 11 March 1867, p. 4.

140 *Freeman's Journal*, 22 August 1871, p. 8.

141 *Dublin Daily Express*, 8 September 1862, p. 1.

142 *Freeman's Journal*, 4 June 1870, p. 2.

143 *Freeman's Journal*, 11 August 1870, p. 2.

local residents in Milltown, but the likelihood is that the take up was poor. The working-class inhabitants in the village would very infrequently have spent their disposable income on the luxury of travelling into town or to the seaside by train. For example, one August weekend in 1899 John Downey of Milltown travelled to Bray without paying his fare and was also charged with being drunk and disorderly.[144] Furthermore, the wealthy professional classes who lived in the large detached villas surrounding Milltown and on Temple Road had their own horse-drawn carriages (and from the Edwardian era onwards, their own motor cars), so the railway would not have been as convenient for them as for the lower middle classes who lived in the redbrick terraced houses of Ranelagh and Rathmines. That said, from the 1860s onwards advertisements for house lettings in the vicinity of Milltown used the proximity to the railway station as an attraction. On 27 March 1867 *Saunders's Newsletter* advertised the following unnamed house to let: 'Milltown – Cheap house, only £35 a year. A very nice house with garden, coach house and stable, having the convenience [of] both railway and omnibus quite close.'[145]

A report of a political nature indirectly supports the view that Milltown station was a backwater on the Harcourt Street line. Arising from the split in the Irish Parliamentary Party (IPP) following the O'Shea divorce case and the death of Parnell, Timothy Healy MP was travelling by train from Arklow to Dublin on 26 June 1892 in very hostile circumstances. According to a newspaper report, Healy needed clerical and police protection from the hostile crowds which met him at each railway station as he made his way back to Dublin on the eight o'clock train. The *Evening Herald* told its readers that 'After arriving at Milltown, Mr Healy sneaked from the train to the great disappointment of his fellow passengers. A large crowd awaited Mr Healy's arrival at Harcourt street station but were also disappointed.'[146] It was ironic that Healy had to alight for his personal safety incognito in the midst of the unionist stronghold of the Rathmines township.

The issue of personal safety for women was also a concern. In 1893 a deputation from the Ranelagh Improvement Association met the directors of the railway company to petition for a station in Ranelagh. Apart from the inconvenience of having to use Milltown station, the Ranelagh residents pointed out that 'no lady would think of going to Milltown station after dark, unless under escort'.[147] Such fears were not unfounded because reports of indecent assault committed against women between the Milltown railway station and the village appear from time to time in the newspapers in the 1890s.[148] Indeed, during a board meeting of the Rathmines township commissioners in 1895, opinion was divided on whether or not to close up the Milltown Path. One commissioner was against the idea because of the inconvenience it would cause to local railway commuters, while another argued for its closure on the grounds that 'it was a scandal to the township from a moral point of view'.[149]

In due course a station was opened in Ranelagh in 1896.[150] This may have caused a further

144 *Rathmines News*, 19 August 1899, p. 5.

145 *Saunders's Newsletter*, 27 March 1867, p. 4.

146 *Evening Herald*, 27 June 1892, p. 2.

147 *Irish Society*, 23 October 1893, p. 19.

148 *Rathmines News*, 18 April 1896, p. 3; 16 April 1898, p. 4.

149 *Dublin Evening Telegraph*, 4 September 1895, p. 3. Ultimately the Milltown Path remained open and was widened between its junction with Palmerston Park and the railway line.

150 *Dublin Evening Mail*, 24 August 1896, p. 3.

reduction of passengers using Milltown because the station master, Mr Anderson, had enough time the following December to very prettily decorate the waiting room for Christmas, according to the *Rathmines News*.[151]

LONG-TERM CONSEQUENCES OF THE RAILWAY

The building of the railway line on the outskirts of Milltown in the mid-nineteenth century had significant long-term consequences for the district, which are not immediately obvious from the historical records. Critically, the railway line created a physical barrier to opening up the agricultural land on the eastern side of the tracks for building. Additionally, access to this landbank from Milltown Road was impeded by the steep embankment on the northern side of the Dodder River floodplain between the descent into the village on Milltown Road and Richmond Avenue South. In contrast, the open and accessible land on the west side of the railway line was, as noted earlier, intensively de veloped from the 1860s onwards. In short, organic housing development from the mid-nineteenth century onwards, which was expanding in an easterly and southerly direction from Upper Rathmines and Ranelagh respectively, was blocked by the railway line and the extensive demesnes and farmland surrounding St Philip's, Milltown House, Milltown Castle, Milltown Park, Sandford Grove and Sandford Hill. These properties formed a green crescent around the northern and western flanks of Milltown village. Consequently, throughout the nineteenth century and for the early decades of the twentieth century Milltown village remained physically cut off and socially separated from the prosperous middle-class suburban villages of Ranelagh and Rathmines, which benefited from their inclusion in the Rathmines township. This in turn created a strong sense of community with a separate identity among the villagers of Milltown.

The changes to the local topography caused by the railway made the Milltown Path redundant. The railway track bisected the path at a point which is still visible today opposite the Brookfield apartment complex and the Alexandra College hockey pitches, where the road veers to the left towards Rathmines, and which before this point is parallel with the Luas tramline. In consequence, Richmond Avenue South was laid out parallel to the railway tracks, and provided access from Temple Road to Milltown Road at its current junction immediately west of the Nine Arches Bridge. Today, Richmond Avenue South also links remnants of the Milltown Path bisecting Temple Villas and Cowper Road.

MILLTOWN CATHOLIC CHAPEL

The relaxation of the penal laws in the third quarter of the eighteenth century gradually saw the Catholic Church in Dublin emerge from the shadows and promote itself more confidently in the public arena. Tradition has it that a stable owned by a Mrs Burke was used to celebrate mass before a chapel was built in the village at the instigation of an activist priest called Fr Henry Young, known as the Apostle of Dublin.[152] However, the first public mention of a chapel in Milltown appeared in the *Freeman's Journal* newspaper of 20 July 1812 when an advertisement was inserted at the bottom of the first page notifying the public that 'a charity sermon will be preached in the chapel of Milltown by Rev. R. Kenrick'.[153] The charity

151 *Rathmines News*, 9 January 1897, p. 4.

152 Murray, 'The Story of Milltown'. Fr Murray sourced this information from a history of Milltown chapel written by Rev. Myles V. Ronan on 1 September 1935 and subsequently reproduced in the winter 1996 edition of the Milltown Parish Newsletter.

153 *Freeman's Journal*, 20 July 1812, p. 1.

sermon was held to raise funds for the Milltown Sunday and Evening Schools for male and female children. This advertisement shows that the local children were working at home or employed in one of the mills nearby such as Burke's or Hunt's woollen mills. The majority of these children were very likely to have been Catholics, whose families formed the bulk of a growing class of factory operatives and agricultural labourers; the latter group employed as gardeners and workmen on the farms and gardens attached to the dozens of villas and their demesnes which were built in the eighteenth and early nineteenth centuries in the townlands of Rathmines South (i.e. Upper Rathmines), Milltown, Farranboley, Clonskeagh and Roebuck.

The precise location of the 1812 chapel in Milltown village is not known but we know for certain that the Catholic chapel was rebuilt in 1819 and the likelihood is that the same site was used. A brass plaque commemorating the new chapel records in Latin that: 'This House of the Lord was consecrated in honour of the Blessed Virgin Mary of the Assumption on the 30 November, the feast of St Andrew the Apostle, in the year of our Lord 1819.'

A map of William Hogan's demesne of Fairyland (later St Philip's, now Alexandra College) drawn up in 1821 shows the new chapel marked with the number two and a cross on his estate map of 1821 (plot 2 on Map 8). This small building is the earliest known record of the chapel building in Milltown village. The siting of the small chapel building discretely behind houses fronting the main street was typical of pre-Catholic emancipation chapels, many of which originated in the eighteenth century. The present Catholic church in Milltown occupies the same site as the 1821 chapel, having been extended in 1935. The footprint of the original chapel of 1819 is retained today in the low rectangular part of the church structure fronting the road, which, in 1845, the surveyors of the Griffith's Valuation recorded as being 80 feet long by 24 feet in breadth and 13.5 feet high.[154] In September 2016 DBFL Consulting Engineers opened up the southern gable wall of this structure revealing the original random rubble wall of 1819, which was found to be in a very poor condition with no evidence of an effective mortar binding.[155]

The Catholic Directory for 1821, which was compiled by the aforementioned Fr Young of Harold's Cross, recorded that devout recital of the rosary was practised every evening at Milltown chapel while the stations of the cross were performed every Friday evening there too.[156]

On Sunday 19 October 1823 solemn benediction of Milltown chapel 'with grand high mass and oratorio' was performed by the archbishop, Dr Murray, following which a charity sermon was preached by Rev. Mr Ward. The newspaper notice advised that 'the collection will go to liquidate the heavy debt incurred by building a chapel in that poor district'.[157] Reflecting the growing population living south of the Grand Canal, in December of the same year Dr Murray constituted the new parish of St Peter of Milltown and Harold's Cross, and appointed Fr William Stafford as parish priest of the new parish.[158]

The debt incurred by the Catholic diocese in building Milltown chapel appears not to have been significantly reduced, for two years later, in September 1825, a further appeal was made for funds to liquidate the debt. On this occasion the Rev. P. Dowling delivered a charity sermon and the public and parishioners who could not attend the sermon were asked to give

154 NAI, VO, OL50945, House Book for Milltown Village 1845, no. 79.

155 Parish Newsletter of the Church of Ss Columbanus and Gall, Milltown, April 2017.

156 Patrick Cunningham, 'The Catholic Directory for 1821', *Reportorium Novum*, ii, no. 2 (1959–1960), p. 359.

157 *Freeman's Journal*, 18 October 1823, p. 1.

158 Rev. William M. O'Riordan, 'The Succession of Parish Priests in the Archdiocese of Dublin, 1771–1851', *Reportorium Novum*, i, no. 2 (1956), p. 423.

'benefactions' to a list of local gentlemen, including Messrs Stapleton, De Veaux, Burke and Hevey, each of whom lived in Milltown or its vicinity.[159]

The small chapel building continued to serve the Catholic inhabitants of the village for the remainder of nineteenth century. In 1863 a charity sermon was preached in St Gall's in aid of a collection to 'defray the expenses of urgent repairs required in the abovenamed church'.[160] Despite the growth of large and elaborately decorated Catholic churches in the Dublin diocese in the second half of the nineteenth century there do not seem ever to have been any proposals to build a new bigger church in Milltown. Indeed, by the end of the nineteenth century the Jesuits at Milltown Park and the Sisters of Charity at Mount St Anne's each had chapels built of granite which were much more lavishly appointed than the village church of Ss Gall and Columbanus.[161]

Milltown Park was the Jesuit headquarters in Ireland where the order's primary focus from 1860 onwards was on training priests and offering retreats, or spiritual exercises as they were sometimes called, to priests and middle-class Catholic men.[162] The following notice in the *Freeman's Journal* was typical of the activity undertaken by the Jesuits at Milltown Park in the nineteenth and twentieth centuries:

> *A spiritual retreat for lay gentlemen will be given next month at Milltown Park by the Rev. Henry Lynch, S.J. It will begin on Sunday the 16th December at six o'clock in the evening and end on the following Sunday the 23 December at eleven in the morning.*[163]

In October 1863 the Jesuits conducted a mission in Milltown village, culminating in a solemn high mass.[164] Thereafter, the Jesuits of Milltown Park very rarely involved themselves in pastoral work in Milltown or with the affairs of St Gall's church. One exception occurred in 1897, when a Milltown church improvement fund was set up to fund the redecoration of St Gall's church. One of the promotors and fundraisers for this initiative was Fr Peter Finlay SJ of Milltown Park.[165]

Fr Peter Finlay and his Jesuit brother Fr Tom Finlay held very strident views on religion and politics. They were both avowedly anti-Parnellite after the latter's divorce scandal, and at times the brothers' views expressed in the Jesuit periodical, the *Lyceum*, led to censure from their clerical superiors. Of the two priests, Fr Peter Finlay was described as being the most inflexible and not 'sensitive to the atmosphere' of the times.[166] It is puzzling why such a remote intellectual priest should be chosen to deliver the homily to the parishioners of St Gall's at Sunday mass as part of the fundraising appeal for the church improvement fund, which was published verbatim the *Rathmines News*.[167] Fr Finlay initially lauded the achievements of Ss Gall

159 *Freeman's Journal*, 17 September 1825, p. 1.

160 *Freeman's Journal*, 17 October 1863, p. 3.

161 *Rathmines News*, 13 March 1897, p. 4 (Milltown Park); 20 January 1887 (Mount St Anne's).

162 *Freeman's Journal*, 20 January 1860, p. 2.

163 *Freeman's Journal*, 29 November 1860, p. 1.

164 *Freeman's Journal*, 17 October 1863, p. 3.

165 *Rathmines News*, 30 October 1897, p. 4.

166 Thomas J. Morrisey, SJ, *Thomas A. Finlay, S.J., 1848–1940 Educationalist, Editor, Social Reformer* (Dublin, 2004), pp. 44–5.

167 *Rathmines News*, 30 October 1897, p. 5. An abbreviated report was published in the *Dublin Daily Nation* on 25 October 1897, at p. 5.

and Columbanus before warning the congregation of the religious perils of the times, some of which resonate in the twenty-first century:

> *It has happened in other lands than our own, where anti-Catholic Catholics have gained the ear of the people, the consequences of their teaching have been distrust first, then dislike of the clergy, neglecting the sacraments, half empty churches, and a gradual decay of Faith. Are we wholly beyond the possibility of such danger among themselves?*

Fr Finlay concluded his sermon with the following exhortation to the men in the congregation:

> *If the Catholic men of Milltown were to stand together and to give each week only half of what they spend on useless or harmful luxuries – on smoking and on drink – how very soon would the improvements be accomplished?*[168]

How well Fr Finlay's sermon was received is not recorded but the men were unlikely to give up their harmful luxuries lightly. It is likely too that by the end of a long mass most of the congregation were impatient to avail of the limited leisure time available to them on Sundays and soon afterwards forgot the injunctions of Fr Finlay – except perhaps for a young man named Patrick Doyle, who was an extremely devout Catholic, a non-smoker and a pioneer.[169] Doyle went on to fight and die in the 1916 Rising. Immediately before he was killed by a sniper's bullet, Doyle reportedly said to his comrade Tom Walsh: 'Did I ever think I'd see a day like this? Shouldn't we all be grateful to the good God that he has allowed us to take part in a fight like this?'[170]

St Gall's church was eventually redecorated in 1905 to a particularly richly coloured and elaborate design under the supervision of the parish priest, Monsignor FitzPatrick.[171] The building was later refurbished and enlarged to its present size in 1935.[172]

THE CHURCH OF IRELAND AND THE ORIGINS OF ST PHILIP'S CHURCH, TEMPLE ROAD

As previously noted, the Catholic chapel in Milltown village was built on land owned by William Hogan of Fairyland. In 1830 William Hogan's second daughter, Mary, married William Henry Flemyng, who later became a Church of Ireland clergyman. Six years later, in 1836, Hogan built a small chapel of ease at his own expense for the convenience of Church of Ireland worshippers in Milltown. This small place of worship was built beyond the northern boundary wall of Hogan's home at Fairyland behind four small cottages in Lee's Lane (Map 16a/29).[173] The *Freeman's Journal* reported the appreciation of the archdeacon of Dublin who noted that 'by this benevolent and generous act a number of Protestant parishioners and the poor of that vicinity are accommodated with a house of worship adjacent to their homes

168 *Rathmines News*, 30 October 1897, p. 5.

169 Patrick Doyle papers, biographical note by Doyle's granddaughter Mrs May Nolan (NLI, MS 46,594).

170 Paul O'Brien, *Blood on the Streets: 1916 and the battle for Mount Street Bridge* (Dublin, 2008), p. 69.

171 *Rathmines News*, 23 December 1905, p. 4.

172 Murray, 'The Story of Milltown', under the section headed Modern Milltown.

173 *Freeman's Journal*, 11 October 1836, p. 3.

and convenient for their families'.[174] The surveyors of the Griffith's Valuation first visited Milltown village in 1845. During their visit they recorded the dimensions of the chapel as being 22 feet by 33 feet, and that it was under the management of the Rev. Mr Hartage.[175]

It is possible that Hogan's act of generosity in building the chapel of ease influenced the appointment of his son-in-law, Rev. William Henry Flemyng, as incumbent (i.e. perpetual curate) of St Philip's parish, Milltown, in 1846. This appointment occurred not long after the St Philip's parish had been created as a parochial district separate from the Parish of St Peter in 1840.[176] During his incumbency at St Philip's, Rev. Flemyng and his family lived in villas on Milltown Road close to Classon's Bridge called Nullamore and Rydalmount.[177]

The chapels of the two religious faiths stood almost side by side for 30 years in Milltown village. During this time relations between the two religious communities seem to have been cordial enough, at least initially. In 1849, when the first national school was being set up in Milltown under the management of Fr William Meagher, an application for aid was supported by Rev. Flemying.[178] However, St Philip's parishioners later made arrangements for separate religious instruction for their own children. In October 1856 the local vestry resolved that:

> *Mr Lee be requested to offer to Mrs Waldron one shilling and six pence a week to come each Sunday to St Peter's Schoolroom [as it was then called] at 1 O'o'clock a.m. and teach catechism ... to the children who present themselves at the Sunday School between 10 a.m. and morning divine service.*[179]

The Sunday school house was located in a small building leased from William Lee on the north side of the village main street beside St Peter's chapel of ease (Map 16a/28).[180]
The fledgling parish of St Philip's began to grow almost as soon as it had been established. In 1851 the chapel of ease was extended with the result that the building could accommodate an organ and 20 pews, each of which were individually allocated to parishioners for £1 per annum in 1856.[181] The following year the parish boundary was enlarged so that its territory now comprised the two civil townlands of Milltown and Rathmines South (Map 15) and, at the same time, the archdeacon of Dublin consented to the parish becoming a perpetual cure. The extent of the parish as delineated in 1857 continued unchanged until modern times, save for some minor boundary adjustments made with the neighbouring parishes of Rathmines

---

174 *Freeman's Journal*, 11 October 1836, p. 3.

175 NAI, VO, OL5945, House Book for Milltown Village 1845, no. 67.

176 J.B. Leslie and W.J.R. Wallace, *The clergy of Dublin and Glendalough* (Ulster Historical Foundation and the Diocesan Councils of Dublin and Glendalough, 2001), pp. 139, 631.

177 Pettigrew and Oulton's Dublin Almanac and General Register of Ireland 1848, p. 855; RCB Library, D6/64.

178 NAI ED1/29/47/1.

179 RCB Library P654, St Philip's Parish Vestry Book.

180 VO, Cancellation Books 1855–1862 for County of Dublin, Barony of Uppercross, Parish of St Peter, Electoral Division of Rathmines, p. 125 at entry 17/28.

181 RCB Library, D6/64, Dublin diocesan papers, St Philip's Parish, Milltown; RCB Library P654, St Philip's Parish Vestry Book, 12 May 1856.

and Sandford in the early twentieth century.[182] The enlargement of St Philip's parish necessitated the appointment two years later of a curate, Rev. Charles Holt Ensell, to assist Rev. Flemying.[183] For a time Rev. Ensell lived in a mid-eighteenth-century detached house located off the main street in Milltown village, called Turret House, until he was promoted to the incumbency in Lucan in 1862.[184]

The tensions between the two majority Christian faiths, particularly concerning proselytism and doctrinal differences, occasionally surfaced in Milltown in the mid-nineteenth century. On 14 August 1859 Rev. Ensell delivered a charity sermon at St Philip's chapel of ease in Milltown in aid of the Protestant Orphan Union. This charity was one of several devoted to saving orphaned children from the clutches of rival Christian faiths. The objects of the Protestant Orphan Union left no doubt as to the primary importance of its missionary intent:

> *A very large class of Protestant Orphans, viz; those who have had only one parent Protestant are throughout the whole North of Ireland, Dublin, Wicklow etc without any Protestant Asylum except that which this Society can afford. The object of the Orphan Refuge is to preserve the Protestantism of those Orphans. While Roman Catholic 'Orphanages', which shelter the offspring of those unhappy marriages have long existed, it is only within the last few years that Protestants have turned their attention to the duty and importance of rescuing these poor children from the dangers to which they are so peculiarly exposed.*[185]

Rev. Ensell, who seems to have been in demand for his public speaking abilities, delivered charity sermons in October 1862, shortly before his relocation to Lucan, at divine services in Clonsilla, Rathcoole and Donard in aid of the Society for the Propagation of the Gospel in Foreign Parts.[186] In June of the following year, the Irish Church Missions to Roman Catholics hosted a sermon by the Rev. Eade, who had apparently attended mass in Rathmines Catholic church celebrated by 'Priest Bentley' for the feast of Corpus Christi. Rev. Eade had, perhaps controversially for the time, deliberately attended mass so that he could later dispute Fr Bentley's sermon on the Catholic doctrine of transubstantiation, as explained in the newspaper advertisement for Rev. Eade's sermon:

182 Leslie and Wallace, *The clergy of Dublin and Glendalough*, p. 139; RCB Library, D6/64 and P654/15/2 (parish maps), RCB Library, P654/27, miscellaneous documents concerning St Philip's Parish, Milltown. In 1982 the Parish of St Philip's was joined with the Parish of Sandford.

183 *Leinster Express*, 1 July 1859, p. 8.

184 Thom's Directory 1862, p. 1354; *Dublin Daily Express*, 21 November 1862, p. 1.

185 *Saunders's Newsletter*, 13 August 1859, p. 4.

186 *Dublin Daily Express*, 18 October 1862, p. 1.

Why is the Rev. Mr Bentley of Milltown, who preached last Thursday evening in Rathmines Chapel, wrong in stating that John vi. 54 – 58 must be taken literally and applied to the Eucharistic Sacrament? Roman Catholic friends, come and hear. Believe the Bible and not your priests.[187]

The opening up of the Palmerston estate in Upper Rathmines for development in the 1860s meant that the chapel in Milltown was no longer able to meet the needs of the growing congregation of St Philip's. Accordingly, a site for a new chapel was donated by Lord Palmerston on Temple Road and the new building was consecrated by the archbishop of Dublin on 1 May 1867.[188] Initially, all did not go smoothly after the move from Milltown village to Temple Road. It would appear that there were differences of opinion or personality clashes among the congregation, which caused the resignation of Rev. Flemying in late January or early February 1871.[189] When Rev. Flemying was handing over the keys of the church to Charles Granby Burke, the churchwarden, he remarked in his covering letter dated 5 May 1871 that:

It is indeed with extreme regret I feel myself through the influence of one man in the parish, a comparative stranger, totally banished from that building which I had taken so lively an interest in rising up.[190]

During the process to replace Rev. Flemying as incumbent of St Philip's several candidates emerged, one of whom was the assistant curate, the Rev. Frederick John Lucas.[191] On 31 March 1871 Rev. Lucas petitioned the archbishop of Dublin for the position vacated by Rev. Flemying with the support of the entire St Philip's congregation, which included (among many others) the following residents of the big houses of Milltown: Richard Warneford Boyle (Milltown House), C.W. McCutcheon (Prospect House/Milltown Hill/The Old House), the Misses Hunt (Elm Hall/Elm House), Charlotte St George (Swiss Cottage/Garrynure), Frederick L'Estrange (Mount Prospect/Grove House), E.H. L'Estrange (Greenmount/Greenfields), John Lee (Rydalmount), Maurice Brooks (Nullamore) and Alfred Henshaw (Hatherton, Richmond Avenue South).[192] Needless to say, when Rev. Lucas was not chosen by the Dublin diocesan board of nomination as Rev. Flemying's successor there was disquiet among parishioners.[193] Rumblings of discontent continued into the summer of 1871 when an anonymous letter writer to *Saunders's Newsletter* complained about some of the design of St Philip's church, which he found too Catholic in its decoration and which he described as 'an attempt being made to force another innovation in the church in this parish'.[194]

By the early 1880s the number of parishioners' children attending the parish Sunday school exceeded 100. The parish had incurred a debt of £400 in building a new school house in the grounds of St Philip's church and sales of work were organised to raise funds

187 *Saunders's Newsletter*, 6 June 1863, p. 4.

188 RCB Library, D6/64; *Saunders's Newsletter*, 27 April 1867, p. 2.

189 *Saunders's Newsletter*, 11 February 1871, p. 3.

190 RCB Library, Miscellaneous Documents, P654/27.

191 *Saunders's Newsletter*, 19 April 1871, p. 2.

192 RCB Library, Miscellaneous Documents, P654/27; *Saunders's Newsletter*, 5 May 1871, p. 2.

193 *Saunders's Newsletter, 5 May 1871*, p. 2; 9 May 1871, p. 2.

194 *Saunders's Newsletter*, 27 June 1871, p. 2.

to clear off this liability.[195] Aside from religious instruction, the children were sometimes brought on day trips to the countryside, such as in May 1899 when the Rev. Moffatt led a trip to Blessington, to which the party had travelled by the steam tram from Terenure.[196] The Rev. Moffatt had been appointed curate and incumbent of St Philip's parish successively in 1885 and 1886. Prior to his ordination as a deacon in 1882, Rev. Moffatt had qualified as a medical doctor and had served in the army medical corps.[197]

Considerable numbers of the residents in the villas and big houses in Milltown and Upper Rathmines were members of the Church of Ireland congregation of St Philip's church on Temple Road. These parishioners took the practice of their faith seriously and supported their small parish by acting as churchwardens, subscribing for pews in the church and supporting parish fundraising and charitable activities.[198] A curious postscript to the relocation of Protestant worship to Temple Road was that the old chapel in Milltown village fell into ruins which were for several decades afterwards recorded on successive OS maps, thereby giving a mistaken impression of antiquity (Maps 18 & 20).

THE KEATINGE SCANDAL

The history of St Philip's parish during the final decades of the nineteenth century is unremarkable save for its unwitting involvement in a clerical scandal during the autumn of 1886, which was widely reported in the national press at the time. In short, the scandal concerned a fraudster and bogus clergyman called Theodore Oswald Keatinge who came to Dublin from England in the spring of 1886 and preached in a number of Dublin Protestant churches, including St Philip's, during the summer of that year. The background to this extraordinary case is as follows.

At the beginning of 1886 Keatinge was living in England under police supervision following his release from prison some years previously.[199] Keatinge now held himself out as having been formerly a Jesuit student and a Catholic priest, but having subsequently converted to Protestantism, he was now subjected to vicious persecution by the Catholic Church and the Vatican. Keatinge embellished his fictitious story to suit his audience and gained the confidence and support of evangelically inclined Protestants in London, including a Colonel Rowe and a Rev. Berguer.[200] Critically, Keatinge managed to secure a meeting in London with the archbishop of Dublin, Dr William Conyngham Plunket, who was taken in by Keatinge's tale.[201] Dr Plunket told Keatinge that should Keatinge be offered employment in his diocese he would give the matter favourable consideration.[202] Thus encouraged, with the help of Colonel Rowe, Keatinge applied in February 1886 for assistance from the Priests' Protection Society. This society was an Irish Protestant charity whose objects were to aid former Catholic priests

195 *Freeman's Journal*, 10 November 1883, p. 3.

196 *Rathmines News*, 20 May 1899, p. 4.

197 Leslie and Wallace, *The Clergy of Dublin and Glendalough*, p. 896.

198 RCB Library, P654, St Philip's Church Vestry Book 12 May 1856; *Dublin Daily Express*, 29 December 1862, p. 3; *Saunders's Newsletter*, 15 June 1870, p. 4; *Dublin Daily Express*, 24 April 1878, p. 6; *Freeman's Journal*, 10 November 1883, p. 3.

199 *Dublin Daily Express*, 26 October 1886, p. 2.

200 *Freeman's Journal*, 8 December 1886, p. 6; 16 December 1886, p. 3.

201 *Dublin Daily Express*, 10 December 1886, p. 8.

202 *Freeman's Journal*, 10 December 1886, p. 5.

who had converted to Protestantism.[203] The secretary of the Society was Captain Robert Wade Thompson of Clonskeagh Castle. Robert's father, Thomas H. Thompson, was a trustee of the Society.[204] Although the Thompsons resided in Taney parish they were active members of St Philip's congregation, Thomas H. Thompson having previously served as the parishioners' churchwarden there.[205]

In May 1886 Keatinge travelled to Ireland for an interview with the committee of the Priests' Protection Society, having previously completed a detailed questionnaire and made a lengthy written submission to the Society.[206] Prior to the interview, Captain Thompson had met with Dr Plunket to discuss Keatinge's application to the Society and to consider the testimonials submitted on his behalf.[207] At the interview, the committee of the Priests' Protection Society was sympathetic to Keatinge's plight and its members were impressed by his testimonials from Colonel Rowe and Rev. Berguer and by credulous letters of authority from the bishop of London and the archbishop of Canterbury, which were later found to be forgeries.[208] The upshot was that the Priests' Protection Society decided to take Keatinge into its care for three months and to pay him a salary of £100 per annum.[209] At the same time, some of the Society's committee members felt it appropriate that Keatinge should be occupied in some clerical capacity and to that end one of the committee members, the Rev. Mills, obtained verbal permission from Dr Plunket for Keating to preach in Rev. Mills' church in Inchicore, provided that a written application was submitted by Rev. Mills stating the grounds on which his Grace's permission was sought.[210]

The necessary formalities having been completed, Keatinge commenced preaching at Inchicore. A short time later Rev. Moffatt contacted the Priests' Protection Society seeking permission to employ Keatinge as a curate at St Philip's.[211] Why Rev. Moffatt made this request is unknown, but it is possible that he was canvassed by one of the Thompsons of Clonskeagh Castle. In any event Rev. Moffatt obtained the necessary permissions from the Priests' Protection Society and the archbishop of Dublin.[212] Keatinge preached his first sermon at St Philip's in the last week of May and following on from that Rev. Moffatt formally employed Keatinge as a curate on an initial salary of 10*s*. a week (later increased to £1) following which Keatinge's contract with the Priests' Protection Society was terminated as he had secured work at St Philip's.[213] By that stage the Society had paid Keatinge £44 in total.[214]

---

203 *Freeman's Journal*, 8 December 1886, p. 6.

204 *Freeman's Journal*, 8 December 1886, p. 6.

205 *Dublin Daily Express*, 24 April 1878.

206 *Freeman's Journal*, 2 November 1886, p. 5; *Dublin Daily Express*, 10 December 1886, p. 8.

207 *Dublin Daily Express*, 10 December 1886, p. 8.

208 *Dublin Evening Mail*, 22 October 1886, p. 3; *Irish Times*, 22 October 1886, p. 5.

209 *Belfast Newsletter*, 9 November 1886, p. 7.

210 *Irish Times*, 22 October 1886, p. 5; *Freeman's Journal*, 9 December 1886, p. 6.

211 *Freeman's Journal*, 8 December 1886, p. 6.

212 *Dublin Daily Express*, 26 October 1886, p. 5; *Belfast Newsletter*, 23 October 1886, p. 8; 9 November 1886, p. 7; *Freeman's Journal*, 9 December 1886, p. 6.

213 *Belfast Newsletter*, 9 November 1886, p. 7; *Freeman's Journal*, 9 November 1886, p. 7; 8 December 1886, p. 6; *Dublin Daily Express*, 10 December 1886, p. 8.

214 *Dublin Daily Express*, 10 December 1886, p. 8.

During the summer of 1886 Keatinge preached frequently to the congregation of St Philip's, whose members were extremely impressed by his oratorical skills. Keatinge's sermons were thus very well attended with the result that the parish debt on the Sunday school was all but paid off. [215] Although Keatinge's official salary was very modest, Captain Robert Wade Thompson gave evidence at Keatinge's trial that Keatinge had received far more money from the parish vestry, including a cheque for a large sum which was signed by Thompson.[216]

While Keatinge was insinuating himself with the parishioners of St Philip's during the summer of 1886 it seems that he was less adroit with managing his relationship with the Rev. Moffatt, for by the middle of August the pair had fallen out. The reasons for this are not at all clear but it seems that Keatinge overplayed his hand and had become too self-confident and assertive for Rev. Moffatt's liking.[217] According to subsequent evidence given in court, Rev. Moffatt stated that their dispute arose over Keatinge's desire to take control of the singing arrangements at St Philip's, which Rev. Moffatt would not allow because Keatinge was not a musician. As a result of their disagreement, Moffatt dismissed Keatinge on 24 August and followed up with a letter on 31 August confirming that their 'temporary engagement' would terminate at the end of September if Keatinge was agreeable to stay on until then.[218] While Keatinge had been employed at St Philip's Rev. Moffatt had paid him a total of £12 10*s*.[219] Rev. Moffatt next wrote to Archbishop Plunket to inform him of these developments and to check if Dr Plunket had any objection to Keatinge continuing his ministrations until the end of September. The archbishop did not object and on 10 September 1886 Dr Plunket wrote to Keatinge informing him it was Keatinge's duty to cooperate with Rev. Moffatt's arrangements, adding 'I feel sure that you will do what you can to quiet any feelings of excitement that may prevail in the parish.'[220] On the following day a notification of Keatinge's sermons to be preached at St Philip's on Sunday 12 September was inserted in the *Dublin Daily Express*.[221]

As his curacy at St Philip's was due to finish at the end of September Keatinge had to find alternative employment. He accordingly made contact with the incumbent of the Old Molyneux church in Bride Street, the Rev. Dr Murphy, with a view to obtaining work.[222] It seems that a large majority of the congregation of St Philip's were very disappointed with Keatinge's departure from the parish and in response they formed a committee to raise subscriptions for a testimonial to Keatinge. The testimonial committee held a public meeting in St Philip's schoolhouse in early October by which stage £67 had been collected for the testimonial fund.[223] In the meantime, Keatinge had managed to secure permission from Rev. Murphy to

215 *Irish Times*, 26 October 1886, p. 6; *Freeman's Journal*, 8 December 1886, p. 6.

216 *Dublin Daily Express*, 10 December 1886, p. 8.

217 The detailed explanations for the dispute 'from reliable sources' given by the *Irish Times* on 21 October 1886 at p. 5 were not substantiated in subsequent court proceedings, and so cannot be relied upon.

218 *Dublin Daily Express*, 26 October 1886, p. 5; *Belfast Newsletter*, 9 November 1886, p. 7.

219 *Dublin Daily Express*, 26 October 1886, p. 5.

220 *Dublin Daily Express*, 26 October 1886, p. 5.

221 *Dublin Daily Express*, 11 September 1886, p.1.

222 *Freeman's Journal*, 2 November 1886, p. 2.

223 *Dublin Daily Express*, 27 September 1886, p. 2; 6 October 1886, p. 2.

preach at the Molyneux church on the 3 October and the 10 October.[224] An indication of the influence over the St Philip's congregation which Keatinge had built up was evident in the advertisement for Keatinge's 'special appeals' in the Molyneux church in Bride Street, which concluded with the following practical information:

By the courtesy of the Dublin United Tramways Company, Special Cars will start from the Palmerston Park Terminus at 10.30, 10.37, 10.45, 10.52 and 11 am, and at 6.30, 6.37 and 6.45 pm.[225]

It was thus apparent that Keatinge was not obeying the archbishop's instructions to 'quiet any feelings of excitement that may prevail in the parish'. In fact Keatinge had been spreading rumours about the circumstances of his departure, the nature of which can only be gleaned from the press report of the testimonial committee, where one individual referred to Keating's severance from the parish, 'the cause of which they all regretted', while another attendee alluded to Keatinge's 'illness which had been induced by worry'.[226]

If anyone had cause to become ill through worry it was Rev. Moffatt, for he had lost the support of many of his parishioners, several of whom now appeared to be switching their allegiance to Keatinge. At this point Rev. Moffatt decided to investigate Keatinge's personal history and to substantiate the claims made by Keatinge as to his clerical background and experiences while a member of the Catholic Church. What prompted Rev. Moffatt to do this is unknown, although the *Irish Times* asserted that Rev. Moffatt had received private intelligence that Keatinge was an imposter. Some credence may be given to this assertion because Rev. Moffatt later confirmed in court that he did not tell the St Philip's vestry of a plans to travel to England.[227] In any event, Rev. Moffatt's investigations in England with the Jesuit and Church of England communities discovered that Keatinge was a complete fraudster with a long criminal record and that he had no genuine clerical background whatsoever, notwithstanding his carefully constructed fictitious past.[228] Rev. Moffatt duly informed the clerical authorities and Keatinge's licence to preach was revoked by the archbishop of Dublin in mid-October. Shortly afterwards Keatinge fled to England.[229] Keatinge was later arrested in Liverpool on 23 October and brought back to Dublin by Irish detectives to stand trial at the suit of the Attorney General on charges of obtaining money by false pretences with intent to defraud, and for failing to report himself to the police. The initial criminal proceedings took place at the northern divisional police court. Despite the overwhelming evidence against him, Keatinge's tactics were to impugn the motives of Rev. Moffatt who, Keatinge alleged, was prosecuting him out of malice and jealousy. Rev. Moffatt denied that he wanted to prosecute Keatinge and the crown solicitor pointed out that the proceedings had been taken by the Attorney General and by no one else.[230] At the conclusion

224 *Freeman's Journal*, 2 November 1886, p. 2.

225 *Dublin Daily Express*, 2 October 1886, p. 2.

226 *Dublin Daily Express*, 6 October 1886, p. 2.

227 *Irish Times*, 21 October 1886, p. 5; *Belfast Newsletter*, 9 November 1886, p. 7.

228 *Freeman's Journal*, 21 October 1886, p. 5; *Dublin Weekly Nation*, 23 October 1886, p. 9.

229 *Dublin Daily Express*, 19 October 1886, p. 4; *Belfast Newsletter*, 23 October 1886, p. 8.

230 *Dublin Evening Telegraph*, 23 October 1886, p. 3; *Irish Times*, 25 October 1886, p. 5; *Dublin Daily Express*, 26 October 1886, p. 5, 29 October 1886, p. 5.

of the police court hearing the magistrate committed Keatinge for trial by jury at the next Commission of Oyer and Terminer on the charges put forward by the Attorney General.[231] Rather surprisingly, the jury at the Commission court failed to reach a verdict because they could not agree whether or not Keatinge had intended to defraud the Priests' Protection Society.[232] As a result, a retrial took place at the Commission of Oyer and Terminer with a new jury, which in the end found Keatinge guilty of defrauding the Priests' Protection Society out of £40. For this conviction Keatinge was sentenced to 18 months' imprisonment with hard labour.[233] Keatinge was released 10 months later in September 1887 by order of the Lord Lieutenant because of poor health.[234] Notwithstanding his very public disgrace, for a brief period after his release Keatinge delivered public lectures in Dublin to his diehard supporters before departing Ireland permanently.[235]

The extensive newspaper reports about the scandal show that Keatinge, like all fraudsters, was an extremely intelligent, articulate and persuasive individual with an ability to forge documents. His chosen methods of deception as a distressed clergyman with an exotic Catholic or Protestant background – as the circumstances and audience dictated – worked extremely well in the Victorian era. This was a time when religious faith and creed was a fundamental component of individual identity, and frequently in Ireland, of one's political identity and social class too. The Keatinge scandal also coincided with a period of increasing sectarian tensions in Ireland as Parnell and the Home Rule movement gathered force. Keatinge skilfully used these tensions to his advantage when he targeted the archbishop of Dublin, Dr Plunket, and the Priests' Protection Society. Both Dr Plunket and the committee of the Priests' Protection Society held strong Protestant evangelical views, so Keatinge's fantastical, fabricated story of Catholic persecution and religious conversion to the Protestant faith would have had an emotional appeal to these men and affirmed whatever anti-Catholic prejudices they held privately.[236]

The Keatinge affair undoubtedly caused much embarrassment to the parishioners of St Philip's, who had been so completely duped by him.[237] It was Keatinge's personal aura which impressed them most and not the fact that he had converted to Protestantism, as an unnamed parishioner of St Philip's explained in the letter columns of the *Freeman's Journal*:

> *And here allow me to correct an idea that he [Keatinge] was taken up by us because he was supposed to be a convert from the Church of Rome. No such thing. Any of us who took and even now take interest in him knew and cared nothing for the Priests' Protection Society (which seem to be a mischievous body), he was introduced to St Philip's by the rector, and the congregation*

231 *Belfast Newsletter*, 9 November 1886, p. 7.

232 *Freeman's Journal*, 9 December 1886, p. 6.

233 *Dublin Daily Express*, 10 December 1886, p. 8; 11 December 1886, p. 6.

234 *Northern Whig*, 3 September 1887, p. 5.

235 *Freeman's Journal*, 14 September 1887, p. 5; 12 October 1887, p. 7; *Dublin Daily Express*, 14 September 1887, p. 3; *Irish Times*, 24 September 1887, p. 4.

236 James McGuire and James Quinn (eds), *Dictionary of Irish Biography* (RIA/Cambridge, 2009), 8, p. 169 for William Conyngham Plunket. Thomas H. Thompson was secretary of the Protestant Defence Association before he died: *Irish Times*, 13 August 1886, p. 3.

237 It is worth noting that no mention is made of the Keatinge scandal in the vestry minute books or parish records of St Philip's deposited in the Representative Church Body's archives.

knew nothing of him till his extraordinary and beautiful delivery in pulpit and reading desk took us, as it were, by storm.[238]

The final word belongs to Keatinge. He died in 1891 in a Sydney gaol, having been sentenced to five years' imprisonment for sexually assaulting a twelve-year-old child.[239]

VICTORIAN PHILANTHROPY: MISS ELIZABETH MAGEOUGH

A very brief mention of the Mageough Home is included here because this residential complex was built at the northern end of Milltown townland at its boundary with Cullenswood townland, and formed part of St Philip's Church of Ireland parish in the nineteenth century (Map 17).

Elizabeth Mageough was a single lady who lived with her parents and siblings in the mid-nineteenth century in a house called Richview, which is still standing on its own grounds at the north-eastern end of Palmerston Park just inside the townland of Rathmines South at its boundary with Milltown townland. Richview was one of the first houses to be built on the W.C. Hogan estate at Fairyland in about 1830 (Map 15). Elizabeth Mageough sold Richview in 1862. She had outlived her parents and siblings by the time of her death in 1869, by which time she had amassed a considerable fortune. By virtue of a complicated set of circumstances the residue of her estate, amounting to over £44,000, was vested in trustees who eventually built the Mageough Home on Cowper Road in 1878 on land purchased from Cowper Temple, a descendant of Lord Palmerston. Although the testamentary intentions expressed by Miss Mageough had been complicated by unforeseen events – primarily the disestablishment of the Church of Ireland in 1870 – it was clear that Miss Mageough had wanted her bequest to go towards establishing a home for 'aged females professing the Protestant faith and of good character and sobriety'. In 2006 the original objects of the trust were extended to include elderly Protestant single men and couples, thus creating a mixed-gender community, residing in a residential complex of 37 individual houses.[240]

A public notice which appeared in the *Rathmines News* in 1904 explained in clear terms how the charity operated:

The Mageough Home, Cowper Road, Rathmines. The trustees will meet in May next for the election of not more than three inmates, each of whom will be allotted a furnished house, rent free, with coals and gas. Each applicant must be over fifty years of age; and must give satisfactory proof that she is without means, or that she has a yearly income not exceeding £31, which must be lodged with the registrar quarterly, in advance, for weekly disbursement by him for her benefit. Each applicant whose income is less than £31, will be on election entitled to an allowance from the funds of the Institution which will make up that sum, but the amount available for this purpose is, on the present occasion, very small ... Elections are made after careful inquiry into the merits of each case, without regard to personal influence, or canvassing.[241]

Over time this financial model became unsustainable and so residents were required to pay their way or make a cash donation to the institution, depending on their circumstances.

238 *Freeman's Journal*, 2 November 1886, p. 2.

239 *Irish Times*, 9 April 1891, p. 6; *Leinster Express*, 11 April 1891, p. 3.

240 Information sourced from the Mageough Home website, www.mageough.ie (accessed on 29 June 2018).

241 *Rathmines News*, 26 March 1904, p. 2.

Fundraising became a constant preoccupation of the management board and it is only in recent times that the finances of the Mageough Home have become relatively secure.[242]

DEVELOPMENTS AT CLASSON'S BRIDGE

At the turn of the nineteenth century the Milltown Road from the Packhorse Bridge to Rathmines was open farmland with very few buildings apart from the woollen mills on the Dodder at Dartry and some cabins along the road. The area to the west and south of Classon's Bridge had, since the beginning of the eighteenth century, been owned by the Temple family, whose family had, in the seventeenth century, originally settled in west Dublin at Palmerstown, and who were ennobled under the tile of Viscount Palmerston in 1723. In 1746 Henry Temple, the first Viscount Palmerston, leased the mansion house of Rathmines to Chief Justice William Yorke.[243] Yorke's name is recorded on Rocque's map of 1760, in an area now synonymous with Dartry (Map 4). By the mid-eighteenth century these lands came into the possession of James Classon of Rathmines, who in 1748 had been granted a lease by Viscount Palmerston of over 69 plantation acres in Rathmines.[244] As previously argued in Chapter 4, James Classon almost certainly gave his name to the eponymous bridge which spans the Dodder beside The Dropping Well pub.

The first sign of new developments beginning to take place beside Classon's Bridge occurs in 1819 when Mr Sweeney (variously spelled Swiney or Swinny) placed an advertisement for a house and 9 [plantation] acres of ground to let 'to a solvent tenant'. The grounds were:

> *situated between Rathmines and Milltown, on the left bank of the Dodder, and although but two miles from the [Dublin] Castle, possesses as much rural beauty, and delightful scenery, as could be enjoyed twenty miles from town.*[245]

Bladen Sweeney had started his business as a linen draper in 1786.[246] The historian John D'Alton, writing in 1837, recorded that 'At Windy Harbour, near Milltown, were the silk works of Mr Sweeney, now also deserted.'[247] Sweeney died in December 1833 at his home in Kildare Street aged seventy-five so the silk works at Windy Arbour may have closed due to his death or possibly because of the decline in the Irish silk industry during the 1820s and 1830s.[248]

The house and lands referred to in the 1819 advertisement made up the demesne called South Hill. This villa appears on a private estate map commissioned by an unknown leaseholder in 1833, by which time South Hill had been leased by Sweeney to Frances Elliott (Map 11).[249] Elliott subsequently sold South Hill in 1856 to a prominent Dublin merchant called James

---

242 *The Story of the Mageough*, Chapter 3, as found on the Mageough Home website.

243 Ball, *History of county Dublin*, ii, p. 106. Nessa O'Connor, *Palmerstown: An ancient place* (Dublin, 2003), p. 18; RD 123/345/84839.

244 RD 357/274/240334. According to a deed of 1856 (RD 1856/34/247), the demesne of South Hill (now the South Hill housing estate on the north side of the Milltown Road opposite The Dropping Well pub) was originally part of James Classon's lands.

245 *Saunders's Newsletter*, 15 April 1819, p. 4.

246 *Saunders's Newsletter*, 9 January 1786, p. 3.

247 D'Alton, *History of County Dublin*, p. 799.

248 *Limerick Chronicle*, 14 December 1833, p. 2.

249 'A map of premises on the north side of the River Dodder between the turn of the road from Rathmines to Milltown and Classon's Bridge, 1833' (NAI, MS 2754).

FitzGerald Lombard.[250] Lombard's daughter married the newspaper and tramway magnate William Martin Murphy, who lived a short distance up the road at Dartry House.[251]

The open space to the west of Classon's Bridge between the Milltown Road and the River Dodder was opened up by Bladen Sweeney for building in 1817 (Map 7). In the 1830s open ground between the Dodder weir and Classon's Bridge was acquired by local builder William Lee, who lived in Milltown village in the first half of the nineteenth century.[252] Lee built 10 labourers' cottages at Classon's Bridge on the flood plain of the River Dodder, which are depicted on the first edition of the six-inch OS map as lying in the townland of Rathmines South (Map 15).[253]

THE ORIGINS OF THE DROPPING WELL PUB

The well-known licensed premises called The Dropping Well, currently owned by publican Charlie Chalke and which is located beside Classon's Bridge on the north bank of the River Dodder between Milltown and Dartry, was established by John Howe in October 1831. Howe was a native of Keswick, a small town in the Lake District of Cumbria, where he had worked as a woollen manufacturer in his father-in-law's firm of John Twentyman and Son. John had married Jane Twentyman on 24 January 1810, so it may reasonably be inferred that he was born in the 1780s. Unfortunately, John Twentyman's business got into financial difficulties in the late 1820s and after it failed Howe and his family migrated to Dublin.[254] It is unknown why John Howe specifically chose to relocate to Dublin, but he may have hoped to pick up employment in one of the woollen mills in the vicinity of Dublin, the largest of which were owned by west Yorkshire families such as the Willans and the Houghtons.[255] As it transpired, Howe became a publican.

John Howe's public house began in controversial circumstances, the extensive details of which are contained among the papers of the Chief Secretary's Office, which are preserved in the National Archives.[256] In short, Howe put down roots in Milltown in October 1831 when he leased a new building beside Classon's Bridge. He successfully applied for a publican's licence at the county magistrates court in Rathfarnham and commenced trading. Soon afterwards, it was brought to Howe's attention that his licence was invalid, and he was advised to apply to the relevant authorities in Dublin city. An explanation for the licence's invalidity is not available, but the cause is probably related to the fact that Howe's pub lay just inside the city's jurisdiction on the north bank of the River Dodder whereas the Rathfarnham licence covered publicans in south county Dublin. Howe applied to the city authorities for a licence to deal in 'malt and spirituous liquors', but one of the presiding magistrates, Alderman Fleming, refused to grant Howe a licence because he (Fleming) was opposed to the establishment of a new public house in the district of Classon's Bridge, as there were already three or four public houses nearby in Milltown village and in Windy Arbour. Howe's failure to obtain a licence

250 RD 1856/34/247.

251 *Rathmines News*, 15 December 1900.

252 *Dublin Evening Post*, 5 October 1830, p. 1; Pettigrew and Oulton's Dublin Almanac and General Register of Ireland, 1843, p. 818; The Post Office and Annual Directory and Calendar for 1843, p. 300.

253 In the twentieth century the houses were called Roberts Cottages.

254 *Lancaster Gazette*, 10 February 1810, p.12; *Cumberland Packet*, 14 March 1826, p. 2; 1 August 1826, p. 2; 4 April 1828, p. 2; 30 October 1855, p. 5.

255 Dickson, *Dublin: The making of a capital city*, p. 283.

256 NAI, CSO/RP/1832/4299.

Plate 17. Classon's Bridge, Milltown, c. 1920 (image courtesy of the National Library of Ireland)

was compounded when he was prosecuted by the excise authorities, and as a result he was fined £12 10*s*. Howe's position was very precarious – he had no contacts, he could not earn a livelihood and he could not afford to pay the fine. A local Protestant clergyman, the Rev. John Prior, who was a curate attached to Taney parish, took up Howe's case and persistently lobbied the authorities on Howe's behalf. Howe's case was referred to the Chief Secretary's Office which determined that it could not overrule the magistrates' decision to refuse Howe's licence; nonetheless a civil servant recommended that the fine imposed by the excise authorities be remitted by the Lord Lieutenant.[257]

Unfortunately, the records do not provide any further information about John Howe's subsequent licence applications, but we know for certain that he was back trading by 1839, in which year his premises was flooded by the River Dodder![258] When the surveyors from the Griffith's Valuation visited Classon's Bridge in 1845, they recorded that William Lee was the landlord of a public house and 10 cottages which he rented out to publican John Howe and other weekly tenants respectively at 2*s*. a week. Apart from the public house, which was two storeys in height (15 feet), all of the cottages were single-storey dwellings.[259] John Howe died sometime between 1850 and 1851, the latter year being the first occasion on which Mrs Howe is recorded as the proprietress of the pub.[260]

257 NAI, CSO/RP/1832/4299; Ball and Hamilton, *Parish of Taney*, p. 76.

258 *Dublin Weekly Herald*, 3 August 1839, p. 3. The Dropping Well was flooded as recently as 2008: *Irish Times*, 6 September 2008.

259 NAI, VO, OL5936, House Book for Townland of Rathmines South 1845, nos 26–9.

260 Thom's Directory 1851, p. 905. Mrs Howe died in 1855 aged seventy: *Saunders's Newsletter*, 9 October 1855, p. 3; *Cumberland Packet*, 30 October 1855, p. 5.

In 1898 the then owner, Mrs Daly, renamed the pub 'The Dropping Well', apparently in reference to an 'an ancient well situated close by on the banks of the river Dodder'.[261] A fine photograph (Pl. 17) taken in about 1920 to the west of Classon's Bridge from the south bank of the River Dodder gives a good view of Classon's Bridge, The Dropping Well (then owned by Patrick Meagher), and the labourers' cottages (then called Roberts Cottages).

MYSTERIOUS DEATH AT CLASSON'S BRIDGE

The rhythm and routine of daily life in Milltown was violently interrupted in the early hours of Sunday 18 December 1842 when a dead body was discovered in suspicious circumstances in the lime kiln on the south bank of the River Dodder a little to the east of Classon's Bridge (Map 19), by a local youth named Patrick Tynan.[262] A short while after Tynan had raised the alarm another local boy named Edward Byrne, who worked in Duffys mills in Ballsbridge, was sent to the local police station in Donnybrook where he reported the incident. The first policeman arrived on the scene at 7 a.m. Constable James Carty had been out on his beat since 6 a.m., which ranged from Donnybrook to the Willans woollen mills at Dartry.[263] This incident was reported extensively in the national newspapers over a two-week period during and after the coroner's inquest which took place over five days from Monday 19 December to Friday 23 December 1842.[264]

The deceased was a man aged about twenty-five. When his body was discovered in the lime kiln on the Sunday morning he was partially burned and his throat had been cut. As the man's identity was unknown the corpse was laid out for public viewing in an outhouse attached to Howe's public house (now The Dropping Well). Over the course of the next few days hundreds of people walked to Milltown from the city and suburbs to view the body. This fact alone shows that news of the incident had spread rapidly around the city via newspaper reports and word of mouth. The deceased was identified on the following Wednesday morning as being a man named Alfred Lynch who lived with his father and siblings at Parnell Place, Harold's Cross, and who worked as a surveyor in the OS office in the Phoenix Park. The critical issue for the jury to determine during the five-day inquest was how Lynch had met his death – had he been murdered or had he committed suicide.

The enquiry was conducted by the Dr James McCarthy, the senior coroner for County Dublin, and took place on the premises of Howe's pub. The jury was composed of 18 or 19 men – the exact number reported varies – some of whom were Milltown residents. These included publicans John Howe and Patrick Hackett and local landowners George F. Mowlds and William McCann.[265] One of the witnesses to give evidence was Richard Charles of Millmount Lodge on the Dundrum Road. Charles's testimony was important because he heard the last cries uttered by Alfred Lynch immediately before his death:

> *I reside at Millmount Lodge, within about two fields of the lime-kiln; I was awoke on yesterday morning, but at what hour I cannot tell, by a bawl or loud noise that died away immediately; it was somewhat like the croaking of a raven, and it was rather loud or it would not have awoke me; I*

---

261 *Rathmines News*, 25 June 1898, p. 4.

262 *Freeman's Journal*, Monday 19 December 1842, p. 3.

263 *Freeman's Journal*, 21 December 1842, p. 3.

264 See especially the *Freeman's Journal*, the *Dublin Evening Post* and *The Nation* for the period 19–31 December 1842.

265 *The Nation*, 24 December 1842, p. 166; *Freeman's Journal*, 20 December 1842, p. 3.

observed to my wife at the time that it could not have been a raven at that hour; it did not last half a minute, and was not repeated; my mother also heard it, and like an old woman appeared to regard it as an omen to herself that she was about to die; my house is not half a quarter of a mile from the kiln, and I think it was from that direction the noise came; no car could pass in the direction of my house [from the direction of the lime kiln], as there is a river [the River Slang] and a large [mill] pond before the door; I have dogs, but they did not bark; the noise was very sudden and rather alarming.[266]

The evidence given by a local youth, Patrick Tynan, described as 'a fat, quiet, heavy looking boy, of about 18 years of age' is valuable because it outlines daily life in Milltown before the Famine. For this reason, extracts from Tynan's testimony are provided below.

I live with Mr Brennan, at Classon's Bridge, and I have lived with him as a servant boy since last May. I lived before that with my father and mother in Milltown. My father is a labouring man. I went to the lime kiln about half past five o'clock on yesterday [Sunday] morning, as near as I can judge. I went there to see if the fire was well up, as I wanted to warm a kettle of wash for one of the cows that was sick ... I went up to the kiln again about six o'clock, or half an hour after. I had been there before I was cutting potatoes in the house. After coming down the first time I went up again in consequence of finding a smell of something roasting. I thought from the smell that some of the boys might have been roasting a duck, as the smell was partly like that of burning feathers. I was in the habit of going up to warm wash for the cows on the kiln. When I saw the body I thought at first that it was a log of wood until I saw that the arm was raised up. I shouted as loud as I could, but nobody came, and then I ran down and called three times at the door for Patrick Callaghan, the lime burner's son ... I heard of a person named Bentley having been burnt in the kiln about four years ago. That man fell in by accident and had not been murdered. To the best of my opinion I got up about four o'clock in the morning. There is a clock in the house, but I do [sic] not mind to look at it before I went out.[267]

Ultimately, the evidence given by the many witnesses over the five-day hearing – family members of the deceased, medical experts, the police and the local inhabitants – all of which was transcribed almost verbatim by the press reporters, was inconclusive. As a result, the jury delivered the following verdict on Friday 23 December:

We find that Alfred Lynch was found dead on the lime kiln, near Classon's Bridge, in the parish of Taney, county Dublin, on Sunday morning, the 18th December, with the wound inflicted on the right side of his throat by a sharp instrument; but how he came to same place, or whether the wound was inflicted there, or by whom said, the jury cannot say, and we further find that said wound was inflicted on Sunday, the 18th December.[268]

Needless to say, such an inconclusive verdict fuelled continuing speculation into the New Year about the cause of Lynch's death.[269] Indeed, Alfred Lynch's boss at the OS office, Thomas Larcom, went as far as to formulate his own conspiracy theory several years later when, after the conviction of William Blake Kirwan for the murder of his wife on

266 *Freeman's Journal*, 20 December 1842, p. 3.

267 *Freeman's Journal*, 20 December 1842, p. 3. For brief details of Bentley's accident see *The Pilot*, 5 March 1838, p. 1.

268 *Freeman's Journal*, 24 December 1842, p. 3.

269 *The Nation*, 7 January 1843, p. 208 where the editor opined that the cause of death was suicide.

Ireland's Eye in 1852, Larcom opined that Kirwan had murdered Alfred Lynch in 1842 (coincidentally Kirwan had been a neighbour of the Lynch family in Parnell Place and also worked in the OS office).[270] Regardless, the case illustrates the primitive state of medical science and criminology at that time. A further sad aspect was that, due to a breakdown in communications over the Christmas weekend, Alfred Lynch's body was brought, on the orders of the coroner, from Classon's Bridge by ass and cart to Taney graveyard for internment on 26 December 1842 without the prior knowledge of his father, and without a funeral mass having been said for the deceased.[271]

The dramatic circumstances of the Lynch case brought Classon's Bridge to national consciousness for two weeks over the Christmas of 1842. That attention can be contrasted with a very brief report of an infanticide that occurred in the same place in April 1847:

> *Another inquest was held yesterday by James McCarthy, esq, at Howe's tavern, Upper Rathmines, on the body of a female child found near the lime kiln, Classon's Bridge. From the medical evidence it was apparent the child was a new born infant and that violence had been used by some persons unknown. The jury found a verdict accordingly.*[272]

The country was in the grip of the Famine when the new-born infant was done to death, which explains the perfunctory notice.

THE MILLTOWN ROAD OUTRAGE

One of the most sensational criminal trials of mid-nineteenth century Ireland had its origins in events close to Classon's Bridge which occurred on the night of 27 September 1861. Miss Louisa Jolly was a young woman of nineteen or twenty years of age who was a native of Portarlington. Since 26 August Louisa had been employed as a governess – today she would be called an au pair – at the Gelston family home in 'Dunlouis', Terenure Road East, Rathgar. On the evening of 27 September Louisa was in town with her younger brother at a religious tea meeting in Lombard Street. When they left at about 10 p.m. the last omnibus to Rathgar had departed Nelson's pillar and so her brother hailed a cab and negotiated a fare of 1*s.* 6*d.* to take his sister home to Rathgar. Louisa was not familiar with the geography of the city or its suburbs. Instead of taking Louisa to Rathgar, the cabman drove her to an isolated part of the Lower Churchtown Road about a quarter of a mile south of Classon's Bridge, at a spot close to where the junction with Churchtown Drive is now (Map 19). The cabman, John Curran, stopped his horse and entered the cab where he tried to kiss Louisa. When Louisa screamed and resisted his advances Curran violently attacked his fare and dragged her onto the ground. After a struggle Louisa broke free and fled into the fields on the left-hand side of the road, where Churchtown Drive and Churchtown Close are now. Curran was momentarily distracted by his horse which had moved off during the commotion, and while he retrieved the animal Louisa attempted to make good her escape. However, Curran pursued Louisa as she stumbled in the dark into water-filled ditches in the fields. At length, Louisa gave Curran some money and agreed to return to the cab on Curran's promise that he would not harm her. While Curran turned back towards the road Louisa made

270 Suzanne Leeson, *The Kirwan murder case, 1852: A glimpse of the Irish Protestant middle class in the mid-nineteenth century* (Dublin, 2019), p. 42 (Alfred Lynch's surname is mistakenly recorded as Byrne).

271 *Freemen's Journal*, 17 April 1843, p. 2 (John Lynch letter to editor). Burial records for Taney Parish on Irishgenealogy.ie website.

272 *Freemen's Journal*, 9 April 1847, p. 3.

Plate 18. Railway viaduct and quarry pond on the south bank of the River Dodder, Milltown, c. 1900 (courtesy of the Irish Architectural Archive)

her second bid to escape and this time she was successful. In the pitch dark, narrowly avoiding death or serious injury from falling over the precipice of the Milltown quarry adjacent to the River Dodder (where Patrick Doyle Road is now), Louisa made her way up the embankment to the railway line and found refuge at Milltown station which was the only lighted building in sight (Pl. 18). There she was kindly assisted and given a bed for the night (it was past 11 p.m.) by the station master, Patrick Healy, and his daughter.[273]

The assault on Miss Jolly made headline news in all of the national and Dublin newspapers for a five-week period during which time the search for the culprit was carried out and, once discovered, the accused (John Curran) was brought to trial, convicted by jury and sentenced to two years' imprisonment with hard labour. The case outraged polite Victorian society which was appalled at the nature of the attack on a young middle-class woman and which, in equal measure, admired Louisa's plucky resistance and escape from her assailant.[274] Numerous correspondence from their outraged readership was published in the letters columns of the press and testimonial funds were raised by the public in sympathy and appreciation for Ms Jolly and the station master, Healy.[275]

273 *Freeman's Journal*, 19 October 1861, pp. 3–4; *Irish Times*, 9 November 1861, p. 4.

274 The national and local newspapers covered the story from 2 October to 16 November 1861, under the headline 'The Milltown Outrage'.

275 See for example, *Dublin Daily Express*, 2 November 1861, p. 3; 13 November 1861, p. 3; *Dublin Evening Mail*, 11 November 1861, p. 1; 16 November 1861, p. 3.

From a local history perspective, the Jolly case provides interesting details about the locality around Milltown and Classon's Bridge in the mid-nineteenth century. Although photography had been invented the technology had not yet advanced to the stage where photographs could be reproduced in newspapers, so the public were reliant on the keen observation, dramatisation, and often the exaggeration, of the journalist. The following extract from the *Freeman's Journal* illustrates this point well:

> *The scene of the outrage is doubtless familiar to many – there are few inhabitants of the city who, in their Summer Sunday rambles, have not passed over Classon's Bridge towards Churchtown or Dundrum, or by it, and along the road that leads to Milltown. The scene from the bridge is picturesque, though lonely. A few hundred yards away in front is the railway viaduct with its lofty arches, under which the Dodder, when flooded by rain, flows with considerable force; the line of the railway is marked by white posts of the telegraph wires; in the distance, rather to the left, lies the village of Milltown, and a vast expanse of pasture land stretches towards the mountain ranges of Dublin and Wicklow which form the background of the scene. At the right-hand corner of the bridge is 'Brownrigg's grocery and provision stores' [successor to John Howe], which, on the night of the occurrence, was closed nearly an hour before the cab passed by. To the left, in a hollow formed by a slope in the ground, is the dairy house and other farm buildings; below them, in front, is an extensive pool of water caused by a dip in the ground, and, still lower, there is a piece of pasture which gradually slopes down till it runs level with the bank of the river at the viaduct.*[276]

The scene described above remained largely unchanged for the next 70 years. At the turn of the twentieth century hopes were entertained that a new bridge across the Dodder at Dartry would be built to replace Classon's Bridge in response to complaints about its unsuitability for modern traffic. This in turn would open up the townlands of Rathmines Great and Rathmines Little for building development, both of which were located on the south bank of the River Dodder and formed part of the extensive estate of Lord Palmerston. A minority of commissioners on the Rathmines UDC opposed the proposed new bridge because they feared it would create competition from external developers by luring potential Rathmines ratepayers outside the township. Despite passing a resolution in 1897 in favour of building the new bridge, no meaningful action was taken by the township to give effect to that resolution apart from contributing £500 to Dublin County Council towards the reconstruction of Classon's Bridge in 1928.[277] It was not until the 1930s that the district to the east of Lower Churchtown Road began to be developed when houses were built on the east side of the road. In the late 1940s and early 1950s the St Columbanus/Farranboley local authority housing estate and the Patrick Doyle Road were laid out between the railway line and the Dundrum Road.[278] In contrast, the land on the west side of the Lower Churchtown Road as far as Orwell Road was, over time, acquired by Milltown Golf Club beginning in 1907.[279]

The Milltown Road outrage became part of local folklore. In the 1940s Milltown children were afraid to walk at night under one of the arches of the railway viaduct which was close to

276 *Freeman's Journal*, 3 October 1861, p. 3.

277 *Rathmines News*, 23 January 1897, p. 4; 6 February 1897, p. 5; 20 February 1897, p. 5; 7 December 1901, p. 4; Dublin City Council Archives, UDC/1/Min 1/10, Rathmines and Rathgar UDC Minute Book, vol. 10, 1927–30, p. 89, Council Meeting 7 March 1928.

278 See Chapter 16.

279 Beale, Gilleece and Redmond, *Milltown Golf Club*, p. 30.

a spot known locally as 'Ms Jolly's leap', where tradition had it that Ms Jolly had fallen off her horse and drowned.[280]

MILLTOWN IN THE THIRD QUARTER OF THE NINETEENTH CENTURY - THE DECADES OF DISTRESS

The impact on Milltown of the major national events of the mid-nineteenth century – the introduction of national primary education, the Famine and the Fenian Rising – are considered in separate chapters devoted to those topics. At this juncture, it is appropriate to investigate the lives of the villagers in Milltown and reveal the steady decline and poverty that prevailed among the ordinary working-class people living in the village.

Many permanent residents and temporary lodgers who had evaded death during the Famine were forced to emigrate or seek employment in the army during the Crimean War of the mid-1850s. Accordingly, by 1861 the population of Milltown townland had declined over the previous 10 years from 863 to 596.[281] Likewise, the population of Farranboley townland reduced from 297 to 271 during the same period.[282] This explains why, for most of the 1850s, the Dublin street directories merely advised that Milltown was a 'dilapidated village' in St Peter's Parish.[283] Less tangible but nonetheless indirect evidence of the poverty prevalent in Milltown is available in the property records of the Valuation Office. The cancellation books for Milltown for the period 1855–62 reveal a trend in occupancy whereby cottages let to individually named tenants were replaced by multiple anonymous occupants described as lodgers.[284] Inhabitants among this class of cottage resident tended to be among the poorest and most vulnerable in society, such as Mrs Maria McGrath, a lodger living in Milltown in 1841, who was charged with infanticide. During McGrath's trial her landlady told the court that the accused appeared deranged in her mind and was very badly off for food.[285] Seasonal migrants and poor individuals who were called strolling beggars or tramps by nineteenth-century commentators, also relied heavily on lodgings. In the Tallaght district of the early 1840s these lodgers commonly paid 2*d.* or 3*d.* a night for a bed.[286]

The livelihoods of some of those inhabitants who remained in Milltown after the Famine can be gleaned from the employment columns in the national newspapers. Advertisements by washerwomen offering to provide laundry services to the local gentry living in the villas surrounding the village were quite common from the late 1840s up until the establishment of the Dublin Laundry Company in Milltown in 1887.[287] The following examples are typical of the laundry services offered by Milltown washerwomen:

---

280 Personal communication from Mrs Bernadette Sheehan (née Purcell) on 27 September 2019.

281 Census of Ireland 1861, County of Dublin, Barony of Uppercross, Parish of St Peter, Townland of Milltown, p. 41 (CD-ROM, Archive CD Books Ireland, Dublin, 2010).

282 Census of Ireland 1861, County of Dublin, Barony of Rathdown, Parish of Taney, Townland of Farranboley, p. 38 (CD-ROM, Archive CD Books Ireland, Dublin, 2010).

283 Thom's Directories from 1850 (p. 837) to 1856 (p. 1092).

284 VO, Cancellation Books, Dublin/Rathmines 1855–1862, p. 120–7.

285 *Dublin Morning Register*, 15 January 1841, p. 3.

286 Séan Bagnal, *Tallaght, 1835–1850: A rural place* (Dublin, 2008), p. 45.

287 *Saunders's Newsletter*, 2 May 1846, p. 3; 22 July 1861, p. 4; 26 September 1866, p. 4; 8 January 1867, p. 4; 13 January 1868, p. 4; 18 October 1869, p. 4; *Irish Times*, 29 March 1875, p. 7.

Washing and Mangling done by Isabella Fogarty, Milltown, on the most reasonable terms. I.F. in presenting herself to her friends and the public hopes to merit a continuance of that support which she has received these years. She pledges herself that all orders shall be attended to with accuracy and correctness; and the most satisfactory references of her ability can be obtained from families of distinction, for whom she works.[288]

A respectable woman has a vacancy for washing from a gentleman's house; has every convenience for the purpose, with a large supply of fresh soft water from the mountains; can be well recommended for strict honesty, regularity, and clothes properly made up; if any commands please address by letter to Mrs Sheridan, 3 Mowlds Cottages, Milltown, County Dublin.[289]

It is noteworthy that Mrs Sheridan referred to her use of the soft Vartry water which since 1877 had been available to inhabitants like her living on the south bank of the River Dodder close to Milltown Bridge, where Mowlds Cottages were situated (Map 21).[290]

Advertisements placed by young men and women living or working in Milltown seeking positions as domestic servants, or by prospective employers looking for household staff, occur frequently throughout the 1860s and 1870s.[291] Most employers were demanding as to the religious affiliation, nationality or social accomplishments of their prospective servants, which generally ruled out prospective employees from the local workforce:

Children's maid – Wanted, a respectable Roman Catholic as above (French or English); must be accustomed to the care and management of children; good temper and accent indispensable; she must understand all kinds of plain work; the youngest child four years old. Address, with copy of last discharge and wages expected, Mrs M. Post Office, Milltown.[292]

Butler or general indoor servant, a respectable Protestant man, who perfectly understands his business in its various branches, and who will be well recommended for civility and general good conduct by a gentleman at present in town; no objection to the country. Address W. W., 6 Hackett's Cottages, Milltown, County Dublin.[293]

Wanted by a lady residing near Dublin, an English housemaid, capable of waiting on a lady, working well with her needle, and of washing and getting up fine things. Apply by letter, stating particulars and terms, to J.E., Post Office, Milltown.[294]

288 *Saunders's Newsletter*, 2 May 1846, p. 3.

289 *Dublin Daily Express*, 5 September 1881, p. 8.

290 *Wicklow Newsletter*, 14 April 1877, p. 1.

291 *Saunders's Newsletter*, 20 February 1861, p. 4; 26 May 1863, p. 4; 19 June 1867, p. 4; 16 February 1869, p. 4; 18 May 1869, p. 4; 2 June 1871, p. 4.

292 *Freeman's Journal*, 15 April 1861, p. 1.

293 *Saunders's Newsletter*, 26 May 1863, p. 4.

294 *Saunders's Newsletter*, 25 October 1858, p. 4.

Many of the laundress and domestic service advertisements use the adjective 'respectable' in their text. Of the 66 job and accommodation newspaper advertisements relating to Milltown reviewed for the period 1846–99, 28 referred either to the applicant or the employer as being respectable. This reflected a growing social trend from the 1840s among the middle class and, notably, the skilled working class, with a greater preoccupation with acquiring social respectability and its traits as identified by polite Victorian society. This phenomenon took firm root in the emerging middle-class suburbs of the Rathmines and Pembroke townships, and was an important factor in the suppression of the ancient Donnybrook Fair in the 1860s.[295]

Outside of laundry work and domestic service advertisements for skilled or semi-skilled jobs in Milltown were very rare during the nineteenth century. In 1870, a local dressmaker offered her services to prospective employers, adding that she had no objection to relocating to the country.[296] Four years later, a young father took the initiative and placed the following advertisement in the *Irish Times*:

> *General man and ploughman – A young man in the prime of his life, wishes for a situation as above; is married, one child; his wife would care a gate lodge if required; can be highly recommended and will be found useful and obliging. Address J.B., Post Office, Milltown.*[297]

Not all of the domestic servants were as honest as they asserted and domestic servants occasionally gave into temptation to steal from their employers. Margaret Shea was charged with stealing money from her employer in Raglan Road while the family were living in Bray during the summer season. Shea was apprehended in Milltown by police detectives and subsequently sentenced to four months' imprisonment with hard labour.[298]

The advertisements quoted above were only relevant to a small proportion of Milltown's workforce. The fact was that many families living in Milltown village consisted of low-skilled general labourers who were frequently underemployed or unemployed. According to the 1841 census, 68 families in Milltown townland were chiefly dependent on their manual labour while 27 men and 168 women had no specified occupation.[299] This situation did not change after the Famine; in fact it got worse as employment in the mills declined or ceased altogether.

The full extent of poverty in Milltown can be found among the records of Milltown's national school which are deposited in the National Archives. When the inspector from the Board of Education visited the national school in Milltown on 16 January 1850 there were 32 boys and 36 girls present.[300] The children were expected to pay one penny a week to the local school committee albeit that half of the children were admitted for free.[301] In supporting the application for aid the inspector made the following comments about Milltown at that time:

295 Fergus A. D'Arcy, 'The Decline and Fall of Donnybrook Fair: Moral Reform and Social Control in Nineteenth Century Dublin', *Saothar: Journal of the Irish Labour History Society*, xiii (1988), pp. 17–19.

296 *Freeman's Journal*, 26 March 1870, p. 1.

297 *Irish Times*, 31 August 1874, p. 7.

298 *Dublin Daily Express*, 3 September 1863, p. 4.

299 Census of Ireland for the year 1841, County Dublin, Barony of Uppercross, Parish of St Peter, Townland of Milltown, pp. 30–1.

300 NAI, National School Papers, Milltown, ED1/29/47/2.

301 NAI, National School Papers, Milltown, ED1/29/47/2B.

> *I beg leave to recommend this application to the Board on the grounds that this is a very poor neighbourhood. Twenty of the more necessitous pupils (male and female) receive their breakfast every morning in the school; Sundays excepted.*[302]

Nine years later, in January 1859 another application for State aid was supported by the local inspector 'on the grounds of the poverty of this village'.[303] During the application process the local curate Rev. Dennan stated that 'on account of the utter poverty of the locality he could not for a moment entertain the idea of promising the teachers anything beyond what the board will give'.[304]

Further indicators of poverty and distress can be found in the admission and discharge registers for the South Dublin Union workhouse. James Neshaw, a fourteen-year-old orphan from Milltown, was admitted to the workhouse on 10 April 1860, where he remained until his discharge on 16 April 1861.[305] A second fourteen-year-old Milltown orphan, Thomas Brien, was admitted to the workhouse on 28 November 1860 for six weeks.[306] Older, unskilled labourers were vulnerable to sickness or downturns in work. Hence sixty-four-year-old widower Peter Kevil and forty-nine-year-old married labourer Patrick Dempsey sought refuge in the workhouse on 1 September 1862 and 16 March 1863 respectively.[307] Kevil and Dempsey were long-term inhabitants of Milltown who can be traced back to the Griffith's Valuation of the 1840s.[308]

The local Protestant community was an important source of charity in combatting the endemic poverty that prevailed in Milltown. On New Year's Eve 1860 Rev. Flemyng thanked his parishioners who had contributed to a fund to buy coal, tea, sugar and bread for the aged, helpless, cold and hungry poor of Milltown parish, and he appealed for further subscriptions 'during this inclement season ... for the numerous poor of this locality'.[309] During a particularly harsh winter spell in January 1867 one of the local clergymen, the Rev. Thomas Scott of 'Barmeen', Dartry, set up a soup kitchen for the poor of the district. According to an anonymous letter writer to *Saunders's Newsletter*, Rev. Scott:

> *had this day a large boiler full of excellent soup prepared, and to a number of the poor of Milltown and Rathmines was given a gallon or more, some meat, and a loaf of bread. This timely boon was received by the poor people most thankfully, as they showered upon him their blessings. Widows with large families, and wives with helpless little ones and sick husbands alike, received what was provided for them. Would that this good example were followed by all the neighbouring gentry.*[310]

This singular act of kindness starkly highlighted the endemic poverty in Milltown village that existed side by side with the Georgian villas and the new luxurious houses being built

302 NAI, National School Papers, Milltown, ED1/29/47/2B.

303 NAI, National School Papers, Milltown, ED1/30/6/2B.

304 NAI, National School Papers, Milltown, ED1/30/6/3, Bernard Dennan, letter dated 11 February 1859.

305 NAI, South Dublin Poor Law Union Workhouse Register, BG 79/G23, no. 1337.

306 NAI, South Dublin Poor Law Union Workhouse Register, BG 79/G23, no. 2358. Brien left the workhouse on 17 January 1861.

307 NAI, South Dublin Poor Law Union Workhouse Register, BG 79/G25, nos 501 and 4669.

308 NAI, VO, OL50945, House Book for Milltown Village 1845, nos 19 and 26.

309 *Saunders's Newsletter*, 31 December 1860, p. 4.

310 *Saunders's Newsletter*, 21 January 1867, p. 3.

on Temple and Palmerston Roads. Conscientious members of the St Philip's congregation continued to relieve the poor, as demonstrated by the following extract from the parish vestry report of Easter 1887:

> *The Report of the Relief and Coal Fund for the Winter of 1886 and '87 has been issued, from which it appears that coal was supplied at reduced rates to 32 families, in all amounting to 479 bags, and that tea, sugar, blankets, and boots were distributed to distressed people in the parish, irrespective of creed, by the ladies who kindly undertake this duty – Mrs Thompson of Clonskeagh Castle, Mrs Henshaw, of St Philip's, Mrs Johnson of Nullamore, and Miss Griffin. A Dorcas Society has also been started with the view of encouraging thrift, and enabling poor people to purchase various articles of clothing at reduced rates, by payments extending over a considerable period.*[311]

Despite the best charitable efforts of the professional classes from the Church of Ireland, chronic poverty and general lack of sufficient economic opportunities continued in Milltown into the 1870s and 1880s due to the high numbers of poor people living in Milltown. This had a knock-on effect on the business of small tradesmen and shopkeepers, some of whom went bankrupt. These unfortunates included the local baker, James Butterly, in 1855, James Campbell, a road contractor and dairyman living in Milltown in 1859, a local dairyman Patrick Murphy, in 1863, and the bootmaker William Clay, in 1870.[312] Other traders cut corners with their customers to get by. John Molloy of Milltown, whose occupation was not stated, was in February 1868 fined half a crown for having one unjust weight and one unjust beam and scales.[313] Thomas Lambert and John Hackett, dairyman and market gardener respectively and both of Milltown, were fined for the same offences five years later.[314]

Relationships among the villagers did not always run smoothly. In 1870 Thomas Franklin, who lived in a cottage on the north side of the village main street opposite Geraldine Terrace and who kept a small shop nearby, paid a high price for losing his temper with a group of young boys who had been in the habit of harassing him. In response to their taunts Franklin flung a chisel at the group seriously injuring a boy named Edward Kenny. Notwithstanding that the master of the Court of Common Pleas, Charles Granby Burke of St Philip's, gave Franklin a good character reference Franklin was found guilty by a jury of assault inflicting actual bodily harm and sentenced to three months' imprisonment.[315] On another occasion a young man called Patrick Murphy was sent to prison for three months for setting his dog at a policeman during a disturbance in the village.[316]

---

311 RCB Library, D6/64, St Philip's Parish Milltown, Report of select vestry, with statement of parochial accounts, for the year 1886–7, p. 5.

312 *Dublin Mercantile and Weekly Price Current*, 10 August 1855, p. 5; 26 August 1859, p. 2; *Saunders's Newsletter*, 3 December 1863, p. 3; *Freeman's Journal*, 28 September 1870, p. 4. The circumstances behind these individual cases are unknown but collectively they do not inspire confidence in the local economy of Milltown village.

313 *Saunders's Newsletter*, 21 February 1868, p. 2.

314 *Freeman's Journal*, 15 February 1873, p. 6; Thom's Directory 1874, p. 1659.

315 *Saunders's Newsletter*, 7 April 1870, p. 2. VO, Cancellation Books, Dublin/Rathmines 1873–1887, p. 196 plots 3, 75, 76; Thom's Directory 1870, p. 1603.

316 *Dublin Evening Telegraph*, 3 July 1880, p. 3.

HEALTH AND MORTALITY IN THE THIRD QUARTER OF THE NINETEENTH CENTURY

Previous discussions of health and mortality in Milltown have up until now dealt with the impact of national crises such as the Famine, the typhus and cholera epidemics and the impact of the South Dublin and Rathdown Union workhouses. Information about the health of the inhabitants of Milltown under normal living conditions is available too, and this provides a more realistic snapshot of people's daily lives and health experiences. Under the Medical Charities (Ireland) Act 1851 all Poor Law Unions were divided into dispensary districts, each of which established a local dispensary staffed by a qualified medical officer and which provided free medical services to the local poor. The dispensary service was initially funded entirely through local taxation (the poor rate) but from 1867 onwards the government paid half the salary of the dispensary doctor and the entire costs of a midwife, if appointed, and of the medicines dispensed.[317]

For the villagers of Milltown who lived on the north bank of the Dodder the local dispensary was in the Meath Hospital. Conversely, Milltown residents living on the south bank of the River Dodder could avail of the local dispensary at Dundrum.[318] A successful medical intervention by the dispensary doctor in the Meath Hospital in the case of a patient named Sarah Byrne of Milltown was reported in the local medical press. Mrs Byrne visited the dispensary on 27 July 1861 complaining of a 'dead aching pain' in her right arm. Neuralgia of the arm was diagnosed and a poultice was applied to Mrs Byrne's arm which successfully relieved her pain. During the course of the treatment the doctor made the following unflattering observations about his patient: 'Her temperament was evidently nervous and excitable; she is subject to leucorrhoea, flatulence, and want of appetite.'[319]

Many outbreaks of illness and infection could not be treated successfully, particularly as the cramped unhygienic housing conditions in the village aided the spread of disease and infections. In April 1869 there was an outbreak of a bad form of measles in Milltown from which three people died.[320] Eleven years later, Cork Street fever hospital reported that it had treated seven patients with smallpox from Milltown during the year ending 31 March 1880.[321] One of the Milltown patients at Cork Street was a woman named Mary Sutton. While she was in hospital the sanitary officer of the Rathdown Union had Sutton's house disinfected and the bedding destroyed and replaced at a cost of £2.[322]

The death of the family breadwinner had devastating financial consequences for a bereaved family. Communities attempted to mitigate the hardships by establishing burial (or tontine) societies. By about 1866 the villagers of Milltown had set up the St Columbaners [*sic*] Friendly Burial Society, later renamed the St Gall's Friendly Christian Burial Society, which provided basic mortality benefits on the death of the husband, wife or a child of the member. According to mortality returns made by the burial society to the Registrar of Friendly Societies in Ireland 117 death benefits had been paid out in the five-year period to 31 December

317 Crossman, *Local Government*, p. 50; Potter, *The municipal revolution in Ireland*, p. 84.

318 *Dublin Medical Press*, 13 November 1861, p. 6; Ball and Hamilton, *Parish of Taney*, pp. 203–6.

319 *Dublin Medical Press*, 13 November 1861, p. 6.

320 *Freeman's Journal*, 28 April 1869, p. 2.

321 *Dublin Evening Mail*, 14 June 1880, p. 4.

322 Rathdown Poor Law Union, Board of Guardians Minute Book 73–78, August 1879–November 1881, Folio 20, p. 580.

1870, i.e. an average of over 23 deaths per annum.[323] The total membership of the Milltown burial society was not supplied to the registrar – it is unlikely to have been more than a few hundred at most – so it is impossible to calculate the mortality rate among the working-class inhabitants of Milltown. Even so the suspicion must be that the Milltown death rate was high by contemporary standards because the average death rate for the city of Dublin during the years 1864–70 based on officially recorded deaths (i.e. deaths registered under compulsory legislation introduced in 1864) was 27.45 deaths per 1,000 people.[324]

CONCLUSION

The inhabitants of Milltown village experienced very high levels of poverty and distress over the course of most of the nineteenth century due to a combination of national and local events over which they had no control. Attempts to ameliorate the conditions of the poor were largely ineffective because the burden of relief was left to local charity which on its own could not cope with the pervasive poverty that prevailed in the district. However, from the 1870s onwards, the poor law guardians began slowly to improve the conditions of the poor in Milltown, particularly in the areas of housing sanitation, cattle disease and the regulation of dairy yards, but the guardians' work tended to be reactive rather than proactive in nature. In short, the situation in Milltown required radical long-term intervention. Three significant events commencing in 1879 brought long-lasting improvements to the lives of the working-class villagers of Milltown; these are the subject of Chapter 11. ■

323 *Report of the Registrar of Friendly Societies in Ireland, 1870*, Appendix (Abstract of quinquennial returns of sickness and mortality in Ireland), pp. 2–3; Rathmines News, 31 May 1902, p. 2.

324 Mary E. Daly, *Dublin: The deposed capital. A social and economic history 1860–1914* (Cork, 1984), p. 242.

Chapter 8:
The Great Famine 1845–50

Chapter 8: The Great Famine 1845–50

INTRODUCTION

Most of the historical studies of the Irish Famine of 1845–50 have, quite naturally, examined its devastating impact on the rural population of Ireland, particularly in the southern and western provinces of the country which were hardest hit. As a result, there are far fewer investigations into the immediate and knock-on effects of the Famine in Dublin, particularly its suburban and rural hinterland. What follows here is an attempt to give some idea how the poorest inhabitants of Milltown and its vicinity were adversely affected by the national catastrophe. Before doing so it is necessary to consider what sort of diet the least affluent inhabitants survived on and the prevalence of potatoes in their daily meals.

THE TYPICAL DIET OF THE POOR

Attention has been drawn in other chapters to the importance of dairy farming to the economy of Milltown and in south county Dublin generally. Nonetheless, one must not lose sight of the fact that crops were grown too. When the taxation for the support of the Church of Ireland, known as tithes, was being assessed for the Church of Ireland parishes of St Mary's (Donnybrook) and St Peter's (Milltown on the north bank of the Dodder) in 1824 and 1833, the main crop grown in each parish was oats and wheat respectively.[1] Potatoes, too, were grown for domestic consumption and as a cash crop. A newspaper advertisement dating from May 1795 offered a property for sale or letting in Milltown village which included:

1 NAI, Tithe Aplotment Books for Diocese of Dublin, Parish of St Mary's Donnybrook (16 June 1833) and Parish of St Peter (30 December 1833).

a large new-built house which, containing six rooms, a kitchen, coal-hole, and small dairy, a good yard, and large walled-in garden, full cropped, and well planted with choice young fruit trees; also, a potato garden, now planted, containing near half an acre.... [2]

Similarly, one of the attractions advertised in August 1835 to potential purchasers of Milltown Lodge on the Dundrum Road was a 'quantity of early potatoes in the ground'.[3] In addition, some of the cottages in Milltown village had small potato gardens which were destroyed by flooding from the River Dodder on 29–30 July 1839, and a farmer named Byrne had lost 'a very large crop of Bangor potatoes' in the same flood at his 4-acre farm at Ballsbridge.[4]

At a coroner's inquest held in December 1842 involving a suspicious death at the lime kiln at Classon's Bridg (an incident discussed in detail in the previous chapter), Patrick Tynan said he had been cutting potatoes before he discovered the body of the dead man.[5] Similarly, at a trial in a case of suspected infanticide, the Milltown landlady of the accused told the court in January 1841 that the prisoner, Mrs Maria McGrath, appeared deranged in her mind and 'had only a herring, a potato and a drink of water'. Another lodger, William Kavanagh, corroborated the evidence given by his landlady, Catherine Smullen, but added that when McGrath returned to her lodgings, she 'took tea and toast too'.[6] The reference to the herring illustrates the Catholic dietary requirement to abstain from eating meat on Fridays.

More importantly, the McGrath case also reveals the extent of poverty that existed in Milltown before the Great Famine. Catherine Smullen was a widow who had been living in Milltown for 40 years when she was called on to give evidence at the trial of Maria McGrath. At the time, Mrs Smullen was renting a small cottage from Patrick Hackett on the south side of Milltown main street and had sublet her house to three lodgers, Maria McGrath, her infant son Billy (Maria was acquitted of killing her nine-month-old child), and William Kavanagh.[7] Mrs Smullen told the court that although she herself was a poor woman, she helped Mrs McGrath who was very badly off for food.[8]

On a broader geographical level, when the Dublin workhouses began operating in 1840 the paupers' diet consisted of 7 ounces of meal and half-a-pint of milk for breakfast, and 2lbs of potatoes and broth or 4lbs of potatoes and 1 pint of buttermilk for dinner.[9] The most compelling evidence of the importance of potatoes in the local economy of Milltown and its vicinity comes from the neighbouring parish of Rathfarnham. At the outset of the Famine a local police constable, reporting in October 1845 to his superiors on the effects of the potato blight in his locality, noted that: 'I have heard that there is a large quantity of the potatoes of this district sold for the foreign market, and that a number of them are used in the starch and other manu-

2 *Saunders's Newsletter*, 26 May 1795 p. 2.

3 *Dublin Morning Register*, 1 August 1835, p. 1.

4 *Dublin Weekly Herald*, Saturday 3 August 1839, p. 3; *Dublin Mercantile Advertiser and Weekly Price Current*, 2 August 1839, p.3.

5 *Freeman's Journal*, 20 December 1842, p. 3.

6 *Dublin Morning Register*, 15 January 1841, p. 3.

7 *Dublin Morning Register*, 15 January 1841, p. 3; Griffith's Valuation, Rateable Valuation of Tenements, County of Dublin, Barony of Uppercross, Parish of St Peter, Townland of Milltown, p. 55 at entry no. 60 (1850).

8 *Dublin Morning Register*, 15 January 1841, p. 3.

9 Gerard O'Brien, 'Workhouse Management in Pre-Famine Ireland', *Proceedings of the Royal Irish Academy, 86C* (1986), pp. 113–34.

factories.'[10] There is no reason to suppose that the commercial usage to which potatoes were put in Rathfarnham parish was unique to that district or radically different to the rural parts of Milltown south of the River Dodder at Farranboley and Windy Harbour, which were located in the neighbouring parish of Taney.[11] According to Lewis's Topographical Dictionary of Ireland, which was published in 1837, a starch and glue mill was operating in Milltown in the 1830s.[12] In actual fact, the starch mill was situated on the River Slang at Windy Arbour.[13]

The importance of the potato in the diet of the labouring classes of rural County Dublin was highlighted in a report given to an official enquiry into the state of poverty in Ireland in the 1830s by a landowner in Balbriggan, County Dublin. George Alexander Hamilton furnished the inquiry with what he believed to be the minimum allowance of food per day for an able-bodied labourer:

BREAKFAST	
1lb of oatmeal (1/14th stone), at 1*s* 6*d*. per stone	one and a quarter pennies
1 quart buttermilk	one halfpenny
DINNER	
¼ stone (3½ lbs. potatoes), at 3*d* per stone at 3*d* per stone	three quarters of a penny
¼ lb butter, or fish to same amount, or ½ lb. of bacon	two and a half pence
SUPPER	
Same as breakfast	one and three quarter pennies
TOTAL:	**six and three quarter pennies.**[14]

An agricultural labourer with a wife and four children employed by Hamilton stated that his family ate potatoes for breakfast and dinner and, when they could afford it, stirabout for supper. In short, Hamilton advised the commissioners of the poor inquiry that a family could not be supported at a cost of less than 1*s*. per week per head.[15] Hamilton's report on the importance of potatoes as the staple food for the Dublin poor was supported by the evidence given to the same inquiry by the secretary of the Association for suppressing street-begging in Dublin, who advised that the numbers of urban poor seeking relief from the mendicity institution fluctuated in accordance with the increase or decrease in the average price of potatoes.[16]

Returning to Milltown, the importance of agriculture to its economy can be seen in the 1841 census which revealed that 56 families out of a total of 150 in Milltown townland (i.e. that part of Milltown on the north bank of the River Dodder) were chiefly employed in agriculture.

10 NAI, Famine Relief Commission Manuscripts, RLFC/2/Z 14282.

11 In October 1830 during a scarcity of potatoes in Cork City, a starch factory was attacked and plundered by a mob due to the large quantities of potatoes consumed in the manufacture of the starch: *Cork Constitution*, 27 October 1830, p. 4.

12 Lewis, *Topographical Dictionary of Ireland*, ii, p. 370.

13 OSI, Co. Dublin, Sheet 22, six inches to one statute mile, surveyed in 1837 and corrected in 1843.

14 *Poor Inquiry, City of Dublin, 1836*, Communications, p. 27.

15 *Poor Inquiry, City of Dublin, 1836*, Communications, p. 27.

16 *Poor Inquiry, City of Dublin, 1836*, p. 34 (evidence of C. Haliday).

The same census also disclosed that 68 families were chiefly dependant on their own manual labour for their livelihood.[17] The poorest and most vulnerable people in this category were the labourers who held conacre holdings. Typically, a conacre holding was one where the farmer or landlord gave their labourers a cabin and a portion of ground, perhaps between three quarters to one acre in size, on which they could grow potatoes for their own consumption. Rent was worked off in days of labour with each labourer receiving two meals a day from his employer. Variations of the basic conacre arrangement involved, for example, cash payments and the renting of enough land to graze a cow, depending on local circumstances.[18] As will be explained presently, the numbers of labourers residing in Milltown and the surrounding districts on the eve of the Famine who held conacre plots planted with potatoes was probably very small. It is, however, worth highlighting a small plot of land in Clonskeagh which was probably a conacre holding. A crown survey of the Roebuck estate in 1832 recorded a small holding of about one statute acre comprising three cottages and a potato garden which was located on a narrow strip of land on the south bank of the River Dodder and parallel with the road from Clonskeagh Bridge to Donnybrook, now called Beaver Row. A middleman landlord, William Kavanagh, held this land on a 99-year lease at an annual rent of £5 5*s.* Kavanagh undoubtedly would have sublet the three cottages and potato ground to labourers at a profit rent.[19] Today, this strip of land together with three derelict cottages is located opposite the David Lloyd sports complex on Beaver Row.

THE ARRIVAL OF THE POTATO BLIGHT IN AUTUMN 1845

The fungal disease *phytophthora infestans* (commonly called the potato blight) which devastated the potato crop in Ireland broke out in the country in September 1845. The initial public reaction to the new mysterious disease was restrained because the late crop of potatoes had yet to be harvested and the blight was to some degree offset by a particularly good oat crop that year.[20] The first reports of potato blight prepared by the police of County Dublin villages have survived among the Famine papers deposited in the National Archives. These reports which date from October 1845 provide very valuable information about local conditions in suburban villages and farms as the potato blight broke out and progressed. The constabulary reports from Rathfarnham and Dundrum are most relevant to understanding the initial impact of the potato blight on Milltown. On 21 October 1845 the Head Constable at Rathfarnham wrote to his superiors in Dublin advising that:

> *Having kept my attention on the state of the potato crop, and lately having made very extensive inquiries relative thereto, I feel pleasure in being enabled to state that generally speaking up to the present time there is but a trifling failure in this district; some parts it extends to one fifth, and some to not more than two potatoes in the stone, and in parts the crop is more than an average one; there does not appear to be much alarm among the people. They say that with a little care and attention that as yet there is no fear, the failure is not in the quantity but in the quality. Some of them are quite rotten, some*

17 Census of Ireland for the year 1841, County of Dublin, Barony of Uppercross, Parish of St Peter, Townland of Milltown, pp. 30–1.

18 Oliver MacDonagh, 'The economy and society, 1830–45' in W.E. Vaughan (ed.), *A new history of Ireland, v: Ireland under the Union 1801–1870* (Oxford, 1989), pp. 218–19; Cecil Woodham-Smith, *The Great Hunger* (New English Library edition, London, 1970), p. 77.

19 'Report and Valuation of the lands of Roebuck in the County of Dublin by Brassington and Gale, 1832' (NAI, QRO 4/3/28).

20 James S. Donnelly, 'Famine and government response, 1845–6' in W.E. Vaughan (ed.), *A new history of Ireland, v: Ireland under the Union 1801–1870* (Oxford, 1989), pp. 272–3.

[have] a rotten crust over them, and some more or less injured with black spots. Parts of them appear so when turned out of the ground, and some [of] them appear quite healthy but in a few days after turn so [i.e. rotten]. The farmers have not commenced digging their entirety out; they only dig what is wanting for the present supply and until they are dug out the extent of the failure cannot be known.[21]

At the same time that the police report was being sent in to Dublin Castle from Rathfarnham the secretary of the Kinsale Poor Law Union reported pessimistically that:

we are completely in the dark as to any remedy for it [the blight], and the farmers in this locality are digging them [potatoes] out and sending them to the starch mill where they get 2d. per weight for them.[22]

The critical issue of finding a remedy to halt or mitigate the spread of the potato blight now became an urgent issue for the Dublin authorities and for well-meaning individuals. Unfortunately, in the absence of any scientific understanding of the potato blight, a variety of putative remedies and thoroughly impractical suggestions for treating diseased potatoes poured forth in official circulars and in letters to the newspapers as the crisis worsened in the autumn of 1845.[23] To take one extreme example, an English correspondent recommended that the cottagers treat their diseased potatoes with chlorine gas, which they were to manufacture by mixing together oil of vitriol, manganese oxide and salt, ingredients that they were expected to obtain themselves for a few shillings![24] Such farcical remedies only served to illustrate the complete ignorance among some of the privileged classes of rural cottiers' lives.

The Rathfarnham police report of 12 November 1845 presented a rather mixed set of circumstances pertaining in that district after the initially sanguine report the previous month. Some farmers were reporting that their potatoes were unaffected by the blight yet others were reporting a total failure in their crop; by all reports it seemed that blight attacked different varieties of potatoes to varying degrees of severity, with apple potatoes being the worst affected. All told, the constable considered that one fifth of the potato crop would be lost in Rathfarnham. In spite of his assessment, the constable opined that 'there will be no want in the district, either as to seed [i.e. seed potatoes for next year's crop] or provisions'. Unsurprisingly, the constable thought that the people were not paying any heed to the advice received from the authorities, which they considered too troublesome and expensive. He concluded by stating that 'they do not appear apprehensive of famine or want'.[25]

Conditions began to worsen nationally and locally over the course of the winter of 1845 and 1846 as the full effects and implications of the potato blight were realised. Local constabulary reports carried out in the spring and summer of 1846 for the parishes of Rathfarnham and Taney show a rather grim situation unfolding. For example, on 16 March 1846 reports from Dundrum advised that half of the potato crop was lost and that three quarters of the labourers were unemployed. As a result, a meeting of the local magistrates and other influential persons was held in Dundrum on 4 April to enquire into the state of the poor and the best mode to

21 NAI, Famine Relief Commission Manuscripts, RLFC/2/Z 14282.

22 *Statesman and Dublin Christian Record*, 28 October 1845, p. 1.

23 Woodham-Smith, *The Great Hunger*, pp. 40–2.

24 *Cork Examiner*, 31 October 1845, p. 3; *Enniskillen Packet and Erne Chronicle*, 6 November 1845, p. 2.

25 NAI, Famine Relief Commission Manuscripts, RLFC/2/Z 15796.

relive distress. In particular, the constabulary reported on 7 April 1846 that 'in the neighbourhood of Dundrum and onto Milltown great destitution prevails, occasioned by want of employment and badness of potatoes'.[26]

In order to obtain a more precise understanding of how events were unfolding on the ground, a one-page questionnaire was circulated nationally from the police headquarters in Dublin Castle on 20 May 1846. The five questions directed to the local constabulary were designed to capture statistical data that was so beloved of Victorian enquiries. Nonetheless, the questionnaires provide very valuable information and so they are transcribed in full below.

PARISH OF RATHFARNHAM, 27 MAY 1846

1. *What extent of land was planted with potatoes, in the above parish, in each of the years 1844, 1845 and 1846? Ans: 65 acres and 1 rood in the year 1844, 78 acres in the year 1845, 53 acres & 3 roods in the year 1846.*
2. *What proportion of the land planted in potatoes was let in conacre? Ans: 8 acres in the year 1844, 17 acres in the year 1845 and 7 acres in the year 1846.*
3. *What is the extent of land planted with potatoes this year? Ans: 53 acres and 3 roods.*
4. *What proportion has been this year let in conacre? Ans: 7 acres.*
5. *What crops have been sown in the land which would under ordinary circumstances have been planted with potatoes? Ans: 11 acres of oats and barley.*
   Note: part of this parish is in the Dublin Metropolitan Police District which I have not included in this return.'[27]

PARISH OF TANEY, 28 MAY 1846

1. *What extent of land was planted with potatoes, in the above parish, in each of the years 1844, 1845 and 1846? Ans: for 1844 – 114 acres, for 1845 – 90 acres, and for 1846 – 100 acres.*
2. *What proportion of the land planted in potatoes was let in conacre? Ans: 1/38.*
3. *What is the extent of land planted with potatoes this year? Ans: 100 acres.*
4. *What proportion has been this year let in conacre? Ans: 1/13*
5. *What crops have been sown in the land which would under ordinary circumstances have been planted with potatoes? Ans: The same as under ordinary circumstances.*[28]

Bearing in mind that the parishes of Rathfarnham and Taney comprised in total over 2,781 and 4,562 acres respectively, [29] the most revealing statistic for both parishes is the tiny proportion of conacre holdings that were sown with potatoes both before and at the onset of the potato blight. Indeed, the total acreage figures for conacre holdings in general are very small relative to the size of the parishes. This might be explained if the constables in these large rural parishes only assessed the local situation close to their barracks, which would alter the picture considerably. Assuming that the data collected by the local constabulary were accurate, it begs the question as to why three quarters of the labourers in the Dundrum area were reported as being unemployed by the middle of March 1846. There is no obvious answer to this question in either the official records or in contemporary newspaper reports. It is possible that some of the un-

26 NAI, Famine Relief Commission Manuscripts, RLFC/3/Z 7014.

27 NAI, Famine Relief Commission Manuscripts, RLFC/5/9/04.

28 NAI, Famine Relief Commission Manuscripts, RLFC/4/9/80.

29 *Parliamentary Gazetteer of Ireland*, iii, pp. 128, 310.

employed labourers were in fact refugees from the mountainous districts of south Dublin and north Wicklow who would likely have flocked to the Dundrum district in search of work on the villas and their home farms. The deteriorating conditions south of the River Dodder had not at this stage impinged on the social life of the well-to-do of Dublin such as William Tighe Hamilton of Milltown Park, who, at the beginning of May 1846, was preoccupied with his garden:

> *Horticultural Improvement Society. The first exhibition of this society will be held at the Rotundo this day. From all that we have heard it is likely to be a most creditable one. Among other flowers of interest there will be exhibited from the unrivalled collection of Orchidaceae of W. Tighe Hamilton esq., of Milltown Park, some beautiful Epiphytes, including two gorgeous specimens of the 'Oncidium papello,' the celebrated butterfly plant Zygopetaton crinitum, Epipendrum crassulatum, etc etc. The fine band of the 70th will play in the garden during the day, and the Society's marquee will be erected there.*[30]

During the week that Hamilton was getting his plants ready for the Rotundo flower show, local laundress Isabella Fogarty was, as we have seen in the previous chapter, advertising for business in *Saunders's Newsletter*:

> *Washing and Mangling done by Isabella Fogarty, Milltown, on the most reasonable terms. I.F. in presenting herself to her friends and the public hopes to merit a continuance of that support which she has received these years. She pledges herself that all orders shall be attended to with accuracy and correctness and the most satisfactory references of her ability can be obtained from families of distinction, for whom she works. Any commands left at Mr Bolton's, 63 Grafton street, or with Isabella Fogarty, Milltown, shall be attended to.*[31]

As the summer of 1846 wore on the rural poor waited apprehensively for the first crop of potatoes to ripen. In this regard, the last constabulary questionnaire to have survived for Rathfarnham dates from late August 1846 and was designed to ascertain the state of the first harvest of the potato crop for the 1846 season in the 'district' of Rathfarnham, as opposed to the previous reports which had referred to the parish of Rathfarnham.

> ***DISTRICT OF RATHFARNHAM, 25 AUGUST 1846***
> 1. *Has the extent of potatoes planted this year equalled that of ordinary years? Ans: Something less than former years.*
> 2. *Has the crop been affected by blight, and in what proportion? Ans: The whole has been affected.*
> 3. *Has the early or late crop been chiefly injured, and to what extent in each of those crops? Ans: Both have been injured but the late seems to have suffered most extent/cannot yet be known.*
> 4. *Has the crop or any portion of it as yet become available for food? Ans: About ¼ available.*[32]

The constable was certainly correct in his assessment that the entire crop for Rathfarnham was lost, for the land agents for the Palmerston estate, Stewart and Kincaid, had written to Lord Palmerston on 20 August 1846 confirming that the potato crop for County Dublin was 'entire-

30 *Saunders's Newsletter*, 7 May 1846, p. 2.

31 *Saunders's Newsletter*, 2 May 1846, p. 2.

32 NAI, Famine Relief Commission Manuscripts, RLFC/5/9/04.

ly gone'.[33] It was strange, therefore, for the constable to state that a quarter of the potato crop was available for food.

The government's response to the now full-blown crisis was to purchase large quantities of maize from America, known as Indian meal or, more infamously, Peel's Brimstone. Initial resistance to this unfamiliar food substitute which entered Ireland from February 1846 was twofold: it was unpalatable to the Irish peasantry and the meal itself had to be ground before it was fit for human consumption, a major difficulty in remote rural areas lacking corn mills. In addition, Prime Minister Peel's primary motivation was to use the Indian meal as a means of controlling food prices rather than feeding the starving. Despite these difficulties, resistance to the new food staple fell away, particularly when it was later discovered that adding oatmeal to the Indian meal made it more palatable.[34] These developments explain why Milltown miller James Henderson inserted the following notice in *Saunders's Newsletter* on 20 October 1846:

> *To corn factors, etc – Indian Corn. James Henderson begs to announce to the public that he has lately fitted up his mill at Milltown, near Dublin, where he will grind Indian Corn on moderate terms. Every attention paid to punctuality and dispatch. Apply to the above at Millmount Lodge, Milltown, or at his office, 29 Richmond Street.*[35]

Replacing potatoes with other food substitutes, temporary or otherwise, was ultimately doomed to failure because all other forms of basic food provisions had to be purchased with cash unless they were grown or farmed by the consumer. This proved to be an insoluble economic conundrum. Prior to the potato blight the rural poor had grown their own food supply, without having to purchase anything additional in order to be largely self-sufficient in normal times. Now, with the potatoes gone the labouring poor needed to earn wages in cash before they could access food for themselves and their dependants. In the absence of potatoes, the demand for other foodstuffs led to massive increases in the price of provisions as market forces took over and unscrupulous merchants took advantage, thereby increasing the levels of poverty and distress among the poor and the unemployed. In Milltown, January 1846 marks the last recorded instance of a collection for the (Catholic) Association for the Propagation of the Faith, when 10*s.* was collected on behalf of Milltown by Andrew Lewis.[36] This minor detail suggests that the Catholic congregation in Milltown had more important domestic priorities during the winter of 1846–7.

The official response to the twin problems of unemployment and increasingly unaffordable provisions was to increase expenditure on public works, particularly road building, from January 1846 onwards. These works were carried out under the direction of the grand juries of the Board of Works. Where the grand juries sponsored a scheme, the entire cost was borne by the ratepayers whereas if the Board of Works sponsored the scheme only half the cost was charged to the taxpayer.[37] A few months later, the government revised its relief programme under the Labour Relief Act, enacted on 28 August 1846, whereby all public relief works were to

33 Desmond Norton, *Landlords, Tenants, Famine: The business of an Irish Land Agency in the 1840s* (Dublin, 2006), p. 64.

34 Donnelly, 'Famine and government response', pp. 278–82; Woodham-Smith, *The Great Hunger*, pp. 48–50.

35 *Saunders's Newsletter*, 20 October 1846, p. 3.

36 *Dublin Evening Post*, 21 January 1847, p. 6.

37 Donnelly, 'Famine and government response', p. 282.

be integrated under the Board of Works and funding was to be an entirely local charge, based on government loans repayable through the county cess (property tax).[38]

The impact of the government's policies can be seen in newspaper reports from October and November 1846 when special measures were adopted to relieve distress in the barony of Uppercross, which included Rathmines and that part of Milltown situate on the north bank of the River Dodder. On 12 October 1846 an extraordinary presentment session of the grand jury was held in Tallaght for the relief of distress in the barony of Uppercross, which resulted in a sum of £10,000 authorised for expenditure on public works throughout the barony. However, the allocation of the funding was completely manipulated by local pressure groups who had formed themselves into a committee. As a consequence, £2,600 alone was given to repairing the Rathmines and Rathgar Road, notwithstanding that an influential ratepayer, Mr T. Dolan, had opined that there were very few able-bodied men in want of employment in Rathmines. As for Milltown, a mere £40 was voted for 'putting in passable condition the road at Milltown hill'.[39]

At an extraordinary meeting of the presentment sessions for the barony of Rathdown held over two days in Dundrum on 29 and 31 October 1846, the cess-payers met to consider constabulary reports on the level of destitution in the barony and to decide whether or not to levy further taxation on cess-payers.[40] At that meeting, the chairman of the presentment sessions, Lord Cloncurry, painted a bleak picture of the conditions pertaining in Rathdown, an area which was, relative to the rest of the country, a very wealth barony:

> *The chairman said he originally thought that from the number of gentry and people of opulence that lived in that barony there would be no necessity for such a call [£3,000] as that ... Yet he felt bound to say that the destitution was much greater than was imagined by many persons, and to lessen its amount or remove it completely should be their undivided object (hear, hear). Constant applications [for charity] were made to him; amongst others, he had been applied to for relief by poor people who had within the last month been discharged by opulent gentlemen who kept up villas and that sort of thing (cries of oh, oh). They had discharged these poor creatures at a time when men ought rather to take in additional hands (hear, hear).*[41]

Despite considerable differences of opinion expressed by the cess-payers, the meeting ultimately approved the adoption of taxation measures which raised £3,000 for expenditure on local works within the barony.[42] On the second day of the presentment session local landowner Arthur Burgh Crofton of Roebuck Castle, Roebuck Road (now part of the UCD Belfield campus), expressed sentiments similar to Lord Cloncurry's:

> *The county surveyor had, by reason of this assessment, a sum of £3,000 at his disposal for works within the barony, and there could not be any question as to the large amount of employment that money would extend to the labouring population – that was to the able bodied, for they should bear in mind that although a great deal of distress prevailed and a lamentable amount of misery and infirmity*

38 Ciarán Ó Murchadha, *The Great Famine: Ireland's agony 1845–1852* (London, 2011), p. 53.

39 *Dublin Evening Post*, 15 October 1846, p. 3.

40 *Saunders's Newsletter*, 30 October 1846, p. 2; 2 November 1842, pp. 1–2.

41 *Saunders's Newsletter*, 30 October 1846, p. 2.

42 *Saunders's Newsletter*, 30 October 1846, p. 2.

> *existed in the various towns and villages throughout the barony, that the presentments they passed that day would only go to the relief of the men who were able to work (hear, hear, hear). Everyone possessed of humanity must deplore the prevalent distress amongst the poor. Relief Committees would be established in each district, and the cess-payers would be expected to subscribe to them, so that irrespective of the coercive tax – that of assessment – they would have the voluntary tax to meet (hear, hear).*[43]

The meeting went on to approve (among other things) the expenditure of £50 and £267 respectively on repairing the road from Churchtown to Classon's Bridge (now called Lower Churchtown Road) and the road from Donnybrook to Clonskeagh (now called Beaver Row).[44]

Notwithstanding the exhortations of Cloncurry and Crofton, some of the local gentry continued to behave in a very unscrupulous manner and used the availability of the public works scheme as an opportunity to dismiss employees, much to the chagrin of the Dundrum Relief Committee:

> *The Committee regret to say that some of the applicants for relief have stated that they had been dismissed from their employment by gentlemen resident in this district and thereby thrown for the means of support upon the Relief Committee, in the hope of being employed on the public works. The Committee would strongly urge upon the respectable and wealthy residents in the district the necessity of giving more employment than usual to the distressed poor at this period of unexampled distress.*[45]

Deplorable though these actions by a minority of the gentry were, their actions probably belie the fact that some people higher up the social chain were feeling the adverse economic effects of the Famine, and were also struggling financially.

LOCAL RELIEF COMMITTEES – RATHMINES AND DUNDRUM

On 26 October 1846 it was reported that a local relief committee had been appointed by the Lieutenant of County Dublin (the Earl of Meath) to assist the poor of Rathmines, Harold's Cross, Milltown, Ranelagh and Cullenswood. The new relief committee provided ledgers for recording the names, addresses and family details of the able bodied and the infirm poor, which were left for completion in various shops and public houses, including Patrick Hackett's public house in Milltown, prior to transmission to the Board of Works.[46] Such an initiative was badly needed because the local unemployed labourers were restless and had to be calmed by the clergy:

> *On yesterday the Roman Catholic clergymen after last mass informed the congregation of what had been done to afford employment and earnestly urged the impropriety of any meeting in large numbers. The multitudes quietly dispersed in the hope of employment being afforded, and it is to be hoped for the peace and relief of the district that the works presented so far back as the 12th inst. will be at once set on foot by the board of works.*[47]

43 *Saunders's Newsletter*, 2 November 1846, pp. 1–2.

44 *Saunders's Newsletter*, 2 November 1846, pp. 1–2.

45 *Saunders's Newsletter*, 28 December 1846, p. 4.

46 *Saunders's Newsletter*, 26 October 1846, p. 2.

47 *Saunders's Newsletter*, 26 October 1846, p. 2.

A week later, the Rathmines Relief Committee met on 3 November 1846 and passed a resolution setting up a relief fund which was to be made up of donations collected by committee members from among their neighbours.[48] The committee's fundraising activity bore fruit and on 22 December 1846 the newspapers reported that:

> *Rathmines – The Relief Committee here are issuing meal and rice to the labouring poor at reduced prices three times a week by which upwards of 100 families are relieved. Fuel has also been distributed at reduced prices. Straw for bedding has been gratuitously distributed at Harold's Cross, Rathmines, Milltown and Cullenswood to 250 families.*[49]

> *A soup kitchen will be opened on Wednesday next and a quart of soup and a piece of bread supplied to every person bringing a ticket, which tickets are sold at convenient places at 1½ d. each; and it is trusted that the charitable will avail themselves of these tickets instead of giving money. The committee earnestly hope that they may be enabled to continue their operations by liberal contributions from the inhabitants of the district.*[50]

There can be no doubt from the above reports that the unfolding disaster of the Famine was causing huge distress to the poor of Dublin's suburban villages due to unemployment and rising food prices. As early as March 1846, 695 poor people in Kingstown (Dún Laoghaire) could not afford adequate food because of rising prices.[51]

In the meantime, while the Rathmines Relief Committee was busy distributing food and organising a soup kitchen, its counterpart in Dundrum had been collecting money from the affluent residents who resided in the numerous villas in the districts of Dundrum, Roebuck and Churchtown. The money collected was to be used to purchase food provisions for distribution among the distressed poor of the district. A list of the donors' names, places of residence together with the amounts contributed was published on 28 December 1846. Among them were James D. Meldon of Casino, who contributed £5 3*s.*, and committee member Richard Ferrall of Milltown Lodge, who contributed £2.[52] To put some context on the contemporary purchasing power of these donations, a tenant renting a cabin with a small garden in Farranboley townland, adjacent to Milltown village on the south bank of the River Dodder, typically paid between 2*s.* and 3*s.* a week in rent.[53] Thus a donation of £2 was the equivalent of between 13 and 20 weeks' rent for a labourer with a cottage and small garden. It is not possible to discover what the typical cost of provisions were at that time in the Dundrum and Milltown districts, unfortunately.

While the initial response to the famine emergency by the majority of the wealthy classes of Rathmines and Dundrum was commendable, the critical question was how long could their local relief efforts be sustained as the national calamity continued to worsen. In this regard,

48 *Saunders's Newsletter*, 4 November 1846, p. 4.

49 *Dublin Evening Post*, 22 December 1846, p. 2.

50 *Saunders's Newsletter*, 22 December 1846, p. 2.

51 Eva Ó Cathaoir, 'The Rathdown Union Workhouse at Loughlinstown, 1838–1923', *Dublin Historical Record*, xlviii, no. 2 (Autumn 1995), pp. 111–24.

52 *Saunders's Newsletter*, 28 December 1846, p. 4.

53 NAI, VO, OL53660, House/Tenure Book for Farranboley townland, 1847 nos 1 and 2.

the next stage of their efforts was focused on applying for government grants which matched the amounts collected by the local relief committees.

The chairman of the Rathmines Relief Committee was a landowner called Sir Robert Shaw who came from a prominent nineteenth-century mercantile family from Terenure. Robert, who lived in Kimmage House, was a son of the MP Frederick Shaw of Bushy Park, Terenure. Frederick Shaw represented Dublin University in the House of Commons during the 1830s and 1840s, where he became the unofficial leader of the Irish Conservative MPs at Westminster.[54] Given his background Robert Shaw was well connected and could expect to be taken seriously by the authorities. On 4 January 1847 he wrote the following letter to the Chief Secretary of Ireland, Henry Labouchere, MP:

> *Kimmage House January 4th 1847*
>
> *Sir, as chairman of the Rathmines Relief Committee I beg to address you for the purpose of ascertaining whether Her Majesty's Government will grant a sum of money in aid of the funds collected by private subscriptions for the relief of the poor. The district for which the committee has been appointed is extensive and comprises two very poor and populous localities – Milltown and Harold's Cross. These contain a large number of labouring and destitute poor. The former in consequence of the extreme dearness of provisions find great difficulty in supporting themselves and [their] families. To enable them to purchase food at something approaching a reasonable price the committee have opened a poor shop where meal and rice are sold on tickets at a small reduction under cost price. All persons to entitle them to this privilege must have their names entered in a Registry kept for that purpose in which all the particulars of their occupation, weekly earnings, number in family etc are carefully entered. The quantity sold to each per week is proportioned to the number in [the] family. By this means upwards of 300 families are relieved weekly. The committee have also opened a soup shop similar to those already established in the metropolis where tickets are sold to the poor who are able to purchase them. They are thus provided with a cheap and nutritious food. The charitably disposed are also enabled to relieve the poor at a small cost. To meet the numerous claims upon them the committee have as yet only been able to collect £240. This fund will soon be exhausted. The committee have been given to understand that [a] large cotton factory in Harold's Cross now giving employment to 500 hands will shortly be closed in consequence of the stagnation in trade and the difficulty of disposing of the manufactured articles. Under the foregoing circumstances the committee would respectively solicit some assistance on the part of her Majesty's Government.*[55]

Shaw's letter was passed by Labouchere to the bureaucrats in the Central Relief Commission, which had been set up by Peel's government in November 1845 to oversee the distribution of food aid as part of the government's famine relief effort.[56] Shaw's application for aid was turned down by the Central Relief Commission 'in consequence of some deviation from the Government instructions of which the Committee had been guilty'. It appears from the correspondence that the Rathmines Relief Committee had not adhered to the Commission's regulations which, among other things, forbade the selling of food at less than cost or giving food

54 Tony McCarthy, *The Shaws of Terenure: A nineteenth century Dublin merchant family* (Dublin, 2010), pp. 52–4.

55 NAI, Famine Relief Commission Manuscripts, RLFC/3/2/9/36.

56 Donnelly, 'Famine and government response', p. 278.

away (except to the infirm) unless the local workhouse was full.[57] Undaunted, Shaw appealed the decision citing new, less stringent regulations in his favour and he enclosed the complete list of donors to the relief fund together with the appropriately worded certificate with his appeal. Shaw reiterated that 'The Rathmines district is large, the pauper population numerous. The funds collected by private subscription [are] totally inadequate to meet the necessary expenses.' [58]

In response, the Central Relief Commissioners sought a breakdown of the Rathmines figures showing the total amount collected (£325 5*s.* 11*d.),* the total amount expended to date (£80 17*s.*, comprising £26 17*s.* spent on turf and straw and an estimated £54 spent on purchasing provisions which were sold to the poor at below cost price), and the balance remaining in hand (£244,8*s.* 11*d.*). Following receipt of the figures the Commissioners awarded a matching grant of £244, i.e. they excluded all of the funds which the Rathmines Relief Committee had spent to date because the funds been not been applied in accordance with the most stringent regulations. The sum settled on, £244, appears to have been personally approved by the most important figure in the Central Relief Commission, Sir Randolph Routh, whose initial 'R' appears beside the final figure awarded in the middle of February, 1847.[59]

One particular piece of bureaucracy was causing considerable difficulties for all relief committees. In October 1846 the Central Relief Commission issued new qualifying criteria for the government's matching grant which forbade the selling of food at less than the wholesale or cost price plus an additional 5 per cent to cover selling and storage costs. These rules were purposely designed to prevent the local relief committees from quickly exhausting the funds by selling provisions below cost price, funds which the Central Relief Commission wanted spent more sparingly over a longer period of time. In desperation, many local relief committees ignored the rules in order to feed their starving local population, even though by doing so they forfeited the matching grant. Indeed, the injustice of the inflexible rules led to the Central Relief Commission receiving dozens of letters in December 1846 seeking permission to sell food to the poor below cost price.[60]

Like its Rathmines counterpart, the Dundrum Relief Committee was busy collecting funds in the winter of 1846 and preparing its application for a matching government grant. The chairman of the Dundrum Relief Committee was Arthur Burgh Crofton, whose comments on the state of the district have been quoted above. Crofton was passionately opposed to the matching funds rules and he personally petitioned the Prime Minister, Lord John Russell, whose Liberal government had succeeded Sir Robert Peel's administration in July 1846.[61] Crofton's letter pointed out that many relief committees had declined to apply for the matching grant because of the authorities' lack of flexibility, and he went on to explain the economic reality of the situation on the ground, as existed in December 1846:

> *Your Lordship is aware that the rate of wages paid to persons employed on the Public Works now being carried on throughout the country never exceeds and is generally less than the customary wages of the district while the price of provisions such as [Indian] meal, flour etc is at least one third higher than it*

---

57 NAI, Famine Relief Commission Manuscripts, RLFC/3/2/9/36.

58 NAI, Famine Relief Commission Manuscripts, RLFC/3/2/9/36.

59 NAI, Famine Relief Commission Manuscripts, RLFC/3/2/9/36.

60 Woodham-Smith, *The Great Hunger*, pp. 127, 161–3.

61 Woodham-Smith, *The Great Hunger*, pp. 81–2; NAI, Famine Relief Commission Manuscripts, RLFC/3/2/9/29.

> *was twelve months ago. Potatoes being lost, the people are thrown for subsistence upon a description of food which formerly formed but a very small item in their consumption. The consequence of this is that those who have large families, although earning full wages, are unable to purchase sufficient meal or flour to support them, while the old and sickly, not able to earn half wages, are almost in a state of starvation. I need scarcely have [to] inform your Lordship that a man earning one shilling a day in former years could purchase therewith (supposing he had none of his own growth) three stones of potatoes for the daily support of his family, while now with the same sum he cannot purchase even half a stone of Indian Meal, the cheapest description of provision to be had now, and I will leave your Lordship to judge how far such a supply would go towards the support of a family.*[62]

Crofton's letter was passed to the Treasury Office in London and the officials there drafted a reply, which was to be issued to Crofton by the Dublin authorities. In short, Crofton's petition to relax the matching grant rules was refused on the basis that:

> *if this precaution were not taken the funds of the [local relief] committees would be soon exhausted and the consumption of the stock of provisions remaining in the country would proceed at a rate which would be productive of much greater distress hereafter.*[63]

Despite the illogicality, not to mention the inhumanity, of its argument in the face of the bald facts explained by Crofton, the Treasury justified its response in line the British political establishment's economic orthodoxy, and its insistence on not interfering with market forces:

> *Their Lordships, however, also consider the encouragement of the private trader to be an object of great public importance because the people cannot permanently be supplied with food through the artificial machinery of the Relief Committees, and until dealers shall have been induced to undertake the collection and distribution of meal and other kinds of food on ordinary mercantile principles this essential branch of social economy cannot be considered as being placed upon a proper footing.*[64]

Despite this cold response, the government soon afterwards radically revised its famine policy in January 1847 and gave up the policy of funding the purchase of meal. Instead, the government decided to replace that scheme with a new measure, popularly called the Soup Kitchen Act. Under this act, new relief committees were to be established tasked with distributing soup but without any work being required from the recipients. On 20 January 1847 relief committees were advised that free distribution of food was now permitted to the infirm, poor widows, orphans and children, provided that the local workhouse was full.[65]

With the new change of policy, the Dundrum Relief Committee decided to apply for a government grant on 19 February 1847. The committee drew up a list of the names and addresses and amounts collected from the residents of their district since 17 November 1846 to 19 February 1847. Why the retrospective cut-off date of 17 November 1846 was chosen is not explained in the surviving files. Nonetheless, the timing of the application was very likely to have been influenced by the fact that the numbers of destitute poor seeking refuge in the Rathdown Union work-

62 NAI, Famine Relief Commission Manuscripts, RLFC/3/2/9/29.

63 NAI, Famine Relief Commission Manuscripts, RLFC/3/2/9/29.

64 NAI, Famine Relief Commission Manuscripts, RLFC/3/2/9/29.

65 Woodham-Smith, *The Great Hunger*, pp. 165–6.

house had by 30 January 1847 exceeded its maximum capacity of 600 inmates by 89.[66] The list of names and the amounts collected submitted with the grant application do not match the data published in *Saunders's Newsletter* on 28 December 1846 because the former data only covered a two-month period whereas the latter data covered the entire amount collected during the calendar year to 28 December 1846. The data accompanying the grant application provide a snapshot of 83 local donors who collectively gave £149 and 9*d.* for the relief of the poor over a two-month period, including the Christmas of 1846. These affluent donors inhabited the villas dotting the rural hinterland of County Dublin south of the River Dodder along the Dundrum Road, Bird Avenue, Roebuck Road, Goatstown Road, Mount Anville Road, Fosters Avenue, Churchtown Road, and further beyond to Dundrum, Balally and Ballinteer.[67]

The application to the Central Relief Commission for the government grant was made by the secretary of the Dundrum Relief Committee, John White of Readsdale House, Dundrum, to Sir Randolph Routh on 19 February 1847. White's letter set out the basis of the committee's application as follows:

> *I am also instructed to state for the information of his excellency that the grounds upon which they rest the reasonableness of their application for the largest amount of money which his excellency is authorised to grant as follows. Firstly, the committee distribute weekly one ton of wheaten meal, charging first, cost price to all who are anyway employed, giving gratuitous relief only to the infirm poor, widows and orphans, of which there are a great number in this district. Secondly, that the amounts received by private subscription is small in comparison to the number of poor resident in the parish, and thirdly, that the committee had been in existence for some months last Spring and contributed much to alleviate the then existing distress without making any application to government for a grant.*[68]

White's assertions that the amounts received by private subscription were small in comparison with the number of poor residents, and that the district contained a 'great number' of infirm poor, widows and orphans are noteworthy given that the Committee's district had such a large concentration of middle- and upper-class residents in comparison with other rural parts of County Dublin. It is possible that the Dundrum Relief Committee felt the need to exaggerate the situation because it was competing for aid with the south and west of Ireland which were in dire straits. On the other hand, the cholera epidemic of the 1830s coupled with the collapse of local manufacturing industries had undoubtedly swelled the numbers of distressed inhabitants. In any event, White's application was successful and the Central Relief Commissioners recommended that Dundrum Relief Committee get a grant of £149, provided that the Committee complied with the latest set of government regulations which had been issued on 20 January 1847. In response, the Dundrum Relief Committee passed a resolution that:

> *the instructions of government be strictly and totally adhered to by the sub-committee in giving orders for meal, and that in no case shall meal be distributed under cost price, except to the really destitute as directed by the 3rd paragraph of the Instruction dated 20 January.*[69]

66 NAI, Famine Relief Commission Manuscripts, RLFC/3/2/9/29.

67 NAI, Famine Relief Commission Manuscripts, RFLC/3/2/9/29.

68 NAI, Famine Relief Commission Manuscripts, RFLC/3/2/9/29.

69 NAI, Famine Relief Commission Manuscripts, RFLC/3/2/9/29.

The government's policy introduced in January 1847 of feeding the poor through soup kitchens was not promptly adopted by the Dundrum Relief Committee. While the reasons for this are unclear due to the incomplete survival of the official records, the Dundrum Relief Committee appears to have had a preference for distributing meal to the poor instead of soup. The final mention in the official records of the Dundrum Relief Committee occurs on 12 March 1847, when the secretary confirmed to the Central Relief Commission that 'there is no soup kitchen in our relief district'.[70] It seems that the Dundrum Relief Committee was not alone in its lack of enthusiasm for soup kitchens. Nationally, many local relief committees wanted to use up their own resources before signing up to the soup kitchen scheme, while other relief committees desired an extension to the public works system of relief for as long as possible.[71]

The government's policy of providing matching funds finally ceased in August 1847 and with it the motivation for retaining local relief committees ended.[72] This explains why press reports and famine relief records for the Dundrum and Rathmines districts are absent after March 1847.

THE WORKHOUSE: THE REFUGE OF LAST RESORT

The government's soup kitchen scheme terminated early in September 1847 and thereafter the Poor Law was used as the principal means of providing relief to the victims of the Famine. This marked a fundamental change in the government's philosophy towards famine relief. State assistance for famine relief measures was ended and henceforth Irish ratepayers would be entirely responsible for providing relief under the Poor Law and the workhouse.[73] The workhouse admission records for the Rathdown and South Dublin poor law unions have survived, and they throw some light on the situation prevailing at Milltown in the period 1848 to 1850. But before examining these records it is necessary to give some background to how the Poor Law operated in practice both before and during the Famine.

By the 1830s the pressure to provide some form of rudimentary relief for the poor in the face of increasing poverty in Ireland led to the introduction of the poor law in 1838. In brief, relief was provided by a countrywide system of workhouses financed by local landlords and ratepayers, in which the indoor assistance available to the inmates was deliberately made as unattractive as possible to deter all but the most desperate and destitute from applying for admission.[74] The funding of the workhouse was structured so that the poor rate in each electoral division was levied according to the proportion of paupers (as the inmates of the workhouses were called) in the workhouse who had previously been resident in that district.[75] The townland of Milltown was part of electoral division 3 (Rathmines) of the South Dublin Poor Law Union, an area comprising 1,200 statute acres, all of which were located to the south of the Grand Canal, and which had a population of 9,973 in

70 NAI, Famine Relief Commission Manuscripts, RFLC/3/2/9/29.

71 James S. Donnelly, 'The soup kitchens' in W.E. Vaughan (ed.), *A new history of Ireland, v: Ireland under the Union 1801–1870* (Oxford, 1989), p. 308.

72 Tim P. O'Neill, 'The charities and famine in mid-nineteenth century Ireland' in Jacqueline Hill and Colm Lennon (eds), *Luxury and Austerity* (Dublin, 1999), p. 143.

73 James S. Donnelly, 'The administration of relief, 1847–51' in W.E. Vaughan (ed.), *A new history of Ireland, v: Ireland under the Union 1801–1870* (Oxford, 1989), p. 316; Christine Kinealy, 'The operation of the Poor Law during the Famine' in John Crowley, William J. Smyth and Mike Murphy (eds), *Atlas of the Great Irish Famine* (Cork, 2012), p. 91.

74 Crossman, *Local Government*, pp. 44–6.

75 Gerard O'Brien, 'The new Poor Law in pre-Famine Ireland: A case history', *Irish Economic and Social History*, 12 (1985), pp. 33–49.

1831. This electoral district was entitled to elect two poor law guardians.[76]

The South Dublin Union workhouse and the Rathdown Union workhouse opened in March 1840 and October 1841 in James's Street and Loughlinstown respectively.[77] The test for admission to the workhouse was strictly applied. Aside from orphans, abandoned children, the infirm and the disabled, only the most destitute of able-bodied adults were admitted to the workhouse. The poor law guardians of the South Dublin Union workhouse thoroughly investigated the background of each applicant to see if he or she had any relatives who could support the individual. Once the paupers gained admission to the workhouse, they were segregated in separate wards according to gender, age, mental disability and physical infirmity. Children were separated from their mothers from as early as two years of age, but this rule was not rigidly enforced. Able-bodied children and adults had to undertake 'irksome' work – a further deterrent – within the confines of the workhouse and its grounds. In addition, the paupers' two daily meals were composed of a diet that was specifically designed to ensure that it was inferior to the diet of the labouring classes living in the poor law union. In practice this was not always the case and the diet varied according to the severity of protests by the paupers (food riots were not unknown) or the philanthropic inclinations of the guardians: at Christmas 1839 the pauper children in the Dublin workhouses dined on beef, mutton, bread and beer. Ordinarily their diet consisted of oatmeal, milk or buttermilk, potatoes and soup.[78]

Paupers were free to leave the workhouse of their own volition or they could be expelled for serious misbehaviour. To take a couple of extreme cases, two female teenagers were expelled from the South Dublin Union workhouse in 1842 for refusing to break stones while in 1845 several runaway boys were caught and imprisoned for six months because they had absconded in their workhouse clothes which belonged to the South Dublin Union.[79] Indeed, the early years of the workhouses in pre-famine Ireland were characterised by shockingly poor standards of behaviour and competency by the staff employed by the poor law guardians. One historian has concluded that life in Irish workhouses was austere to the point where inmates were often in great physical danger, a not unreasonable view considering that the apothecary of the South Dublin Union workhouse sold unclaimed corpses to anatomists for 10*s.* each, including 2*s.* 6*d.* for the porter.[80]

The provision of basic social welfare through the workhouse system was never designed to cope with a calamity as big as the Irish Famine of 1845–50. Inevitably, therefore, as conditions deteriorated the workhouses were overwhelmed by masses of starving malnourished and sick people, conditions which aided the spread of contagious diseases and fatal illnesses. The mortality rate in Irish workhouses rose from 5.4 per 1,000 at the end of April 1846 to 25 per 1,000 April 1847.[81] The following incident illustrates how bad conditions in Dublin were by then. Responding to a widespread fever epidemic prevailing in the city and county during the summer of 1847, the South Dublin Union set up a temporary fever hospital in

---

76 *Freeman's Journal*, 1 May 1839, p. 4.

77 Helen Burke, *The People and the Poor Law in 19th Century Ireland* (The Women's Education Bureau, 1987), p. 64, Eva Ó Cathaoir, 'The Poor Law in County Wicklow' in Ken Hanigan and William Nolan (eds), *Wicklow History and Society* (Dublin, 1994), p. 508.

78 O'Brien 'Workhouse Management in Pre-Famine Ireland', pp. 114–21.

79 O'Brien 'Workhouse Management in Pre-Famine Ireland', pp. 127–8.

80 O'Brien 'Workhouse Management in Pre-Famine Ireland', pp. 128, 132.

81 Burke, *The People and the Poor Law*, p. 130.

Kilmainham, but by September 1847 the fever hospital had become so overcrowded that temporary sheds were erected beside the Grand Canal at Rialto Bridge, where people died for want of treatment and adequate shelter.[82]

The total failure to mitigate the worsening effects of famine distress forced the government to introduce a fundamental change of approach in the summer of 1847. Under the Poor Relief Extension Act of 1847, a new policy was introduced, namely, the provision of outdoor relief. Hitherto assistance under the poor law was only available inside the workhouse, hence the term 'outdoor relief' to distinguish it from assistance provided inside the workhouse.[83] This term is misleading because it gives the impression that outdoor relief involved activity carried outdoors, but this was not the case – outdoor relief could take the form of grants of food or cash. The radical difference in comparison to indoor relief was that the poor could, subject to qualifying criteria, receive assistance in their immediate neighbourhood; i.e. they did not have to enter the workhouse to obtain outdoor relief. In keeping with the prevailing parsimonious ethos of the policy makers in England, very strict rules were laid down to determine who was eligible to apply for outdoor relief, which was restricted to the following three categories of the destitute:

1. destitute poor persons who are permanently disabled from labour by reason of old age, infirmity, or bodily or mental defect,
2. destitute poor persons who being disabled from labour by reason of severe sickness, or serious accident, are thereby deprived of the means of earning a subsistence for themselves and their families, whom they are liable by law to maintain,
3. destitute poor widows having two or more legitimate children dependent upon them.[84]

These unfortunate people – sometimes known as the impotent poor – could be given outdoor relief at the discretion of the local board of guardians. Exceptions were permitted during periods of unusual distress. If the workhouse was full, or if disease was rife inside, the Poor Law Commissioners (the authority having oversight and control of the operation of the poor laws) could authorise local poor law guardians to provide outdoor relief to the able-bodied poor for a maximum of two months, but only in the form of food to individuals willing to engage in hard labour, such as stone breaking.[85]

The Poor Law Guardians were required to employ additional staff to administer outdoor relief at the local level within their poor law union. These new administrators, called relieving officers, became highly important people within their community because of the control they had over the granting or withholding of outdoor relief.[86] Initially, outdoor relief was provided in the form of food rather than cash: in 1849, for example, an unidentified recipient of outdoor relief got an average of less than 1lb of Indian meal per day, but if the recipient was engaged in hard labour he would get up to one-and-three-quarter lbs of meal per day. Outdoor relief was strictly a temporary benefit to tide people over a period of acute distress. The recipient's cir-

82 *Dublin Medical Press*, 1 September 1847, pp. 138–41.

83 Donnelly, 'The administration of relief, 1847–51', pp. 316–7.

84 Burke, *The People and the Poor Law*, p. 130.

85 Donnelly, 'The administration of relief, 1847–51', p. 317.

86 Burke, *The People and the Poor Law*, pp. 130–2.

cumstances were kept under constant review by the local relieving officer. Research has shown that outdoor relief given during the period 1848–51 was most widely availed of in the month of July, at which point in time what was left of the old crop of potatoes had been exhausted prior to the harvesting of the new season's crop.[87]

Under the poor law regulations applying in the South Dublin Union in November 1847, people recovering at home from fever, dysentery and other illnesses were entitled to a daily ration of one pound of bread and one pint of milk from the relieving officer. However, the doctor in charge of the Donnybrook Parochial Dispensary wrote to the guardians opining that this amount of food was insufficient for the effective recovery of the patients or to prevent their relapse, and he requested that the guardians sanction 'a more liberal allowance for those poor creatures, whom it has pleased Providence to afflict with fever'. Dr Quinan's petition was also supported by the local relieving officer for Donnybrook. The issue was discussed at length at a board meeting held on 18 November. After a contentious debate, a motion by one of the guardians, David La Touche, to empower the relieving officers to provide recovering patients with more nutritious food than the standard diet on the direction of the medical officers or the dispensary doctor, was defeated by the casting vote of the chairman.[88] The controversy is noteworthy because it demonstrates that the level of distress prevailing among the poor in the Donnybrook district and beyond (a deceased fever case from Rathfarnham was cited in support of La Touche's motion) in the autumn of 1847 was sufficiently worrisome for Donnybrook's dispensary doctor and relieving officer to petition the guardians to better provide for the dietary needs of recovering fever patients.

MILLTOWN ADMISSIONS TO THE WORKHOUSE

Given the very challenging conditions in the workhouses both before and during the Famine it is perhaps not surprising that the first workhouse admission on record of a person from Milltown occurred as late as 1848. On 19 June 1848 eighteen-year-old Peter Kenny from Milltown entered the South Dublin Union workhouse. The admission clerk for every workhouse was required to note in the ledger 'observations on the condition of the pauper when admitted'. In Peter Kenny's case, he was wearing very old clothes, one of the most commonly used phrases to describe the condition of the paupers who presented themselves for admission to the workhouse.[89] We don't know why Peter Kenny entered the workhouse but he must have been destitute (no occupation is given for him) or else he would not have been let in. In any event, he left the workhouse on 30 June 1848. At the time Peter entered the workhouse there were two households in Milltown village with the Kenny surname – Anne Kenny and Mathew Kenny.[90] Peter Kenny was probably related to Anne or Mathew Kenny, or possibly both. If this was the case, Peter Kenny must have withheld this information as otherwise he would not have been admitted to the workhouse because he had family or relatives in Milltown. Nearly two years later, on 22 April 1850, a Peter Kenny, aged eighteen, from Milltown was admitted to the South Dublin Union workhouse. His occupation was given as a dealer, a commonly used descriptor in the workhouse admission register for the South Dublin Union. This detail

87 Burke, *The People and the Poor Law*, pp. 135–7.

88 *Freeman's Journal*, 19 November 1847, p. 1.

89 NAI, South Dublin Poor Law Union Workhouse Register, BG 79/G4, pp. 199–200, no. 3997.

90 Griffith's Valuation, Primary Valuation of Tenements, County of Dublin, Barony of Uppercross, Parish of St Peter, Townland of Milltown, pp. 58, 60 at entry nos 30, 152 (1847).

suggests that Kenny was a casual trader in Dublin city – a very precarious livelihood at the best of times.[91] Even though the two Peter Kennys birth years do not match (1830 and 1832), the second individual was possibly the same Peter Kenny who was previously admitted to the workhouse in 1848, allowing for errors and inaccuracies in recording dates of birth.

The first four months of 1849 saw the highest numbers of people from Milltown (17) entering the workhouse during the period 1845–50. The reason for the sudden increase in the numbers during that period is not immediately obvious – it predates the cholera epidemic of the summer and autumn of that year – but it is likely that the acute distress was related to the decline and closure of Samuel Moore's woollen mills and the impact that had on the local economy.[92] A second contributory factor was the failure of the potato crop in Milltown once more, in the early autumn of 1848. A Rathmines resident wrote to the *Dublin Evening Post* on 6 September 1848 to inform readers of the situation then prevailing in Milltown:

> *Perceiving by your columns, the interest which you have taken in the state of the potato crop, I take the liberty of sending you a short account of the state of this crop in the vicinity of Miltown [sic], County of Dublin. I have made it my business to go through the above neighbourhood, in which, within the last two years, there has been a large quantity of ground laid under the potato. On the property of one gentleman there are at least seven acres destroyed, which, within the last month, looked quite healthy. The stalks, about a fortnight ago, began to get black, and in a few days after I took up several of the potatoes, and found the inside eaten away, and the skin quite slimy. I visited several other places, and found them in the same state.*[93]

These circumstances provide some explanation for the increase in the number of people from Milltown entering the workhouse in the late winter and early spring of 1849. On 25 January 1849 thirty-three-year-old Cecilia Lambert and her nine-year-old son James were forced to take refuge in the South Dublin Union workhouse because Cecilia had been deserted by her husband.[94] Cecilia's husband was probably the James Lambert who in 1847 was living in a small cottage beside Howe's public house (now The Dropping Well) beside Classon's Bridge which the family rented from William Lee.[95] Cecilia and James Lambert were discharged and readmitted to the workhouse on the same day, 3 February 1849.[96] This detail illustrates a misleading deficiency in workhouse recording procedures. Paupers who were let out on short-term leave – to look for work or make contact with relatives for example – were entered into the workhouse register as new applicants on their return.[97] When the Lamberts first entered

91 NAI, South Dublin Poor Law Union Workhouse Register, BG 79/G7, pp. 59–60, no. 1199. Kenny left the workhouse on 4 May 1850.

92 *General Advertiser for Dublin, and All Ireland*, 1 April 1848, p. 3.

93 *Dublin Evening Post*, 9 September 1848, p. 4.

94 NAI, South Dublin Poor Law Union Workhouse Register, BG 79/G5, nos 3237–38. When Mrs Lambert first entered the workhouse, her Christian name was recorded as Sarah. This is almost certainly an error. When Mrs Lambert re-entered the workhouse her Christian name was given as Celia (entry no. 3377) which very closely matches the baptismal and marriage records for her son James Lambert, who was baptised in Rathmines RC church on 2 July 1839, married in the same place on 19 November 1865, and whose parents were named in both records as James Lambert and Cecilia Doyle.

95 Griffith's Valuation, Primary Valuation of Tenements, County of Dublin, Barony of Uppercross, Parish of St Peter, Townland of Rathmines South, p. 74 at entry no. 47 (1847).

96 NAI, South Dublin Poor Law Union Workhouse Register, BG 79/G5, nos 3237, 3238, 3377 and 3378.

97 O'Brien 'Workhouse Management in Pre-Famine Ireland', p. 131.

the workhouse on 25 January 1849 they were recorded as wearing very old clothes, but when they were readmitted on 3 February 1849 the clerk noted that they were wearing clean clothes.[98] The background to so few details is of course impossible to uncover but the information does provide a human dimension to the bare data in the admissions register. Cecilia and James Lambert left the workhouse for good on 7 February 1849 and resumed their lives in Milltown.[99] Throughout the nineteenth century and up to the mid-twentieth century Lambert families appear very frequently among the civil, Catholic and Church of Ireland parish records for Milltown, Windy Arbour, Classon's Bridge and beyond.

Although desertion is very frequently given as the reason for entering the workhouse during the Famine period, not all cases of desertion involved a deliberate or permanent abandonment of dependants by the male bread winner. In some cases, the husband went in search of work with a view to returning to collect his family.[100] This may well have been the case with Cecelia Lambert and her son James.

Two Milltown families whose circumstances compelled them to enter the South Dublin Union workhouse in the spring of 1849 had very sad outcomes. On 20 March 1849 sixty-one-year-old William FitzGerald, an unemployed labourer, sought admission to the workhouse together with his wife Catherine (thirty-eight) and their four children, Michael (ten), Darby (seven), Mary (three) and Christopher (two months).[101] As William and Catherine's toddler, Mary, had fever, Catherine was discharged from the workhouse the following day and she brought her sick child to the fever hospital in nearby Cork Street where little Mary remained for a week. Following her treatment in Cork Street, Mary FitzGerald was readmitted to the South Dublin Union workhouse. Somehow against all odds Mary survived the fever hospital and the workhouse, and she was discharged from the latter institution on 14 July 1849 with her two brothers.[102] Mary's baby brother Christopher was not so lucky, and he died in the workhouse on 7 April 1849.[103] William FitzGerald left the workhouse on 7 July 1849, presumably to look for work. The FitzGerald's three surviving children were discharged from the workhouse a week later, on 14 July 1849.[104] The surviving members of the FitzGerald family appear to have returned to their home in Milltown, as the following year William FitzGerald was recorded as renting a house with an office and yard from Patrick Hackett worth £7 4*s.*[105]

One of the issues raised by the FitzGerald's case is the very high rate of infant mortality that occurred in workhouses at that time. Social historian Helen Burke has revealed that 38 per cent of all infants aged under two years of age who entered the South Dublin Union workhouse in

98 NAI, South Dublin Poor Law Union Workhouse Register, BG 79/G5, nos 3237, 3238, 3377 and 3378.

99 NAI, South Dublin Poor Law Union Workhouse Register, BG 79/G5, nos 3377 and 3378.

100 Ó Cathaoir, 'The Poor Law in County Wicklow', p. 546.

101 NAI, South Dublin Poor Law Union Workhouse Register, BG 79/G5, nos 4231–36.

102 NAI, South Dublin Poor Law Union Workhouse Register, BG 79/G5, nos 4232, 4235, 4370. A different tenant was living in the house by 1850: Griffith's Valuation, Rateable Valuation of Tenements, County of Dublin, Barony of Uppercross, Parish of St Peter, Townland of Rathmines South, p. 71 at entry no. 20 f (1850).

103 NAI, South Dublin Poor Law Union Workhouse Register, BG 79/G5, no. 4236.

104 NAI, South Dublin Poor Law Union Workhouse Register, BG 79/G5, nos 4231, 4233, 4234, 4370.

105 Griffith's Valuation, Rateable Valuation of Tenements, County of Dublin, Barony of Uppercross, Parish of St Peter, Townland of Milltown, p. 54 at entry no. 11 (1850).

1848 died.[106] It was the unacceptably high levels of infant mortality, particularly among orphaned babies who invariably died in the absence of their birth mothers, which led to reforms of the poor laws. In 1862 the Poor Law Act was amended to facilitate the boarding out of orphans and deserted children under the age of five, which marked the beginning of officially sanctioned foster care in Ireland.[107]

Undoubtedly the saddest case in the Famine records of Milltown concerns the Byrne family. In the late spring of 1849 thirty-year-old Anne Byrne was deserted by her husband, leaving her to rear their four children, Patrick (seven), Mary (five), James (two) and Anne (one month).[108] The Griffith's Valuation records for 1847 record that at least two Byrne families were living in Milltown village, the households being headed by Michael Byrne and Patrick Byrne respectively.[109] Of the two, Patrick Byrne is most likely to have been Anne's husband given that their eldest boy was called Patrick. In the weeks or days prior to 26 April 1849 little Mary became very sick, and this seems to have forced the family to seek relief in the South Dublin Union workhouse. When Anne and her four children arrived at the workhouse the admission clerk noted that they were 'ragged and filthy'. Clearly, the family had either been living rough or had walked to the workhouse along the muddy roads from Milltown to James's Street during inclement weather. The clerk also noted laconically that Mary Byrne was 'apparently dying'.[110] This diagnosis was put beyond doubt when Mary died in the workhouse four days later, on 30 April 1849.[111] Mary's brother James did not survive the rigours of the workhouse and he too died on 12 May 1849.[112] Anne Byrne, her son Patrick and her infant daughter Anne left the workhouse on 8 June 1849.[113] Their fate is unknown.

Some of the Milltown residents who resorted to the South Dublin Union workhouse in 1849 and 1850 were single middle-aged or elderly people (i.e. forty-five years of age or more). Bachelor James Growney, aged fifty-four, entered the workhouse on 26 February 1849. He described himself as a servant and gardener.[114] Growney may have been dismissed from his previous job and found it impossible to find work, or perhaps he was no longer able for the physical demands required. Growney stayed in the workhouse for 10 months before being discharged on 21 December 1849.[115] Another Milltown gardener, John Ryan, was admitted to the workhouse on 10 April 1849 for a very brief period. Ryan, a bachelor, was aged sixty-six. For unknown reasons he was discharged from the workhouse two days later on 12 April 1849.[116]

106 Burke, *The People and the Poor Law*, p. 229.

107 Burke, *The People and the Poor Law*, pp. 230–1.

108 NAI, South Dublin Poor Law Union Workhouse Register, BG 79/G5, nos 4926–30.

109 Griffith's Valuation, Primary Valuation of Tenements, County of Dublin, Barony of Uppercross, Parish of St Peter, Townland of Milltown, p. 59 at entry nos 105, 125, 134 and 142 (1847).

110 NAI, South Dublin Poor Law Union Workhouse Register, BG 79/G5, nos 4926–30.

111 NAI, South Dublin Poor Law Union Workhouse Register, BG 79/G5, no. 4928.

112 NAI, South Dublin Poor Law Union Workhouse Register, BG 79/G5, no. 4929.

113 NAI, South Dublin Poor Law Union Workhouse Register, BG 79/G5, nos 4926, 4927, 4930.

114 NAI, South Dublin Poor Law Union Workhouse Register, BG 79/G5, no. 3846.

115 NAI, South Dublin Poor Law Union Workhouse Register, BG 79/G5, no. 3846.

116 NAI, South Dublin Poor Law Union Workhouse Register, BG 79/G5, no. 4569. The master of the workhouse or the guardians may have discovered that Ryan had relatives who could look after him.

An unemployed widowed dealer, forty-five-year-old Mary Byrne, spent five weeks in the workhouse in the spring of 1849.[117] One year later, widower Myles Doran entered the workhouse on 22 April 1850 when he was recorded as being ninety-two years of age, scarcely credible for the time. Doran had also worked as a gardener, presumably a very long time prior to his admission to the workhouse.[118] As noted earlier, eighteen-year-old Peter Kenny from Milltown was admitted to the South Dublin Union workhouse on two separate occasions. His second admission was on the same day as Doran (their admission numbers are adjacent to one another in the register), so Kenny may have accompanied the elderly man as his minder until they were both safely inside.[119]

Unemployment and desertion by their husbands (either permanent or temporary) continued for the poor women of Milltown for the remainder of 1849 and into 1850. The case of twenty-five-year-old Mary Fyans is an example of the hazards of unemployment during the Famine. Mary Fyans entered the South Dublin Union workhouse in clean old clothes on 8 December 1849 and remained there until 31 December 1849. Mary described herself as single and her occupation as a servant.[120] One interpretation of these details is that Mary Fyans had possibly worked as a domestic servant in one of the villas close to Milltown and, having no family connections in Milltown village, she was forced to seek temporary refuge in the workhouse after she was discharged from service. The fact that Mary arrived at the workhouse in clean clothes suggests that her previous abode was a reasonably comfortable one where clean clothing was required or which had access to laundry facilities.

The final case study concerns the unfortunate Ellen Kerr, a twenty-two-year-old married woman who, like Mary Fyans, was a servant. Kerr was deserted by her husband sometime before 13 May 1850 while she was pregnant with their son James, who was subsequently born in the South Dublin Union workhouse on 28 August 1850.[121] Baby James Kerr did not survive for long in the harsh conditions of the workhouse and he died at three months of age on 3 December 1850.[122] Ellen remained in the workhouse until her death there on 11 July 1851 at the age of twenty-three or twenty-four.[123]

The numbers of people from Milltown entering the workhouse began to fall considerably following the traumatic spring of 1849. During the period 1850 to 1859 only nine people from Milltown are listed among the admissions to the Dublin workhouses compared to 18 admissions for the calendar year 1849.

UNEMPLOYMENT AND FACTORY CLOSURES

Contemporary reports of Dublin suburban villages show that many were in a state of decay by the mid-nineteenth century. One commentator in 1849 remarked that 'Glasnevin, Chapelizod, Milltown, Rathfarnham, Roundtown [Terenure] and Templeogue, furnish special instances of

117 NAI, South Dublin Poor Law Union Workhouse Register, BG 79/G5, no. 4788. Byrne was admitted on 19 April and discharged on 25 May 1849.

118 NAI, South Dublin Poor Law Union Workhouse Register, BG 79/G7, no. 1200. Doran died in the workhouse on 13 August 1854.

119 NAI, South Dublin Poor Law Union Workhouse Register, BG 79/G7, no. 1199. Kenny left the workhouse on 4 May 1850.

120 NAI, South Dublin Poor Law Union Workhouse Register, BG 79/G6, no. 3127.

121 NAI, South Dublin Poor Law Union Workhouse Register, BG 79/G7, nos 1526, 3513.

122 NAI, South Dublin Poor Law Union Workhouse Register, BG 79/G7, no. 3513.

123 NAI, South Dublin Poor Law Union Workhouse Register, BG 79/G7, no. 1526.

evident retrogression in the material and industrial condition of the wealthiest portion of Ireland.'[124] With the exception of Roundtown, all of the aforementioned places were old industrial villages sited on the Liffey, Tolka and Dodder Rivers, and had become impoverished with the gradual closure of the textile factories and industrial mills beginning in the second decade of the nineteenth century.

The Famine had a devastating impact on the cloth mills that employed hundreds of people in Harold's Cross, Dartry and Milltown. As noted earlier, by the beginning of 1847 the Rathmines Relief Committee was very apprehensive that the large cotton factory at Harold's Cross would close with the loss of 500 employees. Similarly, when the surveyors from the Griffith's Valuation visited Samuel Moore's woollen factory at Milltown in July 1847 they reported on the decline in business: 'No trade – nothing done here since the 18th March. Work only 4 days a week during Winter – no prospect of work'; 'Trade is on the decline. No work whatsoever doing here and the cloth manufactured last year is still on hands. In consequence I think the above valuation may be reduced to £50.'[125]

By the spring of 1848 Moore's business at Milltown had closed down and the premises were advertised for sale on 1 April 1848.[126] More tellingly, a subsequent auction of unsold machinery was held the following September, 1849, with everything to be peremptorily sold without any reserve whatsoever.[127] The dire effects of the factory closure can be gauged by the fact that on Sunday 26 August 1849, a charity sermon was preached in Rathmines in support of the local school at Milltown, 'in which one hundred and fifty of the most destitute in the parish are educated'.[128]

It is unsurprising that the Famine had such a negative effect on the cloth mills and factories. Much of the woollen and cotton cloth manufactured at Milltown and elsewhere was predominantly made to clothe the poorer classes of Irish society, most of whom by 1847 were desperately trying to survive on what little money they had or to get together sufficient funds to emigrate. On their visit to Milltown village in 1847 the surveyors from the Griffith's Valuation noted that an erstwhile occupant (and former employee of Moore's woollen mills) of a small house, office and yard beside the mills, William Hunt, 'is gone to England in quest of work', having previously been exempted from paying his rent 'whilst idle'. [129] Hunt was one of the 44 Milltown residents who had subscribed to the National Repeal Association in September 1840.[130]

Another option for young men was to join the armed forces, by either enlisting in Ireland or joining up after emigrating to England. It is impossible to know how many unemployed young men from Milltown chose this route out of poverty. We do know of one youth who joined the army during the Famine. John Donovan was born in Milltown in 1830. His father was almost certainly the James Donovan who was living in a cottage in the main street of Milltown village in 1845.[131]

---

124 *Advocate,* 7 November 1849, p. 7.

125 NAI, VO, OL70089, Quarto Book for Milltown Village 1847, p. 216, no. 40.

126 *General Advertiser for Dublin, and All Ireland,* 1 April 1848, p. 3.

127 *Freeman's Journal,* 16 September 1849, p. 1.

128 *Freeman's Journal,* 24 August 1849, p. 1.

129 NAI, VO, OL70089, Quarto Book for Milltown Village 1847, p. 215, no. 36.

130 *Dublin Morning Register,* 30 September 1840, p. 4.

131 NAI, VO, OL50945, House Book for Milltown Village 1845, no. 29.

CHARITY FATIGUE

As famine continued into the late 1840s, the enthusiasm of the public to continue their charitable donations flagged as donor fatigue set in and frustration with the ineffectiveness of the various publicly funded relief measures mounted. This was especially the case in England where public sympathy for Ireland had run out. The Young Ireland rebellion of 1848 also had the unintended consequences of alienating public opinion in England against the starving Irish who were viewed as a disloyal and undeserving race.[132]

Yet despite these desperate times, ordinary life went on unchecked for the affluent classes of Dublin. William Tighe Hamilton of Milltown Park and Samuel Bewley of Sandford Grove won prizes at the 1848 and 1849 Summer Shows held by the Royal Horticultural Improvement Society of Ireland.[133] At times, some of the Dublin newspapers displayed a complete detachment from the realities of life beyond the metropolis. One Saturday in November 1847 the Lord Lieutenant visited the Royal Dublin Society to view the society's annual prizewinning crops and vegetables. As the potato crop for 1847 was disease free (critically, however, the yield was completely inadequate for the country's needs because very few seed potatoes had been planted), prizes could be awarded to potato growers. The first prize for a seedling potato was awarded to Rev. Flemyng of Nullamore, Classon's Bridge, Milltown. The journalist went on to remark proudly that among the group of prize-winning potatoes, 'one tuber weighed 24 ounces. This beats what our French neighbours state they do'.[134]

CHOLERA AND EMIGRANTS

In the summer and autumn of 1849 Dublin was badly hit by a serious outbreak of cholera. The impact of this short epidemic saw the annual average death rate for the city increase from 9,300 in 1848 to 14,400 in 1849.[135] In June 1849 the first case of fatal cholera was reported in Sandymount, and the disease soon spread to Ballsbridge and Donnybrook.[136] By September cholera had reached Rush in north County Dublin, where 12 people alone died of the illness on 2 September 1849 according to local diarist Ellen Palmer of Kenure Park.[137] Indeed, a total of 369 people died in the Balrothery Poor Law Union in north Dublin in the autumn of 1849.[138] On the other hand, a contemporary magistrate and landlord of cottages in Milltown village, Frank Thorpe Porter, contended that the outbreak of cholera in 1849 was much less severe than it had been in 1832. At the time Porter was living in Roundtown (Terenure). Several years later he somewhat facetiously recounted the following incident which occurred at his house in 1849:

> *My residence at Roundtown was not far from a range of small cottages occupied by the labouring class. One of our female servants alarmed my family by stating that the cholera was very nigh, for*

132 Tim P. O'Neill, 'The charities and famine in mid-nineteenth century Ireland' in Jacqueline Hill and Colm Lennon (eds), *Luxury and Austerity* (Dublin, 1999), p. 146.

133 *Dublin Evening Mail*, 3 May 1848, p. 3; 15 June 1849, p. 1.

134 *The Warder*, 13 November 1847, p. 6.

135 Fergus D'Arcy, 'An age of distress and reform: 1800–1860' in Art Cosgrove (ed.), *Dublin Through the Ages* (Dublin, 1988), p. 102.

136 Blacker, *Brief sketches of the parishes of Donnybrook and Booterstown*, p. 205.

137 Robbins, *The miasma*, pp. 143–8.

138 Sinéad Collins, *Balrothery Poor Law Union, County Dublin, 1839–1851* (Dublin, 2005), p. 54.

> *that she had seen five poor people taken off to hospital from the cottages near the quarry. I mentioned her statement to a police sergeant, and requested him to inquire if it was correct. In about half an hour, he returned and said, 'Your worship, I have good news for you. The cholera has not come near you: it is only typhus fever.'*[139]

It would be naïve to assume that Milltown was not affected by the cholera outbreak of 1849 even though the official records and contemporary newspaper reports are silent on this point. An anonymous pamphlet which briefly sets out the history of The Dropping Well pub at Classon's Bridge from 1847–1997 states that publican John Howe established a community morgue on his premises in 1847 to deal with the increasing numbers of fever victims, and that Howe died of fever in 1850. The unidentified author of the pamphlet did not, unfortunately, provide any contemporary sources for this information, which has proved impossible to substantiate thus far.[140] It is beyond doubt, however, that coroners' inquests into unexplained deaths were held at The Dropping Well during the 1840s and that John Howe's widow died at Classon's Bridge in 1855, aged 70.[141] In addition, on 2 May 1847 John Howe's daughter married a Dundrum native, John Williams, who was the local collector of the poor rate.[142]

Milltown also mirrored Dublin city's growth in population between 1841 and 1851. During the years of the Great Famine the city's population was swollen by refugees seeking relief or waiting to embark on the cross-channel ferries to Liverpool prior to onward emigration to North America.[143] By the later stages of the Famine a huge proportion of the paupers in the city's relieving institutions were famine migrants and beggars.[144] It is quite likely that some of these people took up temporary refuge in the lodging houses of Milltown village due to a shortage of cheap accommodation in the city. It is possible too that the emigrants of Wicklow and south Dublin overnighted in Milltown on their journey to the ships docked on Dublin's quays. Tenants on assisted emigration schemes, such as from the earl of Fitzwilliam's estate in Coolatin, County Wicklow, would have had the funds to pay for lodgings on their arrival in Dublin as they awaited embarkation on the cross-channel ferries.[145] Similarly, the Board of Guardians of the Rathdown Union workhouse in Loughlinstown assisted 154 men, women and children to emigrate to Quebec in the nine-month period from August 1849 to the end of May 1850.[146] These special circumstances, then, most probably explain why the population of Milltown townland grew from 736 in 1841 to 863 in 1851 and why the number of houses increased from 129 to 143.[147] Expansion took place too in the adjacent townland of

---

139 Frank Thorpe Porter, *Gleanings and Reminiscences* (Dublin, 1875), pp. 228–9; Griffith's Valuation, Rateable Valuation of Tenements, County of Dublin, Barony of Uppercross, Parish of St Peter, Townland of Milltown, p. 55 at entry nos 80–83 (1850).

140 The Dropping Well 1847–1997: Celebrating 150 Years of Licenced Heritage (undated, Coachhouse Publications).

141 *Freeman's Journal*, 20 December 1842, p. 3; 9 April 1847, p. 3; *Saunders's Newsletter*, 9 October 1855, p. 3.

142 Marriage register for the Parish of St Peter, p. 58 no. 115, marriage of Mary Anne Howe and John Williams 2 May 1847.

143 *Freeman's Journal*, 14 August 1847, p. 4, Report of South Dublin Union Relief Committee.

144 Dickson, *Dublin: The making of a capital city*, p. 317.

145 *Coolatin House, Shillelagh, County Wicklow*, Souvenir Brochure for Coolatin Open Weekend 9 and 10 July 1994.

146 Burke, *The People and the Poor Law*, p. 343.

147 Census of Ireland 1851, County of Dublin, Barony of Uppercross, Parish of St Peter, Townland of Milltown, p. 41 (CD-ROM, Archive CD Books Ireland, Dublin, 2010).

Farranboley, where the population increased from 208 in 1841 to 297 in 1851.[148] Conversely, the townland of Clonskeagh and its little village experienced a decline in its population from 352 in 1841 to 310 in 1851.[149] The reasons for the drop in numbers in Clonskeagh are not readily apparent but it is likely that factory closures or lay-offs were to blame. Nonetheless, in overall terms the hinterland of Dublin city experienced significant increases of population over the period 1841–51 reflecting an influx of famine refugees and economic migrants.[150]

LONG-TERM EFFECTS OF THE FAMINE ON MILLTOWN

A study of Dublin's monetary economy during and after the Famine has highlighted a significant withdrawal of capital from savings institutions, together with a decline in the cash advances made by Dublin's pawnbrokers. This led to a loss of investment capital and a lack of confidence among benevolent capitalists which delayed the post-Famine recovery in Dublin until well into the 1860s.[151] Support for this thesis can be gleaned from the post-Famine experience in Milltown. As noted above, Samuel Moore's woollen mills on the north bank of the Dodder at Milltown had run into difficulties in 1846 and had closed by April 1848. The premises remained derelict for several years until it was eventually sold to flour millers Robert Gibney senior and Robert Gibney junior in 1858, which illustrates the long-term impact of the economic dislocation caused by the Famine.[152]

Another example of the malign economic effects of the Famine occurs at Lee's saw mills, which were located on the south bank of the Dodder beside the Packhorse Bridge in Milltown. In November of 1849 John Lee surrendered his lease to his landlord, William Heaviside, who in turn leased the mills back to Lee at the greatly reduced rent of £6 9*s.* 6*d.*, i.e. a reduction from £22 15*s.*[153] There is little doubt therefore that industrial activity at Milltown had suffered very badly due to the effects of the Famine and that any prospect of a recovery was very uncertain. The conclusion is reinforced by the fact that when the Leeson estate was put up for sale in 1856, the earl's freehold interest in lot 57 on the south bank of the River Dodder in Milltown and described as 'a desirable estate comprising a building formerly used as an iron mill, several houses, meadow land and premises', did not sell.[154]

By the end of the 1850s the population of Milltown townland had declined quite considerably from its nineteenth century maximum of 863 in 1851, to 596 in 1861.[155] Likewise, the population of the adjacent townland, Farranboley, decreased from 297 to 271 during the same

148 Census of Ireland 1851, County of Dublin, Barony of Rathdown, Parish of Taney, Townland of Farranboley, p. 38 (CD-ROM, Archive CD Books Ireland, Dublin, 2010).

149 Census of Ireland 1851, County of Dublin, Barony of Dublin, Parish of Donnybrook, Townland of Clonskeagh, p. 30 (CD-ROM, Archive CD Books Ireland, Dublin, 2010).

150 William J. Smyth, 'The province of Leinster and the Great Famine' in John Crowley, William J. Smyth and Mike Murphy (eds), *Atlas of the Great Irish Famine* (Cork, 2012), pp. 329 (Fig. 5), 333 (Fig. 8).

151 Raymond J. Raymond, 'Dublin: The Great Famine 1845–1860', *Dublin Historical Record*, xxxiii, no. 3 (June 1978), pp. 98–105.

152 RD 1858/15/80.

153 RD 769/43/521379, RD 1849/20/261, RD 1849/20/263

154 NAI, Landed Estates Court Rental, vol. 38, no. 3, 'Particulars and Conditions of Sale of the Freehold Estate of the Earl of Milltown to be sold on 8 January 1856, lot 57'; *Allnut's Irish Land Schedule,* 15 January 1856, p. 3.

155 Census of Ireland 1861, County of Dublin, Barony of Uppercross, Parish of St Peter, Townland of Milltown, p. 41 (CD-ROM, Archive CD Books Ireland, Dublin, 2010).

period.[156] The declining number of inhabitants was also reflected in the physical conditions of Milltown village. The earliest Valuation Office town plan for Milltown village shows at least 10 ruinous houses at the western end of the village on the north bank of the River Dodder close to the Packhorse Bridge (Map 16b/41–8). The majority of these buildings were part of the landholding of the old derelict woollen mills which had previously belonged to Samuel Moore and had fallen into disrepair.[157] Under the terms of the Hogan-Gibney lease of 1858 the new tenants were required to demolish these buildings.[158] The same town plan depicts a site at the eastern end of Milltown village containing about a dozen dilapidated cottages stood (where nos 4–7 Geraldine Terrace and the public carpark are now). According to a handwritten note inserted on the plan in February 1872, these cottages had all been removed by that date (Map 16a/88–100).[159]

These demolitions are consistent with the Milltown townland census returns for 1861 which recorded that the total number of houses had declined from 143 to 109 since 1851.[160] These pervasive physical changes are a further indication that the population of Milltown had been artificially inflated temporarily during and shortly after the Famine by lodgers who were not native to Milltown and who, along with local economic emigrants such as John Donovan, had permanently left the area by 1861.

CONCLUSION

It would be an injustice to dismiss the effects of the Famine on Milltown merely because there were, as far as is known, no reports of death by starvation in Milltown. The potato blight and the subsequent famine that affected the country in the late 1840s also had an extremely negative and long-lasting impact on Milltown. It is beyond doubt that the privation among the poor of the area caused by the potato blight and the consequential increase in the price of basic food would have caused malnutrition and a greater susceptibility to mortal illnesses such as fever and cholera. These conditions were exacerbated by overcrowded housing filled with temporary lodgers and by high levels of unemployment which peaked in Milltown in the late 1840s when Moore's woollen mills closed.

On the other hand, Milltown's geographical position close to Rathmines worked to its advantage because of the proximity of well-off landowners and professionals living in the new township and further afield in the dozens of villas south of the River Dodder in Roebuck townland. Those families provided charitable donations and acted as volunteers on the local relief committees. The charity available to the multitude of poor inhabitants and economic migrants of Milltown village was not unending and, inevitably, donor fatigue set in and people became desensitised to poverty. Contemporary records prove that the local relief committees in Rathmines and Dundrum could not cope indefinitely with the scale of the national famine disaster as it impacted on the local labouring class from 1846 onwards.

The economic depression that set in after the Famine is evident in the decline of the mills and factories in Milltown. Milltown's industrial base never recovered after the closure of Samuel

156 Census of Ireland 1861, County of Dublin, Barony of Rathdown, Parish of Taney, Townland of Farranboley, p. 38 (CD-ROM, Archive CD Books Ireland, Dublin, 2010).

157 NAI, VO, OL50945, House Book for Milltown Village 1845, no. 10.

158 RD 1858/15/80.

159 The vacant ground subsequently became known locally in Milltown as 'The Strand'.

160 Census of Ireland 1861, County of Dublin, Barony of Uppercross, Parish of St Peter, Townland of Milltown, p. 41 (CD-ROM, Archive CD Books Ireland, Dublin, 2010).

Moore's woollen mills. It was not until the 1890s, when the Dublin Laundry Company began employing large numbers of local inhabitants at its new laundry (located on the site of the old woollen mills) that the economic outlook for Milltown began to improve significantly.

Before quitting this melancholy subject – to use a Victorian turn of phrase – it is worth pondering some national statistics. It has been estimated that the British government contributed about £7 million in famine relief measures between 1845 and 1853, which experience shows was not nearly enough to mitigate the calamity. This sum amounted to less that the total contributions made by Irish ratepayers and Irish landlords under Irish poor laws and other famine relief measures. The parsimony of the British political elite is starkly revealed by the fact that Britain spent just shy of £70 million on the Crimean War in the years 1854–6.[161] Clearly, the Act of Union between Great Britain and Ireland was not a partnership of equals. ■

161 James S. Donnelly, 'The administration of relief, 1847–51' in W.E. Vaughan (ed.), *A new history of Ireland, v: Ireland under the Union 1801–1870* (Oxford, 1989), pp. 328–9.

Chapter 9:
Primary Education in the Nineteenth Century

Chapter 9: Primary Education in the Nineteenth Century

INTRODUCTION

This chapter reviews the introduction of primary level education to Milltown in the early nineteenth century and the experiences of children and teachers under the national school system from its establishment in the 1830s until the outbreak of the First World War.

FIRST SCHOOL IN MILLTOWN

The ending of the penal laws in the last quarter of the eighteenth century, coupled with increasing numbers of Protestant education societies in the early nineteenth century, provided the impetus to the Catholic Church to rebuild its education system in Ireland.[1] The first public notice of this activity in Milltown appeared in the *Freeman's Journal* newspaper of 20 July 1812 which promoted a charity sermon to be preached in Milltown chapel by the Rev. R. Kenrick in aid of the 'Milltown Sunday and Evening Schools for Male and Female Children'. The reference to Sunday and evening schooling is noteworthy because it shows that the children were not available for schooling during the daytime (the law in this regard changed under the Factories Act 1833) because many of them were required to work, either at home or in one of the mills nearby such as Burke's or Hunt's woollen mills. As previously noted in Chapter 6, the growth in employment of large numbers of women and children by suburban manufacturers was due to the employers' desire to operate outside the control of guilds and journeymen organisations in Dublin city.[2] Evidence of this practice was also provided to the Poor Inquiries of 1834 and 1835 by a Dublin papermaker.[3]

It is not known where the school was located originally, but according to a Dublin Catholic Diocesan diary of 1821 it was by then being run by the Franciscans at their monastery called

1 Susan M. Parkes, *A guide to sources for the history of Irish education, 1780–1922* (Dublin, 2010), pp. 23–6.

2 Dickson, *Dublin: The making of a capital city*, p. 282.

3 See quotations from the Poor Inquiry reports in Sean Bagnall, *Tallaght, 1835–50: A rural place* (Dublin, 2008), pp. 17–18.

'Mount Alverne', which was located near Milltown.The Diocesan diary, which was compiled by Fr Henry Young of Harold's Cross, stated that the Franciscans 'govern a day, evening, and Sunday Free School for the poor male children of Milltown and the neighbouring villages. Charity Sermon on the fourth Sunday in July.'[4]

At this time there were a number of schools for Protestant children such as the Erasmus School, which was established in 1814 at the bottom of Beaver Row in Donnybrook[5] and the Vergemount Boarding School, run by Rev. John Crosthwaite at Vergemount House, Clonskeagh Road, in the 1820s and 1830s.[6] There was another Protestant boarding school in Donnybrook run by the Rev. Prince Crawford 'for young gentlemen'. [7] By the mid-1820s an official commission of enquiry calculated that there were about 11,000 schools nationwide catering for upwards of half a million children.[8]

Statutory provision of basic education for children who worked in the mills and factories was introduced in Ireland by the Factories Act of 1833.[9] The Act required that children between the ages of eleven and thirteen employed in such places attend a school of the parents' choice for a minimum of two hours a day, six days a week. As previously noted in Chapter 6, in 1834 Milltown mill owner Maurice Harnett subscribed 10*s*. to the Rathmines Free School, which could accommodate nearly 600 children, some of whom undoubtedly worked in his mills.[10]

The religious tensions caused by proselytism in the 1820s and 1830s were apparently behind one of the local Catholic priests, Fr Young, being assaulted by the teacher of a Protestant school in Milltown when Fr Young attempted to remove the Catholic children from the classroom. This incident, which was passed down in local folklore, holds that the teacher brought an action for assault against Fr Young who was successfully defended by Daniel O'Connell.[11] Neither the alleged assault nor the subsequent court case is mentioned in O'Connell's personal papers, and reports in contemporary newspapers are not forthcoming, so the story remains unsubstantiated. Neither is there any official record of a Protestant school in Milltown in the 1830s. What is beyond doubt is that gains were being made in the provision of basic education for the children of Milltown in the 1820s and 1830s. According to the 1841 Census of Ireland, the townland of Milltown had 158 boys and 139 girls of five or more years of age who could read and write versus 99 boys and 109 girls in the same age category who could do neither.[12] Eight years later, on Sunday 26 August 1849, a charity sermon was preached at the Catholic church, Rathmines, in aid of the local national schools. The funds raised were also to support a day, night and Sunday school at Milltown, 'in which one hundred and fifty of the most destitute in the parish are educated'.[13]

---

4 Patrick Cunningham, 'The Catholic Directory for 1821', in *Reportorium Novum*, ii, no. 2 (1959–1960), p. 338.

5 Holland, *Clonskeagh*, p. 312; in 1837 the school is reported to have been 'in that part of the village which is in Taney parish', i.e. on the south bank of the River Dodder: Lewis, *Topographical Dictionary of Ireland*, ii, p. 370.

6 *The Warder*, 2 August 1823, p. 248; Pettigrew and Oulton's Dublin Almanac and General Register of Ireland 1834, p. 158.

7 Pettigrew and Oulton's Dublin Almanac and General Register of Ireland 1834, p. 157.

8 John Coolahan, *Irish Education: History and Structure* (Dublin, 1981), p. 9.

9 An Act to regulate the Labour of Children and young persons in the mills and factories of the United Kingdom (3 & 4 Will. IV, c. 103) (29 August 1833).

10 *Freeman's Journal*, 8 February 1834, p. 1.

11 *Souvenir of the Blessing and Dedication of the Church of the Immaculate Virgin Mary of the Miraculous Medal at Clonskeagh.*

12 Census of Ireland for the year 1841, County of Dublin, Barony of Uppercross, Parish of St Peter, Townland of Milltown, pp. 30–1.

13 *Freeman's Journal*, 24 August 1849, p. 1.

THE INTRODUCTION OF NATIONAL SCHOOLS

The advent of Catholic emancipation in 1829 created further urgency on the part of the British government to provide a State-sponsored primary education system for the lower classes thereby creating a literate and loyal electorate; accordingly, the national school system of primary education was introduced in Ireland in October 1831. The aim of the new national school system was to provide a non-denominational education for Catholic and Protestant children together, but with separate religious and secular education to prevent proselytism.[14] Needless to say, the attempt to create mixed education was strenuously resisted by the Catholic and Presbyterian Churches and in practice the national schools became denominational.[15] In the 1840s the Board of Education applied a separate set of rules in relation to non-vested national schools, which received State aid for the teacher's salary and school books and equipment but not for the school building which was paid for out of local resources and subscriptions. The rules allowed the school manager (typically the parish priest) to prohibit religious instruction of another denomination in his school while accepting the right of the pupils to opt out of religious instruction.[16]

FIRST NATIONAL SCHOOL IN MILLTOWN

Very extensive records of the operation of individual national schools throughout the country from the mid-nineteenth century have survived and are preserved in the National Archives. Very fortunately, there is a considerable amount of data available for the male and female national schools which were established in Milltown village in the 1840s and 1850s. The first national school was set up in Milltown on 11 December 1849 under the management of Fr William Meagher the parish priest of Rathmines (Map 16a/11).[17] An application for aid towards payment of the teacher's salary and for the supply of books was submitted on 20 December 1849 by four local Catholic landowners with the support of the local Church of Ireland curate, the Rev. William Henry Flemying.[18] The support of the local Protestant clergyman was helpful because the commissioners of education had stated from the beginning that they would look with 'peculiar favour' on joint applications.[19] Rev. Flemying's support for Fr Meagher would seem also to undermine the veracity of the alleged assault on Fr Young some years previously.

As part of the procedure for every application for State aid, an inspector from the Board of Education had to visit the school and complete a standard questionnaire. In true Victorian fashion, the pro-forma questionnaire contained 46 questions (86 by the late 1850s) designed to collect as much data as possible. Space precludes listing all of the data but a few facts are worth noting. When the inspector visited the school in Milltown on 16 January 1850 there were 32 boys and 36 girls present. The two-storey stone and slated building, measuring 34 feet long, 13 feet wide and 20 feet high, contained separate classrooms for boys and girls and was in 'tolerable' repair.[20] The children were expected to pay one penny a week to the local school

---

14 Parkes, *A guide to sources for the history of Irish education*, p. 39.

15 Coolahan, *Irish Education, p. 5; Parkes, A guide to sources for the history of Irish education*, p. 42.

16 Parkes, *A guide to sources for the history of Irish education*, pp. 42, 46.

17 NAI ED1/29/47/1.

18 NAI ED1/29/47/1.

19 Parkes, *A guide to sources for the history of Irish education*, p. 46.

20 NAI ED1/29/47/2.

committee albeit that half of the children were admitted for free.[21] In supporting the application the inspector made the following comments about Milltown at that time:

> *I beg leave to recommend this application to the Board on the grounds that this is a very poor neighbourhood to which the two nearest National Schools are Dundrum – 2 miles – Rathmines 1 ½ miles. Twenty of the more necessitous pupils (male and female) receive their breakfast every morning in the school; Sundays excepted.*

STANDARDS OF TEACHING AND BEHAVIOUR

The new male and female national school ran into serious difficulties from the start due to the poor standard of teachers employed at the school. In the mid-nineteenth century teacher training was very inadequate. The Board of Education offered a short six-month training course for teachers in its Marlborough Street training college. In practice, teacher training was based on the monitorial apprenticeship model whereby older teenage pupils remained on at the school as monitors, helping the adult teachers and learning how to teach.[22] The results, so to speak, of this system are starkly revealed in the very detailed inspectors' reports and the orders of the Board of Education which were recorded throughout the nineteenth century in large bound volumes, now deposited in the National Archives. The following entries for Milltown male national school need no elaboration: 'July 26 1855: Pat Bannon severely admonished on low proficiency of pupils and for failing to maintain becoming discipline and order'; 'December 28 1855: Withdraw salary from Daniel Shea from 31 January '56 being incompetent'; 'March 7 1856: Strike off roll no. 5934 and cancel grants from 31.1.56 school having ceased'.[23]

The school remained closed for the next two years during which time the local children would have had to attend the national schools in Rathmines or Dundrum – if their parents were inclined to send them to school. In any event, the female and male sections of the national school were re-established in 1858 and January 1859 respectively.[24] In addition, a new school house was built with funds from the Catholic archdiocese of Dublin.[25] The original school building is shown on the Valuation Office town plan of Milltown village as being located on the north side of the main street on a site now occupied by the Wilde and Green delicatessen and restaurant (Map 16a/11).[26] The replacement school building was built in 1858, when the re-established school was relocated a few metres further down the village main street directly in front of the Catholic church (Map 18 & Map 20).[27]

An application for aid towards payment of the teacher's salary and for the supply of books was submitted on 13 January 1859 accompanied with the following interesting comments:

21 NAI ED1/29/47/2B.

22 Parkes, *A guide to sources for the history of Irish education*, pp. 42–3.

23 NAI ED2/150 folio 44. Milltown female national school roll no. 5935 was also struck off on 7 March 1856: NAI ED2/150 folio 45.

24 NAI ED2/150 folio 68 and folio 69.

25 NAI ED1/30//1.

26 The post office moved into the premises after the school closed according to the VO plan of 6 April 1852.

27 VO, Cancellation Books, County Dublin, Barony of Uppercross, Parish of St Peter, Townland of Milltown, 1855–1862, p. 123, at nos 17/11, 17/15, 17/16.

The school house has been erected within the last six months with funds chiefly supplied by his Grace the Most Reverend Archbishop Cullen, and is a solid well-furnished and well lighted building consisting of two principal apartments, one over the other, that on the ground floor apportioned for the boys and that above for the girls. There is a yard sufficiently ample and furnished with all necessary appurtenances. The furniture consists of a sufficiency of desks, forms etc. and a good supply of books, maps etc., granted by the National Board to the schools in this village some years ago, has been carefully preserved and answers very well as a stock to commence with. The dimensions of the boys school are 36 feet in length by a median breadth of 13 feet. Height 10&1/2 feet – of the girls 40 by 13 – 10&1/2 high. The system pursued in teaching is that of the National Board – the teachers both trained in its schools and classified. Name of the male teacher – James Vicars aged 40; of the female [teacher] Mary Anne Evers aged 18. The average number of children in daily attendance ranges boys from 40 to 50, girls from 50–60. School hours from ten to three. One hour each day is set apart for religious instruction and every facility afforded to visitors for inspecting and recording their instruction. The parish priest, under whose management the entire concerns of the school are conducted, and who earnestly conjoins [?] the Commissioners to act with all the liberality in their power towards the poor children of a [illegible], he firmly believes, to no others of the county Dublin, in the abject wretchedness of its inhabitants.[28]

In response to question 77 of the application form, which asked if the inspector had communicated with clergymen of different [i.e. non-Catholic] denominations and whether they had objected to the application or not, Mr McDermott, the school inspector, stated that he did not meet any of the local Protestant clergymen when he visited Milltown, but that he would write to them on the subject of the application. However, no such correspondence, if any, has survived.[29]

A Bernard Dennan of Cullenswood subsequently wrote to McDermott, on 11 February 1859 in response to financial queries which the inspector had raised when he had visited the school the previous day:

since I had the pleasure of seeing you yesterday I have informed Fr. Meagher of your visit to Milltown. He desires to state in reply to your enquiries that an annual rent of four pounds is paid for the ground on which the school is built. On account of the utter poverty of the locality he could not for a moment entertain the idea of promising the teachers anything beyond what the Board [of Education] will give. A charity sermon (in case there should be one) will not realise more than that will be sufficient to defray current expenses etc.[30]

McDermott completed his report on 12 February 1859 and recommended acceptance of the application for aid 'on the grounds of the poverty of the village and no N [ational] School nearer than two miles'.[31] On the issue of national school funding, the government intended from the start in 1831 that the system should be financed jointly from central funds and local sources. This never happened as the local funds never matched the central funds and as a re-

28 NAI ED1/30/6/1, roll no. 8082-3.

29 NAI ED1/30/6/1, roll no. 8082-3.

30 NAI ED1/30/6/3.

31 NAI ED1/30/6/2B.

sult the Treasury became increasingly dissatisfied with the heavy reliance on central funding, hence the correspondence between Dennan and McDermott quoted above.[32]

INSPECTORS' REPORTS

By 1858 the Board of Education had appointed 66 school inspectors nationally, organised into head and district inspectors. The district inspectors were responsible for an administrative area covering about 100 schools, and they were instructed to make their visits unexpectedly.[33] The outcomes of these school visits made separately to the male and female classrooms were recorded in large official record books, now deposited in the National Archives, and which are available for Milltown for the period 1859 to 1883.[34] The inspectors' reports for the male school throughout the 1860s reveal a high turnover of teachers and, for the most part, an unsatisfactory level of proficiency, as per the following example of 21 May 1864: 'Attention called to deficiencies of pupils and want of sale stock.'[35] Yet despite these difficulties, which were exacerbated by the poor pay (in 1860 the teacher's annual salary was £15) and challenging conditions which the teachers had to put up with in Milltown, throughout the 1860s the most common answers given by the visiting inspector to the question as to whether he considered the school to be 'stationary', 'retrograde' or 'progressing' , was 'stationary', 'fair', and 'going on fairly'.[36]

On 1 November 1865 a new schoolmaster, John Glennon, took up a teaching position in Milltown boys' national school. An inspector visited the school on 27 February 1866 and found that the supply of books and requisites was adequate, the accounts were neat and accurate and that the school was progressing. This was a rare example of a good report for the school under all three assessment criteria.[37]

The influence of the Catholic Church on the appointment and dismissal of national school teachers and the authorities' concerns about the morals and politics of the school master/mistress is apparent in the outcome of the enquiry into Glennon's departure from Clonshaugh national school in the autumn of 1865:

> *March 7 1866: Inspector waited on Rev. Wm Rooney manager of Clonshaugh NS to ascertain cause of John Glennon's removal from that school who stated that though there was some report of this teacher being a Fenian he (manager) had no proof of it and could not act on it. He removed him because it was believed in the village in which he resided that he had an improper intimacy with a servant woman and though the manager had no actual proof of this yet as he [Glennon] gave bad example by not attending to his religious duties he (manager) thought it his duty to remove him.*
>
> *March 16 1866: H.J. Sheehan directed to wait on Fr Meagher, manager of the [Milltown] school, and communicate substance of above to him.*

32 Coolahan, *Irish Education*, p. 6.

33 Coolahan, *Irish Education*, p. 22.

34 NAI ED2/150 folio 45 and folios 68/69.

35 NAI ED2/150 folio 68.

36 NAI ED2/150 folio 68.

37 NAI ED2/150 folio 68.

April 7 1866: H.J. Sheehan communicated the above to Dr Meagher on 17 March. He then intended to write to Rev. William Rooney on the subject. Teacher is to resign on 1 April. Rev. William Rooney gave Fr Meagher a good character of Glennon before his appointment.[38]

Why Fr Rooney removed Glennon yet gave Fr Meagher a good character reference was not explained or questioned.

Glennon's departure from Milltown and the high turnover in teaching staff throughout the 1860s impacted negatively on the children's education and their attendance at school. At three inspections carried out in 1866 there were 21, 19 and 25 boys present while the average number of pupils on the rolls in the previous three months on the relevant inspection dates was stated to be 78, 75 and 69.[39] These statistics mirror the national trends in the period between 1863 to 1867 when it was estimated that 2,594 teachers either resigned for other jobs, emigrated or were dismissed; in 1871 the average national daily attendance of pupils on the school rolls was about 37 per cent.[40] On 21 April 1872 the inspector asked the school manager, Fr Meagher, to use his influence with the parents of the pupils to induce them to send their children regularly and punctually to school.[41]

There was a marked reduction of inspections of the male school recorded for the 1870s and only one report stands out. When the inspector visited the male school in December 1870, he 'ordered that steps be taken to prevent disorderly conduct on the part of pupils during play hour. Suggested to manager to abolish play hour and shorten school hours by so much.'[42] It is no wonder there was a drop off in attendance as reported in April 1872.

DISHONEST TEACHER

In May 1883 Francis Kavanagh was employed as the school principal by the manager of the boys' national school in Milltown village. Sometime later, Kavanagh was appointed as secretary of the local tontine society, called the St Gall's Friendly Christian Burial Society.[43] To outward appearances Francis Kavanagh was a respectable member of the community. However, in the autumn of 1893 Kavanagh absconded with the tontine fund and left the country. The school manager, the Rev. Patrick Doyle, wrote to the Board of Education in February 1894 claiming Kavanagh's salary for the three months ending 31 December 1893 which, under the terms of his contract, Kavanagh was bound to pay to the manager if he left service without notice. A financial assistant secretary in the Office of National Education declined Rev. Doyle's claim on the basis that the money owed to the school was 'a debt recoverable by law and not from the Commissioners'.[44] On 9 April 1894, Rev. Doyle wrote to the official as follows:

I am sorry I have to object to Kavanagh getting his salary. I cannot answer the query 11 on [the] quarterly return to his advantage. Has he applied for his salary? I think the amount should be given for the school improvements recently made at Milltown.

38 NAI ED2/150 folio 68.

39 NAI ED2/150 folio 44.

40 Coolahan, *Irish Education*, pp. 25, 29.

41 NAI ED2/150 folio 68.

42 NAI ED2/150 folio 68.

43 NAI ED9/9080; *Rathmines News*, 31 May 1902.

44 NAI ED9/9080.

The file is silent thereafter until September 1900, when the manager, Francis O'Loughlin, attempted to reopen the matter. A manuscript note on the file shows that on 21 September 1900 a junior civil servant was directed by his superior to:

> *inform writer in accordance with decision conveyed with regard to salary in letter of 19 February 1894 and with reference to it say that Kavanagh was not employed by the Board. The Commissioners merely granted aid to the school which he was locally appointed.*

The file concludes with the words, 'Done – 17 October, 1900.'

GIRLS' NATIONAL SCHOOL

The girls' experience of school was not much different to that of the boys. On 2 September 1859 the Board of Education withdrew the teacher's salary from Mary Evers because an inspection of 17 August had found that she was 'inefficient, negligent of accounts, and utterly regardless of her duties'.[45] This despite the fact that Evers was supposed to have been trained at the Board of Education's teacher training college in Marlborough Street.[46] Unlike the boys' school, the girls' school from time to time appointed monitors, such as Sarah Doyle and Eliza Murphy who were appointed to those roles on 1 July and 1 October 1860 respectively.[47] School equipment was not neglected and in December 1870 the Board of Education ordered that 'new maps of Europe and Ireland be got'.[48]

The sensitive issue of religious instruction and the national school rules regarding same explains a controversial incident reported in an entry for the female school on 26 October 1872, as follows:

> *on letter 116 d 38 of 72 in which inspector states that two Protestant children were on the rolls and remained in the school during R.C. instruction time and that he directed the teacher she should send for the parents to sign the Certificate Book – (see also letter 88 d.38 of 72) inspector informed that it was altogether wrong for him to suggest to the teacher that she should send for the parents of these children, Sarah and Mary Smith, to sign the Religious Certificate Book: and [inspector] informed [teacher] that the rule requires that these children be excluded from the school during the time of Religious Instruction. Manager requested to caution teacher as regards this rule.*[49]

The attendance of the two Protestant girls at the national school is explained by the fact that Sunday school only was available specifically for Protestant children living in Milltown village at this time.[50]

PROTESTANT SUNDAY SCHOOL

By the third quarter of the nineteenth century national schools in Ireland had long ceased to be multi-denominational, a trend that had been acknowledged in the Powis report of 1872

45 NAI ED2/150 folio 69.

46 NAI ED1/30/6/1.

47 NAI ED2/150 folio 69.

48 NAI ED2/150 folio 69.

49 NAI ED2/150 folio 69.

50 RCB Library P654, St Philip's Parish Vestry Book.

which favoured the recognition of denominational rights in the management of schools, and accepted that the national school system had in practice become denominational.[51] In 1883 a new schoolhouse was built beside St Phillip's Church of Ireland parish church on Temple Road, Upper Rathmines, which was attracting over 100 children to Sunday School.[52] Most of these children would have come from the new wealthier residential districts of Temple Road, Palmerston Road and other parts of Upper Rathmines which, along with Milltown, were part of St Phillip's parish. The lack of contact between children of different religions was also shown in a newspaper report of an excursion of school children to Blessington, led by the local Church of Ireland Clergyman, Rev. John Moffatt, incumbent of St Phillips parish church, Milltown.[53]

ST ANNE'S NATIONAL SCHOOL

Two important developments in education of national importance occurred in 1872 and 1892 when the payment by results system of supplementing teachers' salaries and compulsory school attendance respectively were introduced.[54] Before considering the impact of compulsory school attendance it is necessary to review first a hugely important and beneficial event that occurred in 1879 – the establishment of a convent at Milltown House (renamed Mount St Anne's Convent) by the Sisters of Charity. From an educational viewpoint the Sisters of Charity had a hugely beneficial and long-lasting impact on the education of infants and girls when they established an infants and primary school in the grounds of their new convent at Mount St Anne's in 1883.[55]

A sense of a new beginning is evident in the district inspector's recommendation of 4 September 1883 to grant aid to St Anne's in the following comment:

> *The school house is a beautiful one, and admirably furnished. This school can scarcely be regarded as a new one. It is merely Milltown Female National School transferred to a new house, and placed under [the] Sisters of Charity. I believe an average of from 90 to 110 [children] will be maintained.*[56]

From the answers given to the extensive questionnaire on the grant aid application form some interesting details emerge. The new school house was built by the nuns out of their own funds and they also agreed to contribute £50 per annum towards the teachers' salaries. Children up to third class were required to pay one penny a week in school fees and from third class upwards 2*d*. a week. From 10 a.m. to 12 noon and from 1 p.m. to 3 p.m. the senior pupils received secular education, with the religious instruction taking place between 12 noon and 1 p.m. The same timetable applied to the junior pupils except that their religious instruction was for half an hour.[57]

The school evidently prospered because St Anne's was honoured by a vice-regal visit in 1896 when the Countess of Cadogan spent over an hour in the convent and was greatly pleased with

51 Parkes, *A guide to sources for the history of Irish education*, pp. 47–8.

52 *Freeman's Journal*, 10 November 1883, p. 3.

53 *Rathmines News*, 20 May 1899.

54 Parkes, *A guide to sources for the history of Irish education*, pp. 49–51.

55 Irish Sisters of Charity, *Milltown in Brief… 1879–1995*, Circular Letter 26 April 1995.

56 NAI ED1/32/96.

57 NAI ED1/32/96.

everything she saw there.[58] The school's curriculum had expanded successfully too, as the following editorial in the local newspaper shows:

> *That we are glad to notice that in the musical competitions for primary schools, in the Antient Concert Rooms this week, St Anne's Convent National School, Milltown, (conductor Miss Sarah Feeney), carried off one of the three ten-pound prizes.*[59]

In the absence of official data, it is difficult to assess whether the boys' national school showed such a marked improvement as did St Anne's national school. There are a couple of reports which indicate that things had progressed well since the bad days of the 1850s and 1860s. When, after several years spent teaching in Milltown, the school principal of the boys' national school, Mr O'Sullivan, was promoted in 1905 to the post of headmaster of the Tranquilla Boys School in Upper Rathmines, he was considered 'a most capable and successful teacher'.[60] O'Sullivan was also one of the first teachers to have received an increment to his salary under a new incentive scheme 'for industry and successful work at Milltown'.[61]

EXTRA-CURRICULAR ENTERTAINMENT

By the mid-1890s an annual fete was put on for the schoolboys with a sumptuous tea and a magic lantern show.[62] Notwithstanding its gushing tone, the report on the 1897 fete by the *Rathmines News* is worth quoting in full because of the atmosphere it evokes:

> *Fete at Milltown National School.*
>
> *On Thursday the 14th inst., the annual fete was given to the boys attending the above school by the Manager, the Very Rev. Monsignor Fitzpatrick, P.P. V.G., Rathgar. A large number of the pupils attended to avail of the hospitalities lavishly meted out by the Very Rev. Manager, assisted by Rev. P. Carolan, C.C., and Rev. F. O'Loughlin, C.C. Business commenced at 6 p.m., when a sumptuous tea was served, after which sweetmeats in abundance were distributed, and cheerfully relished by the youthful guests. Next on the programme came the magic lantern performance – the event of the evening – by Father O'Loughlin. The popular and energetic C.C. was fortunate in his selection of a very appropriate set of views, and one at the beginning of the entertainment, that of his Grace Dr Walsh, was very fine, and loudly applauded. A variety of comic scenes were exhibited, and the witty criticisms and ejaculations which they elicited from the juveniles were laughable in the extreme. Some familiar views of picturesque Milltown and its surroundings were also presented, including one of the nine arches, with the stalwart figure of a venerable old man well-known and respected in Milltown in the foreground. This production evoked much laughter and applause. Another, that of the 'New Bridge', Milltown, with the inevitable 'Dew Drop' in the distance, received speedy recognition. The magic lantern performance was a great success, and closed with cheers for Father O'Loughlin. Sweetmeats were again indulged in, and the entertainment terminated with more cheers for the Monsignor, Father Carolan, Father O'Loughlin*

58 *Rathmines News*, 11 January 1896.

59 *Rathmines News*, 8 July 1899.

60 *Rathmines News*, 9 September 1905.

61 *Rathmines News*, 9 September 1905.

62 *Rathmines News*, 23 January 1897; 22 January 1898.

and the Teacher. The children then dispersed for their homes much pleased with the treat, and promising punctual and regular attendance at the school in future.[63]

COMPULSORY ATTENDANCE

The improvement in teaching standards – not to mention the extra-curricular social activities – must have repaired the reputation of the national schools in the parents' eyes and thus improved school attendance. In a separate but related development, the Irish Education Act 1892 made attendance at school compulsory for children aged between six and fourteen years and forbade the employment of children under eleven years of age, except during periods of seasonal labour, such as at harvest time.[64] This legislation required the setting up of a school attendance committee and the appointment of two school attendance inspectors by the Rathmines township, who were responsible for monitoring the attendance of children at school within the township and for prosecuting parents who neglected to send their children regularly to school. For such parents an attendance order was made by the relevant authority – the Dundrum Petty Sessions or Southern Police Courts – or a fine was imposed.[65] For example, John Rawl, who lived in Milltown village, was, in 1903 and 1905, fined 5*s.* for neglecting to send his children regularly to school.[66] No reasons for the non-attendance of his children at school were reported. According to the 1901 census, the Rawls had eight children ranging in ages from seven months to eighteen years of age so it is quite likely that one or more of the children (usually the girls) were kept at home to help their mother with domestic chores and the rearing of the younger children.

Some of the children attending St Anne's national school lived in Farranboley and Windy Arbour and so the Rathmines UDC (as it had become in 1898) regularly liaised with its counterpart on the south side of the River Dodder, the Rathdown RDC, to ensure that the latter body investigated, and if necessary prosecuted, cases of non-attendance in its jurisdiction.[67]

ABSENTEEISM

Some of the young working-class boys of Milltown sought out work as caddies at Milltown Golf Club from an early age as the following letter of 6 April 1916 to the secretary of the Milltown Golf Club illustrates:

Complaints have been made to the Rathdown No. 1 Rural District School Attendance Committee regarding the attendance of boys of a school going age at the Golf Links at Milltown during school hours, particularly on Wednesdays. At the last meeting of my Committee I was directed to bring this matter to your attention in the hope that you and the members of Milltown Golf Club will assist my Committee in enforcing the provisions of the school attendance act by giving instructions not to have the boys under 14 years of age employed on the links during school hours. The children attending school are not allowed out from school until about 3 o'clock in the afternoon so that any children who attend before that hour or half an hour afterwards cannot possibly be in school to meet the requirements of the law for that particular day.[68]

---

63 *Rathmines News*, 23 January 1897.

64 Parkes, *A guide to sources for the history of Irish education*, p. 50.

65 *Rathmines News*, 15 December 1900; 19 January 1901; 14 February 1903; 18 July 1903; 18 November 1905.

66 *Rathmines News*, 18 July 1903; 18 November 1905.

67 See the Outward Letter Books of the Rathdown RDC No. 1 for 1914-1918 (NAI, BG 137 R1 B 15-B 18).

68 Rathdown RDC No. 1 Outward Letter Book for 1916 (NAI BG 137 R1 B16 p. 751).

Obviously, the golf club shared most of the blame for turning a blind eye to members employing boys as caddies, but there was probably some pressure on boys who came from large families to bring in extra household income, even if that forced or encouraged boys into truancy and lying about their age. Regardless, the responsibility for sending their children to school rested with the parents, and the Rathdown school attendance committee was quite prepared to have persistent truants sent to an Industrial School.[69]

CONCLUSION

Although the standard of education experienced by Milltown's children varied quite considerably over the course of the nineteenth century, there is no doubt that education standards began to improve from the 1880s onwards with the establishment by the Sisters of Charity of St Anne's national school and the introduction of compulsory school attendance. By 1911, only 3.9 per cent of children aged nine years and over living in the district electoral division of Milltown were illiterate (74 individuals).[70] Some of the poorest households in Milltown lived in this area,[71] yet through a combination of diligent school attendance inspectors and higher teaching standards in Milltown's boys' and girls' national schools illiteracy levels were kept admirably low. ■

69 Rathdown RDC No. 1 Outward Letter Book for 1916 (NAI BG 137 R1 B16 p. 977, 5 September 1916).

70 Census of Ireland 1911, County of Dublin, population and educational data returns for Milltown District Electoral Division, pp. 89, 99 (CD-ROM, Archive CD Books Ireland, Dublin, 2010).

71 The Milltown D.E.D. lay on the south bank of the River Dodder and comprised the townlands of Churchtown Lower, Churchtown Upper, Rathmines Great, Rathmines Little, Farranboley, Friarland and the congested districts of Rosemount, Windy Arbour and Concrete (Milltown).

Mill

Chapter 10:
The Fenian Rising of 1867

Chapter 10: The Fenian Rising of 1867

INTRODUCTION

The history of the Fenian Rising has received much less attention in comparison to the 1798 and 1916 risings. The Japanese historian Shin-ichi Takagami has investigated the activities of Dublin's Fenians and the military events which took place on the south side of Dublin on the night of 5/6 March 1867.[1] Some of the military engagements recounted by Takagami involved young men from Milltown, Clonskeagh and Windy Arbour. This chapter describes the Fenian activities that took place at Milltown and in south Dublin and examines the involvement of three local protagonists whose names are recorded in the archival records and in contemporary newspapers.

BACKGROUND TO THE FENIAN RISING

A detailed explanation of the reasons for, and the planning of, the Fenian Rising in Dublin is beyond the scope of this book. Very briefly, a two-phased military strategy was devised by a French General, Gustave Cluseret, which involved an initial guerrilla campaign to be followed by a more general war.[2] This plan was drawn up on the assumption that 5,000 armed men would be available to take part in the rising initially centred in Dublin.[3] Part of the first phase of the military plan involved attacks by several hundred Fenians on isolated police barracks in the Dublin mountains with the intention of drawing out the city's military garrison thereby facilitating attacks within Dublin city.[4] About 60 per cent of the Dublin Fenians came from artisan backgrounds.[5]

1 Shinichi Takagami, 'The 'Dublin Fenians' 1858–79' (PhD thesis, University of Dublin, 1990) and Shinichi Takagami, 'The Fenian Rising in Dublin, March 1867', *Irish Historical Studies*, 29, no. 115 (1995), pp. 340–62.

2 Takagami, 'Fenian Rising in Dublin', p. 343; Takagami, 'Dublin Fenians', p. 246.

3 Takagami, 'Fenian Rising in Dublin', p. 343.

4 Takagami, 'Fenian Rising in Dublin', p. 344.

5 Takagami, 'Dublin Fenians', Chapter 4.

In March 1867 Dublin city was protected by over 5,000 well-armed soldiers.[6] Additionally, civilian protection was provided by the DMP which was composed of about 1,100 policemen.[7] Opposing these formidable forces were the Dublin Fenians, whose membership numbers are estimated to have ranged from several thousand to 10,000 men, but who lacked sufficient arms and were infiltrated by police informers.[8]

Most of the important information about the Fenian Rising in Dublin is contained in three contemporary sources – the newspapers, police reports and the Crown's prosecution brief against the Fenians which was prepared for the Fenian Trials (referred to as 'The Special Commission') which took place initially from 8 April to 24 May 1867. On 26 February 1867 the Dublin leaders (called centres) learned that the rising was planned to start a week later on 5 March 1867 but they were ordered not to communicate with their subordinates until 24 hours before the rising.[9] The police had advance warning that a Fenian Rising was planned to take place in 1867 but they were not aware of the actual date – 5 March – until the day beforehand. The police relied on informers and local constabulary intelligence concerning the movement of many young men out of the city on their way to the main *rendezvous* at Tallaght Hill.[10]

LORD PALMERSTON'S FIELDS

The first stage of the action which took place on the night of the 5/6 March, with which this study is concerned, involved a second group of men several hundred strong under the leadership of Patrick Lennon who assembled in the fields belonging to Lord Palmerston at Upper Rathmines, where Palmerston Park and Palmerston Road are now (Map 15). DMP Constable Bryan Kelly 103 gave the following evidence at the trial of Thomas Burke and Patrick Doran:

> *I was on duty in Upper Rathmines in plain clothes; I know Palmerston fields, and was there that night at eleven o'clock; I saw about 500 men there; they arrived there in groups of four and five; I heard the word 'slow' given; I understood it to be a word of command; I heard a noise of swords and the command, 'right-close'; I heard then 'fours'; to the right'; the night was very dark; I heard the word 'quick march'; I left then, the men remaining; I returned in about an hour, and the party had gone away. There were between 400 and 500 men when I first came up; I was in plain clothes, and I was sent with special instructions to watch the Palmerston fields; I received the instructions from the superintendent; I was well acquainted with that part of the country.*[11]

From the Palmerston fields the Fenians proceeded via Milltown and Windy Arbour to attack police barracks at Dundrum, Stepaside and Glencullen.[12] Police sergeant Francis Sheridan of the DMP gave the following evidence to the Special Commission:

6 Takagami, 'Dublin Fenians', p. 240.

7 Takagami, 'Dublin Fenians', p. 186.

8 Takagami, 'Dublin Fenians', pp. 209, 240.

9 Takagami, 'Dublin Fenians', p. 250.

10 Takagami, 'Fenian Rising in Dublin', pp. 346–7, 351; Takagami, 'Dublin Fenians', p. 253.

11 *Freeman's Journal*, 29 April 1867, p. 3.

12 Takagami, 'Fenian Rising in Dublin', pp. 349, 351–5.

I went on duty at nine o'clock on the night of the 5th March, and patrolled in the direction of Milltown; about the railway arches we met a number of men armed with muskets, and fixed bayonets; they were going in the direction of Milltown from the railway; they were about fifteen minutes' walk from the Palmerston fields; I saw them armed; they had pikes, rifles, fixed bayonets and revolvers; many of those who carried pikes had revolvers; ... I was accompanied by Constables Doran, Reilly and Gavan, and this man Lennon told his men to surround us ... and they were ordered to take charge of us. We had revolvers and cutlasses, and Lennon took them from us ... we were marched across Milltown Bridge towards Dundrum; we were kept prisoners; the party consisted of between 800 and 900 persons, and from 500 to 600 were armed.[13]

WINDY ARBOUR TO GLENCULLEN

When the Rathmines Fenians and their four DMP prisoners reached Windy Arbour they were joined by another large group of armed men commanded by John Kirwan who took overall charge. This combined group of Fenians had the benefit of being led by two men with military experience – John Kirwan and Patrick Lennon. Kirwan had served as a sergeant in the Irish Papal Brigade and Patrick Lennon was a deserter from the 9th Lancers. This group achieved the most success compared with the actions of the other Fenian groups.[14] When the Fenians reached Dundrum, they attacked the police barracks there but, encountering stiff resistance from the Irish Constabulary (the district south of the River Dodder was outside the jurisdiction of the DMP and was policed by the Irish Constabulary), they withdrew. Kirwan was wounded during the engagement at Dundrum and he relinquished command to Patrick Lennon.[15]

The men proceeded to Stepaside where they arrived at about 2 a.m. on 6 March. Lennon ordered the constables inside the police barracks to surrender in the name of the Irish Republic. The police refused to surrender following which the Fenians opened fire and attempted to set the building alight. Eventually, the policemen surrendered and the Fenians took the five constables prisoner. The Fenians then marched off towards Bray. When they got to Old Connaught the Fenian scouts discovered that the Bray barracks was too strongly fortified and, more alarmingly, that cavalry was on its way from Dublin to intercept them.[16] In fact the army had hurried out to Rathmines in response to the police reports only to find that the Fenians had dispersed by the time they arrived in Rathmines.[17] In response to the discouraging news from Bray the Fenians divided into two groups, with the larger group moving west via Kiltiernan and Golden Ball (where they raided a bakery) and the second group heading towards Tallaght, presumably with the intention of linking up with the other Fenian groups in Kilakee and on Tallaght Hill. The main group arrived at the police barracks at Glencullen at about 6 a.m. or 7 a.m. and tried to break into it. When they failed the Fenians ordered one of their captives, constable McIlwaine, to persuade his colleagues to surrender the building on pain of being shot. The police surrendered and the Fenians took more arms and ammunition before marching off towards Kilakee and Rockbrook where they eventually dispersed.[18]

---

13 *Freeman's Journal*, 29 April 1867, p. 3.

14 Takagami, 'Fenian Rising in Dublin', p. 352.

15 Takagami, 'Fenian Rising in Dublin', p. 352.

16 Takagami, 'Fenian Rising in Dublin', p. 353.

17 NAI, CSORP/1867/3821.

18 Takagami, 'Fenian Rising in Dublin', pp. 354, 361.

The Fenian Rising in Dublin petered out in the daylight hours of 6 March. It was a complete military failure.[19] Several reasons for this have been identified by Takagami, including a failure on the part of the Fenians to mobilise at Kilakee as originally planned, a lack of organisation and leadership, poor drilling and a failure of communication between the various groups that mobilised on the night of 5 March.[20] In addition, it is clear from contemporary reports that the rank and file Fenians – many of whom were teenage boys – were totally lacking in proper provisions and warm clothing. Accordingly, morale and discipline evaporated as the night went on and, in the absence of leadership and encouragement, the men dispersed at daybreak.

IMMEDIATE AFTERMATH

On 7 March, the following report appeared in the *Freeman's Journal*:

> *The 'insurgents' who marched by Dundrum and Glencullen assembled in the fields near Milltown last night fully provided with arms and ammunition. After some drilling and preparation on the part of the force, numbering about 500 – the greater proportion of whom were rather boys than men – they proceeded to Dundrum police station. In the fields known as Callaghans fields, near Milltown, where the Fenians first assembled, there were found the remains of provisions, bits of paper, a few cartridges, percussion caps, etc.*

In the immediate aftermath of the rising the army and the police detained 207 prisoners and continued to arrest more suspected participants in the following days and weeks.[21] For example, in the early hours of 6 March a man named Michael Walshe was arrested after a struggle on Clonskeagh Road near St James's Terrace and was found to be in possession of a loaded revolver and a powder horn.[22]

A police informer who had accompanied the Fenians from Milltown to Stepaside and Glencullen told his handler on 1 April that a Peter Healy, 'a plasterer of Milltown' was 'the man who thrust some straw into a window of the Stepaside Barracks, and called out for the Greek fire to burn the place'. According to the informer, after the rising Healy left to join his father (also a plasterer) and the rest of the family who had settled in Manchester.[23] The reference to Healy's trade as a plasterer is important in the context of an earlier incident which had taken place the previous year. On 24 March 1866 a police informer reported to his handler that a case of rifles was concealed in a house under construction in Temple Road near Milltown. In a follow-up search conducted on 26 March the police uncovered two wooden cases containing nine rifles with bayonets buried beneath the basement floor of the house.[24] It is thus possible that Peter Healy the 'plasterer of Milltown' was involved in procuring and hiding the guns in Temple Road. Healy does not appear in any other contemporary Fenian records or in newspaper reports of Fenian activity.

19 Curiously, the *Freeman's Journal* reported on 11 March 1867 that the telegraph wires were cut and an attempt made to lift the rails on the Dublin, Wicklow and Wexford Railway midway between the Milltown and Dundrum stations at a point close to the Quaker meeting house on the Lower Churchtown road in the early hours of Saturday 9 March, i.e. three days after the rising in Dublin.

20 Takagami, 'Fenian Rising in Dublin', pp. 360–2.

21 Takagami, 'Fenian Rising in Dublin', p. 359.

22 *Freeman's Journal*, 9 March 1867, p. 3.

23 NAI, CSORP/1867/14141.

24 NAI, CSORP/1866/6322; *Catholic Telegraph*, 31 March 1866, p. 4.

Plate 19. Terence Kelly, Clonskeagh, member of the Fenian Brotherhood (image courtesy of the National Library of Ireland)

It seems that the authorities decided it was not worth trying to track down Healy in Manchester because of the very limited information available as to his actual whereabouts.

ARRESTS AND A STATE TRIAL

The police focused their efforts on tracing Terence Kelly of Clonskeagh and William Cosgrove of Windy Arbour, both of whom had been identified by their police captives as playing prominent roles in the attacks on the police barracks, and who were subsequently charged with High Treason and Whiteboy offences respectively.[25] Terence Kelly was a twenty-three-year-old blacksmith's helper who lived in lodgings in a cottage in Clonskeagh.[26] Kelly was committed to Kilmainham gaol on 2 April 1867 charged with High Treason and on 18 June a warrant under the Habeas Corpus Suspension Act was lodged against him.[27] Kelly was considered important enough to be photographed after his arrest (Pl. 19).[28]

One of the captured DMP, constable Thomas Doran 39 E, gave sworn information to the authorities that:

> *At Glencullen I saw two men, whom I recognized at the moment as John Ward, of Milltown, and Kelly of Clonskea [sic], formerly known there as 'skirts' Kelly. The latter had had a rifle in his hand when he came up from the barrack.*[29]

> *The prisoner now present, Terence Kelly, was at the attack of Glencullen Barrack on the morning of the 6 March ult., and formed one of the armed party of insurgents that assaulted said place, and were in rebellion against the dominion of Her Majesty in Ireland. I arrested him at Clonskeagh, on yesterday, the 1st April, between three and four o'clock.*[30]

Another policeman who had been taken captive at Milltown, sergeant Francis Sheridan 34 A, gave similar evidence under oath on three separate occasions as follows:

> *Terence Kelly, now present, was one of an armed party who attacked Stepaside Barrack, and disarmed the police, on the night of 5th and morning of 6th March ult. My attention was drawn particularly to Kelly on the way to Dundrum, while I, along with Constables Doran, Reilly and Galvin, were prisoners, moving along disarmed in the ranks of the insurgent party ... On the way I heard a voice addressing one of the insurgents, 'Keep up, Skirts'. This I knew to be the familiar designation of a young man who lived in Clonskea; and my attention being thus called, I at once recognized Terence Kelly marching in their ranks ... I saw the prisoner Terence Kelly, while the attack was being*

25 NLI, P 2271, Dublin Special Commission – High Treason Indictment, pp. 18–29; NLI, IR 3431 D4, Dublin Special Commission, Informations and Indictments, April 1867, pp. 241, 797; *Freeman's Journal*, 5 April, p. 3; 6 April, p. 3; 8 May, p. 4; 13 May, p. 7; 21 May, p. 4.

26 NLI, IR 3431 D4, Dublin Special Commission, Informations and Indictments, pp. 241, 625, witness statement of Patrick Robinson of Doyle's Cottages, Clonskeagh.

27 Kilmainham Gaol Registry of Criminal Prisoners for 1867: http://search.findmypast.ie/record?id=ire%2fprisr%2frs00018280%2f4492656%2f00624%2f005 (accessed 30 January 2017).

28 NLI, MS 5957, Members of the Fenian Brotherhood.

29 NLI, IR 3431 D4, Dublin Special Commission, Informations and Indictments, p. 601, statement of Thomas Doran. I have found no further mention of John Ward of Milltown in the Fenian records, which suggests either that the police did not pursue him or that he evaded detection.

30 NLI, IR 3431 D4, Dublin Special Commission, Informations and Indictments, p. 603, statement of Thomas Doran.

made on the barrack at Glencullen ... on the morning of the 6th March ultimo. He was with the party at the front who opened the fire, and I saw him with a gun in his hand actually fire on the barrack at the occasion.[31]

Kelly's legal team produced seven witnesses who contradicted the police statements.[32] The defence case was that Terence Kelly had been at home in bed on the night of the 5/6 March and that the police had mistaken him for his brother Jack, also a blacksmith, who was nicknamed locally as 'Skirts' and who was much taller than his brother Terence. Terence Kelly's employer, Patrick Robinson, swore the following evidence for the defence:

The prisoner, Terence Kelly, came to work about 6.30 on Wednesday morning. It was Ash Wednesday. He was working with me nearly all that week and has been doing so ever since, save an odd Monday. I was in bed about ten o'clock on Monday night – the night of the row. Kelly has two brothers; one of them is called Jack Kelly, and the other Mike. Jack Kelly is called 'Skirts'. He has left work on Monday or Tuesday last. He is taller than the prisoner a good deal, and I could not mistake him for the other.[33]

Kelly's trial was adjourned and postponed on several occasions during the spring and summer of 1867. In the end the Crown decided not to proceed with its prosecution of Kelly with the result that on 7 October Kelly was discharged on entering security to appear and stand trial whenever the Crown should so wish.[34] Kelly continued to live and work in Clonskeagh as a shovel maker (probably in Henshaw's iron works) for many years afterwards. In 1883 he was sentenced to a half crown fine and a day's imprisonment in Grange Gorman gaol for being drunk.[35]

The Windy Arbour Fenian, William Cosgrave, was a thirty-one-year-old married man with three children.[36] Cosgrave was charged with offences under the Whiteboy Act, that is, with having risen in arms and attacked the police barrack at Stepaside, to which he pleaded not guilty.[37] The Crown's case against Cosgrave was based on the sworn testimony of two of the policemen who had been taken prisoner during the night of 5/6 March, Constable John McIlwaine and DMP Sergeant Francis Sheridan.[38] Constable McIlwaine swore:

That on the morning of the 6th March last, the barrack at Stepaside, in the County of Dublin, was attacked by a party of Fenians or insurgents, who took the barrack by force and made prisoners of the

31 NLI, IR 3431 D4, Dublin Special Commission, Informations and Indictments, pp. 603, 605, 623, statements of Francis Sheridan.

32 NLI, IR 3431 D4, Dublin Special Commission, Informations and Indictments, pp. 623–7.

33 NLI, IR 3431 D4, Dublin Special Commission, Informations and Indictments, p. 625. Terence Kelly's height was recorded as 5 feet 3 and a quarter inches: Kilmainham Gaol Register of Prisoners for 1867: http://search.findmypast.ie/record?id=ire%2fprisr%2frs00018280%2f4492656%2f00624%2f005 (accessed 30 January 2017).

34 *Dublin Evening Post*, Tuesday, October 8, 1867; *The Nation*, 12 October 1867, p. 6; Kilmainham Gaol Register of Prisoners for 1867: http://search.findmypast.ie/record?id=ire%2fprisr%2frs00018280%2f4492656%2f00624%2f005 (accessed 30 January 2017).

35 Grange Gorman Gaol Register of Prisoners for 1883: http://search.findmypast.ie/record?id=ire%2fprisr%2frs00018281%2f4492705%2f00441&parentid=ire%2fprisr%2frs00018281%2f4492705%2f00441%2f020 (accessed 30 January 2017).

36 NAI, CSORP/1867/9598, Memorial made by W.S. Purdon on behalf of William Cosgrave.

37 *Freeman's Journal*, 13 May, p.7; 21 May, p. 4; 22 May, p. 4; NLI, IR 3431 D4, Dublin Special Commission, Informations and Indictments, pp. 797, 799.

38 NLI, IR 3431 D4, Dublin Special Commission, Informations and Indictments, p. 797.

> *Constabulary, including myself, who were stationed therein. The prisoners were then marched to Glencullen, and the Constabulary barrack at that place was also attacked by the same body of Fenians, and, after a severe encounter, surrendered. While on the road to Glencullen I heard the name 'Cosgrave' repeatedly called by different men among the insurgents, which caused me to take particular notice of said Cosgrave, and I now identify the prisoner as the same person. He was very active giving orders, and was armed with a rifle. I saw the prisoner Cosgrave during the attack on Glencullen barrack; he was in the front of the insurgents among the firing party, and I saw him actually fire into the barrack.*[39]

Sergeant Sheridan of the DMP also swore the following information against Cosgrave:

> *That, on the night of the 5th March last, I, along with three other Constables of the Dublin Metropolitan Police, were forcibly made prisoners of by a body of 700 or 800 Fenians in the neighbourhood of Milltown, in said County, and disarmed us of our revolvers and swords. We were then marched as prisoners to Stepaside, and subsequently to Glencullen Constabulary Barrack, both of which were attacked and captured by this same body of insurgents. While on the march from Milltown to Stepaside I repeatedly heard the name 'Cosgrave' called out by the insurgents, and I saw the prisoner William Cosgrave, whom I identify, along with them. He took an active part; and, while the attack was going on at Stepaside, he ordered that we (the prisoners) should be brought up to the front, and subjected to opposing fires, if the barrack was not surrendered. I saw him carry a rifle with fixed bayonet on the march, and he was armed with it during the attack on Stepaside Barrack.*[40]

Shortly after the rising Cosgrave fled the country to Oldham, where he was arrested on 16 April following a tipoff from a police informer.[41] Cosgrave's health deteriorated while he was imprisoned in Kilmainham gaol. On 29 April, Cosgrave was visited by his neighbour and occasional employer, W.S. Purdon, proprietor of the *Farmer's Gazette.*[42] Purdon petitioned the under secretary, Sir Thomas Larcom, to admit Cosgrave to bail for which he (Purdon) agreed to go security for any reasonable amount. Purdon stated in his memorial that:

> *I saw the prisoner yesterday and fully believe he is in a dying state, fast hastening to his grave, and that further confinement will deprive him of all chance of ultimate recovery. I may mention that he has been very ill since December last and that on Christmas eve he took to his bed and was attended by the Dispensary Doctor of Dundrum (Dr Bernard) for several weeks, and was only able to creep about at the time of the Fenian outbreak. This I know of my own knowledge as he has lived close to me at Windy Arbour for the last ten years and frequently worked for me. He was always a quiet industrious man but very easily led; he has a wife and 3 young children and will soon have a fourth.*[43]

39 NLI, IR 3431 D4, Dublin Special Commission, Informations and Indictments, p. 797.

40 NLI, IR 3431 D4, Dublin Special Commission, Informations and Indictments, p. 797.

41 NLI, IR 3431 D4, Dublin Special Commission, Informations and Indictments, p. 799; NAI, CSORP/1867/14141, DMP Superintendent Ryan to Commissioners of Police, 2 April 1867; *Freemen's Journal*, 19 April 1867, p. 3.

42 NAI, CSORP/1867/9598, Memorial made by W.S. Purdon on behalf of William Cosgrave.

43 NAI, CSORP/1867/9598, Memorial made by W.S. Purdon on behalf of William Cosgrave.

In response to Purdon's memorial, the Kilmainhan gaol's physician examined Cosgrave and swore a declaration on 1 June 1867 opining that Cosgrave's life 'is not in immediate danger from his confinement, but he is in delicate health and suffers from the effects of a large tumour on his neck'.[44]

Notwithstanding Purdon's memorial and the physician's evidence, Cosgrave was not released and he remained in custody. On 19 June 1867 Cosgrave was brought to court for trial on indictment for an offence under the Whiteboy Act. According to the press report in the *Dublin Evening Post of 20 June, Cosgrave changed his plea to guilty on the advice of his counsel, even though his defence was that Cosgrave had* 'gone out [in the rising] under pressure'. The medical evidence given in court confirmed that Cosgrave's health was very bad and that further confinement would be almost certain to hasten his death. Based on the medical testimony and Cosgrave's guilty plea, the Crown prosecution team decided not to look for an immediate sentence. At the Judge's suggestion, the prosecution agreed to Cosgrave's release on entering full recognisances, with W.S. Purdon becoming bail for Cosgrave's appearance when called upon, and good behaviour for five years.[45] Cosgrave did not live long after his release and his death is recorded as having occurred in 1869 aged thirty-three.[46] In contrast, the police informer whose information was responsible for Cosgrave's conviction was subsequently given a reward of £50 on the recommendation of Superintendent Ryan, who stated that 'Cosgrave I know, from information both prior to, and subsequent to his arrest, to be about as bad a Fenian as was ever inside prison walls.'[47]

The coercion defence put forward by Cosgrave's barrister was also raised by other men charged with Fenian activities.[48] The following witness evidence given by Edward Green at the trial of James Gorman is but one example:

> *I heard the doctor ask him [Gorman] 'where did he leave his friends last night'; the doctor and Gorman spoke together, and Gorman said if he would allow him he would tell him; he said he was taking a walk that evening after his work, and that, as well as he could recollect, he was on the Rathgar road; a party of men, he said, met him there, and told him that he should go with them; they brought him in the direction of Milltown, and there was a number of men on the mountain side of the railway; some parties there said there was no use in fighting unless they had something to fight with; these persons went into a field and handed up some pikes, and they all got orders to march on; they marched on in the direction of Milltown, and a man with a revolver said the first person who would turn back he would shoot him.*[49]

HISTORICAL ASSESSMENT

Takagami's assessment of the Rathmines/Windy Arbour Fenian group is worth quoting as it provides an important understanding of the group's achievements in the context of the Dublin rising as a whole:

---

44 NAI, CSORP/1867/9598, Declaration of William Thornhill.

45 *Dublin Evening Post*, 20 June 1867, p 2.

46 Civil register of deaths, Dublin South, 1869, vol. 7, no. 631 http://search.findmypast.ie/record?id=ire%2fbmd%2fd%2f617137670 (accessed 1 February 2017).

47 NAI, CSORP/1867/14141, DMP Superintendent Ryan to Commissioners of Police, 5 and 9 August 1867.

48 Takagami, 'Dublin Fenians', p. 258.

49 *Freeman's Journal*, 9 May 1867, p. 2.

> *While the action of the Rathmines/Dundrum Fenians ended in dispersal, they had not at any stage been put to flight. In all respects this was the most purposeful action of the night. They had advanced as far as Old Connaught; then withdrew in good order, and in the process took Glencullen barrack. Given the fact that their leader, John Kirwan, was injured in the initial action of the night and replaced as leader, their performance is all the more meritorious, and bears out the comparative competence of Kirwan's B, Lennon, who took over ... The role of this group has been neglected, because its action has been seen as subsidiary to the gathering of the Fenians in the hills at Tallaght. If it is seen as having an independent purpose, then it gains in significance. Indeed, if it is seen somewhat more conjecturally as having had a twofold task of both organizing guerrilla activity on the eastern side of the Dublin/Wicklow hills and of spreading the diversionary action far afield – as far as Arklow – then the importance of its intended role is greatly enhanced.*[50]

Writing five years later on the topic in *Irish Historical Studies,* Takagami had this to say:

> *If the mobilization of manpower was larger than has been believed, and many were ready to turn out despite the inauspicious omens, then the politicisation of the city artisan classes had advanced quite far. The threat represented by the Fenians in 1867 was not in the final analysis a serious military one. However, if not a successful military mobilisation, it was a forceful mobilization of political opinion at the novel level of artisans and skilled workers. The fear the Fenians struck into the minds of the Catholic bishops, most notably the archbishop of Dublin, is proof of that. In that sense, given the fact that the fiasco of 1867 was more one of leadership and planning than of popular readiness to take the field, the Fenians may need to be reassessed, and their place to be seen in a less romantic and more formidable light. In other words, they may deserve more pages than they get in general accounts, and the Fenians and the sympathies they aroused among their supporters may emerge as a more central element in the context of circumstances which changed Ireland in the succeeding two generations.*[51]

Takagami's conclusions are supported by this review of the events in Milltown and neighbouring districts. The local population had been politicised as far back as the 1790s when Henry Jackson of United Irishman fame and the Emmet family resided respectively in Clonskeagh Castle and Casino (now Emmet House, Dundrum Road). Fifty years later in April 1848, at a meeting of the short-lived Irish Confederation, a confederate club was established in Clonskeagh with the pointedly radical name of 'The Jackson Club'.[52] As noted earlier, the local Fenian protagonists came from skilled artisan backgrounds such as a carpenter, a plasterer and a blacksmith. Given the fact that hundreds of men took part in the military operations in south Dublin commencing at Lord Palmerston's fields, it is most likely that several more men from Milltown than have been identified thus far took part in the Fenian Rising.

In terms of a local historical legacy it is the author's opinion that the Fenians had an important influence on the succeeding generations of the working-class inhabitants of Milltown, Windy Arbour and Dundrum when it came to a choice in the autumn of 1914 of joining the National Volunteers and fighting in the Great War, as advocated by John Redmond, or joining (or remaining in) the Irish Volunteers under Eoin McNeill. Members of the local 'E' Company of the Irish Volunteers were recruited from Milltown, Windy Arbour and

50 Takagami, 'Dublin Fenians', pp. 264–5.

51 Takagami, 'Fenian Rising in Dublin', p. 362.

52 *The Nation*, 8 April 1848.

surrounding districts. Among the Patrick Doyle papers in the National Library is an undated newspaper cutting reporting the death of Mr Dick Ruth, a foundation member of the Dundrum (County Dublin) Company, 3rd Battalion of the Irish Volunteers. The report states that Mr Ruth's (unnamed) grand-uncle was transported to Van Diemen's Land after the Fenian Rising of 1867.[53]

In concluding the discussion of the Fenian Rising, the following obituary report in the *Irish Press* of 15 September 1931 is particularly apposite:

> *TRUE TO THE END – DEATH OF DUBLIN FENIAN VETERAN*
>
> *With the death of Mr Joseph Canton, Ross Road, Dublin at the age of eighty-six years, another of the few remaining '67 men passed away. The late Mr Canton joined the Fenian Movement as a young man, and was out with his Company on the memorable Shrove Tuesday in March, 1867, under the command of Patrick Lennon and Michael Lambert. He saw active service in Milltown, Dundrum, Stepaside and Glencullen districts, and assisted in the taking of a police barracks in one of these areas. He remained on service until his Company got orders to disperse on the morning of the 6th March. Throughout his life the late Mr Canton remained steadfast to the Republican cause, and followed with interest every movement for the freedom of the nation.* ■

53 Patrick Doyle papers (NLI, MS 46,594).

Chapter 11: Social and Economic Improvements, 1880–1910

Chapter 11: Social and Economic Improvements, 1880–1910

INTRODUCTION

Previous chapters have exposed the entrenched poverty that existed in Milltown for much of the nineteenth century. Three fortuitous and very significant events took place in the 1880s which greatly improved the outlook for Milltown village and the working-class inhabitants of the surrounding district. The first and perhaps the most significant event was the arrival of the Sisters of Charity in Milltown in 1879–80 with their acquisition of Milltown House and Milltown Castle respectively. Secondly, legislation was passed in 1880 which incorporated the townland of Milltown into the Rathmines and Rathgar township, an event which brought municipal government to Milltown village. Thirdly, the establishment of Dublin Laundry Company in 1887 vies with the arrival of the Sisters of Charity as the most important event to positively impact in the long-term the lives of the working-class inhabitants of Milltown from the end of the nineteenth century and beyond. By the turn of the twentieth century the outlook for Milltown was much better than it had been 25 years previously.

Over time the upturn in fortunes gave the inhabitants of Milltown, especially the Catholic working class living in the village, a greater sense of communal identity and political awareness. In addition, Milltown also benefited from increasing integration with the wider Dublin community through the growth in organised sport and other cultural pastimes. There were, however, intractable social problems associated with poor housing conditions and unemployment among unskilled workers. Higher up the social scale, growing religious, class and political tensions simmered below the surface, mirroring developments on a national level. Each of these topics will be reviewed in this chapter.

THE SISTERS OF CHARITY

The Sisters of Charity put down their roots in Milltown in 1879 and 1880 when they successively bought the Milltown House and Milltown Castle demesnes. An outbreak of smallpox in their novitiate in Harold's Cross – which later became the Hospice for the Dying – was instrumental in their decision to buy Milltown House on 29 August 1879. Over 50 nuns and novices, including the Superior General Mother Francis Scholastica Margison, moved into Milltown House. When Milltown Castle and its grounds were put up for sale a few months later in 1880 the nuns bought the property and demolished the castle. The following year, 1881, the nuns erected a large red-brick building on the castle site to house the novices, which is now converted into private apartments.[1] Six years later, in 1887, the archbishop of Dublin laid the foundation stone for a new chapel constructed of Dublin granite, which was built to commemorate the centenary of the birth of Mother Mary Aikenhead.[2]

The religious order's presence in Milltown was felt immediately. In March 1880 the nuns successfully applied to the Irish National Land League for relief funds, and were granted £15 to support local children.[3] In December 1889 the Sisters of Charity at Mount St Anne's placed the following advertisement in the *Freeman's Journal*:

> *The Sisters of Charity, Mount St Anne's, Milltown, for the first time come forward to ask a share in the alms bestowed by a generous public on the poor at this season. A large district is visited by the Sisters, who are depending entirely on the charity of the public for the wherewith to relieve their crying wants at this inclement time. The smallest help will be most gratefully acknowledged by the Sisters of Charity, Christmas, 1889.*[4]

As noted in Chapter 9, the Sisters of Charity had a hugely beneficial impact on the education of infants and girls when they established an infants and primary school in the grounds of their new convent at Milltown House in 1883.[5] The nuns included music in their curriculum and by 1897 the school choir was receiving commendations from the Royal Academy of Music.[6]

In September 1911 the St Mary's Teacher Training College was opened at Mount St Anne's. Its aim was to train the sisters in methods of teaching and school organisation in order for them to obtain official recognition from the Board of Education.[7] Around the same time, the Leinster College of Irish established an Irish teacher training centre at Mount St Anne's prior to the outbreak of the First World War. Following examinations for diplomas in teaching and in Irish studies distinctions were awarded to Sister Patricia and Sister Colombiene of Mount St Anne's.[8] The consistent quality of the education received by young girls at St Anne's national school enabled the more academically minded girls from working-class backgrounds to pursue better employment opportunities outside traditional jobs in the Dublin Laundry Company or domestic service. Milltown teenagers Anastatia O'Keeffe, Nellie Carpenter, Eileen Heron and Margaret McArdle all won prizes at the Rathmines Technical Institute's annual awards ceremony in 1923 for the shorthand clerks and typists' course and the girls' afternoon commercial course.[9] The nuns also catered for the majority of girls who were not in a position to undertake further education beyond primary level, by providing them with practical skills. For example, 14 girls from St Anne's national school

1 Irish Sisters of Charity, *Milltown in Brief... 1879–1995*, Circular Letter 26 April 1995.

2 *Freeman's Journal*, 20 January 1887, pp. 5–6.

3 *Dublin Evening Telegraph*, 31 March 1880, p. 3.

4 *Freeman's Journal*, 14 December 1881, p. 3; 27 December 1881, p. 1.

5 Irish Sisters of Charity, *Milltown in Brief... 1879–1995*, Circular Letter 26 April 1995.

6 *Dublin Evening Telegraph*, 2 July 1897, p. 4.

7 Irish Sisters of Charity, *Milltown in Brief... 1879–1995*, Circular Letter 26 April 1995.

8 *Irish Independent*, 9 June 1914, p. 9.

9 *Rathmines Free Press*, 27 January 1923, pp. 5–6.

were among 407 Dublin pupils to be awarded prizes for proficiency in cooking by gas in 1930, despite the fact that some of the girls lived in cramped cottages with only very basic cooking facilities.[10]

The Sisters of Charity established connections with the largest employer in Milltown, the Dublin Laundry Company.[11] In 1895 the nuns set up an informal arrangement whereby they could visit the laundry with a view to recommending girls for employment there.[12] Sister Padua of Mount St Anne's obtained £25 from the Dáil Special Fund in 1925 for a terminally ill veteran of the 1916 Rising and the War of Independence, Peter Shortall, of Castlewood Place, Rathmines.[13] When the River Dodder burst its banks on 3 September 1931 and flooded several cottages close to the river bank on the south side of the village main street in Milltown, the nuns provided a temporary refuge in the school buildings for 200 people and provided them with hot food, with the assistance of an unnamed prominent local lady.[14]

Three years later, in 1934, the Sisters of Charity donated part of their property to facilitate the enlargement of the parish church, Ss Gall and Columbanus. The land on which the extension was built was originally part of Luscombe's field, so named after the last owner of Milltown Castle.[15]

The examples given above are only a very small selection of the educational, vocational and practical help that the Sisters of Charity provided for the poor of Milltown at a time when State social welfare was meagre or non-existent. The full extent of the Sisters of Charity's impact on the lives of the people of Milltown and the surrounding district during their nearly 120-year tenure is an untold story. That said, the fact cannot be ignored that some of the Sisters of Charity were guilty of oppression and cruelty in their treatment of the women in the Magdalene laundries, such as their laundry in Donnybrook, which ironically was competing for business with the Dublin Laundry Company in Milltown. Indeed, the head nun of the Donnybrook Magdalene laundry freely admitted in 1887 to deliberately frustrating demands for release by inmates whose period of detention was up and who were entitled to leave the laundry.[16]

MILLTOWN JOINS THE RATHMINES AND RATHGAR TOWNSHIP

The circumstances that led to the inclusion of Milltown in the Rathmines and Rathgar township are rather complicated. In very simple terms, by 1880 Milltown had become a pawn in a long drawn out three-way political conflict between Dublin Corporation, dissenting ratepayers in the Rathmines and Rathgar township and the township's commissioners concerning the township's water supply and sewerage disposal and the threatened extension of the Corporation's jurisdiction over Rathmines and Rathgar.[17] Aside from these issues it also seems that some of the gentry residents of Milltown underwent a change of heart and were now prepared to lobby for the inclusion of Milltown in the township, regardless of the increased rates they would suffer. The reasons for this are not entirely clear but it is likely that an increasing awareness of the hazards to health posed by bad drinking water and poor sanitation arrangements was a factor. Such awareness had built up

10 *Irish Times*, 24 June 1930, p. 5.

11 Hearn, *Thomas Edmondson*, p. 57.

12 NAI, Business Records, Dublin 56, Dublin Laundry Company, letter book 1895–1902, 16 March 1895; 11 October 1898.

13 NAI, Department of the Taoiseach, Cabinet S 7645, file for Peter Shortall, Grant from the Dáil Special Fund.

14 *Irish Independent*, 5 September 1931, p. 9.

15 Irish Sisters of Charity, *Milltown in Brief… 1879–1995*, Circular Letter 26 April 1995.

16 Hearn, *Thomas Edmondson*, pp. 100–1, 123–5.

17 *Freeman's Journal*, 15 January 1880, p. 3; 5 February 1880, p. 2; 2 June 1880, p. 6; *Irish Times*, 2 June 1880, p. 6.

over the nineteenth century due to various outbreaks of cholera and smallpox in Dublin city and its suburbs, and from criticism generated by the Dublin Sanitary Association which was set up in 1872.[18] It was well-known that Milltown village was in a very unsanitary state and that its effluent was discharged into cesspools or into the River Dodder, not alone endangering the health of the villagers but also that of the wealthy professional classes who lived in the big houses on the outskirts of the village.[19] Such concerns are evident in a newspaper advertisement for a detached house on two acres situated close to Milltown railway station which assured prospective tenants that the property had 'excellent sewerage'.[20]

Having laid out the background to the incorporation of Milltown into the Rathmines and Rathgar township it is appropriate now to review the process involved in bringing Milltown within the township. Due to a lack of surviving information it is not possible to state why the inclusion of Milltown in the township became an objective of the township's commissioners in 1879. Although the minute books of the board meetings have survived, the level of detail recorded in them is brief. Added to this, the commissioners were secretive in their affairs and deliberately excluded the public and the press from their meetings, much to the chagrin and annoyance of the ratepayers.[21] This explains why the first mention of Milltown occurs on 15 October 1879 when the board minutes record that:

> *Read letter no. 289 from Messrs D. & T. FitzGerald [township's solicitors] in reference to annexation of Milltown. Copy of letter to be forwarded to Mr Bewley [Sandford Hill] and Mr Luscombe [Milltown Castle]; further arrangements to be left to Parliamentary Committee.*[22]

It appears that the township's solicitors were investigating the possibility of the township taking over Milltown using provisions under the Public Health (Ireland) Act of 1878, but Counsel's opinion recommended against this option.[23] For Milltown to be brought into the Rathmines township it was necessary to initiate a private member's bill to amend the Rathmines and Rathgar township acts. This was no easy task as the sponsors had to navigate their bill through various legal and parliamentary committees and procedures before the bill finally received royal assent. Hence 17 individuals, including Samuel Bewley of Sandford Hill, Tooke C. Luscombe of Milltown Castle, Charles Granby Burke JP of St Philip's and John Drury of Dartry House, put themselves forward in 1879 as promotors and petitioners of a bill entitled The Rathmines and Rathgar Township (Milltown Extension) Bill.[24]

Once the Milltown Extension Bill became public in December 1879, determined opposition was raised against the bill on grounds of cost by an association of disgruntled ratepayers.[25] These ratepayers were also vehemently opposed to the commissioners' water bill, which proposed to secure water for the township by the construction of reservoirs in the Glenasmole valley, County Dublin. To counter the commissioners' water bill, the ratepayers promoted their own water bill which

18 Julianna Adelman, *Civilised by Beasts: Animals and Urban Change in Nineteenth-Century Dublin* (Manchester, 2020) pp. 149–51.

19 *Freeman's Journal*, 28 September 1870, p. 1; 30 January 1871, p. 5; 2 June 1880, p. 6.

20 *Saunders's Newsletter*, 5 February 1867, p. 4.

21 *Freeman's Journal*, 5 February 1880, p. 2; 2 June 1880, p. 6.

22 Dublin City Archives, Rathmines and Rathgar UDC papers, UDC 1/Mins/1/5, Book 1878–85, p. 102.

23 Dublin City Archives, Rathmines and Rathgar UDC papers, UDC 1/List 7/1, Opinion of Pembroke Stephens 30 October 1879.

24 *Freeman's Journal*, 4 December 1897, p. 3; Drury Papers (NAI, Small Accessions no. 1/704, M 1231/3/3) (hereafter cited as the Milltown Extension Bill).

25 *Freeman's Journal*, 13 January 1880, p. 8, 15 January 1880, p. 4, 5 February 1880, p. 2.

involved paying Dublin Corporation to supply water to the township from the River Vartry. This bill also included powers for the creation of 'an efficient Fire Brigade'.[26] In the meantime the Milltown Extension Bill began its progression through the Houses of Parliament.[27] The bill's opponents succeeded in obtaining an interim injunction from the Master of the Rolls on 25 February 1880 restraining the commissioners from promoting the bill in parliament, which was found to be outside their corporate powers.[28] In practical terms, the injunction delayed but did not derail the Milltown Extension Bill, as the injunction restrained the township commissioners in their corporate capacity from promoting the bill but not the individual promotors. Even so, the opposing ratepayers gave notice on 30 March 1880 of their intention to petition against the Milltown Extension Bill, which was then pending in the House of Lords.[29]

The critical juncture for the promotors and the opponents of the Milltown Extension Bill came on 1 June 1880 when a select committee of the House of Lords convened to hear the arguments of the two opposing protagonists. This hearing was reported in detail in the national press but the unexpected outcome was that, at the conclusion of the hearing and after only five minutes of private deliberation, the House of Lords committee decided that the objections were sustained and that the bill could not proceed.[30] On any objective reading of the newspaper reports there was no obvious reason – cost to the ratepayers apart – why the bill should not have gone ahead, and given that it was clearly in the broader public interest that Milltown be taken over by the township and provided with modern public utilities. Undoubtedly, the murky world of parliamentary lobbying and political deal making was behind the outcome. Thus, all appeared to be lost with Milltown remaining without municipal government for the foreseeable future.

On 14 June 1880 a notice appeared in the newspapers advising that 'The Earl of Powis [chairman of the House of Lords select committee] will, on Friday, move that the Rathmines and Rathgar Townships (Milltown Extension) Bill be recommitted.'[31] So what had happened over the previous two weeks for such a volte-face on the committee's part? Surviving information is very limited but it appears that two related factors were responsible. Correspondence from one of the bill's promotors, town commissioner John Drury of Dartry House, indicates that the opposing ratepayer faction may have exhausted their funds fighting the Milltown Extension Bill and the Rathmines Water (Dodder) Bill in parliament. Their solicitor, Mark Bentley, wrote to the township's solicitor, D & T FitzGerald, on 21 July 1880 seeking a contribution of £750 towards their parliamentary expenses as part, it would appear, of negotiations to halt the rate payers' opposition in parliament to the two bills promoted by the commissioners. In his letter to D & T FitzGerald, Bentley included the following threat:

> *I think it is worthy of consideration of your clients whether they will make this concession before it is too late and thus avoid the determined opposition of the Ratepayers Committee at the election next November. Should the 7 outgoing members of the Board be then defeated it must be a deadly blow to the present policy of the Board and may result in the repeal of the Dodder Bill as the Committee are advised such course is open to them.*[32]

---

26 *Freeman's Journal*, 13 January 1880, p. 8, 15 January 1880, p. 4; *Irish Times*, 13 January 1880, p. 4, 15 January 1880, p. 4.

27 *Freeman's Journal*, 10 January 1880, p. 5, 21 January 1880, p. 5, 18 February 1880, p. 5, 23 February 1880, p. 6.

28 *Dublin Evening Telegraph*, 25 February 1880, p. 3; Law Reports (Ireland), Chancery Division, 1880, pp. 114–20.

29 Drury Papers (NAI, Small Accessions no. 1/704, M 1231/3/3).

30 *Freeman's Journal*, 2 June 1880, p. 5; Irish Times, 2 June 1880, p. 6.

31 *Dublin Evening Telegraph*, 14 June 1880, p. 4.

32 Drury Papers (NAI, Small Accessions no. 1/704, M 1231/3/3).

In any event, the township commissioners won the water wars and their bill carried the day, much to the chagrin of the nationalist *Dublin Weekly Nation* newspaper which opined:

> *Nevertheless, Ascendancy dies hard. The Rathmines Commissioners have been able to carry their water bill through Parliament. Happily for them, the opposition to it was led by Maurice Brooks. Who can doubt that if Mr Parnell, or even one of his lieutenants, had that opposition in charge, the commissioners might now be found looking though the largest telescope they could get for the appearance of their water bill as law in some far remote period of the future?*[33]

While the wrangling over the water bill was taking place during June and July 1880 the recommitted Milltown Extension Bill proceeded through parliament without any further opposition and received Royal assent on 2 August 1880.[34] The second factor that had caused a change of mind and removed the ratepayers' opposition to the Milltown Extension Bill was the inclusion in the bill as originally promoted of statutory powers enabling the Rathmines township to establish its own fire brigade. Everyone in the township agreed that a proper fire service was sorely needed, and in light of recent calamitous fires no one wanted to be blamed if the fire brigade became a casualty of the politics affecting the water bills. It seems likely therefore that the township commissioners had decided as a precautionary measure to include the fire brigade clauses in the Milltown Extension Bill instead of their Rathmines Water (Dodder) Bill, in case the latter more contentious bill was defeated in parliament.[35] Of relevance too was the fact that the new water supply under either of the rival water bills would provide increased water pressure to improve the effectiveness of the township's fire-fighting capabilities, as low water pressure was a significant problem affecting the township.[36] However, when the ratepayers' association's rival water bill had been defeated at the instigation of the township's parliamentary sub-committee, its fire brigade provisions had lapsed too.[37] Critically, notwithstanding that the Milltown Extension Bill had been defeated at the House of Lords committee hearing on 1 June 1880, it was ultimately in everyone's greater practical and political interests to expedite and enact the recommitted Milltown Extension Bill to ensure that the township would have its own fire service, even if for the bill's opponents that meant taking on the additional expense of Milltown townland.[38] In summary, it can truthfully be said that the fire brigade came to the rescue of Milltown!

The extent of the lobbying for the Milltown Extension Bill and the two opposing Rathmines Water Bills is instructive of the political power wielded by the Rathmines commissioners which ground down the dissenting ratepayers' association. But this power came at a considerable cost. On 24 November 1880 at their monthly board meeting the township commissioners agreed to borrow £2,000 to pay the costs of the Milltown Extension Bill and the following month they exe-

---

33 *Dublin Weekly Nation*, 31 July 1880, p. 9.

34 *Dublin Daily Express*, 17 July 1880, p. 5; 24 July 1880, p. 4; Drury Papers (NAI, Small Accessions no. 1/704, M 1232). The full title of the Milltown Extension Bill as enacted is 'An Act for extending the Rathmines and Rathgar Township so as to include therein the adjoining townland of Milltown in the County of Dublin for the establishment of a Fire Brigade and for other purposes' (43 & 44 Vict., 2 August 1880). The short title of the act is The Rathmines and Rathgar (Milltown Extension) Act 1880.

35 *Freeman's Journal*, 5 February 1880, p. 2.

36 *Freeman's Journal*, 13 January 1880, p. 8; Irish Times 15 January 1880, p. 4.

37 Dublin City Archives, Rathmines and Rathgar UDC papers, UDC 1/Mins/1/5, Book 1878–85, p. 154.

38 *Irish Times*, 5 June 1880, p. 7 at Colonel Harberd's evidence to the House of Lords on the water bills.

cuted a mortgage with the National Bank for £10,000 to pay the township's legal bills.[39] Another successful lobby group which affected the Milltown Extension Bill was the Dublin, Wicklow and Wexford Railway Company. At their half yearly meeting held on 16 August 1880 the chairman reported that the company had got a clause, called the 'fourth rating clause', inserted into the Milltown Extension Bill whereby the railway would pay reduced rates at 25 per cent of the net annual value of the land over which the railway line passed through Milltown townland.[40]

Sections 15 and 36 of the new Milltown Extension Act empowered the township commissioners to strike an additional special rate on top of the ordinary annual rate to be levied on the ratepayers of Milltown to cover the costs of the act. When the town commissioners met at a board meeting held on 1 January 1881 a special rate of 4*d.* in the pound was struck for 1881, which was to be payable on a total property valuation for Milltown townland of £1,945 10*s.*[41] When the accounts for the year ending 25 March 1881 were published, they disclosed that £22 10*d.* out of the total special rate of £30 1*s.* 6*d* due from Milltown's ratepayers had been paid. The accounts also disclosed that the township had purchased a steam fire engine and carriage costing almost £380, and that £10 7*d.* had already been spent on 'labour at fire'.[42]

Before we examine some of the public utility works undertaken in Milltown after the enactment of the Milltown Extension Act it is worth concluding with the report given by the parliamentary committee to the Rathmines township commissioners at a special board meeting held on 25 August 1880:

> *Your committee have much pleasure in reporting to the Board the success of your water bill which received Royal assent on 6th instant. It will now be your duty to carry its provisions into effect. The Rathmines and Rathgar (Vartry) Water Bill, which if passed into law would have been injurious to your township, was by your wishes and instructions opposed and was thrown out by the House of Lords. With like pleasure your committee report the success of the Rathmines and Rathgar (Milltown Extension) Bill which received the Royal assent on the 2nd instant. This extension will in many respects be advantageous to the township, but it is right that we should remind you that it casts on you the responsibility of taking the same care of Milltown as of the other portions of your township.*[43]

The parliamentary committee's admonishment of the commissioners to take the same care of Milltown as the other parts of the township was very prescient. Certainly, in the short term the commissioners took the message to heart and, as will shortly be shown, quickly introduced public utilities to the village. In the longer term, however, the case in favour of the commissioners turned out not to be strong, particularly as regards the provision of working-class housing and the extension of the electoral franchise to the inhabitants of Milltown village. These topics are addressed in Chapters 12 and 16.

ADMINISTRATION OF MILLTOWN BY THE RATHMINES AND RATHGAR TOWNSHIP

Within three weeks of the Milltown Extension Act becoming law, the Rathmines and Rathgar township's surveyor together with Messrs Bolton, Bewley and Drury had inspected the newly incorpo-

39 Dublin City Archives, Rathmines and Rathgar UDC papers, UDC 1/Mins/1/5, Book 1878–85, pp 174, 180.

40 *Freeman's Journal*, 17 August 1880, p. 4; The Rathmines and Rathgar (Milltown Extension) Act 1880, s. 16.

41 Dublin City Archives, Rathmines and Rathgar UDC papers, UDC 1/Mins/1/5, Book 1878–85, p. 181.

42 *Dublin Daily Express*, 14 June 1881, p. 2.

43 Dublin City Archives, Rathmines and Rathgar UDC papers, UDC 1/Mins/1/5, Book 1878–85, p. 154.

Plate 57. Postcard of Milltown village looking west, c. 1910 (author's collection)

rated townland of Milltown and recommended to the township commissioners that six gas lamps be erected at once. The commissioners agreed to the recommendation at their board meeting of 25 August 1880 and the secretary was instructed to inform the secretary of the Alliance Gas Company. At the same board meeting the surveyor was instructed to submit a report to the next meeting 'as to the best means of giving that district a supply of water'.[44] The information about the gas lamps is useful because it can be used to date the few late nineteenth-century photographs and post cards of Milltown village, all of which include gas lamps (Pl. 57).

At the next township board meeting on 1 September 1880, the commissioners agreed to two requests from Thomas P. Hackett, a publican and a landlord of cottages in Milltown, to relocate a gas lamp to the opposite side of Milltown Bridge and to 'shut up [the] road over the old bridge'. The second request referred to the Packhorse Bridge. The wall which was built in 1880 to block access to vehicular traffic is still in place. The surveyor also submitted his report on the water supply for Milltown and the matter was referred back 'to see if supply can be obtained from Ranelagh road'.[45] On 6 October 1880 the board minutes record that the surveyor had submitted an amended report to the board following which the commissioners ordered that the (unspecified) work be done and

44 Dublin City Archives, Rathmines and Rathgar UDC papers, UDC 1/Mins/1/5, Book 1878–85, p. 155.

45 Dublin City Archives, Rathmines and Rathgar UDC papers, UDC 1/Mins/1/5, Book 1878–85, p. 159. Farranboley townland is located on the south bank of the River Dodder on the Dundrum Road.

that an advertisement for pipes be inserted in the newspapers.[46] Despite these directions progress seems to have stalled, for on 20 July 1881 a memorial from the Milltown rate payers was read at the board meeting following which the board passed a resolution to:

> *refer the matter to Mr Bewley and Mr Henshaw as subcommittee to consult with Mr Johnston, and they be empowered to authorise the laying down of water mains and to order advertisements to be inserted for the supply of pipes.*[47]

No mention of the water supply for Milltown appears in the board minutes after this entry so it is assumed that the work was carried out. This can also be inferred by the fact that references to Milltown in the board minutes were, from 1884 onwards, concerned with laying down sewer pipes in Milltown and surrounding districts as part of the Dodder Valley Drainage Scheme, which was a joint enterprise undertaken by the Rathmines and Pembroke townships under the Public Health (Ireland) Act of 1878. This project involved the construction of a gravity sewer along the River Dodder valley from Orwell Bridge in Rathgar to Ballsbridge to drain the sewage of both townships.[48] These works necessitated the closure of Milltown village main street to traffic for several weeks from January to March 1885 while the sewer pipes were laid and connections made to individual properties.[49] Robert Gibney, the owner of Milltown Flour mills, lodged a claim against the township for compensation totalling £1,815, but he was obviously chancing his luck because he later settled for £458, 5*s*.[50]

It should be explained at this point that the drinking water supplied to Milltown village continued to be sourced from the Grand Canal until the water from the township's Bohernabreena reservoir come on tap in 1887, which coincidentally was the driest year recorded on the Dodder up to that time. Conversely, Dublin Corporation had, since 1867, been able to supply pure soft water from the Vartry reservoir to customers. In 1877 the guardians of the Rathdown Union arranged to take Vartry water to supply the townland of Farranboley at a cost of 6*d*. per 1,000 gallons.[51] By 1880 demand for Vartry drinking water had increased in the Dundrum district to such an extent that Dublin Corporation approved a scheme to lay water mains throughout Dundrum, Windy Arbour and Farranboley.[52] Farranboley townland also included that part of Milltown village lying on the south bank of the River Dodder comprising about two acres which was known locally as Concrete. This meant that because of the political antipathy between Dublin Corporation and the Rathmines township the villagers of Milltown had two different water supplies depending on which side of the river bank they lived. In short, a dysfunctional situation existed for several years whereby Milltown villagers living on the north bank of the River Dodder in the Rathmines township had an inadequate water supply with a modern mains sewer, while the villagers living in Concrete on the south bank of the River Dodder in the Rathdown No. 1 Rural District/Poor Law Union had (where connected) access to good quality water, but without sewage disposal facilities.

46 Dublin City Archives, Rathmines and Rathgar UDC papers, UDC 1/Mins/1/5, Book 1878–85, p. 165.

47 Dublin City Archives, Rathmines and Rathgar UDC papers, UDC 1/Mins/1/5, Book 1878–85, p. 218.

48 *Dublin Daily Express*, 26 January 1884, p. 2.

49 Dublin City Archives, Rathmines and Rathgar UDC papers, UDC 1/Mins/1/5, Book 1878–85, pp. 436 and 441.

50 Dublin City Archives, Rathmines and Rathgar UDC papers, UDC 1/List 1/43, Agreement dated 21 June 1886.

51 *Wicklow Newsletter*, 14 April 1877, p. 1; McEntee and Corcoran, *The Rivers Dodder and Poddle*, pp. 182, 250.

52 *Irish Times*, 19 October 1880, p. 3.

Contemporary letting advertisements in the late Victorian press frequently referred to the source of the available water supply, as a typical advertisement from 1900 in the *Freeman's Journal* explains: 'Dairy premises to let, comprising shop and dwelling house, large well enclosed yard with cowsheds and stables, connected Vartry water. Apply Hackett's Milltown.'[53] The mention of the Vartry water identifies Hackett's property as lying on the south bank of the River Dodder in Concrete, at the northern end of the townland of Farranboley in the Parish of Taney. Concrete also fell within the jurisdiction of the Rathdown No. 1 Rural District Council and the Dundrum Petty Sessions court.

Aside from public utilities, the township made its presence felt in Milltown in other spheres of daily life. At their monthly board meeting held in October 1880 the commissioners passed a resolution to oppose the application for a licence by Edward Daly of Classon's Bridge House (as The Dropping Well pub was then called) which had been refused the previous year. The resolution was proposed by commissioner John Drury, who lived up the road from the pub in Dartry House, for the following reasons:

> *In view of the increase of crime arising from drink, we earnestly deprecate an increase of licensed houses and especially resolve that an earnest representation be made to the magistrates at quarter sessions against granting a licence to a house at Classon's Bridge already refused twelve times in eleven years and which from its position is particularly dangerous as tending to draw objectionable persons to the township and being utterly unnecessary for any useful purpose.*[54]

Despite the longstanding opposition to their public house the Dalys eventually succeeded with their licencing applications, for by 1897 the *Rathmines News* reported that 'Mrs Daly has recently obtained a seven-day licence for her establishment which is favourably situated for the accommodation of the cyclist, the pedestrian and the railway traveller.'[55]

The Rathmines township was responsible for prosecuting offences under an ever-increasing body of legislation and regulations concerning the administration of local government and health laws. Regulation of the livestock and dairy industry was particularly relevant to Milltown. Patrick Murphy of Milltown Hill was fined £2 in 1891 for keeping pigs in his dairy yard following a prosecution by the township's public health inspector.[56] Nine years later the *Rathmines News* reported that 'the Rathmines Urban Council are determined to put an end to the adulteration of milk by dairymen, and several prosecutions have taken place. Fortunately offenders are but few, considering the large number of people engaged in the milk trade.'[57] Aside from the watering down of milk, the insanitary conditions of numerous dairy yards in Dublin city and its suburbs were almost certainly the cause of outbreaks of infectious diseases such as tuberculosis and scarlet fever. Accordingly, effective oversight and regulation of dairy yards and slaughter houses was a constant concern of the municipal authorities.[58]

---

53 *Freeman's Journal*, Tuesday 10 April 1900, p. 1.

54 *Freeman's Journal*, 15 October 1879, p. 3; Dublin City Archives, Rathmines and Rathgar UDC papers, UDC 1/Mins/1/5, Book 1878–85, p. 167.

55 *Rathmines News*, 11 December 1897, p. 4.

56 *Freeman's Journal*, 30 May 1891, p. 3.

57 *Rathmines News*, 15 December 1900, p. 5.

58 Daly, *Dublin: The deposed capital*, pp. 263–4.

Plate 20. Sketch of the Dublin Laundry Company's complex at Milltown, formerly Gibney's Flour Mills, 1888 (courtesy of the National Archives of Ireland)

In the late 1890s the Rathmines township began dumping refuse in a disused quarry on the north bank of the River Dodder beyond Strand Terrace in Milltown village (Map 18).[59] This increased the traffic of heavily laden horse-drawn carts through a densely inhabited area, which tragically led to three separate fatal accidents involving children in August 1899, August 1900 and October 1902.[60] The practice of dumping refuse in Milltown ceased when the Rathmines and Rathgar UDC bought a refuse destructor in 1904.[61]

The sample of activities undertaken by the Rathmines township described above illustrates the gradual increase in the influence of municipal governance on the inhabitants of Milltown over a 20-year period from the townland's incorporation into the Rathmines township in 1880. By the turn of the twentieth century the cost of local government in the township had escalated due to (among other things) increasing payroll costs, legal expenses and interest payable on infrastructure loans. By 1902 the ordinary and special rates for the Milltown district totalled 10*s*. 1*d*. in the pound, an extremely high level of local taxation particularly for the poorer ratepayers of the locality.[62]

59 Recital in a 35-year lease held by Mathew O'Neill of Milltown: RD 1897/47/173; *Rathmines News*, 8 August 1896, p. 3.

60 *Rathmines News*, 12 August 1899, p. 4; 26 August 1899, p. 5; 21 October 1899, p. 5; 4 August 1900, p. 5; 4 October 1902, p. 4.

61 *Rathmines News*, 5 March 1904, p. 3. In 1899 the township was reconstituted as an urban district council under the Local Government (Ireland) Act 1898.

62 *Freeman's Journal*, 16 January 1899, p. 6; *Rathmines News*, 10 May 1902, p. 4.

THE DUBLIN LAUNDRY COMPANY

The foundation of a modern steam laundry in Milltown in 1887 by Thomas Edmondson has been expertly detailed by the late social historian, Mona Hearn.[63] What follows here is a very short examination of the establishment of the Dublin Laundry Company, its impact on the lives of the people of Milltown, and how it transformed their material prosperity.

Thomas Edmondson was an English-born Quaker who came to Ireland in 1858 and subsequently worked in the Manor Mill laundry in Dundrum, which had been set up by his older brother Hewetson Edmondson. Hewetson Edmondson died in 1867 following which Thomas entered into a partnership arrangement with his sister-in-law to run the laundry.[64] Twenty years later Thomas Edmondson was forced out of the Manor Mill Laundry by his unscrupulous nephew George Edmondson, who took advantage of legal flaws in the partnership deeds. This forced Thomas to set up his own laundry business. In this regard the availability of the derelict Gibney flour mills at Milltown beside the Dodder at the railway viaduct was fortuitous (Pl. 20). Edmondson purchased the premises in 1887 and set about converting them into a modern steam laundry with the aid of financial investment from the Quaker community, who were appalled at Thomas's treatment at the hands of his nephew, and who considered Thomas Edmondson to be a better, more experienced businessman.[65] Thomas Edmondson felt the need to inform the public of his change of circumstances and so he inserted the following notice in the *Irish Times* in 1888:

> *An Important Explanation. Thomas Edmondson thinks it desirable to inform his friends and the public that he has now no connection with 'The Manor Mill Laundry.' From shortly after the decease of his brother, Hewetson Edmondson, in 1867, up to July last he [Thomas] acted as managing partner in that concern, but left it owing to the partnership deeds under which he worked for nearly 20 years being found to be invalid. He is now managing director of The Dublin Laundry Company Limited, Milltown, County Dublin, the best equipped public laundry in Ireland.*[66]

The flawed partnership deeds at the Manor Mill laundry obviously did not contain any restrictive clauses to prevent Edmondson from opening a laundry two miles away from the Manor Mill or from soliciting its clients. In contrast, Edmondson ensured that his employees' contracts contained a very restrictive covenant which prevented the employee, on leaving employment with the Dublin Laundry Company, from working in any laundry business in the province of Leinster.[67]

At the beginning the laundry had a workforce of 18 but the business expanded rapidly so that by 1905 it employed over 300 people.[68] In the intervening period the Dublin Laundry Company had in 1895 bought the disused Dartry mills which were fitted up for dyeing, dry cleaning and carpet cleaning, at a cost of £3,000. The improvements included the installation of electric light.[69]

63 Mona Hearn, *Thomas Edmondson and the Dublin Laundry: A Quaker Businessman 1837–1908* (Dublin, 2004).

64 Hearn, *Thomas Edmondson*, pp. 14, 18–19, 25. The plaza and pond in front of the north entrance to the Dundrum shopping centre occupies the site of the Manor Mill laundry.

65 Hearn, *Thomas Edmondson*, pp. 21–5.

66 *Irish Times*, 2 March 1888, p. 1.

67 Hearn, *Thomas Edmondson*, p. 75.

68 *Dublin Daily Express*, 9 September 1905, p. 8.

69 *Dublin Daily Express*, 14 June 1895, p. 1.

Plate 21. Dinner hour at the Dublin Laundry Company, Milltown, c. 1910 (courtesy of Mary Long)

When Edmondson acquired the flourmill complex it contained two back-to-back houses which had formerly been occupied by the manager of the mills. The oldest house faced the entrance gate to the laundry and was called Tinnamullen (the house by the mill). This house is visible in the background of a postcard of laundry girls by the entrance gate which dates from about 1910 (Pl. 21). The house was obviously old by 1900 as it had sash windows of 12 panes, a high-pitched roof with a dormer window and irregular chimney stacks. This building probably dated from the 1760s when John Classon developed the mill complex (see Chapter 6). The second house was built onto the rear of Tinnamullen by the Gibneys sometime between 1850 and 1878 and was called Shanagarry (the old garden), the name given to the apartment complex that occupies the site now.[70] Thomas Edmondson and his wife Anne, who were childless, lived in Shanagarry from 1887 to 1898 after which they rented a large detached house on Temple Road called Thorndale from Mrs Henshaw of St Philip's.[71]

In 1891 Thomas Edmondson specifically recruited a Church of Ireland widow called Jemima McCleery to act as manager of the laundry and its expanding female staff.[72] Mrs McCleery and her adult children Hugh and Kate lived in Tinnamullen. According to the 1901 census taken on

70 Shanagarry is not depicted on the Valuation Office town plan of Milltown of *c.* 1850 (Map 16b) but the house is shown on a later OS map of 1882 (Map 18) where it is slightly offset to the rear of the older, eighteenth-century structure of Tinnamullen.

71 Hearn, *Thomas Edmondson*, pp. 42, 43, 61, 137.

72 Hearn, *Thomas Edmondson*, pp. 73–4.

31 March, thirty-two-year-old Kate was employed as a governess while her brother Hugh was employed in the laundry as an engineer and steam laundry. Both siblings had been born in East India although their mother was a native of Strokestown, County Roscommon. The McCleerys employed a Catholic servant, twenty-five-year-old Bridget Ryan, to look after their domestic needs at Tinnamullen.[73] In December of the same year the workers presented Mrs McCleery with gifts of a gold bracelet, a silver-backed mirror and a silver and tortoiseshell comb to mark their esteem on her completion of 10 years' service with the company. The local newspaper, the *Rathmines News*, reported on the occasion:

> *The gift came as a surprise, not only to Mrs McCleery, but also to the other heads of the establishment, as it was desired that it should be a spontaneous expression of goodwill from the workers themselves, who have always felt that though a strict disciplinarian, Mrs McCleery was fair and just, and in any real trouble could be relied upon for assistance and sympathy. The proceedings were opened by the Dublin Laundry Company's Choral Society, who gave a part song in excellent style, and then the managing director (Mr Thomas Edmondson) made the presentation on behalf of the workers, of whom there were about 300 present, accompanying the gift with a few felicitous words indicative of the cordial relations that had existed between Mrs McCleery and both employer and employees for the past ten years, and hoping for their long continuance.*[74]

The newspaper report did not reveal the true picture about the enforcement of discipline among the workers at the laundry. Money was deducted from employees' wages for various offences such as bad time keeping, talking or singing, careless or bad work or damage to linen. Some of these deductions were found by the Inspector of Factories in 1909 to be contrary to law, including fines imposed for impertinence by employees.[75]

When the Edmondsons moved out of Shanagarry in 1898 the house became the home of the Waring family.[76] Henry Waring was the head mechanical engineer and was in charge of the machinery at Dublin Laundry Company at Milltown. In 1901 forty-five-year-old Henry and his forty-three-year-old wife Kate, both of whom were Quakers from Wexford and Waterford respectively, were living at Shanagarry with their nine-year-old son Noel and their Catholic domestic servant, a thirty-six-year-old native of Wexford.[77] Aside from looking after the boilers and all of the specialist machinery of a modern steam laundry, Waring was also responsible for the company's fleet of Daimler laundry vans which were used to collect and deliver laundry to towns within a radius of about 30 miles of Dublin, stretching from Ashford to the south to Trim in the north, and as far west as Newbridge.[78] The laundry vans (Pl. 63) were the first internal combustion engine vehicles in Milltown when they appeared on the roads in 1901.

Henry Waring supported various charities. On 17 January 1903 he hosted a ping-pong tournament with valuable prizes at Shanagarry to raise funds for the Milltown, Clonskeagh and Dundrum Nursing

73 NAI, 1901 Census, Form A, residents of house no. 99 (Tinnamullen), Milltown Road, Rathmines and Rathgar East Electoral Division, Milltown Townland, Barony of Uppercross, Co. Dublin.

74 *Rathmines News*, 28 December 1901, p. 5.

75 Hearn, *Thomas Edmondson*, pp. 75–6.

76 Hearn, *Thomas Edmondson*, p. 136.

77 NAI, 1901 Census, Form A, residents of house no. 103 (Shanagarry), Milltown Road, Rathmines and Rathgar East Electoral Division, Milltown townland, Dublin.

78 Hearn, *Thomas Edmondson, p. 94; Irish Independent*, 17 September 1901, p. 4.

Plate 63. Van boys at the Dublin Laundry Company, Milltown c.1920 (courtesy of Mary Long)

Association.[79] Two years later in January 1905 an informal gathering of supporters of the 'Stewart Institution for Imbecile Children' was held in Shanagarry and a concert in aid of the Temperance Bazaar.[80] Henry Waring left employment with the Dublin Laundry Company in 1908 to set up his own consultancy business for steam laundry operators.[81] Following the Warings departure Hugh McCleery moved into Shanagarry with his new bride Kathleen Manion, a Catholic from Kilmainham. Hugh and Kathleen's marriage was solemnised in a registry office on 19 August 1908.[82] The reason for this is unclear but it may indicate that either one family was not happy with the mixed marriage or there was an impediment to a Church ceremony. Hugh McCleery was a qualified engineer but on the 1911 census he described himself as a laundry manager. By that time Hugh and Kathleen had a one-year-old infant daughter, Evelyn, who was being raised as a Catholic. The McCleery couple employed a Catholic domestic servant from Limerick, twenty-one-year-old Christina Quinn.[83]

Jemima McCleery continued to live in Tinnamullen with her daughter Kate. As a member of the senior staff, Mrs McCleery was well remunerated by Thomas Edmondson. In 1909, by which time

79 *Rathmines News*, 17 January 1903, p. 3.

80 *Rathmines News*, 21 January 1905, p. 2.

81 *Irish Times*, 4 July 1908, p. 1.

82 Civil registration of marriages, City of Dublin, 19 August 1908, entry no. 78.

83 NAI, 1911 Census, Form A, residents of house no. 41 (Shanagarry), Milltown Road, Rathmines and Rathgar East Electoral Division, Milltown Townland, Barony of Uppercross, Co. Dublin.

Mrs McCleery had accrued 17 years of service with the laundry, her annual salary was £208, a considerable sum given that the salary for a dispensary doctor was £120.[84] By 1911 Mrs McCleery's domestic servant Bridget Ryan had been replaced by a fifty-eight-year-old spinster, a Quaker woman called Bessie Neale from County Laois. Bessie had previously worked as Thomas Edmondson's housekeeper prior to his death in 1908. She was now described more genteelly as a 'lady help'.[85]

Thomas Edmondson preferred to employ workers who lived close to the laundry because of the long hours required of them. Work began at 8 a.m. every morning apart from Mondays which began at 9 a.m. Hearn has carried out a detailed analysis of the 1901 and 1911 census returns and uncovered at least 220 people in 1911 living locally in Milltown, Classon's Bridge, Farranboley, Windy Arbour and Rosemount (Dundrum) who were employed as laundry workers. Most of these people worked in the Dublin Laundry Company in Milltown while the others, probably those living at Rosemount, worked at the Manor Mill laundry in Dundrum. In Concrete there were 46 women and nine men employed in the laundry according to the 1911 census returns. Virtually all of the operative employees were Catholics but the foremen and forewomen were Episcopalians.[86]

During the course of her research Hearn investigated in detail the wages paid to the employees and concluded that on the whole, the employees were fairly paid but never generously so.[87] As was the norm in Victorian times, very unequal treatment in pay rates applied between the sexes and between operatives and managerial staff. Wage rates and grades also varied considerably depending on the age and experience of the employee and the skills required for a particular task. For example, in 1895 there were only two women who earned 16*s.* a week, which was the minimum weekly wage rate for men. In the same year, the largest number of women received weekly wages of between 8*s.* and 8*s.* 6*d.*, remuneration which remained largely unchanged until the First World War.[88] In a gesture that might be regarded as cynical (perhaps unfairly given Edmondson's Quaker credentials), the staff were in 1897 given a presentation, called a 'thrift chat', and provided with literature advising them how to manage their wages.[89] In 1913 the company advertised for a competent millwright with knowledge of laundry machinery who was required to 'take charge of [a] large plant' at a weekly wage of £2.[90] By 1919 the effects of wartime inflation had caused the Dublin Laundry Company's annual wage bill to reach £15,000.[91] The impact of this money in the local economy of Milltown, where it was spent on rent, food, drink and social pastimes cannot be overestimated.

In spite of the modest wage rates available for the majority of the employees it must be noted that many households in Milltown had more than one family member working in the laundry.[92]

---

84 Hearn, *Thomas Edmondson*, p. 74.

85 NAI, 1911 Census, Form A, residents of house no. 40 (Tinnamullen), Milltown Road, Rathmines and Rathgar East Electoral Division, Milltown Townland, Barony of Uppercross, Co. Dublin; Hearn, *Thomas Edmondson*, pp. 155, 159. Bessie Neale was bequeathed a legacy of £50 from Edmondson.

86 Hearn, *Thomas Edmondson*, pp. 60–1.

87 Hearn, *Thomas Edmondson*, pp. 70, 73, 156.

88 Hearn, *Thomas Edmondson*, pp. 70–2.

89 *Dublin Daily Express*, 6 November 1897, p. 3.

90 *Belfast Newsletter*, 18 June 1913, p. 2.

91 *Evening Herald*, 10 March 1920, p. 2.

92 Hearn, *Thomas Edmondson*, p. 61.

At a time of chronic underemployment among Dublin's unskilled labouring classes a family was considered fortunate to have more than one regular wage earner employed in a steady job. This created an imbalance of power in the employer-employee relationship, which the following incident illustrates. In September 1904 the father of a girl employed by the laundry, John Donnelly, got into a row with the company over a letter of complaint which the laundry had allegedly written to him about his daughter. However, the laundry told Donnelly that they had no complaint about his daughter and denied having anything to do with the letter he had received. Furthermore, the company threatened Donnelly that, 'if Miss Perry, or anyone here, is further annoyed by you on this matter, we shall be obliged to discharge your daughter, as to put an end to the unpleasantness'.[93]

John Donnelly, who was described in the census return of 1911 as a general labourer, swallowed his pride and let the matter drop. Donnelly (forty-eight), his wife Eliza (forty-six), and their five children, four of whom were by that stage employed by the laundry, were living in a small four-roomed cottage in Milltown village. The two eldest girls Mary (twenty-two) and Catherine (twenty-one) worked as ironers while their brothers John (seventeen) and James (fifteen) worked as a van driver and van boy respectively. The eldest son, Joseph (eighteen), earned a meagre living as a garden labourer.[94]

Notwithstanding the unpleasant episode with John Donnelly, credit must be given to Thomas Edmondson for the occasions on which he intervened with the authorities on behalf of his employees. In August 1903 Edmondson wrote to the Superintendent at Donnybrook police station as follows:

> *We have to call your attention to the rowdyism which so often prevails in the streets of Milltown at night. One of our employees, Mrs Breen, who lives in the corner cottage next to the bridge, opposite to Mrs Henshaw's gate, is very frequently annoyed by stones being thrown at her door, and in other ways. This was going on last evening from 11 pm to 1 am, and we think it strange that this should have been allowed without any police interference. I shall be very much obliged if you can take stringent measures to repress this sort of thing in our neighbourhood.*[95]

At the time, Edmondson was vice-chairman of the Rathmines and Rathgar UDC so his intervention should have been taken seriously by the police.[96] The problem of antisocial behaviour in Milltown did not abate, for three years later Thomas Edmondson, who by then was chairman of the Rathmines township commissioners, felt compelled to write to the Inspector of the RIC in Dundrum in the following terms:

> *I write to ask you to kindly give your special attention to the rowdyism that too often prevails in Milltown, especially on the county side of the river. Within the last week or two, stones have been thrown and windows broken in the houses of two of our tenants, namely, Mr Cosgrave, who has the shop at the corner [of Bankside Cottages and the Dundrum Road] and our foreman, Mr Taylor, of Bankside Cottages. It appears to me absolutely necessary that there should be one or two of the police constantly on duty at night in that neighbourhood, and perhaps you will allow me to suggest that you might arrange for co-operation with the Dublin Metropolitan Police for the thorough supervision of the whole village of Milltown. I am sure you will do your best in the matter.*[97]

---

93 NAI, Dublin Business Records, Dublin 56, Dublin Laundry Company, letter book 1902–09, p. 595, 22 September 1904.

94 NAI, 1911 Census, Form A and Form B 1, residents of house no. 22, Milltown Road, Rathmines and Rathgar East Electoral Division, Milltown Townland, Barony of Uppercross, Co. Dublin.

95 NAI, Dublin Business Records, Dublin 56, Dublin Laundry Company, letter book 1902–09, 26 August 1903 (see Map 16b, plot 57).

96 Hearn, *Thomas Edmondson*, p. 153.

97 NAI, Dublin Business Records, Dublin 56, Dublin Laundry Company, letter book 1902–09, 13 November 1906; Hearn, *Thomas Edmondson*, p. 153.

If junior staff had cause to grumble about their wages – indeed, one employee was dismissed for what, in Edmondson's view, was the impertinence of looking for an unacceptably high wage increase – there were considerable perks to compensate.[98] Employees could bring their own washing into work and have it cleaned for a nominal sum.[99] The staff were also supplied with uniforms and hot meals.[100] On the social side, the company arranged for a tea and garden party for 150 employees in July 1890, in preparation for which Thomas Edmondson had to ask Rev. Moffatt of St Philip's church if he could borrow some church pews for the occasion.[101] The employees formed a choral society with a musical director and by 1902 the laundry choir was sufficiently accomplished to be invited to take part in the Feis Ceoil week in 1902.[102]

Edmondson was concerned about the health of his workers and he ensured that any sick or injured employee was treated in hospital at the company's expense.[103] In January 1899 the company's altruism was extended to the wider community, as an editorial in the *Rathmines News* reported to its readers:

> *We have pleasure in stating that, having regard to the wants of poor people in the district who are unable to pay a professional nurse in times of sickness, the Dublin Laundry Company Limited have engaged a trained nurse who will attend, subject to doctor's orders, not only the company's own employees but any other persons who may require her services. The district in which this trained nurse will be employed embraces Milltown, Clonskeagh, Windy Arbour, Rosemount and Dundrum. Applications for the services of the nurse may be sent in care of the Dublin Laundry Company Limited addressed to 'The District Nurse,' who will practice under the rules of the Jubilee Association, which strictly forbid her to interfere in any way with the religious opinions of patients or their families.*[104]

Shortly afterwards a Jubilee Nurse was appointed as the district nurse and towards the end of November 1899 she reported to the newly formed Milltown, Clonskeagh and Dundrum Nursing Association that over the previous ten months she had made 2,097 house calls to 172 different patients. The new association was run by a committee made up of local middle-class women, with Miss Victoria Henshaw of St Philip's acting as secretary and Thomas Edmondson acting as president and treasurer. Thomas Edmondson had generously borne the initial 12 months' expenses incurred by his community health initiative, which amounted to about £100 per annum, but in future the wealthier residents of the district were expected to contribute to the expenses of maintaining the district nurse.[105] Thus, for the year ending June 1903 the nursing association managed to raise over £99 through local subscriptions, to which was added £17 17*s.* 6*d.*, the proceeds of a highly successful concert organised by Mrs McCleery.[106]

98 Hearn, *Thomas Edmondson*, pp. 74–5.

99 Hearn, *Thomas Edmondson*, p. 77.

100 Hearn, *Thomas Edmondson*, pp. 76–7, 84.

101 NAI, Business Records, Dublin 56, Dublin Laundry Company, letter book 1887–95, p. 57, 5 July 1890.

102 Hearn, *Thomas Edmondson*, pp. 83–4; NAI, Business Records, Dublin 56, Dublin Laundry Company, letter look 1895–-1902, p. 822, 7 April 1902.

103 Hearn, *Thomas Edmondson*, pp. 77–80.

104 *Rathmines News*, 7 January 1899, p. 4.

105 *Rathmines News*, 25 November 1899, p. 4; 19 May 1900, p. 5; *Freeman's Journal*, 22 November 1899, p. 2.

106 *Rathmines News*, 6 June 1903, p. 3.

It was the provision of workmen's houses that bestowed the greatest credit on Thomas Edmondson. In March 1894, less than five years after setting up business in Milltown, Edmondson wrote to the Rathmines township commissioners to see if they would consider building labourers' cottages at Milltown. Unfortunately for his workforce, Edmondson's approach was poorly timed as the commissioners were preoccupied with building houses for the working-classes at Gullistan in Rathmines, and they did not respond to his request.[107] Having failed to elicit help from the township's commissioners a few months later Edmondson approached his neighbours at Nullamore (Edmund Johnson) and South Hill (J.F. Lombard) to see if they would be willing to sell a small strip of their respective landholdings between the main road and the River Dodder for labourers' cottages.[108] His neighbours did not respond so Edmondson sent a reminder letter two years later and appealed (unsuccessfully) to Johnson in the following terms:

> *I have been waiting now for a very long time to hear from you about the strip of land. Our poor neighbours around us are miserably housed when many of them would gladly pay a little more for better accommodation. Is it not our duty, when we are living in our own comfortable houses, to do what we can for the benefit of those less fortunate ones?*[109]

The failure to get any support for building labourers' cottages, either from the township commissioners or from his neighbours, undoubtedly influenced Edmondson's decision in 1898 to purchase Millmount Lodge with its ground fronting the Dundrum Road. Initially, Millmount was converted into a hostel to accommodate employees but in 1903 Thomas Edmondson let Millmount to the Ryan family, who lived there for several years during which time the house was renamed Clonbeg.[110]

Not long after taking possession of Millmount Edmondson demolished what was left of the derelict mill premises opposite the Packhorse Bridge and built four terraced houses on the site for his employees. These houses form part of the terrace now called Bankside Cottages.[111] Around the same time Edmondson contacted the guardians of the Rathdown Union and Dublin Corporation to arrange the installation of a public water fountain at Concrete, for which he paid £6 to the guardians, and to supply two of his tenants' cottages in Farranboley with Vartry water.[112] In 1903 the Dublin Laundry Company began building several terraced houses for their employees on the grounds of Millmount along the Dundrum Road as far as Windy Arbour. These houses are still standing and are called Coolnahinch and Millmount Terrace (Map 21).[113]

Thomas Edmondson died on 11 February 1908 unexpectedly while on holidays in South Amer-

107 NAI, Business Records, Dublin 56, Dublin Laundry Company, letter book 1895–1902, 13 March 1898; Dublin City Archives, Rathmines and Rathgar UDC papers, UDC/1/Min 1/7, 1893–1902, minutes of meeting 4 April 1894. The meeting did not even record the receipt of Edmondson's letter.

108 NAI, Business Records, Dublin 56, Dublin Laundry Company, letter book 1895–1902, 24 and 28 August 1894.

109 NAI, Business Records, Dublin 56, Dublin Laundry Company, letter book 1895–1902, 28 August 1896.

110 Hearn, *Thomas Edmondson*, pp. 80–1; NAI, 1901 Census, Form A, return for house no. 20 (Millmount house), Dundrum Road, Dundrum Electoral Division, Parish of Taney, Farranboley townland, Dublin; NAI, Dublin Business Records, Dublin 56, Dublin Laundry Company, letter book 1902–09, p. 174, 16 February 1906.

111 Hearn, *Thomas Edmondson*, p. 81.

112 Rathdown Poor Law Union, Board of Guardians Minute Book A111 March–September 1898, Folio 17, p. 665, 28 September 1898, Book A112 March 1898–March 1899, Folio 16, p. 16, 5 October 1898; NAI, Business Records, Dublin 56, Dublin Laundry Company, letter book 1895–1902, 25 July 1998, 11 October 1898.

113 Hearn, *Thomas Edmondson*, pp. 80–2; Rathmines News, 5 September 1903, p. 4; 2 January 1904, p. 2.

Plate 22. Aerial view of the Dublin Laundry Company premises at Milltown, c. 1950 (courtesy of the National Archives of Ireland)

ica, less than a year after his wife Anne's death.[114] Although Edmondson should be credited for bringing lasting material benefits to Milltown, it is striking that his biographer, Mona Hearn, does not appear to have warmed to Edmondson, and was critical of shortcomings in his personality and social attitudes:

> *Thomas was exacting in his expectations of others, and did not readily make allowances for differences in circumstances. While he would have affirmed his belief in the equality of all, men and women, and always tried to be just in his dealings with others, his attitudes often reflected those of his class. He seemed to regard the lower classes, to which the majority of his workers belonged, with a certain amount of suspicion, which may have been partly due to their being Irish and Catholic. He lacked empathy with those outside his own social class and experience. Whereas he was invariably courteous to employees of his own class, nationality and creed, communications with others could be peremptory and brusque. While his treatment of those considered his inferiors, in the rigidly structured society of the day, was tempered by the Quaker philosophy, he was a product of his time. Remarks made about workers often reflected this, and he obviously felt that a strong hand and extreme vigilance were necessary to ensure that they gave of their best.*[115]

After Edmondson's death the laundry business was taken over by a relative, Robert Benson, who had joined the company in 1897 and who now became managing director.[116] Benson seems to

114 Hearn, *Thomas Edmondson*, p. 155.

115 Hearn, *Thomas Edmondson*, pp. 158–9.

116 Hearn, *Thomas Edmondson*, pp. 103–4, 177.

have been a more progressive individual than his predecessor. In February 1914 Benson permitted one of the office staff in the Milltown laundry to give a talk to the entire staff about her visit to Lourdes. After the lecture, which was illustrated with 60 lantern slides, two of the longest-serving employees presented Benson with a solid silver vase. The local priest, Fr Keane, was also present and he contributed a recitation, which was much appreciated.[117] All this took place at the height of the Home Rule crisis when political and religious tensions were running high, yet Benson had the magnanimity and emotional intelligence to maintain good relationships with his staff and the wider community in Milltown.

The laundry business survived the tumultuous decade of world war, revolution and civil war, and following these, the depression of the 1930s and the Second World War. By the 1950s the Dublin Laundry Company's complex at Milltown had increased enormously (Pl. 22). Ultimately, commercial laundry businesses began to decline from the 1960s onwards with the increasing use of the domestic washing machine. In January 1983 the Revenue Commissioners registered a judgement for over £86,000 against the Dublin Laundry Company for unpaid taxes. How this situation arose is unknown but it dealt a critical blow to the business and caused the company to go into voluntary liquidation six months later. The liquidator put up the derelict laundry complex at Milltown for sale by public tender on 21 March 1985. None of the press reports mentioned how many jobs were lost.[118]

COMPETITION FOR ROAD SPACE - HORSES, CARS, BICYCLES AND STEAM ENGINES

The expansion of Dublin's suburbia in Rathmines and Ranelagh in the third quarter of the nineteenth century led to a major increase in the amount and variety of vehicular traffic using the roads around Milltown, as well as the laying down of the electric tramway system terminating in Clonskeagh and Dartry. During the Edwardian era, the risk of accidents increased with the arrival of the motor car and the bicycle.

People driving horse-drawn vehicles such as coaches, vans, drays and floats were at greatest risk due to the increased likelihood of their horse taking fright in the face of an unfamiliar object or noise. The *Rathmines News* published numerous reports of such incidents during its brief period of publication from 1896–1907. Under the arresting heading 'Exciting Runaway at Milltown' a journalist for that newspaper reported how one evening in April 1901 Count and Madame Plunkett were proceeding along Sandford Road in their carriage towards Clonskeagh when their horse took fright at a passing van and dashed off out of control. DMP Constable Crosbie, who happened to be on duty at the crossroads at the Sandford Road and Milltown Road junction, managed to catch hold of the runaway horse and bring the carriage to a halt. Madame Plunkett, who had fainted from her frightening ordeal, was brought into the house at the corner of Milltown Road and Clonskeagh Road, no. 1 St James's Terrace, where she was soon restored to consciousness.[119] Not so lucky was delivery van driver James O'Keeffe. O'Keeffe was driving his van along Richmond Avenue South when his horse took fright at a passing train and bolted out of control. James was thrown from his van and suffered a fractured leg when the wheel ran over it. The runaway horse was eventually stopped at Temple Gardens.[120]

Drivers in charge of horse-drawn vehicles in the nineteenth century were prosecuted for speeding, which is hard to imagine in the twenty-first century. Speeding offences were prosecuted under

---

117 *Dublin Evening Mail*, 23 February 1914, p. 6.

118 *Irish Press*, 28 January 1983, p. 6; *Irish Independent*, 28 January 1983, p. 4; 8 June 1983, p. 19; 1 March 1985, p. 25.

119 *Rathmines News*, 27 April 1901, p. 5.

120 *Rathmines News*, 18 June 1904, p. 3.

the offence of 'furious driving'. On Sunday 11 March 1900, carman Peter Toner was summoned by District Inspector Toppin to appear at the Dundrum petty sessions on a charge of furious driving. Toner did not appear in court, but the Inspector told the court that he saw a car (i.e. a horse-drawn cart) being driven furiously down Milltown Hill by Toner pursuing a man on a bicycle. In his absence, Toner was fined 10*s*. and costs, the indignant magistrate remarking that such conduct was disgraceful as peoples' lives were endangered.[121]

A much more unusual incident occurred in 1903 at Windy Arbour. Hugh O'Rourke was driving a large steam (traction) engine on the Dundrum Road. As required by law, O'Rourke was accompanied by a flagman who was required by law to walk 60 yards ahead of the vehicle and signal to the driver to stop if a horse became frightened at the vehicle's approach. A Colonel Thomas testified to the Dundrum magistrates at the local petty sessions that the flagman was only 15 or 20 yards away from the steam engine, which O'Rourke failed to stop as it approached Thomas's horse-drawn carriage, narrowly avoiding a serious accident. The result was that the owner of the steam engine, Charles Thompson, a previous resident of Vergemount House, Clonskeagh was summoned to court by head constable Plunkett and fined 10*s*. plus costs for breaching the road traffic legislation.[122] The Dundrum police were right to prosecute Thompson for the lax behaviour of his employees. Two years previously, Thompson's steam engine had been involved in a freak accident when the driver ran over and decapitated a man lying on the road in total darkness in the Glen of the Downs early one January morning. The unfortunate victim was suspected of having been in a drunken stupor when he was killed.[123]

A non-fatal accident with a much more modern ring to it involving a bicycle and a motor car occurred at the increasingly busy four-way junction of Sandford Road/Eglinton Road/Clonskeagh Road/Milltown Road on 30 July 1907. In this case, a Ms Norah Phelan of Clonskeagh sued Major A.W. Clarke for £25 for personal injuries and damages, caused by the defendant's motor car knocking her down. Needless to say, the witnesses contradicted each other's evidence completely. Norah Phelan told the court that she was cycling from Clonskeagh to Ranelagh when Major Clarke dashed out in his motor around the corner of Milltown Road and Eglinton Road. She said he was on the wrong side of the road and collided with the back wheel of her bicycle knocking her down. For his part, Major Clarke denied he was on the wrong side of the road; he said he sounded his horn two or three times and Miss Phelan was swerving here and there on her bicycle. The major's passenger and a bystander supported his version of events. In contrast, the plaintiff's case was also supported by an independent witness, Harry L'Estrange of Eglinton Road, who corroborated Phelan's evidence and said that Clarke had not sounded his horn. No medical evidence was mentioned in the press report so it must not have been presented in court even though Miss Phelan was seeking damages for personal injuries. The judge hearing the case then told the parties that he would prefer if they could settle the case because he did not wish to decide it on the conflicting testimony of the defendant and Harry L'Estrange, whose father he knew very well. At this prompting the parties and their legal teams retired and a settlement was subsequently reached whereby Major Clarke agreed to pay Ms Phelan £6 6*s*., and the case was struck out by consent.[124] For the sake of comparison, a contemporary advertisement in the

121 *Rathmines News*, 13 March 1900, p. 5.

122 *Rathmines News*, 9 May 1903, p. 2; *Freeman's Journal*, 12 May 1893, p. 3; 3 January 1901, p. 2.

123 *Kerry Sentinel*, 23 January 1901, p. 3.

124 *Rathmines News*, 16 January 1907, p. 4; NAI, 1901 Census, Form A, residents of house no. 46 on Eglinton Road, Pembroke West Electoral Division, Parish of Donnybrook.

Rathmines News by a bike shop offered bicycles at prices starting at £5 10*s*. or monthly repayments of 8*s*. 8*d*.[125] Thus Norah Phelan's settlement sum would have paid for a new bicycle with little left over, a far cry from her original damages claim for £25. It is worth observing that in the Edwardian era bicycles were unaffordable for working-class men and women and they do not feature in the lives of Milltown's working class at this time.[126]

THE GROWTH OF ORGANISED SPORT AND RECREATIONAL ACTIVITIES

The impact of recreational sport and outdoor activities on the physical landscape and the social history of Milltown since the late nineteenth century has been enormous. Indeed, sport in the form of Shamrock Rovers Football Club (FC) and Milltown Golf Club brought Milltown to the wider public's consciousness from 1923 and 1907 respectively. For the purpose of this history, the activities of other sports and social clubs that established themselves in Milltown at the end of the nineteenth century deserve to be mentioned, albeit very briefly due to space constraints.

The increase in the middle class in the nineteenth century created spare time which became available for recreation in the Victorian era. This led to a growth in organised sports with formal rules, clubs and governing bodies. Initially, these clubs catered for the upper and professional classes, and almost exclusively for men. Probably the earliest formal sporting event to take place under these new conditions was a cricket matched played between Roebuck and a scratch team from Trinity College in the grounds of Casino (Emmet House) on Bird Avenue in July 1862. According to the newspaper report, unfavourable weather brought the game to a premature conclusion.[127] Sometime between 1858 and 1879 the Jesuits built a handball alley on their grounds at Milltown Park behind Milltown Colonnade (Map 17). This structure survived intact until the 1980s when it was demolished.[128]

The increasing expansion of Dublin's suburbs beyond the canals and the setting up of independent townships populated by the middle classes also created demand for playing pitches on undeveloped land close by. The Henshaw family of St Philip's (now Alexandra College) were among the group of early enthusiasts of women's hockey and as a result Alexandra College adopted the fields behind St Philip's beside the railway line on Richmond Avenue South as their home ground in the early 1890s. On 2 March 1896 the first ladies' international hockey match to be played in Ireland was played against England at St Philip's, with Miss F. Henshaw selected for Ireland. In the previous year, the first ladies' international between the two nations had been played in England and had ended in a draw. The international match at Milltown took place in front of a very fashionable gathering, which Ireland won two goals to nil.[129] By the turn of the twentieth century a men's hockey team called the Milltown Magpies were featuring in the middle league, along with Palmerston, at Milltown.[130] Short film clips of hockey matches at Milltown in the 1920s and 1930s are available on the British Pathé website.[131] Hockey has been played uninterrupted at Milltown for over a 126 years – a remarkable sporting continuity – thanks to the Henshaws and Alexandra College.

---

125 *Rathmines News*, 9 March 1907, p. 1.

126 Casual labourer Hugh Doyle of Milltown earned weekly wages of 17*s*. 9*d*: *Rathmines News*, 25 June 1906, p. 4.

127 *Saunders's Newsletter*, 9 July 1862, p. 2.

128 Author's recollection.

129 *Rathmines News*, 29 February 1896, *Dublin Daily Express*, 20 February 1896, p7, 2 March 1896, pp 4,7; Anita Manning, 'The First 100 Years: A history of Irish hockey' in the *Programme for the 8th Women's Hockey World Cup held in UCD*, 1994, pp. 79–81.

130 *Freeman's Journal*, 6 January 1902, p. 7.

131 https://www.britishpathe.com/video/hockey-week/query/hockey+milltown (accessed 3 October 2018).

The grass pitches at Milltown were used for multiple field sports besides hockey. In March 1899 the *Rathmines News* informed its readers that 'the new bicycle polo ground at Milltown will attract a large number of visitors. There are two courts of full size, and play will shortly be commenced.'[132]

It seems that bicycle polo did not take off, for at the start of the 1903/1904 rugby season Palmerston Rugby Club moved to new permanent grounds beside Milltown railway station, at St Philip's. Palmerston RFC remained at the St Philip's grounds until the club moved in the mid-1920s to its penultimate home on Milltown Road beside Prospect Lane, where Millbrook Court and Palmerston Grove are now.[133] On 29 October 1924 the New Zealand 'All Blacks' trained at Palmerston RFC's grounds behind St Philip's on Richmond Avenue South ahead of their international with Ireland, and were photographed by the *Irish Independent.*[134]

The founding of the Gaelic Athletic Association (GAA) in 1884 introduced further sporting options into Irish life which quickly gained in popularity. The first All-Ireland senior football final was played on 29 April 1888 at the grounds of the Benburbs GAA club, which were located off Beaver Row between Clonskeagh and Donnybrook, on land owned by a Clonskeagh dairyman called Corless.[135] The site is commemorated by a plaque at the entrance to the Beech Hill housing estate in Donnybrook. Most of the members of the Benburbs worked in the Henshaw iron mills at Clonskeagh.[136]

Remarkably, Milltown's connections with the GAA predate the first Gaelic football final. On 20 February 1888 the *Freeman's Journal* reported that a Gaelic football game played in Ranelagh between Dauntless and Shelmaliers was refereed by Mr Hackett of Milltown, who 'gave full satisfaction'.[137] Hackett also served on the County Dublin Committee of the GAA for an indeterminate period prior to his resignation in April 1897.[138]

In 1893 Milltown established its own GAA club, which, appropriately enough, was called the Milltown Emmets, in recognition of Robert Emmet's country residence, Casino (Emmet House).[139] The GAA correspondent for the *Irish Independent* was a particular admirer of the Milltown Emmets, and in 1893 he described one of their matches against the Hugh O'Neills club in the following terms:

> *It was one of the very best matches between junior teams that I have ever seen. The Milltown lads played with a free and easy, careless sort of precision that is invariably begot of long and constant training. Yet it cannot have been so, for this club is in existence only a very short time. Judging by the form shown by the juveniles, the First Seventeen must be composed of extra superior footballing material.*[140]

The following year, 1894, the Milltown Emmets won the Dún Laoghaire tournament by beating Shankill Shemaliers in the final.[141] Unfortunately, contemporary newspaper match reports

132 *Rathmines News*, 11 March 1899, p. 4.

133 https://www.dlspfc.ie/about-us/club-history.86.html (accessed 14 April 2015).

134 *Irish Independent, 30 October 1924*, p. 3.

135 *Irish Press, 3 November 1966*, p. 11.

136 Nolan, *Changing Faces*, p. 194.

137 *Freeman's Journal*, 21 February 1888, p. 7.

138 *Freeman's Journal*, 8 April 1897, p. 7.

139 William Nolan (ed.), *The Gaelic Athletic Association in Dublin 1884–2000* (3 vols, Dublin, 2005), iii, p. 1248.

140 *Irish Independent*, 31 October 1893, p. 7.

141 Nolan, *The Gaelic Athletic Association in Dublin*, p. 1248.

of the 1890s do not identify the location of the club's pitches in Milltown. Dublin GAA historians state that the Milltown Emmets grounds were taken over by Shamrock Rovers FC in 1924 at Glenmalure Park, but this assertion is not corroborated by the historians of Shamrock Rovers. When Shamrock Rovers FC was elected to the Leinster Senior League for the 1921/1922 season the club secured the use of a field in Windy Arbour belonging to a farmer, Bernard Rogan, and known locally as 'Rogan's Field'.[142] It is probable that the Milltown Emmets played at Rogan's Field before it was briefly taken over by Shamrock Rovers FC, prior to the soccer club's permanent move to Milltown Road in 1923.

In 1930 junior soccer players from Milltown played in division 3 of the Sunday League. By then they had formed a club called Milltown United, which had its grounds at Classon's Bridge. This short-lived soccer club played against local teams from Windy Arbour, Donnybrook and other parts of south Dublin.[143]

There were alternative activities for those who were not inclined to play team sports. Clonskeagh and Milltown villages were often the point of departure or part of the route for cross country races.[144] In 1889 the County Dublin Harriers advised its members and the public that: 'there will be a run on Saturday next from Milltown to the Meadowbrook course for those members who do not intend competing for the Rowland Cup. 2.30 train, Harcourt Street.'[145]

In the 1890s athletics were held annually in September at Windy Arbour. These were of a much more informal nature and involved local children and adults of all abilities. Aside from the usual disciplines of sprinting, middle-distance running, high jump and shot put, there were tug of war contests which pitted the local Milltown and Windy Arbour teams of 100 stone and 60 stone against competitors from neighbouring villages such as Clonskeagh, Rathfarnham and Harold's Cross.[146] Given that so many men worked in physically demanding manual jobs such as farm labouring and construction, tugs of war were a popular and inexpensive demonstration of physical prowess. More importantly, the Windy Arbour sports days helped to foster community spirit among the villagers and they provided the backdrop to amusing light-hearted incidents which were reported in the local paper from time to time:

> *Great excitement was caused in Milltown on Monday evening. It appears that Mr Mat O'Neill called out the local 'Tug-of-War Team' to remove the root of an ancient sycamore tree which stood for centuries in Elm Hall. The skill displayed by Mr O'Neill in coaching the team was marvellous to behold, so much so, that I would advise the Dublin Metropolitan Police not to lose sight of him in view of the forthcoming military sports. He was very ably assisted by Mr Joseph O'Neill, who, when the team was putting forth its greatest efforts, was seen by them approaching with a half barrel which, at one time contained porter. The root was simply lifted out of the ground in anticipation, when a rush was made for the barrel, but lo! It was empty. For a while the air was blue. At this point Mr Kennedy came on the scene, and by the bare dint of following up Mr O'Neill's tactics, only with more persuasive powers, got the team once more to work as the root had to be moved onto the road. A council of war*

142 Nolan, *The Gaelic Athletic Association in Dublin*, p. 1248; Doolan and Goggins, *The Hoops*, pp. 13–14.

143 *Evening Herald*, 26 April 1930, p. 4, 6 May 1930, p. 8. The club is only mentioned in *Evening Herald* match reports for 1930; however, soccer appears to have been played intermittently at Classon's Bridge since at least 1898: Rathmines News, 9 July 1898, p. 5.

144 *Dublin Daily Express*, 3 December 1886, p. 3; 1 December 1890, p. 6; February 1892, p. 7; *Freeman's Journal*, 6 March 1902, p. 7; 22 December 1904, p. 7.

145 *Dublin Daily Express*, 28 November 1889, p. 21.

146 *Rathmines News*, 18 September 1897, p. 4; 2 October 1897, p. 5; 29 October 1898, p. 4.

was held between 'the boss' and Kennedy as to how the root would be got to its destination, which was negotiated by a float [i.e. a flatbed cart]. The moving of this root must have had a very great interest for the Milltown people, as everyone was at it from the oldest man and woman to the youngest child. Their cheering could be heard for several miles around. I should add that Mr Ned Kane and Mr Tim Fitzpatrick also rendered very valuable aid in the matter.[147]

Much excitement was caused at Milltown on Monday when Mr Laurence O'Rourke of Windy Arbour arrived at the premises of Mr Thomas Murphy, with a large float to claim the prize which he won at the Windy Arbour sports for high jumping. The prize was an enormous pig, valued at £5, which had been fattened for the occasion. A large number of men surrounded the pig to capture it, and after an exciting struggle, the animal was got into the float, amidst great cheering. Mr Murphy wished O'Rourke every success with his prize, and he hoped he would live to win many more.[148]

A more distasteful athleticism in the form of rabbit coursing took place in Windy Arbour in 1897 organised by the Milltown Terrier Coursing Club from its base at the Dew Drop Inn, where 'a good supply of rabbits' could be secured on payment of the entrance fee of 3s.[149]

Reference has been made to the popularity of music and choral singing organised by St Anne's national school and the Dublin Laundry Company. In addition to this predominantly female musical activity, males played in brass and fife bands, which had their origins in the second quarter of the nineteenth century when they became associated with the Fr Mathew temperance society. The popularity of civilian brass bands continued to grow throughout the nineteenth century and by the turn of the twentieth century there were over 20 bands in Dublin alone.[150] Milltown too had its own brass and fife band which can be traced back to 1879.[151] Less than three weeks before he died, Charles Stewart Parnell addressed a large gathering of his supporters in Cabinteely, County Dublin. Among several brass bands which attended the political gathering were bands from Milltown and Dundrum.[152] Nine months later, a public meeting was held in Milltown on 12 June 1892 in support of the Independent Nationalist (Parnellite) candidate for the South Dublin constituency, Dr St Laurence ffrench-Mullen. According to the *Evening Herald*, the presence of bands from Irishtown, Milltown, Dundrum and Rathmines added animation to the demonstration.[153] A Mr J. Walsh represented the St Gall's band at a committee meeting of the organisers of an event called 'Decoration Day' in November 1894. The purpose of this event was for dozens of Dublin's fife and pipe bands to march to Glasnevin cemetery where they would lay wreaths at the graves of Irish patriots.[154] In this way the spirit of Irish patriotism was kept alive in local Dublin communities despite of the divisions in the IPP.

---

147 *Rathmines News*, 15 May 1897, p. 5.

148 *Rathmines News*, 28 October 1899, p. 4.

149 *Irish Independent*, 28 October 1897, p. 1; 29 October 1897, p. 1,14 December 1897, p. 1.

150 Aloys Fleischmann, 'Music and Society' in W.E. Vaughan (ed.), *A new history of Ireland, vi: Ireland under the Union 1870–1921* (Oxford, 1989), pp. 505–6.

151 *The Nation*, 1 February 1879, p. 12.

152 *Freeman's Journal*, 21 September 1891, p. 5.

153 *Evening Herald*, 14 June 1892, p. 2.

154 *Evening Herald*, 24 November 1894, p. 2.

For the next two decades or so, the Milltown brass band would performer regularly at nationalist election rallies in south Dublin. Unfortunately, no information has survived about the members of the band, who held regular practice sessions in a disused mill premises in Windy Arbour.[155] The Milltown band also practised for a time in Old Bridge House beside the Packhorse Bridge on the south bank of the River Dodder.[156]

A branch of the Irish National Foresters' Benefit Society was inaugurated in the Dew Drop Inn, Milltown, on 25 January 1898.[157] This society had been formed in Dublin in 1877 following a split in the Ancient Order of Foresters which was an apolitical, non-sectarian charitable society, whose objects were to pay death benefits and funeral expenses for the poor. In due course the Irish Foresters became highly politicised and members attended patriotic events associated with commemorating the centenary of the 1798 Rebellion and the anniversary of the death of Parnell.[158] It is not surprising therefore that the branch established in Milltown in 1898 was called the United Irishmen branch. According to a newspaper report several nationalistic songs were sung in the Dew Drop Inn as part of the enthusiastic inauguration celebrations:

> *The members who attended the opening were hospitably entertained by Mr Hackett, and the following songs were rendered in capital style: Brother Kirwan sang 'Wolfe tone's Grave', Bother Savage 'Who fears to speak of '98?', Brother Hackett 'A Nation Once again', Brother Keogh recited 'Fontenoy' with fine dramatic effects, and a very enjoyable evening wound up with the singing of 'God Save Ireland' by the company.*[159]

No more information is forthcoming about the Irish National Foresters' Benefit Society's activities in Milltown after the inauguration night because the society's records have not survived, and the contemporary newspapers are silent on the topic. From the description of the entertainment in the Dew Drop Inn it seems doubtful that the poor of Milltown received any material benefits from the Irish National Foresters' Society. In contrast the Milltown tontine society continued to provide mortality benefits irrespective of the arrival of a new benefit society.

THE GAELIC LEAGUE AND THE REVIVAL OF THE IRISH LANGUAGE

The Gaelic League was founded in Dublin in 1893 with the aim of promoting the use of the Irish language. Initially growth in the movement was slow but by the turn of the twentieth century the league began to grow as Irish cultural awareness increased among the general population, enthused by, among other things, the GAA and the centenary celebrations for the 1798 Rebellion. The year 1900 saw a huge upsurge in membership of the league and the founding of over a dozen branches in Dublin alone. Their activities consisted of giving Irish language classes and organising Irish singing and dancing.[160] It was no surprise therefore that a local branch was set up in Milltown on 13 November of that year:

---

155 *Irish Independent*, 14 December 1910, p. 5; *Freeman's Journal*, 14 December 1910, p. 8.

156 *Irish Independent*, 6 February 1952, p. 7.

157 *Irish Independent*, 28 January 1898, p. 6.

158 *Freeman's Journal*, 19 September 1877, p. 2; 28 September 1877, p. 7; 3 October 1877, p. 2; *Irish Times*, 17 July 2017, letters page (David Flood).

159 *Irish Independent*, 28 January 1898, p. 6.

160 Séamas Ó Maitiú, 'A spent force? An Claidheamh Soluis and the Gaelic League in Dublin 1893–1913' in Francis Devine (ed.), *A capital in conflict: Dublin city and the 1913 lock-out* (Dublin, 2013), pp. 281–309.

> *This evening at 8.30 a meeting will be held in the village of Milltown to inaugurate a branch of the Gaelic League. From the promises of support received by the energetic Hon. Secretary, Mr T.P. Hackett, jun., a large influx of members may be expected.*[161]

On 20 December 1900 a large crowd gathered in St Anne's national school for a concert under the auspices of the Donnybrook, Milltown and Dundrum branches of the Gaelic league. This concert had been organised by the Milltown branch of the Gaelic league to benefit the widow and children of a casual labourer, Martin Nolan, who had fallen into the River Dodder and drowned while he was drunk. The relatively expensive prices for admission tickets of one and two shillings reflected the fact that it was a benefit concert. The newspaper report gave a comprehensive list of the Irish songs sung and the jigs danced, including the names of several local participants.[162] One of the Irish teachers was Milltown native Patrick Doyle, who later fought and died in the 1916 Rebellion at Lower Mount Street.[163]

The first suburban Feis Ceoil run by the league took place in Dalkey in 1902 at which participants from Milltown took part, and in the same year it was reported that 30 pupils at St Anne's national school were studying Irish out of a total of 169 children on the rolls.[164] The year 1903 marked the high tide of the Gaelic League's popularity in Dublin. A grand procession through the streets of Dublin was held on 15 March 1903 to open Irish Language Week and among those who took part was T.P. Hackett senior, representing the Board of the Rathdown Guardians.[165] By the end of the year a sub-committee was established to oversee the running of the league's branches in Rathmines, Terenure, Dundrum and Milltown.[166]

The enthusiasm for the Gaelic League was short lived. From about 1905, the league began to decline in Dublin due to a variety of causes, including the monotony of class-work, the failure to progress to conversational Irish, and an excessive emphasis on grammar.[167] That analysis seems to chime with the experience in Milltown as indicated by the fact that only two census forms from Milltown were completed in Irish in 1911 by Tomás Haicead and Ailfrid O' hAirtnéada. Despite the waning of enthusiasm for the Gaelic League, Irish was very much practised and promoted by the nuns at St Anne's national school.[168] In September 1913 several of the Sisters of Charity at Milltown were awarded prizes by the Leinster College of Irish, and in December of that year the nuns hosted an Irish entertainment evening attended by Douglas Hyde who praised the Irish language promotional work done by the school.[169]

In 1908 Patrick Pearse founded St Enda's school in Cullenswood House, a short distance away in Ranelagh. Two years later the school had outgrown that premises so in an ambitious move, Pearse

161 *Irish Independent*, 13 November 1900, p. 2.

162 *Rathmines News*, 24 November 1900, p. 5; 15 December 1900, 29 December 1900, p. 5.

163 Patrick Doyle papers, biographical note by Doyle's granddaughter Mrs May Nolan (NLI, MS 46,594).

164 Ó Maitiú, 'A spent force?', p. 291; *An Claidheamh Soluis*, 11 January 1902, p. 7.

165 *Irish Independent*, 16 March 1903, pp. 5–6.

166 Ó Maitiú, 'A spent force?', p. 289.

167 Ó Maitiú, 'A spent force?', p. 289.

168 *An Claidheamh Soluis*, 15 April 1911, p. 8; 22 April 1911, p. 12; 11 May 1912, p. 7; 28 March 1914, p. 8.

169 *Freeman's Journal*, 6 September 1913, p. 4; 10 December 1913, p. 4.

relocated the school to the Hermitage in Rathfarnham, which was renamed St Enda's.[170] In the spring of 1910 Pearse wrote to potential donors soliciting financial contributions for St Enda's. One of the people he approached was Thomas Hackett of Milltown, who, as noted earlier, had acted as secretary of the Milltown branch of the Gaelic League in 1900. Hackett declined to help but he diplomatically tempered his reply to Pearse:

> *I regret very much that I am unable at present to guarantee any money for the carrying out of your scheme. Nothing could give me greater pleasure than assisting in such useful work, and if circumstances permit, I shall be happy to subscribe at some future date if necessary.*[171]

Thomas Hackett wrote his name and address in Irish but the main body of his letter to Pearse was written in English. This suggests that Hackett may have become less able or confident in using Irish, perhaps through lack of practice. Admittedly, he completed his 1911 census form in Irish using very neat Gaelic script.[172]

SOCIAL PROBLEMS IN CONCRETE AND FARRANBOLEY

The forgoing overview of sporting and cultural activity at Milltown shows that the area was becoming much more integrated with the wider Dublin community as it emerged from the acute poverty and depression of the mid-nineteenth century. Despite the obvious improvements in the material and cultural life of the villagers there were many intractable anti-social problems which stemmed from overcrowded housing conditions (the subject of a separate chapter), alcohol addiction and casual employment among unskilled males, a state of affairs that mirrored conditions in Dublin city's tenements. In turn, women and children frequently bore the brunt of their husband's frustrations through domestic violence, drunkenness and neglect, in what was an extremely patriarchal society. Earlier mention has been made of the requests by Thomas Edmondson to the RIC and the DMP to improve policing in Milltown on behalf of his harassed employees, who were the victims of anti-social behaviour.

The social problems of Dublin tenements at the turn of the twentieth century were examined exhaustively by contemporary officials and are well-known today thanks to extensive research by social historians. The same conditions existed in the poorer suburban villages of Dublin, a fact that is much less well-known. The evidence provided by the Dundrum Petty Sessions (today's equivalent of the District Court) and contemporary newspaper reports shows that the neighbourhood of Milltown around Concrete and Farranboley on the south bank of the River Dodder were blackspots in terms of crime and anti-social behaviour. To highlight these issues, I have used the example of two families – the Doyles and the Leonards – each of whom provided victims and aggressors among a cast of many local protagonists.

Owen and Rose Leonard and their five children lived in a small cottage in Concrete on the

---

170 Elaine Sisson, 'How to make an Irish boy: The founding of Scoil Éanna in Cullenswodd House' in Victoria White (ed.), *Cullenswood House* (Dublin, 2009), pp. 13–24.

171 Patrick Pearse papers (NLI, MS 21,053/10/22).

172 NAI, 1911 Census, Form A, residents of house no. 45 (Tomás Haicead and family), Milltown Road, Rathmines and Rathgar East Electoral Division, Milltown Townland, Barony of Uppercross, Co. Dublin.

south bank of the River Dodder close to the Packhorse Bridge.[173] Owen was a casual labourer with very irregular employment while his wife Rose had a steady job working in the laundry at Milltown. Unfortunately for Rose and her children Owen was a drunkard. On previous occasions he had deserted his family for lengthy periods and had frequently assaulted his wife. After one particularly bad instance of domestic abuse on 17 July 1897 Rose had reached the end of her tether and she summoned her husband to appear at the Dundrum Petty Sessions on charges of assault.[174] Leonard was arrested on the evening of the disturbance but was later released on bail by one of the local justices of the peace, Francis Elrinton Ball, who is better known as the historian of County Dublin.[175] The Leonards' court appearance on 2 August was reported in the *Rathmines News* and the journalist did not spare the readers from the particularly graphic nature of the violence and aggression inflicted on Rose by her husband. During the hearing Rose handed in a letter of support from her employer, signed by Robert Benson, which pleaded her case succinctly:

> *Mrs Leonard has been employed here for some time, and we have always found her a hardworking and industrious woman, anxious to do her best for her children, and we think she deserves all the protections which the law can give her in the matter.*[176]

Mrs Leonard told the court that she wished to separate from her husband as she objected to living with him. Unfortunately, the court did not accede to her wishes. Instead, the magistrates bound Leonard over to the peace for six months with a personal surety of £20 and two independent sureties of £10 each, or three months' imprisonment in default.[177] Owen Leonard continued to beat his wife and terrorise his children and so on 26 October he was summoned again to appear at the Dundrum Petty Sessions on charges of assaulting his wife on 16 October. Leonard failed to appear in court and in his absence the magistrates sentenced him to 14 days' imprisonment.[178] The sentence handed down to Leonard on 30 October was totally inconsistent with the sentence pronounced by the same court on 2 August when he was sentenced to three months' imprisonment if he broke his undertaking to keep the peace. Following Leonard's abscondment his two sureties, one of whom was a local Milltown man named William Dempsey, were summoned to court to pay their forfeited sureties. The magistrates exercised their discretion, however, and reduced the sums due. The chairman of the magistrates took the opportunity to express his surprise that working men were not more careful before consenting to go bail for any person.[179]

After October 1897 Owen Leonard essentially disappears from the historical record. He did not spend the census night of 1901 with his family but in December of that year he was reported as appearing before the northern division of Dublin city police courts for an offence committed

---

173 NAI, 1901 Census, Form A, residents of house no. 15 in Farranboley (Concrete), Dundrum Electoral Division, Farranboley townland, Dublin; VO, Cancellation Books 1878–1903, Dundrum Electoral Division, Rathdown No. 1 RDC, Townland of Farranboley, p. 111, plot 2b.

174 Dundrum Petty Sessions Order Book 19 July 1897, no. 55 (case postponed to 2 August).

175 *Rathmines News*, 24 July 1897, p. 5; 7 August 1897, p. 5.

176 *Rathmines News*, 7 August 1897, p. 5.

177 *Rathmines News*, 7 August 1897, p. 5; Dundrum Petty Sessions Order Book 2 August 1897, no. 63.

178 *Rathmines News*, 30 October 1897, p. 4; Dundrum Petty Sessions Order Book 25 October 1897, no. 16.

179 *Rathmines News*, 13 November 1897, p. 5.

in North Anne Street. Rose Leonard continued to provide for her five children through her employment in Dublin Laundry Company, assisted by her eldest son, fifteen-year-old Patrick Leonard, who also worked in the laundry.[180]

Less than three years later Rose Leonard was the victim of anti-social behaviour in Concrete when four local youths burst in the door of her cottage in a drunken state late at night on 28 December 1903. Two police constables from Dundrum barracks who were on patrol in the vicinity pursued and arrested two of the youths. The four young men were summoned to Dundrum Petty Sessions where Rose Leonard testified that she was subjected to nightly intimidating behaviour. Rather unusually, during the hearing one of the local magistrates, Captain Robert Wade Thompson JP of Clonskeagh Castle took the witness box so that he could appraise his colleagues of the deplorable behaviour in Concrete:

> A*t this stage of the case Captain Thompson, who was on the Bench, stated he wished to bring under the notice of his brother magistrates the intolerable state of affairs created nightly, and especially on Saturday nights, by idle miscreants in this locality. Having been sworn, he said his house was situated only a short distance from this place, and at night time, between 10 and 12 o'clock, horrible cries of murder, and loud and bad expressions filled the air, especially on Saturday nights. He did not blame the police for not effectually stopping this disgraceful conduct, because, as Constable Byrne had stated, Concrete was situated in close proximity to the Metropolitan area, and when the Constabulary [i.e. the RIC] put in an appearance the crowd scampered off across the bridge [to the north bank of the River Dodder], and turned back again when the [Dublin] Metropolitan Police were around.*[181]

Each of the four defendants was fined £1 and 2*s*. 6*d*. costs or 14 days' imprisonment in default.[182] Rose Leonard continued to suffer at the hands of her neighbours, albeit on an infrequent basis. On 11 May 1905 Mathew Davis of Milltown was convicted at the suit of District Inspector Winder at Dundrum Petty Sessions for assaulting Rose Leonard and her daughter Jane at Farranboley on 23 April. The circumstances of this crime were not reported in the press aside from the fact that Davis was ordered to personally provide bail of £5 and two sureties of £2 10*s*. each or in default one month's imprisonment.[183] Thereafter things seem to have settled down for the Leonard family if their absence from the Dundrum Petty Sessions is anything to go by.

On census night 1911 Rose Leonard and her four sons were living together in Concrete. Her daughter Jane, who would have been aged twenty-two, was not listed on the census form so it is likely that she had left home and was probably married at this stage. Tellingly, Rose described herself as a widow which indicates that Owen was dead or that Rose wished to record her status as such in the absence of any information of her estranged husband. Rose's sons Patrick (twenty-three), Hugh (nineteen) and Edward (fifteen) worked as van men, almost certainly in the Milltown laundry (or Darty Dye Works in the case of Edward), while twenty-one-year-old James was described as a labourer, which may suggest that he was unemployed.[184] Edward Leonard was later to join the Irish

180 NAI, 1901 Census, Form A, residents of house no. 15 in Farranboley (Concrete), Dundrum Electoral Division, Farranboley townland; *Dublin Evening Telegraph*, 21 December 1901, p. 2.

181 *Rathmines News*, 16 January 1904, p. 3.

182 Dundrum Petty Sessions Order Book 11 January 1904, nos 22–25.

183 Dundrum Petty Sessions Order Book 11 May 1905, no. 58; *Rathmines News*, 1 May 1905, p. 2.

184 NAI, 1911 Census, Form A, residents of house no. 4 in Milltown (Concrete), Milltown Electoral Division, Parish of Taney.

Volunteers and participate in the 1916 Rising (at Boland's Mills) and the War of Independence.[185]

In July 1912 three of the Leonard boys were summoned to appear at Dundrum Petty Sessions by their neighbour Thomas McArdle who alleged that they had entered his tenement lodgings in Marble Hall, Concrete, and assaulted him. At the court hearing evidence given by McArdle's wife, who was a first cousin of the Leonards, was that her husband arrived home from the pub drunk. He was annoyed with her because earlier that evening she had tried to get him to come home from the pub. As he proceeded to smash the furniture Mrs McArdle cried out for help for herself and her children. Hugh Leonard was first on the scene and he ended up hitting McCardle in self-defence. Mrs McArdle's account was supported by two independent witnesses who had come across the fracas at Concrete on Friday night, 21 June. The magistrates preferred the defendants' evidence and they were acquitted of all charges. The chairman of the magistrates remarked that it was clear that Hugh Leonard entered McCardle's house on a very creditable and humane errand, and the defendants in the case left the court without the smallest stain on their characters.[186]

Just as there were victims of crime and domestic violence in Concrete and Farranboley it followed that the perpetrators were living in the same district. Two of the most disreputable characters living in the area were the Doyle brothers, Mathew and Hugh, of whom the latter was the worst offender of the pair. Mathew Doyle was born in the Coombe Hospital on 2 June 1874, the eldest child of Hugh Doyle and Ellen Dempsey of Milltown.[187] Hugh and Ellen subsequently married on 17 January 1875 and the birth of their second son, Hugh, occurred nine months later 17 October 1875.[188] Nothing is known about Hugh Doyle senior's occupation and he died sometime before 1901 when his widow Ellen was listed in the census returns for Concrete in that year. As a thirteen-year-old boy just out of national school Hugh Doyle junior began getting in trouble with the law from December 1888 onwards, when along with four other Milltown boys and another boy from St Kevin's Park in Upper Rathmines, he was summoned to appear by head constable Thomas Leonard at Dundrum Petty Sessions for throwing stones at a house belonging to Michael and Bridget Drury of Farranboley, throwing human excrement into their house and damaging Drury's cart. These offences occurred on several occasions during the months of December and January 1888/1889.[189] It is impossible to discover why the boys targeted the Drury's house but the speculation must be that the teenagers were acting out of pure malice in targeting a vulnerable couple who, it would appear, were afraid to press charges themselves.

Four years later, Hugh Doyle, by now aged seventeen, was summoned by Patrick Bryan to appear in Dundrum Petty Sessions on 6 March 1893 to face a charge of assault at Farranboley. Doyle did not appear in court on that occasion.[190] Altogether more serious charges were pressed against Doyle on 13 April 1896 when he was accused of robbing groceries from Windy Arbour

185 BMH, MSP34, Ref 458, sworn statement of Edward Leonard, 21 January 1935.

186 *Wicklow Newsletter*, 13 July 1912, p. 4.

187 Baptismal register for St Nicholas (RC) Parish Church 1874, p. 12, no. 191.

188 Marriage register for Rathmines (RC) Parish Church 1875, no. 2378; Baptismal register for St Mary (RC) Parish Church Donnybrook, 1875, no. 278.

189 Dundrum Petty Sessions Order Book 11 February 1889, nos 22–9, 35–9. The boys were each fined 6*d*. for the second, and arguably the worst, offence.

190 Dundrum Petty Sessions Order Book 6 March 1893, no. 50.

woman, Mrs Catherine Reilly, and of attempting to indecently assault her.[191] Doyle was sent forward to a grand jury trial at the Commission of Oyer and Terminer, but he was released after the jury failed to reach a verdict.[192] A few months later, Hugh Doyle, his brother Mathew and a local postman named James Crowley got into a fight in the Dew Drop Inn with Robert and Hugh Carson on 3 August 1896. It was a bank holiday so the men had undoubtedly been drinking heavily before the row started. On this occasion the Dundrum magistrates fined Crowley and the two Doyles 5*s*. plus costs.[193] Given the litany of trouble which Hugh Doyle constantly caused in Milltown and Farranboley it is surprising to discover that he got married to a local girl, Catherine (Kate) McCoy from Byrne's Cottages, Clonskeagh, on 27 September 1896.[194]

Hugh Doyle continued his criminal behaviour despite assuming the responsibilities of marriage and fatherhood. On the evening of 19 July 1897 Hugh and Mathew Doyle assaulted the proprietor of the Dew Drop Inn, Thomas Patrick (T.P.) Hackett senior, his son T.P. Hackett junior and John Hackett while drunk and disorderly. Hugh Doyle had been put out of the pub earlier in the evening but he later returned and assaulted the Hacketts. The disturbance spilled out onto the street close to Milltown Bridge on the south side of the River Dodder. By coincidence, acting Serjeant McGovern and Constable Brunt, who had just arrested Owen Leonard in Concrete arising from the assault on his wife earlier that evening, came upon the melee at Milltown Bridge as they were escorting Leonard to the Dundrum police barracks. The two policemen left Leonard to break up the fight and they arrested Mathew Doyle for assaulting John Hackett. At this point Hugh Doyle attacked the policemen and tried to free his brother. After a further struggle and a chase, the policemen arrested the two Doyle brothers and brought them to Dundrum with Leonard. Ironically, Leonard did not use the diversion to escape and he waited for the police to apprehend the Doyles before resuming the walk to Dundrum.[195] Clearly, Leonard had expended all of his rage and energy on assaulting his wife and breaking up the house and was prepared to spend the night in a police cell. Charges were pressed against the Doyles by both the police and the Hacketts with the result that at the Dundrum Petty Sessions on 2 August 1897 Mathew Doyle was fined 10*s*. plus costs while Hugh Doyle was imprisoned in Kilmainham jail for a month with hard labour for assaulting serjeant McGovern and attempting to free his brother Mathew.[196]

The Doyles appear to have stayed out of trouble for over a year after the fracas at the Dew Drop Inn. However, on 5 November 1900, though, the two brothers were summoned to appear at Dundrum Petty Sessions to face charges made by John and Jane Murphy of Farranboley, who claimed that on 27 October the Doyles had forcibly entered their house and assaulted them. The Doyles did not turn up to court so the background to this incident is unrecorded.[197] None of the records provide any evidence that Hugh Doyle was ever employed. In the absence of a steady job Doyle resorted to burglary. In January 1901 Hugh Doyle and a man named William Dempsey,

191 Dundrum Petty Sessions Order Book 13 February 1896, no. 4.

192 *Dublin Daily Express*, 11 June 1896, p. 2; *Rathmines News*, 7 August 1897, p. 5.

193 Dundrum Petty Sessions Order Book 17 August 1896, nos 23–7; *Rathmines News*, 22 August 1896, p. 3.

194 Marriage register for St Mary (RC) Parish Church Donnybrook 1896, no. 966; Civil register of marriages, District of Dublin South, p. 590, no. 13.

195 *Rathmines News*, 24 July 1897, p. 5; 7 August 1897, p. 5.

196 Dundrum Petty Sessions Order Book 2 August 1897, nos 64–71.

197 Dundrum Petty Sessions Order Book 5 November 1900, nos 52–5.

who was possibly Doyle's first cousin, were arrested and charged with breaking into newly built and unoccupied houses on Victoria Road, Rathgar, and with stealing various property belonging to the residents of the newly completed residences and the workmen who were completing the unfinished houses.[198] Doyle and Dempsey pleaded guilty at the Commission of Oyer and Terminer and they were later sent to prison.[199]

When the 1901 census took place on the night of 31 March Hugh Doyle's wife Kate was living in the Marble Hall tenement with her three children Hugh (six), Kathleen (four) and William (two).[200] Hugh Doyle senior was not recorded on the census form because he was in prison. Thus, as the sole breadwinner Kate's job as a laundress was particularly vital to support her three children. Kate's mother-in-law, the widowed Ellen Doyle (forty-six), was living in a cottage in Milltown village. The household comprised three generations, Ellen Doyle, her daughter Bridget (twenty), son Mathew (twenty-six) and Ellen's father, seventy-nine-year-old William Dempsey. Ellen and her daughter Bridget worked as laundresses while the delinquent Mathew Doyle's occupation was given as a builder's labourer. Their home was part of a terrace of small houses called Hackett's Cottages, whose landlord was T.P. Hackett senior, the proprietor of the Dew Drop Inn.[201]

Hugh Doyle was once again convicted of being drunk and disorderly in Milltown on two occasions in November 1905. On the second court appearance Doyle was given two weeks to pay the fine of 21*s.* plus costs.[202] How Doyle was able to fund his drinking and pay his court fines is a mystery. It is possible that his mother or siblings were prepared to give him money. Kate's wages minus rent and the family's living expenses would not have been enough to fund his lifestyle. Inevitably, drink was the major factor in the incident which caused Hugh Doyle's death, which event was the subject of a coroner's inquest held at Milltown and one that was reported on in great detail in the local newspaper.[203]

On Saturday 16 June 1906 Kate Doyle left her home in Marble Hall at 7 a.m. to go to work in the city where she worked as a laundress. Her brother-in-law, Mathew Doyle, who was currently employed as a builder's labourer, set off for Ringsend. According to her evidence given at the coroner's court Mathew's mother, Mrs Ellen Doyle, went into town where she worked at a market stall. This detail is at odds with the census returns for 1901 and 1911 in which Ellen Doyle gave her occupation as a laundress. Mathew Doyle left work at about 1.30 p.m. on Saturday afternoon with his weekly wages of 16*s.* 11*d.*, and later headed into town. In his evidence, Doyle claimed to have spent 4*s.* 6*d.* on clothes but he also admitted to drinking in three different public houses in Ringsend before he went to Westmoreland Street.[204]

At about 4.30 p.m. Mathew Doyle returned to Milltown by tram, alighting at the Palmerston Park terminus. Shortly afterwards Mathew met up with his brother Hugh, who was currently unem

198 *Rathmines News*, 12 January 1901, p. 4.

199 *Rathmines News*, 9 February 1901, p. 4.

200 NAI, 1901 Census, Form A, residents of house no. 11.9 in Farranboley (Concrete), Dundrum Electoral Division, Farranboley Townland, Co. Dublin.

201 NAI, 1901 Census, Form A, residents of house no. 51 in Milltown Road, Rathmines and Rathgar Electoral Division, Milltown Townland, Barony of Uppercross, Co. Dublin; VO, Cancellation Books, Rathmines and Rathgar East, Milltown 1899–1906, p. 674, no. 56.

202 *Rathmines News*, 2 December 1905, p. 4; *Irish Independent*, 28 November 1905, p. 6; Dundrum Petty Sessions Order Book 27 November 1905, no. 111; 11 December 1905, no. 142.

203 *Rathmines News*, 25 June 1906, p. 4.

204 *Rathmines News*, 25 June 1906, p. 4.

ployed, and another labourer, a local man named James Darcy. Each of the three men proceeded to drink a pint of bottled porter which Darcy had bought from Mrs O'Neill at her off licence on Milltown Hill (currently the site of the Spar shop and off licence). After they had consumed the porter Mathew Doyle attempted to buy more drink in Hackett's pub in the main street of Milltown (the Hacketts owned a second pub as well as the Dew Drop Inn) but he was refused admittance because Hugh and his brother Mathew had been barred on account of the fracas in the Dew Drop Inn several years previously. Later, Hugh Doyle's mother bought a jug of three pints of porter for her sons and their drinking companions with 6*d.* which Mathew had given her. Whether Mrs Doyle did this voluntarily or under duress was not clear because Mathew Doyle claimed, unconvincingly given the circumstances, that his mother had volunteered to buy the drink. Mathew Doyle also testified that he gave his mother 9*s.* 6*d.* out of his wage packet as his contribution towards the family's living expenses. By this stage it was getting late. Hugh Doyle's wife had returned home from her work in a city laundry at 8.30 p.m. Her husband was not at home.[205]

After they had finished drinking the Doyle brothers went to their mother's house at no. 2 Hackett's Cottages where they had tea, bread and butter. It was by now about 10.40 p.m. and getting dark. After finishing their tea, the two brothers decided to go for a swim in the River Dodder to wash themselves. The men brought a towel and soap to a deep part of the river called 'flat' close to the Milltown laundry complex. The evidence concerning the location of the 'flat' is hard to decipher given the changes to the topography, but it is likely that this deep pool was part of a disused quarry pond which was filled in years later when the River Dodder was embanked (Pl. 18). At some point while the two men were swimming Mathew noticed that his brother had disappeared. Hugh had not cried out for help or shown any signs that he was in difficulty; he simply sank without trace and drowned. Hugh's death was only reported to the Dundrum police at 6.15 a.m. the following morning. Kate Doyle told the inquest that after leaving her house on Saturday morning she next saw her husband lying dead in his bed on Sunday morning following his recovery by the Dundrum constabulary. Constable John Walker gave evidence that he located Hugh Doyle's body in seven feet of water following which he and his police colleagues drained the pond and recovered the body. Another constable gave evidence of finding a fishing line entangled in one of Doyle's legs. Only the journalist from the *Rathmines News* attached any significance to this piece of evidence, opining that it caused Hugh Doyle to drown. Following a summing up by the coroner, the jury returned the verdict, 'That the deceased died from suffocation caused by submersion while bathing in the River Dodder.'[206]

Hugh Doyle left behind a wife and four young children.[207] Nobody enquired of the witnesses during the inquest as to who looked after the Doyle children while their parents were absent on Saturday. The children were probably cared for by other relatives as a matter of routine. When the next census was taken on 2 April 1911 the widowed Kate Doyle (thirty-five) was living in the Marble Hall tenement with her five children ranging in ages from sixteen to four. It seems therefore that Kate was pregnant with her fifth child, Mary, when her husband drowned, although the birth and baptismal records for Mary Doyle have proved to be elusive thus far.[208] By 1911 Hugh's mother, Mrs Ellen Doyle (sixty-four), had moved across the river to Concrete and was living in a

205 *Rathmines News*, 25 June 1906, p. 4.

206 *Rathmines News*, 25 June 1906, p. 4.

207 *Rathmines News*, 25 June 1906, p. 4; *Freeman's Journal*, 19 June 1906, p. 5.

208 NAI, 1911 Census, Form A, residents of house no. 29.13 in Milltown (Concrete), Milltown Electoral Division, Parish of Taney.

multi-occupancy house with her unmarried son, Mathew, who was then aged thirty-eight.[209]

It is impossible to assess whether there was more criminal and anti-social behaviour in Concrete than in the main part of Milltown village on the north bank of the River Dodder. This is because the latter area lay in the metropolitan police district of Dublin city. As a result, petty crimes committed in Milltown falling under the city's jurisdiction were underreported in the newspapers in comparison with those committed in Concrete and Farranboley and tried at the Dundrum Petty Sessions. That said, the Kilmainham and Mountjoy prison registers contain numerous entries for the Doyle brothers arising out of convictions which were handed down to them in the city courts, which proves that the Doyles were committing crimes on both sides of the river, along with other Milltown men.[210]

It would be incorrect and unjust to label the inhabitants of Concrete and Farranboley as petty criminals predisposed to drunkenness and anti-social behaviour. In 1901 there were 182 people living in Concrete, the vast majority of whom were doing their best in difficult circumstances and never came to public notice.[211] The purpose of highlighting the experiences of the Leonard and Doyle families is to show that there were blackspots in Milltown, which were not ameliorated by the arrival of the Sisters of Charity and the Dublin Laundry Company in the 1880s. The roots of the anti-social behaviour in Concrete lay in poor living conditions and a patriarchal working-class society whose menfolk were given to excessive drinking and socialising in pubs. This behaviour was exacerbated by overcrowded housing conditions and the chronic underemployment of unskilled workers in the Dublin labour market.

MAINTAINING RESPECTABILITY

All classes of Victorian and Edwardian society were anxious to portray themselves (at least outwardly) as respectable individuals who came from respectable families or in the case of domestic servants, who worked for respectable families. The concept of 'respectability' was very broad, and it encompassed all aspects of personal lifestyle, social class and occupations. Two sample advertisements help explain the point:

> *Wanted, daily, neighbourhood of Milltown, respectable, young Protestant girl, take child to school and help with light housework; 15s. month.*[212]

> *Wanted, a respectable working girl, to share small cottage, Milltown vicinity, with another girl; references exchanged; RC.*[213]

Pregnancy outside marriage was a societal taboo, and for the unfortunate girl involved, her circumstances were the antithesis of respectability. The shame for the girl and her family caused by an illegitimate birth (as it was then described) was hugely damaging to their reputations. The loss of reputation was a major causative factor behind the crimes of infanticide and concealment of birth,

---

209 NAI, 1911 Census, Form A, residents of house no. 22.3 in Milltown (Concrete), Milltown Electoral Division, Parish of Taney.

210 See entries in the Kilmainham Prison Register for 1896–1904 and the Mountjoy Prison Register for 1904 which are searchable on the findmypast.ie website.

211 NAI, 1901 Census, Form N, Enumerator's Abstract of Farranboley (Concrete), Dundrum Electoral Division, Farranboley townland.

212 *Dublin Daily Express*, 14 September 1910, p. 1.

213 *Dublin Daily Express*, 18 March 1913, p. 1.

which desperate women were frequently driven to commit in such a time of crisis.[214] An unmarried female domestic servant was particularly vulnerable if she became pregnant, as she could expect to be dismissed by her employer, usually without any family support network to fall back on. Hence the expectant mother desperately attempted to hide her condition and conceal or kill her new-born baby *in extremis*.[215] Such personal disasters were not unknown in Milltown. In 1906, a girl named Alice Murphy was engaged by the Ryan family of Clonbeg as a domestic servant on 21 September. On 7 November, Mrs Ryan had occasion to enter Alice's bedroom when she was absent, and Mrs Ryan became suspicious when she saw blood-stained bedclothes. Mrs Ryan called the police who carried out a search of the bedroom and found the dead body of a new-born baby concealed in a box. Alice Murphy was taken to the Rathdown Union hospital at the workhouse in Loughlinstown and on her release, she was arrested and charged with concealing the birth of an infant at Milltown on 7 November 1906. However, a post mortem found that the baby was still-born and so the charges against Murphy were later dropped.[216]

Poverty and unmanageable family size also ended in tragic outcomes. On the night of 22/23 October 1914 a six-month-old baby boy was found deserted at Milltown Bridge by a local woman named Kate Russell, who lived nearby in Wright's Cottages on the village main street. Kate brought the small boy to the South Dublin Union workhouse in James's Street, where the pair were admitted at 2 a.m.[217] At their meeting of 28 October the poor law guardians passed the following resolution: 'That this child be registered a Roman Catholic and called by the name of John Thornton. Kate Russell, who brought the child to the Workhouse, to be paid 5s. for loss of time.'[218]

Baby John Thornton died in the workhouse four days later on 3 November from enteritis, an illness which was often caused by contaminated milk and one which was frequently fatal for infants.[219] Apart from the poignancy of the case, what is striking is the name – John Thornton – which the guardians gave to the abandoned child. On the one hand the boy's new name is unremarkable, but on the other hand Thornton is not a typical Irish Catholic surname. Perhaps the guardians deliberately chose a neutral surname with a view to giving the boy a better chance in life growing up in a class conscious and sometimes rather sectarian society.

SUFFRAGIST ACTIVITY

The Irish suffragist movement was active in Ireland in the years before the outbreak of the First World War and its activity in Dublin can be traced through a publication called *The Irish Citizen.* A prominent Dublin suffragette and social campaigner, Louie Bennett, explained to readers of *The Irish Citizen* in May 1913 the latest tactics adopted by the Irishwomen's Reform League:

> *We adopted the idea of the 'Qui Vive' Corps, and have found that the method of visiting a village, having talks with the people there, and distributing literature is one of the most valuable methods of propaganda. In many ways it is more useful than open air meetings, as a quiet talk with individuals gives opportunity for*

---

214 Clíona Rattigan, '*What else could I do?' Single Mothers and Infanticide, Ireland 1900–1950* (Dublin, 2012), pp. 81–4.

215 Elaine Farrell, *A most diabolical deed: Infanticide and Irish society, 1850–1900* (Manchester, 2013), pp. 31–-4.

216 *Rathmines News*, 17 November 1906, p. 3; 24 November 1906, p. 3; 1 December 1906, p. 3; *Dublin Daily Express*, 21 November 1906, p. 7; *Irish Independent*, 21 November 1906, p. 6.

217 South Dublin Poor Law Union, Admission & Discharge Registers, BG 79/G 138, entry no. 1183.

218 South Dublin Poor Law Union, Board of Guardians Minute Book A76 July–December 1914, Folio 9, p. 1417.

219 Register of Deaths for the District of Dublin South City No. 1, 1914, p. 465, entry no.27, 2 November 1914; J.W. Bigger, 'Clean Milk', *Journal of the Statistical and Social Inquiry Society of Ireland*, xiv, no. 2 (1920–23), p. 208.

> *a discussion of difficulties [and] has more lasting effect than ordinary speechifying. It is a slow and tedious method, but the personal effect tells enormously, and does much to dissipate prejudice and embitterment. Our people like better to see us in their homes than engaged in the doubtful business of tub-thumping!*[220]

On 7 August 1913 the Qui Vive Corps of the Irishwomen's Reform League met at Eglinton Road, Donnybrook, at 5 p.m. in preparation for canvassing the inhabitants of Milltown village.[221] Milltown was a good choice given that so many women there were employed as domestic servants, laundry workers and dressmakers, and were probably considered by the Qui Vive Corps to be receptive to their canvassing. Unfortunately Louie Bennet only recorded the fact that 'the Qui Vive did good work in Milltown last Thursday' so it is impossible to gauge the impression that the suffragettes made in Milltown.[222] As we have seen, many working-class women in Milltown were frequently preoccupied with more serious issues closer to home, such as housing conditions, childcare, domestic abuse and unwanted pregnancy. These unfortunate women could not afford to give much thought to breaking down the boundaries of the patriarchal society in which they were reared.

The foundation of Cumann na mBan in April 1914 ushered in a new mixture of Irish feminism and nationalism which acted as a support for the new Irish Volunteer movement. The women of Cumann na mBan became involved in fundraising activities and took lessons in first aid and military tactics, in preparation for armed conflict that might involve the Irish Volunteers. This development created tensions between the suffragette organisations and Cumann na mBan, which was accused of being subservient to the (male) Irish Volunteers and of diverting attention and resources from the cause of female emancipation.[223] Despite these accusations, Cumann na mBan appealed more to the working-class women of Milltown than the Irishwomen's Reform League. Women with a rebellious spirit, such as Ellen (Nellie) and Bridget Lambert who lived in 4 Strand Cottages, joined Cumann na mBan in 1914. These two teenage sisters went on to participate in the 1916 Rising, the War of Independence and the Civil War, which events are discussed in detail in Chapter 13.[224]

EMPLOYMENT CONDITIONS AND THE LABOURING CLASSES

Making a living for unskilled males who were not employed in steady jobs such as van men, coachmen and gardeners was very difficult. In the 1890s the wages paid to unskilled labourers employed by the Rathmines township came in for much criticism. In April 1896 a public meeting was held in Milltown under the auspices of the United Corporation Workmen of Ireland Trade Union, to advocate the claims of the Rathmines township employees for a similar rate of wages to those paid to Dublin Corporation workmen. The Rathmines commissioners were condemned for refusing to grant any increase in the men's wages, although they had sanctioned a salary increase for the township secretary.[225] Fifteen months later, a larger meeting was held at Milltown in July 1897, which was attended by workmen from the Rathmines, Pembroke and Blackrock townships. Workers employed

---

220 *Irish Citizen*, 17 May 1913, p. 419.

221 *Irish Citizen*, 2 August 1913, p. 86. The notice inaccurately locates Eglinton Road at Clonskeagh instead of Donnybrook.

222 *Irish Citizen*, 16 August 1913, p. 102.

223 L.P. Curtis, Junior, 'Ireland in 1914' in W.E. Vaughan (ed.), *A new history of Ireland, vi: Ireland under the Union 1870–1921* (Oxford, 1989), p. 168.

224 NAI, 1911 Census, Form A, residents of house no. 4 in Strand Cottages, Milltown, Electoral Division of Rathmines and Rathgar East, Parish of St Peter, Barony of Uppercross; BMH, MSP34REF56696 (sworn evidence of Ellen Stynes née Lambert on 2 May 1941) and BMH, MSP34REF57178 (sworn evidence of Bridget Doran née Lambert, not dated).

225 *Dublin Evening Telegraph*, 27 April 1896, p. 4.

by those townships were paid weekly wages of 15*s*., compared with Dublin Corporation workmen who earned 17*s*. 6*d*. a week. The speakers argued that the men could not live decently on such wages, yet the Rathmines commissioners had brushed aside their employees' demands for a wage increase, haughtily claiming that other labourers were willing to work for 4*s*. a week less. Even worse, the Rathmines commissioners did not provide any waterproof clothing for their outdoor staff, who, allegedly, were forced to wear old sacks tied with rags in inclement weather. In order to better further the cause of securing fair wages, a resolution was passed calling on all workmen employed by the suburban townships to join the Corporation Workmen's Trade Union. [226] William McCabe from Concrete, Milltown was likely to have been among the crowd of workmen at the meeting. In the 1901 census, William (sixty) described himself as a road labourer, so he was almost certainly employed by the Rathmines or the Pembroke township.[227]

The campaign for improved wages for the Rathmines township workers continued the following year, 1898, with support from sympathetic newspapers such as the *Dublin Daily Nation* and the *Dublin Evening Telegraph*.[228] Although demands for better wages were steadfastly refused by the Rathmines township, the commissioners admitted that their labourers could not afford to pay for accommodation in the township. The example was given of township workers who earned 16*s*. a week, and who had to pay 4*s*. 6*d*. a week for one room and a small one off it; such living quarters were acknowledged as being too expensive.[229] Rather than increasing wages, in 1903 the Rathmines UDC built 102 working-class houses at Holyfields, Upper Rathmines, and a development named Mount Pleasant Buildings off Oxford Road, Ranelagh. The latter consisted of 189 one-, two- and three-roomed flats, which were let out at weekly rents ranging from 1*s*. 6*d*. to 4*s*. 6*d*.[230] Laudable as these developments were, the attention given to providing housing for the working classes in the heart of Rathmines resulted in the housing conditions of Milltown being deprioritised and neglected. Thus, Thomas Edmondson's pleas to the council on Milltown's behalf fell on deaf ears.[231]

The year 1905 was marked by labour unrest, chiefly concerning trade union recognition and work practices.[232] One particularly bitter dispute, involving the Dublin Brick and Stonelayers' Union and the Master Builders' Association, terminated in a victory for the Master Builders' Association after an arbitration award went in their favour.[233] The bitterness of this dispute left its mark on the labourers of Milltown. A local flood relief committee at Classon's Bridge tabled a resolution supporting a decision by the organising committee of the Irish International Exhibition to engage an English building firm to erect the exhibition buildings in Ballsbridge. A labourer named Edward Kinsella seconded the resolution, stating that:

> *it gave him the greatest pleasure, as one who had suffered from the late flood, and knowing as he did the way employment is at the present time. It will help to pay back the men responsible for the late strike in*

226 *Irish Independent, 26 July 1897*, p. 6; 27 July 1897, p. 7.

227 NAI, 1901 Census, Form B1, Residents of a house no. 1 in Farranboley (Concrete), Dundrum Electoral Division, Farranboley townland.

228 *Dublin Evening Telegraph*, 9 July 1898, pp. 3–4; *Dublin Daily Nation*, 26 September 1898, p. 3.

229 *Rathmines News*, 4 December 1897, p. 4.

230 *Rathmines News*, 10 October 1903, p. 3.

231 NAI, Business Records, Dublin 56, Dublin Laundry Company, letter book 1895–1902, 13 March 1898.

232 Daly, *Dublin: The deposed capital*, p. 72.

233 *Irish Independent, 1 July 1905*, p. 5.

> *their own coin for their unjust and slave-driven conduct only a few short months ago in bringing about unwarranted distress and poverty on the poor unfortunate working people of Dublin.*[234]

These handful of press reports concerning trade unionism and the struggles of unskilled labourers in Milltown and Rathmines were overshadowed by the dominant political narrative involving the IPP, its electoral battles with Unionists, and the long campaign at Westminster for Home Rule. Nonetheless, it is important to acknowledge that labour and social issues resonated equally, if not more so, with the labouring classes of Dublin than the national question. In this regard, the working-class men of Milltown were at one with James Connolly, Jim Larkin and their city comrades.

In an attempt to ease the distress caused by the extensive unemployment of the middle years of the Edwardian era, the government introduced the Unemployed Workmen Act of 1905, which made provision for setting up distress committees in urban areas which were required to maintain labour exchanges, whose primary purpose was to direct unskilled workers to jobs.[235] In January 1906 80 unemployed men applied to the Rathmines UDC for relief under the act, but the clerk told a meeting of the councillors that the men could only be relieved by providing work to be paid out of voluntary contributions of the public, and so an appeal was made to the public for funds.[236] When the council met the following month, the councillors were told by the chairman of the Rathmines distress committee, Dr Hillis, that it had only received 10*s.* contributions from the public thus far and that if no more money came in the relief scheme would fall through. To add insult to injury, the committee had expended £25 in putting the act into effect, caused by the 'redtapeism' of the Local Government Board.[237] This unhappy situation suggests either that the relief scheme was not well publicised or that the Rathmines middle class were indifferent to the plight of the unemployed. The latter view is strengthened by the fact that the council could only raise £27 when the scheme was rolled out 12 months later.[238]

RELIGIOUS TENSIONS

The importance of religion to an individual's sense of personal and community identity cannot be overstated in Victorian and Edwardian Ireland. The traditional Protestant/Unionist hegemony faced an increasingly confident Catholic Church and a growing Catholic middle class who were predominantly Nationalist in political outlook. This led to an increase in tensions between the Christian faiths. A peculiar manifestation of this was the practice of a small minority of evangelical Protestants to stage street preaching and hold outdoor religious meetings throughout the country in the 1890s. This activity, termed open-air preaching, was opposed by moderates of all religious persuasion, but especially by the Catholic working class who viewed it as a crude, provocative form of proselytism. Such occasions were frequently an excuse for rougher elements to indulge in public disorder and physically abuse the preachers. Such reaction suited some sections of the unionist political community, who could point to the intolerant responses of local Catholic communities to the preachers as evidence of the undesirability of Home Rule.[239]

234 *Rathmines News, 21 October 1905*, p. 3.

235 Desmond Farley, *Social Insurance and Social Assistance in Ireland* (Dublin, 1964), p. 25.

236 *Irish Times*, 18 January 1906, p. 7.

237 *Dublin Evening Mail*, 7 February 1906, p. 5.

238 *Freeman's Journal*, 5 March 1907, p. 5.

239 Matthew Kelly, 'The Politics of Protestant Street Preaching in 1890s Ireland', *The Historical Journal*, 48, no. 1 (2005), pp. 101–25.

Street preaching took place in the Dublin suburbs of Rathfarnham, Rathmines and Rathgar in the late 1890s.[240] This religious phenomenon was behind several breaches of the peace in Rathmines and Rathgar, so much so that the Rathmines commissioners eventually had to ban these events from public spaces.[241] One of the proponents of open-air preaching was the local incumbent of St Philip's church, Temple Road, the Rev. Moffatt. Rev. Moffatt was a religious conservative; he opposed the sacerdotal party in the Church of England and any attempt to introduce high ritual practice into the Anglican Church.[242] In May 1899 Rev. Moffatt along with members of the Zion Church Men's Association, applied to the Rathmines UDC to erect a gospel tent on open ground in Rathmines called 'The Chains'. This request was turned down and the commissioners decided to fence off 'The Chains' to prevent further outbreaks of public disorder.[243]

Thirteen months later, Rev. Moffatt caused considerable annoyance when he and his supporters conducted open-air preaching on three successive Sundays in June 1900 on open ground known locally as 'The Strand' (Map 18) in Milltown village where the public carpark is now opposite the Wilde and Green delicatessen). There is no evidence that this behaviour was sanctioned or approved of by the parishioners of St Philip's as the parish vestry books do not mention these activities. The first of these controversial events was widely reported in the local and national newspapers. On Sunday afternoon, 10 June 1900, Rev. Moffatt and other lay preachers assembled on 'The Strand' and proceeded to conduct an open-air religious service. The service began peacefully and for a time afterwards but thereafter a large hostile crowd began to assemble. Two young men, Joseph and John Hackett, began kicking a football in the middle of the preachers, one of whom was hit by the ball. The police had been forewarned of the preaching meeting and they were present in Milltown in sufficient numbers – upwards of 25 according to one report – to prevent any serious disturbance breaking out. To the great annoyance of the crowd, a policeman arrested the two Hackett youths, who were subsequently charged before the city's southern police court with assault and obstructing a policeman.

At their trial, the Hackett's lawyer argued that the preachers had acted provocatively in leaving St Philip's church and conducting their preaching on 'The Strand', where it was common practice for children to play football and marbles. The defendants also made the case that when the preachers arrived the police told the locals to stop playing football but they refused, arguing that they had an equal right to be there. On the other hand, the prosecuting barrister opined that Milltown would be all the better for all the teaching it could get regarding morals and good order. He said that there was a 'dead set' made against the clergyman and his friends, who were first on the ground, and had a perfect right to remain there and conduct their service. The presiding magistrate at the police court, Mr Byrne QC, found that the offences had been proved and fined the Hacketts 5*s.* each or seven days' imprisonment.[244] At the same time, Byrne was highly critical of the preachers. Having regard to all the facts, Byrne formed the opinion that the open-air service had been held in anticipation of a breach of the peace, which was, in fact, intended to be provoked because the preachers had called up a large body of policemen as back

---

240 *Rathmines News*, 1 August 1896, p. 3; 3 July 1897, p. 5; 20 May 1899, p. 5; 5 August 1899, p. 5.

241 *Rathmines News*, 20 May 1899, p. 5; 5 August 1899, p. 4; 19 May 1900, p. 5; *Belfast Telegraph*, 24 October 1899, p. 4.

242 *Rathmines News*, 16 February 1904, p. 3; *Irish Independent*, 25 September 1912, p. 6.

243 *Rathmines News*, 5 August 1899, p. 4.

244 *Rathmines News*, 23 June 1900, p. 5; *Dublin Evening Mail*, 11 June 1900, p. 4; *Weekly Irish Times*, 16 June 1900, p. 15; *Evening Herald*, 11 June 1900, p. 4; *Dublin Daily Nation*, 23 June 1900, p. 6.

up. It was therefore improper for the preachers to hold their service in those circumstances.[245]

The preaching controversy at Milltown caused much indignation, particularly as Rev. Moffatt and his preachers continued their occupation of 'The Strand' the following Sunday, notwithstanding the criticism levied against them in the police court. The editorial and correspondence sections of Nationalist newspapers such as the *Dublin Daily Nation* and the *Irish Independent* were especially vocal in their criticism of their action.[246] After the second event, local publican T.P. Hackett, the father of one of defendants and the uncle of the other, eloquently expressed the opinion of the majority of local Catholics and Protestants in a letter published in *Dublin Daily Nation* on Wednesday 21 June 1900:

> *The quietness of this suburban village was again disturbed on last Sunday evening [17 June] by the band of street preachers who created such unusual excitement on the previous Sunday [10 June]. The Rev. Dr Moffatt, Protestant rector of St Philip's Church, Temple Road, appears to be the promotor, or at least the central figure of the intruders. The few Protestant residents of the village were conspicuous by their absence and have since deprecated the wanton innovation [sic] in unmeasured terms. It is not quite clear whether it was the want of an appreciative audience in his church on Sunday evenings that caused the rector and his satellites to take to the highways and bye-ways, or their desire to promote discord and ill-feeling between the Catholic population of this village and the four Protestant families who have lived so long in peace and harmony with their Catholic neighbours. Fortunately, ... the half dozen humble Protestants of the village kept aloof on both days. On the second Sunday, however, about a dozen of the better class, who had been invited by him, viewed the proceedings apparently out of curiosity, and no doubt in disgust, from a distance of several hundred yards and well out of hearing distance.*[247]

The final meeting of the preachers was held on 'The Strand' on Sunday 24 June 1900. On this occasion a force of close to 40 policemen, including two inspectors, provided security for the event. As on previous occasions, the police forcibly stopped the local youths from playing football and held onto the ball until the preachers had left.[248]

The preachers' deliberate goading of the Catholic working-class villagers, backed up by a large body of police, had no positive religious purpose whatsoever. Undoubtedly, there were non-religious motives behind the street preaching activity in Milltown as well as religious ones. It is noteworthy that Rev. Moffatt was a prominent member of the Orange Order. In the politics of the day, the Dublin lodges of the Orange Order opposed the Conservative government's policy of constructive unionism and its local exponent, Sir Horace Plunkett, the Unionist MP for the South Dublin constituency.[249] It was acknowledged by the contemporary unionist press that Rev. Moffatt held very strong political opinions, and he vehemently opposed Home Rule and the establishment of a Catholic university.[250] After Rev. Moffatt's funeral on 24 September 1912, his cortège to Mount Jerome cemetery was accompanied by 800 Orangemen from the City and County of Dublin Grand Lodges.[251] Decades later, in the late 1950s Milltown's Cath-

245 *Rathmines News*, 23 June 1900, p. 5.

246 *Dublin Daily Nation*, 23 June 1900, pp. 5–6; *Irish Independent*, 25 June 1900, p. 3.

247 *Dublin Daily Nation*, 23 June 1900, p. 6.

248 *Dublin Evening Telegraph*, 26 June 1900, p. 2.

249 Alvin Jackson 'The Failure of Unionism in Dublin, 1900', *Irish Historical Studies*, 26, no. 104 (1989), pp. 377–95.

250 *Weekly Irish Times*, 13 February 1904, p. 8; *Dublin Daily Express*, 21 September 1912, p. 5; *Evening Irish Times*, 21 September 1912, p. 7.

251 *Leinster Express*, 28 September 1912, p. 5.

olics could still recall with resentment the attempts at proselytism made by Rev. Moffatt.[252]

Relations between the two major Christian faiths were put under further strain in the early years of the twentieth century by the establishment of a new organisation in 1902, the Catholic Association, whose principal object was to combat perceived Protestant domination and 'jobbery' in business and the professions. The Catholic Association primarily appealed to middle-class Catholics, many of whom felt that their career prospects were being frustrated by a professional, Protestant, hegemony.[253] The Jesuit Fr Peter Finlay of Milltown Park was instrumental is setting up a branch of the Catholic Association for Catholics living in the Rathmines township, in April 1902.[254] The objects of the 'New Catholic Association of the Rathmines and Rathgar Townships' were described as follows:

To make the Catholics of the district known to each other, and to enable them to realise their numbers, their rights, and their powers. To unite them all for the furtherance of their common interests. To secure for them their rightful share in the management of municipal affairs and in the distribution of municipal appointments. For this purpose, to secure that every Catholic man and woman qualified to vote in the District Council Elections shall be placed upon the register. The Association shall be wholly non-political, nor should membership involve abandonment or compromise of any opinions that may be held by a Catholic loyal to his faith.[255]

Religious feelings were particularly inflamed when in late 1903 the Catholic Association published a highly provocative handbook. Its contents were particularly offensive to Protestants because (among other things) it encouraged Catholics to boycott and discriminate against Protestants.[256] The editor of the *Rathmines News* gave his opinion in an editorial published on 2 January 1904:

The Catholic Association handbook business is a very regrettable one, indeed, but thank God it does not affect South Co. Dublin as it may other places. Here Catholics and Protestants work and chum together, and it is not fair that this brand of discord should be thrown amongst them, especially at such a particular time. We notice that the immediate result has been the formation of a Society for the Protection of Protestant Interests, and Captain Robert Wade Thompson, J.P., of Clonskeagh Castle, in announcing this fact writes: 'The Executive will always have in view justice and fair play, and, while seeking to safeguard the liberties of Protestants, will be careful to avoid anything approaching unfairness to Roman Catholics.[257]

Clonskeagh Castle sits on elevated ground on the south bank of the River Dodder directly facing the Catholic church. Although the grounds of Clonskeagh Castle are completely built over now, at the turn of the twentieth century this eighteenth century castellated villa stood in

---

252 G. Murray, 'The Story of Milltown'.

253 Senia Pašeta, *Before the Revolution: Nationalism, Social Change and Ireland's Catholic Elite, 1879–1922* (Cork, 1992), pp. 95, 103, 108, 111.

254 *Rathmines News*, 2 May 1902, p. 3.

255 *Rathmines News*, 2 May 1902, p. 3.

256 *Weekly Irish Times*, 2 January 1904, p. 17.

257 *Rathmines News*, 2 January 1904, p. 2.

wooded grounds of 35 statute acres, bounded by high walls on its northern and western boundaries with the River Dodder and the Dundrum Road respectively (Map 18).[258]

As noted earlier, Captain Robert Wade Thompson dispensed justice at the Dundrum Petty Sessions. The Thompsons were absentee landlords who, in 1876, held extensive estates of over 8,000 acres in Counties Meath, Sligo and Mayo.[259] Thompson's assets and income from his family estates meant that he did not have to work for a living. To the people living in Milltown village, Thompson must have been a remote figure, and his wealth and privileged lifestyle was probably resented by the poor inhabitants of Concrete, who occasionally appeared before him in court. Like his co-religionist and fellow member of the Orange Order, the Rev. Moffatt, Thompson was very committed to his Protestant faith (low-church Anglican), opposing both the establishment of a Catholic university and the Catholic Association, and vigorously defending the union with Great Britain undiluted by any form of devolution or decentralisation to Ireland, however mild.[260] Thompson deprecated perceived concessions made by the Chief Secretary, Gerald Balfour, to Irish nationalists (a conciliation policy commonly referred to as 'Balfourism' or 'killing home rule with kindness') during his term as chief secretary of Ireland and, in the divisions within Dublin unionism during the general election of 1900, opposed the candidacy of the moderate unionist Horace Plunkett for south Dublin.[261]

For several years during the 1890s and 1900s the Thompson family hosted the annual summer gathering of the Protestant Boys' Brigade in the grounds of Clonskeagh Castle. Hundreds of boys, their families and spectators participated at the annual event. Activities partaken of by the boys included playing band music, marching drills and athletics. Important dignitaries attended and delivered speeches which were reported in great detail in the *Rathmines News* and other newspapers. These reports give an idea of the social and class distinctions that permeated Irish society at that time.[262] The noise of the exclusive festivities at Clonskeagh Castle would have carried across the demesne wall and the River Dodder to Milltown village, little more than 100 metres away. These occasions must have reinforced the social, religious and political divisions that existed locally in Milltown, and more broadly in Irish society, in the run up to the Home Rule crisis of 1912–14.

THE DUNDRUM DRAINAGE SCHEME

The availability of piped water from Dublin Corporation's Vartry water supply scheme from the late 1870s onwards was a milestone in the provision of safe drinking water for the city and its southern suburbs, aside from the conspicuous absence of the Rathmines township which for political reasons had declined to avail of the corporation's scheme. Over time, commercial premises in Dundrum village and well-to-do residents in the surrounding roads near Taney church were connected to the water mains. On the face of it, these were all positive developments that typified the engineering prowess of the Victorian age. But a piped water supply without an adequate sewerage system which drains, treats and discharges the waste water creates its own problems. This section examines the challenges of sewage disposal posed by the Vartry water supply, how the

258 Sale advertisement in the *Irish Times*, 6 September 1924, p. 12.

259 Return of Land Owners of Ireland of one acre and upwards (Dublin, 1876), pp. 21, 73, 312, 323.

260 *Dublin Daily Express*, 30 March 1899, p. 8; *Weekly Irish Times*, 13 February 1904, p. 8. For several years Thompson acted as lay honorary secretary of the Church of Ireland Diocesan Synod: *Northern Whig*, 13 February 1919, p. 4.

261 *Irish Times*, 25 August 1900, p. 8; 6 October 1900, p. 6; *Warder and Weekly Dublin Mail*, 22 September 1900, p. 5.

262 *Rathmines News*, 30 May 1896, p. 2; 6 June 1903, p. 3; 17 July 1905, p. 3; 22 May 1907, p. 3; *Weekly Irish Times*, 15 May 1909, p. 21; *Dublin Evening Mail*, 9 May 1914, p. 3.

local authorities dealt with the challenges, and the impact of their actions and inactions on the lives of the residents in Milltown and Farranboley.

The problems caused by the lack of proper sewerage in late nineteenth-century Dublin city and county became increasingly acute as more and more effluent was discharged by property owners into rivers and streams.[263] The Slang river, which ran behind Dundrum village main street on its western side, flowed in a northerly direction through Windy Arbour and Farranboley, until it discharged its contents into the River Dodder about 100 metres upstream from the Packhorse Bridge at Milltown. In addition, water was taken off the River Slang at Windy Arbour to supply the millpond on the south bank of the River Dodder at Milltown. Thereafter the water was discharged into the millrace originating at the Dodder weir which fed the millpond at Clonskeagh that powered the mills at Henshaw's ironworks. These watercourses ran in close proximity to cottages in Windy Arbour, Farranboley and Concrete (Maps 19 & 20). Obviously, then, any sewage discharged into the River Slang would have serious consequences for residents living close to that river and its junction with the Dodder, or who depended on it to water their livestock.

The guardians of the Rathdown Union were responsible for the public health of the district lying on the south bank of the River Dodder at Milltown, and were answerable to the Local Government Board when it came to improving the sewerage of Dundrum and surrounding districts.[264] From the late 1880s reports from the proceedings of the Rathdown board of guardians reveal that complaints had been raised regularly by residents in Rosemount, Dundrum, about pollution of the River Slang. The difficulty for the Rathdown guardians was that the solution to the Dundrum drainage problem lay outside their control. In short, the Rathdown guardians, and from 1899 onwards, the Rathdown No. 1 Rural District Council (Rathdown RDC), wanted to discharge Dundrum's sewage into the Rathmines township's main sewer at Milltown, but the Rathmines township commissioners would not give their consent.[265]

Aside from the lack of co-operation from the Rathmines township, there were other major impediments to a Dundrum drainage scheme. These centred around excessive bureaucracy and political rivalries among several city bodies and local authorities, whose consents were required before any sewerage scheme could proceed. The most important of these were the Rathmines and Pembroke Main Drainage Board, which controlled the main receiving sewer at Milltown, and the Dublin Port and Docks Board, whose authority was required to discharge sewage into Dublin bay.[266]

In addition to the obstacles which lay beyond the control of the Rathdown RDC, inertia and disagreements among the local councillors also delayed matters for years. Several reports and inquiries were carried out during the years 1900 to 1905, including one prepared by Milltown publican T.P. Hackett, who had been co-opted to the Rathdown RDC in 1903.[267] In response to complaints from local ratepayers, the Dundrum drainage nuisance was examined in detail at a sworn public inquiry

263 For a detailed examination of conditions in the South Dublin Union, see Frank Cullen, *Cleansing Rural Dublin: Public Health and Housing Initiatives in the South Dublin Poor Law Union, 1880–1920* (Dublin, 2001), Chapter 2.

264 *Wicklow People*, 11 November 1899, p. 7.

265 *Dublin Daily Express*, 5 July 1888, p. 3.

266 *Rathmines News*, 1 December 1900, p. 5; 6 April 1901, p. 5; 4 January 1902, p. 4; 15 February 1902, p. 4; 8 October 1904, p. 3; *Wicklow Newsletter*, 11 January 1902, p. 4; *Wicklow People*, 7 April 1906, p. 2; NAI, BG 137, R1, BC 3, Correspondence from the Local Government Board to the Rathdown No. 1 RDC, No. 34280/16 June 1903. The city's main sewage treatment works at Ringsend were not completed until 1906.

267 *Wicklow People*, 9 March 1901, p. 2; *Rathmines News*, 5 July 1902, p. 4; *Wicklow Newsletter*, 4 June 1904, p. 8.

chaired by the Local Government Board on 18 April 1905.[268] The inquiry heard evidence that raw sewage from Dundrum village and the surrounding district had been draining into the River Slang for the previous 20 years, and that the river was practically an open sewer. The expert witnesses agreed that the proper solution was to drain the area via a new main sewer running parallel with the Dundrum Road, which would join the Rathmines township main sewer at Milltown. However, due to the impasse that existed between the various city and township authorities, the only alternative then available was for the Rathdown RDC to construct septic tanks on the south bank of the River Dodder at Farranboley. These tanks would treat the Dundrum sewage before discharging it into the River Dodder at Milltown.[269] This option had been investigated previously by the Rathdown RDC's engineer, and was found to be more expensive than the cost of the interconnecting sewerage scheme.[270] Nevertheless, since November 1901 the Local Government Board had, in principle, given loan approval to the Rathdown RDC to implement a remediation scheme using septic tanks.[271]

In spite of the sewage that was flowing into the River Dodder from its tributary, the Dodder somehow managed to support fauna at Milltown. In 1902 four local Milltown men and boys were prosecuted under the Fisheries Acts for damming the River Dodder at Milltown. The evidence given to the Dundrum Petty Sessions by the prosecuting police constable, William Brunt, was that he saw about 20 boys in the bed of the river, one of whom had a basket which contained several eels and a trout. The Dundrum magistrates did not consider that the charge had been sufficiently proven, and the cases against the four defendants, one of whom, Hugh Doyle, was the notorious drunkard and petty criminal, were dismissed.[272]

The outcome of the Local Government Board's inquiry was that the Rathdown RDC was found to be in breach of its statutory duty due under public health legislation. In short, the Rathdown RDC was a sanitary authority under the Public Health (Ireland) Act 1878 and in that capacity the local authority was legally required to provide sewerage for Dundrum. The Local Government Board gave the Rathdown RDC two years to put a proper sewerage system for Dundrum in place.[273] Accordingly, the Rathdown RDC had no choice but to go ahead with the septic tank scheme, at an estimated cost of £13,700.[274]

The Rathdown RDC proceeded to compulsorily acquire a little over two acres of land at Farranboley on which the council proposed to erect the septic tanks. The land in question was situated off the Dundrum Road (at the rear of St Luke's Crescent) and was occupied as tenants by the Milltown publican, T.P. Hackett, and his son-in-law Joseph Field of Donnybrook.[275] The Local Government Board then decided to hold a second inquiry, this time as part of the process of sanctioning a loan of £13,700 to the Rathdown RDC to meet the expenses of the Dundrum drainage scheme.[276] At the inquiry, the council's medical officer Dr Cahill said the drainage scheme was essential. He also gave

268 *Wicklow People*, 4 March 1905, p. 2; 8 April 1905, p. 2; *Dublin Evening Mail*, 18 April 1905, p. 4,

269 *Dublin Evening Mail*, 18 April 1905, p. 4; *Irish Times*, 19 April 1905, p. 5; *Rathmines News*, 22 April 1905, p. 3.

270 *Rathmines News*, 13 August 1904, p. 2.

271 *Wicklow People*, 9 November 1901, p. 5.

272 *Rathmines News*, 21 June 1902, p. 5; Dundrum Petty Sessions Order Book, 2 June 1902, entry nos 160–163.

273 *Dublin Evening Telegraph*, 21 March 1906, p. 4; *Rathmines News*, 24 March 1906, p. 2; 7 April 1906, p. 3; *Dublin Daily Express*, 5 April 1906, p. 7; *Wicklow People*, 7 April 1906, p. 2.

274 *Wicklow People*, 22 September 1906, pp. 2–3.

275 *Freeman's Journal*, 27 October 1906, p. 6; *Irish Independent*, 3 July 1903, p. 1.

276 *Evening Herald*, 5 March 1907, p. 2; *Rathmines News*, 9 March 1907, p. 4.

evidence that the cottages in Milltown (i.e. on the south bank of the Dodder in Concrete) caused nuisances and were injurious to public health. Not one of the cottages was fit for human habitation. If the septic tanks were 190 feet away from the public road and the cottages, the doctor did not believe they would be injurious to health.[277]

Following a tendering process the contractors for the septic tank scheme were appointed in October 1909 and they began site works at Farranboley, Milltown in February 1910.[278] While the Rathdown RDC was progressing with the septic tank scheme at Milltown, some of the councillors had continued to lobby the Dublin Port and Docks Board and Dublin Corporation to obtain their consent for the Dundrum sewage to be piped directly to the city's Ringsend purification works.[279] During these talks the water purification works at Milltown were suspended.[280] The negotiations paid off and the parties agreed terms on 15 September 1910.[281] The new plans now involved the construction of an outfall sewer to carry the sewage of both Dundrum and Rathfarnham (agreement having been reached with the South Dublin RDC in this regard) along the Dodder valley to Ringsend.[282] Although the installation of the septic tanks had more or less been completed before works at Milltown were suspended, the evidence suggests that they were never used. An OS map of 1938 shows the septic tanks located between the River Slang and the millrace attached to Millmount, and records them as disused (Map 21). Like the Rathmines Wards inquiries of 1903 and 1904, this was another example of the waste of public money by local authorities and the Local Government Board.

One might have expected that the sewerage problem had been solved once and for all after the Dundrum main sewer pipe had been laid and connected to Dublin Corporation's sewerage system. Unfortunately, this was not the case because most of the dwellings in Concrete were not promptly connected to the main drainage pipe on the Dundrum Road at Milltown. In October 1915, the Rathdown RDC medical officer for the Dundrum district, Dr Neary, inspected the housing conditions at Concrete and subsequently produced a report which was highly critical of the lack of proper sanitation arrangements at Marble Hall, Old Bridge House and the surrounding cottages (Map 20). In particular, Dr Neary deplored the fact that sewage from houses in Concrete was discharged into a millrace, notwithstanding that the main sewer ran within a few feet of some of the affected houses, such as Mowlds Cottages. The cottages in Concrete were owned by Thomas Hackett, a son of the T.P. Hackett mentioned previously.[283] In a letter to the Rathdown RDC, Hackett brazenly dismissed Dr Neary's criticisms of his tenement properties:

> *The closets do empty into a fast-flowing mill stream, and are consequently the best suited for tenement property. Mr Rogan [grocer/publican at Windy Arbour] can give you first-hand information on this subject, as his public house empties into a mill stream, and not directly, as at Marble Hall; so do several closets in his neighbourhood [Windy Arbour]; and still he is a healthy-looking man.*[284]

277 *Rathmines News*, 9 March 1907, p. 4.

278 *Dublin Evening Telegraph*, 6 October 1909, p. 3; *Wicklow People*, 23 October 1909, p. 2; 19 February 1910, p. 2.

279 *Irish Times*, 17 January 1908, p. 3; *Wicklow People*, 8 February 1908, p. 1; 21 March 1908, p. 2; 24 September 1910, p. 2.

280 *Dublin Evening Mail*, 1 February 1911, p. 1.

281 *Wicklow People*, 24 September 1910, p. 2.

282 *Dublin Daily Express*, 17 November 1910, p. 10; *Wicklow Newsletter*, 21 October 1911, p. 1.

283 *Wicklow Newsletter*, 23 October 1915, p. 8; 6 November 1915, p. 8.

284 *Wicklow Newsletter*, 6 November 1915, p. 8; Thom's Directory 1915, p. 1772.

The sanitation problems at Concrete were but one aspect of the deplorable housing conditions that existed there and at Windy Arbour at that time. In the longer term, the Rathdown RDC wanted to rehouse the inhabitants living in these districts but, due to the out-break of the Great War, the Local Government Board would not sanction any new local authority housing schemes.[285] Instead, the Local Government Board directed the Rathdown RDC to remedy sanitation problems at Concrete using the council's powers under the Public Health acts. Thus, Dr Neary's report was sent to the council's engineer, Mr McCarthy, to carry out an inspection of the sanitary defects at Concrete.[286] McCarthy's report was brought before the bi-monthly meeting of the Rathdown RDC on 15 December 1915. The council ordered that the engineer's report be forwarded to Thomas Hackett and that he be given six months to carry out McCarthy's recommendations.[287]

Thomas Hackett ignored the engineer's report and he did nothing to abate the ongoing sewage pollution at Concrete. Unfortunately, Hackett's inaction was to prove fatal. On 17 May 1916 the Rathdown RDC received a report from Dr Neary of a fatal case of enteric fever at Mowlds Cottages, Milltown. These five houses had no running water or sanitation and the inhabitants had to obtain their water from a spring or well close to their homes which in turn was located very close to the millrace. The well had become contaminated by sewage seeping into it from the polluted millrace. As a result, a seven-year-old boy, Patrick Rorke, became ill on 1 May 1916 and subsequently died in hospital. Dr Neary ordered that the polluted well be closed and that the Rorke's cottage be disinfected.[288]

The death of poor Patrick Rorke was overshadowed by the 1916 Rising and the subsequent arrests that were taking place in its aftermath. Milltown native and Irish Volunteer, Patrick Doyle, had died at the battle of Mount Street Bridge on 26 April 1916, while local men Joseph McKenna, James D'Arcy and Thomas Lambert were subsequently arrested and imprisoned in follow-up operations.[289] In the meantime, the clerk of the Rathdown RDC was ordered to write to Thomas Hackett stating that the matter would be placed in the hands of the council's solicitors.[290] When the Rathdown councillors met on 21 June 1916 the following correspondence was read and noted:

> *From Mr T.J. Cullen architect, Suffolk Street, Dublin, with reference to the sanitary defects at Mr Hackett's Cottages, Milltown, and stating that he (Mr Cullen) has been instructed to inform the Council that he has this matter in hands and will have the work carried out without delay. That Mr Hackett instructed him over a month ago and the cause of the delay was due to the disturbances.*[291]

The sanitation saga of Thomas Hackett's tenement property illustrates the complete disregard that most landlords had for the health and welfare of their tenants, and the contempt in which

285 NAI, BG/137/R1/B16, Rathdown RDC No. 1, outward letter book May 1915–September 1916, p. 386; letter dated 21 October 1915 to Dr Neary, p. 398, letter dated 23 October 1915 to Dr Neary p. 671; letter dated 25 February 1916 to R.M. Butler.

286 *Wicklow People*, 6 November 1915, p. 13; *Wicklow Newsletter*, 6 November 1915, p. 8.

287 NAI, BG/137/R1/A23, Rathdown RDC No. 1 Minute Books April 1915–March 1916, 15 December 1915, p. 629; NAI, BG/137/R1/B16, Rathdown RDC No. 1, Outward Letter Book May 1915–September 1916, p. 516, letter dated 17 December 1915 to Thomas Hackett.

288 NAI, BG/137/R1/A24, Rathdown RDC No. 1 Minute Books April 1916–March 1917, 17 May 1916, p. 116, 7 June 1916, p. 149; NAI, BG/137/R1/BC 13, Local Government Board letters to Rathdown No. 1 UDC 15 & 23 May 1916.

289 O'Brien, *Blood on the Streets*, p. 69; *Weekly Irish Times*, Sinn Fein Rebellion Handbook, pp. 76, 77, 84.

290 NAI, BG/137/R1/A24, Rathdown RDC No. 1 Minute Books April 1916–March 1917, 7 June 1916, p. 151.

291 NAI, BG/137/R1/A24, Rathdown RDC No. 1 Minute Books April 1916–March 1917, 21 June 1916, p. 218.

they held the local sanitary authorities. It is not known which of shame or the threat of legal proceedings was the prime motivator that finally forced Hackett to carry out the remedial work to his cottages. It is revealing too that Hackett could afford to pay an architect to oversee the sanitation works at his tenement property. Despite these vital improvements in sanitation, Concrete continued to be a very unattractive and unhealthy place to live: the sanitary sub-officer for Dundrum reported a few months later in September 1916 that the passage in front of Hackett's Cottages was in a filthy state.[292]

PUBLIC HEALTH IMPROVEMENT INITIATIVES

The improvements made in water supply and sewage disposal in the Milltown district during the period 1880 to 1910 undoubtedly reduced the instances of water-borne infectious diseases. By the turn of the twentieth century the major concern of the health authorities in Ireland was the high incidence of phthisis, better known as consumption or pulmonary tuberculosis (TB). In 1908, a study found that TB was responsible nationally for 50 per cent of the deaths between the ages of fifteen and thirty-five, with the maximum number of deaths occurring around the age of twenty-five.[293] There is sufficient evidence available to suggest that TB was a serious menace in Milltown at this time. When Miss Victoria Henshaw read out the 1903/1904 annual report for the Milltown, Clonskeagh and Dundrum Nursing Association, she referred, by way of example, to three patients who were undergoing treatment for TB.[294] Deaths from the disease were unavoidable, though: Mr and Mrs T.P. Hackett suffered the grievous loss of their eldest son, twenty-eight-year-old Patrick, to TB in 1900.[295] A probable factor in the incidence of TB in Milltown was that, notwithstanding that the disease was most frequently transmitted in enclosed environments, infection could also be caused by consuming infected milk from tuberculous cows.[296]

The severity of the TB problem was such that it was the main item on the agenda of the Rathmines UDC's meeting on New Year's Day, 1908. A motion put forward by the chairman, Thomas Edmondson, to build chalets accommodating 10 to 20 beds in the Clonskeagh isolation hospital at Vergemount (now Clonskeagh Hospital) to treat early cases of TB was defeated. Instead, a revised motion was passed whereby the Royal Hospital, Donnybrook, or other institutions were to be asked to take charge of chronic incurable cases at a fixed charge per capita, and that the district dispensary medical officer be requested to set apart one day per week for special treatment and advice to persons suffering from any form of TB.[297] The council's mean spirited attitude to TB was further in evidence when, three and a half years later, the councillors passed a resolution on 7 June 1911:

> *strongly disapproving of the Royal Hospital's proposal to erect a new wing for patients suffering from advanced tuberculosis as being injurious to the health of the neighbourhood and likely to seriously depreciate the value of property in that portion of the township.*[298]

---

292 NAI, BG/137/R1/A24, Rathdown RDC No. 1 Minute Books April 1916–March 1917, 6 September 1916, p. 389.

293 Jacinta Prunty, *Dublin slums 1800–1925: A study in urban geography* (Dublin, 1999), p. 163.

294 *Rathmines News*, 6 June 1903, p. 3.

295 *Rathmines News*, 15 March 1900, p. 4; Register of Deaths for the District of Rathmines 1900, p. 888, entry no.396, 15 March 1900.

296 Greta Jones, *Captain of all these men of death: The history of tuberculosis in 19th and 20th century Ireland* (Amsterdam, 2001), p. 15; James Deeny, *To Cure and to Care: Memoirs of a Chief Medical Officer* (Dublin, 1989), p. 56.

297 *Belfast Newsletter*, 2 January 1908, p. 7.

298 Dublin City Archives, Rathmines and Rathgar UDC papers, UDC /1/Min/7a, Book 1902–17, pp. 206, 317–18.

Of considerable long-term benefit to public health was the creation in 1907 of the Women's National Heath Association of Ireland, at the instigation of the Countess of Aberdeen. This new body established local branches throughout the country with specific emphasis on preventative medicine, and fighting TB in particular.[299] The work done by the Women's National Heath Association was invaluable in improving the healthcare of babies and children in Milltown and the wider vicinity. At the Association's annual general meeting in 1923 it was reported that the district nurse had carried out 6,156 visits, and that there were no deaths to record amongst the infants and children under her care.[300] A by-product of the Association's public health work was the setting up in Milltown of the St Joseph's Baby Club, which had its premises in a wooden chalet located on 'The Strand' in Milltown Village (Map 21). The baby club opened every Monday, and provided advice and instructions to mothers on nursing and feeding their infants. In May 1922 62 mothers and 82 children were attending the club.[301] The following year, the baby club came under the control of the Rathmines Child Welfare Centre.[302]

THE ENDING OF THE LEESON CONNECTION WITH MILLTOWN

Thus far, this chapter has focused on the lives of the people who lived and worked in Milltown during the nineteenth and early twentieth centuries. At this point it is appropriate to reintroduce the absentee landlords, the earls of Milltown, and explore their changing circumstances.

The acquisition and development of the extensive Leeson landholdings in Milltown in the eighteenth century has been discussed in detail in Chapter 4. By the mid-nineteenth century the Leeson estate in Milltown had become fragmented into multiple landholdings and sub-lettings which were held by middleman, so that the earls ceased to have any control over the physical development of their freehold estate in Milltown. Thus, the land agent for the Leeson estate was responsible for collecting the annual rent from tenants who held their properties under the original Leeson leases of the eighteenth century, and who by now were all absentee middlemen. The Leeson finances had reached a critical condition by the 1850s. This state of affairs was caused by a combination of a loss of rental income during the Famine, difficulties with obtaining credit and the fourth earl's predilection for gambling.[303] These circumstances explain why the fourth earl of Milltown put up his freehold estate for auction on 8 January 1856. Of the 119 lots put forward for auction nine (lots 51 to 59) related to the Leeson estate in Milltown and Clonskeagh.[304]

There is considerable confusion and uncertainty concerning the outcome of the auction vis-à-vis the earl's Milltown and Clonskeagh properties. According to the newspaper reports all of the properties bar lot 57 were sold but these reports were subsequently proven to be inaccurate.[305] In transpired that the sale of lots 51, 52 and 54 did not complete, possibly due to litigation with the earl's creditors which went to court in December 1858.[306] In any event, four of the unsold lots out

299 Prunty, *Dublin slums*, pp. 163, 167.

300 *Irish Times*, 29 May 1923, p. 9.

301 *Freeman's Journal*, 16 May 1922, p. 3.

302 *Rathmines Free Press*, 10 March 1923, p. 2.

303 Laffan and Mulligan, *Russborough*, pp. 173–4.

304 NAI, Landed Estates Court Rental, vol. 38, no. 3, 'Particulars and Conditions of Sale of the Freehold Estate of the Earl of Milltown to be sold on 8 January 1856', lots 51 to 59.

305 *Freeman's Journal*, 10 January 1856, p. 4; *Allnut's Irish Land Schedule*, 15 January 1856, p. 3.

306 *Freeman's Journal*, 15 December 1858, p. 4.

of the original group of nine were put up for auction again on 29 June 1859 but the earl of Milltown withdrew them shortly before the auction day.[307] In short, the Leesons retained their freehold estate (which over time was converted from leases for lives renewable for ever to fee farm grants) in four out of the original nine Milltown and Clonskeagh holdings. These lands were, from time to time, mortgaged as part of the Leeson family's credit arrangements during the second half of the nineteenth century.[308]

It was that lack of a male heir rather than financial woes which eventually extinguished the Leeson peerage. On 30 May 1890 the sixth earl of Milltown, Edward Nugent Leeson, died childless. Edward's brother Henry very briefly succeeded to the title. He, too, died childless ten months later in reduced circumstances in a hotel in Torquay. Consequently, the title became extinct on the death of the seventh earl. The family seat, Russborough House in Blessington, County Wicklow, and the rest of the Leeson estates were inherited by a nephew, Edmund Russborough Turton (1857–1929).[309] In due course Edmund Turton's grandson, Edmund Christopher Turton (1915–1983), succeeded to the family's residual freehold estate in Milltown. Edmund's connection with Ireland effectively ceased when his widowed grandmother, Lady Clementina Turton, sold Russborough House in May 1931.[310]

The vicissitudes of the Leeson and Turton families added another layer of complexity to the freehold title of Milltown. As a result, the timing of the final disappearance of the Leeson estate in Milltown is virtually impossible to pin down. After an existence spanning nearly 250 years, the Leeson's fading shadow in Milltown was just about discernible in the early 1950s. As part of their title investigations, Dublin Corporation's lawyers recorded that Dr Edward [*sic*] Christopher Turton, among others, were the owners or reputed owners of nos 1–4 Strand Cottages in Milltown village, which were compulsorily acquired by the Corporation along with other condemned property in 1952.[311]

CONCLUSION

The 30 years from 1880–1910 were transformational for Milltown in so many ways. In particular, the village emerged from the poverty and isolation of the second and third quarters of the nineteenth century. The overriding impression that emerges time and again is how quickly Milltown became so much more integrated with the outside world. The contending influences of the Catholic Church, the IPP, unionist opposition to Home Rule by local Protestant businessmen and town councillors, and the nascent trade union movement brought Milltown into the wider religious, political and social fabric of Dublin and Ireland during the critical period reviewed in this chapter. These broader developments were nonetheless overshadowed by local poverty in Concrete and Farranboley, localities which were bedevilled by dire housing conditions and anti-social behaviour. ■

307 NAI, Landed Estates Court Rental, vol. 56, no. 17, 'Particulars and Conditions of Sale of the Freehold Estate of the Earl of Milltown to be sold on 29 June 1859', lots 12, 13, 14 and 15; *Allnut's Irish Land Schedule,* 15 June 1859, p. 1.

308 See for example, RD 1859/28/93, RD 1859/34/41, RD 1862/21/119.

309 Laffan and Mulligan, *Russborough*, pp. 189–90, 204.

310 Laffan and Mulligan, *Russborough*, pp. 230–1.

311 Minutes of the Municipal Council of the City of Dublin, 1953, Milltown Village Area Compulsory Purchase Order 1952, pp. 164–5.

MILLTO

Chapter 12: Thomas Hackett, Landlord, Publican and Local Politician

Chapter 12: Thomas Hackett, Landlord, Publican and Local Politician

INTRODUCTION

Of the dozen or so families that can be identified as long-term inhabitants of Milltown – having at least three or more generations of residency – the Hackett family has left behind the greatest impression in the historical record. The most prominent member of this old Milltown family was Thomas Patrick (T.P.) Hackett, who lived all his life in Milltown from his birth in 1833 or 1834 to his death on 25 January 1908. This chapter examines the rise to prominence of the Hackett family in Milltown and the career of T.P. Hackett, who combined several roles as landlord, grocer and publican, local politician and prominent lobbyist for the licensed vintners trade.

THE ORIGINS OF THE HACKETT FAMILY OF MILLTOWN

The Hackett family of Milltown can be traced back to the 1830s. In 1837 Patrick Hackett acquired a 61-year lease of a grocery/pub with living quarters above it and 18 small single-storey cottages, all of which were located on the south side of the village main street backing onto the River Dodder (Map 14). Patrick Hackett was already living on the commercial premises when he signed his lease.[1] Hackett's business evidently thrived. Six years later, in 1843, Patrick acquired a 60-year lease of Old Bridge House together with two acres and three roods of land on which he subsequently built eight cottages. All of the second tranche of property was located to the west of the Packhorse Bridge on the south bank of the Dodder, in Farranboley townland, and later became known locally as Concrete.[2] Patrick Hackett first appears in the Thom's directory for 1846, which describes him as a corn factor and a spirit merchant.[3]

1 Lease dated 4 July 1837 Robert Dry to Patrick Hackett (NAI, MS 999/355/1/10); Griffith Valuation, Primary Valuation of Tenements, Dublin, Barony of Uppercross, Parish of St Peter, Townland of Milltown, nos 57, 66, 67, 68, 95–106, 148, 149–151.

2 RD 1843/15/78. NAI, VO, OL53661, House Book, Townland of Farranboley 1845, no. 2.

3 Thom's Directory 1846, p. 1112.

Patrick Hackett was a firm supporter of Daniel O'Connell. In 1840 he was appointed as a collector of the annual tribute fund for Daniel O'Connell, and throughout the 1840s he actively recruited for the Repeal movement.[4] In October 1840 the *Freeman's Journal* reported that Patrick Hackett had recruited 95 repealers, some of whom resided in Milltown village.[5] By this stage he was married with a large family. His household in Milltown consisted of his wife Charlotte, their children Thomas, John, Teresa, Elizabeth, Anna (or Anastasia), Emma (or Emily) and Martin, and their domestic servant, Bridget Ryan.[6] Another son, James, was born in 1843 or 1844.[7] Most of Patrick and Charlotte's children prospered and married well. Thomas, John and James lived all their lives in Milltown, and will be discussed presently. Elizabeth married a Cork-born builder called John Cunningham and settled in Dalkey, County Dublin.[8] Similarly, another daughter, Charlotte Hackett, also married a Dalkey native, Edward Field, who was a shop keeper.[9] Edward Field's brother, William, was a prominent cattle trader and local politician. William Field became a nationalist MP for Dublin, serving from 1892 to 1918.[10] The Field/Hackett family connection was further strengthened when Patrick Hackett's granddaughter, Charlotte (T.P. Hackett's eldest daughter), married Joseph Field of Donnybrook in 1903.[11]

Emily Hackett married a tailor named John Purcell in 1863 and the couple later emigrated to New York.[12] Emily's brother James also married into the Purcell family when he wedded Teresa Purcell.[13] The Purcell family lived in Windy Arbour and had extensive family and publican business interests in that district.[14] James and Teresa Hackett (née Purcell) lived in a house called Castleview on the north side of the village main street beside the Catholic church at its western end.[15] James was a carpenter who died in 1890 of kidney disease at the relatively young age of forty-six.[16] James was survived by his wife Teresa and a large family of whom

4 *Freeman's Journal*, 1 August 1840, p. 2; 22 October 1842, p. 1; 2 November 1840, p. 1; 16 November 1844, p. 2; 13 November 1845, p. 2.

5 *Freeman's Journal*, 2 October 1840, p. 4. The names of the subscribers published in the newspapers can be matched off against the names listed in the Griffith's Valuation and contemporary Valuation Office records.

6 *Freeman's Journal*, 1 August 1840, p. 2. A daughter named Charlotte is omitted from the 1840 list.

7 Registry of Deaths, District of Dublin South, Rathmines, for 1890, entry no. 339, death of James Hackett 10 November 1890 aged forty-six.

8 *Freeman's Journal*, 11 February 1853, p. 4; Thom's Directory 1868, p. 1560.

9 Marriage register for Rathmines RC church, at entry no. 1611, 4 February 1868. Thom's Directory 1868, p. 1560

10 Obituary of Edward Field in the *Freeman's Journal*, 16 January 1889, p. 7 and obituary of William Field in the *Wicklow People*, 4 May 1935, p. 6.

11 *Irish Independent*, 3 July 1903, p. 1; *Rathmines News*, 4 July 1903, p. 2.

12 Marriage register for Rathmines RC parish church, at entry no. 1132, 29 July 1863; RD 1873/16/210.

13 Birth register for Dublin South, Rathmines, birth of Teresa Hackett at entry no. 369, 29 September 1877; *Rathmines News*, 1 February 1902, p. 3; *Thom's Directory 1879*, p. 1503.

14 *Rathmines News*, 1 February 1902, p. 3.

15 Thom's Directory 1872, p. 1601. Castle View got its name because it faced Clonskeagh Castle across the River Dodder, a prospect now largely obscured by the Dodderview apartment complex on the south bank of the river. In the mid-1950s Castle view, by then numbered 38 Milltown Road, was demolished as part of Dublin Corporation's Compulsory Order for Milltown and the Marian Hall was built on the site. In turn, the Marian Hall was demolished in the early twenty-first century and replaced by a pharmacy and the Marian Hall apartment complex.

16 Civil registration of deaths in the district of Dublin South, Rathmines, 1890, no. 339, 10 November 1890.

four daughters and two sons have been identified.[17] Teresa later became the postmistress for Milltown post office, where her daughter Mary also worked as an assistant postmistress and telegraphist.[18]

When Patrick Hackett died in the late 1850s his widow Charlotte took over the shop on the east side of the main road through Milltown village. The Thom's Directory for 1860 describes Charlotte Hackett as a provision dealer whereas her deceased husband had previously been described as a grocer and nurseryman.[19] After Charlotte Hackett died it appears that her two sons Thomas and John took over the running of the family grocery business and tenement property in Milltown. John Hackett, who remained a lifelong bachelor, worked in the family grocery business.[20] His brother Thomas managed the property side of the family business. The rest of this chapter is devoted to Thomas Hackett's activities, reviewing his roles as a landlord and publican before finally examining his political career.

THOMAS HACKETT'S RECORD AS A LANDLORD

On 6 August 1868 Thomas Hackett married a girl called Mary Anne Dwyer, who was from Thomas Street in Dublin.[21] Thomas and Mary went on to have a large family of four sons and four daughters, and lived over the family's pub and grocery premises on the south side of Milltown village main street, later numbered 90 Milltown Road (Pl. 8).[22] He was thus well located to oversee the several tenement cottages which ran along the village main street as far as the Packhorse Bridge and on the south bank of the River Dodder.

The 1860s and 1870 saw the enactment of new sewerage and sanitation laws which gave additional powers to poor law guardians and urban township commissioners to abate nuisances and carry out disease prevention measures. The Sanitary Act of 1866 required local authorities to appoint a sanitary inspector to advise on the removal of nuisances and the provision of proper drainage and clean water.[23] In January 1871 Thomas Hackett was prosecuted under the Sanitary Act by the Board of Guardians of the South Dublin Union. The sanitary officer sought an order compelling Hackett to cover a drain which flowed in front of his cottages in Milltown into the River Dodder, as the *Evening Freeman* explained:

> *At a place near these cottages the inhabitants of Milltown have been in the habit of procuring water from the Dodder for their domestic purposes, and several communications were made by the guard-*

17 NAI, 1901 Census, Form A and Form B.1, residents of house no. 87 in Milltown Road, Rathmines and Rathgar East Electoral Division, Milltown Townland; NAI, 1911 Census, Form A, residents of house no. 32 in Milltown Road, Rathmines and Rathgar East Electoral Division; *Evening Herald*, 21 April 1893, p. 3 (Death notice for Teresa Mary Hackett junior). Marriage register for Harrington street RC parish church, at entry no. 5, 25 January 1897 (John Hackett and Alice Bell).

18 Thom's Directory 1897, p. 1568; NAI, 1901 Census, Form A, residents of house no. 87 in Milltown Road, Rathmines and Rathgar East Electoral Division, Milltown Townland, Barony of Uppercross, Co. Dublin.

19 Thom's Directory 1857, p. 1175; 1860, p. 1341.

20 NAI, 1901 Census, Form A, residents of house no. 27 in Concrete, Milltown, Dundrum Electoral Division, Farranboley Townland, Half Barony of Rathdown, Co. Dublin; Slater's Royal National Commercial Directory of Ireland 1881, p. 222.

21 Marriage register for St Catherine's RC parish church, 6 August 1868.

22 NAI, 1901 Census, Form A and Form B.1, residents of house no. 45 in Milltown Road, Rathmines and Rathgar East Electoral Division, Milltown Townland, Barony of Uppercross, Co. Dublin; *Irish Independent*, 16 March 1900, p. 1 (Death notice for Patrick Hackett); 14 February 1942, p. 1.

23 Helen Burke, *The People and the Poor Law in Nineteenth Century Ireland* (The Women's Education Bureau, 1987), p. 276.

> *ians to prevent his tenants from using the drain as a common receptacle for sewage matter. A previous summons against Mr Hackett had been dismissed by the magistrate for insufficient evidence.*[24]

The case was adjourned so that an engineer's report could be prepared. Once this had been done, the engineer recommended that it would not be advisable to cover the open drain because this would cause it to overflow into the cottages. The engineer also recommended that a water closet be removed. The magistrate ordered Hackett to abate the nuisance as recommended by the engineer.[25] The most revealing aspect of this case is how reliant the villagers were on the River Dodder for their domestic water supply, and how vulnerable this supply was to contamination. For some inhabitants, such as those living in Mowlds Cottages on the south bank of the River Dodder, this unsatisfactory situation continued to exist as late as 1916, notwithstanding the gradual introduction of piped water to Milltown from the Vartry and Glenasmole reservoirs in the late nineteenth century.[26] The gap between the rich and the poor in Milltown can also be measured in terms of water supply and sanitation. An advertisement in the *Irish Times* in 1879 for a detached house to rent in Temple Road at £130 per annum referred to the availability of hot and cold water throughout the house, and highlighted its shower, reclining baths and good sanitation.[27]

When the townland of Milltown was incorporated into the Rathmines and Rathgar township in 1880 responsibility for sanitary matters in Milltown village switched from the Board of Guardians of the South Dublin Union to the commissioners of the Rathmines and Rathgar township. The Board of Guardians of the Rathdown No. 1 Union remained responsible for sanitary matters on the south bank of the River Dodder at Milltown. In 1885 some of Hackett's Cottages in Milltown village were connected to the township's new main sewer but despite this improvement Thomas Hackett was frequently in trouble with the Rathmines authorities over breaches of sanitary legislation.[28] In his disputes with the sanitary authorities Thomas Hackett revealed an obstinate side to his character. On at least two occasions Hackett was handed down substantial fines for disobeying the magistrates' court orders and on another occasion he unsuccessfully appealed a decision of the magistrates to the Recorder's Court for 'refusal to carry out certain sanitary regulations in respect of nine cottages owned by him'.[29] But perhaps Hackett's most revealing attitude to the sanitary welfare of his tenants can be gleaned from the following advertisement which he placed in the *Freeman's Journal* in September 1890: 'Sewer Pipes: wanted a quantity of 4 and 6-inch, second hand, in good order; state quantity, price and where seen.'[30]

Whatever doubts there may have been about the diameter of the pipes – which probably explains why Hackett was constantly in trouble with the sanitary inspectors – his desire to economise using second-hand sewer pipes is unequivocally damning. In the absence of any satisfactory explanation,

24 *Evening Freeman's Journal*, 16 January 1871, p. 4.

25 *Saunders's Newsletter*, 30 January 1871, p. 3; *Weekly Freeman*, 4 February 1871, p. 8.

26 NAI, BG/137/R1/A24, Rathdown RDC No. 1 Minute Books April 1916–March 1917, 17 May 1916, p. 116 and 7 June 1916, p. 149; NAI, BG/137/R1/BC 13, Local Government Board letters to Rathdown No. 1 UDC 15 & 23 May 1916.

27 *Irish Times*, 11 December 1879, p. 8.

28 Dublin City Archives, Rathmines and Rathgar UDC papers, UDC Minute Books, UDC/1/Mins/1/5, 1878-1885, p. 441 and UDC/1/Mins/1/6, 1886-93, pp. 241, 260, 268; *Freeman's Journal*, 25 May 1901, p. 3.

29 *Dublin Daily Express*, 26 August 1898, p. 6; *Freeman's Journal*, 24 October 1889, p. 3; *Dublin Evening Telegraph*, 11 April 1894, p. 3.

30 *Freeman's Journal*, 20 September 1890, p. 1.

Hackett should also probably be criticised for petitioning the Rathmines UDC to remove a public water fountain on the village main street opposite the post office, a request which was refused because the councillors considered that the fountain was necessary for the inhabitants (Map 18).[31]

The housing conditions of Hackett's tenants on the south bank of the River Dodder were in some respects worse than those living on the north bank of the river in the village. After local millwright John Lee's death, his widow Sarah leased the marble works and saw mills beside the Packhorse Bridge in 1881 to Thomas Hackett at the annual rent of £15.[32] Soon afterwards Hackett converted the buildings into a tenement which was known locally as 'Marble Hall', in reference to its previous use as a marble saw mill by John Lee. The living quarters typically comprised one or two rooms, which Hackett rented to the poorest inhabitants of Milltown.[33] Marble Hall became notorious among the medical officers of health and the sanitary inspectors of the Rathdown Union for its unhealthy overcrowded living conditions. Following an outbreak of scarlatina fever there in August 1892, which resulted in a child being sent to Cork Street fever hospital, the relieving officer of the Rathdown Union reported that he had fumigated the tenement and destroyed the infected bedding, for which he paid 33*s.* compensation to the unfortunate inhabitants.[34]

Six years later, in 1898, the medical officer of health for the Dundrum electoral division of the Rathdown No. 1 Union, Dr Usher, reported that he had 'inspected houses at Milltown the property of Mr Hackett and found certain external defects which tend to make them damp and recommended that the owner be noticed to have them repaired'. Hackett duly complied with the order made by the Board of Guardians of the Rathdown No. 1 Union (who were acting in their capacity as a sanitary authority) and had his cottages repaired.[35] These cottages had been built by Thomas's father, Patrick Hackett, in the 1840s and had not been well maintained. On twentieth-century OS maps the houses are called Field's Cottages, in reference to Thomas Hackett's son-in-law Joseph Field, to whom they were presumably gifted when Joseph Field married Charlotte Hackett in 1903 (Map 20).[36]

When Hackett gave evidence to the Rathmines Wards Inquiry, which was being undertaken by an investigative committee of Dublin County Council in 1903, he was unapologetic about his record as a landlord:

> *Mr T.P. Hackett, who has resided at Milltown for 71 years, was the third witness, and, answering Mr Gordon, he said he did not consider the [Rathmines] Urban Council a 'troublesome body of men' because they had prosecuted him over his tenement property. He had fought the Council, and beaten them in some instances. He admitted that the Urban Council were paying careful attention to proper sanitary accommodation for the artisans and working classes, but they were 'unreasonable.'*[37]

---

31 *Rathmines News*, 4 May 1901, p. 4.

32 RD 1881/11/187.

33 *Freeman's Journal*, 30 September 1881, p. 2.

34 Rathdown Poor Law Union, Board of Guardians Minute Book A99 March–September 1892, Folio 24, p. 456 (10 August 1892) and Folio 17, p. 473 (17 August 1892).

35 Rathdown Poor Law Union, Board of Guardians Minute Book A112 September 1898–March 1899, Folio 17, p. 185 (23 November 1898) and Folio 17, p. 281 (21 December 1898).

36 *Irish Independent*, 3 July 1903, p. 1.

37 *Rathmines News*, 14 November 1903, p. 2.

At this juncture it is appropriate to briefly touch on Thomas Hackett's behaviour in the context of contemporary tenement landlords. The appalling conditions of Dublin city's slums in the nineteenth and twentieth centuries are well-known and have been extensively studied by historians. Mary Daly, for example, concluded that while tenement owners were found at all levels of society, the majority belonged to small businessmen like Thomas Hackett. Furthermore, there seems to have been little social stigma attached to being a tenement landlord, many of whom were members of Dublin Corporation.[38]

From the year 1880 onwards, the records of the Dundrum Petty Sessions court provide information about John and Thomas Hackett's dealings with their tenants who were living on the south bank of the Dodder in Concrete. These cases typically dealt with common landlord and tenant disputes, such as non-payment of rent, trespass and damage to property.[39] Evictions seem to have been very rare but one case involving Thomas Hackett and a tenant called Mary O'Keeffe, who had a turbulent relationship with her neighbours, was reported on extensively in the Rathmines News.[40] Mary O'Keeffe lived with her widowed mother Bridget O'Keeffe in Hackett's Cottages in Concrete.[41] Thomas Hackett got an order for possession of his cottage on 3 June 1901 but the two women refused to leave the house.[42] Hackett went to court again in July to get possession of his property. The press report of the proceedings at the Dundrum Petty Sessions is worth quoting, because it throws some light on contemporary attitudes to landlord and tenant relations and homelessness, issues which are to the fore in modern Ireland:

> *The Clerk informed the magistrates that the defendant [Mary O'Keeffe] was evicted by Mr Hackett, but she only removed her furniture outside the door, and it had remained there ever since. Mr Hackett said on 3 June he obtained a decree for possession in fourteen days, and it was executed. Defendant's things were put outside the house, and she had not taken them away. She had caused a great deal of annoyance to people. She and her mother kept quarrelling late at night and he wanted to ger her removed ... The defendant (crying) said she had lived there 36 years, and she could not get another place. Mr Hackett said the furniture remained outside the door. Defendant said she had been looking for a house, and she was starving. Mr Hackett said sympathising people came to see her, and she appeared to be doing very well.*
>
> *Mr David [presiding magistrate] – Mr Hackett must get his place. Mr Vere Ward Browne [magistrate] – Does she sleep out in all weathers? Head Constable McGowan said she was practically camping out, and the things were placed up against the door of the cottage. The relieving officer[43] was communicated with, and defendant's mother was taken in by a neighbour. Mr Vere Ward Browne – Is the object to prevent the place being taken over by someone else? Head Constable – Well, she is camping out, and furniture is up against the door. Defendant said she would go, as she*

38 Daly, *Dublin: The deposed capital*, pp. 284–6.

39 See for example Dundrum Petty Sessions Order Book 1880, 28 June 1880, no. 179, 18 October 1880, no. 12, 1 November 1880, n. 28; Order Book 1881, 28 November 1881, no. 114; Order Book 1895, 19 August 1895, no. 82, 83 and 84. Records available on-line on https://www.findmypast.ie.

40 *Rathmines News*, 28 April 1900, p. 5; 21 July 1900, p. 4; 4 August 1900, p. 5; 10 November 1900, p. 5; 8 June 1901, p. 5; 20 July 1901, p. 2.

41 NAI, 1901 Census, Form A and Form B.1, residents of house no. 18 in Farranboley (Concrete), Dundrum Electoral Division, Farranboley townland.

42 *Rathmines News*, 8 June 1901, p. 5; 20 July 1901, p. 2; Dundrum Petty Sessions Order Book 1901, 15 July 1901, no. 16.

43 The relieving officer of the Rathdown Union workhouse at Loughlinstown was the nineteenth-century equivalent to a social welfare officer.

thought she had another place to go to. The Chairman said the Bench would adjourn the case for a fortnight to enable her to shift. Mr Hackett said the woman was very unreliable, but he was willing to leave the matter to the magistrates. He did not wish to act harshly. The Chairman said if she did not go something unpleasant would be done towards her. The Clerk (to defendant) – You will be taken out of there if you don't go. The case was then adjourned.[44]

The case was adjourned until 29 July 1901 but Mary O'Keeffe did not turn up to court and so it must be assumed that Hackett got full possession of the cottage.[45]

Four years later, in July 1905 Thomas Hackett summoned two local men to court for taking away stones which he (Hackett) had taken out of the bed of the River Dodder at Milltown. Hackett told the court that 'he would not have prosecuted if the men had not defied him when he cautioned them'.[46] Clearly, Hackett would not tolerate people who challenged his authority. In fairness to Hackett, he dropped the charges against John Rhaul and Arthur Dunbar on receipt of their undertaking not to remove any more stones from the river.[47]

Thomas Hackett had a rocky relationship with his neighbour, the Dublin Laundry Company, which owned Millmount and its extensive grounds on the Dundrum Road above Concrete. The two parties' properties were separated by the millrace which took off water from the River Slang at Windy Arbour to feed the millpond at Milltown (Map 19). At the turn of the twentieth century the water from the millrace was used to water the cattle and pigs that were raised on the grasslands of Farranboley, and to supply water to Hackett's Cottages for domestic purposes. As detailed in the previous chapter in connection with the Dundrum Drainage Scheme, the River Slang and the millrace were heavily polluted and this led to tensions between the two landowners, as the following frosty letter of 8 August 1901 from the Dublin Laundry Company to Thomas Hackett explains:

In reply to your letter about our millrace, it may be well to impress upon you that you have no rights whatsoever in relation to the millrace, as to the control of the water or the discharge into it of sewerage [sic] or rubbish. We intend however for our own sakes shortly to clean up the race, but before doing so, we would ask you on your part to have removed from the overflow channel of the pond the heap of rubbish thrown into it, mostly by your tenants, through the doorway behind our mill [i.e. the derelict Millmount mill complex at Bankside Cottages]. If you do this, we will then build up the doorway to prevent any such trespass in future.[48]

Hackett seems to have ignored the Laundry's letter and so they wrote to him again in October 1901:

We regret you did not as promised clean out the overflow of the Millmount pond, where your tenants had largely helped to fill it up inside of that open doorway. We are however doing this now to save further delay, but we must ask you at once to clean out the channel from the middle of the arch

44 *Rathmines News*, 20 July 1901, p. 2.

45 Dundrum Petty Sessions Order Book 1901, 25 July 1901, no. 22.

46 *Rathmines News*, 29 July 1905, p. 4.

47 *Rathmines News*, 29 July 1905, p. 4.

48 NAI, Dublin Business Records 56, Dublin Laundry Company, Correspondence Out Book, 8 August 1901. The letters from Hackett have not survived.

under the roadway to the outlet under Concrete as there is a large quantity of filth there, thrown into it from your cottages. We intend to cease operations at the point indicated under the middle of the road, so that unless you clear out the remainder, there will be no free access for the water at the back of your cottages. As we are nearly through with the job, you should take the present opportunity, while the race and its contents are dry.[49]

Six years later Hackett complained to the Dublin Laundry Company about the lack of water supply from the millrace, which elicited the following response:

We were much surprised at receiving your letter this afternoon which was evidently written without making any enquiries about the water at your tenement houses in Milltown, as we find on enquiries that the water has been running since yesterday and as none is going over our weir at Windy Arbour you are getting all you can claim from us. We beg to say that we do not put anything more than water into the race and the obstruction is caused by the dam you have on your premises to hold back the water and which is the cause of the objectionable accumulation of filth.[50]

The purpose of quoting these three letters is threefold. Notwithstanding the availability of detailed OS maps, it is necessary to emphasise how completely different the topography of the south bank of the River Dodder at Milltown was 120 years ago. This is all the more important because there are no contemporary photographs of that part of Milltown. The Millmount mill complex, its millpond and millrace were all filled in and built over in the mid-twentieth century by St Luke's Crescent and the landscaping of the Dodder valley walkway. The River Slang was culverted as part of these developments and all of the slum tenements and cottages were swept away. Much later, in the 1990s the Thorncliffe apartment complex was built on the site of Millmount Lodge, which originally stood on elevated ground behind Bankside Cottages. Secondly, the private correspondence between Thomas Hackett and the Dublin Laundry Company complements the official evidence from the municipal and rural authorities concerning the squalid living conditions and the lack of clean water and sanitation in Milltown. Thirdly, the letters add to our knowledge of Thomas Hackett's activity as a landlord in a suburban village of Dublin and the fraught relationship that he had with Milltown's biggest employer. The two protagonists, Thomas Hackett and Thomas Edmondson, although of similar age were from completely different social, religious and political backgrounds. Their fundamental differences in outlook undoubtedly created cool relations between the two men. As a Quaker with strong social principles, Thomas Edmondson would have abhorred Hackett's behaviour as a slum landlord and as a proprietor of the village's two public houses. Added to the mix was the fact that Thomas Hackett would have benefited substantially from the wages paid to the laundry employees, many of whom were his tenants, shopped in his grocery stores, and drank in his public houses.

In today's era (2022) of housing shortages and rising rents, it is appropriate to briefly highlight one instance of how a local landlord like Thomas Hackett was able to exploit market conditions in Milltown. In the mid-nineteenth century Thomas's father Patrick had leased an office (shed), yard and garden at the end of Lee's Lane on the north side of the village main street (Map 16a, plot 25) for which he paid, in 1857, an annual rent of £1 3*s*.[51] By 1887, Thomas Hackett had

49 NAI, Dublin Business Records 56, Dublin Laundry Company, Correspondence Out Book, 5 October 1901.

50 NAI, Dublin Business Records 56, Dublin Laundry Company, Correspondence Out Book, 12 July 1907.

51 VO, Cancellation Books, Dublin, Rathmines, Milltown Road, 1855–62, vol. 1, p. 124, plot 25.

built a cottage on the site and had sublet the property for an annual rent of £26. Hackett was required by law to pay half of the annual poor law valuation of £11 (the occupier paid the other half where the valuation reached or exceeded £4 p.a.), meaning his net annual profit was £19 7*s*. after deducting the head rent and the poor rate.[52] The profits derived from Thomas Hackett's tenement property and his two public houses in Milltown (which will be discussed presently) enabled him to expand his property interests in Milltown at the turn of the twentieth century. By the end of the nineteenth century, the owner of Bawn House, John David Mowlds, appears to have struggled to make ends meet as he entered old age. On 1 June 1900 Mowlds sublet his landholding on the south bank of the River Dodder – which also included an intermediate leasehold interest in the Dew Drop Inn pub and Mowlds Cottages – to Thomas Hackett for £55. In return, Hackett covenanted to spend at least £100 in improvements within five years (Map 21).[53]

In conclusion, Thomas Hackett had built up a considerable property portfolio in Milltown during the last two decades of the nineteenth century. By the turn of the twentieth century Hackett was by far the biggest landlord in the village. He was by no means a perfect landlord but, in comparison with the landlords of Dublin city's tenements, Hackett was not noticeably bad. It must also be borne in mind that insanitary housing conditions existed simultaneously in many of south Dublin's towns and villages, especially in Rathfarnham and Kingstown (Dún Laoghaire), so Milltown was unremarkable in that respect.[54]

THE DEW DROP INN

Thomas and John Hackett expanded their family business in the late 1870s when they bought the licence to the Dew Drop Inn, a commercial venture that turned out to be rather turbulent. The Dew Drop Inn was built on the south bank of the River Dodder on the Dundrum Road opposite Bawn House (now Al Hussain House) and in front of Mowlds Cottages (Map 20). The site is now part of the public park beside the entrance to the Milltown Grove apartment complex. It is not known when the Dew Drop Inn was built but it was probably constructed around 1820, shortly after the realignment of the Dundrum Road and the building of the present Milltown Bridge over the Dodder. The Dew Drop Inn was both a public house and a shop. When the surveyor from the Griffith's Valuation visited the premises in 1847, he recorded that it was situated on an excellent site and did good business. At that time, the pub was operated by a publican named Philip Moran who rented it from Mrs Elizabeth Hunt. Ms Hunt lived across the road from the Dew Drop Inn in Bawn House.[55] By 1857 the Dew Drop Inn was under the management of John Sexton, whose tenure was uneventful.[56] In 1879 Sexton sold the Dew Drop Inn to Thomas Hackett and in October of that year Thomas applied for a licence to sell beer, cider and spiritous liquors by retail. For unknown reasons, the licence was granted to Thomas's brother, John Hackett.[57]

The change of management at the Dew Drop Inn coincided with important developments in Irish licensing laws. In 1878 the Irish Association for the Prevention of Intemperance was

52 VO, Cancellation Books, Dublin, Rathmines East, Milltown Road, 1873–87, vol. 2, p. 198, plot 25.

53 RD 1900/41/73.

54 Cullen, *Cleansing Rural Dublin*, pp. 31–3; Tom Conlon, *Victorian Dún Laoghaire: A Town Divided* (Dublin, 2016), pp. 117–9.

55 NAI, VO, OL70071, Quarto Book, Townland of Farranboley, 1847, p. 29.

56 Thom's Directory 1857, p. 1175.

57 *Freeman's Journal*, 24 September 1879, p. 8; 15 October 1879, p. 3.

established with the aim of securing the enforcement of Sunday closing and a reduction in the number of licences. Following a House of Lords Inquiry on Intemperance which had been set up in 1876, the Sale of Intoxicating Liquors on Sunday (Ireland) Act of 1878 was enacted which forced the closure of pubs on Sundays. However, due to successful lobbying by the powerful licensed vintners trade the metropolitan police district of Dublin and the cities of Belfast, Cork, Limerick and Waterford were permitted to open between 2 and 7 p.m. on Sundays.[58] In practical terms, these changes meant that the Hacketts' pub on the main street of Milltown village could serve alcohol on Sunday afternoons whereas the Hacketts could not serve drink in the Dew Drop Inn on Sundays, which lay beyond the metropolitan police district, except to a limited category of persons called bona fide travellers. In short, the standard closing hours did not apply to a person (the bona fide traveller) consuming alcohol on the licensed premises provided he had travelled a minimum of three miles by public road from his place of abode the previous night. Additional provisions were included to deal with patrons providing false addresses to the police, and to exonerate publicans. The latter were protected from conviction if the publican had taken reasonable precautions to ascertain whether or not the patron was a bona fide traveller and provided the publican truly believed (in the opinion of the magistrates) that the patron was such a traveller.[59]

Unsurprisingly, the licensing laws and their application in respect of bona fide travellers proved to be contentious, and created many difficulties for the police, the publicans and the local magistrates.[60] To illustrate the point, within two years of obtaining his licence for the Dew Drop Inn John Hackett appeared before the magistrates at Dundrum Petty Sessions to answer charges that he had sold alcohol on Sunday 11 September 1881 to persons who were not bona fide travellers. The magistrates were equally divided on the evidence presented and no ruling was made in the case.[61] Throughout the 1880s and into the 1890s the Dew Drop Inn frequently appeared on the charge sheets of the Dundrum Petty Sessions arising from public order offences and licensing law infringements.[62]

At this point it should be pointed out that the Dew Drop Inn was not the only Milltown pub that fell foul of the authorities. At their monthly board meeting of 6 October 1880, the Rathmines township commissioners passed the following resolution deprecating the increase of licensed houses in the area:

> *Resolved that in view of the increase of crime arising from drink, we earnestly deprecate an increase of licensed houses and especially resolve that an earnest representation be made to the magistrates at Quarter Sessions against granting a licence to a house at Classon's Bridge [The Dropping Well pub] already refused twelve times in eleven years and which from its position is particularly*

---

58 Joseph V. O'Brien, *Dear, Dirty Dublin: A city in distress 1899–1916* (University of California Press, 1982), p. 187; Kevin C. Kearns, *Dublin Pub Life and Lore: An oral history* (Dublin, 1996), pp. 21–4; Licensing Act 1872 (35 & 36 Vic., c. 94), s. 78, as amended by s. 1 of the Sale of Intoxicating Liquors on Sunday (Ireland) Act 1878 (41 & 42 Vic., c. 72).

59 The Licensing (Ireland) Act, 1874 (37 & 38 Vic., c. 69), ss. 27–28.

60 *Freeman's Journal*, 17 November 1882, p. 7. In 1896 a court held that a person was not a bona fide traveller when the sole object of his journey, regardless of distance travelled, was to go to a pub to drink: *Parker v the Queen* (1896, 2 Irish Reports, 404).

61 *Dublin Evening Telegraph*, 20 September 1881, p. 3; Dundrum Petty Sessions Order Book 1881, 19 September 1881, no. 114.

62 The Dew Drop Inn is mentioned on more than 20 occasions on the charge sheets for the Dundrum Petty Sessions from 1881 to 1893 inclusive; see also *Sport Dublin*, 4 April 1885, p. 2; 21 December 1889, p. 2; 1 February 1890, p. 2; 30 January 1892, p. 2; 25 November 1893, p. 2; 14 April 1894, p. 2.

> *dangerous as tending to draw objectionable persons to the township and being utterly unnecessary for any useful purpose.*[63]

By the turn of the twentieth century the district around Milltown was dotted with numerous pubs and off licences which were frequently patronised by bogus bona fide travellers.[64] In Milltown village there was O'Neill's off licence at Milltown Hill (now the site of the Spar shopping centre), Hackett's pub on the village main street (originally opposite the Catholic church) and the Dew Drop Inn. Less than a mile away from Milltown Bridge there were another five public houses – Dalys at Classon's Bridge (now The Dropping Well), Clonskeagh House (now Farmer Brown's), Ashtons of Clonskeagh, Delaneys of Windy Arbour and Langans (later Rogans) of Windy Arbour.[65]

Returning to the Dew Drop Inn, the Hacketts' difficulties with bona fide travellers continued unabated. In the months of April and September 1893 Thomas Hackett, who had taken over the licence from his brother John, was convicted of selling drink during Sunday closing hours on the 19 March and 27 August respectively, following which he was, in each case, fined £2 and the convictions were recorded on Thomas Hackett's licence.[66] Hackett decided to appeal his two convictions by case stated, which resulted in a lengthy legal process involving a rehearing in front of the Dundrum magistrates and an appeal at the Kilmainham Quarter Sessions court. During the appeal hearing on 10 April 1894, Hackett volunteered to close the Dew Drop Inn on Sundays even though the terms of his lease obliged him to hold a seven-day licence for the premises. On foot of Hackett's undertaking the Recorder of Dublin reduced the fine in each case to a shilling and removed the endorsements from Hackett's licence.[67]

Following the Recorder's decision handed down in April 1894, the Dew Drop Inn remained closed on Sundays for the rest of that year and during 1895 and 1896. For unknown reasons Thomas Hackett decided in the New Year of 1897 to reopen the Dew Drop Inn on Sundays, specifically to serve drink to bona fide travellers between 11 a.m. and 2 p.m.[68] This action on Hackett's part was clearly a breach of the undertaking he had given to the Recorder of Dublin at the Kilmainham Quarter Sessions in 1894. The editor of the *Rathmines News* jokingly commented on this development, stating that 'the Dew Drop Inn, Milltown, is known to men as the "Do Drop In", an invitation nearly always assented to with remarkable unanimity from each side of the house'.[69] The joke essentially acknowledged how easy it was to get served in the Dew Drop Inn.[70]

The business generated by Thomas Hackett's two strategically placed pubs was evident on a sports day held at Windy Arbour on Sunday 12 September 1897. The programme, which con-

63 Dublin City Council Archives, UDC/1/Min 1/5, Rathmines and Rathgar Township Minute Book, 1878–85, pp. 167–8, Board meeting 6 October 1880.

64 William Lawson, 'Licensing and Public House Reform in Ireland', *Journal of the Statistical and Social Inquiry Society of Ireland*, xi, part 86 (1901–02), p. 116.

65 Thom's Directory 1900, pp. 1580, 1581, 1612.

66 Dundrum Petty Sessions Order Book 1893, 3 April 1893, no. 7, 4 September 1893, no. 89.

67 *Irish Independent*, 20 February 1894, p. 3; *Freeman's Journal*, 11 April 1894, p. 2; *Sport Dublin*, 14 April 1894, p. 2.

68 *Rathmines News*, 9 January 1897, p. 4; 16 January 1897, p. 5.

69 *Rathmines News*, 16 January 1897, p. 4.

70 The littérateur Piaras Béaslaí made the dubious claim that the name was a 'punning play upon the vulgar Dubliner's pronunciation of "Do drop in!"': *Irish Independent*, 30 October 1963, p. 6.

sisted of 16 events, took place in glorious weather and attracted an estimated crowd of 2,000 people. According to the editor of the *Rathmines News*:

> *Mr T P Hackett was largely patronised by those who attended the Windy Arbour Sports on Sunday at both of his houses at Milltown. As the Dew Drop Inn the bona fide travellers were supplied up to 2 o'clock, at which hour Mr Hackett invariably closes, as he did so on this occasion, although the sports were only one hundred yards away. From two o'clock till the closing hour of 7 o'clock, all comers were comfortably provided for at Mr Hackett's other house in the village. The extensive sitting accommodation and improvised bar in his large garden afforded ample room to the crowds that kept coming and going all evening.*[71]

Thomas Hackett was so chuffed with the business generated in his two pubs that he wrote a letter to the *Rathmines News* and jocosely offered two cash prizes to the winners of a slow donkey race, which he suggested should take place at the next Windy Arbour sports day on the following Sunday.[72]

However, his insouciance was misplaced. It was inevitable given the level of drunken behaviour in Concrete during the 1890s that the police would not stand by and allow the Dew Drop Inn to open on Sundays in breach of the publican's undertaking. Indeed, Thomas Hackett had been warned as far back as 12 February 1897 that the police would oppose the renewal of his licence if he continued to open the Dew Drop Inn on Sunday, but he ignored their warnings.[73] The warning issued to Hackett in February 1897 coincided with a direction issued by the Chief Commissioner of the DMP ordering that the objectionable practice of police patrols entering the city's pubs and questioning patrons during normal trading hours was to cease.[74] This may have created a false sense of security for Hackett, even though there is no evidence that the DMP directive was adopted by the RIC under whose jurisdiction the Dew Drop Inn lay. In any event, the Dundrum police successfully opposed the renewal of Hackett's licence for the Dew Drop Inn at the annual licensing sessions in September 1897.[75]

The refusal to renew Hackett's licence prompted a series of court appeals to the Recorder of Dublin and the Queen's Bench, interspersed with rehearings of Hackett's licence application by the Dundrum magistrates. The legal rows went on for nine months. Very briefly, Hackett's legal team argued (among other things) that Hackett's verbal undertaking of 1894 to close on Sundays was void in law, and that Hackett had suffered sufficiently over the last three years by closing the Dew Drop Inn on Sundays. The Dundrum magistrates thought differently. They were of the opinion that Hackett was not a person of good character because he had breached his undertaking and, therefore, he was not fit to hold a publican's licence.[76]

Matters came to a head in the spring of 1898. On 30 March 1898 the Recorder of Dublin offered to grant Hackett a six-day licence for the Dew Drop Inn, but he declined the offer against

71 *Rathmines News*, 18 September 1897, p. 4.

72 *Rathmines News*, 18 September 1897, p. 4.

73 *Irish Independent*, 1 February 1898, p. 7.

74 *Rathmines News*, 6 February 1897, p. 5.

75 *Rathmines News*, 2 October 1897, p. 5.

76 *Rathmines News*, 2 October 1897, p. 5; 4 December 1897, p. 5; 23 January 1898, p. 5; 5 February 1898, p. 5; 2 April 1898, p. 4; 9 April 1898, p. 5; 14 May 1898, p. 4; *Dublin Daily Nation*, 1 November 1897, p. 4; 1 February 1898, p. 7; 7 April 1898, p. 2; 4 May 1898, p. 2; *Evening Herald*, 30 November 1897, p. 3; 30 March 1898, p. 2.

the advice of his legal team, which included Tim Healy, KC MP.[77] For unknown reasons, Hackett compounded matters by writing a personal letter to the Recorder of Dublin disputing the events that had led to Hackett's undertaking of 1894. This was a very foolish act on Thomas Hackett's part because it antagonised the Recorder, who subsequently declined to overturn the decision of the Dundrum magistrates to refuse Hackett a seven-day licence for the Dew Drop Inn.[78] Hackett appealed the Recorder's decision to the Queen's Bench but lost that appeal on 3 May 1898.[79] As a result, Thomas Hackett was forced to shut the Dew Drop Inn indefinitely. At the annual Kilmainham licensing sessions of 1898 and 1899 the magistrates refused to grant a publican's licence to Thomas Hackett's son, John, for the Dew Drop Inn.[80] On the occasion of the latter application, one of the Dundrum magistrates remarked that since the Dew Drop Inn had been closed there had been a great decrease in the number of loafers and corner boys in the neighbourhood.[81] Ultimately, then, the local police won their campaign against the Dew Drop Inn and its bogus bona fide drinkers.[82] Hackett's unethical behaviour had wider consequences for him beyond the confines of Milltown. In handing down his judgement, the Recorder noted that the licensed trade of Dublin had wholly repudiated the course pursued by Hackett, and had assured the Recorder that their members would keep their promises or suffer the consequences.[83] Hackett was persona non grata among the city's publicans.

The Dew Drop Inn affair is revealing on a number of fronts aside from providing a window on contemporary licensing laws and drinking culture. In particular, the events show that Thomas Hackett had enough financial resources to pursue sustained legal proceedings against the licensing authorities, including an appeal to the Queen's Bench. He was also able to afford the legal fees of top barristers, such as Tim Healy. This was possible because Hackett had the benefit of rent from several cottages and tenements in Milltown as well as income from his pub and shop on the main street of Milltown village and, before it was forced to close, from the Dew Drop Inn. Of more human interest, is the glimpse the controversy gives of Thomas Hackett's character.

Thomas Hackett's numerous letters to the newspapers show him to have been an articulate individual. He was certainly educated to secondary level, possibly by the Christian Brothers at Synge Street.[84] Hackett was undoubtedly a successful publican and businessman who, as we have seen, methodically grew his property portfolio in Milltown. Despite these advantages Thomas Hackett had serious flaws, the chief ones being stubbornness and an antagonism towards any authority with which he disagreed. These traits were manifested in Hackett's refusal to accept the Recorder's offer of a six-day licence, which refusal also went against the advice of his legal

77 *Rathmines News*, 2 April 1898, p. 4; 10 October 1898, p. 5.

78 *Rathmines News*, 9 April 1898, p. 5; *Dublin Daily Nation*, 7 April 1898, p. 2.

79 *Rathmines News*, 13 May 1898, p. 4; 30 September 1899, p. 4; *Dublin Daily Nation*, 4 May 1898, p. 2; *Dublin Evening Mail*, 26 September 1899, p. 2; *Irish Independent*, 27 September 1899, p. 8.

80 *Rathmines News*, 10 October 1898, p. 5; 30 September 1899, p. 4.

81 *Rathmines News*, 30 September 1899, p. 4

82 A few years later the premises reopened its grocery business according to the Thom's Directories, but it is unclear whether or not the Hacketts regained their licence to sell alcohol at the Dew Drop Inn because the newspapers and the Valuation Office cancellation books do not confirm the position.

83 *Rathmines News*, 10 October 1898, p. 5.

84 A grandson or grandnephew of Thomas Hackett performed at a CBS Synge street concert for current and former pupils: Rathmines News, 12 February 1898, p. 5.

team. Closely associated with his trait of stubbornness was Hackett's frequent tendency to fall out with peers and colleagues. This aspect of Hackett's character will be uncovered as part of the discussion of his political and lobbying activities.

Before moving on from the Dew Drop Inn, Thomas Hackett's flaws as a publican need to be assessed with his other grocery and licensed premises in the main street of Milltown village and called Hackett's.[85] Unlike the Dew Drop Inn, as far as can be ascertained there was only one publicised prosecution against Hackett's pub in Milltown main street. In July 1896 Thomas Hackett was prosecuted at Dublin city's Northern Police Court for serving alcohol to a drunken man on 7 May 1896 who later, in an inebriated state, had a fatal accident at Palmerston Park after having consumed more alcohol in Daly's public house at Classon's Bridge (subsequently renamed The Dropping Well). Hackett's barrister told the court that Hackett's pub had a clean sheet for the last 60 years. Thomas Hackett's daughter, who had been serving behind the bar on the date of the alleged offence, testified that she served the drunken man soda water and poured a pint for his companion. Based on her evidence and Hackett's clean record, the case against Thomas Hackett was dismissed.[86] In conclusion, it is curious that Thomas Hackett was able to run an orderly house in Milltown village but not, apparently, on the far side of the Dodder at the Dew Drop Inn.

THE COUNTRY VINTNERS' DEFENCE LEAGUE

The changes to the licensing laws brought about by the Sunday closing and bona fide drinking legislation in the 1870s created tensions between Dublin's city and suburban publicans because their business interests diverged. Essentially, the city publicans' priorities were to maintain their privileges under the Sunday opening hours regime and to oppose any changes to the bona fide legislation which was favourable to the suburban and country trade. As a result, Thomas Hackett became a prominent member and secretary of a new licensed trade society which he was involved in setting up in the early 1880s to promote the interests of the suburban and county licensed trade, called the Country Vintners' Defence League.[87] Initially, this organisation was confined to publicans like Hackett, whose licensed premises were within a 10- to 12-mile radius of the city. At a meeting of the League held on 17 November 1882, Hackett expressed the opinion that the city publicans would go so far as to consent to the proposal of the temperance party to allow bona fide travellers to get refreshments in hotels only, and only in case they had travelled seven miles, as opposed to the current three mile requirement.[88] In short, the objects of the League were essentially defensive, to protect members from hostile actions by the city licensed trade and the temperance movement, and to oppose the orders of local magistrates which were antithetical to the business of suburban licensed traders.

From the outset, Thomas Hackett engaged in a campaign of letter writing and lobbying to further the aims of the Country Licensed Vintners' Defence League.[89] Hackett's letters show him to have been a reasonably intelligent man who was well able to articulate his case. On the other

85 By the 1940s the premises had become no. 90 main street and was owned by a family called McKenna: VO, Cancellation Books, County Borough of Dublin, Rathmines and Rathgar East, Town of Milltown, 1940–47, p. 858, no. 90.

86 *Freeman's Journal*, 4 July 1896, p. 6; *Rathmines News*, 11 July 1896, p. 4.

87 *Irish Times*, 9 February 1882, p. 2; *Freeman's Journal, 28 October 1895, p. 7. Hackett had previously been a member of The Licensed Grocers and Vintners ~~Association~~: Evening Freeman*, 13 April 1871, p. 4.

88 *Freeman's Journal*, 17 November 1882, p. 7.

89 *Irish Times*, 9 February 1882, p. 2; 14 April 1882, p. 6; *Freeman's Journal*, 12 August 1883, p. 6; 10 December 1885, p. 7; *Flag of Ireland*, 22 October 1884, p. 2.

hand, his correspondence rarely displayed tolerance of an opposing viewpoint or adopted a subtle approach in rebutting his opponents' arguments. Due to his prolix writing style, Hackett was prone to composing extremely long, punctuated sentences, the effect of which was to dilute the impact of his arguments. The following extract from a letter to the *Irish Times* from 1882 opposing Sunday closing for rural publicans is indicative, and is particularly relevant given Hackett's experience with the Dew Drop Inn:

> *The licenses of country vintners are assessed on the same basis (i.e. the valuation) as those in the places which are exempt from total Sunday closing, and although the holders of them are deprived of the profits to be derived from their best day's business, the Freeman [newspaper] has not sought to obtain either the restoration of the right of Sunday trading, for which they are paying licence duty, or even a reduction of the duty; nor has it shown any disposition to advocate the privilege to which the general public, particularly the working classes, are entitled under the provisions of the bona fide traveller clause, which clause was enacted clearly both in order to compensate to some extent the country traders for the loss sustained by being closed on the Sabbath Day against their local customers, and to give tourists, excursionists, people on business, and those who wished to enjoy a few miles travelling on pleasure, the means of getting refreshments when three miles distant from their residence or last sleeping place, which rights and privileges are now almost a nullity in numerous districts owing to the action of magistrates of extreme and fanatical views on either Sabbatarianism or intemperance who take advantage of the vague discretionary power of deciding who is a bona fide traveller, and which power now appears manifestly to have been foolishly and unfairly entrusted to their discretion, as it can be proved beyond doubt (if an inquiry into the working of the Act be instituted before its renewal is proposed), that this discretionary power has been repeatedly and unmistakably used merely in accordance with the fanatical, intolerant whims of many of those gentlemen, and that appeals against their decisions have proved abortive, owing to the same cause, in a higher court, even in the face of the most conclusive testimony that the requirements of the Act had been observed and complied with, as far as possible to do so, on the part of the publican.*[90]

Despite the impassioned defence of the country vintners as articulated by Thomas Hackett, take up of membership of the Country Licensed Vintners' Defence League was disappointing.[91] This was due to a number of factors. The fledging League had to compete for membership among numerous other trade associations, chief of which was the Licensed Grocers and Vintners' Association.[92] As a result, country and suburban publicans remained apathetic as to the relevance of the League and its ability to influence events. Furthermore, the impression given by the press reports of its proceedings is that the League was largely composed of a clique of Dublin suburban publicans from the south of the county, a group who were especially impacted by the bona fide laws, with few members from the northside of the city or from counties outside Dublin. In an attempt to rectify this situation, the League resolved in September 1883 to send representatives to attend as many of the county licensing sessions as possible to recruit members.[93] Yet, in spite of the unpromising conditions of its early existence, the League remained active during the last two decades of the nineteenth century.

90 *Irish Times*, 14 April 1882, p. 6.

91 *Freeman's Journal*, 8 March 1883, p. 3; 14 March 1883; 23 March 1883, p. 2.

92 *Freeman's Journal*, 14 March 1883, p. 2; 10 December 1885, p. 7; 10 May 1888, p. 5.

93 *Irish Times*, 19 September 1883, p. 6.

In 1888 the Irish licensed trade was under threat from legislation being promoted in Westminster by supporters of the temperance movement and by a parliamentary inquiry into the working of the Sunday Closing Act.[94] In response, the Country Licensed Vintners' Defence League sought a meeting with their Dublin city counterparts to see if the two associations might co-operate in opposing their common enemies. However, the city representatives told a deputation from the League – which included Thomas Hackett – that they would have to look after the bona fide traveller question on their own.[95] Clearly, the city vintners' society was the bigger, dominant party and relations between the two associations remained strained for several years afterwards.[96] The dissention between the two bodies also hampered the League's efforts to solicit financial support from the manufacturing and wholesale traders in Dublin city.[97]

Despite questions hanging over its relevance and influence, the Country Licensed Vintners' Defence League sent its chairman and secretary to London in May 1888 to monitor the progress of the Saturday Early Closing (Ireland) Bill, which was being promoted by the temperance movement.[98] Thus Thomas Hackett got to experience at first hand the political workings of the Imperial Parliament at Westminster and to witness the oratorical skills of Parnell (whom Hackett may have got to meet), Tim Healy (who later acted as his legal counsel in the Dew Drop Inn proceedings) and other IPP members. More impressively, Thomas Hackett was deemed sufficiently capable to represent the League at a Parliamentary inquiry in London which was investigating the working of the Sunday Closing Acts. For several weeks Hackett attended the inquiry at Westminster and reported back to his colleagues in Dublin on its progress and its potential impact on the licensed trade.[99] Two years later, in 1890, Hackett was back in London lobbying against a proposed increase in duties on spirits and beer.[100]

On St Patrick's Day 1893, the following notice of Hackett's lobbying activities appeared in the *Freeman's Journal*:

> *Among the other Irish trade deputations that have been in London for the last week is one from the County Vintners' Defence League, consisting of Mr T.P. Hackett, hon. sec., Mr J.J. Boland, treasurer, and Mr P.J. Hynes, T.C., Kingstown. These gentlemen have been busily engaged all the week interviewing members of the House of Commons, advocating the special interests of the trade of the Sunday closed districts in Ireland. They were also present on the platform at the monster demonstration at St James's Hall.*[101]

On his return to Dublin Hackett briefed the committee members of the Country Licensed Vintners' Defence League of their delegates' lobbying and networking activities in London. At that meeting, which was held at the committee rooms in 80 Grafton Street on 30 March 1893, the

94 *Freeman's Journal*, 13 March 1888, p. 7.

95 *Freeman's Journal*, 13 March 1888, p. 7.

96 *Irish Times*, 14 November 1888, p. 7; *Sport Dublin*, 10 December 1887, p. 2; 17 November 1888, p. 2; 24 November 1888, p. 2; *Freeman's Journal*, 28 November 1888, p. 3; 23 November 1893, p. 2; 29 December 1893, p. 7.

97 *Freeman's Journal*, 28 November 1888, p. 3.

98 *Freeman's Journal*, 10 May 1888, p. 5.

99 *Sport Dublin*, 14 April 1888, p. 2; 5 May 1888, p. 2; 12 May 1888, p. 2; 19 May 1888, p. 2; 31 May 1888, p. 2; 2 June 1888, p. 2;9 June 1888, p. 2; 16 June 1888, p. 2; 23 June 1888, p. 2; *Freeman's Journal*, 12 June 1888, p. 5.

100 *Freeman's Journal*, 21 April 1890, p. 3; 15 May 1890, p. 7; *Sport Dublin*, 26 April 1890, p. 2.

101 *Freeman's Journal*, 17 March 1893, p. 3.

committee passed a resolution calling on all Home Rule supporting MPs to defer the Intoxicating Liquor (Ireland) Bill to a Home Rule parliament in Dublin, which it was widely believed would become a reality following the introduction of Gladstone's second Home Rule Bill.[102]

These were exciting times for Hackett and his experiences in London must have felt far removed from dealing with drunks at the Dew Drop Inn in Milltown. It is not clear to what extent, if any, the League paid for Hackett's expenses while he was lobbying on its behalf in England but it is very likely that he had to pay the majority of the costs out of his own pocket. Assuming this assumption is correct, it once again points to the considerable income that Hackett was making from his two pubs, grocery and rented property in Milltown. From his own viewpoint, Hackett's spells in London and the people he met there, particularly Charles Stuart Parnell, made a lasting impression. His experiences there probably influenced Hackett's decision to enter local politics in support of the IPP (and the Parnellite faction after Charles Stuart's Parnell's death), a subject which will be discussed shortly.

As well as opposing the policies of the temperance movement in parliament, the Country Licensed Vintners' Defence League took a practical interest in the more mundane day-to-day issues that their members had to contend with. On 14 September 1896 a number of publicans were prosecuted and fined 5*s*. at the Dundrum Petty Sessions court for not having their glasses stamped as required with the Weights and Measures Act of 1878.[103] These prosecutions prompted the local publicans, including Thomas Hackett, to hold a meeting in Dundrum to protest against the impracticality of outdated legislation which effectively required every drinking glass to be identified and stamped as being of imperial pint measure. At their meeting the publicans passed a resolution calling on the Country Licensed Vintners' Defence League to lobby the largest national licensed trade association, the Executive Committee of the Liquor Trade of Ireland, to proactively resolve the issues which they had identified.[104] The problem facing the publicans was caused by a new trend in drinking behaviour which was explained in a local press report of 24 October 1896:

> *The public taste developed in recent years for glass in preference to pewter pints has, in itself, vastly increased the cost of public house equipment, owing to the fragile nature of the material, and as glass pints are now made with the denomination 'Imperial Pint' stamped on them we consider it would satisfy the public and the requirements of the law to permit the use of glass measures – of full imperial capacity – with the denomination clearly imprinted on them without the additional cost of a verification stamp on measures glasses which cannot be fraudulently tampered with, and are, moreover, so easily destroyed entirely by breakage, which is of frequent occurrence daily.*[105]

Following the Dundrum meeting, Thomas Hackett wrote to the Executive Committee of the Liquor Trade of Ireland, which after some delay agreed to lobby the chief secretary in accordance with the resolutions passed by the publicans in Dundrum.[106] Separately, the licensed traders from Rathmines, Rathgar and Milltown signed a memorial petitioning the Rathmines township

102 *Freeman's Journal*, 31 March 1893, p. 2.

103 Dundrum Petty Sessions Order Book 1896, 14 September 1896, nos 1–3.

104 *Rathmines News*, 24 October 1896, p. 3.

105 *Rathmines News*, 24 October 1896, p. 3. The horrible modern practice of using glassware to disfigure people in pub brawls was unforeseen and beyond the contemplation of the public and the publicans alike in the 1890s.

106 *Rathmines News*, 21 November 1896, p. 9.

commissioners to postpone, pending the probable amendment of the Weights and Measures' Act, the introduction of a sand blast machine which the commissioners had purchased for stamping the publicans' glassware.[107] In response, the Rathmines commissioners agreed not to stamp the publicans' glasses until the Board of Trade had made a final decision on the controversial issue.[108] Nonetheless, the unilateral action on the part of the Rathmines and Rathgar Commissioners to acquire equipment of dubious utility typified their habit of lavish expenditure which so frequently annoyed local ratepayers.

Dublin's publicans faced a new threat to their livelihood in the spring of 1897 in the form of a bill promoted by Lord Meath to close the city's pubs early on Saturdays and increase the minimum distance required to be travelled by bona fide drinkers, which in practical terms meant the extension of total Sunday closing hours throughout almost the entire area of south County Dublin. In response to this threat, Thomas Hackett and other south Dublin publicans attempted to set up a new organisation of their own in April and May 1897.[109] Why Hackett supported such a move while he was actively involved in Country Licensed Vintners' Defence League is not explained, however the new southside venture did not get off the ground due to lack of support because many suburban publicans were, according to Hackett, content to rely on the Central Committee of the Liquor Trade of Ireland to look after their interests.[110] A second attempt was made in January 1898 by Thomas Hackett and his suburban colleagues to establish another new pressure group called the Dublin Suburban Vintners' Protection Society but this does not appear to have been successful either.[111] These failures point to the limited enthusiasm among the Dublin suburban licensed trade to defend their own interests outside the umbrella of the Central Committee of the Liquor Trade of Ireland.

Yet, despite his policy differences with the city's licensing trade, on several occasions throughout the 1890s Thomas Hackett successfully stood for election to the executive committee of the Central Committee of the Liquor Trade of Ireland either as a representative of the Country Licensed Vintners' Defence League or as one of five members from the Dublin metropolitan suburbs who were entitled to sit on the central committee.[112] If nothing else, this shows Hackett to have been a hard-working activist who was prepared to sit on several committees, thus demonstrating his longstanding commitment to protecting Irish publicans and the interests of the Dublin suburban licensed trade in particular. That said, Hackett's behaviour in relation to the Dew Drop Inn licensing controversy of 1897/1898 damaged his reputation and influence among many Dublin publicans.[113] This objectionable behaviour probably explains why Hackett's name is much less frequently mentioned among the press reports of the activities of the licensed trade associations after 1898.

---

107 *Rathmines News*, 21 November 1896, p. 9.

108 *Rathmines News*, 12 December 1896, p. 4.

109 *Evening Herald*, 12 April 1897, p. 2; *Rathmines News*, 8 May 1897, p. 4.

110 *Rathmines News*, 11 December 1897, p. 5.

111 *Irish Independent*, 25 January 1898, p. 6.

112 *Dublin Evening Telegraph*, 22 January 1895, p. 4; *Freeman's Journal*, 28 October 1895, p. 7; *Dublin Evening Telegraph*, 6 February 1896, p. 2; *Rathmines News*, 11 December 1897, p. 5; *Dublin Daily Nation*, 11 January 1898, p. 7; 14 February 1899, p. 3.

113 *Rathmines News*, 10 October 1898, p. 5.

By the summer of 1906 the health of the septuagenarian Thomas Hackett was beginning to fail and he was no-longer active on behalf of the licensed trade or the IPP.[114] But before departing the subject of Thomas Hackett's lobbying for Dublin suburban publicans, it is appropriate to examine it briefly in the context of the power which the licensed trade in Ireland, and Dublin publicans in particular, held in Irish political life by the end of the nineteenth century. Irish historians have acknowledged that shopkeepers, grocers and publicans were among the most influential group in provincial Irish society in the decades after the Land War, and that over time they became a very influential group in the IPP.[115] This viewpoint is supported by the experience of Milltown and the lobbying activity carried out for over 20 years by Thomas Hackett.

By 1900 publicans and grocers made up the largest occupational group sitting on Dublin Corporation (19 out of 60).[116] Shortly after his election as MP for South Dublin in October 1900, the successful nationalist candidate representing the reunited IPP, a Dublin publican called John J. Mooney, addressed the annual meeting of the Licensed Grocers' and Vintners' Association. At the meeting, Mooney proposed a resolution protesting against the manner in which the licensed trade 'has been again singled out for extra taxation'.[117] Unsurprisingly, the Rathmines News opined that 'the honourable gentleman produced a very favourable impression'.[118] In or around the same time, it was claimed by a witness to a public inquiry to extend Dublin city's boundaries that a petition by some residents of Clontarf for their township to be incorporated into Dublin city (which in the end was successful) was masterminded by local publicans who were anxious to benefit from the city's more liberal licensing laws.[119] These are just a couple of examples of the pervasive influence of Dublin's licensed vintners and grocers at the turn of the twentieth century.

In view of the dominance wielded by the publican trade it is not surprising that supporters of the temperance movement and licensing law reform faced such an uphill battle to pass legislation. They did, however, eventually achieve success in 1906. On 29 November of that year the Intoxicating Liquors (Ireland) Act, 1906 was enacted whereby all pubs in cities and towns with populations exceeding 5,000 people were required to close at 10 p.m. on Sunday nights, and the Sunday opening hours were reduced by two hours to 2 p.m. to 5 p.m.[120] Despite strenuous opposition by the Dublin suburban publicans, the Act also increased the minimum distance for the bona fide traveller from three miles to five.[121] The change in the bona fide law was particularly welcomed by the magistrates of the Dundrum Petty Sessions court, who had, at the instigation of Captain Robert Wade Thompson, passed a resolution on 9 July 1906 stating that:

> *if passed, [the Bill] must prove of great benefit to the public, but specially to neighbourhoods like Dundrum, in close proximity to the city of Dublin, which are over-run on Sunday evenings (after the public houses of the city have been closed) by so called bona fide travellers ...*[122]

114 *Freeman's Journal*, 17 September 1906, p. 11.

115 See for example, Fergus Campbell, *The Irish Establishment 1879–1914* (Oxford, 2009), p. 174.

116 Daly, *Dublin*, The deposed capital, p. 205.

117 *Rathmines News*, 24 November 1900, p. 4.

118 *Rathmines News*, 24 November 1900, p. 4.

119 Daly, *Dublin: The deposed capital*, p. 167.

120 The Intoxicating Liquors (Ireland) Act, 1906 (6 Edw. 7, Ch. 39).

121 The Intoxicating Liquors (Ireland) Act, 1906, section 3; *Freeman's Journal*, 22 June 1906, p. 7; *Rathmines News*, 7 July 1906, p. 2.

122 *Wicklow Newsletter*, 14 July 1906, p. 3.

The reaction of Thomas Hackett to these developments has not survived. Although the evidence is not entirely certain, it would appear that the Dew Drop Inn premises never reopened as a pubic house because of the increase in the bona fide traveller minimum distance limit. In contrast, Hackett's pub on the main street of Milltown village continued to thrive.[123]

POLITICAL SUPPORT FOR THE IRISH PARLIAMENTARY PARTY

Irish political life was completely transformed and reinvigorated in the 1880s. This was due to two things: the setting up of the Irish National League headed by Charles Stuart Parnell and the Representation of the People Act, 1884, which increased the Irish electorate from a little under a quarter of a million (male) voters to a little under three quarters of a million.[124] Given that Thomas Hackett grew up in a family that actively supported the O'Connellite repeal movement of the 1830s and 1840s it was no surprise that Hackett became an activist in nationalist politics as a mature adult. Thomas Hackett's political activity can be divided into two spheres of activity which will be dealt with separately. The first activity concerns Hackett's support for Home Rule candidates who stood for election to Westminster for the South Dublin constituency during the period 1884 to 1906. The second activity relates to Hackett's work in local politics, particularly during municipal elections in the Rathmines township and in the Rathdown No. 1 Rural District of south-east Dublin. In both political theatres, Hackett displayed the same hard work and commitment which characterised his activities for the Dublin suburban licensed trade. Indeed, Hackett's years of lobbying on behalf of the Central Committee of the Liquor Trade of Ireland complemented his involvement with national and local politics because the publicans and the nationalist politicians relied on each other for support.

NATIONAL POLITICS

In the second half of the nineteenth century the (all male) electoral franchise was gradually extended by a series of enactments which also laid down a complex set of conditions governing the right to vote in parliamentary and local elections. In addition, the procedure relating to voter registration, a matter that was particularly important in marginal constituencies was especially complicated.[125] It is appropriate that an explanation of the procedural background and its local context vis-à-vis Milltown and the South Dublin constituency (in which Milltown lay) be provided before reviewing Thomas Hackett's political activities.

Peter Murray, in his excellent article on the politics of working-class Dublin in the Edwardian era, summarises the voter registration process involved in Dublin city elections:

> *The administrative procedures which gave effect to the franchise law were set in motion in April or May of each year with the service of requisition forms by the rate collectors. Those on whom the forms were served, normally the occupier or landlord [of an inhabited property], were legally bound to have them filled in and returned to the town clerk's office. They then formed the basis of the 'Long List' which was published on or before 22 July with the town clerk's objections noted in the margin.*

123 After Thomas Hackett's death in 1908 his son Thomas obtained a transfer of the licence to one pub in Milltown: *Irish Times*, 5 February 1908, p. 5.

124 R.V. Comerford, 'The Parnell era, 1883–91' in W.E. Vaughan (ed.), *A new history of Ireland, vi: Ireland under the Union 1870–1921* (Oxford, 1989), pp. 53–5.

125 Brian M. Walker, 'The Irish Electorate, 1868–1915', *Irish Historical Studies*, 18, no. 71 (March 1973), pp. 359–71. Peter Murray, 'Electoral Politics and the Dublin Working Class before the First World War', *Saothar: Journal of the Irish Labour History Society*, vi (1980), pp. 8–25.

New claims had to be lodged with the town clerk by 4 August and a list of claimants was published by 11 August again with the town clerk's objections noted. Private objections to any name on the list of voters could be lodged up to 20 August and a list of objectors had to be published by 24 August. In September and October the revising barristers adjudicated on the disputed claims [at annual revision court sittings]. The revised register was published in December and came into force on 1 January of the following year. The accuracy and inclusiveness of the register depended on the thoroughness and impartiality with which various officials carried out their duties, on the interpretation of the complex legal requirements of the various franchises by the revising barristers and on the way in which the business of claiming and objecting [to the list of claimants on the register] was managed by the political parties.[126]

Men with a freehold or leasehold interest in a property or who ordinarily paid the property taxes (rated occupiers) made up the vast bulk of the electorate. However, in the Dublin South constituency where the balance between nationalist and unionist voters was quite fine, lodgers (i.e. adults who rented a room in a dwelling on a short-term basis, of which Milltown village had many) became an important sub-group among the electoral franchise during the period under review. Accordingly, each of the two main political parties – the Nationalists and the Conservatives/Unionists – established local registration associations which appointed electoral agents whose job it was to assist constituents with the voter registration process, and distribute and collect voter registration forms as the following notice in the *Freeman's Journal* explains:

Rathmines Nationalists are again reminded that the Registration Offices at 78a Rathmines road are open every week evening, and that the agents and inspectors are in attendance from 7 till 9 p. m. to afford any information regarding the franchise to those requiring it. Persons desirous of being registered as lodgers should communicate at once with the hon secretary or inspectors of the association. Lease holders or free holders of houses or lands within the Rathmines Township (although not themselves resident in the locality) are entitled to vote in respect of such property, and if such persons will forward their names and addresses to the Offices, 78a Rathmines road, together with short particulars of the qualifying property, their cases will be attended to.

All Rathmines residents who have changed their residences within the past twelve months, and especially those who have recently changed, should make a point of calling at 78a Rathmines road some early evening to see that the inspectors have a note of their removal. Neglect of this precaution may lead to the loss of many votes. It is earnestly requested that any Nationalist resident of Rathmines Township having the least doubt of his name appearing on the register, will either call personally at the Office or write to the honorary sec., Mr J.A. Kavanagh.[127]

The revision court was presided over by the revising barrister who heard the claims of people who sought, in the face of objections, to remain on or to be included on the voter registration list, and those who opposed them. Registration agents employed by the main political parties were usually able to identify the political allegiance of claimants and other people already named on the voter registration list. This meant that the agents for one political party frequently challenged the entitlement of claimants of the other party to be included on the electoral register. Each disputed claim was argued before the revising barrister, who had the final say on the

126 Murray, 'Electoral Politics', pp. 11–12.

127 *Freeman's Journal*, 12 July 1904, p. 2.

matter. As a result, the two big political parties sought to influence the appointment of revising barristers who would be sympathetic to their case.[128] Officials from the relevant local authority were usually in attendance too to provide evidence about the rateable value of the property and to confirm if the rates had been paid. The procedure can be appreciated from two typical press reports of 1866 and 1890 with Milltown connections:

> *Parliamentary Revision. The Hon. Charles Trench took his seat on the bench in the court house, Kilmainham, yesterday morning, and proceeded to dispose of the list of voters for the Barony of Uppercross remaining over from the previous day. Mr Granby Burke claimed to be registered out of a house in Milltown [Fairyland/St Philip's], as a rated occupier. Evidence of occupancy having been given. The Liberal [party] Inspector swore that the house had been let to Sir John Kingston James in the month of June of last year, which, however, did not invalidate his [Burke's] claim. The claim was allowed.*[129]

> *South County Dublin. Yesterday, Mr Fleming, revising barrister, sat in the Court House, Dundrum, and resumed the revision of the Parliamentary voters lists for South County Dublin. The Nationalists were represented by Mr H.H. Moran, solicitor, assisted by Messrs P Kearney, objector; P Kearney, jun; J Donovan and J C Caffrey, inspectors. Mr W J Shannon appeared for the Unionists, assisted by Messrs Miller, inspector, and Wm Alexander, objector. Mr J D Cope, clerk of the Rathdown Union; Mr Sutton, collector, Rathdown Union; and Mr Samuel Shelley, South Dublin Union, were in attendance. Mr R H Woods, B. L.; Dr ffench Mullen, and Mr T P Hackett, Milltown, were present during the day on behalf of the central executive of the National Registration Association.*[130]

In summary, the process of getting onto and remaining on the electoral register was anything but straightforward, and highlighted serious shortcomings that undermined the democratic process. Public notice of Thomas Hackett's interest in national politics began when he was named among a long list of delegates who attended the County Dublin Convention of the National League on 30 December 1884.[131] The following year, 1885, saw the creation of the new single seat constituency of South Dublin, in which Milltown lay. The balance of power between the nationalist and the unionist side was quite evenly matched in terms of the number of voters each side could muster. As a result, the seat changed hands on the occasions where there was a split in one side's party or its candidates. At best, by 1900 the South Dublin constituency could be considered as a marginally unionist seat.[132] For this reason, it was vitally important for both sides to ensure that as many of their supporters as possible who were eligible to vote were registered on the voters' list.

The general election of 28 November 1885 saw the election of the first ever Home Rule MP for South Dublin, Sir Grattan Esmonde, who defeated the sitting Conservative MP of 22 years, Ian Trant Hamilton.[133] Not long after his victory, Esmonde addressed the inaugural meeting of the new Rathmines branch of the National League in December 1885, which was attended by

128 Murray, 'Electoral Politics', pp. 12–13.

129 *Saunders's Newsletter*, 19 October 1866, p. 2.

130 *Freeman's Journal*, 13 September 1890, p. 6.

131 *Freeman's Journal*, 31 December 1884, p. 3.

132 Alvin Jackson, 'The Failure of Unionism in Dublin, 1900', *Irish Historical Studies*, 26, no. 104 (1989), p. 378; Liam Clare, *Unionist/Nationalist election campaigns in South County Dublin (1883–1923)*, A talk given to the Foxrock Local History Club on 11 May 1983 (publication no. 13).

133 Clare, *Unionist/Nationalist election campaigns*, pp. 4–6.

Thomas Hackett.[134] Seven months later, on 6 July 1886, a general election was held following the fall of Gladstone's government over the defeat of the first Home Rule Bill. There was no change in South Dublin and Sir Grattan Esmonde retained his seat.[135]

The period between the 1886 general election and the Parnell split in 1890 was largely unremarkable in terms of Thomas Hackett's activity on behalf of the National League. During this period Hackett carried out the unglamorous but important work of ensuring that nationalist voters were included on the register of electors, hence the following notice in the *Freeman's Journal* of 24 May 1886: 'Milltown; Franchise forms; Nationalists can have returns of inhabitant occupiers filled up at Mr Thomas P. Hackett's, Milltown. Negligence now may cause loss of vote hereafter.'[136]

In essence, Thomas Hackett was following in the family tradition begun by his father Patrick 46 years beforehand, when Hackett senior was recruiting members for the National Repeal Association.[137]

The fall-out from the Parnell divorce case and subsequent split in the IPP from 1890 onwards was disastrous for Irish nationalism in south Dublin. Thomas Hackett firmly backed Parnell's leadership and he joined the Parnell leadership committee.[138] In March 1891 Hackett attended a meeting of the Dundrum Registration Association at which Dr ffrench Mullen was elected president and the following resolution was passed:

> *That we, the members of the Dundrum Branch of the South Dublin National Registration Association, declare that in all political matters Charles Stuart Parnell possesses our entire confidence and that our member [of Parliament] Sir Thomas Grattan Esmonde, in seceding from the leadership of Mr Parnell has failed to interpret the feelings of his constituents, and has forfeited their confidence (Applause).*[139]

Hackett attended further meetings in support of Parnell during the summer of 1891, including one of the very last political gatherings addressed by Parnell before his death on 6 October 1891. At the latter event, a monster meeting held at Cabinteely on 20 September 1891, Hackett was accompanied by the Milltown brass band.[140] However, the insurmountable difficulty for Parnell's supporters was that on a countrywide basis they were in a very small minority, despite the fact that Parnellites enjoyed considerable support in Dublin both before and after Parnell's death. These sobering facts were to be borne out in the general election of 7 July 1892.[141]

As part of the preparations for the upcoming general election of 1892 candidates had to be chosen to stand for the South Dublin constituency. There was considerable bitterness and division among the nationalists and, as a result, both the Parnellite and anti-Parnellite factions (each

134 *Freeman's Journal*, 19 December 1885, p. 6.

135 Clare, *Unionist/Nationalist election campaigns*, pp. 6–7.

136 *Freeman's Journal*, 24 May 1886, p. 1.

137 *Freeman's Journal*, 27 August 1840, p. 4.

138 *Flag of Ireland*, 10 January 1891, p. 6.

139 *Freeman's Journal*, 19 March 1891, p. 6.

140 *Freeman's Journal*, 29 May 1891, p. 7; 24 July 1891, p. 5; 21 September 1891, p. 5.

141 F.S.L. Lyons, 'The aftermath of Parnell, 1891–1903' in W.E. Vaughan (ed.), *A new history of Ireland, vi: Ireland under the Union 1870–1921* (Oxford, 1989), p. 82.

reconstituted as the Irish National League and the Irish National Federation, respectively) selected candidates to contest the election in the South Dublin constituency. By a mistake, a letter was sent to Thomas Hackett by David Sheehy on 8 June 1892 inviting him to attend a meeting of anti-Parnellites, who wished to consult with nationalist representatives of south Dublin before deciding whether or not to contest the seat. Hackett duly appeared at the meeting but his presence caused outright hostility when he undiplomatically told the assembled delegates, including John Dillon, Tim Healy, William O'Brien and Sir Thomas Esmonde, that 'a McCarthyite had not the ghost of a chance in South Dublin'.[142] This was too much for some of the anti-Parnellites and Thomas Hackett was physically assaulted by one of the delegates from Dundrum. According to one report, Hackett 'gave a good account of himself and marched off with dignity'.[143] True to form, Hackett wrote long letters to the newspapers setting out his version of events.[144]

Given the turmoil among the nationalists in south Dublin it was inevitable that they would lose the seat to the unionist candidate, Horace Plunkett, particularly as both nationalist factions fielded candidates. Accordingly, following polling on 7 July 1892, Horace Plunkett took the seat for the Unionists with 4,371 votes, followed by the Parnellite candidate, Dundrum resident Dr ffrench Mullen, who amassed 2,261 votes. The anti-Parnellite candidate, Thomas Grattan Esmonde, came home third with 1,452 votes. Three years later, another general election was held on 19 July 1895 which resulted in the unionist candidate, Horace Plunkett, defeating the sole nationalist candidate, the Parnellite Edmund Haviland Burke.[145]

Throughout the period of the Parnellite split Thomas Hackett remained loyal to the Irish National League. The impression gleaned from contemporary press reports is that the majority of nationalists living in Milltown supported the Parnellite cause too. For example, prior to the 1892 general election eight residents of Milltown acting as assenting electors filed nomination papers in support of Dr ffrench Mullen's candidacy.[146] A notice in the *Evening Herald* of 7 July 1892 advised Milltown nationalists that they could obtain information about their votes from Thomas Hackett and at Dr ffrench Mullen's Committee Rooms in Rathmines.[147] The following year a large demonstration in support of the Irish National League was held at Milltown on 22 October 1893, at which speeches were made by Parnellite MPs, including Thomas Hackett's relative through marriage, William Field.[148] One press report stated that the meeting was held on a large common near the Dodder and attended by 'some thousands of people', which was probably an exaggeration designed to impress the anti-Parnellite faction.[149] Another 'monster demonstration' was held at Milltown on 14 July 1895 in support of the Parnellite candidate

142 *Evening Herald*, 10 June 1892, p. 3. Justin McCarthy MP was one of the original founders of the Irish National Federation following the Parnellite split of 1891.

143 *Irish Independent*, 11 June 1892, p. 5. For a different view of the events see the *Freeman's Journal*, 11 June 1892, p. 5.

144 *Irish Independent*, 11 June 1892, p. 5; *Dublin Evening Telegraph*, 18 June 1892, p. 5.

145 Clare, *Unionist/Nationalist election campaigns*, pp. 7–10.

146 *Irish Independent*, 5 July 1892, p. 6.

147 *Evening Herald*, 7 July 1892, p. 1.

148 *Irish Independent*, 23 October 1893, p. 5; *Irish Times*, 23 October 1893, p. 6; *Dublin Daily Express*, 23 October 1893, p. 8; Freeman's Journal, 23 October 1893, p. 2. Field was elected to parliament in 1892 for the St Patrick's division of Dublin city, when, having stood as a Parnellite candidate, he defeated the sitting anti-Parnellite member, William Martin Murphy, who lived near Milltown in Dartry House, Upper Rathmines.

149 *Dublin Daily Express*, 23 October 1893, p. 8.

for South Dublin, Edmund Haviland Burke, which was addressed by Thomas Hackett among many others.[150] In contrast, the only anti-Parnellites living near Milltown in the 1890s identified thus far were William Martin Murphy of Darty House and the president of the Rathmines Branch of the Irish National Federation, W.L. Pearson, who lived in Richmond Lodge on Richmond Avenue South.[151]

For the first five months of 1898 political activity in Milltown centred on preparations to celebrate the centenary of the 1798 Rebellion, which were managed by a central committee in Dublin called the Emerald '98 Club.[152] Thomas Hackett's brother John took the lead in organising the commemorations for Milltown, and he was made president of the local branch of the Emerald '98 club, which was called the Ledwich and Keogh '98 Club, Milltown.[153] Ledwich and Keogh were the leaders of a party of United Irishmen from south Dublin who were attacked by dragoons and yeomanry at Rathfarnham on 24 May 1798. About 100 insurgents were believed to have been killed in the engagement at Rathfarnham, in which Ledwich and Keogh were taken prisoner. Ledwich had previously been a yeoman and so he was convicted for desertion and hanged. The injured Keogh, who was the son of a Rathfarnham farmer, was later pardoned.[154]

John Hackett and his branch committee organised what was described as a monster demonstration of the Emerald '98 Club for Sunday 22 May 1898 at Milltown, where several hundred members would walk in procession to the grounds of Whitehall House, Rathfarnham, via Windy Arbour, Dundrum and Churchtown.[155] The *Irish Independent* described the start of the procession in Milltown very favourably:

> *The gathering was unrivalled in the locality during the past 20 years, so everybody said. The start of the procession was watched in the village by a considerable body of Metropolitan Police, whose duties were relieved by a few men of the Royal Irish Constabulary, as it wended [sic] its way over Milltown Bridge, but their services were unrequired, for one of the most striking features of the whole assemblage was its perfectly orderly demeanour from start to finish.*[156]

At Whitehall three long-worded resolutions were proposed by the treasurer of the Ledwich and Keogh '98 Club, James Dunne, which included the following pronouncement:

> *nothing less than the complete independence of our country will satisfy us, and to achieve our object Irishmen should be prepared to unflinchingly face all dangers whether on the battlefield or the scaffold.*[157]

In seconding the resolutions, John Hackett told his audience that:

---

150 *Irish Independent*, 13 July 1895, p. 5.

151 *Dublin Evening Telegraph*, 23 October 1893, p. 4.

152 *Dublin Daily Nation*, 27 January 1898, p. 3.

153 *Dublin Daily Nation*, 11 May 1898, p. 6.

154 *Irish Independent*, 23 May 1898, p. 6; T.W. Moody, R.B. McDowell and C.J. Woods (eds), *The writings of Theobald Wolfe Tone 1763–98* (3 vols, Oxford, 2007), iii, p. 302.

155 *Irish Independent*, 23 May 1898, pp. 6–7; *Dublin Daily Nation*, 19 May 1898, p. 4; 23 May 1898, p. 6.

156 *Irish Independent*, 23 May 1898, p. 6.

157 *Irish Independent*, 23 May 1898, p. 7

> *he was proud to see there men from the city of Dublin who were not afraid to speak of '98 (hear, hear). They were there that day to assert their right to independence, and to fight for it if necessary, like Ledwich and Keogh in '98 (hear, hear).*[158]

This is the only known example where the Hacketts publicly expressed support for physical violence as a means of achieving independence from Great Britain. At heart, Thomas and John Hackett were constitutional nationalists. John's speech at Rathfarnham was delivered with a specific audience and purpose in mind. Commemorating the centenary of the 1798 Rebellion would have appealed to many of the Milltown and Rathfarnham villagers, especially those with deep-rooted families in their local communities, who had been handed down oral histories of the Irish rebellions of 1798 and 1867. As regards Milltown, the inhabitants would have inherited stories about United Irishmen connected with Milltown, such as Henry Jackson (Clonskeagh Castle and Clonskeagh iron mills), Robert Emmet (Casino/Emmet House) and James 'Napper' Tandy (Milltown iron mills). In the not-too-distant future, some of the young men steeped in this patriotic tradition would be inspired to take up arms as a means of achieving national freedom. The year 1898 was also notable for a notorious scandal concerning the registration of bogus lodgers, which was uncovered by the Dublin *Daily Nation* during a bi-election for the St Stephen's Green Division in January of that year. In short, corrupt electoral agents acting for the Unionist/Conservative party had stuffed the electoral register by filing lodger claim forms of very dubious authenticity. Some of these claim forms were later found to have been forged, to the great indignation of the nationalist-leaning newspapers.[159] The result of the bi-election was that the Unionist candidate, an ambitious lawyer named William Mussen Campbell, was elected despite doubts cast over the validity of the election. In his later years Campbell lived in Milltown, which will be discussed in more detail later.[160]

In the autumn of 1900, the Conservative government called a general election to be held on 9 October. By this stage the split in the IPP had been mended and the nationalists put forward a single candidate, the Dublin publican John J. Mooney. The sitting MP, Horace Plunkett, was also challenged by an independent unionist candidate, Francis Elrington Ball. Ball, who later wrote a six-volume history of County Dublin, lived in Dundrum and sat as a magistrate on the Dundrum Petty Sessions court. He would thus have been familiar to many of Milltown's residents. The split in the unionist vote led to Mooney winning the seat with 3,410 votes to Plunkett's 2,906, a majority of 504 votes.[161] On the night of his election Mooney drove from Milltown to Harold's Cross with a torchlight procession.[162] Thomas Hackett, who had acted as Mooney's election agent for the Rathmines division, was delighted with the result, which he described as a 'glorious victory for Catholicity and Nationality'.[163]

Work on behalf of the Rathmines and Dundrum National Registration associations continued to take up a considerable amount of Thomas Hackett's time in the early years of the new centu-

158 *Dublin Daily Nation*, 23 May 1898, p. 6.

159 *Dublin Daily Nation*, 3 January 1898, p. 4; 5 January 1898, pp. 5–6; 19 January 1898, p. 5; 28 January 1898, pp. 5–6; 2 February 1898, p. 6; *Evening Herald*, 14 March 1899, p. 4. *The Dublin Daily Nation* also claimed that there were over 5,330 lodger voters in the Rathmines polling district, 'of whom the great majority are Tories'.

160 *Dublin Daily Nation*, 19 January 1898, p. 5; *Irish Independent*, 23 March 1931, p. 6.

161 Clare, *Unionist/Nationalist election campaigns*, pp. 10–12. Ball received 1,539 votes.

162 *Rathmines News*, 13 October 1900, p. 4.

163 *Irish Independent*, 10 October 1900, p. 5; *Evening Herald*, 20 October 1900, p. 4.

ry.[164] Registration meetings were held continuously throughout Rathmines, Milltown, Harold's Cross and other adjacent localities, and Hackett was involved in setting up a branch of the South Dublin National Association in Dundrum.[165] A flavour of the typical outdoor political rallies that were held in Edwardian times by the nationalists of south Dublin can be found in the extensive report of one such meeting held at Milltown on Sunday 15 September 1901, as per the following sample extracts:

> *A series of registration meetings were held yesterday in the South Dublin Division, under the auspices of the Rathmines Registration Association, for the purpose of impressing upon the people the great importance of attending the Revision Court, which opens in the Town Hall, Rathmines, today ... The St Gall's Fife and Drum Band, Milltown, attended and accompanied the dray conveying the speakers right round to Harold's Cross, playing selections of music in admirable style along the route. At Milltown, where a fairly large crowd had assembled, Mr T.P. Hackett presided ... Mr William Field, M.P. then addressed the meeting ... He said the register of south Dublin was the most corrupt register in existence in any constituency in Great Britain or Ireland (hear hear). There were more bogus lodger voters in it then in all other constituencies in Ireland except St Stephen's Green (laughter) ... The constitutional Tory Government had entered on the Boer war for the ostensible purpose of giving the Outlanders the franchise, and through their agents there in South Dublin they objected to every working man who claimed a vote, although he resided in it, and had been born in it. Was there ever a greater piece of hypocritical humbug? ... He referred to the exclusive manner in which the Tory Urban Council of Rathmines acted in its official appointments, and pointed out that if every man looked after his vote, they would soon exterminate the corrupt Council of Rathmines (hear hear). He was convinced that the men of Milltown would do their duty, and he called upon them to vindicate their claim to the land which God had sent them (cheers). The proceedings then concluded, and the brake containing the speakers drove leisurely off to Ranelagh, where a large crowd had assembled awaiting their arrival. The brake was preceded by the band, and accompanied from Milltown by many of those attending the meeting there.*[166]

The general election of 1906 saw the Liberals return to power with a large majority. Despite all the fighting talk of the national registration associations in south Dublin, the unionist candidate, William Long, was returned with a sizeable majority, defeating the nationalist candidate, Richard Hazelton, by 5,269 votes to 3,926. The nationalists blamed their defeat on their failure to register a sufficient number of their voters.[167] This begs the question as to how effective the nationalist registration associations in south Dublin actually were in proactively monitoring and updating the electoral register every year. Indeed, the secretary of the South Dublin Nationalist Registration Association, John Kavanagh, publicly admitted in 1904 that the organisation suffered from a lack of funds and voter apathy.[168] Another question concerns the inconvenience that the voting registration process caused for working-class men who could not always take

164 *Rathmines News*, 3 November 1900, p. 5; 20 July 1901, p. 3; *Evening Herald*, 29 July 1901, p. 4; *Rathmines News*, 5 April 1902, p. 5; *Freeman's Journal*, 9 September 1902, p. 5.

165 *Rathmines News*, 1 December 1900, p. 4.

166 *Irish Independent*, 16 September 1901, p. 2. Field's criticism of the Tories and their election agents was not entirely misplaced. In 1904 a registration agent acting on behalf of the Unionist Registration Association was charged with falsifying voter registration papers in respect of voters in Harold's Cross: *Rathmines News*, 30 July 1904; Ó Maitiú, *Dublin's Suburban Towns*, pp. 129–30.

167 Clare, *Unionist/Nationalist election campaigns*, pp. 12–13.

168 *Freeman's Journal*, 21 October 1904, p. 2.

time off to vote, let alone attend the annual revision court. This issue was raised by Thomas Hackett as far back as the Rathmines township elections of 1885.[169]

The indications are that Thomas Hackett's health was declining by the time of the 1906 general election, as he is not mentioned in any of the press reports during the campaign. William Field, addressing another political gathering in Milltown, this time on 16 September 1906, provided further proof of Hackett's demise:

> *Mr Field, M.P., expressed his great regret that their old friend Tom Hackett was not able to take the chair. They all hoped, however, that his illness was only of a temporary character (cheers). He knew Milltown of old, in days of trial, and he knew that in the work which was before them the men of Milltown would do their whole duty, not a part of it but the whole of it.*[170]

Before reviewing Thomas Hackett's work in local politics, it is appropriate to end this section by mentioning a portentous resolution that was passed by the local Orange Order Lodge (Melancthon L.O.L. 1,755), which met in Dundrum in November 1906:

> *That we, the members of the Melancthon L.O.L., in Lodge assembled at Dundrum, Co. Dublin, do hereby place on record our sincere and solemn protest against any form of Home Rule, Devolution, Co-ordination, or any tampering with the Legislative Union of Great Britain and Ireland.*[171]

Clearly, the return of a Liberal government to power after an absence of 13 years was not welcomed by the unionists of south Dublin and was a cause of some apprehension for them.

LOCAL POLITICS AND THE RATHMINES TOWNSHIP

Political discord in the Rathmines township had its origins in the 1870s with the disagreement between the ratepayers and the commissioners about sourcing water for the township. The confidence generated by the ascent of Parnell and the establishment of the Irish National League in the 1880s encouraged nationalists in the township to put forward candidates in the township election of 1885. At a meeting of nationalist voters held at the National Registration Rooms, 4 Duggan Place, Rathmines, seven nationalist candidates (later reduced to six) were selected to contest the township election, which was to be held on 16 November 1885. Thomas Hackett was chosen to stand in the east ward. During their acceptance speeches, Hackett and his fellow candidates criticised the outgoing commissioners on their handling of the water supply issue, and Hackett promised to do his best in the interest of the ratepayers if he was elected.[172] In the east ward there were four commissioners to be elected out of eight candidates, with three of the retiring commissioners seeking re-election. Similarly, all of the three outgoing commissioners in the west ward sought re-election in a field containing six candidates.

The result of the election was a huge disappointment for the nationalists. All of the unionist candidates were elected to the new board of commissioners, including all of the outgoing commissioners who had stood for re-election. Thomas Hackett received 161 votes, the highest number polled by the three nationalists in the east ward (161, 158 and 151), but Hackett's vote was

169 *Freeman's Journal*, 27 November 1885, p. 6.

170 *Freeman's Journal*, 17 September 1906, p. 11. The report names 18 Milltown residents who attended the rally.

171 *Rathmines News*, 24 November 1906, p. 3.

172 *Freeman's Journal*, 5 November 1885, p. 7.

well below the 253 votes secured by the fourth placed unionist candidate, who took the last seat in the east ward. A similar set of results prevailed in the west ward, where the highest vote of the three nationalist candidates (196 versus 194 and 191) was almost 50 per cent less than the vote secured by the third placed unionist candidate (384) who took the final seat there.[173] The municipal election highlighted the fact that the nationalist vote was spread very evenly across each of the six candidates in the township; had the nationalists selected four instead of six candidates, or had one or two candidates secured a large majority of the nationalist vote, then the nationalists would have gained one or possibly two seats on the new board of the township commissioners. Local democracy in Ireland was completely overhauled and reinvigorated by the enactment of the Local Government (Ireland) Act 1898 which became law on 12 August 1898. The primary purpose of this act was to put local government on a representative basis. In short, local government was distributed between county councils, urban and rural district councils and boards of guardians. A whole host of changes in the provision of local government services took place, which among other things, included the extension of the electoral franchise for district councillors to women, the abolition of the grand jury system and the introduction of a democratically elected county council to run Dublin County.

From the point of view of Milltown village, the important changes saw the conversion of the Rathmines township into an urban district council and its electorate brought into line with the (larger) parliamentary franchise.[174] On the south bank of the River Dodder at Concrete, Farranboley and beyond, local government was vested in the Rathdown RDC. Essentially, district councillors elected to the Rathdown RDC took over many of the functions previously exercised by the Rathdown Board of Guardians, the most important of which concerned health, housing and sanitation. Rather confusingly, restructured boards of guardians (also known as poor law guardians or poor law boards) retained responsibility for the provision of medical and poor relief and the management of the workhouses in their poor law union.[175] Under these new arrangements, for example, the Rathdown Poor Law Board now comprised 35 urban district councillors (representing the five townships in the Rathdown Union) and 18 rural district councillors (representing seven electoral rural divisions in the Rathdown Union). The rural electoral division of Dundrum, which included Concrete and Farranboley, was entitled to elect two rural district councillors to the Rathdown RDC.[176]

The impact of the changes to the electoral franchise in the Rathmines UDC wrought by the Local Government Act of 1898 was significant. The electorate had grown to 5,654 voters, which was an increase of 198 per cent over the old franchise. Of these, women voters numbered 1,350 or 23.8 per cent of the new electorate.[177] Emboldened by the extended franchise, Rathmines nationalists mounted another challenge to the status quo among the Rathmines township commissioners when they put forward 13 candidates to contest the township election, which was

173 *Freeman's Journal*, 17 November 1885, p. 7.

174 Although the Rathmines township was reconstituted as an urban district council, its elected representatives continued for a number of years after 1898 to be often referred to as commissioners rather than as councillors, and so the terms were interchangeable at the turn of the twentieth century.

175 Potter, *The municipal revolution in Ireland*, pp. 196–200; Richard Haslam, 'The Origins of Irish Local Government' in Mark Callanan and Justin F. Keogan (eds), *Local Government in Ireland Inside Out* (Dublin, 2003), pp. 25–7; Crossman, Local Government, pp. 92–4.

176 *Wicklow Newsletter*, 18 February 1899, p. 5; *Freeman's Journal*, 17 April 1899, p. 6.

177 Ciarán Wallace, 'Local politics and government in Dublin city and suburbs 1899–1914' (PhD thesis, University of Dublin, 2010), p. 110.

scheduled to take place on 16 January 1899. Once again, Thomas Hackett was selected as a nationalist candidate for the east ward.[178] The Rathmines Registration Association appealed to the Rathmines electorate in mid-December 1898 on the following lines:

> *We trust that in putting forward seven candidates for the East Ward and five for the West Ward, the electors of every class and political section will recognise in a tolerant and practical manner that we are merely seeking what we are justly entitled to, and that they will vote accordingly.*[179]

The nationalists decided to hold their first major meeting of the campaign at Milltown on 1 January 1899. In advance of the big meeting, the *Evening Herald* was optimistic about the nationalists' prospects:

> *Now that the franchise has been extended by reason of the Local Government Act, the Nationalists are about to avail of the opportunity of placing some representatives of their way of thinking on the Council. Tomorrow's meeting will be addressed by several prominent speakers, including the candidates, and should prove one of the largest and most enthusiastic gatherings that has yet assembled in Milltown.*[180]

The *Evening Herald* predictions were later proven wrong. The attendance at the meeting in Milltown on New Year's Day, 1899 was not large because of bitterly cold weather.[181] Nonetheless, the *Rathmines News* reported on the speeches made by candidates in great detail.[182] According to the press report, when Thomas Hackett's turn to speak came he was received with great applause. Hackett was a self-confident and accomplished public speaker, and during his address to the crowd at Milltown his speech was punctuated with applause and cries of 'Hear, hear' and 'You are right there.' All of the candidates were highly critical of the township commissioners, referencing the bad treatment of workmen employed by the township, the lack of provision of affordable working-class housing and the waste of ratepayers' money.[183]

Another nationalist meeting was held in Rathmines on 11 January 1899, at which the perennial topic of the voter registration list was discussed. The secretary of the Rathmines Nationalist Registration Association said the association had succeeded in getting 600 Tory voters removed from the township electoral list at the previous revision court, and that the association had placed a fairly representative number of nationalists on the list of electors. From a superficial glance at the voters' list, the secretary thought the nationalists had a very fair chance of being returned. Thomas Hackett told the meeting that the nationalist candidates could not be accused of having neglected the electoral register, and they had done all in their power to secure every nationalist a vote.[184]

Polling day on 16 January 1899 saw 3,765 votes cast out of a total electorate of 5,654. This amounted to a turnout of 66 per cent.[185] Unfortunately for the nationalists, not one of their 13

---

178 *Rathmines News*, 10 December 1898, p. 4; *Dublin Daily Nation*, 23 December 1898, p. 3.

179 *Dublin Daily Nation*, 17 December 1898, p. 6.

180 *Evening Herald*, 31 December 1898, p. 3.

181 *Freeman's Journal*, 2 January 1899, p. 7.

182 *Rathmines News*, 7 January 1899, p. 5.

183 *Rathmines News*, 7 January 1899, p. 5.

184 *Dublin Daily Nation*, 12 January 1899, p. 6.

185 Wallace, *Local politics*, p. 128.

candidates was elected to fill the 21 seats on the new council. Thomas Hackett received 542 votes, or practically half of the 1,068 votes polled by the twelfth and last candidate to be returned in the east ward. By way of comparison, Milltown's major employer, Thomas Edmondson, the owner of the Dublin Laundry Company, received 1,196 which gained him fourth place in the east ward.[186]

Discontent with the Rathmines township continued to fester. On 20 March 1900 a group of 50 Rathmines township ratepayers signed a lengthy manifesto called, 'Boundaries or Bankruptcy' which criticised the performance of the commissioners and supported the Dublin Corporation Boundaries Extension Bill, which sought to annex the Rathmines township.[187] Although Dublin Corporation's bid to take over the township ultimately failed, the dissident ratepayers' manifesto showed that there was a small cohort of middle-class ratepayers who were dissatisfied with the governance of the township.[188]

In the spring of 1902, the campaign for fairer political representation on the board of the Rathmines UDC was taken up by the Jesuits of Milltown Park. In his address to the inaugural meeting of the Catholic Association of the Rathmines and Rathgar Townships [*sic*] on the subject of Catholicity and Civil Life, Fr Peter Finlay SJ exhorted his audience as follows:

> *We only ask for fair play, and we intend to get it (applause). It is a duty then to organise, to register, to quietly get the civic franchise, and place our members on the Urban Councils, on the Boards of Guardians, in the District Councils, and other local boards and committees where we have a right to be fully represented (applause).*[189]

The nationalists of Rathmines decided on a change of tactics due to their continued failure to secure representation on the Rathmines UDC. Using their influence on Dublin County Council, in 1903 the nationalists petitioned the county council to divide the township into five wards. The proposed redivision, if sanctioned, would include the creation of a municipal ward for Milltown comprising 1,172 inhabited houses, i.e. houses with at least one eligible voter.[190]

A public enquiry was held in the Rathmines Town Hall on 12 November 1903, which was presided over by a sub-committee of Dublin County Council. The petitioners argued that the working classes of the township who predominantly lived in Milltown and Harold's Cross wanted representation on the council but were unable to achieve it. On the other hand, the respondents argued that the township had spent £55,000 in building artisans' dwellings for 1,500 people out of a population of 30,000.[191] Thomas Hackett gave evidence in support of the petition, saying that under the present system of local government in Rathmines there was no chance for a Catholic or a nationalist to get elected. This point was disputed by counsel for the Rathmines UDC, who pointed out that a Catholic (Edward Fottrell) had sat as chairman of the township commissioners for over 20 years. Under cross examination Hackett acknowledged that he owned about 30 tenement houses in Milltown. He admitted too that he had been summoned several times by

186 *Dublin Daily Nation*, 18 January 1899, pp. 5–6; *Rathmines News*, 21 January 1899, p. 5.

187 *Dublin Daily Nation*, 20 March 1900, pp. 6–7; *Rathmines News*, 24 March 1900, p. 5.

188 The group included ex MPs Thomas Mayne and William Martin Murphy JP of Dartry House, James FitzGerald Lombard JP of South Hill and T.P. Hackett of Milltown.

189 *Rathmines News*, 2 May 1902, p. 3.

190 *Freeman's Journal*, 13 November 1903, p. 7, compared with the *Irish Independent*, 13 November 1903, p. 6 where the number of Milltown inhabited houses is put at 1,072.

191 *Irish Independent*, 13 November 1903, p. 6.

the township for offences under the health acts but that the authorities had acted unreasonably and he had defeated them on two or three occasions.[192]

After hearing the witness evidence advanced by the petitioners (who had secured 1,321 signatures in support of the wards' extension) and their opponents (who had secured 1,322 signatures against the petition), the sub-committee of Dublin County Council subsequently found in favour of the extension, recommending that the township be divided into five wards of 21 seats, with the new Milltown ward returning four councillors. Dublin County Council duly adopted the recommendations of its sub-committee on 14 January 1904.[193] Accordingly, Dublin County Council made an order directing the Rathmines UDC to implement the redivision of the wards from two to five, including the new Milltown ward.[194]

Naturally, the order to increase the wards in the township was opposed by the Rathmines councillors. In their opinion, such a change was contrary to the wishes of the large majority of the ratepayers and electors of the district.[195] Unsurprisingly, therefore, the Rathmines UDC appealed the county council's order to the Local Government Board, and a second inquiry was held on 24/25 May 1904.[196] The second enquiry was considered by the editor of the Rathmines News to have been a rather tame affair, although he believed that the number of wards would be increased by the Local Government Board.[197]

Reading the press transcripts of the local government enquiry show that at its heart the dispute was about social class, although politics and religion came into it too. The wealthy middle-class councillors from places like Palmerston and Temple roads did not want to share power with their social inferiors from Milltown and Harold's Cross. From a Milltown perspective, the cross examination of Milltown laundry proprietor and vice-chairman of the Rathmines UDC, Thomas Edmondson, by Timothy Healy, KC, MP provides an amusing vignette. Healy was acting for the Rathmines ratepayers/petitioners. In his cross-examination of Edmondson, Healy tried unsuccessfully to impugn the Quaker businessman:

> *Mr Healy (to Edmondson) – Do you think if Milltown was amalgamated into one ward you would be returned as usual? I won't venture an opinion.*
> *Mr Healy – Why? Because I don't profess to know the unknown.*
> *Mr Healy – What scallywag would take your place? It is not for me to say.*
> *Mr Healy – Do you know of any budding ambition in Milltown amongst the untamed democracy who would oust you? I don't know.*
> *Mr Gordon [counsel for Rathmines UDC] – There is a gentleman named Hackett [i.e. Milltown grocer and publican, T.P. Hackett].*
> *Mr Healy – Rally for Hackett (laughter). Now, as to that laundry of yours, has there been a special varnishing given to it in the matter of footpaths? I never heard of it.*
> *Mr Healy – Never heard that the money of the Council had been expended out there? I presume you refer*

192 *Freeman's Journal*, 13 November 1903, p. 7; *Rathmines News*, 14 November 1903, p. 2.

193 *Irish Independent*, 18 November 1903, p. 6; 15 January 1904, p. 6; *Rathmines News*, 19 December 1903, p. 3. One of the five sub-committee members voted against the extension.

194 *Rathmines News*, 6 February 1904, pp. 2–3.

195 *Dublin Evening Mail*, 3 February 1904, p. 2.

196 *Rathmines News*, 14 May 1904, p. 2; 28 May 1904, p. 3; *Dublin Evening Mail*, 25 May 1904, p. 2; 26 May 1904, pp. 2–3; *Irish Times*, 26 May 1904, p. 7; 27 May 1904, p. 3.

197 *Rathmines News*, 28 May 1904, p. 2.

to the recent removal of the dangerous corner under the arch [i.e. at the railway viaduct].
Mr Healy – How well they saw that. Is it gone? It is gone. We gave the ground free and paid portion of the expense.
Mr Healy – How much did the township expend on that? Probably nearly £100, but our surveyor reported it was the most dangerous corner in Rathmines.
Mr Healy – Of course he did. If you had not been a Commissioner, would he have made that report? [at this point counsel for Rathmines UDC interjected][198]

Healy was more successful in uncovering the snobbery the existed among the Rathmines councillors, as exemplified with this exchange with Councillor W. Carruthers of 10 Palmerston Park:

Mr Healy – You'll agree with me that the electors are entitled to the best means of having their wishes and wants carried out at the council? Certainly, their wishes and wants. Witness, continuing, said he believed that if the division into smaller wards returned more artisans, they would not be so competent to deal with the business of the township as better educated businessmen.
Mr Healy – What persuaded these people to get this petition signed? Well, you know, there are cranks.
Mr Healy – 800 cranks in Rathmines (laughter). I'd advise you to start a lunatic asylum (laughter).[199]

On a broader level, the legal team for the Rathmines UDC argued that the motive behind the ratepayers' petition was purely a religious one, and that no allegation of incompetency or neglect had been proven against the council. The council's lawyers also claimed that the petitioners were using the labouring class as an excuse to justify increased representation, whereas in reality the petitioners wanted to get more Catholics and nationalists onto the council.[200] In the end, it was a technical legal argument which decided the matter. The Solicitor General, acting on behalf of the Rathmines UDC, had argued on the first day of the hearing (25 May 1904) that because the division of the Rathmines township into two wards had been carried out by an Act of Parliament, neither Dublin County Council nor the Local Government Board had the power to make any change to the number of wards.[201] This legal point was eventually conceded by the Local Government Board some months after the public hearing had closed. Accordingly, the order made by Dublin County Council on 14 January 1904 was declared *ultra vires*.[202]

Needless to say, considerable blame was levied by the Rathmines UDC against Dublin County Council and the Local Government Board, deploring how two pointless public inquiries had been held. Not unreasonably, the township's officials and their solicitors queried who was responsible for the waste of time and money, and whether or not the council and its agents would recover their expenses. Allegations were also made about lawyers acting while having a conflict of interest. In truth, the lawyers were very much to blame for what transpired but, in true Irish

198 *Dublin Evening Mail*, 26 May 1904, pp. 2–3.

199 *Irish Times*, 27 May 1904, p. 3.

200 *Irish Times*, 27 May 1904, p. 3; *Dublin Evening Mail*, 1 September 1904, p. 3.

201 *Dublin Evening Mail*, 25 May 1904, p. 2.

202 *Rathmines News*, 3 September 1904, p. 2; *Dublin Evening Mail*, 1 September 1904, p. 3; 8 September 1904, p. 3; Ó Maitiú, *Dublin's Suburban Towns*, pp. 130–2.

fashion, no-one was held accountable.[203] To add insult to injury, the Local Government Board obtained an order from the Lord Lieutenant enabling the Board to recoup its inquiry expenses from the amount due to Dublin County Council from the local taxation account.[204]

The 1904 controversy over the electoral franchise of the Rathmines township extinguished for the foreseeable future the prospect of any meaningful municipal representation for the inhabitants of Milltown.[205] How many of them were bothered by this is a moot point, but the imbroglio undoubtedly reinforced resentment among those nationalist residents in the township who had campaigned to increase the wards, and strengthened their belief that they could never obtain fairness under the unionist-dominated Rathmines Council. The disaffected nationalists did, however, gain some measure of revenge when, in 1906, the IPP with the support of the Liberals successfully defeated a highly controversial Rathmines Extension Bill to annex Terenure.[206] Had their Extension Bill also provided for an increase in the number of electoral wards in the township, the Rathmines councillors may have stood a better chance of getting their legislation through Parliament.

The view has been expressed that the success of the unionist hegemony on the board of the Rathmines UDC was (among other things) due to support from the township's large middle-class Catholic minority who felt well served by the four Catholic councillors and their Protestant colleagues.[207] In supporting this assertion, Ciarán Wallace quotes from a witness statement given to the Bureau of Military History (BMH) by Kevin O'Shiel: 'a very substantial percentage of Catholics voted for the unionist and ratepayers' candidates, not so much of their politics, but rather because they were good men of affairs, and ensured sound, economical urban administration.'[208] The quotation taken from Shiel's witness statement is too simplistic. In reality the Catholic position was more complex. As we have seen, the politics of the Rathmines township was influenced by social class as well as individual or group political and religious affiliation. The priority given to each factor by the voter personal matter. Undoubtedly Catholics prioritised the candidate's administrative ability and record above his political or religious persuasion and voted accordingly. That said, the electoral experience of the Rathmines township in the Edwardian era proves beyond doubt that there was a considerable cohort of Catholic voters who were politically disenfranchised from the unionist-dominated council. Furthermore, scores of potential voters among the lodger franchise, many of whom were working-class Catholics living in old villages such as Milltown and Harold's Cross, were hampered by the complexities of the voter registration system and the machinations of unionist election agents. Historian Mary Daly has also noted how the Rathmines township operated an informal zoning system, which concentrated much of the working-class and lower middle-class housing in the Harold's Cross area. This district was located in the west ward and held only nine council seats compared to the 12 held by the wealthier east ward.[209]

---

203 *Dublin Evening Mail*, 8 September 1904, p. 3; *Rathmines News*, 17 September 1904, p. 4.

204 *Dublin Evening Telegraph*, 12 January 1906, p. 5.

205 Sinn Fein and the IPP eventually won seats on the Rathmines UDC: *Dublin Evening Telegraph*, 17 January 1920, p. 5.

206 *Rathmines News*, 4 November 1905, p. 3; *Dublin Daily Express*, 26 March 1906, p. 8; *Northern Whig*, 26 May 1906, p. 22; Ó Maitiú, *Dublin's Suburban Towns*, pp. 143–4.

207 Wallace, *Local politics*, p. 177.

208 Wallace, *Local politics*, p. 177, quoting from the bureau of military history witness statement of Kevin O'Shiel, NAI, Witness Statement no. 1770, Part 2, p. 60.

209 Mary Daly, 'Late Nineteenth and Early Twentieth Century Dublin' in Harkness and O'Dowd (eds), *The Town in Ireland* (Belfast, 1981), p. 231.

The contemporary opinion (1906) of a middle-class ratepayer, Michael Sullivan living in 'Belclare', Temple Gardens, is worth quoting to counterbalance Shiel's statement:

> *It is a mistake to look on Rathmines as a 'Protestant Township'. In 1901 the population was 32,602, and of these 17,216 – that is 53 per cent. – were Catholics. In Rathmines many Catholics are Conservatives, and some Protestants are Nationalists. Hitherto the Conservative organisation has been by far the most effective, and owing to the division of the township into two unwieldy wards that Conservatives have practically the whole representation in their hands. From this you can see that the Rathmines Bill, proposing to annex Terenure, affected many interests. Its rejection, and by an unprecedented majority [in the House of Commons], gave much satisfaction.*[210]

The charge that the township was dominated by the Conservatives was completely rejected by the council's chairman, the aforementioned Thomas Edmondson, proprietor of the Dublin Laundry Company. Edmondson was interviewed by the *Dublin Daily Express* during which he gave his sincerely held opinion on the absence of political bias on the Rathmines UDC:

> *'I suppose', said Mr Edmondson in conclusion, 'there is little use in reiterating that our Council is a non-political body, composed – as anyone may ascertain who desires to do so – of men of all creeds and politics. We never allow any political discussions in our meetings. I wish to put on record again these absolute facts in the hope that, if they should come before any of those English Liberals who voted against us, they may help to give them a clearer idea of the actual position of affairs in regard to our much abused [Rathmines Extension] Bill.'*[211]

In the final analysis one wonders if the failure to achieve fairer democratic representation among the working-class inhabitants of the township contributed to the political disillusionment of the younger generation of Milltown men and women, some of whom went on to join the Irish/National Volunteers and fight in the 1916 Rising and the War of Independence.

LOCAL POLITICS AND THE RATHDOWN RURAL DISTRICT COUNCIL

As we have seen, Thomas Hackett failed to get elected to the Rathmines UDC in the township elections held on 16 January 1898. A second opportunity presented itself in April 1898, at the local government elections to elect county councillors, rural district councillors and poor law guardians for Dublin city and the Dublin townships.[212] Hackett was duly selected as an Independent Nationalist candidate (Parnellite) for the Dundrum electoral division in the rural district council election for the Rathdown RDC, along with fellow publican James Collins of Uncle Tom's Cabin, Dundrum.[213] Hackett and Collins published a joint election manifesto appealing to nationalist voters by stressing their commitment to addressing the local and national issues of the day. Rather ironically given his poor record as a slum landlord, Hackett promised to give the utmost care and attention to the proper housing of the poor.[214]

---

210 *Northern Whig*, 26 May 1906, p. 22.

211 *Dublin Daily Express*, 26 March 1906, p. 8.

212 *Freeman's Journal*, 7 April 1899, pp. 5–6.

213 *Rathmines News*, 4 March 1899, p. 5; 11 March 1899, p. 4.

214 *Rathmines News*, 11 March 1899, p. 4.

As previously noted, Dundrum had the right to elect two councillors to the Rathdown RDC. Over the course of the campaign it emerged that three nationalist candidates and one unionist candidate would be standing for election on polling day, 6 April 1898. The nationalists' election chances were harmed by infighting and by the fact that, controversially, three nationalist candidates instead of two were standing for election.[215] This explains why the nationalists only returned one candidate (James Collins). Thomas Hackett lost out in fourth place. In contrast, Dundrum resident and local dispensary doctor, Dr Isaac Ussher, topped the poll for the unionists.[216] As a minor consolation, Hackett was subsequently appointed on 19 April 1898 as a poor law warden for the Dundrum district, which included Concrete and Farranboley where some of Hackett's tenement property lay. The local wardens were responsible for distributing medical relief to the poor in the form of dispensary and midwifery tickets.[217]

The next local elections took place in May 1902 but Thomas Hackett was not included among the nationalist ticket for the Rathdown RDC election.[218] Instead, he was co-opted onto the Rathdown RDC on 2 July 1902 to fill a vacancy on the local council. Hackett seems to have owed his appointment as a reward for longstanding service to the nationalist cause rather than for any particular skillset.[219] Once Thomas Hackett became a rural district councillor, he also became an ex officio poor law guardian for the Dundrum electoral division.[220] He thus joined a cohort of over 50 poor law guardians who were responsible for the oversight of the Rathdown Union workhouse and the provision of poor relief.

Hackett's three-year period as a district councillor was marked by controversy rather than by any notable achievement on his part. In 1904 he was appointed to a sub-committee of the Rathdown RDC to report on longstanding problems arising from the absence of proper sewerage arrangements in Dundrum village and along the River Slang valley, a subject discussed in detail in the previous chapter. Rather controversially, Hackett refused to sign the report produced by his colleagues, which caused ongoing friction on the council for several months during that year.[221] Basically, Hackett was opposed to burdening the ratepayers of Dundrum with an expensive septic tank sewerage system, and he largely blamed the Manor Mill Laundry in Dundrum for the pollution of the River Slang.[222] Hackett produced his own detailed written report to support his views. This action on Hackett's part further alienated some of his colleagues who were frustrated with the council's inaction, particularly as it was coming under sustained pressure from the Local Government Board and from local ratepayers to fix Dundrum's drainage problem.[223] Laying the blame for the pollution of the River Slang on the laundry was a convenient excuse to avoid making hard decisions, and as the council was divided on the solution to the drainage issue, the councillors decided at their weekly meeting of 13 July 1904 to commission a report from a

215 *Rathmines News*, 18 March 1899, p. 5; 1 April 1899, p. 5.

216 *Rathmines News*, 15 April 1899, p. 5; *Dublin Daily Express*, 8 April 1899, p. 6.

217 *Rathmines News*, 6 May 1899, p. 4; NAI, Rathdown Poor Law Union, Board of Guardians Minute Book A113, March 1898–October 1899, Folio 14, p. 38.

218 *Rathmines News*, 3 May 1902, p. 4.

219 *Rathmines News*, 5 July 1902, p. 4; *Wicklow Newsletter*, 5 July 1902, p. 3.

220 Wallace, 'Local politics', pp. 201–2.

221 *Wicklow Newsletter*, 16 April 1904, p. 9; 4 June 1904, p. 8; *Rathmines News*, 11 June 1904, p. 2; 9 July 1904, p. 3; 9 July 1904, p. 3.

222 *Wicklow Newsletter*, 25 June 1904, p. 12

223 *Wicklow People*, 9 July 1904, p. 2; *Rathmines News*, 9 July 1904, p. 3; 16 July 1904, p. 3.

civil engineer.[224] This procrastination caused a falling out between Thomas Hackett and his fellow councillor and erstwhile political colleague, John A. Kavanagh, who was the secretary of the Nationalist Registration Association of South Dublin. Kavanagh's home in Dundrum, which he rented from the owner of the Manor Mill Laundry, suffered from the noxious odours emanating from the River Slang at the end of his garden.[225] Thus it would have been very awkward for Kavanagh to side with Hackett and blame his (Kavanagh's) landlord for the pollution. Instead, in a letter to the *Rathmines News* Kavanagh argued passionately that a comprehensive sewerage system should be put in place to mitigate the appalling sanitary conditions of the working-class residents living in Dundrum, Rosemount and Windy Arbour.[226] Hackett viewed Kavanagh's letter as a political stunt. In a typically robust response to Kavanagh, Hackett revealed his inherent bias as a landlord and tenement owner:

> *It is very doubtful if Mr Kavanagh's cheap expressions of philanthropy will succeed in hoodwinking the workingmen of Dundrum to believe in his sincerity for their welfare. I believe the workers of Dundrum are intelligent enough to know that they have all to pay rates, either directly or indirectly with their rents, and that when the rates increase the rents are likely to increase.*
>
> *No doubt Mr Kavanagh can afford to display his magnanimity towards the working classes and his absolute disregard for the ratepayers, as it seems that he is not encumbered with the responsibility of landlordism or the payment of much rates, but as an expert in electioneering tactics he may perhaps be excused on that ground alone for indulging in the hope of years to come.*[227]

The ongoing failure of the Rathdown RDC to solve Dundrum's chronic housing and drainage problems, coupled with petty squabbles exemplified by Hackett and Kavanagh's public spat, was not a good advertisement for local democracy or for nationalist politics in south Dublin. By now Thomas Hackett was into his seventies and losing energy. Hackett's declining powers can be gauged by the lack of press reports of any activity or contributions by him at the weekly meetings of the Rathdown RDC and the Rathdown Board of Guardians. His final reported attendances at the aforementioned boards of management occurred in the last two weeks of April 1905.[228]

CONCLUSION

Thomas Hackett died at home on 25 January 1908 of bronchitis and heart failure, aged seventy-four. According to his death certificate Thomas had also been suffering from prostatic disease for three years prior to his death.[229] This explains why mention of Hackett in the press gradually ceased from 1905 onwards. A relatively perfunctory notice was published in the *Freeman's Journal*, which reported on Hackett's funeral in the following terms:

> *Yesterday the remains of this much esteemed gentleman were removed from the Catholic Church, Milltown, for internment in Glasnevin Cemetery. The funeral was an exceptionally large one – per-*

224 *Rathmines News*, 16 July 1904, p. 3; 23 July 1904, p. 2.

225 *Rathmines News*, 22 April 1905, p. 3.

226 *Rathmines News*, 23 July 1904, p. 3.

227 *Rathmines News*, 6 August 1904, p. 3.

228 *Wicklow Newsletter*, 22 April 1905, p. 2; 29 April 1905, p. 7.

229 Civil registration of deaths in the district of Dublin South, Rathmines, 1908, no. 141, 25 January 1908.

> *haps the largest seen in the district for many years. The numerous friends and members of public bodies who followed the remains to the graveside testified to the esteem and respect in which the deceased was held, and to the sympathy felt for the family in their bereavement.*[230]

As usual, the newspaper published a long list of names of the mourners which as one would expect, was dominated by local publicans, neighbours and councillors. Surprisingly given Hackett's political service to the Home Rule movement, only one MP attended the funeral, William Field, who, as noted earlier, was related to Thomas Hackett through marriage.[231] Noticeable too is the complete absence of information about Hackett's career. Nonetheless, one needs to be careful not to read too much into a short funeral notice. Maybe Hackett had alienated people during his occasionally controversial career as a publican and local politician, or perhaps it was just a case that times (and politicians) had moved on in Edwardian Ireland as Hackett faded from the public arena in his declining years.

One final important point needs to be made about Thomas Hackett. This biographical account of his life has out of necessity relied heavily on contemporary newspapers and official records to build up a profile of his career. Press reports and court records are more likely to present a person in a negative light because, as we have seen, controversies and breaches of the law predominate in those sources. Thus, there is no way of knowing about Hackett's good personal qualities – extension of credit to hard-pressed tenants and mothers buying food 'on tick', for example. Or helping less well-educated villagers to deal with officialdom, or drafting letters for them. Indeed, oral historian Thomas Kearns has shown how Dublin publicans had become leading figures in their local communities in the early twentieth century, a time when they performed valuable services for people in times of need.[232]

No other lifelong inhabitant of Milltown has left behind such an extensive historical record as Thomas Hackett. It is a pity that no photograph of him has come to light which could add some vitality to his personality. His image probably exists in formal group photographs taken at political or vintners' functions, which are more likely to have survived. ■

230 *Freeman's Journal*, 29 January 1908, p. 3.

231 *Freeman's Journal*, 29 January 1908, p. 3. Thomas's sister Charlotte had married William's brother Edward Field in 1868: Marriage register for Rathmines RC church, at entry no. 1611, 4 February 1868.

232 Kevin C. Kearns, *Dublin Pub Life and Lore: An oral history* (Dublin, 1996).

Chapter 13: Politics and Rebellion: From Home Rule to Free State

Chapter 13: Politics and Rebellion: From Home Rule to Free State

INTRODUCTION

This chapter focuses on the political and military developments that saw the country transition from the peaceful pursuit of limited political independence for Ireland in the shape of Home Rule, to the violent struggle for complete separation from Great Britain, which saw the creation of the Irish Free State, and which ultimately led to a civil war among the republican protagonists of the 1916 Rising and the War of Independence. It is also necessary and appropriate to examine local unionist opposition to Home Rule. Unionists had a small but influential presence in Milltown and it is worthwhile reflecting on how that group, opposed as it was to Home Rule, accommodated itself to the changing circumstances of the second and third decades of twentieth-century Ireland. This chapter does not discuss the impact of the First World War on the lives of Milltown people and how it interacted with domestic political developments. Instead, for reasons of space, the Great War, as it was known among contemporaries, and its impact on Milltown is discussed in a separate chapter. It is important to be aware that many of the events discussed in this chapter took place against the background of the Great War and the personal upheavals it caused to dozens of Milltown families.

GENERAL ELECTIONS OF 1910

The genesis of the political revolution in Ireland which occurred over the course of the second decade of the twentieth century has its origins in a constitutional crisis that developed in Westminster in 1909 over a highly contentious budget introduced by the chancellor of the exchequer, Lloyd George, in that year. Although the Liberal government had a sufficient majority in the House of Commons to get its budget passed, it was vetoed by the House of Lords on 30 November. Following this unprecedented action, the Asquith-led government dissolved parliament and called a general election, with the polling day in Ireland set for 28 January 1910.[1]

1 F.S.L. Lyons, 'The developing crisis, 1907–14' in W.E. Vaughan (ed.), *A new history of Ireland, vi: Ireland under the Union 1870–1921* (Oxford, 1989), pp. 126–7; *Clare, Unionist/Nationalist election campaigns*, p. 13.

The outgoing member of parliament for south county Dublin was the Unionist, Walter Long, but he stood for election in an English constituency and so he was replaced by another unionist candidate called Bryan Cooper, of whom more will be presently said. For their part, the nationalists put forward a Dublin corporation councillor, Alderman William Cotton. Cotton, who lived in Hollywood House, Goatstown, was chairman of the Dublin Gas Company and sat at the extreme conservative end of the political spectrum within the IPP.[2]

A nationalist meeting in support of Alderman Cotton was held in Milltown on Sunday 23 January 1910, which was chaired by a local priest, Fr Kean, in the absence of the local Milltown politician Thomas Patrick (T.P.) Hackett, who had died two years previously.[3] According to the *Irish Independent*, the election speeches were attended by a large and enthusiastic crowd, who were addressed initially by Fr Kean in Irish. Fr Kean went on to tell his Milltown audience in English that:

> *the fight was between the man who stood for Ireland and the one who stood against them. The only thing that could beat them was apathy and differences of opinion; but he had no fear that the Unionist would get a vote there, and the National cause was safe in their hands. That place was hallowed by the memory of Robert Emmet, and his spirit would animate them to cast their votes on the side of Ireland (cheers).*[4]

Former IPP MP Pierce O' Mahony, countered some of the arguments made against Home Rule by the unionists:

They were told that Home Rule meant separation, but he was absolutely certain it did not; on the contrary, it was the only way in which they could permanently secure the connection with Great Britain.[5] They were also told that the minority would be persecuted, but, speaking as one of the minority as regarded religion, he never knew a Protestant being unpopular or being persecuted because he was a Protestant.[6]

As will shortly be shown, very many of O'Mahony's co-religionists in the constituency of South Dublin disagreed with his views. The outcome of the election in South Dublin was extremely close. Cooper defeated Cotton by 5,072 votes to 5,006, a majority of just 66.[7] More importantly, the nationalists held the balance of power in the new parliament along with 40 newly elected Labour party members. Negotiations between the Liberals and Conservatives failed to reach a settlement on the constitutional impasse between the upper and lower houses of parliament or the form of Irish self-government, and so the Liberal government called a second general election for December 1910. This second election of 1910 was dominated by the Liberals' threat to create sufficient Liberal peers to swamp the House of Lords, thereby negating its veto.[8]

---

2 Clare, *Unionist/Nationalist election campaigns*, pp. 13–15; Patrick Maume, *The Long Gestation: Irish Nationalist Life 1891–1918* (Dublin, 1999), pp. 106, *224;* https://www.youwho.ie/hollywood.html (accessed 7 March 2022).

3 *Irish Independent*, 24 January 1910, p. 10.

4 *Irish Independent*, 24 January 1910, p. 10.

5 *Dublin Daily Express*, 24 January 1910, p. 8.

6 *Irish Independent*, 24 January 1910, p. 10.

7 Clare, *Unionist/Nationalist election campaigns*, p. 14.

8 Lyons, 'The developing crisis', p. 128.

Alderman Cotton and Bryan Cooper went head-to-head once more in South Dublin on behalf of the nationalists and unionists, respectively. As far as campaigning in Milltown is concerned, the election was dominated by a serious accident which occurred at Windy Arbour rather than by the policies or speeches made by the contestants. On Tuesday evening, 13 December, an election meeting was scheduled to take place outdoors in Windy Arbour. As the weather was bad the organisers decided to hold the meeting in a disused mill building, part of which was used for rehearsals by the local brass band. About 200 members of the public from all age groups – all of whom were described as being from the working classes of the district – were packed into the second storey and stairs of the building. The platform was occupied by the candidate and several local councillors and members of parliament, including T.M. Kettle, William Field MP, Shane Leslie and James Collins, a Dublin county councillor, who was chairing the meeting. One of the speakers, James Cullen, was exhorting the audience to turn out and cast their vote when without warning the floor gave way, sending the audience crashing some 12 feet to the ground. Luckily, no-one was killed although eight people were injured, one seriously.[9] Alderman Cotton visited the injured in St Vincent's Hospital and the Meath Hospital the following day. Another election meeting took place at 9 p.m. in Milltown that Wednesday evening, but its proceedings were only very briefly reported in the press.[10]

As in the previous January, the outcome of the election in South Dublin was extremely close but this time the result was reversed. Cotton defeated Cooper by 5,223 votes to 5,090, a majority of 133.[11] More importantly, the Liberals were returned to power once more with the support of the Irish nationalists, and as a result the Parliament Act of 1911 was brought in. The effect of this act was that the House of Lords could only delay legislation for two years, and any bill passing through the House of Commons in three successive sessions would automatically become law. Thus, with John Redmond and the IPP holding the balance of power, a third attempt could be made to bring in Home Rule.[12] The unionist response to these developments, specifically in Milltown, forms the basis of the next section of this chapter.

UNIONIST OPPOSITION TO HOME RULE

The period of Irish and British history concerning unionist opposition to Home Rule and, in particular, the militant response of the Ulster Loyalists to the Liberal government in the period 1910–14 is one of the most well-known and studied subjects of modern Irish history. What follows here is a brief outline of the local unionist response to the Home Rule crisis (as they saw it) during the period 1910 to 1914 to contrast with the political history of nationalism in Milltown. The discussion also adds to our understanding of the tensions that developed between the two political communities in Milltown during the second decade of the twentieth century, in addition to the pre-existing religious and class divisions which have been explored in other chapters. Before delving into the local details, it is appropriate to comment very briefly on southern unionism (i.e. outside Ulster). Southern unionists were very closely bound up with the Conservative party in England, which included among its leadership the Marquess of Lansdowne and Viscount Midleton. In addition, southern unionists held 86 seats in the House of Lords in 1911. On the wider scale, within the southern unionist community there was much intermarriage and property

9 *Freeman's Journal*, 14 December 1910, p. 8; *Irish Independent*, 14 December 1910, p. 5; *Dublin Daily Express*, 14 December 1910, p. 5.

10 *Irish Independent*, 15 December 1910, p. 6.

11 Clare, *Unionist/Nationalist election campaigns*, p. 15.

12 Lyons, 'The developing crisis', p. 128.

ownership between upper-class British and Irish families. As a result, southern Unionists wielded an influence over the British governing class out of all proportion to their numbers.[13]

This phenomenon was replicated in the South Dublin constituency. When the unionist candidate, Captain Bryan Cooper, filed his nomination papers ahead of the general election of January 1910, the *Dublin Daily Express* newspaper published the names and addresses of 240 of his supporters. The list is a who's who of the military, professional and commercial classes of Dublin's south side coastal townships and their wealthy hinterlands.[14] The south Dublin coastal townships had their own unionist club, called the Kingstown and District Unionist club. From the summer of 1912 onwards, its members began military drilling in imitation of the Ulster Volunteers.[15]

There were half a dozen or so prominent unionists living in Milltown in the Edwardian era. Undoubtedly there were several more, but their historical record is either very slight or remains to be investigated.[16] The handful of men identified thus far all came from professional, military, religious and commercial backgrounds. The activities of some of these individuals are discussed in other chapters, including Thomas Edmondson (Dublin Laundry Company and Chairman of the Rathmines UDC), Captain Robert Wade Thompson JP (Clonskeagh Castle) and Rev. John Moffatt (incumbent, St Philip's church, Milltown). Captain Thompson and Rev. Moffatt were also members of the Orange Order, with the latter acting as Grand Master of the City of Dublin Grand Lodge.[17]

A unionist not previously mentioned in connection with Milltown is Rev. James Fletcher, who lived in a detached house on two acres of grounds called Brookfield on Richmond Avenue South (Map 18). Rev. Fletcher publicly voiced his opposition to Home Rule in the letters pages of the *Dublin Daily Express* in 1911 and 1912.[18] Rev. Fletcher was a supporter of Protestant evangelism and, along with Rev. Moffatt, organised the Dublin Christian Convention of Evangelical Churches in Ireland, in 1906.[19] Rev. Fletcher's opposition to Home Rule was grounded in his religious convictions. He did not put any store in the reassurances given by Redmond and Dillon regarding religious freedom under Home Rule. On the contrary, the Protestant clergyman quoted a passage from the Catholic larger catechism which (on p. 331) defined Protestantism as 'the summary of all the heresies that were before it, that have since, or that can possibly be in the future for the wreck of souls'. Rev. Fletcher challenged Redmond to respond, demanding 'What protection would Protestants have from a Parliament in College Green, dominated by a Party saturated with the teachings of this precious Universal Catechism?'[20] In a continuation of his theme, Rev. Fletcher concluded a second letter to the *Dublin Daily Express* in November 1911 with the following dramatic message:

---

13 Lyons, 'The developing crisis', p. 129.

14 *Dublin Daily Express*, 19 May 1910, p. 2.

15 Buckland, *Irish Unionism*, pp. 153–5.

16 Cross-referencing the names of adult males listed in the Dublin Thom's directories (which contain residency and occupation data) with the names of speakers and attendees at political meetings and election rallies reported in contemporary newspapers would yield useful results.

17 *Dublin Daily Express*, 16 March 1905, p. 6.

18 *Dublin Daily Express*, 13 March 1911, p. 7; 7 November 1911, p. 7; 23 August 1912, p. 4.

19 *Dublin Daily Express*, 8 September 1906, p. 6; *Irish Times*, 17 September 1906, p. 6.

20 *Dublin Daily Express*, 13 March 1911, p. 7.

We want your readers to understand that our struggle is not for supremacy, nor for possessions, nor even for peace, but for what is infinitely more precious to us than all these together – life and liberty, and freedom to worship God according to our conscience. Rather than submit to such a yoke [the Universal Catechism], it would be better to shake Ireland from its centre to its utmost bounds. Our fathers did so at Derry, Aughrim, and the Boyne, and we honour and revere their memory, and shall not we resolve, God helping us, to hand down to our children the priceless heritage they purchased for us with their blood.[21]

Such language is usually associated with denunciations of Home Rule by Ulster Presbyterians and Loyalist politicians such as Edward Carson and James Campbell. At first blush it is surprising to find such sentiment among Dublin's comfortable middle-class Protestants in Milltown and Upper Rathmines. However, Rev. Fletcher was not expressing an isolated or recently developed opinion among the unionists of the Rathmines township. Indeed, in the neighbouring township of Pembroke the local Church of Ireland curate of St Mary's church in Anglesea Road, Donnybrook, Rev. Samuel Sandys, had been rejected and forced out by his parishioners because he attended the inaugural meeting of the Dublin section of the Irish Protestant Home Rule Association, in 1886.[22]

Although preservation of civil and religious liberties was the most often cited reason put forward by unionists and Orangemen to justify their opposition to Home Rule, there was a significant element of social class bias associated with southern unionism. For example, at the annual 12th of July celebrations in 1911, the keynote speaker to the City and County of Dublin Grand Orange Lodges told his enthusiastic audience that: 'It could not be that the enterprising majority would sit down under the chains and slavery of the two-thirds majority, which was so much behind them in education and enterprise (cheers).'[23]

At the same meeting, the Rev. Moffatt proposed several uncompromising resolutions. One of these called on the Orange Order's leaders to 'adopt all necessary measures for resisting Home Rule Government that may be forced upon His Majesty's loyal subjects in Ireland, in view of the conspiracy between His Majesty's Government and the Irish Disloyalists [*sic*] to force Home Rule upon Ireland without an appeal to the electors'.[24]

Some of the 'necessary measures' began to be put in place in earnest in 1912. Following the signing of the Ulster Solemn League and Covenant on 28 September in Belfast by thousands of Ulstermen, a meeting in support of Ulster was held by south Dublin unionists at Dundrum, on 4 October, at which several attendees signed the covenant.[25] In the same month, at the conclusion of the Rathmines voter registration revision sessions – which had taken up a record 21 day sittings and nine night sittings – the revising barrister remarked that 'the revision was fought with unusual keenness on both sides, and apparently no efforts had been spared by the different associations to secure the franchise rights for their clients'.[26]

21 *Dublin Daily Express*, 7 November 1911, p. 7.

22 James Loughlin, 'The Irish Protestant Home Rule Association and nationalist politics, 1886–93', *Irish Historical Studies*, 24, no. 95 (May 1985), pp. 348, 357–8; *Freeman's Journal*, 6 April 1887, p. 7.

23 *Irish Times*, 15 July 1911, p. 9.

24 *Irish Times*, 15 July 1911, p. 9.

25 *Dublin Daily Express*, 5 October 1912, pp. 5–6; *Evening Irish Times*, 5 October 1912, p. 6.

26 *Dublin Daily Express*, 16 October 1912, p. 2.

As the Home Rule crisis deepened, Dublin Orangemen copied their Northern brethren and formed the Loyal Dublin Volunteers (LDV). This volunteer body, which by the second week of November 1913 had enrolled over 2,000 men, was to act as a reserve of the Ulster Volunteers and was intended to be used 'in the preservation of the civil and religious liberties of Protestants in Dublin and the south', should a Home Rule parliament be established in Dublin.[27] The LDV were divided into districts. Rathmines had its own Company ('L' Company, 2nd Battalion) which met in the Protestant Hall in Rathmines, where the men received training in military exercises from numerous retired army officers.[28] Rather ominously, the LDV secretly imported hundreds of rifles and thousands of rounds of ammunition through Kingstown (Dún Laoghaire), some of which were transferred to the Ulster Volunteers. The balance was retained by the LDV and hidden in Fowler Hall, at 10 Rutland (Parnell) Square, which was the headquarters of the Orange Order in Dublin. Five Loyal Dublin Volunteers were subsequently killed while assisting the regular troops in supressing the 1916 Rising.[29]

For several years the focal point for unionists in Milltown centred at Nullamore demesne, the grounds of which are located on the north side of Milltown Road between Classon's Bridge and Richmond Avenue South (Map 18). The circumstances behind this development are as follows. From mid-1906 onwards Nullamore was the residence of a retired British Army officer, Major David Courtney, and his family.[30] Courtney had served in the royal engineers and achieved distinction in the 1879 Zulu war in South Africa and in the Sudan campaign during the River Nile expedition of 1884–5.[31] Courtney's military career was steeped in British imperialism, and anything that undermined the British Empire and Ireland's part in it was anathema. Naturally given his background, Major Courtney was an ardent unionist, and he sat on the executive council of the City of Dublin Unionist Registration Association.[32] Along with Captain Robert Wade Thompson of Clonskeagh Castle, Courtney was a member of the Irish unionist delegation to London that visited the former Conservative prime minister, Arthur Balfour, on 19 March 1907 to lobby for the unionist cause and against the Liberal government's Irish policies.[33]

David Courtney died on 28 November 1909, just as the dispute in Westminster over the House of Lord's veto was becoming critical.[34] Twelve months later, Major Courtney's son Henry contributed £5 to the unionist general election campaign in December 1910, in answer to a clarion call couched in the following dramatic language:

> *A great crisis is upon us. The Conference on the question of the House of Lords has failed. The Radical attack on that House will now be renewed with redoubled vigour. Mr Redmond is confident that the removal of the Veto of the House of Lords means that granting of Home Rule for Ireland. A General*

27 *Irish Times*, 10 November 1913, p. 7.

28 *Irish Times*, 10 November 1913, p. 7; *Dublin Daily Express*, 19 October 1914, p. 7; *Dublin Evening Mail*, 19 November 1914, p. 3.

29 Quincey Dougan, 'Dublin's Loyal Volunteers', *History Ireland*, 22, no. 3 (May–June 2014), pp. 36–8; *Irish Times*, 14 June 1935, p. 8; *Northern Whig*, 14 June 1935, p. 11; *Derry Journal*, 14 June 1935, p. 5.

30 *Irish Times*, 29 August 1906, p. 7; *Northern Whig*, 2 September 1910, p. 1.

31 *Dublin Daily Express*, 6 December 1909, p. 2.

32 *Dublin Daily Express*, 30 November 1909, p. 4.

33 *Irish Times*, 20 March 1907, p. 6; Patrick Buckland (ed.), *Irish Unionism 1885–1923: A Documentary History* (Belfast, 1973), pp. 278–80.

34 *Northern Whig*, 2 December 1909, p. 1.

Election is imminent. In it Home Rule will be brought forward hidden under the constitutional question, and therefore in a more dangerous and insidious form than ever before.[35]

Around this time too Major Courtney's widow decided to vacate Nullamore and lease the demesne to Captain Bryan Cooper, who as we have seen stood twice for election as the unionist candidate for the South Dublin constituency in the two general elections of 1910. Cooper was a native of Sligo and came from a wealthy landed family based at Markree Castle.[36] His arrival at Nullamore was unlikely to have been a random occurrence, however. The Courtneys and the Coopers mixed in the same military, political and social circles so presumably it suited both parties for Cooper to relocate to Milltown as a convenient base for his campaign in South Dublin and to attend unionist demonstrations and lobbying activities in Dublin.[37] Although Cooper lost out to Alderman Cotton in the December 1910 general election, he continued to be extremely active in unionist circles, networking with both Conservative and Liberal politicians who visited Ireland in the years before the outbreak of the Great War.[38]

On 14 September 1912 Captain Cooper threw open his grounds at Nullamore to host a garden fete in aid of the Junior Branch of the Irish Unionist Alliance, of which he was president from 1912–14.[39] The occasion was used to show support and solidarity for the Ulster Unionists who were planning their famous demonstration against Home Rule, the Solemn League Covenant, which was planned for 28 September 1912. The *Dublin Daily Express* reported extensively on the proceedings at Nullamore and the speeches delivered by prominent Unionist and Conservative party members.[40] *The Daily Express*'s reporter gave a vivid description of the scene at Nullamore:

The handsome grounds of Captain Cooper's residence were tastefully decorated with flags and bunting, prominence being given to the Union Jack, and a very numerous company accepted the invitations issued by the president, vice-president, and committee. Visitors were entertained to refreshments in the grounds, and popular and patriotic music was supplied by the band of the Meath School and the Kingstown Protestant Temperance Band. The occasion was favoured with delightful weather, and proved most successful both as a social function and as a rally of the Unionist forces of South County [Dublin].[41]

The *Daily Express* went on to record over several column inches the numerous speeches delivered by the speakers. Lord Farnham gave the keynote address. He was at pains to prove the unity of purpose that existed between the Ulster Unionists and those outside that province:

On the 28th of the present month she [Ulster] would enter into a solemn Covenant. Let everyone to whom she was speaking show their sympathy with Ulster on that day. (A Voice – 'We will'). Let every Unionist who was able to show the true value of Mr Redmond's statement that there was no opposition

35 *Dublin Daily Express*, 5 December 1910, p. 8.

36 Thom's Irish Who's Who 1923, p. 45.

37 *Dublin Evening Telegraph*, 22 September 1911, p. 5; *Irish Independent*, 3 October 1911, p. 4; *Dublin Daily Express*, 5 October 1911, p. 4.

38 *Irish Times*, 2 September 1911, p. 7; 19 September 1911, p. 9; 2 October 1911, p. 4; 'Itinerary of the Eighty Club's visit to Ireland, Saturday 16 September 1911' (NLI, EPH/B441).

39 *Dublin Daily Express*, 13 September 1912, p. 4.

40 *Dublin Daily Express*, 16 September 1912, p. 5.

41 *Dublin Daily Express*, 16 September 1912, p. 5.

to Home Rule outside of Ulster by flying their true colours from every housetop, and let those colours be the Union Jack (applause).[42]

Captain Cooper's activities on behalf of Irish unionism extended to the British mainland. During campaigning in the north-east Derbyshire bye-election in May 1914, Cooper delivered several speeches against Home Rule on behalf of the Unionist Associations of Ireland.[43] It can be seen therefore that some of southern unionism's most active and influential protagonists were living in Milltown during the Home Rule crisis.

The outbreak of the Great War in August 1914 quickly removed the imminent danger of civil war in Ireland between the Irish nationalists and the Ulster unionists. Captain Cooper enlisted with the fifth Battalion of the Connaught Rangers in September 1914 and served with distinction in the ill-fated Gallipoli campaign of 1915.[44] Before Cooper enlisted he had, rather surprisingly, joined the National Volunteers, while they were under the control of John Redmond. This led to friction with his Ulster unionist colleagues as an extract from correspondence written later, in May 1918, by the secretary of the Ulster Unionist Council, explains:

There is one factor which caused a certain amount of feeling between the north and the south. Captain Bryan Cooper, (who, by the way, was a Member of the Joint Committee [of the Unionist Associations of Ireland]) shortly after the outbreak of the war practically repudiated the Irish Unionist Alliance and joined the National Volunteers. This was done at a time when Sir Edward Carson was doing his best to stave off the Home Rule Bill being put on the Statute Book. Captain Bryan Cooper's example was followed by several others, and although the action of these gentlemen may not have resulted in the Bill being put on the Statute Book, at the same time I know it handicapped Sir Edward very much in dealing with the Prime Minister who quoted the action of the south of Ireland Unionists in joining the National Volunteers, as showing how the war had altered entirely the question of Home Rule.[45]

In short, irreconcilable tensions were developing in Irish unionism as well as within Irish nationalism over the Home Rule issue, which eventually saw the Ulster unionists parting company with their southern counterparts.

Sometime in late 1914 Cooper left Nullamore, which was subsequently let by Mrs Courtney to another army officer called Major Fuge.[46] Fuge had served in the Boer War in South Africa following which he joined the Board of Trade in Ireland. He subsequently fought in the Great War, receiving the Legion of Honour from the French president for services rendered during the siege of Arras.[47]

On 24 June 1916 another garden fete was held in the grounds of Nullamore, but the circumstances behind this event were completely different to those pertaining in September 1912. Now the fete was being organised in aid of the Milltown branch of the Irish Sandbag Committee, one of the numerous voluntary groups that had sprung up to aid the war effort.[48]

42 *Dublin Daily Express*, 16 September 1912, p. 5.

43 Buckland, *Irish Unionism*, p. 331.

44 Thom's Irish Who's Who 1923, p. 45.

45 Buckland, *Irish Unionism*, p. 293.

46 Thom's Directory 1915, p. 1868,

47 *Weekly Irish Times*, 23 March 1923, p. 3.

48 *Irish Independent*, 24 June 1916, p. 1.

Mrs Courtney decided to sell Nullamore in the spring of 1917. The reason for her decision is unknown, but possibly Major Fuge had surrendered his tenancy and Mrs Courtney was finding it increasingly difficult to find suitable tenants as the war dragged on. Mrs Courtney sold Nullamore privately to James Campbell, the Lord Chief Justice of Ireland, who soon afterwards renamed the property Glenavy.[49] Campbell was a controversial unionist politician, whose blatant legal careerism and seditious speech making in support of the Ulster Loyalists during the 1912–14 Home Rule crisis made him reviled among the IPP.[50] Campbell delivered a fiery speech in October 1913 which some years later was quoted by Bulmer Hobson when the latter explained the growth of the Irish Volunteers in response to militant loyalism and its Conservative party supporters: 'There have been times in the history of your Nation when rebellion became a sacred duty. That time will arrive for us if we are going to be put under the heel of a Government we hate and abhor.'[51]

Campbell had for many years been an MP successively for the Dublin divisions of St Stephen's Green (1898–1900) and Dublin University (1903–16) before he made these inflammatory remarks, yet they did not do him any harm politically. Quite the contrary, Campbell was appointed successively as Attorney General for Ireland from April–December 1916, Lord Chief Justice of Ireland December 1916–June 1918 and Lord Chancellor of Ireland from June 1918 to June 1921. He was also made a baronet in 1917, and was subsequently raised to the peerage on 30 September 1921 as Baron Glenavy of Milltown.[52] This was the second time that Milltown was used in a peer's tile, the first time being in 1761 when Joseph Leeson was elevated to the earldom of Milltown.

As time went on the diehard unionists mentioned above who survived and remained in the Ireland of the 1920s had to recalibrate their positions on Irish self-government, and this aspect of their careers will be briefly touched on later.

RATHMINES UDC AND DUBLIN COUNTY COUNCIL ELECTIONS OF 1914

Campaigning for the triennial elections for the Rathmines UDC got under way in January 1914. Under the rules of the township, all of the councillors automatically retired after three years. More often than not, all of the individuals stood for re-election (save in cases of genuine retirements) and the same councillors were re-elected *en masse*. This state of affairs was facilitated by the fact that, as detailed in the previous chapter, the township was divided into only two electoral wards and by the rigorous management of the electoral register by unionist election agents.[53] The Rathmines oligarchy did not identify itself with political labels such as independent, home rule or unionist, but at election time it insisted that its members were standing on a 'commercial' ticket and were above party politics and sectarianism.[54] In private, the councillors would have held unionist political sympathies and a large majority would have belonged to non-Catholic faiths.

49 The auctioneering firm of James H. North proudly proclaimed this fact when it advertised an auction of the contents of Nullamore on behalf of Mrs Courtney: *Irish Times*, 30 May 1917, p. 8.

50 Leon Ó Broin, *The Chief Secretary: Augustine Birrell in Ireland (London, 1969)*, pp. 144–5, 168–9.

51 F.X. Martin (ed.), *The Irish Volunteers 1913–1915: Recollections and Documents* (Dublin, 1963), p. 7.

52 Thom's Irish Who's Who 1923, pp. 91–2; *Irish Times*, 1 October 1921, p. 4; *Irish Independent*, 23 March 1931, p. 6 (obituary); *Longford Leader*, 28 March 1931, p. 3 (obituary).

53 *Freeman's Journal*, 7 January 1914, p. 7.

54 *Irish Independent*, 17 January 1914, p. 5; *Dublin Daily Express*, Saturday 17 January 1914, p. 2.

Despite the consistent failure of nationalists to get elected to the Rathmines UDC, in January 1914 the Nationalist party put forward 17 candidates to contest the 21 seats on the council.[55] A large crowd assembled at Milltown on 8 January 1914 to hear election addresses by some of the candidates, who all had active support from the priests of the township's Catholic parishes. The meeting was chaired by a man named Darcy, who was almost certainly a native of the village. Despite the lack of electoral success in the past, candidate Michael Hearn rallied the crowd by telling them that the results of the canvass thus far were very encouraging.[56] In newspaper correspondence Milltown was name-checked among the slums of the township by the nationalists' election agent, who criticised the council for its lack of progress with rehousing the working classes in proper dwellings.[57] Whatever about the validity of this criticism, the *Irish Times* unequivocally urged the Rathmines voters to re-elect the outgoing councillors:

> *We urge the ratepayers of Rathmines to support the policy which has made Rathmines a model of municipal administration in Ireland, and to vote solidly against the political ticket – not because it is Nationalist ticket, but because it is a political ticket.*[58]

Over 80 per cent of the local electorate cast their vote on polling day, Thursday 15 January. The high turn-out reflected political tension concerning the seemingly imminent introduction of Home Rule to Ireland, which was anathema to the unionist voters in the Rathmines township. Accordingly, a show of strength by the unionist voters of Rathmines inflicted a complete defeat on the nationalist candidates.[59] Nonetheless, from studying the results for the two wards it could reasonably be argued that had the nationalists fielded fewer candidates – seats were filled by simple majority – they would have greatly increased their chances of picking up some seats. The *Dublin Daily Express* interpreted the result differently, and claimed that the voters had decisively shown their resentment of the introduction of a (nationalist) political ticket by roundly endorsing the 'business administration' candidates.[60] The *Irish Times* was similarly pleased with the election results in Rathmines:

> *The verdict of the electors of Rathmines is very satisfactory. Municipal government is a business matter, and Rathmines has always conducted it on business lines. This year a deliberate attempt was made to drag the township into the vortex of party politics. A body of candidates came forward, not as businessmen or municipal reformers, but simply and solely on the Nationalist ticket. The experiment is not likely to be repeated.*[61]

---

55 *Dublin Daily Express*, 15 January 1914, p. 8.

56 *Irish Independent*, 8 January 1914, p. 6; *Irish Times*, 8 January 1914, p. 5. A James Darcy who lived in Milltown village was imprisoned in the Frongoch prison camp after the 1916 Rising: NAI, CSOPR/1916/15564/16.

57 *Irish Independent*, 8 January 1914, p. 10.

58 *Irish Times*, 15 January 1914, p. 4.

59 *Irish Independent*, 17 January 1914, p. 5.

60 *Dublin Daily Express*, 17 January 1914, p. 2.

61 *Irish Times*, 17 January 1914, p. 6.

There was some measure of recompense for nationalists when two of their number won seats (out of four available for the Rathmines township) in the Dublin County Council elections held on 8 June 1914. For the first time ever, nationalist candidates topped both of the two seat constituencies of Rathmines West Ward and Rathmines East Ward respectively.[62]

Separately, new electoral developments had taken place on the south bank of the River Dodder in the Rathdown RDC. In May 1910 the Local Government Board made an order dividing the Dundrum electoral division into two divisions, to be named the Dundrum district electoral division and the Milltown district electoral division.[63] The rateable valuation and population of the latter district were £6,351 and 1,970 respectively.[64] The Milltown district electoral division comprised the townlands of Churchtown Lower, Churchtown Upper, Rathmines Great, Rathmines Little, Farranboley, Friarland and the congested districts of Rosemount, Windy Arbour and Concrete.[65] The practical effect of these changes was that the voters in Concrete, Windy Arbour and Rosemount – the vast majority of whom were from working-class backgrounds – could elect two councillors to sit on the Rathdown RDC. In the June 1914 local elections, they re-elected the two outgoing nationalist councillors, James Collins and Bernard Rogan.[66] Collins owned a pub in Dundrum called Uncle Tom's Cabin (which is still trading) while Rogan was a grocer in Windy Arbour.[67]

THE FORMATION OF THE IRISH VOLUNTEERS

The nationalists' success in the local elections of June 1914 was overshadowed by the Home Rule crisis and the threat of armed conflict in Ulster. The formation of the well-armed Ulster Volunteer Force in 1912 to oppose Home Rule by force and the setting up of the Irish Volunteers in November 1913 to counter it had escalated the political situation in Ireland immeasurably by 1914. These militaristic developments would, in the space of a few years, overshadow and render obsolete the years of effort made by constitutional nationalists to obtain self-government for Ireland.

The Rathfarnham branch of the Irish Volunteers was inaugurated on Sunday 7 June 1914 at a meeting chaired by the parish priest of Rathfarnham, Cannon O'Kelly, and addressed by Patrick Pearse and John Joseph (J.J.) Clancy MP among others.[68] At this stage the Irish Volunteers were an unarmed body, but that would change when guns were secretly brought into the country on 26 July at Howth and on 1 August at Kilcoole, County Wicklow. The sense of purpose and excitement of the times can be picked up in the recollections of volunteer, Laurence Nugent:

---

62 *Freeman's Journal*, 10 June 1914, p. 8.

63 The name given to the new Milltown division was misleading because it did not include the townland of Milltown or the bulk of the village, which both lay on the north bank of the River Dodder in the Rathmines township.

64 *Dublin Daily Express*, 19 May 1910, p. 2.

65 Census of Ireland 1911, County of Dublin, housing and population returns for Milltown District Electoral Division, Table VII, p. 32 (CD-ROM, Archive CD Books Ireland, Dublin, 2010).

66 *Freeman's Journal*, 10 June 1914, p. 8.

67 Thom's Directory 1915, pp. 1771–2.

68 *Freeman's Journal*, 8 June 1914, p. 8.

> *In the month of June [1914] we had a great day in South County Dublin. Manoeuvres were arranged. Two columns of volunteers vied with each other for certain important points in the Dublin foot-hills. Pearse was in charge of our party. I was then O/C Dundrum company, when we mobilised around Milltown and marched through Dundrum. We heard Mass in Sandyford and, such were the numbers, that only a fraction of the men could gain admission to the Chapel ... That day was a great success, and the men who took part in the manoeuvres realised their strength in case they ever went into action.*[69]

The optimism of the early days of the Irish Volunteers as vividly conveyed by Laurence Nugent was short-lived. Behind the scenes a power struggle was going on during the late spring and summer of 1914 between the supporters of John Redmond and the more radically minded members of the Irish Volunteers who wanted to keep the Volunteers as an independent domestic military force outside the Redmondites' control.[70] Matters came to a head with the outbreak of the Great War in August and Redmond's subsequent speech at Woodenbridge, County Wicklow on 20 September whereby he encouraged the Irish Volunteers to fight overseas in support of the British war effort. The Volunteers split and as a result approximately 170,000 men, who were renamed the National Volunteers, supported John Redmond while a much smaller minority, numbering about 11,000 volunteers, reorganised themselves as a separate body with the name 'Irish Volunteers' in October 1914.[71] A larger minority of the volunteers from Dublin city (1,900 or 28 per cent) supported the Irish Volunteers.[72] It is this second, smaller force of Dublin volunteers that concerns us as we look ahead to the 1916 Rising.

The split in the Irish Volunteers created considerable ill-feeling between former comrades as explained by Dundrum volunteer, Alex Cullen:

> *I was one of five out of a possible 270 men, who voted against the Redmondite control, so badly were we handicapped that we could not pass up or down the street or we were sneered at, by people who are now super patriots, so I joined up with the old Co. E of Batt 3 [i.e. 'E' Company, third Battalion of the Dublin Brigade of the Irish Volunteers], at the Soup Hall [in] Beaver Row [Donnybrook], where we mustered 10 men ...*[73]

Irish Volunteer Liam Tannam, who went on to play a prominent part in the 1916 Rising and the War of Independence in the Milltown and Dundrum district, also recalled the events surrounding the split among the Donnybrook volunteers:

> *As far as I can recollect the Company was about 150 strong. The majority were present on the night of the split. Eamon de Valera put the matter bluntly that the parting of the ways had come, and he*

---

69 BMH, WS907, p. 11, witness statement of Laurence Nugent 12 November 1953.

70 Lyons, 'The developing crisis, 1907–14' in W.E. Vaughan (ed.), *A new history of Ireland, vi: Ireland under the Union 1870–1921* (Oxford, 1989), p. 143.

71 F.S.L. Lyons, 'The revolution in train, 1914–16' in W.E. Vaughan (ed.), *A new history of Ireland, vi: Ireland under the Union 1870–1921* (Oxford, 1989), pp. 190–1; F.X. Martin (ed.), 'The Irish Volunteers', pp. 169–70. Military historian Richard Grayson puts the numbers of volunteers backing Redmond at 158,360 compared to 12,306 who opposed the call to arms: Grayson, *Dublin's Great Wars*, p. 25.

72 Grayson, *Dublin's Great Wars*, p. 25.

73 NAI, Department of the Taoiseach, S 7696, file for Alex Cullen, Grant from the Dáil Special Fund, 1924.

> *explained the situation and then said, 'Those who side with Ireland will go to that side of the hall, and those who would like to support the British Empire will take the other'. As far as I remember there was no count but I was almost certain that there were two or three of a majority remained with the Irish Volunteers [i.e. before they were renamed the National Volunteers]. The drill hall belonged to the A.O.H. [Ancient Order of Hibernians] which was as you know Redmondite, and, therefore, we had to march out. About fifty on our side were mostly juveniles and their fathers and mothers advised them to keep away from the Irish Volunteers because the old people at the time had been backing Redmond. The next parade mustered about 25 ... Our numbers were then increased by the addition of the remnants of the Dundrum Company. We got a drill hall in Beaver Row when our numbers increased to about 40. We then moved into [Patrick] Pearse's old school [in Cullenswood House] in Oakley Road, Ranelagh.*[74]

The leader of the reconstituted Irish Volunteers was Professor Eoin MacNeill. MacNeill was elected chairman at their first convention, which was held on 25 October 1914, and which among other things adopted policies opposing partition, conscription and the British administration in Dublin Castle. Some two months later, on 16 December 1914, a scheme of military organisation for the Irish Volunteers was adopted. The specifications laid down for the military unit called the Company are particularly relevant to understanding how the Irish Volunteers operated at local level in the Dublin suburbs. At full strength a company comprised three company officers (captain, first and second lieutenants) plus 100 men who were divided into four general sections and other specialised sections.[75]

The pension records and the testimonies of the 1916 Rising veterans indicate that after the split of October 1914 most of the Irish Volunteers living in Milltown joined 'E' Company of the third Battalion of the Dublin Brigade, whose headquarters was in Cullenswood House, Oakley Road, Ranelagh. Other volunteers in 'E' Company lived in Goatstown, Dundrum, Ranelagh, Rathmines, Donnybrook, Ballsbridge and Leeson Street.[76]

The leader of the Irish Volunteers in Milltown village was Patrick Doyle. Patrick Doyle was born in 1879 and lived in a cottage in Milltown on the Dundrum Road. As a young man Patrick worked as a gardener in Gledeswood House, Bird Avenue. He married a local girl, Sarah Byrne, and they went on to have five children. The family lived for a time at 3 Hackett's Cottages in Milltown village. Patrick Doyle was a devout Catholic and a daily communicant. He belonged to the Sacred Heart Sodality and gave great assistance to the local curate for Milltown, Fr Kean. Doyle also gave evening Irish lessons and never smoked or drank.[77]

By 1915 or 1916 Doyle had been appointed section leader of the Milltown section of 'E' Company of the Irish Volunteers. From time to time the Milltown volunteers assembled for parade on 'The Strand' in Milltown village, opposite Redmond's forge. According to local volunteer, Michael Doyle (no relation of Patrick), 'we had a little room in case we wanted to

---

74 BMH, WS242, witness statement of Liam Tannam, pp. 2–3, 30 April 1949.

75 F.X. Martin (ed.), 'The Irish Volunteers', pp. 169–83.

76 BMH, WS242, witness statement of Liam Tannam, p. 3; BMH, WS1768, witness statement of Andrew McDonnell, p. 2.

77 Patrick Doyle papers, biographical note by Doyle's granddaughter Mrs May Nolan (NLI, MS 46,594).

discuss anything in private, he [Patrick Doyle] used to take us there'.[78] Unfortunately no other information has survived about this discrete volunteer meeting place in Milltown and what was discussed there. Drill parades also took place on at least two nights a week in 'E' Company's headquarters at Cullenswood House in Oakley Road. Patrick Doyle acted as a musketry instructor and firing practice took place on Sunday mornings in a large hall in Cullenswood House using a .22 bore rifle.[79]

By 1916 Patrick Doyle was working as a manager in the Dublin Laundry Company in Milltown.[80] It is probable that Doyle promoted the ideals of Irish Volunteers among the workforce, as both male and female employees of the laundry feature among the records of the Bureau of Military History (BMH) and the Military Archives of Ireland (MAI) for the revolutionary period. It is likely too that Doyle recruited youths for the movement among the van boys employed by the laundry in Milltown and Dartry (Pl. 63).

THE 1916 RISING AND THE MILLTOWN VOLUNTEERS

A detailed discussion of the circumstances which led to the Easter rebellion which broke out on Easter Monday 24 April 1916 are beyond the scope of this study. Very briefly, the Irish Volunteers had been thrown into a state of confusion over Holy Week and the Easter weekend of 1916 due to conflict between Eoin MacNeill and a small number of prominent volunteers who were members of the militant Irish Republican Brotherhood (IRB) which had secretly been making plans for a military rebellion against British rule to commence on Easter Sunday. The latter group were determined to launch an armed rebellion in opposition to MacNeill notwithstanding that a large supply of arms from Germany destined for the volunteers had been intercepted by the British off the coast of Kerry on Good Friday. Accordingly, MacNeill issued a countermanding order cancelling all nationwide volunteer manoeuvres which had been planned for Easter Sunday. This was communicated by public notices in the *Irish Independent.* Despite MacNeill's action, the militant volunteer group led by Patrick Pearse and James Connolly decided to proceed with an armed insurrection on Easter Monday with whatever forces they could muster within Dublin city and its suburbs.[81]

The impact of the dramatic series of events of Easter 1916 is well captured in Liam Tannam's witness statement, which he provided to the BMH in 1949. Tannam was the Captain of 'E' Company and therefore was centrally involved with the Irish Volunteers who lived in Milltown and the surrounding districts. His statement is thus worth quoting from in some detail:

> *I went home [on Easter Sunday night] bitterly disappointed, and thinking here is another case of conflicting orders. I went to bed very tired and disappointed that night and did not waken till 10.30 on Easter Monday when I heard a rapping on the door. I ran down to the door and a man named Stephenson was there with an order that 'E' Company was to parade at 10 a.m. at Beresford Place. 'Look here', I said, 'you are handing this to me at 10.35'. 'It can't be helped', he said, 'you are to do the best you can', and he went away ... I had timed the mobilisation for 11.30 at Oakley Road although I knew very well that half the men could not get*

78 MAI, MSP34REF36789, sworn statement of Michael Doyle 30 December 1936. Doyle lived in a cottage in Concrete, on the south bank of the River Dodder in Milltown: NAI, 1911 Census, Form A, residents of house 11 in Milltown (Concrete), Milltown Electoral Division, Parish of Taney, Barony of Rathdown. Before Easter week 1916 Doyle had been making pikes at night; this activity probably took place in Redmond's forge in Milltown village or clandestinely at the Henshaw Ironworks in Clonskeagh.

79 BMH, WS1768, witness statement of Andrew McDonnell, p.2; BMH, WS242, witness statement of Liam Tannam, p. 16.

80 Patrick Doyle papers (NLI, MS 46,594).

81 Grayson, *Dublin's Great Wars*, pp. 115, 119–22.

there. I came back into the house, dressed myself, got my revolver, etc. and went off to Oakley Road. It was just 11.30 when I arrived. I found there about 10 men. In another few minutes a 2nd Lieutenant named Darcy[82] *came along. Paddy Doyle (Milltown), Musketry Instructor, was also there ... I gave Doyle orders to remain in Oakley Road and at 12 o'clock to move off then to Beresford Place with as many men as had reported, leaving one man in Oakley Road to direct late ones. I got Darcy to fetch a hackney car and Darcy and I went on the hackney car to Milltown, Dundrum and Goatstown. The idea was to try and mobilise the outlying districts. I called at Doyle's house in Milltown and collected a Lee Enfield rifle. I went on to Cullens and Dillons of Dundrum. I did not see Company Adjutant, Alec Cullen, but I told his brother and father that the men were to be contacted at once and got into Beresford Place. I then went on to Goatstown and neither of the Cunninghams were in. It must be remembered that in country districts they work on bank holidays and don't work on church holidays so that quite a number of men were working. I found I had no more time and was anxious to get back to command my Company and returned at once to Oakley Road. I found it deserted and then drove straight through the city to Beresford Place. About 25 men had gone in from Oakley Road. A few later reported to Bolands, the G.P.O., the Mail Office and the College of Surgeons.*[83]

While Liam Tannam was seeking out volunteers in Dundrum and Milltown, the men who had mustered earlier at Cullenswood House proceeded to walk into the city amid much uncertainty and confusion about their destination and objectives (which is more generally reflected in the occasionally conflicting recollections of the 'E' Company veterans), as explained by volunteers Andrew McDonnell, Henry Winstanley, Thomas Devine and Alfred Harnett, respectively:

Easter Monday, 24 April, 1916, I was mobilised about 10.30 a.m. by Joe McCormick and told to report to Oakley Road at once with full kit and pike. Reported there about 11 a.m., I found about 12 men and after some little time Captain Liam Tannam arrived on an outside car with Durcan [sic] Darcy. He had a hurried conversation with Paddy Doyle and then left on the car with Darcy to mobilise the Milltown and Dundrum section. Doyle had received instructions to wait about half an hour and then proceed with all available men and arms to Earlsfort Terrace and report to Commandant de Valera. I would say it was about 12.30 p.m. when Paddy Doyle decided to move off with the following members of 'E' Company – Tommy Devine, Michael Tannam, Sean Kinsella, Andy Murphy, Harry Winstanley, Tom Mahon, Mick O'Donovan, Andy McDonnell. There may have been others, but not many. We proceeded through Ranelagh with what arms were available, a few shotguns, pikes and a few small arms. I am sure Paddy Doyle had a rifle ... We were met by a dispatch rider who gave an order to Paddy Doyle, and we were told we were now going to Liberty Hall and the party kept going, much to the amusement of passers-by. How or why we arrived at 144, Pearse Street (then Brunswick Street) I do not know, but arrive we did to find men and arms all over the place and plenty of confusion. I am of the opinion that Paddy Doyle reported to Captain Joe O'Connor while the remainder of 'E' Company was left on the street with other units.[84]

I was mobilised to proceed to Oakley Road. We started with the Company from Oakley Road in charge of Patrick Doyle. At Leeson Street Bridge he despatched me to Liberty Hall with a mes-

82 This was probably James Darcy who lived in Milltown village and who was subsequently imprisoned in Frongoch after the rising: NAI, CSOPR/1916/15564/16.

83 BMH, WS242, witness statement of Liam Tannam, pp. 15–16 (A).

84 BMH, WS1768, witness statement of Andrew McDonnell, pp. 4–5. In 1930 Liam's brother Michael Tannam was living at Classon's Bridge cottages: *Evening Herald*, 16 July 1930, p. 1.

sage to P.H. Pearse to say that 'E' Company was on its way there. When I arrived, I delivered the message and I was told that the Company was to proceed to Liberty Hall. On my way back I missed the Company.[85]

> *On Easter Monday morning Volunteer Alf Harnett and myself turned in to work – Alf to overhaul boilers, myself, a gas plant at the [Milltown] Laundry where we were employed. These tasks we had neglected the previous Saturday, thanks to our faith in an Easter [Sunday] rising. The work engaged us till noon when on our way home to dinner we learned the exciting news that the rising was 'on'. After a hasty conference Alf cycled off to the city; I followed on foot towards Rathmines where later he would meet and tell me the whereabouts of 'E' Company. As it happened our next meeting was as fellow prisoners on the grass patch facing the Rotunda Hospital.*[86]

> *I was a fireman in the Milltown Laundry. I did not turn into work [on Easter Sunday] on account of knowing what was coming off – being a member of the IRB I knew there was to be a Rebellion that time so I turned into work on Easter Monday and finished up what I had to do about mid-day. I then went home and there was a boy working with me [Thomas Devine] belonging to the 3rd Battalion ['E' Company]; we arranged that neither of us would leave our own place. He lived in Milltown and I lived in Windy Arbour. If either of us heard anything we were to let the other know, so in the afternoon he came up to me about three o'clock and told me there was a fight on. I was a member of 'C' Company of the 4th Battalion ... When he told me what was going on he asked me what he would do. He was only about seventeen, so I advised him to make for the G.P.O. He told me G.P.O. was headquarters. I advised him to head there and I was to go on my bicycle and try to get there too. So I went back to the house and got my rifle and equipment – no, I started off towards Portobello Bridge, he told me there was heavy fighting there, and I thought I could get in with the volunteers there. I could not get in because I was held up at Rathmines Catholic Church – the British military were there, but I met Art Neill another member of the 4th Battalion, and he told me there was somebody up in Larkfield [in Kimmage], so we went there ...*[87]

Andrew Cullen from Dundrum was not a volunteer but he knew some of the men of 'E' Company. Cullen later testified (in support of their pension applications) that he met Milltown volunteers Patrick Leonard (who was fully armed) and Michael Murray (armed with a pike) on Easter Monday with about six or eight other volunteers. Cullen accompanied the men to Palmerston Park where there was a car with some ammunition and picks and shovels waiting. The volunteers (but not Cullen) then moved off in the direction of Bolands Mills through Ranelagh.[88]

---

85 MAI, MSP34REF2190, sworn statement of Henry Winstanley, 31 January 1936. Henry Winstanley lived at 30 Millmount Cottages on the Dundrum Road near Windy Arbour. In 1911 Winstanley was working as a van man with his younger brother John while their widowed mother worked as a laundress: NAI, 1911 Census, Form A, residents of house 84 in Windy Arbour Town, Milltown Electoral Division, Parish of Taney, Barony of Rathdown. Thus, Winstanley was likely to have been employed by either the Dublin Laundry Company in Milltown or the Manor Mill Laundry in Dundrum.

86 BMH, WS428, witness statement of Thomas Devine, 22 September 1950, p. 2.

87 MAI, MSP34REF20800, sworn statement of Alfred Harnett, 11 December 1936. Alfred Harnett lived in the Marble Hall Tenement in Concrete on the south bank of the River Dodder in Milltown: NAI, 1911 Census, Form A, residents of house 29.16 in Milltown (Concrete), Milltown Electoral Division, Parish of Taney, Barony of Rathdown.

88 MAI, 24SP2053, pension application of Michael Murray, MAI, 24SP671, pension application of Patrick Leonard.

LACK OF ARMS AND AMMUNITION

It is very apparent from the veterans' testimonies that the volunteers of 'E' Company were chronically short of conventional weaponry when they mustered in Cullenswood House on Easter Monday 1916. Only Patrick Doyle seems to have possessed a rifle, whereas the other men had handguns and shotguns. Some of the teenage volunteers, youths such as Michael Byrne, Michael Murray and Andrew McDonnell, had no conventional weaponry and were only armed with pikes.[89] Milltown volunteer Michael Doyle was armed with a pike and a .22 revolver. Before Easter week 1916 Doyle had been making pikes at night. This clandestine activity probably took place in Redmond's forge in Milltown village, and possibly at the Henshaw Ironworks in Clonskeagh.[90] Andrew McDonnell recalled taking part at a parade of Irish Volunteers on St Patrick's Day 1916:

> *The Company was on parade with arms on the 17th March, 1916, when the salute was taken by Eoin MacNeill in College Green. I was then armed with a 6' pike, as were a number of the men in the company. I well remember the trouble it was to stack the pikes while we attended Mass at S.S. Michael and John's, Exchange St, on our way to the parade at College Green.*[91]

Prior to the outbreak of the 1916 Rebellion the Irish Volunteers carried out bomb making and armaments manufacture at a disused mill premises at Larkfield in Kimmage. The arms made there were used to supply the four Dublin battalions. Part of the activities included fitting six-foot handles to half-inch socket chisels which were to be used as lances.[92] As far as we can tell, pikes were never employed as offensive weapons during the 1916 Rising. At best, these implements could have been used to deter the DMP, which was unarmed apart from carrying police batons. 'E' Company volunteer, Andrew McDonnell, later claimed that he stopped a tram by standing in the street (possibly Brunswick, later Pearse street) with his pike, but this is uncorroborated and may have been exaggerated bravado on his part.[93]

PATRICK DOYLE AND THE BATTLE OF MOUNT STREET BRIDGE

Thanks to the work of John Heuston, the number of men who turned out on Easter Monday with 'E' Company has been identified as being 25 out of a total of 56 who were on the roll.[94] Of the volunteers from 'E' Company who mustered on Easter Monday, at least 11 lived in Milltown village and its vicinity. They were Thomas Devine,[95] Patrick Brennan,[96] Michael Byrne,[97] Michael

---

89 MAI, 24SP2053, MAI, MSP34REF35241, BMH, WS1768, p. 4 (witness statement of Andrew McDonnell).

90 MAI, MSP34REF36789.

91 BMH, WS1768, p. 2, witness statement of Andrew McDonnell.

92 Ann Matthews, *The Kimmage Garrison, 1916: Making billy-can bombs at Larkfield* (Dublin, 2010), p. 24.

93 BMH, WS1768, p. 6.

94 John M. Heuston, *Headquarters Battalion, Army of the Irish Republic, Easter Week 1916* (Carlow, 1966), p. 70. Heuston's list does not include James Darcy of Milltown.

95 MAI, MSP34REF197 and WSO428.

96 MAI, MSP34REF1513. Patrick Brennan worked as a gardener for the Jesuits in Milltown Park. On Easter Sunday he slept in a room over the Milltown Park dairy prior to mobilisation to Cullenswood House.

97 MAI, MSP34REF35241. In 1911 Michael Byrne was living in the Marble Hall tenement in Concrete, Milltown: NAI, 1911 Census, Form A, residents of house 29.11 in Milltown (Concrete), Milltown Electoral Division, Parish of Taney, Barony of Rathdown. Before the Rising Byrne had been employed in Henshaw's Ironworks in Clonskeagh.

Doyle,[98] Patrick Doyle,[99] Patrick and Edward Leonard,[100] John (or Joseph) McKenna,[101] Michael Murray,[102] James Darcy[103] and Henry (Harry) Winstanley.[104] As previously noted, volunteer Alfred Harnett was a member of 'C' Company of the 4th Battalion.

The quotations highlighted above give a very vivid account of how the 1916 Rising unfolded for the ordinary volunteers who lived in Milltown. Given the volume of information available in the 1916 veterans' witness statements and their pension application records it clearly is not feasible to provide a detailed narrative of the entire experiences of each of these men here. An exception needs to be made in the case of Patrick Doyle, the only volunteer from Milltown who died in the 1916 Rising.

Sometime after Doyle arrived at 144 Brunswick Street on Easter Monday afternoon he was ordered to occupy the parochial hall on Northumberland Road with three other volunteers, as part of the defensive arrangements that were being put in place at Mount Street Bridge.[105] In the meantime, Clanwilliam House, which overlooked Mount Street Bridge, had been occupied by five volunteers led by George Reynolds of 'C' Company.[106] The next day, Tuesday, four more volunteers including Doyle, were sent to reinforce Clanwilliam House (Reynolds had by then sent home one of the youngest volunteers who had shown signs of nerves).[107] Doyle and four of his comrades were positioned in the drawing room of Clanwilliam House which had three windows facing the canal.[108]

Military engagements at Mount Street initially with unarmed veteran soldiers (known as the Georgius Rex) and then with British armed troops (Sherwood Foresters) had begun at 4 p.m. on Monday afternoon.[109] Although the volunteers stationed on Northumberland Road and Mount Street Bridge managed to inflict heavy casualties on the inexperienced and ill-deployed Sherwood Foresters, it was only a matter of time before the Irish republican forces would be overwhelmed, particularly as the British began to deploy machine guns and hand grenades.[110] Patrick

98 MAI, MSP34REF36789.

99 MAI, 2D50; Patrick Doyle papers (NLI, MS 46,594).

100 MAI, 24SP671 (Patrick Leonard), MSP34REF458 (Edward Leonard). In 1911 the two brothers were employed as van boys (probably in Milltown laundry) and were living in Concrete, Milltown: NAI, 1911 Census, Form A, residents of house 4 in Milltown (Concrete), Milltown Electoral Division, Parish of Taney, Barony of Rathdown.

101 NAI, CSOPR/1916/15564/16. McKenna gave his address as being care of Redmond's forge, Milltown, and his occupation as a horse shoer: *Weekly Irish Times*, Sinn Féin Rebellion Handbook, Easter 1916, p. 76.

102 MAI, 24SP2053. Michael Murray was living in in the Marble Hall Tenement in Concrete: NAI, 1911 Census, Form A, residents of house 29.16 in Milltown (Concrete), Milltown Electoral Division, Parish of Taney, Barony of Rathdown. Before the 1916 Rising Murray worked as a fitter's helper in the Manor Mill laundry in Dundrum. In 1917 he was living at 4 Hackett's Cottages in Milltown village: *Freeman's Journal*, 20 October 1917, p. 6.

103 MAI, 24SP1779. In the 1920s James Darcy lived at the old Dew Drop Inn (by then a grocery store owned by Thomas Hackett) on the south bank of the River Dodder in Milltown, where he later died in 1952.

104 MAI, MSP34REF2190.

105 O'Brien, *Blood on the streets*, p. 20.

106 O'Brien, *Blood on the streets*, p. 20.

107 O'Brien, *Blood on the streets*, pp. 25, 28.

108 O'Brien, *Blood on the streets*, p. 39.

109 O'Brien, *Blood on the streets*, pp. 22, 42–52.

110 O'Brien, *Blood on the streets*, pp. 67–9.

Doyle was killed in Clanwilliam House during a period of intense fighting on Wednesday evening, 26 April, as recalled by his comrades who survived the battle:

> *Over the din of battle Patrick Doyle shouted, 'Boys, isn't this a great day for Ireland?' Tom Walsh replied, 'Isn't it that!' and continued firing. Doyle then said: 'Did I ever think I'd see a day like this? Shouldn't we all be grateful to the good God that he has allowed us to take part in a fight like this?' The conversation was suddenly cut short as Doyle was shot through the head and killed.*[111]

The number of casualties estimated to have been suffered by the British Army at Mount Street vary considerably according to different historians' estimates. One, citing a contemporary British military source, states that 234 British Army soldiers were killed or injured during the battle of Mount Street Bridge, while military historians who carried out extensive research in 2016, concluded that the British suffered 160 casualties including 26 deaths at that engagement on Wednesday of Easter week.[112] Either way, given Patrick Doyle's expertise with a rifle it is quite likely that he inflicted several casualties (possibly dozens) on the British before he was shot dead. Patrick Doyle's body perished in the conflagration at Clanwilliam House along with those of George Reynolds and Richard Murphy.[113] Doyle was later commemorated with a marble plaque and a holy water font, which were erected outside the side entrance to Ss Gall and Columbanus church in Milltown.

THE IRISH CITIZEN ARMY

The Lambert family were also prominent in the 1916 Rising, but not through the agency of the Irish Volunteers.[114] The family lived for a time at 4 Strand Cottages off the south side of Milltown village main street facing the River Dodder (Map 20), but by 1916 they had moved to larger accommodation in Old Bridge House beside the Packhorse Bridge in Concrete, on the south bank of the River Dodder. The head of the family, Thomas Lambert, was an employee of the Dublin Laundry Company in Milltown. Thomas was a middle-aged married man who had six daughters and a son.[115] In 1913 or 1914 Thomas Lambert and his two daughters Ellen and Bridget joined the Irish Citizen Army (ICA). The two teenage girls regularly attended dramatic classes at the ICA's headquarters in Liberty Hall.[116] The ICA had been established to protect Dublin's labour force who had suffered at the hands of the DMP during the 1913 Lockout. Led by James Connolly and numbering about 200 men in 1914, the ICA had a radical socialist agenda based on the public ownership of the means of production

---

111 O'Brien, *Blood on the streets*, p. 69. O'Brien's footnote references J. McCann's *War by the Irish* (Tralee, The Kerryman Ltd, 1946) but that work does not refer to the utterances allegedly made by Doyle.

112 O'Brien, *Blood on the streets*, p. 80; Brian Hughes, Billy Campbell and Susan Schreibman, 'Contested Memories: Revisiting the Battle of Mount Street Bridge', *British Journal for Military History*, 4, no. 1 (2017), pp. 2–22.

113 O'Brien, *Blood on the streets*, p. 83.

114 This Catholic family was unrelated to the Lamberts who lived in Riversdale at Classon's Bridge, where they owned a dairy farm, and who were Protestants. In 1901 there were 17 Lamberts comprising five households living in Milltown (including Riversdale), some of whom were Catholics and some of whom were Protestants.

115 NAI, 1911 Census, Form A, residents of house 4 in Strand Cottages, Townland of Milltown, Electoral Division of Rathmines and Rathgar East, Parish of St Peter, Barony of Uppercross; *Weekly Irish Times*, Sinn Féin Rebellion Handbook, Easter 1916, p. 77.

116 MAI, MSP34REF56696, sworn statement by Ellen Stynes (née Lambert), 2 May 1941; MSP34REF57178, sworn statement of Bridget Doran (née Lambert).

and exchange.[117] The ICA's working-class roots and radical social reform agenda obviously appealed to Thomas and his two teenage daughters. However, its socialist principles were anathema to Catholic teaching and so it would have been off bounds for Lambert's workmate in the laundry, Patrick Doyle, who channelled his patriotism through the Irish Volunteers instead.

On Easter Monday 1916 Thomas Lambert made his way, armed and in uniform, into the city centre. Later that day, Ellen and Bridget decided to join their father and they made their way to Liberty Hall. As the two girls could not locate their father in Beresford Place, they followed some ICA men to the GPO, where they were put to work in the kitchens. At 9.30 p.m. on Monday evening Ellen and Bridget were allowed to go home to Milltown, where they spent the night. The girls returned to the GPO the following morning. On Tuesday and Wednesday Ellen carried dispatches for Patrick Pearse between the GPO and the College of Surgeons. The Lambert sisters remained in the GPO until midday on Friday, when they left with the other women volunteers. Ellen and Bridget were arrested near Broadstone railway station and interrogated by the British military before being released later on Friday evening with official passes. The two girls spent the night in a safe house and returned home to Milltown on Saturday morning.[118] The Lambert girls' aunt, Mrs Ellen Noone (née Harnett), who was living in Milltown in 1916 and was related to volunteer Alfred Harnett, also joined her nieces in the GPO on the Tuesday of Easter Week 1916 until she left with the other women on Friday.[119]

The 50 or so women from the GPO who had been arrested each obtained a pass from the British to go to 27 Eccles Street, which was the address of the Dominican convent. The women gave this address because they did not want to divulge where they actually lived, but this did not go completely to plan, as Cumann na mBan veteran Áine Ní Rian later explained:

> *Two girls came with me to Eccles Street. They were from Milltown. One of them was Nellie Lambert. The other, whose name I don't remember, was her aunt [Mrs Noone]. We went to Eccles Street and presented a pass to a nun through a grating in the door of the Convent. We said we were sent by the military. She said she could not put us up and did not open the door. We were quite near 15, St Joseph's Street, where I was staying and we went there. Mrs Cleary took us in and made us comfortable. The two others left that evening for home and I stayed on.*[120]

No information has survived about Thomas Lambert's activities during the 1916 Rising because he died in 1919 and so did not have any opportunity to record his experiences in a subsequent pension application or witness statement to the BMH. All we know is that Thomas fought in the City Hall and was later arrested and interned in England.[121]

117 Curtis, 'Ireland in 1914' in Vaughan (ed.), *A new history of Ireland, vi: Ireland under the Union 1870–1921* (Oxford, 1989), p. 183; Lyons, 'The revolution in train' in Vaughan (ed.), *A new history of Ireland, vi: Ireland under the Union 1870–1921* (Oxford, 1989), p. 198.

118 MAI, MSP34REF56696 (Ellen Lambert) and MSP34REF57178 (Bridget Lambert).

119 MAI, MSP34REF25075, sworn statement of Mrs Ellen Noone, 17 June 1940.

120 BMH, WS887, witness statement of Áine Ní Rian, 18 September 1953, pp. 10–11.

121 MAI, MSP34REF56696; *Weekly Irish Times*, Sinn Féin Rebellion Handbook, Easter 1916, p. 77; NAI, CSORP, 1916/15564/16; National Archives, Kew, HO 144/1456/313106, Internment of Irish prisoners 8 June & 11 July 1916.

ARRESTS OF VOLUNTEERS

Although fighting was taking place in Dublin city the military authorities were proactive in securing the suburban villages such as Dundrum. Alex (Alec) Cullen, who was the Company Adjutant of 'E' Company, had failed to meet up with the volunteers in Oakley Road. Although Captain Liam Tannam had left instructions with his father and brother for Alex to try and make his way to Beresford Place, this did not happen, as Cullen later explained:

> *In 1916 Capt [sic] Darcy, never advised us to come to town and when orders did get out, the Lancers were in the occupation of the few big houses in the village [Dundrum], while the R.I.C. were free to attend to such as myself and my two comrades, who were in the same boat. Well we done our best, but could do no more we tried to get in touch up to Wed evening but no use, so we decided to make sure of our stuff. I had equipment for 10 men and I carefully got it off the premises, and well packed and tranced, so that when I was arrested at three a.m. the following morning, only my water bottle and belt could be found.*[122]

Other volunteers from 'E' Company and the Irish Citizen Army were arrested and interned after the 1916 rebellion had been put down, while others managed to avoided capture or were released from detention in Dublin without being sent to England.[123] Dundrum volunteer Alex Cullen and five men from Milltown, James Darcy, John McKenna, Patrick Brennan, Thomas Lambert and Alfred Harnett were interned for several weeks in various prison camps in England and Wales.[124] During this period subscriptions were raised for the families of the internees by the Irish National Aid Association, which included a contribution of 7*s.* and 6 ½ *d.* by sympathisers in Milltown.[125] A telling indication of the gradual swing in public attitude from hostility to sympathy towards the men who fought in the rising – or at least their dependants – can be seen at a meeting of Board of Guardians of the Rathdown Union held on 24 May 1916. During a discussion on the exceptional levels of distress and poverty then prevailing in the union, the chairman, Thomas Clarke JP, opined that:

> *the urban districts within Co. Dublin would be the most likely to suffer exceptional distress owing to arrests and deportations. It was a great pity that anybody should be penalised because one of their family took part in the rising.*[126]

Evidence in support of Clarke's position was provided by the union's relief officers, who confirmed that there were some families in Blackrock, Dundrum and Milltown districts affected by the recent arrests.[127]

---

122 NAI, Department of the Taoiseach, S 7696, file for Alex Cullen, Grant from the Dáil Special Fund. Cullen says he had been promoted to Quartermaster when the volunteers were drilling in Beaver Row but Captain Liam Tannam recalled that Cullen was the Company Adjutant. His mention of Captain Darcy probably refers to James Darcy of Milltown who at that time was an ordinary volunteer in 'E' Company but who later served in the National Army as a sergeant (MAI, 24SP1779).

123 Thomas Devine was imprisoned in Richmond Barracks for eight days and released on account of his youth (MSP34REF197). Michael Doyle, who was wounded in the Rising, spent three weeks in Baggot Street Hospital and as a prisoner in Dublin Castle (MSP34REF36789).

124 NAI, Department of the Taoiseach, S 7696, file for Alex Cullen; *Weekly Irish Times*, Sinn Féin Rebellion Handbook, Easter 1916, pp. 75, 76, 77, 84; NAI, CSORP, 1916/15564/16; MAI, MSP34REF20800, sworn statement of Alfred Harnett.

125 *An Claidheamh Soluis*, 17 August 1916, p. 11.

126 *General Advertiser for Dublin, and All Ireland*, 27 May 1916, p. 7.

127 *General Advertiser for Dublin, and All Ireland*, 27 May 1916, p. 7.

In the longer term, the Irish Volunteers experienced harassment from the police, were dismissed from their jobs or were not re-employed when they were released from prison. Henry Winstanley's home at 30 Millmount Cottages was raided several times by the police and he was forced to move temporarily to England in June 1917.[128] Michael Doyle also sought work in England in January 1919 and took no part in the War of Independence. Doyle returned home in 1922 and joined the anti-Treaty side in the Civil War.[129] Edward Leonard lost his job in the Dartry Dye Works as a consequence of his involvement in the 1916 Rising and was subsequently dismissed from the Royal Hospital Donnybrook when he refused to hoist the Union Jack flag.[130] After the 1916 Rising Michael Murray was employed for short periods by the Dublin Laundry Company in Milltown and by the Dartry Dye Works. Murray was apparently dismissed by the latter company for his involvement with Sinn Féin and the South Armagh bye-election in 1918.[131] At the time of the 1916 Rising James Darcy was employed as a groundsman at the Rathfarnham Golf Club. After Darcy was released from Frongoch prison camp in Wales he was refused re-employment by the golf club because as his former boss put it, he had taken up arms against 'his King and Country'.[132]

In 1917, Bridget Lambert joined the Dundrum branch of Cumann na mBan and was active in that organisation, where she attended first aid lectures, fund raised, and sent parcels to political prisoners.[133] After 1916 Ellen Lambert was victimised by her employer and she emigrated to Scotland in February 1917. While living there Ellen joined the local Sinn Féin clubs. Ellen Lambert returned to Ireland in June 1919 and joined her sisters Bridget, Josephine (Josie) and Kathleen in the Dundrum branch of Cumann na mBan.[134]

RE-EMERGENCE OF THE IRISH VOLUNTEERS

As the internees from England and Wales began to be released in the summer and autumn of 1916 the men began to reorganise and reform their local companies. Meetings and drilling were held secretly in Donnybrook and in the Gaelic League's premises in Ely Place, and these activities attracted new recruits from Milltown and the surrounding districts. By Christmas 1916 all of the Irish Volunteers who had served in 'E' company during the Easter Rising had been released from internment by the British and were in the process of reorganising themselves into new battalions. Captain Liam Tannam was ordered to start a new company in Dundrum to include Irish Volunteers from Milltown, Windy Arbour, Dundrum and Ticknock.[135] This new unit was called 'H' Company. Milltown volunteer Michael Doyle joined the Company as section leader.[136] Charles (Charlie) Noone, a nephew of Thomas Lambert, had been too young to fight in 1916 but he joined 'H' Company in 1918 and served with the IRA until 1924. Charlie was a son of Ellen Noone, who

128 MAI, MSP34REF2190.

129 MAI, MSP34REF36789.

130 MAI, MSP34REF458.

131 MAI, 24SP2053.

132 MAI, 24SP1779.

133 MAI, MSP34REF57178 (Bridget Doran).

134 MAI, MSP34REF56696 (Ellen Stynes) and MSP34REF57178 (Bridget Doran).

135 BMH, WS1768, witness statement of Andrew McDonnell, pp. 23–4.

136 MAI, MSP34REF36789 (Michael Doyle), testimonial of Michael Murray.

had served in the GPO during the 1916 Rising, and a first cousin of Ellen and Bridget Lambert.[137]

The British authorities were not unaware of these developments. Their intelligence officers issued a brief but very informative report on the political situation pertaining in County Dublin towards the end of 1916:

> *Of political societies in county Dublin the United Irish League has lost a good deal of its influence, and its meetings are few and far between. The National Volunteers, who have a nominal membership of 1,289, are a waning force and many of them would break away and join the Sinn Féiners if they saw it was to their advantage to do so: the Irish Volunteers, though their membership is small, have much influence with the labouring classes and shop-boys, and through their relations with the rebels attract the sympathies of the disloyal ... After the rebellion the Sinn Féin movement attracted many new adherents, including some of the younger Roman Catholic clergy. Recruiting [for the Great War] is bad.*[138]

The report's identification of the 'labouring classes' and 'shop boys' as being among the supporters of the Irish Volunteers rings particularly true of those from Milltown and the surrounding districts, many of whom were employed as laundry van boys and general labourers.

During the summer of 1917 a number of significant events took place which increased tensions in Dublin between the DMP and Sinn Féin and their supporters, whose numbers had been growing steadily during this period. More particularly, in June there were sporadic clashes between the police and republican sympathisers which had resulted in a fatal injury to DMP Inspector Mills, who died in hospital after having been struck by a rioter with a hurley stick on 10 June. Concurrently, on the broader national level the last of the republican prisoners arrested after the 1916 Rising were released from English prisons in June, while political talks at the Irish Convention in July 1917 attempted unsuccessfully to resolve Irish constitutional issues – essentially concerning partition – affecting the Home Rule question.[139] By mid-autumn the Irish Volunteers had assumed control of the Sinn Féin party and proceeded to rewrite its constitution and prepare for electoral contests against the increasingly beleaguered IPP.[140] This background then explains the context of an incident that occurred in Milltown in October of 1917 involving two local Irish Volunteers who had fought in the Easter Rising of 1916, Michael Murray and Patrick Leonard.

On a Sunday lunchtime between one and two o'clock on 14 October, a large group of Sinn Féin boy scouts (also known as na Fianna Éireann or the National Boys Scouts) were parading along the main street in Milltown village.[141] Initial reports indicated that two policemen, Sergeant John Walsh and Constable Michael Howard, interfered with the parade following which Sergeant Walsh was allegedly assaulted from behind by Patrick Leonard.[142] As previously discussed, Patrick Leonard had fought in the 1916 Rising at Boland's mills and so there was mutual antagonism

137 MAI, MSP34REF57178 (Bridget Doran née Lambert); Charlie Noone grew up in no. 15 Milltown village. His father was a general labourer and his mother worked as a laundress: NAI, 1911 Census, Form A, house 26.1 Milltown Road, Townland of Milltown, Electoral Division of Rathmines and Rathgar East, Barony of Uppercross, Co. Dublin.

138 'I.O.' [C. J. C. Street], The Administration of Ireland, 1920 (London, April 1921), p. 44. By 1916 the United Irish League had succeeded the Irish National League as the IPP's constituency organisation.

139 Grayson, *Dublin's Great Wars*, p. 232.

140 Yeates, *A City in Wartime*, p. 210.

141 *Freeman's Journal*, 20 October 1917, p. 6; *Weekly Freeman*, 20 October 1917, p. 1.

142 *Irish Examiner*, 16 October 1917, p. 5.

between himself and the DMP.[143] Leonard, who was also injured in the affray, was then arrested by Constable Howard and remanded in custody.[144] More details of the incident were revealed when Leonard's case was tried at the Southern Police Court on 19 October. It soon emerged that the witness evidence was completely at odds with that sworn by the policemen. Michael Murray of 4 Hackett's Cottages gave evidence that he was standing with Leonard on the footpath as the policemen were attempting to disperse the boy scouts. Murray had also fought in 1916 and was involved in recruiting boys to the Fianna Éireann.[145] Suddenly Sergeant Walsh struck Murray and was about to hit him a second time when Leonard assaulted Walsh in defence of his friend. Then Leonard was knocked unconscious by a police constable whom Murray was unable to identify. Murray's version of events was corroborated by Arthur D'Arcy, who lived in Milltown where he worked as a chauffeur. The most credible evidence was provided by the district nurse, Mrs Smithson, who said she saw Leonard get a smashing blow from the fist of a constable. She said Leonard fell to the ground unconscious and was taken away bleeding to hospital.[146]

The presiding magistrate, Mr Drury, was totally unsympathetic to the Milltown men and was clearly biased in favour of the police. Drury said that an attack on police officers carrying out their orders could not be tolerated, and he referenced the tragic death of Inspector Mills in support of his attitude.[147] He completely ignored the evidence of Mrs Smithson and, without any supporting evidence, Drury opined that Leonard's unconsciousness was caused by him hitting his head falling to the ground rather than by the initial blow struck by the policeman.[148] Drury sentenced Patrick Leonard to three months' imprisonment with hard labour.[149] Michael Murray, who had been employed as a van driver by the Dublin Laundry Company, was later dismissed from his job due to his involvement with the Irish Volunteers.[150]

The arrests in Milltown in October 1917 were part of a number made by the authorities that month in Donnybrook, Rathmines and Rathfarnham targeting drilling and parading by the Fianna and the Irish Volunteers.[151]

SOUTH DUBLIN BYE-ELECTION 1917

The death of Alderman Cotton MP in June 1917 precipitated a bye-election contest in the South Dublin constituency. The IPP put forward a candidate called Michael Hearn. Hearn was a solicitor by profession and was widely known in sporting circles. He was also chairman of the *Freeman's Journal*. Hearn lived near Milltown in Temple Gardens, where he resided in a comfortable modern house called 'Waterloo'.[152] Hearn and his wife and three children, who were Catholics, enjoyed a

143 MAI, 24SP671.

144 *Irish Examiner*, 16 October 1917, p. 5.

145 MAI, 24SP2053, Michael Murray, testimony of Joseph Dillon.

146 *Freeman's Journal*, 20 October 1917, p. 6; *Dublin Daily Express*, 20 October 1917, p. 3.

147 *Freeman's Journal*, 20 October 1917, p. 6; *Dublin Daily Express*, 20 October 1917, p. 3.

148 *Dublin Daily Express*, 20 October 1917, p. 3; *Irish Independent*, 20 October 1917, p. 4. This detail was not recorded by the *Freeman's Journal*.

149 *Freeman's Journal*, 20 October 1917, p. 6; *Dublin Daily Express*, 20 October 1917, p. 3. Leonard's conviction was expunged a year later when he paid £10 compensation to Sargent Walsh: *Irish Independent*, 16 October 1918, p. 4.

150 MAI, 24SP2053, Michael Murray, testimonies of Andrew Cullen and Joseph Dillon.

151 BMH, WS907, witness statement of Laurence Nugent, p. 127.

152 *Dublin Daily Express*, 7 July 1917, p. 7.

comfortable lifestyle: in 1911 they employed a cook, a parlour maid and a coachman.[153] Due to a variety of reasons neither the unionists nor Sinn Féin decided to contest the election and so Hearn was returned unopposed the MP for South Dublin on 6 July 1917.[154]

Although Hearn was returned to parliament, an election contest had narrowly been avoided in rather strange circumstances. These involved another Milltown resident, a Miss Fox, who lived in Brookfield on Richmond Avenue South, which was less than a quarter of a mile away from Hearn's home in Temple Gardens. Miss Fox's brother, Major Charles Vincent Fox, had only very recently escaped from a German prisoner of war camp and was making his way back to England.[155] Unbeknownst to Major Fox and for reasons which were never explained, his sister decided to nominate her brother as a candidate for the south Dublin bye-election as a 'non-party Devolutionist'. The Fox family, who were Catholics, were originally from Kingstown (Dún Laoghaire) and were 'well-got' among the township's nationalists. With less than an hour before the closure of nominations, Miss Fox attempted to complete the nomination papers by approaching random members of the public on the street in Kingstown to support Charles's candidacy. By any measure this was rather bizarre behaviour (canvassing or otherwise) yet it almost paid off, though, in the end, Miss Fox ran out of time before she could obtain the requisite numbers of assenting electors to complete the nomination paper.[156]

At this point it is only right to acknowledge that Major Fox was a truly remarkable man whose sporting talents, military service, battlefield bravery and colonial life experiences could not be emulated by any comparable fictional character.[157] Major Fox's association with Milltown was short lived – he retired from his distinguished military career in 1921 and returned from England to live with his sister Mary Valentina at Brookfield until his death in 1928. A brass memorial plaque for Charles Fox is affixed to a pew in Ss Gall and Columbanus church, Milltown, where his funeral took place prior to his burial in Glasnevin cemetery.[158] Charles's sister Mary wrote an unpublished account of her brother's wartime experiences in May 1919 under the pseudonym 'Kilcoursey'. Mary's manuscript, to which she gave the title, *The Boche Baffled – Major Fox's escape from Germany,* surfaced in a second-hand bookstall in Dublin in 1989 but it remains unpublished and its current whereabouts is unclear.[159]

As for Michael Hearn, his parliamentary career was very brief. He failed to get nominated as the IPP candidate for the December 1918 general election, which saw the election of the Sinn Féin candidate, Gavan Duffy (a future signatory of the Anglo-Irish Treaty of 6 December 1921), for the South Dublin constituency.[160]

---

153 NAI, 1911 Census, Form A, residents of house 15 in Temple Gardens, Townland of Milltown, Electoral Division of Rathmines and Rathgar East, Parish of St Peter, Barony of Uppercross.

154 *Dublin Daily Express*, 7 July 1917, p. 7; Clare, Unionist/Nationalist election campaigns, pp. 16 17; *Yeates, A City in Wartime*, pp. 198–9.

155 *Irish Times*, 5 July 1917, p. 5.

156 *Irish Independent*, 7 July 1917, p. 2; *Dublin Daily Express*, 7 July 1917, p. 7; *Clare, Unionist/Nationalist election campaigns*, pp. 16–17.

157 For an outline of Fox's achievements which are too long to record here, see Thom's Irish Who's Who 1923, pp. 86–7; *Irish Times*, 9 November 1928, p. 7 (obituary); and the following link: https://livesofthefirstworldwar.org/lifestorey/5315223 (accessed 2 August 2022).

158 *Irish Times*, 10 November 1928, p. 1. Various siblings of the Fox family continued to live at Brookfield until the late 1950s: *New Ross Standard*, 24 August 24 August 1956, p. 10.

159 *Evening Herald*, 31 August 1989, p. 10.

160 Clare, *Unionist/Nationalist election campaigns*, pp. 17–9.

GENERAL ELECTION OF 1918

Evidence of the solid support for Sinn Féin in Milltown emerged in the autumn of 1918 when Sinn Féin's election agent, Dan McCarthy, was arrested in a safe house at Milltown on 19 September. McCarthy had been on the run for several months from the Dublin Castle authorities over his alleged involvement in the so-called German plot of May 1918. Dan McCarthy was arrested by four police detectives and deported to England where he was imprisoned.[161] McCarthy was released in early December 1918 due to his deteriorating health while in prison, which had been originally caused by wounds received in the 1916 Rising.[162]

The General Election of November 1918 is rightly considered to be a watershed in Irish electoral history for many reasons, not least of all because Sinn Féin took over completely from the IPP and won 73 of the 105 Irish seats in the House of Commons at Westminster. The extension of the electoral franchise to include all males aged over 21 and all females aged over 30 increased the Irish electorate from about 740,000 in 1910 to just shy of 2 million in December 1918.[163]

In 1918, the voters of Milltown found themselves in two new constituencies. Voters living in Milltown village on the north bank of the River Dodder were part of the Rathmines division, which had an electorate of 19,002, while voters living on the south bank in Concrete and Farranboley were included in the Pembroke division, whose electorate was slightly smaller at 17,961.[164] In Rathmines, there was a three-way contest between the unionist candidate, Sir Maurice Dockrell, the IPP candidate, George Moonan BL., and Patrick Little who was Sinn Féin's candidate.[165] Dockrell castigated Sinn Féin's Westminster abstentionist policy and criticised the IPP for its failure to support conscription during the German offensive in the spring of 1918. He supported neither partition nor the coercion of Ulster to Home Rule government, and opined that unionists were best served by MPs who represented people who had shed blood for the British Empire. Dockrell was supported by H.J. McCormick, chairman of the Rathmines UDC, who told the gathering that for the first time in the history of the township they had a parliamentary division, and the unionists there were very anxious that the first representative of the constituency should be a unionist.[166] McCormick's address in support of Dockrell confirmed the popular view that the Rathmines UDC was dominated by Unionists.

At an election address to a large gathering of the working men of Rathmines, Noonan stressed the need for continued parliamentary representation so that the IPP could fight in parliament to secure local authority housing for the Rathmines township and a redrawing of its wards to allow labour to be represented on the council.[167]

On Sunday 24 November 1918, the Sinn Féin candidate Patrick J. Little addressed an election meeting in Milltown. In a reprise of the role occupied by his late father T.P. Hackett in the Parnellite era, Thomas Hackett junior chaired the meeting. Rather tellingly, however, by 1918 the Hackett

---

161 *Irish Independent*, 20 September 1918, p. 3; *Freeman's Journal*, 20 September 1918, p. 2.

162 *Freeman's Journal*, 4 December 1918, p. 4.

163 F.S.L. Lyons, 'The new nationalism, 1916–18' in W.E. Vaughan (ed.), *A new history of Ireland, vi: Ireland under the Union 1870–1921* (Oxford, 1989), pp. 238–9; *Dickson, Dublin: The making of a capital city*, p. 459.

164 *Freeman's Journal*, 18 November 1918, p. 5.

165 Yeates, *A City in Wartime*, pp. 290–1, 294–5.

166 *Irish Independent*, 23 November 1918, p. 6. Dockrell had his Milltown constituency offices in the gate lodge of St Philip's during the election campaign: *Irish Times*, 13 December 1918, p. 4.

167 *Freeman's Journal*, 22 November 1918, p. 4.

family had, sensing the mood among the Milltown villagers, transferred their allegiance from the IPP to Sinn Féin. Little predicted that Sinn Féin would win 65 seats in the general election and said that it was ridiculous for the IPP to tell Sinn Féin to stand aside. When Sinn Féin had suggested to the IPP that the two parties carry out a poll of the nationalists in Rathmines to ascertain who was best placed to oppose the unionist candidate, John Dillon had scornfully refused the proposal.[168]

The 1918 general election was unique because for the first-time women could vote in parliamentary elections (they had been able to vote in local elections In Ireland since 1898). The *Irish Citizen* newspaper remarked on the variety of political creeds held by some prominent women:

> *in Rathmines, for instance, Mrs Kettle and Professor Mary Hayden back one candidate, the Irish party nominee, while Mrs Haslam swears allegiance to the Conservative, Sir Maurice Dockrell, and Mrs Sheehy Skeffington supports Sinn Féin. We understand that all candidates are suffragists – of course, it is a necessity now that women have votes.*[169]

It was estimated that almost 85 per cent of the eligible voters in the Rathmines division cast their vote on election day.[170] The *Larne Times* reported that large numbers of motor cars and taxis were used by all of the parties to convey supporters to the polling stations, and that the women's vote was 'very heavy in Rathmines'. Its journalist predicted that Sir Maurice Dockrell would win the seat.[171] The reporter for the *Irish Independent* remarked on the large number of women voters but noted that many of them had to be shown how to complete their ballot papers. Some of Moonan's supporters felt they had outvoted P.J. Little but were not confident of outright success. For their part, the Sinn Féin supporters claimed to have polled well in Harold's Cross and Terenure but they regarded Milltown as their stronghold.[172] On the other hand, the *Freeman's Journal* was more inclined to talk up the performance of the IPP and play down the electoral performance of Sinn Féin. Its reporter averred that 'even in Milltown and Crumlin which they [Sinn Féin] claimed as their own, the Nationalists scored well'.[173]

A few days later, the *Weekly Freeman* was highly critical of a bogus leaflet distributed by Sinn Féin supporters which purportedly came from the parish priest of Donnybrook, Monsignor Dunne, in which Fr Dunne called for nationalists to vote for Little as the best chance of keeping Dockrell out.[174]

As generally anticipated, Sir Maurice Dockrell won the seat with a majority of 1,834 votes. Nonetheless, the respective votes for the three parties proved beyond doubt that Sinn Féin had overtaken the IPP as the dominant political party for Irish nationalists. The votes cast for each candidate were Dockrell (7,400), Little (5,566) and Moonan (1,780). Thus, the Rathmines division was evenly split between unionists and IPP/Sinn Féin, as the combined nationalist vote was only 54 votes short of the unionist vote.[175]

---

168 *Irish Independent*, 25 November 1918, p. 4.

169 *Irish Citizen*, 7 December 1918, p. 1.

170 *Irish Independent*, 16 December 1918, p. 3; *Freeman's Journal*, 16 December 1918, p. 2.

171 *Larne Times*, 21 December 1918, p. 6.

172 *Irish Independent*, 16 December 1918, p. 3.

173 *Freeman's Journal*, 16 December 1918, p. 5.

174 *Weekly Freeman*, 21 December 1918, p. 2.

175 *Derry Journal*, 25 December 1918, p. 7.

Dockrell and Little were magnanimous in victory and defeat respectively. They both agreed that the campaign had been conducted with mutual respect and good humour. Little said that despite their political differences, the election in Rathmines had proved the capacity of Irish people to manage their own affairs.[176] As a unionist-supporting newspaper, the *Irish Times* was despondent about the success of Sinn Féin. Its editor took solace from the fact that southern unionists were 'less exiguously represented in the new House of Commons than the constitutional nationalists'.[177] The newspaper blamed the demise of the IPP on its failure to recruit younger members and admit new ideas to the party, and was critical of Dillon's failure to support the war effort or offer courageous resistance to Sinn Féin. The editor concluded his piece with the following reflection:

> *From today the country will begin to expect Sinn Féin to fulfil promises that are utterly incapable of fulfilment. Either its new responsibilities will give Sinn Féin some measure of sanity or it will come quickly into grave conflict with the forces of law and order. For the moment sober and patriotic Irishmen can only hope that their country is passing through that darkest hour which precedes the dawn.*[178]

THE WAR OF INDEPENDENCE

One of the seminal periods of Irish history is the transformation of Irish politics in the second decade of the twentieth century which, among other things, led to conditions conducive to bringing about the War of Independence. In later life, General Richard Mulcahy discussed the justification for the War of Independence with his son Risteárd, and told him that Risteárd's generation had 'very little conception of the forces that were operating in Great Britain at the time against this country'.[179] Risteárd Mulcahy's succinct resumé of his discussion with his father is worth quoting in its entirety because it sets the wider context for the evolution of public opinion and the subsequent activities that took place in Milltown during the War of Independence:

> *He [General Mulcahy] mentioned the Ulster Volunteers and the powerful Tory influence supporting the Northern dissidents [Loyalists] which led to Britain changing the rules in relation to Home Rule in 1913 [i.e. the exclusion of Ulster]. He mentioned the conscription issue and the fabricated German Plot in 1918. He stressed the harassment of the Irish political leaders [i.e. republicans] as early as 1917 before the [Irish] Volunteers were officially reorganised in October of that year. Here he referred to [Thomas] Ashe's repeated imprisonment for speaking in public about Ireland's right to freedom and his death in prison in September 1917 from forced feeding as an example of British intransigence. He held that the circumstances of British aggression and harassment of the people and the members of the Dáil was such that local and eventually national reaction in terms of military aggression became inevitable. It would be humanly impossible not to react to the cumulative effect of British aggression which started as early as 1917, and which continued for more than two years before the Volunteers adopted an active policy of military resistance. Until the end of 1919, both the political head (Cathal Brugha) and the military head (Richard Mulcahy) were committed to a defensive policy on the part of the Volunteers, until the suppression of the Dáil in September 1919 was the final provocation.*[180]

---

176 *Belfast Newsletter*, 30 December 1918, p. 3.

177 *Irish Times*, 30 December 1918, p. 4.

178 *Irish Times*, 30 December 1918, p. 4.

179 Risteárd Mulcahy, *Richard Mulcahy (1886–1971): A Family Memoir* (Dublin, 1999), p. 58.

180 Mulcahy, *Richard Mulcahy*, p. 58.

Due to the scarcity or arms and money, in the spring of 1918 the Irish Volunteers resumed manufacturing pikes in expectation of further conflict.[181] A makeshift forge was set up in the Dublin mountains at Ticknock which supplied pikes to the Dundrum volunteers of 'H' Company and beyond in south Dublin and Enniskerry.[182] Viewed in isolation this activity might seem patriotic in a romantic way, harking back to the days of the 1798 Rebellion. But little more than two years later – by the mid-point of the War of Independence – attitudes and tactics among the belligerents had hardened to an unimaginable degree. Papers belonging to Richard Mulcahy captured by the British in November 1920 show that the IRA were investigating the possibilities of using biological warfare against British armed forces, by infecting horses with Glanders and poisoning soldiers' milk and drinking water with typhoid.[183]

Other important events which took place over the course of 1919 accelerated the drift to armed conflict. The failure of the Paris peace conference of 1919 to uphold Ireland's claim to independence, which had formed part of Sinn Féin's 1918 election manifesto, was a major blow to those who hoped for a resolution of the national question without recourse to violence.[184] The possibility of a peaceful solution was further compromised by the outlawing of Sinn Féin, the Gaelic League and the Irish Volunteers in July 1919. Cumulatively, these acts on the part of the British increased the Irish sense of oppression and strengthened the military faction within the republican movement.[185]

Much of the information available about the activities of the Irish Volunteers and the Irish Republican Army (IRA) during the War of Independence in the south County Dublin area, including Milltown, is preserved in the witness statement of Patrick J. Brennan in the archives of the BMH.[186] The organisation of the Irish Volunteers was improved in 1917 when a specific territorial district was allocated to each battalion and to each company within the battalion area. Initially, Milltown was part of the 4th Battalion, though this allocation for Milltown seems to have been rather fluid as new companies became operational.[187] In September 1919 all Irish Volunteer units in south Dublin were reformed into a new battalion of the Dublin Brigade, called the 6th Battalion. Patrick Brennan, who lived on Dundrum main street, and Michael Murray of Concrete, Milltown, were the 1st and 2nd lieutenants respectively in the Brigade's 'A' Company, which encompassed the districts of Balally, Dundrum, Goatstown, Windy Arbour, Churchtown and Milltown. Initially 'A' Company had a strength of 54 active volunteers.[188]

Following their reorganisation in September 1919, the Irish Volunteers in south Dublin began training exercises in the Dublin mountains, consisting of rifle and revolver target practice, grenade throwing and route marches. However, unlike some parts of rural Ireland the Irish Volunteers faced very hostile conditions in south County Dublin from a variety of

---

181 Charles Townsend, *The Republic: The fight for Irish Independence, 1918–1923* (London, 2013), pp. 41–2.

182 BMH, WS1768, witness statement of Andrew McDonnell, pp. 25–6.

183 'I.O.', *Administration of Ireland*, Appendix B.

184 *Freeman's Journal*, 12 October 1918, p. 6.

185 Maryann Gialanella Valiulis, *Portrait of a Revolutionary: General Richard Mulcahy and the founding of the Irish Free State* (Dublin, 1992), pp. 40–1.

186 BMH, WS1773, witness statement of Patrick J. Byrne of 59 Lower Churchtown Road, 31 January 1962.

187 BMH, WS601, witness statement of Henry S. Murray, pp. 6–6a.

188 BMH, WS1773, pp. 1, 3, 4.

different causes. First of all, large portions of the area were inhabited by the wealthy professional and commercial classes who would for the most part have supported the Union with Great Britain or, in the case of many traditional nationalists, the non-violent acquisition of self-government (Home Rule). In addition, all of the RIC Barracks in south Dublin – for example Dundrum which was barely two miles from Milltown – were stoutly built and were well defended and garrisoned. As IRA volunteer Patrick Brennan remarked laconically, 'the areas [where the barracks were located] were thickly populated by a none too friendly people'.[189] Thus, it was deemed too risky to launch all out attacks on the RIC barracks in south Dublin. Furthermore, the elaborate network of main roads, railways, secondary roads and laneways precluded the deployment in the field of a large force of IRA volunteers because of the threat of being cut off or surrounded by the British military which could be called out from Beggars Bush and Portobello barracks at relatively short notice. As a result of these challenging conditions, all local attacks were carried out at the instructions of the Brigade's commanders or General Head Quarters in Dublin for the purposes of relieving pressure on the city at times of acute activity, such as 'Blooding Sunday' (21 November 1920) and the burning of the Customs House.[190]

Aside from the larger attacks carried out on orders from Dublin city, throughout the War of Independence the local IRA units engaged in a wide variety of sabotage and acts of disruption which Brennan listed in detail:

> *sniping of enemy posts, raids for arms, ammunition, mails, supplies, Belfast goods; County Council Rates monies and documents; manufacture of grenades, destruction of telephone and telegraph lines and railway signal cabins; seizure and destruction of enemy property e.g. Post Office bicycles, mails, trucks, telephone linesman's equipment; blocking and trenching bye-roads as well as work undertaken at the instance of Sinn Féin (Parliamentary, Local Elections and Publicity), Dáil Eireann (Courts and Loan) and Chief of Republican Police etc*[191]

During the period January 1921 to 11 July 1921 (the date of the truce with the British), 'A' Company carried out sniping operations almost every night on RIC barracks. This was done with a view to keeping the policemen confined inside the barracks for considerable periods, thereby demoralising them.[192] Finally, it is important to emphasise just how close Milltown village was to major British military barracks such as those at Portobello and Beggars Bush, which respectively housed regular soldiers and the special military police called the Auxiliaries. In addition, the DMP were stationed at Rathmines and Donnybrook police stations, with another force of DMP stationed at Nullamore to protect Lord Glenavy. [193]

Having outlined the situation facing the IRA in south Dublin during the War of Independence we can now review the conduct of the war by both sides in Milltown.

---

189 BMH, WS1773, p. 7.

190 BMH, WS1773, pp. 6–8.

191 BMH, WS1773, p. 6.

192 BMH, WS1773, p. 8

193 BMH, WS1773, p. 9.

SEPARATING FACT FROM FICTION – ATTACKS AT CLASSON'S BRIDGE AND MILLTOWN BRIDGE

Local historian and Dundrum native J. Nolan, who was born in about 1910, recorded valuable information about the 1916 Rising and the War of Independence in the Dundrum and Rathfarnham districts.[194] He had this to say about the activities of the Doyle family of Milltown:

> *Patrick Doyle Road commemorates the father of a large family who left his home in Milltown to participate in the Rising of 1916, and became a member of the garrison at Clanwilliam House where he was killed. His eldest son who was known as 'Tower' took part in the ambush at Classon's Bridge. The bridge was blown up as a lorry of Black-and-Tans was crossing and the lorry ended up in the river [Dodder] bed, where the occupants were picked out by the riflemen overhead. 'Tower' was killed later, and he is buried in Churchtown cemetery [Taney] with four other young men killed during those times. Patrick Doyle is also remembered by a holy water font in the Church of the Assumption [Ss Gall and Columbanus Catholic Church, Milltown].*[195]

Nolan's information about Patrick Doyle is accurate, but what about the ambush at Classon's Bridge? Even allowing for press censorship, the newspapers do not record any disturbances at Classon's Bridge whatsoever. So, what really happened at Classon's Bridge during the War of Independence? Having reviewed the archives of General Richard Mulcahy, the Irish military pension records and the British military archives in the National Archives in Kew, London, it is possible to piece together the events with much greater accuracy than they were recalled by Nolan.

Patrick J. Brennan's statement made to the Bureau of Military History refers to three separate incidents which occurred at Classon's Bridge during the War of Independence.[196] One night in April 1921 the IRA was attempting to demolish Classon's Bridge when they were surprised by a military convoy which had penetrated the IRA's defensive cordon 'owing to the defection of one of our outposts'. According to Brennan, the military attacked the IRA volunteers with machine guns and in the ensuing gunfight that lasted over an hour one IRA member and three British military personnel were injured.[197]

Separately, IRA veteran Andrew McDonnell recalled the same attack in his witness statement:

> *Paddy Brennan moved about with an armed patrol in the hope of meeting up with a military lorry, and met a load of Black and Tans on Classon's Bridge, Milltown. He had with him Dick Doyle (better known as Father), Maurice Kenny (Big Maurice) and Jimmy Lynch. As the tender came on to the bridge, our patrol opened fire and it was returned at once by the Tans. Maurice was hit in the leg, and was carried under cover by Brennan while Dick Doyle kept the enemy at bay, knocking out a few before they decided to get away.*[198]

Some years later when applying for their service pensions, Bridget and Ellen Lambert (by then Mrs Doran and Mrs Stynes) confirmed that Maurice Kenny was brought to their house for first aid before evacuation the following day. During the War of Independence Bridget and

---

194 Nolan, *Changing Faces*, pp. 20–2, 167–8.

195 Nolan, *Changing Faces*, p. 56.

196 BMH, WS1773, pp. 17, 25, 27.

197 BMH, WS1773, p. 17.

198 BMH, WS1768, witness statement of Andrew McDonnell, p. 56.

Ellen lived in a safe house behind Old Bridge House in Concrete, Milltown. The house, probably one of Field's Cottages, was specifically used as a safe house because it was hidden behind Old Bridge House and could not be seen from the main road (Map 20). The Lambert sisters stored arms and fed and sheltered volunteers on the run practically every night. Nonetheless, the day after the attack in which Kenny was wounded the safe house was raided by the military as part of a round-up of the district.[199]

The IRA's Chief of Staff diary records for 16 May 1921 note that a road obstruction was placed at Milltown and 'Constables sniped'.[200] This may refer to a second attack on Classon's Bridge but it most likely refers to activity carried out by the IRA at Milltown Bridge. According to an undated and unnamed newspaper cutting among the Mulcahy papers, an attack took place on Saturday night, 14 May 1921, when:

> *large pieces of masonry were broken from the parapet of the bridge crossing the River Dodder at Milltown and strewn across the road. Traffic to and from Dundrum had to make a wide detour. The obstructions were removed during yesterday.*[201]

The partial demolition of Milltown Bridge was not mentioned by Patrick Brennan or Andrew McDonnell in their witness statements so that incident may have been carried out by a different IRA unit or when the men were absent from active duty.

In June 1921 – the exact date was not given by Brennan – an attempt was made by the IRA to demolish Milltown Bridge but this was again interrupted by the military who arrived in two lorries from Milltown Road. The IRA sentries at the Nine Arches Bridge engaged in a firefight with the soldiers while the demolition party made their escape.[202] Rather confusingly, two pages later Brennan's witness statement provides information about another attack on British forces near Classon's Bridge, this time with the specific date of (Saturday) 4 June 1921.[203] It is thus not clear if the two separately recorded incidents occurred on the same night at one or both bridges (Brennan's memory may be at fault given the passage of time between the events and his statement).

In any event, according to Brennan, on 4 June the IRA attacked a mixed party of Auxiliaries and Black and Tans in lorries near Classon's Bridge, wounding several at no cost to themselves.[204] This attack on Classon's Bridge was reported to IRA headquarters (Chief of Staff, Richard Mulcahy), where it was recorded, 'Auxilliaries attacked [at] Classon's Bridge'.[205] This engagement was also mentioned very briefly in the newspapers, that it happened on Sunday 5 June, and that there were no casualties suffered by the Auxiliaries.[206]

---

199 MAI, MSP34REF57178, sworn evidence of Mrs Bridget Doran (née Lambert); MSP34REF56696, sworn evidence of Mrs Ellen Stynes (née Lambert).

200 UCD Archives, Mulcahy Papers, P7/A/16, pdf 39.

201 UCD Archives, Mulcahy Papers, P7/A/54, pdf 28.

202 BMH, WS1773, p. 23.

203 BMH, WS1773, p. 27.

204 BMH, WS1773, p. 27.

205 UCD Archives, Mulcahy Papers, P7/A/16, pdf 33 and P7/A/57, pdf 6.

206 UCD Archives, Mulcahy Papers, P7/A/55, pdf 50. The discrepancy between the 4 and 5 June dates is explained by the fact that the engagement took place during the night of 4/5 June.

Finally, Brennan stated that a second attempt later in June 1921 was made to demolish Classon's Bridge, and this time the IRA were successful:

> *Demolition of Classon's Bridge, Milltown completed after many operations over a period of three months. On at least four occasions the work was interrupted by approach and subsequent engagement of enemy forces. A new bridge was built in 1926.*[207]

Evidence later sworn by Milltown IRA volunteer and 1916 veteran, Edward Leonard, states that he was on outpost duty 'the night they destroyed Milltown Bridge'.[208] Leonard's evidence must be treated with caution in this regard because Milltown Bridge was never destroyed, although it was damaged on at least one occasion. Furthermore, Leonard was on lookout duty and so he could not have been at the epicentre of the demolition works. Edward Leonard's brother Patrick was also active in the IRA during the War of Independence. In civilian life Patrick Leonard was a van driver in the Dartry Dye Works. According to a testimonial on his military pension application file, Patrick Leonard took part in ambushes at Windy Arbour and Milltown and Classon's Bridges. Leonard's referee, Michael Wedick, deposed that 'I know he took part in an ambush on enemy forces at Windy Arbour Dundrum', also in 'the destruction of Milltown and Classon's Bridges'. Wedick also stated that Patrick Leonard was one of about 15 volunteers who were active in 1920, although acknowledging that Patrick Leonard was not a full-time volunteer. However, Wedick was interned from November 1920 to December 1921 and so, critically, he had to rely on hearsay evidence concerning events at Milltown and Classon's Bridges.[209]

The only evidence about the Classon's Bridge attacks that could be found from the British military side is contained in the National Archives of the United Kingdom at Kew, London. Among their archives is a typed report prepared by Lieutenant Taylor of the Auxiliary division of the RIC on 5 June 1921, which contains the following statement:

> *I beg to report that, acting on information received at about 0.30 hours, 5th inst., I proceeded with two tenders of Cadets towards Classon Bridge – near Dartry Dye Works. On arrival at Dartry road the party debussed and scouts were sent forward, the remainder of the party following close behind. The former, numbering four, succeeded in getting to within thirty or forty yards of the enemy working party before being observed. They were fired upon by sentries, posted at the end of the bridge, after being challenged, and replied to it. A Lewis gun with the main party of cadets was brought into action and fire directed at a range of about seventy yards at the bridge. The enemy quickly decamped, leaving behind a large number of tools and several raincoats. So far as is known, we inflicted no casualties, and suffered none ourselves. The whole of the party engaged in digging, succeeded in getting clear away over the Golf Links situated nearby. From inquiries made, it would appear that the work was commenced at about 10.45 p.m. The bridge had been dug up in several places to a depth of some eight or nine inches, and part of the parapets on either side destroyed, but was still passable. Search of the pockets of one of the raincoats taken, revealed several letters belonging to Charles Buckley, believed to be working for Thomas Kavanagh of Rosy Hill Dairy, Milltown. A letter from C.C. 6th Bn., IRA, Dublin Brigade, addressed to Thomas Kavanagh referring to the employment of Buckley was also found. Nothing else was discovered.*[210]

207 BMH, WS1773, p. 25.

208 MAI, MSP34REF458, sworn statement of Edward Leonard of 277 Farranboley Cottages, Windy Arbour, 21 January 1935.

209 MAI, 24SP671, pdf 13, pp. 18–21.

210 National Archives, Kew, WO 35/85/5664.

Plate 23. Classon's Bridge, Milltown, showing the integration of the eighteenth- and twentieth-century structures (author's collection)

Piecing all of the evidence together, it seems pretty clear that Taylor's report relates to the unsuccessful attempt on the night of 4/5 June 1921 by Brennan and his IRA comrades to demolish Classon's Bridge. Brennan's and Taylor's accounts differ on the question of British casualties. Separately, Brennan stated that the IRA eventually succeeded in destroying the bridge later on in the month of June 1921.[211] In reality, Classon's Bridge was never completely destroyed. This fact can be definitively proven in a number of different ways. During the Horse Show week of 1922, the hackney car marathon was reported to have passed over Classon's Bridge en route to the RDS.[212] In April 1923, the short-lived *Rathmines Free Press* newspaper published an article on the River Dodder. Its reporter stated that 'Classon's Bridge ... is probably the oldest bridge on the Dodder. It is still in perfect condition'.[213] In 1928 the old bridge was repaired and widened incorporating the three arches of the old bridge, an arrangement borne out of economy that still exists today over 90 years later (Pl. 23).[214] A plaque on the pedestrian parapet on the bridge states as follows: 'Classon's Bridge Widened 1928 J A Ryan County Surveyor.'[215]

211 BMH, WS1773, p. 25.

212 *Freeman's Journal*, 11 August 1922, p. 8.

213 *Rathmines Free Press*, 14 April 1923, p. 8.

214 *Irish Times*, 16 October 1928, p. 4; *Wicklow People*, 19 January 1929, p. 10.

215 On 7 March 1928 Rathmines UDC voted to contribute £500 towards the shared costs of 'reconstructing' Classon's Bridge with Dublin County Council: Dublin City Archives, UDC papers, UDC/1/Min 1/10, Rathmines UDC Minute Book, vol. 10, 1927–30, p. 89.

In the end the issue turns on how the various protagonists perceived the attacks at Classon's Bridge and their roles in them. All of the accounts agree that the *modus operandi* used by the IRA volunteers was to post sentries on the roads leading to Classon's Bridge while the other operatives attempted by hand – despite Nolan's account no explosives were ever used – to render the bridge unpassable by digging holes on its road surface and knocking down the parapet walls. The sole British account confirms that the IRA were unable to finish the job on the night of 4/5 June 1921. It is quite possible that the volunteers were finally successful in making the bridge totally unusable for vehicular traffic on completion of their final uninterrupted attack later in June 1921. To that extent, therefore, the IRA succeeded in destroying Classon's Bridge. Once the Truce came into force on 11 July 1921 the relevant authorities could carry out remedial repairs to the bridge before the more permanent reconstruction works of 1928 were put in place. What remains unexplained, and thus more puzzling, is why the IRA went to so much trouble to destroy Classon's Bridge in May/June 1921 when, less than half a mile away, the British forces could cross the Dodder unhindered over the main bridge in Milltown village onto the Dundrum Road.

Several years later, when local IRA veterans were applying for military service pensions some of them referred in their witness statements to the destruction of Classon's and Milltown bridges.[216] This can be explained by the fact that the applicants probably felt the need to exaggerate their military activities to increase their chances of securing a pension; after all, destroying a bridge conveys a much stronger impression than merely damaging it, which is what actually occurred at Classon's Bridge.

COUNTER INTELLIGENCE OPERATIONS

Counter intelligence was vital to all of the protagonists in the War of Independence. According to Patrick Brennan, on several occasions the IRA apprehended British soldiers and their girlfriends along the banks of the River Dodder at Lambert's Lane, which was close to Classon's Bridge on the south bank of the River Dodder opposite The Dropping Well pub, and which was a popular courting spot. The IRA was of the opinion that the soldiers were in fact spying 'in the guise of harmless courting', and so they were held up, ordered to undress, and sent back to barracks 'minus all clothing except trousers and shirt'.[217]

In June 1921 the IRA attempted to stop the civilian occupants of a motorcycle and sidecar on the Lower Churchtown Road close to the entrance to Milltown Golf Club, whom they suspected of being enemy personnel. The sidecar passenger took out a revolver and shot one of the IRA men, wounding him, before the motorcycle sped away to safety, its occupants apparently unharmed despite being fired at by the other IRA men.[218]

Local intelligence almost certainly played a part in several acts of sabotage which took place at the Dublin Laundry Company at Milltown and the Dartry Dye Works, Upper Rathmines, in April and May 1921 respectively.[219] On 9 April six men of the IRA's 'G' Company, 4th Battalion raided the Dartry Dye works and destroyed 300 pairs of military knee breech-

216 BMH, MSP34REF458, sworn statement of Edward Leonard, 21 January 1935; MAI, 24SP671, Patrick Leonard, testimony of Michael Wedick.

217 BMH, WS1773, pp. 17–18. Lambert's lane still exists and forms part of the laneway to Riversdale farmhouse beside Milltown Golf Club.

218 BMH, WS1773, p. 27.

219 UCD Archives, Mulcahy Papers, P7/A/39, pdf 75, 132.

es, which had been sent there from Portobello Barracks.[220]

The following month, the IRA entered the Dartry Dye Works and seized 600 khaki military uniforms which Dublin Castle had sent there to be dyed RIC blue, for use by the Black and Tans. The IRA set the bundle of clothes alight with petrol and benzine but the fire attracted the attention of a party of Auxiliaries who happened to be passing by. A 'sharp engagement' ensued following which the IRA escaped across the River Dodder.[221] The IRA continued their activity on a weekly basis until the military authorities stopped sending their clothing to these suburban laundries.[222] Milltown IRA volunteers, James Darcy and Michael Murray, took part in at least one of these acts of sabotage.[223]

MILITARY RAIDS

The IRA's attacks at Classon's Bridge and the Dartry Dye Works inevitably provoked a reaction and reprisals by the British forces, typically in the form of house-to-house searches by the military who were looking for hidden arms or for men on the run.

Milltown native Mrs Mary Long (née Doyle) recounted to the author the terrifying ordeal experienced by her mother, Maureen Kearns (born in about 1912), during a military raid. One night in 1920 or 1921 the Kearns's house on Milltown main street was raided by the Black and Tans as part of a larger raid on the village. The raid took place when little Maureen was in bed. While the raid was taking place and before the soldiers entered their house, Maureen was given her father's gold fob watch to keep safe under her bedclothes. Eventually the soldiers arrived at the door and burst into their home. Maureen was shaking in terror as the soldiers threw the household furniture and its contents on the floor while searching for arms and valuables. Luckily, the soldiers did not interfere with the children's bedclothes and so the watch remained safe with Maureen.[224]

The trauma caused by such incidents was not restricted to a few unfortunate families. These types of experiences during the War of Independence were widespread, and they entered into the wider Dublin community's consciousness, especially among children, as the following rhyme proves:

Tramp, tramp, tramp the boys are marching,
Cheer up the Bobby's at the door,
If you do not let him in,
He will burst the door in,
And you'll never see your daddy anymore.[225]

Anne Kennedy, who was born in Windy Arbour in 1921, vividly recalls her father speaking of his fear of the 'Black and Tans':

220 UCD Archives, Mulcahy Papers, P7/A/39, pdf 75.

221 BMH, WS1773, p. 21. Fourteen months later, the RIC were awarded £511 in compensation for 350 pairs of pantaloons destroyed in the attack at Dartry: *Freeman's Journal*, 10 June 1921, p. 8.

222 BMH, WS1773, p. 17.

223 MAI, 24SP1779, James Darcy, testimony of Arthur Keogh; MAI, 24SP2053, Michael Murray, testimony of Andrew Cullen.

224 Interviews with Mary Long (née Doyle), formerly of no. 2 Milltown village, on 22 February 2017 and 5 January 2018.

225 Nolan, *Changing Faces*, p. 21.

Plate 24. British military raid on Milltown Park, 21 February 1921 (courtesy of the Jesuit Archives)

> *My father used to say the he was coming up Rosy Hill [i.e. the hill beyond Milltown Bridge on the Dundrum Road – Map 20] – I always remember this story – he was coming up Rosy Hill and he heard the Black and Tans lorry coming. And I remember him saying the hairs stood on the back of his neck with the fright and wondering were they going to shoot him.*[226]

Probably the largest military raid in Milltown during the War of Independence took place during the early hours of 21 February 1921 when the Jesuit headquarters at Milltown Park was searched for individuals wanted by the Dublin Castle authorities (Pl. 24). The military force, estimated to have numbered 250 soldiers, entered Milltown Park at 3 a.m. in a convoy of about a dozen lorries and three armoured cars. All of the priests, staff, laity who were on retreat and the residents of nearby Milltown Colonnade were corralled into the chapel and held there for several hours while the soldiers carried out an extensive search of the large institution.[227] According to most of the newspaper reports the authorities were looking for Michael Collins as part of their search of Milltown Park but, despite failing to find Collins, they arrested an unnamed Dublin official who had been on retreat.[228] It transpired that the arrested individual, a Mr J. Martin, had been

226 Valerie Cox, *Growing Up With Ireland: A century of memories from our oldest and wisest citizens* (Dublin, 2019), p. 111. The lorry was probably on its way to, or coming from, the police barracks in Dundrum village.

227 *Morning Telegraph*, 21 February 1921, p. 1; *Evening Herald*, 21 February 1921, p. 1; *Evening Telegraph*, 21 February 1921, p. 1; *Freeman's Journal*, 22 February 1921, p. 4; *Irish Times*, 22 February 1921, p. 5.

228 *Evening Herald*, 21 February 1921, p. 1; *Evening Telegraph*, 21 February 1921, p. 1; *Freeman's Journal*, 22 February 1921, p. 4.

wanted by the authorities since the previous November and had until then evaded arrest.[229]

Although the conduct of the troops at Milltown Park was reported to have been 'business like, brusque but not discourteous', the interrogation process was a tense occasion for everyone, as made explicitly clear in the *Freeman's Journal*:

> *In the dining hall the Vice-Rector read out the names of the Community, servants and farmhands, who were scrutinised by an intelligence officer and allowed to pass out. The names and addresses of those on retreat were next demanded but the Vice-Rector did not give them. The 24 men on retreat were then questioned as to names, addresses, business, and employer's name. One question asked was, 'Are you a loyalist?'*[230]

Before the soldiers left, cigarettes, personal articles, a razor and a small sum of money were reported as missing to the officer in charge.[231]

Sometimes the Auxiliaries were sent out on raids armed with inaccurate information. On the night of 3 April 1921 Auxiliaries stationed at Portobello Barracks were ordered to search a house called Roebuck Villa in Milltown. When the military convoy got to Milltown at 11.00 p.m., they could not find the house and so they returned to barracks empty handed.[232]

The long-term consequences for the IRA volunteers who had taken part in prison hunger strikes or who had to go on the run to avoid capture were sometimes fatal. Sleeping rough outdoors or in damp barns during all weathers and surviving on infrequent poor-quality food also took its toll on the men's health. Former 1916 Rising participant Peter Shortall had gone on hunger strike with Thomas Ashe in Mountjoy prison in 1920 and had suffered serious damage to his body as a result.[233] By the spring of 1925 Shortall was in the last stages of TB and in financial distress when his case was taken up by Sister Padua of Mount St Anne's convent in Milltown. Sister Padua was a sister-in-law of the President of the Executive Council of the Irish Free State, W.T. Cosgrave, and she used her connections successfully to procure £25 from the Dáil Special Fund for Shortall, who lived in Castlewood Place, Rathmines.[234]

Similarly, Dundrum 1916 and IRA veteran Alex Cullen, who would have fought with, or known, IRA men from Milltown during the War of Independence, was terminally ill with TB when he sought financial help from Batt O'Connor TD in December 1924. As Cullen simply put it, 'Should some assistance not be forthcoming, I must become a burthen [*sic*] on the rates [i.e. enter the workhouse], as I refuse to be a burthen [*sic*] on my people'.[235] O'Connor passed Cullen's letter on to Sister Padua in Milltown, and she managed to obtain three successive special grants for Cullen totalling £60 during 1925 before he died.[236]

---

229 National Archives, Kew, WO 35/83/203, daily raid report by Major Ritchie, 21 February 1921.

230 *Freeman's Journal*, 22 February 1921, p. 4.

231 *Freeman's Journal*, 22 February 1921, p. 4.

232 National Archives, Kew, WO 35/73/159, 3 April 1921.There were several houses in the neighbouring townland of Roebuck with 'Roebuck' in their name, but none were called Roebuck Villa.

233 *Sunday Independent*, 11 April 1920, p. 1; 18 April 1920, p. 5.

234 NAI, Department of the Taoiseach, S 7645, file for Peter Shortall, Grant from the Dáil Special Fund.

235 NAI, Department of the Taoiseach, S 7696, file for Alex Cullen, Grant from the Dáil Special Fund.

236 NAI, Department of the Taoiseach, S 7696, file for Alex Cullen.

SEIZURE OF MAIL BAGS AND ATTACKS ON THE RAILWAY

Disruption of postal services and seizure of mail bags was another tactic used by the IRA to discommode the civil authorities and to uncover or intimidate potential police informants. The relative isolation of Milltown railway station meant that any trains stooping there were vulnerable to attack. At 5 p.m. on Tuesday 17 May 1921 a number of armed men held up the train driver of the Bray to Harcourt Street train and took four post bags, which they placed in a waiting car and drove off. The getaway car, which had been stolen from Milltown Golf Club, was later returned to the club.[237] On 30 May 1921 the *Irish Independent* reported that the DMP found two mail bags at Milltown post office labelled, 'Censored by I.R.A.' The post was believed to have been stolen from the trains at Milltown earlier in the month.[238] Three weeks later two more bags of censored mail were found outside Milltown post office.[239] Milltown IRA man Michael Murray among others took part in these raids.[240] According to one IRA volunteer who was active in the Milltown district during this time, 'the mails produced some startling information from people least suspected'.[241] The IRA veteran, Andrew McDonnell, did not elaborate on what action was taken against those people.

RAIDING FOR ARMS

The IRA was constantly in need of weapons and ammunition with which to carry out its military campaign. The large number of big houses in the vicinity of Milltown and beyond in south Dublin, most of which were inhabited by unionists, became targets for raids by the local volunteer companies during the War of Independence. Milltown native Michael Byrne recalled taking part in raids on about 20 houses in Milltown which the IRA volunteers thought contained arms.[242] Another Milltown volunteer, Michael Murray, also took part in these raids.[243]

CIVILIAN ATTITUDES TO SINN FÉIN AND THE IRA CAMPAIGN

The discussion thus far has centred on the military campaign waged between the IRA and the British military forces and the RIC. It is worth considering how much support for the IRA existed among the non-combatant civilian population living in Milltown. Although there is only a small amount of direct evidence available, the impression formed from that evidence is that a substantial majority of the people of Milltown village supported or were sympathetic towards the republican cause and the IRA campaign against the British. Reference has previously been made to the fracas that occurred between Sinn Féin and the police at a boy scouts' parade in Milltown village on 14 October 1917. Support for the republican cause had, if anything, increased three years later when, on Thursday and Saturday 9 and 11 September 1920, special masses were said for the temporal and spiritual welfare of Cork Lord Mayor Terence MacSwiney, who was on hunger strike.[244] When veteran IRA volunteer, Patrick J. Brennan, was compil-

237 UCD Archives, Mulcahy Papers, P/A/54, p. 34, undated and unnamed newspaper cutting; *Freeman's Journal*, 19 May 1921, p. 6.

238 *Irish Independent*, 30 May 1921, p. 6.

239 *Irish Independent*, 19 June 1921, p. 1.

240 MAI, 24SP2053, Michael Murray, testimonials by Major MacNeill and Andrew Cullen.

241 BMH, WS1768, p. 70, witness statement of Andrew McDonnell.

242 MAI, MSP34REF35241, sworn statement of Michael Byrne 13 September 1937, p. 4.

243 MAI, 24SP2053.

244 *Evening Herald*, Thursday 9 September 1920, p. 1; *Freeman's Journal*, 13 September 1920, p. 6.

ing his witness statement in 1962, he specifically paid tribute to Mrs Tierney of Milltown Hill and Rev. Mother Flanagan of Mount St Anne's convent, for their valuable assistance received by way of meals and, or, shelter.[245]

The night curfew imposed by the military during the War of Independence greatly affected the laundry's business. This was because everyone had to be indoors in their own home by 9 p.m., which meant that there was no social entertainment and consequently few stiff shirts and collars which needed laundering.[246] The destruction of the military uniforms in May and June 1921 at the Dublin Laundry and Dartry Dye Works must also have adversely affected the laundry's business. It is likely that the recent upheavals coupled with the still uncertain outcome of the treaty negotiations were behind the decision made in late 1921 by the laundry's long-serving manager, Sidney Foster, to leave both his job and Ireland. On his last day at work, 23 November 1921, the staff and employees put on a tea and concert for Foster.[247] Given all these difficulties, it was perfectly understandable why businessmen like Robert Benson (the managing director of the Dublin Laundry Company and a Milltown resident), a longstanding councillor on the Rathmines UDC with a unionist outlook, would have abhorred Sinn Féin, the IRA's military campaign, and republicanism in general.

Members of the the small congregation of St Philip's church on Temple Road, the centre of the Church of Ireland parish of Milltown, were quite naturally very apprehensive about recent developments and what the future held for them. In its annual report and accounts for the year ending 31 December 1919, the Select Vestry noted that:

> *Our Parish has had unbroken peace and quietness, but our country, although abounding with material prosperity and plentifulness, has not escaped the epidemic of lawlessness and crime – the aftermath of the Great War.*[248]

Twelve months later the Select Vestry very briefly summarised its experience of 1920 in the following terms:

> *The past year has been one of great difficulty and danger in our beloved land, and although our Parish has been, so far, immune from actual strife, the effect of the awful upheaval throughout the country is reflected in many ways in our Parochial work.*[249]

The Protestant community's heightened sense of insecurity during these turbulent times saw them of necessity adopt a much lower profile than hitherto had been the case in the confident Edwardian era. Thus, a wedding notice in *Irish Society and Social Review* advised that the wedding of Miss A.M. Leachman of Rydalmount 'will take place quietly' at St Philip's Church, Milltown on 8 June 1920.[250]

245 BMH, WS1773, p. 29. Mrs Tierney lived in Milltown Lodge on the Dundrum Road, not Milltown Hill as stated by Brennan.

246 Hearn, *Thomas Edmondson*, p. 173.

247 Hearn, *Thomas Edmondson*, p. 182.

248 RCB Library, Dublin, D6/64, Report of the Select Vestry of St Philip's for the year 1919.

249 RCB Library, Dublin, D6/64, Report of the Select Vestry of St Philip's for the year 1920.

250 *Irish Society and Social Review*, 5 June 1920, p. 3.

LOCAL ELECTIONS OF JANUARY AND JUNE 1920

Local government elections in Ireland, which had been postponed during the Great War, were scheduled to take place in January 1920. In an attempt to mitigate the electoral strength of Sinn Féin the British government introduced proportional representation to the voting process, so that unionist and IPP minority candidates would have some chance of being represented on the boards of local authorities.[251] In the Rathmines township there were 21 outgoing councillors (of whom seven were not seeking re-election), now spread across four electoral areas.[252] Milltown village lay in No. 1 East Ward, which had an electorate of 2,673. Seven candidates – three Unionist, three Sinn Féin and one IPP – were seeking election to four vacant seats.[253] Milltown village was a Sinn Féin stronghold and the party had its committee rooms in 11 Milltown village.[254] Sinn Féin's election manifesto was blunt and to the point:

> *We are vehemently opposed to sectarian bigotry as the enemy of justice, efficiency, and of the fair fame of the Irish Nation. We shall do all in our power to abolish it from Rathmines, where under the late Council, it undoubtedly existed.*[255]

The three Sinn Féin candidates for the Rathmines East No. 1 and Milltown Ward also issued an appeal to the voters of that district based on 'the things you want'. These consisted of six items, namely, Irish Freedom and the Irish Language, a living wage, improved housing, good value for and honest expenditure of ratepayers' money, the support of Irish manufacturers and the abolition of sectarian bigotry.[256]

Polling took place on 15 January and was particularly brisk in Rathmines.[257] In the No. 1 East Ward the total vote polled was 1,974, resulting in the quota required for election being 386 votes. The polarisation of Irish politics was evidenced by the fact that the first preference votes cast were 892 for Sinn Féin, 832 for unionists and 202 for the nationalist candidate, who was not elected.[258] The unionist candidate, William Carruthers, topped the poll with 494 first preference votes followed by Sinn Féin's Dr Kathleen Lynn with 427 first preference votes. Sinn Féin's James Dwyer was elected on the third count with 410 votes, with the final seat being filled by the unionist John Russell on the fourth count with 429 votes.[259] Outgoing Rathmines UDC councillor and managing director of the Dublin Laundry Company, Robert Benson, topped the poll in the No. 2 West Ward with 508 votes.[260]

Overall, 12 Unionist, nine Sinn Féin and one Nationalist (Mrs Tom Kettle) candidates were

---

251 Ó Matiú, *Dublin's Suburban Towns*, p. 198.

252 *Dublin Evening Telegraph*, 6 January 1920, p. 1.

253 *Dublin Evening Telegraph*, 17 January 1920, p. 5.

254 *Irish Independent*, 15 January 1920, p. 2.

255 *Irish Independent*, 12 January 1920, p. 2.

256 Election Handbill dated 15 January 1920 (NLI, EPH C77).

257 *Dublin Evening Mail*, 15 January 1920, p. 4.

258 *Dublin Evening Mail*, 16 January 1920, p. 3.

259 *Dublin Evening Telegraph*, 17 January 1920, p. 5.

260 Ó Matiú, *Dublin's Suburban Towns*, p. 199.

elected to the new Rathmines UDC.[261] This was the first time that the unionist hegemony in Rathmines had been broken – the last attempt by nationalists to win seats on the council in January 1914 had been a total failure.[262] Unsurprisingly, therefore, relationships between the Unionist and the Sinn Féin councillors were hostile at the first sitting of the new council on 30 January 1920, when the Unionists used their majority to re-appoint Robert Benson as chairman and appoint one of their number to the vice-chair.[263]

Elections for county councils, rural district councils and Poor Law guardians took place in June 1920 and further consolidated Sinn Féin in local politics throughout Dublin. Many of the new local authority boards such as the Rathdown Guardians passed resolutions of allegiance to Dáil Éireann, much to the disgust of the unionist minority.[264] Sinn Féin activist Eamonn Martin was elected chairman of the Rathdown RDC on 17 June 1920 when the new council met for the first time after the local elections.[265] Martin, who lived in Churchtown, was also elected as a member of Dublin County Council and the Rathdown Board of Guardians. Inevitably he was targeted by the Dublin Castle authorities and his business premises in the city together with his home in Churchtown were raided by the military three months later, on 9 September 1920.[266]

FROM TRUCE TO TREATY

It is very apparent that the IRA's activities in Milltown took place during a short intense period in the late spring and early summer of 1921. The peak of the War of Independence in Dublin came in May 1921 during which time 107 separate operations were carried out by the IRA's Dublin Brigade, more than any other month of the war.[267] Behind the scenes, international pressure was being brought to bear on the British to reach a settlement with the republicans and simultaneously efforts were being made by the King and to broker a truce.[268] During this time too, the local Dublin IRA units were continuously active in their attacks on the British forces and RIC right up until the Truce of 11 July 1921 was agreed. For example, three days previously, in the middle of the afternoon of Wednesday 8 July, the IRA had attacked a lorry of armed RIC at Windy Arbour, forcing them to drive off hurriedly 'firing indiscriminately'.[269] During the period of the Truce and while negotiations were going on with the British, the IRA continued to drill and procure arms in case conflict with the British resumed. An extensive training camp was established in the Dublin mountains at Barnaculia where all officers of the 6th Battalion received intensive training over several weeks.[270]

By all accounts, the five-month period from the Truce to the signing of the Anglo-Irish Treaty on 6 December 1921 seems to have been peaceful as far as Milltown was concerned save for one

261 Ó Matiú, *Dublin's Suburban Towns*, p. 199.

262 *Irish Independent*, 17 January 1914, p. 5.

263 *Irish Independent*, 31 January 1920, pp. 4, 6; *Dublin Evening Telegraph*, 30 January 1920, p. 16.

264 *Irish Independent*, 9 June 1920, p. 6; 18 June 1920, p. 6; *Wicklow People*, 12 June 1920, p. 8; 19 June 1920, p. 6.

265 *Wicklow People*, Saturday 19 June 1920, p. 6.

266 *Wicklow People*, 11 September 1920, p. 5.

267 Grayson, *Dublin's Great Wars*, p. 291.

268 Grayson, *Dublin's Great Wars*, p. 297.

269 BMH, WS1773, p. 28; UCD Archives, Mulcahy Papers, P7/A/16, pdf 21, P7/A/56, pdf 34 and P7/A/57, pdf 43.

270 BMH, WS1773, p. 28.

incident. On 7 November 1921 two armed and masked men held up the guard and station master at Milltown railway station and robbed the cash box which contained the takings from various stations on the Harcourt Street to Bray line.[271]

CIVIL WAR

The creation of the Irish Free State with dominion status on a partitioned island led, in the absence of the long-fought-for 32-county Irish Republic, to irreconcilable differences of opinion among Sinn Féin politicians and IRA volunteers alike. In military terms, as far as Dublin was concerned the critical developments were that Dublin Castle and the majority of the army barracks gradually vacated by the British forces in Dublin during 1922 were taken over by pro-Treaty forces, which became the nucleus of the new National Army of the Irish Free State.[272]

Clonskeagh Castle had lain empty since the death of Captain Robert Wade Thompson in February 1919 apart from a short time during the War of Independence when it was occupied by Major Fitzjohn.[273] The vacant property was subsequently taken over briefly by the National Army on 1 April 1922 and became the headquarters of the 2nd Dublin Brigade, 2nd Eastern Division until the end of May, when the building was vacated by the National Army.[274] In the same month, Private Nicholas Doyle of The Gardens, Milltown village died from fatal wounds accidentally received while he was stationed at Wicklow Gaol, which was being used as a barracks by the National Army. Tragically, the rifle which accidentally discharged a bullet hitting Doyle was being handled by his best friend Private Michael Bentley, who was subsequently exonerated at a military inquiry which took place in Clonskeagh Castle. Nicholas Doyle was buried in Taney graveyard accompanied by a firing party from Clonskeagh Castle.[275]

During the spring and summer of 1922 Rathfarnham RIC barracks was occupied by anti-Treaty forces. At the beginning of May a party of pro-Treaty troops quartered at Clonskeagh Castle proceeded to Rathfarnham barracks to recover two stolen cars. After negotiations, the anti-Treaty men gave up the two cars and a third touring car which had also been taken and which had arrived back to base just as the pro-Treaty troops were about to leave.[276]

On the political side, the general election held on 18 June 1922 resulted in a very decisive vote in favour of the Treaty in County Dublin, with only one anti-Treaty TD being elected for that constituency. Nationally, the victory of the pro-Treaty side in the June 1922 general election did not prevent the onset of violent conflict between the two sides, however. The artillery bombardment of the Four Courts on 28 June 1922 by pro-Treaty forces (who were under pressure from the British government to evict the anti-Treaty forces) marked the

---

271 *Dublin Evening Telegraph*, 7 November 1921, p. 1.

272 Grayson, *Dublin's Great Wars*, p. 302.

273 BMH, WS956, witness statement of George White, pdf 8–9; BMH, WS535, witness statement of James Francis Hughes, pdf 8.

274 *Northern Whig*, 13 February 1919, p. 4; *Evening Herald*, 31 March 1922, p. 1; *Freeman's Journal*, 29 May 1922, p. 9; NAI, FIN/COMP/2/6/213, financial compensation claim of Colonel Thomas William Thompson of Ditton Hill, Surrey. Thompson claimed £3,889 in reparation for damage to the castle while occupied by the National Army. He was awarded £390. Robert Wade Thompson's children never returned to Clonskeagh Castle after their father's death and the property was eventually sold to the building firm G. & T. Crampton in 1934.

275 *Dublin Evening Telegraph*, 15 May 1922, p. 1; *Irish Independent*, 15 May 1922, p. 7; *Freeman's Journal*, 16 May 1922, pp. 3, 6; 17 May 1922, p. 6; *Weekly Irish Times*, 20 May 1922, p. 4.

276 *Freeman's Journal*, 4 May 1922, p. 6.

beginning of military conflict between the pro- and anti-Treaty sides in Dublin city.[277] Shortly afterwards the three Lambert sisters from Milltown, Bridget, Nellie (Ellen) and Kathleen, whose pre-Treaty republican activities have been discussed earlier in this chapter and who were all members of Cumann na mBan, joined the anti-Treaty forces at Rathfarnham Barracks. Thereafter the sisters helped the anti-Treatyites until, in Nellie's case, she was arrested in February 1923 and interned before being released on 28 September 1923. For several years after the Civil War Bridget and Nellie lived respectively at Old Bridge House and at 17 Farranboley Cottages, Windy Arbour.[278]

It is significant, and perhaps surprising, that Patrick Doyle junior, the eldest son of Patrick Doyle who had died in Clanwilliam House in the 1916 Rising, chose the pro-Treaty side. Given the Doyles' republican pedigree, Patrick junior's example may have persuaded other men and women in Milltown to support the Treaty. Patrick Doyle junior was shot dead by a sniper at Crooksling, County Dublin on 6 July 1922 while serving with the National Army during operations to clear the anti-Treaty forces from the Dublin and Wicklow mountains, and further afield in Blessington.[279] At the time Doyle was killed, Milltown native and 1916 veteran, Alfred Harnett, who had joined the anti-Treaty side, was stationed in Crooksling.[280] Thus six years after fighting together in the 1916 Rising, men from Milltown were shooting at one another, and families and neighbours in Milltown were divided by the Civil War. Patrick Leonard, who lived in Concrete on the south bank of the Dodder at Milltown, supported the pro-Treaty side. He joined the transport section of the National Army in March 1922 as a sergeant where he served for two years.[281] In contrast, Patrick's brother Edward rejected the Treaty and fought with the anti-Treat forces during the Civil War.[282]

Another Milltown 1916 Rising veteran, Michael Byrne, joined the anti-Treaty side when he returned from England in June 1922. Byrne joined an active service unit in the anti-Treatyites which operated in the Foxrock and Stillorgan area, and took part in a raid on Findlaters at Foxrock railway station. Byrne was arrested by the CID in November 1922 and interned until 1924.[283]

For much of 1922 conditions were peaceful in Milltown, save for occasional acts of sabotage by the anti-Treaty forces. For example, on 14 July 1922 an armed man entered a stationary train at Milltown station and destroyed goods in transit from Bray, and in mid-December 1922 three telephone wires in Richmond Avenue South and four wires in Temple Road were cut on two separate nightly occasions.[284] Matters were to take a violent turn for the worse, however, as Milltown prepared for the New Year, 1923.

---

277 Grayson, *Dublin's Great Wars, pp. 302*—3; Dickson, *Dublin: The making of a capital city*, pp. 468–9.

278 MAI, MSP34REF5718, Bridget Doran (née Lambert); MAI, MSP34REF56696, Ellen Stynes (née Lambert).

279 *Freeman's Journal*, Tuesday 11 July 1922, p. 6; John Dorney, *The Civil War in Dublin: The fight for the Irish Capital 1922–1924* (Newbridge, 2017), p. 108.

280 MAI, MSP34REF20800, sworn statement of Alfred Harnett. Harnett was captured by the National Army during a failed attack on Baldonnel Aerodrome and was interned in Hare Park. He was released in November 1923.

281 MAI, 24SP671.

282 MAI, MSP34REF458, sworn statement of Edward Leonard, 21 January 1935.

283 MAI, MSP34REF35241, sworn statement of Michael Byrne. The CID was the Criminal Investigation Department, a plain clothed, armed police unit which was a mainstay of the pro-Treaty forces in Dublin: Dorney, *Civil War in Dublin*, p. 329.

284 NAI, FIN/COMP/2/6/257, financial compensation claim of Grace Cahill; *Freeman's Journal*, 21 December 1922, p. 5.

MURDER OF FRANCIS LALOR

The worst atrocity of the Civil War that took place in the vicinity of Milltown occurred shortly after Christmas 1922. Francis (Frank) Lalor[285] was a young man who worked as an auditor in Plunkett House, the headquarters of the Irish Agricultural Organisation Society.[286] Lalor, a single man aged twenty-six who had grown up in Rugby Road in Ranelagh, was lodging at 6 Castlewood Avenue, Rathmines. Close to midnight on 28 December 1922 two men called to the house and forcibly abducted him. At about 8.30 a.m. the next morning Lalor's body was discovered by two groundsmen employed by Milltown Golf Club a few yards off the Orwell Road on Lambert's Lane (also known as Dan Byrne's Lane). Lalor had been shot several times in the head and abdomen by his abductors. The lane (which still exists) where his corpse was found was then a secluded right of way linking Orwell Road and Classon's Bridge, and ran between the grounds of Milltown Golf Club and Lambert's dairy farm at Riversdale, near Classon's Bridge. An inquest into Lalor's murder was held in Dundrum on 30 December 1922 but neither his father nor his landlord speculated about why Frank was murdered.[287] However, the caretaker at Sir Horace Plunkett's home in Foxrock, Kilteragh (which was later burnt down by anti-Treaty forces), confided in a letter written to Lady Fingal on New Year's day 1923 that, 'I knew all about him [Lalor] and he had been mixed up with a lot of trouble. It was a horrible business.'[288]

Several years after Frank Lalor's death, his mother applied for a dependant's benefit from the Department of Defence in 1932. From investigations made at that time it emerged that Frank had fought in the War of Independence and was an active section commander at the time of the truce in July 1921. His former commanding officer, Joseph O'Connor, advised the authorities that Lalor was on the run when he was abducted and murdered and that he was on duty with the IRA [anti-Treaty forces] at the time of his death. On foot of this information, the Army Pensions Board recommended that Mrs Lalor be awarded a gratuity of £110 and 10*s*, which was subsequently paid to her in 1934. As part of the application process, the Military Service Registration Board issued a posthumous service certificate in respect of Francis Lalor for the period 1917–29 December 1922 with the following concluding statement: 'The Board, from confidential inquiries made, are satisfied that deceased was killed because of his active connection with Oglaigh na h-Eireann.'[289]

According to research by Dublin Civil War historian, John Dorney, Frank Lalor was abducted and killed by an unofficial murder gang in the National Army in reprisal for the murder by anti-Treatyites of Rathmines shopkeeper Séamus Dwyer. There was no proof that Lalor was involved in Dwyer's murder. At the time, Frank Lalor's killing was discussed at a cabinet meeting and referred to General Mulcahy who was absent on military manoeuvres against the anti-Treaty forces, but no further action was apparently taken by the cabinet.[290] A small memorial plaque on the side of the pavement on Orwell Road close to Lambert's Land and

---

285 I have adopted the surname spelling without a 'w' (Lalor) as this spelling was used by Frank's brother in the military service pension application file; other sources spell the surname with a 'w' (Lawlor).

286 *Northern Whig*, 30 December 1922, p. 5.

287 *Freeman's Journal*, 30 December 1922, p. 5; *Irish Times*, 30 December 1922, p. 7; 6 January 1923, p. 2. The Riversdale Lamberts were unrelated to the Lamberts of Old Bridge House.

288 *Seventy Years Young: Memories of Elizabeth, Countess of Fingal told to Pamela Hinckson* (London, 1937, reprinted by Lilliput Press, 1997), p. 416.

289 BMH, DP5250, Francis Lalor, deceased.

290 Dorney, *Civil War in Dublin, pp. 224*–5; UCD Archives, Mulcahy Papers, P7/B/245, pdf 244.

opposite the Russian Embassy recalls Francis Lalor and his violent demise.[291]

The murder of Fank Lalor must have made life very uneasy if not downright terrifying for the non-combatants in the district. At the inquest into Frank Lalor's death, it emerged that the two groundsmen had not gone near the body and had delayed in summoning help because it appears they had been afraid to do so. This explanation was not actually admitted by the men but their discomfiture during questioning at the inquest makes this abundantly clear. Nonetheless, the reluctant witnesses were reprimanded by the coroner for their inaction.[292]

ATTACKS ON HOUSES BY ANTI-TREATY FORCES

As noted earlier, Clonskeagh Castle was occupied briefly by the National Army in the spring of 1922. As the country slid into civil warfare many large houses were burnt down to prevent them being occupied by troops of one side or the other. One such house that fell victim to arson was a large detached house called Errigal, which was situated on the south side of Orwell Road and is now part of the Russian Embassy complex. This house had been derelict for about eighteen months prior to its destruction by anti-Treaty forces. Milltown native Edward Leonard was among the incendiary party, and explained that they burned down the house because 'we got information that the Free State troops were going to occupy it'.[293]

The Chairman of the Free State Senate, James Campbell, Lord Glenavy, was a potential target of the anti-Treatyites during the Civil War. As we have seen, Lord Glenavy lived in a large villa called Nullamore (renamed Glenavy during his residency) opposite Classon's Bridge. During the uneasy period of the truce of July to December 1921, Glenavy had hosted his daughter's wedding reception at Nullamore on 11 October 1921, which displayed a certain degree of insouciance on his part.[294] During the Civil War shots were fired at Nullamore from a distance by anti-Treaty IRA men but without causing any injuries or fatalities.[295] Edward Leonard later confirmed that Lord Glenavy had police protection from the CID Guard, at which the anti-Treaty men used to snipe 'at least one or twice a week'.[296] The robust security at Nullamore undoubtedly explains why they failed to burn the house during their Civil War incendiary campaigns. Instead, the anti-Treaty forces targeted Lord Glenavy's son, Charles Gordon Campbell, and burnt down his house 'Clonard' on the Kimmage Road, Terenure, on 18 December 1922.[297]

The third house to be attacked in the vicinity of Milltown during the Civil War was Dartry House in Upper Rathmines. This was the home of Dr Lombard Murphy, the owner of the *Irish Independent* newspaper, and it was targeted for destruction one Sunday evening in February

291 http://www.irishwarmemorials.ie/Memorials-Detail?memoId=1070 (accessed 22 August 2019).

292 *Irish Times*, 6 January 1923, p. 2.

293 BMH, MSP34REF458, sworn statement of Edward Leonard 21 January 1935; *Freeman's Journal*, 24 May 1924, p. 8. Errigal's owners received £4,000 compensation from the Free State and rebuilt the house: *Freeman's Journal*, 24 May 1924, p. 8; *Irish Times*, 18 December 1937, p. 16. The embassy has received hostile attention on account of the Russian invasion of Ukraine on 24 February 2022.

294 *Freeman's Journal, 12 October 1921, p. 2;* https://www.britishpathe.com/video/marriage-at-milltown/query/marriage+at+milltown (accessed 28 June 2019).

295 *Belfast Newsletter*, 5 February 1923, p. 5; Donal Kerr, *Emmet's Casino and the Marists at Milltown* (Dublin, 1970), p. 9.

296 BMH, MSP34REF458.

297 NAI, Department of Finance, Compensation Files, 2/6/22, Gordon Campbell; *Rathmines Free Press*, 17 February 1923, p. 4.

1923. Five armed men called to the house but were refused admittance by Dr Murphy, who retreated upstairs and blew a whistle. This tactic caused the raiders to panic, and they drove away leaving behind a homemade explosive device.[298]

A history of the Marist Fathers at Milltown which was written in 1970 recalled some local events witnessed by Marist scholastics at Milltown during the Civil War:

> *Occasionally the sound of gunfire rang through Milltown, for the Civil War was on. The Republicans took occasional pot-shots at Lord Glenavy's house across the Dodder. Some eager young novices went out one day hoping to see the new Irish Army. But that same Irish Army was taking no chances. The novices met them just at Milltown Bridge in battle formation: two files of grim-faced men with guns at the ready. The officer cried, 'halt' to the young clerics, came over and quickly frisked them for concealed arms. Later on that same afternoon they were halted again. A third episode as they were returning home was more alarming. They stood to gaze at a lorryload of Free Staters flashing towards them. As the lorry passed, every soldier trained his gun on the young clerics. The moment was tense but no shot was fired. The next morning's newspapers told how a gunman disguised as a cleric tried to penetrate Government Buildings to shoot a Minister of State. It's little wonder the Free Staters were taking no chances with clerics that day.*[299]

ENDING OF THE CIVIL WAR AND ITS AFTERMATH

The *Irish Independent* reported that the Irish Army had been sniped from the railway viaduct while passing Classon's Bridge on the night of Wednesday 21 March 1923. A brisk exchange of fire followed lasting for some minutes but no casualties were reported.[300] However, by the late spring of 1923 it was quite clear that the war was lost as far as the anti-Treaty forces were concerned. By now, the guerrilla columns of the anti-Treaty forces in South Dublin had been reduced to a small poorly armed force. Nationwide, there was no prospect whatsoever that the anti-Treaty side could improve their position, let alone win the Civil War. The conflict ended when Éamon de Valera and Frank Aitken issued the orders on 24 May 1923 for their forces to dump arms and resume civilian life.[301]

Although the Civil War ended with a ceasefire in late May 1923, sporadic armed crimes continued to be committed into the 1920s by disaffected young men with access to guns.[302] On two separate occasions in October 1924 armed raids took place on premises in Milltown. Shortly after 9 p.m. on 6 October two masked and armed men called to a cottage in the grounds of the Milltown laundry and demanded money. When the occupants said they had none, the raiders took away a shotgun and fled in the direction of Churchtown.[303] A little over two weeks later, Mrs O'Neill's shop and off-licence at Milltown Hill was robbed of the contents of the till amounting to 50*s*. by an armed and masked man who rode off on a bicycle in the direction of Clonskeagh.[304]

---

298 *Rathmines Free Press*, 3 March 1923, p. 5.

299 Kerr, *Emmet's Casino*, p. 9.

300 *Irish Independent*, 23 March 1923, p. 6.

301 Dorney, *Civil War in Dublin*, pp. 254–6.

302 Valiulis, *Portrait of a Revolutionary*, p. 199.

303 *Freeman's Journal*, 7 October 1924, p. 6.

304 *Freeman's Journal*, 24 October 1924, p. 5

Unemployment was very prevalent locally and throughout south Dublin during the 1920s and it was probably a major factor behind the armed robberies in Milltown.[305] On 1 March 1922 a deputation of unemployed men from Milltown was received by the councillors of the Rathmines UDC. Following the meeting the councillors resolved that the township's surveyor report to the Public Health Committee as to the pending works in the township and what steps he could advise to be taken to give employment.[306] It seems that the council was not able to alleviate unemployment in Milltown because in December 1923 councillor Madeleine ffrench-Mullen exhorted the council to begin laying the new water main to Milltown which would 'afford some employment, and be of permanent utility'.[307]

Towards the end of 1923 W.T. Cosgrave announced that the government was prepared to provide grants to local authorities to enable them to provide work for the unemployed during the winter months. The Public Health Committee of the Rathmines UDC decided to avail of the grant scheme and in January 1924 offered to pay the men £2 18*s*. a week. However, the trade union representing municipal employees rejected the wages offered by the township because the normal rate for council employees was £3 4*s*. a week, and so the scheme fell through. Not surprisingly, the local councillors and newspaper editorials were highly critical of the union's stance, not least of all because it prevented the unemployed men who wanted to work from doing so.[308] At the beginning of March 1923 the government offered the Rathmines UDC a grant of £12,800 to improve trunk roads in the township, but the councillors were still prevaricating over the terms of the offer five weeks later as the numbers of unemployed continued to increase.[309]

As well as government employment initiatives, brave attempts were made by private enterprise to set up new businesses during the turbulent years of the early 1920s. In late 1921 a small tannery was set up beside the River Dodder close to Classon's Bridge, Milltown on a one-acre site leased to the Dublin Tannery Company by the Dublin Laundry Company.[310] This small business prepared light leathers for boot making, upholstery and bookbinding.[311] The secretary of the new venture, Colm O'Lochlain, gave an optimistic report to the readers of the *Rathmines Free Press* in a letter to the paper which was published on 28 April 1923:

> *There [at Milltown], with a skilled carpenter as foreman, and our three tanners as labourers, we built a neat and useful little tannery, and fitted in with pits, tanning vat, steam heating, drainage, graining machine, etc. Our first skins were ready for sale about ten months ago, and it would be hardly fair to judge progress during this past year of disturbance and stagnation of trade. It should be sufficient to state that the results show limited demand which in normal times should keep about a dozen men employed. We have done a good deal of spade-work in the last two years, and with the skilled co-operation and the appreciation of our goods we are certain of success.*[312]

---

305 Ó Maitiú, *Dublin's Suburban Towns*, pp. 208–9.

306 Dublin City Archives, Rathmines and Rathgar UDC papers, UDC/1/Min 1/9, Minute Book, vol. 9, 1917–27, pp. 313–14.

307 *Rathmines Free Press*, 8 December 1923, p. 6.

308 *Irish Times*, 3 January 1924, p. 4; *Northern Whig*, 3 January 1924, p. 7; *Rathmines Free Press*, 5 January 1924, p. 5.

309 *Rathmines Free Press*, 8 March 1924, p. 5; 12 April 1924, p. 4.

310 *Rathmines Free Press*, 28 April 1923, p. 8.

311 *Rathmines Free Press*, 21 April 1923, p. 5.

312 *Rathmines Free Press*, 28 April 1923, p. 8.

Alas, O'Lochlain's optimism was misplaced, for the tannery in Milltown had closed down 12 months later.[313]

ARMY MUTINY

The demobilisation of thousands of men coupled with efforts to professionalise the National Army in the aftermath of the Civil War created tensions within the military and the Cosgrave cabinet which reached a crisis point by 1924. The editor of the *Rathmines Free Press* reported on 23 February of that year that there were hundreds of disgruntled unemployed young men walking the streets who had been demobilised from the National Army following the ending of the Civil War.[314] Resistance to these developments and the airing of other grievances was led by a group of pre-truce IRA officers, who founded the Irish Republican Army Organisation, better known as the 'Old IRA'.[315] On 6 March 1924 the Old IRA precipitated a crises when they submitted a number of demands to the government concerning political as well as military matters. Unequivocally, this was a mutiny within the national defence forces. Rather than punish the mutineers the government dismissed the Army's top brass, who sat on a body called the army council, and this led to the resignation of General Richard Mulcahy from the cabinet. The reasons behind the government's capitulation to the mutineers are beyond the scope of this study but the essential point is that the country was very nearly plunged into a second civil war.[316]

Milltown native Michael Murray, who lived in 4 Hackett's Cottages, had risen to the rank of captain in the National Army during the Civil War. He resigned from the defence forces on 29 March 1924, apparently due to his involvement with or sympathy towards the mutineers. Less than a year later, Murray applied successfully for an army pension. Accompanying his application was a testimony from Captain Murray's superior, Major Niall MacNeill, who opined rather charitably that 'His [Murray's] action in 1924 I believe to be solely due to his having been fooled by others.' Despite his unspecified misbehaviour, Michael Murray was awarded an annual pension of £100.[317]

COMING TO TERMS WITH THE IRISH FREE STATE - THE EMERGENCE OF FIANNA FÁIL

The formation of a new political party, Fianna Fáil, in 1926 and its participation in the Free State Dáil was a hugely important political development in the aftermath of the Civil War. Within a short space of time Fianna Fáil built up a formidable electoral organisation which was supported and promoted by the *Irish Press* newspaper, which was set up in late 1931. Critically, the party in Dublin gained considerable support from the city's working-classes at the expense of the Labour party.[318] By the early 1930s Fianna Fáil had established a branch in Milltown which met in Old Bridge House beside the Packhorse Bridge.[319] This location strongly suggests that the former Cumann na mBan and anti-Treaty veteran, Mrs Bridget Doran (née Lambert), hosted the

313 *Rathmines Free Press*, 12 April 1924, p. 8.

314 *Rathmines Free Press*, 23 February 1924, p. 4.

315 Valiulis, *Portrait of a Revolutionary*, p. 202.

316 Valiulis, *Portrait of a Revolutionary*, pp. 210–20.

317 MAI, 24SP2053, Michael Murray.

318 Dickson, *Dublin: The making of a capital city*, p. 485.

319 *Irish Press*, 3 February 1933, p. 2; 11 June 1937, p. 5.

branch meetings because she was living in Old Bridge House at that time.[320] Another Milltown resident, George Langan, who lived in a cottage in the laneway known as The Gardens off Milltown village main street (Map 20), was a Fianna Fáil worker during the 1933 general election.[321]

For many years Fianna Fail's TD in the Dublin Townships constituency (replaced by the Dublin South-East constituency in 1947) was Seán MacEntee, who served as Minister for Finance and ran a formidable constituency machine. In the 1938 general election Fianna Fáil won 47.7 per cent of the vote in the Dublin Townships constituency to which Milltown belonged.[322] Years later, his Fine Gael political opponent, John A. Costello, recalled at his retirement party in 1969 that MacEntee was a 'redoubtable warrior, with whom I made [*sic*] many a struggle in the Dáil chamber and on practically every street corner ... in my constituency'.[323]

COMING TO TERMS WITH THE IRISH FREE STATE – FORMER UNIONISTS

The pre-independence activities of a handful of unionists living in Milltown has been reviewed earlier in this chapter. At this juncture, it is instructive to revisit these personalities to see how they coped with the change from the *ancien régime* to Saorstát Éireann. Three of Milltown's oldest unionists of the Edwardian era, the Rev. John Moffatt, the Rev. James Fletcher and Captain Robert Wade Thompson[324], died in succession before the Anglo-Irish treaty was signed, so they can be discounted from this review.[325]

The former and current occupants of Nullamore, Captain Bryan Cooper and Lord Glenavy respectively, accepted political realities and, rather than withdrawing from public life or relocating to Northern Ireland or mainland Britain, they continued to participate in national politics.

Taking Cooper first, he initially regarded the establishment of the Free State as a 'dangerous experiment' but nonetheless he stood as an independent for election to the Dáil, winning a seat in the south County Dublin constituency in the general election of 1923. Cooper was thus one of very few politicians who had sat in both the imperial parliament in Westminster and in the Dáil. Four years later, Cooper joined Cumann na nGaedheal and successfully retained his seat in the general election of 1927.[326] Cooper justified his decision to join W.T. Cosgrave's party in the belief that it was fairer to both himself and to his constituents to stand as a supporter of Cumann na nGaedheal's policy, which in his opinion was working for the restoration of law and order.[327] Indeed, the Rathmines Branch of the new Cumann na nGaedheal party had been set up in April 1923 and it became the political party of choice for the township's erstwhile unionists.[328] Some years after his death in 1929 at his residence in Dalkey, a contemporary political commentator said of Cooper that he had

---

320 MAI, MSP34REF5718, Bridget Doran (née Lambert).

321 *Irish Press*, 3 February 1933, p. 2.

322 Dickson, *Dublin: The making of a capital city*, p. 640, n. 33.

323 David McCullagh, *The reluctant Taoiseach: A biography of John A. Costello* (Dublin, 2010), p. 282.

324 Thompson had been part of the hard-line southern unionist faction opposed to the policy adpoted by the moderate Unionists under Lord Midleton at the Irish Convetion of 1917; *Belfast Newsletter*, 8 June 1918, p. 7; *Larne Times*, 15 June 1918, p. 5; *Irish Independent*, 6 July 1918, p.2.

325 *Leinster Express*, 28 September 1912, p. 5; Northern Whig, 23 May 1917 p. 1; *Irish Independent*, 5 February 1919, p. 4.

326 *Rathmines Free Press*, 25 August 1923, p. 6; Irish Times, 7 July 1930, p. 5; *Belfast Newsletter*, 7 July 1930, p. 5.

327 *Irish Times*, 7 July 1930, p. 5.

328 *Rathmines Free Press*, 21 April 1923, p. 4.

'done more than any other private individual to reconcile the old regime with the new'.[329]

The most remarkable political transformation of all was made by James Mussen Campbell, Lord Glenavy of Milltown. He had made the difficult transition from being a militant unionist to supporting the treaty and taking up a senior position in the Free State legislature in 1922, as chairman of the Senate.[330] Glenavy served for over six years in this role before he retired in 1928, and during his period in office he managed to work in harmony with political colleagues from many different backgrounds.[331] A sign of how far Glenavy's political conversion had taken him can be gauged by the moving tribute that he paid to Kevin O'Higgins after the latter's assassination in 1927.[332] Closer to home, Campbell demonstrated a concern for the poor of Milltown when, in April 1923, he offered to donate part of his ground at Nullamore to the Rathmines UDC to build local authority houses, but his offer was declined.[333] Lord Glenavy died at Nullamore in 1931 and his widow continued to live there after his death.

The most successful and adaptable of Milltown's former unionists living in the Free State were father and son Robert and Ernest Benson, who were the managing director and manger respectively of the Dublin Laundry Company in the 1930s.[334] Robert Benson had, as noted earlier, been a councillor on the Rathmines UDC during the Great War and acted as chairman in 1919 of the local authority at a time when it was dominated by businessmen with a strong unionist outlook.[335] The election of Sinn Féin councillors in January 1920 upset the old status quo and Benson struggled to maintain order at the council's monthly meetings during the first six months of that year.[336] Robert Benson resigned from the council in July because of the political acrimony that had been introduced to the council's meetings, but at their next monthly meeting all of the councillors, including the Sinn Féin members, unanimously agreed that Benson should be co-opted back onto the council if he was agreeable to return.[337] This decision shows that all sides of the political divide valued Benson's experience, business acumen and employment record above short-term political point scoring.[338]

By the late 1920s the Bensons had committed themselves unequivocally to supporting Cumann na nGaedheal. In November 1930 Robert Benson, along with Mrs Lilian Cooper, signed the nomination papers for Thomas Finlay, the Cumann na nGaedheal candidate put forward to contest the bye-election in the Dublin South constituency caused by the death

329 Donal O'Sullivan, *The Irish Free State and its Senate: A study in contemporary politics* (London, 1940), p. 221.

330 O'Sullivan, *Irish Free State*, p. 117; Irish Independent, 23 March 1931, p. 6; *Longford Leader*, 28 March 1931, p. 3.

331 O'Sullivan, *Irish Free State*, pp. 243–5.

332 O'Sullivan, *Irish Free State*, p. 211 which reports Glenavy's address verbatim.

333 Dublin City Archives, Rathmines and Rathgar UDC papers, UDC/1/Min 1/8, UDC Minute Book vol. 8, 25 February 1916–30 November 1925, p. 377.

334 *Irish Times*, 10 January 1935, p. 9. Robert Benson lived inside the grounds of the laundry complex in Milltown in the old manager's house called Shanagarry: *Evening Herald*, 15 September 1930, p. 6.

335 *Dublin Evening Mail*, 7 January 1920, p. 3.

336 *Dublin Evening Telegraph*, 30 January 1920, p. 16; 2 June 1920, p. 1; 10 June 1920, p. 4.

337 *Weekly Irish Times*, 17 July 1920, p. 2; *Dublin Evening Mail*, 30 July 1920, p. 3.

338 Benson had worked in the laundry business for over 20 years and employed about 400 people in the Rathmines township: *Weekly Irish Times*, 17 July 1920, p. 2.

of Major Bryan Cooper.[339] In the same year, when the Rathmines township was abolished, Robert Benson successfully stood for election to the reconstituted Dublin Corporation as the alderman for the Rathmines Ward.[340] In putting himself forward as a candidate, Benson was quoted as saying, 'I am quite optimistic of the future of the Saorstát and I go forward to do my part in its progress.'[341]

It was in fact Robert's son Ernest Edmondson Benson who subsequently went forward to help progress the Saorstát. Robert Benson retired from local politics in 1933 and Ernest successfully stood for election to Dublin Corporation for Cumann na nGaedheal in Rathmines in the same year.[342] Ernest went a step further when he was elected to the ninth Dáil in 1937 for the Dublin Townships constituency, along with his fellow United Ireland Party (later renamed Fine Gael) candidate and future Taoiseach, John A. Costello.[343] Ernest Benson was a popular candidate among Dublin's business community and, most probably, he also enjoyed electoral support from former unionist voters living in the Dublin townships. This was demonstrated by the fact that Benson retained his seat for the Dublin Townships in the general elections of 1938 and 1943, while in contrast John A. Costello failed to get re-elected in the 1943 general election, the only time that Costello lost his seat during his long political career.[344] In that election, Seán MacEntee topped the poll for Fianna Fáil, while Ernest Benson gained a very creditable 8,953 first preference votes to Costello's 7,508 votes.[345] The position was reversed the following year in the 1944 general election, when Costello regained his seat (9,530 first preferences) at the expense of Benson (7,056 first preferences).[346] Following his Dil defeat Ernest Benson retired from politics and concentrated on his business and philanthropic activities, which among others, included serving on the board of the Dublin Chamber of Commerce.[347]

PATRIOTIC SACRIFICES – THE EXAMPLE OF THE DOYLE FAMILY OF MILLTOWN

The death of Patrick Doyle in Clanwilliam House in Mount Street on Wednesday 26 April 1916 has been considered earlier in this chapter as part of the participation of Milltown's men and women in the Easter Rising of 1916. While Patrick Doyle's memory lives on in the eponymous road at Classon's Bridge and the holy water font at Ss Gall and Columbanus's church in Milltown, the misfortunes suffered by Doyle's wife and his five children have long faded from human memory. Among the Doyle family papers in the National Library is a poignant typed message from Patrick to his wife dated Eater Monday 1916. It simply states,

339 *Evening Herald*, 28 November 1930, p. 10.

340 *Evening Herald*, 15 September 1930, p. 6; *Irish Times*, 9 October 1930, p. 5.

341 *Evening Herald*, 15 September 1930, p. 6.

342 *Irish Times*, 15 June 1933, p. 4; 29 June 1933, p. 7.

343 *Irish Times*, 22 June 1937, p. 5; 6 July 1937, p. 5.

344 Members of Dáil Eireann listed on the Oireachtas.ie website: https://www.oireachtas.ie/en/member/Ernest-Edmondson-Benson.D.1937-07-21/ (accessed 20 June 2019).

345 William J. Flynn (ed.), *Irish Parliamentary Handbook 1945* (Dublin, 1945), p. 31.

346 Flynn, *Irish Parliamentary Handbook*, p. 75.

347 *Weekly Irish Times*, 14 September 1940, p. 10; *Dublin Evening Mail*, 26 March 1942, p. 2.

'Sarah. All well, do not fret, will be alright, PAB' [*sic*].[348] Unfortunately, Patrick's reassurance to his wife could not have been more misplaced, as he died in the conflagration of Clanwilliam House and his body was burned to ashes.[349] A few months later, Mrs Doyle and her five children were professionally photographed for the December issue of the *Catholic Bulletin*, which demonstrated how quickly public opinion had changed since the Rising.[350]

The Doyle family suffered a totally unexpected tragedy when six-year-old Charles Doyle was killed in a fall from the Dodder Bridge at Milltown on 3 July 1919 while out walking with a neighbour.[351] Almost three years later to the day, Patrick Doyle junior, aged twenty, was shot dead while serving with the National Army in County Dublin on 7 July 1922.[352] Prior to the truce with the British in July 1921, Patrick had been a member of the Fianna and had fought with the local IRA company.[353] Patrick's death and funeral were reported in the newspapers and a photograph of the funeral cortège approaching Taney cemetery in Dundrum is preserved among the Doyle family papers.[354] Two years later, Sarah Doyle's second son John died on 17 September 1925, at just sixteen years of age.[355] After the Civil War Sarah appears to have given her political allegiance to Cumann na nGaedheal, for a branch – the Patrick Doyle Branch – named after her deceased husband and son Patrick, was active in the early 1930s.[356]

Patrick and Sarah Doyle had one daughter, Mary, who lived to adulthood, married a man by the name of Nolan, and had a family of her own. Before her marriage, Mary had worked in the local laundry earning 30*s.* a week.[357] Very sadly, Mary died on 26 August 1940 following the birth of twins, leaving five children and a widower.[358] Sarah Doyle's five young grandchildren came to live with her in Millmount Terrace, Milltown, with her sole surviving child Joseph, who was then aged twenty-five.[359]

Joseph had inherited his father's rebellious genes, for on 12 May 1941 he was charged in the Special Criminal Court with being a member of an unlawful organisation (which he denied) and with passing on information about local defence measures to other persons.[360] Doyle was subsequently convicted on the charge of passing on the sensitive information and

348 Patrick Doyle papers (NLI, MS 46,594). The word PAB is probably a typo error for PAT.

349 O'Brien, *Blood on the streets*, p. 83.

350 *Catholic Bulletin*, vol. vi, no. 12 (December 1916).

351 Patrick Doyle papers, biographical note by Doyle's granddaughter Mrs May Nolan.

352 Patrick Doyle papers, biographical note; MAI, 2D50A, Patrick Doyle junior, deceased: application for dependant's allowance by Sarah Doyle.

353 MAI, 2D50, Patrick Doyle senior, deceased: application for widow's allowance by Sarah Doyle.

354 Patrick Doyle papers; *Freeman's Journal*, 11 July 1922, p. 6.

355 Patrick Doyle papers, biographical note. The cause of John's death is not explained and it has not been possible to locate John Doyle in the register of deaths.

356 *United Irishman*, 5 August 1933, p. 7.

357 MAI, 2D50, Patrick Doyle senior, deceased: application for widow's allowance by Sarah Doyle.

358 Patrick Doyle papers, biographical note; *Irish Press*, 28 August 1940, p. 11.

359 Patrick Doyle papers, biographical note; NAI, MS TAOIS/S 11443 (political prisoners and internees, 1939–1949).

360 *Irish Examiner*, 12 May 1941, p. 8; *Irish Independent*, 13 May 1941, p. 4; *Dublin Evening Mail*, 13 May 1941, p. 6.

sentenced to 18 months' imprisonment on 23 May 1941.[361] Joseph's incarceration added considerably to the financial strain in the Doyle household due to the loss of his income. Sarah Doyle was receiving a widow's military pension of £90 per annum but this was insufficient to meet her family's basic needs given that she had five young grandchildren to support.[362] Accordingly, Mrs Doyle wrote to the Taoiseach, Éamon de Valera, on 4 June to explain her circumstances and to ask him to release her son. Mrs Doyle thought the fact that her late husband had fought with de Valera in the 1916 Rising might work in her favour, but this was not to be the case and Joseph served out his sentence in Arbour Hill prison.[363]

Joseph Doyle got married sometime in the mid-1940s after his release from gaol, but he continued to cause trouble for his family. In April 1946 Joseph pleaded guilty at the Special Criminal Court to possession of two automatic pistols at his home in Milltown on 1 April without having firearms certificates. Doyle told the court that since his release from prison he had nothing to do with the IRA or any organisation. He said that he had been requested to re-organise the IRA in south County Dublin, but he had refused to have anything to do with it. The court sentenced him to six months' imprisonment, but in view of the fact that he was prepared to give an undertaking as to his future conduct, his release was ordered on his own bail of £25 to keep the peace and be of good behaviour for two years.[364] Sometime afterwards, Joseph Doyle and his wife Norah emigrated to England where Joseph died on 10 January 2000.[365]

Sarah Doyle remained living in Milltown up until her death on 27 December 1958, aged seventy-eight. A few years before she died, her neighbour Mr Kennedy, who lived in a house off the Dundrum Road called Clonbeg (Map 20), wrote to thank her for all the help Sarah had given to his wife while he was often away on business, and to pay tribute to her generous qualities:

> *You must be aware of the fact that you are affectionately regarded as one of those people who has turned their own many sorrows into the everlasting happiness that finds birth in kind turns done to others and I candidly admit it appears to me that whatever goes wrong in the village they run for 'Mrs Doyle'.*[366]

CONCLUSION

The period reviewed above saw the entire island experience an unprecedented degree of violent political upheaval, the like of which had not been seen for such duration and on such a scale since the 1640s. This chapter has attempted to condense Irish history of this period and locate Milltown's place in it – not an easy task. There is also the challenge of interpreting the huge volume of data, making sense of what occurred, and speculating on why events happened in Milltown the way that they did. At a century's remove, it is hard to ignore the criti-

---

361 *Dublin Evening Mail*, 23 May 1941, p. 3.

362 MAI, 2D50, Patrick Doyle senior, deceased, application for a widow's allowance. Mrs Doyle's application for a dependant's allowance on the death of her son was refused: MAI, 2D50A.

363 NAI, MS TAOIS/S 11443 (political prisoners and internees, 1939–1949).

364 *Irish Press*, 18 April 1946, p. 5.

365 *Sunday Independent*, 30 January 2000.

366 Patrick Doyle papers (NLI, MS 46,594).

cal roles played by religion and class in shaping Irish men and women's sense of personal and tribal identity. A toxic mixture of religious and class conflict among Christian denominations, political and labour groups in Ireland (and their respective supporters in England), coupled with personal zealous self-righteousness among the supporters of these groups, degraded the prospects for compromise and peaceful co-existence from 1910 onwards. The outbreak of the First World War ushered in several years of almost unbroken armed conflict successively in Europe and then in Ireland, which desensitised people to death. The country, including the inhabitants of Milltown, were caught in an uncontrollable cycle of violence until, exhausted by armed conflict, the Irish population attained a sullen peace in July 1923. ■

Chapter 14:
The First World War

Chapter 14: The First World War

INTRODUCTION

The First World War, or the Great War as it was called by contemporaries, killed and maimed tens of thousands of Irishmen during four years of bloody conflict on mainland Europe, the high seas around Ireland and the British Isles, and further afield in Gallipoli (Turkey) and Mesopotamia (Egypt and Palestine). It is perhaps surprising that during the course of the war 12 per cent of all those who served in the British armed forces – about three quarters of a million men – died.[1] Given the notorious and well-recorded horrors of trench warfare one might have expected the mortality rate to have been considerably higher. But that seemingly modest percentage rate conceals the physical injuries and psychological trauma that the millions of survivors had to live with for the rest of their lives.

Drilling further down through the statistics reveals that between 35,000 and 40,000 Dublin men served in the British armed forces during the First World War. Out of this group at least 6,568 were killed. Dublin's fatality rate was in the region of 16–19 per cent, which was more than the UK-wide fatality rate of 12 per cent. The higher mortality rate for men who enlisted from Dublin had a number of causes. The bulk of Dublin's recruitment occurred during the early years of the war, and most of those who enlisted (72.2 per cent) served in the infantry. Together, both factors meant that Dubliners served in units which were more likely to face extreme danger, and did so for longer, than the UK average.[2]

This chapter is essentially divided into two sections. The first section reviews the impact of the Great War on the social and economic life of Milltown during the period 1914–18 and into the early 1920s.The second section attempts to compile a roll of honour for Milltown's Great War dead and veterans. At the outset, it must be said that it is impossible to draw up a comprehensive list of Great War combatants from Milltown because of a lack of sufficiently detailed

1 Grayson, *Dublin's Great Wars*, p. 6.

2 Grayson, *Dublin's Great Wars*, p. 339.

and accurate records, particularly concerning men who survived the war. What follows here is therefore only an initial, very incomplete record from the available sources.

MILITARY TRADITION IN MILLTOWN BEFORE THE GREAT WAR

Over the eighteenth and nineteenth centuries Irishmen of every socio-economic and political background served in the British armed forces. From time to time, military veterans who were born in Milltown appear in official records of major military campaigns as the following three examples illustrate. A Philip Hill, who was born in Milltown in 1772, served for 18 months in the infantry during the Napoleonic wars in 1806 and 1807. Hill was invalided out of the army on 7 March 1808 aged thirty-six and retired to live out his days in the Royal Hospital Kilmainham.[3] Another example is John Donovan, who was born in Milltown in 1830. Donovan's distinguished service record was revealed when he was interviewed at considerable length by a journalist from the *Dublin Evening Telegraph* in 1894.[4] His death in poverty two years later was reported in the local paper, the *Rathmines News*, in 1896:

> *Last Thursday Corporal John Donovan of 92 Marlborough Street, a Crimean veteran who took part in the charge of the Light Brigade, died in destitute circumstances after a long illness. Deceased was a native of Milltown, County Dublin, where he was born on 1830. In 1848 he enlisted in the King's Royal Irish Hussars. He was through the entire Crimean War, taking part in the battles of Inkerman and Alma, and the charge of the Light Brigade at Balaclava. On the last-named occasion, a bomb exploded under his horse, and part of his dress was carried away. The reins were also torn out of his hand by a shot and three men in his immediate vicinity were shot dead. Notwithstanding many narrow escapes, he was uninjured. Subsequently he was sent with his regiment to India, and was through the whole of the Sepoy mutiny, being present at the taking of Kotah, Gwalior and Koshama. He was decorated with three medals and four clasps. Despite this honourable record, his pension was only one shilling per day. In the latter years of his life he was only able to eke out a miserable existence; and now he leaves a widow absolutely destitute.*[5]

The outbreak of the Boer War in South Africa in 1899 saw Irishmen fight on both sides of the conflict, which later on created ill-feeling between the war veterans who had fought for the British Empire and some Irish nationalists.[6] On 2 June 1903 Boer war veteran Michael Courtney from Dartry Cottages got into a drunken row in The Dropping Well pub during which 'unpleasant references were also made to his services in the war'.[7]

DISPLAYS OF LOYALTY AND THE BOYS' BRIGADE

As previously mentioned in Chapter 11, during the 1890s and 1900s Captain Robert Wade Thompson JP frequently hosted an annual summer gathering of the Boys' Brigade in the grounds of his home at Clonskeagh Castle. The gathering in Clonskeagh was usually attended each year by the Commander of the Forces in Ireland and the Church of Ireland archbishop of

3 British Army Pensioners, Royal Hospital, Kilmainham: https://search.findmypast.ie/record?id=gbm%2fwo119%2f5145 (accessed 11 October 2017).

4 *Dublin Evening Telegraph*, 7 April 1894, p. 8.

5 *Rathmines News*, 11 April 1896, p. 3.

6 Grayson, *Dublin's Great Wars*, pp. 8–12.

7 *Rathmines News*, 20 June 1903, p. 3; Dundrum Petty Sessions Order Book 1903, 15 June 1905, nos. 166 and 167.

Dublin, both of whom delivered speeches which were reported in great detail in the *Rathmines News* and other newspapers.[8] The boys came from families of staunchly Protestant and unionist backgrounds and collectively they formed a natural source of recruitment for military service in the British Empire.

On a fine spring afternoon on Saturday 2 May 1914 between 700 and 800 boys from the Boys' Brigade met for their annual parade in the grounds of Clonskeagh Castle, at the invitation of Captain Thompson. The boys paraded in three battalion formations and afterwards were addressed by Brigadier General Sandbach, who advised them that:

> *they were just on the threshold of life, and with many of them the time was not far distant when they would have to choose the career they would follow in the future. They would find that the training, both physical and moral, which they had got in the Boys' Brigade would be of the greatest assistance to them. From the bottom of his heart he wished them every success in the future, and congratulated both officers and boys on the splendid work they had already accomplished.*[9]

The terrible unforeseen tragedy was that hundreds of the boys proudly parading at Clonskeagh Castle would be killed and maimed in the Great War.[10]

OUTBREAK OF THE FIRST WORLD WAR

War between Great Britain and Germany broke out on 4 August 1914. Four weeks later, on 2 September 1914 the councillors of the Rathmines UDC passed a resolution, 'that the chairman be requested to call a public meeting in the town hall, Rathmines, to encourage recruiting for Kitchener's army'.[11] At that time, the Rathmines UDC was dominated by professional middle-class Protestant men who opposed the introduction of Home Rule. The outbreak of war was an opportunity for them to demonstrate their loyalty to the Crown and to the union with Great Britain. Later that same month the officers and past members of the Dublin Battalion of the Boys' Brigade met in Molesworth Hall on 18 September to form a Volunteer Company. This new company had been given permission to be attached to the Irish Rugby Football Union Volunteer corps.[12] On a Saturday afternoon in early October the IRFU Volunteer corps held a route march which proceeded by Milltown to Dundrum and returned by Clonskeagh to Lansdowne Road, in which about 350 men took part.[13]

In contrast, the war with Germany caused irreconcilable tensions within the Irish Volunteer movement, which had begun in November 1913 in response to the formation of the Ulster Volunteers. Matters came to a head as a result of a speech made by John Redmond at Woodenbridge, County Wicklow on 20 September 1914 in which he encouraged the Irish Volunteers to fight overseas in support of the British war effort. The volunteers split and as a result approximately 170,000 men, who were renamed the National Volunteers, supported Redmond while a much smaller minority, numbering about 11,000 volunteers, reorganised themselves as

---

8 *Rathmines News*, 30 May 1896, p. 2; 6 June 1903, p. 3; 17 July 1905, p. 3; 22 May 1907, p. 3; *Weekly Irish Times*, 15 May 1909, p. 21; *Dublin Evening Mail*, 9 May 1914, p. 3.

9 *Dublin Evening Mail*, 9 May 1914, p. 3.

10 *Church of Ireland Gazette*, 20 October 1916, p. 747.

11 Ó Maitiú, *Dublin's Suburban Towns*, p. 194.

12 *Irish Times*, 16 September 1914, p. 6.

13 *Dublin Daily Express*, 5 October 1914, p. 6.

a separate body with the name 'Irish Volunteers' in October 1914.[14] At least 2,000 Dubliners enlisted with the 16th (Irish) Division in the British army in response to John Redmond's call to arms in late September 1914, which reflected the high watermark of his popularity and that of the IPP.[15] Indeed, the peak month for army recruitment in Dublin was September 1914 during which month 3,091 men enlisted.[16]

The awful reality of the Great War soon became apparent with the high number of casualties suffered by the British Expeditionary Force at the battles of Mons and Ypres, and the adoption of trench warfare in the military stalemate that followed. The Select Vestry of St Philip's Church, Milltown parish opened its report for the year ending 31 December 1914 with the following paragraph:

> *The past year closed with our beloved country darkened with the gloom of the most devastating and terrible war known in history. A good number of our parishioners have answered the call of their King and Country, and we pray for their safe return, and that, God, in His own time, will grant to our arms victory, and to the nations of Europe an enduring peace. An Intercession Service for the War is held in the Church every Wednesday evening at 6.30 o'clock, and lasts for less than half an hour.*[17]

INCREASE IN FOOD PRICES

A very undesirable impact of the outbreak of the war for the civilian population was the instantaneous increase in food prices. The prices of basic foodstuffs such as tea, sugar, butter, flour and bacon all became much more expensive. To take one extreme example, the price of sugar rose from 2½*d.* a pound to as much as *6d.* a pound. The authorities were very slow to interfere with the market in response to the price inflation. Statutory price controls were introduced in 1916 but for many items the price controls only became effective from mid-1917. This meant that Dubliners experienced increases in the price of bread, meat and potatoes of 70 per cent, 190 per cent and 250 per cent respectively in the first three years of the war.[18] In addition, the war budget of November 1914 exacerbated the cost of living further by increasing taxes and duties on tea, porter, stout and strong ales.[19] In short, high food prices and food shortages forced many unemployed and casually employed unskilled labourers from Dublin's slums to enlist out of economic necessity.[20]

The increase in food prices had a knock-on effect on other household outgoings. During the winter of 1915–16 Rathdown RDC had trouble collecting rates from the council's cottage tenants, some of whom were refusing to pay. By early January 1916 the council's clerk reported to the councillors that out of a total of 296 cottage occupants, 34 tenants were in arrears in the

---

14 F.S.L. Lyons, 'The revolution in train, in Vaughan (ed.), *A new history of Ireland, vi, pp. 190*–1; Martin (ed.), *The Irish Volunteers*, pp. 169–70. Military historian Richard S. Grayson puts the numbers of volunteers backing Redmond at 158,360 to 12,306 against: Grayson, *Dublin's Great Wars*, p. 25.

15 Grayson, *Dublin's Great Wars*, p. 3.

16 Grayson, *Dublin's Great Wars*, p. 38.

17 RCB Library, Dublin, D6/64, Report of the Select Vestry of St Philip's Church, Parish of Milltown, for the year ending 31 December 1914, p. 4.

18 Yeates, *A City in Wartime*, pp. 28–30.

19 Yeates, *A City in Wartime*, p. 50.

20 Yeates, *A City in Wartime*, pp. 43–4.

Rathdown union and, more specifically, that 'in Farranboley there was a regular colony of tenants who had not paid their rates'. The clerk reported that the majority of the 34 defaulters were in constant employment, remarking that one individual was earning £2 per week; the implication being that a weekly wage of that sum was more than sufficient to cover both household necessities and the rates due to the council. The two rate collectors were then called in to the council meeting and asked to give their opinions as to the ability of the 34 defaulting tenants to pay their rates, following which the councillors resolved to issue final payment notices to 10 households that were in arrears and in default to issue legal proceedings to repossess the cottages.[21]

RECRUITMENT DRIVES AND VOLUNTARY AID INITIATIVES 1915–16

In September 1915, Robert Benson, the managing director of the Dublin Laundry Company, was approached along with other major Dublin employers by the City and County of Dublin Recruiting Committee as part of an initiative to get employers to undertake to re-instate their employees who volunteered for the war. The Committee hoped that if the undertaking was given, 'many men who are now hanging back will come forward'. The fact that hundreds of Dubliners had already been slaughtered as part of the ill-fated Gallipoli campaign was not mentioned. Robert Benson agreed to the Committee's request to give the undertaking.[22] Closer to home, the Rathmines Recruiting Committee held a week of recruitment meetings throughout the township in the first and second weeks of December 1915. On Wednesday evening 8 December its chairman, Robert Benson, along with high-ranking officers and justices of the peace addressed a recruitment meeting in Milltown village.[23] It is not known if the meeting made any impression on the villagers of Milltown.[24]

By the close of 1915, the Church of Ireland parish of St Philip's, Milltown recorded that:

> *Many of our parishioners have lost relatives and dear friends, and to them we extend our sincere sympathy. A large number is still fighting or in training, and we pray for God's protection over them.*[25]

In the third week of April 1916 the Rathmines Recruitment Committee held a further series of public meetings in the township. An open-air recruitment meeting was scheduled to take place in Milltown on Saturday 6 May; almost certainly this meeting never took place due to the outbreak of the 1916 Rising on Easter Monday, 24 April.[26]

Indeed, in the spring of 1916 young men were being canvassed to join the Irish Volunteers. On 5 April 1916 meetings were held in Ringsend and Donnybrook to protest against the deportation of Ernest Blythe and Liam Mellows, and it was reported that about 100 men joined the

21 *Wicklow Newsletter*, 8 January 1916, p. 2.

22 Hearn, *Thomas Edmondson*, pp. 169–70.

23 *Irish Times*, 6 December 1915, p. 8.

24 Recruiting numbers for December 1915 reached a new monthly low of 1,297 (excluding Ulster), and stayed poor thereafter: Timothy Bowman, William Butler and Michael Wheatley, *The Disparity of Sacrifice: Irish Recruitment to the British Armed Forces, 1914–1918* (Liverpool, 2020), p. 75.

25 RCB Library, Dublin, D6/64, Report of the Select Vestry of St Philip's Church, Parish of Milltown, for the year ending 31 December 1915, p. 4.

26 *Irish Independent*, 16 April 1916, p. 2; *Dublin Daily Express*, 21 April 1916, p. 14.

Irish Volunteers that day.[27] It must be remembered that at that time only a handful of people in the Irish Volunteers knew that an armed insurrection was being planned. In the context of the outbreak of the 1916 Rising, over 1,000 men who lived in streets close to where the rebellion took place in Dublin city centre served in the British armed forces during the Great War. During Easter Week 1916, the Royal Dublin Fusiliers suffered heavy casualties on the Western Front. In fact, during Easter Week 1916 almost three times more Dubliners were killed in that theatre of war than the number of insurgents killed in Dublin. This explains why there was so much hostility in Dublin towards the rebels in the immediate aftermath of the 1916 Rising.[28]

As noted in the previous chapter when discussing the political activities of Major Brian Cooper, on 24 June 1916 a garden fete was held in the grounds of Nullamore, Classon's Bridge, which was organised in aid of the Milltown branch of the Irish Sandbag Committee, one of the numerous women's voluntary groups that had sprung up to aid the war effort.[29] Among the usual attractions such as military band performances and dramatic shows, visitors to Nullamore could inspect trenches and dug-outs.[30] Two ladies from Eglinton Road, Donnybrook were instrumental in setting up the Sandbag Committee in June 1915, while the treasurer lived in Orwell Park, Rathmines.[31] This illustrates the fact that only women from affluent middle-class backgrounds and with free time could afford to organise voluntary war support work. Even so, nearly 4,000 Dubliners, 90 per cent of them women, served in the Red Cross.[32]

Renewed efforts were made in the summer and autumn of 1916 by the City and County of Dublin Recruiting Committee to replace the casualties at the front and to replenish the seriously depleted Irish regiments. These efforts were unsuccessful and by October 1916 the *Dublin Evening Mail* noted that practically no new recruits were forthcoming.[33] In the same month, as the Battle of the Somme was heading towards a bloody stalemate on the Western Front, Milltown Golf Club held a mixed foursome which attracted 51 entries. After the event the Club Captain gave a donation of £12 to the British Red Cross Society.[34] Clearly, Dublin's middle classes tried to retain some normality and routine in their lives as the war dragged on. Viewed in isolation this little vignette might suggest that the Milltown golfers were cushioned from the horrors of the war. In reality, many members of the club had volunteered for service. By the end of the Great War 48 members of Milltown Golf Club had died in the conflict.[35]

THE DUBLIN LAUNDRY COMPANY

In December 1914 a collection was taken up from employees in the Dublin Laundry Company, many of whom lived in Milltown, for their colleagues who had enlisted with the Royal Dublin Fusiliers. The 'magnificent sum' of £10 was raised which was used to buy 22,000 cigarettes

27 *Irish Independent*, 6 April 1916, p. 4.

28 Grayson, *Dublin's Great Wars*, p. 3.

29 *Irish Independent*, 24 June 1916, p. 1; *Yeates, A City in Wartime*, pp. 32–3.

30 *Irish Times*, 21 June 1916, p. 6.

31 *Irish Times*, 28 June 1915, p. 8; *Dublin Daily Express*, 31 July 1915, p. 8.

32 Grayson, *Dublin's Great Wars*, p. 339.

33 Grayson, *Dublin's Great Wars*, p. 231.

34 Beale, Gilleece and Redmond, *Milltown Golf Club*, p. 23.

35 Milltown Golf Club Roll of Honour: Irish War Memorials website: http://www.irishwarmemorials.ie/Memorials-Detail?memoId=603 (accessed 22 August 2019).

for the men. Packages were made up with a card enclosed with the words 'Good luck and safe return, from the staff and employees of the D.L.C.'[36]

On the domestic front, the war caused many difficulties for the Dublin Laundry Company and its operations at Milltown and Dartry. From the outset, there was a decline in turnover of about £30 a week, while the cost of coal and other materials rose. The decline in turnover was caused by a myriad of factors such as the large numbers of men wearing khaki shirts and collars, the lack of fashionable entertainments and a need for economy in general. However, the falling off of work was most sorely felt in the shirts and collars department, which was the backbone of the laundry industry.[37] From October 1914 the reduction in business made it extremely difficult for the Company to continue to keep all of its staff in employment, and by January 1916 the Company had reduced staff in all departments.[38] Yet, despite these reductions in staff, the Dublin Laundry Company was still able to provide employment for up to 300 people in May 1917.[39]

COAL AND PETROL SHORTAGES

Difficulty with obtaining sufficient quantity of coal from England and having to make do with poor quality fuel caused much disruption to business and ordinary life. The Dublin Laundry Company experienced constant difficulties with obtaining coal and having to make do with poor quality anthracite and slack instead. The problem of obtaining coal became so acute that in 1918 the boiler in the Milltown laundry was shut down on Friday nights to save fuel. Similar problems were caused by petrol rationing, with the result that two of the laundry's four motor vans were laid up, and the company was forced to give up much of its country work and reduce its staff accordingly. It was particularly galling that at the start of the war the army had commandeered the laundry's best horses which had then had to be replaced with two motor vans.[40] Fuel shortages impacted society in other ways. For a few weeks in the spring of 1919 pedestrians travelling at night time on the Milltown Road and the surrounding districts were subjected to muggings by a 'big powerful ruffian' who took advantage of the unlit street lamps when carrying out his crimes.[41] The Dublin United Tramways Company announced that it would be suspending all services after 8.30 p.m. with effect from 2 October 1919 and that the tram service from Clonskeagh to the Finglas Road would go only as far as Nelson's Pillar.[42]

FODDER AND FOOD SHORTAGES

During the Great War the military authorities requisitioned all hay crops within a 10-mile radius of Dublin to meet the needs of cavalry regiments, and fodder shortage remained a serious issue for the duration of the war. This had serious knock-on effects on Dublin's dairymen, who desperately needed fodder for their cattle. From the summer of 1916 onwards the city's cow-keepers had to compete for fodder on the open market at high prices, which caused a decrease in

36 Hearn, *Thomas Edmondson*, p. 169.

37 Hearn, *Thomas Edmondson* pp. 168–9.

38 Hearn, *Thomas Edmondson*, p. 170.

39 Hearn, *Thomas Edmondson*, p. 171.

40 Hearn, *Thomas Edmondson*, pp. 170–2.

41 *Irish Independent*, 25 March 1919, p. 6.

42 *Freeman's Journal*, 4 October 1919, p. 1.

milk yields and a consequential increase in the price for the consumer.[43] Milltown dairyman, Thomas Kavanagh, proprietor of the Rosy Hill dairy on the Dundrum Road (Map 20) was prosecuted for having removed hay from his land without a military permit. As the hay was of poor quality the magistrates at the Dundrum Petty Sessions only imposed a fine of 1*s*.[44]

Constant increases in the price of milk – it rose from 3*d*. a quart in October 1916 to 6*d*. a quart 12 months later – outraged the city's poor, who relied on affordable milk to feed their infants. Eventually, in December 1917 the Department of Agriculture intervened to stop the dairymen's naked profiteering and fixed the price of milk at 4*d*. or 5*d*. a quart, depending on its quality.[45] Despite the imposition of price controls and the high cost of fodder, dairymen had other nefarious ways of making profits. Milk was routinely diluted with water and the fat content abstracted. For example, Thomas Kavanagh of Rosy Hill dairy was in July 1917 fined 10*s*. for adding 6.25 per cent of water to his milk.[46] Two months later, William Kavanagh of Milltown Hill dairy, had a very stiff penalty of £10 imposed on him for selling meat to an abattoir that was unfit for human consumption.[47]

A far more insidious problem was the high levels of contamination of Dublin's milk supply. Scientific knowledge and understanding about germs and bacteria and their causation of illness was only beginning to be fully understood in the first and second decades of the twentieth century. A scientific study of Dublin milk samples in 1921 found that 8 per cent were contaminated with tuberculosis (TB). Even though TB contaminated milk was only responsible for 6 per cent of all deaths from TB, many children who survived infection were weakened for life. The same study found that 382 babies in Dublin city died from enteritis in 1921, and that dirty milk due to unhygienic milking practices was the cause of death in the majority of those cases.[48]

Aside from dairy products, there were widespread shortages of other basic foodstuffs during the war and this accelerated an increase in the number of suburban allotments, on which a wide variety of crops and vegetables were grown.[49] In January 1917 the Rathdown RDC availed of a Local Government Board scheme to provide supplies of seed potatoes, oats and artificial manure which would be given to allotment holders throughout the Rathdown rural district. In this regard, the council owned about three acres of land on the west side of the Dundrum Road on which it leased out allotments at 10*s*. per plot to 29 appointed local families, most of whom lived in Millmount Terrace and Millmount Cottages (Map 21). A few individuals declined to take up their allotments and they were replaced by new, willing applicants. The reasons for refusing allotments were not recorded but it is possible that the men concerned were bachelors in full-time employment who had no interest in the scheme.[50]

43 Yeates, *A City in Wartime*, pp. 133, 134, 188.

44 *Irish Independent*, 3 October 1916, p. 4.

45 Yeates, *A City in Wartime*, pp. 187–8.

46 Yeates, *A City in Wartime*, p. 187; *Dublin Daily Express*, 12 July 1917, p. 3.

47 *Dublin Daily Express*, 15 September 1917, p. 3.

48 J.W. Bigger, 'Clean Milk', *Journal of the Statistical and Social Inquiry Society of Ireland*, xiv, no. 2 (1920–1923), pp. 199–208.

49 Yeates, *A City in Wartime*, pp. 181–4.

50 NAI/BG/137/R1/A24, Rathdown No. 1 RDC Minute Book, April 1916–March 1917, special minutes re food production supply 24 January 1917, 21 February 1917, 7 March 1917; *Wicklow People*, 24 February 1917, p.5; *Wicklow Newsletter*, 10 March 1917, p. 3; OSI, County Dublin, Dublin/Rathdown, Sheet 22. IV, 25 inches to one statute mile (edition of 1938), surveyed in 1837, revised in 1936.

SPRING 1918 – CONSCRIPTION AND RECRUITMENT MEASURES

Opposition to the war by the Irish Volunteers took the form of disrupting recruitment meetings. An IRA veteran, Alex Cullen of Dundrum, recalled that when he and his colleagues in the Irish Volunteers were breaking up recruiting meetings in Dublin, they sang a song which included the following lines: 'And when the war is over/If they want you anymore/They'll find you in the S.D.U.'[51]

The German offensive launched in the spring of 1918 brought immense pressure to bear on the British government which responded (along with other measures) by introducing a conscription bill in parliament on 9 April 1918, which was to apply to Ireland. This measure provoked an unprecedent level of sustained, united, nationwide opposition to conscription from across a broad spectrum of national and republican political parties and the Catholic Church.[52] Local parish defence committees were set up to oppose conscription, including one by Beechwood Parish, the Catholic parish to which Milltown belonged at this time.[53] The worst of the conscription crisis had, however, passed by June 1918 due to several external factors including (among other things) the failure of the German spring offensive, the arrival of American troops to the European front and new recruits from England.[54]

The government had, simultaneously with the conscription bill, launched a voluntary recruitment scheme in Ireland in the spring of 1918. This had the hopelessly optimistic target of recruiting 20,000 new men by 1 August and 3,000 a month thereafter. In practice, the initiative only raised a further 10,000 recruits by October 1918, of whom nearly half joined the Royal Air Force.[55]

Nonetheless, despite general war weariness, women from the affluent classes in Rathmines continued to carry out charitable work in aid of the soldiers at the front and their dependants. On a sunny Saturday at the beginning of June 1918, a 'large and brilliant' gathering assembled for a summer fundraising fete in the grounds of Dartry House (the home of William Martin Murphy) in Upper Rathmines. Among the numerous stallholders manned by a strong contingent of ladies was one selling country produce in aid of the Milltown Work Party, which knitted woollen garments for the troops at the front. One of their number was Miss Henshaw of St Philip's, Milltown. As was typical of the times, entertainment consisted of outdoor games, competitions and pony rides accompanied by a musical programme performed by the band of the Royal Berkshire Regiment.[56]

OCTOBER 1918 – THE GRIMMEST OF ALL MONTHS

October 1918 stands out as possibly the worst month experienced by Dubliners in terms of fatalities caused by war and disease during the period under review in this chapter, including the 1916 Rising. Although the Great War had entered its final phase beginning with the crucial allied victory at the battle of Amiens on 8 August and ending on 11 November, this period, which

51 NAI, Department of the Taoiseach, S 7696, file for Alex Cullen, Grant from the Dáil Special Fund, 1924. The SDU was the South Dublin Union workhouse in James's Street.

52 Grayson, *Dublin's Great Wars*, pp. 258–9.

53 *Freeman's Journal*, 3 December 1918, p. 3.

54 Grayson, *Dublin's Great Wars*, p. 260.

55 Grayson, *Dublin's Great Wars*, pp. 259–60.

56 *Irish Independent*, 3 June 1918, p. 2.

became known as the 'Hundred Days', comprised a succession of bloody allied advances at a cost of scores of fatalities among Irishmen serving in the war.[57] For instance, the 6th Battalion of the Royal Dublin Fusiliers lost 33 men alone on 7 October 1918.[58] Three days later, Dublin was shocked to its core when the RMS *Leinster* was torpedoed off Kingstown (Dún Laoghaire) at about 10 a.m. on the morning of the 10 October with the loss of over 500 lives.[59]

The sinking of the *Leinster* appalled Irish men and women of all creeds and political opinion. No evidence has come to light indicating that anyone from Milltown was caught up in the October war deaths but the psychological impact on the local population must nonetheless have been profoundly negative given that many casualties were from Dublin city and county, some of whom had lived not far from Milltown. On Saturday 12 October the *Freeman's Journal* reported that the body of Mr Tom Foley of 51 Leinster Road, Rathmines had been washed ashore at Ringsend; his wife's body had been recovered earlier and removed to the city's morgue.[60] The same newspaper also reported that Milltown Golf Club had abandoned its October Medal competition which had been due to take place that Saturday.[61]

There was an altogether different menace stalking Dublin's populace on dry land. The great influenza pandemic of 1918 to 1919 first arrived in Ireland in early June 1918. The initial outbreak lasted about six weeks before petering out about eight weeks later.[62] However, the second wave of the pandemic broke out in Dublin in early October. This second outbreak was much more disruptive than the June outbreak, and resulted in a much higher mortality rate.[63] For the week ending 23 October 1918, the *Irish Independent* reported that 101 and 58 people in Dublin city and townships had died of influenza and pneumonia respectively. In addition, the number of burials in Glasnevin cemetery from 1–21 October was 490, as compared with 243 for the corresponding period in 1917. A peculiar feature of the October influenza outbreak was that more deaths occurred in the Dublin townships than in the city.[64]

Aside from the deaths, huge numbers of people were incapacitated and so schools and businesses had to close or curtail their activities.[65] The manager of the Dublin Laundry Company reported that 80 employees were out sick during one week in October and only three regular van drivers out of 12 were available for work. Accordingly, the manager was forced to lend a hand by operating the washing machines, a job which would normally be left to female operatives.[66] This anecdote gives some idea of how badly Milltown was affected by the October influenza outbreak. It is very difficult to identify specific cases of 'flu related deaths among the inhabitants of Milltown, although the likelihood is that some inhabitants did die of the disease, or complications flowing from it, such as pneumonia. Forty-four-year-old bachelor Thomas

57 Grayson, *Dublin's Great Wars*, pp. 263–9.

58 Grayson, *Dublin's Great Wars*, p. 265.

59 Grayson, *Dublin's Great Wars*, p. 261.

60 *Freeman's Journal*, 12 October 1918, pp. 3, 5.

61 *Freeman's Journal*, 12 October 1918, p. 3.

62 Ida Milne, *Stacking the coffins: Influenza, war and revolution in Ireland, 1918–19* (Manchester, 2018), pp. 21–5.

63 Milne, *Stacking the coffins*, pp. 27, 60–1.

64 *Irish Independent, 23 October 1918, p. 2.*

65 *Irish Times*, 23 October 1918, p. 4; *Freeman's Journal*, 22 October 1918, p. 5.

66 Hearn, *Thomas Edmondson*, p. 173.

Singleton, who worked in O'Neill's off-licence on Milltown Hill, was admitted to the infirmary of the South Dublin Union workhouse on 26 October suffering from the effects of 'post influenza'. Singleton was discharged two days later on 28 October which probably indicates that the workhouse was under severe pressure to provide beds for the acute influenza cases.[67] The unfortune nineteen-year-old Walter Caddle of 11 Classon's Bridge was recorded as dying on 24 October 1918 of cardiac failure following seven days of pneumonia. Walter had been employed as a van man and was almost certainly one of the employees who fell sick at the Dublin Laundry Company in October 1918. He had been taken to the Vergemount Hospital in Clonskeagh where he died.[68] Although Caddle's death was recorded as being caused by cardiac arrest, pneumonia was an additional complicating illness that often resulted from severe cases of influenza.[69]

In its end of year report, the Select Vestry of St Philip's church made a brief mention of the influenza outbreak, as follows: 'The Vestry are grateful to Almighty God for His goodness to all during the late serious epidemic of influenza.' Although the wording is somewhat ambiguous, it would seem that there were no influenza deaths among the parishioners of St Philip's in 1918.[70]

The dark mood engendered by the war and disease was made worse by the final misfortune to be endured by the inhabitants of Milltown village in October 1918. Writing to the *Irish Independent* on 16 October, a correspondent signing himself 'In the Dark' complained that ever since the Rathmines UDC had decided that only every third gas lamp should be lighted, 'working-class districts are still left in total darkness'.[71]

WAGE INFLATION AND INDUSTRIAL UNREST

The economic benefits of wartime prosperity, which were primarily concentrated in the agricultural sector, were unevenly distributed across all sections of Irish society. Those who had skills which were in demand either at home or in England benefitted the most.[72] Taking examples of inflation which affected employers in Milltown and Clonskeagh, on 17 November 1917 the Clonskeagh Isolation Hospital at Vergemount sought to appoint a qualified nurse on an annual salary of £35, inclusive of wartime food rations and an indoor uniform.[73] Nineteen months later, in June 1919, the hospital advertised for two trained nurses with experience of treating fever patients. The salary advertised was '£35 progressive'.[74] By the end of October 1919 the hospital had to adjust its pay offer and training expectations. This time the hospital stated that a nurse who had 'just finished training would do' provided she held a fever certificate, in which case the hospital was prepared to pay her £35–£45.[75]

---

67 NAI, South Dublin Poor Law Union Workhouse Register, BG 79/G 149, no. 1981, 26 October 1918.

68 Registration of Deaths for the district of Donnybrook, no. 318, Walter Caddle 24 October 1918.

69 Milne, *Stacking the coffins*, pp. 57, 122–3.

70 RCB Library, Dublin, D6/64, Report of the Select Vestry of St Philip's Church, Parish of Milltown, for the year ending 31 December 1918, p. 4.

71 *Irish Independent*, 16 October 1918, p. 4.

72 Dickson, *Dublin: The making of a capital city*, pp. 457–8; H.D. Gribbon, 'Economic and social history, 1850–1921' in W.E. Vaughan (ed.), *A new history of Ireland, vi: Ireland under the Union 1870–1921* (Oxford, 1989), p. 349.

73 *Irish Independent*, 17 November 1917, p. 2.

74 *Irish Independent*, 19 June 1919, p. 3.

75 *Irish Independent*, 30 October 1919, p. 8.

The Henshaw ironworks at Clonskeagh seems to have suffered from a shortage of men or a high turnover of staff judging by the number of job advertisements that appeared on several separate occasions for various skilled positions during the period October 1915 to December 1919. The jobs mainly involved plating and finishing spades and shovels, which were the mainstay of Henshaw's manufacturing business in Clonskeagh, although axel turners, blacksmiths, carpenters and a gas engine supervisor were also required from time to time.[76] The likelihood is that most, if not all, of the workers who left Henshaws went to work in England as war munitions volunteers in response to various recruiting campaigns begun by the Ministry of Munitions in June 1915. Not alone was the work well paid, of greater significance was the fact that munitions workers were exempted from military service and from conscription.[77]

The men were well organised when it came to labour and industrial disputes. In July 1918 about 100 of the Henshaw workers at the Clonskeagh works and the commercial premises in Christchurch Place went on strike for higher wages, a demand which was refused by their employer.[78] This strike was settled after negotiation, and by October 1918 a competent spade plater was earning 60*s.* a week plus a 5*s.* war bonus.[79] Nonetheless, a second strike which lasted for two weeks in March 1919 saw Henshaws give in to the men's demands for further wage increases.[80]

Industrial relations at the Dublin Laundry Company were also evolving rapidly. In late August 1917 management at the laundry became aware that their van men were either forming or joining a trade union, and that all of the Milltown men were involved.[81] In the same year, 1917, the Irish Women Workers' Union (IWWU) was rekindled by suffragette Louie Bennett after its collapse during the 1916 Rising. The two strongest trades that joined the new trade union were the women who worked in the printing and laundry trades. The manager of the Dublin Laundry Company, Sidney Foster, was quite sanguine about the arrival of the IWWU. It appears that Foster thought that having the laundry women in a less militant female trade union was better than if they joined the more militant Irish Transport and General Workers' Union (ITGWU). Foster also felt it was preferable to tolerate a unionised workforce, as the possible alternative was the imposition of a government-controlled laundry industry, a fear which eventually materialised in 1920 with the establishment of a Laundry Trade Board for Ireland.[82]

However, Foster had not reckoned with the dynamism of Louie Bennett. By March 1918 Bennett had secured a guaranteed rate of 5*s.* 6*d.* a week for workers over fourteen, for a 50-hour week; 6*s.* 6*d.* for girls aged over fifteen years of age, 8*s.* for girls aged over sixteen years of age, increasing to a top weekly wage of 16*s.* for women aged over twenty-one years of age. Overtime rates were fixed at 5*d.* per hour. By 1919 Bennett was claiming that the IWWU had reduced the hours of the laundry workers by five and doubled their wages.[83] All of these

76 *Irish Independent*, 5 October 1915, p. 6; 30 October 1915, p. 3; *Irish Examiner*, 24 March 1917, p. 2; *Freeman's Journal*, 24 August 1917, p. 1; *Anglo-Celt*, 26 October 1918, p. 5; *Freeman's Journal*, 29 November 1919, p. 7.

77 Bowman, Butler and Wheatley, *The Disparity of Sacrifice*, pp. 68–9.

78 *Evening Herald*, 8 July 1918, p. 1; *Freeman's Journal*, 9 July 1918, p. 4.

79 *Evening Herald*, 11 July 1918, p. 1, 13 July 1918, p. 1; *Anglo Celt*, 26 October 1918, p. 5.

80 *Sunday Independent*, 23 March 1919, p. 4; *Irish Independent*, 24 March 1919, p. 3.

81 Hearn, *Thomas Edmondson*, p. 165.

82 Hearn, *Thomas Edmondson, pp. 166, 173*–4. Trade boards were committees of conciliation and arbitration for the regulation of hours of work and wages between masters and men across low paid manual industries for which they were initially established.

83 Hearn, *Thomas Edmondson*, pp. 164–5.

Plate 25. Great War Memorial Window, St Philip's Church, Temple Road, Milltown (author's collection)

improvements would have greatly benefitted the scores of laundry workers living in Milltown and its vicinity. Indeed, the chairman of the Dublin Laundry Company ruefully remarked at the Company's AGM on 25 March 1919 that, 'demands for increased wages and shorter hours are constantly being made on us by the unions, and there seems to be no finality about them'.[84] Twelve months later, the Dublin Laundry Company ran advertisements in the evening papers on 10 March 1920 stating that, 'Fifteen Thousand Pounds was paid by us in wages last year. Good work merits good wages. That is why our wage bill is so high.'[85]

ST PHILIP'S CHURCH GREAT WAR MEMORIAL

The ending of the Great War with the victory for Britain and its allies was received with great relief by the parishioners of St Philip's, whose congregation had suffered several casualties during the conflict. In response, the Select Vestry decided to erect a memorial window to perpetuate 'for all time the names of the gallant men who fell for honour and for right' (Pl. 25).[86]

84 Hearn, *Thomas Edmondson*, p. 169.

85 *Evening Herald*, 10 March 1920, p. 2; *Dublin Evening Telegraph*, 10 March 1920, p. 2.

86 RCB Library, Dublin, D6/64, Report of the Select Vestry of St Philip's Church, Parish of Milltown, for the year ending 31 December 1919, p. 4.

The window was designed by Alfred Ernest Child who worked as the part-time manager in Sarah Purser's stained-glass workshop in Upper Pembroke Street.[87] Almost £450 was raised among parishioners and supporters of the parish, and the memorial was dedicated by the archbishop of Dublin on Advent Sunday, 28 November 1920. A list of the 136 donors was published in the vestry report for the year ending 31 December 1920. Unfortunately Sarah Purser lost money on the contract, as a note appended to the memorial fund account stated that 'any other subscriptions that may come in are to be handed to Miss Purser to assist her to meet the loss on her contract due to the greatly increased cost of labour and materials'.[88]

The memorial window comprises three lancets with a rose above of four circles and one quatrefoil. The lancets contain the figure of a soldier with an angel representing sacrifice, Christ and an angel holding a laurel wreath both representing victory and an angel holding a laurel wreath representing peace. Above the figures are roundels with the Royal coat of arms and badge of the Royal Artillery, the badge of the Royal Navy, cross of St George, the badge of the Royal Medical corps and the badge of the Royal Air Force.[89] The names of the 19 deceased parishioners together with a precis of their service record follows later.

CLUB FOR RATHMINES EX-SERVICEMEN

Given its social and political complexion the Rathmines township produced a considerable number of Great War veterans. In the general election of December 1918, there were apparently more than 1,500 former soldiers and sailors entitled to vote.[90] With such numbers it was logical that a branch of the Legion of Irish Ex-Service Men was established in Rathmines. The new branch was inaugurated on Wednesday 3 October 1923 at 53B Rathmines Road. The keynote address was given by Great War veteran, Major Bryan Cooper TD, who had previously lived in Milltown at Nullamore before the outbreak of hostilities in 1914. These were challenging times for demobilised military men of all political backgrounds, but Cooper remained relatively upbeat in his message to them:

> *Things would not be entirely easy for them, but he was one who did not despair of Ireland. They had only to put their claims regarding pensions and housing fairly before their countrymen. So far as lay in his power, he would serve ex-service men in every part of the Free State. (Applause.).*[91]

HOMES FOR HEROES

One of the most unusual housing developments that took place in Milltown after the First World War was the provision by the Irish Sailors' and Soldiers' Land Trust (ISSLT) of houses for rent by ex-servicemen who had fought in the Great War. The historical background to the ISSLT and its housing schemes in Ireland is a rather neglected but nonetheless interesting

---

87 *St Philip's Church, Milltown Parish – A ten-minute tour* (parish leaflet, 2016); *Irish Architectural Archive, Dictionary of Irish Architects 1720–1940:* https://www.dia.ie/architects/view/1063/CHILD%2C+ALFRED+ERNEST+%2A (accessed 21 August 2019).

88 RCB Library, Dublin, D6/64, Report of the Select Vestry of St Philip's Church, Parish of Milltown, for the year ending 31 December 1920, pp. 10–11.

89 *St Philip's Church, Milltown Parish – A ten-minute tour;* images of the window can be seen on the Irish War Memorials website at: http://www.irishwarmemorials.ie/Memorials-Detail?memoId=618 (accessed 22 August 2019).

90 Yeates, *A City in Wartime*, pp. 294–5: Yeates does not provide any source for his figures.

91 *Rathmines Free Press*, 6 October 1923, p. 4.

subject.[92] Very briefly, the ISSLT had its origins in the 'homes for heroes' campaign that developed towards the end of the Great War in Great Britain and Ireland. After the ending of the First World War the initiative became hugely political in Ireland because the British government was desperately keen to reward the thousands of Irishmen who had fought in the Great War and to retain their continued loyalty to the British State by providing them with houses. The British administration in Ireland fervently hoped that this policy would prevent the battled hardened men from joining Sinn Féin and participating in the War of Independence. These objectives were to be achieved over time by providing the demobbed soldiers with good-quality housing in low-density developments (such as was built in Killester, north Dublin). All of the costs and expenses were to be paid for by the British government, albeit that the soldiers and seamen were required to pay quite high rent for their new homes in order to provide a sufficiently resourced sinking fund.

When the Free State came into existence in December 1922 the Cosgrave government, quite naturally given the political climate of the time, wanted to have nothing to do with housing veterans of the Great War. Accordingly, the controversial project, which had its genesis in the Irish Land (Provision for Soldiers and Sailors) Act of 1919, was reorganised under a trust (the ISSLT) administered from London with a governing board made up of trustee representatives from the Free State and Northern Irish governments, and chaired by an Englishman. The Cosgrave government could thus obtain a tangible benefit for Irish society in the form of much needed housing but without being tainted by political or financial association with the controversial housing scheme.

The target set by the ISSLT was to build 2,626 cottages in the Irish Free State, a figure that was based on its available funding from the British Treasury but which fell well short of the demand given the tens of thousands of ex-servicemen who had fought in the Great War.[93] Progress was rather slow, but in the late 1920s the ISSLT acquired a site on the east side of the Lower Churchtown Road opposite Milltown Golf Club where it built 58 houses.[94] The houses on the Lower Churchtown Road were all two storeys high and thus were much bigger than the labourers' cottages which had been built by the Rathdown RDC nearby in Farranboley in 1913. The ISSLT ceased its building operations in the Irish Fee State in 1933 due to a Supreme Court decision which held that the organisation did not have the power to charge rent for its houses.[95] By that time the trust had built or acquired 2,719 houses, almost 35 per cent of which were in the city and county of Dublin.[96] The Supreme Court decision meant that the ex-servicemen could continue to occupy their cottages without paying rent, although they became liable for rates from 1941 onwards.[97] Finally, in 1951 the Irish and British governments agreed to give ex-servicemen or their widows an option to buy their homes at a purchase price of roughly £550 in urban areas.[98]

---

92 What follows is largely taken from Fraser, *John Bull's Other Homes*, Chapter 7 (Post-war housing for Irish ex-servicemen) and Joseph Brady and Patrick Lynch, 'The Irish Sailors' and Soldiers' Land Trust and its Killester nemesis', *Irish Geography*, 42, no. 3 (November 2009), pp. 261–92 (hereafter cited as Brady and Lynch, 'ISSLT').

93 Brady and Lynch, 'ISSLT', pp. 265, 269–70.

94 *Irish Times*, 16 October 1928, p. 4; 27 June 1929, p. 3.

95 Joseph Brady, *Dublin, 1930–1950: The Emergence of The Modern City* (Dublin, 2014), p. 212.

96 Brady and Lynch, 'ISSLT', pp. 289–90.

97 *Irish Times*, 9 May 1951, p. 7.

98 *Irish Times*, 9 May 1951, p. 7.

Research is needed to identify the backgrounds of the ex-servicemen who were housed by the ISSLT in Milltown, whether or not they had any connections with the area prior to joining the armed forces, and how they integrated with the local community in the 1930s. Military historian Richard Grayson has identified 149 and 122 Great War recruits who came from Rathfarnham and Dundrum respectively.[99] In addition, investigations into the residency of the Royal Dublin Fusiliers who died in the Great War has revealed that 50 men serving in the ordinary ranks were living in the modern postal district of Dublin 6 – essentially the old Rathmines and Rathgar township –when they enlisted.[100] More specifically, in October 1930 the Dundrum Branch of the British Legion (Ireland) had 85 members.[101] Some of the Great War survivors from Rathmines, Rathfarnham and Dundrum must surely have lived on Lower Churchtown Road.

Ex-servicemen of the First World War continued to live out their lives unobtrusively into the third quarter of the twentieth century in Milltown and its environs. When the post office in Milltown was burgled in 1958, among the items stolen were British Army and Navy pension orders.[102]

MILLTOWN'S GREAT WAR SERVICEMEN: TOWARDS A ROLL OF HONOUR

The critical obstacle towards identifying men from Milltown who fought in the Great War is insufficiently detailed personal addresses among the surviving service and casualty records. The British Army's service records, officially called Short Service Attestation forms, originally contained the largest amount of personal data for men who served in the Great War. In 1940 to 1941 about two thirds of all service records were destroyed in the London blitz, so that only 2.5 million of the 6.5 million original records remain, many of which are badly fire damaged. These surviving Short Service Attestation records, informally known as the 'burnt records', have recently been catalogued and digitised for military and genealogical research purposes.[103] The original Short Service Attestation records are preserved in the National Archives of the United Kingdom.

The other important source material is contained among the contemporary casualties lists of the Great War dead. Although there are considerable data among casualty lists, the big stumbling block for researchers is that many of the thousands of contemporary casualty notices only record the county where the deceased soldier was born or where his next of kin were residing at the time of his death. A casualty recorded solely as being from Dublin often cannot be located with absolute certainty to a specific city street or suburban village unless he had an unusual surname or his age at death was given. In other instances, the deceased soldier had originally provided or was mistakenly assigned an incorrect or approximate place of birth. This error typically emerges when attempting to tally a casualty and birth location with the civil register of births. For example, on investigation a small number of individuals who completed their enlistment form put down Milltown as their place of birth, but a search of the register of births shows them to have been born somewhere else. This can probably be explained by the

---

99 Grayson, *Dublin's Great Wars*, p. 368. Grayson des not supply figures for Milltown or any of the villages within the Rathmines and Pembroke townships.

100 Tom Burke, 'The Royal Dublin Fusiliers in the Great War', *History Ireland*, 13, no. 5 (September/October 2005), p. 31.

101 *Irish Independent*, 9 October 1930, p. 8.

102 *Dublin Evening Mail*, 15 February 1958, p. 5.

103 Fiona Fitzsimons, 'Tracing First World War Ancestors', *History Ireland, 22, no. 4* (July–August 2014), p. 31. Another study suggests that the survival rate of the service records may be as high as sixty percent: Bowman, Butler and Wheatley, *The Disparity of Sacrifice*, p. 210.

fact that families in Dublin – particularly very poor ones – moved residence frequently and so by the time the adult male enlisted for service he may not have known exactly where he was born, or cared for that matter. If a recruit's earliest memories of family life were in Milltown (or close by), then it was logical for him to put that down on the form.

The approach adopted here – with the exception of the St Philip's War Memorial – is to record only men who had a proven substantial connection with Milltown village or its immediate vicinity. Thus, soldiers who were born in Milltown or who were living there for a long period before they enlisted are included in the roll of honour. Establishing the facts is made more complicated because individuals and families moved residence frequently and are hard to keep track of. Other servicemen were identified with Milltown in contemporary records via family or next of kin. Some of these men were living in Milltown according to the 1901 or 1911 census. In other instances, such as the case of James Niven, deaths were memorialised in separate parish churches by the deceased serviceman's parents and his widow or in-laws.

A small number of individuals to whom connection with Milltown was made have not been listed here where further investigation has shown them to have none, unproven or the most tenuous short-term links with Milltown. Great War veterans who came to live in Milltown after their discharge from the armed forces have not been included either. Inevitably, there is an element of personal subjectivity in the inclusion/exclusion process.[104]

ST PHILIP'S CHURCH WAR MEMORIAL WINDOW

The 19 servicemen commemorated by this memorial are as follow:

Maurice Ashley: 2nd Lieutenant. On census night, 2 April 1911, fourteen-year-old Maurice Ashley was living with his parents, Thomas and Anna Ashley, his sister and extended family in Gracepark Gardens Drumcondra. By 1915 the Ashley family had relocated to the south side of Dublin, and were living in a house called 'Lismoy' on Temple Gardens, Upper Rathmines.[105] Maurice graduated from the Royal Military School in April 1917 and was appointed 2nd Lieutenant with the Royal Dublin Fusiliers, serving with the 1st Battalion. Maurice Ashley was killed in action on 23 November 1917 while leading his platoon. He was twenty years old. Cambrai Memorial, Louveral.[106]

William Ormsby Wyndham Ball: Lieutenant. William Ball MB, RAMC, was the younger son of the late Henry Wyndham Ball and of Mrs Ball, 5 Palmerston Park, Upper Rathmines. William had a distinguished career in Trinity College, Dublin, entering in 1907 and obtaining his medical degree in 1912. While in College he was well-known in the hockey world, he played two seasons in the colours team, and represented Ireland six times in international matches. He entered the Royal Army Medical Corps in January, 1913, as a Lieutenant. On the outbreak of the war he was attached to the 2nd Battalion South Staffordshire Regiment, and left England on the 13th August 1914. On 26 September, when the British position on the Aisne was being

104 The excluded soldiers are William Cassidy, Owen Thomas, Michael Paisley, John McGuinness, Charles Vincent Fox, Daniel Hayden, Francis Farrell, Henry Hawkins and Thomas Henshaw of St Philip's who served as a non-combatant in the Royal Army Service Corps.

105 NAI, 1911 Census, Form A, residents of house 6 in Gracepark Gardens, Drumcondra; Thom's Directory 1915, p. 1883.

106 *Freeman's Journal*, 1 May 1917, p. 6; *Northern Whig*, 10 December 1917, p. 5; Ireland, National Roll Of Honour 1914–1921: https://www.findmypast.ie/transcript?id=IRE%2FMIL%2FNATROLLHONO%2F1000295 (accessed 13 August 2019); Ireland's Memorial Record: World War 1: 1914–1918: https://www.findmypast.ie/transcript?id=IRE/ENEC011/00000060/001 (accessed 14 August 2019).

shelled, William Ball went out to attend a wounded soldier. When kneeling beside him he was killed by a shell which burst close to him. He was aged twenty-four.[107]

Philip Sydney Campbell: Lieutenant-Commander. Philip Campbell was the son of James Henry Campbell, the Lord Chief Justice of Ireland, who took up residence in Nullamore, Classon's Bridge, Milltown in 1917 and renamed it Glenavy. Philip Campbell joined the Royal Naval Volunteer Reserve, Royal Navy Division, Drake Battalion, in September 1914 as a sub-Lieutenant. He was later promoted to Lieutenant-Commander and was wounded in May 1915 while fighting in the Dardanelles. Campbell recovered and was mentioned in despatches on 11 December 1915 for gallant and distinguished conduct. Philip Campbell was killed in action on 13 November 1916, aged twenty-three and is buried in plot II. D. 44. Ancre British Cemetery, Beaumont-Hamel, Somme, France.[108]

Hedley W. Craig: 2nd Lieutenant. Son of Mrs Craig of 'Kenmare', Orwell Park, Dublin and Thomas Craig, of Novara House, Bray, County Wicklow. 30th Squadron Royal Navy Flying Corps and Royal Engineers. Killed in air combat 15 April 1917, aged twenty-seven. XIV.K.14., Baghdad (North Gate) War Cemetery, Iraq.[109]

Robert Kildahl Dilworth: Second-Lieutenant. Born in Sutton, County Dublin. Son of Mr and Mrs W.T. Dilworth of 17 Palmerston Road, Upper Rathmines. Graduate of Trinity College Dublin. 2nd Battalion, Royal Munster Fusiliers. Died 28 December 1916, aged nineteen. Pier and Face 16 C, Thiepval Memorial, Somme, France.[110]

George Eric Burroughs Dobbs: Lieutenant Colonel (Brevet Major). George Dobbs was born in 1884 at Coolbawn House, Castlecomer, and educated at St Stephen's Green Schools (Strangways) Dublin and at Shrewsbury. He was the second surviving son of Mr and Mrs Joseph Dobbs, 'The Chalet', Temple Road, Upper Rathmines. George Dobbs passed from Shrewsbury directly to Woolwich, and was gazetted to the Royal Engineers on 23 March 1904. At the outbreak of the war he went to France as a 1st lieutenant, and was awarded the Legion of Honour for his valuable work during the retreat from Mons, and later he was mentioned three times in despatches. He became Captain before the end of 1914, and got his Brevet majority the following year. In 1916, on account at his excellent service, he was promoted to the position of Assistant Director of Signals with a corps, and became temporary Lieutenant Colonel in November. He was fatally wounded prospecting a new cable trench in the front line, and died of his wounds 17 June 1917, aged thirty-two. He was a well-known rugby player. George Dobbs is buried in plot XIII.A.25., Lijssenthoek Military Cemetery, Poperinge, West-Vlaanderen, Belgium. Awarded Legion of Honour, Chevalier (France).[111]

107 *Irish Life*, 'Our Heroes', 4 December 1914: http://ourheroes.southdublinlibraries.ie/node/16625 (accessed 15 August 2019).

108 NAI, 1901 Census, Form A, residents of house 30 Upper Pembroke Street; *Irish Times*, 30 May 1917, p. 8; *National Book of Honour Committee, Dublin City and County Book of Honour* (Dublin, 2004), p. 86 (hereafter cited as *Dublin Book of Honour*); *Irish Times*, 13 May 1915, p. 6; 7 November 1916, p. 4; 20 November 1916, p. 6.

109 *Dublin Book of Honour*, p. 491.

110 *Dublin Book of Honour*, p. 493; Thom's Directory 1915, p. 1874.

111 *Dublin Book of Honour*, p. 493; *Irish Life*, 'Our Heroes' 25 July 1917: http://ourheroes.southdublinlibraries.ie/node/17185 (accessed 15 August 2019); Thom's Directory of Dublin 1918, p. 782.

George Grant Duggan: Captain. Husband of Dorothy Duggan of 'Glenvar', St Kevin's Park, Upper Rathmines. Graduate of Trinity College Dublin. Irish International cross-country runner. 5th Battalion, Royal Irish Fusiliers. Died 16 August 1915, aged twenty-nine. Panel 178 to 180, Helles Memorial, Turkey.[112]

Robin C. Fausset: Lieutenant. Royal Field Artillery. Wounded in action and died on 17 November 1916, aged twenty-five. Robin Fausset was born in Cork but was living in Mullingar, County Westmeath in 1901 where his father William Fausset was stationed as a RIC Inspector. By 1918 Inspector Fausset had retired and was living in a house called 'Dochas', Cowper Road, Upper Rathmines, which provides the family connection with St Philip's church and the Great War memorial.[113]

Edward Stokes Hatte: 2nd Lieutenant. Son of William and Lucy Hatte of 'Kingston', Cowper Road, Upper Rathmines. 7th Battalion, Royal Irish Rifles. Joined the Ceylon Planters' Rifle Corps, August 1914. Also served in Egypt and the Dardanelles (Turkey). Died 16 August 1917, aged twenty-nine. Panel 138 to 140 and 162 to 162A and 163A, Tyne Cot Memorial, Zonnebeke, West Vlaanderen, Belgium.[114]

Cyril F. Gordon Hensler: Private (Signaller). Son of Clare Mary Watson (formerly Hensler), of 5 Mount Temple Terrace, Dartry Road, Upper Rathmines and of John Gordon Hensler. 436418. 7th Battalion (formerly 51st Bn.), Canadian Infantry (British Columbia Regiment). Died 25 September 1916, aged twenty-six. XVII. C. 16., Serre Road Cemetery No. 2, Somme, France.[115]

Arthur Douglas Homan: Major. Native of Dublin. Son of W.S.B. and Rina Homan of 'Chudleigh', Park Drive, Cowper Gardens Estate. Major Homan served with the 1st Battalion, Royal Irish Regiment; attached 7th Battalion, Oxfordshire and Buckinghamshire Light Infantry. Died 9 May 1917 of wounds received on the Balkan Front, aged thirty-three. C. 406., Sarigol Military Cemetery, Kriston, Greece.[116]

Ernest Walter Vindin Leach: Captain. Ernest Leach was the son of Ernest and Madelina Leach of Prospect House, Milltown Road. Ernest served with the 3rd Battalion of the Royal Irish Rifles. In January 1916 the *Irish Independent* reported that 'A son of Mr E.W. Leach, Prospect House, Milltown, County Dublin, in the 2nd Batt. Royal Irish Rifles, writes home to say the men are cheerful and always singing. They are getting up a small band, and he ask s for some flutes or a kettle-drum, which may be sent to his father at the above address.'[117] In the

---

112 *Dublin Book of Honour*, p. 494.

113 Ireland's Memorial Record: World War 1: 1914–1918: https://www.findmypast.ie/transcript?id=IRE%2FENEC011%2F00000923%2F015 (accessed 14 August 2019); NAI, 1901 Census, Form A, residents of house 4 in Mullingar town; Thom's Directory of Dublin 1918, p. 883.

114 *Dublin Book of Honour*, p. 501.

115 *Dublin Book of Honour*, p. 225.

116 *Dublin Book of Honour*, p. 502; Thom's Directory 1915, p. 1853.

117 *Irish Independent*, 18 January 1916, p. 6.

same month Leach was reported to have been wounded at the front.[118] A year later Captain Leach was killed in action on 2 January 1917 at the age of twenty. He is buried in grave H 10 in Hyde Park Corner (Royal Berks) Cemetery in Hainault, Belgium.[119]

Harold Barton Mansfield: Second Lieutenant. Husband of Eveleen M. Mansfield, 11 Grosvenor Square, Rathmines. 10th Battalion, Royal Dublin Fusiliers. Killed in action 13 November 1916, aged thirty-six. C. 3., Knightsbridge Cemetery, Mesnil-Martinsart, Somme, France.[120]

George Wyndham Maunsell: 2nd Lieutenant. Son of Richard and Elizabeth Maunsell of 'Islandmore', St Kevin's Park, Upper Rathmines. Indian Army Reserve of Officers, attached 2nd Queen Victoria's Own Sappers and Miners. Died 23 February 1917, aged twenty-eight. Panel 43 and 65, Basra Memorial, Iraq.[121]

James Douglas Niven: Royal Navy Engineer, Lieutenant-Commander. James Niven was born on 17 November 1882 at 83 Marlborough Road, Donnybrook. After school James studied to become a professional naval officer, and in 1904 he entered the Royal Navy as sub-Lieutenant. In April 1911 James Niven married Norah Symes of Glenageary, County Dublin. At the time of his marriage and subsequent death in action in 1916, James's father, Ninian C. Niven, was living at 'Craignure', Cowper Road, Upper Rathmines. James Niven was appointed Lieutenant-Commander on 1 May 1915 while serving aboard HMS *Black Prince*. Niven was killed in action at Battle of Jutland on 31 May 1916, aged thirty-four, leaving a widow and a young son, Cyril. James Niven is also commemorated on the Great War memorial in St Paul's Church, Silchester Road, Glenageary, County Dublin.[122]

Henry William Potter: Private. In 1911 twenty-nine-year-old Henry William (Harry) Potter, an assistant in a seed shop, was boarding in a house in Castlewood Avenue, in Rathmines. Harry, who was single, had been born in Cambridge, England. Harry Potter enlisted with the 2nd Leinster Regiment and was killed in action in France on 7 June 1917. A Mrs Potter, possibly Henry's mother, was living at 41 Rathmines Road in 1918. Apart from having lived for a time in Rathmines, Harry Potter's connection with St Philip's parish is unclear.[123]

William Hubert Potterton: Lieutenant. Born in Dublin. Son of William and Kathleen Potterton of 'Ardeen' 11 Palmerston Park, Upper Rathmines. He was educated at St Andrew's College

118 *Irish Independent*, 11 January 1916, p. 4; 12 January 1916, p. 4 (includes a photograph of Leach).

119 Commonwealth War Graves Commission: https://www.cwgc.org/find-war-dead/casualty/94446/leach,-/#&gid=null&pid=1 (accessed 13 December 2017); *Larne Times*, 13 January 1917, p. 7; *Irish Independent*, 12 January 1916, p. 2.

120 *Dublin Book of Honour*, p. 509.

121 *Dublin Book of Honour*, p. 509.

122 Register of Births for Dublin south, District of Donnybrook p. 653, no.270; *Wicklow Newsletter*, 4 February 1911, p. 8; Biographical notice prepared by the British Foreign Legion and deposited in St Paul's Church, Parish of Glenageary, Church of Ireland Diocese of Dublin.

123 NAI, 1911 Census, Form A, residents of house 17.1 in Castlewood Avenue, Rathmines UDC, Electoral Division of Rathmines and Rathgar East, Parish of St Peter, Barony of Uppercross; Ireland's Memorial Record: World War 1: 1914–1918: https://www.findmypast.ie/transcript?id=IRE%2FENEC011%2F00002630%2F004 (accessed 14 August 2019); Thom's Directory of Dublin 1918, p. 1027.

and Trinity College Dublin, where he graduated in Arts and Engineering. He was in the Engineering Unit of Dublin University Officers' Training Corps, and played rugby for St Andrew's cup team, and was later a member of Wanderers Rugby Club. He obtained a commission as Temporary Lieutenant in the Royal Engineers (23 Field Company) in May, 1915. In July 1915 he married Adelaide Elizabeth, daughter of Marcus B. Mathews, Northern Bank, Dublin. William Potterton died in action near Martinpuich 24 July 1916, aged twenty-four. I. K. 29., Albert Communal Cemetery Extension, Somme, France.[124]

Noel Edmond Scott: Lieutenant. Born Monasterevin, County Kildare. Youngest son of Thomas and Elizabeth Scott of 6 Fortfield Villas, Upper Rathmines. Scott obtained his commission in the 422nd (West Lancashire) Field Company, Royal Engineers in 1915, and was sent to France in July, 1916. Mentioned in Despatches. Died of wounds 21 September 1917, aged twenty-four. V.D. 14., Mendinghem Military Cemetery, Poperinge, West Vlaanderen, Belgium.[125]

Thomas V. T. Thacker Neville: Captain. Thomas Thacker was born in Kilkenny in 1880 and joined the army in 1900. Thomas was the eldest son of Joseph and Anne Thacker who lived at 40 Upper FitzWilliam Street before the outbreak of the Great War. In 1914 Thomas was serving in the Household Cavalry of the 3rd Dragoon Guards (Prince of Wales), the year in which he adopted the surname of his maternal grandfather, Thomas Neville of Borrismore, County Kilkenny. Thomas Neville was killed in action on 13 May 1915, near Ypres. He is buried at Bedford House Cemetery, Ypres, Belgium in enclosure n. 4 XII.L. 24.[126] In the same year a Mrs Thacker – almost certainly Thomas's widowed mother – was living in 'Montrose', Temple Gardens, Upper Rathmines, which provides the family's connection with St Philip's parish and its Great War memorial.[127]

OTHER FATALITIES FROM MILLTOWN

Andrew Ennis: Private. Andrew Ennis was born in Windy Arbour on 29 April 1886 to John and Margaret Ennis. At the time the 1911 census was taken, the Ennis family were living in the gate lodge of Milltown Lodge, which they rented from the Tierney family. John and his two adult sons, Edward and Andrew, worked as gardeners. At an unknown date Andrew Ennis enlisted with the Royal Dublin Fusiliers and later served with the 8th Battalion of the Royal Inniskilling Fusiliers. Andrew Ennis died in France on 18 April 1918 in circumstances that are not recorded. He is buried in Le Cateau Military Cemetery in France.[128]

---

124 *Dublin Book of Honour*, p. 515; Thom's Directory 1915, p. 1874; *Irish Life*, 'Our Heroes' 29 September 1916: http://ourheroes.southdublinlibraries.ie/node/16855 (accessed 15 August 2019).

125 *Dublin Book of Honour*, p. 518; *Irish Life, 'Our Heroes'* 26 October 1917: http://ourheroes.southdublinlibraries.ie/node/17265 (accessed 15 August 2019).

126 Ireland, National Roll of Honour 1914–1921: https://www.findmypast.ie/transcript?id=IRE%2FMIL%2FNATROLL-HONO%2F1017933 (accessed 14 August 2019).

127 Thom's Directory 1915, p. 1883.

128 Register of Births for Rathdown, District of Dundrum, p. 823, no. 443; NAI, 1911 Census, Form A, NAI, 1911 Census, Form A, residents for house 15 in Farranboley townland, Milltown Electoral Division, Parish of Taney, Dublin; Ireland, National Roll Of Honour 1914–1921: https://www.findmypast.ie/transcript?id=IRE%2FMIL%2FNATROLLHONO%2F1007395 (accessed 17 August 2019).

Michael Fitzharris: Private. Michael Fitzharris, a Catholic, was born on 24 June 1894 in 9 Clonskeagh village, the home of his mother's family, the Campbells. Michael's parents, Joseph and Kate, lived half a mile away in Milltown village where Joseph worked as labourer. At the time of their marriage on 4 February 1892, Joseph Fitzharris was recorded as living in Milltown while his wife Kate Campbell was living in Clonskeagh. By 1901 the Fitzharris family had left Milltown and were living with relatives in Dundrum village. Michael Fitzharris served with the 1st Battalion of the Royal Dublin Fusiliers and was killed in action in Gallipoli on 15 June 1915. Helles Memorial, Turkey, panel 190–196.[129]

Thomas Lambert: Private. Thomas Lambert was born in Milltown on 1 October 1892 and came from a Catholic branch of the wider Lambert clan, whose origins in Milltown and its environs go back to the early nineteenth century among the Catholic and Church of Ireland communities. Thomas was the son of Thomas and Mary Lambert who at various times lived in Milltown village and in Old Bridge House (Pl. 51). Thomas enlisted with the Royal Dublin Fusiliers and served with 'A' Company of the 1st Battalion. He was killed in action at Gallipoli on 2 October 1915, and is buried at plot I.C. 20. Azmak Cemetery, Suvla in Turkey.[130] Six months before he died, Thomas signed an informal will on 15 May 1915 leaving his property to his father, Thomas senior.[131] Thomas senior and his daughters Ellen and Bridget took part in the 1916 Rising. Their service with the Irish Citizens Army and Cumann na mBan are discussed in Chapter 13.

John Lambert: Private. John Lambert was born in Milltown on 8 April 1891 to James Lambert and Margaret Lambert (née Dunn) who were born in Milltown and Clonskeagh respectively. At that time the family were living at Hackett's Cottages in Concrete, Milltown. By 1895 the family had left Milltown and were living at 13 Mount Pleasant Place in Ranelagh where their third son Edward was born on 1 April of that year. According to the 1901 and the 1911 census returns, the Lamberts, who were Catholics, were living consecutively in tenements in McGee's Court and Digges Street. John Lambert joined the 1st Battalion of the Royal Dublin Fusiliers. He died of his wounds at Gallipoli on 29 April 1915. Helles Memorial, Turkey, panel 190–196.[132]

Joseph Lambert: Private. Joseph Lambert was a younger brother of John Lambert. Joseph was born in Milltown on 2 June 1892. Joseph enlisted with the 1st Battalion of the Connaught Rangers. He was killed in action in Mesopotamia (Iraq) on 11 July 1917. Basra Memorial, panel 40 and 64.[133]

---

129 Parish marriage register for St Mary's Parish (RC), Donnybrook, no. 419, 4 February 1892; Register of births for Dublin South, District of Donnybrook, p. 517, no. 281; NAI, 1901 Census, Form A, residents for house 19 in Dundrum town, Dundrum Electoral Division, Parish of Taney, Dublin; Ireland, National Roll Of Honour 1914–1921: https://www.findmypast.ie/transcript?id=IRE%2FMIL%2FNATROLLHONO%2F1008025 (accessed 16 August 2019).

130 Register of Births for Dublin South, District of Rathmines, p. 512, no. 475; NAI, 1901 Census, Form A, residents of house 23 in Milltown Road, Electoral Division of Rathmines and Rathgar East, Barony of Uppercross, County Dublin; Ireland, National Roll Of Honour 1914–1921: https://www.findmypast.ie/transcript?id=IRE%2FMIL%2FNATROLLHONO%2F1013334 (accessed 15 August 2019).

131 NAI,2002/119, Informal Will of Thomas Lambert, W.O. no. E/173503/1: http://soldierswills.nationalarchives.ie/reels/sw/LambertT_E173503.pdf (accessed 29 November 2019).

132 Marriage Register for Dublin South, District of Donnybrook, p. 620, no. 121; Register of Births for Rathdown, District of Dundrum, p. 869, no. 333; Register of Births for Dublin South, District of Rathmines, p. 593, no. 293; Ireland's Memorial Record: World War 1: 1914–1918: https://www.findmypast.ie/transcript?id=IRE%2FENEC011%2F00001634%2F008 (accessed 15 August 2019).

133 Register of Births for Rathdown, District of Dundrum, p. 777, no. 437; Ireland's Memorial Record: World War 1: 1914–1918: https://www.findmypast.ie/transcript?id=IRE%2FENEC011%2F00001634%2F013 (accessed 15 August 2019).

Arnold Wilson Moss: Lance-Corporal. Arnold Moss was born in Kilgobbin, County Dublin on 15 April 1896, the youngest son of Mr and Mrs Henry William Moss. By 1901 the Moss family were living at Greenmount (now Greenfields), Milltown Road. On 16 September 1914 Arnold joined the 7th Battalion 'D' Company (the 'Pals' Battalion) of the Royal Dublin Fusiliers. He was recommended for the distinguished conduct medal after his first engagement at Suvla Bay in the Dardanelles, where he was later reported missing on 16 August 1915 and presumed dead. He was just eighteen years old. Arnold Moss and his family were members of the Church of Ireland and attended Sandford Parish Church, Sandford Road, Ranelagh, where Arnold is named among the members of the congregation who fell during the Great War.[134]

Joseph Valentine Tierney: Corporal. Joseph Tierney was the eldest son of John and Mary Tierney of Milltown Lodge. On 11 August 1915 Joseph joined the Signal Depot of the Royal Engineers. He was then aged twenty-four and his height was recorded as being five feet seven-and-three-quarter inches. After initial training Corporal Joseph Tierney was sent to France on 6 October [1915.] He died in a Glasgow hospital on 5 January 1916 as a result of injuries accidentally received while on active service as a dispatch rider in France. Tierney's body was repatriated for his funeral in Dublin following which his remains were interred in Dean's Grange cemetery at plot N. H1. 109.[135]

Archibald Roche Toomey: 2nd Lieutenant. Archibald Roche Toomey was born on 17 December 1891 at 2 Beechwood Road, Ranelagh, the eldest son of Archibald and Nina Toomey. On census night, 1911, the Archibald family were living at 20 Palmerston Park, Upper Rathmines, at which time nineteen-year-old Archibald was a scholar in Trinity College Dublin. On the outbreak of the Great War Archibald applied for and was granted a commission in the 6th Battalion Leinster Regiment from the Officers' Training Corps, TCD. Second Lieutenant Archibald was killed in action at the Dardanelles on 10 August 1915. Archibald Roche Toomey is one of 20 names listed on the Roll of Honour for St Philip's church. Toomey is the only one of the 20 deceased servicemen on the Roll of Honour who is not commemorated on the St Philip's Great War Memorial window.[136]

MILLTOWN'S GREAT WAR VETERANS

David Rowat Chapman: 2nd Lieutenant. Lieutenant Chapman married Doris Telford on 25 September 1918 at St Philip's church, Temple Road. At the time of their marriage, both spouses were stated to be residing at 'Northcote', Temple Gardens, Upper Rathmines, where David's father John Henderson Chapman lived.[137]

---

134 *Dublin Daily Express*, 9 September 1915, p. 8; NAI, 1901 Census, Form A, residents of house no. 69, Milltown Road, Rathmines & Rathgar East Electoral Division, Milltown Townland, Barony of Uppercross, County Dublin; Ken Kinsella, *Out of the Dark 1914–1918: South Dubliners who fell in the Great War* (Sallins, 2014), pp. 94–6; Irish War Memorials website: http://www.irishwarmemorials.ie/Memorials-Detail?memoId=344 (accessed 23 August 2019).

135 NAI, 1911 Census, Form A, residents for house 13 in Farranboley Townland, Milltown Electoral Division, Barony of Rathdown, County Dublin; *Dublin Book of Honour*, p. 450; *Freeman's Journal*, 7 January 1916, p. 1; *Evening Herald*, 8 January 1916, p. 6 (has photograph of Tierney), 10 January 1916, p. 6; National Archives, Kew, British Army World War I Service Records, Short Service Form no. 73108 for J.V. Tierney (accessed from Ancestry.com on 3 January 2017).

136 Marriage Register for Dublin South, District of Rathmines, p. 581, no. 48; NAI, 1911 Census, residents for house 20 Palmerston Park, Rathmines and Rathgar East Electoral Division, Dublin; *Irish Times*, 18 August 1915, p. 6; *Irish Life*, 'Our Heroes', 24 September 1915: https://ourheroes.southdublin.ie/Serviceman/Show/16293 (accessed 23 August 2019); Irish War Memorials, St Philip's Church Great War Roll of Honour: http://www.irishwarmemorials.ie/Memorials-Detail?memoId=619 (accessed 22 August 2019).

137 St Philip's Parish Marriage Register, p. 84, no. 167.

Michael Cullen: Private. Michael Cullen was born in 41 Quinn's Lane off Pembroke Street on 13 November 1894. By 1901 Michael's father had died, his widowed mother Jane had remarried a man called Samuel Conles, and the family had moved to Hackett's Cottages in Concrete, Milltown. Ten years later, on 2 April 1911, Michael Cullen was aged seventeen, unemployed, and living with his mother (who had been widowed for a second time) and his two elder sisters, all three of whom worked as laundresses. In August 1914 Cullen was working as a shop assistant but on the outbreak of the war he enlisted with the Royal Irish Regiment. Michael saw active service in France, Salonica and Egypt for which he was awarded campaign medals. He continued to serve in the British Army for a number of years after the Great War had ended. It is not known if Michael Cullen ever returned to Milltown.[138]

Mathew Doyle: Private. Mathew Doyle was born on 2 June 1874 and lived in Hackett's Cottages and in Old Bridge House, Concrete, Milltown and was living in the latter place with his widowed mother Ellen in 1911. Mrs Doyle worked as a laundress while Mathew worked as a bricklayer's labourer. On 7 May 1915 forty-year-old Mathew enlisted with the Royal Dublin Fusiliers. Mathew's enlistment form recorded that he had several scars on the back of his hand, no doubt due to his bricklaying work. Mathew Doyle survived the war and was discharged from service (demobbed) on 30 October 1919 with four years and 177 days military service. Sadly Mathew died in Grangegorman Mental Hospital in 1941 and is buried in Taney cemetery.[139]

George White Kelly: 2nd Lieutenant. George Kelly was the son of O'Neill Fergusson Kelly, a County Inspector of the RIC, who in 1915 was living in 'Craiglea', Temple Gardens, Upper Rathmines. Lieutenant Kelly married Olive Coleman of 78 Palmerston Road, Upper Rathmines on 9 August 1915 at St Philip's church, Temple Road.[140]

Geoffrey Lawton Moss: Sub-Lieutenant. Geoffrey Moss of Greenmount (Greenfields) Milltown Road was the older brother of Arnold Moss who was killed in Suvla Bay on 16 August 1915.[141]

John Redmond. Private. John Redmond was born in Milltown in 1886, and was a blacksmith (farrier) by trade. John married Mary Connell at the Church of the Sacred Heart, Donnybrook, on 30 July 1905 and went on to have three children. The Redmond family lived in 2 Byrne's Cottages, Milltown main street. John worked with his father (also named John) and his older brother Thomas in the village forge. John Redmond enlisted in the army in Dublin on 20 May 1915, aged twenty-nine. He was recorded as being five feet five inches in height. It is not clear

138 Register of Births for Dublin City District No. 4, Union of South Dublin for 1894, no. 244; NAI, 1901 Census, Form A, residents for house 22 in Concrete, Milltown, Parish of Taney, Farranboley townland, Dublin; NAI, 1911 Census, Form A, residents for house 23 in Concrete, Milltown, Parish of Taney, Farranboley townland, Dublin; National Army Museum (UK) website: https://www.nam.ac.uk/soldiers-records/persons (accessed 18 August 2019).

139 Baptismal register for St Nichols Parish (RC), 15 June 1874, p. 12, no. 191; NAI, 1911 Census, Form A, residents for house 22.3 in Concrete, Millown Electoral Division, Parish of Taney, Farranboley townload, Dublin; Short Service Attestation retrieved from Ancestry.com website on 3 January 2017; *Irish Press*, 10 September 1941, p. 4. Mathew was the elder brother of Hugh Doyle whose untimely death has been detailed in Chapter 11.

140 St Philip's Parish Marriage Register, p. 81 no. 161; Thom's Directory 1915, p. 1883.

141 *Dublin Daily Express*, 9 September 1915, p. 8; NAI, 1901 Census, Form A, residents of house no. 69, Milltown Road, Rathmines & Rathgar East Electoral Division, Parish of St Peter, Milltown townland, Dublin.

what regiment John joined because his enlistment form is partially burnt.[142] John Redmond survived the war but he had suffered a complete loss of hearing. After the war Redmond was employed by the Johnson, Mooney and O'Brien bakery in Ballsbridge to look after their horses.[143]

William Roberts: Private. William Roberts was the eldest of six children of Samuel and Elizabeth Roberts, a Quaker family who lived in a detached house called Ardlevin on the west side of the Dundrum Road, near Milltown. William enlisted with the Royal Dublin Fusiliers on 13 July 1916. He was twenty-seven years old and stood five feet six inches high, and had been employed as a clerk before he signed up. William Roberts was discharged from service the following year, probably as a result of wounds received while on active service. His character was recorded as being 'very good'.[144]

BRIEF OBSERVATIONS

When one looks down the addresses of the casualties listed on the St Philip's War Memorial the very close geographic proximity of the families of the 19 men is striking. In particular, four families lived on Temple Gardens, a development of 21 houses located off Palmerston Road. With the exception of Henry Potter and Cyril Hensler, all of the men were officers. In contrast none of the Catholics from Milltown who fought in the Great War were officers, Corporal Tierney holding the highest rank among that cohort.

It is appropriate at this point to recall that the territory of St Philip's parish had, since 1857, comprised the two townlands of Milltown and Rathmines South (Map 15) save for some minor boundary adjustments made with the neighbouring Church of Ireland parishes of Rathmines and Sandford in 1907.[145] As a result of extensive building on the Palmerston and Hogan estates which had begun in the 1860s, by 1914 the majority of St Philip's parishioners were affluent middle-class professionals who lived in the large houses of Temple Road, Temple Gardens, Palmerston Road, Palmerston Park and Cowper Road, and these addresses feature prominently among the families of the deceased servicemen. The families whose loved ones are recorded on the war memorial would have strongly identified themselves from a social, economic and political outlook with the Rathmines township, and on a broader level, with Great Britain and the British Empire. Parishioners of St Philip's would have had very little in common with Milltown village, its Catholic working-class inhabitants, or their nationalist – later republican – politics. That said, it is very likely that Milltown villagers worked as domestic servants, chauffeurs and gardeners in the big houses of Upper Rathmines. This may explain why, Lord Glenavy and William Martin Murphy apart, there was no recorded violence directed against the well-to-do inhabitants of this area during the War of Independence.

While it is always risky to assign personal motives, it is not unreasonable to speculate that forty-year-old bricklayer Mathew Doyle and twenty-nine-year-old farrier John Redmond,

142 NAI, 1911 Census, Form A, residents for no. 2 Byrne's Cottages and no. 25 in Milltown Road, Rathmines Electoral Division, Parish of St Peter, Dublin; Short Service Attestation form retrieved from Ancestry.com website on 3 January 2017.

143 Personal communication from Tom Feerick on 12 October 2016, a resident of Milltown since 1929.

144 NAI, 1911 Census, Form A, residents for house 18 in Farranboley townland, Milltown Electoral Division, Parish of Taney, Dublin; Short Service Attestation form retrieved from Ancestry.com website on 3 January 2017.

145 Leslie and Wallace, *The clergy of Dublin and Glendalough*, p. 139; parochial maps in the RCB Library, D6/64 and P654/15/2 and miscellaneous correspondence P654/27. In 1982 the Parish of St Philip's was joined with the Parish of Sandford.

who joined the Army on 7 and 20 May 1915 respectively, did so for economic reasons. Before August 1914 Doyle had worked intermittently as a bricklayer but this work dried up when the war broke out. In Redmond's case, the commandeering of horses by the British military authorities may have adversely impacted his work at the forge in Milltown, thus forcing him into the armed forces out of economic necessity.

Some of the skills the the Great War veterans acquired during the conflict were useful in their post-war civilian lives. In October 1928 as the electricity infastructure acommpanying the Shannon hydro-electric scheme was being laid down on Palmerstown Road, a correspondent from the *Irish Times* remarked that 'looking at the men at work on Palmerstown Road, I could see most of them were accustomed to trench-digging.'[146]

CONCLUSION

There is nothing to suggest that the experience of Milltown during the First World War differed greatly from the rest of Dublin City and County. The historical narrative laid out in this chapter is, however, a very incomplete record of the trauma suffered by numerous families and war veterans from Milltown, and the difficulties encountered by those who remained at home. It is regrettable that there are no surviving personal testimonies from the Great War veterans of Milltown. We know nothing about the Great War soldiers who returned to Milltown, how they were received, or how they adjusted to changing public opinion in Ireland towards war veterans. Unlike the IRA veterans of the 1916 Rising and the War of Independence whose testimonies appear in the previous chapter, the survivors of the Great War are the silent majority of the men who fought in the military conflicts that engulfed Ireland in the second decade of the twentieth century. ■

146 *Irish Times*, 16 October 1928, p. 4. The large nondescript ESB substation at the top of Park Drive standing on the east side of the Luas tram track at the Cowper stop dates from this time.

Chapter 15:
The Villas and Larger Houses of Milltown

Chapter 15: The Villas and Larger Houses of Milltown

INTRODUCTION

This chapter covers the history of 18 villas and large houses which were built in Milltown and its vicinity in the eighteenth and nineteenth centuries, and complements the earlier chapters on the Leeson estate and the social history of Milltown in the eighteenth and nineteenth centuries. A subjective approach has had to be taken on the amount of information to provide (or omit) about each house, all the more so because the level of historically interesting information about each property varies greatly. An additional consideration is that the history of some of the villas, including Casino (Emmett House) and Clonskeagh Castle, have been published elsewhere.[1] Rather than repeating that information the reader is referred to the relevant publications or provided with new information not previously covered by other historians. For reasons of space, separate house histories of individual properties on Richmond Avenue South, Upper Rathmines and Classon's Bridge have been omitted. However, many of those houses, e.g. Nullamore, are mentioned throughout this book as required.

An important factor in approaching the compilation of suburban house histories is the fact that until comparatively recently the concept of home ownership was completely different compared to now. In the eighteenth and nineteenth centuries the norm was to rent one's home. The purpose of buying and building houses was, in the absence of pensions and other financial investments, to provide an income from rent. In the case of late nineteenth-century Rathmines for example, renting a house could yield a return of 9 per cent per annum on the purchase price.[2] To underline the point, in 1922 outright home ownership in Ireland was less than 10 per cent, with the trend towards owner occupation in urban areas not accelerating significantly until the second half of

---

1 See for example Patrick Salmon, 'The lost village of Milltown and its houses', *Dublin Historical Record, lxxi*, no. 1 (Spring/Summer 2018), *pp. 17*–31; Martin Holland, *Clonskeagh: A place in history* (Dublin, 2007).

2 Farmar, *Privileged Lives*, pp. 11–13.

Plate 26. Milltown Colonnade, Milltown Road, 2017 (author's collection)

the twentieth century.[3] This meant that there was a wide availability of properties to rent in the Victorian and Edwardian eras (and beyond) thereby resulting in greater mobility of residents. Apart from those who could afford to rent one of the detached villas, middle-class housing for rent in Milltown was limited to Milltown Colonnade and Rydalmount Villas (Pl. 26 & Pl. 27). This explains why the occupants listed in the Dublin street directories changed so frequently. In practice, this meant that most of the houses discussed below were often inhabited on a short-term basis and so no or very little historical information has survived about these ephemeral occupants. Accordingly, there is no value in providing a bare list of the mostly historically anonymous people who lived in the houses. Attention has instead been focused on those residents who either left an interesting historical record or who had a long-term connection with Milltown. Despite these limitations it will be shown that, generally speaking, from the early nineteenth century onwards, the 'big houses' of Milltown tended to be inhabited by stolid middle-class Protestant merchants and professionals who were not inclined towards leaving a legacy of fame or infamy, unlike some of their eighteenth-century predecessors whose careers are discussed below.

It must be acknowledged with some regret that the sparsity of information about the origins of the oldest houses of Milltown means that some of the opinions and supporting factual information set out below has to be qualified, particularly in the absence of corroborating sources such as deed maps and estate records. Inevitably, therefore, there are some factual inaccuracies which may be uncovered at a later date by future local and architectural historians. Never-

3 Ruth McManus, 'Suburban and urban housing in the twentieth century', *Proceedings of the Royal Irish Academy*, 111C (2011), p. 265.

Plate 27. Rydalmount Villas, Milltown Road, 2017 (author's collection)

theless, the information presented here will hopefully provide a solid foundation for further research of the house histories undertaken thus far.

It is a great pity that there are so few photographs of the old houses and the families who lived in them, especially of those houses that no longer survive. Indeed, for many of the house histories there are no known visual records whatsoever. This may seem surprising given that their inhabitants were well to do and undoubtedly owned cameras in the late nineteenth and early twentieth centuries. Regrettably, old family photograph albums rarely survive beyond a generation or two, and those that do are not available in public archive collections except in very rare instances. In my experience, most old family albums with their sepia-toned photographs ended up being lost or discarded as part of a house clearance on the death of an elderly relative.

POLITICAL AND SOCIAL BACKGROUND TO THE VILLA BUILDING BOOM IN MILLTOWN

The political stability that followed the Williamite victory of 1691 laid the foundations for the spread of suburban development in the environs of Dublin city. One of the principal factors in this phenomenon was the attraction of the three Dublin river valleys, the Liffey, Tolka and Dodder with their attractive prospects and healthy air. In this regard, Finola O'Kane has drawn attention to the growth of suburban settlement along the Tolka river at Drumcondra during then eighteenth century, and the fine houses that were built on the north bank of the Tolka to avail of the best views of Dublin bay and the coast.[4] For those that could afford it, the new fashion for suburban living as exemplified by the Delaneys at Delville, Glasnevin, encouraged the building of hundreds of suburban villas in Dublin's environs during the course of the eighteenth and nineteenth centuries.[5] The key differences between villas and country houses is that the villa was not built solely for agricultural, management and landowning purposes. As such, the suburban villa dweller was not bothered by the typical concerns of the rural country house owner, such as tenants, rents and regional politics, for example, and could indulge in new landscaping and architectural projects.[6]

O'Kane has opined that Drumcondra and the Tolka valley have retained the imprint of an eighteenth-century-villa landscape to a greater degree than the Dodder valley.[7] This chapter will hopefully add to that debate, with its focus on the villas and larger houses which sprang up along Milltown and Dundrum Roads with prospects of Dublin bay and the Dublin mountains and on choice sites overlooking the Dodder valley.

ST JAMES'S

St James's originally stood at the eastern end of Milltown Road where the Mount Sandford townhouse complex is now (Map 17). The house was built in 1862 by a wealthy house painter and decorator, James Boswell of 28 Bachelors Walk, at a cost of £9,500 to a design by the architect E.H. Carson.[8] Boswell had, in 1855, acquired the freehold of the land on which St James's house and St James's Terrace were built, and which originally was part of the Mowlds' farm in the eighteenth century.[9] St James's was a typical mid-Victorian detached villa of two storeys over basement with a projecting staircase return on the east side of the house (Pl. 28 & Pl. 55).

James Boswell married Annie Sloane Johnston in 1846 and the couple went on to have a very large family of 13 children, seven of whom died before adulthood during the years 1848 to 1869.[10] In July 1862 Boswell sold his painting and decorating business to the firm William Fry and Company. According to a press announcement, he was retiring from business 'owing to continued ill health'.[11] This explanation was likely to be incorrect as James Boswell was busy developing St James's Terrace on Clonskeagh Road in the 1860s. Furthermore, in February 1863 Annie Boswell gave birth to a daughter, Margaret, who unfortunately only lived for two weeks.[12]

4 Finola O'Kane, 'The appearance of a continued city: Dublin's Georgian suburbia' in Gillian O'Brien and Finola O'Kane (eds), *Georgian Dublin* (Dublin, 2008), pp. 110–26.

5 See for example, Peter Pearson, *Between the Mountains and the Sea: Dun Laoghaire-Rathdown County* (Dublin, 1998).

6 O'Kane, 'Dublin's Georgian suburbia', pp. 118–9.

7 O'Kane, 'Dublin's Georgian suburbia', p. 120.

8 *Freeman's Journal*, 12 July 1862, p. 2; *Irish Builder*, 15 February 1863 (no. 76), p. 30; VO, Cancellation Books 1855-68, Parish of Donnybrook, Clonskeagh townland.

9 Copy transcript of Deed of Fee Farm Grant dated 14 December 1855 and accompanying map in author's possession.

10 John Rutherford Gibb, 'The Boswell family of Dublin, Ireland', http://web.onetel.com/~johngibb/family/genealogy/boswellfamily.html (last updated November 9, 2004, accessed 2 November 2017); Ireland Genealogy Projects Archives (IGPA), Mount Jerome cemetery, http://www.igp-web.com/IGPArchives/ire/dublin/photos/tombstones/1headstones/mt-jerome26.txt headstone entry no. 3864 (accessed 2 November 2017).

11 *Freeman's Journal*, 12 July 1862, p. 2.

12 VO, Cancellation Books 1855-68, Parish of Donnybrook, Clonskeagh townland; IGPA, Mount Jerome cemetery, headstone entry no. 3864.

Plate 28. St James's House, Milltown Road, 1984 (author's collection)

As a consequence of selling his business, Boswell lived off the rental income of his property investments, such as St James's Terrace, which the *Irish Builder* described as being of a 'a very superior character'.[13] In the case of St James's Terrace, the initial phase of the development comprising house nos 1 to 8, were built together in four semi-detached pairs in 1861 and were listed in Thom's Directory from 1862 onwards. Each house could expect to be rented for about £84 per annum, as was the case for no. 3 St James's Terrace.[14] Such speculative building projects were not without risk, and unforeseen difficulties arose from time to time. In November 1863 Boswell was taken to court by his building contractor, Maurice Tracy, over a dispute concerning work and labour.[15] Of much more serious concern was a private bill introduced in parliament in 1865 to build a new railway line called the Dublin South Suburban Railway, which, if built, would run directly opposite St James's Terrace on an embankment thereby depreciating the value of Boswell's investments.[16] Boswell was obliged to travel to London to attend a select committee of the House of Lords, where he gave the following evidence in opposition to the proposed legislation:

> *Mr James Boswell deposed that he had property at Clonskeagh, where he had built a row of houses called James's Terrace; the proposed line would pass in front of these houses at a distance of fifty feet*

13 *Irish Builder*, 15 February 1863 (no. 76), p. 30.

14 VO, Cancellation Books 1855–68, Parish of Donnybrook, Clonskeagh townland.

15 *Freeman's Journal*, 24 November 1863, p. 4.

16 *Freeman's Journal*, 4 April 1865, p. 4.

> *from the gardens; he had expended about £12,000 in building the houses; the property would be considerably diminished in value by the proposed line; he had not received any notice of removal from his tenants, but one of his tenants had spoken to him on the subject; he was of the opinion that such a line was not required in the district; a line of omnibuses was tried, but failed from want of traffic; most of the residents there kept carriages, and would continue to do so even if the company [sic] were constructed; he would not be entitled to compensation for the injury done to his property.*[17]

Boswell's dispute with his former contractor coupled with the proposed railway bill (which did not progress) explains why nos 9 to 12 St James's Terrace were not built until 1868.[18] In October 1868, Boswell wrote to the Pembroke township commissioners asking for an exemption from local taxes on three of the newly built houses at the end of the terrace. The commissioners exempted Boswell from paying water rates but not the other taxes.[19] Not long afterwards, James and Annie suffered a very sad bereavement when their eldest son George Duncan died on 14 March 1869 aged just seventeen.[20] Thereafter James Boswell led a quiet life out of the public eye save for occasional reports of his donations to various charitable and philanthropic causes.[21] James Boswell died at home in St James on 13 March 1882 aged seventy-four, leaving an estate valued at over £44,000.[22] James's widow, Annie, continued to live in St James until her death in 1907.[23]

When the 1901 census was taken on 31 March of that year, Annie Boswell was living in St James with her daughter and son-in-law Josephine and William Gordon together with two Catholic servants, Lizzie Anderson and Mary Clarke. Annie and her daughter Josephine were members of the Church of Ireland and William Gordon was a Presbyterian. The gate lodge was occupied by their gardener, John Nolan, his wife and two daughters aged twelve and nine, all of whom were Catholics.[24]

Although the Boswells had managed to avoid the intrusion of a railway opposite St James's Terrace, they faced another threat in 1901 in the form of an isolation hospital for the treatment of smallpox and other infectious diseases, which was to be built in the grounds of Vergemount House by the Rathmines and Pembroke Joint Hospital Board.[25] Annie Boswell and other

---

17 *Freeman's Journal*, 5 April 1865, p. 4.

18 VO, Cancellation Books 1855–68, Parish of Donnybrook, Clonskeagh townland.

19 Dublin City Council Library and Archive, Pearse Street, Archives of the Pembroke Township, Minute Book vol. 1, 1863–68, p. 129, 11 October 1869. St James's house and terrace were part of Clonskeagh townland in the Parish of Donnybrook, which had been incorporated into the Pembroke Township in 1863.

20 IGPA, Mount Jerome cemetery, headstone entry no. 3864.

21 *Freeman's Journal*, 2 March 1871, p. 1; 20 December 1872, p. 5; 21 December 1875, p. 8; 13 October 1877, p. 2; 6 February 1879, p. 8; 9 January 1880, p. 2; 31 December 1880, p. 3.

22 Certified Copy Death Certificate for James Boswell registered on 17 March 1882; NAI, Wills and Administration Abstracts, no. 119, 21 April 1882.

23 Certified Copy Death Certificate for Annie Sloane Boswell registered on 27 February 1907; NAI, Wills and Administration Abstracts, no. 215, 23 March 1907.

24 NAI, 1901 Census, Form A, residents of house nos 56 and 57, Milltown Road, Pembroke West Electoral Division, Parish of Donnybrook, Clonskeagh townland, Dublin.

25 Holland, *Clonskeagh*, pp. 340–3; *Rathmines News*, 6 February 1904, p. 2. The site is now occupied by the Clonskeagh Hospital campus which provides psychiatric and geriatric residential and daycare services.

local residents formed a committee to oppose the scheme on grounds of public health and depreciation of property, in which Captain Robert Wade Thompson of Clonskeagh Castle and solicitor Michael Cartan O'Meara of 11 St James's Terrace were prominent.[26] As is often the case, the opponents of the hospital were from wealthy backgrounds with substantial property interests to protect. In contrast, the opinions of the working-class families who lived beside the hospital in Byrnes Cottages, Henshaw's Cottages and Beaver Row did not count. Those families had more pressing day-to-day concerns than worrying about depreciating property values and the possibility of contracting smallpox – four boys from the aforementioned cottages were charged with trespassing on the hospital grounds and damaging apple trees in September 1902 and were each fined a shilling.[27]

The upshot of the residents' opposition was that Annie Boswell applied for an injunction against the Joint Hospital Board in July 1903. This was granted by the Vice Chancellor but only as regards the reception and treatment of patients in the hospital with smallpox.[28] In her evidence, Boswell said that she derived a profit rent of £655 per annum out of St James's Terrace from tenants living there but that several of her tenants had said they would leave if the hospital went ahead.[29] However, the injunction was lifted on 1 February 1904, no doubt leaving Boswell with large legal fees to discharge.[30] The disappointing outcome caused additional fall out for the plaintiff because Annie Boswell's solicitor, Michael Cartan O'Meara, was a tenant of hers in 11 St James's Terrace before and during the court case but he had left the terrace by 1906.[31] Two other houses out of a total of 12, nos 5 and 7, were recorded as vacant in 1905, so the fall out in terms of surrenders of leases was not as bad as feared.[32] As for Boswell, she seems genuinely to have worried about her health because numerous Victorian and Edwardian glass medicine bottles were subsequently uncovered in the grounds of St James with exotic names such as 'Dr Adolph Hommel's Haematogen' and 'Fellows Syrup of Hypophosphites'![33] Death when it came for eighty-three-year-old Annie Boswell on 22 February 1907 was by heart attack. She left an estate valued at almost £8,000, a sum which was considerably less than her late husband's estate of £44,000.[34]

The history of St James's and its occupants after the Boswell era becomes more elusive and mundane. Josephine and William Gordon continued living at St James's until their deaths on 2 January 1915 and 17 November 1917 respectively.[35] The Gordons had no children and we have no information about their lives apart from the fact that William (and possibly Josephine

---

26 *Freeman's Journal*, 9 May 1901, p. 6; 5 April 1902, p. 6; Thom's Directory 1902, p. 1593.

27 *Rathmines News*, 6 September 1902.

28 *Rathmines News*, 17 January 1903, p. 3; 4 July 1903, p. 2; 6 February 1904, p. 2.

29 *Attorney-General (Boswell) v Rathmines & Pembroke Joint Hospital Board*, Irish Reports Chancery Division, 1 (1904), pp. 161, 162.

30 The judgement runs to 45 pages but a brief summary of the main legal principles is provided by W.N. Osborough, *Law and the emergence of modern Dublin (Dublin, 1996), pp. 67*–8.

31 Thom's Directory 1902, p. 1593; 1903, p. 1654; 1904, p. 1660; 1905, p. 1713; 1906, p. 1712.

32 Thom's Directory 1905, p. 1713.

33 The bottles were recovered by the author from the grounds of St Jame's in the 1970s and 1980s prior to its demolition in 1989.

34 Certified Copy Death Certificate for Annie Sloane Boswell registered on 27 February 1907; NAI, Wills and Administration Abstracts, no. 215, 23 March 1907.

35 IGPA, Mount Jerome cemetery, headstone entry nos 3862 and 3863.

too) enjoyed attending race meetings at Leopardstown and the Phoenix Park.[36] The only differences of note between the 1901 and 1911 censuses were turnovers in the servants and the occupants of the gate lodge, all of whom were members of the Church of Ireland in 1911. These were respectively a cook and a housemaid and a family comprising of forty-two-year-old DMP John Somerville, his wife and four-year-old daughter. William Gordon gave his occupation as 'proprietor of houses and provident investments'.[37]

After William Gordon's death in November 1917 St James's was bought by a Mrs Sarah Handcock-Glen who in turn sold the house to a Mrs Anne Fogarty in 1926, by which stage the rateable valuation of the property had been reduced from £101 to £83 10*s*.[38] Anne Fogarty was the widow of William Fogarty, formerly of Artane House.[39] In the 1920s a field adjacent to St James's grounds on Milltown Road (now Millbrook Court and Palmerston Grove) was still undeveloped, having remained part of the Boswell/Gordon landholding on Milltown Road since its acquisition by James Boswell from the Leeson estate in 1855. In 1925 the field was leased to Palmerston Rugby Football Club and in 1937 Mrs Fogarty sold her freehold interest in the rugby grounds to the Jesuits across the road in Milltown Park.[40] Palmerston RFC appear not to have been able to afford grass cutting machinery and were relying on sheep to keep the grass down, as is implied by the following letter of 23 February 1956 from the Jesuits to the club secretary, R.T. Jolly:

> *Mrs Fogarty, of St James', Milltown Road, tells me that she has had trouble on several occasions with sheep from the football field invading her garden and doing damage. It would seem that the hedge between the garden and the football field is in need of repair. At her request, I write to ask you kindly to do what is necessary.*[41]

In 1938 Mrs Fogarty was living alone in St James with three maids, and in March of that year she placed an advertisement seeking a good cook to start work immediately.[42] Despite her affluent lifestyle Mrs Fogarty was a deeply religious lady who gave generously to Catholic charities and missions. In recognition of her good works in 1937 Pope Pius XI conferred the papal decoration Pro Ecclesia et Pontifice on Mrs Fogarty. She died at St James's aged ninety-five on 31 October 1957 having outlived her children.[43]

In the 1960s, St James's was occupied by a convent, the Religious Society of Jesus and Mary, which succeeded Mrs Fogarty at the property.[44] The nuns subsequently put up St James's and

---

36 Membership badges for 1909–10, 1910–11 and 1914–15 were recovered by the author while digging for bottles in the 1980s.

37 NAI, 1901 Census, Form A, residents of house nos 1a and 1b, Milltown Road, Pembroke West Electoral Division, Parish of Donnybrook, Clonskeagh townland, Dublin.

38 Thom's Directory 1919, p. 1891; 1927, p. 1743.

39 *Irish Times,* 1 November 1958, p. 10.

40 Jesuit Archives, IE IJA/FM/Mill/5/2/3 (27) and FM/Mill/247 (1). The reason for the purchase is unrecorded but the Jesuits retained their freehold interest up until the mid-1970s; 'De La Salle Palmerston FC: A Brief History': http://www.dlspfc.ie/about-us/club-history.86.html (accessed 14 April 2015).

41 Jesuit Archives, IE IJA/FM/Mill/5/2/3 (33).

42 *Irish Independent*, 14 March 1938, p. 17; *Irish Press*, 16 March 1938, p. 15.

43 *Catholic Standard*, 3 January 1958, p. 5.

44 *Irish Independent*, 8 February 1958, p. 17; Thom's Directory 1962, p. 336.

its grounds of two and a half acres for sale by auction on 1 April 1969.[45] In a sign of the changing times, the newspaper advertisements referred to the development potential of the property, which under the planning regulations of the time potentially permitted the building of 90 flats on the site.[46] St James's was bought prior to the auction by the Institute of Public Administration (IPA) for an undisclosed sum, which was believed to have been a 'near record figure'.[47]

In the late 1970s the IPA had very ambitious plans to build a large expensive training centre on the site, at a cost of £2 million, to meet the increased demand for courses for civil servants.[48] According to a report in the *Irish Examiner* of 6 June 1980, the site was to be cleared shortly with the building being ready for occupation in 1983.[49] Although the Minister for Public Service, Gene FitzGerald, had turned the sod on the new site in June 1980, the IPA's development never went ahead due to the recession of the 1980s. The IPA's development plans were also opposed by the residents of St James's Terrace whose rear gardens would have been overlooked and dwarfed by the IPA's buildings, which were completely out of scale with the residential environment.[50] Instead, the IPA erected a small number of prefabs in the orchard at the back of St Jame's, which are still in place, and which are accessed from Vergemount Hall off the Clonskeagh Road.

During the 1980s, St James's house was allowed to deteriorate and it was vandalised on several occasions. An elderly couple, Mr & Mrs Murphy, continued to live in the gate lodge until the late 1970s but they were powerless to secure the house or the grounds notwithstanding that St James was in the charge of the Office of Public Works (OPW). During the 1970s and 1980s public money was wasted on paying a caretaker to stay overnight in the house, bricking up all of the basement windows and cutting down diseased trees while the State procrastinated over the house's future.[51] Eventually, in 1988 the OPW put St James's up for sale by public tender, with bids closing at noon on 3 June 1988.[52] The winning bid was made by Shannon Homes who applied successfully for planning permission to build four three-storey duplex apartment blocks of 48 units together with a bungalow to replace the gate lodge.[53] On 22 May 1989 the bulldozers moved in and demolished the house and the Mount Sandford apartment complex was built on the site (Pl. 55).

COLDBLOW/MILLTOWN PARK

The first large house to be built on the Milltown Park lands was, according to research carried out by the Jesuits in 1914, built sometime during the third quarter of the eighteenth century when it was called Coldblow.[54] This conclusion is consistent with the architectural evidence of

45 *Irish Independent*, 21 March 1969, p. 30.

46 Irish *Independent*, 21 March 1969, p. 30; *Irish Times*, 14 March 1969, p. 25.

47 *Irish Independent*, 15 April 1969, p. 11.

48 *Irish Press*, 11 May 1979, p. 10.

49 *Irish Examiner*, 6 June 1980, p. 5.

50 Personal recollections of the author.

51 Personal recollections of the author.

52 *Irish Press*, 13 May 1988, p. 29.

53 *Irish Times*, 8 October 1988; *Evening Herald*, 21 June 1989, p. 18. St James's was not listed for preservation.

54 'Milltown Park and some of its owners', pp. 7–8.

Plate 29. Milltown Park College, Milltown, Co. Dublin, c. 1890 (image courtesy of the National Library of Ireland)

the oldest surviving structure (as of 2022), a Georgian house, which is embedded in the Milltown Park complex (Pl. 29). The principal architectural feature of the three-storey-over-basement villa is the entrance doorcase flanked by columns with Ionic capitals, which is surmounted by a narrow semi-elliptical fanlight (Pl. 30). The entrance hall and ground-floor reception rooms retain their original window architraves and shutters.

The early history of the Coldblow demesne is unclear and at times is rather complicated. In 1776, a villa was advertised to be let by the year, or for the summer season, at the following location:

> *To be let on Milltown Road, opposite Clonskeagh lane, a large and convenient house, with coach house, stable, and a large garden; it is pleasantly situated, and commands a most delightful prospect of the harbour of Dublin.*[55]

The location of the house – opposite Prospect Lane – is an important identifier because it distinguishes this substantial villa from the original early eighteenth-century Coldblow House which stood at the top of Belmont Avenue on the corner with Sandford Road.[56] Donnybrook historian Beatrice Doran has stated that Milltown Park was originally an estate at the top of Belmont Avenue owned by a Colonel Coldblow in the eighteenth century, but she did not

55 *Saunders's Newsletter*, Friday 12 to Monday 15 April, 1776, p. 4.

56 NAI, Landed Estates Court Rental, vol. 123, no. 41, 'Rental & Particulars of Sale of Properties in Dublin to be sold on 5 May 1876 for William Radcliff', lot 16.

Plate 30. Milltown Park, entrance doorway with fanlight, 2019 (author's collection)

provide any sources for her assertion.[57] More importantly, the place-name 'Coldblow' existed at the turn of the eighteenth century, a timeframe which predates the creation of the Coldblow demesne (later Milltown Park) by several decades.[58]

Although the builder of Coldblow is unknown, in the opinion of the Jesuit historian of Milltown Park, the house and its pleasure grounds were developed by John Roberts of Old Connaught, and this is most probably correct.[59] John Roberts was a descendant of Lewis Roberts whose ownership of the lands at Coldblow is confirmed by the Leeson estate map of 1718 (Map 3). On 3 February 1796, John Roberts conveyed the following property to the Hon. Denis George:

> *the dwelling house, outhouses, gardens ... and lands situate on the road leading from Dublin to Milltown by Cullenswood and Coldblow containing seven acres, three roods and sixteen perches Irish plantation measure ... and as late in the possession of John Robinson, merchant, which lands are part of the thirty acres of land called Luntsland being part of Donnybrook ... and a plot of ground at the rere of a small house ... then in the possession of John Roberts near Milltown.*[60]

57 Beatrice M. Doran, *Donnybrook: A history* (Dublin, 2013), p. 149. There are no records in the Registry of Deeds or contemporary newspapers of a Colonel Coldblow at this location.

58 Blacker, *Brief sketches of the parishes of Donnybrook and Booterstown*, p. 125.

59 'Milltown Park and some of its owners', pp. 7–8.

60 RD 496/437/32007. The landholding equates to 12 statute acres, 2 roods and 34 perches.

Notwithstanding that the location of the large house mentioned in the 1796 deed is quite different to that given in the *Saunders's Newsletter* advertisement of 1776, both records probably relate to the same property. The first edition of the six-inch OS map of County Dublin confirms that the Coldblow villa (by then called Milltown Park) was situated about 400 metres at the end of an avenue from the main entrance gate opposite Belmont Avenue, to a point on the Milltown Road almost opposite Prospect Lane (Map 15).[61]

Prior to buying the villa and 7 acres, 3 roods and 16 perches from John Roberts in 1796, Denis George bought two other parcels of land and buildings in 1795 in the Milltown/Coldblow area. The first parcel of 7 acres, 2 roods and 28 perches was sold by Robert Keeling of Harold's Cross. This landholding appears to have included a farmhouse but no building as substantial as a villa.[62] The second parcel concerned 12 acres of land, together with a house and garden, which were sold to Denis George by John Hewetson of Rathmines Road.[63] Joseph Leeson had originally leased the second parcel to Robert Harris in 1741 which confirms that it formed part of the Leeson estate immediately adjacent to the Roberts' estate at Coldblow.[64]

It is likely that two of the three property transactions from 1795–6 described above related to the same parcel of land but concerned separate legal interests (sub-lettings) which Denis George wanted to consolidate. The absence of deed maps makes it impossible to be certain about this, unfortunately. More importantly, the Jesuits could confirm that the 12-acre landholding with its house and garden purchased from John Hewetson in 1795, together with the house and 7 acres, 2 roods and 28 perches acquired from John Roberts in 1796, comprised the entirety of Denis George's Coldblow demesne.[65] In short, by the late 1790s the consolidated Coldblow demesne incorporated separate landholdings deriving from the Leeson and Roberts estates.

Rocque's Survey of County Dublin of 1760 depicts three buildings and gardens opposite Clonskeagh Lane, but his map is not always reliable and the number of houses in that location may be exaggerated (Map 4).[66] In summary, the evidence indicates that the Coldblow villa was built on land owned by the Roberts's estate in about 1760 and that there were separate farmhouses or modest dwellings included with Denis George's consolidated landholdings of the mid-1790s.

At the turn of the nineteenth century, Joseph Archer praised George's property as 'a good house, well situated; a small demesne, well wooded, good gardens, and all well enclosed with a stone wall'.[67] A considerable portion of the eighteenth-century demesne wall of the original Coldblow estate together with the entrance gates are still intact, and enclose the property from the top of Belmont Avenue westward along Milltown Road as far as the new main entrance gate which was built in 2016 opposite Prospect Lane. The entrance gates to Milltown Park opposite Belmont Avenue are of a graceful quality, employing decorative iron work and cut granite stone. The individual who commissioned these impressive gates was prepared to go to

61 The house currently (September 2022) faces the Rowan Hall apartments in Millbrook Court on the opposite side of Milltown Road but is scheduled to be demolished.

62 RD 482/444/312578 (deed dated 7 March 1795).

63 RD 481/435/318612 (deed dated 8 December 1795).

64 RD 102/337/71029.

65 'Milltown Park and some of its owners', p. 8.

66 J.H. Andrews, '*Two maps of Dublin and its surroundings by John Rocque*' (Kent, 1977, unpaginated).

67 Archer, *Statistical Survey of the County of Dublin*, p. 108. Archer's critic, Hely Dutton, thought the house was not worthy of public attention: Dutton, *Observations on Mr. Archer's Statistical Survey*, p. 119.

extra expense because it was more costly to transport the masonry from granite quarries in the Dublin/Wicklow mountains than using the calp (limestone) from the local quarries in Milltown.

Of all the owners of Coldblow, Denis George has left the largest historical legacy. Denis George had a long and successful legal career which began when he was called to the bar in 1776.[68] In December 1785 George was elected to the position of Recorder of Dublin at an annual salary of £350 plus perquisites.[69] By some accounts, George dispensed harsh justice as Recorder. To take two examples, in December 1791 George ignored a recommendation of mercy from the jury and passed the death sentence on a felon for stealing a coat and hat. In July 1793 he ordered that Francis Webb be burned in the hand and imprisoned for six months for stealing a silver cream ewer and a silver teaspoon, the property of Michael Keogh.[70] In contrast, on a previous occasion in October 1788, George dismissed the testimony of a police inspector who had arrested and charged 21 women with prostitution, referring to 'the cruelty of confining persons in prison, without sufficient charge being produced against them'.[71]

On 2 June 1794 Denis George was elevated to the bench and created a baron of the Court of the Exchequer in place of Richard Power, deceased.[72] This promotion was probably behind George's decision to acquire the Coldblow demesne in 1796. Shortly before his appointment to the Exchequer court, George had formally resigned as Recorder of Dublin on 30 May 1794.[73] As a mark of their appreciation, the Corporation presented George:

> *with a piece of plate not exceeding in value fifty guineas, as a mark of the grateful sense they entertain of the very able and distinguished manner in which he discharged the important office of Recorder of this city.*[74]

To put this gift in context, the labourers working in the Corporation's store yard were paid wages of 13*d.* per day at that time.[75]

Baron George had a distinguished career of almost twenty-seven years on the bench before he retired in 1821 during which time he served on special commissions after the 1798 Rebellion and after Robert Emmet's Rising of 1803.[76] In a critical review of the Irish Bench in 1808, George emerged with credit, the unnamed critic deeming him to be above criticism and, perhaps more contentiously, having no rival in humanity.[77]

The fields of the Coldblow demesne and those further to the west towards Rathmines, known locally as the Bloody Fields, were sparsely populated. In the eighteenth and early nineteenth century these fields were popular for shooting game, such as snipe, hare and rab-

---

68 Francis Elrington Ball, *The Judges in Ireland, 1221–1921* (London, 1926), ii, p. 229.

69 CARD, xiii (Dublin, 1907), p. 455.

70 Henry, *Dublin Hanged*, p. 30; *Saunders's Newsletter*, 22 June 1793, p. 2.

71 Henry, *Dublin Hanged*, p. 144.

72 *Dublin Evening Post*, 22 June 1794, p. 2.

73 CARD, xiv (Dublin, 1909), p. 364.

74 CARD, xiv (Dublin, 1909), p. 371.

75 CARD, xiv (Dublin, 1909), pp. 442–3.

76 Ball, *The Judges in Ireland*, ii, pp. 229, 259.

77 Ball, *The Judges in Ireland*, ii, p. 225.

bit.[78] In 1813 Baron George and his sons Edward and George junior each held game licences so the Georges presumably hunted on their extensive land at Coldblow in their leisure time.[79] On 4 June 1821 Baron George had the pleasure of giving away his youngest daughter, Dorothea, in marriage by special licence at Coldblow.[80] Less than three weeks later, he died at home in Coldblow on 20 June 1821.[81]

Coldblow was inherited by Baron George's eldest son, Edward George, who was a clergyman.[82] A year after his father's death, the Reverend George put up the extensive contents of Coldblow for auction and sold the house and its demesne to a timber merchant, Richard Connery.[83] Among the long list of household items being auctioned, there are a few small details about the house itself: it had a total of 10 bedrooms, including the servants' bedrooms, a dining room and drawing rooms.[84]

Connery's tenure at Coldblow was short; he became bankrupt in 1831 and thereafter the house passed through a number of short-term owners in the 1830s and 1840s during which time the property was renamed Milltown Park.[85] Two of these, Francis Hodgkinson and George FitzJames Russell built Milltown Colonnade and Milltown Cottage in the late 1830s.[86] In the late 1820s a family named Carty lived in the gate lodge and on one occasion Mrs Carty advertised her services as a wet nurse in the following terms:

> *A wholesome, clean countrywoman, of her third child, wishes for the situation of a wet nurse, having a clean, comfortable lodge, a short distance from the city, situate at Coldblow House, the residence of the late Baron George, and can be highly recommended. Please address Ellen Carty, at Coldblow House lodge, opposite Coldblow lane.*[87]

In the late 1840s and early 1850s Milltown Park was owned by William Tighe Hamilton, who, coincidentally, was a descendant of the Tighe family that Hugh Leeson, grandfather of the first earl of Milltown, had married into in the seventeenth century.[88] In 1850 Milltown Park comprised 24 acres, 2 roods and 27 perches statute measure and was assessed for rates at £203, the highest property valuation in the townland of Milltown.[89] William Tighe Hamilton held an obscure legal position in the Court of Exchequer called the Second Remembrancer, where,

---

78 *Pue's Occurrences, 3 August 1756*, p. 2; Walter Thomas Meyler, *St Catherine's Bells-an autobiography* (Dublin, 1868), p. 40.

79 *Saunders's Newsletter*, 11 November 1813, p. 3.

80 *Saunders's Newsletter*, 4 June 1821, p. 2.

81 *Freeman's Journal*, 25 June 1821, p. 1.

82 'Milltown Park and some of its owners', p. 10.

83 *Saunders's Newsletter*, 8 July 1822, p. 4; 'Milltown Park and some of its owners', p. 10.

84 *Saunders's Newsletter*, 8 July 1822, p. 4.

85 *Saunders's Newsletter*, 16 April 1832, p. 4. 'Milltown Park and some of its owners', p. 10.

86 Milltown Park title deeds, lease dated 6 December 1836, Francis Hodgkinson to George FitzJames Russell.

87 *Saunders's Newsletter*, 14 September 1827, p. 4.

88 'Milltown Park and some of its owners', pp. 5, 11; Griffith's Valuation, Rateable Valuation of Tenements, Co. Dublin, Barony of Uppercross, Parish of St Peter, Townland of Milltown, 1850, p. 54, lot 3a.

89 Griffith's Valuation, Rateable Valuation of Tenements, Co. Dublin, Barony of Uppercross, Parish of St Peter, Townland of Milltown, 1850, p. 54.

among other duties, he was responsible for assessing legal costs in his role as taxing master.[90] In his leisure time Hamilton was a successful horticulturalist and together with his gardener, Mr Gannon, he won several prizes at the Summer Show of the Royal Horticultural Improvement Society of Ireland in 1848 and 1849.[91]

Hamilton sold Milltown Park to John Calvert Stronge in 1853, apparently because of financial difficulties.[92] Stronge was a justice of the peace and in his spare time he was also a keen florist specialising in rare hothouse plants. During the summer of 1857 Stronge, assisted by his gardener at Milltown Park, Thomas Byrne, won a number of first prizes at the Rathmines Floricultural Society.[93] The first OS map depicts the house as essentially a square block (as it still remains today), with a range of buildings to the rear (probably the hothouses) together with a serpentine-shaped pond (Map 15).

In 1858 Milltown Park was put up for sale by John Calvert Stronge. At that time, the Irish vice-province of the Jesuits was looking for a suitable property in which to establish a novitiate. However, because of the religious tensions of the time the Jesuits could not openly approach Stronge to buy Milltown Park. Instead, Denis Redmond of Belmont Lodge acted as a trustee and agent on behalf of the Jesuits and purchased the property from an unsuspecting Stronge on 9 June 1858 for £4,500.[94] The following day, a miscellaneous collection of household furniture, plants, dairy equipment and livestock were auctioned at Milltown Park, including two first-rate milch cows, some true Aylesbury ducks and, more exotically, Spanish and Cochin China fowl.[95] The sale of Milltown Park to the Jesuits raised concerns among some sections of the Irish Protestant community. The editor of *The Warder* remarked that, 'in this mansion they [the Jesuits] will have full scope and calm retirement for carrying on their designs of further aggression on the Protestant demesnes and Christian liberties of the kingdom'.[96]

The history of Milltown Park under the ownership of the Jesuits is beyond the scope of this study. The main Jesuit complex at Milltown Park and over 10 acres of its extensive grounds were put up for sale in June 2019, and subsequently sold to Ardstone Capital for about €65 million.[97] On 23 December 2021 a planning application involving (among other things) the demolition of Milltown Park House (Coldblow) was approved by An Bord Pleanála.[98]

GARRYNURE (PREVIOUSLY MILLTOWN COTTAGE AND SWISS COTTAGE)

Milltown Cottage was a detached two-storey house that was built on part of the extensive landholding of Milltown Park by its owner in the late 1830s, George FitzJames Russell, togeth-

90 Pettigrew & Oulton's Dublin Almanac and General Register of Ireland 1845, p. 509; *Freeman's Journal*, 13 December 1848, p. 3. The closest equivalent body today is the Office of the Legal Cost Adjudicators which replaced the Office of the Taxing Master.

91 *Dublin Evening Mail*, 3 May 1848, p. 3; 15 June 1849, p. 1.

92 'Milltown Park and some of its owners', p. 12.

93 'Milltown Park and some of its owners', p. 12; *Freeman's Journal*, 22 May 1857, p. 3; 11 July 1857, p. 3; *Dublin Evening Mail*, 3 May 1858, p. 8.

94 'Milltown Park and some of its owners', p. 12. It was alleged that an influential Protestant had told Redmond that, 'I would give my last farthing to prevent Milltown Park going to those devils the Jesuits.'

95 *Freeman's Journal*, 9 June 1858, p. 1.

96 *The Warder*, 7 August 1858, p. 5.

97 *Irish Times*, 5 June 2019; Jesuits in Ireland (online newsletter) 11 June 2019: https://www.jesuit.ie/news/sale-of-milltown-park-land/ (accessed 20 January 2020); Sunday Times, 1 September 2019.

98 https://planning.agileapplications.ie/dublincity/application-details/145989 (accessed 28 January 2022).

Plate 31. Garrynure, Milltown Road, 1984 (author's collection)

er with a terrace of four houses called Milltown Colonnade.[99] Milltown Cottage was built in the cottage-orné style with a high gabled roof decorated with ornate carvings, called bargeboards (Pl. 31).[100]A short time later, in the 1840s the house was renamed Swiss Cottage and later still, in the early 1900s, Garrynure (the garden of the yew trees). Both names were apt as the house had an alpine feel to it and yew trees grew in the garden. In 1850 the house was let to a Mrs St George and was taxed at £26 18*s*. The gardens were about a third of an acre in extent and were walled off from the Milltown Park lands (Map 17).[101]

Throughout the nineteenth century Milltown Cottage was rented out to tenants. One of these, Captain Henry Goold, was taken to task by the editor of the *Freeman's Journal* for publishing a pamphlet in April 1847 in which he advocated mass clearances of the peasantry from uneconomic landholdings and their replacement with farms of 30 acres, on the basis that it was desirable to reconstruct Irish rural society on a 30-acre landholding model. The editor sarcastically hoped that Goold's callous sentiments were confined to the Swiss Cottage and 'that romantic locality'.[102]

99 'Milltown Park and some of its owners', pp. 10–11; Milltown Park title deeds, lease dated 6 December 1836, Francis Hodgkinson to George FitzJames Russell; *Dublin Evening Packet and Correspondent*, 1 December 1840, p. 2.

100 Bargeboards are carved or pierced wooden boards which are fixed beneath the eaves of a gable to protect the rafters: *Pevsner's Architectural Glossary* (Yale, 2010), p. 32.

101 Griffith's Valuation, Rateable Valuation of Tenements, Co. Dublin, Barony of Uppercross, Parish of St Peter, Townland of Milltown, 1850, p. 54.

102 *Freeman's Journal*, 16 July 1847, p. 2; Pettigrew and Oulton's Dublin Almanac and General Register of Ireland 1847, p. 843.

A successor to Captain Goold at Swiss Cottage, Miss Frances Cash, in October 1858 confronted a burglar who was attempting to steal two of her dresses. Patrick Long pleaded guilty and was sentenced to four months' imprisonment with hard labour.[103] Long was fortunate in his sentence; had he committed his crime a few years earlier he would undoubtedly have been transported to Australia, but this form of sentencing, with a few exceptions, had ended by 1857.[104] Frances's brush with Patrick Long did not dissuade her religious convictions that criminals could be rehabilitated, for in 1889 she raised over £5 among like-minded people in Milltown for the Dublin Prison Gate Mission.[105] Sixty-six-year-old Frances Cash was still living in Swiss Cottage with her fifty-five-year-old domestic servant, Mary Monks, on the night of the 1901 census, which was taken on 31 March 1901.[106]

Throughout its existence, Swiss Cottage very rarely came up for public sale and on the one publicised occasion that it did, it caused great local interest. In May 1902 Swiss Cottage was put up for auction in what was described as a mortgagee's sale – i.e. a distressed sale. A contemporary newspaper advertisement from this time is the only surviving description of the property and is worth quoting in full:

> *Mortgagee's sale. Pretty detached house Swiss Cottage, Milltown. Beside Milltown Colonnade – a few minutes' walk of Clonskeagh tram. The dwelling house, which is handsomely built in Swiss style, contains handsome porched entrance, two sitting rooms, four bedrooms, kitchen, servants' apartments, storeroom, pantries, etc., lock-up yard, coach house and stabling, large garden front and rear, well walled-in and nicely laid out. The premises are let to a yearly tenant (old letting) at £10 and taxes. Head rent £3. Lease 900 years.*[107]

The auction took place on 23 May 1902 at which the house was sold for an undisclosed sum 'after a very spirited competition'.[108] The sale of Swiss Cottage did not disturb Miss Cash's tenancy, as she died there on 3 October 1904.[109]

The next resident of Swiss Cottage was William Battersby, a prominent Freemason and the head of the longstanding eponymous auctioneering firm. Battersby died suddenly at his home in Milltown on 15 October 1908, which by then had been renamed Garrynure.[110] The following year a Mr Gorevan was living in Garrynure. He was the first Catholic tenant to live there.[111] Two years later the occupants had changed again. On the night of the 1911 census, forty-six-year-old spinster Elizabeth Kiely was living in Garrynure with her unmarried sister Margaret, their servant Annie Howe, and two children named Estella and Valentine Hardy aged six and

---

103 *Evening Freeman*, 14 October 1858, *p. 3; Saunders's Newsletter*, 14 October 1858, *p. 3; Dublin Daily Express*, 14 October 1858, p. 4.

104 Patrick J. O'Farrell, 'The Irish in Australia and New Zealand, 1791–1870' in W.E. Vaughan (ed.), *'A new history of Ireland', v: Ireland under the Union 1801–1870* (Oxford, 1989), p. 661. In the 1820s and 1830s, about 1,000 convicts a year were being sent to Australia.

105 *Dublin Daily Express*, 8 July 1889, p. 6.

106 NAI, 1901 Census, Form A, residents of house no. 7, Milltown Road, Rathmines & Rathgar East Electoral Division, Parish of St Peter, Milltown townland, Dublin.

107 *Freeman's Journal*, 10 May 1902, p. 8.

108 *Rathmines News*, 31 May 1902, p. 4.

109 *Weekly Irish Times*, 8 October 1904, p. 1.

110 *Freeman's Journal*, 16 October 1908, p. 6; *Irish Independent*, 16 October 1908, p. 4.

111 *Freeman's Journal*, 31 July 1909, p. 4. Gorevan gave 3s. to the annual collection for Pope Pius X held that year in the local Catholic church.

eight respectively who were boarders. Curiously, all of the adults in the household on census night were Catholics but the two Hardy children were members of the Church of Ireland.[112]

It would appear from a map in the Jesuit archives that the Jesuits bought Garrynure at the auction of 23 May 1902.[113] As was frequently the case with old properties in Milltown, the leasehold interests attached to Garrynure were complicated. An undated file note in the Jesuit archives from 1952 records that, 'as far as I can make out Miss Kiely paid us £60 per annum but from some notes I have seen I think she also paid £5 annually for ground rent'.[114] The Jesuit archives do not explain why the order purchased Garrynure but their archives furnish more information about the house and its tenants in the twentieth century. In the 1920s a tenant called Mrs Ada Connolly 'raised the kitchen by lowering the floor, put in a lift from kitchen to dining room, put in electric light, built a small room off the lavatory outside the dining room'.[115] Mrs Connolly was a wealthy widow who had been married to a Limerick solicitor. When she died in 1945, Mrs Connolly left an estate of over £55,000. Her will made the news because she bequeathed £5,000 to her faithful housekeeper of 42 years' service, Miss Rose Sheridan, aged sixty. Ms Sheridan told reporters that she had no plans for the future apart from taking 'a much needed rest'.[116] Mrs Connolly was an example of someone who could easily have afforded a substantial home of her own with freehold title but she seems to have been quite happy to rent her home on a yearly lease instead. In fact, Connolly had been a protected tenant under various Rent Acts and had been paying a fixed annual rent of £100 to the Jesuits since 1920. Thus, she had spent £2,500 on rent during her 25-year tenure of Garrynure, small beer when compared to the size of her estate.[117]

Following Mrs Connolly's death, the Jesuits let Garrynure to the Koenigs sisters, Olga, Brenda and Gwendolene at an annual rent of £120.[118] Very little information is available about these ladies apart from the fact that Ms Olga Koenigs was appointed as a personal assistant to an unnamed minister in the Interparty Government of 1948, at a weekly wage of £6 10*s*.[119] The last of the Koenigs sisters died in 1972.[120] Afterwards Garrynure became derelict although it continued in Jesuit ownership until the mid-1990s, at which point the house was demolished prior to the site's sale to Jackson Properties. In November 1995 Jackson Properties applied for planning permission to build 13 apartments following which the current townhouse development, also called Garrynure, was built on the site.[121]

---

112 NAI, 1911 Census, Form A, residents of house no. 3, Milltown Road, Rathmines & Rathgar East Electoral Division, Parish of St Peter, Milltown townland, Dublin.

113 Jesuit Archives, IE IJA/FM/Mill/5/1/7, Map of Milltown Park 3 April 1903.

114 Jesuit Archives, IE IJA/FM/Mill/5/2/4 (199).

115 Jesuit Archives, IE IJA/FM/Mill/5/2/4 (199).

116 *Irish Press*, 22 August 1945, p. 2; *Sunday Independent*, 19 August 1945, p. 1.

117 Jesuit Archives, IE IJA/FM/Mill/5/2/4 (159).

118 Jesuit Archives, IE IJA/FM/Mill/5/2/4 (159, 161, 199); *Irish Press, 2 July 1948, p. 6; 6 April 1963, p. 2; 2 October 1972, p. 2.*

119 *Irish Press*, 2 July 1948, p. 5.

120 *Irish Press*, 2 October 1972.

121 *Irish Independent*, 24 November 1995, p. 19; Dublin City Council Planning Department, plan no. 2129/95.

Plate 32. Elm House, Milltown Road, 2017 (author's collection)

ELM HOUSE AND ELM GROVE HOUSE (PREVIOUSLY ELMFIELD AND ELM HALL)

Elm House is a two-storey five-bay semi-detached house with a double pitched roof and its neighbour, Elm Grove House, is a smaller two-storey four-bay house with a single pitched roof (Pl. 32 & Pl. 33). An unusual feature of Elm House is that the ground floor windows are narrower than those on the first floor on the front façade while the reverse applies at the rear front. The two houses are opposite the row of shops on the south side of Milltown Road on Milltown Hill.

During the eighteenth and nineteenth centuries Elm House and Elm Grove House were inhabited as a single structured dwelling house, successively called Elmfield and Elm Hall, which was surrounded by pleasure grounds and farmland extending to eight statute acres (Map 15 & Map 17). In the early twentieth century Elm Hall (as Elm House was then called) was subdivided into two unequally sized semi-detached residences called Elm House and Elm Grove House.[122] These structures have been rebuilt, extended and renamed on several occasions over the centuries and as a result they have a complicated history. In particular, from the 1890s onwards the names given to the two dwelling houses becomes very confusing, especially as the contemporary records such as the VO cancellation books, the newspapers, the Thom's directories and the Jesuit archives often apply different names and are inconsistent with each other. Furthermore, the home farm attached to the bigger of the two houses (Elm House) continued to be called Elm Hall into the 1920s.

122 *Rathmines News*, 23 July 1904, p. 2; *Sunday Independent*, 13 August 1911, p. 7; Thom's Directory 1915, p. 1868.

Plate 33. Elm Grove House, Milltown Road, 2017 (author's collection)

What follows, therefore, is an attempt to piece together an incomplete jigsaw puzzle of two buildings that at various times have been occupied either as a single detached family home or as two semi-detached properties. In an attempt to avoid as much confusion as possible caused by the many name changes and redevelopment, the approach I have adopted is to refer to the entire property as Elm House except when quoting from contemporary sources or where the context requires that one or other name be used.

In 1731 part of the land on which Elm House was later built was let by Joseph Leeson's tenants, the Allens, to a Dublin merchant called John Adamson. The property amounted to one and a half acres plantation measure and included 'the houses thereon which was formerly in the possession of John Magennis, gardener and now in the occupation of John Adamson'.[123]

It is unclear if any of these houses related to Elm House but it seems they did not for the following reasons. On 19 September 1733 Adamson sublet part of his landholding to the banker David La Touche, junior, which was described as: 'all that and those that piece of ground then in the possession of the said David La Touche containing three roods and eighteen perches.'[124]

Notably, this grant to La Touche did not mention a dwelling house. Three years later Adam-

123 RD 69/29/47040. RD 1869/17/208 converted the 1731 lease to a fee farm grant.

124 'Milltown Park and some of its owners', pp. 5–6; RD 1906/22/195. The original lease of 1733 was held by the Jesuits during their ownership of the property in the nineteenth and twentieth centuries; however, no record of that deed could be found in the Registry of Deeds; A Directory of Dublin for the year 1738 (Dublin Corporation Public Libraries, 2000), p. 1.

son the granted a lease to Alderman William Walker of Dublin on 5 July 1736 of another plot of land described as:

> *that lot of ground situate on the road leading from Dublin to Milltown being part of some lands in the said lease recited containing in front to the road sixty feet or thereabouts and in the rear ninety four feet or thereabouts together with a new house and stable built thereon bounded on the south and west by Mr Johnston's wall [i.e. the wall separating the new house from Milltown Castle grounds] and on the north side bounded by a stone wall ... and also all that house and garden then in the said John Adamson's possession being part of the said recited lands situate between the last mentioned premises and a house and garden belonging to Mr David La Touche.*[125]

The premises recited at the end of the extract belonging to David La Touche is the property now called Elm House.[126] It is impossible to identify the builder of Elm House but the likelihood is that it was David La Touche rather than his landlord John Adamson. The two properties mentioned in the Walker lease adjacent to Elm House have not survived. They appear to have originally been built on ground to the south of Elm House now occupied by the entrance to the Mount St Anne's apartments and town houses.

In 1741 David La Touche extended his landholding beside Elm House to the north and west. In June of that year Robert Harris leased the following plot of land to La Touche:

> *all that piece or parcel of land being part of the lands of Milltown in the county of Dublin containing in breadth on the south east side fronting the high road leading from Dublin to Milltown 359 feet, on the north west side adjoining to other land in the possession of Robert Harris 388 feet, on the north east side adjoining other land in the possession of Robert Harris 724 feet, on the south west side adjoining partly to the then present holding of the said David Digges La Touche and partly to the holding of Mr Dobson 737 feet or thereabouts ... and bounded in a map thereof containing according to the said survey four acres plantation measure more or less.*[127]

This description together with the description of the 3 roods and 18 perches leased to La Touche in 1733 was repeated verbatim in succeeding property deeds down to the twentieth century and formed the landholding of the Elm House demesne as depicted on the first edition of the OS map (Map 15).[128] A small fragment of the original eighteenth-century limestone boundary wall at its northern extremity survives today on the laneway adjacent to the Autovision car dealership on Milltown Road.

In 1769 David La Touche sold all of his property in Milltown to a Dublin jeweller, Francis Smyth, for £1,000, which was a very considerable sum for the time.[129] By 1791 Elm House had come into the possession of Joseph Madden of Donnybrook, who was described as a lime burner. Madden in turn leased the property the following year to a barrister, Robert John-

---

125 RD 85/42/58964.

126 The maps and deeds held in the Jesuit archives put the matter beyond all reasonable doubt.

127 RD 102/457/71781.The four acres was part of the 12-acre holding which Joseph Leeson let to Harris on 9 April 1741: RD 102/337/71029.

128 RD 1901/34/14, RD 1906/22/195.

129 RD 275/106/175335.

son, at the yearly rent of £125.[130] It was while under Johnson's ownership that the property acquired the name Elmfield.[131]

In 1800 and in 1802 Johnson carried out extensive repairs and alterations to his property at Milltown, which are recorded in great detail by the quantity surveyor Bryan Bolger, whose papers are deposited in the National Archives. The work included 'whitening the ceiling of 4 rooms in the new addition', supplying 'the coping on parapets front and rear of the new addition in mountain stone' and repairing 'half the party gutter adjoining Judge Chamberlain's offices.'[132]

A two-bay extension was made to the eastern end of Elm House, which probabbly explains why the hall door is located asymmetrically in the front façade of the house.[133] The different dimensions of the extended dwelling house are recorded in the Griffith's Valuation house book survey of 1845.[134] The granite mountain stone coping referred to in the Bryan Bolger papers can still be seen on the parapet of the current structure, which was extensively renovated in 2016. The reference to 'Judge Chamberlain's offices' is to Judge William Tankerville Chamberlain of the King's Bench, who was living next door to Judge Johnson in Milltown House (later Mount St Anne's).[135]

Of all the owners of Elm House, Robert Johnson has left the most colourful historical legacy. He was born about 1745 and was called to the Irish bar in 1776. He became a member of the Irish parliament in 1788 for Hillsborough under the patronage of the Marquess of Downshire, and was appointed to lucrative positions including the recorder of Hillsborough, counsel to the Linen Board and the revenue, and barrack master of Dublin. Johnson was re-elected as an MP for Hillsborough in 1797. He supported the Act of Union and received compensation for the loss of his various offices of almost £1,400. In 1801 he was rewarded for his support of the Act of Union by being appointed as a judge of the Common Pleas on a salary of £2,500.[136] No doubt these financial rewards facilitated the improvements made to Elm House by Johnson.

For reasons which have never been explained, using the pseudonym 'Juverna' Judge Johnson decided to launch a scathing and libellous attack on the Irish executive, including the Lord Lieutenant and the Lord Chancellor. Johnson made his attacks in the autumn of 1803 in a series of letters which were published in England in Cobbett's Political Register. In due course, Johnson's authorship was revealed when the publisher (Cobbett) was forced to hand over the original manuscript to the English authorities and Johnson's handwriting was identified. In view of the seriousness of the material the English government decided to issue proceedings against Johnson for libel.[137] On 24 November 1804 Johnson was indicted in Middlesex for libel by Lord Ellenborough, the Lord Chief Justice of England and a warrant for his arrest was issued.[138]

---

130 RD 456/485/293715, RD 456/485/293715.

131 *Saunders's Newsletter*, 20 April 1810, p. 4.

132 Bryan Bolger Papers (NAI, MS 2/476/15-16).

133 This detail is confirmed by an estate agent's plan of the house from September/October 2007.

134 NAI, VO, OL50945, House Book for Milltown Village 1845, no. 98.

135 RD 528/4/344352.

136 Ball, *The Judges in Ireland*, ii, p. 333; James McGuire and James Quinn (eds), *A Dictionary of Irish Biography from the earliest times to the year 2002* (Cambridge, 2009), iv, p. 998.

137 Ball, *The Judges in Ireland*, ii, p. 247; Sir Spencer Walpole, *The Life of the Right Honourable Spencer Percival* (London, 1874), pp. 118–20.

138 Walpole, *Life of Spencer Percival*, p. 124.

During the following year, 1805, the pace of the political and legal events quickened against Johnson and what follows here is a brief summary.[139]

During December 1804 and early January 1805 Johnson refused to accede to the government's demands to travel to England to stand trial in the following law term. He justified his position on grounds of ill health – he apparently had suffered a stroke four months previously which left him paralysed on his left side – and Johnson argued (among many other points) that he did not have enough time to prepare his defence. In view of his resistance the Irish authorities had little alternative but to arrest Johnson. Two peace officers arrived at Elm House late on the evening of the 17 January 1805 to execute the arrest warrant. Johnson managed to postpone his arrest that night by writing to the Irish attorney general. Nonetheless, the following day a peace officer and a police constable returned to Elm House with instructions from the attorney general to arrest Johnson and bring him to the city in advance of sailing to England forthwith. In the attorney general's opinion, this course of action was necessary in order for the arrest warrant to comply with the wording of the relevant legislation.[140] On his way to the ship, Judge Johnson called to his brother's house in Harcourt Street so that he could make some hasty domestic arrangements for his family, who were at home in Elm House and were unaware of the critical situation now facing him. In the meantime, Johnson's legal team had been preparing a writ of *habeus corpus* and had arranged for the Chief Justice, Lord Downes, to remain on standby to grant the application. However, Johnson had to get from Harcourt Street to the Chief Justice's house in Merrion square without opposition from the police constable, whose orders were to sail immediately to England with him. Johnson managed to persuade the constable to accompany him in his carriage while he made one final stop on the way to the docks. Before they left Harcourt Street and unbeknownst to the constable, Johnson's private physician Sir Henry Jebb, who was in the house in Harcourt Street, spoke to Johnson's coachman and instructed him to drive directly to the Chief Justice's house in Merrion square. The ruse worked and Johnson successfully sought refuge with the Chief Justice until the writ of *habeus corpus* was obtained.[141] The conspiracy to dupe the police constable was later recalled by Sir Henry Jebb in the following terms:

> *I accordingly desired Mick to bring the carriage to the door, and not to heed any directions that might be given to him as to where he should go; but whenever you [Johnson] got in, to drive directly to Judge Downes, in Merrion square. Mick did his business very well, and saved you a disagreeable passage in a wherry, that I understand was kept in waiting in deep water, to avoid the delay of a few hours for the packet, which was to sail with the next tide.*[142]

Although Johnson had succeeded in avoiding arrest and transportation to England in mid-winter 1805–6, he lost three subsequent court hearings concerning the validity of the arrest war-

139 Those events are recorded in voluminous detail in contemporary manuscript correspondence and publications, e.g. 'R v Johnson' in William Cobbett, *Complete Collection of State Trials*, xxix, no. 672, pp. 81–506 (London, 1821); John Swift Emerson, *A full and faithful report of the proceedings in His Majesty's Court of the Exchequer in Ireland in the case of the Honourable Mr Justice Robert Johnson* (Dublin, 1805); Sir Spencer Walpole, *The Life of the Right Honourable Spencer Percival* (London, 1874), pp. 118–20.

140 The legislation concerned was the English statute of 44 George 3, cap. 92, 'An Act to render more easy the apprehending and brining to trial offenders escaping from one part of the United Kingdom to the other'.

141 'R v Johnson' in Cobbett, *State Trials*, xxix, no. 672, pp. 95–100; Emerson, *Report of the case of the Honourable Mr Justice Robert Johnson*, Postscript (unpaginated).

142 Emerson, *Report of the case of the Honourable Mr Justice Robert Johnson*, Postscript (last page).

rant and his extradition proceedings, which took place successively in the Irish King's Bench, the Court of Exchequer and the Court of Common Pleas. In short, Johnson argued unsuccessfully that his extradition to England for a crime committed there was unlawful because he had never physically been present in England when the crime was committed.[143] These hearings were awkward for the main legal protagonists for several reasons: the case involved a judicial colleague, Baron George, who sat in the Court of the Exchequer, and Prime Sergeant Arthur Browne, a prosecuting counsel, both of whom were neighbours of Johnson on Milltown Road. The end result was that Johnson's libel case went to trial in the English King's Bench in London on 23 November 1805, where he was convicted of libel by the jury at the end of a hearing that lasted all day.[144]

The consequence for Johnson's conviction was that he faced receiving a gaol sentence at a subsequent prosecution on indictment, which was due to take place later in 1806. A notice in *Saunders's Newsletter* of 18 January 1806 advertised a one day's sale of furniture at 'Elm Lodge, Milltown Hill'.[145] Assuming the notice refers to Johnson's house, the timing of the sale is puzzling given that his future was very uncertain at that time. Furthermore, in April 1806 Johnson was reported to be 'at a little distance from Dublin, very unwell'.[146] A change of government improved Johnson's position and he was eventually allowed to retire from the bench on a reduced pension, the attorney general having entered a *nolle prosequi* in the Trinity law term of 1806. Notwithstanding Johnson's bouts of sickness in 1805 and 1806, he lived on in retirement well into his eighties until his death in 1833.[147]

Judge Johnson and his family left Elm House (then named Elmfield) sometime 1810, if not before. In that year a notice appeared in the newspapers advertising the sale of 'Elmfield ... wherein Robert Johnson, esq. lately resided.'[148]

Elm House was bought by Samuel Bruce on 4 July in 1810. Bruce was a public notary and stockbroker who specialised in the negotiation and sale of government and public securities.[149] Seven years later Bruce put Elm House up for sale. The advertisement described the property as consisting of a roomy dwelling house and offices and a good walled garden, all on five acres of land. The advertisement went on to state that if the property did not sell, Bruce would set it partly furnished for the summer season or for a year.[150] There was insufficient interest in Elm House and it was still in Bruce's ownership when he died in August 1834, following which his executors put up the property for sale in accordance with Bruce's will.[151] One of the property's attractions was that 'as this property is held for lives renewable forever, it affords an opportunity seldom offered to builders and others for speculation'. The market thought differently and the house was re-advertised for sale 12 months later when it failed to find a buyer for the

143 Paul O'Higgins, 'Arthur Browne (1756–1805): An Irish Civilian', *Northern Ireland Legal Quarterly*, 20, no. 3 (September 1969), p. 269.

144 Walpole, *Life of Spencer Percival, p. 125; Belfast Newsletter*, 10 May 1805, p. 2; *Finn's Leinster Journal*, 4 December 1805, p. 2.

145 *Saunders's Newsletter*, 18 January 1806, p. 3.

146 *Fortesque Manuscripts*, Historical Manuscripts Commission, viii (London, 1912), p. 99.

147 'R v Johnson' in Cobbett, *State Trials*, xxix, no. 672, p. 502; Ball, *The Judges in Ireland*, ii, p. 253; *Dublin Morning Register*, 22 March 1833, p. 1; 26 June 1833, p. 4.

148 *Saunders's Newsletter*, 20 April 1810, p. 4.

149 *Saunders's Newsletter*, 24 July 1810, p. 4; RD 1846/5/244 (recital in deed).

150 *Saunders's Newsletter*, 30 April 1817, p. 4.

151 *Saunders's Newsletter*, 12 May 1835, p. 1; RD 1846/5/244.

second time.[152] Elm House was retained by Bruce's estate for several years – a deed of 1846 recites that 'his [Bruce's] executors immediately after his decease and from time to time since offered the said premises for sale without effect, no person having proposed to purchase the same'.[153] This suggests that either the property market was in the doldrums or that the rent of £125 negotiated for Elm House in 1792 had become too expensive by the 1830s. Possibly both negative conditions applied.

Elm House was eventually sold in December 1845 to the Misses Hunt, who were descendants of Percival Hunt the younger who died in Milltown in 1776.[154] These four ladies, Mary Anne Hunt, Charlotte Hunt, Amelia Hunt and Helena Louisa Hunt, who were living in Milltown Castle in the 1830s had apparently decided to acquire Elm House as a residence for themselves and generate additional rental income from their erstwhile home, Milltown Castle.[155] The Misses Hunt struck a hard bargain with the Bruce estate. The lease of 25 March 1792 from Joseph Madden to Judge Johnson was surrendered and the Bruce estate paid the Misses Hunt £200 to take the property off their hands.[156] In addition, John Madden of Donnybrook granted a new lease for lives renewable forever to the Misses Hunt at an annual rent of £115 *7s. 8d.* sterling (equivalent to £125 old currency under the 1792 lease) for the lives of Queen Victoria, Prince Albert and Princess Victoria.[157] For whatever reason, the Hunts were unable to negotiate a rent reduction for Elm House but the £200 from the Bruce estate was useful compensation that enabled the ladies to redecorate and furnish the house which, as we have seen, had not been renovated since 1802. An additional benefit was that the three royal lives named in the new lease were all aged under the age of thirty so a renewal fine on the death of one of the lives would not likely occur for a long time into the future.

The Hunts' tenure at Elm House was uneventful. The Hunt ladies were members of the local Church of Ireland congregation and from time to time contributed to charitable collections for the poor of Milltown (£1 each), the City of Dublin Hospital (£1) and the Association for the Relief of Distressed Protestants (£1).[158] None of the four sisters ever married, the last of whom, Charlotte, died on 26 February 1874 aged eighty-three leaving an estate of over £8,000. Charlotte Hunt appointed a distant relative, John Lombard Hunt, as her residual legatee and he inherited Elm House. During their ownership the Misses Hunt had changed the name of their home from Elmfield to Elm Hall.[159] Charlotte Hunt's extensive possessions were auctioned on 16 March 1874.[160] The lease for Elm House was put up for auction two months later, on 25 May 1874. The estate agent provided a detailed description of the property as well as trying to arouse the interest of builders:

---

152 *Saunders's Newsletter*, 30 May 1836, p. 4.

153 RD 1846/5/244.

154 RD 1846/5/244; *Freeman's Journal*, 12 October 1776, p. 3; Patrick Salmon, 'The Hunt Family and Milltown Castle', *Dublin Historical Record*, lxxiii (2020), pp. 98–9.

155 Lewis, *Topographical Dictionary of Ireland*, ii, 370.

156 RD 1846/5/244.

157 RD 1846/5/300.

158 *Daily Express*, 29 December 1862, p. 3; *Saunders's Newsletter*, 4 October 1853, p. 3; 23 July 1856, p. 3.

159 NAI, Will Registers of Ireland, 1874, Surnames G-W, Folio 95-96, Transcript of the original will of Ms Charlotte Hunt, deceased. Transcription from the Register of Births, Marriages and Deaths for 1874, Dublin South, vol. 2, p. 655 as recorded on www.findmypast.ie.

160 *Irish Times*, 13 March 1874, p. 8.

> *The house contains 3 sitting rooms, 5 bedrooms, servants' rooms, spacious hall, kitchen, and pantries, with gate lodge entrance, carriage drive, coach house, stabling, and large garden. The entire stands on about eight acres of land, all under grass, admitted to be the very choicest for dairy cattle. There is a pretty boating pond in one of the lawn fields, supplied by a never-failing stream of the purest water. The frontage, presented for building sites, extends for several hundred feet, on the public road leading from Sandford to Milltown, commanding most magnificent and charming views of the Dublin mountains, etc; situate within three miles of the city, and only a few minutes' walk from the Dublin and Bray railway station at Milltown, on the one side, and an equal distance from the tram terminus, at Donnybrook, on the other side. The entire is held on lease of lives renewable for ever, subject to the low yearly head rent of £1 1 0 [sic]*[161]

Despite this promising advertisement with its curious reference to a boating pond, the house did not sell. Another auction notice appeared 13 months later on 12 June 1875 following which Elm House was sold by John Lombard Hunt to a hotel proprietor, Richard Healy, for £200.[162] Some 13 years later, a very brief notice appeared in the *Irish Times* in May 1888 advertising (unsuccessfully) Elm House for sale: 'Elm Hall, Milltown, large gentlemanly residence (out of repair), standing on six acres.'[163] The following year on 1 July 1889 an auction was held at Elm House of 'about 80 cocks [of] prime strong old meadow hay'.[164] Thus, the Elm House fields continued to be farmed while the house was left unoccupied and allowed to fall into disrepair.

Over the next decade, the ownership of Elm House becomes very complicated as various leasehold interests were consolidated and converted into fee farm grants in the 1890s.[165] In short, Elm House and its farmland came into the dual ownership of the Jesuits of Milltown Park and a local family called the O'Neills, both of whom had separate legal title to the property. Taking the Jesuit interest first, according to a history of Milltown Park written in 1914 the Jesuits bought Elm House from a Richard Healy in 1884.[166] This date is supported by the records of the Valuation Office, which show the Rev. Patrick Hughes as being the occupier and immediate lessor of Elm Hall in December 1885.[167] Turning to the O'Neill's title, in May 1895 John Lombard Hunt sold his remaining legal interest in Elm House to Mathew O'Neill, whose activities will be discussed shortly.[168] In the meantime, Elm House remained unoccupied and fell into further dilapidation in the 1890s.[169]

Mathew O'Neill was a market gardener, dairy farmer and publican who, prior to acquiring Elm House, lived on the opposite side of Milltown Road above a grocery shop and off-licence.[170] As well as these concerns, O'Neill bred prize-winning Jersey cattle that were considered to be among

---

161 *Freeman's Journal*, 22 May 1874, p. 8.

162 *Irish Times*, 12 June 1875, p. 8; RD 1875/35/137.

163 *Irish Times*, 19 May 1888, p. 8.

164 *Freeman's Journal*, 29 June 1889, p. 8.

165 RD 1894/44/59, RD 1894/53/267, RD 1895/35/92.

166 'Milltown Park and some of its owners', p. 12.

167 VO, Cancellation Books, Dublin, Rathmines East, Milltown Road, 1873–87, vol. 2, p. 191.

168 RD 1895/35/92. The property was then called Elm Hall (Map 18).

169 Thom's Directory 1892, p. 1550; VO, Cancellation Books, Dublin, Rathmines East, Milltown Road, 1887–99, vol. 2, p. 239.

170 Thom's Directory 1892, p. 1550; *Rathmines News*, 6 November 1897, p. 5; 29 December 1900, p. 5.

the best herds of the type in the country.[171] O'Neill's principal grazing grounds were on the south side of Milltown Road on what is now the Ramleh Park housing estate. In 1897 O'Neill signed a 35-year lease of 21 acres and 19 perches statute measure with the dwelling houses, shop, offices, buildings and cottages thereon.[172] These buildings were situated where the Spar shop and row of commercial premises at the top of Milltown Hill are now (Map 18).

Mathew O'Neill married a local widow, Mary Ann Doyle, of Milltown Hill in the mid-1890s.[173] In April 1901 the O'Neills mortgaged their legal interest in Elm House for £250, possibly to raise money to refurbish the property, since the Valuation Office had noted in December 1899 that Elm House was to be rebuilt.[174] In any event, Elm House was sufficiently habitable on the 1901 census night of 31 March, when it was then occupied by seven members of the Barlee family and their two domestic servants.[175] The census form for the houses and buildings return records the house as having nine front windows, the same number of front windows that Elm House currently has.

It was sometime during the first decade of the twentieth century that Elm House was divided in two by Mathew O'Neill and became two separate semi-detached properties, the one on the left (west) currently called Elm Grove House and the larger one on the right (east) named Elm House. According to a newspaper report of 13 August 1911, 'Mr O'Neill slept at night in a newly built and partially furnished residence, which he named Elm Hall, and which is situated directly opposite his licenced premises in Milltown.'[176] The circumstances of this information are tragic. O'Neill had been suffering for some years with kidney disease and he may have become estranged from his wife Mary Ann due to his heavy drinking. By February 1911 he had taken to sleeping alone in his new house, Elm Hall (as it was then identified in the newspapers), before he committed suicide by poisoning on 11 August 1911.[177] The coroner's inquest was held in Elm Hall during which Mrs O'Neill denied that her husband had any financial trouble or other worry apart from his health. Mrs O'Neill is likely to have been economical with the truth in giving her evidence. In February 1910 a Thomas O'Neill had successfully prosecuted a claim for £140 and 19*s*. against Mathew O'Neill.[178] Then, during the following October, he had sold off his entire herd of prize-winning Jersey herd on the pretext that he wanted to retire from the dairy business.[179] Clearly, there must have been an accumulation of difficulties that led to Mathew O'Neill taking his life, which his wife may have been unwilling or unable to disclose at the coroner's inquest.

The press report of 1911 refers to O'Neill as having built himself a new residence but this statement is somewhat misleading.[180] From a careful study of the cartographic evidence in

171 *Dublin Daily Nation*, 23 August 1900; *Freeman's Journal*, 22 October 1910, p. 12.

172 RD 1897/47/173.

173 RD 1895/35/114, RD1896/10/134.

174 RD 1901/34/14; VO, Cancellation Books, Dublin, Rathmines East, Milltown Road, 1887–89, vol. 2, p. 239.

175 NAI, 1901 Census, Form A, residents of house no. 70, Milltown Road, Rathmines and Rathgar East Electoral Division, Milltown townland, Dublin. The head of the household was a fifty-nine-year-old Dublin solicitor, Arthur Lee Barlee.

176 *Sunday Independent*, 13 August 1911, p. 7.

177 *Sunday Independent*, 13 August 1911, p. 7.

178 *Irish Independent*, 21 February 1910, p. 6.

179 *Freeman's Journal*, 22 October 1910, p. 12; *Dublin Daily Express*, 27 October 1910, p. 10.

180 *Sunday Independent*, 13 August 1911, p. 7.

the Jesuit archives,[181] the OS maps and the Valuation Office cancellation books, it is beyond doubt that the Elm House property was divided in two rather than replaced with a completely new building. What happened was that the left-hand (western) part of the dilapidated Elm House, perhaps containing offices and servants' quarters, was refurbished and converted into a separate dwelling house by O'Neill, and later renamed Elm Grove House.[182] O'Neill converted part of his Elm Hall property into a small shop, which in the 1960s was called the Barn Stores and contained Milltown post office.[183] The shop is currently a floristry, called the Enchanted Florist. The larger right-hand (eastern) part of Elm House was never occupied by the O'Neills. Instead, they renamed the property Elm House and let it on short-term leases to middle-class families such as the Barlees.[184]

In 1924, the Jesuits bought out the O'Neill freehold interest in Elm House, 'save and except the houses [*sic*] known as Elm Hall'. A note in the Jesuit archives from May 1924 states that 'part of the lands are let to a Football Club for the football season at a rent of £75'.[185] The football field was called 'Elm Park' and was used by the O'Neills for grazing their cattle. The field called Elm Park had been rented to Shamrock Rovers FC since 7 September 1923. Shamrock Rovers' origins lay in Ringsend, but the club is more popularly associated with Milltown. In 1926 the club moved to an adjacent site beside the Elm Park field on a short-term renewable sporting lease at an annual rent of £130. The new site was later named Glenmalure Park.[186] Shamrock Rovers FC member Billy Behan recalled the club's move to Milltown:

> *They moved to Milltown to a pitch which was at the back of the last ground which they had there. You actually walked over that last ground to get to the original pitch [Elm Park field], you went up a laneway which was located along the wall where the [BMW] garage is now and the pitch was just up at the back of that. Then they got the second ground [Glenmalure Park] and all the Ringsend men went up and helped to build it up. It was a real Ringsend Club.*[187]

Originally, the second ground was called Milltown Park but the Jesuits objected to the club's use of that name because the Jesuits did not want people to think they were responsible for organising soccer matches at Shamrock Rover's new grounds! The two parties eventually agreed to rename the new soccer venue Glenmalure Park, the name 'Glenmalure' originating from the Ringsend residence of one of the club's prominent families.[188] In 1988 Glenmalure Park was sold to developers by the Kilcoyne family, who had acquired the ground from the Jesuits two years previously in 1986, and in 1990 the Glenmalure Square estate was built on the site.[189]

181 'Map of Lands at Elm Hall, Milltown, Co. Dublin', 1 October 1923 (Jesuit Archives IJA IE/FM/Mill 39).

182 Thom's Directory 1915, p. 1869.

183 Thom's Directory 1967, p. 408.

184 Thom's Directory 1902, p. 1592.

185 'Statement re Elm Park, 17 May 1924' (Jesuit Archives, IE IJA/FM/Mill/39).

186 Doolan and Goggins, *The Hoops*, p. 14.

187 Doolan and Goggins, *The Hoops*, p. 14.

188 Doolan and Goggins, *The Hoops*, p. 18.

189 Doolan and Goggins, *The Hoops*, pp. 279–317; Irish Independent, Friday 12 July 1991 p. 47. The Glenmalure Park grounds formed part of the four plantation acres of land originally owned by David La Touche in the 1730s.

The residents of Elm House and Elm Grove House changed frequently over the course of the twentieth century. Due to space constraints it is only possible to very briefly touch on some of these. A William Pollitt succeeded Arthur Barlee as resident of Elm House, and he died there in December 1925.[190] In the following decade, the Fianna Fáil TD, Seán O'Grady, was living there in 1938.[191] O'Grady was a native of Clare and had been a commanding officer of the IRA mid-Clare Brigade during the War of Independence. He was parliamentary secretary to the Minister for Lands and Fisheries from 1932 to 1943.[192]

On 8 May 1941 Elm House was put up for auction by Battersby's, whose advertisement advised prospective purchasers that the house had air-raid accommodation.[193] Reference to this feature turned out to be rather prophetic because the devastating bombing of the North Strand in Dublin took place three weeks' later on the night of 31 May 1941. Milltown resident and chief air raid warden Alec King attended the aftermath of that event and has left an extremely powerful oral testimony of the appalling things that he saw.[194]

PROSPECT

Prospect was a two-storey farmhouse which was built probably in the late eighteenth century on farmland to the south of Clonskeagh Lane that was part of George Frederick Mowlds' holding in Milltown of 9 acres and 1 rood plantation measure.[195] Clonskeagh Lane was renamed Prospect Lane in the nineteenth century (Map 17) and now provides access to Millbrook Court, the Crannagh town houses and Palmerston Grove. Prospect farmhouse was often confused in contemporary records and Dublin street directories with its neighbour, a villa called Prospect House (later, Grove House) that stood on the corner of Milltown Road and Prospect Lane, which will be discussed presently.

The early history of Prospect is very sketchy. The farmhouse was likely to have been built in the penultimate or last decade of the eighteenth century by one of George Mowlds' tenants, Joseph Madden, who was leasing land in Milltown and Clonskeagh at that time.[196] Prospect was owned by Joseph Madden's son, Peter, in the 1830s who then held 10 acres and 13 perches of land in Milltown.[197] By 1850 Prospect was the residence of Bartholemew Walker, a seedsman and florist, who held the house and 3 acres, 2 roods and 19 perches statute measure from John Madden.[198] The Madden legal interest in Prospect later devolved to a Richard Butler of Ballyslatter, County Tipperary, and he in turn leased Prospect farm to Daniel Byrne of Milltown in 1862.[199]

---

190 *Irish Times*, 10 December 1925, p. 3.

191 *Weekly Irish Times*, Saturday 23 July 1938, p. 13.

192 William J. Flynn (ed.), *Irish Parliamentary Handbook 1945* (Dublin, 1945), pp. 133–4.

193 *Dublin Evening Mail*, 3 May 1941, p. 6. This probably explains the house's unusual basement arrangement.

194 Kevin C. Kearns, *Dublin Voices: An oral folk history* (Dublin, 1998), pp. 16–21.

195 RD 1862/15/98.

196 RD 386/361/258792, RD 416/62/273539, RD 434/130/280717.

197 NAI, Tithe Aplotment Book, Diocese of Dublin, Parish of St Peter, Ranelagh and Milltown Road, assessed 30 December 1833 http://titheapplotmentbooks.nationalarchives.ie/reels/tab//004625716/004625716_00438.pdf (accessed 24 December 2019).

198 Griffith's Valuation, Rateable Valuation of Tenements, Co. Dublin, Barony of Uppercross, Parish of St Peter, Townland of Milltown, 1850, p. 54; Thom's Directory 1850, p. 837.

199 RD 1862/15/98, RD 1863/40/91; VO, Cancellation Books, Dublin, Rathmines East, Milltown Road, 1873–87, vol. 2, p. 193.

Byrne was a common family name in nineteenth-century Milltown and it is likely that Daniel Byrne's roots in Milltown go back a long way. In 1813 a William Byrne took a lease of 77 years of a small plot of land on the south side of Milltown main street close to 'The Strand'. William was a dairyman and his newly acquired property included a plot of ground with a rebuilt house or lodge.[200] In 1949 when this property was compulsorily acquired by Dublin Corporation, one of the old lessees recorded on the title was Daniel J. Byrne, the same person who took over Prospect farm in 1862.[201]

Daniel Byrne's principal livelihood was that of a horse trainer. In the 1870s Byrne was advertising hunters and harness horses for sale in the *Irish Times* which he sourced 'fresh from the counties Tipperary and Wexford, worthy for the attention of gentlemen'.[202] The horses were 'to be seen at Daniel Byrne's stables, Prospect, Milltown, within five minutes' walk of Donnybrook tramway terminus'.[203] A typical description of one of the hunters provided precise and essential information for a prospective, well-heeled gentleman or lady: 'Bay mare, by Welland, 5 years old, 15 2&1/2 hands high, clever huntress, well up to 13 stone, has been hunted with the Wexford hounds, perfectly steady in harness.'[204]

Byrne's clientele included the son of Field Marshal Lord Roberts, the Hon. Frederick Hugh Sherston Roberts, who sustained a serious head injury at Prospect when, as the *Rathmines News* unfortunately put it, 'Mr Roberts took a fancy to a hunter which was being exercised in Mr Byrne's grounds, and obtained permission to mount it.' The accident to Roberts was caused by the horse overjumping itself, with the result that Roberts was thrown off and sustained a severe concussion. Roberts was brought unconscious to the Royal Hospital Kilmainham where after three days he recovered consciousness. [205]

By the turn of the twentieth century Daniel Byrne had won a reputation as one of the most well-known horse breeders, trainers and dealers in the country, and was a prize winner at the Dublin Horse Show.[206] As well as his successful horse-dealing business, Byrne carried out extensive and diversified farming activities. In 1870 he was advertising for sale a large quantity of 'the best red mangold' at 30*s*. per ton which he would deliver within three miles of Dublin.[207] However, Byrne's dairy business was probably second only to the horse dealing in terms of importance. Byrne's main grazing fields were situated on the south bank of the River Dodder on land between the railway track (now the Luas tramline) and the Lower Churchtown Road and ground on the opposite side of the road which later became part of Milltown Golf Club.[208] In 1890, Daniel Byrne advertised to let at Milltown, a large dairy yard capable of holding 20 cows together with a

---

200 NAI, MS 999/355/1-12.

201 Minutes of the Municipal Council of the City of Dublin, 1953, p. 167 and 168 (Schedule to Milltown Village Area Compulsory Purchase Order, 1952).

202 *Irish Times*, 16 May 1870, p. 1.

203 *Irish Times*, 22 July 1876, p. 1.

204 *Irish Times*, 22 July 1876, p. 1.

205 *Rathmines News*, 22 February 1896, p. 1.

206 *Rathmines News*, 21 December 1901; *Evening Herald*, 26 August 1896, p. 3; *Irish Independent*, 12 July 1900, p. 7.

207 *Irish Times*, 5 December 1870, p. 1.

208 Hearn, *Thomas Edmondson*, p. 229. *Rathmines News*, 29 March 1902, p. 5; 16 July 1902, p. 3.

three-roomed cottage.[209] These dairy premises were probably located near Classon's Bridge and close to the Byrne grazing fields. Byrne also held land in Rowlestown, where he grazed sheep, and had farms in Lispople, St Margarets and Finglas.[210]

Byrne invested his agricultural profits in the local property market. He owned several houses in Ranelagh, Bushfield Avenue (Marlborough Road) and Beechwood Avenue which he advertised for rent on short-term lettings from time to time.[211] A correspondent of the *Rathmines News* from 1896 enthused about Byrne's building activities:

> *The Ranelagh people should be greatly pleased at the fact that Mr Dan Byrne, of Milltown, is opening up his grounds for building. I understand he intends making quite a town from Beechwood road to Milltown. We wish him every good luck.*[212]

The correspondent was a bit premature with his announcement. Two years later the same newspaper reported that Byrne had appeared before the commissioners of the Rathmines township and obtained permission to build two houses on Beechwood Road, Ranelagh. Byrne informed the commissioners that he was going to build a square of houses there, and he undertook to complete the road within a fortnight.[213]

Daniel Byrne's wife died in August 1898 and an extensive list of the mourners' who attended the funeral was published in the *Rathmines News*, which stated that 'the very large attendance testified to the great respect in which Mr Daniel Byrne and his family are held'.[214] Mrs Byrne was survived by four sons and five daughters, one of whom lived next door in Vergemount House with her husband, Charles Thompson, who was a cattle breeder.[215]

Given his extensive building operations it is surprising that on census night, 31 March 1901, Daniel Byrne was living in Prospect in somewhat crowded conditions amid a household of nine people.[216] Daniel Byrne described himself as being a widowed farmer aged sixty. Byrne's twenty-five-year-old daughter Bridget was the housekeeper, a role she inherited when her mother died. Bridget's younger brothers Thomas, aged twenty-two, and John, aged twenty, were also living with their father and described themselves as farmers. Their eight-year-old niece Margaret Murray was also staying over in Prospect on census night. A domestic servant, Ann Jenkinson, two grooms named John Wallis and Michael Phillips and a farm servant called Lawrence Mangan completed the household. The house and buildings census return form reveals that Prospect had five windows on its front elevation and that the house contained a total of seven rooms – a fairly

---

209 *Freeman's Journal*, 29 October 1890, p. 1.

210 *Rathmines News*, 16 February 1907, p. 4; *Dublin Daily Express*, 19 October 1908, p. 8; *Irish Independent*, 1 December 1914, p.2.

211 *Irish Times*, 11 January 1879, p. 8; *Freeman's Journal*, 29 October 1890, p. 1; *Rathmines News*, 29 February 1896, p. 2 and 5 March 1898, p. 5.

212 *Rathmines News*, 29 February 1896, p. 2.

213 *Rathmines News*, 5 March 1898, p. 5.

214 *Rathmines News*, 13 August 1898, p.5.

215 *Rathmines News*, 13 August 1898, p. 5; Thom's Directory 1895, p. 1561; 1897, p. 1569; *Evening Herald*, 7 June 1893, p. 2. This Thompson family was not related to Robert Wade Thompson who was living nearby in Clonskeagh Castle.

216 NAI, 1901 Census, Form A, residents of house no. 68, Milltown Road, Rathmines & Rathgar East Electoral Division, Parish of St Peter, Milltown townland, Dublin.

modest dwelling.[217] The out offices and farm buildings comprised six stables, three cow houses and a shed.[218] Ten years later the Byrne household had reduced to four people, Daniel, Bridget and John Byrne and a twenty-three-year-old domestic servant, Ellen Carroll. More significantly, by 1911 Daniel Byrne had retired from horse training and his son John now described himself as a builder/contactor.[219]

Daniel Byrne died on 26 August 1914 aged seventy-four. As a testament to his business acumen Byrne left an estate initially valued at just under £60,000, which was a colossal sum for the time.[220] Byrne's assets dwarfed the estate of his erstwhile neighbour, Annie Boswell of St James's, who had died in 1907 leaving an estate of under £8,000.[221] Put in another context, in 1904 Daniel Byrne's next door neighbours, the Rathmines and Pembroke Joint Hospital Board, advertised for two nurses to join the new isolation hospital on an annual salary of £30 each.[222] Ironically, Byrne's executors challenged the valuation assessed by the Commissioner of Valuation (£59,880) and on appeal, Byrne's real property valuation was reduced to £49,681 for estate duty purposes.[223]

Daniel Byrne was almost certainly the wealthiest private individual living in Milltown before he died.[224] He could easily have built or bought himself a trophy home but he chose instead to live in unassuming comfort in Prospect, his family home of over 50 years. Byrne came from a very modest Catholic background, yet during his lifetime he accumulated wealth that surpassed the vast majority of professionals and businessmen of the Rathmines township, many of whom came from privileged Protestant families. Aside from leaving bequests to his three sons and three daughters, Daniel Byrne bequeathed a house and premises beside the Catholic Church in the main street of Milltown to the parish clergy, or in the alternative, for use in connection with the national schools.[225]

Siblings John and Bridget Byrne continued living in Prospect after their father's death.[226] Sometime later, their brother Thomas Byrne took over the farmhouse and continued the family business of dairy farming. A photograph taken in about 1940 in the grounds of Vergemount Hospital shows the house and its extensive farm being encroached upon by the new hospi-

217 NAI, 1901 Census, Form B 1, house and buildings return for house no. 68, Milltown Road, Rathmines & Rathgar East Electoral Division, Parish of St Peter, Milltown townland, Dublin.

218 NAI, 1901 Census, Form B 2, out-offices and farm-steads return for house no. 68, Milltown Road, Rathmines & Rathgar East Electoral Division, Parish of St Peter, Milltown townland, Dublin.

219 NAI, 1911 Census, Form A, household return for house no. 1, Milltown Road, Rathmines & Rathgar East Electoral Division, Parish of St Peter, Milltown townland, Dublin on 2 April 1911.

220 *Irish Independent*, 1 December 1914, p. 2; 2 December 1914, p. 1. In 1913 only 1,425 deceased in the entire country left estates worth over £1,000: Peter Hession, 'The Irish Establishment: Continuity and change' in John Crowley, Donal Ó'Drisceoil and Mike Murphy (eds), *The Atlas of the Irish Revolution* (Cork, 2017), pp. 67–8.

221 NAI, Wills and Administration Abstracts, no. 215, 23 March 1907.

222 *Rathmines News*, 17 December 1904, p. 2. There is no information as to whether or not Byrne opposed the location of the hospital at Vergemount in 1902.

223 *Irish Independent*, 25 January 1916, p. 6; *General Advertiser for Dublin, and All Ireland*, 1 April 1916, p. 1.

224 The only known wealthier contemporary comparator, Milltown resident and Clonskeagh ironmonger Alfred Henshaw JP of St Philip's, left an estate worth over £109,000 when he died in 1897: NAI, Calendar of Wills and Administrations for 1897, p. 194.

225 *Irish Independent*, 1 December 1914, p. 2.

226 VO, Cancellation Books, Dublin, Rathmines East, Milltown Road, 1915–1929, vol. 3–4, p. 798.

Plate 34. Vergemount Hospital, Clonskeagh, held by G. & T. Crampton © unknown. Digital content by Dr Joseph Brady, published by UCD Library, University College Dublin http://digital.ucd.ie/view/ucdlib:47130

tal buildings and the houses of Ramleh Park (Pl. 34). In April 1941, a case of foot and mouth disease was discovered in one of Thomas Byrne's cattle herd at Prospect Dairy.[227] Despite this serious setback for his herd, Thomas Byrne was still farming at Prospect in 1945.[228] Thomas died on 31 May 1949. His address was recorded as formerly of Prospect, Milltown and late of 'Talna', Newtown Villas, Rathgar.[229]

After Byrne's death Prospect came into the ownership of W. O'Doherty, who carried on small-scale dairy or pig farming in the farmyard yard and field attached to Prospect farmhouse.[230] Prospect was demolished in the late 1960s to make way for Ramleh Close, a small cul-de-sac of 24 detached houses accessed from Ramleh Park.[231]

GROVE HOUSE (PREVIOUSLY MOUNT PROSPECT)

Mount Prospect was built on the corner of Prospect Lane and Milltown Road in the mid-eighteenth century. It has not proved possible to identify the builder of Mount Prospect or pro-

227 *Irish Independent*, 18 April 1941, p. 6.

228 Jesuit Archives, IE IJA/FM/Mill/5/2/3 (26).

229 NAI, calendar of grants of probate of wills and letters of administration, CS/HC/PO/4/102/109 (Thomas Byrne).

230 Thom's Directory 1952, p. 1271.

231 Dublin City Council Planning Department, plan no. 441/68, reg. no. 376/68.

Plate 35. Grove House, Milltown Road, road frontage, c. 1974 (courtesy of the Irish Architectural Archive)

vide a definite date for when it was built. However, there is evidence indicating that the house was built in the mid-1740s and was occupied by a John Bayly until his death in 1753. Mount Prospect's name was changed in the late nineteenth century to Grove House. Grove House was demolished in 1974 and the eponymous apartment complex was built on the site. Before reviewing the history of the house, it is appropriate to highlight its architectural and decorative features, thanks to the valuable photographic record of the house that is preserved in the Irish Architectural Archive.

Mount Prospect was a large three-storey house with an irregular, asymmetric plan. The house comprises a rectangular five-bay entrance front with a symmetrically placed doorway on the first floor together with a projecting two-storey extension at its eastern end with a Venetian window and a balustrade (Pl. 35). The villa underwent a major redevelopment in the fourth quarter of the eighteenth century which probably explains the irregular layout of the house at its eastern end that features an elevated turret with three windows facing east. In the mid- to late nineteenth century changes were made to the windows of the first-floor reception rooms, and 17 chimney pots were added to the chimney stacks. The rear of the house faced onto Milltown Road and the original narrow entrance to what was then Clonskeagh Lane (now Prospect Lane) is clearly visible between the boundary wall of the house and that of the Palmerston Rugby Club, now the Millbrook Court estate (Pl. 36).

Given the unpretentious exterior of Mount Prospect it is a surprise to discover an interior of very high quality, the most important feature being the plasterwork in the main reception

Plate 36. Grove House, Milltown Road, garden frontage, c. 1974 (courtesy of the Irish Architectural Archive)

room (Pl. 37). When C.P. Curran, the noted expert on Dublin plasterwork, visited Grove House in 1939 or 1940 to photograph the fine stuccowork, he was very taken with the quality of the work, to which he assigned a date of *c.* 1750. This is how Curran contextualised Grove House in the evolution of Irish rococo plasterwork in mid-eighteenth-century Dublin:

> *Grove House, Milltown, has a coved ceiling of approximately this date [1750]. With birds and flowers but without figures it is a very charming and lucid example of pure rococo. The suave elegance of these floral ceilings in Grove House, Mayo House, Mornington House and other houses in Merrion Street and on the north side of Merrion Square realise so completely the intention of their designers that it is irrelevant to put them in competition with their figured elders.*[232]

When Curran published his lifetime's research 27 years later in 1967, he was still enthused by Grove House, and was inclined to assign its plasterwork to one of Dublin's most important mid-eighteenth-century stuccodores, Robert West.[233]

The acclamation given to Grove House's plasterwork eclipses the quality of the eighteenth-century joinery. The hall doorway is particularly elegant, with its fine six-panelled door and delicate fanlight surmounted by a broken pediment. The elaborate joinery of the reception room doors

232 C.P. Curran, 'Dublin Plasterwork', *Journal of the Royal Society of Antiquaries of Ireland*, seventh series, 10, no. 1 (March 1940), pp. 22, 23, 32, 33, 49.

233 C.P. Curran, *Dublin Decorative Plasterwork of the seventeenth and eighteenth centuries* (London, 1967), p. 64.

Plate 37. Grove House, Milltown Road, plasterwork, c. 1974 (courtesy of the Irish Architectural Archive)

and windows with their shouldered architraves are admirable too (Pl. 38). It is of course very regrettable that the house and its fine interior were demolished in the 1970s, a period when there was no planning protection for Dublin's suburban villas. Despite this, the rococo ceiling in Grove House was salvaged and reinstated in Ballyorney House, Enniskerry, County Wicklow.[234]

The land on which Mount Prospect was built formed the northernmost part of the 13½ plantation acres of land at the corner of Milltown Road and Clonskeagh Lane and which was leased by Joseph Leeson to John Kerr in 1725.[235] Kerr in turn sublet all of his holding to four subtenants, one of whom was a Dublin silk weaver, William Cole. In September 1747, a six-acre plot located in the southern half of the 13½ acres was leased to David La Touche, who was required to pay his rent to John Watson in trust for Hannah Cole, William Cole's widow.[236] The lease described the property's northern boundary as being 'another part of the thirteen and a half acres now in the possession of John Baily, esq'.[237] Bayly's land was very close to if not the actual site on which Mount Prospect was built.

John Bayly's wife Katherine kept a diary during the eighteenth century after she married, which refers to the family living in Milltown in the 1740s and buying articles to furnish their house there

234 Walter Pfeifer and Mairanne Heron, *In the Houses of Ireland* (London, 1988), pp. 157–8.

235 RD 47/307/30741.

236 RD 128/199/86582.

237 RD 128/199/86582. John's surname is spelt Bayly in his wife's diary.

Plate 38. Grove House, Milltown Road, interior joinery, c. 1974 (courtesy of the Irish Architectural Archive)

in 1745.[238] The diary and the detail quoted from the La Touche lease of 1747 suggest that the Baylys were living in the house that became known as Mount Prospect. The year when the Baylys furnished their new home in Milltown (1745) coupled with C.P. Curran's dating of Mount Prospect's plasterwork to *c.* 1750 are sufficiently compatible in timeline to support this proposition. John Bayly died in 1753 and the following year Hannah Cole leased Mount Prospect to James Southern at an annual rent of £25.[239] The concurrence of these last two events provides additional evidence that the Baylys lived in Mount Prospect in the 1740s and 1750s as tenants of the Cole family.

The memorial of Hannah Cole's lease of 15 May 1754 to James Southern gives us the first description of Mount Prospect and its grounds and proves that the house had been built before 1754:

> *that dwelling house or tenement situate at the corner of Clonskeagh lane on the great road leading from Dublin to Milltown together with the garden, field and also the outhouses, offices and appurtenances.*[240]

238 H.F. Berry, 'Notes from the diary of a Dublin lady in the reign of George II', *Journal of the Royal Society of Antiquaries of Ireland* (1898), 28, pp. 141–54. The surname is spelt Bayly in the diary and Bailey in the Registry of Deeds. Unfortunately, Katherine Bayly's diary does not give a specific location or name for their house in Milltown and there are no memorials in the Registry of Deeds that refer to the Baylys leasing land there.

239 Berry, 'Notes from the diary of a Dublin lady', p. 141; RD 168/306/113315. The basis of Hannah Cole's title to Mount Prospect is unknown because of insufficient detail in the memorial.

240 RD 168/306/113315.

James Southern died in Mount Prospect in June 1757. The death notice in the newspaper described him as 'formerly an eminent dealer in Chancery lane, and a man of very fair character'.[241] Following Southern's death, William Cole junior granted a new lease of Mount Prospect in 1761 to Southern's son-in-law, Robert Madder, who in turn sold the property in 1764 to Paul Seguin, a Dublin merchant, for £200.[242]

The pattern of frequent changes in ownership and occupation of Mount Prospect continued for the remainder of the eighteenth century. The house was advertised for sale in 1776 and again in 1777 with the following descriptive particulars:

> *A Villa. To be sold, the interest of Mount Prospect, near Milltown, in the County of Dublin, most beautifully situated, with a good house and every accommodation; the garden is very extensive, and well cropped and planted with all kinds of choice fruit trees; the whole containing about six acres, part of which is held by virtue of a lease of lives renewable for ever, and on which considerable improvements have been lately made. For particulars inquire of Lady Cox, No. 13, Molesworth Street, or Mess. Scriven and Glascock, Dawson Street.*[243]

Mount Prospect was put up for sale in April 1786 and attracted the interest of Colonel Charles Vallencey, who on 21 May 1786 executed a lease for lives renewable for ever with Rachel Pilkington, spinster, then of Mount Prospect.[244] Vallencey's lease went into considerable detail about the improvements that had been made to Mount Prospect, referring to 'all fixtures, urns, figures, globes, irons, ornaments and embellishments mentioned in an inventory ... and all buildings, espalier hedges, garden walls, all fruit trees and gravel walks'. Clearly, Mount Prospect now had gardens that matched the quality of the house's interior.

Charles Vallencey is one of the more historic figures to have lived in Milltown. Vallencey was born in Flanders in the 1720s and moved to England at an early age where in adulthood he joined the royal engineers in the British Army, eventually attaining the rank of general. Vallencey was posted to Ireland in the 1750s, which became his adopted home until his death in 1812. Aside from his army career as an engineer and cartographer, during his time in Ireland Vallencey became a committed Hibernophile. He developed a scholarly interest in the Irish language and in Irish antiquities and was active in the Dublin Society and the Royal Irish Academy.[245]

In her biographical article on Vallencey, published in the *Journal of the Royal Society of Antiquaries of Ireland* in 1993, Monica Nevin mistakenly attributes Vallencey's home in Milltown to another house previously called Prospect House (originally called Milltown Hill and now called the Old House) located beside the Spar shop on Milltown Road at the top of its descent into Milltown village.[246] This mistake is understandable because Nevin based her information on OS maps from the mid-nineteenth century, a time when the house at the top of the hill changed its name from Milltown Hill to Prospect House. This is confirmed by a manuscript amendment to a Valuation Office town plan of Milltown village dated 6 April 1852 where the name Milltown Hill is crossed

241 *Pue's Occurrences*, 14 June 1757, p. 2.

242 RD 168/306/113315, RD 213/159/140463, RD 238/33/152106.

243 *Saunders's Newsletter*, 18 September 1776, p. 4; 25 April 1777, p. 4.

244 *Saunders's Newsletter*, 10 April 1786, p. 4; RD 381/299/252002.

245 Levin, 'General Vallencey', pp. 19–58.

246 Levin, 'General Vallencey', pp. 39–40, 48.

out and replaced with the name Prospect House. More importantly, Nevin cites correspondence dating from 1780 between Vallencey and Lord Charlemont, when Vallencey wrote to Charlemont from Milltown. That correspondence is problematic because it predates Vallencey's 1786 lease of Mount Prospect. However, it is quite possible that Vallencey was renting Mount Prospect on short 12-month leases (which typically would not have been registered in the Registry of Deeds) before purchasing the lease for lives renewable forever from Mrs Pilkington when the opportunity arose to do so in 1786.

In 1790 Vallencey was appointed commander of the forts in Cork harbour and so was forced to give up Mount Prospect. Vallencey wrote regretfully to a friend that, 'I must bid adieu to all my improvements at Prospect.'[247] Vallencey did not keep a record of his improvements to the house but it is possible that he built the viewing turret at its northern end. Vallencey moved among an elite group of learned cultural men who were active in societies such as the Dublin Society and the Royal Irish Academy, and who developed their Dublin suburban estates in the third quarter of the eighteenth century. Such persons included Lords Charlemont and Fitzwilliam who carried out extensive improvements at Marino and Mount Merrion, respectively, admittedly on a much larger scale to what was carried out by Vallencey at Milltown.

In any event, on 8 June 1791 Vallencey assigned his lease of Mount Prospect to a barrister, Richard Coles, together with assignments of two adjoining fields which Vallencey had previously leased from David FitzGerald in 1789 and 1790.[248] Coles soon sold on the property in 1792 to the Ranelagh nursery and seedsman, Charles Toole, who in turn assigned the property three years later to Joseph Madden of Donnybrook. Madden, as we have already seen, also acquired farmland to the east of Mount Prospect where Prospect farmhouse was located.[249] Madden lost no time after concluding his contract with Toole by advertising Mount Prospect to let for the summer season of 1795; in fact his advertisement predated the execution of his deed of assignment from Toole in September of that year.[250]

By the 1790s the Mount Prospect demesne comprised three separate but adjacent parcels of land – the house and its garden, a field in Clonskeagh Lane behind the house and garden of 2 acres, 1 rood and 17 perches and another field off Milltown Road of 2 acres and 3 roods, all plantation measure.[251] The additional green space could be used to graze livestock in order to provide milk and butter for the Mount Prospect household or it could be subdivided for building. Joseph Madden chose the latter option and sometime between September 1795 and March 1796 he built a new house on Milltown Road to the west of Mount Prospect, which was originally called Greenmount and later renamed Greenfields.[252] In 1796 Madden sold his interest in Mount Prospect, the two fields, and Greenmount for £500 to a distinguished lawyer and legal academic, Arthur Browne, whose career will be covered shortly under the history of Greenmount.[253] Browne carried out some repairs to Mount Prospect and its gate lodge before he died in 1805.[254]

---

247 Levin, 'General Vallencey', p. 39.

248 RD 437/251/282693.

249 RD 447/530/290820, RD 498/200/316732.

250 *Saunders's Newsletter*, 12 June 1795, p.4; RD498/200/316732.

251 RD 437/251/282693.

252 RD 494/76/320859.

253 RD 494/76/320859, RD 503/25/320860.

254 Bryan Bolger Papers (NAI, MS 2/476/15-16).

Arthur Browne's widow, Bridget, was living in Mount Prospect in January 1814 when she mortgaged it and the field in Clonskeagh Lane to a barrister, Henry Ellis, for £200.[255] Notwithstanding that she was in receipt of two government pensions totalling over £138, it seems that Bridget Browne's financial circumstances eventually forced her to give up the house, for in March the following year Mount Prospect was advertised to be let furnished on a six-month lease.[256]

After the departure of Mrs Browne, tracing the occupants of Grove House becomes more difficult. In 1836 an unnamed military officer attached to the Royal Engineers' Stable at Dublin Castle sought a tenant to take over the remainder of his tenancy (four months) at Mount Prospect, as he had been ordered abroad.[257] Like his predecessor at Mount Prospect, General Vallencey, the officer lived in some style, as evidenced by an interesting advertisement that he placed in *Saunders's Newsletter*:

> *To be sold, together or separate, a light Britzka complete, with a set of pair-horse harness, all in perfect order. Also, a pair of Bay Horses, about 15 ½ hands high, in good condition, and perfectly sound, gentle, and free from blemish, with the exception of a speck on one eye, which does not injure the sight; seven and eight years old, but quite fresh, having had no work beyond moderate daily exercise, and well accustomed to single and double harness; one of them a good roadster and field horse for light weight. ... N.B. The Advertiser wishes to procure a good situation for his coachman, (who shows the above), a native of the North, and who has lived with him above 3 years.*[258]

The history of Mount Prospect during the remainder of the nineteenth century is uneventful. The legal interests of the middlemen landlords, which became more obscure as the century wore on, continued to be bought and sold, albeit much less frequently than in the eighteenth century.[259] At the same time, the villa and its grounds were sublet on short-term leases to solid middle-class tenants who, for the most part, had an ephemeral presence in Milltown and left very little by way of historical record behind them.[260]

At the turn of the twentieth century, Mount Prospect was the home of George Beebe and his wife Margaret Anne, who had been living there since the early 1870s.[261] Beebe was originally from Surrey where he grew up in a house called Grove House.[262] It is not known what brought George Beebe to Ireland but on 10 November 1857 he married Margaret Anne L'Estrange, the daughter of

---

255 RD 673/35/462852.

256 *The Pilot*, 12 October 1829, p. 1; *Saunders's Newsletter*, 15 March 1815, p. 4.

257 *Saunders's Newsletter*, 13 August 1836, p. 4.

258 *Saunders's Newsletter*, 27 August 1836, p. 4. A Britzka was a long horse-drawn carriage with a folding top over the rear seat and a rear-facing front seat.

259 RD 1833/5/111, RD 1859/34/33; *Saunders's Newsletter*, 2 March 1861, p. 3; NAI, Landed Estates Court Rental, vol. 61, no. 30, 'In the matter of the estate of Charles Cottingham Johnstone ... to be sold by auction in one lot ... on 1 March 1861' and NAI, Landed Estates Court Rental, vol. 138, no. 18, 'In the matter of the estate of Maria Moyles ... which will be sold by public auction in three lots ... on 2 March 1880.'

260 The exception was Dr Thomas Prior, Vice-Provost of Trinity College, who died at Mount Prospect in September 1843: *Freeman's Journal*, 19 September 1843, p. 3.

261 NAI, 1901 Census, Form A, residents of house no. 100, Milltown Road, Rathmines & Rathgar East Electoral Division, Parish of St Peter, Milltown townland, Dublin; VO, Cancellation Books, Dublin, Rathmines East, Milltown Road, 1873–87, vol. 2, p. 192.

262 Death notice in the *Weekly Irish Times*, 12 November 1904, p. 1.

Frederick L'Estrange of Belgrave Road, Rathmines, in St Peter's Church.[263] In 1871 George Beebe's father-in-law was living in Mount Prospect but by 1873 George Beebe had taken possession of the property and his widowed mother-in-law had moved next door to Greenmount (Greenfields).[264]

Childhood nostalgia probably prompted George Beebe to change the name of his home in Milltown from Mount Prospect to Grove House sometime in the 1870s, a name the property retained until its demolition in the 1970s.[265] On census night, 31 March 1901, Grove House was occupied by Mr and Mrs Beebe (seventy-five and seventy respectively), George Beebe's unmarried sister-in-law, Elizabeth L'Estrange (sixty-seven), and an unmarried Catholic domestic servant, Anne Nolan (fifty-five) who could not read. George Beebe described himself as an owner of house property and his sister-in-law described herself as a house owner.[266] Grove House was recorded in the 1901 census as having 16 front windows and more than 13 rooms.[267]

George Beebe died on 4 November 1904 at Grove House, apparently childless.[268] By the time of the 1911 census, Grove House was occupied by a widower, John Ryan (fifty-six), his widowed mother Elizabeth Ryan ('aged 86 probably'), and two domestic servants, Bridget Hart (twenty-seven) and Mary Hart (twenty-four). All of the household were Catholics. John Ryan was a barrister who lectured or tutored at the Dublin Technical School.[269] Although he lived in one of Milltown's finest houses, Ryan was not indifferent to the poverty that prevailed generally in Milltown village, as this charitable appeal shows:

> *Sir- Will you permit me to bring a case of acute distress to the notice of your readers? A few weeks ago a respectable lawyer's clerk, named Patrick Ryan, came to live at Milltown, in the house adjoining the Post Office. In a few days he died, leaving a widow and seven young children to the charity of strangers. The crusts of Milltown are more readily shared than they are easily divided, but this pitiful case is beyond the resources of the village. The elder boys are aged 10, 6, and 5, while there is a little girl of 9. If the poor widow could find a decent home for three of the elder children, she might face the odds with the four little ones. I write in hope that some of your readers may be in a position to recommend the elder children for admission to better class orphanages. – Yours truly, John Ryan, Grove House, Milltown, Feb. 15, 1910.*[270]

When C.P. Curran visited Grove House in 1939/40 it was owned by Louis Webb, who apparently told him that the house was said to have begun its existence as an inn.[271] Without doubt

263 *Freeman's Journal*, 12 November 1857, p. 3.

264 RCB Library Miscellaneous Documents P654/27 (list of parishioners and accustomed members of St Philip's Parish, Milltown on 31 March 1871); Thom's Directory 1872, p. 1601; VO, Cancellation Books, Dublin, Rathmines East, Milltown Road, 1873–87, vol. 2, p. 192.

265 Thom's Directory 1881, p. 1512.

266 NAI, 1901 Census, Form A, residents of house no. 100, Milltown Road, Rathmines & Rathgar East Electoral Division, Parish of St Peter, Milltown townland, Dublin.

267 NAI, 1901 Census, Form B 1, house and buildings return for house no. 100, Milltown Road, Rathmines & Rathgar East Electoral Division, Parish of St Peter, Milltown townland, Dublin.

268 Death notice in the *Weekly Irish Times*, 12 November 1904, p. 1.

269 NAI, 1911 Census, Form A, household return for house no. 2, Milltown Road, Rathmines & Rathgar East Electoral Division, Parish of St Peter, Milltown townland, Dublin on 2 April 1911.

270 *Dublin Daily Express*, 16 February 1910, p. 7.

271 Curran, *Dublin Plaster Work*, p. 22 (footnote); VO, Cancellation Books, Dublin, Rathmines East, Milltown Road, 1940-1947, vol. 4, p. 870.

Webb was mistaken in this regard. During the Webbs' ownership of Grove House Milltown Road between their house and Milltown Park was widened in 1936. As a result, Dublin Corporation erected a new boundary wall at the northern boundary of Grove House, for which they paid the Webbs £210 in compensation.[272] In the late 1940s and 1950s a Miss M. Webb was a frequent prize winner at the annual Ramleh Horticultural Show, where she exhibited flowers, fruit and vegetables.[273]

After Louis Webb's death his widow Alicia continued living at Grove House until the 1970s, when it was advertised for sale in April 1973. Although the house was described as a distinctive period residence of character and charm, its developmental potential could not be ignored and the site was described as being a 'superb setting for flat development, zone B'.[274] The Grove House site was bought by Sheelin Homes Limited, who demolished the house and built the Grove House apartment block on the site in the late 1970s.[275] Around the same time, a bungalow was built on Grove House's walled garden for the former owners of Grove House. The bungalow was demolished in about 2015 and its site was redeveloped a second time with four new detached houses fronting the Milltown Road. In 1980, a smaller apartment complex called The Orchard was built on the former grounds of Grove House and later still, a town house development of 17 dwellings called Crannagh was built in 1990 on the south-eastern corner of the former grounds of Grove House on Prospect Lane, in place of another short-lived bungalow called Cranagh/146 Milltown Road.[276]

GREENFIELDS (PREVIOUSLY GREENMOUNT)

Greenfields, originally called Greenmount, is a detached Georgian house of three storeys, with slightly projecting breakfronts at either end of the front façade (Pl. 39). A particularly attractive feature is the granite steps and pillared portico behind which sits an elliptical fanlight. The building's graceful symmetry is maintained by the central chimney stack, which is constructed in an unusual lozenge pattern and topped with ten identical chimney pots. This feature caught the attention of the eminent architectural historian, Dr Maurice Craig, who noted that:

> *the setting of lofty shafts diagonally in a stack, found so late as Greenfield [sic] at Milltown Co Dublin, which from its plan can hardly be much before 1700, goes back in Irish usage at least to Derryhivenny (1643) and no doubt to the 16th century, when it is, of course, commonplace in England.*[277]

Very uncharacteristically, Craig was mistaken in his dating of Greenfields by almost a century, as will now be shown.

---

272 Minutes of the Municipal Council of the City of Dublin, 1936, p. 209.

273 *Irish Press*, 6 September 1948, p. 2; *Irish Independent*, 15 September 1952, p. 8; *Irish Times*, 13 September 1954, p. 7; 14 September 1959, p. 9.

274 Thom's Directory 1967, p. 408; 1974, p. 528; *Irish Independent*, 13 April 1973, p. 6.

275 *Irish Independent*, 1 April 1977, Property Supplement, p. 2.

276 *Irish Independent*, 6 May 1980, p. 18, 28 October 1988 (property supplement), p. 2; 27 April 1990, p. 26; personal knowledge of the author and personal communication from Taffina Farrington.

277 Maurice Craig, *Classic Irish Houses of the Middle Size* (London, 1976), p. 4.

Plate 39. Greenfields, Milltown Road, 2017 (author's collection)

Greenmount was built to the west of Grove House on Milltown Road by Joseph Madden of Donnybrook in the mid-1790s.[278] As noted earlier, Madden sold his leasehold interest in Mount Prospect (Grove House), two adjacent fields, and Greenmount for £500 in 1796 to Arthur Browne.[279] Browne used Mount Prospect as his suburban residence and it seems he intended to rent out the newly built Greenmount before he died unexpectedly in June 1805 at his city residence in Clare Street.[280] In March 1807 Browne's estate was billed for carpentry and plasterwork done 'for The Late Mr Brown at his new built house Greenmount'.[281] The itemised bill, which runs to nine pages, records the work carried out by bricklayers, stone cutters, plasterers and carpenters, all of which cost over £47. Although Browne's lease from Madden refers to 'the house lately erected and built and now standing', it appears that Joseph Madden had not finished Greenmount when he sold it to Browne in 1796, and that Browne completed the job sometime afterwards.[282] One of the items which was supplied to Browne was 'a framed hall door 7' – 0' by 3' – 3 ½' and 2½ inches thick with 8 raised panels and back lined'.[283]

---

278 RD 494/76/320859.

279 RD 494/76/320859, RD 503/25/320860.

280 Bryan Bolger Papers (NAI, MS 2/476/15-16); *Belfast Newsletter*, 13 June 1805, p. 2.

281 Bryan Bolger Papers (NAI, MS 2/476/15-16).

282 RD 494/76/320859.

283 Bryan Bolger Papers (NAI, MS 2/476/15-16).

Arthur Browne was born in about 1756 in Rhode Island, his grandfather having emigrated there from Drogheda in 1699. Browne entered Trinity College Dublin, in 1772, where he excelled academically. Browne later became a barrister in May 1777. He combined a successful legal practice with politics, and Browne became an MP of the Irish House of Commons for the Dublin University constituency in 1783, a position he held until the Act of Union in 1801. Browne was a highly distinguished academic, teacher and publisher of legal textbooks, having become Professor of Laws at Trinity in 1785. In 1799, Browne opposed the Act of Union but thereafter he underwent 'a real change of opinion after twelve months' reflection' and voted in favour of the Union in 1800. Browne's erstwhile political friends and his constituents in Trinity College were appalled at his volte face, and although he always strenuously denied receiving any government bribe, he was nonetheless appointed first to the Board of Accounts in 1801 and, on 29 December 1801, to the position of prime serjeant.[284] The post of prime serjeant had essentially become an archaic political office by the end of the eighteenth century, with the anomaly that the officeholder had precedence over the attorney general and the solicitor general. The office was abolished after Browne's death and replaced by a new office of first serjeant, which ranked immediately after that of the solicitor general.[285]

An obituary notice of Browne in the *Belfast Newsletter* recorded that he was 'a man of refined taste, a highly cultivated understanding, and peculiarly mild and engaging manners ... he has left a widow and five children bereaved of the protection of the tenderest of husbands and fathers'.[286]

Browne's legal and academic achievements have until very recently been overshadowed by his decision to vote in favour of the Act of Union. In 2017 Browne became the subject of a full-length biography which provides a much broader and dispassionate consideration of Browne's life and distinguished career.[287] His contribution to legal learning was honoured by the King's Inns in 2010 when that society instituted the Arthur Browne Prize, which is awarded for the highest grade in the entrance examination to the barrister-at-law degree course. In 2016 the school of law at Trinity College Dublin named a new annual lecture series after him.[288]

Information about Greenmount after the departure of the Browne family is very hard to come by until the 1840s. As with Mount Prospect, the middlemen landlords changed and there was quite a high turnover of Greemount's tenants in the mid-1840s.[289] The reason for the short stays of the tenants is unknown, but in 1848 Greenmount's landlord secured a long-term tenancy for the property. From that year until 1860 a Dublin solicitor, William Thompson, and his family rented Greenmount on a 31-year lease for £60 per annum from Richard Austin and subsequently from Austin's successor, Charles Cottingham Johnstone. William Thompson surrendered his lease in 1860 and the following year Charles Johnstone sold his legal interest in Greenmount (a lease for lives renewable for ever) in the landed estates court. At the time of the sale, Johnstone, who was also selling his interest in the adjacent property (Mount Prospect) derived a profit rent of £74 and 14*s*. The purchaser, Thomas

284 Paul O'Higgins, 'Arthur Browne (1756-1805): An Irish Civilian', *Northern Ireland Legal Quarterly*, 20, no. 3 (September 1969), pp. 255–73; A.R. Hart, *A history of the King's Serjeants at Law in Ireland: Honour rather than Advantage?* (Dublin, 2000), p. 153.

285 Hart, *A history of the King's Serjeants at Law*, pp. 106, 108, 109, 153, 165.

286 *Belfast Newsletter*, 13 June 1805, p. 2.

287 Joseph C. Sweeney, *The life and times of Arthur Browne in Ireland and America, 1756–1805* (Dublin, 2017).

288 Sweeney, *The life and times of Arthur Browne*, p. ix (Foreword by Dr Patrick Geoghegan, TCD).

289 RD 1833/5/111, RD 1859/34/23; Pettigrew and Oulton's Dublin Almanac and General Register of Ireland 1845, p. 825 (James Boyd), 1846, p. 841 (Mrs McKenzie), 1847, p. 843 (Rev. Samuel Medlicott & John Hoskyns, M.D).

Frewen of Buckwall House, Sussex, England, paid £900 for the two villas, a purchase price of about 12 times the annual profit rent.[290]

For several years in the latter part of the nineteenth century the L'Estrange family lived in Greenmount.[291] As previously noted, the L'Estranges were in-laws of George Beebe who was living next door in Grove House. In 1897 Greenmount was burgled and several articles of clothing worth £25 were stolen from Mrs L'Estrange, including two opera cloaks and a cape. The burglars were later apprehended and brought to court by the police, who, to much laughter, told the court that when arrested, the prisoner was wearing Mrs L'Estrange's muffler, dancing shoes and two stockings on one foot![292]

At the turn of the twentieth century Greenmount was the family home of a wholesale chemist, Henry Moss. Moss was married with three sons and a daughter. On census night 1901, the household comprised the Moss family of six, Henry's unmarried brother, Thomas, who was a visitor and two domestic servants. All of the household bar one domestic servant were members of the Church of Ireland.[293] The Moss family were still in situ ten years later but Henry Moss was now a director of a company called Woods Webb and Company, a wholesale business importing fruit, coffee and spices. Moss's eldest son, twenty-one-year-old Henry, had qualified as a chemist by 1911. Henry Moss's two single sisters-in-law (forty-eight and forty) were now living in Greenmount, one of whom supported herself through ownership of house property and teaching.[294] In their leisure time, Henry junior acted as scoutmaster for the Donnybrook Troop of the Dublin Boys' Scouts, while his sister Aileen became a prize-winning cook.[295]

Two of Henry Moss's sons, Arnold and Geoffrey, enlisted for service on the outbreak of the First World War. Corporal Arnold Moss of the Royal Dublin Fusiliers was reported missing after action in Suvla Bay in the Dardanelles on 16 August 1915, having previously been recommended for a distinguished conduct medal after his first engagement at Suvla Bay.[296] Arnold was eighteen years old when he died and his death is commemorated on the Helles Memorial in Turkey.[297]

Several years later Greenmount was put up for auction in 1938 when it was described as having a good walled-in garden well stocked with fruit trees, greenhouse with vinery, tennis court and fowl run. Another attraction was that the house was 'on 'bus route – about seven

---

290 RD 1833/5/111, RD 1846/1/182; Griffith's Valuation, Rateable Valuation of Tenements, Co. Dublin, Barony of Uppercross, Parish of St Peter, Townland of Milltown, 1850, p. 54; *Freeman's Journal*, 25 October 1859, p. 1; *Dublin Evening Mail*, 19 February 1861, p. 1; NAI, Landed Estates Court Rental, vol. 61, no. 30, 'In the matter of the estate of Charles Cottingham Johnstone ... to be sold by auction in one lot .... on 1 March 1861'; *Saunders's Newsletter*, 2 March 1861, p. 3; RD 1861/14/123.

291 The Thom's Directories list the residents as being Mrs L'Estrange (in 1872) and thereafter Edgar W. L'Estrange, solicitor.

292 *Rathmines News*, 11 September 1897, p. 4.

293 NAI, 1901 Census, Form A, residents of house no. 69, Milltown Road, Rathmines & Rathgar East Electoral Division, Parish of St Peter, Milltown townland, Dublin.

294 NAI, 1911 Census, Form A, residents of house no. 4, Milltown Road, Rathmines & Rathgar East Electoral Division, Parish of St Peter, Milltown townland, Dublin.

295 *Dublin Evening Mail*, 19 August 1911, p. 3; *Dublin Daily Express*, 19 November 1910, p. 9.

296 *Dublin Daily Express*, 9 September 1915, p. 8.

297 Commonwealth War Graves Commission: https://www.cwgc.org/find-war-dead/casualty/688981/moss,-arnold-wilson/ (accessed 13 December 2017).

minutes from O'Connell Bridge – and a few minutes' walk from the tram'.[298] The new owners changed the name of the house from Greenmount to Greenfields in about 1942.[299]

By the 1970s the large grounds accompanying the old villas on Milltown Road became increasingly attractive to developers which, as noted previously, sealed the fate of Grove House. Fortunately, Greenfields was spared from the wrecking ball and the house was sensitively converted into self-contained flats in the 1970s. It is now a preserved structure and is currently well maintained by its owners.[300]

THE OLD HOUSE (PREVIOUSLY MILLTOWN HILL AND PROSPECT HOUSE)

The Old House is a pretty, well-proportioned two-storey mid-eighteenth-century house of five bays with a taller three-storey square extension at its southern end (Pl. 40). Internally, the house has changed considerably, but it contains good window architraves and shutters, corner fireplaces and an old pine staircase. Unusually, the house is only one room deep from front to rear and, apart from two or three very small first-floor windows overlooking a garden in Ramleh Park, the entire east (rear) elevation is windowless.

As its original name, Milltown Hill, signifies, the Old House was built at the top of the hill facing west on the descent into Milltown village (Map 15). Over the last 200 years or so the house has had at least three name changes. The property is easily confused with other contemporary villas on Milltown Road, which from time to time also adopted the word 'prospect' in their names. In the early 1980s the Milltown Hill town house development was built on the grounds of the house, with the result that the Old House is now rather hemmed in by the town houses and the Spar shop to the rear.

Milltown Hill was most likely built by a Dublin gentleman, William Hawker, in about 1760 on a site which included an older property described as a 'small slate house and garden' – presumably to distinguish it from its bigger neighbour, Geraldine House. The origins of Milltown Hill begin in 1746, when John Kerr granted a lease for lives renewable forever to William Gunn of Dublin, gentleman, of property described as: 'All that and those the small slate house and garden in Milltown ... then in the possession of William Gunn and then late in the tenure and occupation of Theodore Stones deceased ...'[301]

Gunn in turn sublet this property for 90 years to William Hawker in 1752, when it was described as 'the small slate house and garden in Milltown then in the possession of William Gunn and now in the possession of William Hawker'.[302] Hawker was the accounts supervisor at Dublin's Foundling Hospital and Workhouse.[303] Some years later, in 1766, William Gunn granted a lease for lives renewable forever of the same property to Hawker, including 'all buildings and improvements made or erected thereon'.[304]

---

298 *Irish Press*, 18 June 1938, p. 18.

299 VO, Cancellation Books, Dublin, Rathmines East, Milltown Road, 1940–47, vol. 4, p. 870.

300 *Irish Independent*, 15 September 1976, p. 2; personal knowledge of the author and personal communication from Taffina Farrington.

301 Recital in copy fee farm grant deed 18 March 1878 in the possession of Sheila Dubel.

302 RD 150/527/103703.

303 *Finn's Leinster Journal*, 23 January 1773; *Hibernian Journal*, 3 February 1773, p. 2.

304 RD 253/31/161543.

Plate 40. The Old House, Milltown Road, c. 1980, Patrick Healy Collection (courtesy of South Dublin Libraries)

On the death of William Hawker in 1773, Milltown was inherited by his daughter, Frances Bourne.[305] In 1777 Frances and her husband Richard Edwards Bourne sold their interest in Milltown Hill for £227 10*s*. to John Edwards of Old Court, County Wicklow, which by then included a new house that had been built by William Hawker during his occupation of the premises:

> *all that and those the small slate house and garden then formerly in the tenure and occupation of Theodore Stones deceased and then lately in the possession of William Gunn and then in the possession of James Darby together with the dwelling house messuage or tenement erected and built by William Hawker then lately of Milltown in the County of Dublin, gentleman, deceased and the garden thereto belonging then in the tenure and occupation of Luke Heron.*[306]

The dwelling house 'erected and built by William Hawker' survives today as that part of the Milltown Hill building complex, comprising the two-storey, five-bay entrance front (Pl. 40).[307] It is possible that the earliest surviving structure includes the 'small slate house'

305 *Finn's Leinster Journal*, 23 January 1773; RD 305/606/203980.

306 RD 322/106/212352. Luke Heron's surname was misspelt in the memorial as 'Hearn'. James Darby vacated Milltown Hill in December 1787 following which his household furniture was auctioned off: *Saunders's Newsletter*, 15 December 1787, p. 4.

307 It is conceivable that the present structure is actually the 'small slate house' referred to in the 1746 lease but the mention in the 1777 lease of a dwelling house built by Hawker suggests otherwise.

referred to in the 1746 lease from Kerr to Gunn, but this seems unlikely given that William Hawker had, according to the recitals in the 1766 and 1777 deeds, built a new house during his tenure.

Taking advantage of Milltown's popularity with the Dublin gentry and nobility, Luke Heron, who had also acquired a leasehold interest in Milltown Hill from Frances and Edward Bourne in 1776,[308] advertised Milltown Hill for letting during the summer season of 1778:

> *To be set for the Summer, furnished or on other terms, a house, with coach house and stable, and beautiful garden, in Milltown, not two miles from Dublin; the situation not to be excelled; the garden noted for the choiceness of its fruits; with a green house and hot house in which the finest grapes are produced. Inquire of Mr Heron, at Mr Ward's, watchmaker, No. 11 Exchange Street.*[309]

Fourteen years later Heron was living in Milltown Hill when he advertised his house for letting once more:

> *Heronhausen. A house etc on the top of the descent going into Milltown, inhabited for some years by Lady Cox, at present by Mr Heron; the situation cannot be excelled for health or beauty; to be let for any term, furnished or unfurnished – Goats whey passes the door.*[310]

In 1800 Luke Heron conveyed the property to his daughter Ann who was living with her father in Great Britain Street in Dublin. The conveyance included a separate parcel of adjacent ground fronting the Milltown Road on which three houses, probably small cottages, had been built.[311] Shortly before Ann's marriage in Finglas to George Taylor Owen, attorney at law, in March 1802, Milltown Hill was conveyed to her brother William Heron in trust for Ann as part of her marriage settlement.[312] Two years later Milltown Hill was put up for auction in July 1804 and thereafter passed out of the Herons' ownership.[313]

There is little surviving history about Milltown Hill in the early decades of the nineteenth century, by which time the 1746 lease/root of title had become vested in Rebecca Pineau.[314] The registrar of the Admiralty Court, Daniel Pineau, died in Milltown aged sixty-nine in 1837. He had served as registrar for 31 years 'with honour, and to the satisfaction of the professional gentlemen attached to the Courts'.[315] The Pineau family's interest in Milltown Hill was bequeathed by Rebecca Pineau to Robert Daniel Fitzpatrick, who took up residence in Milltown Hill and married a local girl, Jane Anne Lee, on 2 October 1838.[316]

---

308 RD 310/507/207583. It appears that the Bournes inherited two separate leasehold interests in Milltown Hill which were acquired by Luke Heron.

309 *Saunders's Newsletter*, 10 April 1778, p. 4.

310 *Saunders's Newsletter*, 12 April 1794, p. 4.

311 RD 534/134/349593.

312 RD 542/519/359259; *Saunders's Newsletter*, 4 March 1802, p. 1.

313 *Saunders's Newsletter*, 12 July 1804, p. 3.

314 RD 1876/39/287 (recital in deed).

315 *Dublin Evening Packet and Correspondent*, 23 March 1837, p. 3.

316 RD 1876/39/287 (recital in deed); Marriage records for St Peter's Church (Church of Ireland) contained on the website Irishgenealogy.ie. Jane Lee was almost certainly related to the contemporary Milltown builders and millwrights John and William Lee.

In 1841 Robert Fitzpatrick leased Milltown Hill to George Cowell, a tobacco and snuff manufacturer whose business was in 34 Capel Street.[317] It was Cowell who changed the name of his home from Milltown Hill to Prospect House in 1847, thereby creating more confusion about the names and locations of Milltown's detached houses shown on the nineteenth-century maps and listed in the Dublin directories, which, as we have seen earlier, already included Prospect farm and Mount Prospect on Prospect Lane.[318] Like his predecessor Robert Fitzpatrick, George Cowell married a local girl, Charlotte Hodges, who was the eldest daughter of William Hodges of Milltown House.[319]

In June 1853 George Cowell advertised Prospect House to let in the following advertisement which appeared in *Saunders's Newsletter*:

> *To be let, with or without a fine, Prospect House, Milltown, containing parlour, drawing room, and five bedrooms, kitchen, pantry, etc with stable, mangle room, henhouse etc, beautifully situated on a hill overlooking the River Dodder, in the centre of a large garden, containing nearly an English acre; gate entrance with drive up to the house, which stands detached, and commands unrivalled views of the surrounding country. Lease forever. Fine £250 and £30 [rent] per annum. Apply to George Cowell esq, Killeen, Ballicmoyler [sic], Carlow, or at No. 9 Middle Gardiner Street, Dublin.*[320]

George Cowell died on 11 June 1859 and afterwards Prospect House was occupied intermittently by his widow Charlotte and short-term tenants.[321] Nonetheless, during this period an extension was added to the house in 1864 thereby increasing its rateable valuation from £16 10*s*. to £22.[322]

The next long-term occupants of Prospect House were the Somers family who took over in 1876 and consolidated various legal interests affecting the property.[323] John Somers was a businessman who invested in rental properties.[324] In politics Somers supported the candidacy of the Independent Nationalist (Parnellite) candidate for the South Dublin constituency, Dr ffrench-Mullen, in the General Election of 1892.[325]

The Somers family were living in Prospect House on the night of the 1901 census, when the household comprised John Somers (seventy) who lived off the rental income from investment properties, his wife Anne (seventy-three), a cousin Jane Cullen (twelve according to the cen-

---

317 RD 1841/9/155, RD 1867/28/152 (conversion of leasehold interest to fee farm grant); Pettigrew and Oulton's Dublin Almanac and General Register of Ireland 1845, p. 669.

318 Pettigrew and Oulton's Dublin Almanac and General Register of Ireland 1848, p. 855.

319 *Dublin Evening Post*, 21 December 1848, p. 3. George Clayton Cowell had a son from a previous marriage, George Young Cowell: *Irish Times*, 5 April 1930, p. 6.

320 *Saunders's Newsletter*, 14 June 1853, p. 2. Cowell had previously advertised to let Milltown Hill in April 1846: *General Advertiser for Dublin, and All Ireland*, 25 April 1846, p. 4.

321 *Evening News*, 17 June 1859, p. 4; *Thom's Directories 1860*–76. Charlotte Cowell (née Hodges) died in 1868: *Cork Examiner*, 11 November 1868, p. 4.

322 VO, Cancellation Books, Rathmines Ward 1862–3, bk. 1, p. 135, no. 17/104.

323 RD 1876/29/78, RD 1876/39/287; Recital in copy fee farm grant deed 18 March 1878 in the possession of Sheila Dubel; NAI, Landed Estates Court Rental, vol. 138, no. 18, 'In the matter of the estate of Maria Moyles ... which will be sold by public auction in three lots ... on 2 March 1880', p. 18.

324 *Irish Independent*, 25 March 1898, p. 1.

325 *Irish Independent*, 5 July 1892, p. 6.

sus form) and their domestic servant, Elizabeth Gibson (thirty-eight). In a reversal of the usual religious affiliations of employer and employee in the professional upper middle-class Dublin homes of the time, the Somers were Roman Catholics and their domestic servant was a member of the Church of Ireland.[326] John and Anne Somers had both died by 4 August 1904 but unfortunately a family dispute concerning the payment of annuities and legacies under John Somers's will ended up in the Chancery Court the following year.[327]

The Leach family succeeded John and Anne Somers in Prospect House. On 2 April 1911 Ernest Leach (fifty-one), his wife Madeline (forty-six) and their five children Noelle (seventeen), Ernest (fifteen), Madeline (ten), Edith (eight) and Jack (four) were living in Prospect House, while their domestic servant, Maria Norton (sixty-five and who could not read), was living in the gate lodge. According to the 1911 census return, Ernest Leach was employed in the Local Government Board as a principal clerk.[328] Like their neighbours the Moss family in Greenmount, Ernest and Madeline Leach suffered the loss of a son, Ernest Walter Vinden, in the First World War.[329]

In 1921 Mrs Leach sold Prospect House and its gate lodge, which was let at 3*s*. 6*d*. a week, to Mrs Mary Musters for £1,145. Mrs Musters, who was a widow, renamed the property 'The Old House', its third name change. Musters lived in Garvagh House, Edgeworthstown, County Longford before moving to Milltown in November 1921.[330] County Longford was one of the most disturbed counties during the War of Independence, which probably explains why Mrs Musters moved to Dublin.[331] Mrs Musters was a keen gardener and for a number of years during the 1930s she raised money for the Jubilee Nurses pension fund by opening her garden to the public for 1*s*. entrance fee and 1*s*. for tea.[332] The Royal Horticultural Society of Ireland awarded Mrs Musters its bronze medal in 1937 for the 'most decorative vase of hardy spring flowers'.[333] Mrs Musters died on 16 December 1954 aged ninety-one and afterwards the Old House was sold by her beneficiaries and executors to a Dublin solicitor, Walter P. McGuire.[334]

The Old House and its gardens of three quarters of an acre were put up for auction on 8 July 1981.[335] Subsequently, the garden of the Old House and the neighbouring property, Geraldine House, were acquired by a developer who built the Milltown Hill and Milltown Court apartment

---

326 NAI, 1901 Census, Form A, residents of house no. 16, Milltown Road, Rathmines and Rathgar East Electoral Division, Milltown townland, Dublin.

327 *Freeman's Journal*, 23 January 1905, p. 3.

328 NAI, 1911 Census, Form A, household return for house nos 12 and 12A, Milltown Road, Rathmines & Rathgar East Electoral Division, Parish of St Peter, Milltown townland, Dublin on 2 April 1911.

329 *Larne Times*, 13 January 1917, p. 7.

330 Copy deed of conveyance dated 22 July 1921 in the possession of Sheila Dubel; *Irish Times*, 14 March 1921, p. 10; 23 November 1921, p. 4.

331 Marie Coleman, 'Longford' in John Crowley, Donal Ó'Drisceoil and Mike Murphy (eds), *The Atlas of the Irish Revolution* (Cork, 2017), p. 597. Musters was probably related by marriage with the Musters of Brianstown House, Co. Longford.

332 *Irish Independent*, 4 May 1931, p. 4; 11 May 1936, p. 8.

333 *Irish Times*, 8 April 1837, p. 4.

334 Register of Deaths for Dublin, Donnybrook No. 1 District, p. 306, entry no. 138, death of Mary Elizabeth Musters on 16 December 1954; Copy deed of conveyance dated 11 March 1955 in the possession of Sheila Dubel.

335 *Irish Independent*, 26 June 1981, p. 31.

Plate 41. Geraldine House, Milltown Road, c. 1980 (courtesy of the Irish Architectural Archive)

and town house complex on part of the combined site.[336] Unfortunately Geraldine House was demolished but thankfully the Old House was spared. It remains in use as a private residence and is well maintained at present.

GERALDINE HOUSE

Geraldine House was a large two-to-three-storey over-basement detached house that stood next door to the Old House on Milltown Road (Map 18). The front elevation comprised a five-bay entrance front surmounted by an imposing triangular gable, and flanked at either end by massive square chimney stacks (Pl. 41). The rear elevation was made up of four projecting stepped extensions of four and three floors respectively, each with its own attic gable (Pl. 42). This unusual and elaborate plan probably evolved over the course of the eighteenth century.

The origins of Geraldine House are unknown but the thick chimney stacks and the prominent pitched gables suggest that the house was built in the first quarter of the eighteenth century, or

336 *Irish Independent*, 17 February 1984, p. 29; Dublin City Council Planning Department, plan no. 3381/82, reg. no. 3381/82 (Kaylan Ltd).

Plate 42. Geraldine House, Milltown Road, rear elevation, c. 1980 (courtesy of the Irish Architectural Archive)

potentially as far back as the late seventeenth century. The information available in the Registry of Deeds about the property in the early eighteenth century is hard to interpret because Geraldine House was unnamed at that time. In January 1725 Geraldine House was leased to one of Joseph Leeson's tenants, John Kerr, as part of a 13½-acre landholding on the east side of Milltown Road.[337] Kerr in turn sublet four parcels of the 13½ acres, one of which included 'all that dwelling house and garden situate in Milltown where William Hewston, gardener, lately dwelt'.[338] This property was let to William Cole senior in 1731 at an annual rent of £5, and included a right for Cole to quarry stone for building on and improving the property.[339] Cole subsequently mortgaged the property to David La Touche the elder in 1742, and before his death in February 1745 Cole had spent at least £800 on building and improvements.[340] It is likely therefore that Cole redeveloped or extended Hewston's house using building material sourced from the immediately adjacent limestone quarry beside the River Dodder (now Scully's Field). In short, the available evidence strongly indicates that the Hewston/Cole house was the property that became known as Geraldine House.

337 RD 47/307/30741.

338 RD 70/178/47904. Hewston was likely to have been a market gardener who grew fruit and vegetables for the Dublin market, just as his neighbour across the road, John Magennis, was doing in the 1720s: RD 50/340/33274.

339 RD 70/178/47904.

340 RD 111/64/75630; RSAI, Francis Elrington Ball MSS, vol. 4, p. 64.

William Cole's legal interest in Geraldine House devolved to his widow Hannah Cole and his son William Cole junior. In 1784 William Cole was forced to sell his property in Milltown as a result of a judgement which was issued against him from Luke Heron, who lived next door in Milltown Hill (now called the Old House). The upshot of this was that a David Fitz-Gerald bought the property and renamed it Geraldine House. During the last two decades of the eighteenth century Geraldine House was inhabited at various times by David FitzGerald or his tenants Colonel Madden and the Honourable Philip Tisdall.[341] An advertisement from 1799 provides a useful description of the property:

> *To be let, and entered upon immediately, the large house in Milltown, formerly inhabited by the Right Hon. Philip Tisdall, and the late Col Madden, together with an excellent garden, in full bearing, with coach-house and large stable yard. The house is very roomy, containing two kitchens and other offices on the ground floor; four rooms and two closets on the first; ditto on the second, and good garrets for servants; would answer very well for a large family, academy, or boarding school. Application to be made to Mr Fitzgerald, No. 7, Beaux-walk, Stephen's-green.*[342]

In the 1830s and 1840s Geraldine House was let to the Fox family who at various times operated a florist business and a bakery from a small shop on the grounds of the property.[343] The flowers were grown in the Fox's garden behind Geraldine House and from time to time their plants won prizes at shows run by the Practical Floral Horticultural Society of Ireland.[344] The Griffith's Valuation surveyors visited Geraldine House twice, in 1845. They recorded that the property contained a bake house, a shop, several sheds and offices together with 'a good yard and garden'.[345] Writing over 50 years later in 1901, the Dodder historian John Christopher FitzAchary recalled that 'at the rear of Geraldine House stood Foxe's [*sic*] celebrated silk weaving manufactory'.[346] In this instance the normally accurate FitzAchary mistakenly associated the Fox family with silk weaving when in actual fact they were florists.

By the mid-nineteenth century David FitzGerald's interest in Geraldine House had devolved successively to Jane FitzGerald and to the trustees of her estate.[347] In 1855 Miss Maria Troy, inherited a life interest in Geraldine House from her former employer, spinster Jane Fitz-Gerald, who prior to her death had held the intermediate legal interest (originally a lease

---

341 RD 360/417/244131, RD 579/185/390198; *Saunders's Newsletter*, 8 March 1785, p. 2; 11 July 1786, p. 3; 25 April 1787, p. 4; 12 June 1799, p. 4.

342 *Saunders's Newsletter*, 12 June 1799, p. 4.

343 *Dublin Mercantile Advertiser and Weekly Price Current*, 31 May 1830, p. 3; Pettigrew and Oulton's Dublin Almanac and General Register of Ireland 1847, p. 843.

344 *Freeman's Journal*, 8 July 1837, p. 2; 14 July 1838, p. 3 and 21 April 1842, p. 1, when 'B. Fox, florist, Milltown' won the first prize for his double blue and double red hyacinths.

345 NAI, VO, OL52714, House Book for Milltown Village 1845, p. 571, no. 119; NAI, VO, OL50945, House Book for Milltown Village 1845, no. 59.

346 *Rathmines News*, 14 December 1901.

347 RD1863/34/96; NAI, Landed Estates Court Rental, vol.138, no. 18, 'In the matter of the estate of Maria Moyles ... which will be sold by public auction in three lots ... on 2 March 1880.'

for lives renewable for ever, later converted to fee farm grant) from Lord Milltown.[348] Troy moved into the Milltown property and in 1860 placed the following advertisement in the *Freeman's Journal*:

> *To be let, fully and fashionably furnished, in a large and commodious house, with good attendance, three suites of apartments, consisting of two separate drawing-rooms and a parlour, to each of which are attached a good bedroom and closet. There is a large well walled garden attached to the house, opening out on the River Dodder, the unrestricted use of which would be given to any family living in the house. There is also a stable and coach house. The beauty of the neighbourhood and the salubrity of the air being well known need no comment. The house is situate on the Dublin side, and may be said not to be in the village at all so completely is it detached, and within five minutes' walk of the omnibus and railway stations. The apartments will be set separately or together, as may suit respectable parties requiring accommodation. Apply to Geraldine House, Milltown.*[349]

The success of the advertisement in attracting respectable parties to Milltown is unknown, however, two years later the executors and trustees of the FitzGerald estate leased Geraldine House to Maria Troy for one hundred years at an annual rent of £22.[350] Subsequently, in December 1863 Maria Troy sublet that part of her property which included the outbuildings and other offices attached to Geraldine House to a local dairyman, John Wilmer, for £10 per annum.[351] Finally, Troy mortgaged Geraldine House for £300 in 1864.[352] Some years later, the outbuildings sublet to John Wilmer were replaced by a terrace of three two-storey houses, nos 1–3 Geraldine Terrace, which still exists today. In addition, four small labourers' cottages stood at the end of the rear garden of Geraldine House facing onto the banks of the River Dodder (Map 18).

Maria Troy married coachmaker William Moyles of 20 Upper Dorset Street in 1865, who died the following year.[353] Over the years the widowed Mrs Moyles continued her attempts to derive an income from Geraldine House by advertising accommodation with 'good cooking' and 'pure spring water' laid on, at monthly rents varying between £3 10s. and £2. From time to time the apartments were advertised as being suitable for convalescents or desirable for delicate persons on account of the 'balmy air' close to the River Dodder![354] In short, unlike its neighbour Prospect House, Geraldine House gradually declined in status as its grounds and outbuildings were developed to meet local housing needs notwithstanding the advertisements which attempted to distance the property from the decay and poverty of Milltown village.

For a period in the late 1870s the journalist (and later, nationalist politician) Thomas Sexton took lodgings at Geraldine House.[355] In 1878 Sexton, who was on the staff of The Nation

348 *Irish Independent*, 26 April 1897, p. 8; *Freeman's Journal*, 8 December 1898, p. 7.

349 *Freeman's Journal*, 22 August 1860, p. 1.

350 RD 1863/34/96.

351 RD 1863/39/41.

352 RD 1864/1/220.

353 Civil registration of marriages in the district of Dublin South, Rathmines 1865, no. 57, 1 June 1865; civil registration of deaths in the district of Dublin North, no. 494, 26 February 1866; NAI, Calendar of Wills and Administrations for 1866, p. 160; *Irish Times*, 21 February 1878, p. 3.

354 *Irish Times*, 9 October 1878, p. 8; 16 December 1879, p. 8; 11 May 1880, p. 8; *Dublin Daily Express*, 29 September 1882, p. 8.

355 *Rathmines News*, 14 December 1901.

newspaper, intervened successfully to appeal the sentences imposed on four young men from Milltown who had been convicted of assaulting two policemen in Clonskeagh in June 1877. The prisoners – Abraham Meates, Joseph Neill, John and Joseph Raul – had been sentenced to two years' imprisonment with hard labour. The Raul's mother was a widow who was a tenant of John Wilmer's living in Geraldine Terrace. She depended on her sons for support, and her plight probably prompted Sexton to take up the men's case. A mitigating factor which prompted the Lord Lieutenant to grant remission of their sentences was that one of the policemen was in plain clothes when he was assaulted, and was not recognised as such by his assailants.[356] The following self-congratulatory report appeared in *The Nation* on 25 January following the men's release:

> *The four young men of Milltown, county Dublin, who had been sentenced, at the Commission Court, in June, '77, by Mr Baron Dowse (with whom Judge Keogh was adjudicating) to two years imprisonment, with hard labour, for an assault on two policemen, and whose case was brought up recently by a letter in the press from Mr Thomas sexton, a member of the staff of this journal, were on Wednesday last set at liberty by command of the Lord Lieutenant. The people of Milltown welcomed them home with illuminations, bonfires, and a band of music. A deputation from Milltown, including all of the men released, called yesterday at our office to acknowledge the successful efforts of Mr Sexton in their behalf, and also to offer their thanks to Mr T.D. Sullivan, for the action of this journal in their favour.*[357]

The various tenancies, inheritances, mortgages and complicated legal interests affecting Geraldine House in the mid- to late nineteenth century following Jane FitzGerald's death eventually led to conflict.[358] By the late 1870s Mrs Moyles had run into financial difficulties and she was forced by a mortgagee, John Trafford Gough, to dispose of her legal interests in Geraldine House and other property by auction in the landed estates court on 2 March 1880.[359] Geraldine House failed to sell despite attracting a bid of £140, and over a year later the house was advertised to be let pending the resolution of the dispute between Maria Moyles and Gough in the landed estates court.[360] During this uncertain period, Mrs Moyles composed the following Limerick which she included in her advertisement in the *Irish Times* for furnished apartments at Geraldine House:

> *Ladies and gentlemen whose health is not strong,*
> *Should quickly come here, you need not stay long,*
> *Without pill or powder, physician or quack,*
> *In good health and spirits you'll surely go back,*
> *The charges are small, the advantages great,*
> *And you'll help a poor widow to redeem her estate.*[361]

356 *Freeman's Journal*, 20 December 1878, p. 8; *The Nation*, 28 December 1878, p. 4; 1 February 1879, p. 12; VO, Cancellation Books, Dublin, Rathmines East, Milltown Road, 1873–87, vol. 2, p. 204.

357 *The Nation*, 1 February 1879, p. 12.

358 *Dublin Evening Mail*, 21 February 1878, p. 4; *Irish Times*, 21 February 1878, p. 3; *Freeman's Journal*, 28 March 1879, p. 1 (missing deed).

359 *Dublin Evening Mail*, 21 February 1878, p. 4; NAI, Landed Estates Court Rental, vol. 138, no. 18, 'In the matter of the estate of Maria Moyles ... which will be sold by public auction in three lots ... on 2 March 1880.' Moyles was 'now aged about 58 years'.

360 *Freeman's Journal*, 3 March 1880, p. 2; *Dublin Daily Express*, 18 August 1881, p. 8.

361 *Irish Times*, 4 September 1880, p. 8.

Despite her troubles, Mrs Moyles managed to continue living in Geraldine House until her death on 17 June 1893.[362]

For many years prior to her death, Mrs Moyles's elderly spinster sister, Miss Anne Troy, had also lived in Geraldine House with her bachelor brother John Troy, who died there in 1887.[363] In the late 1890s Anne Troy became embroiled in legal proceedings with John Wilmer over their respective legal titles to Geraldine House deriving from Jane FitzGerald's and Maria Moyles's estates.[364] Matters came to a head in late November/early December 1898 when the bailiffs arrived on at least two occasions to evict Miss Troy, who apparently resisted them with a pitch fork. The nonagenarian was overpowered and removed from her home along with her possessions.[365] That was not the end of the matter, as the following dramatic report in the *Rathmines News* explained:

> *The whole village rose up in arms against the eviction of the venerable old lady, and gathering in front of the house began such a bombardment with every conceivable kind of missile, that the bailiffs were soon in a state of terror lying inside on the floor. Daybreak saw their flight, and they will never forget the bombardment of Geraldine House. The old lady has re-entered possession. She is to appear at the Police Court on remand for taking forcible possession. Whatever the legal rights of the matter may be, one thing is certain that the old lady, whose popularity with the villagers roused such a fiery demonstration, is deserving of the utmost sympathy in her sad plight. The house presented an extraordinary sight, every window broken and the poor lady's furniture thrown about close to the road.*[366]

There was much public sympathy for Anne Troy beyond the confines of Milltown village. An editorial in the *Dublin Evening Telegraph* evinced feelings that resonate in the third decade of twenty-first century Ireland:

> *The poor old lady had neither the legal assistance nor the money to fight Chancery action, otherwise it is possible she might have been able to spend the evening of her days unmolested in her home. She has now been rendered completely destitute, and ought to be an object of the bounty of the benevolent. The courts have, of course, to enforce legal rights, but the enforcement of them very often means, as we all know, the infliction of a moral wrong – a wrong by which the claims of humanity, charity, and mercy are outraged and the weak and innocent crushed and ruined. If there ever was a case in which the demon litigation has claimed an unoffending and undeserving victim it is the case of poor Miss Troy, who has seen prosperous days, who clung to a house which a charitable donor provided for her and her aged sister, and who now finds herself on the brink of starvation owing to a series of mysterious legal proceedings which she could neither understand nor defend and which have undone her.*[367]

---

362 *Irish Independent*, 26 April 1897, p. 8.

363 *Freeman's Journal*, 13 June 1885, p. 1; 4 June 1891, p. 3; Civil registration of deaths in the district of Dublin South, Rathmines, 1887, no. 152, 16 February 1887.

364 This individual was a son of the dairyman John Wilmer who in 1863 held a leasehold interest in part of the Geraldine House property, including Geraldine Terrace: RD 1863/39/41. John senior died in Milltown on 19 January 1889.The family's surname is spelt 'Willmore' in the 1901 Census for house no. 40 South Circular Road, having previously been spelt 'Wilmer'.

365 *Dublin Evening Mail*, 1 December 1898, p. 3; *Freeman's Journal*, 8 December 1898, p. 7; *Dublin Evening Telegraph*, 8 December 1898, p. 3; 9 December 1898, p. 3; *Rathmines News*, 10 December 1898, p. 4; 17 December 1898, p. 5.

366 *Rathmines News*, 10 December 1898, p. 4.

367 *Dublin Evening Telegraph*, 8 December 1898, p. 3.

After a number of adjournments at Dublin's northern police court, Anne Troy was finally given an ultimatum by the judge in mid-December 1898 to give up possession of Geraldine House or face imprisonment.[368] However, Troy was still in situ on 18 February 1899 when she appeared in court again charged with throwing water over bailiff John Williams who had called to the front door of Geraldine House to take possession of the property.[369] Ultimately, Anne Troy was forced to vacate the property and she died in 1900 aged ninety-seven in St Patrick's House for the Aged in Kilmainham.[370] Geraldine House was marked down as vacant when the 1901 census took place on 31 March of that year.[371]

Prior to the eviction proceedings against Anne Troy in the winter of 1898, John Wilmer had, on 29 October 1898, secured a 200-year term lease from her erstwhile landlords comprising Geraldine House and four labourers' cottages to the rear together with an unenclosed piece of waste ground to the south of nos 1–3 Geraldine Terrace.[372] This plot of waste ground had originally formed the small triangular plot of land located at the bottom of the Leeson Estate Map of 1718 and which had subsequently been leased by William Cole to John Barker in April 1768 (Map 3).[373] By the early 1870s several ruined cottages had been cleared from this small parcel of land which was now available for redevelopment (Map 16a). Hence Wilmer was required by his landlord to spend £200 in building new cottages on the property on or before 1 November 1899, and a further £200 on or before 1 November 1900.[374] For unknown reasons, Wilmer failed to fulfil on time the building terms of his lease but in 1909 he temporarily disposed of his interest in his Milltown property for six months to a Rathgar builder, George Kelly, to enable Kelly to carry out construction work.[375] The result was that four new labourers' cottages were built at the rear of Geraldine House to replace much older cottages that had stood there for years. These new homes became known locally as Wilmer's or Strand Cottages.[376] A housing survey carried out in 1919 by the Rathmines UDC recorded that these two-roomed cottages had one bedroom and a kitchen, and 'are always kept in good condition'.[377] Less positively, the housing officer also noted that the tenants threw their ashes and rubbish into the River Dodder!

Geraldine House was repaired and let to various tenants during the first decade of the twentieth century. On census night 1911 it was inhabited by fifty-two-year-old John Battersby, an estate agent, his forty-eight-year-old wife Emily, and their twenty-three-year-old domestic servant, Elizabeth Kelly. John Battersby was related to William Maxwell Battersby who had died nearby

---

368 *Dublin Evening Telegraph*, 8 December 1898, p. 3; *Freeman's Journal*, 10 December 1898, p. 2; *Rathmines News*, 17 December 1898, p. 5.

369 *Rathmines News*, 18 February 1899, p. 5.

370 Civil registration of deaths in the district of South Dublin, South City No. 1, 1900, no. 293, 22 November 1900.

371 NAI, 1901 Census, Form B1, House and Building Return, house no. 17, Milltown Road, Rathmines and Rathgar East Electoral Division, Milltown townland, Dublin.

372 RD 1899/44/199.

373 RD 265/220/174912, RD 1899/44/199.

374 RD 1899/44/199.

375 RD 1909/90/132, RD 1909/90/133, RD 1909/90/134, RD 1910/43/250.

376 A photograph in the *Evening Herald* of 4 September 1931 shows these cottages flooded by the River Dodder.

377 Dublin City Archives, Rathmines and Rathgar UDC papers, UDC/1/14/1, Housing Survey 3 November 1919. It is unclear if Willmore was also responsible for building nos 5–8 Strand Terrace, which were of a superior design to nos 1–4 Strand Cottages, comprising three rooms.

in Garrynure on Milltown Road in 1908.[378] John Battersby lived in Geraldine House during the First World War and during this period he changed the name of his home to a somewhat bizarre name, The Ranch.[379] Battersby or his landlord was probably responsible for building the redbrick two-storey terraced extension to Geraldine Terrace, nos 4–7, during the First World War.[380]

The Battersbys had ceased living in Milltown by 1928 when, thankfully, their former home reverted to its old historic name, Geraldine House.[381] Geraldine House appears to have continued in use as a family home for some time afterwards but by the 1940s the house was being let out again in flats with board and lodgings.[382] The Harmon family were the last long-term occupants of the house.[383]

Geraldine House was demolished in the early 1980s to make way for the development of the Milltown Hill and Milltown Court apartment and town house complex. Dublin Corporation (as Dublin City Council was then called) was also anxious to use the opportunity afforded by the proposed development to widen and straighten the Milltown Road at this narrow point in its descent into Milltown, and this undoubtedly sealed Geraldine House's fate (the unkept grass verge on the left of the pavement is an ugly reminder of the Corporation's traffic management policies of the 1960s and 1970s which prioritised private motorists ahead of historic streetscapes). It was nonetheless very regrettable that such an old historic house was not saved for preservation. Prior to its demolition Dublin artist and historian Peter Pearson salvaged some of the interior fixtures and plasterwork.[384]

MILLTOWN HOUSE (PREVIOUSLY MOUNT ST ANNE'S CONVENT)

Milltown House is a very fine mid-eighteenth-century villa of extremely high quality and craftsmanship. The front elevation, which uniquely among Milltown villas is built with redbrick, comprises a three-storey over-basement entrance front of five bays. The main entrance is through an exceptionally fine tripartite pedimented doorcase of carved granite, flanked by pretty sidelights with elaborate glazing (Pl. 43). The interior of the house matches the exterior in its quality, and contains superb plasterwork and joinery in the entrance hall, main and service staircases and reception rooms (Pl. 44 & Pl. 45). The Dublin stuccodore Robert West (active 1750–90) has been suggested as the creator of the fine plasterwork in Milltown House.[385] In overall terms, Milltown House ranks high among the group of premier quality redbrick suburban villas of eighteenth-century Dublin, such as Glasnevin House and Loreto Abbey, Rathfarnham, to take two examples.

---

378 *Freeman's Journal*, 16 October 1908, p. 8.

379 VO, Cancellation Books, Rathmines and Rathgar East 1906–15, vol. 3–4, p. 743; The Post Office Dublin Directory and Calendar for 1918, p. 767.

380 Thom's Directories for 1917 and 1918, at pp. 1862 and 768 respectively, list no. 5 in 1917 and nos 7 and 8 in 1918, each house having a valuation of £10.

381 Thom's Directory 1928, p. 1751.

382 *Dublin Evening Mail*, 28 February 1941, p. 2; Thom's Directory 1952, p. 816, Thom's Directory 1957, p. 1271, Thom's Directory 1967, p. 408.

383 *Dublin Evening Mail*, 8 February 1956, p. 3; *Irish Independent*, 3 November 1971, p. 8.

384 Personal communication to the author by Peter Pearson in August 1996.

385 David Slattery, Architect and Historic Buildings Consultant, *Assessment of St Anne's House and Former Chapel, Milltown, Dublin 6* (undated report commissioned by O'Mahony Pike Architects).

Plate 43. Milltown House, Milltown Road, entrance front, 2017 (author's collection)

Plate 44. Milltown House, Milltown Road, plasterwork, 2019 (author's collection)

Plate 45. Milltown House, Milltown Road, interior joinery, 2019 (author's collection)

The dating of Milltown House and the identity of its builder has proved to be very elusive thus far and so its early history is conjectural. In September 1725 Edward Allen's executors granted a lease of 41 years to Hugh Johnston of Dublin for the following property:

> *all that the castle commonly called the castle of Milltown together with the new dwelling house, messuage or tenement thereunto adjoining together with the garden, stables, coach house, out houses ... as the enclosed ... and also ... two parks containing thirteen acres, two roods and thirty nine perches with the use and privilege of a way of passage twelve foot wide through the piece of waste ground on the south side of the barn to the field commonly called the six acres.*[386]

On the first edition of the six-inch OS map for County Dublin Milltown House is sited beside the square-shaped Milltown Castle to the east (Map 15). Based on the words 'new dwelling house thereunto adjoining' in the Johnston lease of 1725 and the buildings depicted on the OS map it would be reasonable to assume that Johnston's new house was Milltown House. However, taking into account its design and interior decoration, Milltown House could not have been built as early as the mid-1720s, so Johnston's lease must relate to different property, perhaps the buildings at the rear of the castle shown on the OS map.

386 RD 44/351/29734.

Milltown House would have been expensive to build and its builder/landlord was likely to have been a wealthy Dublin merchant. Based on these criteria another lease from 1751 assumes greater importance in attempting to identify the origins of Milltown House. On 3 August 1751, the widow and son of the late Alderman William Walker sold the following property to George Morgan of Newlands, County Dublin, for £700:

> *All that and those the lot of ground situate on the road leading from Dublin to Milltown together with the new house and stable thereupon and also the house and garden in the possession of John Adamson with all buildings and improvements thereon ... And Rebecca Walker did also grant, bargain and sell all that two fields containing seven [plantation] acres, two roods and twenty five perches part of Milltown with all buildings and improvements thereon and appurtenances to hold for the residue of a term of ninety nine years.*[387]

The references to the 'new house and stable' plus the expensive purchase price of £700 are potentially significant. Three and a half years later, in February 1754, the recorder of Dublin, Thomas Morgan, mortgaged 'part of the lands and houses of Milltown' to Alderman Percival Hunt the elder.[388]

The Morgan property is depicted on the northern side of Milltown village on Rocque's Survey of County Dublin of 1760, but it is impossible to identify Milltown House with complete certainty among the various buildings and properties on the north side of the village main street (Map 4). Indeed, Rocque's map has been found to be inaccurate in its recording of houses in the vicinity of Dundrum, and so his map should be treated cautiously when interpreting its depiction of Milltown village.[389]

All of the Morgan property in Milltown was acquired by Alderman Percival Hunt the younger in 1763 arising from debts owed by Thomas Morgan to Alderman Percival Hunt the elder, both of whom were, by then, deceased.[390] The significance of the property transactions between Morgan and Hunt is that the Hunt connection with Milltown House is later confirmed by the Griffith's Valuation records of 1850, when Miss Charlotte Hunt was recorded as the immediate lessor of the property, her tenant being Nicholas W. Monsarrat.[391] Furthermore, a recital in a renewal lease of 1831 from the descendants of the original Leeson tenant (Edward Allen) to Charlotte Hunt and her sisters, refers to a 99-year lease of 1735 made to William Walker, which had vested in the Misses Hunt by 1831.[392] All of these different strands of information put together suggest that Milltown House was built in around 1750 by either William Walker or Thomas Morgan, with the most likely candidate being Alderman William Walker.[393]

---

387 RD 149/294/99787.

388 RD 166/533/112471. The succession of the Milltown property from George Morgan to Thomas Morgan is not explained in the recitals of any of the deeds so a mistake may have been made in recording the Morgan first names in the memorial records.

389 Andrews, '*Two maps of Dublin*'.

390 RD 166/533/112471, RD 223/163/147771.

391 Griffith's Valuation, Rateable Valuation of Tenements, Co. Dublin, Barony of Uppercross, Parish of St Peter, Townland of Milltown, 1850, p. 54, at entry no. 13, Milltown House.

392 RD 887/444/587444.

393 According to newspaper reports Alderman Percival Hunt was living in Milltown by the late 1760s (*Freeman's Journal*, 1 April 1766, p. 3; 2 May 1769, p. 3) but there is nothing to suggest that he built Milltown House which, on stylistic grounds and the cartographic evidence, probably predates Hunt's arrival in Milltown.

Although contemporary newspapers did not provide the name of the house where he lived in Milltown, it is most likely that Alderman Hunt took up residence in Milltown House sometime after he acquired the various leasehold interests in the house and its demesne from John Selling Allen and the Thomas Morgan estate in 1760 and 1763 respectively.[394] Percival Hunt the younger died in Milltown on 11 October 1776, and subsequently, in May 1778, the following advertisement appeared in *Saunders's Newsletter*:

> *To be let, furnished or unfurnished, for any term (or the interest of the lease to be sold, being for lives renewable forever) the house and demesne at Milltown wherein the late Alderman Hunt lived. The house is large and elegantly furnished, situated within a mile and a half of Dublin. The tenant may have any quantity of land from six acres to twenty. The house may be seen every day (Sundays excepted) from twelve till four. Application to be made to Mrs Hunt at Milltown, or to John Hunt, esq. no. 31 Bride Street.*[395]

The mention of the house being 'large and elegantly furnished' would strongly suggest that the advertisement referred to Milltown House.

On 1 May 1785 Percival Hunt's son, Captain Benjamin Hunt, leased Milltown House and its demesne for lives renewable forever at the annual rent of £150 to the Reverend James Drought, a senior fellow of Trinity College Dublin, which included:

> *the dwelling house, out houses, garden lawn, shrubbery and demesne land of Milltown with four large fields or parks adjoining the rere of the house and garden containing fourteen [plantation] acres, two roods and thirty perches of land part of Milltown bounded on the east by the road leading from Dublin to Milltown, on the south by the castle house of Milltown and fields thereto belonging ...*[396]

Four years later, the Reverend Drought sold his lease for £568 15*s.* to a Dublin widow, Mrs Lettice Walcot.[397] Mrs Walcot in turn bequeathed Milltown House to Lady Elizabeth Eleanor King, who was the second daughter of Edward King, the earl of Kingston, of Rockingham, Roscommon. Shortly after their father died in November 1797 Elizabeth and her sister Isabelle were staying at Milltown House where they were visited by the diarist, Alexander Hamilton, who rode out to the property in a green chaise.[398]

In March 1800 Lady Elizabeth King sold Milltown House to Judge William Tankerville Chamberlain, who was the third justice of the King's Bench.[399] Chamberlain was the third of the triumvirate of judges to take up residency on Milltown Road, the others being his next-door neighbour Judge Robert Johnson of Elm House and Baron George of Coldblow (Milltown Park). Chamberlain was considered by his legal peers to be an able and upright judge and a sound lawyer. His tenure in Milltown was short lived, as he died aged fifty in Milltown House on 12 May 1802, possibly

394 RD 203/492/136431, RD 223/163/147771.

395 *Freeman's Journal*, 12 October 1776, p. 3; *Saunders's Newsletter*, 1 May 1778, p. 2.

396 RD 369/191/246877.

397 RD 412/191/268864.

398 Copy of the diary of Alexander Hamilton, K.C. of Newtownhamilton (3 vols, 1793–1807), at p. 111, entry for 24 November 1797 (Armagh Public Library, MS Johnston Collection no. 8); Ball, *History of county Dublin*, ii, p. 113.

399 RD 528/4/344352.

due to him having been 'a martyr to gout'.[400] A typically effusive obituary followed in the *Gentleman and London Magazine*, which noted that Chamberlain had displayed 'an inflexible integrity and firmness of mind, which were so eminently displayed in the late unfortunate rebellion that he will live forever in the hearts of a grateful nation'.[401] During Chamberlain's brief residence in Milltown his home was visited by the Dublin Society's statistician, Joseph Archer, who described the property as 'a capital house, pleasantly situated, with a beautiful small demesne, well wooded, good gardens, etc'.[402]

Six months after Chamberlain's death Milltown House was put up for sale in December 1802 and the following short advertisement was published in *Saunders's Newsletter*:

> *To be Let or Sold, the house and offices, at Milltown, the residence of the late Mr Justice Chamberlain, together with the garden and fields thereto belonging, the whole containing about 15 acres. The house, gardens, etc may be seen on Mondays only, from 11 until 3 o'clock. For terms apply to Robert Maddock, 52, Camden Street.*[403]

The sale of Milltown House did not take place until 14 months later, when the property was sold for an undisclosed sum to Alexander Crawford of Dublin on 28 February 1804.[404] The length of time it took to sell Milltown House after Chamberlain's death may reflect a softening of the Dublin housing market in the wake of the Act of Union or, more likely, the first signs of the decline in popularity of Milltown as a residential suburb of choice for Dublin's nobility and gentry.

The history of Milltown House in the first quarter of the nineteenth century is unremarkable. The house was offered for sale or short-term lettings sporadically in the early decades of that century, and newspaper advertisements appeared in 1813, 1828 and 1837.[405] In the mid-1830s one of these short-term tenants, woollen merchant Thomas Lyster, renamed the property 'Lyster Wood' and spent his leisure time growing rare green-house plants and keeping bees. He was also a council member of the Horticultural Society of Ireland. Unfortunately, Lyster was declared bankrupt in 1835 and was forced to vacate Milltown House and sell his personal possessions.[406]

In 1838 Milltown House was sold for £1,000 to Alderman William Hodges JP who was previously an ironmonger with offices in lower Sackville (O'Connell) Street. The purchase price included a discharge of all rent arrears owed by Thomas Lyster.[407] In December 1839 Hodges took a lease for lives renewable forever of two fields totalling 7 acres and 18 perches from

---

400 Ball, *The Judges in Ireland*, ii, p. 242; Ball and Hamilton, *The Parish of Taney*, p. 103, which mistakenly states that Chamberlain died at his residence in Churchtown.

401 *Gentleman and London Magazine 1802*, Obituary, p. 585.

402 Archer, *Statistical Survey of the County of Dublin*, p. 108. Archer's critic, Hely Dutton, opined that Milltown House was unworthy of public attention: Dutton, *Observations on Mr. Archer's Statistical Survey*, p. 119.

403 *Saunders's Newsletter*, 24 December 1802, p. 4.

404 RD 562/261/374092.

405 *Saunders's Newsletter*, 12 April 1813, p. 4; *Dublin Evening Mail*, 24 March 1828, p. 2; *The Pilot*, 18 October 1837, p. 1.

406 *Saunders's Newsletter*, 16 April 1835, p. 4; 17 May 1836, p. 3; 24 March 1837, p. 4; Pettigrew and Oulton's Dublin Almanac and General Register of Ireland 1835, pp. 160, 229.

407 RD 1838/8/97; Pigot & Co. City of Dublin Directory 1824, p. 7.

the Hunt sisters, who were then living in Milltown Castle. The annual rent was £21, 19*s*.[408] The previous year, the Hunts had commissioned a survey of this part of their property which shows the pair of pasture and tillage fields on elevated ground above the north side of Milltown village where the Alexandra School's hockey pitches are now. A third irregular-shaped pasture field directly behind the north side of main street, and appropriately named the 'hill field', was retained by the Misses Hunt for their own use and now forms part of the St Anne's apartment complex (Map 13).

William Hodges served as Lord Mayor of Dublin in 1837 and as an alderman of Dublin Corporation.[409] He was also an ex-officio guardian of the South Dublin Union workhouse.[410] Later still, Hodges became a director of the Dublin and Drogheda Railway Company and the Dublin, Dundrum and Rathfarnham Railway Company in the 1840s, a time when investing in railways was all the rage.[411] Like his neighbour Bernard Fox of Geraldine House, Alderman Hodges was a keen gardener and he won second prize from the Practical Floral and Horticultural Society for black grapes grown in the glasshouses of Milltown House which were cultivated by his gardener, Martin Leacy.[412] He also exhibited livestock at the Royal Agricultural Society's Cattle Show in 1844.[413] Romance blossomed too when Hodges' eldest daughter Charlotte married George Clayton Cowell, who lived across the road in Prospect House (Milltown Hill/The Old House).[414]

When a surveyor from the Griffith's Valuation visited Milltown House in 1845, he noted that the house had been given a new roof. What is much more puzzling is his recording of a lead factory on the grounds of Milltown House, which, according to the surveyor, had very recently been erected. The factory was a substantial building of both one and two storeys, the two-storey structure measuring 26' by 21' and being 19' tall; the single-storey structure having the dimensions 29' by 14' by 6.6'.[415] There is no record of this factory in any other contemporary nineteenth-century sources and neither was the factory mentioned when the Griffith's Valuation surveyors revisited Milltown House in 1847.[416] It is therefore very likely that the house book entry recording a lead factory in the grounds of Milltown House was made in error, unless it was a temporary structure associated with the reroofing works.

Alderman Hodges left Milltown House in January 1849 and was replaced by Nicholas W. Monsarrat as tenant of Miss Charlotte Hunt.[417] Monsarrat was briefly succeeded in Milltown House by the 3rd Viscount Avonmore, Barry John Yelverton from 1855–7. Avonmore's son, Major William Yelverton, was a defendant in one of the most infamous bigamy cases of the

408 RD 1839/22/284. The deed was witnessed by Hodges' gardener, William Roper.

409 *Freeman's Journal*, 25 March 1837, p. 1; 5 June 1871, p. 6 (Death notice).

410 Helen Burke, *The People and the Poor Law in 19th century Ireland* (The Women's Education Bureau, 1987), p. 342.

411 *Saunders's Newsletter*, 29 December 1846, p. 1; *Freeman's Journal*, 12 March 1847, p. 3; Thom's Directory 1847, p. 443.

412 *Freeman's Journal*, 14 July 1838, p. 3.

413 *Dublin Monitor*, 16 August 1844, p. 3.

414 *Leinster Express*, 23 December 1848, p. 2; Pettigrew and Oulton's Dublin Almanac and General Register of Ireland 1848, p. 855.

415 NAI, VO, OL50945, House Book for Milltown Village 1845, no. 97.

416 NAI, VO, OL70088, Quarto Book, Townland of Milltown, 1847, p. 210, no. 39.

417 *Freeman's Journal*, 22 January 1849, p. 1; Griffith's Valuation, Rateable Valuation of Tenements, Co. Dublin, Barony of Uppercross, Parish of St Peter, Townland of Milltown, 1850, p. 54, at entry no. 13, Milltown House. The Thom's Directory for 1850 (at p. 837) mistakenly names the property as Milltown Abbey.

nineteenth century. Although the case went through five trials culminating in a decision in favour of Yelverton in the House of Lords, the Major was completely discredited in the eyes of Irish public opinion because the House of Lords held that William Yelverton's first marriage to Theresa Longworth, an Irish Catholic, and which had been officiated on two separate occasions by a Catholic priest in Scotland and Ireland, was invalid, and thus his second marriage to Emily Forbes was lawful (Yelverton had initially hidden his relationship with Longworth from his family and his second spouse and then denied that he had married Longworth notwithstanding that the couple had lived together after the Scottish marriage ceremony). During the trial in the Irish court of common pleas, letters written by Yelverton to Theresa Longworth while he was temporarily residing with his father at Milltown House were produced in evidence.[418]

After Viscount Avonmore's departure the Monsarrat family reoccupied Milltown House until they too departed in 1871.[419] The property also experienced a change of landlord after the last of the Hunt spinsters died in 1874. During the 1860s or 1870s two three-sided bow windows were inserted in the north elevation of the house on the ground and first floors. The last private individual to live in Milltown House was Richard Warneford Boyle JP who took up residence there in 1871, and it was he who sold the property to the Sisters of Charity in 1879.[420] On 21 and 22 August 1879 the home farm livestock, which included among other things a 'useful donkey', prize poultry and large York pigs, were put up for auction. In addition to the livestock, Boyle's collection of stove and greenhouse plants were sold off with the auctioneer stating that 'Comment on its rare excellence is unnecessary, the collection being so well-known to horticulturalists in every part of the kingdom.'[421]

A few months later, on 2 July 1880 the Sisters of Charity bought the adjoining Milltown Castle and its grounds of about six statute acres from Tooke Cumming Luscombe, together with the ground on which Turret House had stood previously.[422] Luscombe had been one of the promotors of the Rathmines and Rathgar (Milltown Extension) Bill which, after much opposition by several ratepayers in the Rathmines township, became law on 2 August 1880.[423] The circumstances behind Luscombe's departure from Milltown and the sale of Milltown Castle to the Sisters of Charity are unknown.

The nuns quickly went about developing their extensive property in Milltown for their needs; they renamed it Mount St Anne's convent. In 1881 Milltown Castle was demolished and the construction of the novitiate building began. Two years later, St Anne's primary school for girls was opened in 1883.[424] To celebrate the centenary of the birth of Mary Aikenhead, the foundress of the Sisters of Charity, the nuns commissioned the architect W.H. Byrne to design a chap-

---

418 Thom's Directories 1855, p. 1052; 1856, p. 1092 and 1857, p. 1175; *Dublin Evening Mail*, 27 February 1861, p. 4; *Rathmines News*, 14 December 1901; *Weekly Irish Times*, 7 May 1938, p. 7; Maria Luddy and Mary O'Dowd, *Marriage in Ireland*, 1660–1925 (Cambridge, 2020), p. 294.

419 Thom's Directory 1870, p. 1603.

420 RD 1879/41/287.

421 *Dublin Daily Express*, 7 August 1879, p. 8.

422 RD 1880/42/282. See Maps 13 & 16a and Chapter 4 where the origins of Turret House are set out in the context of the mid-eighteenth-century development of the village. By the 1870s the Turret House had fallen into ruin and was demolished in 1873: VO, Cancellation Books, Rathmines Ward 1862-3, bk. 1, p. 144, no. 17/9.

423 See Chapter 11 for a detailed discussion of this important event.

424 Irish Sisters of Charity, *Milltown in brief... 1879–1995*, Circular Letter 26 April 1995.

Plate 46. Milltown House, Milltown Road, c. 1887 (image courtesy of the National Library of Ireland)

el and round tower. The foundation stone was laid by the archbishop of Dublin on 19 January 1887 and the chapel was officially opened by Dr Walsh on 15 August 1888.[425] A photograph of Mount St Anne's, most probably taken in the summer of 1887, shows the scaffolding for the chapel building works to the extreme right of the image (Pl. 46).[426]

Although the loss of the medieval Milltown Castle was regrettable, the Sisters of Charity more than compensated for this by maintaining Milltown House to a high standard and preserving its period features throughout their 116 years of ownership from 1879 to 1995. The principal change made to the house by the nuns was the addition of a third storey to the main block sometime after 1957.[427] Thankfully, the new alterations were sensitively carried out. In conclusion, it is worth noting that the acquisition of the two demesnes of Milltown House and Milltown Castle by the Sisters of Charity in the late nineteenth century had the unintended effect of preserving an historical landbank, originating with Alderman Percival Hunt in the 1750s and continuing largely intact until the turn of the twenty-first century, when the grounds were built over by Park Developments in the first decade of this century.

---

425 *Freeman's Journal*, 20 January 1887, p. 6; Irish Sisters of Charity, *Milltown in brief... 1879–1995*, Circular Letter 26 April 1995.

426 NLI, The Lawrence Photographic Collection, L ROY 01122, St Anne's, Milltown, Co. Dublin, photographed by Robert French, c. 1887.

427 The house had its front elevation of two storeys over basement when it was photographed in 1957 for the booklet dedicating the new 'Church of the Immaculate Virgin Mary of the Miraculous Medal Clonskeagh', on Bird Avenue.

MILLTOWN CASTLE

The origins of Milltown Castle and its history before 1700 has been dealt with in previous chapters, and this section briefly covers developments affecting the property in the eighteenth and nineteenth centuries. In the mid-to late 1720s Milltown Castle and a newly built house adjoining the castle was the home of Hugh Johnston for a brief period.[428] Johnston assigned his 41-year lease to Isaac Dobson who in turn sold the property for £200in 1750 to a widow named Patience Howard.[429] Thirteen years later in 1763 the earl of Leeson's principal tenant in Milltown, John Selling Allen, let Milltown Castle and the adjoining dwelling house together with 15 acres and 21 perches (plantation measure) to Alderman Percival Hunt the younger for £90 sterling, under a lease for lives renewable forever.[430] Milltown Castle remained in the ownership of the Hunt family for over a century, during which time it was frequently sublet on short-term leases.

In June 1828 Milltown Castle was advertised for short-term letting in *Saunders's Newsletter* with the following brief description:

> *Milltown Castle. To be let, furnished, with about eight acres of prime land. The situation is most desirable, being within two miles of the City, with every convenience within itself that can be required, and surrounded by gentleman's seats. It will be let for the year, or for five years certain.*[431]

Two years later, a more informative advertisement appeared in the same newspaper:

> *To be let furnished for the season, the house and ground at Milltown, called Milltown Castle. There is a well-furnished garden with coach house, stable and lock up yard etc and about thirteen statute acres of prime land.*[432]

The difference in the acreage figures can be accounted for by the fact that the extensive farmland attaching to both Milltown House and Milltown Castle was all under the control of the four Hunt sisters who leased it separately in varying amounts with each property according to their needs.

Milltown Castle was mentioned briefly again in 1837 when it was the residence of the Misses Hunt and was described as the 'partly repaired edifice of Milltown Castle'.[433] This description and the absence of property advertisements suggests that Milltown Castle may have lain unoccupied for several decades until it was recommissioned before being put on the rental market in 1828. This theory is supported by the recollections of local historian, John Christopher FitzAchary, who described some of the building work that took place.[434]

The indications are, however, that the refurbished dwelling was a fairly modest one. During the occupancy of its final tenant, Tooke Cumming Luscombe, Milltown Castle and its grounds

428 RD 44/351/29734.

429 RD 143/520/98035.

430 RD 223/28/146305. The first four years' rent was initially £59 10*s*. per annum and thereafter £90.

431 *Saunders's Newsletter*, 23 June 1828, p. 4.

432 *Saunders's Newsletter*, 19 May 1830, p. 3.

433 Lewis, *Topographical Dictionary of Ireland*, ii, 370.

434 *Rathmines News*, 14 December 1901. See the discussion about the castle's medieval origins and FitzAchary's recollections in Chapter 2.

Plate 47. River Dodder at Milltown with St Philip's House in the background (now Alexandra College grounds), c. 1950 (courtesy of Mary Long)

of six statute acres was rated for local taxation purposes at £43, which was considerably less than the tax applying to Milltown House and its demesne of just under 24 statute acres, which was rated at £122 15*s*.[435]

As noted previously under the discussion of Milltown House, on 2 July 1880 the Sisters of Charity bought the adjoining Milltown Castle from Tooke Cumming Luscombe and shortly afterwards demolished the castle to make way for their novitiate building.[436]

ST PHILIP'S (PREVIOUSLY FAIRYLAND)

This extensive eighteenth-century property, originally called Fairyland and, from the 1860s onwards, St Philip's, is now the site of Alexandra College (opposite Milltown Bridge), which relocated from Earlsfort Terrace to Milltown in 1972 when the house was demolished to make way for the school buildings. Despite its longevity only a few photographs of St Philip's are known to exist, and none of them show the actual villa in any great detail (Pl. 47).[437]

The Fairyland property was a subdivision of the original 51-plantation-acre landholding granted by Joseph Leeson to Edward Allen in 1720, which by the late 1770s had been let by

435 VO, Cancellation Books, Dublin, Rathmines Electoral Division, Milltown Road, 1855–62, vol. 1, p. 121.

436 RD 1880/42/282.

437 My thanks are due to Mary Long for this photograph and for sharing other family photographs of her father and grandparents, who lived in the gate lodge of St Philip's in the 1930s.

Allen's descendants to a Milltown farmer, James Pagett.[438] The full extent of Fairyland and its adjoining farm land is difficult to discern because of the extensive changes that took place to the original landholding, particularly when the railway (now the Luas tramline) cut through it in 1850 and the land on the western side of the railway was developed afterwards. In spite of this, a map of 1821 confirms that the Fairyland property comprised just under 26 plantation acres of ground extending on the north side of Milltown Road from the present entrance to Alexandra College on the east as far as Classon's Bridge on the west (Map 8). The house and its extensive gardens were located at the western end of Milltown village adjoining the Hunt family's landholding in Milltown, with the remainder of the estate made up of eight fields and a couple of small gardens. The property extended considerably back from the road northwards on the western side of the Milltown Path, an area that in the 1830s was incorporated into the new townland of Rathmines South (Map 15). This western part of the property was laid out in villas from the 1830s onwards and developed intensively from the 1860s onwards when Temple Road and Richmond Avenue South were built (Map 18).[439]

The early history of the house that became known as Fairyland is extremely difficult to pin down because several people held different leases of varying duration and subdivisions over the same property in quick succession in the 1780s.[440] An additional complicating factor is that another house called Richmond Hill (renamed Rydalmount) was built beside Fairyland in the eighteenth century, and that property also formed part of the Fairyland estate (plot 10 on Map 8).[441] As a result, it is often impossible to distinguish between the two houses and disentangle the complicated landownership from the data provided by contemporary newspaper advertisements and property deeds of the late eighteenth century. It is necessary to be mindful of these points, therefore, when considering the following extensive advertisements which appeared in *Saunders's Newsletter* in 1778, 1783 and 1785:

> *To be sold, or the interest of the lease sold, of which 30 years will be unexpired on the 25th March inst., a neat small house, in thorough good repair, which has been inhabited the whole year, situate on the bank above Milltown, on the road leading from thence to Rathmines, with front and rear gardens, extremely well cropped with all kinds of vegetables, and planted with choice fruit trees, enclosed with a stone wall, ten feet high, together with a yard in which there are three out-offices; there is a very good stable for three horses with coach house for two carriages and large hay loft over both, and also a cow house for three cows in an enclosed stable yard; there is also a choice meadow [of] three acres and a half adjoining the house and gardens; the situation is truly desirable, commanding a full view of the bay of Dublin, mountains etc. A servant attends in the house who will show the whole. For further particulars enquire of Mr Thomas Gibbons, No. 6, Suffolk Street, Dublin.*[442]

---

438 RD 27/221/16698, RD 326/459/216623. See Chapter 4 for a detailed discussion of the eighteenth century rural origins of the Fairyland demesne.

439 Dublin City Council Legal Department, Civic Offices, which holds copies of deeds relating to the Hogan estate, including a deed of trust dated 1 June 1909 which contains extensive information about the multiple properties that made up the Hogan estate in Milltown and Rathmines at that time.

440 *Saunders's Newsletter,* 19 December 1781, p. 4; 18 April 1782, p. 4; 30 July 1782, p. 4; 1 March 1783, p. 4; 9 March 1784, p. 4; 6 July 1785, p. 4; 22 May 1786, p. 4.

441 RD 644/123/441040. Plots 10, 11, 12 and 13 of the Hogan estate map comprised the Richmond Hill property.

442 *Saunders's Newsletter*, 8 April 1778, p. 4.

> *To be sold, or the interest of the lease sold, of which 25 years will be unexpired on the 25th March inst., a neat house, in thorough repair, situated on the bank above Milltown, on the road leading from thence to Rathmines, with a well enclosed yard, in which are a stable for three horses, coach house for two carriages, hay loft over both, cow house for three cows. There are two gardens, one in front the other in the rear, well enclosed, cropped with all kinds of vegetables, and planted with some of the choicest wall and other fruit trees; there is a highly manured and well enclosed meadow adjoining, containing three acres two roods, the whole of which may be seen from the front and back windows. The situation speaks for itself, having from all parts beautiful and extensive prospects; the front commanding a view of the bay of Dublin and parts adjacent, the rear, Rathfarnham Castle, and country adjacent. The house has been constantly inhabited, and a servant attends who will show the whole.*[443]

> *A neat house beautifully situated on the hill of Milltown, near the bridge [the Packhorse Bridge]. It commands a most extensive prospect of the sea, the mountains, and the improvements in that neighbourhood, with a large garden, stable, and any number of acres that may be agreeable. There is the convenience of goats whey, and a fine pathway [Milltown Path] through the fields to Camden Street, computed to be not more than a mile and a quarter. Inquire of John Percevall Hunte [sic], esq. at his house in Ship Street or of John Donnellan, at his house in Milltown.*[444]

The John Donnellan of Milltown mentioned in the third advertisement can be linked to a lease of 1786, whereby Peter Healy, a Dublin grocer, leased the following property to John Donnellan of Milltown, farmer, for 77 years at an annual rent of £126:

> *the dwelling house, stable, garden and six fields being part of Milltown containing twenty acres three roods and twenty eight perches bounded on the north by lands demised to Alderman Percival Hunt, on the west by the stone wall that divides the premises from the lands of Rathmines and on the south by the road that leads from Milltown to Rathfarnham [sic] and partly by a millrace and on the east partly by Mr Gibbons and partly by Mr Hunt's holding.*[445]

A second sublease for 72 years from Peter Healy to Christopher Sheil of Milltown in 1789 related to a subplot of Fairyland where the entrance gate and perimeter wall of Alexandra College on Milltown Road now stand:

> *those dwelling houses, messuages or tenements with all that the plot of ground on which the houses were then erected commonly called and known as the Quarry opposite the bridge of Milltown [the Packhorse Bridge] bounded on the east and south by the road from Dublin leading to Rathmines and on the north by a field called the bridge field held by Mr Thomas Gibbons and on the west by a garden held by Thomas Gibbons.*[446]

---

443 *Saunders's Newsletter*, 1 March 1783, p. 4.

444 *Saunders's Newsletter*, 6 July 1785, p. 4. John Percival Hunt was a son of Alderman Percival Hunt who died at his home in Milltown in 1774.

445 RD 364/511/249575.

446 RD 403/524/270209. The deed was witnessed by John Denny of Milltown, yeoman, and by John Brennan, gardener to William Sankey.

The properties described in the two leases quoted above along with several others eventually came into the ownership of Edward Sankey, a wealthy barrister who set about enlarging and developing his property at Fairyland.[447] From 1790 to 1797 Sankey spent hundreds of pounds enlarging the house and gardens and its out offices. The details of the work carried out were recorded meticulously by the Dublin quantity surveyor, Bryan Bolger, whose papers are kept in the National Archives.[448] The extent of Sankey's improvements can also be gauged from the Hogan estate map of 1821 (Map 8). Despite his improvements to Fairyland Sankey put his home up for sale in 1803. The property was advertised in *Saunders's Newsletter* in the following terms:

> *Fairyland, Milltown, two miles from the castle of Dublin. To be let, for a long term of years, that delightfully situated house, walled in gardens, shrubberies, and upwards of thirteen acres of land, highly improved, and richly manured last Winter, the house lately the residence of Counsellor Sankey, who expended a very large sum of money on the improvements, it is in perfect order, newly slated. It is requested none but principals will apply, as the family are residing there at present. Tickets of admission may be had at 10, Leinster Street, where the terms may be known.*[449]

Whatever the reason, Fairyland did not sell and Sankey had to wait until 1810 before disposing of his several leasehold interests at great loss to a Dublin solicitor named William Caldwell Hogan. Hogan paid £160 for the Fairyland subleases, most of which were of a relatively short duration. At the same time, he took a lease for lives renewable forever from Peter Healy of 25 plantation acres of farmland at Milltown at an annual rent of £181.[450] In the process, Hogan was acquiring the freehold interest in Fairyland whereas the Healy lease previously held by John Donnellan (and subsequently by William Sankey) was for 77 years. Over the course of the nineteenth century, William Hogan and his sons continuously bought up and consolidated the various leasehold interests affecting Fairyland, including premises on the north side of the main street of Milltown village (Map 8).[451]

As previously noted in Chapter 4, William Hogan was a committed member of the Church of Ireland and was instrumental in building a chapel of ease in Milltown village. At a meeting held at the vestry room of St Peter's parish church in 1818 Hogan was appointed an overseer to 'enforce a due observance of the Sabbath Day'.[452] The purpose of overseers was to ensure that the laws relating to Sunday observance were obeyed and to prevent drinking in pubs, as explained by the following extract from a history of Taney parish, which included that part of Milltown (i.e. Farranboley) which lay on the south bank of the River Dodder:

> *At a Vestry held on March 9, 1829, to appoint overseer to assist the churchwardens and civil officers in preventing the profanation of the Sabbath, fourteen leading parishioners were nominated under 55 Geo. III; chap. 19, and 100 copies of their nomination were ordered to be printed and*

447 RD 403/524/270210, RD 547/109/360241, RD 560/170/374439, RD 622/456/430260.

448 Bryan Bolger papers (NAI, MS 2/476/15-16).

449 *Saunders's Newsletter*, 29 July 1803, p. 4.

450 RD 631/173/432324. This Healy is likely to be the same lessor recorded in the 1786/89 leases.

451 RD 778/58/526794, RD 1837/22/200, RD 1860/26/258.

452 *Freeman's Journal*, 7 September 1818, p. 2.

> *served in all the public-houses, and also posted in the most conspicuous places, in the parish. A report of the houses where spirits were retailed was also ordered to be made to the churchwardens every month, in order that they might see how they were conducted.*[453]

William Hogan had three sons, two of whom became solicitors and joined their father's practice at 48 York Street.[454] Hogan's eldest son, William junior, qualified as a barrister and on his marriage in 1822 to Ms Ann Lea, Fairyland was charged with an annuity of £200 payable annually to William and Ann.[455]

In the 1830s Hogan began developing the western extremity of the Fairyland demesne which lay on the western side of the Milltown Path. In less than a decade, new avenues were laid out across the fields and four villas were built on the estate, all of which are marked on the first edition of the OS six-inch map (Map 15). The residents of these villas, who were listed in Lewis's *Topographical Dictionary* of 1837, included W.H. Flemyng of Nullamore, Rev. S.W. Fox of Rich View, W. McCann of Richmond Park (later renamed Noursdale) and J. Smith of Brookfield. With the exception of Brookfield, these houses are still standing off Richmond Avenue South.[456] As well as the four villas, three small detached cottages had been built by about 1840 opposite Richview and fronting the Milltown Path, one of which (Richmond Cottage) was leased to an ironmonger and hardware merchant named David FitzHenry (Map 18).[457] These three houses were demolished at some stage in the late nineteenth or early twentieth century to facilitate more intensive building development and road widening on Richmond Avenue South.[458] When William Hogan senior made his will in 1849 he arranged for his extensive property portfolio to be put into a trust for various family members.[459] Hogan died aged eighty-six at Fairyland on 23 July 1853. His death notice recorded that he had been for many years an active and zealous member of several religious and charitable societies.[460]

After William Hogan's death in 1853 Fairyland was leased to Protestant middle-class gentry, professionals and affluent merchants such as Charles Granby Burke JP who was master of the Court of Common Pleas and a director of the Colonial Life Assurance Company, Sir John Kingston James (in 1865) and ironmonger Alfred Henshaw, whose family will be discussed shortly.[461] At some time in the early 1860s Fairyland was renamed St Philip's, probably by the Hogan estate tenant, Charles Granby Burke.[462]

Some idea of the wealth of this class of resident can be gauged from a reported theft at St Philip's in which Mrs Burke's French housemaid was charged with stealing jewellery and dress-

453 Ball and Hamilton, *The Parish of Taney*, p. 219.

454 Pettigrew and Oulton's Dublin Almanac and General Register of Ireland 1845, p. 806.

455 RD 778/58/526794.

456 Lewis, *Topographical Dictionary of Ireland*, ii, 370; Deeds and legal papers in the law department of Dublin City Council offices, Wood Quay, relating to Milltown, inc. Hogan Estate Trust Deed dated 1 June 1909.

457 *Freeman's Journal*, 18 January 1858, p. 1. The three properties are named Richmond Cottage, Richmond Ville and Richview Lodge on the map.

458 A house called Ardvarna stands on the site now.

459 Dublin City Council Housing Files for Milltown, extract from abstract of title for William Caldwell Hogan (undated).

460 *Saunders's Newsletter*, 25 July 1853, p. 5; 26 July 1853, p. 3.

461 Hogan Estate Trust Deed dated 1 June 1909; VO, Cancellation Books, Dublin, Rathmines East, Milltown Road, 1873–1887, vol. 2, p. 198; *Saunders's Newsletter*, 21 April 1863, p. 4; *Dublin Builder*, 1 January 1865, p. 1; *Evening Freeman*, 19 October 1866, p. 2.

462 Thom's Directory 1862, p. 1351.

es to the value of £100, a very considerable amount of money in 1864.[463] Notwithstanding this theft, Mrs Granby Burke's fashionable attire caught the attention of an *Irish Times* reporter when she attended a vice regal Drawing Room at Dublin Castle on 29 January 1873 and was reported to be wearing the following outfit:

> *train, corsage, panier and petticoat of the richest gros grain violet, lined with marcelline, and trimmed with fine point lace, headed with swansdown, corsage and panier trimmed to correspond; petticoat trimmed with flounces of old point, looped with violets and primroses. Headdress, flowers, lappets, and court plumes; ornaments, diamonds and topaz.*[464]

Alfred Henshaw was a Dublin ironmonger who in the 1860s acquired and successfully built up the ailing iron mills at Clonskeagh, specialising in manufacturing spades and other agricultural and industrial tools.[465] In 1867 Henshaw acquired from the Hogan estate a 900-year lease of just under two acres opposite Milltown railway station (now the Milltown Luas stop) on Richmond Avenue South. Under the terms of his lease Henshaw was required within two years to spend £800 in building a substantial house and to pay annual ground rent of £25. By December 1869 Henshaw had built a fine Victorian villa called Hatherton.[466]

The Henshaw family purchased St Philip's from Charles Granby Burke in 1882 and it remained the family home for nearly 80 years.[467] Over time Alfred Henshaw acquired the long leasehold interests of St Philip's and other adjoining properties from the Hogan estate. As well as Hatherton, Henshaw invested the profits of his business in buying or building several houses on Temple Road in the late 1860s.[468] To take one example, from 1898 to 1904 Alicia Henshaw (Alfred's widow) let one of these big Temple Road houses, Thorndale, for an annual rent of £120 to Thomas Edmondson, the owner of the Dublin Laundry, whose career is discussed in Chapter 11.[469] Alicia Henshaw paid annual ground rent of £29 4*s*. 6*d*. to the Hogan estate, so she was making a good profit from her late husband's property investments.[470]

As befitting his station in life, Alfred Henshaw was active in local affairs. As well as being a justice of the peace, for over 22 years Henshaw served on the board of the Rathmines and Rathgar Township before retiring due to poor health in 1894.[471] Henshaw was also prominent in the affairs of his local parish church, St Philip's, where he acted as a churchwarden.[472] Alfred Henshaw died in Greystones

463 *Saunders's Newsletter*, 18 January 1864, p. 2.

464 *Irish Times*, 30 January 1873, p. 3; 31 January 1873, p. 5.

465 A separate history could be written about the Henshaw ironworks at Clonskeagh but for a good introduction see Holland, *Clonskeagh*, pp. 362–64.

466 Extracted from a copy of the lease of Hatherton dated 14 October 1867 in the possession of Mrs Anne O'Byrne; *Saunders's Newsletter*, 17 December 1869, p. 3.

467 RD 1882/28/186, RD 1882/28/187; NAI, Probate Office Records, Will Calendar for 1961, Probate registry 3042 (Annie Henshaw).

468 Hogan Estate Trust Deed dated 1 June 1909; *Irish Press*, 21 July1945, p. 6 (sale of profit rents).

469 Edmondson complained that the selection of wallpaper which Mrs Henshaw allowed him to choose from was 'very poor for such a house': Hearn, *Thomas Edmondson*, p. 137.

470 Hogan Estate Trust Deed dated 1 June 1909.

471 Dublin City Archives, Rathmines and Rathgar UDC papers, UDC/1/Min/1/7, 1893-1902, p. 108.

472 *Freeman's Journal*, 20 April 1881, p. 3.

on 12 October 1897 leaving behind him an estate worth over £109,000.[473] After his death the Henshaw family presented a large brass lectern in his memory to St Philip's which is still in use today.[474]

Alfred Henshaw was survived by his wife Alicia, his son Thomas, and his eight daughters.[475] During the Edwardian era three of the Henshaw sisters – Alberta, Alfreda and Victoria – were married at St Philip's church and afterwards the wedding receptions were held at St Philip's.[476] These happy family occasions were reported in great detail in the local newspapers and the accounts give a glimpse into the affluent lives of the privileged classes of Edwardian Dublin, as the following extract illustrates:

> *The bride was attended by her sister, Miss Margaret Henshaw, who wore a picturesque dress of cream cashmere de soie with bretelles of Chantilly lace, net chemisette, and bands of black satin finished at the high waist with tiny buttons and loops; large cavalier hat of grey satin with large osprey. Her bouquet of roses and dragon-fly brooch of diamonds and pearls were gifts of the bridegroom, who was supported by his brother, the Rev. H. Orpen. After the ceremony the wedding party which was restricted to close relatives of the families, repaired to St. Philip's, where the usual cake cutting and other formalities were duly gone through. At 1 pm Mr and Mrs Orpen motored to Kingstown en route for London, the latter wearing a long mole motor coat over a blue cloth dress, and a motor hat and veil. The end of the honeymoon will be spent motoring through the south of Ireland.*[477]

By the time of the 1911 census the Henshaw household at St Philip's had reduced to three family members – Alicia (seventy-one), Anne (forty-three) and Thomas (thirty) – and their four Catholic domestic servants. To compensate for the lack of photographs, the size of St Philip's can be gleaned by the fact that the house had 20 front windows.[478] The property had extensive out offices, including a stable and coach house, a cow house, a fowl house and two motor houses.[479] In the absence of contemporary records to the contrary, the Henshaws were almost certainly the first people in Milltown to own a private motor car, which was a very expensive luxury in Edwardian times. In fact, the scion of the family, Thomas Henshaw, was an enthusiastic amateur racing driver who successfully competed in his 28 h.p. Daimler throughout Ireland in 1906 and 1907.[480]

Thomas Henshaw was the managing director of the family ironmongery wholesale business Thomas Henshaw and Company, which for years had its offices in Christ Church Place,

---

473 NAI, Calendar of Wills and Administrations for 1897, p. 194.

474 *St Philip's Church Milltown Parish: A Ten Minute Tour,* a pamphlet prepared by the Parish Development Committee in 2016.

475 *Dublin Daily Nation*, 18 October 1897, p. 2; *Rathmines News*, 21 September 1901, p. 2; Register of Marriages for St Philip's Church, Parish of Milltown (Church of Ireland), 1882, no. 10, 1894, nos 78 and 80, 1901, no. 110, 1902, no. 113, 1909, no. 138, 1913, no. 154; NAI, 1911 Census, Form A, residents of house no. 46, Milltown Road, Rathmines & Rathgar East Electoral Division, Parish of St Peter, Milltown townland, Dublin.

476 *Rathmines News,* 21 September 1901, p. 2; 26 July 1902, p. 5; *Irish Independent*, 30 July 1909, p. 4.

477 *Irish Independent*, 30 July 1909, p. 4.

478 NAI, 1911 Census, Form A, residents of house no. 46, Milltown Road, Rathmines & Rathgar East Electoral Division, Parish of St Peter, Milltown townland, Dublin.

479 NAI, 1901 Census, Form B 2, out-offices and farm-steads return for house no. 46, Milltown Road, Rathmines & Rathgar East Electoral Division, Parish of St. Peter, Milltown townland, Dublin.

480 *Wicklow Newsletter*, 2 November 1905, p. 2, *Weekly Irish Times*, 22 August 1931, p. 12; Brendan Lynch, *Green Dust: Ireland's Unique Motor Racing History*, 1900–1939 (Dublin 1988), pp. 36–41.

as well as its manufacturing operations in Clonskeagh where spades and shovels were made. Thomas died on 14 August 1931 leaving a wife and two young children.[481] In late 1931 or early 1932 the factory at Clonskeagh closed down, apparently due to the effectd of foreign competition, but the wholesale business in the city continued nonetheless. A short time later the government introduced a protective tariff of 50% on imported ironomngery and this development led to the former workforce taking over the factory under a new co-operative venture with the encouragement of Thomas Henshaw and Company. Unfortunately, this venture did not work out and by the mid-1930s the Clonskeagh ironworks had closed for good.[482] Thomas Henshaw and Company continued to trade at Christchurch Place until the business went into voluntary liquidation in 1963, its demise hastened by alleged professional negligence on the part of a foreign firm of managment consutlants that had been brought in the previous year to advise the business.[483]

Anne Henshaw, known locally as Miss Annie Henshaw, lived at St Philip's for the rest of her life until her death on 10 February 1961.[484] By all accounts Annie Henshaw was liked by the villagers in Milltown and was not in any way aloof. Her continued residence in St Philip's provided local employment. For many years the Doyle family lived in the gate lodge of St Philip's and worked as gardeners for Miss Henshaw.[485] During the 1930s and 1940s Anne Henshaw's widowed sister Alberta Pringle and her son Alfred Pringle BL lived in St Philip's where they continued the family tradition of engaging in charitable and philanthropic work.[486]

In the early 1950s Dublin Corporation attempted to compulsorily acquire the walled garden and orchard at St Philip's as part of its plans to demolish Milltown village main street which was considered unfit for human habitation. The reason for including the garden in the compulsory purchase order was that the Corporation wanted to build shops on the garden, which was located at the northern end of St Philip's grounds where the entrance gates to Alexandra College are now.[487] During cross examination by Miss Henshaw's barrister (Mr Miley), the city's planning inspector (Mr O'Brien) revealed his prejudices against the type of property – a period house on large grounds – under threat:

O'Brien: My observation is that it is not an economic holding at the moment, St Philip's private residence.
Miley: What do you mean?
O'Brien: This type of dwelling is fast fading out.
Miley: You would not agree that in the interests of the State they should be preserved as long as possible?
O'Brien: Not for this type of house. This type of house is an embarrassment to most type of owners.[488]

---

481 *Irish Independent*, 15 August 1931, p. 1; *Weekly Irish Times*, 22 August 1931, p.12.

482 *Irish Independent*, 18 January 1932, p. 1; *Irish Times*, 27 April 1932, p. 3; *Irish Press*, 25 March 1932, p 7, 18 May 1932, p. 8, 27 May 1932, p7, 25 April 1933, p.9, 22 July 1937, p. 3.

483 *Irish Time*, 16 January 1963, p. 1, 21 January 1963, p. 8, 18 May 1963, p. 21, 15 June 1963, p. 19, 1 February 1964, p. 13.

484 NAI, Probate Office Records, Will Calendar for 1961, Probate registry 3042.

485 Personal recollections of Tommy Feerick, Benny McGuirk and Mary Long (née Doyle) in conversation with the author.

486 Thom's Directory 1941, p. 1225; *Irish Times*, 24 June 1935, p. 4; 2 February 1953, p. 6; Register of Deaths for Dublin South District, death of Alberta Pringle on 1 September 1950 at St Philip's.

487 Milltown Village CPO Inquiry, pp. 103–18.

488 Milltown Village CPO Inquiry, p. 107.

Plate 48. Rydalmount House, Milltown Road, entrance front, 2019 (author's collection)

Ultimately, Miss Henshaw's counsel was successful in saving his client's property and in the end the garden at St Philip's was excluded from the compulsory purchase area that was finally confirmed by the Minister for Local Government.[489]

On 29 September 1960 St Philip's and eight acres of grounds – the residue of the original eighteenth-century Fairyland demesne and its farmland of 25 plantation acres – were put up for auction and subsequently sold for over £17,000.[490] Not long afterwards, the last of Alfred Henshaw's children, Miss Annie Henshaw, died on 4 July 1961.[491] The fact that Alexandra College had their hockey grounds in St Philip's was probably a factor in the school's decision to leave Earlsfort Terrace and move to a new 12-acre school campus in Milltown in 1972. This resulted in the demolition of St Philip's after 200 years of existence.

RYDALMOUNT (PREVIOUSLY RICHMOND HILL)

In many respects Rydalmount has been overshadowed by its erstwhile neighbour, Fairyland/St Philip's. As noted earlier, Rydalmount formed part of the Hogan estate in the nineteenth

489 Annotated map relating to the Milltown Village Area CPO 1952 retained by the legal department of Dublin City Council, Civic Offices.

490 *Irish Times*, 3 September 1960, p. 16; Irish Architectural Archive, Roseanne Dunne papers, undated newspaper cutting of St Philip's House, Milltown.

491 NAI, Probate Office, Wills Calendar for 1961, probate registry 3042.

century when it was called Richmond Hill and as such was let out to tenants, none of whom appear to have left much in the way of historical record. For these reasons, Rydalmount's history is brief in comparison with its neighbouring villas.

Richmond Hill was built on the top of the north bank of the River Dodder at the junction of the Milltown Path and the Milltown Road, to the west of Milltown village and the Packhorse Bridge (Map 8). The house as originally built was a compact building of three storeys with a two-bay entrance front. The entrance front was later enhanced by the addition of a crenelated entrance porch with the hall door approached by a short flight of steps. In the early 1860s a two-storey extension overlooking the main road and the Dodder valley was added at right angles to the south gable of the main block (Pl. 48).[492]

Richmond Hill was probably built in the last or penultimate decade of the eighteenth century. The house can first be definitively traced back to a deed of 1795 whereby John Keeling of Dublin, distiller, conveyed to Jonathan Wilson of Dublin, confectioner:

> *all the dwelling house, stable, garden and two fields adjoining thereto containing five acres and thirty one perches bounded on the north by ground in the possession of John Donnellan of Milltown, on the west by a stone wall that divides the premises from the lands of Rathmines, on the south by the road that leads from Milltown to Rathfarnham and partly by a millrace and on the east by [ground in the possession of] William Sankey esq. [i.e. Fairyland].*[493]

Two years later, in 1797 Richmond Hill was advertised for sale when more revealing particulars about the property were provided in *Saunders's Newsletter*:

> *To be sold the interest in the lease of a house and garden, with a new coach house and stable, and two fields adjoining, containing 5 [plantation] acres and 31 perches, or thereabouts. The house consists of 5 rooms and a kitchen, and cannot be exceeded for beauty of prospect, both sea and land, adjoining Counsellor Sankey's beautiful improvements [Fairyland], near Milltown, and known by the name of Richmond Hill. The gardens are well stocked with fruit trees, and well cropped with vegetables, on which there have been laid out upwards of two hundred guineas in useful and lasting improvements. There are 63 years of the lease unexpired. Inquire at said place, or the printer's hereof. If not disposed by private contract [it] will be sold by auction on 8 May.*[494]

In 1811 William Hogan leased the property for lives renewable forever to a woollen manufacturer, Walter Burke, at the annual rent of £68 5*s*.[495] As previously noted in Chapter 6, Burke was the proprietor of a cloth mill on the north bank of the Dodder located immediately across from Richmond Hill, where the Shanagarry apartment complex is now (Map 7). When Walter Burke went bankrupt in 1816 Richmond Hill was put up for auction.[496]

Richmond Hill, its gardens and two fields were included in the Fairyland estate map commissioned by William Hogan in 1821, at which time Richmond Hill was leased to a William Thom-

---

492 VO, Cancellation Books, Rathmines Ward 1862–3, bk. 1, p. 128.

493 RD 499/350/316768.

494 *Saunders's Newsletter*, 28 April 1797, p. 4.

495 RD 644/441040/123.

496 *Belfast Newsletter*, 19 November 1816, p. 3.

as at the annual rent of £68 5*s.* (Map 8, plots 10–13).[497] From the Fairyland map we can identify Richmond Hill and its outbuildings immediately to the west of the Milltown Path, at its junction with the road from Milltown to Classon's Bridge and Upper Rathmines, and that the rear of the house backed onto the Milltown Path. Two fields belonging to Richmond Hill's pleasure grounds extended in a westerly direction parallel with the road to Classon's Bridge, terminating in a walled garden which abutted the boundary wall with the demesne of South Hill which was located on the lands of the Palmerston estate in Upper Rathmines and identified as 'Mr Sweeney's Ground' on the Fairyland map.

Within the space of 30 years the whole landscape around Richmond Hill changed radically. As previously noted in Chapter 7, William Hogan began developing his landholding to the west of the Milltown Path in the 1830s. This involved appropriating the two fields and the walled garden attached to Richmond Hill (Map 8, plots 11–13) and converting them into parkland for the new villa of Nullamore which was later inhabited by his son-in-law William Henry Flemying in the mid-1830s.[498] At the same time the Milltown Path was realigned to run by the front of Richmond Hill by creating a dog-leg at the rear, and an avenue to Nullamore and Richmond Park was laid out (Maps 15 & 16b). In the months of May and June 1836 Richmond Hill was advertised for sale and was described as being located between the demesne of Nullamore, then inhabited by the Rev. William Flemying (Hogan's son-in-law), and Mr Hogan's demesne of Fairyland. The accommodation at Richmond Hill included a drawing room and dining room, three bedrooms, a servant's room, kitchen and pantry together with a large fruit and vegetable garden.[499]

In the 1840s Richmond Hill was inhabited by John Somers. The valuator from the Griffith's Valuation recorded the house as being 43 feet long, 17 feet broad and 26 feet high.[500] The laying out of the railway line and viaduct in 1850, together with the realignment of Milltown Road and the Milltown Path as Richmond Avenue South, changed the grounds of Richmond Hill again, and the current entrance gate and driveway probably date from that period (Map 16b).

In 1862 the Hogan estate granted John Lee a 300-year lease of Richmond Hill from 1 January 1862 at an annual rent of £34 4*s.*[501] John Lee was for many years the proprietor of a saw mill and marble cutting works which was located on the south bank of the Dodder beside the Packhorse Bridge.[502] The Lees improved the house and added an extension with the result that in September 1864 the rateable valuation of the property increased from £20 to £25.[503] At the same time, John and Sarah Lee renamed their home Rydalmount. Rydalmount was the name of the poet William Wordsworth's country cottage, but it is impossible to say whether or not this influenced the Lees' choice of name for their home. On 30 April 1870 John and Sarah Lee's only daughter Mary Ida was married at St Philip's church to William Clayton of Bushfield Avenue (now Marlborough Road), Ranelagh. Almost a year to the day later, on 25 April 1871 Mary gave birth to a son at Rydalmount. Perhaps the young couple wanted to have their baby with the extra family support available in Rydalmount.[504]

---

497 *Freeman's Journal*, 10 January 1826, p. 2.

498 RD 1833/6/61, RD 1833/6/78, RD 1833/16/95.

499 *Saunders's Newsletter*, 31 May 1836, p. 3; 20 June 1836, p. 4.

500 NAI, VO, OL50945, House Book for Milltown Village 1845, no. 5.

501 Hogan Estate Trust Deed dated 1 June 1909.

502 RD 1849/20/2623; Thom's Directory 1872, p. 1601.

503 VO, Cancellation Books, Rathmines Ward 1862–3, bk. 1, p. 128, no. 17/35.

504 *Cork Examiner*, 4 May 1870; The Nation, 29 April 1871, p. 28.

Now armed with his new lease from the Hogan estate, William Lee decided to take advantage of the new railway station at Milltown by building a pair of semi-detached houses of two storeys over basement in the grounds of Richmond Hill beside the railway line (Pl. 27 & Map 18). The new houses, which were built in the early 1860s, were variously named as nos 1 and 2 Rydalmount Terrace (also known as Rydalmount Villas or 1 and 2 Rydalmount). Lee, and subsequently his widow Sarah, in turn sublet the two terraced houses on short-term leases.[505] Sarah Lee died intestate at Rydalmount in 1893 after a short illness, following which the property was sold to Henry Frazer Leachman for £1,800.[506] Leachman lived in Rydalmount until 1897 when he moved next door to no. 1 Rydalmount Terrace and let Rydalmount to tenants.[507] Leachman lived in Rydalmount Terrace for several decades and so it is worthwhile pausing to mention his achievements briefly before returning to Rydalmount.

Henry Leachman was a Dublin solicitor whose offices were in Westmoreland Street.[508] Evidently, Leachman was not prepared to accept the occasional inconveniences of living at the interface between the city's suburbs and the countryside. In 1899 he sued a Milltown dairyman, Thomas Kavanagh of Rosy Hill, for damages caused by Kavanagh's donkey, which had persistently trespassed and caused damage to his property.[509]

Leachman was a bachelor and on census night, 31 March 1901 his thirteen-year-old niece Sarah, who was born in Tipperary, spent the night in Rydalmount. According to the census form Sarah Leachman was attending school so it is possible that she was living with her uncle while she was attending secondary school in Dublin. Apart from Henry and Sarah Leachman the only other resident was their twenty-two-year-old Catholic housekeeper and domestic servant, Mary Bevin who was born in Kingstown (Dún Laoghaire).[510] Ten years later, on the night of 2 April 1911, Sarah Leachman, who by now was aged twenty-three, was still living in Rydalmount with her uncle Henry (seventy-four) and their housekeeper, Mary Bevin (thirty-three). That night the pair were joined by a visitor, twenty-five-year-old Helen Leachman, who was probably Sarah's sister.[511]

Henry Leachman was a very private individual and he eschewed public service of any kind. His claim to fame was his extreme longevity as an individual and as a practising solicitor. He died at Rydalmount in February 1936 aged ninety-eight. Reports of his length of service as a practising solicitor vary, with two reports stating that he had practiced for 79 years and two others stating that he had practiced for over 60 years.[512] Either way, it was a remarkably long career. According to one obituary:

---

505 Hogan Estate Trust Deed dated 1 June 1909; Thom's Directory 1872, p. 1602; VO, Cancellation Books, Dublin, Rathmines East, Milltown Road, 1873–1887, vol. 2, p. 199.

506 *Daily Express*, 11 December 1893, p. 1; RD 1894/32/251.

507 Thom's Directory 1895, p. 1562; 1896, p. 1564; 1899, p. 1576.

508 Thom's Directory 1896, p. 1390.

509 *Rathmines News*, 1 April 1899, p. 4.

510 NAI, 1901 Census, Form A, residents of house no. 766, Milltown Road, Rathmines and Rathgar East Electoral Division, Milltown townland, Dublin.

511 NAI, 1911 Census, Form A, residents of house no. 45, Milltown Road, Rathmines and Rathgar East Electoral Division, Milltown townland, Dublin.

512 *Derry Journal*, 21 February 1936, p. 7; *Irish Examiner*, 18 February 1936, p. 13; *Belfast Newsletter*, 19 February 1936, p. 6; *Irish Press*, 18 February 1936, p. 7.

in his early days Mr Leachman was a noted cricketer and made many high scores for the Leinster Club. He later became a keen yachtsman and was a prominent member of the Royal Irish Yacht Club. He cycled until he was 90 years of age, and even in the middle of Winter was in the habit of riding to his office in College Green. He was a most genial man in disposition and had a fund of good stories relating to his experiences, but he shunned publicity.[513]

Returning now to Rydalmount, after the Lee family the next long-term occupants of the property were Mrs Susan Anne Jackson and her daughter Sydney Jackson. Mrs Jackson was the widow of a Church of Ireland clergyman. On the night of the 1901 census seventy-one-year-old annuitant Mrs Jackson, a native of County Mayo, was residing at Rydalmount with her twenty-eight-year-old daughter who was born in County Sligo and whose occupation was described as a landowner. Mother and daughter employed two domestic servants, fifty-three-year-old Ellen Healy from County Roscommon and Lily Begley from County Cork, both of whom were members of the Church of Ireland.[514] Ten years later, the 1911 census reveals that Mrs Jackson's eighty-five-year-old unmarried sister, Sarah Louisa Kenny also a native of Mayo, had come to live with her sister and niece. The two Protestant servants had been replaced by two Catholics, fifty-year-old Mary O'Brien from County Dublin and thirty-eight-year-old Kate O'Brien from County Wexford.[515]

In June 1914 an official notice addressed to potential claimants and objectors appeared in the *Irish Times* stating that the High Court had ordered the sale of Rydalmount and Rydalmount Terrace following a petition of Robert and Rowland Wade.[516] The circumstances that gave rise to this development are unknown but it appears that the sale of Rydalmount was never completed because the Jackson family and Henry Jackson continued to live at Rydalmount and no. 1 Rydalmount Terrace respectively for many more years.

Mrs Jackson died of senility on the 7 December 1923 at the advanced age of ninety-three.[517] Thereafter there is very little history available about Rydalmount. In 1951 the owners built a detached house on part of the grounds called Dunelm.[518] The most recent advertisement for Rydalmount that can be found in the newspapers dates to September 1972 when the house and its grounds of about half an acre were put up for auction on 11 October 1972 by the then owner Mr Ian Byrne, who had previously made public his concerns about the number of road traffic accidents taking place at the blind junction at the end of the driveway to Rydalmount and Richmond Avenue South.[519]

513 'Veteran Solicitor's Death', *Irish Examiner*, 18 February 1936, p. 13.

514 NAI, 1901 Census, Form A, residents of house no. 62, Milltown Road, Rathmines and Rathgar East Electoral Division, Milltown townland, Dublin. Extract from Registration of Deaths, District of Dublin South, 7 December 1923 for Susan Anne Jackson, no. 238 and no. 334 (the death was recorded twice in 1923 and 1924, the second entry was obviously an error).

515 NAI, 1911 Census, Form A, residents of house no. 43, Milltown Road, Rathmines and Rathgar East Electoral Division, Milltown townland, Dublin.

516 *Irish Times*, 11 June 1914, p. 6.

517 Extract from Registration of Deaths, District of Dublin South, 7 December 1923 for Susan Anne Jackson, no. 238.

518 *Irish Independent*, 10 November 1956, p. 20.

519 *Sunday Independent*, 6 September 1970, p. 7; *Irish Times*, 22 September 1972, p. 28.

MILLTOWN LODGE

Milltown Lodge was an early nineteenth-century villa that originally stood on the Dundrum Road close to Milltown Bridge. The structure was a two-storey over-basement house with a three-bay entrance front of seven windows; the hall door was approached by a flight of steps (Map 18).[520] The house was demolished in about 1939 and replaced by a large detached residence called Dodder Ground when Milltown Bridge Road was laid out.[521]

Unfortunately no visual records have survived of Milltown Lodge, but an advertisement from 1835 gives a good impression of the house and its grounds:

> *Sale at Milltown Lodge. The lodge or house is situated immediately beyond the bridge, on an eminence adjoining the castle [Clonskeagh Castle], having a splendid view of its tasteful and well arranged garden. Attached to it is from four to five acres of prime land, tastefully laid out in flower and kitchen gardens, with large meadow, and a quantity of early potatoes in the ground; coach house and stable, with a lodge at the gate. The house consists of dining parlour, drawing room, breakfast room, with suitable bedchambers, and excellent accommodation in the basement storey. In short, the situation, with its proximity to the city, and salubrity of air, is such as renders further comment unnecessary.*[522]

A country villa such as Milltown Lodge typically had extensive gardens, stables, dairy and outhouses so that the household could be supplied with a very varied selection of food and produce, which as noted above, included potatoes. In the 1901 census reports, Milltown Lodge's offices included a stable and coach house, one cow house, one calf house, a piggery, two fowl houses and a shed, giving a total of eight out offices.[523] The ubiquity of dairy farming in Milltown and its vicinity, especially on the south bank of the Dodder at Farranboley townland is again evident in the following notice which appeared in the *Freeman's Journal* in 1887: 'Calves, three for sale, in good condition; and a good milch cow. Milltown Lodge, Milltown, County Dublin.'[524]

Research in the Registry of Deeds confirms that Milltown Lodge was originally called Gaymount, and was built in about 1800, probably by James Kenny who was living in Milltown at that time.[525] A lease dated 30 October 1812 recited that in 1807: 'James Kenny demised to Arthur Stanly a house, garden, offices and land called Gaymount, being part of the lands of Clonskeagh.'[526] A contemporary undated map of Clonskeagh Castle demesne shows the boundary with Stanly's property which equates to the location of Milltown Lodge.[527]
Notwithstanding the deed's references to Gaymount and Clonskeagh the description of the

520 NAI, 1901 Census, Form B 1, house and buildings return for house no. 21, Dundrum Road, Dundrum Electoral Division, Parish of Taney, Farranboley townland, Dublin.

521 Ruth McManus, *Crampton Built* (Dublin, 2008), p. 98.

522 *Dublin Morning Register*, 1 August 1835, p. 1.

523 NAI, 1901 Census, Form B 2, out offices and farm steadings return for house no. 21, Dundrum Road, Dundrum Electoral Division, Parish of Taney, Farranboley townland, Dublin.

524 *Freeman's Journal*, 29 July 1887, p. 1.

525 James Kenny of Milltown died on 10 September 1809 aged seventy-three and is buried in Taney graveyard, Churchtown: Ball and Hamilton, *Parish of Taney*, pp. 40–1.

526 RD 656/258/450956.

527 'A survey of the Demesne of Clonskeagh in the Co. Dublin belonging to Geo. Thompson Esq' (NLI, Longfield map collection, MS 21 F. 52(021)).

property's boundaries puts it beyond doubt that the lease related to the property which later came to be called Milltown Lodge:

> *the house, offices, garden and lands of Gaymount, Clonskeagh containing four [plantation] acres and eight perches bounded on the north by Hugh Jackson's concerns and garden [i.e. Clonskeagh Castle], on the south by Mr Mowld's land [i.e. Casino, Dundrum Road], on the east by Mr Frank's land [i.e. Springmount, later St Bridgets, Clonskeagh Road] and on the west by the high road leading from Dublin to Dundrum with the [gate] lodge adjoining to the high road and the passage leading from thence to said dwelling house which said premises are lying and being near Milltown ... to hold to Arthur Stanley from 25 March 1812 for 61 years.*[528]

Milltown Lodge originally formed part of the Trimleston estate of Roebuck and adjoined the earl of Milltown's estate in Milltown to the south (Map 10). However, Lord Trimlestown sold his entire freehold estate at Roebuck, including Milltown Lodge, in 1812 to a wealthy surgeon called Solomon Richards for almost £30,000.[529] When the Roebuck estate was surveyed in 1832, Milltown Lodge comprised 6 statute acres, 2 roods and 5 perches, and was then leased to a Mr Nolan at an annual rent of £120.[530] This compact demesne was included in the townland of Roebuck when the OS townland boundaries were laid down in the 1830s, and its southern boundary divided Roebuck townland from the townland of Farranboley (Map 15). Milltown Lodge changed hands very frequently throughout the nineteenth century, as attested by the innumerable entries in the Thom's Dublin Directories, the Roebuck estate records in the National Library and the cancellation books in the Valuation Office. As such it is impossible to build a worthwhile profile of the villa's residents, apart from a couple of staff advertisements from conscientious employers:

> *Children's maid, or Housemaid or Parlourmaid – A lady is anxious to procure a situation in either station for a young girl, still in her service; she is most trustworthy and cleanly, and works very well; she can attend table nicely. Address BB, Milltown Lodge, Milltown, near Dublin.*[531]

> *Housemaid or Parlourmaid. – A lady wishes to procure a situation for a young girl as above, or she is well suited to take charge of a couple of grown children, as her manners and accent are good; she also sews neatly, and is in every respect a good servant; she remains in her present situation until comfortably settled. Address T.C. Milltown Lodge.*[532]

In 1889, Arthur Richards created a new leasehold interest when he leased Milltown Lodge to Patrick Kelly for 99 years.[533] The, by the turn of the twentieth century a family called Gourley was living there. Samuel Gourley worked in the wholesale tobacco business and was instru-

528 RD 656/258/450956.

529 *The Pilot*, 13 November 1835, p. 1; *Lessee of the Right Hon, John Thomas Baron Trimlestown and others v Henry Kemis*, 5 Irish Law Reports 1842–43, pp. 384–5.

530 'Report and Valuation of the lands of Roebuck in the County of Dublin by Brassington and Gale, 1832' (NAI, QRO, MS 4/3/28).

531 *Saunders's Newsletter*, 28 January 1861, p. 4.

532 *Saunders's Newsletter*, 16 February 1863, p. 4.

533 Recital in a deed of conveyance of Milltown Lodge dated 9 February 1938 from Elizabeth Richards and others to G. & T. Crampton Ltd (copy in author's possession).

mental in establishing a trade association called the Dublin United Tobacconists' Association. After 16 years in the tobacco business Gourley, who was by then in his early forties, decided to change career and become an insurance agent.[534] An unusual aspect of an otherwise unremarkable change of circumstances was that a deputation from the Dublin United Tobacconists' Association visited Gourley at Milltown Lodge and presented him with a formal written address of appreciation. In their address to Gourley, the members of the association, among whom included A.K. Kapp and C. Peterson who later established the well-known tobacconist on Nassau Street called Knapp and Peterson, had this to say of their erstwhile colleague:

> *We the members of the Dublin United Tobacconists' Association, having learned of the severance of your connection with the firm of Messrs. Murray & Co. with whom you have been for nearly 16 years, cannot allow the occasion to pass without marking in some tangible way their great appreciation of your excellent qualities, their pleasant recollections of your kindly and courteous manner through the many long years of your commercial career, and their sincere regard for your future welfare. We are not unmindful of the great interest and ability displayed by you in the formation of the Tobacconists' Association, and feel that it was mainly through your efforts that it is in its present flourishing condition, which enables us to watch and protect the numerous interests of the retail traders.*[535]

The Gourley family were Presbyterians. Samuel Gourley had been born in County Armagh and his wife Jane had been born in County Wicklow. The Gourleys had a large family of five sons and three daughters ranging in ages from one year to fourteen years of age. A Catholic youth, John Scully, aged sixteen and described as a servant lived with the Gourleys at Milltown Lodge.[536] In addition, the Gourleys could call upon help from their tenants, the Ennis family, one of whom was their gardener. The Ennis family lived in the gate lodge, which had five rooms and three front windows.[537]

A few months after the 1901 census was taken the Gourleys put Milltown Lodge and all of its contents up for auction in November 1901. Included among the contents were:

> *eight milch cows, 3 yearling calves, 2 draught mares, 1 pony (quiet in harness, winner of races), 1 pony in foal, 1 yearling foal, a waggonette by Denehey, Raleigh car by Colclough, a governess car by Lates, grains cart, wash balloon, 3 farm carts, about 7 tons of well saved hay ...*[538]

These details are a reminder of how ubiquitous and important farm animals were in everyday life 120 years ago, providing personal transport and milk for larger households lying outside Dublin city's suburbs.

For whatever reason, the sale of Milltown Lodge was postponed until 30 July 1902. The

534 *Rathmines News*, 21 July 1900, p. 4; NAI, 1901 Census, Form A, return for house no. 22, Dundrum Road, Dundrum Electoral Division, Parish of Taney, Farranboley townland, Dublin. (Note: The household Form A incorrectly numbered Milltown Lodge as no. 22 whereas the buildings Forms B1 and B2 correctly numbered Milltown Lodge as no. 21.)

535 *Rathmines News*, 21 July 1900, p. 4.

536 NAI, 1901 Census, Form A, return for house no. 22, Dundrum Road, Dundrum Electoral Division, Parish of Taney, Farranboley townland, Dublin.

537 NAI, 1901 Census, Form A, return for house no. 21, Dundrum Road, Dundrum Electoral Division, Parish of Taney, Farranboley townland, Dublin. (Note: The household Form A incorrectly numbered the Ennis dwelling as no. 21 whereas the buildings Forms B1 and B2 correctly number it as 22.)

538 *Freeman's Journal*, 26 October 1901, p. 4.

editor of the *Rathmines News*, who was typically bullish about suburban development reaching Milltown and beyond the south bank of the River Dodder, opined that:

> *There should be a brisk competition for this property, as in view of the great probability of large commercial undertakings being started in the immediate neighbourhood within a short time, it should eventually prove a very profitable investment.*[539]

In the event, Milltown Lodge and its six and a half acres was sold to the Tierney family for £370.[540] The Dublin street directories record that Patrick Tierney had a business in 5 Chatham Street, where he is described as being a 'purveyor'.[541]

Patrick and Mary Tierney were the parents of a large family of seven sons and a daughter ranging in ages from twenty years of age to three years of age when the census was taken on 2 April 1911. The Tierneys employed three domestic servants, one of whom was only fourteen years of age. All members of the household were Catholics. The eldest son, Joseph Tierney (twenty), worked as an assistant, while the second and third sons (nineteen and eighteen) were, respectively, an apprentice engineer and a scholar.[542] Joseph was an accomplished rugby player who played for St Mary's College Rathmines.[543] This level of education proves that the Tierneys were a well-off family who were part of the rising Catholic middle class that emerged in greater numbers in the late nineteenth century and beyond.

The Tierneys' comfortable circumstances contrasted sharply with the Ennis family. John Ennis was still the gardener to Milltown Lodge and his two adult, Edward and Andrew, also worked as gardeners. For the first time the census recorded that John and Margaret Ennis had had eight children in total, of whom only five were living, which demonstrates the high level of infant mortality among the labouring classes of Dublin. Much less obvious is the reason why all of the ages given for the Ennis family in the 1911 census do not tally with the ages provided in the 1901 census; the age differences are quite marked and cannot be explained by the introduction of the old age pension in 1907 (some people exaggerated their ages in order to qualify for the pension which is one reason why inconsistencies in ages can occur between the two censuses).[544]

The Tierneys' eldest son, Joseph, enlisted for service in the Great War and, as noted in Chapter 14, was fatally injured while on active service in France as a despatch rider and died on 5 January 1916. The Tierney family's political sympathies changed over the remaining course of the decade. Years later, veteran IRA volunteer, Patrick J. Brennan, specifically paid tribute to Mrs Tierney for her valuable assistance received 'by way of meals and, or, shelter' during the War of Independence.[545]

Mary Tierney continued living at Milltown Lodge into the late 1920s when she would have been aged in her early sixties and all of her children had grown up. She put Milltown Lodge

---

539 *Rathmines News*, 26 July 1902, p. 7.

540 *Rathmines News*, 2 August 1902, p. 2.

541 The Post Office Dublin Directory and Calendar for 1908, p. 352.

542 NAI, 1911 Census, Form A, NAI, 1911 Census, Form A, residents for house 13 in Farranboley townland, Milltown Electoral Division, Parish of Taney, Dublin.

543 *Dublin Daily Express*, 18 January 1912, p. 9; *Evening Herald*, 10 January, p. 6.

544 NAI, 1911 Census, Form A, NAI, 1911 Census, Form A, residents for house 15 in Farranboley townland, Milltown Electoral Division, Parish of Taney, Dublin.

545 BMH, WS1773, p. 29. Mrs Tierney lived in Milltown Lodge on the Dundrum Road, not Milltown Hill as stated by Brennan.

Plate 49. Milltown Bridge and the River Dodder, c. 1820 (courtesy of the Gorry Gallery)

up for auction on 3 November 1927. The newspaper advertisement shows how some things remained unchanged at Milltown Lodge compared with the sale advertisement from 1901, but the notice also reveals the impact of modern transport developments, which were incomprehensible a quarter of a century previously:

> *The residence contains 9 apartments, all in good order. The out offices are extensive, and comprise horse stabling, cow sheds, piggeries, barn, lofts, motor house, etc. There is also a neat gate lodge, containing 4 apartments, let at 5s. weekly. The property is situated on the Dublin to Enniskerry road, in a charming locality, about ten minutes' drive from the city, with several bus services passing the entrance gate, and constitutes a most attractive and desirable residence.*[546]

The sale of Milltown Lodge did not go ahead. Ten years later a very significant development occurred when Mrs Tierney managed to sell her property to the building firm, G. & T. Crampton Limited, in September 1937 for £1,077 *2d.*[547] Five months later, the Cramptons bought out the freehold interest in Milltown Lodge from the Richards family for £1,730.[548]

The Cramptons had already acquired the freehold of the neighbouring Clonskeagh Castle demesne and its 35 acres from the Thompson family in 1934 for £7,000.[549] Now, with the addition

546 *Irish Independent*, 24 October 1927, p. 14.

547 McManus, *Crampton Built*, p. 98.

548 Deed of Conveyance of Milltown Lodge dated 9 February 1938 from Elizabeth Richards and others to G. & T. Crampton Ltd (copy in author's possession).

549 Deed of Conveyance of Clonskeagh Castle dated 23 October 1934 from Thomas William Thompson to G. & T. Crampton Limited (copy in author's possession).

of Milltown Lodge, they could lay out an access road (Dodder Bridge Road) through the grounds of Milltown Lodge to their new developments of Whitebeam and Whitethorn Roads. In addition, the Cramptons demolished Milltown Lodge in 1938 or 1939 and replaced it with a detached house called Dodder Ground. This house became the home of Cecil and Doris Crampton and later served as the residence of the Argentinian ambassador.[550] The fields attached to the south of Milltown Lodge were developed after the Second World War when Maple Road was laid out.[551] The most recent evolution of the old Milltown Lodge demesne occurred in the late 1990s when the owner of Dodder Ground built the Woodhaven apartment complex, which is located opposite the junction of Dodder Bridge Road and Maple Road at the mini-roundabout.[552]

BAWN HOUSE

Bawn House was a medium-sized early nineteenth-century two-storey, three-bay detached house that stood on the south bank of the River Dodder beside Milltown Bridge (Pl. 49 & Map 21). Bawn House was demolished in the mid-1990s and the site is now occupied by the Shi'a Muslim Islamic centre of worship in Ireland, Al Hussain House, which opened in 1996.[553]

The ground on which Bawn House was built has an interesting but rather complicated history. In the late eighteenth century the land was owned by the Beeby (also spelt Beebey or Bibby) and Heaviside families, both of whom also who owned various industrial concerns on the south bank of the River Dodder which are discussed in Chapter 6. A deed from 1797 records the assignment by John Heaviside of his share in the property to William, Thomas and John Beeby of:

> *part of the lands of Milltown in the parish of Taney then called and known by the name of the Bawn field, formerly in the possession of William Beeby then deceased and the said John Heavisid [sic] containing by a survey thereof one [plantation] acre and thirty perches bounded on the north west by the River Dodder on the west by a Boreing and Grinding mill in the possession of John Heavisid on the south by the road leading from Milltown Bridge [i.e. Packhorse Bridge] to the road of Dundrum and on the south east by the road leading from Dundrum to the River Dodder.*[554]

The Bawn field took its name from a rath which stood in the field up until the end of the eighteenth century.[555] When attempting to visualise the eighteenth-century boundaries with the modern topography it is critical to understand that the current bridge spanning the Dodder at Milltown had not been built in 1797 so all of the space to the east of Al Hussain House including the public park and the pathway as far as its closest point to the Dodder – opposite the public carpark on the north bank (the ancient fording point) – was open land. The 'road leading from Milltown Bridge to the road of Dundrum' is now a cul-de-sac accessed from the Dundrum Road at the south corner of Al Hussain House, where Bankside Cottages are now and which leads to

550 McManus, *Crampton Built*, pp. 98–9.

551 McManus, *Crampton Built*, pp. 155–9.

552 *Irish Independent*, 11 July 1997.

553 Dún Laoghaire Rathdown County Council Planning Department, file D94A/0548, 27 October 1994. http://homepage.tinet.ie/~ahlulbyteassociation/ (accessed 3 May 2021).

554 RD 511/8/327979.

555 D'Alton, *History of County Dublin*, p. 798. See discussion of the rath's significance in Chapter 1.

the Packhorse Bridge. The 'road leading from Dundrum to the River Dodder' refers to the old road which forded the Dodder at a point about 100 metres east of the pedestrian lights on Milltown Bridge (Map 4).

In 1820 Thomas Beeby granted a lease for lives renewable for ever to Elizabeth Mowlds of Milltown, spinster, of:

> *all that farm or parcel of ground situate on the south east side of the River Dodder in Milltown called the Bawn field together with the millpond thereon and the ground on which two cabins formerly stood which now forms part of the mill adjoining said premises containing in the entire one acre and sixteen perches ... at the yearly rent of fourteen pounds and fourteen shillings.*[556]

The Beeby's retained their leasehold interest in the Bawn field until 1919 when they sold their annual ground rent profit of £1 14*s*., but for now we are concerned with the Mowlds' involvement in the premises.[557]

Elizabeth Mowlds, who was born sometime in the 1780s, was a daughter of George Frederick Mowlds, originally of Milltown, and who practised as a solicitor in Montague Street where the family subsequently went to live. In 1805 Elizabeth had the misfortune of having her engagement to Robert Burke broken off which resulted in her father, 'an eminent attorney of Dublin', instituting proceedings against Burke for breach of promise of marriage.[558] Breach of promise cases were widely reported in the contemporary newspapers because their readership avidly consumed the usually scandalous behaviour that such cases brought to the public's attention.[559] In Elizabeth Mowlds' case, her fiancé retracted the marriage, allegedly because he was dissatisfied with her dowry, and he ceased to call on Elizabeth. According to one report, 'it appeared that in consequence of this disappointment, the young lady suffered extreme indisposition and torture approaching to delirium'. The upshot was that the jury in the case awarded £150 damages to Elizabeth's father George Frederick Mowlds in December 1805.[560] Interestingly, a different version of events had emerged earlier in a prequel to the civil action, when Elizabeth's three brothers were tried in September in a criminal case involving charges of riot and assault. During the criminal trial it was alleged that Burke had been keeping company with another woman while purportedly being engaged to Elizabeth. When Elizabeth found out she told her brothers, who, to avenge her dishonourable treatment at Burke's hands, tracked him down and beat him up. The three fraternal defendants were later acquitted at the criminal trial thanks to the powerful testimony given by Elizabeth.[561] Some months previously, the press had also reported that Elizabeth's brother John David Mowlds had seriously injured Burke in a duel in the Phoenix Park in May.[562]

---

556 RD 766/432/519967. The deed was witnessed by George Frederick Mowlds who was Elizabeth's father or brother.

557 Sale of the Beeby Estate, advertisement in the *Irish Times*, 24 June 1919, p. 12.

558 *Dublin Evening Post*, 7 December 1805, p. 2.

559 Maria Luddy, *Matters of deceit: Breach of promise to marry cases in nineteenth and twentieth century Limerick* (Dublin, 2011), p. 12.

560 *Dublin Evening Post*, 7 December 1805, p. 2.

561 *Belfast Commercial Chronicle*, 23 September 1805, p. 4.

562 *Faulkner's Dublin Journal*, 1 June 1805, p. 2. The accuracy of this incident must be doubted as it was not mentioned in the subsequent press reports in September and December 1805.

While Elizabeth Mowlds may have been bruised by her romantic experience in 1805 it did not deter her from getting married. In 1825 she married a John Hunt of Milltown, who was probably related to the woollen merchant family of that surname.[563] As part of her marriage settlement, Elizabeth agreed to transfer her land at the Bawn Field, which she had acquired from Thomas Beeby in 1820, into a trust of whom her brothers George Frederick Mowlds junior and John David Mowlds were the trustees. The settlement deed recited that Elizabeth had obtained a judgement in 1812 against her father George Frederick Mowlds, senior, for £370, but as part of the marriage settlement Elizabeth agreed not to execute the judgement until both of her parents had died.[564] In broad terms, such details give some idea of the complicated legal and financial affairs and the vicissitudes that often befell middle-class families, where land was central to maintaining or increasing their income, wealth and status. More specifically, the marriage settlement shows Elizabeth to have been a capable and pragmatic middle-aged woman who was no longer the young innocent victim portrayed in 1805.

Taking all of the above into account it is quite likely that Bawn House was built by Elizabeth Mowlds sometime between 1820 and her marriage to John Hunt in 1825. It is possible that the house was built after the marriage but this is less likely. Bawn House, its garden and out offices were built within enclosed grounds of about three quarters of a statute acre. When the surveyors from the Griffith's Valuation visited Milltown in the mid-1840s Elizabeth Mowlds had by then been widowed and was referred to as Mrs Eliza Hunt .[565] Eliza was the occupant of Bawn House and the landlady of six small cottages.[566] As regards Bawn House, the surveyor opined that it had 'a good situation in some respects but [is] surrounded by too many cabins'. The surveyor omitted to mention that John Lee's saw mill was located immediately behind the garden of Bawn House beside the Packhorse Bridge (now open grassland behind Al Hussain House), which must have been rather noisy to live beside.[567] Elizabeth Hunt subsequently moved to Manchester where she died on 11 December 1858.[568]

By the 1840s further developments had taken place on the Bawn Field. Following a presentment made at the County Dublin Grand Jury in 1816, a new bridge across the Dodder (Milltown Bridge – see Pl. 11 & Pl. 49) was erected at a cost of £1,662 & 6*s*. and the current road was laid out (i.e. the Dundrum Road outside the main entrance to Al Hussain House).[569] Thus, after centuries of use the old fording point of the Dodder was now redundant and the old Bawn Field was cut in two. Arising from these developments a terrace of cabins called Mowlds Cottages, a shop, and pubic house, later called the Dew Drop Inn (discussed in Chapter 12), were built to the east of the new road on the south bank of the River Dodder

---

563 RD 803/273/542009. John Hunt was not related to the Hunt family who owned extensive property on the north side of Milltown main street including Milltown Castle and Milltown House.

564 RD 803/273/542009.

565 John Hunt died at Bawn House on 3 August 1842 aged forty-eight: *Dublin Evening Packet and Correspondent*, 9 August 1842, p. 3.

566 Griffith's Valuation, Rateable Valuation of Tenements, Co. Dublin, Barony of Rathdown, Parish of Taney, townland of Farranboley, 1849, p. 149, at entry nos 1–10. Eliza Hunt was unrelated to the contemporary Milltown landowner, Charlotte Hunt.

567 Griffith's Valuation, Rateable Valuation of Tenements, Co. Dublin, Barony of Rathdown, Parish of Taney, townland of Farranboley, 1849, p. 149, at entry no. 11.

568 *Dublin Daily Express*, 15 December 1854, p. 4. The newspaper incorrectly names Eliza's late husband as Nicholas Hunt instead of John Hunt.

569 Ball and Hamilton, *Parish of Taney*, p. 222.

Plate 50. River Dodder and Milltown Bridge, c. 1890, Charles Russell Collection (courtesy of South Dublin Libraries)

where the entrance to the Milltown Grove apartments is now (Map 18).[570] These early nineteenth-century buildings are visible in an old photograph of Milltown Bridge taken about 1890 (Pl. 50). The four Mowlds Cottages faced onto the millrace leading from the Dodder weir at Milltown to the iron mills at Clonskeagh.[571]

Various members of the extended Mowlds family resided at Bawn House in the mid-nineteenth century. A baby girl called Elizabeth Moulds was born to George Frederick Moulds, who was a law agent, and his wife Mary at Bawn House on 4 August 1857.[572] A few years later, Eliza Mowlds died at Bawn House in 1866 leaving her estate of under £200 to her sole executor, John David Mowlds.[573] John David subsequently obtained a fee farm grant of Bawn House in 1863 from the Beeby estate.[574]

570 NAI, VO, OL70071, Quarto Book, Townland of Farranboley, 1847, p. 29.

571 Remnants of this millrace, including a small footbridge, can be seen parallel to the bank of the River Dodder beside the boundary wall of Al Hussain House; the millrace is shown for the first time on Bernard Scale's map of 1773 (Map 5) which updated John Rocque's Survey of County of Dublin of 1760.

572 Transcription of baptism records of Taney Parish (Church of Ireland) available online at Irishgenealogy.ie.

573 NAI, Calendar of Wills and Administrations for 1866, p. 248.

574 RD 1863/34/182.

John David Mowlds, a bachelor, was a market gardener who was still living in Bawn House at the turn of the twentieth century.[575] There are indications that he was struggling to make ends meet as he entered old age. On 1 June 1900 Mowlds sublet his entire landholding in Milltown, including the Dew Drop Inn, to local publican and landlord, Thomas Hackett (see Chapter 12) for £55, while retaining a right of residence at Bawn House. In return, Hackett agreed to spend at least £100 on improvements within five years.[576] After deducting the ground rent to the Beeby estate (£14 3*s*. 6*d*.) John David's annual profit rent (essentially his pension) was a modest £40 15*s*. 6*d*. before payment of local taxes.[577]

At the time of the 1901 census John David Mowlds stated on his census return form that he spent the night alone in Bawn House and occupied five rooms in the building. In addition, John David Mowlds or Thomas Hackett had sublet a room to a Catholic couple, Charles and Esther Byrne, who were aged thirty-seven and twenty-four respectively. Charles gave his occupation as a van driver, a strong indication that he worked for the Dublin Laundry Company in Milltown.[578] Esther Byrne did not give any occupation on the census form but she may have provided domestic help on a casual basis to John David Mowlds, who was by then aged in his seventies.

Much more pertinently, a notice appeared in the *Irish Times* advising that the High Court had ordered that Bawn House, the Dew Drop Inn and several small cottages be sold by auction on 22 March 1905 on foot of proceedings taken by Bridget O'Malley against John David Mowlds, Samuel Johnson Mowlds (heir at law of Eliza Hunt, deceased) and William Henry Mowlds.[579] Due to a lack of contemporary information the cause of the action against the Mowlds and the outcome of the auction are unknown. In any event, John David Mowlds died at Bawn House on 17 April 1909 aged eighty-two in the presence of Mary Singleton.[580] His death brought an end to the Mowlds family's connection with Milltown that had existed for 200 years without interruption.

After John David Mowlds died, Bawn House was converted into a tenement house for lodgers by Thomas Hackett who, as noted earlier, held the property under a sublease from John David Mowlds.[581] By the time of the next census which was taken on the night of 2 April 1911, the house was inhabited by three separate Catholic family units comprising a total of eight persons, with each family renting two rooms in the building. Two single women, Mary Dunne (twenty-eight) and Mary Byrne (thirty), who were both laundresses, lived in the house, as well as Edward Geraghty, (twenty-five, a general labourer) and his wife Annie (twenty-two, who was also a laundress) and their seven-month-old son Edward. The third family residing in Bawn House comprised fifty-year-old spinster Eliza Darcy, who did not specify

575 NAI, 1901 Census, Form A, return for house no. 37 (John D. Mowlds), Dundrum Road, Dundrum Electoral Division, Parish of Taney, Farranboley townland, Dublin.

576 RD 1900/41/73. The activities of Thomas Hackett are discussed in a separate chapter.

577 *Irish Times*, 18 March 1905, p. 4.

578 NAI, 1901 Census, Form A, return for house no. 37 (Charles and Esther Byrne), Dundrum Road, Dundrum Electoral Division, Parish of Taney, Farranboley townland, Dublin.

579 *Irish Times*, 18 March 1905, p. 4.

580 Register of Deaths for Rathdown District, Dundrum, County Dublin, for 1909 at entry no. 486.

581 VO, Cancellation Books, Dundrum Book 1878–1903, Rathdown No. 1 RDC, Electoral Division of Dundrum, Townland of Farranboley, p. 110, no. 1a.

any occupation, and her two teenage nieces, Mary Ennis who was an apprentice dress maker and her sister Julia Ennis who was a scholar.[582]

The rate of turnover of tenants and lodgers at Bawn House is very difficult to quantify. In 1913 the *Freeman's Journal* reported that:

> *a respectable looking young man named Patrick A. Nolan, described as a commercial traveller, residing at Bawn House, Milltown, County Dublin, was charged with obtaining sums of money by false pretences and by means of bogus cheques.*[583]

Nolan was remanded in custody pending his trial. Prior to residing in Bawn House Nolan had been living in a small cottage nearby with his wife Margaret and their seven-year-old daughter, Rosanna.[584] Patrick Nolan's imprisonment would have had devastating consequences for his family notwithstanding that his work as a commercial traveller had probably been very precarious (on the 1911 census form Patrick Nolan described himself as a commission agent).

At some stage after the First World War, probably not long after the sale of Beeby leasehold interest in 1919, Bawn House reverted to single family occupancy. In the 1940s a family called D'Arcy lived in the property where they bred poultry.[585] On 14 March 1945 Mrs D'Arcy placed an advertisement in the *Irish Independent* for a 'Country girl for working class home, fond of children. 10*s*. weekly'.[586] Given that the D'Arcys were living in a house on an acre of grounds and could afford to employ a childminder their definition of a working-class home seems rather unusual, even more so given that Michael D'Arcy later advertised his 1938 Morris 8 car for sale, which had a sunroof and was 'in splendid condition'![587] Michael D'Arcy died on 9 December 1948 leaving an estate worth almost £1,500.[588] In 1952 the D'Arcys put Bawn House up for sale by private treaty for £1,400.[589] Thereafter, the last family to live in Bawn House comprised Tom and Avril Hingerty and their six children.[590]

In the early 1970s Dublin County Council began acquiring land on the south bank of the Dodder at Milltown in order to create the current linear park that is enjoyed by walkers today, a process which involved the compulsory purchase of land belonging to Bawn House adjacent to the river.[591] By the late 1980s Bawn House had become extremely valuable because of its development potential and a number of planning applications to build apartments and town houses on the site were

---

582 NAI, 1911 Census, Form A, return for house no. 3.1/3.2/3.3 (Bawn House), Dundrum Road, Dundrum Electoral Division, Parish of Taney, Farranboley townland, Dublin.

583 *Freeman's Journal*, 14 August 1913, p. 4.

584 NAI, 1911 Census, Form A, return for house no. 25 (Patrick Nolan), Dundrum Road, Dundrum Electoral Division, Parish of Taney, Farranboley townland, Dublin.

585 *Irish Independent*, 14 March 1945, p. 1; 10 May 1945, p. 1; 10 August 1945, p. 1; 14 November 1945, p. 6.

586 *Irish Independent*, 14 March 1945, p. 1.

587 *Irish Independent*, 22 March 1947, p. 1.

588 NAI, calendar of grants of probate of wills and letters of administration, CS/HC/PO/4/102/2356 (Michael D'Arcy, retired van driver).

589 *Irish Independent*, 10 March 1952, p. 2; *Irish Press*, 22 March 1952, p. 11.

590 *Irish Independent, 11 January 1965, p. 20; Evening Herald*, 6 December 1968, p. 22.

591 *IIrish Press*, 28 March 1973, p. 14; 1 August 1975, p. 13.

submitted to Dublin Corporation.[592] However, plans for a residential development at Bawn House did not proceed because the proposed development was a material contravention of the zoning of the site for open space and recreational purposes.[593] Ultimately, the property was acquired by the Irish Shi'a Islamic community, who subsequently built the Ahlul Bayt Islamic Centre of Ireland (Al Hussain House) on the site following the granting of planning permission in October 1994.[594]

OLD BRIDGE HOUSE (SOUTH)

Old Bridge House, as its name suggests, was located immediately beside the Packhorse Bridge on the south bank of the River Dodder (Pl. 51). This house was a plain two-storey five-bay early or mid-eighteenth-century structure which was built as part of the industrial buildings that grew up on the south bank of the River Dodder from the 1720s onwards. The house was never given a name in the eighteenth or nineteenth centuries, and it seems that the building was informally named Old Bridge House in the late nineteenth century when it had become a tenement.

The earliest documentary information about the house has not survived but the building was undoubtedly associated with either the papermill or the iron mills which were located beside the Packhorse Bridge from the mid-1720s onwards (see Chapter 6). In February 1724 William Ford granted a lease to Robert Randal of Milltown, whereby Randal was required to build a good paper mill and a dwelling house, with Ford agreeing to contribute £80 towards the cost of the new buildings.[595] Randal's new papermill was built on the south bank of the River Dodder close to the Packhorse Bridge, so it is possible that the house built by Randal under the terms of the 1724 lease was the building that became known as Old Bridge House. Some 35 years later, in December 1759, *Pue's Occurrences* reported the death in Milltown of an ironmonger called Dogherty, who has previously been mentioned in Chapter 6.[596] Although it is impossible to link Dogherty to Old Bridge House it is not fanciful to suggest that the two were connected.

More definite information begins to emerge in the 1770s when Joseph Chappell set up his linen printing business on the south bank of the River Dodder beside the Packhorse Bridge. In August 1771 the ironmongers James Tandy and Thomas Cavanagh, who had succeeded to Dogherty's iron mills, granted a lease for lives renewable for ever to 'Joseph Chappell of Milltown, Linen Printer'. Of particular relevance among the property leased to Chappell are two houses, one of which was almost certainly Old Bridge House:

> *all that the two houses with the stable and coach house and small garden with two acres and twelve perches [plantation measure] of land in Milltown as marked out to Rose's Ground as appeared by map to said deed ... together with such a supply of water from the watercourse belonging to the said James Tandy and Thomas Cavanagh as shall flow or proceed through the bore or pipe of one inch diameter then laid down and fixed into the said watercourse for the supplying of Joseph Chappell with water and Joseph Chappell and his heirs or assigns are in no ways to disturb or remove the same.*[597]

592 *Irish Press*, 18 September 1987, p. 11 (application made by T. Hingerty); *Evening Herald*, 15 June 1992, p. 25 (application made by Glenbard Inns Ltd).

593 Dún Laoghaire Rathdown County Council Planning Department, file 92A/1043, 17 June 1992.

594 Dún Laoghaire Rathdown County Council Planning Department, file D94A/0548, 27 October 1994.

595 RD 62/285/42895.

596 *Pue's Occurrences*, 4 December 1759.

597 RD 290/120/189337.

In 1843 a successor to the Tandy and Cavanagh lease, James Harvey, let the 2 acre and 12 perches, on which Old Bridge house Stood, to Patrick Hackett of Milltown, on the understanding that he would develop the premises.[598] The Griffith's Valuation records reveal that in the late 1840s Old Bridge House was occupied by Patrick Hackett and his lodgers (from whom Hackett derived a gross weekly rent of 6*s.* 4*d.*) and was rated for local tax purposes at £10 10*s.*[599]

In 1911 Old Bridge House was inhabited by four families – 12 persons in total – all of whom were Catholics. The largest of the four families was the McArdles who lived in three rooms in the house. Forty-six-year-old Patrick McArdle worked as a coal factor and his forty-four-year-old wife Mary worked as a house keeper. The McArdles had three sons and a daughter, Michael, John, Maggie and Patrick, all of whom were under thirteen years of age.[600] Bessie Dowling and her niece Fannie Redmond lived in one room and both worked as laundresses. The two unmarried women were aged forty and seventeen years of age respectively.[601] A sixty-four-year-old widow, Ellen Doyle, and her unmarried son Mathew, aged thirty-eight, lived in two rooms. Ellen worked as a laundress while her son was a bricklayer's labourer.[602] Finally, twenty-three-year-old Thomas Bennett and his wife Kitty, aged twenty-five, lived in one room. Kitty was also a laundress while her husband worked as a labourer in a brick works. According to their census return, the Bennett's had an infant child but for whatever reason it did not spend the census night with its parents.[603]

At the time of the 1916 Rising a young woman called Bridget Lambert (Mrs Bridget Doran) lived in Old Bridge House. Bridget, who was born in 1897, was a member of Cumann na mBan and the Irish Citizen Army and, as discussed in Chapter 13, saw active service in the GPO during the Rising. She was also active in the War of Independence, supported the anti-Treaty side in the Civil War.[604] Mrs Doran was living in Old Bridge House up to the early 1940s prior to emigrating to England.[605] In the 1930s branch meetings of the local Fianna Fáil Cumann were held in Old Bridge House, attended by Seán MacEntee TD.[606]

Two of the last residents to live in Old Bridge House were Desmond Grogan and Mrs Catherine Doyle. Grogan was the producer of a Dublin drama group called the Phoenix Theatre Group which won a 100-guinea prize at the Isle of Man Drama Festival in 1951.[607] The following

---

598 RD 1843/15/78.

599 Griffith's Valuation, Rateable Valuation of Tenements, Co. Dublin, Barony of Rathdown, Parish of Taney, Townland of Farranboley, 1849, p. 149, at entry no. 2/12; NAI, VO, OL70071, Quarto Book, Townland of Farranboley, p. 30, plot 2/12, 1847.

600 NAI, 1911 Census, Form A, return for house no. 22.1, Milltown/Concrete town, Dundrum Electoral Division, Parish of Taney, Farranboley townland, Dublin.

601 NAI, 1911 Census, Form A, return for house no. 22.2, Milltown/Concrete town, Dundrum Electoral Division, Parish of Taney, Farranboley townland, Dublin.

602 NAI, 1911 Census, Form A, return for house no. 22.3, Milltown/Concrete town, Dundrum Electoral Division, Parish of Taney, Farranboley townland, Dublin.

603 NAI, 1911 Census, Form A, return for house no. 22.4, Milltown/Concrete town, Dundrum Electoral Division, Parish of Taney, Farranboley townland, Dublin.

604 BMH, MSP34REF57178 (sworn evidence of Bridget Doran née Lambert, not dated).

605 *Irish Press*, 19 January 1961, p. 2.

606 *Irish Press*, 11 June 1937, p. 5.

607 *Irish Press*, 18 June 1951, p. 5.

year, 1952, Mrs Doyle was interviewed by the *Irish Independent* as part of its coverage of the decision by Dublin Corporation to declare Milltown village a slum clearance area, by which time Old Bridge House was earmarked for demolition. According to Mrs Doyle her mother-in-law, who had died 13 years previously aged ninety-three, was born in Old Bridge House.[608] This would mean that Doyle's mother-in-law had been born in the house at the time of the Famine, in 1845 or 1846.

Old Bridge House survived the slum clearance of Milltown village of the 1950s but was eventually demolished in 1964.[609] Like many of its Dublin city-centre Georgian counterparts, Old Bridge House had been a tenement house for at least 100 years. During that time the house provided a home for scores of people whose life stories – Bridget Lambert apart – will never be known.

OLD BRIDGE HOUSE (NORTH)

This house was never given a specific name but because it was located immediately beside the Packhorse Bridge at its north-west corner, thus mirroring Old Bridge House on the south-west side of the bridge, it is appropriate for our purposes to refer to the structure as Old Bridge House north to distinguish it from its twin on the opposite side of the bridge and the River Dodder, both of which are recorded on Rocque's Survey of County Dublin (Map 4).

Old Bridge House north was a good quality mid-eighteenth-century residence of two or three storeys. The building features in an early nineteenth-century pencil drawing of the Packhorse Bridge by Samuel Brocas, standing on the right-hand side of the composition behind a stone wall embankment (Pl. 52).[610] The old buildings on the left-hand side on the south bank of the River Dodder were part of one of the eighteenth-century mill complexes, and should not be confused with Old Bridge House on the south bank (Pl. 51), which Brocas omitted from his drawing. Old Bridge House north is first encountered in *Faulkner's Dublin Journal* where in 1742 James Hamill of Chancery Lane advertised the following property to be let: 'A house near the Bridge of Miltown [*sic*] within a mile and a half of Dublin, with a coach house and stable, and other conveniences.'[611]

The house was subsequently let to John Church, but in 1764 the property was then included with part of the extensive mill holding acquired by John Classon from John Wallis of Dublin.[612] In December 1772 John Classon let Old Bridge House north to Dixie Coddington for 31½ years at £20 rent per annum. Coddington paid Classon an entry fine of £80 for the lease wherein the property was described as:

> *All that dwelling house or tenement situate lying and being in Milltown in the county of Dublin formerly in the tenure and occupation of James Hamill and then in the occupation of Dixie Coddington with the two gardens one of which is behind the said house and the other behind the concerns lately belonging to Cornelius Egan, deceased and are both enclosed with stone walls ...*[613]

608 *Irish Independent*, 6 February 1952, p. 7.

609 Personal information kindly given to the author by Milltown resident and local historian, Barry Farrell.

610 Samuel Brocas, *Figures crossing the old bridge at Milltown* (NLI, Prints and Drawings, PD 2064 TX 92).

611 *Faulkner's Dublin Journal,* 11 May 1742, p. 3.

612 RD 246/324/158097.

613 RD 294/152/194176.

Plate 52. Figures crossing the Old Bridge (Packhorse Bridge), Milltown, pencil drawing by Samuel Brocas, c. 1820 (image courtesy of the National Library of Ireland)

Coddington had been appointed as principal sergeant-at-arms by royal letters patent in January 1768.[614] This was a well-paid position, and in 1773 the accounts committee of the Irish house of commons awarded him an annual salary of £800.[615] Dixie's city residence was in Queen Street where his first wife died in 1768, before he moved to Milltown in 1772 on a more permanent basis.[616] Dixie Coddington died in September 1776 at his town house in Queen Street in his eighty-third year.[617] Old Bridge House north and its contents were advertised for auction on 19 August 1777 but neither the house nor its contents sold, and so the house was readvertised for sale in July 1778. At that time it was described as being in good repair, with a garden that was planted with the best kinds of fruit trees in full bearing.[618] The following month, the contents of Old Bridge House north were put up for auction without reserve.[619] Dix-

614 *Freeman's Journal*, 19 March 1768, p. 2.

615 *Freeman's Journal*, 8 November 1773, p. 3.

616 *Freeman's Journal*, 30 January 1768, p. 3.

617 *Hibernian Journal*, 20 September 1776, p. 3; *Journal of the Association for the Preservation of the Memorials of the Dead*, vii, no. 1, part 1 (1907), p. 63.

618 *Saunders's Newsletter*, 18 August 1777, p. 3; 6 July 1778, p. 1.

619 *Saunders's Newsletter*, 20 August 1778, p. 3.

ie's Coddington's extensive effects provide a rare insight into the wealthy lifestyle enjoyed by the gentry and professional classes in Milltown in the late eighteenth century:

> *To be sold by auction ... the entire household furniture, etc, etc, of the late Dixie Coddington, esq; at his house in Milltown, adjoining the bridge, consisting of cheque four post beds lined, filed, press, and tallboy beds, with ditto curtains, seasoned feather beds, blankets, matrasses [sic], quilts, and counterpanes, servants beds upon a new construction and bedding, 12 Chinese mahogany parlour chairs, covered with English hair cloth and double nailed, drawing room, back and seat chairs, and a sofa, with cheque covers, and window curtains to match, fancy painted rush chairs with cushions and Damascus cases, ornamented with knotted fringe, two arm chairs to match, and window curtains completely finished, painted chairs to match the bedroom furniture, mahogany bureaus with bookcases, nobbies, tallboys, glass and tea trays, coopers and commodes, fine old Jamaica mahogany dining, voidore, tea and card tables, large Scotch and Irish carpets, glass bells and shades, a toilet table furnished, a dressing glass in a japanned frame, a rolling stone and garden utensils, a jack, and some kitchen furniture.*[620]

Dixie's second wife and widow, Catherine Coddington, assigned the lease of Old Bridge House north to John Bird for £70 in September 1778.[621] Bird went on to build himself a house on the south side of a new avenue linking the Dundrum Road with the Clonskeagh Road, which was later named Bird Avenue.[622] Thereafter Old Bridge House north appears to have been sublet on short-term leases, and by the 1820s employees of Burke's woollen mills were living in it when the building had essentially become a tenement (Map 7). By the time the mills closed in the late 1840s Old Bridge House north had fallen into disrepair and was partly ruinous.[623] When the derelict mill complex was bought by two flour millers named Gibney in 1856, the landlord inserted a covenant in the lease requiring the derelict Old Bridge House north and the adjoining houses at the northern end of the site to be demolished (Map 16b).[624]

ROSY HILL AND EMMET HOUSE (FORMERLY CASINO AND MOUNT ST MARYS)

As previously discussed in Chapter 4, the Mowlds family held extensive farmland in Milltown from the Leeson estate on the south bank of the River Dodder on both sides of the Dundrum Road in the eighteenth century. In the third quarter of the eighteenth century George Mowlds owned two houses called Rosy Hill and Casino, which stood on the east side of the Dundrum Road between Milltown Bridge Road and Bird Avenue. Of the two, Rosy Hill was the older and smaller property. A third house, Violet Lodge, was built on a smaller site to the north of Rosy Hill beside the entrance to Milltown Lodge, roughly where the junction of Milltown Bridge Road and the Dundrum Road is now (Map 21). The boundary between Rosy Hill/Violet Lodge (on the southern side) and Milltown Lodge (on the northern side) was also the boundary between the Leeson and Timleston estates and the townlands of Farranboley and Roebuck respectively (Map 10). Rosy Hill and Violet Lodge have long since been demolished and their lands

620 *Saunders's Newsletter*, 20 August 1778, p. 3.

621 RD 324/459/217492.

622 RD 342/538/231418, RD 841/255/564255. Bird's house was originally called Bloomville, and is now called Gledswood House.

623 NAI, VO, OL50945, House Book for Milltown Village 1845, no. 10; Griffith's Rateable Valuation of Tenements Co. Dublin, Barony of Uppercross, Parish of St Peter, Townland of Milltown, 1850, p. 55, lot 48.

624 RD 1858/15/80.

Plate 53. Emmet House, Dundrum Road, 2019 (author's collection)

built upon, but Emmet House still stands (Pl. 53) and is currently occupied by the Joint Managerial Body (JMB) Secretariat of Secondary Schools.[625] In the early twentieth century Casino changed its name to Mount St Mary's but it is now called Emmet House, in recognition of its historical association with the patriot, Robert Emmet, who lived there in the 1790s.

Rosy Hill can be traced back to a lease from 1 April 1765 when John Mowlds of Churchtown leased 5 plantation acres and 4 perches of land (8 acres and 33 perches statute measure) to George Mowlds of Milltown together with the dwelling house and all other houses and improvements made and to be made thereon.[626] This plot of land formed the basis of Rosy Hill farm, part of which was later used to lay out the walled garden of Casino.[627] No photographs of Rosy Hill have survived. When Rosy Hill was sold in 1953 and subsequently demolished, it was described as a 'substantial 2-storey dwelling, with entrance hall, dining room, sitting room, 3 bedrooms, bathroom kitchen and scullery'.[628]

Over time George Mowlds acquired more land on the Dundrum Road on which he built a beautifully proportioned neo classical villa called Casino, which is best appreciated in a late nine-

625 See also photograph at https://www.jmb.ie/Contacts (accessed 28 January 2022).

626 RD 309/586/207363.

627 NAI, Landed Estate Court Rental, vol.140, no. 32, 'In the matter of the estate of George Frederick Mowlds ... which will be sold by public auction in one lot ... on 3 December 1880.'

628 *Irish Times*, 24 January 1953, p. 11.

Plate 54. Casino, Dundrum Road and Bird Avenue, c. 1900 (courtesy of South Dublin Libraries)

teenth-/early twentieth-century photograph (Pl. 54).[629] That George Mowlds was the builder of Casino is confirmed by an advertisement which he placed in *Saunders's Newsletter* in March 1776:

> *To be let for any term, or for lives renewable for ever, a small, neat convenient house, with coach house, out offices and stabling for six horses, and a good garden, with or without land, situate at the summit of the hill of Milltown, two miles from Dublin [Rosy Hill]; or the large commodious house wherein Mr George Mowlds now dwells [Casino] a little above the two mile stone on said road, furnished or unfurnished, for any term not exceeding five years; there is a coach house, stabling for 16 horses and all necessary out offices, a large garden enclosed with a high wall, well cropped; the whole concerns in good repair, and fit for the immediate reception of any nobleman or gentleman, who will not have a shilling to lay out on improvements; the tenant may be accommodated with any quantity of meadow land under fifteen [plantation] acres. The prospect and situation of this concern, and the air, is equal to any about Dublin. For particulars apply to Mr Mowlds, near Milltown, or Mr Meredith in Crampton court.*[630]

The reference to the two-mile stone is critical because Rocque's Survey of County Dublin of 1760 (Map 4) records this marker on the Dundrum Road opposite to where Rosy Hill is

629 The difference in the appearance of the house in the late nineteenth century compared to today is explained by the fact that the Marist Fathers carried out extensive repairs in the 1950s which necessitated replacing the old roof with a flat one.

630 *Saunders's Newsletter*, 27 March 1776, p. 2.

shown on the later OS maps (Map 20). This detail also confirms that the 'summit of the hill of Milltown' contained in the advertisement refers to the elevated ground on the Dundrum Road on the south bank of the River Dodder, and not the elevated part of Milltown Road (somewhat confusingly called Milltown Hill in the nineteenth and twentieth centuries) before the descent to Milltown village on the city side of the river.

The reference to the 'small, neat, convenient house' can only refer to the house acquired by George Mowlds in the lease of 1 April 1765, i.e. Rosy Hill, while the 'large commodious house wherein Mr George Mowlds now dwells' must be Casino. Finally, the availability of just under 15 plantation acres of meadow land is persuasive too because the Casino demesne comprised almost 18 statute acres when it was surveyed for the Griffith's Valuation in the 1840s, and Mary Anne Mowlds was recorded as the immediate lessor of the property.[631]

Lettings for Casino and Rosy Hill were advertised again in *Saunders's Newsletter* in April 1781 and in January 1782.[632] The second advertisement omitted any reference to Rosy Hill which suggests that George Mowlds had managed to let that property in the intervening eight months. The second advertisement eventually yielded a tenant for Casino. On 25 May 1782 George Mowlds' eldest son, George Frederick Mowlds, who had acquired the property from his father, leased Casino to Thomas Andrews of the Coombe for 99 years at the extremely low rent of £8 per annum.[633] The deed described the property as follows:

> *the large house, garden and out offices and eight [plantation] acres and two roods of land ... bounded on the north by fields in the possession of George Frederick Mowlds, on the east by fields in the possession of William Slater, on the south by the avenue leading from the Blackrock [sic] [i.e. Bird Avenue] and on the west by the great road leading from Dublin to Dundrum ... being near the village of Milltown.*[634]

It is impossible to discover why the rent charged to Andrews was so low. Perhaps Mowlds owed money to Andrews or Andrews had paid a large up-front lump sum payment, known as an entry fine, in return for a reduced rent. However, all was not so prosperous with the Mowlds family as suggested by their building and leasing activities in Milltown. By 1783 four separate judgements arising from debts had been registered against John Mowlds (who had died in Churchtown on 4 March 1787 aged forty-three),[635] George Mowlds of Milltown, his widowed daughter Mary Bell and his son George Frederick Mowlds. All of the debts were assigned by the creditors – Dublin merchants James Costello, Bartholemew Delander and Richard Cox – to another merchant, Archibald Armstrong, whose name appears alongside that of George Frederick Mowlds in an advertisement of Rosy Hill from 26 October 1787.[636] The situation appears to have become even worse for George Frederick Mowlds because two years later he was forced to sell his household furniture, cattle and farming utensils at Mill-

631 Griffith's Valuation, Rateable Valuation of Tenements, Co. Dublin, Barony of Rathdown, Parish of Taney, Townland of Farranboley, 1849, p. 149, at entry nos 5a/5b and 6a/6c where Mary Anne Mowlds is named as the immediate lessor.

632 *Saunders's Newsletter*, 3 April 1781, p. 3; 29 January 1782, p. 4.

633 RD 347/123/231374, RD 345/228/232935.

634 RD 345/228/232935.

635 Transcript of Mowlds family gravestone in Donnybrook cemetery, in Blacker, *Brief sketches of the parishes of Donnybrook and Booterstown, p. 129.*

636 *Saunders's Newsletter*, 26 October 1787, p. 4

town to settle a debt of £41 18*s*. owed to Henry Hawker Browne.[637] The furniture, household goods and farm items comprised:

> *twenty rush chairs, three mahogany tables, one mahogany desk, one mahogany field bedhead, four feather beds, four pairs of blankets, one mahogany fire screen, one looking glass, two milch cows, three draught horses, two cars and gear, one cart, one mahogany working table, one deal kitchen table, one deal settle bed, four tin saucepans and two brass candlesticks.*

It has not been possible to uncover the causes of the Mowlds' financial difficulties but George Frederick Mowlds survived and passed on his landholding in Milltown to the next generation.[638]

The Emmet family's association with Casino can be traced back to the early 1790s when Dr Robert Emmet (the patriot's father) acquired by assignment two leasehold interests in the property from Alderman Thomas Andrews.[639] Casino and its demesne was assigned by Thomas Andrews to Dr Robert Emmet in 1792, when the property was described as:

> *the large house, garden and out offices and eight [plantation] acres and two roods of land bounded on the north by fields in the possession of George Frederick Mowlds, on the east by fields in the possession of William Slater, on the south by the avenue leading from the Blackrock [sic] i.e. Bird Avenue] and on the west by the great road leading from Dublin to Dundrum being near the village of Milltown ... and also the field part of the lands of Milltown in the parish of Taney situated at the corner of the road or avenue leading from Milltown Road to Roebuck [i.e. Bird Avenue] containing two acres one rood and eight perches plantation measure.*[640]

In 1799 George Frederick Mowlds and his wife Mary Anne Mowlds granted a lease of three other small parcels of ground on the boundary of Casino and Rosy Hill to Robert Emmet for 82 years at the annual rent of £22 9*s*. 6*d*.[641]

The history of the Emmet family's residency at Casino has been extensively researched. The older histories focus a lot of fruitless speculation and investigation on the existence of secret passages and bolt holes in the house and its grounds, and other fanciful stories associating Casino with Robert Emmet's flight from his failed rebellion of 1803 and his nemesis, Henry Sirr. The history of Casino after the Emmets' tenure has been well documented in recent times and it is not proposed to repeat that information here.[642]

---

637 RD 401/519/269383. The memorial incorrectly records the surname as Bourne but the will of Anne Elizabeth Mowlds confirms it as Browne (NAI, T 19297).

638 Griffith's Valuation, Rateable Valuation of Tenements, Co. Dublin, Barony of Rathdown, Parish of Taney, Townland of Farranboley, 1849, p. 149.

639 RD 453/133/289401, RD 495/50/321029.

640 RD 453/113/289401.

641 RD 537/558/354638. The memorial does not state if it was Dr Emmet or his son Robert who was the lessee but the lease was probably executed by the patriot's father, Dr Robert Emmet.

642 See for example, J.J. Reynolds, *Footprints of Emmet* (Dublin, 1903), John Christopher FitzAchary, 'The Dodder; its history, traditions, and associations', *Rathmines News*, 14 December 1901. On the other hand, Kerr, *Emmet's Casino* and Holland, *Clonskeagh*, pp. 47–55, give a more balanced view of this aspect of the Emmet association with Casino. Both books provide a good history of the house after the Emmets' occupancy.

Unlike Casino, Rosy Hill continued in the Mowlds' family ownership for several generations until the late nineteenth century. Miss Mary Anne Mowlds, who was born in 1790, lived in Rosy Hill until her death in 1864 when the house was inherited by her nephew, George Frederick Mowlds.[643] He was the third or fourth generation of the family to have been given those two first names. Like his forbears, George Frederick ran into financial difficulties and he was forced to mortgage Rosy Hill to his neighbour, David Thompson of Clonskeagh Castle in 1871.[644] Around this time George Frederick was speculating in land in America as part of a consortium and, in 1878, offered over 1,000 acres of grazing land for sale in Illinois State.[645] When David Thompson died his sons and executors George William Thompson and Robert Wade Thompson called in a debt of £410 owed to their father's estate by George Frederick Mowlds.[646] Accordingly, Rosy Hill was put up for sale in the landed estates court on 3 December 1880 when it was bought by the Thompson executors for £810, the actual purchase price being reduced to £400 after it was set off against the debts owed to the Thompson estate by George Frederick Mowlds.[647]

The two Thompson brothers subsequently granted Mowlds a fee farm grant of Rosy Hill and an acre of gardens at a modest annual rent of £12 10*s*.[648] A month after signing his lease with the Thompsons Mowlds mortgaged the property to an Anne Ryan of Rathgar on 23 August 1883.[649] It seems that George's finances were in such bad shape that he could not obtain a commercial loan, and he was forced to apply to private individuals and his neighbours for financial assistance. Five years later, Rosy Hill was put up for auction on 29 September 1888.[650] It is unclear if the property was sold but in any event George continued residing in the house for another two or three years before moving to nearby Bawn House, which was owned by his bachelor brother John David Mowlds.[651] George Frederick Mowlds died aged seventy-five in Bawn House on 10 January 1897.[652] He was survived by his widow Mary and his unmarried daughter Bessie, both of whom subsequently found accommodation in the Mageough Home on Cowper Road.[653]

By 1891 Rosy Hill was occupied by the Kavanagh family who operated a dairy farm on the premises.[654] On census night 1901, Thomas Kavanagh (sixty and a native of Wexford) and his wife Margaret (fifty-five) were living at Rosy Hill with their four adult children, John (thir-

643 NAI, Calendar of Wills and Administrations for 1864, p. 263.

644 RD 1871/27/287.

645 *Freeman's Journal*, 26 October 1876, p. 1.

646 RD 1881/23/109.

647 NAI, Landed Estates Court Rental, vol. 140, no. 32, 'In the matter of the estate of George Frederick Mowlds ... which will be sold by public auction in one lot ... on 3 December 1880.'

648 RD 1883/30/94; *Freeman's Journal*, 27 September 1888, p. 8.

649 RD 1883/35/181.

650 *Freeman's Journal*, 27 September 1888, p. 8.

651 The Thom's Directories for 1889, 1890 and 1891 (at pp. 1543, 1543, 1550) list 'George F. Moulds' [*sic*] as the occupier of Rosy Hill. Thereafter only John David Moulds [sic] is listed at Milltown; he was living in Bawn House: Thom's Directory 1892, p. 1550.

652 Register of Deaths for Rathdown District, County Dublin, for 1897 at entry no. 215.

653 NAI, 1911 Census, Form A, return for house no. 38 Cowper Road, Rathmines & Rathgar East Electoral Division, Dublin.

654 Thom's Directory, 1892, p. 1550.

ty), Thomas (twenty-seven), Bridget (twenty-two), Margaret (nineteen) and their employee, Thomas Singleton (twenty-five) who was described as a dairy assistant. All of the householders were Catholics.[655] Two years later the Kavanagh's second eldest daughter, Bridget, married George Lambert, who was the second son of another Milltown dairyman, George Lambert of Riversdale, Classon's Bridge. The wedding, which took place at the Church of the Sacred Heart, Donnybrook, was reported in detail by the local press, and among other things the reporter noted that the Kavanagh's next-door neighbour at Casino, Sir Henry Harty, 'kindly presented the bridal party with special bouquets from his flower gardens'.[656]

By the time of the next census on 2 April 1911 the Kavanagh family's circumstances had changed considerably. Thomas Kavanagh senior had died and Mrs Kavanagh's widowed daughter, Mrs Susanna Hurley (forty-four), spent the night at Rosy Hill with her widowed mother and her unmarried brothers Thomas and John, Mrs Kavanagh's granddaughter, Holly Nolan (six) and their dairy assistants John Smith (forty-two) and Peter Drury (forty and illiterate).[657] The Kavanaghs continued farming at Rosy Hill for several years until Thomas Kavanagh's retirement due to ill health in April 1937, at which time his livestock and farming implements were sold.[658] Thomas died in Delaford House, Templeogue, the following November and was buried in Taney graveyard.[659]

The Armstrong family took over Rosy Hill and the dairy business from the Kavnaghs and renamed it Primrose Dairy. The Armstrongs sold the property in January 1953 at which time the house was described as a '2-storey dwelling with enterance hall, dining room, sitting room, 3 bedrooms, bathroom, kitchen and scullery.[660] Subsequently, Rosy Hill was demolished and new houses were built on part of the property fronting on the main road to Dundrum. Much later, in the 1990s the Churchfields housing estate was built on the original five plantation acres of farmland at the rear. In 2015 a small developtment of townhouses called Richmond Court was built on the road frontage of the old Rosy Hill site colse to the side entrance of Emmet House.

VIOLET LODGE

Although it is not entirely certain, it is very likely that George Frederick Mowlds was responsible for building Violet Lodge in the 1780s, on farmland to the north of Rosy Hill (Map 21).[661] As with its neighbour Rosy Hill, there are no surviving visual records of Violet Lodge. A mortgage from 1836 provides a few details about the location of the property:

---

655 NAI, 1901 Census, Form A, return for house no. 25, Dundrum Road, Dundrum Electoral Division, Parish of Taney, Farranboley townland, Dublin.

656 *Rathmines News*, 4 July 1903, p. 2.

657 NAI, 1911 Census, Form A, return for house no. 16, Dundrum Road, Dundrum Electoral Division, Parish of Taney, Farranboley townland, Dublin.

658 *Irish Press*, 13 April 1937, p. 16.

659 *Evening Herald*, 22 November 1937, p. 4.

660 *Irish Times*, 24 January 1953, p. 11

661 *Saunders's Newsletter*, 26 October 1787, p. 4 where two houses and gardens and five acres held under the original 1 April 1765 lease for lives were advertised for sale. The advertisement described George Frederick Mowlds as an attorney; NAI, VO, OL53660, Tenure Book, Townland of Farranboley, 1847, p. 12, no.4.

the dwelling house and garden on the summit of the hill of Milltown bounded on the north by ground in the possession of Arthur Stanley [Milltown Lodge] on the east by the hedge dividing the garden from the garden in the possession of George Frederick Mowlds [Rosy Hill] and on the south by premises also in the possession of the said George Frederick Mowlds [Rosy Hill] and on the west partly by the high road leading from Dublin to Dundrum and partly by a house in the possession of Miss Bridget Byrne.[662]

In the 1840s Violet Lodge was the home of William Thomas Mowlds, a solicitor, who had a town house and office at 6 Digges Street.[663] William Thomas Mowlds had become insolvent in 1844 and he appears to have vacated Violet Lodge at this time or not long afterwards, as thereafter the Dublin street directories record William Thomas (still a solicitor) as residing in the city.[664] In spite of these developments the Mowlds family continued to retain an intermediate leasehold interest in Violet Lodge until 20 July 1883, when George Frederick Mowlds sold his interest in the property to George William Thompson and Robert Wade Thompson.[665] The deed of sale for Violet Lodge was executed simultaneously with the Thompsons' lease of Rosy Hill to George Frederick Mowlds, the circumstances of which have been discussed earlier.[666] Notwithstanding that the Thom's Directory for 1862 records that George and Thomas Mowlds were living in Violet Lodge, in actual fact the property had by then been sublet on short-term leases and continued to be inhabited by various subtenants up until 1894.[667] In March 1894 Thomas Richardson advertised his leasehold interest in Violet Lodge for sale in the *Freeman's Journal*. The property was described as 'a cottage, seven apartments, large garden, coach house ... five minutes from Milltown railway station, on the Dundrum Road'.[668] A few months later, Richardson was advertising for sale 21 cocks of well-saved hay at Violet Lodge farm.[669]

Although Violet Lodge had been a working dairy farm under the Richardsons, not all of the tenants who lived in the house were farmers. On census night 1901 Violet Lodge was inhabited by Albert and Sophia Lindop (forty-three and forty), their son Albert (three) and two daughters, Violet (five) and Sophia (eight months) together with their seventeen-year-old domestic servant, Harriet Ferguson. Albert Lindop worked as an insurance agent and an accountant. All of the residents were members of the Church of Ireland.[670] By the time of the next census in 1911, Violet Lodge had been leased by the Thompsons to a widowed dairy farmer, John Timmons (38), and his four children Anna (?) (seventeen), Thomas (sixteen), John (thirteen) and Albert (eleven), all of

662 RD 1836/22/262.

663 *Dublin Morning Register*, 11March 1841, p. 3;Thom's Directory 1846, p. 1112; NAI, VO, OL53660, Tenure Book, Townland of Farranboley, 1847, p. 12, no,. 4; Griffith's Valuation, Rateable Valuation of Tenements, Co. Dublin, Barony of Rathdown, Parish of Taney, Townland of Farranboley, 1849, p. 149, at entry no. 4.

664 *Freeman's Journal*, 3 February 1844, p. 1; Thom's Directory 1846, p. 1112. The directories and the valuation records are inconsistent with each other as to Mowlds' occupation at Violet Lodge so the exact position is unclear.

665 RD 1883/30/93.

666 RD 1883/30/94.

667 *Freeman's Journal*, 11 March 1861, p. 3 (Joshua Fox); Leinster Express, 28 September 1867, p. 4 (John Keatinge); *Wexford People*, 23 April 1885, p. 7 (John O'Donnell); *Freeman's Journal*, 13 January 1890, p. 1 (T. Richardson) and *Freeman's Journal*, 26 March 1894, p. 1.

668 *Freeman's Journal*, 26, 27 and 28 March 1894, p. 1.

669 *Freeman's Journal*, 19 July 1894, p. 1.

670 NAI, 1901 Census, Form A, return for house no. 23, Dundrum Road, Dundrum Electoral Division, Parish of Taney, Farranboley townland, Dublin.

whom were members of the Church of Ireland. Interestingly, the eldest girl Anna was described as a domestic servant yet two men, Hugh Singleton (thirty-six) and James Walsh (twenty-eight), were living at Violet Lodge and also working as domestic servants.[671] It seems likely that Hugh Singleton and James Walsh worked in the dairy alongside their employer, John Timmons. The Timmons family continued their thriving dairy business at Violet Lodge for several years. They made good profits during the Great War, and by 1919 John Timmons was in a position to purchase 48 acres of grazing land from the Pembroke estate in Dundrum.[672]

John Timmons was an unattractive character. In 1920 he paid Elizabeth Doyle of Rosebuck Dairy, Clonskeagh, £50 to settle slander proceedings which Doyle had brought against Timmons in the King's Bench division of the High Court.[673] In 1923 Timmons was fined £2 fo diluting his milk with water to the extent that the water made up almost 25% of the liquid sample.[674] He had been found guilty of the same offence in 1907 while supplying milk to the Dundrum Lunatic Asylum.[675] Such nefarious trading practices no doubt helped Timmons to fund the purchase of his motor car, and in 1930 he was put off the road for three years dangerous driving on Milltown Road.[676] John Timmons died on 28 March 1931 and is buried with his second wife Margaret in Taney cemetery.[677] Violet Lodge and its farm buildings were demolished in the 1950s and 1960s to make way for suburban housing on the east side of the Dundrum Road. A bungalow from that era still retains the name Violet Lodge.

CLOSING COMMENTS

This chapter's review of 18 detached villas and farmhouses on the Milltown and Dundrum roads reveals a number of interesting observations. Fourteen of the 18 properties surveyed were built before 1800 and this supports the impression that Milltown's heyday was in the eighteenth century, with the finest villas such as Milltown House, Grove House and Casino having been built in a narrow timeframe from about 1745 to 1775, a time when Milltown was at its most popular as both a resort and a suburban residence for Dublin's nobility and gentry. Conversely, only four of the houses surveyed were built after 1800. This shows that there was little or no demand for middle-class suburban housing in Milltown in the nineteenth century, excluding limited building on the Hogan estate at Fairyland to the west of Milltown in the 1830s. This was especially so from 1847 onwards with the arrival of the Rathmines and Pembroke townships, which Milltown could not compete with.

A striking feature is the many instances of continuity of ownership and residency among the families of these properties, in one instance lasting 200 years. Families such as the Mowlds, the Hunts, the Henshaws and the Byrnes crop up time and again among the records. On the other hand, the commonplace practice of renting out houses on short-term lettings provided flexibility, which in several instances allowed extended families and in-laws to live beside or close to

671 RD 1903/9/278; NAI, 1911 Census, Form A, return for house no. 17, Dundrum Road, Dundrum Electoral Division, Parish of Taney, Farranboley townland, Dublin.

672 RD 1919/11/206.

673 *Evening Herald*, 10 November 1920, p. 4.

674 *Freeman's Journal*, 7 March 1923, p. 7.

675 *Wicklow Newsletter*, 7 March 1907, p. 11.

676 *Irish Times*, 27 November 1930, p. 2.

677 IGPA, Taney cemetery, headstone entry no, 205.

each other. In other cases, this practice reflected the management of a property portfolio by landlords such as the Hogan estate and James and Annie Boswell of St James's house.

All of the houses were capable of producing food for the household. It was normal for their owners to keep cows, poultry, and sometimes pigs or goats, for domestic consumption with the excess produce (milk and hay) being sold locally or in the city. The bigger villas had extensive walled gardens and glass houses which enabled their residents to grow a wide variety of fruit and vegetables as well as cultivate prize-winning flowers and hothouse plants. Horses, ponies and donkeys were essential for personal transport, ploughing and draught purposes and so crops such as oats and barley were grown alongside the pasture and meadow lands which predominated on the dairy farms at Prospect, Rosy Hill and Violet Lodge.

All of the houses under review employed domestic servants, gardeners, farm labourers, stable hands and laundresses. It is difficult to assess what proportion of this labour was sourced locally or from further afield. Indoor domestic servants with specialist skills such as cooks, butlers and children's maids would not have been sourced from people living locally in Milltown. On the other hand, outdoor labour needs could be, and indeed were, supplied by the local villagers. At least 26 separate newspaper advertisements from the second half of the nineteenth century have been identified so far relating to employment vacancies, where the contact address given was the post office in Milltown. Naturally, this does not mean that all of the vacancies advertised related to the big houses of Milltown; however, a small number of the advertisements specifically gave the names of people who lived in the village, to take two examples:

> *Laundry. – A respectable, steady, honest woman, who has an excellent place for bleaching and drying at Milltown, Dodder bridge, is anxious to obtain the washing and making up of clothes for ladies and gentlemen. Her residence is well adapted for the above. All order will be punctually attended to. The very best references. Address E.B. Byrne, Milltown, Dodder bridge, county Dublin.*[678]

> *Thorough Servant – A young girl wants a situation as above in a small family; is a good plain cook and laundress; can be well recommended by her last mistress. Address Kate Byrne, Post Office, Milltown.*[679]

Aside from the long hours, hard physical work and modest wages, a servant's livelihood was precarious and they could be dismissed at short notice for trivial reasons:

> *Butler or Indoor Servant – A smart, active man, who will be disengaged in eight days, in consequence of the family going to the Continent for a few months; he thoroughly understands his business, having lived in highly respectable families both in town and the country; perfectly understands the care of plate, and all kinds of lamps and furniture; his discharge will bear strict investigation, and will be highly recommended by the gentleman he is about to leave; is a Protestant, a native of the North of Ireland; the country preferred. Address M.C., Butler, Post Office, Milltown, near Dublin.*[680]

The employer-servant relationship worked both ways. An employer could get more than he bargained for with an employee, as was the case for Mr Hugh Stafford, who employed a

678 *Saunders's Newsletter*, 8 January 1867, p. 4.

679 *Irish Times*, 7 March 1878, p. 7.

680 *Dublin Evening Mail*, 7 July 1863, p. 2.

Plate 55. Demolition of St James, Milltown Road, 1989 (author's collection)

dishonest youth named John Coyle, at his home in Milltown Village in 1840.[681] Coyle was brought to court for the following disorderly behaviour:

> *John Coyle, a rakish looking lad, about 17 or 18 years old, was brought up in custody charged by Mr Hugh Stafford of Milltown, in whose service he had been, with absenting himself from his house without leave. It appeared that the prisoner left his master's house on Monday week, and induced a son of Mr Stafford's, aged 14 years, to go with him to the review in the [Phoenix] Park, in celebration of the Queen's birthday. Besides the clothes the boy had on at the time he prevailed on him to take another suit with him. The prisoner also made free with a shirt belonging to his master. The boy remained away from home till the following day, when he was restored through the police to his parents. The faithful servant pawned the extra suit and the shirt, kicked up a spree on the proceeds, and remained away several days until apprehended by the police. The bench sentenced him to spend ten days in the Bridewell, as a disorderly servant, and to fourteen additional days' imprisonment for the pawning without consent.*[682]

It is a truism that people generally marry within their own social class. The nineteenth-century marriage register for St Philip's church in Temple Road contains a few examples of marriages

681 *Freeman's Journal*, 6 June 1840, p. 3; Stafford lived in Turret House off the north side of the village main street (Map 13).

682 *Freeman's Journal*, 6 June 1840, p. 3.

between domestic servants who worked in some of the villas in the Church of Ireland parish of Milltown. Thus, we find that the coachman employed at St Philip's (formerly Fairyland), David McConnell, married Mary Anne Ferris, a domestic servant also employed at St Philip's, on 9 September 1873.[683]

CONCLUSION

The demand for high-density suburban housing for Dublin's expanding population created irresistible pressure to redevelop the low-density land along Milltown Road. This pressure became pronounced after 1960 and unfortunately resulted in the loss of many important historic properties in the area in the 1970s and 1980s (Pl. 55). Indeed, there are currently plans (September 2022) to build high density apartments on the grounds of Milltown Park and Nullamore which will result in the demolition of the remaining eighteenth-century structure of Milltown Park House (Coldblow House) which was not listed for protection. The small number of historic houses that remain in Milltown – Milltown House, Emmet House, Greenfields, The Old House, Elm House, Elm Grove House, Rydalmount and Clonskeagh Castle – are well maintained and have belatedly benefited from protection under more stringent planning laws. The owners of these properties are the temporary custodians of Milltown's architectural heritage. They need to be encouraged and supported by the relevant local and government authorities to ensure these vulnerable structures survive long into the future. ■

683 Register of Marriages for St Philip's Church, Parish of Milltown (Church of Ireland) for 1873 at p. 5, no. 10, available online at irishgenealogy.ie/churchrecords.

Chapter 16:
Housing Conditions in the Nineteenth and Twentieth Centuries

Chapter 16: Housing Conditions in the Nineteenth and Twentieth Centuries

INTRODUCTION

This chapter considers the housing and infrastructure of Milltown village in the nineteenth and twentieth centuries and the official responses to the poor housing conditions encountered there. In particular, attempts to introduce local authority housing to Milltown by the Rathmines UDC and the Rathdown RDC and their successors, Dublin Corporation and Dublin County Council will be critically examined. Private and philanthropic housing initiatives which were undertaken in Milltown in the 1930s will be considered as a counterpoint to the ineffectiveness of local government at that time. The chapter will conclude with a brief reflection on the emergence of Milltown as a modern middle-class Dublin suburb.

MILLTOWN VILLAGE IN THE 1830S AND 1840S

The first visual depiction of Milltown village was published in the *Dublin Penny Journal* on 23 May 1835 (Pl. 56).[1] Unlike some of the contemporary nineteenth-century paintings and prints of the old Packhorse Bridge at Milltown, which are often inaccurate in their detail or employ artistic licence, this print of the village is very realistic in its portrayal of the location and the daily lives of the inhabitants. In the foreground two women with milk or water pails are chatting in front of a thatched cabin or outhouse while two children play beside the trunk of a long dead tree. On the left of the picture, a workman proceeds down the village towards Hackett's spirit stores, with the left-hand turn to the River Dodder bridge and the Dundrum Road just visible at the far end of the terrace of cottages beyond the stores. The languid smoke issuing from the chimney of the corner house behind the two women fits the mood of the times; there is not much going on in Milltown in the 1830s. Yet despite the seemingly nondescript scene, it is possible to identify most of the families who occupied the houses thanks to the survival of contemporary estate maps and the records of the Griffith's Valuation, which were produced over the course of the 1840s for Milltown.

1 *Dublin Penny Journal*, no. 151, vol. 3, 23 May 1835, p. 372.

Plate 56. Milltown village, Dublin Penny Journal, *23 May 1835 (author's collection)*

Not long after the print of Milltown was published, the ruins fronting the north side of the main street (in the foreground on the right-hand side behind the two women) were demolished, as proven by an estate map of 1838 (Map 12). The landlord of the yard and houses depicted on the map, Miss Charlotte Hunt, leased the property to a solicitor, Mr Rooke, who lived in Monkstown.[2] Rook was a middleman landlord who had no connection with Milltown. Of greater interest are the tenants who lived in two of the cottages, George and Daniel O'Brien. The map depicts two buildings beside the O'Brien's cottages which are described as a hatters' workshop. In the early nineteenth century hat manufacturing was a thriving business and a large hat factory was set up in Donnybrook by the Wright brothers. This factory specialised in making beaver hats and gave its name to the road from Clonskeagh to Donnybrook on the south bank of the River Dodder, called Beaver Row.[3] The Wrights' factory was located on the north bank of the River Dodder opposite the footbridge (which was originally erected for the factory workers) and was operating there in 1829.[4] By 1835 the factory had relocated to Mespil Road.[5] This was a time when Irish hat manufacturers were coming under increasing pressure from English

2 The Post Office Annual Directory and Calendar for Dublin 1843, p. 499.

3 Doran, *Donnybrook*, pp. 109–11.

4 The Treble Almanac 1829, p. 137.

5 Pettigrew and Oulton's Dublin Almanac and General Register of Ireland 1835, p. 151.

imports.[6] In spite of these pressures, earnings for journeymen hatters had improved over the previous 20 years. In the mid-1830s an operative in the hatter trade could expect to earn an average of £1. 4*s.* *to* £1. 10*s.* per week, or up to £2 per week for finishing work, and sometimes considerably more.[7] Such wages compared very favourably with the agricultural labourer in Balbriggan who was then earning 4*s.* 6*d.* per week plus his meals.[8]

It is possible that George and Daniel O'Brien had previously worked for the Wrights before setting up their own workshops in Milltown in the mid- to late 1830s. By 1845 Daniel O'Brien had been succeeded by Thomas O'Brien and both he and George O'Brien were living and working in Milltown during the late 1840s.[9] George's cottage and workshop were given the superior quality mark '1a' by the surveyor from the Griffith's Valuation, meaning that the buildings were new or recently built slated structures constructed of stone or brick. His premises also included a thatch roofed office or shed.[10] The O'Brien's hat-making business does not seem to have survived beyond the early 1850s, albeit that Thomas O'Brien (but not George) continued to live in Milltown into the 1860s.[11]

Beyond the O'Briens' property, a laneway off the main street led to the grounds of Milltown Castle, then located on an elevation above the village (Map 13). The lane also provided access to a detached Georgian house called Turret House (demolished in the 1870s), which was built behind the terraced houses on the village main street (Map 16a).[12] A postcard of Milltown village dating from about 1910 (Pl. 57) makes for an interesting comparison with the 1835 print. Apart from the gas lamps the streetscape remains unchanged. The laneway remains in situ, and today provides access to the Wilde and Green carpark behind the grocery and restaurant and the Mount St Anne's apartment complex further to the rear (Pl. 58).

The ground floor of the two-storey house on the corner of the lane was used as a shop for over 100 years during the course of the nineteenth and twentieth centuries. The shop formed part of a terrace of six two-storey houses, most of which were built in the mid-eighteenth century by George Casson, as outlined in Chapter 4.[13] In the 1840s the business was run by John Waldron and the premises, which included a good-sized yard, were valued at £9 and 9*s.* for local taxation purposes (Map 16a/10). In practice, the turnover of retail tenants was quite high during the nineteenth century which reflected the difficult economic circumstances prevailing in the village at that time.[14]

---

6 *Poor Inquiry, City of Dublin, 1836*, Evidence on Combination, pp. 26–7; *Freeman's Journal*, 22 March 1838, p. 1; 6 November 1838, p. 1; 24 December 1838, p. 2.

7 *Poor Inquiry, City of Dublin, 1836*, Evidence on Combination, pp. 25–6.

8 *Poor Inquiry, City of Dublin, 1836*, Evidence on Combination, p. 27.

9 Griffith's Valuation, Primary Valuation of Tenements, Co. Dublin, Barony of Uppercross, Parish of St Peter, Townland of Milltown, 1847, p. 58, at entry nos 51–52.

10 NAI, VO, OL50945, House Book for Milltown Village 1845, no. 90; McGee, *Archives of the valuation of Ireland*, pp. 214–15.

11 The last mention of the hat business is in Thom's Directory of 1852 at p. 903; VO, Cancellation Books, County of Dublin, Barony of Uppercross, Parish of St Peter, Townland of Milltown, 1855–62, p. 122.

12 RD 124/208/84348; VO, Cancellation Books, Rathmines Ward 1862–3, bk. 1, p. 144, no. 17/9.

13 RD 167/197/111944, RD 167/197/111945.

14 NAI, VO, OL70089, Quarto Book for Milltown Village 1847, p. 213, no. 10; Griffith's Valuation, Rateable Valuation of Tenements, Co. Dublin, Barony of Uppercross, Parish of St Peter, Townland of Milltown, 1850, p. 54, at entry no. 17/10; VO, Cancellation Books for Milltown.

The building next to Waldron's shop was used for a brief period in the late 1840s to accommodate the first national school in Milltown (Map 16a/11) and subsequently became the village post office under the charge of the postmistress Mrs Anna Waldron.[15] The Waldrons were succeeded in 1866 by Michael Kavanagh who became the new postmaster and took over the corner shop.[16] In October 1870 residents living in Milltown and Clonskeagh gained an extra postal delivery in the evenings, which presumably increased the workload.[17] After Michael Kavanagh's death in 1893, the post office was run by a Miss Courtenay before being taken over by Mrs Teresa Hackett and her daughter Mary in 1896. At this point in time it relocated further down the street just beyond the Catholic church to a house called Castleview.[18] The Hackett family retained the position of postmistress up to the late 1940s.[19]

Two doors down from the 1840s post office building Robert Bell occupied a house and forge in 1845, where he lived and worked as the village blacksmith for several decades (Map 16a/13).[20] He was also the occupier of the terraced house next to the forge which he was subletting to lodgers at a weekly rent of 3*s.*, just as the worst effects of the Famine were taking hold and people were on the move.[21] The last house in the terrace of six mid-eighteenth-century houses was occupied in the 1840s by a dairyman called Loftus Buckley, when it was described as being a very old house (Map 16a/15).[22] The national school was rebuilt in 1858 on a new site in front of the Catholic chapel (Map 16a/16). As previously noted, the former schoolhouse building became the post office.[23]

Returning to the 1835 print, a number of buildings of irregular height extend into the middle distance on the right-hand side of the street, beyond the uniform two-storey terrace of houses. The Catholic chapel, which was built in 1819, was not visible from the road because it was erected behind a house which fronted onto the main street (Map 16a/17). Immediately next to the Catholic chapel was a pair of two-storey semi-detached houses 18 feet tall, subsequently named Castleview, which were likely to have been built by local builder William Lee in about 1820 (Map 8 & Map 16a/18–19).[24] The gable wall of this pair of houses is just visible in the *Dublin Penny Journal* print of 1835 (Pl. 56). Beyond Castleview and largely out of sight, there were five small cottages in a short laneway off the street, called Lee's Lane. Finally, the trees on the right of the street in the middle distance mark the village boundary with

15 Thom's Directory 1864, p. 1476.

16 Thom's Directory 1866, p. 1568.

17 *Freeman's Journal*, 24 August 1871, p. 7.

18 Register of Deaths for Rathmines District in 1893, p. 516, entry 341 (17 January); Thom's Directories 1894, p. 1553; 1895, p. 1562; 1896, p. 1564; 1897, p. 1568; NAI, 1901 Census, Form A, Return of residents for house no. 87 Milltown Road, Rathmines & Rathgar East.

19 VO, Cancellation Books, Rathmines & Rathgar East, Milltown Road, 1940–1947, p. 851, entry no. 38.

20 NAI, VO, OL50945, House Book for Milltown Village 1845, no. 83. The last entry for Robert Bell is in Thom's Directory 1880, p. 1510, following which Patrick Bell took over the forge for two years only: Thom's Directory 1881, p. 1512; 1882, p. 1512.

21 NAI, VO, OL70089, Quarto Book for Milltown Village 1847, p. 213, no. 14.

22 NAI, VO, OL70089, Quarto Book for Milltown Village 1847, p. 213, no. 15; Thom's Directory 1856, p. 1129 (22 Cullenswood).

23 VO, Cancellation Books, County Dublin, Barony of Uppercross, Parish of St Peter, Townland of Milltown, 1855–62, p. 123, nos 17/11, 17/15, 17/16.

24 NAI, VO, OL50945, House Book for Milltown Village 1845, nos 77 and 78; Pettigrew and Oulton's Dublin Almanac and General Register of Ireland 1846, p. 841.The houses are shown on the W.C. Hogan estate map of Fairyland demesne of 1821 (Map 8).

Plate 58. Milltown village, 2017 (author's collection)

the demesne of Fairyland, later known as St Philip's. Today, Alexandra College girls' school occupies the site.

In contrast to the north side of the village main street there were very few buildings of consequence on its south side. In the immediate foreground of the 1835 print three small cottages – or cabins as they were called in the nineteenth century – are visible before the road branches to the left down to the ancient fording point of the River Dodder. These three decrepit cabins were removed later in the nineteenth century (Map 16a). The tall building with 'spirit stores' painted on its gable was the only three-storey building in the village. It contained Patrick Hackett's pub and grocery stores with living quarters overhead.[25] Apart from Hackett's pub most of the buildings on the south side of the village were single-storey cottages with two to four small rooms, some of which had yards. These small structures stretched beyond the left-hand turn to the Dundrum Road as far as the Packhorse Bridge and beyond. In addition, a small laneway leading off the south side of the main street provided access to six small cottages known locally as The Gardens. By 1850 just under 60 cottages had been built between the River Dodder and the village, including cottages on the river bank as far as the townland boundary with Clonskeagh to the east and as far west as Moore's woollen mills (now the Shanagarry apartment complex).[26]

25 NAI, VO, OL50945, House Book for Milltown Village 1845, no. 23, where the height of the house is recorded as being 25 feet tall.

26 Griffith's Valuation, Rateable Valuation of Tenements, Co. Dublin, Barony of Uppercross, Parish of St Peter, Townland of Milltown, 1850, pp. 55–6, nos 42–101.

The records of the Griffith's Valuation, which date from 1845 to 1850 for Milltown, provide a wealth of detail about the physical environment of Milltown village, particularly the housebooks which were compiled in 1845.[27] The surveyors noted down the dimensions of every structure, the materials used in its construction and its general age and condition. A series of numbers and letters were used to grade each building under a nationwide uniform set of instructions which were compiled by Richard Griffith and issued to the local surveyors. A total of 256 separate structures were recorded by the surveyors in Milltown village. These ranged from mansions, factories and chapels to cow houses and sheds. All of the buildings surveyed were constructed using stone or brick and lime and mortar, which is unsurprising given the proximity of the limestone quarries. Space constraints preclude a detailed review of every building but the following statistics give an indication of the physical fabric of the village:

(a) 34 structures in new or nearly new condition
(b) 91 structures of medium age and in good repair
(c) 45 structures classified as old but in good repair
(d) 63 structures in disrepair or deteriorated by age
(e) 22 structures with thatched roofs
(f) 1 structure with a wooden roof

What is perhaps the most striking feature of these statistics is the survival into the 1840s of thatched buildings so close to the city of Dublin. Oat and wheat straw would likely have been used as roofing material in Milltown as these crops were the most commonly grown in the vicinity at that time.[28] Most of Milltown's 22 thatched buildings were outhouses, sheds and cowhouses, but seven of them were dwelling houses. To take one example, Patrick Condron lived in a thatched cottage which he rented from John Madden for 1*s.* a week.[29] Condron's thatched cottage was old but in good repair when the surveyor from the Griffith's Valuation visited it in 1845, when it was recorded as being 20 feet long, 17 feet deep, and 6½ feet tall.[30] The little cottage had been built very close to the River Dodder on the old street which led down to the fording point (Map 16a/88). Condron's house had almost certainly been built in the previous century, and was possibly recorded on Rocque's Survey of County Dublin of 1760 (Map 4). It would also have been very vulnerable to regular flooding by the Dodder.

In summary, all of the buildings providing public services were located close together on the north side of the village main street with the exception of Hackett's pub. Additionally,

27 There are three sets of (digitised, on-line) house books for Milltown village and Milltown townland: the house book for Houses in the Town of Miltown [*sic*] (July 1845) OL52714, the house book for Houses in the Town of Milltown OL50945 (November 1845) and the house book for Houses in the Townland of Milltown OL50936 (November 1845). Confusingly, the earliest house book (OL52714) uses the placename 'Miltown', records the quality letter data in column 1 and uses a different numbering system to the later house books (OL50945, OL50936) which refer to the placename 'Milltown' and record the quality letter data in column 4. Throughout the nineteenth century especially, the interchangeable spelling of Miltown/Milltown was commonplace. Awareness of the two different spellings is critical (not to mention infuriating!) when carrying out online searches, especially on Findmypast.ie and the NAI Genealogy websites.

28 NAI, Tithe Aplotment Books for Diocese of Dublin, Parish of St Mary's Donnybrook (16 June 1833) and Parish of St Peter (30 December 1833).

29 NAI, VO, OL70089, Quarto Book for Milltown Village 1847, p. 22, no. 88.

30 NAI, VO, OL50945, House Book for Milltown Village 1845, no. 46.

there were roughly 15 one- and two-storey residential cottages on the north side of the village main street (Map 16a). In the mid-nineteenth century the majority of the village's inhabitants lived in cramped terraces of single-storey cottages on the south side of the village main street and further along the banks of the Dodder.

POST-FAMINE DECAY

By 1851 Milltown townland had reached perhaps its maximum nineteenth-century population of 863, but by 1861 this figure had reduced to 596.[31] The declining number of inhabitants was also reflected in the physical condition of the village as depicted on the Valuation Office town plan of 1850 (Map 16a/16b). The presence of several ruinous buildings is consistent with the townland census returns for 1861 which show that the total number of houses recorded for Milltown townland had declined from 143 in 1851 to 109 in 1861.[32] Nonetheless, the south side of the village main street continued to suffer from overcrowding. In 1880 a small plot of ground opposite Milltown Catholic chapel with 50 feet of road frontage measuring 19 perches in total and extending back to the River Dodder was advertised as follows:

> *Six cottages are erected on the plot of ground and are occupied by weekly tenants, and after payment of outgoings produce a net yearly rental of £27. There is room for building other houses on a part of the said plot of ground, which is unbuilt on, and which extends from the road to the River Dodder.*[33]

No thought was given to the consequences of building cottages so close to the Dodder which was notoriously prone to flooding. Flooding was a specific worry for those who lived close to the River Dodder, a concern that did not afflict the tenement dwellers in Dublin city's slums. Indeed, the residents of the 11 the cottages (Roberts Cottages) beside the River Dodder at Classon's Bridge were very vulnerable to flooding (Pl. 17).[34]

In contrast to the decrepitude of the housing stock in Milltown village, the Palmerston and Hogan estates began to develop their respective landholdings on the western end of Milltown townland, where large houses were laid out at Rydalmount Villas, Temple Road, Palmerston Road and Palmerston Villas, beginning in the early 1860s. These developments are reflected in the 1871 census, when the number of houses had increased by 16 (from 109 to 125) and the population by 98 persons (from 596 to 694).[35]

---

31 Census of Ireland 1861, County of Dublin, Barony of Uppercross, Parish of St Peter, Townland of Milltown, p. 41 (CD-ROM, Archive CD Books Ireland, Dublin, 2010).

32 Census of Ireland 1861, County of Dublin, Barony of Uppercross, Parish of St Peter, Townland of Milltown, p. 41 (CD-ROM, Archive CD Books Ireland, Dublin, 2010).

33 *Freeman's Journal*, 2 December 1880, p. 8.

34 *Dublin Daily Express*, 1 September 1905, p. 6; *Irish Times*, 4 September 1931, p. 7; *Dublin Evening Mail*, 13 August 1946, p. 4. The carpark of The Dropping Well pub where the cottages originally stood is occasionally flooded in modern times: *Irish Times*, 6 September 2008.

35 Census of Ireland 1871, County of Dublin, Barony of Uppercross, Parish of St Peter, Townland of Milltown, p. 103 (CD-ROM, Archive CD Books Ireland, Dublin, 2010). A possible increase in the number of permanent and temporary residents in the new Jesuit headquarters in Milltown Park may also explain the increase in population.

THE RATHMINES TOWNSHIP AND THE PROVISION OF WORKING-CLASS HOUSING IN MILLTOWN VILLAGE

It might have been expected that the incorporation of Milltown townland into the Rathmines township in 1880 would see an improvement in the housing conditions of the labouring class in Milltown village and the introduction of proper planning controls. However, for reasons which will be explained presently, this expectation was never realised during the 50 years that Milltown was controlled by the Rathmines township.

When James Drury was preparing his evidence for the Royal Commission for the Housing of the Working Classes in 1885, he included the following opinion in his draft statement of proofs:

> *There is not in the Township what may be called an unhealthy area, and so, the provisions of the Artisans Dwellings Act 1875 scarcely applies to the Township. There are a number no doubt of unhealthy houses, but they are scattered over the Township. These unhealthy houses are some of them old stables, or parts of stables and old agricultural cottage dwellings that have been in evidence for many years.*[36]

Drury was the secretary to the township commissioners and was also the township's executive sanitary officer. Under the act referred to by Drury (known as the Cross Act), urban authorities were granted powers to raise loans for clearing slum areas and building working-class housing, subject to the consent of the Local Government Board. Given his position, Drury could have been expected to be familiar with the housing conditions of Milltown but he obviously did not consider the conditions in the village sufficiently bad to fall within the remit of the Cross Act, but in any event the act was not used much in practice.[37]

In 1885 the Rathmines township obtained Counsel's opinion on the powers of the township to acquire land compulsorily for building working-class housing. This was done with a view to acquiring a site called Gullistan on which to build housing for the labourers living in Rathmines.[38] Better housing for the villagers for Milltown was not a priority for the township commissioners and it was left to private individuals to make the running. Hence, in March 1894, less than five years after setting up the Dublin Laundry Company in Milltown, Thomas Edmondson wrote to the secretary of the Rathmines township and asked him 'to bring the matter definitely before the Commissioners as there is really an urgent need for the improved accommodation of the working classes of this neighbourhood'.[39]

The Rathmines township commissioners did not respond to Edmondson's petition, probably because they were more concerned with providing working-class housing closer to Rathmines in the new housing scheme at the Gullistan site which they had acquired in 1891.[40] Edmondson was not put off by the lack of support, and he stood successfully as a candidate in the Rathmines township elections in November 1894. During his time as a township commissioner Thomas Ed-

36 Dublin City Archives, Rathmines and Rathgar UDC papers, UDC/List 1/8/8, *The Royal Commission for the Housing of the Working Classes*, Proof belonging to James W. Drury, May 1888, pp. 2–3.

37 Prunty, *Dublin slums*, p. 118; Murray Fraser, *John Bull's Other Homes: State housing and British Policy in Ireland, 1883–1922* (Liverpool, 1996), pp. 70, 74.

38 Dublin City Archives, Rathmines and Rathgar UDC papers, UDC/List 1/8/9, *Case for Counsel, 3 September 1885.*

39 NAI, Dublin Business Records, Dublin 56, Dublin Laundry Company, letter book 1887–95, letter dated 13 March 1894.

40 Dublin City Archives, Rathmines and Rathgar UDC papers, UDC/1Min 1/6, 1886–1893, pp. 293, 293; UDC/1/Min 1/7, 1893–1902, minutes of commissioners' meeting 4 April 1894: the minutes of the board meeting did not even record the receipt of Edmondson's letter of 13 March.

mondson campaigned for the provision of working-class housing in the township.[41]

The Housing of the Working Classes Act, 1890 and the Housing of the Working Classes (Ireland) Act 1908 (the Clancy Act) provided additional powers regarding the provision and financing of local authority housing. The Clancy Act proved to be a milestone because for the first time a government subsidy was made available to municipal authorities as part of the financial assistance provisions for large-scale social housing schemes.[42] The impetus provided by these measures meant that by 1908 the Rathmines UDC had built 355 working-class dwellings, however none of these were close to Milltown.[43]

The first detailed investigation into the housing conditions of Milltown village did not occur until after the Great War, with the enactment of the Housing (Ireland) Act, 1919. This act was brought in as part of a commitment made by the British government's post-war building programme to build 50,000 urban cottages in Ireland. By this stage, the housing problems for agricultural labourers had largely been tackled – 48,000 rural cottages had been built by 1919 – so that attention could now be focused on the problems of urban housing.[44] A critical feature of the 1919 act was that, for the first time, municipal authorities were compelled to meet the working-class housing needs in their area. As a result, all municipal authorities were required to prepare a housing scheme for submission to the Local Government Board before 15 November 1919. For this purpose, survey forms were prepared by the Local Government Board for completion by the relevant municipal authority.[45]

The housing survey forms for the Rathmines UDC were completed on 2 November 1919.[46] The pages for Milltown and Classon's Bridge contain a wealth of data about the individuals and families who lived in the small cottages, including details of the numbers of rooms and families in each dwelling, the amount of rent paid, the sanitary, ventilation and waste disposal arrangements and whether the house was unfit for human habitation or could be made fit. Perhaps the most interesting facts are contained in the remarks section, which were carefully and scrupulously filled in by the surveyor, Frederick Jackson. The houses in the village were divided into groups by the surveyor according to the names by which they were known locally (usually by reference to the landlord) or by reference to a particular landmark. For example, the tenants of 10 cottages on the south side of the village main street called Byrne's Cottages were recorded as paying rent varying from 2*s*. to 4*s*. per week. All bar one cottage had two rooms only, a bedroom and a living room. Seven cottages shared one outside toilet. The surveyor noted that two of the ten cottages had their front doors over the bank of the River Dodder in a dangerous position. The floors of the five cottages which fronted onto the main street were 18 inches below the level of the footpath and the height from the footpath to the eaves was just six feet. In addition, the surveyor remarked that 'roofs of all these cottages (except nos 9 & 10) are always out of order'. Needless to say, Jackson determined that Byrne's Cottages were unfit for human habitation and could not be made habitable.[47]

---

41 *Irish Independent*, 22 November 1894, p. 2; *Rathmines News*, 4 December 1897, p. 4; 22 February 1902, p. 5.

42 Fraser, *John Bull's Other Homes*, pp. 77–95.

43 Fraser, *John Bull's Other Homes*, p. 79.

44 Fraser, *John Bull's Other Homes*, p. 199.

45 Dublin City Archives, Rathmines and Rathgar UDC papers, UDC/1/C/389, Housing Department, LGB, 22 September 1919 (No. 170: M: 1919) and Memorandum 19 August 1919 (No. 40579:1919. M).

46 Dublin City Archives, Rathmines and Rathgar UDC papers, UDC/1/14/vol. 1.

47 Dublin City Archives, Rathmines and Rathgar UDC papers, UDC/1/14/vol. 1.

As explained in Chapter 12, the Hackett family was one of the most prominent families of Milltown village, having been landlords of multiple properties since the 1830s. Of particular interest therefore are the remarks which the surveyor made in 1919 about some of the Hackett's tenement cottages in the village (Map 18). The six cottages known as The Gardens, which were owned by the Hacketts, were noted as being very damp due to the roofs always being out of order and there being no eave gutters at the back. The landlord received from 2*s.* to 5*s.* a week in rent from each tenant. As for Hackett's five cottages adjoining the post office on the north side of the village main street, the surveyor noted a general state of decay and that the houses were very confined at the back with old high walls. Mrs Hackett lived above the post office (which was also called Castleview, in reference to the building's dual use as a private dwelling house) in accommodation consisting of six rooms, which included its own water closet. Her property was considered habitable but her tenants' cottages adjoining the post office in Lee's Lane were not.[48]

Moving westwards to Classon's Bridge, Mr Jackson had this to say about the 12 houses known as Roberts Cottages, in which each of the 12 tenants paid a weekly rent of 3*s.* for accommodation consisting of two rooms:

> *Each cottage consists of [a] small bedroom and a living room, no fireplace in any bedroom, no back windows or [back] doors to any of the cottages. Walls and floors are damp, and roofs (except nos 1 & 2) are always out of order. Cottages at lower end often are flooded when the River Dodder overflows. The Council have had to alter [the] footpath to prevent them being flooded from the main road. There are four W.C.s for 11 families. Open ashpit common to the 12 cottages.*[49]

These extracts from the Housing Survey for Milltown comprise a small sample of the data contained therein. The remarks by the surveyor give a vivid description of the housing conditions, and this complements the visual imagery of the early twentieth-century postcards of Milltown village.

For the first time, the Rathmines UDC now had the full facts concerning the housing conditions of Milltown village and in other congested areas of the township. Following the completion of Mr Jackson's report, in November 1919, the council approved a new housing scheme for 239 new houses whereby the council was to acquire new housing sites at Church Avenue Rathmines, Kimmage and Milltown, and demolish the houses which were unfit for habitation.[50] Two alternative locations were selected for the housing scheme in Milltown.[51] The site was a 16-acre site of land owned by the Jesuits on Milltown Road, which included part of Milltown Park and the farm attached to Elm House (referred to as the Elm Hall site) run by Mrs Mary O'Neill. The second location was a 28-acre site on the opposite side of the road, which the planners called 'Milltown Hill' (not to be confused with the eighteenth-century house of that

48 Dublin City Archives, Rathmines and Rathgar UDC papers, UDC/1/14/vol. 1.

49 Dublin City Archives, Rathmines and Rathgar UDC papers, UDC/1/14/vol. 1.

50 *Irish Independent*, 15 November 1919, p. 6; Dublin City Archives, Rathmines and Rathgar UDC papers, UDC/1/C/389, engineer's report dated 10 June 1920.

51 Dublin City Archives, Rathmines and Rathgar UDC papers, UDC/1/C/542/2, Local Government Board Report 26 March 1920.

name), where the Ramleh Park estate is now.[52] The Local Government Board's inspector visited the sites in Milltown and had the following to say about their suitability:

> *Site No. 2. Milltown Hill. 28 acres. 77 houses proposed on portion of the site. On the east side of Milltown Road, includes seven acres of waste land some of which is used as a refuse depot. About 14 acres are used as a market garden [by Mrs O'Neill of Milltown Hill] and the remainder is in part occupied by the home farm of Mt. Prospect [the Byrne dairy farm], a licensed house [actually a shop and off-licence later called the Barn Stores], cattle sheds and small cottages and the houses known as Prospect House [now the Old House] and The Ranch [Geraldine House] both of which are in good repair. It is intended to rehouse here or on No. 4 the persons displaced by the clearance of the unhealthy area in Milltown.*

> *Site No. 4. Elm Hall. 16 acres. Alternative to Site No. 2 and situated between Milltown Road and the Dublin and South Eastern Railway [now the Luas line]. It is a desirable site in every way with convenient sewer and water service. The necessary means of access to Park Drive is not clearly shown on [the] map and it should be now defined.*[53]

Following the inspector's preference for the Elm Hall site, the council's engineer served site survey notices on the Jesuit fathers and Mrs O'Neill on 28 May 1920.[54] A housing lay-out plan for the Elm Hall site was drawn up by the Rathmines UDC's architect, Edwin Bradbury, on 2 August 1920 and later submitted to the Local Government Board on 22 January 1921 (Pl. 59).[55] The plan provided for 72 terraced and semi-detached two-storey houses which were designed in accordance with the Local Government Board's recommended housing templates known as Type A to Type D. The lay-out also included allotments, a playground and shops fronting the main road next door to Elm House. The entrance to the proposed housing scheme was sited where the entrance to Glenmalure Square is now.

From the outset, the Jesuits and Mrs O'Neill strenuously opposed the council's proposal to acquire their land and engaged solicitors to oppose the council's proposal (formally drawn up on 12 January 1921) to take and compulsorily acquire the Elm Hall site.[56] The reasons for their opposition differed and it is worth exploring why the two landowners – particularly the Jesuits – were so opposed to the housing scheme. Mrs O'Neill argued that her farm at Elm Hall was her 'home farm' and was thus precluded by law from compulsory acquisition.[57] For their part, the

52 Dublin City Archives, Rathmines and Rathgar UDC papers, UDC/1/C/389 and UDC/1/9/1, *Map E*: OSI sheets XXII.3 and XXII.4. The 16-acre site (officially called No. 4 Elm Hall) is now covered by the Churchfield and Glenmalure housing estates and the Gonzaga College ruby pitches, while the Ramleh Park estate and the waste ground known as Scully's Field now makes up the 28-acre site (officially called No. 2 Milltown Hill).

53 Dublin City Archives, Rathmines and Rathgar UDC papers, UDC/1/C/542/2 Local Government Board Report 26 March 1920.

54 Dublin City Archives, Rathmines and Rathgar UDC papers, UDC/1/C/389, engineer's report of 10 June 1920.

55 Dublin City Archives, Rathmines and Rathgar UDC papers, UDC/1/9/13, lay-out plan for Milltown housing scheme, 2 August 1920.

56 Dublin City Archives, Rathmines and Rathgar UDC papers, UDC/1/C/524, CPO 12 January 1921, UDC/1/C/389, inter-party correspondence dated 29 May 1920 and 8 February 1921; letter dated 3 March 1921 McDonald to Local Government Board (Jesuit Archives, IE IJA/FM/Mill/39 (1/2).

57 Dublin City Archives, Rathmines and Rathgar UDC papers, UDC/1/C/389, letter of 29 May 1920. Section 9 of the Housing (Ireland) Act 1919 prohibited a local authority from including in a petition for compulsory powers to acquire lands any portion of a home-farm, park, garden, pleasure ground or other land required for the amenity or convenience of a dwelling house, if suitable sites could be obtained on other land: Housing Department, LGB Memorandum 19 August 1919 (No. 40579:1919. M).

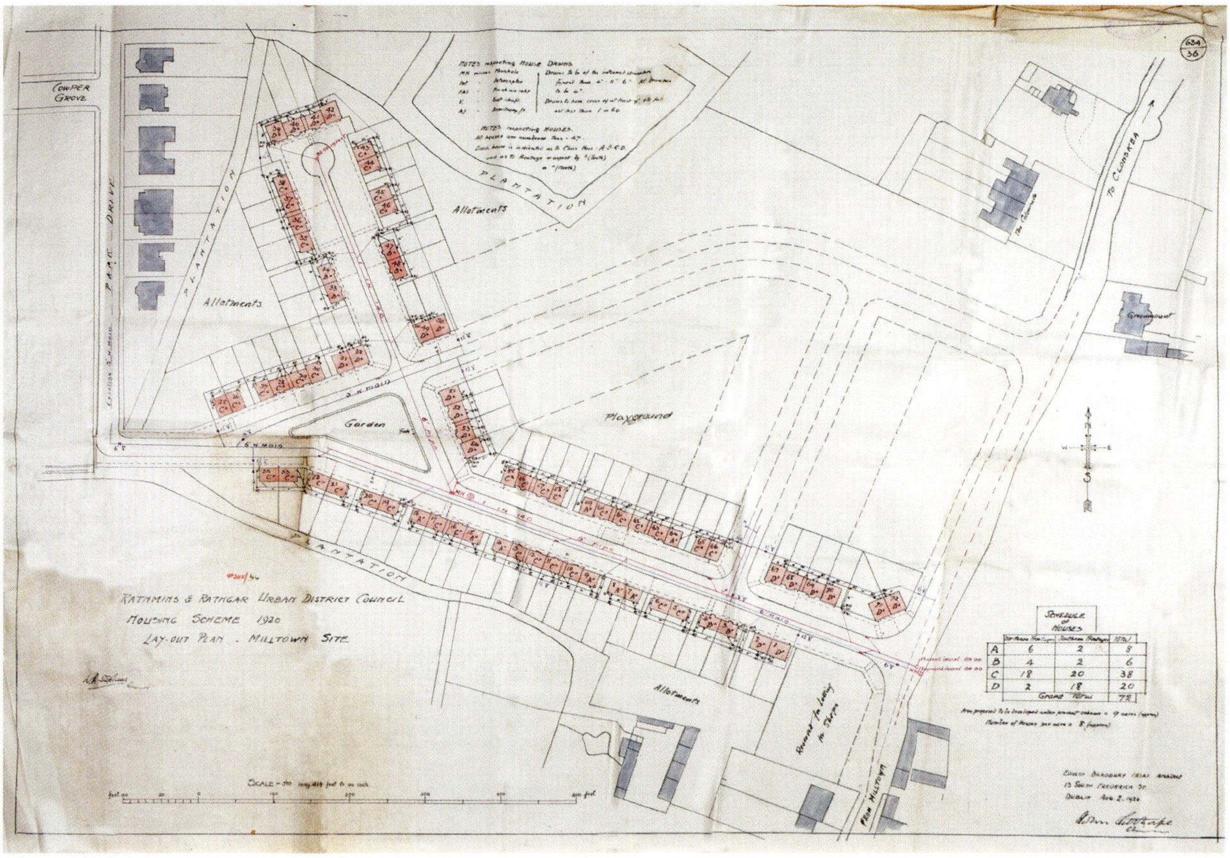

Plate 59. Rathmines and Rathgar UDC, plan for proposed Milltown housing scheme, 1920 (with kind permission of Dublin City Council Archives)

Jesuits opposed the Elm Hall housing scheme for several reasons, each of which were set out in a letter from Fr Martin Maher SJ to the members of the Rathmines UDC in May 1921 as follows:

> *Milltown Park College, whose land it is proposed to take, is an Educational Establishment, numbering nearly one hundred members – professors, clerical students, and servants. The Students are being educated for priestly work in Ireland and in foreign Missions. It is also a house of Retreats.*
>
> *The land in question is urgently required for the work of the College –*
>
> - *To provide necessary milk and garden produce.*
> - *As a place for exercise and games for the Students.*
> - *As affording the aloofness and quiet necessary for study; which would be quite destroyed by the proximity of the suggested dwellings.*
> - *For the convenience of the retreatants – clergy and lay Catholics – many hundreds of whom come annually to Milltown Park, and use the land in question to walk and read and pray in. The peace and silence of a retreat are not consistent with the immediate neighbourhood of a number of such buildings as the Council propose to erect.*

The objects, therefore, for which Milltown Park was acquired by the Jesuit Fathers, and for which very many thousands of pounds have been since expended by them on the property, would be gravely hindered by depriving them of this land; and the work of the College would be seriously hampered. The Fathers of Milltown Park are, I understand, and have been for many years, the largest ratepayers in the Rathmines Township; and may consequently look confidently to the Council for consideration and assistance in carrying on the work of the College.

An alternative site at least equally suitable for the contemplated buildings, on the opposite side of the Milltown Road, may be acquired at a cheaper rate, and by agreement with the present occupier, Mrs O'Neill, who has so informed the Fathers.[58]

Around the same time that Fr Maher wrote his letter to the Rathmines UDC, the Jesuits' solicitor wrote to the council's solicitor on 4 May 1921 stating that his clients could not under any circumstances enter into negotiations for the acquisition of the Jesuits' lands.[59] The solicitor briefly restated the reasons for his clients' opposition, which differ in some respects to those in Fr Maher's letter, as follows:

There is a site on the opposite side of the road much more suitable for Artisans' dwellings, which could be acquired at one half the cost of the lands comprised in the present Scheme. I have reason to believe that this alternative site could be acquired by agreement and the great expense of inquiry avoided. I have reason to know that the owners of houses in Park Drive, the adjoining property, will strongly oppose the Scheme on the grounds that their valuable property will be depreciated if the Scheme is adopted. My clients will be most seriously affected if the present Scheme goes through, as the very object for which their Institution exists will be nullified, and the rest of their property on which they have expended a great deal of money will be valueless to them.[60]

Fr Maher's argument that the housing development would destroy the aloofness and silence necessary for spiritual contemplation rings hollow given that two years later, on 7 September 1923, the Jesuits leased part of their land (a field called 'Elm Park') to Shamrock Rovers FC.[61] When the first game was played at Rovers' new ground, Glenmalure Park, on Saturday 11 September 1926 a crowd of 18,000 spectators turned up, and 'the quiet sleepy village of Milltown, hitherto unknown amongst the masses, was never to be the same again'.[62]

Notwithstanding the opposition of the Jesuits and Mrs O'Neill in 1920 and 1921 to the Milltown housing scheme at the Elm Hall site, the Rathmines UDC had, as we have just seen, pressed ahead and submitted architects' plans and engineering drawings to the Local Government Board for approval in early 1921. During the spring of 1921 attempts were made by the Rathmines UDC to reach agreement with the Jesuits and Mrs O'Neill about a purchase price for their respective properties, which the council's valuer had assessed at £5,183 11*s.* 8*d.*, while at the same time

58 Fr Martin Maher SJ, letter dated May 1921 to Rathmines UDC (Jesuit Archives, IE IJA/FM/Mill/39 (3/4). According to correspondence in the Rathmines township archives, Fr Maher's letter was written on 18 May 1921.

59 Dublin City Archives, Rathmines and Rathgar UDC papers, UDC/1/C/389, letter of 4 May 1921 McDonald to Shannon.

60 Dublin City Archives, Rathmines and Rathgar UDC papers, UDC/1/C/389, letter of 4 May 1921 McDonald to Shannon. It is ironic that 101 years later a dispute over the rezoning of Milltown Park erupted between Dublin City Council and Ardstone Capital regarding planning permission to build 667 apartments on the former Jesuit lands: *Irish Times*, 2 March 2022.

61 Doolin and Goggins, *The Hoops*, p. 14.

62 Doolin and Goggins, *The Hoops*, pp. 29–30.

the council's solicitor was instructed to prepare the paperwork to petition the Local Government Board for a compulsory purchase order for the Elm Hall site.[63] The council's housing committee met on 4 May 1921 and passed a resolution to the effect that if the Jesuits and Mrs O'Neill declined the council's offer of £5,183 11*s.* 8*d.* for the Elm Hall site, 'within seven days proceedings to be taken to acquire the site compulsorily be referred back to the Housing Committee'.[64]

The councillors appear to have had a change of mind, for when the Rathmines UDC met again at the end of May they deliberated on Fr Maher SJ's letter of 18 May 1921, and at his suggestion the councillors decided to pursue the alternative option of building on the Milltown Hill site.[65] Accordingly, on 2 June 1921 the council sought permission from the Local Government Board – which was subsequently granted – to proceed with the alternative site.[66] A revised set of maps and plans for the Milltown Hill site were submitted to the Local Government Board in July 1921, and a revised valuation of the site with proposed compensation for each of the several landowners was prepared for the Rathmines UDC on 28 December 1921.[67]

The valuation report of 28 December 1921 uncovered a complicated pyramid of parties with legal interests in the alternative site at Milltown Hill. One of these was Mrs O'Neill who, in addition to her home farm at Elm Hall, held 19 acres on the Milltown Hill site (where the Ramleh Park housing estate is now) under a 35-year lease which her late husband Mathew O'Neill had acquired in 1897.[68] On 22 April 1922, a minute of the council's housing committee meeting of 28 April 1922 contained the briefest of record: 'Milltown area deferred.'[69] The outlook for the Milltown housing scheme became even bleaker on 25 April 1923 when the council's housing committee turned down an offer from Lord Glenavy of a strip of land in front of his residence at Nullamore, the minutes instructing the clerk to 'thank him for his offer and inform him that there is no intention to build in Milltown at present'.[70]

What brought the Milltown housing scheme to a halt? Unfortunately, the correspondence in the Rathmines township archives relating to the Milltown housing scheme virtually ceases after 12 July 1921 and so it is impossible to discover precisely why the council never proceeded with the alternative Milltown housing scheme at Milltown Hill.[71] Nonetheless, the surviving paperwork points to the failure of the Rathmines UDC to agree compensation terms among the various land-

63 Dublin City Archives, Rathmines and Rathgar UDC papers, UDC/1/C/389, letters 16 and 26 April 1921 to E. Bradbury, letter 3 May 1921 to W.J. Shannon.

64 Dublin City Archives, Rathmines and Rathgar UDC papers, UDC/1/Min 1/8, Minute Book vol. 9, 25 February 1916–30 November 1925, p. 250.

65 Dublin City Archives, Rathmines and Rathgar UDC papers, UDC/1/C/389, letter 2 June 1921 to W.J. Shannon.

66 Dublin City Archives, Rathmines and Rathgar UDC papers, UDC/1/C/389, interparty correspondence 2, 3, 7, 22, 24 June 1921 and 11, 12 July 1921.

67 Dublin City Archives, Rathmines and Rathgar UDC papers, UDC/1/C/389, letter dated 11 July 1921; UDC/1/12/9, valuation schedule for alternative housing site on Milltown Hill, 28 December 1921.

68 Dublin City Archives, Rathmines and Rathgar UDC papers, UDC/1/9/1 *Map E:* OSI sheet XXII.4 and UDC/1/12/9, valuation schedule for Milltown Hill site.

69 Dublin City Archives, Rathmines and Rathgar UDC papers, UDC/1/Min 1/8, UDC Minute Book vol. 8, 25 February 1916–30 November 1925, p. 300.

70 Dublin City Archives, Rathmines and Rathgar UDC papers, UDC/1/Min 1/8, UDC Minute Book vol. 8, 25 February 1916–30 November 1925, p. 377.

71 The lack of surviving correspondence from the Milltown Hill landowners' legal representatives is also a major hindrance.

owners of the Milltown Hill site in the early 1920s as being primarily responsible for stopping the development.[72] In addition, it seems that by the late 1920s financial constraints and a lack of energy on the part of the council's housing committee were also to blame.[73]

An undated note among the council's archives, which nonetheless can confidently be assigned to January 1929, states that when officials went to inspect Mrs O'Neill's ground in 1920, 'Mrs O'Neill refused to meet the Council and the matter was left in abeyance.'[74] This explanation is unsatisfactory and is not supported by the surviving evidence. It is true that Mrs O'Neill refused to allow the council access to her land, but her refusal was in relation to her home farm at Elm Hall on the north side of Milltown Road (the preferred no. 4 site). By May 1921 Mrs O'Neill was open to the possibility of selling her land on the south side of the road at Milltown Hill (the alternative no. 2 site), but the parties were ultimately unable to agree on the price.[75] It is noteworthy that Mrs O'Neill's interest in Milltown Hill derived from a lease executed by her husband in 1896 which was due to expire in 1931. It was critical, therefore, for the council to strike an agreement with Mrs O'Neill's landlord (the Butler Trust Estate) and with the other freeholders and fee farm grantors with an interest in the Milltown Hill site. It is obvious from reading the surveyor's report that negotiations between the Rathmines UDC and the landowners to agree sale terms would not have been straightforward.[76] Legal difficulties aside, this explanation does not explain why the Rathmines UDC did not apply for a compulsory purchase order to acquire the Milltown Hill site.

In 1923 the Rathmines UDC applied to the Department of Local Government (successor to the Local Government Board) for sanction for a loan of £10,000 to expend on laying a new nine-inch water main for Milltown and Sandford.[77] The new main was to replace the inadequate three-inch pipe and alleviate the low water pressure experienced by consumers. During evidence given to an inquiry into the proposed water main by the Department of Local Government, the Rathmines UDC stated that it was interested in building a working-class housing scheme in the district.[78] The editor of the short-lived *Rathmines Free Press* admitted that the people of Milltown should have had better living conditions 'years ago', but was nonetheless of the opinion that the Rathmines UDC was not entirely responsible for this state of affairs.[79] Loan approval for the Milltown watermain was given by the Department of Local Government and Public Health in November 1923, with the tendering process being completed in March 1924 when the contract was awarded to a builder from Ranelagh.[80] In spite of the expressions of interest made at the public enquiry in October 1923, the Rathmines UDC never followed through

72 Dublin City Archives, Rathmines and Rathgar UDC papers, UDC/1/9/13, interparty correspondence dated 11 July 1921.

73 *Irish Times*, 5 September 1929, p. 4.

74 Dublin City Archives, Rathmines and Rathgar UDC papers, UDC, UDC/1/C/524, undated memo from W.H. Lambert to Mr Mason.

75 Dublin City Archives, Rathmines and Rathgar UDC papers, UDC/1/C/389 letter dated 11 May 1921, Shannon to Mason wherein it appears that O'Neill's solicitor made a counter offer; Fr Martin Maher SJ, letter dated May 1921 to Rathmines UDC (Jesuit Archives, IE IJA/FM/Mill/39 (3/4).

76 Dublin City Archives, Rathmines and Rathgar UDC papers, UDC/1/12/9, valuation schedule for Milltown Hill site dated 28 December 1921.

77 *Rathmines Free Press*, 22 September 1923, p. 4.

78 *Evening Herald*, 8 October 1923, p. 1; *Rathmines Free Press*, 13 October 1923, p. 6.

79 *Rathmines Free Press*, 22 September 1923, p. 6.

80 *Rathmines Free Press*, 10 November 1923, p. 6; 8 March 1924, p. 5.

with its intention of building houses at Milltown, even after Mrs O'Neill died in 1926.[81] Instead, the evidence from the *Rathmines Free Press* strongly indicates that the council's housing committee was very much preoccupied with the Kimmage Housing Scheme in 1923 and 1924, to the neglect of Milltown's needs.[82]

Rathmines UDC's aborted housing scheme in Milltown contrasts with the council's successes in improving working-class housing in other parts of the township. During the early and mid-1920s the council successfully progressed its housing schemes at Church Place, Rathmines, Madigan's farm, Harold's Cross and Bedford Lodge in Kimmage.[83] When the council's finances became tighter in the late 1920s it continued to prioritise housing in Kimmage and Harold's Cross at the expense of Milltown.[84] Around this time too, the Rathmines Public Utility Society was formed to complete further housing schemes in Kimmage that had been initiated there by the Rathmines UDC.[85]

The demand for local authority housing in the Rathmines township was such that in 1923 700 applications were made for 124 houses in the Kimmage Housing Scheme, and allegations were subsequently made in March 1924 that people from outside the township had obtained tenancies under false pretences.[86] A schedule with data for 20 applicants for working-class housing, drawn up in February 1927, has survived among the archives of the Rathmines township papers.[87] The document reveals some truly deplorable cases of overcrowding in Milltown. The Davis family lived in Roberts Cottages in Milltown village. The household consisted of eight adults and a twelve-year-old boy, all of whom were living in two-roomed accommodation comprising a kitchen and bedroom. The data collector was particularly concerned with recording the weekly wages of the inhabitants, important information indicating how much rent the family could afford to pay if they were granted a local authority house. Thus, we find that Mr and Mrs Davis were employed by a Mrs Reilly (the Davis's occupations are not stated) and earned £1 10*s*. a week. The Davis's two adult sons aged twenty-four and twenty were earning £3 and £1 a week respectively. The couple had four adult daughters ranging in ages from eighteen to twenty-eight, three of whom were stated to be bringing in 16*s*. a week each (possibly as employees of the Dublin Laundry Company). However, it is the remarks made by the enumerator that catch the attention: '3 beds in one room. Father and boy [12-year-old] in one bed. 2 boys in one bed. 2 girls and mother in one bed. 2 girls in bed in kitchen.'[88]

---

81 Mrs O'Neill died on 19 December 1924 and her property was put up for auction by her executors on 24 August 1925: Register of Deaths for Rathmines No. 1 District in 1924, p. 288, entry no. 443; *Irish Times*, 18 August 1925, p. 10.

82 *Rathmines Free Press*, 6 January 1923, p. 5; 2 June 1923, p. 4; 15 September 1923, p. 4; 8 December 1923, p. 6; 8 March 1924, p. 5; 8 May 1924, p. 4.

83 *Irish Times*, 27 October 1921, p. 2; 28 August 1924, p. 4; *Dublin Evening Telegraph*, 5 March 1924, p. 4; 1 October 1924, p. 1; *Weekly Irish Times*, 19 September 1925, p. 12; Dublin City Archives, Rathmines and Rathgar UDC papers, UDC/1/C/542, Kimmage housing scheme files 1920–1930.

84 The Council were able to raise a commercial loan in 1928 for £5,000 for works at the Kimmage Road site as part of conditions for receiving a government relief grant of £1,000: *Irish Times*, 22 December 1927, p. 2; Dublin City Archives, Rathmines and Rathgar UDC papers, UDC/1/12/23.

85 Brady, *Dublin*, 1930–1950, p. 209.

86 *Rathmines Free Press*, 12 May 1923, p. 3; 2 June 1923, p. 8; 8 March 1924, p. 5; *Dublin Evening Telegraph*, 5 March 1924, p. 4.

87 Dublin City Archives, Rathmines and Rathgar UDC papers, UDC/1/C/524, schedule in manuscript of housing applications dated 25 February 1927. This handwritten document was probably prepared for the housing sub-committee.

88 Dublin City Archives, Rathmines and Rathgar UDC papers, UDC/1/C/524, schedule in manuscript of housing applications dated 25 February 1927, applicant no. 2 (Davis. M).

The Murray family of ten were living in the same overcrowded conditions as the Davis family. In the Murray's cottage in Milltown, the four males slept in one room and the six females slept in the other. Mr Murray worked as a civil servant in the stationary office, apparently earning £7 5*s.* a week. Two of the Murrays' adult sons and four of their daughters were also working, so cumulatively the weekly household income would have been higher than many other households in the village. This explains why the housing official recorded that Murray 'wants a 15*s.* 9*d.* house'.[89]

The third family applicant from Milltown was the Doyle family who were living in Old Bridge House on the south bank of the River Dodder beside the Packhorse Bridge. A widow, Mrs Catherine Doyle, and her seven children lived in a bedsitting room and a very small attic. There were two beds in an attic which had a leaking roof and a skylight with a broken pane of glass.[90]

It is not possible to confirm whether or not any of the three Milltown families named in the housing application list of February 1927 obtained a local authority house from the Rathmines UDC. What we do know is that by the end of November 1927 the council had 1,000 applicants on its housing list, so an applicant's chances of securing a house were rather slim.[91]

On 9 October 1928 a concerned member of the public, John McGlew (address unknown), wrote to the secretary of the Department of Local Government to express his concerns about the living conditions in Milltown village.[92] McGlew was obviously well acquainted with the area, as proven by his letter:

> *I will thank you to ask the Minister for Health to have inquiries made regarding Housing conditions existing in Milltown Village, Rathmines U.D.C. There are at least twenty-five families living in hovels a disgrace [with] neither air, light nor sanitary accommodation and its [sic] really wonderful how they are able to do so. Most of these are employed in the Laundry, earn good wages and could pay a fair rent for healthy houses if erected for them. They are paying a big rent for the hovels at present any sanitary Inspector would say they are not fit for human habitation particularly on the east side from Baby Club [i.e. a temporary wooden building originally built c. 1910 on 'The Strand', where the carpark opposite Wilde and Green is now] to [Dundrum Road] Bridge over Dodder at the south end, and looking round a very cheap and suitable place for erecting houses appears to be going to waste along the Bank of [the] Dodder from Baby Club to Clonskeagh Bridge, a waste ground belonging to the R.U.D.C. I believe [i.e. the area now known as Scully's field which was formerly used as a dumping ground by the Rathmines RDC]. This would give a chance to have [a] road made wide thro' [the] village as at present it is really [a] perfect death trap with the bus and motor traffic, anyone can tell its [sic] nothing short of a miracle that an awful accident involving serious loss of life does not occur. Should a skid or other unforeseen accident happen these buses any time nothing could save the occupiers on the East Side and they are living in daily terror of this. Trusting you will see your way to have this much wanted improvement carried out by whoever is the proper parties in the not distant future.*[93]

---

89 Dublin City Archives, Rathmines and Rathgar UDC papers, UDC/1/C/524, schedule in manuscript of housing applications dated 25 February 1927, applicant no. 18 (Murray. P).

90 Dublin City Archives, Rathmines and Rathgar UDC papers, UDC/1/C/524, schedule in manuscript of housing applications dated 25 February 1927, applicant no. 22 (Doyle. Catherine).

91 *Irish Times*, 30 November 1927, p. 5.

92 Dublin City Archives, Rathmines and Rathgar UDC papers, UDC/1/C/389, letter dated 9 October 1928 McGlew to McCarron.

93 Dublin City Archives, Rathmines and Rathgar UDC papers, UDC/1/C/389, letter dated 9 October 1928 McGlew to McCarron.

In response to Mr McGlew's letter, the Department of Local Government sent one of its engineers, Mr Strahan, to Milltown to inspect the conditions there and to report on potential sites for local authority housing.[94] Among other things, the engineer's report of 24 November 1928 highlighted the following points of interest:

> *Later I interviewed the Chairman [of Rathmines UDC], Town Clerk and District Surveyor as to the possibility of dealing in part or whole with the inferior housing conditions which are so well-known to exist here. The Council, I was informed, are only too well aware of the circumstances generally and would like to improve them but are also aware of the difficulties, economic and otherwise.*
>
> *The dwellings on the right bank of the river and situated in Rathdown No. 1 Rural District [i.e. in the area known locally as Concrete] are even more inferior and include a number of two and three storey tenements [Marble Hall and Old Bridge House] of low standard. It will be seen, therefore, that the existing conditions concern two authorities who should be encouraged to collaborate towards the preparation of a lay-out plan which on completion would present an efficiently planned conjoint endeavour. The presence in the neighbourhood of a dyeworks [at Dartry], laundry and other industrial concerns [the Henshaw ironworks at Clonskeagh] would appear to denote a capacity to pay for better homes than those so unfortunately evident to the passer-by.*[95]

The Department of Local Government sent copies of Mr McGlew's letter and Strahan's report to the Rathmines UDC for its comments, but a formal written response has not survived.[96] An *Irish Times* report of 5 September 1929 briefly mentioned the Rathmines UDC's housing committee's minutes which had discussed the reasons for the delay in the Milltown development scheme. Apparently, financial constraints and a lack of co-ordination between the housing committee and the council's officials were to blame for the lack of progress.[97]

On 4 November 1929 the Rathmines UDC prepared an updated housing survey of the township's working-class housing. The council's report for Milltown village was almost identical to the 1919 housing survey, but with much less information in the 'remarks' column than the earlier report.[98] Three weeks later, on 27 November 1929, the Rathmines UDC town clerk, Seacome Mason, completed a housing needs questionnaire for submission to the Department of Local Government. In his report Mason stated that one of the four unhealthy areas in the township included three acres in Milltown village containing 50 houses inhabited by approximately 218 people.[99] Mason advised that 'the Council propose erecting blocks of buildings containing 66 two bedroomed flats'.[100] The proposal never went ahead and on 8 October 1930

94 Dublin City Archives, Rathmines and Rathgar UDC papers, UDC/1/C/389 report dated 24 November 1928 and Department of Local Government letter to Rathmines UDC dated 4 December 1928.

95 Dublin City Archives, Rathmines and Rathgar UDC papers, UDC/1/C/389, report dated 24 November 1928.

96 Dublin City Archives, Rathmines and Rathgar UDC papers, UDC/1/C/389.

97 *Irish Times,* 5 September 1929, p. 4.

98 Dublin City Archives, Rathmines and Rathgar UDC papers, UDC/1/14/2, vol. 1, report by Lilian O'Ratigan, 4 November 1929.

99 Dublin City Archives, Rathmines and Rathgar UDC papers, UDC/1/14/3, circular of 20 July 1929 from the Department of Local Government to local authorities and completed questionnaire by Seacome Mason dated 27 November 1929. The other unhealthy areas were in Rathmines Avenue, Union Place and Harold's Cross.

100 Dublin City Archives, Rathmines and Rathgar UDC papers, UDC/1/14/3, completed questionnaire by Seacome Mason dated 27 November 1929.

the councillors of the Rathmines UDC held their last meeting. Shortly afterwards the township was dissolved and its territory taken over by Dublin Corporation.[101]

To sum up, during Milltown's half-century under the municipal control of the Rathmines township none of the various private petitions, working-class housing schemes and official recommendations to alleviate the housing conditions in the village ever bore fruit. At no stage did the Rathmines UDC show a firm commitment to compulsorily purchasing a housing site at Milltown. As a consequence, the opportunity to build local authority houses on the Milltown Hill site was lost completely when the site was acquired by a public utility society to build larger houses for the middle classes in about 1930.[102] This is a pretty damning indictment of Dublin's wealthiest township.

The consequences for failing to provide adequate housing for the villagers of Milltown were brought home when, on 3 September 1931, the village suffered one of its worst ever floods; without warning the River Dodder burst its banks and flooded the cottages on the south side of the village main street. Low-lying cottages at Classon's Bridge and in Clonskeagh and Windy Arbour were also devastated, and in Windy Arbour houses were washed away by the River Slang. The damage caused by rainstorm that hit Dublin that day was recorded in great detail by all of the main newspapers and, for the first time, the reports were accompanied by dramatic photographs.[103] The Sisters of Charity at Mount St Anne's convent spearheaded the relief efforts and provided food and shelter to the 20 unfortunate families from Milltown who were flooded out of their homes.[104] In addition, Dublin's Lord Mayor, Alfie Byrne, set up a flood relief fund to which Milltown Golf Club contributed £20.[105] Byrne was later photographed distributing bedding to Milltown residents.[106] Following the floods, the Dublin Board of Health decided to send a deputation to the Minister for Local Government and Public Health to seek permission to build temporary huts for the displaced families of Milltown and Windy Arbour, but nothing seems to have come of this initiative.[107]

The Dodder claimed a fatality in Milltown on St Patrick's Day 1937 when a seven-year-old boy, Noel Kane of Roberts Cottages, fell into the river while playing and drowned.[108] The Lord Mayor visited the Kane family to offer his condolences on the drowning of the little boy, whose body was not recovered from the river until 16 April, at Fitzwilliam Quay.[109] The tragedy prompted the headmaster of Milltown boys' national school to call for the construction of a wall and railings along the Dodder river bank as a safety measure, which would also provide

101 Ó Maitiú, *Dublin's Suburban Towns*, p. 215.

102 From 1931 onwards Ramleh Villas and Ramleh Park were built on the site by the Saorstát Civil Service Utility Society. It has proved impossible to identify the relevant conveyancing transactions in the Registry of Deeds, but given the timing and the earlier departure of Mrs O'Neill in 1925/26 it is likely that the Butler Trusts Estate was responsible for selling the land.

103 *Irish Independent*, 4 September 1931, pp. 9, 11 and 5 September p. 9; *Irish Times*, 4 September 1931, p. 7; *Evening Herald*, 4 September 1931, p. 1; *Irish Press*, 5 September 1931, pp. 1, 4.

104 *Irish Times*, 4 September 1931, p. 7; *Irish Independent*, 5 September 1931, p. 9; *Irish Press*, 5 September 1931, p. 1; *The Watchword*, 12 September 1931, p. 7.

105 *Irish Press*, 7 September 1931, p. 2. The members also donated £30 to the Sisters of Charity: *Irish Independent*, 7 September 1931, p. 6.

106 *Irish Press*, 11 September 1931.

107 *Irish Press*, 12 September 1931, p. 12.

108 *Irish Independent*, 18 March 1937, p. 14; *Evening Herald*, 18 March 1937, p. 2.

109 *Irish Press*, 24 March 1937, p. 11; 17 April 1937, p. 6.

'much needed employment for many of the unemployed in the district'.[110] Nothing came of this call for assistance either. Indeed, given the unrealised expectations of municipal housing experienced under the Rathmines township, the people of Milltown must have wondered whether Dublin Corporation would ever improve on the efforts of the former municipal authority to provide them with affordable local authority housing. Before discussing this issue, it is appropriate to examine the attempts made to improve housing conditions on the south bank of the River Dodder, in the Rathdown RDC.

HOUSING CONDITIONS ON THE SOUTH BANK OF THE RIVER DODDER

That part of Milltown village lying on the south bank of the River Dodder adjacent to the Dundrum Road was, as explained in previous chapters, known locally as 'Concrete' in the nineteenth and twentieth centuries. The 1901 Census described this small but congested neighbourhood in the following terms: 'Milltown, now known as Concrete Town, stands on the townland of Farranboley, in which its area and valuation are included; its estimated area is 2 acres.' For local government purposes, Concrete came under the jurisdiction of the Rathdown No. 1 RDC/Poor Law Union and the district electoral division of Dundrum.[111] By the 1900s most of Concrete had degenerated into a dilapidated area of slum dwellings and cottages which were owned by the Hackett family of Milltown. The poverty of the inhabitants and the poor housing and sanitary conditions which they had to endure gave rise to anti-social behaviour, drunkenness and domestic abuse, issues which have been examined in detail in Chapter 11. The overcrowding in Concrete continued to increase at each decennial census, from 161 persons in 1891 to 182 individuals in 1901, with the pace of growth quickening so that by 1911 238 people were crowded into an area of about two acres, living in 28 dwellings.[112]

This unhappy state of affairs was not just confined to Concrete. Similar conditions existed in other parts of the Milltown district electoral division, especially in Windy Arbour, which was less than a mile south of Concrete on the Dundrum Road.[113] There, during the course of the nineteenth century between 40 and 50 tiny crowded cottages had grown up around a disused mill premises on the River Slang, which had originally been built as a papermill in the eighteenth century.[114] In 1911 52 inhabitants in Milltown district electoral division were living in tenements of one room.[115]

During the 1880s Michael Davitt campaigned to improve the housing conditions for rural labourers and as a result the Labourers' (Ireland) Acts of 1883 and 1885 were passed at the Westminster parliament. These acts enabled Poor Law Guardians in rural areas to build cot-

110 *Evening Herald*, 22 March 1937, p. 5.

111 Census of Ireland 1901, County of Dublin, Table VII, housing and population returns for Concrete Town, p. 34 (CD-ROM, Archive CD Books Ireland, Dublin, 2010).

112 Census of Ireland 1911, County of Dublin, Table VII, housing and population returns for Concrete Town, p. 32 (CD-ROM, Archive CD Books Ireland, Dublin, 2010).

113 The Milltown District Electoral Division comprised the townlands of Churchtown Lower, Churchtown Upper, Rathmines Great, Rathmines Little, Farranboley, Friarland [*sic*] and the congested districts of Rosemount, Windy Arbour and Concrete: Census of Ireland 1911, County of Dublin, Table VII, p. 32 (CD-ROM, Archive CD Books Ireland, Dublin, 2010).

114 OSI, Co. Dublin, Rathmines and Rathgar Township, Sheet XXII.28, five feet to one statute mile, surveyed in 1879 and revised in 1882; *Pue's Occurrences*, 22 October 1754.

115 Census of Ireland 1911, County of Dublin, tenement returns for Milltown District Electoral Division, Table X, p. 38 (CD-ROM, Archive CD Books Ireland, Dublin, 2010).

tages on half-acre plots of land for agricultural labourers, most of whom were housed in sub-standard cabins.[116] Unfortunately this legislation was of limited use as far as Concrete and Windy Arbour were concerned because the acts defined an agricultural labourer as (among other things) a herdsman or a man or woman who does agricultural work for hire at any season of the year on the land of some other person(s).[117] This meant that those inhabitants of Concrete, Roebuck, Windy Arbour and Dundrum who were unemployed or who worked as gardeners or outdoor servants at the local gentry's villas were ineligible for labourers' cottages. In short, inappropriate rural housing laws were applied in Concrete to housing and employment conditions which were much more urban in their characteristics. This unsatisfactory situation was recognised by the councillors of the Rathdown RDC when they met in April 1900, as reported in the *Rathmines News*:

> *The Local Government Board wrote stating that the report for the sanitary sub-officer with reference to the overcrowding of dwellings in Dundrum district required the immediate attention of the Council.*
> *Mr Reilly said that if they closed the houses where were the people to go?*
> *Mr Rafferty – To South Africa [i.e. to fight in the Boer war].*
> *Mr Collins – Could the Local Government Board invest us with urban powers to build artisan dwellings?*
> *Mr Rafferty – You will have to get a larger population.*
> *Mr Collins – I do not know.*
> *Mr Smith – You will have to form Dundrum into a township.*
> *Mr Collins – I wish it was, and not have this Council peddling with it.*
> *After some discussion it was decided to refer the report of the sanitary sub-officer back to him for alteration.*[118]

This vignette of the Rathdown RDC's proceedings illustrates the practical difficulties facing the councillors when it came to rehousing the poorer inhabitants of the Dundrum district. As a result, a repetitive circular process evolved over several years whereby the council's sanitary officer filed reports of unhealthy housing conditions in his district with the Local Government Board, which in turn forwarded the sanitary officer's report to the local councillors for action. For their part, the councillors usually complained about insufficient finance or legal powers, or sometimes both, and generally procrastinated on the housing issues affecting the Dundrum district.[119] This was particularly so in the case of Concrete and Windy Arbour because the large number of new houses required for these districts would create a prohibitively expensive burden on the local ratepayers, despite Rathdown RDC being one of the wealthiest rural districts in the country. Admittedly, the Rathdown Union did not have the concentrated wealth of the Rathmines township which, as we have seen, failed to provide artisans' dwellings for the inhabitants of Milltown village and Classon's Bridge. Despite their faults, credit should be given to the Rathdown councillors where it is due. In 1901 the Rathdown RDC embarked on labourers' cottages schemes in the south County Dublin townlands of Ballyogan, Rathmichael, Shankill, Ballyman, Kilgobbin, Murphystown, Cornelscourt and Dean's Grange.[120]

---

116 McKay, Enda. 'The Housing of the Rural Labourer, 1883–1916', *Saothar: Journal of the Irish Labour History Society*, xvii (1992), pp. 27–8.

117 McKay, *Housing of the Rural Labourer*, p. 28.

118 *Rathmines News*, 21 April 1900, p. 5.

119 See for example, *Wicklow People*, 9 March 1901, supplement, p. 2; 6 November 1915, p. 13; *Wicklow Newsletter*, 18 November 1916, p. 7.

120 *Wicklow People*, 7 December 1901, p. 10.

Two important developments took place in the first decade of the twentieth century which strengthened the rural district councils' ability to provide rural housing for labourers. The first development took place in 1906 when the definition of an agricultural labourer was widened in the Labourers Act 1906 to cover any person (excluding domestic servants) working for hire in a rural district whose average wages in the preceding year did not exceed 2*s.* 6*d.* per day, and who did not occupy land above a quarter of an acre in extent. This definition broadened the scope of people who qualified for rural cottages beyond the traditional agricultural labourer.[121] Secondly, and more importantly, the Labourers Act of 1906 also provided generous loan terms for rural councils to finance rural housing schemes, including a direct subsidy whereby the state paid 36 per cent of the loan repayments.[122]

The process of building labourers' cottages was a lengthy one. An initial representation was made to the RDC by a minimum of three ratepayers or agricultural labourers. A report from the sanitary officer was carried out and the building site or sites were selected. Next, the proposed cottage scheme was publicised in the newspapers and the land was acquired by the rural authority. A local inquiry was held following which an order confirming the scheme was made by the Local Government Board. Such orders could be contested by disgruntled objectors petitioning the local county court.[123] Despite the bureaucracy, the financial terms were so attractive that by the outbreak of the First World War virtually every rural council in the country had availed of the 1906 Act.[124]

LABOURERS' COTTAGES IN FARRANBOLEY

In September 1909 a Local Government Board inquiry was held into an application by Rathdown RDC for a loan of £28,200 to finance the building of 119 labourers' cottages throughout the entire rural district. As part of the housing schemes, the council proposed to secure 13 acres of land occupied by Mrs Langan in Farranboley townland, to the north of Windy Arbour, on which to build 26 cottages. In addition, a further 16 cottages were planned for the townlands of Churchtown Lower and Churchtown Upper (both of which covered Windy Arbour which was not a separate townland), bringing the total number of labourers' cottages for the Dundrum electoral district to 42.[125] Following the public hearing the Local Government Board issued confirmation orders in October 1909 for two of the three housing schemes proposed for the Dundrum electoral division. By way of compensation, the Local Government Board authorised the Rathdown RDC to acquire additional land in Farranboley in lieu of a disallowed site of 3 acres and 3 roods for ten cottages and owned by Mrs O'Rourke at Churchtown Lower townland, thereby increasing the number of cottages in the Farranboley housing scheme to 36.[126]

The process from official approval to actual occupation of the labourers' cottages in Farranboley took a long time to complete. Although the Local Government Board had sanctioned the Dundrum housing schemes in the autumn of 1909, the Rathdown RDC reported in late August

121 McKay, *Housing of the Rural Labourer*, p. 34.

122 Fraser, *John Bull's Other Homes*, p. 46.

123 McKay, *Housing of the Rural Labourer*, pp. 34–6.

124 Fraser, *John Bull's Other Homes*, pp. 41–2.

125 *Irish Times*, 25 September 1909, p. 5

126 *Dublin Daily Express*, 21 October 1909, p. 2; *Wicklow Newsletter*, 23 October 1909, p. 5.

1911 that 63 applicants had applied for cottages in Farranboley.[127] These cottages were still at the drawing board stage, for the following June the local authority gave a short-term grazing contract in respect of five acres of land at Windy Arbour to the contractor who had won the tender to build the cottages.[128] Eventually, it was reported on 15 March 1913 that the Rathdown RDC 'will consider tenders for completion of the building of eighteen pairs of labourers' cottages at Farranboley, Windy Arbour, Dundrum'.[129] The delays were not explained but in due course 36 cottages were duly completed in 18 semi-detached pairs (Pl. 60). Each cottage was provided with a garden of a quarter of an acre in size (Map 21).[130] Even so, the insatiable demand for housing in Windy Arbour and the surrounding district coupled with the delay in building the council cottages had encouraged a private landlord (probably Patrick O'Rourke) to build over 30 cottages (now Millmount Grove) in January 1910 on an unsuitable site between the Dundrum Road and the River Slang much to the dismay of the medical officer of health for Dundrum and the Rathdown RDC's engineer.[131]

DEPLORABLE CONDITIONS IN CONCRETE

It is impossible to ascertain if any families from Concrete were rehoused in the cottages in Farranboley, although it is known that two or three people living in the Marble Hall tenement in 1915 were on the Rathdown RDC housing list.[132] What is beyond doubt is that the housing requirements of the Dundrum electoral district far exceeded the 36 local authority cottages built in Farranboley before the outbreak of the First World War brought a halt to local authority housing schemes.[133] But even if tenants in places like Concrete were able to move on to better accommodation, that did not solve the problem of insanitary housing because the departed tenants were quickly replaced. To counteract this practice, a rural district council could apply to the Local Government Board for an order compelling the owner (landlord) of a condemned building to demolish it, provided suitable accommodation had been obtained or was obtainable elsewhere by the agricultural labourer occupying the condemned dwelling.[134] However, these powers were never used in Concrete by the Rathdown RDC because no suitable alternative accommodation was available locally. So instead of ordering the landlord to demolish tenements such as Marble Hall and Old Bridge House, the council made orders – usually ignored – requiring the landlord to remedy sanitation defects in their tenement property. Once a moratorium on government loans for housing schemes took effect on the outbreak of the Great War, a sanitation remedy order was the only punitive action available to local authorities faced with housing unfit for human habitation.[135]

---

127 *Dublin Evening Mail*, 30 August 1911, p. 5.

128 *Wicklow People*, 22 June 1912, p. 2.

129 *Wicklow Newsletter*, 15 March 1913, p. 1.

130 VO, Cancellation Books, Dublin, Milltown, 1910–38, bk. 1, pp. 109–14.

131 *Wicklow Newsletter*, 29 January 1910, p. 11; 5 February 1910, p. 8. The cottages are 1–37 Millmount Grove.

132 *Wicklow Newsletter*, 23 October 1915, p. 8.

133 In 1901 the Rathdown No. 1 UDC had estimated that there were 150 cottages unfit for human habitation in the Dundrum district alone: *Wicklow Newsletter*, 24 November 1917, p. 10.

134 *Wicklow Newsletter*, 23 September 1911, p. 5.

135 *Wicklow Newsletter*, 23 October 1915, p. 8; 6 November 1915, p. 8; 15 July 1916, p. 10; 18 November 1916, p. 7; *Wicklow People*, 6 November 1915, p. 13.

Plate 60. Cottages in Farranboley Park, Dundrum Road, 2019 (author's collection)

The bureaucratic impasse described above is illustrated in the case of the Hackett tenement in Concrete called Marble Hall. In October 1915 the medical officer for health for Dundrum, Dr Neary, submitted his report to the Rathdown RDC on the property:

> *I have inspected the premises known as Marble Hall, Farranbolie [sic], Milltown, set out in apartments as a tenement house. It contains 29 rooms, all of which are at present let, except 8. In the 21 occupied apartments there are eleven separate tenants, comprising with their families a total of 51 persons. Sometime ago all the rooms were let, I am informed, so that then the total number of inhabitants would have been proportionately greater. The rooms are small and totally unsuited for such purposes. There are no sanitary conveniences, nor is the water supply on the landings. There are closets in the yard discharging directly into a millrace, which arrangement is unsatisfactory and insufficient. That this over-crowding should exist in a rural district, even in the close proximity of the city, is very regrettable. I consider that the overcrowding in this case is a grave menace to the public health of the district, and that it is a matter of extreme urgency in the interest of the public health that proper housing accommodation be provided for those people. The premises, on account of situation, site, size, and number of apartments, and lack of proper conveniences, are unsuitable for tenements, and I recommend that they be no longer used as such.*[136]

The councillors discussed Dr Neary's report at their board meeting of 20 October 1915, and the steps they could take to ameliorate the situation at Marble Hall. Some councillors were in

136 *Wicklow Newsletter*, 23 October 1915, p. 8.

favour of applying to the Local Government Board for a housing loan because of the exceptional circumstances of the case. Others doubted such an approach would work, and that instead they should force the landlord, Thomas Hackett (son of T. P. Hackett, Milltown publican and local politician whose career is discussed in Chapter 12), to provide proper sanitary accommodation. The council's clerk feared that Hackett would retaliate against the council's sanitary order by evicting his tenants. The clerk opined that there was a very strong case to be made to the Local Government Board for a housing loan, and so the councillors made an order that Dr Neary's report be sent to the Local Government Board with a request for authority to build more cottages in the district.[137]

The housing conditions at Concrete came up for discussion again at the next meeting of the Rathdown councillors in early November 1915.[138] After reading the press reports of the board meeting of 20 October, Thomas Hackett had written to the council ahead of the next board meeting refuting the charges made against his tenement property, and making self-serving allegations against Dr Neary:

> *There has been less sickness in Marble Hall for the past thirty years than in any other part of the barony, which is reply enough to Dr Neary's statement that the place is a menace to public health. Dr Neary called on me some time ago and told me not to issue any visiting tickets [i.e. tickets for free medical appointments available under the poor laws] for children or old people except in the mornings, as he could not be bothered coming so far out of his way in the evenings. I believe it is because I refused to obey this cheeky order that he has reported these premises ...*[139]

However, since the previous council meeting, Dr Neary had submitted a second medical report to the Rathdown RDC, which took into account the housing conditions in the extended districts of Farranboley and Concrete, and which contradicted Hackett's blithe dismissals:

> *Dr Neary's report referred to the housing conditions in Farranboley, Milltown. There was considerable overcrowding in the district as a whole. In a space he would calculate to be under two acres there were about seventeen houses with 154 inhabitants.*[140] *Considering that in no single instance are there proper sanitary conveniences (all closets discharge directly into the millrace, except two discharging into a filthy cesspool), and that in many cases there are families of 8 or 10 persons inhabiting two small rooms. It was a state of affairs requiring urgent and immediate attention.*[141]

The *Wicklow People* quoted further extracts from Dr Neary's extensive report, which were critical of conditions at Mowlds Cottages, Hackett's (later Field's) Cottages and Old Bridge House. Unfortunately, Dr Neary's efforts to expose the conditions in Concrete were of little practical value because the Local Government Board had replied to the council and refused to sanction a housing loan. Instead, the Local Government Board suggested that the insanitary conditions reported by Dr Neary be remedied using the Rathdown RDC's powers under the Public Health Acts. As

137 *Wicklow Newsletter*, 23 October 1915, p. 8.

138 *Wicklow People*, 6 November 1915, p. 13.

139 *Wicklow People*, 6 November 1915, p. 13.

140 The 1901 census recorded 182 inhabitants in Concrete: NAI, 1901 Census, Form N, Enumerator's Abstract of Farranboley (Concrete), Dundrum Electoral Division, Farranboley townland.

141 *Wicklow People*, 6 November 1915, p. 13.

usual, the councillors resigned themselves to the situation – which one remarked was nothing more serious than had existed for the last 40 years – and referred Dr Neary's report to the council's engineer for his opinion.[142] Fifteen months later nothing had changed. In February 1917 the medical officer reported to the Local Government Board that landlords were ignoring the council's sanitary orders, and, in exasperation, he suggested that the Rathdown RDC insist that the landlords reduce their rents by half.[143]

AFTER THE GREAT WAR

Six weeks after the end of the First World War the government announced its intention to introduce funding and loans on a limited scale for essential public utilities works, including the building of labourers' cottages.[144] Seven months later, on 29 July 1919, the Rathdown RDC completed a housing return showing the number of labourers' cottages provided under the Labourers Acts in and in the immediate vicinity of small towns having a population of 500 or upwards. The return stated that 68 labourers' cottages had been built by the council in the three districts of Dundrum (estimated population 600), Rosemount (estimated population 500) and Windy Arbour (estimated population 550).[145] In short, by 1919 the Council had built 68 labourers' cottages to service the needs of a population of roughly 1,650 living in the villages of Dundrum and Windy Arbour and their immediate vicinity. In particular, a large majority of the inhabitants of Rosemount and Windy Arbour were from working-class industrial, domestic and agricultural backgrounds, and lived in substandard accommodation.

The scale of the housing problem facing the Rathdown RDC emerged at a council meeting in December 1919 which noted that there were 447 applicants alone from the Stillorgan district looking for labourers' cottages, at a cost of £450 per cottage.[146] In addition, 160 people from the Dundrum district had applied for houses, most of whom were living in accommodation that had been condemned by the council's medical officer. Aside from increased building and labour costs, the principal difficulty was that only 56 housing sites were available in the Dundrum district on land currently occupied by the council.[147] Clearly, the council could not satisfy all demands for labourers' cottages. Nonetheless the councillors passed a resolution requiring all condemned dwellings to be closed or demolished as soon as they were vacated by tenants.[148] The worst places in the Dundrum district name-checked by the councillors during their discussion included Woodbine Terrace, Majenta Lane, Rourke's Cottages (Windy Arbour), Delaney's Cottages (Windy Arbour) and Concrete in Milltown, which 'was also very bad'.[149] In addition to

142 *Wicklow People*, 6 November 1915, p. 13.

143 NAI, BG 137, R1, BC 14, Correspondence from the Local Government Board to the Rathdown No. 1 RDC, 19 February 1917; *Wicklow People*, 4 August 1917, p. 6.

144 NAI, BG 137, R1, BC 15, Correspondence from the Local Government Board to the Rathdown No. 1 RDC, 23 December 1918.

145 NAI, BG 137, R1, BC 16, Housing Return Form L 5985/215/19, Rathdown No. 1 RDC, 29 July 1919. It is possible that the population for Windy Arbour included people living in Concrete but this is not certain.

146 *Wicklow People*, 6 December 1919, p. 3. The Local Government Board gave £270 for each cottage at 3.25 per cent interest p.a. but the government subsidy paid 36 per cent of the £270. The balance (£180) had to be funded on the open market at an interest rate of 6 per cent p.a.

147 *Wicklow People*, 6 December 1919, p. 3.

148 *Wicklow People*, 6 December 1919, p. 3. This resolution was meant to be strictly enforced but this did not happen because condemned housing remained in Windy Arbour and Concrete up until the 1950s.

149 *Wicklow People*, 6 December 1919, p. 3.

an insufficiency of cottages and building sites, a critical obstacle facing the Rathdown RDC and all local authorities after the Great War was the effects of inflation and the high cost of borrowing on the commercial markets, and the negative impact this had on the rents which were charged to the local authority tenants. When the issue of rents was discussed by the Rathdown RDC meeting in December 1919, the clerk estimated that the weekly rent for a new cottage would be 6*s*. 6*d*., excluding the cost of repairs, insurance and rent collection. In contrast tenants were currently paying between 2*s*. and 2*s*. 9*d*. a week for their cottages.[150]

The twin problems of inflated building costs and their knock-on effects on setting rents seems to have paralysed the Rathdown RDC as regards making any decisions to build new cottages in the Dundrum, Windy Arbour and Concrete districts under the government's post-war housing initiatives. The council's attitude is neatly captured in a report of their proceedings in March 1920 concerning a joint housing initiative with the Rathmines UDC:

> *The town clerk, Rathmines, wrote stating the urban council have under consideration a labouring scheme for the district of Milltown, and he was directed to suggest that Rathdown Rural Council might at the same time take steps to improve the housing accommodation of that portion of Milltown situated in your district. The clerk said that the rural counsel had taken up the matter long ago, but were up against the same difficulty which Rathmines would encounter in regard to the cost of building. The clerk was directed to reply.*[151]

Aside from financial constraints, deteriorating working conditions during the War of Independence undoubtedly impacted on the day-to-day administration and efficiency of the Rathmines and Rathdown local authorities. That said, this factor was not as disruptive in comparison with local councils that were controlled or boycotted by Sinn Féin and their republican supporters.

LIVING CONDITIONS IN THE FREE STATE

The housing conditions at Concrete and Farranboley remained unchanged throughout the 1920s and beyond. During this period the Free State embarked on a policy of centralising local government at the expense of the Victorian devolved model of district councils and poor law guardians, which had reached its apogee under the Local Government (Ireland) Act 1898. Among other things, this policy was behind the abolition of poor law unions in 1923 and their replacement with county boards of health, which now had responsibility for local health and social welfare services and the provision of local authority housing. Under the Local Government Act of 1925, every rural district council was abolished (with the exception of those in County Dublin, which continued until 1930). Needless to say, the new centralised system of control over local government was unpopular with local politicians who had become accustomed to considerable local autonomy before 1922. Nevertheless, despite the loss of local powers the public benefited by the Local Government (Extension of Franchise) Act 1935, which extended the local franchise (essentially reduced to electing county or town councillors) to all adults over the age of twenty-one.[152]

The introduction of County Boards of Health brought little improvement to the housing problems of Concrete and Farranboley. In February 1933 the Dublin County Board of Health

150 *Wicklow People*, 6 December 1919, p. 3.

151 *Wicklow People*, 20 March 1920, p. 3.

152 Potter, *The municipal revolution in Ireland*, pp. 289–93.

advertised for tenders for the building of 115 labourers' cottages in south County Dublin, including 34 cottages at Farranboley. Twelve months later, the medical officer for the Dublin County Board of Health reported that the housing conditions in Dundrum, Windy Arbour and Milltown areas required the Board's most serious consideration.[153] In response, a resolution put forward at a meeting of the Dublin County Board of Health in April 1934 proposing to obtain demolition orders against Marble Hall, tenements in Concrete and Rourke's Cottages in Windy Arbour was defeated by six votes to four.[154] The more things changed the more they remained the same.

The completion of the 34 new labourers' cottages in Farranboley in March 1935 brought the total number of local authority houses in Farranboley to 70, inclusive of the 1909 to 1913 scheme of 36 houses.[155] Welcome as these houses were, these two schemes did not bring an end to the deplorable housing conditions in Windy Arbour, Farranboley and Concrete.[156] For example, in February 1934 it was reported by the County Medical Officer that at Hackett's Cottages in Milltown, a family of nine occupied two rooms, another family of six occupied one room and two families of five each also occupied a single room.[157] The housing issue came up for discussion once again by the Dublin County Board of Health in September 1936 when, as had happened many times before, opinions as what to do were split between those who favoured closing and demolishing the condemned properties, thereby making the unfortunate inhabitants homeless, and those who favoured doing nothing until alternative accommodation was available. The only action taken was that the Dublin County Board of Health decided to enter into negotiations with the landlord of Marble Hall (still Thomas Hackett apparently) to demolish the building.[158]

During the autumn of 1936 the *Irish Press* ran a series of investigative reports exposing the worst of Dublin city slums, accompanied by oral testimonies and stark pictures of urban poverty. As part of the investigation, a small number of politicians brought two journalists from the *Irish Press* to view housing conditions in Milltown and Dundrum.[159] Under a column titled 'South Co. Dublin's Shame', the newspaper laid bare the following conditions in Marble Hall and in Rourke's Cottages in Windy Arbour:

> *South Co. Dublin has a slum problem, limited, but challenging Dublin's in kind. Mr Sean Brady, T.D., Councillor Clare and Miss [Margaret] Pearse, T.D., proved this when they took with them Irish Press investigators T. O'Brien and S. Hughes. Next the greenest of fields are the most squalid shacks. 'Marble Hall', Milltown, once a mill, is now a typical tenement, in galloping decay and ruin. Here in smoke-filled rooms – some of them with no windows and none with proper ventilation – adults and children, down to the tenderest years, were found clinging to life. The 'ground*

153 *Evening Herald*, 21 February 1934, p. 8; 22 February 1934, p. 11.

154 *Irish Independent*, 11 April 1934, p. 4.

155 *Leinster Leader*, 2 March 1935, p. 2. In due course the roads for the two schemes were named Farranboley Cottages and Farranboley Park.

156 An indication of the scarcity of available building land and as a consequence a requirement for a higher density development, was that the garden plots for the 1935 housing scheme were smaller (18–35 perches) than those of the 1913 scheme (1 rood): VO, Cancellation Books, Dublin, Milltown, 1910–38, bk. 1, pp. 150–3.

157 *Irish Times*, 21 February 1934, p. 11.

158 *Irish Times*, 23 September 1936, p. 2; Irish Independent, 23 September 1936, p. 5; Irish Press, 23 September 1936, p. 4.

159 *Irish Press*, 24 October 1936, p. 9.

floor' of Marble Hall is below ground level. Some of the occupants have lived here for 20 years. One visitor had to climb, crablike, up the moving wooden stairway. At the top he entered a room where an infant lay in a bed, inhaling foul air and smoke from the chimney. 'I wonder how the people have the heart to keep the rooms so nice and clean,' said Miss Pearse, emerging from the place.' Rourke's Cottages [at Windy Arbour], once closed as unfit for habitation, are occupied. 'Why do you go into this place?' repeated a woman. 'We have to, or sleep on the road.' At the home of Mrs Kenny were two babies in bed with measles. They had not been visited by a doctor – the mother was afraid the doctor would order her to leave the house.

Margaret Pearse's slightly gauche remarks on leaving Marble Hall betrayed her own personal circumstances of domestic luxury and isolation, which could not have been more different to those of the Marble Hall tenants.[160] On the death of her mother Mrs Margaret Pearse in 1932, Margaret, whose brothers Patrick and William Pearse had died in the 1916 Rising, inherited a life interest in St Enda's in Rathfarnham. Had she been minded to do so, Margaret Pearse was not in a position to donate land from St Enda's for labourers' cottages because she held a life interest in the property. Nonetheless, after the boarding school at St Enda's closed in 1935, she continued to live alone in the beautiful granite villa and its 30 acres of walled grounds until her death in 1969, when the property passed to the State.[161]

The extract quoted from the *Irish Press* was the final mention in the newspapers of housing conditions in Milltown in the 1930s. Silence prevailed for the next 13 years until the problem was tackled once and for all by Dublin Corporation in 1949. Before examining that momentous development in the evolution of Milltown, it is appropriate to review briefly some of the other housing initiatives that took place in the environs of Milltown between the two world wars.

PRIVATE HOUSING SCHEMES IN MILLTOWN PRIOR TO THE SECOND WORLD WAR

As noted earlier, the area between the south side of Milltown Road and the River Dodder to the north of the village known as Milltown Hill was earmarked for local authority housing by the Rathmines UDC. Those plans fell through and later, in 1931, part of Milltown Hill was acquired for development by a body called the Saorstát Civil Service Public Utility Society Limited.[162] In simple terms, a public utility society was a co-partnership society made up of private individuals with the object of pooling their resources in order to build houses for the working-classes. The concept of the public utility society was given a statutory basis by the Housing Act of 1919, but it was the introduction of generous State grants and other relief measures under the 1925 Housing Act which greatly boosted their popularity. For example, a public utility society that built a five-roomed house at a cost of £600 in the County Borough of Dublin (after 1930 the reconstituted Dublin Corporation) received State and municipal grants totalling £200 as well as a remission of rates.[163] In 1931 the Saorstát Civil Service Public Utility Society Limited developed 20 two-storey houses comprising 10 semi-detached pairs along the Milltown Road, which were advertised for sale at £730. Each house had two reception rooms, three bedrooms, a bathroom and a small garage to the side. The houses were also fitted out with electricity and

160 According to the *Irish Parliamentary Handbook 1945*, at p. 173, Ms Pearse's recreations were reading and travel.

161 *Scéal Scoil Éanna: The story of an educational adventure* (Office of Public Works, 1986), pp. 44–5.

162 *Irish Independent*, 3 September 1931, p. 13.

163 Brady, *Dublin, 1930–1950*, p. 207.

gas and were built by the well-known firm of G. & T. Crampton.[164] This new development was named Ramleh Villas. In the 1930s Ramleh was a town in Palestine which, among other things, contained the Christian pilgrimage site known as the house of Joseph of Arimathea.[165] How a small suburban housing development in Dublin acquired the name Ramleh remains unexplained.

Ramleh Villas were priced for the middle classes and would have been unaffordable for the majority of the inhabitants who lived in the cramped cottages of Milltown village. The public utility societies operating in the Rathmines township in the 1920s predominantly catered for the middle classes and were not resourced to provide houses for the poorest inhabitants of the township. This limitation was made clear by a Mr Thomas Johnson in November 1927 at a public meeting held in the Rathmines Town Hall to establish the Rathmines Public Utility Society:

> *The meeting ought not to break up without understanding that the utility society will do something to ease the pressure, but it will not build houses for the poor, and it cannot, in its present form, or in the near future. That will remain a problem for the State and for the municipality. While it was very desirable that the work of the society should go on, there should not be a misapprehension that it was going to provide houses for men who are out of work or only earning 16s to 25s a week. The immediate value of the building society was that it would absorb a considerable amount of the unemployed, and it was on that score that he thought an urgent call to action should be taken from that meeting.*[166]

Soon after Ramleh Villas were completed in 1931, building began to the rear in a new development called Ramleh Park, and over the course of the 1930s 106 houses were built on the old O'Neill farm.[167] Unlike Ramleh Villas, several individuals and builders were involved in this housing scheme, many of whom submitted planning applications to Dublin Corporation to build single pairs of houses.[168] Two of the main builders at Ramleh Park were firms called Donnelly and O'Brien and Elgin Contractors Ltd.[169] O'Donnelly and O'Brien advertised their houses in the *Irish Press* in February 1935 in the following terms:

> *Semi-detached Houses of quality and distinction, ideally situated in a picturesque suburban area within a 3d. Tram and 'Bus Fare to City. Soundly constructed residences, with slated roofs, containing 2 large Reception Rooms, sliding doors; Kitchen, with modern fireplace, built-in cupboard, and having Terazzo floors: Porch Entrance to Hall, with lead lights; 3 Bedrooms; Bathroom, separate W.C.; Electric heating plugs and provision for Gas Fires fitted in all rooms: Garage, Coal House; large front, rere and side Gardens. We invite you to inspect these modern houses with their labour-saving devices.*[170]

---

164 *Irish Independent*, 3 September 1931, p. 13; McManus, *Crampton Built*, pp. 108–9.

165 See the *Irish Press* of 25 March 1935, p. 7 which reported on an Irish pilgrimage to the Holy Land. Ramleh is now called Ramla and is part of the State of Israel.

166 *Irish Times*, 30 November 1927, p. 5.

167 By 1941 all 106 houses were occupied according to the 1941 edition of Thom's Directory (p. 1233).

168 *Irish Times*, 25 June 1936, p. 3; 12 July 1935, p. 13; 3 August 1935, p. 5; 9 April 1936, p. 3.

169 *Irish Times*, 4 October 1934, p. 5; *Irish Press*, 23 February 1935, p. 2.

170 *Irish Press*, 23 February 1935, p. 2.

Houses at Ramleh Park could be purchased outright for £795 or acquired with a small deposit with the balance of the purchase price paid as rent.[171] A sign of the developing community spirit at Ramleh Park was the inauguration of the annual Ramleh Horticultural Show in 1946, which by 1952 had grown to such an extent that it attracted 300 entries.[172] Although the Ramleh show attracted gardeners from all over Dublin the event showcased Milltown's gardeners, thus following in the tradition set by Fox's florists of Milltown and other Milltown prize winners of the Rathmines Horticultural Society Show in the 1840s.[173]

By the mid-1920s the boys' national school in the village main street beside Ss Gall and Columbanus church was severely overcrowded with 75 children packed into a space scarcely sufficient for half that number, a situation which prompted the editor of the *Rathmines Free Press* to describe the congestion as a disgrace to civilisation.[174] The chronic overcrowding was not remedied for 19 years until a new boys' primary school was opened in January 1943. The building was erected on a site adjacent to 20 Ramleh Villas on Milltown Road. By 1957 the school had 231 boys on the roll, some of whom were on Gaelic football, hurling and athletic teams.[175]

BREAKING THE CYCLE IN MILLTOWN – DUBLIN CORPORATION HOUSING INITIATIVES AFTER THE SECOND WORLD WAR

The change of government in February 1948 heralded in a new determination by the Inter-Party administration and Dublin Corporation to eradicate Dublin's slums. To this end Dublin Corporation agreed to a target of building 3,000 houses a year, which was about double the rate achieved in the 1930s.[176] In the spring of 1949 Dublin Corporation began the process of compulsorily acquiring about 40 acres of land on the south bank of the River Dodder at Milltown where it planned to build 354 two-storey houses, eight residential shops and school buildings.[177] As nearly all of the land lay in the Dublin County Council's area its consent to the development had to be obtained first before the Corporation could proceed to acquire the lands from the landowners.[178] Almost 30 acres of pasture lands were acquired from a single landowner, dairyman Laurence Byrne, for which he received £12,000 in compensation.[179] By September 1949 the last of the cattle had been removed

---

171 *Irish Press*, 26 January 1935, p. 14; 23 February 1935, p. 2. The houses also qualified for a two thirds remission of rates for seven years.

172 *Irish Press*, 6 September 1948, p. 2; *Irish Independent*, 15 September 1952, p. 8; *Irish Times*, 13 September 1954, p. 4.

173 *Freeman's Journal*, 8 July 1837, p. 2; 14 July 1838, p. 3; 21 April 1842, p. 1; 8 August 1845, p. 4; *Saunders's Newsletter*, 7 May 1846, p. 2; *Dublin Evening Mail*, 15 June 1849, p. 1.

174 *Rathmines Free Press*, 12 April 1924, p. 4.

175 *Souvenir of the Blessing and Dedication of the Church of the Immaculate Virgin Mary of the Miraculous Medal at Clonskeagh*. The building is currently (September 2022) used by the HSE for Milltown Mental Health Services.

176 Dickson, *Dublin: The making of a capital city*, p. 514.

177 *Irish Independent*, 16 April 1949, p. 9; *Dublin Evening Mail*, 29 April 1949, p. 6. Dublin City Council Law Department Housing Files (hereafter cited as DCC Housing Files), Transcript of the Public Inquiry into the Milltown Area Compulsory Purchaser Order 1949 held on 29 April 1949, p. 6. Simultaneously, Dublin County Council was preparing its own local authority housing scheme at Mulvey Park, Windy Arbour.

178 *Dublin Evening Mail*, 29 April 1949, p. 6. DCC Housing Files, Transcript of the Public Inquiry into the Milltown Area Compulsory Purchaser Order 1949 held on 29 April 1949.

179 DCC Housing Files, Milltown CPO 1949, Department of Local Government letter dated 8 December 1949.

from the new housing site, thus bringing to an end cattle farming at Farranboley after more than a millennium.[180] The new housing estate was called the Milltown (Farranboley) Scheme although most of the houses were actually built in the adjacent townland of Rathmines Great on land lying between the Dundrum Road and the Harcourt Street railway line.[181]

During the years 1949–52 a new network of roads was laid out over the old pasturelands of Farranboley and Rathmines Great townlands comprising St Columbanus Road, St Columbanus Avenue, St Columbanus place, Patrick Doyle Road, St Gall's Gardens North and South and St Luke's Crescent.[182] By the end of the building works for the Farranboley Scheme 328 houses and six residential shops had been built which was slightly less than the numbers (354 and eight respectively) which had been planned originally.[183] The new scheme included 31 maisonettes comprising two flats, each with a separate entrance.[184] More importantly, a playground and a new primary school, now called Our Lady's Clonskeagh Parish National School, was built on St Columbanus Road in 1957.[185]

In a further development, on 14 March 1952 Dublin Corporation decided to allocate at least 40 houses in Farranboley for its tenant-purchase scheme.[186] This was part of a policy decision on the Corporation's part to offset the burden on tax and rate payers of keeping thousands of local authority houses under repair.[187] From 1955 onwards tenants in the Farranboley Scheme could apply to purchase a small number of houses on St Columbanus Road from Dublin Corporation subject to a deposit of £50 plus legal fees. The weekly repayments for the houses varied between £1 14*s.* 9*d.* for nos 9, 32 and 50 St Columbanus Road and £1 16*s.* 11*d.* for nos 8 and 15.[188] By the end of 1957 Dublin Corporation had allocated 42 houses in Farranboley to the Milltown Tenant Purchase Scheme. By then, defects had already arisen in some of these houses which had to be put right, and at the same time the Corporation took the opportunity to add fuel stores and rear entrances to the dwellings.[189]

A small number of the new Corporation tenants were not appreciative of their new environment. In September 1952 a despondent writer to the *Irish Independent* informed readers that 22 of the 44 blossom trees planted along Patrick Doyle Road had been destroyed by vandals.[190] Things eventually settled down and the Milltown-Farranboley tenants association, inaugurated in 1953, began liaising with Dublin Corporation on issues of local con-

180 DCC Housing Files, Milltown CPO 1949, letter dated 18 July 1950.

181 DCC Housing Files, Land Registry Folio 3496 Co. Dublin.

182 The names of several of the earliest occupants are listed in Holland, *Clonskeagh*, pp. 283–8.

183 *Irish Press*, 8 October 1952, p. 6; Minutes of the Municipal Council of the City of Dublin, 1952, pp. 302–3; *Irish Times*, 26 March 1953, p. 10.

184 *Irish Independent*, 6 February 1952, p. 7.

185 *Irish Times*, 9 November 1954, p. 9; *Dublin Evening Mail*, 19 September 1957, p. 4.

186 *Irish Times*, 15 March 1952, p. 4.

187 *Irish Times*, 1 January 1953, Supplement, p. 25.

188 *Irish Independent*, 23 March 1955, p. 3.

189 Minutes of the Municipal Council of the City of Dublin, 1957, p. 428 and 1958, p. 18.

190 *Irish Independent*, 17 September 1952, p. 6.

cern.[191] In a further effort to promote pride of place in the new housing developments, the Ramleh Horticultural Society introduced two new competitions in September 1954 for the best kept front gardens in Mulvey Park and the Farranboley area.[192]

The rehousing of the villagers of Milltown necessitated a separate procedure under the Housing Acts which delayed their move to the new local authority houses in Farranboley. Firstly, Dublin Corporation decided to deal with the insanitary and unhealthy houses by way of a clearance order under section 23 of the Housing Act of 1931. This type of order was designed to deal with large slum areas and was infrequently used in practice.[193] In conjunction with the clearance order, Dublin Corporation proposed to compulsorily purchase land and buildings surrounding the clearance area in the village which it deemed reasonably necessary for the satisfactory development or use of the cleared area.[194] In effect, this meant that some houses in Milltown village which were fit for habitation were to be compulsorily acquired and demolished to facilitate the redevelopment of the village following the removal of the unhealthy houses under the clearance order. As we shall see shortly, this was to lead to several objections by disgruntled landlords, publicans and shop owners.

The process was initiated by the Medical Officer of Health for Dublin Corporation, Dr Harbison, who on 22 May 1951 reported to the Corporation's housing committee on the conditions pertaining at Milltown. In short, 54 homes in the heart of Milltown village were deemed unfit for human habitation by Dr Harbison: nos 1–4 Strand Cottages, 1–10 Byrne's Cottages, 1 and 2 Roberts Cottages East and 1 and 2 Roberts Cottages West, 1–6 The Gardens (off main street), 1–3 Milltown Hill, Main Street nos 6, 7, 29–34, 75–78, 80–84, 91, 100 and 101, 1 and 2 Castleview, 1–3 Hackett's Cottages West and a gate lodge adjoining 2 Hackett's Cottages West.[195] Most of the condemned properties are visible in a contemporary photograph taken shortly before the area was cleared (Pl. 3).

On foot of Dr Harbison's report the housing committee recommended on 14 December 1951 that the village should be declared a clearance area, as a preliminary step to rehousing the residents.[196] Dublin Corporation formally adopted the housing committee's recommendation on 4 February 1952, the Lord Mayor having noted that there were already sufficient houses built in Farranboley to house the Milltown people.[197] This decision prompted a reporter from the *Irish Independent* to visit Milltown to interview some of the villagers whose homes were due to be demolished. The opinions proffered by the inhabitants reveal a mixture of anticipation and loss as one ancient community contemplated its imminent demise:

> *Mrs Catherine Doyle of the Old Bridge House, one of the oldest houses in the area, told me that it was the first big change she would witness after living there for over 50 years. 'My mother-in-law was born here', she told me, 'she died at the age of 93, and she is 13 years dead. I believe that*

191 *Dublin Evening Mail*, 11 November 1953, p. 6.

192 *Irish Times*, 13 September 1954, p. 7.

193 DCC Housing Files, Transcript of the Public Inquiry into the Milltown Village Area Compulsory Purchase Order 1952 held on 7, 17 and 18 October 1952 (hereafter cited as Milltown village inquiry), p. 125.

194 Milltown village inquiry, pp. 104–5.

195 Minutes of the Municipal Council of the City of Dublin, 1951, no. 141, pp. 344–6.

196 Minutes of the Municipal Council of the City of Dublin, 1951, no. 141, p. 349.

197 *Irish Press*, 5 February 1952, p. 1

this house will be included in the demolition scheme, which is a pity. It is a fine old house and you won't get rooms in the new houses like those we have here.

Down in the main street I stepped off the narrow pavement into one of the little cottages that will be among the first to feel the blows of the demolition gangs. Inside I met Mrs Julia Kavanagh who, with her husband Bob, has lived there since she was married over 40 years ago. Mrs Kavanagh is 77 years of age and her husband is 83. 'I was born in Milltown,' she replied to my question, 'and I moved into this house when I got married. There were people living here for years before we moved in.' Mrs Kavanagh is, I think, torn between two conflicts. The prospect of living in a new house attracts her, but she will grieve for the old house which has been home for her and her family for so long. 'I would rather stay here but it is an awful area and should have been done away with years ago. But you will never get the like of these cottages again for 3/6 a week,' she added.

Mr Tom Singleton, Mrs Kavanagh's brother, told me that most of the people in the area welcomed the news that they were to move into the new houses. A loss which some of the people will experience is that they will no longer be so convenient to the church and the school. One of the interesting things about Milltown is its rather colourful place names. One of the areas is known merely as 'Concrete', but if you should be writing to one of the people who live there you would address the letter to 'Marble Hall.' 'The Strand', 'The Bottoms', 'The Coach Road' are other examples.[198]

The slow pace of the Corporation's bureaucracy created unease among the many inhabitants who were waiting to be rehoused. By the end of May 1952, the editor of the *Irish Press* sought to assuage their worries about the availability of houses in Farranboley:

Residents of old Milltown village need not be uneasy, because numbers of new houses in the nearby scheme have been tenanted by applicants who formerly lived in other parts of the city. A complete section of the new estate is being reserved for the Milltown people; but the Corporation are meeting with legal difficulties, outside their control, which are causing a hold-up in the procedure necessary to make their condemnation order of the village property absolute.[199]

The date 20 June 1952 stands out as a critical date in the history of Milltown. On that date Dublin Corporation made the compulsory purchase order under Part II of the Housing (Miscellaneous Provisions) Act, 1931, thereby acquiring virtually the entire village area of Milltown. The Corporation's order was subject to confirmation by the Minister for Local Government and Public Health.[200] With the exception of Ss Gall and Columbanus Catholic church every building on the west (or north) side of the village main street from St Anne's national school as far as the grounds of St Philip's was scheduled to be demolished. Similarly, the entire built-up area of the village on the east (or south) side of the main street from Geraldine Terrace to the Packhorse Bridge was also scheduled to be demolished, with the exception of nos 5–8 Strand Terrace at the rear of Geraldine House.[201]

198 *Irish Independent*, 6 February 1952, p. 7.

199 *Irish Press*, 30 May 1952, p. 5.

200 *Irish Press*, 25 June 1952, p. 4.

201 *Irish Press*, 25 June 1952, p. 4. The total area being acquired was about five and a half acres: *Evening Herald*, 7 October 1952, p. 3.

By the second week of September 1952 some residents in the clearance area began to leave their old homes and move into their new Corporation dwellings.[202] About half a dozen landlords and small businesses whose properties were affected by the compulsory purchase order had objected, and so a public inquiry was planned for 7 October 1952 at which a local government inspector would hear their objections and determine if the Corporation's order should be made with or without modifications by the Minister for Local Government and Public Health.[203]

PUBLIC INQUIRY INTO THE MILLTOWN VILLAGE AREA COMPULSORY PURCHASE ORDER

The sworn public inquiry into the Milltown village area compulsory purchase order 1952 opened at the City Hall on 7 October 1952 and was subsequently adjourned until 17 October.[204] The transcript of the oral evidence given over the three-day hearing in October 1952 runs to 129 pages and provides an unprecedented level of detail about individuals' homes and businesses in 1950s Milltown.[205]

The director of housing for Dublin Corporation, Mr O'Mahony, opened the hearing by giving the background to the compulsory purchase order. He said that the Corporation had long been aware of the housing conditions in Milltown village but had had to postpone action until a suitable building site had been secured in the locality. Mr O'Mahony told the inquiry that the Corporation had built most of the 328 houses authorised in 1949 for the Farranboley Scheme and that the remainder were nearing completion.[206]

The Corporation's officials told the inquiry that a census carried out on 4 December 1951 had identified 247 people comprising 60 separate families living in the Milltown village compulsory purchase area.[207] Dr Harbison gave evidence that he had inspected 54 houses and concluded that none of them were fit for human habitation. In a similar vein the assistant city architect opined that the condemned houses could not be made fit for human habitation at a reasonable cost and, accordingly, they should be demolished.[208] In addition, the redevelopment plan for the village planned to widen Milltown Road to 50 feet, with a 30-foot roadway and two footpaths 10 feet wide on either side. As the land between the main road and the River Dodder was unsuitable for housing (it was part of the flood plain), it would be made into a public park.[209]

An important aspect of the scheme was the acquisition of two sites on either side of the Catholic church and a walled orchard attached to St Philip's (now the main entrance to Alexandra College) on which 20 new houses and six residential shops were to be built as part

---

202 *Irish Independent*, 12 September 1952, p. 4.

203 *Irish Press*, 4 October 1952, p. 6.

204 The proceedings are reported in the *Evening Herald*, 7 October 1952, p. 3; 17 October 1952, p. 3; 18 October 1952, p. 7; *Irish Press*, 8 October 1952, p. 6; *Irish Times*, 8 October 1952, p. 8; 18 October 1952, p. 4; *Irish Independent*, 18 October 1952, p. 8.

205 DCC Housing Files, Milltown village inquiry.

206 Milltown village inquiry, p. 2.

207 Milltown village inquiry, p. 38.

208 Milltown village inquiry, pp. 33–5.

209 *Irish Times*, 8 October 1952, p. 8.

of the redevelopment of the village.[210] However, the compulsory purchase of St Philip's orchard was successfully opposed by Miss Henshaw and the residential and commercial redevelopment of the village on the north side of the main street never took place as originally planned.[211]

The bulk of the inquiry's time over the course of the three-day hearing was spent examining and cross-examining expert witnesses and objectors to the scheme. What emerges from the evidence is that all of the houses in the clearance area failed the Corporation's by-laws and modern planning policy as well as statutory health and sanitation requirements.[212] Inadequate ventilation and light, rising damp, leaking roofs and inadequate sanitary accommodation in contravention of the Housing Acts were frequently cited by the Corporation's health and housing officials as reasons why the houses were not fit for habitation. An example of a condemned property was no. 29 Main Street in Milltown village, which contained a shop on the ground floor. The shop appears in Edwardian postcards of the area when it was owned by the Gormley family (Pl. 57). The Wilde and Green café and delicatessen stands on the site now (Pl. 58). In the 1950s the property was owned by James Donegan whose parents had purchased the property some 26 years previously.[213] The Corporation's medical officer of health gave the following evidence about the building which was typical of housing conditions in Milltown:

> *There is a dwelling house with a lock-up shop and yard. The dwelling house comprises 5 rooms, 2 on the ground floor and 3 upstairs apartments. The kitchen floor is 3 feet below the road level. The floors are concrete and the walls show evidence of dampness. The premises are in a general state of disrepair, the plaster work is broken and the premises are old and the upper floor rooms are a little off level. I consider that the upstairs rooms are deficient in lighting and ventilation. The ground floor is 2 or 3 feet below street level, and is less well lighted than upstairs. The roof and plaster work inside has been broken in parts. The sanitary accommodation consists of one water closet in the yard. There is a tap over a sink inside and there is a tap outside as well. There are two families of seven persons [living in the house].*[214]

Donegan's property was 200 years old – it was the corner building in a terrace of four two-storey houses which had been built by George Casson on the north side of the village main street in the late 1740s or early 1750s – so its dilapidated condition was hardly surprising.[215] Nonetheless, Donegan let the shop, the living quarters and several out offices to tenants for which he made a net profit of £4 and 15*s*. a week after deducting rates and ground rent.[216] In mitigation, Donegan's tenants had access to a kitchen with a good range and a gas cooker.[217]

---

210 Milltown village inquiry, pp. 17, 104–5; *Irish Times*, 8 October 1952, p. 8.

211 DCC Housing Files, OSI map accompanying the Milltown Village Area Compulsory Purchaser Order 1952.

212 Milltown village inquiry, p. 22.

213 Milltown village inquiry, pp. 88, 90.

214 Milltown village inquiry, p. 82.

215 RD 167/197/111944, RD 167/197/111945. See Chapter 4 for the origins of this and other property in Milltown village.

216 Milltown village inquiry, pp. 89–91.

217 Milltown village inquiry, p. 86.

Objector and publican Frank McKenna had bought the old Hackett's public house (no. 90 Main Street, Milltown) and 17 cottages in 1943 (Pl. 9). According to his legal counsel, Liam Cosgrave TD, the pub had been closed for 12 months before McKenna bought it and renovated it. The new owner built up a very substantial trade and established a good clientele as well as demolishing five of the old cottages adjacent to the pub.[218] As the McKenna's pub was not listed in the clearance area Cosgrave argued that it could be left out of the village redevelopment scheme. This point was rebutted by the Corporation's chief planning officer, who stated that the pub had to be demolished to facilitate the Milltown Road widening scheme.[219]

The inquiry also gives interesting insights into contemporary attitudes among the inhabitants and the bureaucrats towards poverty and the level of State intervention that should be undertaken to relieve it. The following extract from the Corporation's health inspector concerning an elderly couple reveals a complete absence of any sense of entitlement on their part, an attitude that has practically died out in Irish society today:

> *I would also like to say that strange as it may appear local officers do have a little sentiment in their make-up. I have a great deal of sympathy with the Grant family. They are of a type that is fast disappearing in this country. The two old people are nearly 80 years of age and they have never sought anything either from the State or from the Local Authority and all they ask now is to be left alone. There is no doubt whatever that the house is not fit for human habitation if it ever could have been described as being fit, but the question of the small garden from which these people derive their living [rearing pigs] is another matter.*[220]

The Corporation's medical officer of health placed considerable importance on providing good ventilation by having adequate windows and fireplaces in living accommodation. Such contemporary concerns are somewhat ironic given the modern preoccupation with draught exclusion and energy efficiency ratings. During cross examination Dr Harbison was asked for his opinion on the accommodation in no. 30 Main Street, which was owned by Patrick O'Neill:

> *When you said the house was unfit for human habitation, would you consider if you had three rooms with two people in them, that there was adequate ventilation with three rooms, three windows and three fireplaces? [Answer] If I was asked if these rooms were adequate for a couple married six months ago, I would object, but if I was asked about a couple 25 years married and no children I might take a very different view of it.*[221]

Miss Elizabeth Bradfield was the landlady of three terraced houses and a shop (called the Mascot) which were located between the main bridge over the River Dodder and the Packhorse Bridge on the south side of Milltown Road heading towards Dartry, which she had purchased for £300 in January 1952. These four properties were nos 75, 76, 77 and 79 Milltown village. Three of the residential cottages had yards backing onto the River Dodder but otherwise they were well elevated from the river. Miss Bradfield's solicitor told the inquiry that his client's property was occupied by

218 Milltown village inquiry, pp. 60–1.

219 Milltown village inquiry, pp. 63–4.

220 Milltown village inquiry, p. 26. The Grants' house and garden were located at the end of a laneway (Lee's Lane) off the north side of the village main street where the Riverside apartments are now.

221 Milltown village inquiry, pp. 74–5.

weekly tenants. Nos 75, 76 and 77 were each let at 9*s*. a week while no. 79 was let at 10*s*. a week.[222]

When Miss Bradfield was cross examined by Counsel for Dublin Corporation, she was taken to task for reletting the houses when she was aware that they had been condemned by the Corporation. The following evidence neatly illustrates the economics and housing demands that were at play in Milltown in the early 1950s:

Mr McGonigal S.C. Were these houses occupied by tenants when you bought them?
Miss Bradfield: Yes
Were they the same tenants? – I have two the same. The other two did not want to leave, but they felt that they might have to move out and that they should ask for houses in the district.
They went to Corporation houses? – Yes.
Since you purchased two of the houses were vacant? – Three were vacant.
Then you agree that at one time all three houses were vacant? – Yes
When did you make those new lettings? - About six weeks ago.
That is since the question of acquisition by the Corporation became a really live issue? – Yes
How long were they vacant? – One was vacant a week and the other people went in straight away.
There was no great interval? – No.
What is the head rent you pay? – I pay £13 on the lot, but I recover £4 from the shop [i.e. no. 78 Main Street, called the 'Mascot'].
You really pay £9 head rent and the rates on £13? – Yes.
Mr Arnold [Bradfield's solicitor]: Would you tell the inspector what profit you have out of the four houses at present? – Up to £60 [per annum].
Explain why you relet the houses after you got possession? – I realised that it would be better to put people into them, and it would be better than if they were not occupied.[223]

The main concern raised by Dr Harbison about Miss Bradfield's properties was the sleeping arrangements in three of her houses. The sleeping quarters were located in attic space in the roofs with very low ceilings and accessed by extremely steep stairs.[224] He had this to say about house no. 75 Milltown Road which was at the end of the terrace beside the Packhorse Bridge:

From the area of cubic capacity of these attic sleeping rooms I do consider, as they are at present, that they are definitely unfit for sleeping accommodation. Especially if they are depending on rooflight or skylight, the probability is that if the weather is bad it will be kept closed and that would cause serious interference with ventilation. I am uneasy about the question of such houses let to families with young children. I don't think it is a very safe approach to the bedroom.[225]

The final comment by Dr Harbison is the only time during the inquiry where safety concerns were raised, in this case the risk of an accident to a child caused by climbing steep stairs. The issue of fire safety was never once mentioned by any of the architects or health inspectors, yet in many cases families were crowded into multi-unit accommodation with totally inadequate emergency egress and with no means of extinguishing a fire (an outside tap hardly

222 Milltown village inquiry, pp. 46–8.

223 Milltown village inquiry, p. 48.

224 Milltown village inquiry, pp. 49–50.

225 Milltown village inquiry, p. 53.

counts). Perhaps the pervasive dampness of the houses and the proximity of the River Dodder led to insouciance. Remarkably, there are no newspaper reports of any fires occurring in Milltown village in the eighteenth, nineteenth or early twentieth centuries. It is very unlikely that such absence reflects historical experience. In fact, on two separate occasions serious fires broke out at religious institutions in the 1930s and 1940s. In 1936 a fire caused extensive damage to an annex attached to the Marists' College at Mount St Mary's (Casino/Emmet House) in 1936.[226] A few years later a fatal fire broke out at Milltown Park in the early morning of 11 February 1949 which destroyed the Finlay wing of the Jesuit headquarters and resulted in the death of thirty-three-year-old Fr James Johnston SJ who was cut off from the stairs by the fire. Several more of the 32 priests and scholastics who were sleeping in their dormitories would have been killed had the alarm not been raised by one of their number shortly after 5 a.m.[227]

The public inquiry into the Milltown village compulsory purchase order concluded on 18 October 1952. The upshot was that on 28 May 1953 the Minister for Local Government and Public Health confirmed the order (with modifications) with effect from 19 August 1953.[228] The most important modifications made to the order was that St Philip's orchard, the terrace of houses nos 1 to 3 Milltown Hill and other properties and yards on the north side of the main street were excluded altogether from the compulsory purchase order.[229] The final designation of properties to be included in the clearance and redevelopment areas or excluded from the order altogether was drawn up by hand on a large-scale plan of the village (Map 22).[230] The area marked blue on the north side of the main street was excluded from the order. The open spaces marked yellow adjacent to the River Dodder were acquired for road widening, a public carpark and for amenity purposes as part of the redevelopment of the clearance area. All of the buildings coloured pink which had been condemned as uninhabitable by Dr Harbison made up the clearance area.[231]

An arbitration hearing was fixed for 28 June 1955 at City Hall:

> *to ascertain the amount of compensation demanded by the several claimants in disputed cases and the amount which the Corporation will be willing to pay, and to hear all parties interested as may appear before him [the arbitrator].*[232]

The arbitration proceedings were only covered very briefly by one national newspaper. The *Irish Times* reported that a claim for £900 had been made by the representatives of James Donegan, late of 29 Main Street, but that the Corporation had offered £500 for the property. The arbitrator reserved his decision which was not subsequently made public.[233]

Aside from arbitration, Dublin Corporation was able to reach satisfactory arrangements

---

226 *Irish Press*, 30 January 1936, p. 1; *Irish Times*, 30 January 1936, p.5

227 *Evening Herald*, 11 February 1949, p. 1; Irish Press, 12 February 1949, p. 1; *Irish Independent*, 12 February 1949, p. 7.

228 *Irish Times*, 31 July 1953, p. 9.

229 Minutes of the Municipal Council of the City of Dublin, 1953, pp. 156–77.

230 Milltown Village Area Compulsory Purchase Order 1952, map index no. 5982, plan no. 3440A dated 20 July 1953.

231 Minutes of the Municipal Council of the City of Dublin, 1953, pp. 156–7.

232 *Irish Times*, 27 May 1955, p. 9.

233 *Irish Times*, 29 June 1955, p. 7. Donegan was survived by five children (four of whom were minors) who had no source of income apart from 29 Main Street.

with other interested parties in the village. For example, two friendly societies, the Milltown Tontine and Benefit Society and the St Gall's Friendly Christian Burial Society, had to vacate no. 38A Main Street (also known as Castleview) as it was scheduled for demolition. In 1954 the Corporation compensated the two societies by granting them a long lease (150 years at £1 rent p.a.) over a site comprising 540 square yards where nos 1–4 Strand Cottages were due to be demolished.[234] Three years later, in response to an application received from the parish priest of Donnybrook, Fr Condon, Dublin Corporation proposed to sell a small plot of two perches of ground to the Dublin archdiocese to facilitate the erection of a suitable entrance to the Church of Ss Gall and Columbanus.[235]

THE END OF OLD MILLTOWN VILLAGE

The villagers of old Milltown were conscious of the end of an era and the dawning of a new one in their lives. A photograph taken in the 1950s gives some idea of the community spirit that existed at that time, as well as highlighting the decrepitude that had descended on the old village buildings (Pl. 61).

Dublin Corporation housing officials began removing the last of the village's inhabitants in the summer of 1955. One local woman, Mrs Donnelly, refused to leave and so the workmen removed her furniture and left it outside her cottage on the pavement. Thankfully, the situation was resolved later on the same day when the Corporation gave her the key to a new home and transported her belongs there.[236] On 1 September 1955 the *Irish Times* reported that all the villagers had in recent weeks moved to their new Corporation homes as the process of demolishing the old cottages progressed.[237] Although the journalist highlighted the benefits that would accrue to motorists after the village was cleared and the main road was widened, he spared a thought for the old community life that was about to vanish for good:

> *Transporting the people of Milltown from their old, condemned cottages to the housing schemes in other parts of Dublin has been no easy task, for the villagers clung tenaciously to the claim that they were a community apart from Dublin. Although the expanding city engulfed their village, they still referred to those not born in the village as 'runners-in'. An 80-year-old woman who had lived there most of her life was still regarded as a 'runner-in' up to the time of her death, which took place recently.*[238]

Demolition work continued apace. On 14 September 1955 the *Irish Examiner* reported that 'at the moment, the demolition squads are hard at it changing the landscape. Already the greater portion of the age-old village has disappeared and the residents have moved to other districts.'[239] When the demolition squads had finished their work only a handful of the pre-demolition houses were left in the village area on the north bank of the River Dodder: Geraldine

---

234 Minutes of the Municipal Council of the City of Dublin, 1954, p. 127; Milltown Village Area Compulsory Purchase Order 1952, map index no. 5982, plan no. 3440A dated 20 July 1953 (manuscript note).

235 Minutes of the Municipal Council of the City of Dublin, 1957, p. 50.

236 *Irish Press*, 6 August 1955, p. 2.

237 *Irish Times*, 1 September 1955, p. 7.

238 *Irish Times*, 1 September 1955, p. 7. A photograph accompanying the report shows that most of the south side of the main street had been cleared by this time.

239 *Irish Examiner*, 14 September 1955, p. 4.

Plate 61. Milltown village main street and villagers prior to clearance work, c. 1952 (courtesy of Mary Long)

House, nos 1–7 Geraldine Terrace and nos 5–8 Strand Terrace behind Geraldine House. On the south bank of the River Dodder at Concrete, Mowlds Cottages, the Dew Drop Inn, Marble Hall and Field's (formerly Hackett's) Cottages were demolished at the behest of Dublin County Council. Bankside Cottages were left in situ and Old Bridge House managed to survive the wrecking ball until 1962.[240]

Although Milltown village was cleared by October 1955 it took several years for the road widening to happen. It seems that cutbacks in Dublin Corporation's budget were responsible. In October 1954 the Corporation's housing committee had proposed to spend £33,000 on demolition and road widening in Milltown, but as late as 1961 Alderman Sean Moore was advised by the City Manager that 'a local widening scheme opposite the Marian Hall and the Church is envisaged for construction next year subject to provision being made in the estimates'.[241] The official change of attitude is rather ironic given the Corporation's insistence during the 1952 public inquiry that the road widening was an urgent traffic safety requirement, and could not be held up under any circumstances.

AFTERMATH OF DEMOLITION

As we have seen, Dublin Corporation had been planning since the late 1940s for the future housing needs of the wider Milltown and Farranboley community. The Corporation's task

240 Interview with Barry Farrell, 30 December 2016.

241 *Irish Press*, 26 October 1954, p. 7; Minutes of the Municipal Council of the City of Dublin 1961, p. 221.

was essentially completed by the autumn 1955 with the rehousing of the last of the villagers. Thereafter the Catholic Church took over as the most important agent of change in Milltown for the remainder of the decade.

Since 1953 plans had been put in train to build a parish hall and theatre on a site which lay to the west of Ss Gall and Columbanus church on which terraced cottages and Castleview had previously stood. The site had been excluded from the Corporation's compulsory purchase order and now benefited from additional land to the rear in Mount St Anne's convent which was donated by the Sisters of Charity. The extent of the Church's input and control over the project can be gleaned from the fact that the design for the hall was submitted to Archbishop McQuaid for his approval.[242] The extra ground furnished by the Sisters of Charity enabled the architect to design a large building fully equipped along modern lines, as the following contemporary account explains:

> *The finished building has evoked much appreciation. The hall has a cream and blue interior, red curtains, tip-up seats and is oil heated. The stage would do honour to any big picture theatre, with 'flies' for scenery, a modern electric dimming system, and – above all – plenty of space for big productions. The seating capacity is five hundred. This – the Marian Hall – was opened on Sunday, 28 November 1955, and since that night has been used for social, dramatic and musical gatherings, almost non-stop.*[243]

The Marian Hall became the second home of an amateur dramatic society, called the Bernadette Players, which recruited roughly 30 local people to the stage.[244] Some 50 years later the Marian Hall was demolished in the first decade of the twenty-first century as part of the development of the Sisters of Charity's extensive lands in Milltown. A block of apartments and a pharmacy stand on the site today.

Another development of considerable long-term benefit for Milltown and the surrounding area was the opening of a senior school for girls on 3 September 1956 by the nuns at Mount St Anne's. Initally, 22 girls enrolled in the new secondary school, but numbers grew and so in 1959 the nuns built a large modern three-storey school block on the north side of Milltown Road, just below St Anne's girls' primary school, that was capable of accommodating 300 pupils.[245] Besides their secondary school the Sisters of Charity undertook an impressive array of philanthropic and community work at St Anne's:

> *The Irish Sisters of Charity have encouraged an integration policy with other students which, over the years, has led to the inclusion of partially sighted girls from the Merrion School for the Blind, children with learning difficulties, overseas students from Africa and Asia and a more recent development in the school's curriculum is the inclusion of a Vocational Preparation Training Programme which aims to bridge a gap between traditional academic programme and the world of work. Within this diverse educational establishment, the Irish Sisters of Charity sees its primary*

242 *Souvenir of the Blessing and Dedication of the Church of the Immaculate Virgin Mary of the Miraculous Medal at Clonskeagh.*

243 *Souvenir of the Blessing and Dedication of the Church of the Immaculate Virgin Mary of the Miraculous Medal at Clonskeagh.*

244 The names of 29 Milltown/Farranboley members are listed in the *Souvenir of the Blessing and Dedication of the Church of the Immaculate Virgin Mary of the Miraculous Medal at Clonskeagh.*

245 *Souvenir of the Blessing and Dedication of the Church of the Immaculate Virgin Mary of the Miraculous Medal at Clonskeagh; Catholic Standard,* 16 October 1959, p. 8.

function as providing a centre of Catholic formation by means of spiritual, academic, cultural and athletic programmes where students are educated for life.[246]

All of this activity was very impressive. Yet, with the benefit of social progress and, critically, twenty-first century research and investigation, we now know that Irish social mores and Catholic religiosity – which were at their apogee in the mid-twentieth century – were very harmful to some unfortunate groups in Irish society. The same publication that so praised the educational efforts of the Sisters of Charity at St Anne's had this to say about the Order's Magdalen laundry in nearby Donnybrook:

The women are occupied in laundry-work, which helps to support the home, but no press of work is ever allowed to interfere with the spiritual duties of the day, or the annual retreat. Not all the inmates are 'penitents' in the sense usually understood, but all are souls who, for one reason or another, need the safeguard of an institution such as this. Under the same roof with their loving Saviour, and provided with every spiritual help, they are enabled to lead better lives.[247]

The *pièce de résistance* in the ecclesiastical building programme was the dedication on 8 September 1957 of the new Catholic church on Bird Avenue, Clonskeagh, its site having been donated by the Marist fathers of Mount St Mary's (formerly Casino, now Emmet House). This massive redbrick building was designed in a hybrid style of Romanesque architecture that was commonly adopted by the Catholic church at this time. Bird Avenue and its environs were then part of the parish of Donnybrook, but a little later Clonskeagh became a parish in its own right in 1965.[248] The new church, which was formally named the Church of the Immaculate Virgin Mary of the Miraculous Medal, became the focal point for Catholic worship for inhabitants in the new housing estates at Farranboley and Windy Arbour. The massive, confident structure must have made the old pre-emancipation church of Ss Gall and Columbanus in Milltown seem very outdated, standing rather forlornly in open space formerly occupied by a vibrant village community.

New Catholic religious congregations and educational institutions moved to Milltown in the 1950s too. In 1950 the Jesuits acquired the two Bewley residences, Sandford Hill and Sandford Grove, and established Gonzaga College on the extensive grounds.[249] Opus Dei acquired Nullamore and seven acres of grounds at Classon's Bridge in 1953, and in the early 1960s the Religious Society of Jesus and Mary bought St James's House at the eastern end of Milltown Road.[250] Thus by the middle of the 1950s a huge portion of the land on the northern side of Milltown Road from Sandford Road as far as South Hill (opposite The Dropping Well pub) was occupied or owned by the Catholic Church, with the exception of

246 *Souvenir of the Blessing and Dedication of the Church of the Immaculate Virgin Mary of the Miraculous Medal at Clonskeagh.*

247 *Souvenir of the Blessing and Dedication of the Church of the Immaculate Virgin Mary of the Miraculous Medal at Clonskeagh.* The author is unknown but it may have been Fr T.B. Condon, PP of Donnybrook.

248 *Souvenir of the Blessing and Dedication of the Church of the Immaculate Virgin Mary of the Miraculous Medal at Clonskeagh;* Peter Costello, *Dublin Churches* (Dublin, 1989), p. 190; Holland, Clonskeagh, pp. 305–9.

249 The two demesnes had formed the northern end of Milltown townland in the 1830s but by 1950 they had long since become associated with Ranelagh.

250 *Souvenir of the Blessing and Dedication of the Church of the Immaculate Virgin Mary of the Miraculous Medal at Clonskeagh;* Thom's Directory 1962, p. 336. The Mount Sandford townhouse complex replaced St James's House in 1989.

Milltown Colonnade, Elm House, Elm Grove House, Rydalmount and St Philip's, which was later acquired by Alexandra College. Lastly, the Marist fathers owned several acres of land fronting the Dundrum Road between Milltown Bridge Road and Bird Avenue, which they had acquired in 1920 with Casino, which were renamed by them Mount St Mary's.[251]

The focus of what was left of old Milltown was now on the summit of Milltown Road before its descent to Geraldine Terrace. Milltown post office was relocated from Castleview to the rear of a newsagents and tobacconists called The Barn (now the Enchanted Florist).[252] In the 1950s and 1960s The Barn was owned by Michael Brennan.[253] Michael's brother Thomas owned the grocery store and off-licence across the road at no. 137 Milltown Road, which had also been owned by the O'Neill family.[254] Rather confusingly, Thomas Brennan's licensed premises was variously named The Barn Stores or The Park Stores.[255] Thomas's sons Francis and John are well-known hoteliers and television personalities. As children they lived in Milltown in the 1950s before their father took over a new commercial venture in Sandyford. Their cousin Michael Brennan still lives in Milltown and sells Christmas trees every December at Milltown Colonnade.[256]

The two Barn shops on Milltown Hill were advantageously located to benefit from the school children of St Anne's girls' schools and the boys' national school beside Ramleh Villas. The regular large crowds attending Shamrock Rovers FC's games in Glenmalure Park would have provided plenty of regular customers too. For a brief period in the late 1950s a ladies' hair stylist called Phyleen operated out of a small house beside The Barn Stores off-licence, at no. 134 Milltown Road.[257] This establishment might have expected to pick up custom from the women of Ramleh Park and Ramleh Villas, but for whatever reason the business ceased and the house became derelict (Pl. 62). The Spar shopping centre stands on the site now.

MODERN TIMES

The 1960s turned out to be a very quiet decade for Milltown after the eventful changes of the 1950s. The only visible development on Milltown Road that took place in the 1960s occurred in 1960. In that year a petrol station and car dealership were built by Autocars Ireland Limited on a site beside Shamrock Rovers FC's grounds at Glenmalure Park, which had originally formed part of the grounds of Elm House.[258] In the following decade the Gheel training centre for autistic adults and the St Joseph's school for Travellers were set up in new premises built behind the car dealership.

The growth of primary and secondary schools such as St Anne's (1956), Gonzaga College

251 Kerr, *Emmet's Casino*, p. 8.

252 Thom's Directory 1952, p. 816; *Souvenir of the Blessing and Dedication of the Church of the Immaculate Virgin Mary of the Miraculous Medal at Clonskeagh.*

253 Thom's Directory 1952, p. 816 and 1967, p. 408.

254 Thom's Directory 1952, p. 816.

255 Thom's Directory 1952, p. 816, 1967, p. 408; *Evening Herald*, 21 April 1961, p. 17.

256 RTE Radio broadcast, 'Sunday with Miriam', 21 January 2018.

257 Thom's Directory 1952, p. 816. *Souvenir of the Blessing and Dedication of the Church of the Immaculate Virgin Mary of the Miraculous Medal at Clonskeagh.*

258 *Irish Independent*, 4 March 1960, p. 8.

Plate 62. Derelict houses on Milltown Hill, Milltown Road, c. 1960 (courtesy of the Irish Architectural Archive)

(1950) and Alexandra College (1972), coupled with the introduction of State-funded secondary education and the relocation of University College Dublin to the Belfield campus in Clonskeagh, laid the foundations for the development of Milltown as a firmly middle-class suburb. The increasing numbers of private cars and commuter traffic from the 1960s onwards meant that Dublin Corporation developed a policy of widening the Milltown Road from its junction with Sandford and Clonskeagh roads in the east, to Classon's Bridge at its western end, whenever planning permission was sought for a housing development along the road. The effects of the Corporation's incomplete road strategy in Milltown can be seen by the number of green verges between the road and boundary walls and the irregular width of the road. Dublin Corporation had more ambitious plans than widening Milltown Road, though. In 1975 Dublin Corporation refused to grant planning permission to the Jesuits of Milltown Park, who wanted to build eight houses on Milltown Road beyond Milltown Colonnade (where Abbeyfield is now), because 'the development would prevent the attainment of the planned road from Palmerston Park to Milltown Road'.[259] Thankfully the proposed road never progressed beyond the drawing board. Had it gone ahead the link road would have added considerably to traffic congestion at the eastern end of Milltown Road as well as taking away a considerable portion of the grounds of Gonzaga College and Milltown Park. More positively, in the 1970s Dublin Corporation compulsorily acquired derelict land where the old Henshaw iron mills and millpond formerly stood on the south bank of the River Dodder (Pl. 13)

259 Dublin City Council Planning Files, plan no. 2560/75.

and laid out the linear park which now extends from Clonskeagh Bridge to Classon's Bridge.

Just as the 1950s was a watershed for the inhabitants of Milltown village, the 50-year period beginning in 1968 has been hugely transformative for Milltown with the growth of high-density infill developments of apartments and town houses, as the table below shows.

Table 2. Apartments and town houses built in Milltown since 1968

Year	Name	Location	Development	Units
1968	Ramleh Close	Milltown Road	Detached houses	25
1975	Richmond Court	Richmond Avenue South	Apartments	70
1977	Grove House	Milltown Road	Apartments	20
1978	Milltown Grove	Dundrum Road	Apartments	48
1980	Rowan & Cedar Hall	Prospect Lane	Apartments	72
1980	The Orchard, Grove House	Milltown Road	Apartments	20
1984	Milltown Hill & Court	Milltown Road	Apartments & town houses	40
1985	Millbrook Village	Prospect Lane	Town houses	53
1985	Palmerston Grove	Prospect Lane	Detached houses	20
1989	Mount Sandford	Milltown Road	Town houses & bungalow	44
1989	Crannagh	Prospect Lane	Town houses	17
1989	Thorncliff	Dundrum Road	Apartments	20
1991	Glenmalure Square	Milltown Road	Town houses & detached houses	76
1994	Riverside	Milltown Road	Apartments	14
1994	Churchfields	Dundrum Road	Detached & semi-detached houses	76
1995	Abbeyfield	Milltown Road	Town houses	88
1996	Garrynure	Milltown Road	Town houses	13
1996	Shanagarry	Milltown Road	Apartments	105
1997	Woodhaven	Milltown Bridge Road	Apartments	21
2000	Mount St Anne's	Milltown Road	Apartments and town houses	458
2002	Dodderbank	Dundrum Road	Apartments	45
2004	Marian & Maple Hall	Milltown Road	Apartments	217
2015	Richmond Close	Dundrum Road	Terraced houses	6

Note: The year given to some developments and the stated number of units may vary slightly.

All of the homes built since 1968 are located within a half mile radius of the Catholic church, Ss Gall and Columbanus, in what was once the heart of the old village of Milltown.

CONCLUSION

In the modern age, with its emphasis on personal privacy and self-containment, there is an ongoing need to develop and foster a real sense of community in Milltown among the thousands of new residents.[260] Milltown and the surrounding areas are well served by secondary schools but there is a chronic shortage of primary school places. Arising from this the Milltown School Initiative was set up in March 2015.[261] In 2017 St Philip's church, Temple Road, celebrated its sesquicentennial and, two years later, the bicentenary of the old Catholic chapel in Milltown was commemorated after that building had undergone extensive refurbishment. Both occasions were marked by a large attendance by their respective parishioners, with a varied programme of liturgical and social celebrations and historical exhibitions.

There are plenty of other challenges – traffic congestion, overcapacity on the Luas green line at peak times and a lack of affordable housing in Milltown.[262] Scully's Field remains derelict despite years of optimistic plans and promises made by local politicians. Yet despite these problems, if the earl of Milltown, Joseph Leeson, was alive today he could truthfully repeat his assertion made in 1751 that Milltown was a 'flourishing town'.[263] The wheel has turned full circle. ■

260 In 2016 the population of Rathmines East B Electoral Division, which includes the part of Milltown on the north bank of the River Dodder as well as parts of Clonskeagh, Donnybrook and Ranelagh, had over 6,000 inhabitants: http://www.citypopulation.de/php/ireland-dublin.php?cityid=02135 (accessed 17 April 2019).

261 Letter from Kevin Humphries TD to local residents/constituents dated 15 July 2015.

262 According to the Central Statistics Office, the average monthly rent for a two-bedroom property in Milltown in 2018 was €1,904.75: https://www.cso.ie/px/pxeirestat/Statire/SelectVarVal/saveselections.asp (accessed 17 April 2019).

263 Letter from Joseph Leeson to Sir Robert Wilmot, 15 July 1751 (Derbyshire Record Office, D3155/WH/3442).

Bibliography

A PRIMARY SOURCES

1. MANUSCRIPTS

Derbyshire Record Office, D3155/WH/3442, Sir Robert Wilmot papers.

Dublin City Archives, Rathmines and Rathgar UDC minute books and miscellaneous papers.

NAI, MS 2/476/15-16, Bryan Bolger Papers.

NAI, Business Records 56, Dublin Laundry Company Limited.

NAI, Cholera Papers, MS 2/440/8.

NAI, Famine Relief Commission Manuscripts.

NAI, Landed Estates Court Rentals.

NAI, QRO/4/3/28, 'Report and Valuation of the Lands of Roebuck in the Parish of Taney Barony of Rathdown and County of Dublin made by order of the Right Honourable and the Honourable the Commissioners of his Majesty's Woods Forests Lnd Revenues Works and Building By Brassington and Gale 1832'.

NAI, VO/3.1583, Boundary Register of Donnybrook Parish in the Barony of Rathdown and County of the City of Dublin, 31 March 1837.

NAI, MS M/4912, 'List of Freeholders in Dublin, 1767'.

NAI, Tithe Aplotment Book, Diocese of Dublin, Parish of St Peter, Ranelagh and Milltown Road, assessed 30 December 1833, pp. 17–18.

NAI, MS CRF 1848/O/16, 'William Smith O'Brien Petition, 1848–49'.

NAI, ED1/29/47/2, National School Papers, Milltown County Dublin.

NAI, Small Accessions no. 1/704, Drury Papers.

NLI, MS 5957, Members of the Fenian Brotherhood (Terence Kelly).

NLI, MS 46,594, Patrick Doyle papers.

NLI, Prints and Drawings 1969 TX 26, Cecilia Margaret Nairn née Campbell, 'Old Clonskeagh Bridge' and 'Clonskeagh Bridge'.

NLI, Prints and Drawings ET A354, 'Old Bridge at Clonskeagh', unsigned and undated hand-coloured etching *c.* 1800–20.

NLI, Prints and Drawings PD 2084 (TX) 1, 'Two figures on a bridge with single arch at Milltown', pencil drawing by Samuel Brocas.

NLI, Prints and Drawings, PD 2064 TX 92, 'Figures crossing the old bridge at Milltown', pencil drawing by Samuel Brocas.

RIA, MS 24E37, Minute Book of the Florists' Club of Dublin.

RCB Library P654, St Philip's Parish Vestry Book.

RCB Library, D6/64, Dublin diocesan papers, St Philip's Parish, Milltown.

RCB Library, P654/15/2, parish maps of St Philip's, Milltown.

RCB Library, P654/27, miscellaneous documents concerning St Philip's Parish, Milltown.

Jesuit Archives, IE IJA/FM/Mill/5/2/, Milltown Park papers.

Trinity College, Dublin, MS 809, fols 295r-295v, deposition of John Bacon, 29 January 1641.

Trinity College, Dublin, MS 810, fols 230r-230v, deposition of Hugh Booth, 6 January 1644.

UCD Archives, Mulcahy Papers.

UCD, Department of Folklore, County Dublin Book 795, Milltown, Uppercross, County Dublin.

2. REPORTS AND ACTS OF PARLIAMENT

Report from the Committee on the Alnage Laws of Ireland: Appendix: Minutes of Evidence, H.C. 1817 (315), viii, 5.

Grand Jury Presentments, Dublin: Accounts of All Sums presented to be raised off the City of Dublin by the different term Grand Juries from the year 1807 inclusive, to the 1st January 1821, H.C. 1821 (477), xx, 325.

An Act to regulate the Labour of Children and young persons in the mills and factories of the United Kingdom (3 & 4 Will IV, c. 103) (29 August 1833).

Appendix to the First Report of the Commissioners appointed to inquire into the corporations in Ireland: Report on the City of Dublin, Part 1, H.C. 1835 (25), xxvii.

First report from his Majesty's Commissioners for inquiring into the poorer classes in Ireland: Appendix C, Part II, Report on the City of Dublin and Supplement containing answers to queries, with Addenda to Appendix (A), and Communications, H.C. 1836 (35), xxx.

Reports from the Assistant Hand-Loom Weavers Commissioners; viz. Report by C.G. Otway, Esq; on Ireland, Part III, H.C. 1840, (43), xxiii.

An Act to alter the Number and define the Boundaries of the several Baronies of the County of Dublin (5 & 6 Vict. c. xcvi) (10 August 1842).

Local Acts – Preliminary Inquiries: 9 & 10 Vict. C. 106. Report by A. Hayward and C.P. Brassington on the Rathmines Improvement Bill to the Commissioners of Her Majesty's Woods, Forests, Land Revenues, Works and Buildings, H.C. 1847 (124), xxvi.

An Act for extending the Rathmines and Rathgar Township so as to include therein the adjoining townland of Milltown in the County of Dublin for the establishment of a Fire Brigade and for other purposes (43 & 44 Vict.) (2 August 1880).

3. MAPS

Down Survey, 'The Barony of 1/2 Rathdowne in the County of Dublin by Williem Farrand and Williem Storck' (copied by the Ordnance Survey Office, Southampton in 1908 and reprinted by the Ordnance Survey of Ireland in 1927).

Down Survey, 'The Parishes of Doonabrooke & Tannee in the 1/2 Barony of Rathdowne by Wm Farrand'.

'A Survey of the above Denominations being part of the Estate of Joseph Leeson Esq in the Parishes of Donnybrook and St Kevins and County of Dublin: Miltown *[sic] and its parts in the Parish of St Kevins and Mouls holding in the Parish of Donnybrook Containing in the whole as in the particulars may appear Surveyed on the 22 day of March in the year of our Lord God 1718/9'.*

'An Actual Survey of the County of Dublin, on the same scale as those of Middlesex, Oxford, Barks, & Buckinghamshire, by John Rocque; 1760'.

'A Plan of the City Suburbs and Environs of Dublin by John Rocque ... with additions and improvements by Mr Bernard Scale 1773'.

NLI, Longfield map collection, MS 21 F. 52/021, 'A survey of the Demesne of Clonskeagh in the Co. Dublin belonging to Geo. Thompson Esq'.

NLI, Longfield map collection, MS 21 F. 52/41a, 'A survey of part of the River Dodder between Milltown and Clonskeagh done for Geo. Thompson Esq by J.L. 1812 Nov'.

NLI, Longfield map collection, MS 21 F. 53/125, 'A survey of the demesne of Fairyland at Milltown in the County of Dublin belonging to W.C. Hogan esq by J Longfield, 1821'.

NLI, Longfield map collection, MS 21 F. 53/123, 'A map of the woollen factory at Milltown, County Dublin belonging to Burke, esq. Surveyed by Jn. Longfield, 1821'.

NAI, MS 2574, 'Survey of part of the farm of St Sepulchre by Brassington and Greene, 1826'.

NAI, VO/3.1584, Sketch map of the parish of Donnybrook in the Barony of Rathdown and County of the City of Dublin, 23 August 1830 by the Boundary Department of the Ordnance Survey of Ireland.

NAI, QRO/4/3/28, 'Map of the Lands of Roebuck in the Parish of Taney Barony of Rathdown and County of Dublin made by order of the Right Honourable and the Honourable the Commissioners of his Majesty's Woods Forests Land Revenues Works and Building By Brassington and Gale 1832'.

NAI, MS 2754, 'A map of premises on the north side of the River Dodder between the turn of the road from Rathmines to Milltown and Classon's Bridge, 1833'.

NAI, MS 999/355/1/10, Map of Milltown village appended to lease dated 4 July 1837 Robert Dry to Patrick Hackett.

NLI, Longfield map collection, MS 21 F. 53/126, 'Map of premises at Milltown for Mr Rooke by William Longfield, 1838'.

NLI, Longfield map collection, MS 21 F.53/124, 'A survey of ground at Milltown for Miss Hunt, 1839'.

OSI, Co. Dublin, Sheet 22, six inches to one statute mile, surveyed in 1837 and corrected in 1843.

NLI, MS 16.G.49 (17), 'Map and survey of that part of the estate of the Right Hon. Viscount Palmerston situate at Rathmines in the County of Dublin, surveyed in June 1861, by William Gartland'.

NLI, MS 16.G. 49 (18), 'Ground design for an arrangement of small villas etc occupying about seventy acres of land situated between Rathmines, Milltown and Sandford in the County of the city of Dublin, the property of the Right Hon. the Viscount Palmerston' (unsigned and undated).

Valuation Office, Town Plans, Plan 17, South Dublin Union, Milltown, scale 5 feet to one statute mile, one undated and the other dated 6 April 1852.

OSI, Co. Dublin, Rathmines and Rathgar and Pembroke Townships, Sheet XXII.8, five feet to one statute mile, surveyed in 1865 and revised in 1879.

OSI, Co. Dublin, Rathmines and Rathgar Township, Sheet XXII.18, five feet to one statute mile, surveyed in 1878 and revised in 1882.

OSI, Co. Dublin, Rathmines and Rathgar Township, Sheet XXII.28, five feet to one statute mile, surveyed in 1879 and revised in 1882.

OSI, Co. Dublin, Dublin/Rathdown/Uppercross, Sheet XII.4, 25 inches to one statute mile (edition of 1911), surveyed in 1837, revised in 1908.

OSI, Co. Dublin, Dublin/Rathdown, Sheet 22. IV, 25 inches to one statute mile (edition of 1938), surveyed in 1837, revised in 1936.

Dublin City Archives, Rathmines and Rathgar UDC papers, UDC/1/9/13, lay-out plan for Milltown housing scheme, 2 August 1920.

Dublin City Archives, Milltown Village Area Compulsory Purchase Order 1952, map index no. 5982, plan no. 3440A dated 20 July 1953.

B SECONDARY WORKS

Adelman, Julianna, *Civilised by Beasts: Animals and Urban Change in Nineteenth-Century Dublin* (Manchester, 2020).

Andrews, J.H., *Two maps of Dublin and its surroundings by John Rocque* (Kent, 1977, unpaginated).

Anon., *The Dropping Well 1847–1997: Celebrating 150 Years of Licenced Heritage* (undated, Coachhouse Publications).

Anon., *'Archbishop Bulkeley's report on the diocese of Dublin, 1630', Irish Ecclesiastical Record, 5*, (Dublin, 1869), pp. 145–66.

Anon., *Milltown in Brief ... 1879–1995*, Irish Sisters of Charity, Circular Letter 26 April 1995.

Anon., *'Milltown Park and some of its owners' in Memorials of the Irish Province S.J. Centenary Year 1814–1914* (Dublin, 1914), pp. 3–24.

Anon., 'New Discoveries at Rathfarnham Castle', *Archaeology Ireland*, 28, no. 4, issue 110 (Winter 2014), pp. 4–5.

Anon., *Souvenir of the Blessing and Dedication of the Church of the Immaculate Virgin Mary of the Miraculous Medal at Clonskeagh* (Dublin, 1957).

Archer, Joseph, *Statistical Survey of the County of Dublin with observations on the means of improvement; drawn up for the consideration, and by order of the Dublin Society* (Dublin, 1801).

Armstrong, E.C.R., *Catalogue of Irish gold ornaments in the collection of the Royal Irish Academy* (Dublin, 1920).

Ball, Francis Elrington, *'The Battle of Rathmines', Journal of the Royal Society of Antiquaries of Ireland*, 32, no. 3 (1902), pp. 246–56.

Ball, Francis Elrington, *The history of the county of Dublin*, Parts 1–6 (Dublin, 1903–1920).

Ball, Francis Elrington, *The Judges in Ireland, 1221–1921* (2 vols, London, 1926).

Ball, Francis Elrington and Hamilton, Everard, *The Parish of Taney* (Dublin, 1895).

Bagnal, Sean, *Tallaght, 1835–50: A rural place* (Dublin, 2008).

Beale, Eamonn, Gilleece, Dermot, and Redmond, John, *Milltown Golf Club: An illustrated centenary history 1907–2007* (Dublin, 2007).

Berry, H.F., *'Notes from the diary of a Dublin lady in the reign of George II', Journal of the Royal Society of Antiquaries of Ireland* (1898), 28, pp. 141–54.

Berry, H.F. (ed.), *Statute rolls of the parliament of Ireland, reign of Henry VI* (Dublin, 1910).

Betham, William, 'On the Account of Thomas de Chaddisworth, Custodee of the Temporalities of the Archbishop of Dublin', *Proceedings of the Royal Irish Academy*, 5C (1850–3), pp. 145–62.

Bigger, J.W., 'Clean Milk', *Journal of the Statistical and Social Inquiry Society of Ireland*, xiv, no. 2 (1920–23), pp. 199–208.

Blacker, Beaver H., *Brief sketches of the parishes of Donnybrook and Booterstown in the county of Dublin* (Dublin, 1874).

Bowman, Timothy, Butler, William and Wheatley, Michael, *The Disparity of Sacrifice: Irish Recruitment to the British Armed Forces, 1914 – 1918* (Liverpool, 2020).

Bradley, John, 'Some reflections on the problem of Scandinavian settlement in the hinterland of Dublin during the ninth century' in John Bradley and others (eds), *Dublin in the Medieval World: Studies in Honour of Howard B. Clarke* (Dublin, 2009), pp. 39–62.

Brady, Joseph, *Dublin, 1930–1950: The Emergence of The Modern City* (Dublin, 2014).

Brady, Joseph and Lynch, Patrick, 'The Irish Sailors' and Soldiers' Land Trust and its Killester nemesis', *Irish Geography*, 42, no. 3 (November 2009), pp. 261–92.

Briggs, Stephen C., 'Dealing with Antiquities in 19th Century Dublin', *Dublin Historical Record*, xxxi, no. 4 (September 1978), pp. 146–8.

Broderick, David, *Local government in nineteenth century County Dublin: The Grand Jury* (Dublin, 2007).

Brophy, Imelda, *'Women in the Workforce' in David Dickson (ed.), The Gorgeous Mask: Dublin 1700–1850* (Dublin, 1987), pp. 51–63.

Buckland, Patrick (ed.), *Irish Unionism 1885–1923: A Documentary History* (Belfast, 1973).

Burke, Helen, *The People and the Poor Law in 19th Century Ireland* (The Women's Education Bureau, 1987).

Burke, Tom, 'The Royal Dublin Fusiliers in the Great War', *History Ireland, 13, no. 5* (September/October 2005), pp. 29–33.

Butlin, R.A., 'Agriculture in County Dublin in the late eighteenth century', *Studia Hibernica*, no. 9 (1969), pp. 98–101.

Campbell, Fergus, *The Irish Establishment 1879–1914* (Oxford, 2009).

Canny, Nicholas, 'What really happened in 1641?' in Jane H. Ohlmeyer (ed.), Ireland from independence to occupation 1641–1660 (Cambridge, 1995), pp. 24–42.

Casey, Christine, *The Buildings of Dublin* (Yale, 2005).

Clare, Liam, *Unionist/Nationalist election campaigns in South County Dublin (1883–1923),* A talk given to the Foxrock Local History Club on 11 May 1983 (publication no. 13).

Clarke, Aidan, *The old English in Ireland, 1625–42* (Dublin, 1966).

Clarke, Howard B., 'Urbs et suburbinem: Beyond the walls of medieval Dublin' in Conleth Manning (ed.), *Dublin and beyond the Pale: Studies in honour of Patrick Healy* (Wicklow, 1998), pp. 45–58.

Cleary, Arthur P., *The Law of Parliamentary Registration of Voters in Ireland* (2nd edition, Dublin, 1868).

Clinton, Mark, Fibiger, Linda and Shiels, Damian, 'Archaeology of massacre: The Carrickmines mass grave and the siege of March 1642' in David Edwards, Padraig Lenihan & Clodagh Tait (eds), *Age of atrocity: Violence and political conflict in early modern Ireland* (Dublin, 2007), pp. 192–218.

Colgan, Edward, *For want of good money: The story of Ireland's coinage* (Bray, 2003).

Comerford, R.V., 'The Parnell era, 1883–91' in W.E. Vaughan (ed.), *A new history of Ireland, vi: Ireland under the Union 1870–1921* (Oxford, 1989), pp. 53–80.

Collins, Sinéad, *Balrothery Poor Law Union, County Dublin, 1839–1851* (Dublin, 2005).

Conlon, Tom, *Victorian Dún Laoghaire: A Town Divided* (Dublin, 2016).

Connolly, S.J., 'Union Government, 1812–23' in W.E. Vaughan (ed.), *A new history of Ireland, v: Ireland under the Union 1801–1870* (Oxford, 1989), pp. 48–73.

Coolahan, John, *Irish Education: History and Structure* (Dublin, 1981).

Corcoran, Michael, *Through Streets Broad and Narrow: A history of Dublin Trams* (Leicester, 2000).

Corlett, Christiaan, *Antiquities of old Rathdown* (Bray, 1999).

Costello, David, '*The political and topographical history of the half barony of Rathdown, county Dublin in the seventeenth century*' (MA thesis, University College, Dublin, 1990).

Costello, Peter, *Dublin Churches* (Dublin, 1989).

Coughlan, Rupert J., *Napper Tandy* (Dublin, 1976).

Craig, Maurice, *Classic Irish Houses of the Middle Size* (London, 1976).

Crossman, Virginia, *Local Government in Nineteenth Century Ireland* (Belfast, 1994).

Cullen, Frank, Cleansing Rural Dublin: Public Health and Housing Initiatives in the South Dublin Poor Law Union, 1880–1920 (Dublin, 2001).

Cullen, L.M., 'Economic development, 1691–1750' in T.W. Moody and W.E. Vaughan (eds), *A new history of Ireland, iv: Eighteenth century Ireland 1691–1800* (Oxford, 1986), pp. 123–95.

Cunningham, Patrick, 'The Catholic Directory for 1821', *Reportorium Novum*, ii, no. 2 (1959–1960), pp. 324–63.

Curran, C.P., 'Dublin Plasterwork', *Journal of the Royal Society of Antiquaries of Ireland*, 7th Series, 10, no. 1 (March, 1940), pp. 1–56.

Curran, C.P., *Dublin Decorative Plasterwork of the seventeenth and eighteenth centuries* (London, 1967).

Curtis, L.P., Junior, 'Ireland in 1914' in W.E. Vaughan (ed.), *A new history of Ireland, vi: Ireland under the Union 1870–1921* (Oxford, 1989), pp. 145–88.

Daly, Mary, 'Late Nineteenth and Early Twentieth Century Dublin' in Harkness and O'Dowd (eds), *The Town in Ireland* (Belfast, 1981), pp. 221–52.

Daly, Mary, *Dublin: The deposed capital: A social and economic history 1860–1914* (Cork, 1985).

D'Alton, John, *A History of the County of Dublin* (Dublin, 1838).

D'Arcy, Fergus A., 'The Decline and Fall of Donnybrook Fair: Moral Reform and Social Control in Nineteenth Century Dublin', *Saothar: Journal of the Irish Labour History Society*, xiii (1988), pp. 7–21.

D'Arcy, Fergus, 'An age of distress and reform: 1800–1860' in Art Cosgrove (ed.), *Dublin Through the Ages* (Dublin, 1988), pp. 93–112.

Dickson, David and English, Richard, 'The La Touche Dynasty' in David Dickson (ed.), *The Gorgeous Mask*, Dublin 1700–1850 (Dublin, 1987), pp. 17–29.

Dickson, David, *Dublin, the making of a capital city* (Dublin, 2014).

Donnelly, James S., 'Famine and government response, 1845–6' in W.E. Vaughan (ed.), *A new history of Ireland, v: Ireland under the Union 1801–1870* (Oxford, 1989), pp. 272–85.

Donnelly, James S., 'The administration of relief, 1846–7' in W.E. Vaughan (ed.), *A new history of Ireland, v: Ireland under the Union 1801–1870* (Oxford, 1989), pp. 294–306.

Donnelly, James S., 'The soup kitchens' in W.E. Vaughan (ed.), *A new history of Ireland, v: Ireland under the Union 1801–1870* (Oxford, 1989), pp. 307–15.

Donnelly, James S., 'The administration of relief, 1847–51' in W.E. Vaughan (ed.), *A new history of Ireland, v: Ireland under the Union 1801–1870* (Oxford, 1989), pp. 316–31.

Donnelly, James S., 'A famine in Irish politics' in W.E. Vaughan (ed.), *A new history of Ireland, v: Ireland under the Union 1801–1870* (Oxford, 1989), pp. 357–71.

Doolan, Paul and Goggins, Robert, *The Hoops: A history of Shamrock Rovers* (Dublin, 1993).

Doran, Beatrice M., *Donnybrook: A history* (Dublin, 2013).

Dorney, John, *The Civil War in Dublin: The fight for the Irish Capital 1922–1924* (Newbridge, 2017).

Dougan, Quincey, 'Dublin's Loyal Volunteers', *History Ireland, 22, no. 3 (May*–June 2014), pp. 36–8.

Dublin Special Commission: High Treason Indictment (NLI, P 2271).

Dublin Special Commission, Informations and Indictments, April 1867 (NLI, IR 3431 D4).

Dutton, Heley, *Observations on Mr Archer's Statistical Survey of the County of Dublin* (Dublin, 1802).

Farley, Desmond, *Social Insurance and Social Assistance in Ireland* (Dublin, 1964).

Farmar, Tony, Privileged Lives: A social history of middle-class Ireland 1882–1989 (Dublin, 2010).

Farrell, Elaine, *A most diabolical eed: Infanticide and Irish society, 1850–1900* (Manchester, 2013).

FitzAchary, John Christopher, *'The Dodder; its history, traditions, and associations', Rathmines News and Dublin Lantern,* November 1901–January 1902.

FitzPatrick, W.J., *History of the Dublin Catholic Cemeteries* (Dublin, 1900).

Fitzsimons, Fiona, *'Tracing First World War Ancestors', History Ireland, 22, no. 4 (July*–August 2014), p. 31.

Fleischmann, Aloys, 'Music and Society' in W.E. Vaughan (ed.), *A new history of Ireland, vi: Ireland under the Union 1870–1921* (Oxford, 1989).

Flynn, William J. (ed.), *Irish Parliamentary Handbook 1945* (Dublin, 1945).

Foley, Áine, *The Royal Manors of Medieval Dublin: Crown and Community* (Dublin, 2013).

Frazer, William, 'Description of a Great Sepulchral Mound at Aylesbury', *Proceedings of the Royal Irish Academy, 2C* (1880), pp. 29–55.

Giacometti, Antoine and MacGowan, Alva, *Rathfarnham Castle Excavations 2014* (Dublin, 2015).

Gillespie, Raymond (ed.), *The first chapter act book of Christ Church cathedral, Dublin, 1574–1634* (Dublin, 1997).

Gilbert, John T. (ed.), *Calendar of ancient records of Dublin* (19 vols, Dublin, 1889–1944).

Graham, B.J. and Proudfoot, L.J., Urban Improvement in Provincial Ireland 1700–1840, *Irish Settlement Studies* No. 4 (The Group for the Study of Irish Historic Settlement, 1994).

Gribbon, H.D., 'Economic and social history, 1850–1921' in W.E. Vaughan (ed.), *A new history of Ireland, vi: Ireland under the Union 1870–1921* (Oxford, 1989), pp. 260–356.

Griffith, Margaret C., *Calendar of Inquisitions formerly in the office of the Chief Remembrancer of the Exchequer prepared from the MSS of the Irish Record Commission* (Dublin, 1991).

Haden, Christopher W. and O'Malley, Catherine, *The Demesne of Old Rathmines: An historical survey of Upper Rathmines, Dartry and Milltown* (Dublin, 1988).

Harrison, Richard S., *Irish Insurance: Historical Perspectives 1650–1939* (published privately by the author, 1992).

Hart, A.R., *A history of the King's Serjeants at Law in Ireland: Honour rather than Advantage?* (Dublin, 2000).

Haslam, Richard, 'The Origins of Irish Local Government' in Mark Callanan and Justin F. Keogan (eds), *Local Government in Ireland Inside Out* (Dublin, 2003), pp. 14–40.

Hearn, Mona, *Thomas Edmondson and the Dublin Laundry: A Quaker Businessman 1837–1908* (Dublin, 2004).

Henry, Brian, Dublin Hanged: *Crime, law enforcement and punishment in late eighteenth century Dublin* (Dublin, 1994).

Hession, Peter, 'The Irish Establishment: Continuity and change' in John Crowley, Donal Ó'Drisceoil and Mike Murphy (eds), *The Atlas of the Irish Revolution* (Cork, 2017), pp. 67–73.

Heuston, John M., *Headquarters Battalion, Army of the Irish Republic, Easter Week 1916* (Carlow, 1966).

Holland, Martin, *Clonskeagh: A Place in History* (Dublin, 2007).

Hughes, Brian, Campbell, Billy and Schreibman, Susan, 'Contested Memories: Revisiting the Battle of Mount Street Bridge', *British Journal for Military History*, 4, no. 1 (2017), pp. 2–22.

Jackson, Alvin, 'The Failure of Unionism in Dublin, 1900', *Irish Historical Studies*, 26, no. 104 (1989) pp. 377–95.

Johnston, Declan, 'Black Monday: The power of myth in medieval Dublin' in Sean Duffy (ed.), *Medieval Dublin XIII* (Dublin, 2013), pp. 139–49.

Jones, Greta, *Captain of all these men of death: The history of tuberculosis in 19th and 20th century Ireland* (Amsterdam, 2001).

Kearns, Kevin C., *Dublin Pub Life and Lore: An oral history* (Dublin, 1996).

Kearns, Kevin C., *Dublin Voices: An oral folk history* (Dublin, 1998).

Kelly, David, 'The conditions of debtors and insolvents in eighteenth century Dublin' in David Dickson (ed.), *The Gorgeous Mask: Dublin 1700–1850* (Dublin, 1987), pp. 98–120.

Kelly, Deirdre, *Four Roads to Dublin: The History of Ranelagh, Rathmines and Leeson Street* (Dublin, 1995).

Kelly, James, *'That Damn'd Thing Called Honour': Duelling in Ireland 1570–1860* (Cork, 1995).

Kelly, Matthew, 'The Politics of Protestant Street Preaching in 1890s Ireland', *The Historical Journal*, 48, no. 1 (2005), pp. 101–25.

Kerr, Donal, *Emmet's Casino and the Marists at Milltown* (Dublin, 1970).

Keyes, Michael J., 'Money and Nationalist politics in nineteenth century Ireland: From O'Connell to Parnell' (PhD thesis, NUI Maynooth, 2009).

Kinealy, Christine, 'The operation of the Poor Law during the Famine' in John Crowley, William J. Smyth and Mike Murphy (eds), *Atlas of the Great Irish Famine* (Cork, 2012), pp. 87–95.

Kinsella, Ken, *Out of the Dark 1914–1918: South Dubliners who fell in the Great War* (Sallins, 2014).

La Touche, Edmund R. Digues, *The Law of Landlord and Tenant as administered in Ireland* (2nd Eedition, 2 vols, Dublin, 1869).

Laffan, William Laffan and Mulligan, Kevin, *Russborough: A great Irish house, its families and collections* (Blessington, 2014).

Lawson, William, 'Licensing and Public House Reform in Ireland', *Journal of the Statistical and Social Inquiry Society of Ireland*, xi, part 86 (1901–1902), pp. 106–19.

Lenihan, Pádraig, 'War and Population, 1649–52', *Irish Economic and Social History*, 24 (1997), pp. 1–21.

Lennon, Colm, *The lords of Dublin in the age of the Reformation* (Dublin, 1989).

Leslie, J.B. and Wallace, W.J.R., *The clergy of Dublin and Glendalough* (Ulster Historical Foundation and the Diocesan Councils of Dublin and Glendalough, 2001).

Lodge, John, *The Peerage of Ireland* (7 vols, Dublin, 1789).

Longfield, Ada K., 'History of the Irish Linen and Cotton Printing Industry in the 18th Century', *Journal of the Royal Society of Antiquaries of Ireland*, 7, no. 1 (June 1937), pp. 26–56.

Loughlin, James, 'The Irish Protestant Home Rule Association and nationalist politics, 1886-93', *Irish Historical Studies*, 24, no. 95 (May 1985), pp. 341–60.

Lydon, James F., *The Lordship of Ireland in the Middle Ages* (2nd edition, Dublin, 2003).

Lydon, James F. 'Medieval Wicklow – A Land of War' in Ken Hannigan and William Nolan (eds), *Wicklow History and Society* (Dublin, 1994), pp. 151–89.

Lyons, F.S.L., 'The aftermath of Parnell, 1891–1903' in W.E. Vaughan (ed.), A new history of Ireland, vi: Ireland under the Union 1870–1921 (Oxford, 1989), pp. 81–110.

Lyons, F.S.L., 'The Watershed, 1903–1907' in W.E. Vaughan (ed.), *'A new history of Ireland', vi: Ireland under the Union 1870–1921* (Oxford, 1989), pp. 111–22.

Lyons, F.S.L., 'The developing crisis, 1907–14' in W.E. Vaughan (ed.), *A new history of Ireland, vi: Ireland under the Union 1870–1921* (Oxford, 1989), pp. 123–44.

Lyons, F.S.L., 'The revolution in train, 1914–16' in W.E. Vaughan (ed.), *A new history of Ireland, vi: Ireland under the Union 1870–1921* (Oxford, 1989), pp. 189–206.

Lyons, F.S.L., 'The new nationalism, 1916–18' in W.E. Vaughan (ed.), *A new history of Ireland, vi: Ireland under the Union 1870–1921* (Oxford, 1989), pp. 224–39.

MacCotter, Paul, 'The church lands of the diocese of Dublin: Reconstruction and history' in Sean Duffy (ed.), *Medieval Dublin XIII* (Dublin, 2013), pp. 81–107.

MacDonagh, Oliver, 'Ideas and institutions, 1830–45' in W.E. Vaughan (ed.), *A new history of Ireland, v: Ireland under the Union 1801–1870* (Oxford, 1989), pp. 193–217.

MacDonagh, Oliver, 'The economy and society, 1830–45' in W.E. Vaughan (ed.), *A new history of Ireland, v: Ireland under the Union 1801–1870* (Oxford, 1989), pp. 218–41.

Maginn, Christopher, 'English marcher lineages in south Dublin in the late middle ages', *Irish Historical Studies*, 34, no. 134 (November 2004), pp. 113–36.

McCullagh, David, *The reluctant Taoiseach: A biography of John A. Costello* (Dublin, 2010).

McDowell, R.B., 'The Irish courts of law, 1801–1914', *Irish Historical Studies*, 10, no. 40 (September, 1957), pp. 263–91.

McDowell, R.B., *The Irish Administration 1801–1914* (London, 1964).

McEntee, Don and Corcoran, Michael, *The Rivers Dodder and Poddle: Mills, Storms, Droughts and the Public Water Supply* (Dublin, 2016).

McGee, Frances, *The archives of the valuation of Ireland, 1830–1865* (Dublin, 2018).

McGuire, James and Quinn, James (eds), *A Dictionary of Irish Biography from the earliest times to the year 2002* (9 vols, Cambridge, 2009).

McKay, Enda, 'The Housing of the Rural Labourer, 1883–1916', *Saothar: Journal of the Irish Labour History Society*, xvii (1992), pp. 27–38.

McManus, Ruth, *Crampton Built* (Dublin, 2008).

McManus, Ruth, 'Suburban and urban housing in the twentieth century', *Proceedings of the Royal Irish Academy*, 111C (2011), pp. 253–86.

McNeill, Charles (ed.), *Calendar of Archbishop Alen's Register c. 1172–1534* (Dublin, 1950).

Mallet, Robert, *Report on the proposed formation of reservoirs on the River Dodder* (Dublin, 1844).

Matthews, Ann, *The Kimmage Garrison, 1916: Making billy-can bombs at Larkfield* (Dublin, 2010).

Martin, F.X. (ed.), *The Irish Volunteers 1913–1915: Recollections and Documents* (Dublin, 1963).

Meyler, Walter Thomas, *St Catherine's Bells – An autobiography* (Dublin, 1868).

Mills, James, 'Notices of the manor of St Sepulchre, Dublin, in the fourteenth century', *Journal of the Royal Society of Antiquaries of Ireland*, 19 (1889), pp. 31–41.

Mills, James, 'The Norman settlement in Leinster: The cantreds near Dublin', *Journal of the Royal Society of Antiquaries of Ireland*, 2, no. 4 (1894), pp. 161–75.

Mills, James, *The register of the Parish of St. Peter and St. Kevin 1669–1761* (Parish Register Society of Dublin, 1911).

Milne, Ida, *Stacking the coffins: Influenza, war and revolution in Ireland, 1918–19* (Manchester, 2018).

Moriarty, Christopher, *Down the Dodder* (Dublin, 1991).

Morrill, John, 'The Drogheda massacre in Cromwellian context' in David Edwards, Padraig Lenihan & Clodagh Tait (eds), *Age of atrocity: Violence and political conflict in early modern Ireland* (Dublin, 2007), pp. 242–65.

Morrisey, Thomas J., S.J., *Thomas A. Finlay, S.J., 1848–1940 Educationalist, Editor, Social Reformer* (Dublin, 2004).

Mulcahy, Risteárd, *Richard Mulcahy (1886–1971): A Family Memoir* (Dublin, 1999).

Murphy, Margaret and Potterton, Michael, *The Dublin region in the Middle Ages: Settlement, land-use and economy* (Dublin, 2010).

Murphy, Sean, 'The Corporation of Dublin 1660–1760', *Dublin Historical Studies*, xxxviii, no. 1 (December 1984), pp. 22–35.

Murray, Rev. Michael G., 'The Story of Milltown', in *Souvenir of the Blessing and Dedication of the Church of the Immaculate Virgin Mary of the Miraculous Medal at Clonskeagh* (Dublin, 1957).

Murray, Peter, 'Electoral Politics and the Dublin Working Class before the First World War', *Saothar: Journal of the Irish Labour History Society*, vi (1980), pp. 8–25.

Nelson, E. Charles, 'The Dublin Florists' Club in the Mid-eighteenth Century', *Garden History*, 10, no. 2 (Autumn 1982), pp. 142–8.

Nevin, Monica, 'General Charles Vallencey 1725–1812', *Journal of the Royal Society of Antiquaries of Ireland*, 123 (1993), pp. 19–58.

Nolan, J., *Changing Faces* (Dublin, 1982).

Nolan, William (ed.), *The Gaelic Athletic Association in Dublin 1884–2000* (3 vols, Dublin, 2005).

Norton, Desmond, *Landlords, Tenants, Famine: The business of an Irish Land Agency in the 1840s* (Dublin, 2006).

Nugent, Brian, *A guide to the 18th century records in the Irish Registry of Deeds* (privately published, Corstown, 2012).

'I.O.' [C.J.C. Street], *The Administration of Ireland, 1920* (London, April 1921).

O'Brien, Elizabeth, 'Churches of South-East County Dublin, Seventh to Twelfth Century' in G. MacNiocaill and P.F. Wallace (eds), Keimelia, *Studies in medieval archaeology and history in memory of Tom Delaney* (Galway, 1988), pp. 504–24.

O'Brien, Elizabeth, 'Excavations at Dundrum Castle' in Christiaan Corlett (ed.), *Unearthing the Archaeology of Dún Laoghaire-Rathdown* (Dublin, 2013), pp. 114–23.

O'Brien, George, *The Economic History of Ireland in the Eighteenth Century* (Dublin, 1918).

O'Brien, Gerard, 'The Establishment of Poor-Law Unions in Ireland, 1838–43', *Irish Historical Studies*, 23, no. 90 (November 1982), pp. 97–120.

O'Brien, Gerard, 'The new Poor Law in pre-Famine Ireland: A case history', *Irish Economic and Social History*, 12 (1985), pp. 33–49.

O'Brien, Gerard, 'Workhouse Management in Pre-Famine Ireland', *Proceedings of the Royal Irish Academy, 86C* (1986), pp. 113–34.

O'Brien, Joseph V., *Dear, Dirty Dublin: A city in distress 1899–1916* (California, 1982).

O'Brien, Paul, *Blood on the Streets: 1916 and the battle for Mount Street Bridge* (Dublin, 2008).

Ó Broin, Leon, *The Chief Secretary: Augustine Birrell in Ireland* (London, 1969).

O'Byrne, Emmet, 'A much disputed land: Carrickmines and the Dublin marches' in Sean Duffy (ed.), *Medieval Dublin IV* (Dublin, 2003), wpp. 229–52.

O'Byrne, Emmet, 'Cultures in contact in the Leinster and Dublin marches, 1170–1400' in Sean Duffy (ed.), *Medieval Dublin V* (Dublin, 2004), pp. 111–48.

Ó Cathaoir, Eva, 'The Poor Law in County Wicklow' in Ken Hanigan and William Nolan (eds), *Wicklow History and Society* (Dublin, 1994), pp. 503–79.

Ó Cathaoir, Eva, 'The Rathdown Union Workhouse at Loughlinstown, 1838–1923', *Dublin Historical Record*, xlviii, no. 2 (Autumn 1995), pp. 111–24.

O'Connor, Nessa, *Palmerstown: An ancient place* (Dublin, 2003).

O'Donnell, E.E., *The Annals of Dublin* (Dublin, 1987).

O'Donovan, Edmond, 'Early Christian and medieval excavations at Teach Naithí: The changing morphology of a church site in Dundrum, County Dublin' in Sean Duffy (ed.), *Medieval Dublin XXII* (Dublin, 2012), pp. 9–93.

O'Donovan, Edmond, 'Early Christian Remains at St Nahí's Church, Churchtown Upper' in Christiaan Corlett (ed.), *Unearthing the Archaeology of Dún Laoghaire-Rathdown* (Dublin, 2013), pp. 91–4.

O'Donovan, Edmond, 'Medieval Remains at St Nahí's Church, Churchtown Upper' in Christiaan Corlett (ed.), *Unearthing the Archaeology of Dún Laoghaire-Rathdown* (Dublin, 2013), pp. 129–32.

O'Farrell, Patrick J., 'The Irish in Australia and New Zealand, 1791–1870' in W.E. Vaughan (ed.), *'A new history of Ireland', v: Ireland under the Union 1801–1870* (Oxford, 1989), pp. 661–81.

Ó Gráda, Diarmuid, 'The rocky road to Dublin: Transport modes and urban growth in the Georgian Age, with particular reference to the turnpike roads', *Studia Hibernica*, 22/23 (1982–1983), pp. 128–48.

Ó Gráda, Diarmuid, *Georgian Dublin: The forces that shaped the city* (Cork, 2015).

O'Higgins, Paul, 'Arthur Browne (1756–1805): An Irish Civilian', *Northern Ireland Legal Quarterly*, 20, no. 3 (September 1969), pp. 255–73.

O'Kane, Finola, 'The appearance of a continued city: Dublin's Georgian suburbia' in Gillian O'Brien and Finola O'Kane (eds), *Georgian Dublin* (Dublin, 2008), pp. 110–26.

O'Kelly, Michael J., *Early Ireland: An Introduction to Irish Prehistory* (Cambridge, 1989).

Ó Maitiú, Séamas, *Dublin's Suburban Towns 1834–1930* (Dublin, 2003).

Ó Maitiú, Séamas, 'A spent force? An Claidheamh Soluis and the Gaelic League in Dublin 1893–1913' in Francis Devine (ed.), *A capital in conflict: Dublin city and the 1913 lock-out* (Dublin, 2013), pp. 281–309.

Ó Maitiú, Séamas, *Rathmines*, Irish Historic Towns Atlas: Dublin Suburbs No. 2 (Dublin, 2021).

O'Neill, Tim P., 'The charities and famine in mid-nineteenth century Ireland' in Jacqueline Hill and Colm Lennon (eds), *Luxury and Austerity* (Dublin, 1999), pp. 137–64.

O'Riordan, Rev. William M., 'The Succession of Parish Priests in the Archdiocese of Dublin, 1771–1851', *Reportorium Novum*, i, no. 2 (1956), pp. 406–33.

Osborough, W.N., *Law and the emergence of modern Dublin* (Dublin, 1996).

O'Sullivan, Aidan, McCormick, Finbar, Kerr, Thomas R. and Harney, Lorcan, *Early Medieval Ireland, AD 400–1100* (Dublin, 2013).

O'Sullivan, Donal, *The Irish Free State and its Senate: A study in contemporary politics* (London, 1940).

O'Sullivan, Muiris and Downey, Liam, 'Lime kilns', *Archaeology Ireland*, 19, no. 2, issue 72 (Summer 2005), pp. 18–22.

Otway-Ruthven, Jocelyn, 'The organization of Anglo-Irish agriculture in the middle ages', *Journal of the Royal Society of Antiquaries of Ireland*, 81, no. 1 (1951), pp. 1–13.

Otway-Ruthven, Jocelyn, 'The church lands of medieval county Dublin' in J.A. Watt, J. Morral and F.X. Martin (eds), *Medieval Studies presented to Aubrey Gwynn S.J.* (Dublin, 1961), pp. 54–73.

Parkes, Susan M., *A guide to sources for the history of Irish education, 1780–1922* (Dublin, 2010).

Pašeta, Senia, *Before the Revolution: Nationalism, Social Change and Ireland's Catholic Elite, 1879–1922* (Cork, 1992).

Pearson, Peter, *Between the Mountains and the Sea: Dun Laoghaire-Rathdown County* (Dublin, 1998).

Pender, Séamus (ed.), *A census of Ireland circa 1659 with a new introduction by William J Smyth* (Dublin, 2002).

Porter, Frank Thorpe, *Gleanings and Reminiscences* (Dublin, 1875).

Potter, Matthew, *The municipal revolution in Ireland: A handbook of urban government in Ireland since 1800* (Dublin, 2011).

Prunty, Jacinta, *Dublin slums 1800–1925: A study in urban geography* (Dublin, 1999).

Prunty, Jacinta, *Maps and map-making in local history* (Dublin, 2004).

Rattigan, Clíona, *'What else could I do?' Single Mothers and Infanticide, Ireland 1900–1950* (Dublin, 2012).

Raymond, Raymond J., 'Dublin: The Great Famine 1845–1860', *Dublin Historical Record*, xxxiii, no. 3 (June 1978), pp. 98–105.

Refaussé, Raymond and Clark, Mary, *A catalogue of the maps of the estates of the archbishop of Dublin 1654–1850* (Dublin, 2000).

Reynolds, J.J., *Footprints of Emmet* (Dublin, 1903).

Return of Land Owners of Ireland of one acre and upwards (Dublin, 1876).

Report of the Deputy Keeper of the Public Records of Ireland, *Index to the Act or Grant Books, and to original Wills, of the Diocese of Dublin 1272–1858* (Dublin, 1894).

Robbins, Joseph, *The miasma: Epidemic and panic in nineteenth century Ireland* (Dublin, 1995).

Rutty, John, *An Essay towards a Natural History of County Dublin* (2 vols, Dublin, 1772).

St Philip's Church, *Milltown Parish: A ten-minute tour* (parish leaflet, 2016).

St John Joyce, *Weston, The neighbourhood of Dublin* (2nd edition, Dublin, 1913).

Salmon, Patrick, 'The lost village of Milltown and its houses', *Dublin Historical Record*, lxx, no. 1 (Spring/Summer 2018), pp. 17–31.

Salmon, Patrick, 'The Hunt Family and Milltown Castle', *Dublin Historical Record*, lxxiii (2020), pp. 95–104.

Salmon, Patrick, 'Notable houses in Eighteenth and Nineteenth Century Milltown', *Dublin Historical Record*, lxxv (2022), pp. 97–106.

Scantlebury, C., SJ, 'Rathfarnham Castle', *Dublin Historical Record*, xxii, no.1 (February 1951), pp. 20–30.

Simington, Robert C., *The Civil Survey of County Dublin AD 1654–1656* (Dublin, 1945).

Simms, Angret and Flanagan, Patricia, 'Villages in county Dublin: Their Origins and Inheritance' in Aalen and Whelan (eds), *Dublin City and County: From Prehistory to Present* (Dublin, 1992), pp. 79–119.

Simms, J.G., 'The establishment of protestant ascendancy, 1691–1714', in T.W. Moody and W.E. Vaughan (eds), *A new history of Ireland, iv: Eighteenth century Ireland 1691–1800* (Oxford, 1986), pp. 1–30.

Sisson, Elaine, 'How to make an Irish boy: The founding of Scoil Éanna in Cullenswood House' in Victoria White (ed.), *Cullenswood House* (Dublin, 2009).

Smyth, William J., 'Society and settlement in seventeenth century Ireland: The evidence of the "1659 Census"' in W.J. Smyth and K. Whelan (eds), *Common Ground: Essays on the historical geography of Ireland* (Cork, 1988), pp. 55–83.

Smyth, William J., 'Exploring the social and cultural topographies of sixteenth and seventeenth century county Dublin' in F.H.A. Allen and Kevin Whelan (eds), *Dublin City and County: From Prehistory to Present* (Dublin, 1992), pp. 121–79.

Smyth, William J., 'The province of Leinster and the Great Famine' in John Crowley, William J. Smyth and Mike Murphy (eds), *Atlas of the Great Irish Famine* (Cork, 2012), pp. 325–33.

Stout, Geraldine and Stout, Matthew, 'Patterns in the Past: County Dublin 5,000 BC to 1,000 AD' in F.H.A. Allen and Kevin Whelan (eds), *Dublin City and County: From Prehistory to Present* (Dublin, 1992), pp. 5–42.

Sweeney, Joseph C., *The life and times of Arthur Browne in Ireland and America, 1756–1805* (Dublin, 2017).

Takagami, Shinichi, 'The Dublin Fenians 1858–1879' (PhD thesis, University of Dublin, 1990).

Takagami, Shinichi, 'The Fenian Rising in Dublin, March 1867', *Irish Historical Studies*, 29, no. 115 (1995), pp. 340–62.

Townsend, Charles, *The Republic: The fight for Irish Independence, 1918–1923* (London, 2013).

Valiulis, Maryann Gialanella, *Portrait of a Revolutionary: General Richard Mulcahy and the founding of the Irish Free State* (Dublin, 1992).

Walker, Brian M., 'The Irish Electorate, 1868–1915', *Irish Historical Studies*, 18, no. 71 (March 1973), pp. 359–71.

Wall, Maureen, 'The Catholic Merchants, Manufacturers and Traders of Dublin, 1778–1782', *Reportorium Novum*, ii, no. 2 (1959–1960), pp. 298–323.

Wallace, Ciarán, 'Local politics and government in Dublin city and suburbs 1899–1914' (PhD thesis, University of Dublin, 2010).

Walsh, Ged, *On the Banks of the Dodder, Rathgar and Churchtown: An Illustrated History* (Dublin, 2019).

Woodham-Smith, Cecil, *The Great Hunger* (New English Library edition, London, 1970).

Yeates, Pádraig, *A City in Wartime*: Dublin 1914–1918 (Dublin, 2011)

3. DIRECTORIES AND TOPOGRAPHICAL GUIDES

A Directory of Dublin for the year 1738 (Dublin Corporation Public Libraries, 2000).

Lewis, Samuel, *Topographical Dictionary of Ireland* (2 vols, Dublin, 1837).

Pettigrew and Oulton, The Dublin Almanac and General Register of Ireland, 1835–1848.

Pigot & Co. City of Dublin and Hibernian Provincial Directory (Dublin, 1824).

The Parliamentary Gazetteer of Ireland, 1845–45 (3 vols, Dublin, 1846).

The Post Office Annual Directory and Calendar for 1843.

The Post Office Dublin Directory and Calendar for 1908.

The Treble Almanac 1818, 1829.

Thom's Directories 1844 to date.

Thom's Irish Who's Who 1923.

4. NEWSPAPERS

An Claidheamh Soluis
Anglo Celt
Belfast Commercial Chronicle
Belfast Newsletter
Catholic Bulletin
Catholic Standard
Church of Ireland Gazette
Cork Examiner
Cumberland Packet
Derry Journal
Drogheda Journal
Dublin Builder
Dublin Chronicle
Dublin Courier
Dublin Daily Express
Dublin Daily Telegraph
Dublin Evening Telegraph
Dublin Evening Mail
Dublin Evening Packet and Correspondent
Dublin Evening Post
Dublin Journal
Dublin Medical Press
Dublin Mercantile and Weekly Adviser
Dublin Mercantile and Weekly Price Current
Dublin Monitor
Dublin Morning Post
Dublin Morning Register
Dublin Observer
Dublin Penny Journal
Dublin Weekly Herald
Dublin Weekly Nation
Dublin Weekly Register
Enniskillen Chronicle
Evening Herald
Evening News
Evening Packet
Faulkner's Journal
Finn's Leinster Journal
Flag of Ireland
Freeman's Journal
General Advertiser for Dublin, and All Ireland
Gentleman's and London Magazine
Hibernian Journal
Irish Builder
Irish Citizen
Irish Independent
Irish Penny Journal
Irish Press
Irish Society
Irish Times
Kerry Sentinel
Lancaster Gazette
Larne Times
Leinster Express
Limerick Chronicle
Londonderry Sentinel and North West Advertiser
Longford Leader
Nenagh Guardian
Northern Whig
Pue's Occurrences
Rathmines Free Press
Rathmines News and Dublin Lantern
Saunders's Newsletter
Sport Dublin
Statesman and Dublin Christian Record
The Advocate
The Daily Nation
The Nation
The Pilot
The Vindicator
The Warder
The Watchword
United Irishman
Waterford Mail
Weekly Freeman's Journal
Weekly Irish Times
Westmeath Journal
Wexford Independent
Wexford People
Wicklow Newsletter
Wicklow People

Index

Italic page numbers indicate illustrations and captions.
Mc and Mac are both treated as Mac.
St and Ss are treated as Saint and Saints.